Houghton
Mifflin
Harcourt

collections

GRADE 9

Program Consultants:

Kylene Beers

Martha Hougen

Carol Jago

William L. McBride

Erik Palmer

Lydia Stack

A&E   H HISTORY.   bio.

Printed in the U.S.A.

ISBN 978-0-544-56971-3

2 3 4 5 6 7 8 9 10   0868   24 23 22 21 20 19 18 17 16 15

4500545846 · A B C D E F G

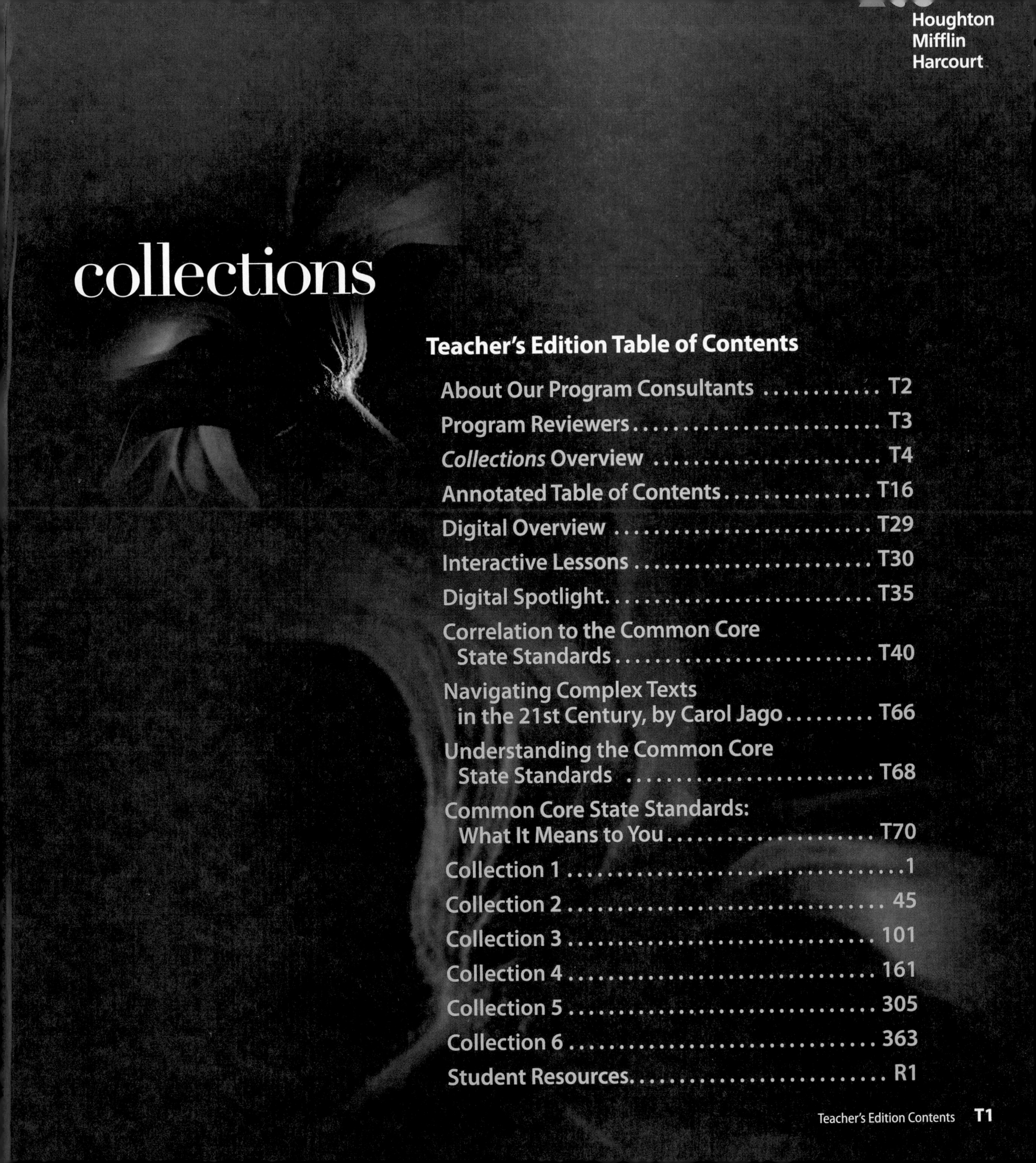

Houghton
Mifflin
Harcourt

collections

Teacher's Edition Table of Contents

Kylene Beers Nationally known lecturer and author on reading and literacy; 2011 recipient of the Conference on English Leadership Exemplary Leader Award; coauthor of *Notice and Note: Strategies for Close Reading*; former president of the National Council of Teachers of English. Dr. Beers is the nationally known author of *When Kids Can't Read: What Teachers Can Do* and coeditor of *Adolescent Literacy: Turning Promise into Practice*, as well as articles in the *Journal of Adolescent and Adult Literacy*. Former editor of *Voices from the Middle*, she is the 2001 recipient of NCTE's Richard W. Halley Award, given for outstanding contributions to middle-school literacy. She recently served as Senior Reading Researcher at the Comer School Development Program at Yale University as well as Senior Reading Advisor to Secondary Schools for the Reading and Writing Project at Teachers College.

Martha Hougen National consultant, presenter, researcher, and author. Areas of expertise include differentiating instruction for students with learning difficulties, including those with learning disabilities and dyslexia; and teacher and leader preparation improvement. Dr. Hougen has taught at the middle school through graduate levels. Recently her focus has been on working with teacher educators to enhance teacher and leader preparation to better meet the needs of all students. Currently she is working with the University of Florida at the Collaboration for Effective Educator Development, Accountability, and Reform Center (CEEDAR Center) to improve the achievement of students with disabilities by reforming teacher and leader licensure, evaluation, and preparation. She has led similar efforts in Texas with the Higher Education Collaborative and the College & Career Readiness Initiative Faculty Collaboratives. In addition to peer-reviewed articles, curricular documents, and presentations, Dr. Hougen has published two college textbooks: *The Fundamentals of Literacy Assessment and Instruction Pre-K–6* (2012) and *The Fundamentals of Literacy Assessment and Instruction 6–12* (2014).

Carol Jago Teacher of English with 32 years of experience at Santa Monica High School in California; author and nationally known lecturer; and former president of the National Council of Teachers of English. Currently serves as Associate Director of the California Reading and Literature Project at UCLA. With expertise in standards assessment and secondary education, Ms. Jago is the author of numerous books on education, including *With Rigor for All* and *Papers, Papers, Papers*, and is active with the California Association of Teachers of English, editing its scholarly journal *California English* since 1996. Ms. Jago also served on the planning committee for the 2009 NAEP Framework and the 2011 NAEP Writing Framework.

William L. McBride Curriculum specialist. Dr. McBride is a nationally known speaker, educator, and author who now trains teachers in instructional methodologies. He is coauthor of *What's Happening?*, an innovative, high-interest text for middle-grade readers, and author of *If They Can Argue Well, They Can Write Well*. A former reading specialist, English teacher, and social studies teacher, he holds a master's degree in reading and a doctorate in curriculum and instruction from the University of North Carolina at Chapel Hill. Dr. McBride has contributed to the development of textbook series in language arts, social studies, science, and vocabulary. He is also known for his novel *Entertaining an Elephant*, which tells the story of a veteran teacher who becomes reinspired with both his profession and his life.

Erik Palmer Veteran teacher and education consultant based in Denver, Colorado. Author of *Well Spoken: Teaching Speaking to All Students* and *Digitally Speaking: How to Improve Student Presentations*. His areas of focus include improving oral communication, promoting technology in classroom presentations, and updating instruction through the use of digital tools. He holds a bachelor's degree from Oberlin College and a master's degree in curriculum and instruction from the University of Colorado.

Lydia Stack Internationally known teacher educator and author. She is involved in a Stanford University project to support English Language Learners, *Understanding Language*. The goal of this project is to enrich academic content and language instruction for English Language Learners (ELLs) in grades K-12 by making explicit the language and literacy skills necessary to meet the Common Core State Standards (CCSS) and Next Generation Science Standards. Her teaching experience includes twenty-five years as an elementary and high school ESL teacher, and she is a past president of Teachers of English to Speakers of Other Languages (TESOL). Her awards include the TESOL James E. Alatis Award and the San Francisco STAR Teacher Award. Her publications include *On Our Way to English, Visions: Language, Literature, Content,* and *American Themes,* a literature anthology for high school students in the ACCESS program of the U.S. State Department's Office of English Language Programs.

Additional thanks to the following Program Reviewers

Rosemary Asquino

Sylvia B. Bennett

Yvonne Bradley

Leslie Brown

Haley Carroll

Caitlin Chalmers

Emily Colley-King

Stacy Collins

Denise DeBonis

Courtney Dickerson

Sarah Easley

Phyllis J. Everette

Peter J. Foy Sr.

Carol M. Gibby

Angie Gill

Mary K. Goff

Saira Haas

Lisa M. Janeway

Robert V. Kidd Jr.

Kim Lilley

John C. Lowe

Taryn Curtis MacGee

Meredith S. Maddox

Cynthia Martin

Kelli M. McDonough

Megan Pankiewicz

Linda Beck Pieplow

Molly Pieplow

Mary-Sarah Proctor

Jessica A. Stith

Peter Swartley

Pamela Thomas

Linda A. Tobias

Rachel Ukleja

Lauren Vint

Heather Lynn York

Leigh Ann Zerr

Collections provides students with the tools to succeed in the classroom and beyond.

Student Dashboard

All of the resources that each student needs are accessible from the *Collections* Student Dashboard.

HMH Player App provides innovative features supporting instruction both in class and outside of class, synchronizing online and offline work.

available in iOS® and Google Chrome™ formats

Teachers can plan lessons, customize content, present instruction, assign assessments and activities, and review student progress.

Students can download content to their devices and fully use *Collections* without an Internet connection. When back online, all student work is saved and available.

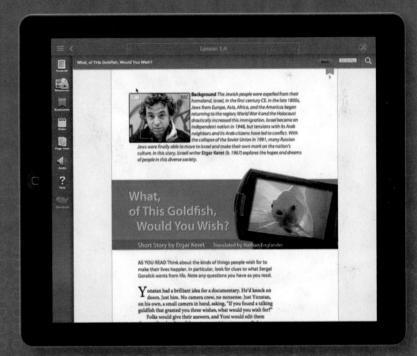

Supporting students' individual strengths, *Collections* integrates scaffolds that build competencies.

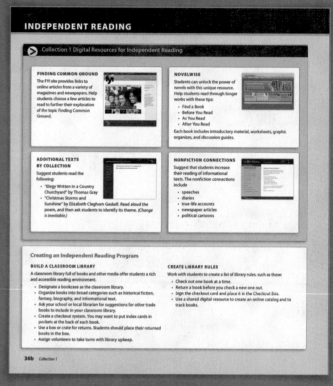

Independent Reading

Independent reading customizes learning for each student, tapping personal interests and matching appropriate reading levels. Resources in *Collections* are easily accessible and complement learning.

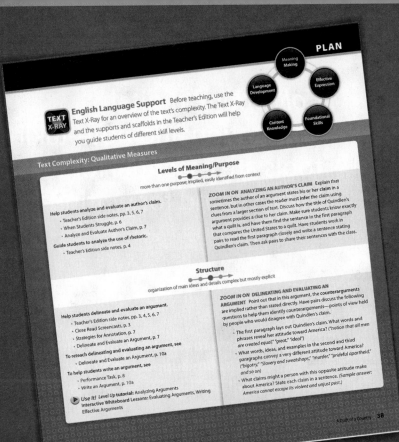

Integrated English Language Development

Integrated ELD instruction is woven seamlessly throughout *Collections*, providing directions for teachers and scaffolding for students.

Level Up Interactive Tutorials

Tutorials escalate learning with new digital instruction and feedback for critical learning objectives.

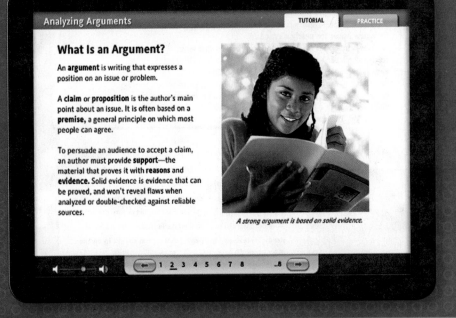

Analyzing Arguments

TUTORIAL | PRACTICE

What Is an Argument?

An **argument** is writing that expresses a position on an issue or problem.

A **claim** or **proposition** is the author's main point about an issue. It is often based on a **premise**, a general principle on which most people can agree.

To persuade an audience to accept a claim, an author must provide **support**—the material that proves it with **reasons** and **evidence.** Solid evidence is evidence that can be proved, and won't reveal flaws when analyzed or double-checked against reliable sources.

A strong argument is based on solid evidence.

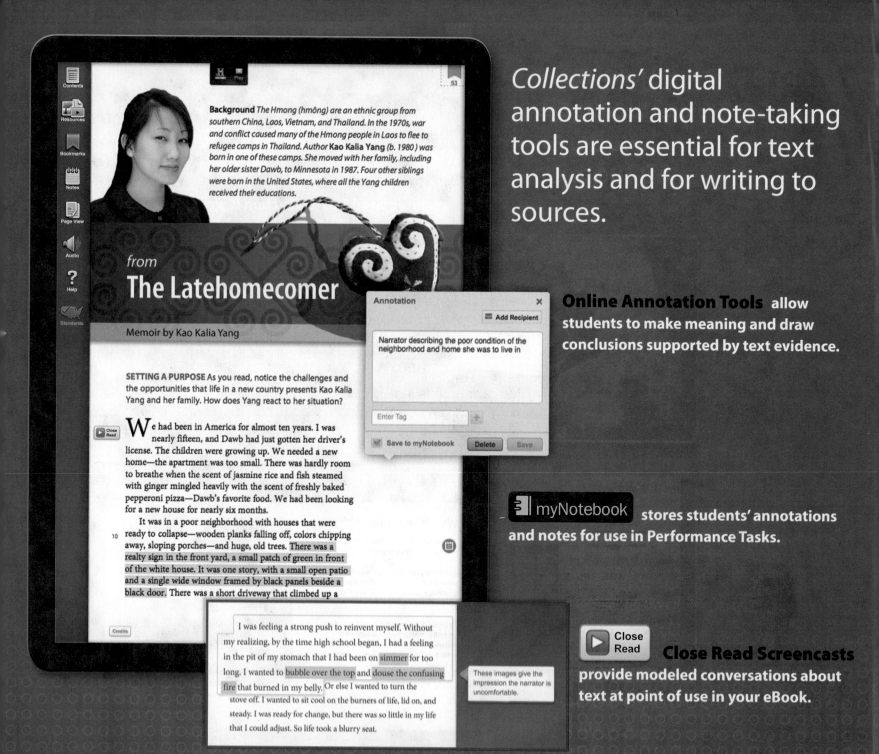

Collections' digital annotation and note-taking tools are essential for text analysis and for writing to sources.

Online Annotation Tools allow students to make meaning and draw conclusions supported by text evidence.

myNotebook stores students' annotations and notes for use in Performance Tasks.

Close Read Screencasts provide modeled conversations about text at point of use in your eBook.

Does love look with the eyes. . .

Stream to Start

Stream to Start Videos delight and instruct with engaging digital explanations of each collection's theme.

Close Reader allows students to apply standards and practice close-reading strategies in a digital or consumable print format.

Background *A member of the Standing Rock Sioux,* **Susan Power** *was born in 1961 and grew up in Chicago. She spent her childhood listening to her mother tell stories about their American Indian heritage. These stories later served as inspiration for Power's writing. As a young girl, Power made frequent visits with her mother to local museums—trips that inspired her memoir "Museum Indians."*

Museum Indians

Memoir by Susan Power

CLOSE READ
Notes

1. **READD** As you read lines 1–16, begin to cite text evidence.

   • Underline a metaphor in the first paragraph that describes the mother's braid.
   • Underline a metaphor in the second paragraph that describes the mother's braid differently.
   • In the margin, note the adjectives the narrator uses to describe the

coils in my mother's dresser drawer; it is thick and black,
as sequins. My mother cut her hair several years ago,
s born, but she kept one heavy braid. It is the three-foot
from its nest and handle as if it were alive.
why did you cut your hair?" I ask. I am a little girl lifting a
river into the light that streams through the kitchen
om turns to me.
me headaches. Now put that away and wash your hands

n't cut *my* hair, will you?" I'm sure this is a whine.
t a little trim now and then to even the ends."
the dark snake to its nest among my mother's slips,
s so that its thin tail hides beneath the wide mouth sheared

*thick
black
glossy*

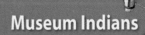

13

Anchor Texts drive each collection and have related selections in the Close Reader.

Background *A member of the Standing Rock Sioux,* **Susan Power** *was born in 1961 and grew up in Chicago. She spent her childhood listening to her mother tell stories about their American Indian heritage. These stories later served as inspiration for Power's writing. As a young girl, Power made frequent visits with her mother to local museums—trips that inspired her memoir "Museum Indians."*

Museum Indians

Memoir by Susan Power

The March on Washington

I Have a Dream
Speech by Martin Luther King Jr.

from Nobody Turn Me Around: A History of the 1963 March on Washington
History Writing by Charles Euchner

MEDIA

AMERICA The Story of Us: March on Washington
Video by HISTORY®

Background *On August 28, 1963, thousands of Americans marched on Washington, D.C., to urge Congress to pass a civil rights bill. Martin Luther King Jr. delivered his "I Have a Dream" speech on the steps of the Lincoln Memorial before more than 250,000 people. After you read and analyze the speech, you will read an excerpt from a history text which describes the historic speech in detail and includes first-hand accounts from people who were on the National Mall that day. Then you will watch a short video about the march and compare the two accounts.*

Martin Luther King Jr. *(1929–1968) became a catalyst for social change in the 1950s and 1960s. Preaching a philosophy of nonviolence, he galvanized people of all races to participate in boycotts, marches, and demonstrations against racial injustice. His moral leadership stirred the conscience of the nation and helped bring about the passage of the Civil Rights Act of 1964. In that same year, he was awarded the Nobel Peace Prize. King continued his work for justice and equality until he was assassinated in 1968.*

Compare Anchor Texts

Transcending time and place, media resources enrich informational and literary text throughout *Collections*.

Voices and images from A&E®, Bio®, and HISTORY® transport students to different times and places.

Informational text on *FYI* is linked to each collection topic and is curated and updated monthly.

Channel One News®

Channel One helps students become global citizens in a digital world.

Media Lessons prompt students to read news reports, literary adaptations, ads, and websites as complex texts.

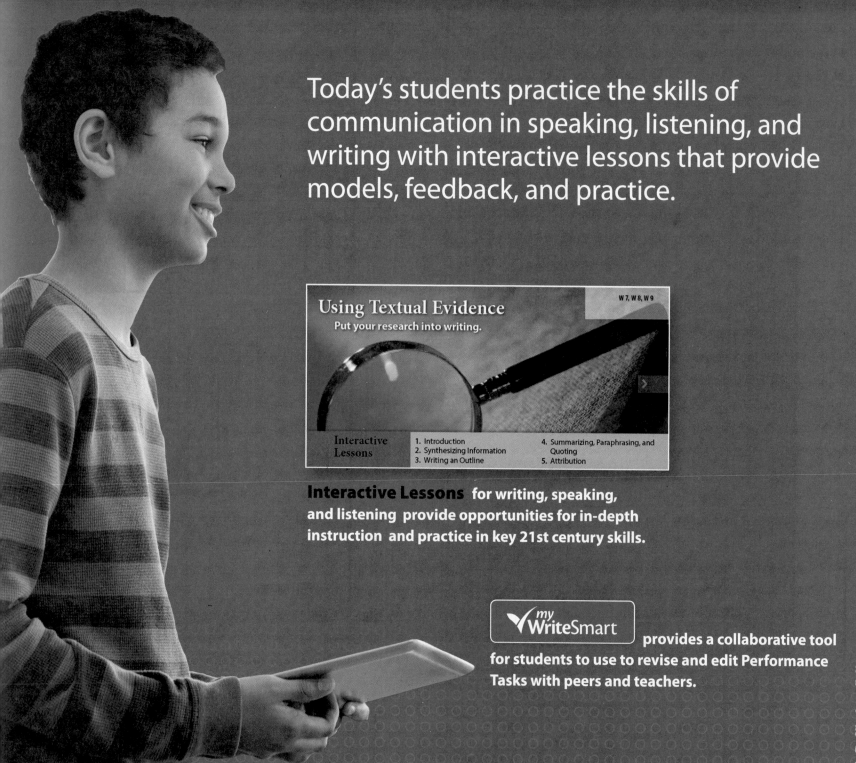

Today's students practice the skills of communication in speaking, listening, and writing with interactive lessons that provide models, feedback, and practice.

Using Textual Evidence
Put your research into writing.

W 7, W 8, W 9

Interactive Lessons

1. Introduction
2. Synthesizing Information
3. Writing an Outline
4. Summarizing, Paraphrasing, and Quoting
5. Attribution

Interactive Lessons for writing, speaking, and listening provide opportunities for in-depth instruction and practice in key 21st century skills.

my WriteSmart provides a collaborative tool for students to use to revise and edit Performance Tasks with peers and teachers.

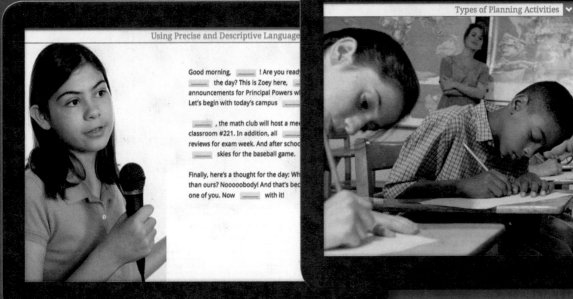

Speaking and Listening

Interactive lessons provide audio and video speeches and class discussions for students to critique using rubrics for each activity.

Writing

Models, rubrics, direct instruction, and ongoing feedback provide quality interactive instruction in each of the primary writing types.

Performance Tasks for each collection provide explicit writing process instruction and links to *my*Notebook and to related Interactive Lessons.

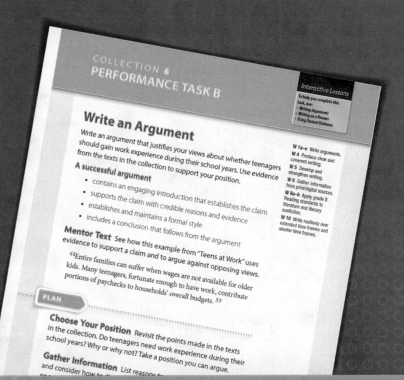

COLLECTION 6
PERFORMANCE TASK B

Interactive Lessons
To help you complete this task, use:
• *Writing Arguments*
• *Writing as a Process*
• *Using Textual Evidence*

Write an Argument

Write an argument that justifies your views about whether teenagers should gain work experience during their school years. Use evidence from the texts in the collection to support your position.

A successful argument
• contains an engaging introduction that establishes the claim
• supports the claim with credible reasons and evidence
• establishes and maintains a formal style
• includes a conclusion that follows from the argument

Mentor Text See how this example from "Teens at Work" uses evidence to support a claim and to argue against opposing views.

"Entire families can suffer when wages are not available for older kids. Many teenagers, fortunate enough to have work, contribute portions of paychecks to households' overall budgets."

PLAN

Choose Your Position Revisit the points made in the texts in the collection. Do teenagers need work experience during their school years? Why or why not? Take a position you can argue.

Gather Information List reasons to

W 1a–e Write arguments.
W 4 Produce clear and coherent writing.
W 5 Develop and strengthen writing.
W 8 Gather information from print/digital sources.
W 9a–b Apply grade 8 Reading standards to literature and literary nonfiction.
W 10 Write routinely over extended time frames and shorter time frames.

Collections provides 21st century resources supporting teachers and students in achieving their learning goals.

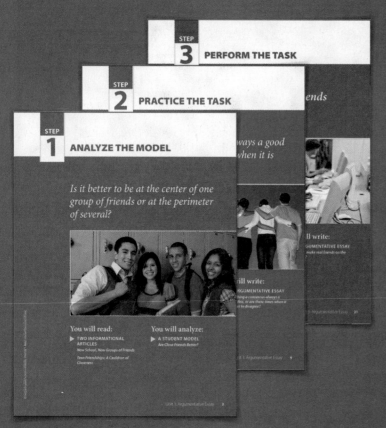

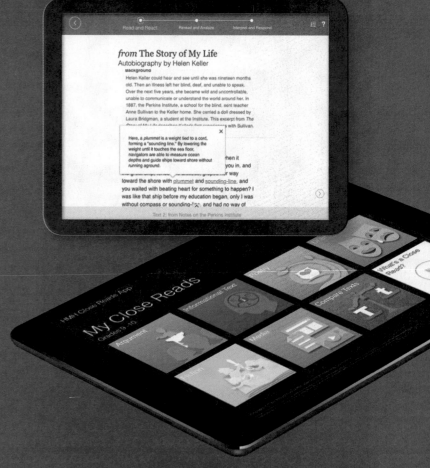

Performance Assessment

Guided instruction and practice performance tasks prepare students for reading and writing tasks in state and national assessments. Three detailed steps—Analyze the Model, Practice the Task, and Perform the Task—lead students to confidence and success.

HMH Close Reads App engages learners with appealing digital instruction in close reading, informing learning with instant feedback as students practice.

Professional Development for Language Arts

The world around us is constantly changing. Current and timely on-going professional development can help you prepare your students for whatever comes their way.

Close Reading

Choosing Complex Texts

Writing & Language

Vocabulary

Speaking & Listening

Media Literacy & Technology

Differentiation

Reading Support

Engagement & Motivation

Performance Task Assessments

HMH Professional Development Website provides teachers with instructional videos by our authors and with podcasts, teaching resources, and more to enhance classroom success.

Assessment Drives Informed Instruction

- **Diagnostic tests with Lexile® scores**
- **Selection and collection tests**
- **ExamView® customization**
- **Selection and collection performance tasks**
- **Benchmark tests**
- **Summative evaluation**

Collection Overviews

Each collection provides overviews of digital resources, key learning objectives, instructional topics for selections, and student support.

Topical Organization

Each collection reflects an engaging topic that connects selections for discussion and analysis so students can integrate and synthesize evidence as they explore several dimensions of the topic.

COLLECTION **1**

Finding Common Ground

KEY LEARNING OBJECTIVES		
Cite text evidence.	Analyze and evaluate author's claim.
Support inferences about theme.	Analyze author's purpose and rhetoric.
Analyze author's choices about structure.	Delineate and evaluate an argument.
Analyze representations in different mediums.	Analyze seminal U.S. documents.
Determine central idea.	

Close Reader

Image Credits: (c) ©Diana Ong/Superstock

eBook *Explore It!*

 ▶ Video Links   Visit **hmhfyi.com** for current articles and informational texts.

Standards Coverage

Each collection addresses a range of standards, ensuring coverage of Reading Literature and Reading Informational Texts standards.

Close Reader

The **Close Reader** provides selections related to the collection topic for additional practice and application of close reading skills and annotation strategies.

The Struggle for Freedom

INTEGRATED PROGRAM CONTENTS

COLLECTION PERFORMANCE TASK

Student Edition + Close Reader

In each collection, the collection topic is explored in both the **Student Edition** and **Close Reader** selections. This page shows how the two components are integrated.

Anchor Texts

Complex and intellectually challenging, the anchor texts provide a cornerstone for exploring the collection topic and completing the Collection Performance Task. Close Reader selections relate to the Student Edition anchor texts.

Informational Texts

From speeches to history writing to diaries to memoirs, students read and analyze a variety of informational texts.

COLLECTION **2**

The Struggle for Freedom

COMPARE ANCHOR TEXTS AND MEDIA

COMPARE TEXT AND MEDIA

Close Reader

KEY LEARNING OBJECTIVES
Analyze author's choices about style and structure.
Analyze author's point of view and cultural background.
Analyze how an author unfolds events.
Analyze connections between ideas and events.
Analyze impact of word choice on tone.
Determine author's point of view.
Analyze author's use of rhetoric.
Analyze accounts in different mediums.
Analyze seminal U.S. documents.

eBook *Explore It!*

▶ Video Links

Visit hmhfyi.com for current articles and informational texts.

Compare Text and Media

To underscore that textual analysis applies to media as well as print, a rich variety of media is compared to other texts for close reading, analysis, and meaning making.

COLLECTION 3
The Bonds Between Us

Cultural Diversity

To enrich students' perspectives, both the Student Edition and the Close Reader include selections by writers from diverse cultures.

COLLECTION PERFORMANCE TASKS

Variety of Genres

Both the Student Edition and the Close Reader include a variety of genres of literary texts, informational texts, and media. The genre of each selection is clearly labeled.

COLLECTION 3

The Bonds Between Us

KEY LEARNING OBJECTIVES
Cite text evidence.
Support inferences about theme.
Analyze character and theme.
Interpret figurative language.
Analyze the impact of word choice on tone.
Analyze author's point of view and cultural background.

Analyze ideas in informational text.
Analyze the purpose and development of ideas in media.
Determine technical meanings of words.
Analyze and evaluate author's claims.

Close Reader

Image Credits: ©Carlos Sanchez Pereyra/Alamy Images

 eBook *Explore It!*

 Video Links   **Visit hmhfyi.com** for current articles and informational texts.

Collection Performance Tasks

Collection Performance Tasks present a cumulative task for students. To develop writing or speaking products, students draw on their reading and analysis of the collection's selections, as well as additional research.

eBook

The eBook, both Student Edition and Teacher's Edition, is your entryway to a full complement of digital resources that promote 21st century skills.

COLLECTION **4**
Sweet Sorrow

Contemporary Selections

Selections by contemporary writers promote new insights into classic selections, enriching students' understanding of both old and new.

Image Credits: ©Sandy MacKenzie/Shutterstock

Media Analysis

Lessons based on media provide opportunities for students to apply analysis and techniques of close reading to other kinds of texts.

COLLECTION 4

Sweet Sorrow

Close Reader

Image Credits: ©Sandy MacKenzie/Shutterstock

eBook *Explore It!*

KEY LEARNING OBJECTIVES   Analyze character motivations.
Analyze parallel plots.
Analyze point of view.
Analyze source material.

Analyze interpretations of Shakespeare.
Determine word meanings.
Analyze ideas presented in an essay.

▶ Video Links   **Visit hmhfyi.com** for current articles and informational texts.

Complex Texts

Complex texts from a variety of genres and content areas include rich themes, sophisticated concepts, and high knowledge demands that challenge students to make meaning as readers and thinkers.

Digital Resources

From video links to additional literary and informational texts, a range of digital resources in the eBook enriches students' reading and supports technology skills.

A Matter of Life or Death

Prize-Winning Writers

Selections by internationally and nationally recognized prize-winning writers expose students to the very best in literary and nonfiction texts.

Image Credits: ©The Asahi Shimbun/Getty Images

Collection Performance Tasks

Collection Performance Tasks require students to develop a variety of writing and speaking products, working through the process of planning, producing, revising, and presenting for each task.

Focus on Argument

Through a range of content-rich informational texts, students analyze claims and supporting evidence.

COLLECTION 5

A Matter of Life or Death

Close Reader

Image Credits: ©The Asahi Shimbun/Getty Images

KEY LEARNING OBJECTIVES
Support inferences about theme.
Determine figurative meanings and tone.
Analyze effects of author's choices about structure.
Determine central idea of a text.
Summarize the text.
Analyze ideas and events presented in a text.
Analyze impact of word choice on tone.
Analyze author's purpose and use of rhetoric.
Delineate and evaluate an argument.

 eBook *Explore It!*

 Video Links   Visit hmhfyi.com for current articles and informational texts.

HISTORY® and A&E®

Adding the images and voices that make selections and time periods come alive, these video assets are available at point of use in the eBook.

Classic + Contemporary

Classic and contemporary selections illustrate how themes and topics transcend time and remain relevant to today's readers.

Annotated Student Edition Table of Contents

Supplemental Video

▶ This icon indicates supplementary video that accompanies selections.

Text-Dependent Questions

Both the Student Edition and the Close Reader include a range of text-dependent questions that ask students to engage with the text, make inferences, and cite textual evidence to support their claims.

COLLECTION 6

Heroes and Quests

Close Reader

eBook *Explore It!*

▶ Video Links — HISTORY · A&E · Channel One News® · fyi hmhfyi.com · **Visit hmhfyi.com** for current articles and informational texts.

KEY LEARNING OBJECTIVES	Analyze character.	Cite text evidence.
	Analyze epic poems.	Determine central idea of a text.
	Analyze figurative meanings.	Analyze ideas and events presented in a text.
	Interpret figurative language.	Delineate and evaluate an argument.

Image Credits: ©Oliver Burston/Ikon Images/Getty Images

FYI

The *FYI* website at hmhfyi.com provides additional contemporary informational texts to enhance each collection. Updated regularly, this site expands background knowledge and enhances discussion and research.

Student Resources

Information, Please

When students have questions, they can turn to Student Resources for answers. This section includes information about performance tasks; the nature of argument; vocabulary and spelling; and grammar, usage, and mechanics.

Word Knowledge

The Glossaries provide definitions for selection, academic, and domain-specific vocabulary, conveniently compiled in a single location.

Connecting to Your World

Every time you read something, view something, write to someone, or react to what you've read or seen, you're participating in a world of ideas. You do this every day, inside the classroom and out. These skills will serve you not only at home and at school, but eventually, in your career.

The digital tools in this program will tap into the skills you already use and help you sharpen those skills for the future.

Start your exploration at my.hrw.com

Start with the Dashboard

Get one-stop access to the complete digital program for *Collections,* as well as management and assessment tools.

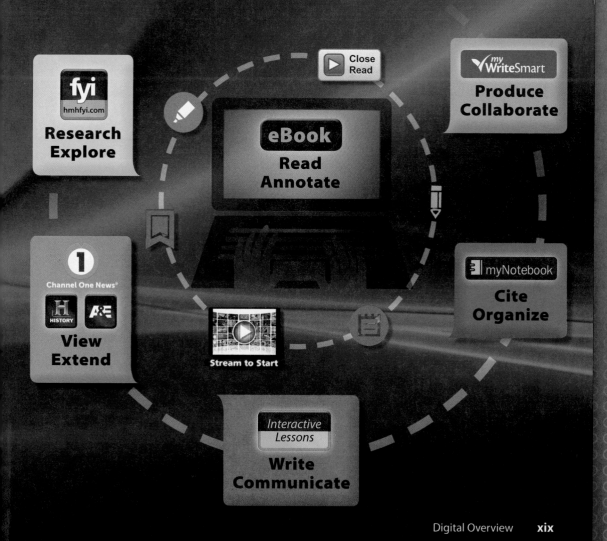

- fyi hmhfyi.com — **Research Explore**
- **Close Read**
- **my WriteSmart** — **Produce Collaborate**
- **eBook** — **Read Annotate**
- Channel One News® HISTORY A&E — **View Extend**
- **Stream to Start**
- myNotebook — **Cite Organize**
- *Interactive Lessons* — **Write Communicate**

Writing and
Speaking & Listening

Communication in today's world requires quite a variety of skills. To express yourself and win people over, you have to be able to write for print, for online media, and for spoken presentations. To collaborate, you have to work with people who might be sitting right next to you or at the other end of an Internet connection.

Comprehensive Standards Coverage
Twelve interactive lessons provide thorough coverage of all Writing and Speaking and Listening standards.

Available Only in Your eBook

Interactive Lessons

These interactive lessons will help you master the skills needed to become an expert communicator.

What Does a Strong Argument Look Like?

Read this argument and answer the questions about how the writer states and supports his position.

Tip

Pitching Perfect Pitch
by José Alvarez

Did you know that when you are listening to your favorite vocalist, you might be hearing a computer-generated pitch? Many record companies use pitch-correction software to ensure that their performers are pitch-perfect. While perfectionism is an admirable goal, there is a fine line between using technology to enhance music and using it to make performers into something they're not. Whether recording in the studio or playing a live performance, musicians should not use pitch-correction software. ●

Music production has become a digital experience. Producers use software to cut and paste pieces of music together, just like you cut and paste words together in your word-processing software. ○ When editing these different things together digitally, slight imperfections can occur where the pieces are joined. Enter the correction software. What began as a method to streamline the digital editing process has turned into an almost industry-wide standard of altering a musician"s work. "Think of it like plastic surgery," says a Grammy-winning recording engineer.

What is the writer's position, or **claim**, on the use of pitch-correction software?

- Musicians should learn to live with their imperfections.
- ✓ Musicians should never use the software.
- Musicians should use the software to enhance live performances only.

Writing Arguments
Master the art of proving your point.

W 1, W 10

Interactive Lessons

1. Introduction
2. What Is a Claim?
3. Support: Reasons and Evidence
4. Building Effective Support
5. Creating a Coherent Argument
6. Persuasive Techniques
7. Formal Style
8. Concluding Your Argument

Student-Directed Lessons
Though primarily intended for individual student use, these interactive lessons also offer opportunities for whole-class and small-group instruction and practice.

Writing Informative Texts
Shed light on complex ideas and topics.

W 2, W 10

Interactive Lessons

1. Introduction
2. Developing a Topic
3. Organizing Ideas
4. Introductions and Conclusions
5. Elaboration
6. Using Graphics and Multimedia
7. Precise Language and Vocabulary
8. Formal Style

Writing Narratives
A good storyteller can always capture an audience.

W 3, W 10

Interactive Lessons

1. Introduction
2. Narrative Context
3. Point of View and Characters
4. Narrative Structure
5. Narrative Techniques
6. The Language of Narrative

Writing as a Process

W 4, W 5, W 10

Get from the first twinkle of an idea to a sparkling final draft.

Interactive Lessons

1. Introduction
2. Task, Purpose, and Audience
3. Planning and Drafting
4. Revising and Editing
5. Trying a New Approach

Teacher Support

Each collection in your teacher eBook includes

- support for English language learners and less-proficient writers
- instructional and management tips for every screen
- a rubric
- additional writing applications

Producing and Publishing with Technology

W 6

Learn how to write for an online audience.

Interactive Lessons

1. Introduction
2. Writing for the Internet
3. Interacting with Your Online Audience
4. Using Technology to Collaborate

Conducting Research

W 6, W 7, W 8
W 9, W 10

There's a world of information out there. How do you find it?

Interactive Lessons

1. Introduction
2. Starting Your Research
3. Types of Sources
4. Using the Library for Research
5. Conducting Field Research
6. Using the Internet for Research
7. Taking Notes
8. Refocusing Your Inquiry

Evaluating Sources

Approach all sources with a critical eye.

W 8

Interactive Lessons

1. Introduction
2. Evaluating Sources for Usefulness
3. Evaluating Sources for Reliability

Authentic Practice of 21st Century Skills

Students have ample opportunities to evaluate real websites, engage in digital collaboration, conduct Web research, and critique student discussions.

Using Textual Evidence

Put your research into writing.

W 7, W 8, W 9

Interactive Lessons

1. Introduction
2. Synthesizing Information
3. Writing an Outline
4. Summarizing, Paraphrasing, and Quoting
5. Attribution

Participating in Collaborative Discussions

There's power in putting your heads together.

SL 1

Interactive Lessons

1. Introduction
2. Preparing for Discussion
3. Establishing and Following Procedure
4. Speaking Constructively
5. Listening and Responding
6. Wrapping Up Your Discussion

Analyzing and Evaluating Presentations

Is there substance behind the style?

SL 2, SL 3

Interactive Lessons	1. Introduction	4. Tracing a Speaker's Argument
	2. Analyzing a Presentation	5. Rhetoric and Delivery
	3. Evaluating a Speaker's Reliability	6. Synthesizing Media Sources

Assessments in *my*WriteSmart

Test students' mastery of the standards covered in each digital collection by assigning the accompanying assessment in *my*WriteSmart.

Giving a Presentation

Learn how to talk to a roomful of people.

SL 4, SL 6

Interactive Lessons	1. Introduction	4. Style in Presentation
	2. Knowing Your Audience	5. Delivering Your Presentation
	3. The Content of Your Presentation	6. Presenting a Recitation

Using Media in a Presentation

If a picture is worth a thousand words, just think what you can do with a video.

SL 5

| **Interactive Lessons** | 1. Introduction | 3. Using Presentation Software |
| | 2. Types of Media: Audio, Video, and Images | 4. Practicing Your Presentation |

DIGITAL SPOTLIGHT

eBook | **myNotebook** | **fyi** | **my WriteSmart**

Supporting 21st-Century Skills

The amount of information people encounter each day keeps increasing. Whether you're working alone or collaborating with others, it takes effort to analyze the complex texts and competing ideas that bombard us in this fast-paced world. What can allow you to succeed? Staying engaged and organized. The digital tools in this program will help you to think critically and take charge of your learning.

Integrated Digital Suite

The digital resources and tools in *Collections* are designed to support students in grappling with complex text and formulating interpretations from text evidence.

Stream to Start

Ignite your Investigation

You learn best when you're engaged. The **Stream to Start** video at the beginning of each collection is designed to inspire interest in the topics being explored. Watch it and then let your curiosity lead your investigations.

Videos to Motivate and Engage

Spark student curiosity and conversation by viewing short, engaging videos at the start of each collection.

and how do we cope?

Digital Spotlight **xxv**

Close Read Screencasts

For each anchor text, students can access modeled conversations in which readers analyze and annotate key passages.

Close Read

Learn How to Do a Close Read

An effective close read is all about the details; you have to examine the language and ideas a writer includes. See how it's done by accessing the **Close Read Screencasts** in your eBook. Hear modeled conversations about anchor texts.

Who, almost dead for breath, had scarcely more
Than would make up his message.

Lady Macbeth.   Give him tending.

35 He brings great news.

[Messenger *exits*.]

                    The raven himself is hoarse
That croaks the fatal entrance of Duncan
Under my battlements. Come, you spirits
That tend on mortal thoughts, unsex me here,

The Tragedy of Macbeth
by William Shakespeare

The raven himself is hoarse
That croaksthe fatal entrance of Duncan
Under my battlements. Come, you spirits
Thattend on mortalthoughts, unsex me here,
And fill me from the crown to the toe top-full
Of direst cruelty. Make thick my blood.
Stop up th' access and passage to remorse,
That no compunctious visitings of nature

The raven is a symbol of death and evil.

Annotate the Texts

Practice close reading by utilizing the powerful annotation tools in your eBook. Mark up key ideas and observations using highlighters and sticky notes. Tag unfamiliar words to create a personal word list in *my*Notebook.

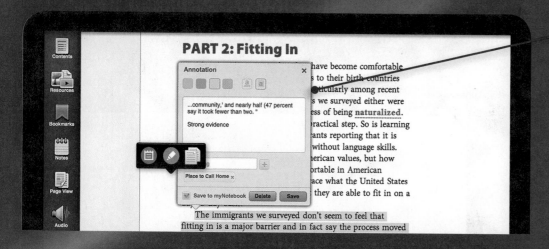

Digital Tools for Close Reading

Annotation tools allow students to note central ideas and details as they gather evidence from the text.

Find More Text Evidence on the Web

Tap into the *FYI* website for links to high-interest informational texts about collection topics. Synthesize information and connect notes and text evidence from any Web source by including it in *my*Notebook.

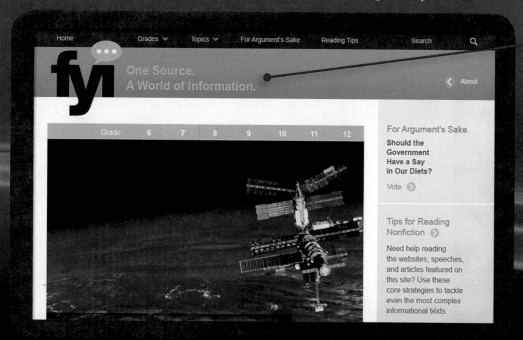

High-Interest Informational Text

Updated monthly, *FYI* features links to reputable sources of informational text.

myNotebook

Save and Organize Your Notes

Save your annotations to *my*Notebook, where you can organize them to use as text evidence in performance tasks and other writing assignments. You can also organize the unfamiliar words you tagged by creating word lists, which will help you grow your vocabulary.

Digital Notebook

Students can save their annotations to *my*Notebook, tag them to particular performance tasks, and create word lists for vocabulary development.

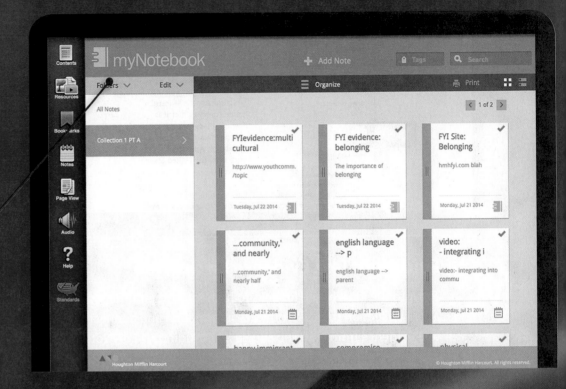

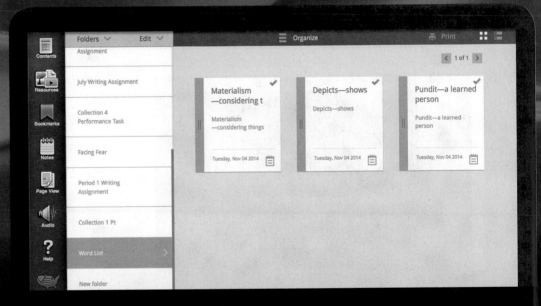

Create, Communicate, and Collaborate

Use the technology provided by the **myWriteSmart** tool to keep track of your writing assignments, create drafts, and collaborate and communicate with peers and your teacher. Use the evidence you've gathered in *my*Notebook to support your ideas.

Tools for Writing

Assign and manage performance tasks in *my*WriteSmart. Students can use the annotations they've gathered and tools for writing and collaboration to complete each task.

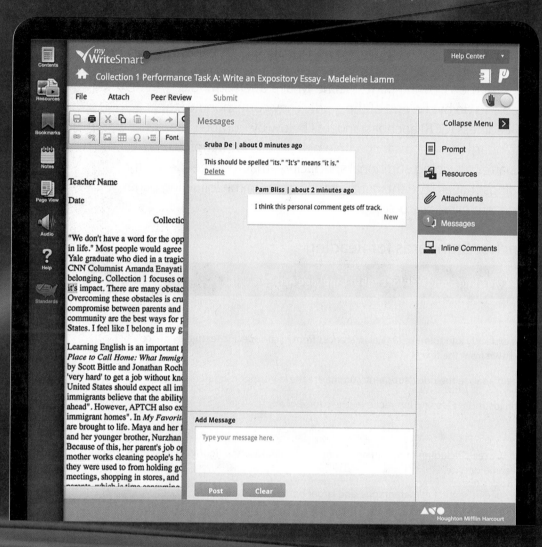

Correlation of *Collections*, Grade 9, to the English Language Arts Common Core State Standards

The grade 9 standards on the following pages define what students should understand and be able to do by the end of the grade. They correspond to the College and Career Readiness (CCR) anchor standards below by number. The CCR and grade-specific standards are necessary complements—the former providing broad standards, the latter providing additional specificity—that together define the skills and understandings that all students must demonstrate. In the following pages, Teacher's Edition page references are boldfaced.

College and Career Readiness Anchor Standards for Reading

Common Core State Standards for English Language Arts
KEY IDEAS AND DETAILS
1. Read closely to determine what the text says explicitly and to make logical inferences from it; cite specific textual evidence when writing or speaking to support conclusions drawn from the text.
2. Determine central ideas or themes of a text and analyze their development; summarize the key supporting details and ideas.
3. Analyze how and why individuals, events, and ideas develop and interact over the course of a text.
CRAFT AND STRUCTURE
4. Interpret words and phrases as they are used in a text, including determining technical, connotative, and figurative meanings, and analyze how specific word choices shape meaning or tone.
5. Analyze the structure of texts, including how specific sentences, paragraphs, and larger portions of the text (e.g., a section, chapter, scene, or stanza) relate to each other and the whole.
6. Assess how point of view or purpose shapes the content and style of a text.
INTEGRATION OF KNOWLEDGE AND IDEAS
7. Integrate and evaluate content presented in diverse formats and media, including visually and quantitatively, as well as in words.
8. Delineate and evaluate the argument and specific claims in a text, including the validity of the reasoning as well as the relevance and sufficiency of the evidence.
9. Analyze how two or more texts address similar themes or topics in order to build knowledge or to compare the approaches the authors take.
RANGE OF READING AND LEVEL OF COMPLEXITY
10. Read and comprehend complex literary and informational texts independently and proficiently.

Reading Standards for Literature, Grades 9–10 Students

Standard	Where Taught
KEY IDEAS AND DETAILS	

RL 1
Cite strong and thorough textual evidence to support analysis of what the text says explicitly as well as inferences drawn from the text.

INSTRUCTION
Student Edition/**Teacher's Edition**
11, **13**, **14**, **15**, 17, **17**, **20a**, 33, 34, 35, 105, 106, 109, 110, 118, 119, **119**, 135, 136, 148, **175**, **185**, **189**, **195**, **196**, **198**, 202, 210, 215, 219, 220, 239, 245, 273, 339, 340, 341, 345, 347, **347**, **350a**, 387, **389**, **404**

APPLICATION
Student Edition/**Teacher's Edition**
11–16, **11–16**, **20a**, 33–35, **33–35**, 103–118, **103–118**, 133–136, **133–136**, 149–150, **149–150**, 173–175, **173–175**, 181–205, **181–205**, 207–226, **207–226**, 228–251, **228–251**, 253–264, **253–264**, 266–278, **266–278**, 283–287, **283–287**, 339–346, **339–346**, **350a**, 369–398, **369–398**, 401–416, **401–416**

Close Reader/**Teacher's Edition**
9–18, **20b–20i**, 29–36, **96b–96g**, 39–52, **122b–122k**, 57–60, **150b–150e**, 63–74, **282b–282i**, 91–94, **354b–354e**, 97–112, **420b–420k**

INSTRUCTION/APPLICATION
Standards Support and Enrichment
• CIting Text Evidence

ASSESSMENT
Student Edition/**Teacher's Edition**
18, **18**, 36, **36**, 94, **94**, 120, **120**, 138, **138**, 150, **150**, 176, **176**, 227, **227**, 252, **252**, 280, **280**, 288, **288**, 348, **348**, 354, **354**, 399, **399**, 418, **418**, 444, **444**

RL 2
Determine a theme or central idea of text and analyze in detail its development over the course of the text, including how it emerges and is shaped and refined by specific details; provide an objective summary of the text.

INSTRUCTION
Student Edition/**Teacher's Edition**
11, 12, **13**, **14**, **15**, 17, **17**, 33, 35, **36a**, 105, 106, 109, 110, 111, 118, 119, **119**, **122a**, 174, **214**, 226, 278, 287, 294, 295, 339, 340, 341, 343, 344, 345, 347, **347**, **350a**, 352, **354a**, 384, 395, 414

APPLICATION
Student Edition/**Teacher's Edition**
11–16, **11–16**, **20a**, 33–35, **33–35**, **36a**, 103–118, **103–118**, **122a**, 133–136, **133–136**, 173–175, **173–175**, **181–205**, 207–226, **207–226**, 228–251, **228–251**, 253–264, **253–264**, 266–278, **266–278**, 289–296, **289–296**, **300a**, 339–346, **339–346**, **350a**, **354a**

Close Reader/**Teacher's Edition**
9–18, **20b–20i**, 39–52, **122b–122k**

ASSESSMENT
Student Edition/**Teacher's Edition**
18, **18**, 36, **36**, 94, **94**, 120, **120**, 138, **138**, 176, **176**, 206, **206**, 227, **227**, 252, **252**, 265, **265**, 280, **280**, 288, **288**, 298, **298**, 348, **348**, 354, **354**, 399, **399**, 418, **418**, 444, **444**

CORRELATION

Standard	Where Taught
RL 3 Analyze how complex characters (e.g., those with multiple or conflicting motivations) develop over the course of a text, interact with other characters, and advance the plot or develop the theme.	**INSTRUCTION** Student Edition/**Teacher's Edition** **90, 103, 104, 106, 107, 108, 109, 110, 111, 112, 113, 114, 115, 116, 117,** 119, **119, 122a,** 177–180, **177–180, 185, 187, 188, 193, 194, 196,** 197, **199, 205, 208, 209, 211, 213, 214,** **215, 217, 219, 222, 228, 229, 230, 231, 233, 236, 237, 238, 239, 241, 246, 248, 249, 250,** **251, 253, 254, 255, 258, 259, 262, 267, 269, 270, 271, 272, 273, 274, 276, 277, 279,** 279, **282a, 291, 294,** 348, **348, 350a,** 365–368, **365–368, 371, 372, 373, 374, 375, 376, 377,** **379, 381, 383, 390, 391, 394, 395, 396, 397,** 399, **399, 402, 403, 405, 410, 420a** **APPLICATION** Student Edition/**Teacher's Edition** 103–118, **103–118, 122a, 181–205,** 207–226, **207–226, 221,** 228–251, **228–251,** 253– 264, **253–264,** 266–278, **266–278, 282a, 350a,** 365, **365,** 369–398, **369–398,** 401–416, **401–416, 420a** Close Reader/**Teacher's Edition** 9–18, **20b–20i,** 29–36, **96b–96g,** 39–52, **122b–122k,** 63–74, **282b–282i,** 97–12, **420b–420k** **ASSESSMENT** Student Edition/**Teacher's Edition** 94, **94,** 120, **120,** 206, **206,** 227, **227,** 252, **252,** 265, **265,** 280, **280,** 288, **288,** 298, **298,** 348, **348,** 399, **399,** 418, **418**

CRAFT AND STRUCTURE

Standard	Where Taught
RL 4 Determine the meaning of words and phrases as they are used in the text, including figurative and connotative meanings; analyze the cumulative impact of specific word choices on meaning and tone (e.g., how the language evokes a sense of time and place; how it sets a formal or informal tone.)	**INSTRUCTION** Student Edition/**Teacher's Edition** **14, 34, 35, 36a, 90, 108, 117, 133, 134, 136,** 137, **137, 140a, 148,** 149, **149, 150a, 174,** **175, 176a,** 177–180, **177–180, 183, 186, 197, 200, 201, 203, 204, 207, 212, 216, 218,** **223, 231, 234, 236, 245, 247, 253, 261, 263, 268, 284, 286, 289, 342, 351, 352,** 353, **353,** **354a,** 365–368, **365–368, 374, 378, 380, 386, 393, 407, 413, 415,** 417, **417, 442,** 443, **443, 444a,** R48, R49, R51 **APPLICATION** Student Edition/**Teacher's Edition** 33–35, **33–35, 36a,** 133–136, **133–136, 140a,** 147–148, **147–148, 150a, 176a, 181–205,** 207–226, **207–226, 209,** 228–251, **228–251,** 253–264, **253–264,** 266–278, **266–278,** 351–352, **351–352, 354a,** 401–416, **401–416,** 441–442, **441–442, 444a** Close Reader/**Teacher's Edition** 9–18, **20b–20i,** 57–60, **150b–150e,** 63–74, **282b–282i,** 91–94, **354b–354e,** 97–112, **420b–420k** **ASSESSMENT** Student Edition/**Teacher's Edition** 36, **36,** 94, **94,** 138, **138,** 150, **150,** 206, **206,** 227, **227,** 252, **252,** 265, **265,** 354, **354,** 418, **418,** 444, **444**

Standard	Where Taught
RL 5 Analyze how an author's choices concerning how to structure a text, order events within it (e.g., parallel plots), and manipulate time (e.g., pacing, flashbacks) create such effects as mystery, tension, or surprise.	**INSTRUCTION** Student Edition/**Teacher's Edition** **12, 13, 16**, 17, **17, 89, 90, 91, 92**, 93, **93, 96a, 116**, 177–180, **177–180, 183, 184, 186, 189, 190, 191, 192, 193, 200, 201, 203, 204, 207, 208, 210, 211, 216, 217, 220, 221, 228, 229, 232, 233, 234, 235, 238, 240, 242, 243, 244, 245, 246, 249, 251, 256, 257, 260, 261, 264, 266, 267, 268, 269, 272, 275**, 279, **279, 285, 289, 292, 293, 294, 296**, 297, **297, 300a, 340, 341, 342, 344, 346**, 347, **347, 365–368, 365–368, 371, 373, 375, 376, 377, 378, 381, 382, 384, 385, 386, 387, 388, 392, 393, 401, 402, 403, 404, 405, 406, 407, 408, 409, 410, 411, 412, 413, 414**, 417, **417, 420a, 442, 444a** **APPLICATION** Student Edition/**Teacher's Edition** 11–16, **11–16**, 89–92, **89–92, 96a**, 181–205, **181–205**, 207–226, **207–226**, 228–251, **228–251**, 253–264, **253–264**, 266–278, **266–278**, 289–296, **289–296, 300a**, 339–346, **339–346**, 369–398, **369–398**, 401–416, **401–416, 420a, 444a** Close Reader/**Teacher's Edition** 29–36, **96b–96g**, 39–52, **122b–122k**, 63–74, **282b–282i** **ASSESSMENT** Student Edition/**Teacher's Edition** 18, **18**, 94, **94**, 206, **206**, 227, **227**, 252, **252**, 265, **265**, 280, **280**, 288, **288**, 298, **298**, 348, **348**, 418, **418**, 444, **444**
RL 6 Analyze a particular point of view or cultural experience reflected in a work of literature from outside the United States, drawing on a wide reading of world literature.	**INSTRUCTION** Student Edition/**Teacher's Edition** **12, 15**, 18, **18, 89, 91**, 93, **93, 96a, 133, 135, 136**, 137, **137**, 354, **354**, 365–368, **365–368, 371, 373, 375, 376, 377, 378, 381, 382, 384, 385, 386, 387, 388, 392, 393, 401, 402, 403, 404, 405, 406, 407, 408, 409, 410, 411, 412, 413, 414**, 417, **417, 420a** **APPLICATION** Student Edition/**Teacher's Edition** 11–16, **11–16**, 89–92, **89–92, 96a**, 133–136, **133–136**, 351–352, **351–352**, 369–398, **369–398**, 401–416, **401–416, 420a** Close Reader/**Teacher's Edition** 29–6, **96b–96g**, 57–60, **150b–150e** **ASSESSMENT** Student Edition/**Teacher's Edition** 18, **18**, 94, **94**, 138, **138**, 354, **354**, 418, **418**

Standard	Where Taught

INTEGRATION OF KNOWLEDGE AND IDEAS

RL 7
Analyze the representation of a subject or a key scene in two different artistic mediums, including what is emphasized or absent in each treatment (e.g., Auden's "Musée de Beaux Arts" and Breughel's *Landscape with the Fall of Icarus*).

INSTRUCTION
Student Edition/**Teacher's Edition**
33, **34**, **35**, 36, **36**, 173, 175, 198, 215, 219, 225, **300a**, 369

APPLICATION
Student Edition/**Teacher's Edition**
33–35, **33–35**, 219, **300a**, 369–398, **369–398**, 401–416, **401–416**

ASSESSMENT
Student Edition/**Teacher's Edition**
36, **36**

RL 8
(Not applicable to literature)

N/A

RL 9
Analyze how an author draws on and transforms source material in a specific work (e.g., how Shakespeare treats a theme or topic from Ovid or the Bible or how a later author draws on a play by Shakespeare).

INSTRUCTION
Student Edition/**Teacher's Edition**
173, 175, 176, **176**, **283**, **284**, **285**, **286**, **287**, 288, **288**, **288a**, 289, **290**, 292, **293**, 296, 297, **297**

APPLICATION
Student Edition/**Teacher's Edition**
173–175, **173–175**, **176a**, 283–287, **283–287**, 289–296, **289–296**

INSTRUCTION/APPLICATION
Standards Support and Enrichment
• Analyzing Literary Sources

ASSESSMENT
Student Edition/**Teacher's Edition**
176, **176**, 288, **288**, 298, **298**

RANGE OF READING AND LEVEL OF TEXT COMPLEXITY

RL 10
By the end of grade 9, read and comprehend literature, including stories, dramas, and poems, in the grades 9-10 text complexity band proficiently, with scaffolding as needed at the high end of the range.

APPLICATION
Student Edition/**Teacher's Edition**
36b, 89–94, **89A**, **89–94**, **96h**, 103–120, **103A**, **103–120**, **152b**, **177A**, 181–280, **181–280**, **300b**, 339–348, **339A**, **339–348**, 351–354, **351A**, **351–354**, **355f**, **365A**, 369–418, **369–418**, **444b**

Close Reader/**Teacher's Edition**
39–52, **122b–122k**, 63–74, **282b–282i**, 91–94, **354b–354e**, 97–112, **420b–420k**

Reading Standards for Informational Text, Grades 9–10 Students

Standard	Where Taught
KEY IDEAS AND DETAILS	

RI 1
Cite strong and thorough textual evidence to support analysis of what the text says explicitly as well as inferences drawn from the text.

INSTRUCTION
Student Edition/**Teacher's Edition**
3, 4, 22, 23, 25, **25, 26a, 27, 28, 123, 124, 125, 126, 141, 142, 143, 166, 168, 169, 307, 308, 325, 327, 328, 329, 330, 333, 334**, 335, **335, 338a, 421, 422, 423, 424, 426, 427, 428**, 429, **429, 432a**

APPLICATION
Student Edition/**Teacher's Edition**
3–6, **3–6**, 21–24, **21–24, 26a**, 47–51, **47–51**, 123–128, **123–128**, 307–312, **307–312**, 325–334, **325–334, 338a**, 421–428, **421–428, 432a**, 433–436, **433–436**

Close Reader/**Teacher's Edition:**
3–8, **10b–10g**, 19–22, **32b–32e**, 25–28, **72b–72e**, 53–56, **132b–132e**, 77–84, **316b–316g**, 85–90, **324b–324g**, 113–120, **432b–432g**

INSTRUCTION/APPLICATION
Standards Support and Enrichment
• Citing Text Evidence

ASSESSMENT
Student Edition/**Teacher's Edition**
8, **8**, 25, **25**, 30, **30**, 53, **53**, 69, **69**, 72, **72**, 78, **78**, 86, **86**, 130, **130**, 144, **144**, 170, **170**, 314, **314**, 336, **336**, 430, **430**, 438, **438**

RI 2
Determine a central idea of a text and analyze its development over the course of the text, including how it emerges and is shaped and refined by specific details; provide an objective summary of the text.

INSTRUCTION
Student Edition/**Teacher's Edition**
22, 23, 24, 25, **25, 26a, 88a, 326, 327, 328, 329, 331, 333, 334**, 335, **335, 338a**, 422, 423, **425, 426, 427, 428**, 429, **429**

APPLICATION
Student Edition/**Teacher's Edition**
21–24, **21–24, 26a**, 47–51, **47–51, 88a**, 163–168, **163–168, 172a**, 325–334, **325–334, 338a**, 421–428, **421–428**

Close Reader/**Teacher's Edition:**
3–8, **10b–10g**, 113–120, **432b–432g**

ASSESSMENT
Student Edition/**Teacher's Edition**
25, **25**, 53, **53**, 69, **69**, 86, **86**, 152, **152**, 170, **170**, 314, **314**, 322, **322**, 336, **336**, 430, **430**, 438, **438**

Standard	Where Taught

RI 3
Analyze how the author unfolds an analysis or series of ideas or events, including the order in which the points are made, how they are introduced and developed, and the connections that are drawn between them.

INSTRUCTION
Student Edition/**Teacher's Edition**
55, 56, 57, 59, **60, 63, 64, 65**, 67, **68**, 69, **69, 72a, 73, 74, 75, 76**, 77, **77, 80a, 141, 142, 143**, 144, **144, 146a, 163, 164**, 166, **169**, 169, **172a, 325, 326, 327, 328, 330, 332, 333, 334**, 335, **335, 421, 422, 423, 424, 425, 426, 427, 428**, 429, **429, 432a**

APPLICATION
Student Edition/**Teacher's Edition**
55–68, **55–68, 72a**, 73–76, **73–76, 80a**, 141–143, **141–143, 146a**, 163–168, **163–168, 172a**, 325–334, **325–334**, 421–428, **421–428, 432a**

Close Reader/**Teacher's Edition:**
25–28, **72b–72e**, 85–90, **324b–324g**, 113–120, **432b–432g**

ASSESSMENT
Student Edition/**Teacher's Edition**
53, **53**, 69, **69**, 72, **72**, 78, **78**, 144, **144**, 170, **170**, 336, **336**, 430, **430**, 438, **438**

CRAFT AND STRUCTURE

RI 4
Determine the meaning of words and phrases as they are used in a text, including figurative, connotative, and technical meanings; analyze the cumulative impact of specific word choices on meaning and tone (e.g., how the language of a court opinion differs from that of a newspaper).

INSTRUCTION
Student Edition/**Teacher's Edition**
5, 6, 21, 23, 26a, 55, 56, 57, 58, 60, 61, 62, 63, 64, 65, 66, 67, 68, 73, 74, 75, 77, **77, 123, 124, 125, 126, 127, 128, 129, 129, 141, 142, 146a, 163, 164, 165**, 167, **169**, 169, **307, 308, 309, 310, 311**, 313, **313, 320, 329, 330, 331, 434, 436, 440a**, R48, R49, R51, R52

APPLICATION
Student Edition/**Teacher's Edition**
26a, 54, **54**, 55–68, **55–68**, 73–76, **73–76**, 123–128, **123–128, 146a**, 163–168, **163–168**, 307–312, **307–312**, 325–334, **325–334, 440a**

Close Reader/**Teacher's Edition**
53–56, **132b–132e**, 77–84, **316b–316g**

ASSESSMENT
Student Edition/**Teacher's Edition**
8, **8**, 25, **25**, 53, **53**, 69, **69**, 78, **78**, 130, **130**, 144, **144**, 170, **170**, 314, **314**, 336, **336**

RI 5
Analyze in detail how an author's ideas or claims are developed and refined by particular sentences, paragraphs, or larger portions of a text (e.g., a section or chapter).

INSTRUCTION
Student Edition/**Teacher's Edition**
3, 5, 6, 7, 7, 123, 125, 126, 127, 129, **129, 132a, 151**, 164, **325, 326, 327, 328, 330, 332, 333, 334**, 335, **335**, R16–R21

APPLICATION
Student Edition/**Teacher's Edition**
3–6, **3–6**, 123–128, **123–128, 132a**, 151–152, **151–152**, 325–334, **325–334**, R16, **R16**, R21, **R21**

Close Reader/**Teacher's Edition**
3–8, **10b–10g**, 19–22, **32b–32e**, 53–56, **132b–132e**

ASSESSMENT
Student Edition/**Teacher's Edition**
8, **8**, 53, **53**, 69, **69**, 130, **130**, 152, **152**, 170, **170**, 314, **314**, 336, **336**, 430, **430**, 438, **438**

Standard	Where Taught

RI 6
Determine an author's point of view or purpose in a text and analyze how an author uses rhetoric to advance that point of view or purpose.

INSTRUCTION
Student Edition/**Teacher's Edition**
4, 6, 21, 23, 24, 27, 28, 29, **29, 48, 49, 50, 51,** 52, **52, 61, 81, 82, 83, 84,** 85, **85, 88a,** 151, **151,** 152, **152, 152b, 307, 308, 309, 310, 311, 312,** 313, **313, 316a, 319, 424, 436,** R16–R21

APPLICATION
Student Edition/**Teacher's Edition**
27–28, **27–28,** 47–51, **47–51,** 81–84, **81–84, 88a,** 151–152, **151–152, 152a,** 307–312, **307–312, 316a,** R17, **R17,** R21, **R21**

Close Reader/**Teacher's Edition**
19–22, **32b–32e,** 25–28, **72b–72e,** 77–84, **316b–316g**

ASSESSMENT
Student Edition/**Teacher's Edition**
8, **8,** 25, **25,** 30, **30,** 53, **53,** 86, **86,** 151, **151,** 152, **152,** 314, **314,** 336, **336,** 438, **438**

INTEGRATION OF KNOWLEDGE AND IDEAS

RI 7
Analyze various accounts of a subject told in different mediums (e.g., a person's life story in print and multimedia), determining which details are emphasized in each account.

INSTRUCTION
Student Edition/**Teacher's Edition**
47, 71, **71,** 72, **72, 81, 82,** 85, **85,** 181, **181**

APPLICATION
Student Edition/**Teacher's Edition**
55–68, **55–68,** 71–72, **71–72,** 81–84, **81–84,** 181, **181**

Close Reader/**Teacher's Edition:**
432g

ASSESSMENT
Student Edition/**Teacher's Edition**
72, **72,** 86, **86**

RI 8
Delineate and evaluate the argument and specific claims in a text, assessing whether the reasoning is valid and the evidence is relevant and sufficient; identify false statements and fallacious reasoning.

INSTRUCTION
Student Edition/**Teacher's Edition**
3, 4, 5, 6, 7, **7, 10a, 123, 125, 126, 127,** 129, **129, 132a, 317, 318, 319, 320,** 321, **321, 324a, 433, 434, 435, 436,** 437, **437, 440a,** R16–R21

APPLICATION
Student Edition/**Teacher's Edition**
3–6, **3–6, 10a,** 123–128, **123–128, 132a,** 317–320, **317–320, 324a,** 433–436, **433–436, 440a,** R16, **R16,** R18, **R18,** R20, **R20,** R21, **R21**

Close Reader/**Teacher's Edition:**
3–8, **10b–10g,** 53–56, **132b–132e,** 85–90, **324b–324g**

ASSESSMENT
Student Edition/**Teacher's Edition**
8, **8,** 130, **130,** 322, **322,** 438, **438**

Standard	Where Taught
RI 9 Analyze seminal U.S. documents of historical and literary significance (e.g., Washington's Farewell Address, the Gettysburg Address, Roosevelt's Four Freedoms speech, King's "Letter from Birmingham Jail"), including how they address related themes and concepts.	**INSTRUCTION** Student Edition/**Teacher's Edition** **27, 28,** 29, **29, 48, 49, 51,** 52, **52** **APPLICATION** Student Edition/**Teacher's Edition** 27–28, **27–28,** 47–51, **47–51** Close Reader/**Teacher's Edition** 25–28, **72b–72e** **INSTRUCTION/APPLICATION** **Standards Support and Enrichment** • Analyzing Seminal U.S. Documents **ASSESSMENT** Student Edition/**Teacher's Edition** 30, **30,** 53, **53**

RANGE OF READING AND LEVEL OF TEXT COMPLEXITY

Standard	Where Taught
RI 10 By the end of grade 9, read and comprehend literary nonfiction in the grades 9–10 text complexity band proficiently, with scaffolding as needed at the high end of the range.	**APPLICATION** Student Edition/**Teacher's Edition** 3–8, **3A, 3–8,** 27–30, **27A, 27–30, 36b,** 47–53, **47A, 47–53, 96h,** 123–130, **123A, 123–130, 152b, 300b,** 317–322, **317A, 317–322, 355f,** 421–430, **421A, 421–430,** 433–438, **433A, 433–438, 444b** Close Reader/**Teacher's Edition** 3–8, **10b–10g,** 25–28, **72b–72e,** 85–90, **324b–324g,** 113–120, **432b–432g**

College and Career Readiness Anchor Standards for Writing

Common Core State Standards for English Language Arts

TEXT TYPES AND PURPOSES

1. Write arguments to support claims in an analysis of substantive topics or texts, using valid reasoning and relevant and sufficient evidence.

2. Write informative/explanatory texts to examine and convey complex ideas and information clearly and accurately through the effective selection, organization, and analysis of content.

3. Write narratives to develop real or imagined experiences or events using effective technique, well–chosen details, and well–structured event sequences.

PRODUCTION AND DISTRIBUTION OF WRITING

4. Produce clear and coherent writing in which the development, organization, and style are appropriate to task, purpose, and audience.

5. Develop and strengthen writing as needed by planning, revising, editing, rewriting, or trying a new approach.

6. Use technology, including the Internet, to produce and publish writing and to interact and collaborate with others.

RESEARCH TO BUILD AND PRESENT KNOWLEDGE

7. Conduct short as well as more sustained research projects based on focused questions, demonstrating understanding of the subject under investigation.

8. Gather relevant information from multiple print and digital sources, assess the credibility and accuracy of each source, and integrate the information while avoiding plagiarism.

9. Draw evidence from literary or informational texts to support analysis, reflection, and research.

RANGE OF WRITING

10. Write routinely over extended time frames (time for research, reflection, and revision) and shorter time frames (a single sitting or a day or two) for a range of tasks, purposes, and audiences.

Writing Standards, Grades 9–10 Students

Standard	Where Taught
TEXT TYPES AND PURPOSES	
W 1 Write arguments to support claims in an analysis of substantive topics or texts, using valid reasoning and relevant and sufficient evidence.	**INSTRUCTION/APPLICATION** **Interactive Lessons:** Writing Arguments • Introduction • What Is a Claim? • Support: Reasons and Evidence • Building Effective Support • Creating a Coherent Argument • Persuasive Techniques • Formal Style • Concluding Your Argument Student Edition/**Teacher's Edition:** **10a,** 97–100, **97–100,** 355–358, **355–358,** R2–R3 **ASSESSMENT** Student Edition/**Teacher's Edition:** 8, **8,** 97–100, **97–100,** 336, **336,** 355–358, **355–358,** 438, **438**
a. Introduce precise claim(s), distinguish the claim(s) from alternate or opposing claims, and create an organization that establishes clear relationships among claim(s), counterclaims, reasons, and evidence.	**INSTRUCTION/APPLICATION** **Interactive Lessons:** Writing Arguments • What Is a Claim? • Creating a Coherent Argument Student Edition/**Teacher's Edition:** 97–100, **97–100,** 355–358, **355–358,** R2–R3 **ASSESSMENT** Student Edition/**Teacher's Edition** 8, **8,** 97–100, **97–100,** 355–358, **355–358**

Standard	Where Taught
b. Develop claim(s) and counterclaims fairly, supplying evidence for each while pointing out the strengths and limitations of both in a manner that anticipates the audience's knowledge level and concerns.	**INSTRUCTION/APPLICATION** **Interactive Lessons:** Writing Arguments • Support: Reasons and Evidence • Building Effective Support Student Edition/**Teacher's Edition:** 97–100, **97–100**, 355–358, **355–358**, R2–R3 **ASSESSMENT** Student Edition/**Teacher's Edition** 8, **8**, 97–100, **97–100**, 355–358, **355–358**
c. Use words, phrases, and clauses to link the major sections of the text, create cohesion, and clarify the relationships between claim(s) and reasons, between reasons and evidence, and between claim(s) and counterclaims.	**INSTRUCTION/APPLICATION** **Interactive Lessons:** Writing Arguments • Creating a Coherent Argument Student Edition/**Teacher's Edition:** 97–100, **97–100**, 355–358, **355–358**, R2–R3 **ASSESSMENT** Student Edition/**Teacher's Edition:** 97–100, **97–100**, 355–358, **355–358**
d. Establish and maintain a formal style and objective tone while attending to the norms and conventions of the discipline in which they are writing.	**INSTRUCTION/APPLICATION** **Interactive Lessons:** Writing Arguments • Formal Style Student Edition/**Teacher's Edition:** 97–100, **97–100**, 355–358, **355–358**, R2–R3 **ASSESSMENT** Student Edition/**Teacher's Edition:** 97–100, **97–100**, 355–358, **355–358**
e. Provide a concluding statement or section that follows from and supports the argument presented.	**INSTRUCTION/APPLICATION** **Interactive Lessons:** Writing Arguments • Concluding Your Argument Student Edition/**Teacher's Edition:** 97–100, **97–100**, 355–358, **355–358**, R2–R3 **ASSESSMENT** Student Edition/**Teacher's Edition:** 97–100, **97–100**, 355–358, **355–358**

Standard	Where Taught
W 2 Write informative/explanatory texts to examine and convey complex ideas, concepts, and information clearly and accurately through the effective selection, organization, and analysis of content.	**INSTRUCTION/APPLICATION** **Interactive Lessons:** Writing Informative Texts • Introduction • Developing a Topic • Organizing Ideas • Introductions and Conclusions • Elaboration • Using Graphics and Multimedia • Precise Language and Vocabulary • Formal Style Using Textual Evidence • Writing an Outline Student Edition/**Teacher's Edition:** 41–44, **41–44,** 301–304, **301–304, 432a,** 445–448, **445–448,** R4–R5, R8–R11 **ASSESSMENT** Student Edition/**Teacher's Edition:** 41–44, **41–44,** 53, **53,** 301–304, **301–304,** 314, **314,** 430, **430,** 445–448, **445–448**
a. Introduce a topic; organize complex ideas, concepts, and information to make important connections and distinctions; include formatting (e.g., headings), graphics (e.g., figures, tables), and multimedia when useful to aiding comprehension.	**INSTRUCTION/APPLICATION** **Interactive Lessons:** Writing Informative Texts • Developing a Topic • Organizing Ideas • Introductions and Conclusions • Using Graphics and Multimedia Student Edition/**Teacher's Edition:** 41–44, **41–44,** 301–304, **301–304,** 445–448, **445–448,** R4–R5, R8–R11 **Standards Support and Enrichment** • Using Digital Media • Creating a Class Blog **ASSESSMENT** Student Edition/**Teacher's Edition:** 41–44, **41–44,** 301–304, **301–304,** 445–448, **445–448**
b. Develop the topic with well-chosen, relevant, and sufficient facts, extended definitions, concrete details, quotations, or other information and examples appropriate to the audience's knowledge of the topic.	**INSTRUCTION/APPLICATION** **Interactive Lessons:** Writing Informative Texts • Elaboration Student Edition/**Teacher's Edition:** 41–44, **41–44,** 301–304, **301–304,** 445–448, **445–448,** R4–R5, R8–R11 **ASSESSMENT** Student Edition/**Teacher's Edition:** 41–44, **41–44,** 78, **78,** 301–304, **301–304,** 445–448, **445–448**

Standard	Where Taught
c. Use appropriate and varied transitions to link the major sections of the text, create cohesion, and clarify the relationships among complex ideas and concepts.	**INSTRUCTION/APPLICATION** **Interactive Lessons:** Writing Informative Texts • Organizing Ideas Student Edition/**Teacher's Edition:** 41–44, **41–44,** 301–304, **301–304,** 445–448, **445–448,** R4–R5, R8–R11 **ASSESSMENT** Student Edition/**Teacher's Edition:** 41–44, **41–44,** 301–304, **301–304,** 445–448, **445–448**
d. Use precise language and domain-specific vocabulary to manage the complexity of the topic.	**INSTRUCTION/APPLICATION** **Interactive Lessons:** Writing Informative Texts • Precise Language and Vocabulary Student Edition/**Teacher's Edition:** 41–44, **41–44,** 301–304, **301–304,** 445–448, **445–448,** R4–R5, R8–R11 **ASSESSMENT** Student Edition/**Teacher's Edition:** 41–44, **41–44,** 301–304, **301–304,** 445–448, **445–448**
e. Establish and maintain a formal style and objective tone while attending to the norms and conventions of the discipline in which they are writing.	**INSTRUCTION/APPLICATION** **Interactive Lessons:** Writing Informative Texts • Formal Style Student Edition/**Teacher's Edition:** 41–44, **41–44,** 301–304, **301–304,** 445–448, **445–448,** R4–R5, R8–R11 **ASSESSMENT** Student Edition/**Teacher's Edition:** 41–44, **41–44,** 301–304, **301–304,** 445–448, **445–448**
f. Provide a concluding statement or section that follows from and supports the information or explanation presented (e.g., articulating implications or the significance of the topic).	**INSTRUCTION/APPLICATION** **Interactive Lessons:** Writing Informative Texts • Introductions and Conclusions Student Edition/**Teacher's Edition:** 41–44, **41–44,** 301–304, **301–304,** 445–448, **445–448,** R4–R5, R8–R11 **ASSESSMENT** Student Edition/**Teacher's Edition:** 41–44, **41–44,** 301–304, **301–304,** 445–448, **445–448**

Standard	Where Taught
W 3 Write narratives to develop real or imagined experiences or events using effective technique, well-chosen details, and well-structured event sequences.	**INSTRUCTION/APPLICATION** **Interactive Lessons:** Writing Narratives • Introduction • Narrative Context • Point of View and Characters • Narrative Structure • Narrative Techniques • The Language of Narrative Student Edition/**Teacher's Edition:** **20a, 140a,** 153–156, **153–156,** R6–R7 **ASSESSMENT** Student Edition/**Teacher's Edition:** 18, **18,** 72, **72,** 86, **86,** 120, **120,** 153–156, **153–156,** 280, **280,** 298, **298,** 418, **418**
a. Engage and orient the reader by setting out a problem, situation, or observation, establishing one or multiple point(s) of view, and introducing a narrator and/or characters; create a smooth progression of experiences or events.	**INSTRUCTION/APPLICATION** **Interactive Lessons:** Writing Narratives • Narrative Context • Point of View and Characters • Narrative Structure Student Edition/**Teacher's Edition:** 153–156, **153–156,** R6–R7 **ASSESSMENT** Student Edition/**Teacher's Edition:** 153–156, **153–156,** 418, **418**
b. Use narrative techniques, such as dialogue, pacing, description, reflection, and multiple plot lines, to develop experiences, events, and/or characters.	**INSTRUCTION/APPLICATION** **Interactive Lessons:** Writing Narratives • Narrative Structure • Narrative Techniques • The Language of Narrative Student Edition/**Teacher's Edition:** 153–156, **153–156,** R6–R7 **ASSESSMENT** Student Edition/**Teacher's Edition:** 153–156, **153–156**

Standard	Where Taught
c. Use a variety of techniques to sequence events so that they build on one another to create a coherent whole.	**INSTRUCTION/APPLICATION** **Interactive Lessons:** Writing Narratives • Narrative Structure Student Edition/**Teacher's Edition:** 153–156, **153–156,** R6–R7 **ASSESSMENT** Student Edition/**Teacher's Edition:** 153–156, **153–156**
d. Use precise words and phrases, telling details, and sensory language to convey a vivid picture of the experiences, events, setting, and/or characters.	**INSTRUCTION/APPLICATION** **Interactive Lessons:** Writing Narratives • The Language of Narrative Student Edition/**Teacher's Edition:** **72a,** 153–156, **153–156,** R6–R7 **ASSESSMENT** Student Edition/**Teacher's Edition:** 138, **138,** 153–156, **153–156,** 418, **418**
e. Provide a conclusion that follows from and reflects on what is experienced, observed, or resolved over the course of the narrative.	**INSTRUCTION/APPLICATION** **Interactive Lessons:** Writing Narratives • Narrative Structure Student Edition/**Teacher's Edition:** 153–156, **153–156,** R6–R7 **ASSESSMENT** Student Edition/**Teacher's Edition:** 153–156, **153–156**
PRODUCTION AND DISTRIBUTION OF WRITING	
W 4 Produce clear and coherent writing in which the development, organization, and style are appropriate to task, purpose, and audience. (Grade-specific expectations for writing types are defined in Standards 1–3 above.)	**INSTRUCTION/APPLICATION** **Interactive Lessons:** Writing as a Process • Task, Purpose, and Audience Student Edition/**Teacher's Edition:** 41–44, **41–44,** 97–100, **97–100,** 153–156, **153–156,** 301–304, **301–304,** 355–358, **355–358,** 445–448, **445–448** **INSTRUCTION/APPLICATION** **Standards Support and Enrichment** • Writing Clearly and Coherently **ASSESSMENT** Student Edition/**Teacher's Edition:** 41–44, **41–44,** 97–100, **97–100,** 153–156, **153–156,** 301–304, **301–304,** 355–358, **355–358,** 445–448, **445–448**

Standard	Where Taught
W 5 Develop and strengthen writing as needed by planning, revising, editing, rewriting, or trying a new approach, focusing on addressing what is most significant for a specific purpose and audience. (Editing for conventions should demonstrate command of Language standards 1–3 up to and including grades 9–10.)	**INSTRUCTION/APPLICATION** **Interactive Lessons:** Writing as a Process • Introduction • Task, Purpose, and Audience • Planning and Drafting • Revising and Editing • Trying a New Approach Student Edition/**Teacher's Edition:** 41–44, **41–44,** 97–100, **97–100,** 153–156, **153–156,** 301–304, **301–304,** 355–358, **355–358,** 445–448, **445–448** **ASSESSMENT** Student Edition/**Teacher's Edition:** 41–44, **41–44,** 97–100, **97–100,** 153–156, **153–156,** 301–304, **301–304,** 355–358, **355–358,** 445–448, **445–448**
W 6 Use technology, including the Internet, to produce, publish, and update individual or shared writing products, taking advantage of technology's capacity to link to other information and to display information flexibly and dynamically.	**INSTRUCTION/APPLICATION** **Interactive Lessons:** Producing and Publishing with Technology • Introduction • Writing for the Internet • Interacting with Your Online Audience • Using Technology to Collaborate Student Edition/**Teacher's Edition:** 37–40, **37–40,** 41–44, **41–44,** 97–100, **97–100,** 153–156, **153–156,** 157–160, **157–160,** 301–304, **301–304,** 355–358, **355–358,** 445–448, **445–448** **Standards Support and Enrichment** • Using Digital Media • Creating a Class Blog **ASSESSMENT** Student Edition/**Teacher's Edition:** 37–40, **37–40,** 41–44, **41–44,** 86, **86,** 97–100, **97–100,** 152, **152,** 153–156, **153–156,** 157–160, **157–160,** 171, **171,** 176, **176,** 301–304, **301–304,** 355–358, **355–358,** 445–448, **445–448**

Standard	Where Taught

RESEARCH TO BUILD AND PRESENT KNOWLEDGE

W 7
Conduct short as well as more sustained research projects to answer a question (including a self-generated question) or solve a problem; narrow or broaden the inquiry when appropriate; synthesize multiple sources on the subject, demonstrating understanding of the subject under investigation.

INSTRUCTION/APPLICATION
Interactive Lessons:
Conducting Research
• Introduction
• Starting Your Research
• Refocusing Your Inquiry

Using Textual Evidence
• Synthesizing Information

Student Edition/**Teacher's Edition:**
80a, 96a, 152a, 152b, 445–448, **445–448,** R8–R11

Standards Support and Enrichment
• Using Library and Media Sources

ASSESSMENT
Student Edition/**Teacher's Edition:**
78, **78,** 445–448, **445–448**

W 8
Gather relevant information from multiple authoritative print and digital sources, using advanced searches effectively; assess the usefulness of each source in answering the research question; integrate information into the text selectively to maintain the flow of ideas, avoiding plagiarism and following a standard format for citation.

INSTRUCTION/APPLICATION
Interactive Lessons:
Conducting Research
• Types of Sources
• Using the Library for Research
• Using the Internet for Research

Evaluating Sources
• Introduction
• Evaluating Sources for Usefulness
• Evaluating Sources for Reliability

Student Edition/**Teacher's Edition:**
80a, 96a, 445–448, **445–448,** R8–R11

Standards Support and Enrichment
• Using Footnotes and Endnotes

ASSESSMENT
Student Edition/**Teacher's Edition:**
78, **78,** 445–448, **445–448**

Standard	Where Taught

W 9
Draw evidence from literary or informational texts to support analysis, reflection, and research.

INSTRUCTION/APPLICATION
Interactive Lessons:
Writing Informative Texts
• Elaboration

Conducting Research
• Taking Notes

Using Textual Evidence
• Introduction
• Synthesizing Information
• Summarizing, Paraphrasing, and Quoting

Student Edition/**Teacher's Edition:**
41–44, **41–44,** 97–100, **97–100,** 153–156, **153–156,** 301–304, **301–304,** 355–358, **355–358,** 445–448, **445–448**

ASSESSMENT
Student Edition/**Teacher's Edition:**
41–44, **41–44,** 94, **94,** 97–100, **97–100,** 153–156, **153–156,** 288, **288,** 301–304, **301–304,** 354, **354,** 355–358, **355–358,** 445–448, **445–448**

---

a. Apply *grades 9–10 Reading Standards* to literature (e.g., "Analyze how an author draws on and transforms source material in a specific work [e.g., how Shakespeare treats a theme or topic from Ovid or the Bible or how a later author draws on a play by Shakespeare]").

INSTRUCTION/APPLICATION
Student Edition/**Teacher's Edition:**
41–44, **41–44,** 97–100, **97–100,** 153–156, **153–156,** 301–304, **301–304,** 355–358, **355–358,** 445–448, **445–448**

ASSESSMENT
Student Edition/**Teacher's Edition:**
41–44, **41–44,** 97–100, **97–100,** 153–156, **153–156,** 288, **288,** 301–304, **301–304,** 354, **354,** 355–358, **355–358,** 445–448, **445–448**

---

b. Apply *grades 9–10 Reading Standards* to literary nonfiction (e.g., "Delineate and evaluate the argument and specific claims in a text, assessing whether the reasoning is valid and the evidence is relevant and sufficient; identify false statements and fallacious reasoning").

INSTRUCTION/APPLICATION
Student Edition/**Teacher's Edition:**
41–44, **41–44,** 97–100, **97–100,** 153–156, **153–156,** 301–304, **301–304,** 355–358, **355–358,** 445–448, **445–448**

ASSESSMENT
Student Edition/**Teacher's Edition:**
41–44, **41–44,** 97–100, **97–100,** 153–156, **153–156,** 301–304, **301–304,** 355–358, **355–358,** 445–448, **445–448**

Standard	Where Taught

RANGE OF WRITING

W 10
Write routinely over extended time frames (time for research, reflection, and revision) and shorter time frames (a single sitting or a day or two) for a range of tasks, purposes, and audiences.

INSTRUCTION/APPLICATION
Interactive Lessons:
Writing as a Process
• Task, Purpose, and Audience

Writing Arguments

Writing Informative Texts

Writing Narratives

Using Textual Evidence

Student Edition/**Teacher's Edition:**
41–44, **41–44,** 97–100, **97–100,** 153–156, **153–156,** 301–304, **301–304,** 355–358, **355–358,** 445–448, **445–448**

ASSESSMENT
Student Edition/**Teacher's Edition:**
8, **8, 18,** 18, 41–44, **41–44,** 53, **53,** 72, **72,** 78, **78,** 86, **86,** 94, **94,** 97–100, **97–100,** 120, **120,** 138, **138,** 152, **152,** 153–156, **153–156,** 170, **170,** 176, **176,** 252, **252,** 265, **265,** 280, **280,** 288, **288,** 298, **298,** 301–304, **301–304,** 314, **314,** 336, **336,** 354, **354,** 355–358, **355–358,** 418, **418,** 430, **430,** 438, **438,** 445–448, **445–448**

College and Career Readiness Anchor Standards for Speaking and Listening

Common Core State Standards for English Language Arts

COMPREHENSION AND COLLABORATION

1. Prepare for and participate effectively in a range of conversations and collaborations with diverse partners, building on others' ideas and expressing their own clearly and persuasively.

2. Integrate and evaluate information presented in diverse media and formats, including visually, quantitatively, and orally.

3. Evaluate a speaker's point of view, reasoning, and use of evidence and rhetoric.

PRESENTATION OF KNOWLEDGE AND IDEAS

4. Present information, findings, and supporting evidence such that listeners can follow the line of reasoning and the organization, development, and style are appropriate to task, purpose, and audience.

5. Make strategic use of digital media and visual displays of data to express information and enhance understanding of presentations.

6. Adapt speech to a variety of contexts and communicative tasks, demonstrating command of formal English when indicated or appropriate.

Speaking and Listening Standards, Grades 9–10 Students

Standard	Where Taught

COMPREHENSION AND COLLABORATION

SL 1
Initiate and participate effectively in a range of collaborative discussions (one-on-one, in groups, and teacher-led) with diverse partners on *grades 9–10 topics, texts, and issues,* building on others' ideas and expressing their own clearly and persuasively.

INSTRUCTION/APPLICATION
Interactive Lessons:
Participating in Collaborative Discussions
- Introduction
- Preparing for Discussion
- Establishing and Following Procedure
- Speaking Constructively
- Listening and Responding
- Wrapping Up Your Discussion

Student Edition/**Teacher's Edition:**
6, **6**, 16, **16**, 24, **24**, 28, **28**, 35, **35**, 68, **68**, 76, **76**, 84, **84**, 92, **92**, 118, **118**, 128, **128**, 136, **136**, 143, **143**, 148, **148**, 151, **151**, 157–160, **157–160**, 168, **168**, 172a, 175, **175**, 205, **205**, 226, **226**, 251, **251**, 264, **264**, 265, **265**, 278, **278**, 287, **287**, 296, **296**, 312, **312**, 320, **320**, 334, **334**, 346, **346**, 352, **352**, 359–362, **359–362**, 398, **398**, 428, **428**, 436, **436**, 442, **442**, **444b**, R12–R13, R14–R15

Close Reader/**Teacher's Edition:**
10b–10g, 420b–420k, 432b–432g

ASSESSMENT
Student Edition/**Teacher's Edition:**
25, **25**, 30, **30**, 130, **130**, 144, **144**, 150, **150**, 157–160, **157–160**, 170, **170**, 206, **206**, 227, **227**, 322, **322**, 348, **348**, 354, **354**, 359–362, **359–362**, 444, **444**

---

a. Come to discussions prepared, having read and researched material under study; explicitly draw on that preparation by referring to evidence from texts and other research on the topic or issue to stimulate a thoughtful, well-reasoned exchange of ideas.

INSTRUCTION/APPLICATION
Interactive Lessons:
Participating in Collaborative Discussions
- Preparing for Discussion
- Speaking Constructively

Student Edition/**Teacher's Edition:**
16, **16**, 24, **24**, 28, **28**, 35, **35**, 51, **51**, 68, **68**, 76, **76**, 84, **84**, 92, **92**, 118, **118**, 136, **136**, 143, **143**, 151, **151**, 157–160, **157–160**, 168, **168**, 175, **175**, 251, **251**, 264, **264**, 287, **287**, 296, **296**, 312, **312**, 320, **320**, 334, **334**, 346, **346**, 352, **352**, 359–362, **359–362**, 398, **398**, 416, **416**, 428, **428**, 436, **436**, R12–R13, R14–R15

Close Reader/**Teacher's Edition:**
10b–10g, 420b–420k, 432b–432g

ASSESSMENT
Student Edition/**Teacher's Edition:**
144, **144**, 157–160, **157–160**, 170, **170**, 227, **227**, 322, **322**, 348, **348**, 359–362, **359–362**, 444, **444**

Standard	Where Taught

b. Work with peers to set rules for collegial discussions and decision-making (e.g., informal consensus, taking votes on key issues, presentation of alternate views), clear goals and deadlines, and individual roles as needed.

INSTRUCTION/APPLICATION
Interactive Lessons:
Participating in Collaborative Discussions
- Establishing and Following Procedure

Student Edition/**Teacher's Edition:**
157–160, **157–160**, 359–362, **359–362**, R12–R13, R14–R15

ASSESSMENT
Student Edition/**Teacher's Edition:**
157–160, **157–160**, 359–362, **359–362**

c. Propel conversations by posing and responding to questions that relate the current discussion to broader themes or larger ideas; actively incorporate others into the discussion; and clarify, verify, or challenge ideas and conclusions.

INSTRUCTION/APPLICATION
Interactive Lessons:
Participating in Collaborative Discussions
- Speaking Constructively
- Listening and Responding

Student Edition/**Teacher's Edition:**
157–160, **157–160**, 359–362, **359–362**, R12–R13, R14–R15

ASSESSMENT
Student Edition/**Teacher's Edition:**
157–160, **157–160**, 359–362, **359–362**

d. Respond thoughtfully to diverse perspectives, summarize points of agreement and disagreement, and, when warranted, qualify or justify their own views and understanding and make new connections in light of the evidence and reasoning presented.

INSTRUCTION/APPLICATION
Interactive Lessons:
Participating in Collaborative Discussions
- Listening and Responding
- Wrapping Up Your Discussion

Student Edition/**Teacher's Edition:**
132a, 157–160, **157–160**, **324a**, 359–362, **359–362**, R12–R13

Close Reader/**Teacher's Edition:**
10b–10g, 420b–420k, 432b–432g

ASSESSMENT
Student Edition/**Teacher's Edition:**
30, **30**, 130, **130**, 157–160, **157–160**, 359–362, **359–362**

SL 2
Integrate multiple sources of information presented in diverse media or formats (e.g., visually, quantitatively, orally) evaluating the credibility and accuracy of each source.

INSTRUCTION/APPLICATION
Interactive Lessons:
Analyzing and Evaluating Presentations
- Introduction
- Evaluating a Speaker's Reliability
- Synthesizing Media Sources

Student Edition/**Teacher's Edition:**
157–160, **157–160**

Standards Support and Enrichment
- Using Digital Media

ASSESSMENT
Student Edition/**Teacher's Edition:**
157–160, **157–160**

Standard	Where Taught

SL 3
Evaluate a speaker's point of view, reasoning, and use of evidence and rhetoric, identifying any fallacious reasoning or exaggerated or distorted evidence.

INSTRUCTION/APPLICATION
Interactive Lessons:
Analyzing and Evaluating Presentations
- Tracing a Speaker's Argument
- Rhetoric and Delivery

Student Edition/**Teacher's Edition:**
152a, 359–362, **359–362**

Standards Support and Enrichment
- Debating an Issue

ASSESSMENT
Student Edition/**Teacher's Edition:**
130, **130**, 359–362, **359–362**

PRESENTATION OF KNOWLEDGE AND IDEAS

SL 4
Present information, findings, and supporting evidence clearly, concisely, and logically such that listeners can follow the line of reasoning and the organization, development, substance, and style are appropriate to purpose, audience, and task.

INSTRUCTION/APPLICATION
Interactive Lessons:
Giving a Presentation
- Introduction
- Knowing Your Audience
- The Content of Your Presentation
- Style in Presentation
- Delivering Your Presentation

Student Edition/**Teacher's Edition:**
37–40, **37–40**, 157–160, **157–160**, 359–362, **359–362**, R14–R15

Standards Support and Enrichment
- Debating an Issue
- Creating a Class Blog
- Presenting Research

ASSESSMENT
Student Edition/**Teacher's Edition:**
78, **78**, 157–160, **157–160**, 322, **322**, 359–362, **359–362**

SL 5
Make strategic use of digital media (e.g., textual, graphical, audio, visual, and interactive elements) in presentations to enhance understanding of findings, reasoning, and evidence and to add interest.

INSTRUCTION/APPLICATION
Interactive Lessons:
Using Media in a Presentation
- Introduction
- Types of Media: Audio, Video, and Images
- Using Presentation Software
- Practicing Your Presentation

Student Edition/**Teacher's Edition:**
157–160, **157–160**

ASSESSMENT
Student Edition/**Teacher's Edition:**
36, **36**, 152, **152**, 157–160, **157–160**, 176, **176**

Standard	Where Taught
SL 6 Adapt speech to a variety of contexts and tasks, demonstrating command of formal English when indicated or appropriate. (See grades 9–10 Language standards 1 and 3 for specific expectations.)	**INSTRUCTION/APPLICATION** **Interactive Lessons:** Participating in Collaborative Discussions • Speaking Constructively Giving a Presentation • Style in Presentation Student Edition/**Teacher's Edition:** 37–40, **37–40**, 157–160, **157–160**, 359–362, **359–362**, R14–R15 **ASSESSMENT** Student Edition/**Teacher's Edition:** 18, **18**, 30, **30**, 37–40, **37–40**, 78, **78**, 144, **144**, 150, **150**, 157–160, **157–160**, 170, **170**, 206, **206**, 227, **227**, 265, **265**, 322, **322**, 348, **348**, 359–362, **359–362**, 444, **444**

College and Career Readiness Anchor Standards for Language

Common Core State Standards for English Language Arts

CONVENTIONS OF STANDARD ENGLISH

1. Demonstrate command of the conventions of standard English grammar and usage when writing or speaking.

2. Demonstrate command of the conventions of standard English capitalization, punctuation, and spelling when writing.

KNOWLEDGE OF LANGUAGE

3. Apply knowledge of language to understand how language functions in different contexts, to make effective choices for meaning or style, and to comprehend more fully when reading or listening.

VOCABULARY ACQUISITION AND USE

4. Determine or clarify the meaning of unknown and multiple-meaning words and phrases by using context clues, analyzing meaningful word parts, and consulting general and specialized reference materials, as appropriate.

5. Demonstrate understanding of word relationships, and nuances in word meanings.

6. Acquire and use accurately a range of general academic and domain-specific words and phrases sufficient for reading, writing, speaking, and listening at the college and career readiness level; demonstrate independence in gathering vocabulary knowledge when considering a word or phrase important to comprehension or expression.

Language Standards, Grades 9–10 Students

Standard	Where Taught
CONVENTIONS OF STANDARD ENGLISH	

L 1
Demonstrate command of the conventions of standard English grammar and usage when writing or speaking.

INSTRUCTION/APPLICATION

Student Edition/**Teacher's Edition:**
10, **10**, 20, **20**, 32, **32**, 38, **38**, 40, **40**, 43, **43**, 44, **44**, 54, **54**, 80, **80**, 94, **94**, 99, **99**, 100, **100**, 122, **122**, 140, **140**, 146, **146**, 156, **156**, 159, **159**, 160, **160**, 172, **172**, 282, **282**, 300, **300**, 303, **303**, 304, **304**, 350, **350**, 357, **357**, 358, **358**, 362, **362**, 420, **420**, 447, **447**, 448, **448**, R22–R47, **R30, R32, R34, R37, R38, R39, R40, R41, R42, R43, R47**

Standards Support and Enrichment
- Nouns and Noun Phrases
- Combining Sentences
- Condensing Ideas

a. Use parallel structure.

INSTRUCTION/APPLICATION

Student Edition/**Teacher's Edition:**
32, **32**, 54, **54**, 282, **282**, R22, R44

b. Use various types of phrases (noun, verb, adjectival, adverbial, participial, prepositional, absolute) and clauses (independent, dependent; noun, relative, adverbial) to convey specific meanings and add variety and interest to writing or presentations.

INSTRUCTION/APPLICATION

Student Edition/**Teacher's Edition:**
10, **10**, 20, **20**, 80, **80**, 122, **122**, 140, **140**, 146, **146**, 172, **172**, 300, **300**, 350, **350**, 420, **420**, R22, R38–R41, **R38–R41**, R41–R43, **R41–R43**

Standards Support and Enrichment
- Nouns and Noun Phrases
- Combining Sentences
- Condensing Ideas

L 2
Demonstrate command of the conventions of standard English capitalization, punctuation, and spelling when writing.

INSTRUCTION/APPLICATION

Student Edition/**Teacher's Edition:**
44, **44**, 96, **96**, 100, **100**, 132, **132**, 156, **156**, 304, **304**, 338, **338**, 448, **448**, R22, R25–R28, R41, **R41**, R45, R48, R53–R56

a. Use a semicolon (and perhaps a conjunctive adverb) to link two or more closely related independent clauses.

INSTRUCTION/APPLICATION

Student Edition/**Teacher's Edition:**
96, **96**, 338, **338**, R22, R26, R41, **R41**, R45

b. Use a colon to introduce a list or quotation.

INSTRUCTION/APPLICATION

Student Edition/**Teacher's Edition:**
96, **96**, 132, **132**, 338, **338**, R22, R26

c. Spell correctly.

INSTRUCTION/APPLICATION

Student Edition/**Teacher's Edition:**
44, **44**, 100, **100**, 156, **156**, 304, **304**, 448, **448**, R48, R53–R56

Standard	Where Taught

KNOWLEDGE OF LANGUAGE

L 3
Apply knowledge of language to understand how language functions in different contexts, to make effective choices for meaning or style, and to comprehend more fully when reading or listening.

INSTRUCTION/APPLICATION

Student Edition/**Teacher's Edition:**
20, **20**, 83, 88, **88**, 300, **300**, 316, **316**, **316a**, 324, **324**, **432**, 432, **434**, 440, **440**, R22, R24, R29–R47, **R30**, **R32**, **R34**, **R37–R43**, **R47**, R48–R52

---

a. Write and edit work so that it conforms to the guidelines in a style manual (e.g., *MLA Handbook*, Turabian's *Manual for Writers*) appropriate for the discipline and writing type.

INSTRUCTION/APPLICATION

Student Edition/**Teacher's Edition:**
447, **447**, R8–R11

Standards Support and Enrichment
• Documenting Sources

VOCABULARY ACQUISITION AND USE

L 4
Determine or clarify the meaning of unknown and multiple-meaning words and phrases based on *grades 9–10 reading and content*, choosing flexibly from a range of strategies.

INSTRUCTION/APPLICATION

Student Edition/**Teacher's Edition:**
9, **9**, 19, **19**, 31, **31**, 70, **70**, 79, **79**, 87, **87**, 95, **95**, 121, **121**, 131, **131**, 139, **139**, 145, **145**, 171, **171**, 299, **299**, 315, **315**, 323, **323**, 337, **337**, 349, **349**, 400, **400**, 419, **419**, 439, **439**, R48–R53, R52

---

a. Use context (e.g., the overall meaning of a sentence, paragraph, or text; a word's position or function in a sentence) as a clue to the meaning of a word or phrase.

INSTRUCTION/APPLICATION

Student Edition/**Teacher's Edition:**
31, **31**, 139, **139**, 171, **171**, 299, **299**, 337, **337**, R48

---

b. Identify and correctly use patterns of word changes that indicate different meanings or parts of speech (e.g., *analyze, analysis, analytical; advocate, advocacy*).

INSTRUCTION/APPLICATION

Student Edition/**Teacher's Edition:**
9, **9**, 19, **19**, 95, **95**, 121, **121**, 145, **145**, R48, R49–R50

Standards Support and Enrichment
• Using Greek and Latin Roots and Affixes

---

c. Consult general and specialized reference materials (e.g., dictionaries, glossaries, thesauruses), both print and digital, to find the pronunciation of a word or determine or clarify its precise meaning, its part of speech, or its etymology.

INSTRUCTION/APPLICATION

Student Edition/**Teacher's Edition:**
19, **19**, 70, **70**, 79, **79**, 131, **131**, 171, **171**, 315, **315**, 323, **323**, 349, **349**, 400, **400**, 419, **419**, 439, **439**, R48, R52

Standards Support and Enrichment
• Using Reference Aids

Standard	Where Taught
d. Verify the preliminary determination of the meaning of a word or phrase (e.g., by checking the inferred meaning in context or in a dictionary).	**INSTRUCTION/APPLICATION** Student Edition/**Teacher's Edition:** 79, **79**, 139, **139**, 171, **171**, 299, **299**, R48, R52
L 5 Demonstrate understanding of figurative language, word relationships, and nuances in word meanings.	**INSTRUCTION/APPLICATION** Student Edition/**Teacher's Edition:** 26, **26**, 87, **87**, **148**, 149, **149**, 150, **150**, **150a**, **175**, **183**, **186**, **197**, 207, **207**, **236**, **245**, 281, **281**, 353, **353**, 354, **354**, **354a**, **374**, **378**, **380**, **386**, **393**, **407**, **408**, **413**, **415**, 417, **417**, 418, **418**, 431, **431**, 443, **443**, 444, **444**, R48–R49, R51–R52
a. Interpret figures of speech (e.g., euphemism, oxymoron) in context and analyze their role in the text.	**INSTRUCTION/APPLICATION** Student Edition/**Teacher's Edition:** **148**, 149, **149**, 150, **150**, **150a**, **175**, **183**, **186**, **197**, **236**, **245**, 281, **281**, 353, **353**, 354, **354**, **354a**, **374**, **378**, **380**, **386**, **393**, **407**, **408**, **413**, **415**, 417, **417**, 418, **418**, 442, **442**, 443, **443**, 444, **444**, **444a**, R48–R49
b. Analyze nuances in the meaning of words with similar denotations.	**INSTRUCTION/APPLICATION** Student Edition/**Teacher's Edition:** 26, **26**, 87, **87**, 121, **121**, 323, **323**, 431, **431**, R48, R51
L 6 Acquire and use accurately general academic and domain-specific words and phrases, sufficient for reading, writing, speaking, and listening at the college and career readiness level; demonstrate independence in gathering vocabulary knowledge when considering a word or phrase important to comprehension or expression.	**INSTRUCTION/APPLICATION** Student Edition/**Teacher's Edition:** 2, **2**, **5**, **13**, **22**, **31**, **34**, 37, **37**, 41, **41**, 46, **46**, **50**, **57**, **60**, **66**, **74**, 79, **79**, 83, **91**, 97, **97**, 102, **102**, **109**, **112**, **118**, **134**, **142**, **148**, 153, **153**, 157, **157**, 162, **162**, **165**, **175**, **182**, **211**, **237**, **258**, **275**, **286**, **290**, **295**, 301, **301**, 306, **306**, **309**, **319**, **326**, **341**, 355, **355**, 359, **359**, 364, **364**, **376**, **389**, **412**, **422**, **426**, **434**, **442**, 446, **446**, R48–R53

Navigating Complex Texts in the 21st Century

By Carol Jago

Reading complex literature and nonfiction doesn't need to be painful.

But to enjoy great poetry and prose you are going to have to do more than skim and scan. You will need to develop the habit of paying attention to the particular words on the page closely, systematically, even lovingly. Just because a text isn't easy doesn't mean there is something wrong with it or something wrong with you. Understanding complex text takes effort and focused attention. Do you sometimes wish writers would just say what they have to say more simply or with fewer words? I assure you that writers don't use long sentences and unfamiliar words to annoy their readers or make readers feel dumb. They employ complex syntax and rich language because they have complex ideas about complex issues that they want to communicate. Simple language and structures just aren't up to the task.

Excellent literature and nonfiction—the kind you will be reading over the course of the year—challenge readers in many ways. Sometimes the background of a story or the content of an essay is so unfamiliar that it can be difficult to understand why characters are behaving as they do or to follow the argument a writer is making. By persevering—reading like a detective and following clues in the text—you will find that your store of background knowledge grows. As a result, the next time you read about global issues, financial matters, political events, environmental news, (like the California drought), or health research, the text won't seem nearly as hard. Navigating a terrain you have been over once before never seems quite as rugged the second time through. The more you read, the better reader you become.

Good readers aren't scared off by challenging text. When the going gets rough, they know what to do. Let's take vocabulary, a common measure of text complexity, as an example. Learning new words is the business of a lifetime. Rather than shutting down when you meet a word you don't know, take a moment to think about the word. Is any part of the word familiar to you? Is there something in the context of the sentence or paragraph that can help you figure out its meaning? Is there someone or something that can provide you with a definition? When we read literature or nonfiction from a time period other than our own, the text is often full of words we don't know. Each time you meet those words in succeeding readings you will be adding to your understanding of the word and its use. Your brain is a natural word-learning machine. The more you feed it complex text, the larger vocabulary you'll have and as a result, the easier navigating the next book will be.

Have you ever been reading a long, complicated sentence and discovered that by the time you reached the end you had forgotten the beginning? Unlike the sentences we speak or dash off in a note to a friend, complex text is often full of sentences that are not only lengthy but also constructed in intricate ways. Such sentences require readers to slow down and figure out how phrases relate to one another as well as who is doing what to whom. Remember, rereading isn't cheating. It is exactly what experienced readers know to do when they meet dense text on the page. On the pages that follow you will find stories and articles that challenge you at a sentence level. Don't be intimidated. By paying careful attention to how those sentences are constructed, you will see their meanings unfold before your eyes.

That same kind of attention is required for reading the media. Every day you are bombarded with messages—online, offline, everywhere you look. These, too, are complex texts that you want to be able to see through; that is, to be able to recognize the message's source, purpose, context, intended audience, and appeals. Another way text can be complex is in terms of the density of ideas. Sometimes a writer piles on so much information that you find even if your eyes continue to move down the page, your brain has stopped taking in anything. At times like this, turning to a peer and discussing particular lines or concepts can help you pay closer attention and begin to unpack the text. Sharing questions and ideas, exploring a difficult passage together, makes it possible to tease out the meaning of even the most difficult text.

> "Your brain is a natural word-learning machine. The more you feed it complex text, the larger a vocabulary you'll have."

Poetry is by its nature particularly dense and for that reason poses particular challenges for casual readers. Don't ever assume that once through a poem is enough. Often, a seemingly simple poem in terms of word choice and length—for example an Emily Dickinson, Mary Oliver, or W.H. Auden poem—expresses extremely complex feelings and insights. Poets also often make reference to mythological and Biblical allusions which contemporary readers are not always familiar with. Skipping over such references robs your reading of the richness the poet intended. Look up that bird. Check out the note on the page. Ask your teacher.

You will notice a range of complexity within each collection of readings. This spectrum reflects the range of texts that surround us: some easy, some hard, some seemingly easy but hard, some seemingly hard but easy. Navigating this sea of texts should stretch you as a reader and a thinker. How could it be otherwise when your journey is in the realms of gold? Please accept this invitation to an intellectual voyage I think you will enjoy.

Understanding the Common Core State Standards

What are the English Language Arts Common Core State Standards?

The Common Core State Standards for English Language Arts indicate what you should know and be able to do by the end of your grade level. These understandings and skills will help you be better prepared for future classes, college courses, and a career. For this reason, the standards for each strand in English Language Arts (such as Reading Informational Text or Writing) directly relate to the College and Career Readiness Anchor Standards for each strand. The Anchor Standards broadly outline the understandings and skills you should master by the end of high school so that you are well prepared for college or for a career.

How do I learn the English Language Arts Common Core State Standards?

Your textbook is closely aligned to the English Language Arts Common Core State Standards. Every time you learn a concept or practice a skill, you are working on mastery of one of the standards. Each collection, each selection, and each performance task in your textbook connects to one or more of the standards for English Language Arts listed on the following pages.

The English Language Arts Common Core State Standards are divided into five strands: Reading Literature, Reading Informational Text, Writing, Speaking and Listening, and Language.

xxxii   Grade 9

Strand	What It Means to You
Reading Literature (RL)	This strand concerns the literary texts you will read at this grade level: stories, drama, and poetry. The Common Core State Standards stress that you should read a range of texts of increasing complexity as you progress through high school.
Reading Informational Text (RI)	Informational text includes a broad range of literary nonfiction, including exposition, argument, and functional text, in such genres as personal essays, speeches, opinion pieces, memoirs, and historical and scientific accounts. The Common Core State Standards stress that you will read a range of informational texts of increasing complexity as you progress from grade to grade.
Writing (W)	The Writing strand focuses on your generating three types of texts—arguments, informative or explanatory texts, and narratives—while using the writing process and technology to develop and share your writing. The Common Core State Standards also emphasize research and specify that you should write routinely for both short and extended time frames.
Speaking and Listening (SL)	The Common Core State Standards focus on comprehending information presented in a variety of media and formats, on participating in collaborative discussions, and on presenting knowledge and ideas clearly.
Language (L)	The standards in the Language strand address the conventions of standard English grammar, usage, and mechanics; knowledge of language; and vocabulary acquisition and use.

Common Core Code Decoder

The codes you find on the pages of your textbook identify the specific knowledge or skill for the standard addressed in the text.

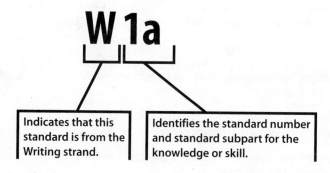

W 1a

| Indicates that this standard is from the Writing strand. | Identifies the standard number and standard subpart for the knowledge or skill. |

English Language Arts
Common Core State Standards

Listed below are the English Language Arts Common Core State Standards that you are required to master by the end of grade 9. We have provided a summary of the concepts you will learn on your way to mastering each standard. The CCR anchor standards and high school grade-specific standards for each strand work together to define college and career readiness expectations—the former providing broad standards, the latter providing additional specificity.

College and Career Readiness Anchor Standards for Reading

Common Core State Standards

KEY IDEAS AND DETAILS

1. Read closely to determine what the text says explicitly and to make logical inferences from it; cite specific textual evidence when writing or speaking to support conclusions drawn from the text.

2. Determine central ideas or themes of a text and analyze their development; summarize the key supporting details and ideas.

3. Analyze how and why individuals, events, and ideas develop and interact over the course of a text.

CRAFT AND STRUCTURE

4. Interpret words and phrases as they are used in a text, including determining technical, connotative, and figurative meanings, and analyze how specific word choices shape meaning or tone.

5. Analyze the structure of texts, including how specific sentences, paragraphs, and larger portions of the text (e.g., a section, chapter, scene, or stanza) relate to each other and the whole.

6. Assess how point of view or purpose shapes the content and style of a text.

INTEGRATION OF KNOWLEDGE AND IDEAS

7. Integrate and evaluate content presented in diverse formats and media, including visually and quantitatively, as well as in words.

8. Delineate and evaluate the argument and specific claims in a text, including the validity of the reasoning as well as the relevance and sufficiency of the evidence.

9. Analyze how two or more texts address similar themes or topics in order to build knowledge or to compare the approaches the authors take.

RANGE OF READING AND LEVEL OF TEXT COMPLEXITY

10. Read and comprehend complex literary and informational texts independently and proficiently.

Reading Standards for Literature, Grades 9–10 Students

The College and Career Readiness Anchor Standards for Reading apply to both literature and informational text.

Common Core State Standards	What It Means to You
KEY IDEAS AND DETAILS	
1. Cite strong and thorough textual evidence to support analysis of what the text says explicitly as well as inferences drawn from the text.	You will use details and information from the text to support your understanding of its main ideas—both those that are stated directly and those that are suggested.
2. Determine a theme or central idea of a text and analyze in detail its development over the course of the text, including how it emerges and is shaped and refined by specific details; provide an objective summary of the text.	You will analyze the development of a text's main ideas and themes by showing how they progress throughout the text. You will also summarize the main idea of the text as a whole without adding your own ideas or opinions.
3. Analyze how complex characters (e.g., those with multiple or conflicting motivations) develop over the course of a text, interact with other characters, and advance the plot or develop the theme.	You will analyze the development of a text's characters and how their actions, thoughts, and words contribute to the story's plot or themes.
CRAFT AND STRUCTURE	
4. Determine the meaning of words and phrases as they are used in the text, including figurative and connotative meanings; analyze the cumulative impact of specific word choices on meaning and tone (e.g., how the language evokes a sense of time and place; how it sets a formal or informal tone).	You will analyze specific words and phrases in the text to determine both what they mean individually as well as how they contribute to the text's tone and meaning as a whole.
5. Analyze how an author's choices concerning how to structure a text, order events within it (e.g., parallel plots), and manipulate time (e.g., pacing, flashbacks) create such effects as mystery, tension, or surprise.	You will analyze the ways in which the author has chosen to structure and order the text and determine how those choices affect the text's mood or tone.
6. Analyze a particular point of view or cultural experience reflected in a work of literature from outside the United States, drawing on a wide reading of world literature.	You will analyze the point of view or cultural experience of a work of literature from outside the United States.

Common Core State Standards	What It Means to You
INTEGRATION OF KNOWLEDGE AND IDEAS	
7. Analyze the representation of a subject or a key scene in two different artistic mediums, including what is emphasized or absent in each treatment (e.g., Auden's "Musée des Beaux Arts" and Breughel's *Landscape with the Fall of Icarus)*.	You will compare and contrast how events and information are presented in visual and non-visual texts.
8. (Not applicable to literature)	
9. Analyze how an author draws on and transforms source material in a specific work (e.g., how Shakespeare treats a theme or topic from Ovid or the Bible or how a later author draws on a play by Shakespeare).	You will recognize and analyze how an author draws from and uses source material from other texts or other types of sources.
RANGE OF READING AND LEVEL OF TEXT COMPLEXITY	
10. By the end of grade 9, read and comprehend literature, including stories, dramas, and poems, in the grades 9–10 text complexity band proficiently, with scaffolding as needed at the high end of the range.	You will demonstrate the ability to read and understand grade-level appropriate literary texts by the end of grade 9.

Reading Standards for Informational Text, Grades 9–10 Students

Common Core State Standards	What It Means to You
KEY IDEAS AND DETAILS	
1. Cite strong and thorough textual evidence to support analysis of what the text says explicitly as well as inferences drawn from the text.	You will use details and information from the text to support your understanding of its main ideas—both those that are stated directly and those that are suggested.
2. Determine a central idea of a text and analyze its development over the course of the text, including how it emerges and is shaped and refined by specific details; provide an objective summary of the text.	You will analyze the development of a text's main ideas and themes by showing how they progress throughout the text. You will also summarize the main idea of the text as a whole without adding your own ideas or opinions.

Common Core State Standards	What It Means to You
3. Analyze how the author unfolds an analysis or series of ideas or events, including the order in which the points are made, how they are introduced and developed, and the connections that are drawn between them.	You will analyze the ways in which the author has chosen to structure and order the text and determine how those choices affect the text's central ideas.

CRAFT AND STRUCTURE

Common Core State Standards	What It Means to You
4. Determine the meaning of words and phrases as they are used in a text, including figurative, connotative, and technical meanings; analyze the cumulative impact of specific word choices on meaning and tone (e.g., how the language of a court opinion differs from that of a newspaper).	You will analyze specific words and phrases in the text to determine both what they mean individually as well as how they contribute to the text's tone and meaning as a whole.
5. Analyze in detail how an author's ideas or claims are developed and refined by particular sentences, paragraphs, or larger portions of a text (e.g., a section or chapter).	You will examine specific portions of the text (sentences, paragraphs, or larger sections) to understand how they develop the author's ideas and claims.
6. Determine an author's point of view or purpose in a text and analyze how an author uses rhetoric to advance that point of view or purpose.	You will understand the author's purpose and analyze how the author uses language to effectively communicate that purpose.

INTEGRATION OF KNOWLEDGE AND IDEAS

Common Core State Standards	What It Means to You
7. Analyze various accounts of a subject told in different mediums (e.g., a person's life story in both print and multimedia), determining which details are emphasized in each account.	You will compare and contrast the ways in which various media, such as newspapers, television, documentaries, blogs, and the Internet, portray the same events.
8. Delineate and evaluate the argument and specific claims in a text, assessing whether the reasoning is valid and the evidence is relevant and sufficient; identify false statements and fallacious reasoning.	You will evaluate the strength of the author's claims by examining the supporting details and reasoning and identifying any faults or weaknesses in them.
9. Analyze seminal U.S. documents of historical and literary significance (e.g., Washington's Farewell Address, the Gettysburg Address, Roosevelt's Four Freedoms speech, King's "Letter from Birmingham Jail"), including how they address related themes and concepts.	You will read and analyze influential documents and explain how they address important themes related to United States history and culture.

Common Core State Standards **xxxvii**

Common Core State Standards	What It Means to You

RANGE OF READING AND LEVEL OF TEXT COMPLEXITY

10. By the end of grade 9, read and comprehend literary nonfiction in the grades 9–10 text complexity band proficiently, with scaffolding as needed at the high end of the range.	You will demonstrate the ability to read and understand grade-level appropriate literary nonfiction texts by the end of grade 9.

College and Career Readiness Anchor Standards for Writing

Common Core State Standards

TEXT TYPES AND PURPOSES

1. Write arguments to support claims in an analysis of substantive topics or texts, using valid reasoning and relevant and sufficient evidence.

2. Write informative/explanatory texts to examine and convey complex ideas and information clearly and accurately through the effective selection, organization, and analysis of content.

3. Write narratives to develop real or imagined experiences or events using effective technique, well-chosen details, and well-structured event sequences.

PRODUCTION AND DISTRIBUTION OF WRITING

4. Produce clear and coherent writing in which the development, organization, and style are appropriate to task, purpose, and audience.

5. Develop and strengthen writing as needed by planning, revising, editing, rewriting, or trying a new approach.

6. Use technology, including the Internet, to produce and publish writing and to interact and collaborate with others.

RESEARCH TO BUILD AND PRESENT KNOWLEDGE

7. Conduct short as well as more sustained research projects based on focused questions, demonstrating understanding of the subject under investigation.

8. Gather relevant information from multiple print and digital sources, assess the credibility and accuracy of each source, and integrate the information while avoiding plagiarism.

9. Draw evidence from literary or informational texts to support analysis, reflection, and research.

RANGE OF WRITING

10. Write routinely over extended time frames (time for research, reflection, and revision) and shorter time frames (a single sitting or a day or two) for a range of tasks, purposes, and audiences.

Writing Standards, Grades 9–10 Students

Common Core State Standards	What It Means to You
TEXT TYPES AND PURPOSES	
1. Write arguments to support claims in an analysis of substantive topics or texts, using valid reasoning and relevant and sufficient evidence.	You will write and develop arguments with strong evidence and valid reasoning that include
a. Introduce precise claim(s), distinguish the claim(s) from alternate or opposing claims, and create an organization that establishes clear relationships among claim(s), counterclaims, reasons, and evidence.	a. a clear organization of precise claims and counterclaims
b. Develop claim(s) and counterclaims fairly, supplying evidence for each while pointing out the strengths and limitations of both in a manner that anticipates the audience's knowledge level and concerns.	b. relevant and unbiased support for claims
c. Use words, phrases, and clauses to link the major sections of the text, create cohesion, and clarify the relationships between claim(s) and reasons, between reasons and evidence, and between claim(s) and counterclaims.	c. use of transitional words, phrases, and clauses to link information
d. Establish and maintain a formal style and objective tone while attending to the norms and conventions of the discipline in which they are writing.	d. a tone and style appropriate to the task
e. Provide a concluding statement or section that follows from and supports the argument presented.	e. a strong concluding statement or section that summarizes the evidence presented
2. Write informative/explanatory texts to examine and convey complex ideas, concepts, and information clearly and accurately through the effective selection, organization, and analysis of content.	You will write clear, well-organized, and thoughtful informative and explanatory texts with
a. Introduce a topic; organize complex ideas, concepts, and information to make important connections and distinctions; include formatting (e.g., headings), graphics (e.g., figures, tables), and multimedia when useful to aiding comprehension.	a. a clear introduction and organization, including headings and graphic organizers (when appropriate)

Common Core State Standards	What It Means to You
b. Develop the topic with well-chosen, relevant, and sufficient facts, extended definitions, concrete details, quotations, or other information and examples appropriate to the audience's knowledge of the topic.	**b.** sufficient supporting details and background information
c. Use appropriate and varied transitions to link the major sections of the text, create cohesion, and clarify the relationships among complex ideas and concepts.	**c.** appropriate transitions
d. Use precise language and domain-specific vocabulary to manage the complexity of the topic.	**d.** precise language and relevant vocabulary
e. Establish and maintain a formal style and objective tone while attending to the norms and conventions of the discipline in which they are writing.	**e.** a tone and style appropriate to the task
f. Provide a concluding statement or section that follows from and supports the information or explanation presented (e.g., articulating implications or the significance of the topic).	**f.** a strong concluding statement or section that restates the importance or relevance of the topic
3. Write narratives to develop real or imagined experiences or events using effective technique, well-chosen details, and well-structured event sequences.	You will write clear, well-structured, detailed narrative texts that
a. Engage and orient the reader by setting out a problem, situation, or observation, establishing one or multiple point(s) of view, and introducing a narrator and/or characters; create a smooth progression of experiences or events.	**a.** draw your readers in with a clear topic and an interesting progression of events or ideas
b. Use narrative techniques, such as dialogue, pacing, description, reflection, and multiple plot lines, to develop experiences, events, and/or characters.	**b.** use literary techniques to develop and expand on events and/or characters
c. Use a variety of techniques to sequence events so that they build on one another to create a coherent whole.	**c.** have a coherent sequence and structure
d. Use precise words and phrases, telling details, and sensory language to convey a vivid picture of the experiences, events, setting, and/or characters.	**d.** use precise words and sensory details that keep readers interested
e. Provide a conclusion that follows from and reflects on what is experienced, observed, or resolved over the course of the narrative.	**e.** have a strong conclusion that reflects on the topic

Common Core State Standards	What It Means to You

PRODUCTION AND DISTRIBUTION OF WRITING

Common Core State Standards	What It Means to You
4. Produce clear and coherent writing in which the development, organization, and style are appropriate to task, purpose, and audience. (Grade-specific expectations for writing types are defined in standards 1–3 above.)	You will produce writing that is appropriate to the task, purpose, and audience for whom you are writing.
5. Develop and strengthen writing as needed by planning, revising, editing, rewriting, or trying a new approach, focusing on addressing what is most significant for a specific purpose and audience. (Editing for conventions should demonstrate command of Language standards 1–3 up to and including grades 9–10.)	You will revise and refine your writing to address what is most important for your purpose and audience.
6. Use technology, including the Internet, to produce, publish, and update individual or shared writing products, taking advantage of technology's capacity to link to other information and to display information flexibly and dynamically.	You will use technology to share your writing and to provide links to other relevant information.

RESEARCH TO BUILD AND PRESENT KNOWLEDGE

Common Core State Standards	What It Means to You
7. Conduct short as well as more sustained research projects to answer a question (including a self-generated question) or solve a problem; narrow or broaden the inquiry when appropriate; synthesize multiple sources on the subject, demonstrating understanding of the subject under investigation.	You will engage in short and more complex research tasks that include answering a question or solving a problem by using multiple sources. The product of your research will demonstrate your understanding of the subject.
8. Gather relevant information from multiple authoritative print and digital sources, using advanced searches effectively; assess the usefulness of each source in answering the research question; integrate information into the text selectively to maintain the flow of ideas, avoiding plagiarism and following a standard format for citation.	You will effectively conduct searches to gather information from different sources and assess the relevance of each source, following a standard format for citation.

Common Core State Standards	What It Means to You

9. Draw evidence from literary or informational texts to support analysis, reflection, and research.
 	
   a. Apply grades 9–10 Reading standards to literature (e.g., "Analyze how an author draws on and transforms source material in a specific work [e.g., how Shakespeare treats a theme or topic from Ovid or the Bible or how a later author draws on a play by Shakespeare]").
 	
   b. Apply grades 9–10 Reading standards to literary nonfiction (e.g., "Delineate and evaluate the argument and specific claims in a text, assessing whether the reasoning is valid and the evidence is relevant and sufficient; identify false statements and fallacious reasoning").
	You will paraphrase, summarize, quote, and cite primary and secondary sources, using both literary and informational texts, to support your analysis, reflection, and research.

RANGE OF WRITING

Common Core State Standards	What It Means to You
10. Write routinely over extended time frames (time for research, reflection, and revision) and shorter time frames (a single sitting or a day or two) for a range of tasks, purposes, and audiences.	You will write for many different purposes and audiences both over short and extended periods of time.

College and Career Readiness Anchor Standards for Speaking and Listening

Common Core State Standards

COMPREHENSION AND COLLABORATION

Common Core State Standards
1. Prepare for and participate effectively in a range of conversations and collaborations with diverse partners, building on others' ideas and expressing their own clearly and persuasively.
2. Integrate and evaluate information presented in diverse media and formats, including visually, quantitatively, and orally.
3. Evaluate a speaker's point of view, reasoning, and use of evidence and rhetoric.

PRESENTATION OF KNOWLEDGE AND IDEAS

Common Core State Standards
4. Present information, findings, and supporting evidence such that listeners can follow the line of reasoning and the organization, development, and style are appropriate to task, purpose, and audience.
5. Make strategic use of digital media and visual displays of data to express information and enhance understanding of presentations.
6. Adapt speech to a variety of contexts and communicative tasks, demonstrating command of formal English when indicated or appropriate.

Speaking and Listening Standards, Grades 9–10 Students

Common Core State Standards	What It Means to You
COMPREHENSION AND COLLABORATION	
1. Initiate and participate effectively in a range of collaborative discussions (one-on-one, in groups, and teacher-led) with diverse partners on grades 9–10 topics, texts, and issues, building on others' ideas and expressing their own clearly and persuasively.	You will actively participate in a variety of discussions in which you
a. Come to discussions prepared, having read and researched material under study; explicitly draw on that preparation by referring to evidence from texts and other research on the topic or issue to stimulate a thoughtful, well-reasoned exchange of ideas.	a. have read any relevant material beforehand and have come to the discussion prepared
b. Work with peers to set rules for collegial discussions and decision-making (e.g., informal consensus, taking votes on key issues, presentation of alternate views), clear goals and deadlines, and individual roles as needed.	b. work with others to establish goals and processes within the group
c. Propel conversations by posing and responding to questions that relate the current discussion to broader themes or larger ideas; actively incorporate others into the discussion; and clarify, verify, or challenge ideas and conclusions.	c. initiate dialogue by asking and responding to questions and by relating the current topic to other relevant information
d. Respond thoughtfully to diverse perspectives, summarize points of agreement and disagreement, and, when warranted, qualify or justify their own views and understanding and make new connections in light of the evidence and reasoning presented.	d. respond to different perspectives and summarize points of agreement or disagreement when needed
2. Integrate multiple sources of information presented in diverse media or formats (e.g., visually, quantitatively, orally) evaluating the credibility and accuracy of each source.	You will integrate multiple sources of information, assessing the credibility and accuracy of each source.
3. Evaluate a speaker's point of view, reasoning, and use of evidence and rhetoric, identifying any fallacious reasoning or exaggerated or distorted evidence.	You will evaluate a speaker's argument and identify any false reasoning or evidence.

Common Core State Standards	What It Means to You
PRESENTATION OF KNOWLEDGE AND IDEAS	
4. Present information, findings, and supporting evidence clearly, concisely, and logically such that listeners can follow the line of reasoning and the organization, development, substance, and style are appropriate to purpose, audience, and task.	You will organize and present information to your listeners in a logical sequence and style that are appropriate to your task and audience.
5. Make strategic use of digital media (e.g., textual, graphical, audio, visual, and interactive elements) in presentations to enhance understanding of findings, reasoning, and evidence and to add interest.	You will use digital media to enhance and add interest to presentations.
6. Adapt speech to a variety of contexts and tasks, demonstrating command of formal English when indicated or appropriate. (See grades 9–10 Language standards 1 and 3 for specific expectations.)	You will adapt the formality of your speech appropriately, depending on its context and purpose.

College and Career Readiness Anchor Standards for Language

Common Core State Standards
CONVENTIONS OF STANDARD ENGLISH
1. Demonstrate command of the conventions of standard English grammar and usage when writing or speaking.
2. Demonstrate command of the conventions of standard English capitalization, punctuation, and spelling when writing.
KNOWLEDGE OF LANGUAGE
3. Apply knowledge of language to understand how language functions in different contexts, to make effective choices for meaning or style, and to comprehend more fully when reading or listening.
VOCABULARY ACQUISITION AND USE
4. Determine or clarify the meaning of unknown and multiple-meaning words and phrases by using context clues, analyzing meaningful word parts, and consulting general and specialized reference materials, as appropriate.
5. Demonstrate understanding of word relationships and nuances in word meanings.
6. Acquire and use accurately a range of general academic and domain-specific words and phrases sufficient for reading, writing, speaking, and listening at the college and career readiness level; demonstrate independence in gathering vocabulary knowledge when considering a word or phrase important to comprehension or expression.

Language Standards, Grades 9–10 Students

Common Core State Standards	What It Means to You
CONVENTIONS OF STANDARD ENGLISH	
1. Demonstrate command of the conventions of standard English grammar and usage when writing or speaking.	You will correctly use the conventions of English grammar and usage, including
a. Use parallel structure.	**a.** parallel structure
b. Use various types of phrases (noun, verb, adjectival, adverbial, participial, prepositional, absolute) and clauses (independent, dependent; noun, relative, adverbial) to convey specific meanings and add variety and interest to writing or presentations.	**b.** phrases and clauses
2. Demonstrate command of the conventions of standard English capitalization, punctuation, and spelling when writing.	You will correctly use the conventions of English capitalization, punctuation, and spelling, including
a. Use a semicolon (and perhaps a conjunctive adverb) to link two or more closely related independent clauses.	**a.** semicolons
b. Use a colon to introduce a list or quotation.	**b.** colons
c. Spell correctly.	**c.** spelling
KNOWLEDGE OF LANGUAGE	
3. Apply knowledge of language to understand how language functions in different contexts, to make effective choices for meaning or style, and to comprehend more fully when reading or listening.	You will apply your knowledge of language in different contexts by
a. Write and edit work so that it conforms to the guidelines in a style manual (e.g., *MLA Handbook,* Turabian's *Manual for Writers*) appropriate for the discipline and writing type.	**a.** conforming to a style manual when writing and editing

Common Core State Standards	What It Means to You
VOCABULARY ACQUISITION AND USE	
4. Determine or clarify the meaning of unknown and multiple-meaning words and phrases based on grades 9–10 reading and content, choosing flexibly from a range of strategies.	You will understand the meaning of grade-level appropriate words and phrases by
a. Use context (e.g., the overall meaning of a sentence, paragraph, or text; a word's position or function in a sentence) as a clue to the meaning of a word or phrase.	a. using context clues
b. Identify and correctly use patterns of word changes that indicate different meanings or parts of speech (e.g., *analyze, analysis, analytical; advocate, advocacy*).	b. recognizing and adapting root words according to meaning or part of speech
c. Consult general and specialized reference materials (e.g., dictionaries, glossaries, thesauruses), both print and digital, to find the pronunciation of a word or determine or clarify its precise meaning, its part of speech, or its etymology.	c. using reference materials
d. Verify the preliminary determination of the meaning of a word or phrase (e.g., by checking the inferred meaning in context or in a dictionary).	d. inferring and verifying the meanings of words in context
5. Demonstrate understanding of figurative language, word relationships, and nuances in word meanings.	You will understand figurative language, word relationships, and slight differences in word meanings by
a. Interpret figures of speech (e.g., euphemism, oxymoron) in context and analyze their role in the text.	a. interpreting figures of speech in context
b. Analyze nuances in the meaning of words with similar denotations.	b. analyzing slight differences in the meanings of similar words
6. Acquire and use accurately general academic and domain-specific words and phrases, sufficient for reading, writing, speaking, and listening at the college and career readiness level; demonstrate independence in gathering vocabulary knowledge when considering a word or phrase important to comprehension or expression.	You will develop vocabulary knowledge at the college and career readiness level and demonstrate confidence in using it appropriately.

Finding Common Ground

" We may have different religions, different languages, different colored skin, but we all belong to one human race. "

STREAM TO START

Motivate students to read the collection texts and spark their curiosity about the collection by playing the video and watching it in class. After students view the video, ask them to think about two things they hope to learn from reading Finding Common Ground. Call on volunteers to share their response.

PERFORMANCE TASK PREVIEW

Point out to students that they will complete two performance tasks at the end of the collection. The performance tasks will require them to further analyze the selections in the collection and to synthesize ideas about these analyses. They will present their findings in a variety of products.

ACADEMIC VOCABULARY

Students can acquire facility with the academic vocabulary words through frequent, repeated exposure as they analyze and discuss the selections in the collection. Academic vocabulary can be used in the following instructional contexts. This will enable students to incorporate the academic vocabulary words into their working vocabulary.

- Collaborative Discussion at the end of each selection
- Analyzing the Text questions for each selection
- Selection-level Performance Task
- Vocabulary instruction (for Critical Vocabulary and/or for Vocabulary Strategy)
- Language and Style
- End-of-collection Performance Task for all selections in the collection

ASK STUDENTS to review the Academic Vocabulary word list for this collection. You may wish to pronounce each word aloud so students hear the

The focus of this collection is the individual and society—from the individual's struggle to be a part of a society to a nation's struggle to unite for a common cause.

Stream to Start   hmhfyi.com   Channel One News®

COLLECTION
PERFORMANCE TASK Preview

At the end of this collection, you will have the opportunity to complete two tasks:

- Plan and deliver a speech about whether people can learn to live together.
- Write an essay about an individual's role in society.

ACADEMIC VOCABULARY

Study the words and their definitions in the chart below. You will use these words as you discuss and write about the texts in this collection.

Word	Definition	Related Forms
enforce (ĕn-fôrs´) *tr v.*	to compel observance of or obedience to	enforceable, enforcer, enforcement
entity (ĕn´ tĭ-tē) *n.*	a thing that exists as a unit	entities
internal (ĭn-tûr´nəl) *adj.*	inner; located within something or someone	internality, internally
presume (prĭ-zoōm´) *v.*	to take for granted as being true; to assume something is true	presumably, presumption, presumed
resolve (rĭ-zŏlv´) *v.*	to decide or become determined	resolution, resolvable

📖 myNotebook

As students read, analyze, and discuss the texts in this collection, encourage them to use the *my*WordList folder in *my*Notebook to build their own personal word lists.

- **Annotate** Students can highlight vocabulary terms and other

English Language Support

▶ **View It!**

Professional Development Podcast:
English Language Learners

ENGAGE WITH THE COLLECTION TOPIC

Draw students' attention to the title of the collection, Finding Common Ground. Explain that people find "common ground" when they discover a point of agreement. Tell students that this collection focuses on how people of different backgrounds find common ground.

ACCESS PRIOR KNOWLEDGE Ask students to think of a time when they had to find "common ground" with someone else—a teammate, a parent, or an opponent. How did it play out? Discuss why it's important for people to find mutual understanding.

FIVE-WORD SUMMARY

Use this strategy to help students determine the central idea of the texts in this collection.

- *First*, have students read a paragraph and create a list of what they consider its five most important words, words that best explain and clarify its main idea.
- *Then,* have pairs compare and discuss their individual lists. Tell each pair to create a single list of the five most important words, selecting only from words that appear on their individual lists. Remind students that they should discuss and defend their word choices as they work to synthesize their lists.

- *Next,* gather pairs into groups of four and have them share, discuss, and defend their word choices. Ask groups to work together to synthesize their lists, forming a single list of the text's most important words.
- *Finally,* have students work individually to summarize the paragraph. Tell them to include each of the five key words on their group's final list and to underline each of those words.

 Collection 1 Digital Resources for English Language Support

INTERACTIVE WHITEBOARD LESSONS

Use the Interactive Whiteboard Lessons for additional support on:
- citing textual evidence
- theme/central idea
- text structure and meaning

LEVEL UP TUTORIALS

Students can access *Level Up* Tutorials from the eBooks to get additional help on analyzing literature, analyzing informational text, reading skills, vocabulary skills, and language conventions.

 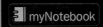
Collection 1 Lessons	**Media**	**Teach and Practice**
Student Edition | eBook	▶ **Video Links** HISTORY A&E Channel One News	**Close Reading and Evidence Tracking**

ANCHOR TEXT **Argument by Anna Quindlen** "A Quilt of a Country"	🔊 **Audio** "A Quilt of a Country"	**Close Read Screencasts** • Modeled Discussion 1 (lines 22–28) • Modeled Discussion 2 (lines 72–79) • Close Read application pdf (lines 94–103) **Strategies for Annotation** • Delineate and Evaluate an Argument • Patterns of Word Change
CLOSE READER **Blog by Eboo Patel** "Making the Future Better, Together"	🔊 **Audio** "Making the Future Better, Together"	
ANCHOR TEXT **Short Story by Nadine Gordimer** "Once Upon a Time"	🔊 **Audio** "Once Upon a Time"	**Close Read Screencasts** • Modeled Discussion 1 (lines 1–10) • Modeled Discussion 2 (lines 121–130) • Close Read application pdf (lines 181–188) **Strategies for Annotation** • Analyze Author's Choices: Text Structure
CLOSE READER **Short Story by Lisa Fugard** "Night Calls"	🔊 **Audio** "Night Calls"	
Essay by Kimberly M. Blaeser "Rituals of Memory"	🔊 **Audio** from "Rituals of Memory"	**Strategies for Annotation** • Determine Central Idea • Denotation and Connotation
Speech by Abraham Lincoln **The Gettysburg Address**	▶ **Video HISTORY®** *The Gettysburg Address: A New Declaration of Independence* 🔊 **Audio** The Gettysburg Address	**Strategies for Annotation** • Analyze Seminal U.S. Documents
CLOSE READER **Speech by Bill Clinton** **Oklahoma Bombing Memorial Address**	🔊 **Audio** Oklahoma Bombing Memorial Address	
Photo Essay "Views of the Wall" **Poem by Alberto Ríos** "The Vietnam Wall"	▶ **Photo Essay** "Views of the Wall" ▶ **Video HISTORY®** *Remembering Fallen Friends* 🔊 **Audio** "The Vietnam Wall"	**Strategies for Annotation** • Analyze Representations in Different Mediums
Collection 1 Performance Tasks: **A** Present a Speech **B** Write an Analytical Essay	**fyi** hmhfyi.com	**Interactive Lessons** **A** Writing Arguments **A** Giving a Presentation **B** Writing Informative Texts **B** Using Textual Evidence

For Systematic Coverage of Writing and Speaking & Listening Standards

Interactive Lessons

Writing as a Process

Participating in Collaborative Discussions

Assess		Extend	Reteach
Performance Task	✓ *Assess It Online!*	**Teacher eBook**	**Teacher eBook**
Writing Activity: Argument	Selection Test	**Write an Argument > Interactive Lessons >** Writing Arguments	**Delineate and Evaluate an Argument >** *Level Up* **Tutorial >** Analyzing Arguments
Speaking Activity: Fairy Tale	Selection Test	**Write a Narrative > Interactive Lesson >** Writing Narratives	**Support Inferences About Theme >** *Level Up* **Tutorial >** Theme
Speaking Activity: Discussion	Selection Test	**Analyze Language**	**Determine Central Idea >** *Level Up* **Tutorial >** Main Idea and Supporting Details
Speaking Activity: Presentation	Selection Test	**Present a Speech > Interactive Lessons >** Analyzing and Evaluating Presentations	**Analyze Seminal U.S. Documents >** *Level Up* **Tutorial >** Evaluate an Argument
Media Activity: Reflection	Selection Test	**Conduct Research > Interactive Whiteboard Lesson >** How to Conduct an Effective Web Search	**Determine a Central Idea >** *Level Up* **Tutorial >** Theme
A Present a Speech **B** Write an Analytical Essay	Collection Test		

| **Lesson Assessments**
Writing as a Process
Participating in Collaborative Discussions | **Standards Support and Enrichment** | For more instruction and practice in reading literary and informational texts, language, spelling, and speaking and listening, see Teacher Resources > Standards Support and Enrichment. | |

Collection 1 Lessons	Key Learning Objective	Performance Task
ANCHOR TEXT **EXEMPLAR** **Argument by Anna Quindlen** "A Quilt of a Country," p. 3 A **Lexile 1260L**	**The student will be able to…** analyze and evaluate an author's claim and delineate and evaluate an argument	Writing Activity: Argument
ANCHOR TEXT **Short Story by Nadine Gordimer** "Once Upon a Time," p. 11A **Lexile 1390L**	**The student will be able to…** analyze author's choices concerning text structure; determine and support inferences about the theme; and cite text evidence to support analysis of the text	Speaking Activity: Fairy Tale
Essay by Kimberly M. Blaeser "Rituals of Memory," p. 21A **Lexile 1380L**	**The student will be able to…** determine a central idea and analyze its development over the course of a text	Speaking Activity: Discussion
EXEMPLAR **Speech by Abraham Lincoln** The Gettysburg Address, p. 27A **Lexile 1170L**	**The student will be able to…** analyze an author's purpose and the use of rhetorical devices in a seminal U.S. document	Speaking Activity: Presentation
Photo Essay "Views of the Wall," p. 33A **Poem by Alberto Ríos** "The Vietnam Wall" p. 33A	**The student will be able to…** analyze the representation of a subject in two different mediums	Media Activity: Reflection

Collection 1 Performance Tasks:

A Present a Speech
B Write an Analytical Essay

Vocabulary Strategy	Language and Style	Differentiated Instruction	CLOSE READER Selection
Patterns of Word Changes	Noun Clauses	**English Language Support:** Understand Cultural References **When Students Struggle:** Summarize	Blog by Eboo Patel "Making the Future Better, Together," p. 10b **Lexile 1170L**
Words from Latin	Prepositional Phrases	**English Language Support:** Analyze Language **When Students Struggle:** • Theme • Words from Latin **To Challenge Students:** Write from Author's Perspective	Short Story by Lisa Fugard "Night Calls," p. 20b **Lexile 1110L**
Denotations and Connotations		**English Language Support:** Analyze Language **When Students Struggle:** Main Idea and Supporting Details	
Multiple–Meaning Words	Parallel Structure	**English Language Support:** Analyze Language **When Students Struggle:** Comprehension **To Challenge Students:** Compare Speeches	Speech by Bill Clinton Oklahoma Bombing Memorial Address, p. 32b **Lexile 1060L**
		English Language Support: Build Background **When Students Struggle:** Compare Text and Photo	
	A Transition Words **B** Combine Ideas	**A English Language Support:** Adapt Language Choices **When Students Struggle:** Analyze the Text **To Challenge Students:** Add Media Features **B English Language Support:** Condense Ideas **When Students Struggle:** Write a Thesis Statement **To Challenge Students:** Broaden the Discussion	

A Quilt of a Country

ANCHOR TEXT EXEMPLAR

Argument by Anna Quindlen

Why This Text?

Students regularly encounter formal and informal arguments in media, in conversations, and in text materials. This lesson explores the argument that America is both a unified and fractured country that has been this way throughout history.

▶ **View It!**
Professional Development Podcast:
Teaching Argument

Key Learning Objective: The student will be able to analyze and evaluate an author's claim and delineate and evaluate an argument.

For additional practice:

Close Reader selection
"Making the Future Better, Together"
Blog by Eboo Patel

RI 1 Cite textual evidence.
RI 4 Determine the meaning of words and phrases.
RI 5 Analyze how an author's claims are developed.
RI 6 Determine an author's point of view and analyze how an author uses rhetoric.
RI 8 Delineate and evaluate the argument and claims in a text.
W 1 Write arguments.
W 1a Introduce precise claim(s).
W 1b Develop claim(s) and counterclaims.
L 1b Use various phrases and clauses.
L 4b Identify and use patterns of word changes.

▲ Text Complexity Rubric

Quantitative Measures	**A Quilt of a Country** Lexile: 1260L
Qualitative Measures	**Levels of Meaning/Purpose**  more than one purpose; implied, easily identified from context
	Structure organization of main ideas and details complex but mostly explicit
	Language Conventionality and Clarity some unfamiliar, academic, or domain-specific words
	Knowledge Demands  extensive knowledge of history required
Reader/Task Considerations	• Teacher determined • Vary by individual reader and type of text • See the Text X-Ray for suggested Reader/Task Considerations.

English Language Support Before teaching, use the Text X-Ray below for an overview of the text's complexity. The Text X-Ray and the supports and scaffolds in the Teacher's Edition will help you guide students of different skill levels.

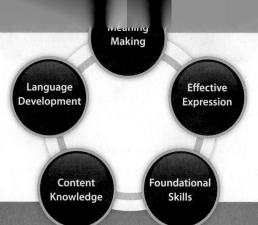

Text Complexity: Qualitative Measures

Levels of Meaning/Purpose

more than one purpose; implied, easily identified from context

Help students analyze and evaluate an author's claim.

- Teacher's Edition side notes, pp. 3, 5, 6, 7
- When Students Struggle, p. 6
- Analyze and Evaluate Author's Claim, p. 7

Guide students to analyze the use of rhetoric.

- Teacher's Edition side notes, p. 4

***ZOOM IN ON* ANALYZING AN AUTHOR'S CLAIM** Explain that sometimes the author of an argument states his or her **claim** in a sentence, but in other cases the reader must **infer** the claim using clues from a larger section of text. Discuss how the title of Quindlen's argument provides a clue to her claim. Make sure students know exactly what a quilt is, and have them find the sentence in the first paragraph that compares the United States to a quilt. Have students work in pairs to read the first paragraph closely and write a sentence stating Quindlen's claim. Then ask pairs to share their sentences with the class.

Structure

organization of main ideas and details complex but mostly explicit

Help students delineate and evaluate an argument.

- Teacher's Edition side notes, pp. 3, 4, 5, 6, 7
- Close Read Screencasts, p. 3
- Strategies for Annotation, p. 7
- Delineate and Evaluate an Argument, p. 7

To reteach delineating and evaluating an argument, see

- Delineate and Evaluate an Argument, p. 10a

To help students write an argument, see

- Performance Task, p. 8
- Write an Argument, p. 10a

▶ *Use It! Level Up* **tutorial:** Analyzing Arguments
Interactive Whiteboard Lessons: Evaluating Arguments, Writing Effective Arguments

***ZOOM IN ON* DELINEATING AND EVALUATING AN ARGUMENT** Point out that in this argument, the **counterarguments** are implied rather than stated directly. Have pairs discuss the following questions to help them identify counterarguments—points of view held by people who would disagree with Quindlen's claim.

- The first paragraph lays out Quindlen's claim. What words and phrases reveal her attitude toward America? *("notion that all men are created equal," "great," "ideal")*
- What words, ideas, and examples in the second and third paragraphs convey a very different attitude toward America? *("bigotry," "Slavery and sweatshops," "murder," "prideful apartheid," and so on)*
- What claims might a person with this opposite attitude make about America? State each claim in a sentence. *(Sample answer: America cannot escape its violent and unjust past.)*

Language Conventionality and Clarity

some unfamiliar, academic, or domain-specific words

Teach unfamiliar vocabulary in context.

- Teacher's Edition Critical Vocabulary notes, pp. 3, 4, 5, 9
- Applying Academic Vocabulary, p. 5
- Strategies for Annotation, p. 9

Help students determine the meaning of phrases.

- Teacher's Edition side notes, pp. 5, 6

Support students in recognizing patterns of word changes.

- Teacher's Edition side note, p. 9
- Strategies for Annotation, p. 9

Teach the correct use of noun clauses.

- Teacher's Edition side note, p. 10

ZOOM IN ON **USING CONTEXT** Remind students that **antonyms**, words with opposite or nearly opposite meanings, can provide **context clues** to the meaning of an unfamiliar word. Have pairs locate each of the following words, find an antonym in the surrounding text, and define both words.

- *tolerance*, line 12 (*bigotry*)
- *tragedy*, line 20 (*blessings*)
- *quaint*, line 33 (*incendiary*)
- *disparate*, line 50 (*common*)

Ask pairs to share their definitions. Then discuss the **oxymoron** "fractured coalescing" (line 75). This creative phrase combines words with opposite meanings into a single idea.

Knowledge Demands

extensive knowledge of history required

Support English Learners in understanding the historical and cultural references in the text.

- Teacher's Edition Background note, p. 3
- English Language Support, p. 4

ZOOM IN ON **BUILDING HISTORICAL KNOWLEDGE** Help students understand references to American history in the text.

- In lines 13–15, "the burning of crosses" and "the lynching of blacks" refer to the violence and intimidation African Americans faced after slavery ended in 1865.
- In line 16, "the murders of gay men" refers to the victimization of gay men, like Matthew Shepard, a 21-year old who was beaten and left to die near Laramie, Wyoming in 1988.
- Lines 78–87 reflect the fact that immigrants have come to the United States in waves. The first waves were from European countries, but today more immigrants come from Asia, the Middle East, and Latin America.

Suggested Reader/Task Considerations

You might consider the following before assigning this argument to students.

- Will students develop an interest in the topic as a result of reading the text?
- Do students have prior experience with the **genre** that will help them manage the content?

ZOOM IN ON **SUPPORTING COMPREHENSION**

- Ask small groups to discuss the forces that bring people together and those that tear them apart.
- Remind students that this piece is selection is an argument. As they read, suggest students take notes when they disagree with the author.

Background Have students read the background note. Tell students that the attacks of September 11, 2001, brought expressions of sympathy from around the world. The attacks sparked feelings of patriotism among many Americans, but some became distrustful of Arab immigrants and others of perceived Middle Eastern descent. Many Americans also questioned the nation's immigration and visitation policies.

AS YOU READ Direct students to use the As You Read statement to focus their reading. Remind students to write down any questions they generate during reading.

Analyze and Evaluate an Author's Claim (LINES 4–6)   RI 5

Note that one way authors can support their position, or **claim,** is by using quotations or references from other respected writers.

A **ASK STUDENTS** what idea the Daniel Boorstin quotation in lines 4–6 supports. *(The idea that America is built from parts that do not easily fit.)*

Delineate and Evaluate an Argument (LINES 1–13)   RI 1, RI 8

Explain that when writers introduce an argument, they need to define, or **delineate,** the issues and ideas they will develop over the course of the text.

B **CITE TEXT EVIDENCE** Have students reread lines 1–13 and identify two ideas that readers can expect Quindlen to develop in the text. *(The American ideal is like a patchwork quilt that unifies ideas, but the society has often failed to find unity.)*

CRITICAL VOCABULARY

discordant: Quindlen suggests that the United States has been constructed in an uneven manner unlike that of a harmonious melody. **ASK STUDENTS** to describe how a "crazy quilt" might seem discordant. *(The fabrics may clash.)*

pluralistic: Quindlen notes that the United States combines many ethnic and cultural groups. **ASK STUDENTS** to provide an example of how American society is pluralistic. *(Americans' religious beliefs vary widely.)*

Background *Author **Anna Quindlen** (b. 1953) was born in Philadelphia. She is a columnist and author who has been described as having a "common touch" because so many people relate to her writings about politics and gender-specific issues. In 1992, she became the third woman to win a Pulitzer Prize for commentary. "A Quilt of a Country" was published after the World Trade Center attacks of September 11, 2001. The argument was written at a time when many people were thinking about what it means to be an American.*

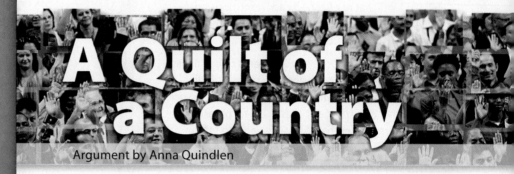

A Quilt of a Country

Argument by Anna Quindlen

AS YOU READ Pay attention to how the details in the text support the idea of America as "an improbable idea." Write down any questions you generate during reading.

myNotebook

As you read, mark up the text. Save your work to *my*Notebook.
- Highlight details.
- Add notes and questions.
- Add new words to *my*WordList.

America is an improbable idea. A mongrel[1] nation built of ever-changing disparate[2] parts, it is held together by a notion, the notion that all men are created equal, though everyone knows that most men consider themselves better than someone. "Of all the nations in the world, the United States was built in nobody's image," the historian Daniel Boorstin wrote. That's because it was built of bits and pieces that seem **discordant**, like the crazy quilts that have been one of its great folk-art forms, velvet and calico and checks and brocades. Out of many, one. That is the ideal.

10   The reality is often quite different, a great national striving consisting frequently of failure. Many of the oft-told stories of the most **pluralistic** nation on earth are stories not of tolerance, but of bigotry. Slavery and sweatshops, the burning of crosses

discordant
(dĭ-skôr´dnt) *adj.* conflicting or not harmonious.

pluralistic
(plŏŏr´ə-lĭs´tĭc) *adj.* consisting of many ethnic and cultural groups.

---

[1] **mongrel:** something produced by mixing different breeds.
[2] **disparate:** distinct or not alike.

Image Credits: (c) ©Boston Globe via Getty Images; (tr) ©Bobby Bank/WireImage/Getty Images

A Quilt of a Country   **3**

Close Read Screencasts   Close Read

Modeled Discussions

Have students click the Close Read icons in their eBooks to access the two screencasts in which readers discuss and annotate the following key passages:

- statement of inherent conflicts within American ideals (lines 22–28)
- statement of two basic American attitudes (lines 72–79)

As a class, view and discuss at least one of these videos. Then have students pair up to do an independent close read of an additional passage—Quindlen's concluding sentences (lines 94–103).

Delineate and Evaluate an Argument (LINES 14–29)   RI 8

Tell students that to effectively address opposing viewpoints, authors often use **counterarguments** supported by **evidence.**

C CITE TEXT EVIDENCE Have students reread lines 14–19 to identify the opposing viewpoint Quindlen wants to address. *(It is difficult to know how to convince them … that amid all the failures …)* What phrases lead readers to infer that Quindlen wants to refute that viewpoint? *(In lines 18–19, she suggests there is "something spectacularly successful" in America. She then refers to "enormous blessings" [line 21] and goes on to present her counterargument [lines 22–28].)*

Analyze Use of Rhetoric   RI 1, RI 6
(LINES 29–39)

Note that Quindlen ends this section with a question [lines 37–39], suggesting readers know the answer.

D CITE TEXT EVIDENCE Have students identify the evidence Quindlen provides to answer the question in lines 37–39. *(She cites instances from New York and Philadelphia of conflicts between different ethnic groups. She references literature to support her claim.)*

Analyze Use of Rhetoric (LINES 40–49)   RI 1, RI 6

Explain that writers can emphasize ideas with a **rhetorical question** that doesn't expect an answer.

E CITE TEXT EVIDENCE Ask what ideas Quindlen stresses with the rhetorical questions in lines 40–49. *(There are extensive ethnic divisions within America.)*

CRITICAL VOCABULARY

interwoven: Quindlen suggests America could not be split into countries because it is like a piece of cloth with threads woven together.
ASK STUDENTS how ideals and beliefs might be interwoven. *(People's religious beliefs are sometimes closely blended with their political ideals.)*

---

and the ostracism[3] of the other. Children learn in social-studies class and in the news of the lynching of blacks, the denial of rights to women, the murders of gay men. It is difficult to know how to convince them that this amounts to "crown thy good with brotherhood," that amid all the failures is something spectacularly successful. Perhaps they understand it at this

20   moment, when enormous tragedy, as it so often does, demands a time of reflection on enormous blessings.

This is a nation founded on a conundrum,[4] what Mario Cuomo[5] has characterized as "community added to individualism." These two are our defining ideals; they are also in constant conflict. Historians today bemoan the ascendancy of a kind of prideful apartheid[6] in America, saying that the clinging to ethnicity, in background and custom, has undermined the concept of unity. These historians must have forgotten the past, or have gilded it. The New York of my children is no more Balkanized,[7] probably

30   less so, than the Philadelphia of my father, in which Jewish boys would walk several blocks out of their way to avoid the Irish divide of Chester Avenue. (I was the product of a mixed marriage, across barely bridgeable lines: an Italian girl, an Irish boy. How quaint it seems now, how incendiary then.) The Brooklyn of Francie Nolan's famous tree, the Newark of which Portnoy complained, even the uninflected WASP suburbs of Cheever's characters:[8] they are ghettos, pure and simple. Do the Cambodians and the Mexicans in California coexist less easily today than did the Irish and Italians of Massachusetts a century ago? You know the answer.

40   What is the point of this splintered whole? What is the point of a nation in which Arab cabbies chauffeur Jewish passengers through the streets of New York—and in which Jewish cabbies chauffeur Arab passengers, too, and yet speak in theory of hatred, one for the other? What is the point of a nation in which one part seems to be always on the verge of fisticuffs with another, blacks and whites, gays and straights, left and right, Pole and Chinese and Puerto Rican and Slovenian? Other countries with such divisions have in fact divided into new nations with new names, but not this one, impossibly **interwoven** even in its hostilities.

interwoven
(ĭn´tər-wō´vən) *adj.*
blended or laced together.

---

[3] **ostracism:** exclusion or separation from society.
[4] **conundrum:** a riddle or a puzzle.
[5] **Mario Cuomo:** Governor of New York from 1983 until 1994.
[6] **apartheid:** a political system of racial or ethnic separation and discrimination.
[7] **Balkanized:** divided into small, uncooperative groups like countries on the Balkan Peninsula in the early 20th century.
[8] **Francie Nolan's . . . WASP suburbs of Cheever's characters:** characters in the novels *A Tree Grows in Brooklyn* and *Portnoy's Complaint*; John Cheever's characters were generally White Anglo-Saxon Protestants, or WASPs.

ENGLISH LANGUAGE SUPPORT

Understand Cultural References Help students understand the phrase "Out of many, one" based on context clues. *(one nation made up of diverse groups)* Explain that the phrase is a translation of the Latin motto *E Pluribus Unum*, which appears on U.S. currency.

ASK STUDENTS to repeat the exercise with "crown thy good with brotherhood" in lines 17–18. *(Honor righteousness with camaraderie, solidarity, and compassion.)* Point out that the author quotes the patriotic song "America the Beautiful."

"What is the point of this splintered whole?"

50   Once these disparate parts were held together by a common enemy, by the fault lines of world wars and the electrified fence of communism. With the end of the cold war[9] there was the creeping concern that without a focus for hatred and distrust, a sense of national identity would evaporate, that the left side of the hyphen— African-American, Mexican-American, Irish-American—would overwhelm the right. And slow-growing domestic traumas like economic unrest and increasing crime seemed more likely to emphasize division than community. Today the citizens of the United States have come together once more because of armed conflict and
60 enemy attack. Terrorism has led to devastation—and unity.

    Yet even in 1994, the overwhelming majority of those surveyed by the National Opinion Research Center agreed with this statement: "The U.S. is a unique country that stands for something special in the world." One of the things that it stands for is this vexing notion that a great nation can consist entirely of refugees from other nations, that people of different, even warring religions and cultures can live, if not side by side, then on either side of the country's Chester Avenues. Faced with this **diversity** there is little point in trying to isolate anything remotely resembling a national
70 character, but there are two strains of behavior that, however tenuously, abet the concept of unity.

diversity
(dĭ-vûr´sĭ-tē) *n.*
having varied
social and/or ethnic
backgrounds.

[9] **cold war:** diplomatic and economic hostility between the United States and the Soviet Union and their respective allies in the decades following World War II.

A Quilt of a Country   **5**

APPLYING ACADEMIC VOCABULARY

entity	internal

As you discuss the Quindlen argument, incorporate the following Collection 1 academic vocabulary words: *entity* and *internal*. To consider Quindlen's claims, ask students to determine if Quindlen describes America as a single **entity** or more as a collection of disparate cultural groups. In examining paragraph 5, ask students to compare the **internal** forces that separate groups with the external forces that draw them together.

CLOSE READ

Analyze and Evaluate Author's Claim (LINES 50–60)   RI 5

Note that strong arguments use **evidence** that connects claims and other widely accepted ideas.

(F) CITE TEXT EVIDENCE Direct students to reread lines 50–60 and identify the connection the author draws between the past and the present. *(Quindlen connects the period just after the 9/11 attacks with the cold war because Americans were united against a common enemy during both periods.)*

Determine the Meaning of Phrases (LINES 53–56)   RI 4

Tell students that authors often restate or define the meanings of phrases in adjacent phrases and clauses.

(G) CITE TEXT EVIDENCE Have students identify the idea that Quindlen restates in lines 53–56. *("the left side of the hyphen . . . would overwhelm the right" restates the idea that "a sense of national identity would evaporate" by implying people would identify more with their ethnic backgrounds than their nationality.)*

Delineate and Evaluate an Argument (LINES 61–71)   RI 8

Point out that Quindlen uses a public opinion poll as **evidence** to support her argument.

(H) ASK STUDENTS to reread lines 61–71 and identify the idea that this evidence supports. *(Americans possess a "concept of unity" even when they are not focused against a common enemy. A large majority felt so in 1994—after the cold war ended and before 9/11.)*

CRITICAL VOCABULARY

diversity: Quindlen refers to the differences within the United States because it has grown as a country of refugees from opposing countries and religions. **ASK STUDENTS** how diversity could strengthen and weaken a nation. *(Different beliefs could spur innovation and conflicts.)*

Delineate and Evaluate an Argument (LINES 72–87) RI 8

Point out the Leonel Castillo quotation that Quindlen uses to support her argument.

(I) ASK STUDENTS Direct students to reread lines 79–87 to determine if the quotation is relevant to Quindlen's claims and, if so, to cite the lines it supports. *(Castillo's quotation is relevant to lines 75–79, which suggest that "new immigrants are not so different . . .")*

Determine the Meaning of Phrases (LINE 89) RI 4, RI 6

Note the phrase Quindlen uses to describe tolerance.

(J) CITE TEXT EVIDENCE Have students look for context clues in lines 88–91 to help them determine the meaning of the phrase. Ask what viewpoint Quindlen suggests by using this description in connection with successful coexistence. *(She uses the phrase to indicate a minimal description of the triumph of coexistence. She believes that there is much more to Americans' acceptance of others than just "tolerance.")*

Analyze and Evaluate Author's Claim (LINES 97–100) RI 5

Explain that in a conclusion, writers often restate claims presented at the beginning of an argument.

(J) ASK STUDENTS to reread lines 97–103 to explain what evidence Quindlen uses to restate her claim. *(She uses the fact that immigrants from all over the world were victims of the terrorist attacks to lead to the restatement of her claim that America has for many years accepted immigrants from everywhere.)*

COLLABORATIVE DISCUSSION Have pairs discuss the quotations, references, facts, and other information Quindlen uses to support her argument. Have them share their ideas with the class.

ASK STUDENTS to share any questions they generated in the course of reading and discussing the selection.

There is that Calvinist undercurrent[10] in the American psyche that loves the difficult, the demanding, that sees mastering the impossible, whether it be prairie or subway, as a test of character, and so glories in the struggle of this fractured coalescing. And there is a grudging fairness among the citizens of the United States that eventually leads most to admit that, no matter what the English-only advocates try to suggest, the new immigrants are not so different from our own parents or grandparents. Leonel Castillo,
80 former director of the Immigration and Naturalization Service and himself the grandson of Mexican immigrants, once told the writer Studs Terkel proudly, "The old neighborhood Ma-Pa stores are still around. They are not Italian or Jewish or Eastern European any more. Ma and Pa are now Korean, Vietnamese, Iraqi, Jordanian, Latin American. They live in the store. They work seven days a week. Their kids are doing well in school. They're making it. Sound familiar?"

Tolerance is the word used most often when this kind of coexistence succeeds, but tolerance is a vanilla-pudding word, **(J)**
90 standing for little more than the allowance of letting others live unremarked and unmolested. Pride seems excessive, given the American willingness to endlessly complain about them, them being whoever is new, different, unknown, or currently under suspicion. But patriotism is partly taking pride in this unlikely ability to throw all of us together in a country that across its length and breadth is as different as a dozen countries, and still be able to call it by one name. When photographs of the faces of all those who died in the World Trade Center destruction are assembled in one place, it will be possible to trace in the skin color, the shape of **(K)**
100 the eyes and the noses, the texture of the hair, a map of the world. These are the representatives of a mongrel nation that somehow, at times like this, has one spirit. Like many improbable ideas, when it actually works, it's a wonder.

COLLABORATIVE DISCUSSION Why does Anna Quindlen consider America to be "an improbable idea"? Discuss Quindlen's argument with a partner.

[10] **Calvinist undercurrent:** the social influence of Calvinism, a Christian religion with a strict moral code and a belief in God as absolutely sovereign.

WHEN STUDENTS STRUGGLE...

To increase students' comprehension, have students work in pairs to write a one-sentence summary of each paragraph of Quindlen's argument in a chart like the one shown. Then have students use the chart to write a two-sentence summary of the entire article.

Paragraph	Summary Sentence
1	*The American ideal is to create unity out of many different and sometimes conflicting parts.*
2	

Delineate and Evaluate an Argument

RI 8

In "A Quilt of a Country," Anna Quindlen presents an **argument** about how America works as a country. An argument presents a claim, or position, on an issue and supports it with reasons and evidence. To evaluate the strength of Quindlen's argument, you must **delineate,** or describe in detail, these elements:

- Identify the **claim,** or Quindlen's position, on the issue.
- Look for the **reasons** Quindlen uses to support her claim. Reasons should be valid and logical.
- Evaluate whether the **evidence** Quindlen cites for each reason is credible, or believable, and relevant to the claim. Evidence can include facts, statistics, examples, anecdotes, or quotations.
- Look for **counterarguments,** which are statements that address opposing viewpoints. Does Quindlen anticipate opposing viewpoints and provide counterarguments to disprove them?

Analyze and Evaluate Author's Claim

RI 5

To support a **claim,** authors develop and refine their ideas throughout the text. An author may use a particular sentence to develop a claim, or use an entire paragraph or larger section of the text to develop a claim with reasons and evidence.

Use a chart to help you analyze and evaluate how Anna Quindlen develops her claim in "A Quilt of a Country." First, identify the claim. Then, list specific reasons or evidence from the text. Finally, evaluate if the reason or evidence supports the claim. Read this example from a student newspaper editorial.

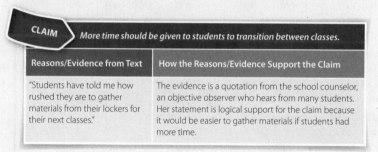

CLAIM *More time should be given to students to transition between classes.*

Reasons/Evidence from Text	How the Reasons/Evidence Support the Claim
"Students have told me how rushed they are to gather materials from their lockers for their next classes."	The evidence is a quotation from the school counselor, an objective observer who hears from many students. Her statement is logical support for the claim because it would be easier to gather materials if students had more time.

TEACH

CLOSE READ

Delineate and Evaluate an Argument

RI 8

Discuss the key terms related to argument. Number the paragraphs 1–8 and have students identify whether each paragraph presents a claim, supports a claim with reasons and evidence, or addresses a counterargument. *(Paragraph 1 presents the claim; paragraphs 2-3 address counterarguments; paragraphs 4–8 support the claim with reasons and evidence.)*

Analyze and Evaluate Author's Claim

RI 5

Discuss the differences between a reason and evidence when a writer supports a claim. *(A reason describes a general principle that supports a claim; evidence helps prove a claim.)* Have students work in groups to identify Quindlen's claim. *(America is united despite conflicts that have arisen as a result of its diverse population.)* Guide groups to complete a chart like the one shown, using paragraph 5 as an example that presents reasons and evidence to refute a counterargument. *(Reasons/Evidence from Text: Historians have forgotten conflicts of the past. How the Reasons/Evidence Support the Claim: Descriptions of earlier Philadelphia and other areas show that cultural divisions have been a regular part of the American past, just as they are today.)* Direct students to complete the chart for the rest of Quindlen's reason and evidence. They should note whether the reasons and evidence are logical and sufficient to support Quindlen's claim.

Strategies for Annotation 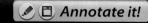 *Annotate it!*

Delineate and Evaluate an Argument

RI 8

Share these strategies for guided or independent analysis:

- Review the claim that Quindlen makes in her argument.
- Highlight in green the counterarguments Quindlen gives to address opposing views.
- Highlight in blue each reason and evidence that Quindlen provides to support her claims.

rights to women, the murders of gay men. It is difficult to know how to convince them that this amounts to "crown thy good with brotherhood," that amid all the failures is something spectacularly successful. Perhaps they understand it at this moment, when enormous tragedy, as it so often does, demands a time of reflection on enormous blessings.

Analyzing the Text
RI 1, RI 4, RI 5, RI 6, RI 8

Possible answers:

1. *Quindlen claims that the United States is an idea/concept that works despite the fact that it shouldn't. It is unique because the country perseveres even though other countries with similar challenges have dissolved.*

2. *She indicates that America is made up of many different pieces that do not resemble each other yet are stitched together into a unified whole. This supports the claim that Americans have ties that bind them in spite of their differences.*

3. *Quindlen explores the opposing claim that the nation fails more than it succeeds. She cites examples such as bigotry, slavery, sweatshops, and ostracism. Her counterargument is that the United States is "spectacularly successful" because it is "enormously blessed." While the evidence is relevant and seems to speak to the reader emotionally, it is not sufficient, because it does not provide specifics about how the United States is blessed.*

4. *She repeats the rhetorical question "What is the point of . . ." three times in the paragraph. Her repetition emphasizes the power of the cultural divisions and challenges America faces in trying to create and maintain a unified country.*

5. *She repeats the phrases "a mongrel nation" and "an improbable idea." By repeating these phrases in reference to the people killed in the terrorist attacks, she supports the idea that American society includes diverse members who manage to function alongside each other in many areas, such as working together at the World Trade Center in New York City.*

6. *The quotation in lines 4–6 supports Quindlen's claim that the pieces of America are extremely varied and not designed to fit together. Lines 61–64 cite a public opinion poll that supports the claim that Americans' ability to live together is special. The quotation in lines 82–87 supports the claim that today's immigrants are not very different from immigrants a few generations before.*

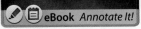
eBook *Annotate It!*

Analyzing the Text
RI 1, RI 4, RI 5, RI 6, RI 8, W 1a–b

Cite Text Evidence Support your responses with evidence from the selection.

1. **Summarize** What is Anna Quindlen's claim in "A Quilt of a Country"? Summarize her claim in your own words.

2. **Interpret** In lines 7–8, what does Quindlen mean when she describes America as being "like the crazy quilts that have been one of its great folk-art forms"? How does this description support her claim?

3. **Evaluate** What opposing viewpoint does Quindlen respond to in paragraph 3? What counterargument does she offer to it? List the reasons and evidence she includes in her counterargument and evaluate if it is relevant and sufficient.

4. **Analyze** In paragraph 4, Quindlen uses **repetition** and **parallelism**—expressing related ideas using similar grammatical constructions. What sentence structure and words does she repeat? What is the effect of this repetition?

5. **Analyze** Reread Quindlen's conclusion. What specific words and phrases does she use to link the conclusion to her introduction? How do these words and phrases support her argument?

6. **Evaluate** Quindlen uses many different types of evidence throughout the argument to support her claim, for example, facts, statistics, and quotations. Identity at least three examples of evidence and evaluate how she uses each one to support her claim.

PERFORMANCE TASK

Writing Activity: Argument Using what you have learned about how to develop an argument, write and support a claim about a positive aspect of your school or community.

1. Think about something you feel is an important, positive feature of your school or community. Write a claim about it.

2. Make notes about the reasons that support your claim. Then collect evidence that supports your reasons. Consider an opposing claim and list valid counterarguments.

3. Write the draft of your argument. Work carefully to present your reasons and evidence in a logical order.

4. Revise your draft to eliminate unrelated or illogical evidence. Finally, check your work to make sure you have used the conventions of standard English.

Assign this performance task.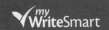

PERFORMANCE TASK
W 1a-b

Writing Activity: Argument Have students work in pairs or small groups. Remind them that gathering evidence for a claim related to their school or community may involve further research such as finding statistics, quoting from a newspaper or other written reports, or conducting personal interviews. See page 10a for further instruction on citing evidence to support an argument.

Critical Vocabulary

Practice and Apply Answer the following questions and explain your ideas.

discordant	pluralistic	interwoven	diversity

1. If a piece of music is **discordant**, do you want to continue listening or not? Why?

2. Is a society made up of one cultural group a **pluralistic** society, or not? Why?

3. Is an all-school assembly an example of an **interwoven** school community? Explain.

4. What is one way that **diversity** strengthens a community? Explain your idea.

Vocabulary Strategy: Patterns of Word Changes

Words can have different meanings or be different parts of speech. Many words have several different meanings listed in the dictionary. For example, the word *equal*, as used in "A Quilt of a Country," means "having the same privileges or rights." However, it also means "being the same or identical." Knowing the different meanings of words can help you become an effective reader.

Words also change depending on the part of speech to which they belong. The Critical Vocabulary words *discordant* and *pluralistic* change spelling and meaning when the part of speech changes. Knowing how a word functions in a sentence will help you gain a complete understanding of the word's meaning.

Practice and Apply Complete the sentences with the correct word from the chart.

Noun	Verb	Adjective
discord—lack of agreement	**pluralize**—to engage in pluralism	**discordant**—conflicting
pluralism—a condition of society where many groups coexist		**pluralistic**—consisting of many ethnic and cultural groups

1. The people shouting indicated the level of _____ during the meeting.

2. Some governmental entities claim to be _____ because people of different ethnic groups work together.

3. The _____ parts of the book made it difficult to understand.

4. Even when a country tries to have _____, there can be unfairness and resentment.

Critical Vocabulary

Possible answers:

1. *No, because a discordant piece of music is probably made up of notes that don't sound pleasant together.*

2. *No, because pluralistic is an adjective that describes a society made up of many groups.*

3. *Yes, an all-school assembly would be an example of the students being interwoven because all the classrooms would be blended together at the assembly.*

4. *One example of strength through diversity would be that different points of view from people of varied social backgrounds lead to more appropriate solutions to issues.*

Vocabulary Strategy: Patterns of Word Changes

Answers:

1. *discord*

2. *pluralistic*

3. *discordant*

4. *pluralism*

Strategies for Annotation 🖊 🗐 *Annotate it!*

Patterns of Word Change

Have students locate the sentences containing *discordant, pluralistic, interwoven,* and *diversity* in the article. Encourage them to use their eBook annotation tools to do the following:

- Highlight in yellow each of the Critical Vocabulary words.
- Use the notes tool to rewrite the sentence or phrase using another form of the Critical Vocabulary word.

image," the historian Daniel Boorstin wrote. That's because it was built of bits and pieces that seem discordant, like the crazy quilts

> to cause discord

PRACTICE & APPLY

Language and Style: Noun Clauses

L 1b

Remind students that there is no single correct way to use a noun clause and that the varied use of noun clauses is a way for students to experiment with their writing and refine it to make it lively and interesting. This can be true in both fiction and nonfiction and may be a way for them to construct a unique and interesting style of writing.

Possible answers: *Answers will vary because of the unique writing done by each student. When students have completed the exercise, they should be able to point to at least one example in their writing of a noun clause used as a subject, direct object, predicate nominative, and object of a preposition.*

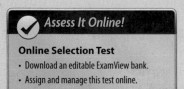

✓ Assess It Online!

Online Selection Test
- Download an editable ExamView bank.
- Assign and manage this test online.

Language and Style: Noun Clauses

L 1b

A subordinate clause contains a subject and a verb, but it cannot stand alone in a sentence. A **noun clause** is a subordinate clause that takes the place of a noun in a sentence. It usually begins with *that, what, whatever, why, whether, how, who, whom, whoever,* or *whomever.*

A noun clause may function in a sentence as the subject, the direct object, the predicate nominative, or the object of a preposition.

Examples of Noun Clauses	
subject	**What Anna Quindlen wrote** was very thoughtful.
direct object	Many people don't appreciate **that America is made up of many diverse cultures.**
predicate nominative	My suggestion is **that we learn how to live together peacefully.**
object of a preposition	I will share my ideas with **whoever will listen.**

Writers use noun clauses to convey precise meanings and to add variety and interest to their writing. Read this sentence from the text in which Anna Quindlen strings together multiple noun clauses:

> It is difficult to know how to convince them that this amounts to "crown thy good with brotherhood," that amid all the failures is something spectacularly successful.

In this sentence, the first noun clause, *how to convince,* is the direct object of *know.* The second two noun clauses that begin with *that* are direct objects of *convince.* This sentence has a different structure from surrounding sentences in the paragraph. By using noun clauses to vary sentence structures, Quindlen keeps her readers engaged and interested.

Practice and Apply Look back at the argument about a positive aspect of your school or community you created in this selection's Performance Task. Revise your argument to include at least one noun clause for each of the four functions listed in the chart above. Then, discuss with a partner how the noun clauses add variety and interest to your writing.

Write an Argument

W 1

TEACH

This selection's Performance Task asks students to write an argument that supports a claim about a positive aspect of their school or community. Tell students that an effective argument will contain a precise claim and relevant evidence.

Remind students that a **claim** presents a position, and it should make clear to the reader what the writer thinks about an issue. Remind them also that each reason given to support a claim will need **evidence** that is not only believable but is also related to the issue.

PRACTICE AND APPLY

Display an example of a claim that may name a positive aspect but does not express a position. Invite students to revise the claim so that is it more precise. Explain that a specific position should be obvious.

Example: *My community has a recreational center.*

Revised example: *The recreational center in my community benefits many people.*

Next, present two examples of evidence, one that is unrelated to a claim and reason, and one that is relevant. Ask students to identify the evidence that best supports the claim and reason.

Claim and Reason: *The recreational center in my community benefits many people. People of all ages can take classes at the center.*

Evidence: *Doctors say that children should receive at least one hour of exercise each day.* (unrelated) *My younger brother participates in a karate class each week, and my mother takes a yoga class every Tuesday.* (relevant)

Direct students to utilize these strategies as they write or revise the arguments they create in response to the Performance Task.

Before students write or revise their arguments, have them complete the appropriate interactive lessons within **Writing Arguments.**

Delineate and Evaluate an Argument

RI 8

RETEACH

Review the terms *claim, reasons, evidence,* and *counterarguments.* Then give an example of a claim, such as, "To improve learning, student homework should be reduced."

- Ask students to provide examples of types of reasons and evidence that might be used to support the claim. *(Sample reason: Too much homework can reduce student interest in a subject.)*
- Provide the following opposing claim: "Homework helps improve test scores." Ask students how they might refute this opposing view. *(Sample counterargument: Test scores show the level of test preparation, not the true level of learning.)*

 LEVEL UP TUTORIALS Assign the following *Level Up* tutorial: **Analyzing Arguments**

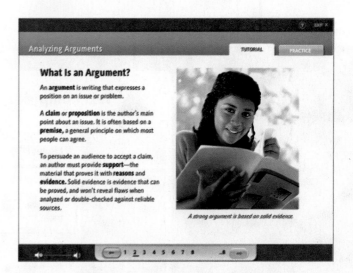

A strong argument is based on solid evidence.

INDEPENDENT READING

Students can apply the skill to a current magazine or newspaper editorial or Internet blog. Have them work independently to outline the claim, reasons and evidence, and counterargument. Ask: Does the writer include enough support to prove the claim? Does the argument adequately address opposing viewpoints?

Making the Future Better, Together

Blog by Eboo Patel

Why This Text

Students may have difficulty thoroughly understanding the writer's ideas and evidence in an argument. The following argument by Eboo Patel cites complex reasoning and difficult quotations that become clear only with careful study. With the help of the close-reading questions, students will trace and evaluate Patel's argument that claims that the United States is a nation that cherishes its diversity. This close reading will guide students to comprehend Patel's argument.

Background Have students read the background and biographical information about Eboo Patel, the founder and president of the Interfaith Youth Core. That organization brings together people of all faiths to work together to build a better future. Patel has written for numerous publications and has spoken at universities around the world. His blog *The Faith Divide* examines religious issues that unite people—and issues that drive them apart.

AS YOU READ Ask students to pay close attention to the reasons Patel gives to support his position about diversity in America. How soon into Patel's blog can they begin to identify his point of view?

Standards Support

- cite strong and thorough textual evidence
- analyze how an author's ideas or claims are developed and refined
- trace and evaluate an argument
- assess an author's claims and reasoning

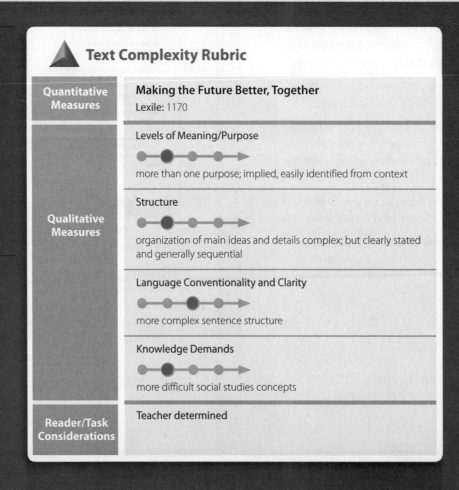

▲ Text Complexity Rubric

Quantitative Measures	**Making the Future Better, Together** Lexile: 1170
Qualitative Measures	**Levels of Meaning/Purpose** more than one purpose; implied, easily identified from context
	Structure organization of main ideas and details complex; but clearly stated and generally sequential
	Language Conventionality and Clarity more complex sentence structure
	Knowledge Demands more difficult social studies concepts
Reader/Task Considerations	Teacher determined

Strategies for CLOSE READING

Trace and Evaluate an Argument

Students should read this blog carefully all the way through. Close-reading questions at the bottom of the page will help them focus on a thorough analysis of the argument and the evidence, including details, facts, quotations, and examples that support them. As they read, students should record comments or questions about the text in the side margins.

WHEN STUDENTS STRUGGLE . . .

To help students follow the reasons Patel gives to support his claim about our nation's respect for diversity, have students work in a small group to fill out a chart such as the one shown below as they analyze the blog entry.

CITE TEXT EVIDENCE For practice in tracing an argument, ask students to cite the evidence Patel uses to support each reason.

CLAIM: *The United States is a nation that cherishes its diversity.*

SUPPORT:

Reason 1: He cites George Washington's view that the nation needed to be built without bigotry or ethnic or religious persecution.

Reason 2: He agrees with Washington that a diverse democracy based on respect, relationship, and service to the common good will thrive.

Reason 3: He states that the "essence of our nation" is still that people's identities will be respected, their freedoms protected, and their safety secured.

Reason 4: He agrees with the idea of Dr. Martin Luther King Jr. that for real change to occur, people must work together to build bridges, community, and the future.

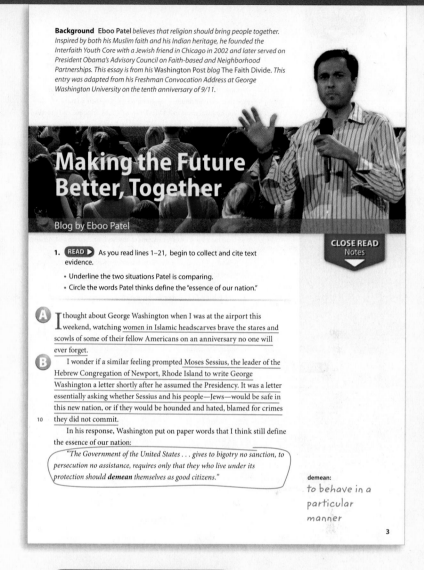

Background Eboo Patel *believes that religion should bring people together. Inspired by both his Muslim faith and his Indian heritage, he founded the Interfaith Youth Core with a Jewish friend in Chicago in 2002 and later served on President Obama's Advisory Council on Faith-based and Neighborhood Partnerships. This essay is from his Washington Post blog* The Faith Divide. *This entry was adapted from his Freshman Convocation Address at George Washington University on the tenth anniversary of 9/11.*

Making the Future Better, Together

Blog by Eboo Patel

CLOSE READ Notes

1. **READ ▶** As you read lines 1–21, begin to collect and cite text evidence.

   • Underline the two situations Patel is comparing.
   • Circle the words Patel thinks define the "essence of our nation."

A I thought about George Washington when I was at the airport this weekend, watching <u>women in Islamic headscarves brave the stares and scowls of some of their fellow Americans on an anniversary no one will ever forget.</u>

B I wonder if a similar feeling prompted <u>Moses Sessius, the leader of the Hebrew Congregation of Newport, Rhode Island to write George Washington a letter shortly after he assumed the Presidency. It was a letter essentially asking whether Sessius and his people—Jews—would be safe in this new nation, or if they would be hounded and hated, blamed for crimes</u>
10 they did not commit.

In his response, Washington put on paper words that I think still define the essence of our nation:

*"The Government of the United States . . . gives to bigotry no sanction, to persecution no assistance, requires only that they who live under its protection should **demean** themselves as good citizens."*

demean:
to behave in a particular manner

3

---

1. **READ AND CITE TEXT EVIDENCE** Explain that Patel compares two situations to open his blog—one from the present, the other from the past—prefacing the situations with a reference to George Washington to get the reader's attention.

A **ASK STUDENTS** to identify the two situations Patel is comparing, citing evidence from lines 1–21, and citing words and sentences from Washington that Patel thinks define the "essence of our nation." *Responses may include specific references to lines 2–4 and 5–10, and to lines 11–15 and 16–21.*

Critical Vocabulary: demean (line 15) Have students share their definitions of *demean* as Washington used it in the text cited by Patel. *Washington used it to mean "to behave in a particular manner."* Point out that *demean* is a word with multiple meanings. The same word from a different origin is more commonly used today. Ask students what this word means. *It means "to degrade."*

In this new nation, the new president was saying, people would have their identities respected, their freedoms protected, their safety secured. They would be encouraged to cultivate good relationships with fellow citizens from other backgrounds, no matter the tensions and conflicts in
20   the lands from which they came. And they would be invited—and expected—to contribute to the common good of their country.

Washington came to his views through both principle and practical experience. As the leader of the Continental Army, the first truly national
C   institution, Washington recognized he was going to need the contributions of all willing groups in America. Back then, it was a common anti-Catholic practice to burn the Pope in effigy. Washington banned this, and other anti-Catholic insults within the Continental Army, and wrote: "At such a juncture, and in such circumstances, to be insulting their Religion, is so monstrous, as not to be suffered or excused."

30   Washington brought this ethic to his private life. When seeking a carpenter and a bricklayer for his Mount Vernon estate, he remarked: "If they are good workmen, they may be of Asia, Africa, or Europe. They may be Mohometans,[1] Jews or Christians of any Sect, or they may be Atheists." What mattered is what they could build.

Wars between clans and tribes, tension between sects and groups, prejudice directed at religion or nationality—those were the problems of past centuries. And whether you are reading the news about Somalia or Libya or Europe or Oklahoma, those are the problems of our time.

[1] **Mohometans:** another term for Muslims.

D   Washington wanted America to stand for something different: not the
40   old idea that we are better apart, but the high hope that people from the four corners of the earth could do remarkable things together, even build a nation, and show humanity that we are better together. Respect, relationship and service to the common good—that was Washington's ethic, the three pillars on which he believed a diverse democracy would thrive.

F   In a too-seldom read sermon called "Remaining Awake Through A Great Revolution," Martin Luther King Jr. summarized the story of Rip Van Winkle. He mentioned the details we all know—old man goes up the
E   mountain, falls asleep for many years, grows a long beard. But King pauses
50   on one detail we might have passed over: When Rip Van Winkle went up the mountain, he passed an Inn with a picture of King George III, the English monarch. When he came down the mountain some years later, the Inn was still there, but the picture had changed: it was now of George Washington. America had gone from living under a dictator to living in a democracy.

What strikes me about King's use of George Washington as a symbol of democracy is that King's great-great grandparents could well have been owned by General Washington. The man who welcomed Jews and Catholics into the nation, the man who spoke of a government that gave bigotry no
60   sanction and persecution no assistance, he was a slaveholder.

---

2.   **◀ REREAD**   Reread lines 1–21. Explain how starting his article with George Washington's views on bigotry helps establish Patel's point of view. Support your answer with explicit textual evidence.

Starting the article with a quotation from Washington helps to establish Patel's point of view that people of different faiths can work together. He uses Washington as an example of people overcoming their differences to work together.

3.   **READ ▶**   As you read lines 22–45, underline the details that explain Washington's reasoning.

4.   **◀ REREAD**   Reread lines 39–45. Explain how the author supports his opinion about Washington's view of people's freedom and identity. Support your answer with explicit textual evidence.

He notes that Washington recognized that all willing groups were needed in the fight for independence. Washington believed in "respect, relationship and service to the common good."

5.   **READ ▶**   As you read lines 46–64, explain King's outlook for America in the margin.

4

5

---

2. **REREAD AND CITE TEXT EVIDENCE**   By opening his blog with a reference to George Washington's views about bigotry, Patel grabs the reader's interest and introduces the topic and point of view he will be presenting in his blog.

B **ASK STUDENTS**   to state Patel's point of view and to support it with Washington's intolerance of bigotry, citing specific evidence from the text. *Students should recognize that Patel's point of view is similar to Washington's in that both believe that people of different backgrounds, faiths, and ethnicities can overcome their differences and work together to contribute to "the common good."*

3. **READ AND CITE TEXT EVIDENCE**

C **ASK STUDENTS**   to cite specific details or textual evidence that explains Washington's reasoning and views concerning America's refusal to sanction bigotry. *Students should cite specific references to lines 24–25 and 39–45.*

4. **REREAD AND CITE TEXT EVIDENCE**

D **ASK STUDENTS**   to cite explicit textual evidence that shows how Patel supports his opinion about Washington's point of view concerning freedom and personal identity. *Students should cite explicit textual evidence from lines 39–45.*

5. **READ AND CITE TEXT EVIDENCE**

E **ASK STUDENTS**   to read their margin notes to a partner and then write one response that best states King's outlook for the United States, citing specific textual evidence. *Students should point out that King's outlook for the nation includes putting the past behind and working together as one people toward a better future.*

FOR ELL STUDENTS   Tell students that Rip Van Winkle was a fictitious character from a celebrated short story written in 1819. Rip Van Winkle slept for 20 years and saw great changes once he awoke—the American Revolution had taken place and the nation had become independent.

cynical:
scornfully
negative

King has great
hope for the
future because
so much has
changed
already.

King knew this. But it neither paralyzed him nor made him **cynical.** He didn't tie himself into knots trying to untie that mother of all contradictions. Instead, he committed himself, body and soul, to shaping the future.

America's genius is to give its diversity of citizens a stake in the well-being of the nation. That's what keeps us facing forward, seeking inspiration from the past when possible, correcting mistakes when necessary. This nation could well have been a house divided, but today we stand as one—and that has everything to do with how a previous generation, led by

70 Abraham Lincoln, acted. This nation could easily have been declared a lie by an entire race of people—kidnapped and enslaved, separated out and hunted down. Instead King and his movement termed it a broken promise, one that the people on the receiving end of the breach took actions to mend.

As a nation, we've spent the last several weeks trying to decipher the meaning of 9/11. That's as it should be; those who were lost on that day deserve that and much much more.

As I looked out at the Freshman Class at George Washington University on the 10th Anniversary of 9/11, they represented for me the next ten years, and the decades after. Here was my message to them:

6. **◀ REREAD** Reread lines 46–64. What point about change was Martin Luther King, Jr. making by telling the story of Rip Van Winkle? Support your answer with explicit textual evidence.

King tells the story of Rip Van Winkle to emphasize the extreme shift
in the country that happened during Washington's time. America
was now a democracy. King wants to point out that for real change to
occur, people must look forward and not backward. Using Washington
as an example, even though Washington was a slaveowner, shows how
King was able to put the past behind him and work toward a better
future.

6

" " When you serve, you are part of the future. " "

Patel is asking
for the
freshmen to
participate in
meaningful
discussions, to
make a
commitment,
and to shape
the future.

80 **G** **I** Yes, be a part of the conversation, but more importantly, take part in action. Don't forget, the people who talk for a living talk about the people who act.

For sure, ask big questions; but also make deep commitments—to your faith or philosophy, to the nation and the world, to the earth and to each other.

Debate the meaning of the events of past decades and centuries, but above all, shape the arc of the future.

H When you serve, you are part of the future. When you dream, you are part of the future. When you build bridges that show we are better together

90 you lower the barriers that make people believe we are better apart.

7. **READ ▶** As you read lines 65–87, continue to cite textual evidence.
- Underline the claims Patel makes.
- Circle the evidence he gives to support his claims.
- In the margin, explain what Patel is asking the Freshman Class at George Washington University to do.

8. **READ ▶** As you read lines 88–97, underline Patel's advice for students and their futures.

7

6. **REREAD AND CITE TEXT EVIDENCE**

F **ASK STUDENTS** how Patel uses King's retelling of the story of Rip Van Winkle to make a point about change. How does Patel's use of King's retelling of the story support his own argument about working together toward change? *Students should cite explicit textual evidence from lines 56–60. Responses may include the idea that for real change to occur, people must put the past behind and look toward the future.*

Critical Vocabulary: cynical (line 61) Have students share their definitions of *cynical*. Ask volunteers to give examples of cynical behavior. *Students may suggest people thinking or expecting the worst, or expecting everyone to have a selfish motivation.*

7. **READ AND CITE TEXT EVIDENCE**

G **ASK STUDENTS** to read their margin notes to a partner and then write one response, using explicit textual evidence, that explains what Patel is asking the Freshman class at George Washington University to do on the 10th anniversary of 9/11. *Students should cite explicit textual evidence from lines 80–87, pointing to the details that state that students should participate in discussion, make commitments, and take part in action in order to shape the future together.*

8. **READ AND CITE TEXT EVIDENCE**

H **ASK STUDENTS** how Patel's advice supports his own claim that by working together, we can shape the future. *Students should cite specific textual evidence from lines 91–97. Patel believes that taking part in action and working together can help shape a positive future.*

King looks
forward to
reconciliation
and building
community.

When you are wronged, in ways both small and large, remember what
Martin Luther King Jr. said in the waning days of the Montgomery Bus
Boycott, after the African-Americans of that city had endured a year of
walking to work, of facing false arrests and very real death threats, King
gave a speech about looking forward, about building the nation: "Now is the
time for redemption, now is the time for reconciliation, now is the time to
build the beloved community."

9. ◀ **REREAD AND DISCUSS** Reread lines 80–97. In the margin of lines
91–97, summarize King's hopes. Then, with a small group, discuss the
kind of world Patel envisions for the future.

SHORT RESPONSE

Cite Text Evidence Explain whether or not Patel convinced you that the
United States is a nation that cherishes its diversity. Review your reading
notes, and evaluate the effectiveness of the examples and evidence. Be
sure to **cite text evidence** from the blog in your response.

Responses may vary but students should explain that Eboo Patel gives
examples from both George Washington and Martin Luther King Jr.
to support his view of the U.S. He quotes Washington as saying, "...
the United States... gives to bigotry no sanction, to persecution no
assistance..." And he notes that Washington understood that he
needed contributions from all willing groups in America. He explains
that Martin Luther King Jr. was willing to use Washington, a
slaveholder, as a symbol of democracy, and that King was committed
to mending the past and shaping the future.

8

TO CHALLENGE STUDENTS . . .

For more context about Patel's blog entry, students should read
Dr. Martin Luther King Jr.'s complete address in which he talked
about Rip Van Winkle. It is the Commencement Address for
Oberlin College from 1965, entitled "Remaining Awake Through a
Great Revolution," and it can be found online.

ASK STUDENTS to read King's commencement address and
to reread Patel's blog entry. Encourage students to work in
small groups to write an essay or blog entry that compares and
contrasts King's address with Patel's advice in "Making the Future
Better, Together." With the class, discuss the elements of writing a
compare-and-contrast essay or blog, eliciting these points:

- Prepare one list of your subjects' similarities and another list
  of their differences.

- Write your central idea in a sentence that clearly states what
  you are comparing and contrasting.

- Write supporting sentences that include details, facts,
  examples, and quotations to explain how the two subjects are
  alike and different.

- Use words and phrases to show similarities, such as *similarly,
  like, in the same way,* and others to show differences, such as
  unlike, however, but, and *on the contrary.*

- Organize your writing in one of two ways: by presenting one
  paragraph about similarities and another about differences,
  or by describing the key characteristics of your first subject
  in one paragraph and then the key characteristics of your
  second subject in another paragraph. As you describe the
  second subject, point out similarities and differences with the
  first subject.

Have group members plan, write, revise, and proofread their
essay or blog, publishing and sharing their essay with the class or
posting their blog for everyone to read.

9. **REREAD AND DISCUSS USING TEXT EVIDENCE**

🔵 **ASK STUDENTS** to appoint a reporter for each group to cite
specific textual evidence and line numbers to support their
discussion of Patel's vision for the future. *Students should cite
explicit textual evidence from lines 80–90.*

SHORT RESPONSE

Cite Text Evidence Student responses will vary, but students
should cite specific examples and evidence from the text to support
their positions. Students should:

- explain whether or not they were convinced by Patel's argument.
- give reasons for their position on Patel's claim.
- cite specific evidence from the text to support their reasons.

DIG DEEPER

With the class, return to Question 9, Reread and Discuss. Have students share their summaries about the hopes expressed by Dr. Martin Luther King Jr. Then have them share the results of their group discussion about the kind of world Eboo Patel envisions for the future.

ASK STUDENTS whether they were satisfied with their summaries of King's hopes and with the outcome of their small-group discussions. Have each group share what they saw as Patel's vision for the future. Did they agree or disagree with his vision? What convincing evidence did the groups cite from Patel's blog to support this opinion?

- Guide students to assess their summaries by checking to see that they include only the most important facts, details, and examples concerning Dr. King's hopes.

- Encourage groups to tell whether there was any compelling evidence cited by group members holding a different view of Patel's vision for the world of the future. Ask why the textual evidence cited wasn't strong enough to sway the group's position.

- Have groups explain how they determined whether or not they had found sufficient evidence to support what they saw as Patel's vision for the future. Did everyone in the group agree as to what made the evidence sufficient? How did the group resolve any conflicts or disagreements?

- After students have shared the results of their group's discussion, ask whether another group shared any ideas they wish they had considered.

ASK STUDENTS to return to their Short Response answer to revise it based on the class discussion concerning Patel's vision for the future.

CLOSE READING NOTES

ANCHOR TEXT

Once Upon a Time

Short Story by Nadine Gordimer

Why This Text?

The tension between being safe and being open to new experiences is one students have probably encountered, particularly as they have grown older and more independent. This lesson explores that tension in the context of a deeply divided society in a time of historical upheaval.

▶ **View It!**

Professional Development Podcast:

Text Complexity

Key Learning Objective: The student will be able to analyze author's choices concerning text structure; determine and support inferences about the theme; and cite text evidence to support analysis of the text.

For additional practice:

Close Reader selection
"Night Call"
Short Story by Lisa Fugard

RL 1 Cite textual evidence to support analysis of the text.

RL 2 Determine a theme or central idea.

RL 4 Determine the meaning of words and analyze the impact of specific word choices on meaning.

RL 5 Analyze how an author's choices concerning structure create effects.

RL 6 Analyze a point of view reflected in a work of literature from outside the United States.

W 3 Write narratives using effective technique, well-chosen details, and well-structured event sequences.

L 1b Use various types of phrases.

L 3 Understand how language functions in different contexts.

L 4c Consult reference materials to find the pronunciation of a word or determine its meaning, part of speech or etymology.

 **Text Complexity Rubric**

Quantitative Measures	**Once Upon a Time** Lexile: 1390L
Qualitative Measures	**Levels of Meaning/Purpose** single level of complex meaning
	Structure somewhat complex story concepts
	Language Conventionality and Clarity complex and varied sentence structure
	Knowledge Demands cultural and literary knowledge essential to understanding
Reader/Task Considerations	• Teacher determined • Vary by individual reader and type of text • See the Text X-Ray for suggested Reader/Task Considerations.

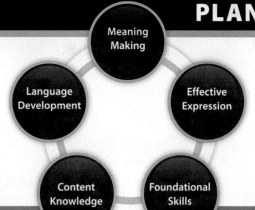

TEXT X-RAY

English Language Support Before teaching, use the Text X-Ray below for an overview of the text's complexity. The Text X-Ray and the supports and scaffolds in the Teacher's Edition will help you guide students of different skill levels.

Text Complexity: Qualitative Measures

Levels of Meaning/Purpose

single level of complex meaning

Help students support inferences about theme.
- Teacher's Edition side notes, pp. 11, 12, 13, 14, 15, 16, 17
- When Students Struggle, pp. 14–15
- Support Inferences About Theme, p. 17

To reteach supporting inferences about theme, see
- Support Inferences About Theme, p. 20a

 Use It! *Level Up* **tutorial:** Theme

Interactive Whiteboard Lesson: Theme/Central Idea

ZOOM IN ON **SUPPORTING INFERENCES ABOUT THEME** Explain that a story's **theme** is a message about life that the author wants to share with readers. Traditional stories such as fairy tales often teach a lesson, such as "Being too greedy can cause a person to lose everything." Characters' actions and their consequences often provide clues to the lesson or theme. Use these questions to help students infer the theme of Gordimer's story.

- What happens to the boy at the end of the story? *(He gets tangled in the barbed wire and dies a horrible death.)*
- Why did the parents put up the barbed wire? *(They were afraid that other people would hurt them or steal from them if they didn't go to great lengths to protect themselves.)*
- What lesson can readers learn from what happened to the family? *(When we are overly fearful of others, we may end up hurting ourselves.)*

Structure

somewhat complex story concepts

Help students analyze the author's choices surrounding text structure.
- Teacher's Edition side notes, pp. 12, 13, 16, 17
- Close Read Screencasts, p. 11
- Strategies for Annotation, p. 17
- Analyze Author's Choices: Text Structure, p. 17

To help students write and perform a fairy tale, see
- Performance Task, p. 18
- Write a Narrative, p. 20a

 Use It! **Interactive Whiteboard Lesson:** Writing Narratives

ZOOM IN ON **ANALYZING AUTHOR'S CHOICES**

Use these questions to help students explore the fairy-tale **structure**.
- When and where does the story take place? *(The time and place are not unspecified.)*
- Who are the main characters? *(a man, his wife, their little boy, their pets, their "trusted housemaid," and their gardener)*
- In what way do the **author's choices** about the setting and characters contribute to the fairy-tale structure? *(In fairy tales, the setting is usually vague and the characters are described as "the handsome prince" or "the evil queen" rather than by name.)*

Language Conventionality and Clarity

complex and varied sentence structure

Teach unfamiliar vocabulary in context.

- Teacher's Edition Critical Vocabulary notes, pp. 11, 13, 14, 15, 16, 19
- English Language Support, p. 12
- Applying Academic Vocabulary, p. 13

Help students analyze sensory language.

- Teacher's Edition side note, p. 14

Support students in analyzing words with Latin etymologies.

- Vocabulary Strategy: Words from Latin, p. 19
- When Students Struggle, p. 19

Guide students to analyze the use of prepositional phrases.

- Language and Style: Prepositional Phrases, p. 20

ZOOM IN ON **UNPACKING SENTENCES** Display sentences such as the one in lines 59–64 and help students define unfamiliar vocabulary. For example, in the first clause, guide students to use **context clues** to define *inscribed ("enrolled as members")*. Also point out that the phrase "in a medical benefit society" modifies *inscribed* and means that the family has health insurance. When students have discussed each part of the sentence, have them **summarize** its overall meaning. *(The man and wife have taken all the usual steps to keep the family safe.)*

Knowledge Demands

cultural and literary knowledge essential to understanding

Support English Learners in understanding the historical and cultural context of the story.

- Teacher's Edition Background note, p. 11

ZOOM IN ON **BUILDING BACKGROUND KNOWLEDGE** Tell students that while Nadine Gordimer is best known for her works exploring South African apartheid, she did not set out to be a political writer. Instead, she found that in learning to become a writer—to examine the details that reveal the truth about human life—she could not ignore the political situation in her country. White Afrikaner nationalists took power in 1948, when Gordimer was in her twenties, and she saw the repression of black South Africans gradually increase over the years. She was actively involved in the anti-apartheid movement, not only through her writing, but also as a secret member of Nelson Mandela's African National Congress party. Mandela was finally freed from prison in 1990, about a year before Gordimer won her Nobel Prize. She continued to write for years after apartheid ended; she was 90 years old when she died in 2014.

Suggested Reader/Task Considerations

You might consider the following before assigning this short story to students.

- Do students have the ability to **visualize** text details and imagine the story's setting and events?

ZOOM IN ON **SUPPORTING COMPREHENSION**

- Read aloud lines 1–48. Use your voice to convey the author's attitude toward the idea of writing a children's story and her fear of noises in the night. Discuss with students what kind of "bedtime story" they expect her to tell.
- Ask students to **visualize** the gradual transformation of the family's house, focusing on lines 49–57, lines 75–83, lines 90–98, lines 135–138, and lines 181–185. Have them point out details in the text that help them imagine the setting. Discuss how the "razor-bladed coils" create a feeling of danger that leads into the story's final scene.

Background Have students read the background and information about the author. Tell students that when this story was published in 1989, South Africa was still under apartheid. White families lived in desirable neighborhoods, and many nonwhites (Africans, Indians, and people of mixed race) lived in segregated areas called townships. Nonwhites only came to white neighborhoods to work, for example as housemaids and gardeners.

AS YOU READ Direct students to use the As You Read question to focus their reading. Remind them to write down any questions they generate during reading.

Support Inferences About Themes (LINES 11–17)   RL 1, RL 2

Point out that the initial paragraphs of a text often give clues to the **theme,** or underlying message, of the story that follows. Read aloud the first paragraphs of the selection. Discuss with students their impressions of the details in lines 11–17. *(The theme has to do with fear and how different people in a community react to fear.)*

Ⓐ CITE TEXT EVIDENCE Have students reread lines 11–17 and identify the reason the narrator is afraid and the ways in which she is similar to and different from other people in her community. *(She is afraid someone is breaking into her home because she hears a creaking sound, and crimes have happened in her area. She does not have extra security in her home even though others do. However, she is explaining that she has the same fears in common with people who do have extra security.)*

> #### CRITICAL VOCABULARY
>
> **distend**: Explain that Gordimer uses this word figuratively here; the narrator's ears do not actually physically bulge or expand when concentrating on a sound.
>
> **ASK STUDENTS** to make up a simile that explains what the narrator means when she writes that she "felt the apertures of my ears distend." *(Example answer: Her ears would distend as a dog's ears perk up when it hears an interesting sound.)*

Nadine Gordimer (1923–2014) *was born in South Africa. Her family was privileged and white in a country that practiced apartheid—an official policy of segregation of nonwhite South Africans enforced by the government. Nadine Gordimer became politically opposed to the policy. Her early works, such as* The Soft Voice of the Serpent *and* The Lying Days, *explore themes of exile and the effects of apartheid on internal life in South Africa. Before apartheid ended in 1994, some of Gordimer's writings were banned by the South African government; however, these texts were appreciated in other parts of the world. She has been awarded many literary prizes, including the Nobel Prize for Literature in 1991.*

Once Upon a Time

Short Story by Nadine Gordimer

AS YOU READ Pay attention to the relationship of the characters to the community in which they live. What steps do the parents take to ensure their family's safety?

Someone has written to ask me to contribute to an anthology of stories for children. I reply that I don't write children's stories; and he writes back that at a recent congress/book fair/seminar a certain novelist said every writer ought to write at least one story for children. I think of sending a postcard saying I don't accept that I "ought" to write anything.

And then last night I woke up—or rather was wakened without knowing what had roused me.

A voice in the echo chamber of the subconscious?

A sound.

10   A creaking of the kind made by the weight carried by one foot after another along a wooden floor. I listened. I felt the apertures of my ears **distend** with concentration. Again: the creaking. I was waiting for it; waiting to hear if it indicated that feet were moving from room to room, coming up the passage—to my door. I have no burglar bars, no gun under the pillow, but I have the same fears as people who do take these precautions, and my windowpanes

distend
(dĭ-stĕnd´) *v.*
to bulge or expand.

Image Credits: (tr) ©Tiziana Fabi/AFP/Getty Images; (c) ©Simon Potter/Cultura/Getty Images

Once Upon a Time   **11**

Close Read Screencasts

Modeled Discussions

Have students click the *Close Read* icons in their eBooks to access two screencasts in which readers discuss and annotate the following key passages:

- introduction where the author explains how she came to write the story that follows (lines 1–10)
- description of different classes, the unemployed, the trusted employee, and the sheltered family (lines 121–130)

As a class, discuss at least one video. Then have pairs do an independent close read of a third passage—description of a security measure the family takes (lines 181–188).

Support Inferences About Themes (LINES 30–45)

RL 2, RL 6

Have students reread lines 30–45. Tell students that gold and diamond mining is an important part of South Africa's economy. In the past, most mine workers were African men who left their families in rural areas and worked under brutal conditions for white bosses.

B ASK STUDENTS why Gordimer mentions her house's location above a mine here. *(Gordimer is explaining what woke her up and frightened her.)* Discuss how Gordimer's inclusion of the description of the miners is also an explanation of why people are afraid in South African society. *(The lines illustrate the point that South African whites cannot isolate themselves from the oppression and suffering they have imposed on non-whites. It is all around them and under them, affecting them at unexpected moments.)*

Analyze Author's Choices

RL 5

(LINES 46–53)

Point out that lines 46–48 provide a transition from the narrator's autobiographical story to a fictional one about a family. The narrator uses these lines to help her readers understand how she came to imagine the story of the family.

C ASK STUDENTS how the shift in structure from an autobiographical tale to a "bedtime story" affects the reader. *(By moving from her own feelings of lying sleepless and fearful in bed to descriptions of a family living hapily ever after, the narrator may cause the reader to think that the bedtime story will be a soothing one.)*

are thin as rime,[1] could shatter like a wineglass. A woman was murdered (how do they put it) in broad daylight in a house two
20 blocks away, last year, and the fierce dogs who guarded an old widower and his collection of antique clocks were strangled before he was knifed by a casual laborer he had dismissed without pay.

I was staring at the door, making it out in my mind rather than seeing it, in the dark. I lay quite still—a victim already—but the arrhythmia[2] of my heart was fleeing, knocking this way and that against its body-cage. How finely tuned the senses are, just out of rest, sleep! I could never listen intently as that in the distractions of the day; I was reading every faintest sound, identifying and classifying its possible threat.
30 But I learned that I was to be neither threatened nor spared. There was no human weight pressing on the boards, the creaking was a buckling, an epicenter[3] of stress. I was in it. The house that surrounds me while I sleep is built on undermined ground; far beneath my bed, the floor, the house's foundations, the stopes[4] and passages of gold mines have hollowed the rock, and when some face trembles, detaches, and falls, three thousand feet below, the whole house shifts slightly, bringing uneasy strain to the balance and counterbalance of brick, cement, wood, and glass that hold it as a structure around me. The misbeats of my heart tailed off like the
40 last muffled flourishes on one of the wooden xylophones made by the Chopi and Tsonga[5] migrant miners who might have been down there, under me in the earth at that moment. The stope where the fall was could have been disused, dripping water from its ruptured veins; or men might now be interred there in the most profound of tombs.

I couldn't find a position in which my mind would let go of my body—release me to sleep again. So I began to tell myself a story; a bedtime story.

In a house, in a suburb, in a city, there were a man and his wife
50 who loved each other very much and were living happily ever after. They had a little boy, and they loved him very much. They had a cat and a dog that the little boy loved very much. They had a car and a caravan trailer for holidays, and a swimming pool which was fenced so that the little boy and his playmates would not fall in and drown. They had a housemaid who was absolutely trustworthy

---

[1] **rime:** a coating of frost.
[2] **arrhythmia:** an irregular heartbeat.
[3] **epicenter:** the focal point.
[4] **stopes:** step-like holes or trenches made by miners.
[5] **Chopi and Tsonga:** (chō′pē and tsôn′ga) ethnic groups that live in Mozambique.

ENGLISH LANGUAGE SUPPORT

Analyze Language The word *holiday* (line 53) is an example of regional speech or dialect. In the United States, this word is used to mean special religious or cultural celebrations, such as Thanksgiving or Independence Day. In other parts of the world, such as South Africa, *holiday* is also used to mean "vacation." Remind students that when they are unclear about the meaning of a word, they can look for context clues in the text by rereading surrounding sentences for words that offer clues about meaning.

ASK STUDENTS which meaning of *holiday* the author intends. *(vacations)* Which words provide clues to the correct meaning? *(caravan trailer)*

and an itinerant[6] gardener who was highly recommended by the
neighbors. For when they began to live happily ever after they were
warned, by that wise old witch, the husband's mother, not to take
on anyone off the street. They were inscribed in a medical benefit
60 society, their pet dog was licensed, they were insured against fire,
flood damage, and theft, and subscribed to the local Neighborhood
Watch, which supplied them with a plaque for their gates lettered
YOU HAVE BEEN WARNED over the silhouette of a would-be
intruder. He was masked; it could not be said if he was black or
white, and therefore proved the property owner was no racist.

It was not possible to insure the house, the swimming pool,
or the car against riot damage. There were riots, but these were
outside the city, where people of another color were quartered.
These people were not allowed into the suburb except as reliable
70 housemaids and gardeners, so there was nothing to fear, the
husband told the wife. Yet she was afraid that some day such people
might come up the street and tear off the plaque YOU HAVE
BEEN WARNED and open the gates and stream in. . . . Nonsense,
my dear, said the husband, there are police and soldiers and tear
gas and guns to keep them away. But to please her—for he loved
her very much and buses were being burned, cars stoned, and
schoolchildren shot by the police in those quarters out of sight and
hearing of the suburb—he had electronically controlled gates fitted.
Anyone who pulled off the sign YOU HAVE BEEN WARNED and
80 tried to open the gates would have to announce his **intentions** by
pressing a button and speaking into a receiver relayed to the house.
The little boy was fascinated by the device and used it as a walkie-
talkie in cops and robbers play with his small friends.

The riots were suppressed, but there were many burglaries in
the suburb and somebody's trusted housemaid was tied up and shut
in a cupboard by thieves while she was in charge of her employers'
house. The trusted housemaid of the man and wife and little boy
was so upset by this misfortune befalling a friend left, as she herself
often was, with responsibility for the possessions of the man and
90 his wife and the little boy that she implored her employers to have
burglar bars attached to the doors and windows of the house, and
an alarm system installed. The wife said, She is right, let us take
heed of her advice. So from every window and door in the house
where they were living happily ever after they now saw the trees
and sky through bars, and when the little boy's pet cat tried to
climb in by the fanlight[7] to keep him company in his little bed

intention
(ĭn-tĕn′shən) *n.*
purpose or plan.

---

[6] **itinerant:** frequently traveling to different places.
[7] **fanlight:** an arched window, usually over a door.

APPLYING ACADEMIC VOCABULARY

internal	presume

As you discuss Gordimer's short story, incorporate the following Collection
1 academic vocabulary words: *internal* and *presume*. To analyze the message
of the story, ask students what the narrrator's **internal** struggle is regarding
safety and security. As you dig deeper into the story the narrator tells, ask
students what the family **presumes** about people "of another color" from
outside their neighborhood.

CLOSE READ

Analyze Author's Choices (LINES 57–65)   RL 1, RL 5

Point out that the story contains elements of a fairy
tale, such as "happily ever after" and "wise old witch,"
to convey the narrator's ideas in the story. These
elements help Gordimer express ideas in a way
readers will understand.

D CITE TEXT EVIDENCE Have students cite the
warning the "wise old witch" gives to her son and
his wife. *("not to take on anyone off the street")* Ask
students to explain the role witches usually play in
fairy tales. *(Witches are usually troublemakers.)* Then
ask them to infer, or make an educated guess about,
the witch's purpose in this story. *(The witch's advice
might cause trouble.)*

Support Inferences About Theme (LINES 66–78)   RL 2

Have students reread lines 66–78. Tell students that
this passage contains key information about the
story's theme. It suggests how segregation and the
resulting racial tensions might have fueled the wife's
fear of a break-in and also tells how the husband tries
to dispel her fear.

F ASK STUDENTS what the wife is worried about.
What specific details explain how the husband is
trying to reassure her that she need not be fearful?
*(The wife is worried about the riots making their way to
the suburbs. The husband tells her in lines 68–71 that the
people "of another color" are not allowed in the suburbs
except as employees of residents. He goes on to say in
lines 73–75 that the police and soldiers will keep the
rioters away. The narrator goes on to say the husband
has additional security measures installed to allay his
wife's fears.)*

CRITICAL VOCABULARY

intentions: The intercom system forces visitors to
announce their presence and say why they are at
the house before they can gain entry.

ASK STUDENTS what the real intention is of the
intercom system. *(The intercom system gives the
family control over who gains entry to the house.)*

Analyze Language   RL 1, RL 4

(LINES 99–110)

Tell students that authors sometimes use **sensory language,** words that appeal to readers' senses, to help express ideas.

F **CITE TEXT EVIDENCE** Have students look for words in lines 99–110 that appeal to certain senses. (*shrills, bleats, wails, grating*) What does the writer express about the neighborhood alarms in her use of sensory language? How does this description help you understand the time and place, or the society of South Africa? (*The writer describes the neighborhood alarms as if they are noisy animals that the people no longer pay attention to. In this way, the writer expresses the futility of the neighborhood's efforts to protect itself from the change in society.*)

Support Inferences About   RL 2

Theme (LINES 114–130)

Tell students that authors sometimes use characters' actions, thoughts, and feelings to help express a theme about a society.

G **ASK STUDENTS** what Gordimer expresses about South African society by giving details in lines 114–130 about the attitudes of the housemaid and the wife toward the unemployed people. (*In expressing the housemaid's fear about the unemployed people and the wife's concern about their hunger, Gordimer is showing that while there is hope in the society because the wife cares, it is a hope that is being overwhelmed and crushed by fear.*)

CRITICAL VOCABULARY

audaciously: The intruders' boldness in stopping to drink from the liquor cabinets showed that they were not afraid of being caught by the home owners.

ASK STUDENTS why Gordimer included the detail about the intruders behaving audaciously. (*It shows that the security measures people put in their homes were not effective.*)

---

at night, as it customarily had done, it set off the alarm keening[8] through the house.

100   The alarm was often answered—it seemed—by other burglar alarms, in other houses, that had been triggered by pet cats or nibbling mice. The alarms called to one another across the gardens in shrills and bleats and wails that everyone soon became accustomed to, so that the din roused the inhabitants of the suburb no more than the croak of frogs and musical grating of cicadas'[9] legs. Under cover of the electronic harpies'[10] discourse intruders sawed the iron bars and broke into homes, taking away hi-fi equipment, television sets, cassette players, cameras and radios, jewelry and clothing, and sometimes were hungry enough to devour everything in the refrigerator or paused **audaciously**
110   to drink the whiskey in the cabinets or patio bars. Insurance companies paid no compensation for single malt, a loss made keener by the property owner's knowledge that the thieves wouldn't even have been able to appreciate what it was they were drinking.

Then the time came when many of the people who were not trusted housemaids and gardeners hung about the suburb because they were unemployed. Some importuned for a job: weeding or painting a roof; anything, *baas*,[11] madam. But the man and his wife remembered the warning about taking on anyone off the street. Some drank liquor and fouled the street with discarded bottles.
120   Some begged, waiting for the man or his wife to drive the car out of the electronically operated gates. They sat about with their feet in the gutters, under the jacaranda trees that made a green tunnel of the street—for it was a beautiful suburb, spoiled only by their presence—and sometimes they fell asleep lying right before the gates in the midday sun. The wife could never see anyone go hungry. She sent the trusted housemaid out with bread and tea, but the trusted housemaid said these were loafers and *tsotsis*,[12] who would come and tie her up and shut her in a cupboard. The husband said, She's right. Take heed of her advice. You only encourage them
130   with your bread and tea. They are looking for their chance. . . . And he brought the little boy's tricycle from the garden into the house every night, because if the house was surely secure, once locked and with the alarm set, someone might still be able to climb over the wall or the electronically closed gates into the garden.

You are right, said the wife, then the wall should be higher. And the wise old witch, the husband's mother, paid for the extra bricks

audacious
(ô-dā´shəs) *n.*
bold, rebellious.

---

[8] **keening:** wailing or crying.
[9] **cicadas:** large, loud insects.
[10] **harpies:** mythological creatures who were part woman and part bird.
[11] *baas:* (bäs) a white person in a position of authority in relation to nonwhites.
[12] *tsotsis:* (tsō´´tsēs) dishonest, untrustworthy people.

WHEN STUDENTS STRUGGLE. . .

To help students understand the **theme**, or underlying purpose, of the story, have them compare the choices the writer makes about her own security with the choices the family in her story make. Ask: What do the writer and the family have in common? (*They are both afraid of intruders.*) What do they do differently? (*The writer chooses to live normally; she doesn't have extra security measures to protect herself. The family allows fear to dictate their life; they keep adding more and more "security" measures.*) Have partners fill out a Venn diagram like the one shown and discuss what the results were for the author and the family. (*The writer remains safe while the family is harmed by the very things that were meant to keep them safe.*) Guide students to surmise that the theme of the story is fear and how the various characters choose to confront it.

as her Christmas present to her son and his wife—the little boy got a Space Man outfit and a book of fairy tales.

140 But every week there were more reports of **intrusion**: in broad daylight and the dead of night, in the early hours of the morning, and even in the lovely summer twilight—a certain family was at dinner while the bedrooms were being ransacked upstairs. The man and his wife, talking of the latest armed robbery in the suburb, were distracted by the sight of the little boy's pet cat effortlessly arriving over the seven-foot wall, descending first with a rapid bracing of extended forepaws down on the sheer vertical surface, and then a graceful launch, landing with swishing tail within the property. The whitewashed wall was marked with the cat's comings and goings; and on the street side of the wall there were larger red-earth smudges that

150 could have been made by the kind of broken running shoes, seen on the feet of unemployed loiterers, that had no innocent destination.

H When the man and wife and little boy took the pet dog for its walk round the neighborhood streets they no longer paused to admire this show of roses or that perfect lawn; these were hidden behind an array of different varieties of security fences, walls, and devices. The man, wife, little boy, and dog passed a remarkable choice: there was the low-cost option of pieces of broken glass embedded in cement along the top of walls, there were iron grilles ending in lance points, there were attempts at reconciling the

160 aesthetics of prison architecture with the Spanish Villa style (spikes painted pink) and with the plastic urns of neoclassical façades (twelve-inch pikes finned like zigzags of lightning and painted pure white). Some walls had a small board affixed, giving the name and telephone number of the firm responsible for the installation of the devices. **I** While the little boy and the pet dog raced ahead, the husband and wife found themselves comparing the possible effectiveness of each style against its appearance; and after several weeks when they paused before this barricade or that without

intrusion
(ĭn-trōo′shən) *n.*
act of trespass or invasion.

Once Upon a Time   **15**

Image Credits: ©Jane Burton/Dorling Kindersley/Getty Images

Narrator	Both	Family
no bars on windows; no alarm system; no weapons;	fear of intruders	fence, barbed wire; intercom system; neighborhood watch

LEVEL UP TUTORIALS Assign the following *Level Up* tutorial: **Theme.**

Support Inferences About Theme (LINES 152–165)   RL 1, RL 6

Discuss that this passage describes how the once-visible, manicured gardens of neighborhood homes are hidden by fences and iron grilles. Have students think about how the description relates to the theme.

H **CITE TEXT EVIDENCE** Have students read lines 152–165. What do the changes to the neighborhood, including Gordimer's description of the "prison architecture," suggest about residents' feelings? Have students support their inferences with specific details. *(The former beauty of the neighborhood's gardens and yards is now hidden behind an array of barricades [lines 154–155]. The residents' fear of burglary has prompted them to fortify their homes with menacing features such as broken glass on walls and spiked fences, intended to keep intruders at bay.)*

Support Inferences About Theme (LINES 165–167)   RL 1, RL 2

Explain to students that a **symbol**—an object, a character, or a place that suggests a meaning beyond itself—can help illustrate a story's theme. Examine how the boy serves as a symbol.

I **CITE TEXT EVIDENCE** What is different about the boy's approach to life versus his parents? What does the boy symbolize? Cite specific details to support your answer. *(The boy is a symbol of innocence and happiness. In lines 165–167, the boy continues to run and play like a normal child while the parents are consumed with the subject of security. The boy enjoys his life while his parents plan fearfully for what could happen.)*

CRITICAL VOCABULARY

intrusion: Gordimer is referring to the act of burglars breaking into homes in the family's neighborhood.

ASK STUDENTS the difference between the family cat jumping over the high wall and a burglar entering the home. *(The cat is a family member and is welcome to come and go. The burglar is unwelcome, and entering the house is an intrusion.)*

CLOSE READ

Analyze Author's Choices RL 5

(LINES 193–203)

Discuss with students how the final scene introduces **irony**, or a contrast between what is expected and what occurs, to the story. Have students consider the roles of the witch, the boy's grandmother, and the gardener.

Ⓙ ASK STUDENTS who they would expect to care about the boy more, his grandmother or the gardener. Then ask whose actions hurt the boy and whose actions helped him. *(The witch's actions ultimately destroyed the family because her advice and gifts led to the boy being seriously injured. The gardener cut his own hands trying to save the boy, so he helped the family more than the witch did.)* Is this outcome what a reader might expect? *(Most students will say that they expected or would have expected the actions of the boy's grandmother to be in the boy's best interest, while the gardener might not have been expected to help.)*

CRITICAL VOCABULARY

serrated: Gordimer uses this word to describe the sharp, jagged edge of the wire used to make the wall secure.

ASK STUDENTS why a serrated edge would make the barricade more effective. *(The jagged blades would cut a person if he or she tried to climb over or through the fence.)*

COLLABORATIVE DISCUSSION Have students pair up and discuss the precautions the parents took to protect the family. Tell them to look for specific details in the story in order to draw a conclusion. Then have them share their conclusions with the class as a whole.

ASK STUDENTS to share any questions they generated in the course of reading and discussing the selection.

---

needing to speak, both came out with the conclusion that only one
170 was worth considering. It was the ugliest but the most honest in its suggestion of the pure concentration-camp style, no frills, all evident efficacy. Placed the length of walls, it consisted of a continuous coil of stiff and shining metal **serrated** into jagged blades, so that there would be no way of climbing over it and no way through its tunnel without getting entangled in its fangs. There would be no way out, only a struggle getting bloodier and bloodier, a deeper and sharper hooking and tearing of flesh. The wife shuddered to look at it. You're right, said the husband, anyone would think twice. . . . And they took heed of the advice on a small board fixed to the wall: Consult
180 DRAGON'S TEETH The People For Total Security.

> **serrate**
> (sĕrʹāt´) *adj.*
> having a jagged, saw-toothed edge.

Next day a gang of workmen came and stretched the razor-bladed coils all round the walls of the house where the husband and wife and little boy and pet dog and cat were living happily ever after. The sunlight flashed and slashed, off the serrations, the cornice of razor thorns encircled the home, shining. The husband said, Never mind. It will weather. The wife said, You're wrong. They guarantee it's rustproof. And she waited until the little boy had run off to play before she said, I hope the cat will take heed. . . . The husband said, Don't worry, my dear, cats always look before they
190 leap. And it was true that from that day on the cat slept in the little boy's bed and kept to the garden, never risking a try at breaching security.

Ⓙ One evening, the mother read the little boy to sleep with a fairy story from the book the wise old witch had given him at Christmas. Next day he pretended to be the Prince who braves the terrible thicket of thorns to enter the palace and kiss the Sleeping Beauty back to life: he dragged a ladder to the wall, the shining coiled tunnel was just wide enough for his little body to creep in, and with the first fixing of its razor teeth in his knees and hands and
200 head he screamed and struggled deeper into its tangle. The trusted housemaid and the itinerant gardener, whose "day" it was, came running, the first to see and to scream with him, and the itinerant gardener tore his hands trying to get at the little boy. Then the man and his wife burst wildly into the garden and for some reason (the cat, probably) the alarm set up wailing against the screams while the bleeding mass of the little boy was hacked out of the security coil with saws, wire cutters, choppers, and they carried it—the man, the wife, the hysterical trusted housemaid, and the weeping gardener—into the house.

COLLABORATIVE DISCUSSION Was the boy safer because of the precautions his parents took to protect the family? Discuss your thoughts with a partner using details from the story to support your ideas.

TO CHALLENGE STUDENTS...

Write from Author's Perspective What does Nadine Gordimer think about the society of South Africa at the time the story was written? Explain that Gordimer is expressing her attitudes and beliefs through her writing. Challenge students to write a continuation of the story that describes a conversation the parents have the next day about what has happened and what they are thinking (or have learned) about their security systems. Some students may find it intriguing to include the "wise old witch" character in their descriptions. Encourage students to try to write in the same tone and style as Gordimer. Give students the opportunity to share their writing in a small group or with the class.

Analyze Author's Choices: Text Structure

RL 5

Nadine Gordimer's "Once Upon a Time" was originally published in 1989. The late 1980s were a period of internal unrest in South Africa and this story reflects the fear and isolation that people felt as the policy of apartheid continued to be enforced. To convey her ideas, Gordimer structured her story using some of the traditional elements of fairy tales. For example, the title "Once Upon a Time" and the fact that the family is "living happily ever after" are both traditional elements of fairy tales. This **structure**, or arrangement of the parts of the story, holds together the elements of the story. The choices that Gordimer made about the structure of her story help create effects such as tension and surprise, as in a fairy tale. As you analyze the structure, look for other fairy tale elements as shown in the chart and think about how this story is similar to and different from other fairy tales you have read.

Elements of a Fairy Tale
• The main characters are opposed by an evil force.
• Animals have special abilities.
• The story is used to teach a lesson.
• Good characters have bad things happen to them.
• The setting does not seem quite real.
• Details in the story foreshadow that the problem, or conflict, will be resolved in a "happily ever after" ending.

Support Inferences About Theme

RL 1, RL 2

Gordimer develops the **theme,** or the underlying message, through the details and symbols she includes in the story. An author can use all the elements of a story to develop a theme, including the characters, plot, and setting. For example, to convey a theme about the rewards of working hard, an author might relate a story about a hockey team that finally wins a championship. As the story develops, the players discover each other's strengths and weaknesses and learn that working together brings success to everyone.

An author might also develop the theme through the use of a **symbol**—a person, a place, or an object that stands for something beyond itself. In the hockey team story, the author might use the symbol of a trophy to represent the team's success.

As you analyze "Once Upon a Time," make **inferences,** or logical guesses, about the theme by considering the details and symbols Gordimer includes. Pay particular attention to the characters' actions and motivations, as well as the setting—including the historical background—to help you infer the theme.

TEACH

CLOSE READ

Analyze Author's Choices: Text Structure

RL 1, RL 5

As a class, work through the chart and identify each fairy tale element that this story contains. Ask students to discuss how the elements work to create mystery, tension, or surprise. Remind students to support their ideas with evidence from the story. *(Sample answer: There is considerable tension created by the fact that each time the parents deal with the security of their family, the story also mentions that they are living "happily ever after" even when they aren't.)*

Support Inferences About Theme

RL 1, RL 2

Help students make inferences about the theme by having them analyze the characters' actions and motivations. Ask students to identify repeated actions and their causes. *(Sample answer: The family's fear of being burglarized and physically harmed motivates them to add progressively stronger safety features around their home—electronically controlled gates, burglar bars, and eventually barbed wire—to give them a sense of security.)* Guide students to connect the characters' actions to the events taking place in South Africa during apartheid to identify a theme. *(Sample answer: The theme is fear and the resulting desire to protect oneself from danger. The references to burglaries, riots, the burning and stoning of vehicles, and the shooting of schoolchildren are clues to the level of violence that a politically and racially divided South African society faced under apartheid.)*

Strategies for Annotation   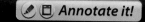 Annotate it!

Analyze Author's Choices: Text Structure

RL 5

Share these strategies for guided or independent analysis:

- Highlight in yellow the main characters.
- Underline evidence that the main characters are good people.
- Highlight the "evil forces," or the fears the characters face, in blue.
- Highlight examples of bad things happening to good characters in green.
- On a note, record the conflict and whether the ending was happy or not.

In a house, in a suburb, in a city, there were a man and his wife who loved each other very much and were living happily ever after. They had a little boy, and they loved him very much. They had a cat and a dog that the little boy loved very much. They had a car

Analyzing the Text   RL 1, RL 2, RL 5, RL 6

Possible answers:

1. The story uses language common in fairy tales, such as "once upon a time" and "happily ever after." The story also has good characters, the family members, who are up against an evil force. The family learns a lesson in the end.

2. Gordimer's story reflects her view that apartheid causes fear and isolation. The family's fear of the people "of another color" ends up imprisoning the family and ultimately hurts them irreparably.

3. At the end of the story, it is unclear whether the boy has been killed, although the phrase "the bleeding mass of the little boy" suggests he has been gravely hurt. Readers also don't know for sure whether the family learns a lesson from the boy's accident.

4. The first two times the witch is mentioned, she is acting to keep the family isolated from the outside world. Similar to the way that the government was trying to keep the policy of apartheid in place, the witch works to convince the family that living separately from people of "other colors" is the key to happiness. The third time the witch is mentioned, she gives the boy a book of fairy tales. This is also symbolic of the apartheid government's efforts to convince whites that a "separate but equal" society is the key to living "happily ever after."

5. The cat symbolizes freedom because it moves through the barriers that the family erects between themselves and those outside. However, once the barbed wire goes up, the cat is also trapped, another victim of the family's misguided attempts to be happy and secure.

6. One theme is that people shouldn't allow fear to dictate their actions and isolate them from the community. Gordimer uses the structure of a fairy tale in which good people struggle against an evil force, but in this case the evil force is their own fear rather than en external foe such as a wolf or a dragon. Because the characters succumb to their fears, the happy ending readers expect does not happen. Gordimer uses the "wise old witch" to symbolize the evil power of irrational fears. The "witch" is the boy's grandmother who only wants the family to be safe, but the evil power of fear and prejudice undermines her good intentions.

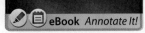
eBook *Annotate It!*

Analyzing the Text

RL 1, RL 2,
RL 5, RL 6,
W 3, SL 4

Cite Text Evidence Support your responses with evidence from the selection.

1. **Identify Patterns** How is the structure of this story similar to a fairy tale? What elements do they share? Cite details from the text to support your analysis.

2. **Connect** Nadine Gordimer wrote many stories about the injustices of apartheid. She was also active in bringing change to the political entities of South Africa. Even though her books were banned in South Africa for a time, she resolved to stay instead of living in exile. What do you learn about Gordimer's political point of view by reading this story? Explain your ideas using evidence from the story.

3. **Infer** Authors often leave things unstated in a story, leaving the reader with questions about the outcome. What can you infer about what Gordimer leaves unstated at the end of her story? How does it relate to her statements about the family living "happily ever after"?

4. **Evaluate** In lines 58, 136, and 194, the phrase "wise old witch" is used to describe the husband's mother. Explain how the wise old witch can be interpreted to symbolize the government of South Africa.

5. **Draw Conclusions** How does the cat symbolize and support the theme of this story? Explain.

6. **Infer** What is the theme of this story? Explain how Gordimer develops this theme through the story's elements, such as structure and symbols.

PERFORMANCE TASK

Speaking Activity: Fairy Tale Nadine Gordimer uses her writing to convey ideas about the society and country she lives in. Explore this idea by developing a modern fairy tale that you can perform with a partner.

1. Identify a community or school event that has happened or that you have observed. Then make notes about the two characters and plot of your fairy tale.

2. Think about a theme for your fairy tale. For example, you might consider the themes of fairness, justice, or equality. What important symbols can you include to convey your theme?

3. Combine your ideas to write a short fairy tale that conveys a message.

Refer back to "Once Upon a Time" to examine how Nadine Gordimer wrote a powerful political commentary using a fairy tale structure.

4. Perform your fairy tale with your partner. Use appropriate eye contact, adequate volume, and clear pronunciation as you perform. Ask your audience to evaluate if you were successful in conveying your underlying message.

Assign this performance task.

PERFORMANCE TASK   W 3

Speaking Activity: Fairy Tale Have students work in pairs or small groups. Direct them to reread "Once Upon a Time" and other stories with fairy tale elements for examples of how they can develop their own fairy tale. Instruct students to discuss the theme, characters, and plot they would like to convey through their writing and performance. Remind students to practice their performance concentrating on using their voices and expressions to help convey their ideas.

Critical Vocabulary

distend   intention   audacious   intrusion   serrate

Practice and Apply Choose which of the two situations best fits the word's meaning.

1. **distend**
   a. The bicyclist will inflate the tires on her bike.
   b. The wheel rim bent when the bicyclist hit a pothole.

2. **intention**
   a. The soccer player showed his determination to shoot for the goal.
   b. The soccer player's purpose was to play better in the next game.

3. **audacious**
   a. The daring boy brought gum to the computer lab.
   b. The mischievous boy was caught by his teacher.

4. **intrusion**
   a. The newspaper talked about the girl's wrongful entrance into the clubhouse.
   b. The girl's interruption of the conversation made the club members unhappy.

5. **serrate**
   a. The edge of the paper was cut into a decorative pattern.
   b. The toothed edge of the paper looked like a set of teeth.

Vocabulary Strategy: Words from Latin

Word and Dictionary Definition	Etymology	Latin Definition
surround (line 33) "to enclose on all sides"	from the Latin *super-* + *unda*	*unda* means "wave"

Etymologies show the origin and historical development of a word. For example, the Critical Vocabulary word *distend* comes from the Latin word *distendere*, which means "to stretch." Exploring the etymology of words can help you clarify their precise meanings. It can also help you expand your vocabulary.

Practice and Apply Follow these steps for each Critical Vocabulary word:

- Look up the word in a dictionary.

- Find the etymology of each word. If you are not sure how to read the etymology, look at the front or the back of your dictionary. There will be a section that explains how the etymology is noted and what the abbreviations mean.

- Compare the Latin definition of each word with the English definition. Are they the same? How does the English definition relate to the Latin meaning?

WHEN STUDENTS STRUGGLE...

To help students work through the Vocabulary Strategy activity, have them fill out a chart like this one.

Word	Latin definition	English definition	
distend	*to stretch out, extend*	*to bulge or expand*	
intention	*act of stretching out*	*a purpose or plan*	
audacious(ly)	*brave, bold, daring*	*bold, rebellious*	
intrusion	*to thrust in*	*act of trespass or invasion*	
serrate(d)	*to saw*	*having a jagged, saw-toothed edge*	

Critical Vocabulary

Answers:

1. *a*

2. *b*

3. *a*

4. *a*

5. *b*

Vocabulary Strategy: Words from Latin

Students should compare the English definitions to the Latin definitions.

distend—The definitions are similar in that the Latin definition includes "extend" while the English means "expand."

intention—The Latin and the English are not similar.

audacious—Both the Latin and the English contain the concept of "bold." The definitions seem to suggest action.

intrusion—The definitions are not similar, but the English definition includes the idea of invasion, which is related to the idea of something being "thrust in" as in the Latin definition.

serrate—Both definitions include an idea of a saw, but the Latin is about the action of sawing while the English is about the form of a saw.

 LEVEL UP TUTORIALS For additional support, assign the following *Level Up* tutorials: **Greek and Latin Word Roots**

PRACTICE & APPLY

Language and Style: Prepositional Phrases

Tell students that while adding prepositional phrases can add rhythm and interest to a piece of writing, it is also possible to overuse them. Ask students to consider situations in which too many prepositional phrases may detract from the meaning instead of adding to it. *(Instructional or expository writing is often better served by more concise language.)* Discuss how a careful writer chooses language and style to support the purpose and goals of the piece of writing.

Remind students that there are many prepositions other than the ones listed in the chart. As a class, brainstorm additional prepositions that students can use in their writing. Invite students to complete a sentence stem, such as "__ the mountain," in order to identify prepositions. *(across, below, toward, over, beyond, after, against)*

Answers: *Answers will vary because of the unique writing done by each student. When students have completed the exercise, have pairs share their revisions and discuss the reasons for them.*

Assess It Online!

Online Selection Test
- Download an editable ExamView bank.
- Assign and manage this test online.

Language and Style: Prepositional Phrases

Authors use various types of phrases to convey specific meanings and to add variety and interest to their writing. **Prepositional phrases** are phrases consisting of a preposition and an object of the preposition, usually a noun or a pronoun. Here are some common prepositions and phrases that can be created with them.

Preposition	Object of Preposition	Prepositional Phrase
from	the street	from the street
before	the rain	before the rain
during	the game	during the game
until	her test	until her test
outside	the gate	outside the gate

Read the following sentence from the story.

> **In a house, in a suburb, in a city,** there were a man and his wife who loved each other very much and were living happily ever after.

Nadine Gordimer might have written the sentence this way:

> In a suburban house, there were a man and his wife who loved each other very much and were living happily ever after.

While this sentence conveys the same meaning, it doesn't have the same interest as the original sentence. The prepositional phrases used one after another, *in a house, in a suburb, in a city,* help the author change gears from a story about something that happened to her to a story about another family. The phrases mimic the way a storyteller might use a steady beat or rhythm to start a story.

Examine another sentence from "Once Upon a Time":

> One evening, the mother read the little boy to sleep **with a fairy tale from the book** the wise old witch had given him at Christmas.

Although Gordimer could have written several shorter sentences, this sentence with a series of prepositional phrases conveys the sense of a fairy tale.

Practice and Apply Review the modern fairy tale that you created about a current event for this selection's Performance Task. Working independently, revise your fairy tale to include prepositional phrases that clarify your ideas and that add variety and interest to your sentences. Compare your revisions to those of your partner.

Write a Narrative

W 3

TEACH

Before students begin writing the fairy tale in response to this selection's Performance Task, offer these guidelines:

- **Choose an event or situation that can teach the characters a lesson** Explain that this is a key element of most fairy tales.
- **Create an outline or a storyboard** Tell students that planning the story's main elements will help the writing go more smoothly. Before they begin writing the narrative, they should answer the following questions:
  - Where will the story take place (setting)?
  - Who are the main protagonists and antagonists (the good characters and the evil force)?
  - What is the conflict between them?
  - What is the story's theme? What lesson will the characters learn?
  - What symbols will you use to support the story's theme?
  - How will the conflict be resolved?

 INTERACTIVE LESSON Before students begin the assignment, have them complete appropriate interactive lessons within **Writing Narratives.**

COLLABORATIVE DISCUSSION

When students have performed their fairy tales, lead the class in a discussion evaluating the effectiveness of the narratives. Remind students that a well-written, effective fairy tale should exhibit the following characteristics: a consistent narrative structure and language commonly used in fairy tales; a vividly described setting; clearly defined characters who develop over the course of the narrative; a well-developed, recurring theme that is supported by details and symbols; and a conflict or a plot that progresses logically and is resolved at the end.

Have students consider the following as they evaluate narratives:

- Is the story setting described in detail?
- Are the main characters clearly described? Do they develop throughout the story? Do their actions and motivations help the audience better understand them?
- Is the theme supported by details and symbols?
- Does the plot or conflict progress logically? Is it resolved at the end? Does it allow the audience to figure out the "lesson" or "moral" of the fairy tale?

Support Inferences About Theme

RL 1, RL 2

RETEACH

Review the concept of theme in a work of fiction. A **theme** can be a purpose or message the author wants to convey.

- Ask students to provide examples of well-known fairy tales or fables that have a clear theme or message. Examples may include "The Tortoise and the Hare," "Cinderella," or "Hansel and Gretel."
- Examine one or more of the stories that students suggest. Ask: How does the author convey the story's message? What clues do you receive about the theme throughout the story?

 LEVEL UP TUTORIALS Assign the following *Level Up* tutorial: **Theme.**

INDEPENDENT READING

Students can apply the skill to other works of fiction. Have them work independently to read or reread another work of fiction to identify a theme, or underlying message. Ask: What is the story's theme? What evidence from the story supports the theme you identified? Remind students that different people may identify different themes in a text based on their personal perspectives.

Night Calls

Short Story by Lisa Fugard

Why This Text

Students sometimes find it difficult to infer the theme of a story. "Night Calls" provides an opportunity to analyze character development and interpret symbols in order to determine the story's theme. With the help of the close-reading questions, students will support their inferences about the characters with textual evidence. This close reading will lead students to determine the theme of "Night Calls."

Background Have students read the background and the information about the author. "Night Calls" develops the central idea of a daughter's yearning to connect with a distant father. Introduce the selection by telling students that Lisa Fugard grew up in South Africa, where the story is set. Tell students to be on the lookout for a key event we learn in a flashback near the start of the story.

AS YOU READ Ask students to pay attention to clues to the story's theme: its underlying message. Remind them to look for clues to the theme in what the text says explicitly and to draw inferences about the theme based on the text.

Standards Support

- cite strong and thorough textual evidence
- determine a theme or central idea of a text
- analyze how complex characters develop over the course of a text
- determine the meaning of words and phrases as they are used in the text

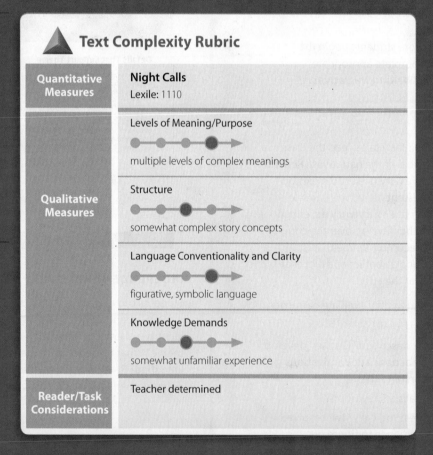

Text Complexity Rubric

Quantitative Measures

Night Calls
Lexile: 1110

Qualitative Measures

Levels of Meaning/Purpose

multiple levels of complex meanings

Structure

somewhat complex story concepts

Language Conventionality and Clarity

figurative, symbolic language

Knowledge Demands

somewhat unfamiliar experience

Reader/Task Considerations

Teacher determined

Strategies for CLOSE READING

Support Inferences About Theme

Students should read this story carefully all the way through. Close-reading questions at the bottom of the page will help them focus on a thorough analysis of the story. As they read, students should jot down comments or questions about the text in the side margins.

WHEN STUDENTS STRUGGLE . . .

To help students make and support inferences about the theme, have them work in a small group to fill out a chart, such as the one shown below, as they analyze the story.

CITE TEXT EVIDENCE For practice in supporting inferences about the theme of "Night Calls," ask students to cite evidence from the text to support their answers to the questions about Marlene, her father, and the heron.

	TEXTUAL EVIDENCE
What does Marlene want at the beginning of the story?	She wants to be close to her father. She offers to do bird calls at night at the foot of his bed.
What is Marlene's father like at the beginning of the story?	Marlene's father is distant. He is neglecting his work and his daughter.
How does the father's life change when the heron comes to the sanctuary?	The heron gives the father hope after he loses his wife. He shares news about the heron with Marlene.
How does the relationship between Marlene and her father change after the heron is freed?	After the heron is free, the father feels hopeful again. Father and daughter grow closer. They work together making repairs to the compound.
Why does Marlene imitate the heron's call at the end of the story?	Marlene wants to protect her father's feelings. She has been trying to reach out to him throughout the whole story.

Inferred Theme: Giving and receiving love can be challenging.

Background *Lisa Fugard grew up in South Africa, the daughter of the playwright and actor Athol Fugard and Sheila Fugard, a novelist and poet. Fugard came to the United States in 1980 and worked as an actress before she turned to writing. The following story is set in South Africa, though the red-crested heron Fugard describes does not actually exist.*

Night Calls

Short Story by Lisa Fugard

CLOSE READ
Notes

1. **READ ▶** As you read lines 1–26, begin to collect and cite text evidence.

• Underline text that describes the narrator's father.
• Circle text that hints at the narrator's feelings toward her father.

My father's hands were huge. Slablike. When he was idle, they seemed to hang off the ends of his arms like two chunks of meat. He sat on his hands during the months he courted my mother.

When I was thirteen, I watched my thin hand disappear into his. It was at the train station at Modder River. I'd come home for the September holidays. It was hot, and the only other car at the small station pulled away. The siding at Modder River, 150 miles north of Johannesburg, was busy. I remember it all clearly, standing in the dust, watching him get out of the truck and walk toward me, noticing that there was no smile on his face but still feeling my body move toward him, my arms opening for an embrace, something rising in my throat. My father stopped and held out his right hand.

Once in the truck, I was filled with anxiety about how close to him I could sit. I settled in the middle of my half of the bench seat and watched his large, brown hand move from the steering wheel to the gearshift and back. I breathed deeply. Suddenly I was filled with the smell of him:

The narrator wants a hug from her father, but instead she gets a handshake.

9

---

1. **READ AND CITE TEXT EVIDENCE** Point out to students that the narrator's descriptions of her father and of herself help establish the characters and their interactions.

Ⓐ ASK STUDENTS to find text that gives hints about how the narrator feels toward her father. *Students should notice that the narrator wants his affection (lines 10–11) and she is nervous in his company (line 13). These feelings are mirrored in line 18 ("I felt like a thief") and in line 25 ("Laughingly, I turned to find my father's smile").*

FOR ELL STUDENTS Clarify the multiple meanings of the noun *calls*. Ask volunteers to provide the meaning they already probably know. Then explain that in the context of this selection, *calls* means "cries that animals make to alert others."

She wants
his approval
for her guinea
fowl call,
but he does
not respond.

Borkum Riff tobacco, sweat, the sweet odor of cheap Cape brandy. Filled
with his secrets, I felt like a thief and moved a little closer to the window.

20 Then we were at the entrance to the Modder River Wildlife Sanctuary,
and I jumped out of the car to open the gate. It swung easily, once I
unlatched it, and banged against the wooden fence post, startling several
guinea fowl that scampered into the veld.[1] "Krrdll . . . krrdll . . . krrdll," I
called, and they slowed down. I mimicked their rattling cry again, and they
stopped. Again, and a few of them stepped hesitantly toward me.
Laughingly, I turned to find my father's smile, but his face was gone, blotted
out by the expanse of blue sky reflected in the windshield.

I have a gift for mimicking bird and animal calls. During my third year
C at boarding school I'd finally made myself popular and gained the respect
of Wendy Venter, the bully of our dorm, by doing several calls late one
30 night. It became a ritual, and every couple of weeks, around midnight, I'd
hear rustling and whispering from the eleven other girls in the dormitory;
then a balled-up sock would land on my bed, usually right next to my head,
and Wendy would call my name in a sly whisper, "Marlene." The dorm
would fall silent. Lying back in the darkness I'd start with the deep moan of
the spotted eagle owl; then the high-pitched yip of the black-backed jackal;
the low snuffle and violent laugh of the hyena; and then a deadly
combination: the rasping, half-swallowed growl of the leopard, followed by
the wild scream of the chacma baboon. Inevitably one of the younger girls
would begin to cry, and I'd hear Wendy snickering in the darkness.

The narrator
probably felt
disappointed
and rejected.

40 I'd told my father about this during my next trip home, about how much
the other girls had enjoyed it, and I offered to do it for him one evening,
offered to steal into his room at midnight, crouch at the foot of his bed, and
D make the calls for him. He'd shaken his head ever so slightly. "I've got the
real thing right outside my window," he said.

E As we drove up to our house now, I noticed the shabby state of the
compound. The road was rutted and washed-out in many places by the
spring rains. The visitors' kiosk was boarded up, and the map of the
sanctuary had been knocked off its post and lay on the ground. Even the

---

[1] **veld:** in South Africa, open grassy country with few bushes and almost no trees.

2. ◀ REREAD   Reread lines 4–12 and lines 19–26. In the margins, explain
what the narrator wants from her father and what she gets instead.

3. READ ▶   As you read lines 27–44, continue to cite textual evidence.
• Circle the reason why the narrator describes her ability to mimic bird and
animal calls "a gift."
• Underline her father's response to her calls.

10

pond had been neglected. When my parents had first come to Modder
50 River, five years before I was born, my father had had the pond dug out for
my mother. An avid botanist,[2] she'd planted it with indigenous water lilies
that she collected, along with bulrushes, seven-weeks ferns, and floating
hearts. During the two years when the Modder River was reduced to a
trickle by the drought, the local farmers had been astonished to hear that
my father was actually pumping precious water from our borehole into the
pond to prevent it from drying up. An **opulent** jewel in the dusty, cracked
landscape, it became a haven for birds, being visited by pied kingfishers,
mountain chats, spoonbills, bokmakieries, a pair of black-shouldered
kites—all told, my mother counted 107 different species. Now a thick layer
60 of brown scum covered the shallow, stagnant water. I remembered a letter
that I'd received from my father several months before. The scrawled
handwriting hadn't even looked like his. I'd read it once and then hidden it
away, scared by the loneliness that the words hinted at.

None of this seemed to matter, however, when I stood among our dogs,
being pelted with paws and tails and long pink tongues: King, with his tail
plumed like an ostrich feather, and Blitz, a lean, black shadow. They
clattered behind me as I went into my bedroom. The room was still and
dark and smelled musty. Quickly I opened the wooden shutters. I moved to
the chest of drawers and found the large framed photograph of my mother,
70 frozen at age thirty-two. She was laughing, and her head was turned slightly
as a lock of hair blew across her face. I traced her jaw line with my finger
and moved to the mirror with the photograph, but the dogs were
demanding, barking and pawing at my legs.

I ran outside with them and chased them up and down the cool stone
lengths of the veranda, flying past the living room and the dining room,
screeching past my father's study and back again with the dogs racing
behind me. Back and forth I went, until the force of motion made me round
the corner past my parents' old bedroom. I stopped, panting, trying to catch
my breath. I stared at the large fenced-in area under the blue gum tree. It

opulent:
having or
showing great
wealth or
value

---

[2] **botanist:** a scientist who studies plant life.

4. ◀ REREAD   Reread lines 27–44. In the margin, make an inference
about how the narrator probably felt about her father's response to her
new talent.

5. READ ▶   As you read lines 45–94, underline details that describe how
the compound at Modder River has changed. Circle words that describe
changes in Marlene's father.

11

---

2. **REREAD AND CITE TEXT EVIDENCE**   Students have noted that
the narrator is nervous around her father, and that she seeks his
affection.

B **ASK STUDENTS** to cite evidence that shows that the
narrator is probably disappointed by her father's actions. *Students
should cite text in lines 9–12, where the narrator wants a hug but
gets a handshake, and lines 25–26, where she expects approval for
her birdcall but is ignored.*

3. **READ AND CITE TEXT EVIDENCE**

C **ASK STUDENTS** to explain in their own words why the
narrator considers her ability to mimic animals a gift. Point out
that she is in boarding school, and have students focus on the
words *finally, respect,* and *bully* in lines 28–29 to give more
context to the narrator's appreciation of her gift.

4. **REREAD AND CITE TEXT EVIDENCE**

D **ASK STUDENTS** to cite textual evidence to support their
inferences about the narrator's feelings. *Students may cite the text
that shows how proud the narrator is of her talent, and how she
wants to share it with her father. His reaction—implying that her
ability is worthless—would make the narrator feel rejected.*

5. **READ AND CITE TEXT EVIDENCE**

E **ASK STUDENTS** to compare the changes in the compound
with the changes in Marlene's father, using the text evidence they
have identified. *Students will probably note that both the
compound and Marlene's father have deteriorated.*

Critical Vocabulary: opulent (line 56) Have students compare
definitions for *opulent* and then explain the antonyms *opulent*
and *shabby* (line 45) in the context of the story.

Marlene's mother died in a car crash. Marlene was sent to boarding school. Her father was ready to resign.

80 was where my father kept the red-crested night heron, one of the last of its kind.

F The year that the park officials brought the bird to Modder River had been a difficult one. My mother was killed in a car accident just before my eighth birthday. Numbly, I watched my father make funeral arrangements with the help of his sister, Annette, who drove up from Johannesburg. She was adamant: There was no way I could stay at Modder River. It was too remote, and there was my schooling to consider; my mother had been my tutor. As for my father, it made no sense for him to remain, grieving, in a place so closely associated with his wife. My father was on the verge of 90 resigning as warden of the small sanctuary when park officials telephoned about the bird. The red-crested night heron had been captured at the vlei³ on Nie Te Ver, the farm abutting the sanctuary's eastern border, and the National Parks Board wanted the heron kept at Modder River on the slim chance that they might find a mate for it.

A Mr. Vanjaarsveld arrived with the bird. "We had to tie the bugger's beak up, otherwise he'd have cut us to ribbons," he said, as he placed a large burlap bag in (the pen that my father had hastily constructed.) He opened the bag and then quickly stepped out and shut the gate. A few moments of silence—then a (wild flurry of wings,) the sound of the air being thumped, 100 and the heron hit the wire at the top of the pen and came crashing down. Again and again, till (the bird lay in the dust exhausted, its wings useless.) Quietly my father opened the gate and stepped inside the pen. For several minutes he squatted on his haunches in the corner and then slowly he inched his way toward the bird. Kneeling alongside it, he checked the feathers for damage, spreading the wings on the ground in front of him, like a fan. Then, making soft noises in the back of his throat, he untied the strip **G** of burlap around the heron's beak. My father stayed on at Modder River, and arrangements were made for me to go to boarding school.

³ **vlei:** in South Africa, a temporary lake formed in a marshy area during the rainy season.

---

6. ◀ REREAD Reread lines 82–94. The narrator describes the year as "difficult." In the margin, explain in your own words what happened.

7. READ ▶ As you read lines 95–139, continue to cite textual evidence.

• Underline the changes the heron brought to Modder River.
• Circle text that describes the heron and its surroundings.

12

> Then, making soft noises in the back of his throat, he untied the strip of burlap around the heron's beak.

H During holidays I came home, and my father would share the latest 110 news about the heron with me. He showed me articles from the local papers **lauding** the conservation efforts surrounding the bird, as well as articles from foreign countries in languages we couldn't understand. He showed me the stamp that the South African government issued—a thirty-seven-cent stamp with the heron's lean profile and brilliant crest. And once he gave me a feather, a long, steel-gray feather from the tip of the heron's wing, a flight feather, and it was smooth as I stroked it against my cheek during the overnight train ride back to boarding school. But after two or three years, interest in the heron faded. The articles died down, and in private the National Parks Board expressed their doubts to my father that they would 120 ever find a mate for the bird. The sanctuary was small, and apart from a secretive leopard we didn't have any of the Big Five—animals like elephants and lions that attracted tourists. Modder River returned to the way it used to be, a trickle of visitors on the occasional weekend.

I stared at the pen for a long time now. I knew what was in there. A (large gray bird, with ugly hooked feet, a long slithery neck that gave me nightmares, and a red crest that was raised during the courtship ritual.) I had never seen the crest, but once I'd caught a glimpse of a small red feather that had escaped from the heron's crown. There was no need to walk

lauding: praising

The heron might symbolize hope for the father and the sanctuary.

---

8. ◀ REREAD Reread lines 109–136. In the margin, explain what the heron might symbolize.

13

---

6. **REREAD AND CITE TEXT EVIDENCE** Students may have already inferred that Marlene's mother had died. (Her photograph showed her "frozen at age thirty-two.")

F ASK STUDENTS to note Marlene's mother's death and other events mentioned in lines 82–94 that contributed to the year being "difficult" and to summarize the events in the margin.

7. **READ AND CITE TEXT EVIDENCE** The narrator has explained why the year was difficult, and that her father was ready to resign.

G ASK STUDENTS to underline the changes that happen after the heron is brought to Modder River. *Students should cite specific evidence about Marlene's father deciding to stay at the sanctuary (lines 107–108) and his interest in the attention the bird brought (lines 109–113).*

8. **REREAD AND CITE TEXT EVIDENCE** Remind students that writers often develop themes through the use of symbols.

H ASK STUDENTS to read their margin notes to a partner, discuss the heron as a symbol, and revise their margin notes citing text evidence. *Students may conclude that the heron is a symbol of hope, citing evidence from lines 109–116.*

Critical Vocabulary: lauding (line 111) Have students compare their definitions. Point out that a more common word from the same root is *laudable*, meaning "praiseworthy."

through the dust to look at the bird under the swaying blue gum tree
130 branches. I went anyway. Effortlessly, I climbed the blue gum tree, but now
it was difficult for me to squeeze into the small fork halfway up. The heron
pecked listlessly at a dried-out fish, and I noticed that the pen hadn't been
cleaned in quite a while. I'd spent many school holidays in the tree watching
my father as he fed the bird, collected the feathers during the molt,[4] and
proudly chatted with visitors. Maybe he'd known that I was up there
all the time.

I shivered. The sun had set, taking all the warmth with it, and a thin
veil of light pressed against our house and the Modder River as it crawled
like a fat brown snake out of the mountains.

140 Walking back down the length of the veranda, I peered through the
windows of the rooms we'd stopped using, the dining room with its yellow
wood table, the living room where my mother's desk was still piled high
with the field guides and books she'd used to identify unknown plants she'd
come across. The outside light flickered on, and I found my father in the
kitchen, heating up a tin of curry. We ate our dinner in silence, and then he
read a book and I listened to the radio. I felt uncomfortable in the house
and longed for the morning, when I could go racing through the veld with
the dogs, go out looking for tracks and walk far into the sanctuary. At
10 P.M., as was custom, my father switched off the electricity generator and
150 went to his study, where he slept.

The low hum now gone, I lay in bed and let the night overtake me,
hungrily following the calls in the darkness. A jackal marking his territory,
the rhythmic eruptions of spring bullfrogs, the steady breath of King at the
foot of my bed. And then I heard another familiar sound, the creaking of
the gate on the heron's pen. Gently I felt my way down the hall and into my
parents' old bedroom. I hid behind the soft lace curtains, and as my eyes
grew accustomed to the night, I saw my father move slowly across the
compound carrying the heron gently under his arm, its long legs dangling
at his side. The heron's neck was liquid in the moonlight, curving and
160 swaying, at times seeming to entwine my father. Its beak glinted like a

It has been five years, and Marlene's father has not moved his dead wife's books from her desk.

---
[4] **molt:** shedding of feathers at certain intervals, prior to replacement by new growth.

dagger. One of my father's hands followed the bird's neck, lightly touching it
at times, while the other was sunk deep into the heron's soft breast, pale
gray feathers around his wrist. My father slipped by with the heron, and I
went back to bed and stared into the darkness. Later on I heard a **tremulous**
wail repeated several times. It came from the river. I knew it was the
red-crested night heron, even though I'd never heard its call before, and I
thought about my father in the darkness on the banks of the Modder River
with the bird.

At breakfast the next morning, my father told me that a hyena had
170 gotten the best of us, had finally broken into the heron's pen, because the
bird had disappeared. Under the blue gum tree we examined a huge hole in
the fence. "Yes, I think so, Dad," I said, and nodded in agreement as we
watched King and Blitz sniff inside the pen. He seemed lighter and chatted
with me about school as I helped him dismantle the fence. "Hyena," he had
said with such authority. He told me that now he might even be able to
come to the end-of-the-year recital at my school. That night I made fried
bananas and ice cream for dessert, and we listened to a radio play together.
At ten, just before he switched off the generator, I looked in the mirror and
thought, I have his eyes.

180 In bed, in the blackness, I listened to the night again. The jackal that
had been barking the previous night had moved on, and it seemed quiet out
there. It wasn't long before I heard the heron calling. I knew my father heard
it as well, and I tried to picture him in his bed. I wondered if his heart beat
like mine, an urgent knocking in my chest. I rolled over and thought of the
red-crested night heron, alone by the river, the last of its kind, and I
imagined that its crest was raised and that it picked its way delicately
through the muddy water, lifting its feet up like wet handkerchiefs.

The following night I heard the heron's call again, and I also heard
footsteps leaving our house. I knew it was my father going down to the
190 river. For ten nights the heron called and my father followed. During the
days we worked on repairing things around the compound. We cleaned up
the pond and made a day trip to the western corner of the sanctuary, where
the Modder River dropped abruptly into a densely forested ravine—gnarled
trees hung with a thick gray moss that I called "old man's beard." We

tremulous:
shaky, fearful, or nervous

Marlene's father seems more engaged. They are doing more things together.

---

9. **READ** ▶ As you read lines 140–179, underline language that describes how the father seems to be changing. Make notes in the margin in lines 140–150 about what hasn't changed.

10. **READ** ▶ As you read lines 180–205, circle the unfolding events.

---

9. **READ AND CITE TEXT EVIDENCE**

I **ASK STUDENTS** to compare their notes about what has not changed (the mother's books are still on her desk). Have students figure out how long the books must have been there. *Students should find that the books have been there at least five years, citing evidence from lines 4 and 83–84, showing that the mother died just before Marlene was eight; she is now thirteen.*

10. **READ AND CITE TEXT EVIDENCE** Marlene's father has secretly released the heron, and his mood has changed for the better.

J **ASK STUDENTS** to summarize what happens in lines 180–205, and to discuss with a partner what they think the father is doing as he leaves the house. *The father is keeping track of the heron and making sure that it is all right.*

Critical Vocabulary: tremulous (line 164) Ask volunteers to read their definitions. Have students discuss why the narrator uses the phrase *tremulous wail* to refer to the heron's call. *Students may suggest that the phrase sounds sad, or foreshadows danger for the heron.*

collected water lilies from the dappled pools, wrapping their roots in damp newspaper and placing them in our packs. Baboons barked from the rocky ledges. We saw the spoor of the leopard, two pugmarks⁵ in the rich black mud. For the drive home I sat in the back of the truck. As my father shifted to low gear and negotiated the sandy part of the road that ran alongside the river, I scanned the banks, hoping to catch a glimpse of the heron roosting, waiting for nightfall. I spent a day repairing the signs along the Succulent Trail, a one-mile loop that wound through an area that my father had filled with rare plants—aloe albida, aloe monotropa, a lydenberg cycad. We put the map back on its post and touched it up with small pots of paint, the Modder River a blue vein in the brown landscape.

Then, one long night, I didn't hear the heron's call. The bird had disappeared, and when I got out of bed the next morning, I saw that (my father's eyes had gone dull like a dead animal's.) I knew why but couldn't say anything. Then (he started walking all the time,) often coming home only for an hour or two in the early dawn. I'd hear the creak of the floorboards near the kitchen and the thud of Blitz's tail on the floor. I'd hear my father pacing, and then, eventually, stillness. He's lying on the sofa in his study, he's asleep now, I'd say to myself. Then the pacing again and the soft slam of the screen door. From the blue gum tree I'd see him crisscrossing the veld, like a rabid dog, always coming back to touch the river. Straining my eyes, I'd watch him walk (farther and farther away,) until he vanished into the landscape.

⁵ **spoor ... pugmarks:** *Spoor* is the track or trail of a wild animal. *Pugmarks* are the footprints or trail of an animal.

The bird might symbolize hope to the father: it's the only thing he cares about since his wife died.

11. ◀ **REREAD** Reread lines 169–205. In the margin, explain how Marlene's relationship with her father has changed. What is her father doing at night? Support your answer with explicit textual evidence.

Marlene's father is looking for the bird who has gone missing. He said a hyena "had finally broken into the heron's pen."

12. **READ ▶** As you read lines 206–231, continue to cite textual evidence.
• Circle language that describes the father in lines 206–217.
• In the margin, make an inference about what the bird might mean to the father.

Accidentally, I found the heron's remains. I was out late one afternoon, looking for a snakeskin for my next school biology project. I had chosen a rocky area, where I'd seen cobras and puff adders sunning themselves, and as I moved slowly through it, poking into crevices with a stick, I came across a broken fan of bloodied feathers. The steel-gray patina was unmistakable, and I knew it was part of the heron's wing. I scratched out a hole with my stick and buried the feathers, pushing a large rock over the small grave.

I made sandwiches for supper that night. I made extra ones for my father, but he didn't come home. I sat on the veranda with King and Blitz until ten o'clock, when I switched off the generator. Swiftly, silently, I

The heron was probably killed by snakes. Marlene doesn't want her father to find the bird; she knows he will be devastated.

13. ◀ **REREAD** Reread lines 218–225. In the margin, explain what happened to the heron. Why does the narrator bury it?

11. **REREAD AND CITE TEXT EVIDENCE**

K **ASK STUDENTS** to compare their responses about Marlene's relationship with her father. *Students should see that Marlene and her father are now doing things together and are cleaning up the sanctuary.* Ask what the father does at night, and what it may have to do with his changed mood. *Students should cite evidence from lines 188–190 to explain that the father follows the heron at night. They may see some connection between the bird's freedom from the pen and the father's freedom from his despair.*

12. **READ AND CITE TEXT EVIDENCE**

L **ASK STUDENTS** to describe the father's behavior that they have circled in lines 206–231. How does it compare to his behavior when he was able to hear the heron's call? Have students write what the bird might mean to the father. *Students may think that the heron symbolizes hope to the father; he rejoices in its (and his) freedom, and he is troubled by its disappearance.*

13. **REREAD AND CITE TEXT EVIDENCE** Marlene has been paying close attention to her father's behavior since the heron has gone.

M **ASK STUDENTS** to cite evidence that lets them know that the heron has died. *In line 218, the narrator says that she finds the heron's remains. In the same paragraph, she recognizes the bloodied feathers of the heron.*

FOR ELL STUDENTS Point out that in South Africa—where the story is set—the English that is spoken has been influenced by the British. The use of "supper" here is equivalent to "dinner" in American English.

followed the footpath down to the far bank of the river, pushing my way
230   through the warm water that came up to my waist. I hid in the reeds and
waited.

    An hour later I saw my father on the opposite bank, looking, listening.
He sat down on the dark sand and rolled a pebble in his large palms. I
crouched even lower. <u>Slowly I tilted my head back until my throat was wide
open and a tremulous wail slid out. My father stood up and looked across
the water to where I was crouched. Again I made the sound, again and
again.</u> He took three more small steps toward my side of the river and his
hands fluttered like giant, tawny moths in the moonlight.

---

14. **READ ▶** Read lines 232–238. Underline text describing Marlene's
action and her father's response. What does she do, and why? Support
your answer with explicit textual evidence.

Marlene imitates the heron's call with the intention of making her
father think it is still alive. She wants to give him hope that the
heron is still out there.

SHORT RESPONSE

Cite Text Evidence   Think about Marlene's relationship with her father
and what it reveals about the story's theme. Review your reading notes. Be
sure to **cite text evidence** to explain your response.

At the beginning of the story, Marlene returns home and hopes for a
close relationship with her father. However, he remains distant and
seems to connect only with the heron. As Marlene begins to work
with her father fixing up the compound, he starts to warm up, but
when the bird goes missing he retreats into himself again. By the end
of the story, Marlene and her father have switched roles—she is
taking care of him. The theme of the story is about the challenges
of giving and receiving love.

18

---

14. READ AND CITE TEXT EVIDENCE

 ASK STUDENTS to find the text that describes what
Marlene does and how her father reacts. Have them explain
Marlene's action. *Marlene uses her ability as a mimic to imitate the
heron call, knowing that her father desperately hopes that the heron
is still alive (lines 233–236). She feeds his hope.*

SHORT RESPONSE

Cite Text Evidence   Student responses will vary, but they should
cite evidence from the text to support their inferences. Students
should:

- provide text-based insights into the relationship between Marlene
and her father.
- focus on details of their relationship that develop the theme.
- determine a theme of the story that is supported by the
relationship details.

TO CHALLENGE STUDENTS . . .

Remind students that writers often use symbols to develop their
themes. In "Night Calls," Lisa Fugard uses the red-crested heron
as a symbol of hope for the father. Have students research how
certain birds have been used as symbols in the past, and how
they are used today. For example, people think of owls as symbols
of wisdom, but in the past, writers such as William Shakespeare
used them as symbols of impending death. The dove has been
almost universally considered a symbol of peace since ancient
Egyptian times.

ASK STUDENTS to research birds as symbols in mythology,
cultures, or literature. Each student should find out about at least
one bird. Have students share the results of their research with
the class, and discuss how several of the birds might be used as
symbols in a short story.

DIG DEEPER

1. With the class, return to Question 8, Reread. Have students share their responses.

ASK STUDENTS to cite the text evidence that led to their inferences about what the heron might symbolize.

- Point out that lines 109–136 provide details about an earlier time, before Marlene's trip home at age thirteen. Ask students how the compound has changed since then. *The compound has not been well maintained. It is looking shabby and the pond is stagnant.*

- Have students cite text that shows that the father was energized by the heron's presence. *He showed Marlene articles about the bird and a stamp with the heron on it.*

- Have students cite text that shows that things changed. *The interest in the heron faded, and there were fewer visitors to the sanctuary.*

- Have students compare the father's behavior—and the condition of the compound—when the heron first arrived and in the present setting. *Students may point out that her father was happier earlier, chatting proudly about the bird to visitors, but has now lost interest.*

- Ask students what the heron might have meant to the father when it first lived at the sanctuary. *Students may consider the heron to be symbol of hope for the future.*

2. With the class, return to Question 11, Reread. Have students share their responses.

ASK STUDENTS to discuss how the father acts after he releases the heron. Remind them to cite textual evidence in their discussion.

- What clues let you know that the father is happier? *He chats with Marlene, suggests visiting her at school, and listens to the radio with her.*

- What does the father do at night, and during the day? *He follows the bird at night. During the day he works with Marlene and seems much happier.*

- Ask students how the heron being a symbol of hope might account for the father's behavior. *The father is happy to have set the heron free. He has also set free his own sadness, but he still somehow depends on the heron's existence.*

ASK STUDENTS to return to their Short Response answer and revise it based on the class discussion.

CLOSE READING NOTES

Rituals of Memory

Essay by Kimberly M. Blaeser

Why This Text?

Memory is a universal human experience that is shaped by individual and community events and by culture. This autobiographical essay explores how the ceremonies and stories from Kimberly Blaeser's dual cultural heritage shaped her memories and her identity.

Key Learning Objective: The student will be able to determine a central idea and analyze its development over the course of a text.

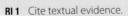

RI 1 Cite textual evidence.
RI 2 Determine a central idea of a text and analyze its development.
RI 4 Determine the meaning of words and phrases.
RI 6 Analyze how an author uses rhetoric to advance point of view or purpose.
SL 1 Participate effectively in collaborative discussions.
L 5b Analyze nuances in the meaning of words with similar denotations.

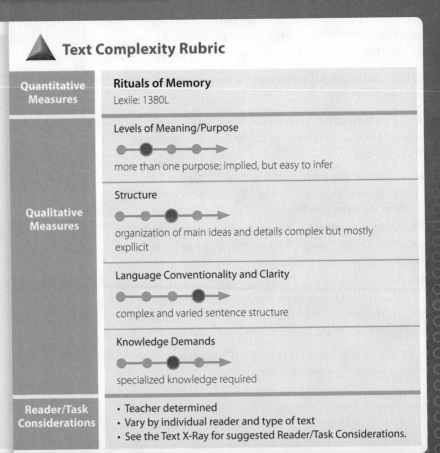

▲ Text Complexity Rubric

	Rituals of Memory
Quantitative Measures	Lexile: 1380L

Levels of Meaning/Purpose

more than one purpose; implied, but easy to infer

Structure

organization of main ideas and details complex but mostly explicit

Language Conventionality and Clarity

complex and varied sentence structure

Knowledge Demands

specialized knowledge required

Qualitative Measures

Reader/Task Considerations
- Teacher determined
- Vary by individual reader and type of text
- See the Text X-Ray for suggested Reader/Task Considerations.

Meaning Making

Language Development

Effective Expression

Content Knowledge

Foundational Skills

English Language Support Before teaching, use the Text X-Ray below for an overview of the text's complexity. The Text X-Ray and the supports and scaffolds in the Teacher's Edition will help you guide students of different skill levels.

Text Complexity: Qualitative Measures

Levels of Meaning/Purpose

more than one purpose; implied, but easy to infer

Help students determine the central idea of the text.
- Teacher's Edition side notes, pp. 23, 24
- When Students Struggle, p. 23
- Strategies for Annotation, p. 24
- Determine Central Idea, p. 25

To reteach determining central idea, see
- Determine Central Idea, p. 26a

 Use It! **Interactive Whiteboard Lesson:** Theme/Central Idea

ZOOM IN ON **DETERMINING CENTRAL IDEA** After students have read the essay, have them use the following sentence frames to discuss it with a partner. Have each pair then develop a sentence stating the **central idea** of the essay. (Clarify that this idea should apply to all people, not just the author.) Ask pairs to share their sentences, and work with them to refine the language as needed.

- "Rituals of memory" (line 24) are ___.
- The author's memories of Memorial Day are important to her because ___.
- The author led a "double life" (line 81) because ___.
- Stories and memories were important to her education because ___.

Structure

organization of main ideas and details complex but mostly explicit

Help students analyze the text structure of the essay.
- Teacher's Edition side notes, pp. 22, 25
- When Students Struggle, p. 23
- Strategies for Annotation, p. 24
- Determine Central Idea, p. 25

 Use It! *Level Up* tutorial: Main Idea and Supporting Details

ZOOM IN ON **ANALYZING TEXT STRUCTURE** After students read the essay, have them form small groups to apply the strategy described on Student Edition page 25.

- Assign several paragraphs to each group. For each paragraph, have them identify the **topic**, examine specific **details**, determine the **main idea**, and state this idea in a sentence.
- Ask groups to share their main-idea sentences with the whole class. Write each sentence on the board in order.
- Discuss how all the paragraph statements relate to the **central idea** of the essay.

Language Conventionality and Clarity

complex and varied sentence structure

Teach unfamiliar vocabulary in context.

- Teacher's Edition Critical Vocabulary notes, pp. 21, 22, 23, 24, 26
- Applying Academic Vocabulary, p. 22

Help students analyze language.

- Teacher's Edition side notes, pp. 21, 22, 23, 24
- English Language Support, p. 21
- Analyze Language, p. 26a
- Vocabulary Strategy: Denotations and Connotations, p. 26
- Strategies for Annotation, p. 26

ZOOM IN ON **UNPACKING SENTENCES** Display the compound sentence below. Point out the conjunction *and*, which divides it into two clauses. Guide students to identify the subjects and verbs.

> Uniformed, sometimes sweating in the early summer heat, they marched to the sites, stood at attention as taps was played, and then, as a gesture of salute to the fallen veterans, they shot over the graves. (lines 33–36)

Note that the basic frame of this sentence is *They marched, [they] stood, and they shot*. Discuss how words and phrases add detail.

Knowledge Demands

specialized knowledge required

Support English Learners in understanding the author's cultural background.

- Teacher's Edition Background note, p. 21

ZOOM IN ON **BUILDING CULTURAL KNOWLEDGE** Students may benefit from knowing more about these references.

- Ed Castillo (line 80), born in 1948 in California, is a professor of Native American Studies and a long-time Native American activist.
- The "Hail Mary [and] the Our Father" (line 99) are prayers that all Catholic children learn. The author compares these prayers to the natural phenomena appreciated by her Native American relatives.
- "Baptism, First Communion, and confirmation" (lines 105–106) are rituals that mark a Catholic child's development.

Suggested Reader/Task Considerations

You might consider the following before assigning this essay to students.

- Will students be interested in the topic and content of the essay?
- Will students **make connections** between details presented in different parts of the text?

ZOOM IN ON **SUPPORTING COMPREHENSION**

- Before students read, ask them to think about traditions and customs that come from various relatives, from their native cultures, and from American culture. Encourage students to make connections to their own experiences as they read the essay.
- Review with students the **metaphor** of the loops in Mary's hair (lines 1–7). Ask: How does the loop metaphor relate to the author's memory of Memorial Day? *(She often "loops back" to the memory of people from different backgrounds coming together.)* How does this memory help her keep the two strands of her background together (lines 68–74)? *(It reminds her that all people are connected by their common humanity.)*

Kimberly M. Blaeser Have students read the information about the author. Explain that Blaeser grew up on the White Earth Reservation in northwest Minnesota, which covers about 1,300 square miles and currently has a population of about 20,000 people. *Anishinaabe* is the name that the largest Indian group in Minnesota call themselves; the word means "original people." Europeans called these people Ojibwe (or Ojibwa) or Chippewa; both names are now used by tribal members in Canada. The essay "Rituals of Memory" appeared in the anthology *Here First: Autobiographical Essays by Native American Writers* (2000).

AS YOU READ Instruct students to use the As You Read note to focus their reading.

Analyze Language
RI 4, RI 6

(LINES 1–16)

Inform students that a **metaphor** is a type of figurative language in which an author compares two things without using the word *like* or *as*.

A CITE TEXT EVIDENCE Ask students to reread lines 1–16, identify where Blaeser uses the term *metaphor*, and explain what she is comparing. *(She uses the term in line 11, comparing her friend Mary's belief about her hair growing in loops [lines 5–7] to the "looped relationships of family, place, and community.")* Then ask students to summarize the central idea in lines 9–16, based on this metaphor. *(Possible answer: People's relationships and memories tend to circle back to the central experiences of their origins.)*

CRITICAL VOCABULARY

innate: Blaeser says our "looped relationships" are innate patterns that keep us returning to our origins. **ASK STUDENTS** how innate patterns are connected with family. *(Patterns that exist at birth come from our ancestors and their experiences that get passed down through the generations.)*

Kimberly M. Blaeser (b. 1955), *of German and Anishinaabe ancestry, is a member of the Minnesota Chippewa tribe. Blaeser began her career as a journalist but is now a professor at the University of Wisconsin-Milwaukee. Blaeser is also a writer whose work includes poetry, personal essays, short stories, and reviews. Her first collection of poems,* Trailing You, *won the First Book Award in Poetry from the Native Writer's Circle of Americas in 1993. In her work, Blaeser often alludes to her dual heritage and to the collective nature of the human experience.*

Rituals of Memory

Essay by Kimberly M. Blaeser

Image Credits: (c) ©Franek Strzeszewski/Image Source/Corbis; (cr) ©Laurence Mouton and Isabelle Rozenbaum/PhotoAlto/Corbis

AS YOU READ Look for evidence about how Blaeser's mixed ancestry shapes her experiences and her ideas on memories. Write down any questions you generate during reading.

Memory begins with various wonders. For my friend Mary, it began with hair. Her hair grew tightly curled, so strong the spirals defied taming. Brushing and combing brought tears. When Mary tried to run her fingers through her hair as she saw others do, her fingers became hopelessly captured by the curls. Hair, she deduced, must grow in loops, out of our head at one point, back into it at another. Because her locks had never been cut, the loops never broken, her fingers became entangled in the loops.

Perhaps that story delights me because it stands as a wonderful
10 example of our always innocent attempts to explain the world. Or perhaps because it seems a fine metaphor for the looped relationships of family, place, and community, the **innate** patterns of ourselves that always keep us returning. No matter how long our lives, no matter how far our experience takes us from our origins, our lives remain connected, always loop back to that center of our identity, our spirit.

innate
(ĭ-nāt´) *adj.* inborn; existing at birth.

ENGLISH LANGUAGE SUPPORT

Analyze Language Help students understand the metaphor introduced in lines 1–16. Call on volunteers to identify all the words used to refer to hair in lines 1–8. *(tightly curled, spirals, curls, loops, locks)* Have them explain or draw the image of the hair described. Then ask volunteers to find the word *loop* in lines 9–16. *("looped relationships"; "our lives . . . always loop back")* Ask: How are loops of hair like relationships? *(They entangle us; they connect back to a central place.)* As they continue reading, encourage students to notice other places in the essay where the words *loop* and *circle* are used.

Determine Central Idea

RI 1, RI 2

(LINES 17–24)

Explain that in order to determine the central idea—the most important point—of a text, it helps to identify the main idea of each paragraph. Review these strategies:

- Identify the topic or subject of each paragraph.
- See how each topic relates to the selection title.
- Look for a topic sentence that states the main idea or main message of the paragraph. Often it is the first or last sentence of the paragraph.
- If there is no explicit topic sentence, infer the main idea from the details presented about the topic.

B **CITE TEXT EVIDENCE** Ask students to reread lines 17–24 and identify where Blaeser defines rituals of memory. *("storytelling and ceremonies that feed" memory [lines 23–24])* Then ask them to state the main idea in their own words. *(Rituals of memory such as storytelling and ceremonies are the strongest way to stay connected to our sense of who we are.)*

Analyze Language

RI 1, RI 6

(LINES 29–45)

Tell students that an author's purpose can be implied in the details that he or she presents. **Rhetoric** is the effective use of language that allows an author to advance his or her purpose.

C **CITE TEXT EVIDENCE** Have students infer Blaeser's purpose in lines 29–45. *(She wants to show that the different cultures in her life were sometimes mixed together [lines 29–31].)* Then have them cite the rhetoric that helps her advance that purpose. *(She provides vivid details about how people with different backgrounds joined together to honor the deceased veterans on Memorial Day.)*

CRITICAL VOCABULARY

foremost: Blaeser says her Native American culture may be foremost in her mind.

ASK STUDENTS why Blaeser's Native American culture might be foremost in her mind. *(because some of her memories, like the one described in lines 41–51, remind her of her heritage)*

> "*My memories entangle themselves oddly among the roots of several cultures.*"

B   I believe we belong to the circle and, for our survival, we will return in one way or another to renew those rhythms of life out of which our sense of self has emerged. Some of us have a physical

20 place and a people we return to. We also have what Gerald Vizenor calls the "interior landscapes" of our imaginative and spiritual lives. Perhaps our strongest link to the sacred center, the pulsing core of being, is memory and the storytelling and ceremonies that feed it— our own rituals of memory.

    My memories entangle themselves oddly among the roots of several cultures: Native American, perhaps **foremost** in my mind, but also a German Catholic background, the culture of rural America, the close looping of small towns in the Midwest, and what I guess could be called Minnesota wilderness culture. But these

30 several cultures did not always exist in opposition or in isolation from one another. I remember Memorial Day celebrations when my father joined the Legionnaires[1] in their visits to all the graveyards in Mahnomen and Nay-Tah-Waush.[2] Uniformed, sometimes sweating in the early summer heat, they marched to the sites, stood at attention as taps was played, and then, as a gesture of salute to the fallen veterans, they shot over the graves. Each year, through late morning and early afternoon, we followed the men on these tours. We stood, moved to goose bumps by the lonely trumpet tune, scrambling with all the other children for spent casings when each

40 ceremony was concluded.

    The last site on their schedule was the Indian burial grounds close to the BAB landing. As a child I saw nothing unusual about a dozen American Legionnaires marching back on the little wooded

foremost

(fôr´mōst´) *adv.* most importantly.

---

[1] **Legionnaires:** members of the American Legion, a social, service-based organization of American veterans.

[2] **Mahnomen and Nay-Tah-Waush:** cities in northwestern Minnesota.

22   Collection 1

APPLYING ACADEMIC VOCABULARY

internal	presume

As you discuss the essay, incorporate the Collection 1 academic vocabulary words **internal** and **presume**. To explore Blaeser's ideas about memory, invite students to cite evidence of how **internal** rituals of memory help shape a person's awareness of self. In addition, ask students to explain why it might be incorrect to **presume** that Blaeser's different cultures were isolated from one another.

path and paying solemn respect to those Indian warriors who I would later realize were really of another nation. On this march through the tall grasses and hazelnut bushes that crowded the path, my older brother and I often fell in step. Several times I marched beside Sig Tveit and his trumpet, his arm linked through mine. We stood, all of us—those descended from settlers of Norwegian, German, or other European origins, and those descended from Anishinaabe or other Indian people. Together in a moment out of ordinary time, we paused in the little opening at the wooden grave houses, oblivious to the wood ticks, which must later be picked carefully from our clothes and our flesh, oblivious to the buzzing of mosquitoes or sand flies, oblivious as well to the more trivial tensions of contemporary politics. We stood together in a great ceremonial loop of our humanity, in our need to remember our ancestors and the lives they lived, together in our desire to **immerse** ourselves in their honor, to always carry those memories forward with us, to be ourselves somehow made holy by the ritual of those memories. We emerged quiet from those little woods, from that darker place of memory, into the too bright sunshine of a late May day in the twentieth century.

And then we arrived back at the sandy beach. The men brought out drinks from the trunks of their cars, laughter and talk sprang up, picnic foods came out, and people would disperse again—to their own families.

I don't know if the Legionnaires still march back into the woods each year. I like to believe they do. For that kind of experience has helped me keep balance when the strands of my mixed heritage seem to pull one against another. However unconscious, it was a moment of crossover, a moment when the borders of culture were **nullified** by the greater instincts of humanity to remember and to give honor.

Perhaps the Memorial Days of those early years have become one of the watermarks[3] of my life because they brought to ceremonial focus the many tellings of the past that filled up the hours and days of my childhood. As children, we were never so much taught as storied. All work and play had memories attached.

"Indians," Ed Castillo says, "can hold more than one thing sacred." With school began my double life. I went to Catholic grade school, where I earned a reputation for being quiet, obedient, pious, and bright. I learned my Baltimore Catechism[4]—*Who made you?*

---

[3] **watermarks:** marks impressed in paper that can be viewed when the paper is held up to the light.

[4] **Baltimore Catechism:** a summary of Christian beliefs in a question-and-answer format that was taught in Catholic schools until the late 1960s.

immerse

(ĭ-mûrs´) *v.* to absorb or involve deeply.

nullify

(nŭl´ə-fī´) *v.* to make of no value or consequence.

Rituals of Memory   23

WHEN STUDENTS STRUGGLE . . .

Have students work in pairs and use reciprocal teaching with each paragraph of the essay.

- Students take turns reading paragraphs aloud and listening.
- The reading partner asks the listening partner to summarize the main idea and identify important details.
- Students record their conclusions in a chart like this one.

Central Idea	Supporting Details
Memorial Day ceremonies are rituals to honor the memory of veterans.	People of different backgrounds visit graveyards, play taps, and fire rifles over graves.

CLOSE READ

Analyze Language   RI 4, RI 6

(LINES 56–63)

Explain that one way authors use language to convey their point of view is by creating imagery that appeals to readers' senses and makes abstract ideas concrete.

D CITE TEXT EVIDENCE Ask students to reread lines 56–63 and give examples of Blaeser's language that creates imagery. (*"We emerged quiet . . . from that darker place of memory, into the too bright sunshine . . . ."[lines 61–62]*) Then ask students to cite evidence to explain what Blaeser means by "We stood together in a great ceremonial loop of our humanity" (lines 56–57). (*They were part of the great human circle that continuously brings past and present together through ritual; they desire to "always carry those memories forward . . . made holy by the ritual of those memories."*)

Determine Central Idea   RI 1, RI 2

(LINES 75–79)

Tell students that an author shapes a central idea by adding specific details over the course of a text.

E ASK STUDENTS to reread lines 75–79 and explain how Blaeser develops a central idea introduced earlier (lines 23–24). (*She says that her memories of Memorial Day ceremonies are key because they illustrate how the stories of her childhood have shaped her. This develops the central idea that "rituals of memory," storytelling, and ceremony, help us understand who we are.*)

CRITICAL VOCABULARY

immerse: Participants in the Memorial Day ceremonies wanted to immerse themselves in the honor of the deceased veterans.
ASK STUDENTS how the people at the Memorial Day ceremonies showed their desire to immerse themselves to honor their ancestors. (*They focused on their ancestors' lives with respect, ignoring ordinary concerns such as ticks, flies, and politics.*)

nullified: Blaeser says the differences among cultures were overcome by common human instincts. **ASK STUDENTS** how Memorial Day activities nullified differences among the people in Blaeser's community. (*People from different backgrounds came together to honor the dead.*)

Analyze Language

RI 6

(LINES 97–103)

Encourage students to continue to look for examples of metaphor as they read.

F **CITE TEXT EVIDENCE** Ask students to reread lines 97–103 and identify two examples of metaphor. How do the metaphors help Blaeser achieve her purpose? *(The metaphors are "the misty prayers water gives off at dawn" [line 100] and "the intricate language of a beaver's teeth and tail" [lines 102–103]. They support Blaeser's purpose of revealing the education she received in the woods.)*

CRITICAL VOCABULARY

tangibles: Blaeser says she has some tangibles of her Native American education. **ASK STUDENTS** to to explain how the tangibles related to Blaeser's Native American education are different from "stories, dreams, and memories." *(She can touch objects like her jingle dress and feather fans, but most of what she learned is not documented by physical objects.)*

COLLABORATIVE DISCUSSION Have students pair up and discuss Blaeser's views on memories. Then have them share their conclusions with the whole class. Accept all reasonable responses.

ASK STUDENTS to share any questions they generated in the course of reading and discussing the selection.

"God made me." "Why did God make you?" "God made me because he loves me."—learned my singsong phonics—*ba be bi ba bu, ca ce ci ca cu, da de di da du*—studied my spelling—*i before e, except after c, or when it sounds like a as in neighbor and weigh.* In between school days, we gathered hazelnuts, went partridge hunting, fished, had long deer-hunting weekends, went to powwows,[5] went spearing
90 and ice fishing, played canasta and whist, learned the daisy chain, beaded on looms, made fish house candles, sausage, and quilts. No one then questioned the necessity or value of our school education, but somehow I grew up knowing it wasn't the only—maybe not even the most important— education I would need, and sometimes we stole time from that education for the other one. My parents might keep us home from school or come and get us midday for some more lovely adventure on a lake or in the woods. I'm still thankful for those stolen moments, because now I know by heart not only the Hail Mary, the Our Father, and the National Anthem,
100 but the misty prayers water gives off at dawn and the ancient song of the loon; I recognize not only the alphabet and the parts of the English sentence, but the silhouetted form of the shipoke and the intricate language of a beaver's teeth and tail.

My life at school and in the Catholic Church is officially recorded and documented—dates of baptism, First Communion and confirmation, quarterly grade reports, attendance records— just as my academic life is later documented at universities in Minnesota, Indiana, and Wisconsin. But for my other education, practical and spiritual, I have no grades or degrees, no certificates
110 to commemorate the annual rituals. I have some **tangibles** of those processes—a jingle dress, fans of feathers, sometimes photos—but mostly I have stories, dreams, and memories.

tangible
(tăn′jə-bəl) *n.* something that can be touched.

COLLABORATIVE DISCUSSION With a partner, discuss Blaeser's views on how memories are formed. What does she believe influences her memories? In your discussion, cite evidence from the text.

---

[5] **powwows:** a celebration of Native American culture in which diverse nations gather for the purpose of singing, dancing, and honoring their ancestors.

Strategies for Annotation 🖉 🗒 *Annotate it!*

Determine Central Idea

RI 2

Share these strategies for guided or independent analysis:

- Highlight in yellow any words or phrases that relate to the topic of each paragraph.
- Underline specific details related to the topic.
- Highlight in blue an explicit topic sentence if there is one.
- On a note, write a sentence stating the main idea in your own words.

My life at school and in the Catholic Church is officially recorded and documented—dates of baptism, First Communion and confirmation, quarterly grade reports, attendance records—

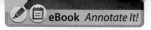

Determine Central Idea

RI 2

The **central idea** of an essay is the most important point conveyed in the essay. Sometimes the central idea is stated in the first paragraph, but more often, you will need to infer the central idea that is implied by specific details. As you analyze "Rituals of Memory," keep notes using these strategies to help you understand how Blaeser develops the central idea over the course of the text:

- Identify the topic of each paragraph.
- Examine the specific details the author includes in the paragraph.
- Ask what idea or message the details convey about the topic.
- Write a sentence that states the idea or message in your own words.

Analyzing the Text

RI 1, RI 2,
RI 4, RI 6, SL 1

Cite Text Evidence Support your responses with evidence from the selection.

1. **Analyze** An extended metaphor compares two unlike things at length and in a number of different ways. In the first four paragraphs, Blaeser provides an extended metaphor for rituals. To what does she compare rituals? Explain how the comparisons relate to the idea that rituals are connected and repeated.

2. **Identify Patterns** In lines 51–56, Blaeser uses repetition, or phrases that repeat the same pattern, to describe the annoyances she and the others ignored during their tribute. What is the purpose of this repetition?

3. **Connect** In line 81, Blaeser says, "With school began my double life." Explain how Blaeser has two lives. How do her two lives relate to her previous statement, "My memories entangle themselves oddly among the roots of several cultures"?

4. **Infer** What is the central idea that Blaeser develops in "Rituals of Memory"? Cite details from the text that helped you determine the central idea.

PERFORMANCE TASK

Speaking Activity: Response to Literature In her essay, Blaeser lists a few mementoes that are linked to memorable events in her life. What connections can you make between objects and memories? Share your reflections in a group discussion.

1. Collect two keepsakes or souvenirs that represent meaningful events from your life, events that you are willing to discuss. Make notes on how these objects serve as reminders and why the events are important to you.

2. Bring your notes to a group discussion along with your mementoes, if you can. If not, take a photograph or video recording of the objects to show. Share your objects, describe your events, and explain their significance.

Assign this performance task.

PERFORMANCE TASK

SL 1

Speaking Activity: Discussion Have students look around their homes for two objects that represent meaningful events that they could share with peers. Have students make notes about the objects to bring to a group discussion. Encourage students to incorporate into their discussions Blaeser's ideas about rituals of memory and their role in connecting us to our origins.

Determine Central Idea

RI 2

Call on volunteers to read the definition of a central idea and the strategies for determining it. Explain that the main idea of a paragraph may be stated in a topic sentence or implied by details.

Then display the first paragraph of Blaeser's essay, and model the strategies by doing a read-aloud/think-aloud. Show how to determine the topic by looking for important and repeated words or phrases ("*memory*," "*hair*," and "*loops*"), identify details (*the descriptions of Mary's hair*), and state the main idea. (*One of Mary's first memories was a belief her hair grew in loops on her head*)

Analyzing the Text

RI 1, RI 2, RI 4, RI 6

Possible answers:

1. *She compares rituals to loops of curly hair that seem to grow from the head in one place and grow back into the head in another place. Like the loops of hair, rituals come from our origins and return us to them. Rituals are often repeated year after year, returning to the same events and memories and connecting people to one another in a circle.*

2. *By repeating the phrase "oblivious to," Blaeser emphasizes how absorbed all the participants were in the ritual. They recognized that honoring the ancestors was more important than any small annoyances in the present.*

3. *Blaeser has two lives because she received a Native American education from her parents in the woods and in the stories of her ancestors, and she received another education at school based on her German Catholic background. These are two of the several cultures that form the roots of her memories and that sometimes get tangled together.*

4. *Rituals of memory such as stories and ceremonies help us stay connected to our deepest and most central self. Text details: lines 13–16; lines 22–24; description of the Memorial Day rituals involving people of different origins (lines 29–74); descriptions of the different things she learned at school and outside of school (lines 80–103); official records and physical objects are less important to her sense of self than "stories, dreams, and memories" (lines 110–112).*

Critical Vocabulary   L 5b

Possible answers:

1. *planning an outdoor activity.*

2. *had resulted in higher grades.*

3. *improve their relationship.*

4. *her childhood drawings.*

5. *making them feel they are in the scene.*

Vocabulary Strategy: Denotations and Connotations

Possible answers:

1. *delights* suggests fun; *intrigues* suggests mystery

2. *oddly* suggests unusual; *ridiculously* suggests silly or unreasonable

3. *scrambling* suggests spontaneous and disorganized; *pushing* suggests aggressive

4. *questioned* suggests intellectual curiosity; *challenged* suggests a stronger disagreement

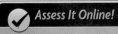

Assess It Online!

Online Selection Test
- Download an editable ExamView bank.
- Assign and manage this test online.

Critical Vocabulary   L 5b

innate   foremost   immerse   nullify   tangible

Practice and Apply Complete each phrase with your ideas about the Critical Vocabulary word. Share your work with a partner.

1. Weather conditions should be a **foremost** consideration when . . .

2. Her improved report card was **tangible** evidence that her extra study hours . . .

3. The sisters' bickering will **nullify** the efforts of their parents to . . .

4. Her **innate** creativity is revealed through . . .

5. 3D movies **immerse** the audience in the action by . . .

Vocabulary Strategy: Denotations and Connotations

A word may have different meanings. The literal definition of a word found in a dictionary is called the **denotation**. A **connotation** is what a word implies or suggests in addition to its literal meaning. This means that words with the same or similar denotations may have different connotations, or shades of meaning. A connotation may be positive or negative.

Kimberly Blaeser uses specific words to convey certain meanings. For example, the Critical Vocabulary word *immerse* (line 58) has a positive connotation and suggests that Blaeser's family and friends engaged themselves deeply in their tribute to their ancestors. However, notice how the connotation changes if you replace the word *immerse* with the word *involve*. The connotation of the word *involve* is also positive, but it suggests something less dedicated than *immerse*.

Practice and Apply Read each example from the text. Write an explanation of the connotation of the underlined word. Then, replace the underlined word with the word in parentheses, which has a similar denotation. Explain how the connotation of the new word changes the meaning of the sentence.

1. Line 9: "Perhaps the story <u>delights</u> me because it stands as a wonderful example of our always innocent attempts to explain the world." (intrigues)

2. Line 25: "My memories entangle themselves <u>oddly</u> among the roots of several cultures . . . ." (ridiculously)

3. Line 38: "We stood, moved to goose bumps by the lonely trumpet tune, <u>scrambling</u> with all the other children for spent casings when each ceremony was concluded." (pushing)

4. Line 91: "No one then <u>questioned</u> the necessity or value of our school education . . . ." (challenged)

Strategies for Annotation   ✎ 📋 **Annotate it!**

Denotation and Connotation   L 5b

Have students locate the passages that contain each example in the Practice and Apply activity. Encourage them to use their eBook annotation tools to do the following:

- Highlight in green each underlined word in the question.
- Underline any context clues that help them understand the connotation of the word.
- On a note, write the connotation of the underlined word and of the replacement word shown in parentheses.

Perhaps that story delights me because it stands as a <u>wonderful</u> example of our always <u>innocent</u> attempts to explain the world.

Analyze Language

RI 4

TEACH

Kimberly Blaeser uses language creatively to convey her ideas. Tell students that informational texts can include figurative language just as well as literary ones. Remind students that one type of figurative language they may encounter in an informational piece is an extended metaphor. A **metaphor** is a comparison of two dissimilar things; an **extended metaphor** is a comparison that, after being introduced, reappears intermittently and develops throughout a work.

Because an extended metaphor is carried throughout a text and not simply stated in a sentence, its meaning is understood over time. Provide these steps to help students locate and analyze an extended metaphor:

- Note repeated or synonymous words in a text that create images and any comparison between the images.
- Determine the purpose of the comparison.
- Think of the text's overall meaning or central idea and how the comparison relates to the idea

PRACTICE AND APPLY

Have students return to Blaeser's essay in their books. Read the first paragraph aloud. Invite students to point out the repeated or synonymous words that create an image, and ask them to describe the image. *(hair, defied taming/hopelessly captured/ entangled, curled/curls, loops/looped; tangled curly hair)* Read paragraph 2 aloud, and ask students to identify to what the girl's hair is being compared. *(relationships to family, place, and community)*

Have students work in small groups to analyze the remaining paragraphs of the essay, noting repeated words, the images the words create, and the comparison between them. When groups are finished, bring students together as a class to discuss their findings.

Then examine the purpose of the comparison and how it relates to the essay's central idea. Ask: What point is Blaeser making by returning to images of circles and relationships? *(Relationships are circular, connecting a person's past to her present and creating the person's identity.)* What message does Blaesar convey is her essay? *(She says that her dual heritage formed her identity.)* How is the comparison related to her message? *(The comparison supports her idea that relationships to the past help shape a person's identity.)*

Determine Central Idea

RI 2

RETEACH

Explain that the central idea is the most important idea or the main message that an author conveys in a piece of writing.

- Tell students that sometimes a writer will state the central idea of an essay in an introduction. Titles and headings often give clues to the central idea. However, when a central idea is not explicitly stated, readers may need to review the main ideas presented in paragraphs to infer the central idea. The main idea of a paragraph may be stated as a topic sentence that summarizes the details presented in the paragraph. It is often the first or last sentence of a paragraph.
- Explain that often the central idea needs to be inferred from the details an author presents. Tell students they should look at the details and see what big picture they create. That big picture is the central idea.

 LEVEL UP TUTORIALS Assign the following *Level Up* tutorial: **Main Idea and Supporting Details**

INDEPENDENT READING

Students can apply the skill to a selection from a textbook or to a current magazine or newspaper article. Have them work independently to identify the central idea of a text by analyzing the main ideas and details of each paragraph. Ask: What is this piece about? How does the author develop the central idea throughout the piece?

The Gettysburg Address

Speech by Abraham Lincoln

Why This Text?

The Gettysburg Address captures the essence of the United States and its principles as put forth in the Declaration of Independence. Lincoln's argument in the speech includes rhetorical devices that students will learn to recognize and appreciate in other texts.

View It!

Professional Development Podcast:

Teaching Argument

Key Learning Objective: The student will analyze an author's purpose and the use of rhetorical devices in a seminal U.S. document.

For additional practice:

Close Reader selection
Oklahoma Bombing Memorial Address
Speech by Bill Clinton

RI 1	Cite textual evidence.
RI 6	Determine author's purpose and analyze rhetoric.
RI 9	Analyze seminal U.S. documents.
SL 1d	Respond thoughtfully to diverse perspectives.
SL 6	Adapt speech to a variety of contexts and tasks.
L 1a	Use parallel structure.
L 4a	Use context as a clue to the meaning of a word or phrase.

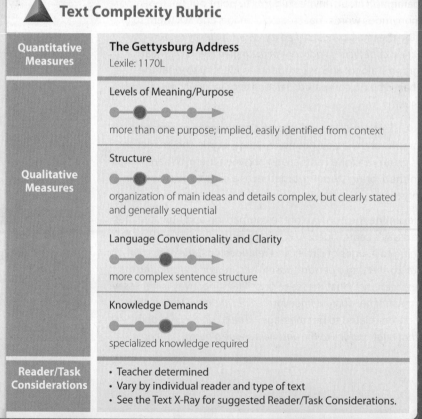

▲ Text Complexity Rubric

Quantitative Measures

The Gettysburg Address
Lexile: 1170L

Qualitative Measures

Levels of Meaning/Purpose

more than one purpose; implied, easily identified from context

Structure

organization of main ideas and details complex, but clearly stated and generally sequential

Language Conventionality and Clarity

more complex sentence structure

Knowledge Demands

specialized knowledge required

Reader/Task Considerations

• Teacher determined
• Vary by individual reader and type of text
• See the Text X-Ray for suggested Reader/Task Considerations.

English Language Support Before teaching, use the Text X-Ray below for an overview of the text's complexity. The Text X-Ray and the supports and scaffolds in the Teacher's Edition will help you guide students of different skill levels.

Meaning Making

Language Development

Effective Expression

Content Knowledge

Foundational Skills

Text Complexity: Qualitative Measures

Levels of Meaning/Purpose

more than one purpose; implied, easily identified from context

Help students analyze seminal U.S. documents.
- Teacher's Edition side notes, pp. 27, 28, 29
- English Language Support, p. 27
- Analyze Seminal U.S. Documents, p. 29

Help students prepare an oral presentation of the Gettysburg Address.
- Performance Task, p. 30
- Present a Speech, p. 32a

To reteach analyzing seminal U.S. documents, see
- Analyze Seminal U.S. Documents, p. 32a

 Use It! Level Up tutorial: Elements of an Argument

ZOOM IN ON ANALYZING SEMINAL U.S. DOCUMENTS Divide students into small groups, and assign each group one of the four characteristics of **seminal documents** in the diagram on Student Edition page 29.

- Have each group review the speech and find examples in the text that demonstrate their characteristic.
- Invite groups to share their examples with the entire class.

Structure

organization of main ideas and details complex, but clearly stated and generally sequential

Help students analyze author's purpose and rhetoric.
- Teacher's Edition side notes, pp. 27, 28, 29
- When Students Struggle, p. 28
- Strategies for Annotation, p. 29
- Analyze Author's Purpose and Rhetoric, p. 29

ZOOM IN ON ANALYZING AUTHOR'S PURPOSE Remind students that Lincoln gave his speech, in part, to stir people's emotions and move them to action. Use these questions to analyze how the **author's purpose** is accomplished.

- Are the first two paragraphs very emotional? Explain. *(No. Lincoln describes the context of the ceremony in dignified language.)*
- How does Lincoln grab the audience's attention at the beginning of the third paragraph? *(He implies that the ceremony is useless because the ground has already been dedicated by the soldiers' sacrifice.)*
- How does he build to an emotional **call to action,** urging his audience to do something? *(He says that what the living can do to honor the dead is win the war, and he ends by describing a government worth fighting for—"of the people, by the people, for the people.")*

Language Conventionality and Clarity

more complex sentence structure

Teach unfamiliar vocabulary in context.

- Teacher's Edition Critical Vocabulary notes, pp. 27, 28, 31
- Applying Academic Vocabulary, p. 31

Help students determine the correct meanings of multiple-meaning words.

- Vocabulary Strategy: Multiple-Meaning Words, p. 31

Guide students to recognize parallel structure.

- Language and Style: Parallel Structure, p. 32

ZOOM IN ON **ANALYZING MULTIPLE-MEANING WORDS** Point out that *dedicate* is a **multiple-meaning word,** and display the following two definitions.

- to set something apart as a sign of special respect
- to commit to a specific purpose

Have pairs of students locate "dedicated" in line 2 and "dedicate" in line 7. Ask them to use context clues to determine which is the correct definition in each sentence. Then have them explain their answers to the class.

Knowledge Demands

specialized knowledge required

Support English Learners in understanding the historical context and significance of the speech.

- Teacher's Edition Background note, p. 27

For more context and historical background, students can view the video "The Gettysburg Address: A New Declaration of Independence" in their eBooks.

ZOOM IN ON **DEFINING DEMOCRACY** The familiar phrase "of the people, by the people, for the people" is described at the end of the History video as "as good a definition as we have of what a republic [or democracy] actually is." Have small groups of students discuss what each part of this phrase means in terms of how the United States government is meant to work. Then have groups share their ideas with the class. *(Sample answers: "Of the people" means that the government is made up of ordinary citizens; "by the people" means that citizens have the power to elect their representatives; "for the people" means that the government works for the benefit of all citizens.)*

Suggested Reader/Task Consideration

You might consider the following before assigning this speech to students.

- Do students have the comprehension strategies they will need to understand the text?
- Will students recognize enough of the vocabulary in the text to understand its **central ideas**?

ZOOM IN ON **SUPPORTING COMPREHENSION**

- Before students read, advise them to look for **transition words** that bind sentences and paragraphs together. Display the phrase "so conceived and so dedicated" (line 5). Explain that the word *so* refers to earlier descriptions of exactly how the nation was conceived and dedicated. Words such as *that* and *here* serve a similar function.
- Have small groups read the text together, taking turns reading aloud each paragraph or section (lines 1–3, 4–9, 10–15, 15–23). When each student finishes reading, the group should pause to discuss any difficult vocabulary and look it up as needed. Students should then **paraphrase** the text using simpler words and state the **main idea** of each section in one sentence.

CLOSE READ

 For more context and historical background, students can view the video "The Gettysburg Address: A New Declaration of Independence" in their eBooks.

Background Have students read the background. Explain that the Civil War resulted from issues not resolved during the ratification of the U.S. Constitution in 1788–1789, particularly the constitutionality of slavery and the rights of states to secede. At the end of the Civil War, the Union was preserved, and slaves emancipated. But the human cost was high. About 620,000 soldiers died (perhaps as many as 750,000), and the economy of the South was devastated.

AS YOU READ Direct students to use the As You Read suggestion to focus their reading. Encourage them to generate questions as they read.

Analyze Seminal U.S. Documents (LINES 1–3) RI 9, RI 1

Explain that the Gettysburg Address references another seminal U.S. document—the Declaration of Independence—signed eighty-seven years previously.

Ⓐ CITE TEXT EVIDENCE Have students read the first paragraph and identify the theme of the Declaration of Independence. (*"[A]ll men are created equal"*)

Analyze Author's Purpose and Rhetoric (LINES 1–9) RI 6

Discuss how authors use **rhetoric**—the art of using specific words—and **rhetorical devices** lke repetition.

Ⓐ ASK STUDENTS what might Lincoln's purpose have been in repeating a certain word? (*Nation is repeated four times; the repetition emphasizes what is at stake in the war.*)

> #### CRITICAL VOCABULARY
>
> **conceived**: Lincoln explains that the new nation was formed on the foundation of liberty. **ASK STUDENTS** to explain the relationship between a nation conceived in liberty and the proposition that all men are created equal. (*Because the nation was conceived in liberty, its citizens are free and equal.*)
>
> **detract**: Lincoln's use of a contrasting clue, "add," helps make the meaning of *detract* clear. **ASK STUDENTS** how Lincoln might have detracted from the soldiers' actions. (*by criticizing them, or somehow minimizing their value*)

Background *President **Abraham Lincoln** (1809–1865) is considered an American hero for preserving the Union and emancipating the slaves. He was a skillful politician, leader, and orator. One of his most famous speeches was delivered at the dedication of the National Cemetery at Gettysburg, Pennsylvania, in 1863, site of one of the most deadly battles of the Civil War. The victory for the Union forces marked a turning point in the Civil War, but losses on both sides at Gettysburg were staggering: 28,000 Confederate soldiers and 23,000 Union soldiers were killed or wounded. Lincoln was assassinated by John Wilkes Booth in 1865. Lincoln's dedication to the ideals of freedom and equality continue to inspire people around the world.*

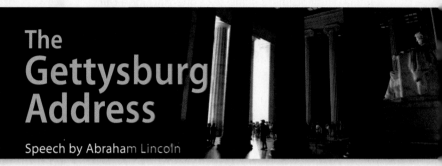

The Gettysburg Address

Speech by Abraham Lincoln

AS YOU READ Pay attention to how Lincoln's speech emphasizes the importance of ending the Civil War and reuniting the country.

Four score and seven[1] years ago our fathers brought forth on this continent, a new nation, **conceived** in liberty, and dedicated to the proposition that all men are created equal. Ⓐ

Now we are engaged in a great civil war, testing whether that nation, or any nation so conceived and so dedicated, can long endure. We are met on a great battle field of that war. We have come to dedicate a portion of that field, as a final resting place for those who here gave their lives that that nation might live. It is altogether fitting and proper that we should do this.

10 But, in a larger sense, we cannot dedicate—we cannot consecrate[2]—we cannot hallow[3]—this ground. The brave men, living and dead, who struggled here have consecrated it, far above our poor power to add or **detract**. The world will little note, nor long remember what we say here, but it can never forget what they did here. It is for us, the living, rather, to be dedicated here to the

conceive
(kən-sēv´) *v.*
to form or develop in the mind; devise.

detract
(dĭ-trăkt´) *v.*
to take away from.

[1] **four score and seven:** eighty-seven.
[2] **consecrate:** to dedicate as sacred.
[3] **hallow:** define as holy.

Image Credits: (c) ©The Washington Post/Getty Images

ENGLISH LANGUAGE SUPPORT

certain speeches, are important and influential texts. Explain that the Gettysburg Address was delivered at a turning point of the Civil War. Have students choral read the first two paragraphs of the speech. Reread the text one sentence at a time and ask students to identify words that indicate why the subject of this speech is important. (*Sample words:* liberty, equal, dedicate, brave)

ASK STUDENTS why this speech is influential. Encourage them to read aloud parts of the text that support their answers.

Analyze Seminal U.S. Documents (LINES 18–21)

RI 9

Inform students that seminal texts often include a **call to action,** a request to do or take part in something.

C **CITE TEXT EVIDENCE** Have students cite the lines that state the actions the speaker believes should be taken. *(lines 18–21)*

Analyze Author's Purpose and Rhetoric (LINES 22–23)

RI 6, RI 1

Explain that Lincoln uses **parallel structure** in his speech. This rhetorical device, which uses a grammatical pattern to create rhythm, can evoke emotion in an audience.

D **CITE TEXT EVIDENCE** Have students identify the example of parallel structure in lines 22–23, and to explain what emotion it evokes. *("of the people, by the people, for the people"; hope and pride)*

> ### CRITICAL VOCABULARY
>
> **resolve**: Lincoln wants us to *resolve*, or determine, that "the dead shall not have died in vain."
>
> **ASK STUDENTS** how Lincoln's enemies might react to the way he has resolved to honor the dead. *(They might feel threatened by the intensity of his resolve and redouble their efforts to defeat the Union.)*
>
> **perish**: Lincoln believes that there is a danger that the United States will come to an end.
>
> **ASK STUDENTS** to discuss the connection between *conceive* in the first sentence of the speech and *perish* in the last sentence. *(What is conceived, or created, can also perish, or be destroyed.)*

COLLABORATIVE DISCUSSION Have partners identify two or more of Lincoln's beliefs about why it was important to reunite the nation. Have them cite the lines where these beliefs are expressed.

ASK STUDENTS to share any questions they generated in the course of reading and discussing the speech.

---

unfinished work which they who fought here have thus far so nobly advanced. It is rather for us to be here dedicated to the great task remaining before us—that from these honored dead we take increased devotion to that cause for which they gave the last full
20 measure of devotion—that we here highly **resolve** that these dead shall not have died in vain—that this nation, under God, shall have a new birth of freedom—and that government of the people, by the people, for the people, shall not **perish** from the earth.

resolve
(rĭ-zŏlv´) *v.*
to decide or become determined.

perish
(pĕr´ĭsh) *v.*
to die or come to an end.

COLLABORATIVE DISCUSSION With a partner, discuss Lincoln's beliefs about the importance of reuniting the country. Cite specific evidence from the speech to support your ideas.

WHEN STUDENTS STRUGGLE . . .

Have students reread the final sentence in the speech (lines 17–23). Point out that the dedication to the *great task* Lincoln refers to is multi-faceted, and that the dashes in the sentence eill help students understand what the different pars of the task involve. Explain that each phrase between dashes signals a part of the task that awaits the nation.

Have students reread the speech in groups and list or paraphrase what the great task is that remains before the people Lincoln is addressing.

LEVEL UP TUTORIALS For additional support, assign the following *Level Up* tutorial: **Elements of an Argument.**

Analyze Seminal U.S. Documents

RI 9

Speeches, essays, and other texts that have great historical and literary significance are called **seminal documents.** In the United States, the Gettysburg Address is a seminal document, as are George Washington's Farewell Address, Franklin D. Roosevelt's Four Freedoms Speech, and Martin Luther King Jr.'s "Letter from Birmingham Jail." As you analyze the speech, look for these characteristics that can help you recognize and analyze seminal documents:

Strong themes such as freedom, equality, strength, democracy

Concepts such as fairness, justice, respect, honor

Seminal Documents

Engaging ideas presented in an original way

Themes and concepts that encourage the audience to take action

Analyze Author's Purpose and Rhetoric

RI 6

An author may write a speech for one or more reasons. These reasons are called the **author's purpose.** An author's purpose might be to inform or explain, to persuade, to express thoughts or feelings, or to entertain.

To help advance a purpose, an author will often use **rhetoric,** or the art of using specific words and language structures to make the message memorable. In the Gettysburg Address, Lincoln makes effective use of two rhetorical devices:

- **Repetition** is the use of the same word or words more than once. Repetition is used to emphasize key ideas.
- **Parallelism** is a form of repetition in which a grammatical pattern is repeated. Parallelism is used to create rhythm and evoke emotions.

Look at this example from President Ronald Reagan's Remarks at Moscow State University. Notice how he repeats the word *freedom* and uses parallelism to emphasize a key idea:

> "The key is freedom—freedom of thought, freedom of information, freedom of communication."

As you analyze the Gettysburg Address, notice the repeated words and parallel clauses and phrases, such as *we are engaged, we are met, we have come.* Think about how Lincoln uses both repetition and parallelism to advance his purpose.

The Gettysburg Address **29**

CLOSE READ

Analyze Seminal U.S. Documents

RI 9

Review the characteristics of seminal documents presented in the diagram and help students think about why it is important to recognize and analyze these documents. Have them locate examples from the speech of each characteristic presented in the diagram.

- The nation was founded on liberty.
- Lincoln believes we should honor the soldiers.
- Lincoln begins and ends the speech with the suggestion of birth and death.
- The concept of devotion to the cause encourages the audience to take action.

Analyze Author's Purpose and Rhetoric

RI 6

Review with students examples of repetition and parallelism in the speech and have volunteers explain why the devices are effective in helping Lincoln achieve his purpose. Show students that parallelism is used in other seminal U.S. documents by providing the following examples from Patrick Henry's "Speech to the Virginia Convention."

"The battle, sir, is not to the strong alone; it is to the <u>vigilant, the active, the brave.</u>"

"... those who, <u>having eyes, see not,</u> and, <u>having ears, hear not.</u>"

Strategies for Annotation   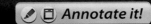 *Annotate it!*

Analyze Seminal U.S. Documents

RI 9

Have students use their eBook annotation tools to analyze the text. Ask them to do the following:

- Highlight in yellow words that show the concepts of respect and honor.
- Underline the words that describe the idea of freedom in a new way.
- Highlight in blue statements of action for the audience to take.

nobly advanced. It is rather for us to be here dedicated to the great task remaining before us—that from these honored dead we take increased devotion to that cause for which they gave the last full measure of devotion—that we here highly resolve that these dead shall not have died in vain—that this nation, under God, shall have a <u>new birth</u> of freedom—and that government of the people, by the

The Gettysburg Address **29**

PRACTICE & APPLY

Analyzing the Text   RI 1, RI 6, RI 9

Possible answers:

1. *Lincoln delivered the speech at the dedication of a military cemetery. His main purposes were to persuade his listeners to respect the fallen by continuing to support the nation and to express his thoughts and feelings about the consequences of the war. He reminds his audience of America's early history in the first paragraph and uses the word we to encourage the audience to share his beliefs about the importance of preserving the nation.*

2. *The "unfinished work" mentioned is to preserve the nation.*

3. *Lincoln means that the nation can survive only if it retains the principles, such as freedom, upon which it was founded. The first "birth of freedom" is referred to in the opening paragraph: "a nation so conceived and so dedicated."*

4. *In line 2, "dedicated" means "committed to a particular course of action," while in line 5, the adjective "dedicated" means "wholly committed." In line 7, the word is used in the sense of "opening a cemetery in a formal ceremony"; in line 10, it means "to set apart or consecrate." The repetition of this word strengthens Lincoln's message of being committed to restoring the nation.*

5. *In paragraph two, the statements "we are engaged," "we are met," and "we have come" are positive statements that can draw the audience into agreement. In lines 10–11, the statements are negative ("we cannot dedicate—we cannot consecrate—we cannot hallow"). Both examples of parallelism emphasize that the audience and Lincoln are on the same side, working together.*

6. *The theme of the speech is that the ideals upon which the nation was created are worth preserving. It supports the ideals of freedom, democracy, and equality, not only for the United States, but also for all nations built on the same pattern.*

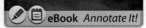

Analyzing the Text   RI 1, RI 6, RI 9, SL 1d, SL 6

Cite Text Evidence   Support your responses with evidence from the selection.

1. **Analyze** Why did Lincoln write and deliver the Gettysburg Address? What were his two main purposes? Explain using evidence from the speech.

2. **Infer** What is "the unfinished work" of those who died (line 16)?

3. **Infer** What does Lincoln mean when he refers to "a new birth of freedom" (line 22)? Explain your response with evidence from the text.

4. **Identify Patterns** The word *dedicate* is repeated several times in the speech. What does *dedicate* mean? What idea does Lincoln emphasize with the repetition of this word?

5. **Identify Patterns** Identify two examples of parallelism in the speech. How does Lincoln use parallel structure to persuade the audience to accept his message?

6. **Draw Conclusions** Seminal U.S. documents often refer to themes and ideals that are important to the audience they address. What is the **theme,** or underlying message, of the Gettysburg Address? Are those themes still important today? Explain the underlying message and the American ideals that the speech upholds.

PERFORMANCE TASK

Speaking Activity: Informative Presentation The Gettysburg Address is one of the most famous speeches in U. S. history. Work in a small group to prepare an oral presentation of the speech. Follow these steps:

1. Reread the speech silently to yourself, making notes about pacing and emphasis. Pay particular attention to the effects of punctuation on your presentation.

2. In a small group, have a volunteer read the speech aloud. Discuss any questions about the meaning of the speech and the best way to present it. Summarize in writing points of agreement and disagreement,

   acknowledging that different people may want to emphasize different words or phrases in the speech.

3. Practice your speech with a partner. After each partner has delivered the speech, discuss what was effective in the performance. Use your summary to help guide your constructive criticism.

4. Use the feedback from your partner to deliver the speech to your class.

Assign this performance task.

PERFORMANCE TASK   SL 1d, SL 6

Speaking Activity: Presentation As students work in small groups, challenge them to explore different views and perspectives about Lincoln's purpose and the meaning of certain passages. Encourage them to respond thoughtfully to other group members' suggestions about the best way to prepare the presentation. Have students make eye contact with their audience and adjust pace and volume as they deliver their speeches.

Critical Vocabulary

conceive   detract   resolve   perish

Practice and Apply Choose which Critical Vocabulary word is most closely associated with the underlined word or phrase in each sentence.

1. Additional details in a speech sometimes take away from the whole message.

2. A special election can be used to decide a tie in the vote for the student body president.

3. It takes a creative person to form an idea in his or her mind about an important issue and then convey that message to an audience.

4. Sometimes organizations such as clubs come to an end when the members are no longer interested.

Vocabulary Strategy: Multiple-Meaning Words

Words that have more than one definition are considered **multiple-meaning words.** To determine a word's appropriate meaning within a text, you need to look for context clues in the words, sentences, and paragraphs that surround it. Look at the word *fitting* in this sentence from the Gettysburg Address:

It is altogether fitting and proper that we should do this. (lines 8–9)

The word *fitting* can mean "the act of trying on clothes" or "a small part for a machine." However, the word *proper* is a context clue that the tells you the correct meaning of *fitting* in this sentence is "appropriate."

Practice and Apply Find these multiple-meaning words in the speech: *engaged* (line 4), *testing* (line 4), *poor* (line 13), *measure* (line 20). Working with a partner, use context clues to determine each word's meaning as it is used in the speech.

1. Determine how the word functions in the sentence. Is it a noun, an adjective, a verb, or an adverb?

2. If the sentence does not provide enough information, read the paragraph in which the word appears and consider the larger context of the speech.

3. Write down your definition and the clues you used to determine the correct meaning of each word.

Critical Vocabulary

Answers:

1. *detract*

2. *resolve*

3. *conceive*

4. *perish*

Vocabulary Strategy: Multiple Meaning Words

Possible answers:

1. *engaged (verb); testing (verb); poor (adjective); measure (noun)*

2. *Students should examine the immediate and larger contexts to identify each word's function and meaning.*

3. *Definitions and clues:*

   - **engaged:** *involved (clue: The word is followed by "great civil war"; people are involved in wars.)*

   - **testing:** *trying to find out (clue: The sentence suggests that the nation might not endure; the outcome of the war will give the answer.)*

   - **poor:** *limited (clue: The adjective modifies the word power; within the context of the sentence, it suggests that only the men who fought had the power to consecrate the ground; civilians cannot do so)*

   - **measure:** *portion; amount (clue: The word is modified by the word full and modifies the phrase of devotion; here, it expresses a quantity of something valuable.)*

APPLYING ACADEMIC VOCABULARY

resolve	internal	presume

As you discuss the speech, incorporate the following Collection 1 academic vocabulary words: *resolve, internal,* and *presume.* Point out that while Lincoln must have had an **internal** conflict about sending soldiers to their deaths, he was **resolved** that the war's casualties could inspire a "new birth of freedom." As they read and think about the speech, ask students what values and expectations Lincoln might be **presuming** about his audience.

Language and Style: Parallel Structure

L 1a

Review the grammatical forms in the chart. Read the examples aloud, and ask students to listen for the different rhythm created by each form.

Before writing their letters, have students brainstorm other parallel constructions or find other examples in the speech. (lines 14–15: "what we say here, . . . what they did here")

Possible answers: *Answers will vary. When students have completed the activity, they should be able to point to at least two examples of parallel structure in their letters. Invite students to share their letters with a partner, discussing the effects of each example.*

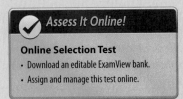

✓ Assess It Online!

Online Selection Test
• Download an editable ExamView bank.
• Assign and manage this test online.

Language and Style: Parallel Structure

L 1a

One grammatical feature that makes Abraham Lincoln's rhetoric so effective is his use of **parallel structure**, or the repetition of grammatical forms within a sentence. The repetition can occur at the word, phrase, or clause level. Lincoln uses parallel structure to express and connect ideas that are related or equal in importance and to create rhythm and evoke emotions. Consider these examples from the Gettysburg Address:

Type of Structure	Example from the Gettysburg Address
parallel words	living and dead (line 12)

Type of Structure	Example from the Gettysburg Address
parallel phrases	of the people, by the people, for the people (lines 22–23)

Type of Structure	Example from the Gettysburg Address
parallel clauses	we cannot dedicate—we cannot consecrate—we cannot hallow (lines 10–11)

Practice and Apply With a partner, look back at the Gettysburg Address and identify additional examples of parallel structure. Then imagine you were at Gettysburg on the day President Lincoln delivered his speech. Write a brief letter to Lincoln explaining how you were affected by his remarks. Use at least two examples of parallel structure in your letter. Exchange letters with a partner and discuss how effectively you each used parallel structure to communicate your message to Lincoln.

TO CHALLENGE STUDENTS. . .

Compare Speeches Have pairs compare the tone, or manner of expression, and structure of the Gettysburg Address to a speech Lincoln gave two years earlier in Philadelphia. Lincoln gave the address at Independence Hall at his stop in that city during his inaugural journey from Springfield, Illinois, to Washington, D.C.

ASK STUDENTS to look for the speech on the Internet. After reading the speech, have students discuss the following, citing evidence from the text to support their ideas:

• How does the tone of the address at Independence Hall compare to the Gettysburg Address? Is one more hopeful than the other? Why?

• Does Lincoln use parallel structure in the address at Independence Hall? Is the use of this structure effective in creating rhythm and evoking emotions?

Present a Speech

RI 9, SL 1d, SL 5, SL 6, W 7

TEACH

Point out that the effectiveness of a speech is not only dependent on the words a speaker uses but also on the speaker's delivery of those words. Before students complete the Performance Task for this selection, review the following delivery techniques with them.

Verbal Techniques

- **Tone:** Maintain a formal and somber tone in order to convey an attitude of seriousness and respect.
- **Volume:** Speak loudly enough to be heard. Consider speaking with more force when making a point.
- **Pauses:** Pause after important details to emphasize their value.
- **Rate:** Speak slowly enough for an audience to understand what is being said. Vary the rate of speech so an audience does not get bored.

Nonverbal Techniques

- **Eye contact:** Involve an audience by making eye contact with listeners.
- **Gestures:** Use natural gestures that match what is being said. Be careful not to fidget.
- **Facial expressions:** Allow your face to express your feelings and attitude.
- Before students begin the practice activity, have them complete the appropriate interactive lessons within Analyzing and Evaluating Presentations.

PRACTICE AND APPLY

Provide students with an evaluation chart like the one that follows. Model a presentation of the Gettysburg Address or another speech of your choice, incorporating a few of the delivery techniques discussed above. Have students rate your delivery using the evaluation chart. Then discuss the areas that need improvement.

Students may use the evaluation chart during the creation of their speech for the Performance Task.

Technique	Evaluation (Rate from 1–10.)
Tone:	
Volume	
Pauses	
Rate	
Eye contact	
Gestures	
Facial expressions	

Analyze Seminal U.S. Documents

RI 9

RETEACH

Remind students that **seminal U.S. documents** such as the ones cited on page 29 are ones that greatly influenced key events in U.S. history. Students should look for key words associated with concepts usually found in U.S. seminal documents. For example, the words *just, fair, equal,* and *equitable* all relate to *justice,* a concept upon which the nation was built. Concepts can help determine the theme, or underlying message, of a document. Have students reread the Gettysburg Address. Ask them to consider these questions in their rereading:

- What key words in the speech help you identify a key concept? *(The words* dedicated *and* devotion *refer to concepts of courage and loyalty to one's nation.)*
- How does the concept relate to the theme? *(The concept of loyalty to the nation relates to the theme of a nation remaining united despite conflict amongst its citizens.)*

 LEVEL UP TUTORIALS Assign the following *Level Up* tutorial: **Elements of an Argument.**

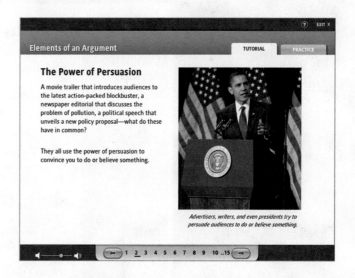

INDEPENDENT READING

Students can apply the skill to another important speech or letter. Have them work independently to note concepts, theme, and specific language used to construct a clear, succinct argument intended to influence and persuade an audience. Ask: How did the author create a convincing argument? Who was the audience?

Oklahoma Bombing Memorial Address

Speech by Bill Clinton

Why This Text

Readers of the text of a speech may not have the same reactions as those who hear the speech. A good speaker can advance the purpose of a speech effectively—but the words of a good speech can stand on their own. With the help of the close-reading questions, students will analyze the purpose and effectiveness of Clinton's "Oklahoma Bombing Memorial Address." This close reading will lead students to understand the purpose, rhetoric, and themes of the speech.

Background Have students read the background information about Bill Clinton and the Oklahoma City bombing. Many of the people who worked at the Alfred P. Murrah Federal Building had not yet arrived at work when the truck bomb exploded, but 168 people were killed. Point out that the Oklahoma City bombing was the most deadly attack by domestic terrorists in U.S. history.

AS YOU READ Ask students to pay attention to the rhetorical devices used in this speech. How do they help the speaker advance his purpose?

Standards Support

- cite strong and thorough textual evidence
- analyze how an author's ideas are developed
- determine an author's point of view or purpose
- analyze how an author uses rhetoric to advance his or her purpose

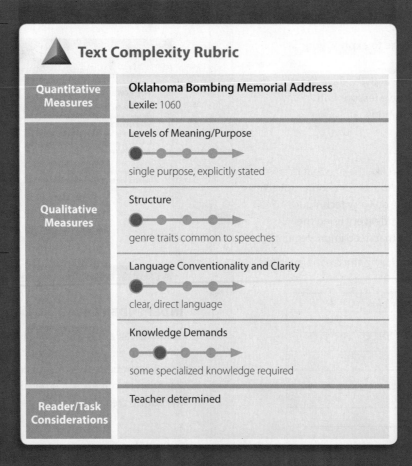

Text Complexity Rubric

Quantitative Measures	**Oklahoma Bombing Memorial Address** Lexile: 1060
Qualitative Measures	Levels of Meaning/Purpose — single purpose, explicitly stated
	Structure — genre traits common to speeches
	Language Conventionality and Clarity — clear, direct language
	Knowledge Demands — some specialized knowledge required
Reader/Task Considerations	Teacher determined

Strategies for CLOSE READING

Analyze Author's Purpose and Rhetoric

Students should read this speech carefully all the way through. Close-reading questions at the bottom of the page will help them focus on a thorough analysis of the author's purpose. As they read, students should jot down comments or questions about the text in the margins.

WHEN STUDENTS STRUGGLE . . .

To help students analyze the "Oklahoma Bombing Memorial Address," have them work in small groups to fill out a chart like the one shown below.

CITE TEXT EVIDENCE For practice in analyzing an author's purpose and rhetoric, ask students to cite text evidence for each section of the chart.

Purpose	Rhetoric
to show support for the grieving	"Today our nation joins with you in grief."
	"We pledge to do all we can . . ."
	". . . your pain is unimaginable, and we know that."
Purpose	Rhetoric
to thank those who helped	"We thank all those who have worked so heroically . . ."
	"Let us say clearly, they served us well, and we are grateful."
	". . . many who left their own lives to come here . . ."
Purpose	Rhetoric
to connect with his audience	". . . also come as parents, as husband and wife . . ."
	". . . we will stand with you for as many tomorrows as it takes."
	"My fellow Americans . . ."
Purpose	Rhetoric
to influence people's actions	". . . you must try to pay tribute to your loved ones . . ."
	"In the face of death, let us honor life."
	"The hurt you feel must not be allowed to turn into hate . . ."

Background William [Bill] Jefferson Clinton *was president of the United States when, on April 19, 1995, the Alfred P. Murrah Federal Building in Oklahoma City was bombed by the domestic terrorists Timothy McVeigh and Terry Nichols. The blast killed 168 people, including 19 children under the age of 6, and injured more than 680. At first, it was not clear who had set off the bomb, or why. The FBI thought it might be international terrorists. But they quickly discovered that the people who caused this massive destruction were actually citizens of this country.*

Oklahoma Bombing Memorial Address

Speech by Bill Clinton

CLOSE READ
Notes

1. **READ ▶** As you read lines 1–15, begin to collect and cite text evidence.
   - Circle the language President Clinton uses to introduce himself.
   - Underline the words Clinton uses to describe himself and Hillary.
   - In the margin, explain the purpose for his speech.

Thank you very much, Governor Keating and Mrs. Keating, Reverend Graham, to the families of those who have been lost and wounded, to the people of Oklahoma City, who have endured so much, and the people of this wonderful state, to all of you who are here as our fellow Americans.
A (I am honored to be here today to represent the American people.) But I have to tell you that Hillary and I also come as parents, as husband and wife, as people who were your neighbors for some of the best years of our lives.

B Today our nation joins with you in grief. We mourn with you. We share
10 your hope against hope that some may still survive. We thank all those who have worked so heroically to save lives and to solve this crime—those here in Oklahoma and those who are all across this great land, and many who left their own lives to come here to work hand in hand with you. We pledge to do all we can to help you heal the injured, to rebuild this city, and to bring to justice those who did this evil.

He is there to show support for the grieving, to mourn with them, and to thank those who helped with the rescue efforts.

19

1. **READ AND CITE TEXT EVIDENCE** Tell students that Clinton made his speech in Oklahoma City four days after the bombing took place. The people he names are the Governor of Oklahoma and his wife, and the Reverend Billy Graham, who also spoke at the memorial. Clinton had lived in—and been governor of—Arkansas, a state that adjoins Oklahoma.

A **ASK STUDENTS** to compare what they wrote describing the purpose of the speech. Have them cite the text evidence supporting their descriptions. *Students may point out that Clinton represents the American people (line 5), identifies with the people who suffered (lines 6–7), and thanks those who worked to help (lines 10–13). He promises to bring justice to those responsible (line 15).*

His purpose here is to acknowledge the tragedy and offer his sympathy.

C This terrible sin took the lives of our American family, innocent children in that building, only because their parents were trying to be good parents as well as good workers; citizens in the building going about their 20 daily business; and many there who served the rest of us—who worked to help the elderly and the disabled, who worked to support our farmers and our veterans, who worked to enforce our laws and to protect us. Let us say clearly, they served us well, and we are grateful.

But for so many of you they were also neighbors and friends. You saw them at church or the PTA meetings, at the civic clubs, at the ball park. You know them in ways that all the rest of America could not. And to all the members of the families here present who have suffered loss, though we share your grief, your pain is unimaginable, and we know that. We cannot undo it. That is God's work.

Our words seem small beside the loss you have endured. But I found a 30 few I wanted to share today. I've received a lot of letters in these last terrible days. **D** One stood out because it came from a young widow and a mother of three whose own husband was murdered with over 200 other Americans when Pan Am 103[1] was shot down. Here is what that woman said I should say to you today:

The anger you feel is valid, but you must not allow yourselves to be consumed by it. The hurt you feel must not be allowed to turn into hate, but instead into the search for justice. The loss you feel must not paralyze your own lives. Instead, you must try to pay tribute to your loved ones by continuing to do all the things they left undone, thus ensuring they did not 40 die in vain.

[1] **Pan Am 103:** transatlantic flight from London to New York, bombed by terrorists over Lockerbie, Scotland, on December 21, 1988.

2. ◀ REREAD Reread lines 9–15. Make an inference about why Clinton began his speech by speaking about grief.

Clinton wanted to connect emotionally with his audience, most of whom had suffered a great loss.

3. READ ▶ As you read lines 16–49, continue to cite textual evidence.
- Underline descriptive language that describes the tragedy.
- Circle examples of advice Clinton gave his audience.
- In the margin, explain Clinton's purpose in lines 16–28.

20

"You have lost too much, but you have not lost everything."

Wise words from one who also knows.

You have lost too much, but you have not lost everything. And you have certainly not lost America, for we will stand with you for as many tomorrows as it takes.

If ever we needed evidence of that, I could only recall the words of Governor and Mrs. Keating: "If anybody thinks that Americans are mostly mean and selfish, they ought to come to Oklahoma. If anybody thinks Americans have lost the capacity for love and caring and courage, they ought to come to Oklahoma."

50 To all my fellow Americans beyond this hall, I say, one thing we owe those who have sacrificed is the duty to **purge** ourselves of the dark forces which gave rise to this evil. They are forces that threaten our common peace, our freedom, our way of life. Let us teach our children that the God of comfort is also the God of righteousness: Those who trouble their own house will inherit the wind. Justice will prevail.

E Let us let our own children know that we will stand against the forces of fear. When there is talk of hatred, let us stand up and talk against it. When there is talk of violence, let us stand up and talk against it. In the face of death, let us honor life. As St. Paul admonished us, Let us "not be overcome 60 by evil, but overcome evil with good."

purge:
to purify; to rid of sin, guilt

admonished:
cautioned against

4. ◀ REREAD AND DISCUSS Reread lines 29–40. With a small group, discuss why the letter from the widow stood out to Clinton and why he chose to include it in his speech.

5. READ ▶ As you read lines 50–74, underline the phrases that Clinton repeats.

21

2. **REREAD AND CITE TEXT EVIDENCE**

B **ASK STUDENTS** to infer what feelings most of Clinton's audience would have had just a few days after the bombing. *They would probably be shocked at what had happened in their city and devastated about the victims.* Why might Clinton have started his speech talking about their grief? *He wanted to first acknowledge their feelings and show that the nation supports them in their grief.*

3. **READ AND CITE TEXT EVIDENCE**

C **ASK STUDENTS** why Clinton identified the kinds of people who worked in the building and how they affected others' lives (lines 16–28). *Clinton describes the victims as parents, workers, and children. He then goes on to describe them in more personal terms, to show how they touched the lives of the people of Oklahoma.*

FOR ELL STUDENTS Explain to students that the abbreviation "PTA" in line 24 stands for Parent-Teacher Association.

4. **REREAD AND DISCUSS USING TEXT EVIDENCE**

D **ASK STUDENTS** why the letter from the widow had such an impact on Clinton. *The widow had overcome the extreme anger she would be expected to feel.* Why did Clinton include the widow's advice in his speech? *The advice came from someone who had been through a similar experience.*

5. **READ AND CITE TEXT EVIDENCE**

E **ASK STUDENTS** what effect the repetition has. *The repetition reinforces the idea that people are not alone.*

Critical Vocabulary: purge (line 51) Have students share their definitions of *purge*, and ask volunteers to use the verb.

Critical Vocabulary: admonished (line 59) Have students suggest several synonyms for the verb *admonish*. Possible synonyms are *warn, advise, encourage, recommend, exhort.*

Yesterday, Hillary and I had the privilege of speaking with some children of other federal employees—children like those who were lost here. And one little girl said something we will never forget. She said, "We should all plant a tree in memory of the children." So this morning before we got on the plane to come here, at the White House, we planted that tree in honor of the children of Oklahoma. It was a dogwood with its wonderful spring flower and its deep, enduring roots. It embodies the lesson of the Psalms[2]—that the life of a good person is like a tree whose leaf does not wither.

70   My fellow Americans, a tree takes a long time to grow, and wounds take a long time to heal. But we must begin. Those who are lost now belong to God. Some day we will be with them. But until that happens, their legacy must be our lives.

Thank you all, and God bless you.

[2] **Psalms:** a section of the Bible.

6. ◀ **REREAD AND DISCUSS** Reread lines 61–74. With a small group, discuss Clinton's story of the tree. What does the tree symbolize? Why does he mention the planting of the tree to his audience?

SHORT RESPONSE

Cite Text Evidence   Do you think Clinton's speech was effective in showing support for the American people during this tragedy? How does his use of language and parallelism help advance his purpose? Explain, **citing text evidence** in your response.

Possible response: Clinton's speech was very effective. He shared the grief of those who had lost loved ones, those affected by the tragedy, and all of the United States citizens. At the same time, he appealed to the people to follow the values they have as Americans, and he read a message from a woman whose husband had been killed in a terrorist bombing, exhorting people not to be "consumed" by anger, but to "search for justice." By demonstrating a deep understanding of people's feelings and giving advice for moving on, he made an emotional connection to all who heard him.

22

6.   **REREAD AND CITE TEXT EVIDENCE**

F **ASK STUDENTS** to look closely at what the girl suggested, what the Clintons did, and what a tree symbolizes. Have groups share their responses. *Students may point out that the Clintons planted a tree in memory at the White House, to honor the children in the nation's symbolic center. Clinton points out that "a tree takes a long time to grow" and compares that time with wounds that take a long time to heal. He says that we have to begin healing, and planting the tree is a symbolic beginning.*

SHORT RESPONSE

Cite Text Evidence   Students' responses should include text evidence that supports their positions. They should:

- determine whether or not they find the speech effective.
- give examples of rhetorical devices that further Clinton's points.
- explain Clinton's use of parallelism to evoke emotions.

TO CHALLENGE STUDENTS . . .

When Clinton made the "Oklahoma Bombing Memorial Address," the audience did not know who was responsible for the terrorist act. Many people assumed that it was international terrorists.

ASK STUDENTS to reread the speech and discuss whether or not any passages might have been worded differently had it been common knowledge that the crime was committed by an American. *Students may suggest that the passages that include "our American family" (line 16) and "If anybody thinks that Americans are mostly mean" (lines 46–47) might have been worded differently. They might suggest that Clinton would have included specific thoughts and advice about dealing with domestic terrorism.*

DIG DEEPER

With the class, return to Question 4, Reread and Discuss. Have groups share their responses to the question.

ASK STUDENTS about the letter that Clinton shared with his audience.

- Have students discuss why the widow's words were relevant in the situation. *She had lost her husband in a terrorist attack and must have felt the same emotions that people in Oklahoma City were feeling.*
- Ask students why Clinton thought that the widow's advice was meaningful. *People's anger could turn to hate, but that would not solve anything. The widow pointed out that hate could ruin the lives of the survivors.*
- Ask students what effect the widow's letter might have had on the audience. *The letter from the widow showed that someone who had gone through a similar experience had coped and been able to live through the pain. The letter might have given the survivors hope.*

ASK STUDENTS to return to their Short Response answer and revise it based on the class discussion.

COMPARE TEXT AND MEDIA

MEDIA **Views of the Wall**

The Vietnam Wall

Photo Essay

Poem by Alberto Ríos

Why These Texts?

Students frequently encounter a subject that is explored in different ways through various mediums. This lesson explores the reaction of visitors to the Vietnam Veterans Memorial in both photographs and poetry.

Key Learning Objective: The student will be able to analyze the representation of a subject in two different mediums.

RL 1 Cite textual evidence.
RL 2 Determine a central idea.
RL 4 Determine the meaning of words and phrases, including figurative meanings.
RL 5 Analyze author's choices.
RL 7 Analyze representation of a subject in different mediums.

▲ Text Complexity Rubric

	Views of the Wall Lexile: N/A	The Vietnam Wall Lexile: N/A
Quantitative Measures		
Qualitative Measures	**Levels of Meaning/Purpose** more than one purpose; implied, easily identified from context	**Levels of Meaning/Purpose** multiple levels of meaning (multiple themes)
	Structure less conventional	**Structure** free verse, no particular patterns
	Language Conventionality and Clarity N/A	**Language Conventionality and Clarity** clear, direct language
	Knowledge Demands moderately complex theme	**Knowledge Demands** some specialized knowledge required
Reader/Task Considerations	• Teacher determined • Vary by individual reader and type of text • See the Text X-Ray for suggested Reader/Task Considerations.	

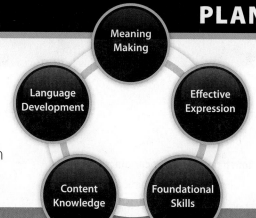

Meaning Making

Language Development

Effective Expression

Content Knowledge

Foundational Skills

English Language Support Before teaching, use the Text X-Ray below for an overview of the text's complexity. The Text X-Ray and the supports and scaffolds in the Teacher's Edition will help you guide students of different skill levels.

Text Complexity: Qualitative Measures

 Levels of Meaning/Purpose

Help students determine the central idea in a photo essay and in a poem.

- Teacher's Edition side note, p. 33
- Determine a Central Idea, p. 36a

To reteach determining a central idea, see

- Determine a Central Idea, p. 36b

▶ *Use It!* *Level Up* tutorial: Theme

Interactive Whiteboard Lesson: Theme/Central Idea

ZOOM IN ON **DETERMINING A CENTRAL IDEA** Have pairs use the following sentence starters to discuss the meaning of key details in the poem and to **draw** conclusions about its **central idea**.

- The "magic" in line 3 is ___.
- Little kids and boys at the memorial ___.
- The speaker points out that men sometimes cry at the wall because ___.
- A central idea of the poem is that the memorial ___.

(Sample central idea: The memorial has a powerful and unexpected effect on people who visit it.)

▲ Structure

Help students analyze representations in different mediums.

- Teacher's Edition side notes, pp. 33, 34, 35, 36
- When Students Struggle, p. 35
- Strategies for Annotation, p. 36
- Analyze Representations in Different Mediums, p. 36

Guide students to express ideas in their choice of mediums.

- Performance Task, p. 36

To help students analyze the poem, see

- Analyze a Free-Verse Poem, p. 36b

ZOOM IN ON **ANALYZING REPRESENTATIONS IN DIFFERENT MEDIUMS** Tell students that a **metaphor** often compares the subject of a poem to something familiar so that readers can better understand or imagine it. Have pairs of students match each of the following metaphorical descriptions to an image in the photo essay. Ask them to evaluate whether each metaphor does a good job of describing the actual memorial, based on what they see in the photos.

- "a scar / Into the skin of the ground" (lines 6–7)
- "a black winding / Appendix line" (lines 8–9)
- "a little black marble wall / Of a dollhouse" (lines 13–14)

▲ Language Conventionality and Clarity

Teach unfamiliar vocabulary in context.

- Applying Academic Vocabulary, p. 34

Help students analyze metaphors.

- Teacher's Edition side note, p. 34

Guide students to analyze a poet's choice of a speaker.

- Teacher's Edition side note, p. 35

Help students analyze a poet's use of precise words.

- Teacher's Edition side note, p. 35

ZOOM IN ON **ANALYZING PRECISE WORD CHOICES** Remind students that poets choose precise words to convey meaning. In some cases, a **multiple-meaning word** can suggest more than one meaning in the same context. Discuss these examples with students.

- The word *appendix* (line 9) can mean a section at the end of a book that provides additional information, often in the form of a list. It can also refer to an internal organ, often surgically removed, leaving a scar on the abdomen. In the poem, the word *appendix* provides a transition from the scar imagery to a description of the wall's list of names.)
- In the field of archaeology, a "dig" (line 10) is a place where scientists dig up clues left behind by human activity. The memorial is like a dig because it descends into the ground.

▲ Knowledge Demands

Support English Learners in understanding the historical context of the photo essay and the poem.

- Teacher's Edition Background note, p. 33
- English Language Support, p. 33

To help students learn more about the Vietnam Veterans Memorial, see

- Conduct Research, p. 36a

 For more context and historical background, students can view the video "Remembering Fallen Friends" in their eBooks.

ZOOM IN ON **BUILDING CULTURAL KNOWLEDGE** Share the following information with students who may not be familiar with the cultural references.

- Lines 15–16 refer to shoeshine boys. In the early to mid-1900s, boys could earn money in American cities by shining people's shoes. They walked the streets looking for customers, carrying their polish and brushes in wooden boxes.
- Lines 34–35 refer to the custom of wearing green clothing on St. Patrick's Day, a March 17 holiday celebrating Irish culture. People who do not wear green might be punished with a pinch.

▲ Suggested Reader/Task Considerations

You might consider the following before assigning this poem to students.

- Do students have the skills to make **inferences** based on details in the text?
- Do students have access to the technology needed to view the photo essay independently?

ZOOM IN ON **SUPPORTING COMPREHENSION**

- Have students work with partners to **infer** the meaning of "The magic, / The way like cutting onions / It brings water out of nowhere" (lines 3–5). Then invite pairs to share their inferences.
- View the photo essay in class with students. If possible, allow individual students or pairs to take turns reviewing the photos at their own pace.

CLOSE READ

 For more context and historical background, students can view the video "Remembering Fallen Friends" in their eBooks.

Background Have students read the background. Explain that the Vietnam War was one of the longest and most contentious conflicts in U.S. history, lasting from 1964 until 1973. The war resulted in the deaths of almost 60,000 U.S. soldiers and more than a million Vietnamese, who still refer to the war as "the American War." The war's casualties and costs divided the people of the United States; protests erupted around the country. The Vietnam Veterans Memorial sought to bring Americans together and heal the wounds caused by the war.

AS YOU VIEW AND READ Direct students to use the As You View and Read note to focus their viewing and reading.

Analyze Representations in Different Mediums
RL 1, RL 7

(PHOTOS 1–8; LINES 1–43)

Explain that identifying a target audience helps artists and writers decide how to portray their subjects to achieve their **purposes,** or reasons they create a work.

ASK STUDENTS if they think the photo essay and poem have the same target audience. *(Yes, both likely have a wide target audience. The photographs show people of different age groups, and the poet refers to children and adults responding to the memorial.)* Ask students which medium would likely appeal to a wider audience. *(Answers will vary, but students will likely point to the photo essay as having a wider appeal because people are often moved more by images than by words.)*

Determine a Central Idea
RL 1, RL 2

(PHOTOS 1–8)

Tell students that the **central idea** is the point or message the author or artist wants to convey.

ASK STUDENTS why they think these particular photographs were chosen for the photo essay. Encourage them to explain how the photographs, viewed together, have a meaning that is not necessarily the same when viewed separately. *(The photographs show different views of the wall and different age groups responding to the wall. This emphasizes the idea that the wall brings out an emotional response in people of all ages.)*

Background *The Vietnam Veterans Memorial was dedicated in 1982 to commemorate the 2.7 million military men and women who served in the conflict. There are approximately 58, 272 names inscribed on the wall in chronological order from the first death, injury, or missing-in-action date to the last. The polished black granite V-shaped wall was designed by Maya Lin and was intended to be a place of reflection and harmony without any political message.*

MEDIA

Views of the Wall
Photo Essay

The Vietnam Wall
Poem by Alberto Ríos

AS YOU VIEW AND READ Consider how both the photographs and the poem express the reactions of visitors to the Vietnam Veterans Memorial. Write down any questions you generate.

Views of the Wall
Photo Essay

Image Credits: (t) ©Nicholas Kamm/AFP/Getty Images (b) ©James P. Blair/Corbis

ENGLISH LANGUAGE SUPPORT

Build Background Many English language learners may be unfamiliar with the Vietnam Veterans Memorial. As you discuss the Background in class, provide definitions of terms such as *veterans* and *memorial.* Then list key points about the memorial, including who it commemorates and what it is made of. You may also want to add information about the Vietnam War and the conflicts it generated in the United States.

ASK STUDENTS why people might experience the wide range of responses to the memorial that the photo essay and poem portray.

CLOSE READ

Analyze Language (LINES 6–7) RL 4

Explain that a **metaphor** is a figure of speech in which one thing is referred to as another to suggest a comparison. Writers use metaphors to make their writing more descriptive and interesting.

(A) CITE TEXT EVIDENCE Ask students to identify the metaphor Ríos uses in lines 6–7. Ask them to explain why the author might have used this particular metaphor and how it relates to the subject matter. *(Ríos compares the wall to a scar on skin. He uses the metaphor of a scar because the Vietnam War was seen by many to have wounded and divided the nation. The wall represents the scar that comes when a wound heals.)*

Analyze Representations in Different Mediums RL 1, RL 7

(LINES 1–25)

Tell students that an **artistic medium** is the method or material used to tell a story. Artistic mediums may include paintings, plays, songs, works of fiction, poetry, photographs, and many more. Point out that each artistic medium allows an artist to emphasize a particular aspect of a subject in a certain way.

(B) ASK STUDENTS to examine the poem's narrative movement. The poem tells a story, with the poet as the main character, walking to the wall, examining it, looking at others who have come to look at the wall. Then ask students how the poem's narrative differs from the experience presented by the photo essay. *(With the poem, there is the continuous movement of a story with a narrator. By contrast, the photo essay presents separate images with no connecting narrative. The viewer must find the story in them.)*

Point out that analyzing how different artistic mediums treat a particular subject helps you more carefully judge and evaluate what you read and view.

CITE TEXT EVIDENCE Have students identify places in the poem where the author mentions other people's reactions to the memorial. *(Lines 16, 30, 31, 40)* Then ask them how these descriptions compare to photographs of individuals viewing the wall. *(The author tells you how people feel, whereas the photographs leave you to infer.)*

The Vietnam Wall
Poem by Alberto Ríos

I
Have seen it
And I like it: The magic,
The way like cutting onions
5   It brings water out of nowhere.
Invisible from one side, a scar   **(A)**
Into the skin of the ground
From the other, a black winding
Appendix line.
10   A dig.
         An archaeologist can explain.
The walk is slow at first
Easy, a little black marble wall
Of a dollhouse,
15 A smoothness, a shine
The boys in the street want to give.
One name. And then more
Names, long lines, lines of names until
They are the shape of the U.N. building[1]
20 Taller than I am: I have walked
Into a grave.
And everything I expect has been taken away, like that, quick:
        The names are not alphabetized.
        They are in the order of dying.
25   An alphabet of—somewhere—screaming.
I start to walk out. I almost leave
But stop to look up names of friends,
My own name. There is somebody
Severiano Ríos.
30 Little kids do not make the same noise
Here, junior high school boys don't run
Or hold each other in headlocks.
No rules, something just persists
Like pinching on St. Patrick's Day
35 Every year for no green.
        No one knows why.

---

[1] **U. N. Building:** headquarters of the United Nations in New York City.

APPLYING ACADEMIC VOCABULARY

presume	enforce

As you discuss the photo essay and the poem, incorporate the Collection 1 academic vocabulary words *presume* and *enforce*. In discussing artistic mediums, ask students why they might **presume** that a photo essay offers more opportunities to show physical details of a subject than a poem would. Then ask them how the visuals in the photo essay and poem help to **enforce** each artist's message or main idea.

Flowers are forced
Into the cracks
Between sections.
40　Men have cried
At this wall.
I have
Seen them.

COLLABORATIVE DISCUSSION In a small group, discuss how the photographs and the poem depict visitors' reactions to the Vietnam Veterans Memorial. What details are emphasized in each? Use details from the photo essay and the poem to support your discussion.

WHEN STUDENTS STRUGGLE...

To guide students' analyses of the photo essay and poem, juxtapose specific photographs with lines from the poem that relate to the subject matter in the photographs. Make a two-column chart, and encourage students to fill it in by describing what they see in the photograph and what they read and interpret in related lines of the poem.

 LEVEL UP TUTORIALS For additional support, assign the following *Level Up* tutorial: **Analyzing Visuals.**

CLOSE READ

Analyze Author's Choices　RL 4
(LINES 1–43)

Explain that the **speaker** of a poem may be the author or someone else whom the author chooses to share the message of the poem.

CITE TEXT EVIDENCE Ask how the author reveals the identity of the poem's speaker and what readers can learn about the speaker from the poem. *(The speaker is the author. He narrates in the first person and refers to finding his last name in line 29. The reader can tell he is touched by the memorial and surprised by it.)* Ask how the impact of the poem might differ if it were written in the third person. *(Students may suggest that a detached speaker would have less of an impact.)*

Analyze Representations in Different Mediums　RL 1, RL 7

Explain that the order of ideas in a poem or photo essay helps the author or artist develop a message.

CITE TEXT EVIDENCE Have students look back at the poem and the photo essay and explain how the order of ideas progresses in both works. *(Both progress from general to more specific. The poet first describes the wall, while the first photograph shows a view of the wall. Then the poem and the essay show people's reactions to the wall.)*

Analyze Language　RL 2, RL 4
(LINES 37–39)

Explain that poets use precise words to convey ideas.

C **ASK STUDENTS** to reread lines 37–39. Have them explain the image these lines evoke. Ask: Do any of the photos capture a similar image? Which image is more powerful? *(The poem evokes an image of flowers jutting out from sections of the memorial. A photograph also shows flowers left by people.)*
COLLABORATIVE DISCUSSION Have students work in groups to discuss lines from the poem and photos that depict visitors' reactions to the memorial.

ASK STUDENTS to share questions they generated as they viewed, read, and discussed the selection.

CLOSE READ

Analyze Representations in Different Mediums

RL 7

Help students understand artistic mediums and how the nature of each medium determines subject treatment. Display a chart of different types of mediums and encourage students to fill in the chart with the characteristics of each.

Analyzing Text and Media

RL 1, RL 2, RL 4, RL 7

Possible answers:

1. *The subject of both the photo essay and the poem is the Vietnam Veterans Memorial. Both convey the importance of honoring those who fought in the war.*

2. *The simile helps the reader understand the sudden onset of emotion that the wall can evoke by comparing how it induces tears just like the act of cutting onions. The photos do not show a similar comparison; however, viewers can compare their own experiences to the ones depicted in the photos.*

3. *Both the photographs and poem portray emotional responses to the wall. The photographs provide exact visual information, but viewers must interpret the emotions of the people in the photos. The poem uses description to help readers visualize the wall, but the poet also shares his personal feelings about the wall.*

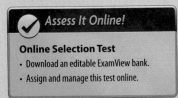

Assess It Online!

Online Selection Test
- Download an editable ExamView bank.
- Assign and manage this test online.

A subject, such as the Vietnam Veterans Memorial, can be represented in different **artistic mediums,** such as poems, stories, paintings, or photographs. Each artistic medium can emphasize certain aspects of the subject. For example, an author might emphasize an emotion evoked by the subject and give a personal, internal reaction. A visual artist, on the other hand, may show intricate, physical details of the subject that a writer might not be able to express. Rather than using words to describe people's emotions, an artist shows them using visual images. Analyzing how different mediums express the same or similar ideas can help you become a more critical reader and viewer.

Analyzing Text and Media

RL 1, RL 2, RL 4, RL 7, SL 4

Cite Text Evidence Support your responses with evidence from the selections.

1. **Draw Conclusions** What is the central idea of both the photo essay and the poem? How is the subject matter related to the central idea that the photographs and the poem convey?

2. **Analyze** A **simile** makes a comparison between two unlike things, using the words *like* or *as*. Explain the simile Ríos uses in lines 3–4. Are the photographs in the photo essay able to show this kind comparison? Explain.

3. **Compare** What are the similarities and differences between presenting ideas in photographs versus a poem? What does each emphasize or leave out?

PERFORMANCE TASK

Media Activity: Reflection Choose between two mediums (Activity A or B) to express ideas about the value of war memorials.

A. Think about the ideas expressed in the poem and the photo essay. Draw a picture or paint a scene to express similar ideas. Then write a short description of the difference between what a painting or drawing can express as compared to photographs or a poem.

B. Work with a partner to produce a short video interviewing classmates and teachers about the memorial. Include a final scene in which you and your partner discuss the advantages and disadvantages of using film to capture emotions about the memorial.

36   Collection 1

Strategies for Annotation

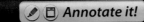 *Annotate it!*

Analyze Representations in Different Mediums

RL 7

Share these strategies for guided or independent analysis:
- Highlight in blue the author's descriptions of the wall. (*Example: lines 19–20, 23–24*)
- Highlight in yellow the responses the wall evokes. (*Example: line 22*)
- On a note, describe the subject of each photo.
- Reread your highlighted material and notes and compare the two.

Assign this performance task.

PERFORMANCE TASK

Media Activity: Reflection Have students review the poem and the photo essay, noting the ideas expressed in each. For option A, have them work alone to express similar ideas through drawing or painting. For option B, have pairs work together to list questions and advantages/disadvantages in preparation for filming.

Conduct Research

RL 2

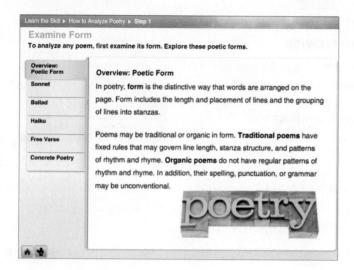

TEACH

Tell students that the memorial was dedicated in 1982. Maya Lin designed the wall of names that was originally intended as the entire memorial, though a sculpture of three soldiers was added before the dedication, and a Vietnam Women's Memorial was added in 1993. Lin was a student at Yale University when she won the design competition. Although her design was meant to be a tribute to American soldiers lost in the Vietnam War, her vision became controversial. Some objected to the design itself; some to the color of the black granite wall. Even Lin's ethnicity became a source of controversy (she is Chinese American). Today, the controversy has faded. Millions have visited the memorial. It is considered a national shrine to soldiers lost in the war.

PRACTICE AND APPLY

Brainstorm a list of subjects about the memorial that interest your students. (This list might include Maya Lin, the original controversy, the decision to include a sculpture of three soldiers, the experiences of veterans who have visited the memorial, and the building of the Vietnam Women's Memorial.)

- Divide students into small groups and have each group conduct research about one of the brainstormed topics.
- Consider using the Interactive Whiteboard Lesson, "How to Conduct an Effective Web Search."
- Schedule at least one day where students have access to the Web for a search for information about their topic.
- Have student groups report back to the class on their findings.

Determine a Central Idea

RL 4

RETEACH

Review what a **central idea** is—the point or message the writer or artists wants to convey—and point out that to identify the central idea of a piece, students must look carefully for details to determine the message. Provide students with a short poem that contains several details, such as the poem "Nothing Gold Can Stay" by Robert Frost.

- Read aloud the poem, and then ask students to identify its theme. *(Change is inevitable.)*
- Ask students to name details that help to support this theme. *(Sample answer: The line "only so an hour" refers to change, as does "So dawn goes down to day" and "nothing gold can stay.")*

 LEVEL UP TUTORIALS Assign the following *Level Up* tutorial: **Theme**

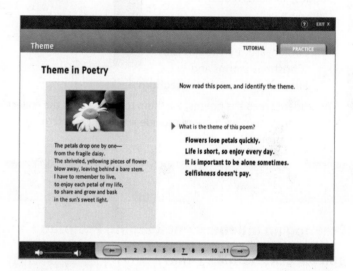

INDEPENDENT READING

Students can apply the skill to other short poems, including Robert Frost's "Stopping by Woods on a Snowy Evening." Provide a copy of the poem, and have them work independently to highlight details that help them determine theme. Suggest that students also look at paintings and photo essays, listing details they observe and then using those details to determine the theme or central idea of the piece.

FINDING COMMON GROUND

The *FYI* site provides links to online articles from a variety of magazines and newspapers. Help students choose a few articles to read to further their exploration of the topic "finding common ground."

NOVELWISE

Students can unlock the power of novels with this unique resource. Help students read through longer works with these tips:

- Find a Book
- Before You Read
- As You Read
- After You Read

Each book includes introductory material, worksheets, graphic organizers, and discussion guides.

ADDITIONAL TEXTS BY COLLECTION

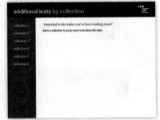

Suggest students read the following:

- "Elegy Written in a Country Churchyard" by Thomas Gray
- "Christmas Storms and Sunshine" by Elizabeth Cleghorn Gaskell

As students read the poems, ask them to think about the collecion theme. How does each poem provide an insight into finding common ground?

NONFICTION CONNECTIONS

Suggest that students increase their reading of informational texts. The nonfiction connections include

- speeches
- diaries
- true-life accounts
- newspaper articles
- political cartoons

Creating an Independent Reading Program

BUILD A CLASSROOM LIBRARY

A classroom library full of books and other media offer students a rich and accessible reading environment.

- Designate a bookcase as the classroom library.
- Organize books into broad categories such as historical fiction, fantasy, biography, and informational text.
- Ask your school or local librarian to recommend other trade books you could include in your classroom library.
- Create a checkout system. You may want to put an index card in a pocket at the back of each book or use a digital library app to track checkouts and returns.
- Ask volunteers to take turns with library upkeep.

CREATE LIBRARY RULES

Work with students to create a list of library rules, such as these:

- Check out one book at a time.
- Return a book before you check a new one out.
- Sign the checkout card and place it in the Checkout Box or use a digital tracking device to record checkouts and returns.
- Use a shared digital spreadsheet to create an online catalog and to track books.

Present a Speech

SL 4 Present information, findings, and evidence.
SL 6 Adapt speech to a variety of contexts and tasks.

Recall the quotation from Kofi Annan that opened this collection: "We may have different religions, different languages, different colored skin, but we all belong to one human race." Do you think individuals can live together as "one human race"? Using evidence from the collection texts, you will present your ideas on this topic in a speech.

An effective speech

- has a clear, logical thesis statement supported by reasons and evidence
- includes an introduction, a logically structured body including connecting and transitional words, and a conclusion
- demonstrates appropriate and clear use of language
- uses suitable expression, volume, and pronunciation
- engages listeners through gestures and eye contact

PLAN

Analyze the Text Choose three texts from this collection, including "A Quilt of a Country," and identify what each author suggests about whether individuals can live together as members of "one human race." Look for examples of the difficulties that arise because of people's differences. Find examples of and details about whether these differences can be overcome. Use the annotation tools in your eBook to help you. Save each piece of evidence to *my*Notebook in a file titled *Collection 1 Performance Task A.*

ACADEMIC VOCABULARY

As you share your ideas about how individuals live together, be sure to use these words.

enforce
entity
internal
presume
resolve

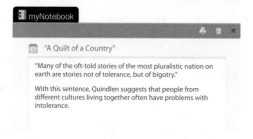

myNotebook

"A Quilt of a Country"

"Many of the oft-told stories of the most pluralistic nation on earth are stories not of tolerance, but of bigotry."

With this sentence, Quindlen suggests that people from different cultures living together often have problems with intolerance.

PRESENT A SPEECH

SL 4, SL 6

Introduce students to the Performance Task by reading the introductory paragraph with them and reviewing the criteria for what makes an effective speech. Remind students that a speech needs to be written well, in the same way that an essay does, but that the delivery of the speech is of equal importance.

PLAN

ANALYZE THE TEXT

Remind students to review the quotation from Kofi Annan and to determine how the quotation applies to the anchor text and to two other selections in the collection. Tell students to analyze how each text explores the relationship of the individual to society and to synthesize ideas common to all three texts.

View It!

Professional Development Podcast:

Performance Task

WHEN STUDENTS STRUGGLE

Analyze the Text Suggest that students work in small groups to analyze the texts. Have each group focus on one text. Provide students with the following questions to guide their analyses:

- Who is the main character or individual in the text?
- What role does society play in the text?
- What conflict does the main character or individual face?

PERFORMANCE TASK A

PLAN

WRITE A THESIS STATEMENT

Review with students the characteristics of an effective thesis statement: It clearly and objectively states the writer's position on a topic and can be supported with evidence from the texts. Students' thesis statements should state their position on whether individuals can live together "as one human race."

PRODUCE

PLAN YOUR PRESENTATION

Suggest to students that they write their speeches with their audience in mind. They should incorporate enough text evidence to support their claim and present their ideas in a way that will engage their listeners.

Write a Thesis Statement Based on these texts and your own experience, write a thesis statement presenting your position on whether individuals can live as "one human race." For example, you might state that people can live together as one human race when they are united by a common purpose. Remember that you will need to provide sufficient evidence to support your thesis statement. Review the details you gathered in *my*Notebook to find evidence that supports your thesis statement.

Get Organized Organize your notes in an outline.

- Write your thesis statement about whether individuals can live as "one human race" in the introduction section of your outline.
- In the body section, list reasons and evidence that support your thesis statement.
- Summarize your main points in the concluding section.

> *Interactive Lessons*
> To help you plan your speech, complete the following lesson:
> - Writing Arguments: Support: Reasons and Evidence

PRODUCE

Write Your Speech Use your notes to write a clearly organized speech. Keep in mind the purpose of your speech and your audience. Remember to include

- quotations and examples from the texts and your own experience to support your thesis statement
- connecting and transitional words or phrases to link your ideas
- language choices appropriate for an oral presentation
- a variety of grammatical structures that will help keep your audience interested in your speech

Plan Your Presentation When you deliver your speech to an audience, use appropriate expression, volume, and gestures. Mark places in the text where you might want to

- adjust your volume to emphasize a word or phrase
- pause to give the audience time to consider an important idea
- use gestures to convey meaning or emotion
- make eye contact to engage your listeners

> **WriteSmart**
> Write your rough draft in *my*WriteSmart. Focus on getting your ideas down rather than perfecting your choice of language.
>
> *Interactive Lessons*
> To help you plan your presentation, complete the following lesson:
> - Giving a Presentation: Knowing Your Audience

ENGLISH LANGUAGE SUPPORT

Adapt Language Choices Remind students that their speeches should be written as formal oral presentations, using formal language. For this speech, the audience is their peers, people who are familiar with the texts being discussed. Encourage students to practice their presentations with a partner, paying special attention to the following:

- appropriate eye contact
- adequate volume
- clear pronunciation

Review Your Draft
Use the following chart to revise your draft.

myWriteSmart

Have your partner or a group of peers review your draft in *my*WriteSmart. Ask your reviewers to note places where you should add emphasis or gestures when you deliver your speech.

Questions	Tips	Revision Techniques
Does the introduction include a clear thesis statement?	**Highlight** the thesis statement.	**Clarify** your thesis statement so it clearly expresses your thoughts on the issue.
Does evidence from the text support the thesis?	**Underline** at least three examples of text evidence that support the thesis.	**Add** evidence from the text that supports your thesis.
Do connecting and transitional words or phrases link ideas throughout the speech?	**Highlight** connecting and transitional words or phrases that link ideas.	**Add** connecting and transitional words or phrases that link ideas.
Is the language used appropriate for the purpose and task?	**Underline** examples of formal language that is appropriate for a speech to your classmates.	**Revise** as needed, adapting language choices so that they are appropriate.
Does the conclusion summarize the main points?	**Highlight** the summary of your main points.	**Add** a summary of your main points to your conclusion.

Language and Style: Understand Cohesion

Look for places where you can use connecting and transitional words or phrases to increase cohesion. Read the following example from "The Gettysburg Address."

> " We have come to dedicate a portion of that field, as a final resting place . . . But, in a larger sense, we cannot dedicate—we cannot hallow this ground. "

Note how Lincoln uses the transition word *but* to suggest a contrast with his first statement. Using a transition in this way adds cohesion to Lincoln's speech.

Interactive Lessons
To help you deliver your presentation, complete the following lesson:
• Giving a Presentation: Delivering Your Presentation

Practice Your Delivery
Before presenting to the class, practice with a partner.

- Mark your text to show where you will adjust your volume or use a gesture to emphasize a point.
- Use correct pronunciation so your audience understands you.
- Maintain appropriate eye contact to engage your audience.
- Allow your partner to give you feedback, and then make any changes to your speech before presenting to the whole class.

PERFORMANCE TASK A

REVISE

LANGUAGE AND STYLE

Tell students that connecting or transition words and phrases an be used to link ideas, events, or reasons throughout a text. Provide students with more examples of transitional words and phrases, including: *first, second, meanwhile, however, on the other hand, on the contrary, moreover,* and *in addition.*

PRESENT

PRACTICE YOUR DELIVERY

Students may present their speeches directly to the whole class or to a small group, or they may want to videotape their presentations. Videotaping will allow them to critique themselves on their delivery and to focus on their use of text evidence to support the claim.

PERFORMANCE TASK A

USE THE SCORING RUBRIC

Have students use the rubric to assess each other's presentations. In particular, ask students to note the tone and register of the language they used in their speeches. Was it more formal or informal? If students answer more informal, have them replace instances of informal language with formal words and phrases. Encourage them to consult reference materials such as a dictionary or thesaurus during the revision process.

REFLECT ON THE PROCESS

Tell students that thinking about how they presented their speeches will help them complete other performance tasks. Ask students to think about how well they engaged their audience. Then, ask students to answer the following questions.

- When did you feel most confident delivering your speech, and why?
- What would you add to your draft to create more audience engagement?
- How did writing this speech help you to better understand the relationships between individuals and their role in society?

PERFORMANCE TASK A RUBRIC
SPEECH

	Ideas and Evidence	Organization	Language
4	• The introduction immediately engages the audience; the thesis statement clearly states the speaker's position. • Valid reasons and relevant evidence from the texts and from the speaker's experience strongly support the speaker's thesis statement. • The concluding section effectively summarizes the main points.	• The reasons and evidence are organized consistently and logically throughout the speech. • Varied connecting and transitional words and phrases link ideas and add cohesion.	• The speech reflects a formal style and an objective, or controlled, tone. • Sentence beginnings, lengths, and structures vary and have a rhythmic flow. • Grammar, usage, and mechanics are correct.
3	• The introduction could do more to capture the audience's attention; the speaker's thesis statement states a position. • Most reasons and evidence from the texts and from the speaker's experience support the speaker's thesis statement, but they could be more substantial. • The concluding section restates the main points.	• The organization of reasons and evidence is confusing in a few places. • Some connecting and transitional words and phrases are needed to link ideas and add cohesion.	• The style is informal in a few places, and the tone is defensive at times. • Sentence beginnings, lengths, and structures vary somewhat. • Some grammatical and usage errors are repeated in the speech.
2	• The introduction is ordinary; the speaker's thesis statement identifies an issue, but the position is not clearly stated. • The reasons and evidence from the texts and from the speaker's experience are not always logical or relevant. • The concluding section includes an incomplete summary of the main points.	• The organization of reasons and evidence is logical in some places, but it often doesn't follow a pattern. • Many more connecting and transitional words and phrases are needed to link ideas and add cohesion.	• The style becomes informal in many places, and the tone is often dismissive of other viewpoints. • Sentence structures barely vary, and some fragments or run-on sentences are evident. • Grammar and usage are incorrect in many places, but the speaker's ideas are still clear.
1	• The introduction is confusing. • Significant supporting reasons and evidence from the texts and from the speaker's experience are missing. • The concluding section is missing.	• A logical organization is not used; reasons and evidence are presented randomly. • Connecting and transitional words and phrases are not used, making the speech difficult to understand.	• The style is inappropriate, and the tone is disrespectful. • Repetitive sentence structure, fragments, and run-on sentences make the speech monotonous and hard to follow. • Many grammatical and usage errors change the meaning of the speaker's ideas.

TO CHALLENGE STUDENTS...

Add Media Features Challenge students to add media features to enhance their presentations. Encourage them to use digital media or visual displays to engage their audience. After they have given their speeches, ask students to discuss which media elements worked best and why.

Write an Analytical Essay

W 2 a–f Write informative/explanatory texts.
W 4 Produce writing appropriate to task, purpose, and audience.
W 5 Develop and strengthen writing.
W 9 a–b Draw evidence from literary or informational texts.

The texts in this collection focus on the tension between individuals and society. Look back at the anchor text "Once Upon a Time" and at the other texts you have read in this collection. You will discuss the ideas they present about an individual's role in society in an analytical essay.

An effective analytical essay

- clearly and accurately analyzes the texts
- provides quotations or examples to support main points
- has an introduction, a logically structured body including transitions, and a conclusion
- follows the conventions of written English

Mentor Text In this excerpt from "Rituals of Memory," note how the author uses a description of her friend Mary to illustrate her ideas about memory.

> " Memory begins with various wonders. For my friend Mary, it began with hair. Her hair grew tightly curled, so strong the spirals defied taming. Brushing and combing brought tears. When Mary tried to run her fingers through her hair as she saw others do, her fingers became hopelessly captured by the curls. "

 myNotebook

Use the annotation tools in your eBook to locate evidence that supports your thesis statement. Save each piece of evidence to your notebook.

> **PLAN**

Analyze the Text Choose three texts from this collection, including "Once Upon a Time," and analyze the ideas they convey about the individual's role in society.

- Take notes on the relationship between the individual and society presented in each text. Is the relationship agreeable, combative, or something else?
- What is the most important idea expressed in each text? Think about what this idea suggests about an individual's role in society.

Develop a Thesis Statement Once you have analyzed your chosen texts, you will need to develop a thesis statement. A thesis statement states your point of view on a subject. In this case, your thesis will express your ideas about the way an individual's role in society is presented in the texts you have read.

ACADEMIC VOCABULARY

As you share your ideas about the role of individuals in society, be sure to use these words.

enforce
entity
internal
presume
resolve

WHEN STUDENTS STRUGGLE . . .

Write a Thesis Statement Display or print out the Student Model that accompanies *Interactive Lessons*: Writing Informative Texts. Help students identify the thesis statement in the first paragraph. ("*He uses repetition and figurative language throughout the story to show. . . .*") Then have partners review the notes they took about the collection texts and help each other write clear thesis statements. Remind them that their sentences should state the main idea they intend to write about, an idea that relates to *all* the texts. Let pairs join small groups to share and discuss their thesis statements as you circulate to monitor progress and provide support.

WRITE AN ANALYTICAL ESSAY

W 2 a–f, W 4, W 5, W 9 a–b

Point out to students the qualities of an effective analytical essay. Note that their completed essays should reflect accurate analysis, sufficient textual evidence to support their ideas, a clear organizational structure, and correct use of language conventions.

> **PLAN**

ANALYZE THE TEXT

Suggest that students review any notes they made while reading the texts they have chosen to write about, as well as their answers to the "Analyzing the Text" questions for each selection. Since this performance task depends on careful analysis of each text, remind students to devote their planning time to reviewing and analyzing the texts.

> *View It!*
> Professional Development Podcast:
> **Performance Task**

DEVELOP A THESIS STATEMENT

Explain that the thesis statement will become the main idea of the essay. It should state an idea about the individual's role in society that applies to all three of their selected texts without citing specific details from any of them.

PERFORMANCE TASK B

PRODUCE

WRITE A DRAFT

Suggest to students that they read their essays aloud to gauge the level of language they have used. An analytical essay should observe the formal requirements for writing of this type. Remind students to avoid slang, colloquialisms, and nonstandard forms, as well as to convey a respectful, academic tone.

PRODUCE

LANGUAGE AND STYLE

Remind students that they can combine two clauses to form a complex sentence using a subordinating conjunction, such as *after, although, because, before, even though, when,* or *while*. Sometimes a clause can be rewritten as a phrase and combined with another clause. For example, "The author describes the wall. She is showing the characters' fear" can be condensed as follows: "The author describes the wall to show the characters' fear."

Gather Evidence You will need to support your thesis by citing text evidence, including quotations and examples from the text. For literary texts, you might focus your analysis on the conflict the main character faces or on the theme of the work. For informational texts, analyze the writer's claim and the evidence that supports the claim.

Interactive Lessons
To help you plan your essay, complete the following lesson:
· Writing Informative Texts: Organizing Ideas

Organize Your Essay Your essay should include an introduction, a body, and a conclusion.

- Your introduction should include your thesis statement and the titles and authors of the works you are discussing.
- The body of your essay should present evidence in support of your thesis. Each paragraph in the body of your essay should focus on a main point that supports your thesis.
- The conclusion summarizes the main points in your essay and includes an original insight.

PRODUCE

my WriteSmart
Write your rough draft in *my*WriteSmart. Focus on getting your ideas down rather than perfecting your choice of language.

Write a Draft Use your outline to write an analytical essay explaining how the authors express ideas about the individual and society. Remember to

- provide a clear and cohesive introduction, body, and conclusion
- support your main points with evidence from the text
- explain how the evidence supports your ideas
- use language that is appropriate for your audience
- connect related ideas within a paragraph by combining clauses
- include transitions to link the major sections of the text

Interactive Lessons
To help you cite text evidence in your essay, complete the following lesson:
· Using Textual Evidence: Summarizing, Paraphrasing, and Quoting

As you draft your analytical essay, remember that this kind of writing requires formal language and a respectful tone. Essays that analyze texts are expected to be appropriate for an academic context.

Language Conventions: Combine Ideas

Look for places where you can combine clauses to make connections between or join ideas. Read the following passage from Anna Quindlen's "A Quilt of a Country."

> Today the citizens of the United States have come together once more because of armed conflict and enemy attack.

In this example, Quindlen joins two clauses to explain the cause that leads the citizens of the United States to come together.

ENGLISH LANGUAGE SUPPORT

Condense Ideas In the Student Model for *Interactive Lessons*: Writing Informative Texts, have students locate this sentence: "The Red Room is the bedroom where a young man once slept—that is, until he died after falling down a spiral staircase."

Discuss how the writer combined the sentences with an embedded clause ("where a young man once slept"), the conjunction *until*, and the phrase "after falling down a spiral staircase" to replace the clause "he fell

down a spiral staircase." The combined sentence shows how all the ideas are related. Then have pairs locate this sentence and discuss how ideas are connected:

- Though the man relights each one, he has a hard time keeping up, saying, "the shadows. . . ." (*conjunction though; phrase "saying . . ." instead of clause "he says . . ."*)

Encourage students to combine ideas in similar ways in their essays.

REVISE

Review Your Draft Have your partner or group of peers review your draft. Use the following chart to revise your draft.

Questions	Tips	Revision Techniques
Does the introduction include a clear thesis statement?	**Underline** the thesis statement.	**Add** or **clarify** the thesis statement.
Are there quotations and examples to support the main points?	**Underline** quotations and **highlight** examples that support the main points.	**Add** quotations and examples to support the main points.
Are ideas linked in the essay by combined clauses?	**Underline** sentences in which clauses are combined to link ideas.	**Combine** clauses from two sentences to link ideas.
Do transitions link the major ideas in the text?	**Highlight** transitions used between paragraphs and key points.	**Add** transitional words or phrases or direct references between key points, if needed.
Is appropriate language and a respectful tone used throughout the essay?	**Highlight** instances of formal language and a respectful tone.	**Delete** instances where the language is informal and the tone is not respectful.
Does the conclusion summarize the main points of the essay?	**Highlight** the summary of the key points.	**Add** one or more sentences that summarize the key points of the essay.

myWriteSmart

Have your partner or a group of peers review your draft in *my*WriteSmart. Ask your reviewers to note any main points that are not adequately supported with text evidence.

Interactive Lessons
To help you revise your essay, complete the following lesson:
· Writing Informative Texts: Formal Style

PRESENT

Create a Finished Copy Once you have revised your draft, choose a way to share your analytical essay with your audience.

- Submit your essay to the school newspaper or literary magazine.
- If your class has a Web page, find out if you can post it there.
- Hold a meetup in the school library. You and your fellow students can exchange papers and discuss your views on the topic.

PERFORMANCE TASK B

REVISE

REVIEW YOUR DRAFT

As students apply the revision chart to their drafts, point out that an effective analysis includes a mix of direct quotations and examples. Suggest that they review their drafts and ask themselves whether a wordy quotation could be replaced by a summarized example, or if a vague example could be replaced by a striking quotation. Remind them that quotations can be anything from a whole sentence to a brief, meaningful phrase.

PRESENT

CREATE A FINISHED COPY

Provide students with other options for presenting their essays, such as making videos of themselves reading the essays aloud. Students could then collaborate on a class video about the individual's role in society, using audio clips from the individual readings as voice-over for images relevant to the topic.

TO CHALLENGE STUDENTS . . .

Broaden the Discussion When students have finished their essays, have small groups meet to share the insights they gained from analyzing the texts and writing their analyses. Then have them discuss one of the following:

- What other stories, books, movies, or television shows do you know that express ideas about the individual's role in society? How are these ideas similar to or different from the ones in the collection texts?
- What impact do social media have on the individual's role in society? Relate your ideas about social media to those you analyzed in the collection texts.

PERFORMANCE TASK B

USE THE SCORING RUBRIC

Have partners use the rubric to evaluate their essays. To check whether they have combined clauses to show how details are connected, suggest that they read their essays aloud to each other. Listening partners should point out when sentences seem short, choppy, and disjointed, or when the relationships between ideas are unclear. Have students discuss how to combine sentences with appropriate conjunctions to clarify the writer's meaning.

REFLECT ON THE PROCESS

Tell students that thinking about their work on the analytical essay will help them tackle future writing assignments. Ask students to think about how well they supported their ideas with evidence from the texts. Then have them answer the following questions.

- What part of the writing process went the most smoothly, and why?
- What part of the process was the most difficult? What tips or techniques did you learn to get through this stage successfully?
- How will you approach your next writing assignment differently, if at all?
- How did writing this essay affect your thinking about the tension between an individual and the society in which he or she lives? Explain.

PERFORMANCE TASK B RUBRIC
ANALYTICAL ESSAY

	Ideas and Evidence	Organization	Language
4	• An eloquent introduction includes the titles and authors of the works; the thesis statement presents a unique idea about the texts. • Specific, relevant evidence from the texts supports the key points. • A satisfying concluding section synthesizes the ideas, summarizes the analysis, and offers a unique insight into the texts.	• Key points and supporting details are organized effectively and logically throughout the analysis. • Varied transitions successfully show the relationships between ideas.	• The analysis has an appropriately formal style and a knowledgeable, objective tone. • Language is precise and captures the writer's thoughts with originality. • Clauses are combined to connect ideas in a variety of ways. • Grammar and usage are correct.
3	• The introduction identifies the titles and authors of the works but could be more engaging; the thesis statement presents a clear idea about the texts. • One or two key points need more support. • The concluding section synthesizes most of the ideas and summarizes most of the analysis, but it doesn't provide an original insight.	• The organization of key points and supporting details is confusing in a few places. • A few more transitions are needed to clarify the relationships between ideas.	• The style becomes informal in a few places, and the tone does not always communicate confidence. • Most language is precise. • Some clauses are joined to connect ideas. • Some grammatical and usage errors are repeated in the literary analysis.
2	• The introduction identifies the titles and the authors of the works; the thesis statement only hints at the main idea of the analysis. • Details support some key points but are often too general. • The concluding section gives an incomplete summary of the analysis and restates the thesis statement.	• Most key points are organized logically, but many supporting details are out of place. • More transitions are needed throughout the analysis to connect ideas.	• The style is informal in many places, and the tone reflects a superficial understanding of the works. • Language is repetitive or vague at times. • Few clauses are joined to connect ideas. • Grammar and usage are incorrect in many places, but the writer's ideas are still clear.
1	• The appropriate elements of an introduction are missing. • Details and evidence are irrelevant or missing. • The analysis lacks a concluding section.	• A logical organization is not used; ideas are presented randomly. • Transitions are not used, making the analysis difficult to understand.	• The style and tone are inappropriate for the analysis. • Language is inaccurate, repetitive, and vague. • Clauses are not joined to connect ideas. • Many grammatical and usage errors change the meaning of the writer's ideas.

The Struggle for Freedom

"If there is no struggle, there is no progress.**"**

—Frederick Douglass

PLAN

STREAM TO START

Motivate students to read the collection texts, and spark their curiosity about the collection by playing the video and watching it in class. After students view the video, ask them to think about two things they hope to learn about people's desire for freedom. Call on volunteers to share their responses.

PERFORMANCE TASK PREVIEW

Point out to students that they will complete two performance tasks at the end of the collection. The performance tasks will require them to further analyze the selections in the collection and to synthesize ideas about these analyses. They will present their findings in a variety of products.

ACADEMIC VOCABULARY

Students can acquire facility with the academic vocabulary words through frequent, repeated exposure as they analyze and discuss the selections in the collection. Academic vocabulary can be used in the following instructional contexts. This will enable students to incorporate the academic vocabulary words into their working vocabulary.

- Collaborative Discussion at the end of each selection
- Analyzing the Text questions for each selection
- Selection-level Performance Task
- Vocabulary instruction (for Critical Vocabulary and/or for Vocabulary Strategy)
- Language and Style
- End-of-collection Performance Task for all selections in the collection

ASK STUDENTS to review the Academic Vocabulary word list for this collection. You may wish to pronounce each word aloud, so students hear the correct pronunciation. Then, discuss the definitions and the related forms for each word. Remind students that they will encounter these five academic vocabulary words throughout the collection.

The Struggle for Freedom

From the American civil rights movement to the Middle East and Latin America, this collection explores the universal desire for freedom.

Stream to Start   hmhfyi.com   Channel One News®

COLLECTION
PERFORMANCE TASK Preview

At the end of this collection, you will have the opportunity to complete a task:

- Write an argumentative essay about whether freedom should be given or must be demanded.

ACADEMIC VOCABULARY

Study the words and their definitions in the chart below. You will use these words as you discuss and write about the texts in this collection.

Word	Definition	Related Forms
decline (dĭ-klīn´) *v.*	to fall apart or deteriorate slowly	declinable, decliner
enable (ĕ-nā´bəl) *tr.v.*	to give the means or opportunity	enabler
impose (ĭm-pōz´) *v.*	to bring about by force	imposer, imposition
integrate (ĭn´tĭ-grāt´) *v.*	to pull together into a whole; unify	integration, disintegrate
reveal (rĭ-vēl´) *tr.v.*	to show or make known	revealable, revealment

46

---

myNotebook

As students read, analyze, and discuss the texts in this collection, encourage them to use the *my*WordList folder in *my*Notebook to build their own personal word lists.

- **Annotate** Students can highlight vocabulary terms and other unfamiliar words and save each highlighted term to *my*Notebook.
- **Organize** Within *my*Notebook, students can drag each word into the *my*WordList folder.
- **Elaborate** Ask students to add details to the entry for each word, such as a definition, other forms of the word, and a sample sentence.

English Language Support

▶ View It!
Professional Development Podcast:
English Language Learners

ENGAGE WITH THE COLLECTION TOPIC

Draw students' attention to the title, The Struggle for Freedom. Discuss that all over the world, people work to gain freedom from political and other types of oppression. Tell students that this collection focuses on how people find freedom in difficult circumstances.

ACCESS PRIOR KNOWLEDGE Ask students to think about what they consider freedom to mean. Does freedom mean being able to do what you want all the time? Discuss why it is important to think about freedom and the responsibilities that freedom brings.

SOCRATIC SEMINAR

Use this strategy to deepen students' understanding of the ideals of freedom as presented in the texts in this collection.

- **First**, have students annotate a text as they read, noting interesting ideas, questions they may have, and difficult or tricky passages. Students can use *my*Notebook in the eBook to record their annotations.
- **Then,** introduce the discussion by explaining that students should not only answer questions, but should also respond to what's said, building on each other's ideas. Explain that they are free to take sides in the discussion, to persuade each other, and to pose

additional follow-up questions. Remind them to use textual evidence to support what they say.

- **Next,** begin a discussion by posing open-ended questions, such as: "How does [*an aspect of the text*] relate to your own experience? What does your own experience tell you about [*a character's experience*]?"
- **Finally,** when discussion has ended, have students write short responses to the discussion, describing their own participation, as well as personal goals for future seminars.

Collection 2 Digital Resources for English Language Support

INTERACTIVE WHITEBOARD LESSONS

Use the Interactive Whiteboard Lessons to provide additional support on

- word choice and tone
- point of view
- historical and cultural context

LEVEL UP TUTORIALS

Students can access *Level Up* Tutorials from the eBooks to get additional help on analyzing literature, analyzing informational text, reading skills, vocabulary skills, and language conventions.

my SmartPlanner **eBook** **myNotebook** **my WriteSmart** **fyi** hmhfyi.com

Collection 2 Lessons	Media	Teach and Practice
**Student Edition	eBook**	**Video Links** HISTORY A&E Channel One News®	**Close Reading and Evidence Tracking**
ANCHOR TEXT Speech by Martin Luther King Jr. **"I Have a Dream"**	Audio "I Have a Dream"	**Close Read Screencasts** • Modeled Discussion 1 (lines 10–16) • Modeled Discussion 2 (lines 34–45) • Close Read application pdf (lines 69–83) — **Strategies for Annotation** • Analyze Author's Use of Rhetoric
ANCHOR TEXT History Writing by Charles Euchner from *Nobody Turn Me Around: A People's History of the 1963 March on Washington* **Video** *AMERICA The Story of Us: March on Washington*	Audio from *Nobody Turn Me Around: A People's History of the 1963 March on Washington* — Video **HISTORY®** *AMERICA The Story of Us: March on Washington*	**Close Read Screencasts** • Modeled Discussion 1 (lines 33–40) • Close Read application pdf (lines 313–318) — **Strategies for Annotation** • Analyze Ideas and Events
CLOSE READER Speech by Robert F. Kennedy **"A Eulogy for Dr. Martin Luther King Jr."**	Audio "A Eulogy for Dr. Martin Luther King Jr." Video **A&E®** *Class of the 20th Century: 1963–1968*	
Diary by Ahdaf Soueif from *Cairo: My City, Our Revolution*	Audio from *Cairo: My City, Our Revolution*	**Strategies for Annotation** • Analyze the Impact of Word Choice on Tone • Reference Sources
Memoir by Azar Nafisi from *Reading Lolita in Tehran* **Graphic Novel by Marjane Satrapi** from *Persepolis 2*	Audio from *Reading Lolita in Tehran* — Audio from *Persepolis 2*	**Strategies for Annotation** • Determine Author's Point of View
Short Story by Luisa Valenzuela **"The Censors"**	Audio "The Censors"	**Strategies for Annotation** • Analyze Author's Choices • Suffixes That Form Nouns
CLOSE READER Short Story by Bessie Head **"The Prisoner Who Wore Glasses"**	Audio "The Prisoner Who Wore Glasses"	
Collection 2 Performance Task: **Write an Argument**	**fyi** hmhfyi.com	**Interactive Lessons** Writing an Argument
	For Systematic Coverage of Writing and Speaking & Listening Standards	**Interactive Lessons** Writing an Argument Analyzing and Evaluating Presentations

Assess		Extend	Reteach
Performance Task	✔ *Assess It Online!*	**Teacher eBook**	**Teacher eBook**
Writing Activity: Analysis	Selection Test	**Analyze Language**	**Analyze Seminal U.S. Documents >** *Level Up* **Tutorial >** Primary and Secondary Sources
Writing Activity: Account	Selection Test	**Write a Narrative**	**Analyze Ideas and Events >** *Level Up* **Tutorial >** Point-by-Point Organization
Research Activity: Oral Report	Selection Test	**Conduct Research on the Web > Interactive Whiteboard Lesson >** Conduct Research on the Web	**Analyze Ideas and Events >** *Level Up* **Tutorial >** Chronological Order
Media Activity: Graphic Novel	Selection Test	**Synthesize Information**	**Determine Point of View > Interactive Whiteboard Lesson >** Historical and Cultural Contexts
Writing Activity: Letter	Selection Test	**Analyze Point of View: Cultural Background**	**Analyze Author's Choices: Irony > Interactive Whiteboard Lesson >** Analyze Author's Choices: Irony
Write an Argument	Collection Test		
Lesson Assessments Writing an Argument Analyzing and Evaluating Presentations	**Standards Support and Enrichment**	For more instruction and practice in reading literary and informational texts, language, spelling, and speaking and listening, see Teacher Resources > Standards Support and Enrichment.	

Collection 1 Lessons		Key Learning Objective	Performance Task
ANCHOR TEXT EXEMPLAR Speech by Martin Luther King Jr. "I Have a Dream," p. 47A	Lexile 1120L	**The student will be able to...** analyze a seminal U.S. document and the impact of its rhetoric	Writing Activity: Analysis
ANCHOR TEXT History Writing by Charles Euchner from *Nobody Turn Me Around: A People's History of the 1963 March on Washington*, p. 55A Video *AMERICA The Story of Us: March on Washington*, p. 55A	Lexile 1030L	**The student will be able to...** analyze connections between ideas and events and analyze accounts in different mediums	Writing Activity: Account
Diary by Ahdaf Soueif from *Cairo: My City, Our Revolution*, p. 73A	Lexile 990L	**The student will be able to...** analyze how an author unfolds events in a diary and analyze the impact of word choice on tone	Research Activity: Oral Report
Memoir by Azar Nafisi from *Reading Lolita in Tehran*, p. 81A Graphic Novel by Marjane Satrapi from *Persepolis 2*, p. 81A	Lexile 1150L	**The student will be able to...** determine author's point of view and analyze accounts in different mediums	Media Activity: Graphic Novel
Short Story by Luisa Valenzuela "The Censors," p. 89A	Lexile 1200L	**The student will be able to...** analyze an author's point of view and cultural background, and also analyze an author's choices about style and structure	Writing Activity: Letter

Collection 2 Performance Task:

Write an Argument

Vocabulary Strategy	Language and Style	Differentiated Instruction	CLOSE READER Selection
	Repetition and Parallelism	**English Language Support:** • Analyze Figurative Language • Develop Reading Fluency **When Students Struggle:** Identify Audience **To Challenge Students:** Evaluate Effects of a Speech	Speech by Robert F. Kennedy "A Eulogy for Dr. Martin Luther King Jr.," p. 72b **Lexile 1290L**
Words from Greek and Latin		**English Language Support:** • Language: Print Cues • Language: Modifiers • Vocabulary: Affixes • Language: Pronoun Referents • Comprehension Support **When Students Struggle:** • Analyze Impact of Word Choice • Examine Supporting Sentences • Analyze Purpose • Develop Reading Fluency **To Challenge Students:** Evaluate the Selection	
Reference Sources	Noun Phrases	**English Language Support:** Organizational Patterns: Time Sequence **When Students Struggle:** Synonym and Paraphrase **To Challenge Students:** Analyze Ideas and Events	
Denotations and Connotations	Rhetorical Questions	**English Language Support:** • Language: Context Clues • Language: Verb Tenses **When Students Struggle:** Compare and Contrast **To Challenge Students:** Analyze Nuance	
Suffixes That Form Nouns	Colons and Semicolons	**English Language Support:** Vocabulary: Idioms **When Students Struggle:** Comprehension: Summarize **To Challenge Students:** Draw Conclusions	Short Story by Bessie Head "The Prisoner Who Wore Glasses," p. 96b **Lexile 970L**
	Paraphrase or Summarize	**English Language Support:** Understand Text Structure **When Students Struggle:** Develop Claims **To Challenge Students:** Online Debate	

COMPARE ANCHOR TEXTS AND MEDIA

I Have a Dream

Speech by Martin Luther King Jr.

Why This Text?

Great leaders through the centuries have influenced American thought and actions. This lesson explores the literary and historical value of a speech from one such leader that galvanized Americans to fight for equality.

Key Learning Objective: The student will be able to analyze a seminal U.S. document and the impact of its rhetoric.

For additional practice:

Close Reader selection
"A Eulogy for Dr. Martin Luther King Jr."
Speech by Robert F. Kennedy

Text Complexity Rubric

RI 1 Cite textual evidence.
RI 2 Determine a central idea.
RI 3 Analyze how the author unfolds ideas or events.
RI 4 Analyze the impact of word choices on meaning and tone.
RI 5 Analyze how ideas or claims are developed.
RI 6 Determine an author's point of view or purpose and analyze rhetoric.
RI 7 Analyze various accounts of a subject told in different mediums.
RI 9 Analyze seminal U.S. documents.
W 2 Write informative/explanatory texts.
L 1a Use parallel structure.

Quantitative Measures	**I Have a Dream** Lexile: 1120L
Qualitative Measures	**Levels of Meaning/Purpose** single purpose, explicitly stated
	Structure more than one text structure
	Language Conventionality and Clarity more complex sentence structure
	Knowledge Demands some specialized knowledge required
Reader/Task Considerations	• Teacher determined • Vary by individual reader and type of text • See the Text X-Ray for suggested Reader/Task Considerations.

English Language Support Before teaching, use the Text X-Ray below for an overview of the text's complexity. The Text X-Ray and the supports and scaffolds in the Teacher's Edition will help you guide students of different skill levels.

Meaning Making

Language Development

Effective Expression

Content Knowledge

Foundational Skills

Text Complexity: Qualitative Measures

Levels of Meaning/Purpose

single purpose, explicitly stated

Help students analyze seminal U.S. documents.

- Teacher's Edition side notes, pp. 48, 49, 51, 52
- Close Read Screencasts, p. 47
- When Students Struggle, p. 49
- Analyze Seminal U.S. Documents, p. 52
- Performance Task, p. 53

Help students evaluate how well an author achieved his purpose.

- To Challenge Students, p. 54

To reteach analyzing seminal documents, see

- Analyze Seminal U.S. Documents, p. 54a

 Use It! *Level Up* Tutorial: Primary and Secondary Sources

ZOOM IN ON **ANALYZING SEMINAL U.S. DOCUMENTS** King's speech refers back to Lincoln's Gettysburg Address (line 4), in which Lincoln described the U.S. government as "of the people, by the people, for the people." Use the following questions to help students analyze lines 69–82 in light of Lincoln's description.

- What details suggest that the government is not working "for" African Americans? *(They suffer police brutality and discrimination.)*
- How would you **summarize** the connection between the two **seminal documents**? *(King's speech says that more change is needed to fulfill the promise of Lincoln's address.)*

Structure

more than one text structure

Help students analyze an author's use of rhetoric.

- Teacher's Edition side notes, pp. 48, 49, 50, 51, 52
- Analyze Author's Use of Rhetoric, p. 52
- Strategies for Annotation, p. 52

Prepare students to analyze accounts in different mediums.

- Teacher's Edition side note, p. 47

ZOOM IN ON **ANALYZING RHETORIC** Point out that King wrote his **speech** knowing that he would read it aloud. He used **rhetorical devices** because he knew they would increase the power of his words for listeners. Help students understand the effect of the rhetoric.

- Ask students to read lines 10–16 silently.
- Point out that the repetition of "one hundred years later" does not affect the meaning of the paragraph. Then read it aloud, omitting this phrase after the first instance.
- Read the paragraph again, including the repeated phrase. Discuss how this rhetorical device makes the language more powerful and memorable.

Language Conventionality and Clarity

more complex sentence structure

Teach unfamiliar vocabulary in context.

- Teacher's Edition Critical Vocabulary notes, pp. 48, 49, 50, 54
- Applying Academic Vocabulary, p. 50

Help students analyze figurative language.

- English Language Support, p. 48

Help students develop reading fluency.

- English Language Support, p. 51

Guide students to analyze repetition and parallelism.

- Teacher's Edition side note, p. 54

ZOOM IN ON **PREVIEWING VOCABULARY**

- Distribute these words among pairs of students: *momentous, captivity, segregation, discrimination, poverty, prosperity, exile, unalienable.* Have pairs look up their words in a **reference source** and report back to the class on their definitions.
- Have pairs read lines 1–24 together, pausing at the end of each paragraph to discuss the meaning. Circulate to clarify any sentences students cannot figure out on their own.
- As a class, discuss the ideas King lays out in the first part of his speech, and elicit predictions as to what the remainder of the speech will be about.

Knowledge Demands

some specialized knowledge required

Support English Learners in understanding the historical context of the speech.

- Teacher's Edition Background note, p. 47

ZOOM IN ON **BUILDING HISTORICAL KNOWLEDGE** King says although the Emancipation Proclamation freed African Americans from slavery, in 1963 they were still not free. Clarify for students what he means by "the manacles of segregation and the chains of discrimination" (line 12).

- *Segregation* means "separation." In the South, black and white people were separated in public places, such as restaurants. Facilities for African Americans were invariably of poorer quality.
- *Discrimination* means "treating one person or group differently than others." African Americans faced discrimination when they applied for jobs, schools, housing, and so on.

Suggested Reader/Task Considerations

You might consider the following before assigning this speech to students.

- Do students have the necessary attention to read and understand the speech?
- Do students have enough experience with the language to interpret **metaphors** in the text?

ZOOM IN ON **SUPPORTING COMPREHENSION**

- Divide the speech into manageable sections. Place students in mixed-ability groups. After students read each section, have them pause to discuss any questions with their group.
- To help students interpret the **extended metaphor** in lines 17–33, review the meanings of words and phrases related to money and banking: *cash a check, signing a promissory note, to fall heir, defaulted, bad check . . . marked "insufficient funds," bankrupt, great vaults.*

TEACH

CLOSE READ

Background Have students read the background note and the biographical information about Martin Luther King Jr. Explain that in 1955 Dr. King led the greatest nonviolent demonstration of its kind in the United States—the Montgomery Bus Boycott against segregated busing. The boycott lasted for 382 days, ending when the Supreme Court ruled that segregated busing was (and is) unconstitutional. The ruling showed that nonviolent actions can achieve results. It also established King as the foremost leader of the civil rights movement.

An ordained Baptist minister, King was committed to nonviolent protest as a way of achieving social justice. With the eyes of the country and the world on the organizers of the Montgomery Bus Boycott, King stirred protesters with powerful speeches and strong words of encouragement. His prominent role came with a price. King's home was bombed and he himself was arrested and threatened. Nevertheless, he remained committed to the cause of social justice, a commitment that eventually led to the March on Washington.

Analyze Accounts in Different Mediums
RI 7

Tell students that factual information about historic events can be presented in different ways. Point out that

- a written history of the event may include details and even photographs that help readers understand the event
- a documentary film may include video and audio footage of the event, as well as narration

Explain that each medium has both advantages and disadvantages and that to thoroughly analyze historic events, students should consider accounts in different mediums. Tell students that they will read the entire speech, as well as an analysis of the speech, and then they will watch a short video about the March on Washington.

ASK STUDENTS why it might be important for them to read the text of King's speech, rather than simply read an analysis and watch a video about it. *(Reading the text of the speech will enable them to examine what King actually said, rather than how he said it or the effects of what he said.)*

HISTORY VIDEO

The March on Washington

I Have a Dream
Speech by Martin Luther King Jr.

from Nobody Turn Me Around: A History of the 1963 March on Washington
History Writing by Charles Euchner

MEDIA

AMERICA The Story of Us: March on Washington
Video by HISTORY®

Background *On August 28, 1963, thousands of Americans marched on Washington, D.C., to urge Congress to pass a civil rights bill. Martin Luther King Jr. delivered his "I Have a Dream" speech on the steps of the Lincoln Memorial before more than 250,000 people. After you read and analyze the speech, you will read an excerpt from a history text which describes the historic speech in detail and includes first-hand accounts from people who were on the National Mall that day. Then you will watch a short video about the march and compare the two accounts.*

Martin Luther King Jr. *(1929–1968) became a catalyst for social change in the 1950s and 1960s. Preaching a philosophy of nonviolence, he galvanized people of all races to participate in boycotts, marches, and demonstrations against racial injustice. His moral leadership stirred the conscience of the nation and helped bring about the passage of the Civil Rights Act of 1964. In that same year, he was awarded the Nobel Peace Prize. King continued his work for justice and equality until he was assassinated in 1968.*

Compare Anchor Texts and Media **47**

Close Read Screencasts
 Close Read

Modeled Discussions

Have students click the *Close Read* icons in their eBooks to access two screencasts in which readers discuss and annotate the following key passages:

- King says that 100 years after the Emancipation Proclamation, African Americans still are not free (lines 10–16).
- King stresses the need for immediate action (lines 34–45).

As a class, view and discuss at least one of these videos. Then have pairs do an independent close read of an additional passage—King tells why he is not satisfied with the present situation (lines 69–83).

Compare Anchor Texts and Media **47**

AS YOU READ Direct students to use the As You Read note to focus their reading.

Analyze Seminal U.S. Documents (LINES 1–16)   RI 9

Explain that a **seminal U.S. document** is a document or speech that has helped shape the country and its people. Point out that King's speech helped propel the civil rights movement, changing our laws and our ideas about equality. Tell students that in analyzing the speech, they must determine its **purpose**, or the reason the speaker delivered the speech.

A **CITE TEXT EVIDENCE** Have students cite the lines that state King's purpose. *(In lines 1–3, King states it as demonstrating for freedom. In line 17, he states he will "dramatize a shameful condition.")* Ask what other seminal U.S. documents King cites in his speech. *(the Emancipation Proclamation [line 5], the Constitution [line 20], the Declaration of Independence [line 20])*

Analyze Author's Use of Rhetoric (LINES 17–31)   RI 6

Point out to students that **rhetorical devices** appear throughout King's speech. Define rhetorical devices as techniques that writers use to enhance arguments and convey ideas. Explain that one such device is an **extended metaphor,** or a comparison between two unlike things that is explored in some depth.

B **ASK STUDENTS** to reread lines 17–31 and notice the extended metaphor King uses. What is the meaning of this metaphor? *(King uses the metaphor of a bad check to explain that the U.S. government has failed in its obligation to its African American citizens.)*

> **CRITICAL VOCABULARY**
>
> **defaulted**: King says that the country has failed to honor its promises to African Americans.
>
> **ASK STUDENTS** why King says that the country has defaulted on its promise to African Americans. *(The Constitution and the Declaration of Independence promised freedom and equality to Americans, but these rights were not extended to African Americans.)*

I Have a Dream
Speech by Martin Luther King Jr.

AS YOU READ Note ways in which Dr. King uses words and phrases to inspire his audience. Write down any questions you have.

 myNotebook

As you read, mark up the text. Save your work to *myNotebook*.
- Highlight details.
- Add notes and questions.
- Add new words to *myWordList*.

I am happy to join with you today in what will go down in history as the greatest demonstration for freedom in the history of our nation.

    Five score[1] years ago, a great American, in whose symbolic shadow we stand today, signed the Emancipation Proclamation.[2] This momentous decree came as a great beacon light of hope to millions of Negro slaves who had been seared in the flames of withering injustice. It came as a joyous daybreak to end the long night of their captivity.

10   But one hundred years later, the Negro still is not free; one hundred years later, the life of the Negro is still sadly crippled by the manacles of segregation and the chains of discrimination; one hundred years later, the Negro lives on a lonely island of poverty in the midst of a vast ocean of material prosperity; one hundred years later, the Negro is still languishing in the corners of American society and finds himself in exile in his own land.

    So we've come here today to dramatize a shameful condition. In a sense we've come to our nation's capital to cash a check. When the architects of our republic wrote the magnificent words of the
20 Constitution and the Declaration of Independence, they were signing a promissory note[3] to which every American was to fall heir. This note was the promise that all men, yes, black men as well as white men, would be guaranteed the unalienable rights of life, liberty, and the pursuit of happiness.

    It is obvious today that America has **defaulted** on this promissory note insofar as her citizens of color are concerned. Instead of honoring this sacred obligation, America has given the Negro people a bad check, a check which has come back marked "insufficient funds." But we refuse to believe that the bank of justice
30 is bankrupt. We refuse to believe that there are insufficient funds in the great vaults of opportunity of this nation. And so we've come to

> **default**
> (dĭ-fôlt´) *v.*
> to fail to keep a promise to repay a loan.

---

[1] **five score:** 100; *score* means "twenty." (This phrasing recalls the beginning of Abraham Lincoln's Gettysburg Address: "Four score and seven years ago . . .")

[2] **Emancipation Proclamation:** a document signed by President Lincoln in 1863, during the Civil War, declaring that all slaves in states still at war with the Union were free.

[3] **promissory note:** a written promise to repay a loan.

English Language Support

Analyze Figurative Language Read aloud the third paragraph of the speech. Focus students' attention on "the Negro lives on a lonely island of poverty in the midst of a vast ocean of material prosperity."

- Explain that this is figurative language and that the Negro (a term used at the time to mean African American) did not really live on an island. King means that African Americans were poor and separated from wealthier white Americans.

- Help students interpret other instances of figurative language, including the metaphors in lines 6–9 and lines 11–12.

- Point out that figurative language helps the author create a picture in the minds of the reader or listener.

cash this check, a check that will give us upon demand the riches of freedom and the security of justice.

We have also come to this hallowed spot to remind America of the fierce urgency of now. This is no time to engage in the luxury of cooling off or to take the tranquilizing drug of gradualism. Now is the time to make real the promises of democracy; now is the time to rise from the dark and **desolate** valley of segregation to the sunlit path of racial justice; now is the time to lift our nation from
40 the quicksands of racial injustice to the solid rock of brotherhood; now is the time to make justice a reality for all of God's children. It would be fatal for the nation to overlook the urgency of the moment. This sweltering summer of the Negro's legitimate discontent will not pass until there is an invigorating autumn of freedom and equality.

Nineteen sixty-three is not an end, but a beginning. And those who hope that the Negro needed to blow off steam and will now be content will have a rude awakening if the nation returns to business as usual. There will be neither rest nor tranquility in America until
50 the Negro is granted his citizenship rights. The whirlwinds of revolt will continue to shake the foundations of our nation until the bright day of justice emerges.

But there is something that I must say to my people, who stand on the worn threshold which leads into the palace of justice. In the process of gaining our rightful place, we must not be guilty of wrongful deeds. Let us not seek to satisfy our thirst for freedom by drinking from the cup of bitterness and hatred. We must forever conduct our struggle on the high plain of dignity and discipline. We must not allow our creative protests to **degenerate** into physical
60 violence. Again and again we must rise to the majestic heights of meeting physical force with soul force. The marvelous new militancy, which has engulfed the Negro community, must not lead us to a distrust of all white people. For many of our white brothers, as evidenced by their presence here today, have come to realize that their destiny is tied up with our destiny. And they have come to realize that their freedom is **inextricably** bound to our freedom. We cannot walk alone. And as we walk, we must make the pledge that we shall always march ahead. We cannot turn back.

There are those who are asking the devotees of civil rights,
70 "When will you be satisfied?" We can never be satisfied as long as the Negro is the victim of the unspeakable horrors of police brutality; we can never be satisfied as long as our bodies, heavy with the fatigue of travel, cannot gain lodging in the motels of the highways and the hotels of the cities; we cannot be satisfied as long as the Negro's basic mobility is from a smaller ghetto to a larger one; we can never be satisfied as long as our children are

C

desolate
(dĕs′ə-lĭt) *adj.*
unhappy; lonely.

degenerate
(dĭ-jĕn′ər-āt) *v.*
to decline morally.

inextricably
(ĭn-ĕk′strĭ-kə-blē)
adv. in a way
impossible to
untangle.

D

I Have a Dream   **49**

WHEN STUDENTS STRUGGLE...

Direct students to lines 46–52 and lines 53–68. Ask them to reread the first passage and explain who King is addressing. How do they know? *(King is addressing all Americans; he warns that the nation will experience no peace until African Americans attain justice.)* Then have students reread the second passage and explain why King now addresses African Americans. *(He is urging them to maintain their nonviolent approach and to see white Americans as partners in the struggle for freedom.)*

LEVEL UP TUTORIALS For additional support, assign the following *Level Up* tutorial: **Primary and Secondary Sources.**

Analyze Seminal U.S. Documents (LINES 34–35)   RI 9

Explain that King's speech is especially significant because it was made in 1963 on the steps of the Lincoln Memorial, one hundred years after Lincoln signed the Emancipation Proclamation.

C **CITE TEXT EVIDENCE** Have students cite the line in which King refers to where he is giving the speech. *(line 34)* Ask them what he means by the reference. *(The phrase "this hallowed spot" means that King believes the Lincoln Memorial is a sacred place. It represents the promise of African American equality.)*

Analyze Author's Use of Rhetoric (LINES 70–80)   RI 6

Explain that another rhetorical device is **repetition**. Point out that in his speech, King uses repetition, saying a word or phrase over and over for emphasis.

D **CITE TEXT EVIDENCE** Ask students to cite the repeated phrase in lines 70–80. *("We can never [or cannot] be satisfied")* Ask what effect this repetition has. *(It emphasizes that there are many examples of injustice, not just one or two. It strengthens King's argument by indicating a wealth of evidence.)*

CRITICAL VOCABULARY

desolate: King describes segregation as a dark and depressing valley. **ASK STUDENTS** how a desolate person might feel. *(Possible answers: sad, lonely)*

degenerate: King beseeches activists not to allow the nonviolent protests to become violent. **ASK STUDENTS** why King does not want the creative protests to degenerate. *(He thinks the protesters should be dignified and moral.)*

inextricably: King explains that many white Americans realize their freedom is tied to the freedom of African Americans. **ASK STUDENTS** how the freedoms of white and black Americans might be inextricably bound. *(The absence of freedom for one group could lead to loss of freedom for another group.)*

Analyze Author's Use of Rhetoric (LINES 83–116)

RI 6

Tell students that throughout his speech, King employs another rhetorical device called **parallelism.** Explain that parallelism is the repeated use of the same grammatical construction to express ideas that are equal in importance. As an example, tell students that King uses parallelism in lines 78–81: "we cannot be satisfied . . . we are not satisfied . . . we will not be satisfied." Point out that parallelism often employs repetition.

E **CITE TEXT EVIDENCE** Have students point to other uses of parallelism on the page. *(lines 83–85: "Some of you have come"; lines 89–91: "Go back to"; lines 96–116: "I have a dream that one day")* Then ask them to explain what King's use of parallelism and repetition in lines 89–91 emphasizes. *(King uses repetition and parallelism to emphasize that each place—Alabama, Mississippi, South Carolina, and so on—is equally difficult for African Americans.)*

Explain that the use of parallelism and repetition can affect the meaning and tone of a speech. **Tone** is the author's attitude toward the subject and the audience. Point out that the tone of a speech can be angry, encouraging, even funny.

F **ASK STUDENTS** what tone is apparent in the most famous section of King's speech, in which he repeats "I have a dream." *(The tone is uplifting and encouraging.)* Have students explain how this tone affects the meaning of the speech. *(The uplifting tone gives the speech a meaning that is more encouraging and hopeful than it might otherwise be.)*

CRITICAL VOCABULARY

redemptive: King assures African Americans that the suffering they endure as a result of segregation will not be in vain.

ASK STUDENTS in what way unjust suffering might be redemptive. *(It makes people stronger, and the injustice of it will eventually be apparent and lead to justice.)*

---

stripped of their selfhood and robbed of their dignity by signs stating For Whites Only; we cannot be satisfied as long as the Negro in Mississippi cannot vote and a Negro in New York believes he has nothing for which to vote. No! No, we are not satisfied, and we will not be satisfied until "justice rolls down like waters and righteousness like a mighty stream."

E I am not unmindful that some of you have come here out of great trials and tribulations. Some of you have come fresh from narrow jail cells. Some of you have come from areas where your quest for freedom left you battered by the storms of persecution and staggered by the winds of police brutality. You have been the veterans of creative suffering. Continue to work with the faith that unearned suffering is **redemptive.** Go back to Mississippi. Go back to Alabama. Go back to South Carolina. Go back to Georgia. Go back to Louisiana. Go back to the slums and ghettos of our Northern cities, knowing that somehow this situation can and will be changed. Let us not wallow in the valley of despair.

I say to you today, my friends, even though we face the difficulties of today and tomorrow, I still have a dream. It is a dream deeply rooted in the American dream. **F** I have a dream that one day this nation will rise up and live out the true meaning of its creed, "We hold these truths to be self-evident; that all men are created equal." I have a dream that one day on the red hills of Georgia, sons of former slaves and the sons of former slave owners will be able to sit down together at the table of brotherhood. I have a dream that one day even the state of Mississippi, a state sweltering with the heat of injustice, sweltering with the heat of oppression, will be transformed into an oasis of freedom and justice. I have a dream that my four little children will one day live in a nation where they will not be judged by the color of their skin, but by the content of their character.

I have a dream today!

I have a dream that one day down in Alabama—with its vicious racists, with its Governor having his lips dripping with the words of interposition and nullification[4]—one day right there in Alabama, little black boys and black girls will be able to join hands with little white boys and white girls as sisters and brothers.

I have a dream today!

I have a dream that one day every valley shall be exalted, and every hill and mountain shall be made low. The rough places will be plain and the crooked places will be made straight, "and

redemptive
(rĭ-dĕmpˈtĭv) *adj.* causing freedom or salvation.

---

[4] **Governor . . . nullification:** Rejecting a federal order to desegregate the University of Alabama, Governor George Wallace claimed that the principle of nullification (a state's alleged right to refuse a federal law) allowed him to resist federal "interposition," or interference, in state affairs.

APPLYING ACADEMIC VOCABULARY

reveal	integrate

THINK-PAIR-SHARE Have students turn to a partner to discuss the following questions. Guide students to include the academic vocabulary words *reveal* and *integrate* in their responses. Ask volunteers to share their responses with the class.

- What does King's tone **reveal** about his hopes and expectations regarding justice for African Americans?
- Does King believe **integration** is attainable?

the glory of the Lord shall be revealed, and all flesh shall see it together."

120   This is our hope. This is the faith that I go back to the South with. With this faith we will be able to hew out of the mountain of despair a stone of hope. With this faith we will be able to transform the jangling discords of our nation into a beautiful symphony of brotherhood. With this faith we will be able to work together, to pray together, to struggle together, to go to jail together, to stand up for freedom together, knowing that we will be free one day. And this will be the day. This will be the day when all of God's children will be able to sing with new meaning, "My country 'tis of thee, sweet land of liberty, of thee I sing. Land where my fathers died,
130 land of the pilgrims' pride, from every mountainside, let freedom ring." And if America is to be a great nation, this must become true.

    So let freedom ring from the prodigious hilltops of New Hampshire; let freedom ring from the mighty mountains of New York; let freedom ring from the heightening Alleghenies of Pennsylvania; let freedom ring from the snowcapped Rockies of Colorado; let freedom ring from the curvaceous slopes of California. But not only that. Let freedom ring from Stone Mountain of Georgia; let freedom ring from Lookout Mountain of Tennessee; let freedom ring from every hill and molehill of
140 Mississippi. "From every mountainside, let freedom ring."

    And when this happens, and when we allow freedom to ring, when we let it ring from every village and every hamlet, from every state and every city, we will be able to speed up that day when all of God's children—black men and white men, Jews and Gentiles, Protestants and Catholics—will be able to join hands and sing in the words of the old Negro spiritual, "Free at last. Free at last. Thank God Almighty, we are free at last."

COLLABORATIVE DISCUSSION Which parts of the speech did you find the most inspiring? With a partner, discuss how King uses words and phrases to support his argument. Cite specific textual evidence from the speech in your discussion.

English Language Support

Develop Reading Fluency Use King's soaring words from lines 132–140 to help students practice reading a speech. Remind them that a speech should be delivered with expression and with emphasis on repeated words and phrases, using punctuation marks as a guide to when to pause and when to begin a new thought.

First, model for students an effective reading of the speech, or show them a video of King delivering the specific lines they will be practicing. Then, read each sentence or clause and have students echo read.

TEACH

CLOSE READ

Analyze Seminal U.S. Documents (LINES 120–131)
RI 9

Tell students that analyzing a seminal speech involves determining its **theme** or themes, or the central message(s) the speaker wants to convey. Explain that determining a speech's theme requires them to think about the speech's context as they analyze the words.

G **ASK STUDENTS** to look at lines 120–131. Ask them what "faith" King is referring to. (*faith in the notion that all people will be free and equal one day*) Ask what new meaning King expects Americans to find in the words of "My Country, 'Tis of Thee"? (*He expects them to find new meaning in the idea of liberty once all Americans are free.*) Discuss how the context of the speech, including years of inequality and nonviolent resistance, coupled with an analysis of his words, helps illuminate a theme. (*The oppression of African Americans and King's focus on freedom and equality suggests the theme that while everyone deserves freedom, some people must fight for it.*)

Analyze Author's Use of Rhetoric (LINES 132–140)
RI 6

Have students continue looking for examples of repetition and parallelism.

H **ASK STUDENTS** to look at the repetition in lines 132–140 of "let freedom ring." Discuss how the repetition of these words and the parallelism of the clauses affect the meaning of the passage. (*The repetition emphasizes the call for freedom and justice, but the parallelism suggests that King believes justice for African Americans is possible in the Southern states as well as in other parts of the country.*)

COLLABORATIVE DISCUSSION Have students pair up and discuss specific sections of the speech that they felt were inspiring, as well as lines and phrases that resonated with them. Ask them to discuss which rhetorical devices they found most effective and why. Then have them share their conclusions with the class.

ASK STUDENTS to share any questions they generated in the course of reading and discussing the selection.

TEACH

CLOSE READ

Analyze Author's Use of Rhetoric

RI 6

Explain that rhetorical devices help keep the audience's attention, and they allow the speaker to impart words and phrases that stay with the audience long after the speech has ended. Discuss the rhetorical devices used frequently in the speech:

- **Repetition** helps King emphasize important words and phrases and it creates a rhythm that makes the words pleasant to listen to and memorable.
- **Parallelism** often employs repetition by setting up grammatical constructions that begin with the same word or phrase.
- To follow King's **extended metaphors**, students must determine what two things are being compared and what they have in common.

Analyze Seminal U.S. Documents

RI 9

Point out that seminal documents are not only important for understanding history. They are referenced frequently in the media, in speeches, and in popular culture. Therefore, understanding their significance helps us understand our own culture and values. Review the bulleted questions with students and make sure they understand the role of historical context in analyzing a seminal document or speech.

Analyze Author's Use of Rhetoric

RI 6

To establish a point of view or purpose, authors and speakers like Martin Luther King Jr. use **rhetorical devices** to shape the structure of sentences and paragraphs within a work. Rhetorical devices can evoke an emotional response in an audience and make the message memorable. Here are some examples.

Repetition	Parallelism	Extended Metaphor
Uses the same word or words more than once for emphasis	Uses similar grammatical constructions to express ideas that are related or equal in importance. It often creates a rhythm.	Makes a comparison between two unlike things that continues at some length
"Let there be justice for all. Let there be peace for all. Let there be work, bread, water, and salt for all."	"We cannot, we must not, refuse to protect the right of every American to vote in every election. . . . And we ought not, and we cannot, and we must not wait another eight months before we get a bill."	"'A house divided against itself cannot stand.' I believe this government cannot endure permanently half slave and half free. I do not expect the Union to be dissolved; I do not expect the house to fall; but I do expect it will cease to be divided. It will become all one thing, or all the other.
—from "Glory and Hope" by Nelson Mandela	—from "We Shall Overcome" by Lyndon Baines Johnson	— from "A House Divided" by Abraham Lincoln

Analyze Seminal U.S. Documents

RI 9

A **seminal U. S. document** is a document or speech from which a change in our nation's laws, society, or ideas about itself grew. Reading and analyzing important speeches like "I Have a Dream" is one of the best ways to understand our history and our national experience. To understand a speech's importance, you need to know something about its background, or **historical context.** Asking questions will help you understand its context better. To answer some of these questions, you may need to research information about the speaker and the events and attitudes of the day.

- Who is the speaker?
- Who was the audience?
- When and where was the speech presented?
- What was the purpose of the speech?
- How did the speech contribute to our national experience?

Strategies for Annotation    *Annotate it!*

Analyze Author's Use of Rhetoric

RI 6

Share these strategies for guided or independent analysis:
- Find the extended metaphor in the speech.
- Use two colors of highlighting to show the two parts of the metaphor: the real historical situation King is talking about, and the familiar thing to which he compares it.
- On notes, record the meaning of the extended metaphor, including how it helps you understand the speech.

It is obvious today that America has defaulted on this promissory note insofar as her citizens of color are concerned. Instead of honoring this sacred obligation, America has given the Negro people a bad check, a check which has come back marked "insufficient funds." But we refuse to believe that the bank of justice is bankrupt. We refuse to believe that there are insufficient

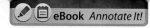

Analyzing the Text

RI 1, RI 2, RI 3,
RI 4, RI 5, RI 6,
RI 9, W 2

Cite Text Evidence Support your responses with evidence from the selection.

1. **Infer** The central point of an **argument** is the **claim,** or proposition. What is King's claim in this speech? What evidence does he cite to support his claim?

2. **Analyze** How does King structure, or organize, his speech? Explain how each section integrates his ideas and advances his argument.

3. **Interpret** An **allusion** is an indirect reference to something that the audience is expected to know. In his speech, King makes more than one allusion to the Declaration of Independence. Identify the allusions and explain how they advance King's argument.

4. **Interpret** King uses an extended metaphor to compare a familiar object—a bad check—to an abstract idea. How does King develop the metaphor? What does he believe was promised to African Americans? How has America given African Americans a "bad check?"

5. **Analyze** Find examples of parallelism in lines 36–41. What effect does the parallel structure create? What point is King emphasizing?

6. **Analyze** Identify two examples of repetition in the speech. Explain why these words or phrases are important and how they advance King's argument.

7. **Evaluate** Why do you think King's "I Have a Dream" speech is remembered as one of the most significant speeches in American history? Explain what makes the speech memorable and how it contributes to the ideal of an American society.

PERFORMANCE TASK

Writing Activity: Analysis In Collection 1, you read another seminal United States speech, Abraham Lincoln's Gettysburg Address. Compare the ideas in Lincoln's speech to "I Have a Dream." Write a one- to two-page analytical essay in which you compare how Lincoln and King address the theme of freedom.

1. Identify each speaker's purpose.

2. Evaluate how the idea of freedom is articulated in each speech.

3. Give examples of how each speaker uses rhetorical devices to achieve his purpose.

4. Use the conventions of standard English.

Assign this
performance task.

PERFORMANCE TASK

W 2

Writing Activity: Analysis Have students work independently to write a draft of their analytical essay. Suggest that they review the three points that must be covered in their essay: the speaker's purpose or reason for making the speech, how each speaker frames the idea of freedom, and how each speaker uses rhetorical devices to make his points. When students have completed their draft, have them exchange papers with a partner and give each other constructive feedback. Then ask them to share their essays in small groups.

PRACTICE & APPLY

Analyzing the Text

RI 1, RI 2, RI 3,
RI 4, RI 5, RI 6,
RI 9

Possible answers:

1. *King's central claim is that "the Negro still is not free" (line 10). He supports the claim that African Americans do not enjoy complete freedom by pointing out that segregation, discrimination, and poverty still exist for the majority of African Americans (lines 12–13).*

2. *King structures his speech with topic sentences followed by evidence that provides examples of the statement. All of the evidence supports his claim and his argument. For example, in paragraph three, he talks about a "shameful condition" and then tells what the shameful condition is. To make his meaning clear, King uses an extended metaphor.*

3. *King mentions the Declaration of Independence directly in line 20, alludes to it in lines 23–24 ("unalienable rights"), and quotes from it in lines 98–99 ("We hold these truths . . ."). These allusions advance his argument by pointing out that the nation is failing to keep its promise and also by holding it up as an ideal that Americans can still choose to fulfill.*

4. *King develops this metaphor by relating common ideas of everyday banking to the more abstract ideas of "sacred obligation," "justice," "opportunity," and "freedom." He believes that African Americans were promised "unalienable rights," but that instead America has segregated African Americans and treated them unfairly.*

5. *"This is no time to…" and "Now is the time to…" are examples of parallel structure. King is using the structure to stress the concept of time and the urgency of the situation.*

6. *In paragraph three, King repeats "one hundred years later" four times. This emphasizes the length of the problem and the lack of solution. It shows that African Americans have already been patient and that there is little reason for them to continue waiting.*

7. *Answers will vary. King's speech is remembered because it encouraged people to change direction when it came to civil rights. King was "dreaming" of the ideal United States where all of the promises of freedom and human rights were kept. He invited all the nation's people to share that dream and live up to our potential as a society.*

PRACTICE & APPLY

Critical Vocabulary
RI 4, L 1a

Possible answers:

1. *King says that America has failed to keep a promise to guarantee the rights of people.* Defaulted *carries the connotation that the American people have failed to keep a binding agreement.*

2. Segregation *is empty of hope and barren in its loneliness. Many in the audience have experienced the desolation of segregation and can relate to the need to abolish the practice.*

3. Degenerate *means to deteriorate and worsen. King's view is that violence is not a path to a solution, and that he would consider physical violence a deterioration in the power of the protests.*

4. *The freedom of white people and black people is inextricably bound because if all Americans are not free then no one's freedom is safe. If the government does not protect your neighbor's freedom, there's no guarantee it will protect yours, either.*

5. *A faithful person may suffer in this world, but the suffering is* redemptive *if the person is rewarded in heaven. Similarly, King suggests that people who suffer undeservedly while fighting for freedom will ultimately be rewarded.*

Language and Style: Repetition and Parallelism

Tell students that the examples on this page are just two of the many examples of repetition and parallelism in King's speech. Point out that many of the most famous lines in the speech use repetition and parallelism, and therein lies one of the most important reasons for these devices: they make an impact so that people remember the ideas.

Possible answers:

Students' revisions should focus on using repetition and parallelism to emphasize key words and phrases that clearly and forcefully express their thesis.

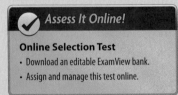

Assess It Online!

Online Selection Test
- Download an editable ExamView bank.
- Assign and manage this test online.

Critical Vocabulary
RI 4, L 1a

default   desolate   degenerate   inextricably   redemptive

Practice and Apply Answer the following questions in complete sentences, incorporating the Critical Vocabulary words and their meanings.

1. Look back at line 25. Why does King say that America has **defaulted,** and what makes this word choice especially effective?

2. Look back at line 38. In what ways is segregation **desolate**? How might referring to segregation as **desolate** help persuade listeners?

3. Look back at line 59. How is physical violence a good example of how protests might **degenerate**? How does this reflect King's views?

4. Look back at line 66. How is the freedom of white people **inextricably** bound to that of black people?

5. Look back at line 89. How and why does King use the word **redemptive** to link the concepts of freedom and religious faith?

Language and Style: Repetition and Parallelism

One grammatical feature that makes King's rhetoric so effective is his use of **repetition** and **parallelism**—expressing related ideas using similar grammatical constructions. By creating a pattern through repeated phrases and structures, King both creates a strong rhythm in his speech and links his ideas in listeners' minds. Here are some examples from "I Have a Dream":

Repetition

<u>We can never be satisfied</u> as long as the Negro is the victim of the unspeakable horrors of police brutality; <u>we can never be satisfied</u> as long as our bodies, heavy with the fatigue of travel, cannot gain lodging in the motels of the highways and the hotels of the cities; . . .

Parallelism

". . . we will be able <u>to work together</u>, <u>to pray together</u>, <u>to struggle together</u>, <u>to go to jail together</u>, <u>to stand up for freedom together</u> . . ."

Practice and Apply Look back at the essay you wrote for this selection's Performance Task. Find two places where you can revise your wording to make it parallel. Then, locate two places where you can use repetition for effect. Finally, write two sentences explaining how repetition and parallel structure helped you communicate your ideas to readers.

TO CHALLENGE STUDENTS . . .

Evaluate Effects of a Speech Would Martin Luther King Jr. be satisfied with the progress that he helped make? Have students think about King's purpose for writing and delivering his "I Have a Dream" speech. Point out that King was assassinated in 1968, four years after President Johnson signed significant civil rights legislation but before society as a whole made huge strides toward equality. Then have them write a brief analytical essay addressing these points:

- the purpose of King's "I Have a Dream" speech
- whether King achieved the goals he laid out in his speech
- examples from today that help support the argument that King did or did not achieve his goals

Analyze Language

RI 4

TEACH

Tell students that Martin Luther King Jr. is speaking from a platform of certainty. He knows that what he is saying is nothing less than the truth. To help his audience feel this same conviction, he weaves **allusions** into his speech. Explain that allusions are references to well-known people, places, events, or literary works. Discuss with students the reasons why King uses allusions in his speech:

- to prompt his audience to think of a particular idea, concept, or principle without having to explain it
- to evoke feelings in his audience, such as pride, patriotism, and desire for justice
- to offer authoritative proof in support of his argument
- to characterize people or situations in order to help the audience see a similarity or difference

Explain that the quotations in King's speech are a form of allusion. The quotations jog listeners' memories, making them think of the works from which they are taken and what those works represent. For example, King quotes from the Bible in lines 80–82; he uses the recognized authority of this work to support what he is saying.

Point out that King also alludes to images or ideas, expecting that the audience will recognize his reference. For example, the speech takes place at the Lincoln Memorial; he refers to "this hallowed spot," an allusion to the ideal of freedom for all Americans that Lincoln represents.

COLLABORATIVE DISCUSSION

Display these sets of lines on the board: 1–9, 17–24, 120–140. Organize students into groups and ask them to identify the allusion in each passage. Have them discuss what purpose each allusion has and how it helps to intensify King's meaning in that part of the speech or the speech as a whole. Invite groups to contribute their insights to the class.

Analyze Seminal U.S. Documents

RI 9

RETEACH

Remind students that U.S. seminal documents are those that set forth principles and ideals that become the foundation for the philosophy, laws, and values by which we define ourselves as Americans. Explain that although seminal documents may arise from different historical contexts, they can have similar purposes and express related themes and concepts. Have students review King's speech and the Gettysburg Address in Collection 1.

- Ask: How is the purpose of both speeches similar? *(Both encourage Americans to fight for freedom and equality.)*
- Have students consider these lines from the Gettysburg Address: "Four score and seven years ago our fathers brought forth on this continent, a new nation conceived in Liberty, and dedicated to the proposition that all men are created equal." What lines from King's speech echo this ideal? *(Accept any lines that reflect the idea that to be great, all must be free.)* How might you sum up the themes of both speeches? *(Freedom is worth fighting for; without equality there can be no true freedom.)*

 LEVEL UP TUTORIALS Assign the following *Level Up* tutorial: **Primary and Secondary Sources.**

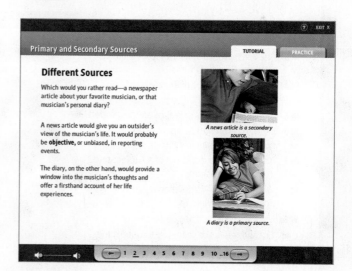

INDEPENDENT READING

Have students apply what they have learned to another speech or document. Ask: What is the purpose of the document? What theme does it convey?

COMPARE ANCHOR TEXTS AND MEDIA

ANCHOR TEXT

from Nobody Turn Me Around: A People's History of the 1963 March on Washington

MEDIA   **AMERICA The Story of Us: March on Washington**

History Writing by Charles Euchner   Video

Why These Texts?

Students often encounter a subject that is explored in different ways through various mediums. This lesson explores the March on Washington through a third-person account of the march and through a video explaining the march and its significance.

Key Learning Objective: The student will be able to analyze connections between ideas and events and analyze accounts in different mediums.

▲ Text Complexity Rubric

RI 1 Cite textual evidence.

RI 2 Determine a central idea.

RI 3 Analyze how the author unfolds ideas or events.

RI 4 Analyze the impact of word choices on meaning and tone.

RI 5 Analyze how ideas or claims are developed.

RI 6 Determine an author's point of view or purpose and analyze rhetoric.

RI 7 Analyze various accounts of a subject told in different mediums.

W 3 Write narratives to develop real or imagined experiences.

W 3d Use precise words and phrases.

L 4c Consult reference materials to determine etymology.

	from Nobody Turn Me Around	AMERICA The Story of Us: March on Washington
Quantitative Measures	Lexile: 1030L	Lexile: N/A
Qualitative Measures	**Levels of Meaning/Purpose** more than one purpose; implied, easily identified from context	**Levels of Meaning/Purpose** implied, but easy to infer
	Structure genre traits less common to informational text	**Structure** less conventional
	Language Conventionality and Clarity more complex sentence structure	**Language Conventionality and Clarity** some unfamiliar or academic words
	Knowledge Demands a number of references to other texts	**Knowledge Demands** specialized knowledge required
Reader/Task Considerations	• Teacher determined • Vary by individual reader and type of text • See the Text X-Ray for suggested Reader/Task Considerations.	

English Language Support Before teaching, use the Text X-Ray below for an overview of the text's complexity. The Text X-Ray and the supports and scaffolds in the Teacher's Edition will help you guide students of different skill levels.

Meaning Making

Language Development

Effective Expression

Content Knowledge

Foundational Skills

Text Complexity: Qualitative Measures

▲ Levels of Meaning/Purpose

Help students analyze accounts in different mediums.
- Teacher's Edition side notes, pp. 71, 72
- Close Read Screencasts, p. 55
- Analyze Accounts in Different Mediums, p. 72

Support students in identifying central ideas.
- When Students Struggle, pp. 58, 63

Help students determine an author's point of view.
- Teacher's Edition side note, p. 61

Help students analyze the audio portion of a video.
- English Language Support, p. 71

ZOOM IN ON **ANALYZING A VIDEO ACCOUNT** Some students may struggle to understand the information in the video as it plays in real time. Place students in mixed-ability pairs or small groups. Have them watch the video once and then play it again, pausing at logical points. During the pauses, students should ask and answer questions about the preceding segment and take notes. Encourage them to replay portions of the video as many times as necessary until they feel confident in their comprehension.

▲ Structure

Help students analyze ideas and events.
- Teacher's Edition side notes, pp. 55, 56, 57, 59, 60, 63, 64, 65, 67, 68, 69
- When Students Struggle, p. 61
- Strategies for Annotation, p. 69
- Analyze Ideas and Events, p. 69

Prompt students to evaluate the structure of the text.
- To Challenge Students, p. 64

To reteach analyzing ideas and events, see
- Analyze Ideas and Events, p. 72a

▶ *Use It!* *Level Up* **Tutorial:** Point-by-Point Organization

ZOOM IN ON **ANALYZING STRUCTURE** Tell students that the history text has an unusual **structure** that alternates between several different types of text. Have them imagine that the author took a printed copy of King's speech, cut it into sections, and then inserted his own comments and other information between the sections. Have pairs skim the text and label each section with the following categories or others that they create.

- text from King's speech
- description of the setting at the National Mall
- analysis of King's text
- description of King
- description of people's reactions to the speech

▲ Language Conventionality and Clarity

Teach unfamiliar vocabulary in context.

- Teacher's Edition Critical Vocabulary notes, pp. 55, 56, 58, 61, 62, 67, 70
- English Language Support, p. 62
- Applying Academic Vocabulary, pp. 57, 66

Help students analyze the impact of word choice.

- Teacher's Edition side notes, pp. 55, 56, 57, 58, 60, 61, 62, 63, 64, 65, 66, 67, 68

Guide students to interpret print cues.

- English Language Support, p. 56
- When Students Struggle, p. 67

Help students define words with Greek and Latin roots.

- Teacher's Edition side note, p. 70

ZOOM IN ON ANALYZING WORD CHOICE Point out that in line 45, Euchner writes that "the oration becomes poetry." Discuss what students can **infer** from **print cues** in the remainder of the history text.

- Compare lines 46–55 to the same words in "I Have a Dream." What is different? *(The actual speech is in prose, but Euchner sets these lines as if they are poetry, with a line break at the end of each sentence.)*
- What does the poetry format help you notice about King's words? *(The repetition of "one hundred years later" is more obvious because it appears at the beginning of each new line. The rhythm of the speech is emphasized.)*

Ask students to notice what other sections of the speech are set as poetry and to think about Euchner's reason in each case.

▲ Knowledge Demands

Support English Learners in understanding the historical context of the text and the video.

- Teacher's Edition Background note, p. 55

ZOOM IN ON BUILDING HISTORICAL KNOWLEDGE Make sure students understand Euchner's reference to Lincoln's "freeing the slaves, with the simple stroke of a pen in the middle of a bloody war" (lines 41–42). The "stroke of a pen" is Lincoln's signing his name to the Emancipation Proclamation, which officially freed all slaves in the Confederate states. Lincoln's signature was enough because he used his authority as commander in chief to enact the proclamation—it was not passed by Congress. The "bloody war" is the Civil War, which took place between 1861 and 1865.

▲ Suggested Reader/Task Considerations

You might consider the following before assigning this text and video to students.

- Will students understand their **purpose for reading** the history text?
- Will students struggle with complex questions asked about the text?

ZOOM IN ON SUPPORTING COMPREHENSION

- Students may question the purpose of reading Euchner's account, which repeats much of Dr. King's speech. Explain that they should read this account to compare Euchner's analysis to their own and also to learn how listeners responded to each part of the speech.
- Support students in responding to question 4 on page 69 by identifying possible examples of historic events and biblical allusions: lines 23–29, 138–143, 144–147, 164–171, 246–248.

TEACH

CLOSE READ

Background Have students read the background information here and also review the background information for the "I Have a Dream" speech.

AS YOU READ Direct students to use the As You Read note to focus their reading.

Analyze Ideas and Events (LINES 1–22)

RI 3

Explain that authors often structure an analysis of an event by providing background in the introduction. Point out that Euchner offers background information that includes details about the way King spoke.

A **ASK STUDENTS** to reread lines 1–22 and notice the details about King's accent and how he pronounced specific words. Then have them explain what Euchner accomplishes by providing these details. *(He appeals to the reader's senses, helping the reader to "hear" King.)*

Analyze Impact of Word Choice (LINES 1–2)

RI 4

Point out that Euchner opens the selection with a **simile**, a figure of speech that compares two dissimilar things using the word *like* or *as*.

B **ASK STUDENTS** to read lines 1–2 and explain what the simile means. *(It compares King's voice to thunder, meaning he begins speaking slowly but builds up speed and volume. It emphasizes the power of King's speech.)*

CRITICAL VOCABULARY

cadence: Euchner explains that King creates rhythm in his speech by emphasizing certain syllables. **ASK STUDENTS** why creating his own cadence might capture the audience's attention. *(King did not speak in a monotone. His rhythmic speech engaged the audience and emphasized powerful words.)*

parallel: Euchner describes two similar stories of exile and return: one about the Jews in Egypt and one about blacks in America. **ASK STUDENTS** how the story of the Jews' exile is parallel to that of black people's exile in America. *(Both groups were held as slaves, both struggled to maintain their identity; both endured because of their faith in God.)*

Background *This excerpt from* Nobody Turn Me Around: A People's History of the 1963 March on Washington *provides a detailed account of one of the most iconic days in American history.*

from Nobody Turn Me Around: A People's History of the 1963 March on Washington
History Writing by Charles Euchner

AS YOU READ Note how the author structures the text to help you visualize the event. Write down any questions you generate.

Always, he begins slowly, like thunder rolling from a distance before a great storm.

Martin Luther King speaks deliberately, like a 45 rpm record being played at 33⅓ rpm speed.[1] His long, thick, baritone words stretch out to establish a new mood. In a low drawl, he emphasizes syllables to create his own **cadence**, to bring his audience into the flow of emotions.

"I am *happy* to *join* with you to*day*," he says, sounding mournful, "in what will go *down* in *his*tory as the *greatest* demonstration for *freedom* in the *his*tory of our *nation*."

Martin Luther King invokes Abraham Lincoln and tells the long, hard story of the subjection of American blacks.

"Five score years ago, a great American, in whose symbolic shadow we stand today, signed the Emancipation Proclamation. This momentous decree came as a great beacon light of hope to millions of Negro slaves who had been seared in the flames of withering injustice. It came as a joyous daybreak to end the long night of their captivity."

King's Southern accent, softened by time spent in his family's bourgeois circles[2] and tempered by years in the North, put a special emphasis on his words: "in the *his-tor-eh* of our *ow-a* nation" . . . "a *gret* American" . . . "symbolic *shadda*" . . . "*gret beckon* light."

Long night of captivity. King's brooding voice tells two **parallel** stories of exile and return. For hundreds of years, Jews were held in captivity, as slaves, in Egypt—like blacks in America. They struggled to maintain their own identity—like blacks in America. They endured because of their faith in God—like blacks in

cadence
(kād′ns) *n.* lyrical rhythm.

parallel
(păr′ə-lĕl′) *adj.* related; corresponding.

---

[1] **45 rpm record . . . 33 ½ speed:** a recorded disc, designed to spin on a turntable at 45 revolutions per minute, playing at a slower speed (33 ½ rpm), which produces a deeper, drawn-out sound.
[2] **bourgeois circles** (bŏŏr-zhwä′): middle-class group of friends.

Nobody Turn Me Around **55**

Close Read Screencasts ▶ *View It!*

Modeled Discussions

Have students click the *Close Read* icons in their eBooks to access the screencast in which readers discuss and annotate the following key passage:

• Euchner describes King's use of anaphora (lines 33–40).

As a class, view and discuss this video. Then have students pair up to do an independent close read of an additional passage—a white minister in the audience connects with King's discussion of his "dream" (lines 313–318).

Analyze Impact of Word Choice (LINES 33–40)

RI 4

Reiterate that **anaphora** is a type of repetition in which the first word or words are repeated in a series of statements.

C **CITE TEXT EVIDENCE** Point out that in analyzing King's use of anaphora, Euchner himself uses this rhetorical device. Ask students to cite the lines in which Euchner uses anaphora. *(In lines 34–39, Euchner begins each statement with the word repetition.)* Ask students why they think Euchner used anaphora here. *(to demonstrate the use of anaphora; to keep his audience involved)*

Analyze Ideas and Events (LINES 41–57)

RI 3

Point out that analysis of an historical event usually depends on **primary sources**—materials from the time the event happened. These include speeches, documents, and firsthand accounts such as interviews, television footage, photographs, and news reports.

D **ASK STUDENTS** what main primary source Euchner uses for his analysis. *(King's speech)* Then ask them if they think Euchner used other primary sources and how they know. *(Euchner probably used firsthand accounts of the event and film footage to be able to describe how King spoke and how he delivered his speech. Euchner probably interviewed people who attended the speech, as well.)*

CRITICAL VOCABULARY

invocation: Euchner describes how King repeats the phrase "one hundred years" as if he is asking for help or beginning a prayer.

ASK STUDENTS why Euchner describes King's repetition of "one hundred years" as an invocation. *(Each repetition of the phrase introduces a way in which African Americans have suffered, making the passage sound like a prayer asking for deliverance.)*

America. And then one day, they freed themselves from bondage—like blacks will, one day, as well.

30   His voice is steady, but King wants to find his pacing. If he moves slowly, he will not falter, and he will find a way to bring the crowd with him.

C   Right away, King uses anaphora, the repetition of key words and phrases at the beginning of successive statements. Repetition brings the listener back to a familiar place, then connects to a new thought or image. Repetition keeps the audience involved. Repetition makes it easy to remember the words and to get into a rhythm, as they become familiar. Repetition invites the call and response in black churches across the South. *Yeah! Uh-huh! Amen!*
40 *That's right!*

D   After recalling the story of Lincoln freeing the slaves, with the simple stroke of a pen in the middle of a bloody war, King laments the inferior position of blacks a century later. Each mournful repetition deepens the pain, raises the dramatic tension. Each repetition condemns the oppressor. The oration becomes poetry:

> But one hundred years later, the Negro still is not free.
> One hundred years later, the life of the Negro is still
>   sadly crippled by the manacles of segregation and
>   the chains of discrimination.
50 One hundred years later, the Negro lives on a lonely
>   island of poverty in the midst of a vast ocean of
>   material prosperity.
> One hundred years later, the Negro is still languished
>   in the corners of American society and finds
>   himself in exile in his own country.

King looks down at his text, shakes his head as he speaks. He rocks back and forth on the balls of his feet as he finds his rhythm.
Every **invocation** of "one hundred years" emphasizes the horrors of the black's position in American life. *Not free. Crippled.*
60 *Manacles. Chains. Lonely island of poverty. Languished in the corners. Exile in his own country.*

E   And then King introduces Clarence Jones's[3] metaphor of the bad check, so simple and so basic. A bad check represents bad faith, failed promises, broken contracts.

> In a sense we have come to our nation's capital to cash
>   a check. When the architects of our republic wrote
>   the magnificent words of the Constitution and the

invocation
(ĭn′və-kā′shən) *n.* a formal appeal, often used in prayer.

---

[3] **Clarence Jones:** (b. 1931) King's attorney and advisor, who helped prepare many speeches.

English Language Support

Language: Print Cues Point to lines 39–40 and 59–61 and explain that italics are used for different purposes, including the following:

- to indicate speech
- to indicate key themes or ideas
- to emphasize important words or phrases

ASK STUDENTS to reread the paragraphs that include lines 39–40 and lines 59–61 and use context clues to determine what the italics indicate. *(In lines 39–40, Euchner uses italics to indicate speech, specifically the responses from black congregations in the South. In lines 59–61, Euchner uses italics to indicate key ideas that represent the horrors of black people's position in American life.)*

Declaration of Independence, they were signing a promissory note to which every American was to fall heir. This note was a promise that all men— yes, black men as well as white men—would be guaranteed the unalienable rights of life, liberty, and the pursuit of happiness.

It is obvious today that America has defaulted on this promissory note insofar as her citizens of color are concerned. Instead of honoring this sacred obligation, America has given the Negro people a bad check, a check which has come back marked "insufficient funds."

The first burst of applauses rises up from the crowd.
"But we *refuse* to believe that the bank of justice is bankrupt. We *refuse* to believe that there are insufficient funds in the great vaults of opportunity of this nation."

APPLYING ACADEMIC VOCABULARY

entity	internal

THINK-PAIR-SHARE Have students discuss the following questions with a partner. Guide them to include the academic vocabulary words *enable* and *integrate* in their responses. Ask volunteers to share their responses.

- How do Eucher's descriptions of King's speaking patterns **enable** you to "hear" how king spoke?

- How does Eucher **integrate** the crowd's reaction with his analysis of King's words and their meaning?

CLOSE READ

Analyze Ideas and Events (LINES 62–80)   RI 3

Tell students that the **structure** of an informational text is the order in which the author presents ideas. The author must make the connections between ideas, sentences, and paragraphs clear. Point out that in lines 62–64, Euchner explains King's metaphor of a bad check.

E   CITE TEXT EVIDENCE Have students point to the text that Euchner uses to support his analysis of the bad check metaphor. *(lines 65–79; they are excerpts from King's speech)* Ask students how providing this excerpt after his analysis helps readers understand his point. *(Euchner reproduces the exact lines he has analyzed, allowing readers to read King's words with the analysis fresh in their minds.)*

Explain that Euchner's analysis of King's speech is unusual in that he does not simply provide a line-by-line interpretation of King's words. He also weaves in audience reactions.

F   CITE TEXT EVIDENCE Have students indicate where Euchner describes the audience's reaction to King's idea of the "bad check." *(line 80)* What is the effect of providing the audience's reaction? *(It helps readers understand the effect that King's words had on people that day.)*

Analyze Impact of Word Choice (LINES 81–83)   RI 4

Point out that **print cues** include punctuation as well as italics and boldface type. Explain that Euchner reproduces some of King's words in italics, even though most copies of the speech do not show words in italics.

G   ASK STUDENTS which word appears in italics, and why. *(The word* refuse *appears in italics to emphasize the stress that King likely put on the word as he pronounced it.)*

Analyze Impact of Word Choice (LINES 95–99)

RI 4

Point out that Euchner uses descriptive words and **figurative language**, or words and phrases whose meaning is not literal, to help convey the power of King's words and the atmosphere on the National Mall on the day that King delivered his speech.

Ⓗ ASK STUDENTS to reread lines 95–99 and explain why Euchner chose the verb *ripples*. What does he mean when he says King's line "releases some toxin from the body"? (Ripples *suggests that people did not respond with laughter all at once, but a little at a time. The reference to the toxin means that the man's laughter is a therapeutic counterpoint to the anger that had built up over racism.*)

Analyze Impact of Word Choice (LINES 114–118)

RI 4

Tell students that **mood** is the atmosphere or general feeling conveyed by the details an author includes. Point out that the mood can refer to the entire work or to one particular part of a work.

Ⓘ CITE TEXT EVIDENCE Have students reread lines 114–118 and describe the mood that Euchner creates in the paragraph, citing specific words that help create the mood. (The words quieted down, tinny sounds of the loudspeakers, whispers, soft breeze, *and* rippling *all help establish a mood of quiet anticipation and peacefulness.*)

CRITICAL VOCABULARY

civic: King calls attention to the Lincoln Memorial's power to make people feel a sense of community and citizenship.

ASK STUDENTS why the Lincoln Memorial might have a civic power. (*It reminds people of the struggle of African Americans and also the shared struggle of Americans during the Civil War. It is a reminder of our common history.*)

Laughter from the crowd. Shouts: "Uh huh!" "Yeah!" "Sure enough!"

"So we have come to cash this check—a check that will give us upon demand the riches of freedom and the security of justice."

A second, greater burst of applause.

Now King honors his country, calling attention to the **civic** power of Lincoln's monument. He rejects calls to "go slow" and "cool off."

"We have also come to this hallowed spot to remind America of *the fierce urgency of now*. This is no time to engage in the luxury of cooling off or to take the tranquilizing drug of gradualism."

The crowd ripples with recognition, then knowing laughter. A thin black man sitting close to the stage hears the tranquilizer reference, looks down for a moment, thoughtfully, then looks up and explodes in laughter. King's line releases some toxin from the body.

For this one moment, the stubbornness of racism lifts and the people revel in a moment of integrated community.

> Now is the time to make real the promises of democracy.
> Now is the time to rise from the dark and desolate valley of segregation to the sunlit path of racial justice.
> Now is the time to lift our nation from the quicksands of racial injustice to the solid rock of brotherhood.
> Now is the time to make justice a reality for all of God's children.

Each invocation pulls the audience into the future. And people in the crowd respond. *You got it! Yes it is! Yeah! Amen! Now is the time! Now! That's right!*

Across the Mall, people have quieted down. King's voice echoes, his baritone voice triumphing over the tinny sounds of the loudspeakers. Whispers can be heard in spots. A soft breeze, occasionally rippling over the crowd, is louder than the sounds of the masses below.

King now warns the Washington establishment—and the vast middle class, what one politician would call the "forgotten middle class" and the "silent majority"—that gradual improvements will not satisfy blacks anymore. Conflict could turn into a bloodbath unless the American people redeem the promise of freedom.

> It would be fatal for the nation to overlook the urgency of the moment.

civic
(sĭv′ĭk) *adj.* related to community and citizenship.

WHEN STUDENTS STRUGGLE...

After students read lines 119–123, discuss how King is speaking not only to the people in the audience, who for the most part agree with him, but also to the rest of the nation, including politicians and the white majority. Ask them how Euchner uses this passage to help convey one of the main points in King's speech. (*King wanted to warn the rest of the nation that African Americans would not be content until there was justice for them.*)

If students have trouble with the political vocabulary, help them define the words, including *establishment*, *middle class*, and *silent majority*, using the context of the paragraph.

This sweltering summer of the Negro's legitimate
    discontent will not pass until there is an
    invigorating autumn of freedom and equality.
Nineteen sixty-three is not an end, but a beginning.
130 Those who hope that the Negro needed to blow off
    steam and will now be content will have a rude
    awakening if the nation returns to business as usual.
There will be neither rest nor tranquility in America
    until the Negro is granted his citizenship rights.
The whirlwinds of revolt will continue to shake the
    foundations of our nation until the bright day of
    justice emerges.

Subtly, King conjures images of apocalypse. The "whirlwinds
of revolt" echo the countless moments where the Bible talks about
140 staggering catastrophe, when evil brings forth flood, famine,
drought, a plague of locusts, and the chaos of the Tower of Babel.[4]
As Jeremiah (4:20) teaches: "Disaster on disaster is proclaimed / For
the whole land is devastated."

" For this one moment, the stubbornness of racism lifts and the people revel in a moment of integrated community. "

King warns his people to maintain their own dignity, to avoid
the temptation to embrace bitterness or violence. He speaks to the
followers of Malcolm X, who offers a simpler, purer, solution—
fighting back, by any means necessary.[5]

---

[4] **Tower of Babel:** according to the bible, a tall structure built when people all
   spoke the same language. God disrupted the work by so confusing the language
   of the workers they could no longer work together.

[5] **Malcolm X...necessary:** (1925–1965) African American activist who believed
   that people should demand and protect their human rights in any way they can.

Image Credits:

CLOSE READ

Analyze Ideas and Events (LINES 138–143; 144–147)   RI 3

Tell students that the author of an informational text develops ideas with supporting details and examples. These may include direct quotes from other sources.

J   CITE TEXT EVIDENCE Have students identify the details Euchner uses to support his idea that King conjures images of apocalypse in his speech. *(He points out the phrase "whirlwinds of revolt" in King's speech and he says it echoes moments of catastrophe in the Bible, including "the chaos of the Tower of Babel.")*

Explain that authors often weave in **allusions**, or references to well-known people, events, or literary works that the author expects the audience to know. Point to the mention of Malcolm X in line 146 and encourage students to read the footnote at the bottom of the page.

K   ASK STUDENTS how mentioning Malcolm X helps underscore Euchner's point that King was warning people to reject violence. *(Euchner is contrasting the philosophy of Malcolm X with that of Martin Luther King Jr., suggesting that Malcolm X's followers, specifically, needed to heed King's message of nonviolence.)*

English Language Support

Language: Modifiers Explain that a **modifier** is a word or phrase that adds information. Modifiers can be **adjectives,** which tell more about a noun or pronoun, or **adverbs,** which tell more about a verb or adjective. For example, the adverb *subtly* in line 138 modifies the verb *conjures* and tells *how* King conjures images. The adjective *staggering* in line 140 modifies the noun *catastrophe.*

ASK STUDENTS to reread lines 138–147 and identify adjectives and adverbs and the words they modify. *(countless: adjective modifying moments; forth: adverb modifying brings; whole: adjective modifying land; their, own: adjectives modifying dignity; simpler, purer: adjectives modifying solution; any: adjective modifying means)*

Analyze Impact of Word Choice (LINES 152–158)

RI 4

Explain that in the tradition of black churches in the South, ministers use a technique of call and response, to which Euchner earlier alluded. The minister speaks, and congregants shout back words of agreement and encouragement.

 CITE TEXT EVIDENCE Have students reread lines 152–158 and cite the instance of call and response. *(King speaks in lines 152–153, and the audience responds with "O Lord! Amen! Yes! Sure enough!" in line 154.)* Ask students what the effect is of including this call and response in the text. *(It helps readers "hear" the exchange and visualize the atmosphere in the crowd that day and thus understand how King engaged the audience.)*

Analyze Ideas and Events

RI 3

(LINES 179–186)

Remind students that Euchner uses primary sources to support his analysis of events during the March on Washington.

M CITE TEXT EVIDENCE Point to lines 179–186 and have students reread the paragraph. Then ask them to cite the primary source Euchner uses to support his contention that not everyone could hear King's words. *(In lines 182–186, Euchner quotes Elsa Rael, who attended the speech.)* Ask students to explain the effect of including Ms. Rael's words. *(Readers feel as if they are listening to an interview. The quotation helps readers see and understand events from the perspective of the audience, and it also helps support Euchner's analysis.)*

"But there is something that I must say to my people who stand on the warm threshold which leads into the palace of justice. In the process of gaining our rightful place, we must not be guilty of wrongful deeds.

"Let us not seek to satisfy our thirst for freedom by drinking from the cup of bitterness and hatred."

O Lord! Amen! Yes! Sure enough!

"We must forever conduct our struggle on the high plane of dignity and discipline. We must not allow our creative protest to degenerate into physical violence. Again and again, we must rise to the majestic heights of meeting physical force with soul force.

"The marvelous new militancy which has engulfed the Negro community must not lead us to a distrust of all white people, for many of our white brothers, as evidenced by their presence here today, have come to realize"—his voice rises—"that their destiny is tied up with our destiny."

Marvelous militancy. All summer, critics of the civil rights movement have wondered why blacks cannot be more patient. The president, congressmen, newspaper publishers, TV commentators, professors, mayors, unions, corporate CEOs, churches, social organizations—everyone seemed to be saying to go slow. But the time for patience is over. Militancy—*marvelous militancy,* borne of great patience and suffering, expressed with love, and applied with the tools of nonviolence—is now the movement's watchword.

Cheers rise up, louder and more sustained than before. People smile.

"They have come to realize that their freedom is inextricably bound to our freedom. We cannot walk alone.

"As we walk, we must make the pledge that we shall always march ahead. We cannot turn back. There are those who are asking the devotees of civil rights, 'When will you be satisfied?'"

Not everyone could hear King's words. The sound system, the best available, still crackled and blanked out. Far from the Lincoln Memorial, people followed the words on transistor radios—and by watching the movement of bodies ahead. "Down near the front there were people jumping up, waving hands and flags and signs," Elsa Rael said. "We were a little out of it, so we had to make our own joy—so we were singing. We got small bursts of words from King and shut up."

We can never be satisfied as long as the Negro is
the victim of the unspeakable horrors of police
brutality.

APPLYING ACADEMIC VOCABULARY

decline	impose

THINK-PAIR-SHARE Have students turn to a partner to discuss the following questions. Guide students to include the academic vocabulary words *decline* and *impose* in their responses. Ask volunteers to share their responses with the class.

- Does King believe that the movement will **decline** if protesters resort to violence? Cite text evidence in your discussion.
- How did the brutality that police **imposed** on the African American community likely affect King?

190   We can never be satisfied, as long as our bodies, heavy
        with the fatigue of travel, cannot gain lodging in the
        motels of the highways and the hotels of the cities.
    We cannot be satisfied as long as the Negro's basic
        mobility is from a smaller ghetto to a larger one.
    We can never be satisfied as long as our children
        are stripped of their selfhood and robbed of their
        dignity by signs stating "For Whites Only."
    We cannot be satisfied as long as a Negro in
        Mississippi cannot vote and a Negro in New York
200   believes he has nothing for which to vote.
    No, no, we are not satisfied, and we will not be
        satisfied until justice rolls down like waters and
        righteousness like a mighty stream.

        With each line, King increases the stakes for his movement. He
begins with police brutality, the search for night lodging and food,
and life in the ghetto. He moves on to children's dignity and the
right to vote. He ends with the prophet Amos's great image of the
Kingdom of Heaven on earth.
        Each round gets cheers. First scattered clapping and cheers and
210 calls. *Yes!* Then more. *That's right!* Finally, huge applause. *My Lord!*
        Every good preacher—every good leader—connects with the
real circumstances of his audience's lives. *I know your pain. I have
shared in your pain. I have been beaten and jailed and* **reviled**. *I have
not forgotten how you have suffered. I know, so you can trust me.*
King has spent a decade learning about the problems of the people
assembled before him. He has worked, intimately, with people at
the highest and lowest levels of society.

revile
(rĭ-vīl′) *v.* to
condemn or insult.

        I am not unmindful that some of you have come here
        out of great trials and tribulations.
220   Some of you have come fresh from narrow jail cells.
    Some of you have come from areas where your quest
        for freedom left you battered by the storms of
        persecution and staggered by the winds of police
        brutality.
    You have been the veterans of creative suffering.
    Continue to work with the faith that unearned
        suffering is redemptive.

        That brief phrase—*unearned suffering is redemptive*—strikes
Harold Bragg "like an electric shock."
230   Harold and his wife, Lynn, traveled all night from Kent, Ohio,
in their VW Beetle. Harold sits on a stool, holding an umbrella over

WHEN STUDENTS STRUGGLE...

Direct students to lines 211–217. Point out that Euchner introduces his topic
in the first sentence and then uses subsequent sentences to support the
topic sentence. If a paragraph is not clear, students should focus on the first
sentence and then determine whether subsequent sentences support it.

ASK STUDENTS how the last sentence in the paragraph helps support the
first. *(The fact that King has worked with people in all levels of society supports
the idea that he connects with real circumstances.)*

LEVEL UP TUTORIALS For additional support, assign the
following *Level Up* tutorial: **Main Idea and Supporting Details.**

TEACH

CLOSE READ

Determine Point of View (LINES 211–217)
RI 6

Tell students that understanding an author's
perspective or point of view can help them analyze a
text.

ASK STUDENTS to reread lines 211–217 and then
to explain how the lines provide clues to the author's
perspective on Martin Luther King Jr. *(Phrases like
"every good preacher" and "every good leader" and
sentences like "He has worked, intimately, with people
at the highest and lowest levels of society." indicate
that Euchner admires King.)* Then ask students how
knowing the author's perspective might help them
evaluate his analysis. *(They might look for instances in
which Euchner's admiration has influenced his analysis,
perhaps by making him inclined only to praise and not
to criticize King's work.)*

Analyze Impact of Word Choice (LINES 212–214)
RI 4

Point out that in lines 212–214, Euchner adds in italics
the sentiments that he believes King signals with his
words, his style, and the work he has done.

ASK STUDENTS why Euchner included these
sentences. *(They help demonstrate the point that King
is a good preacher who connects with and understands
his people.)* How does the repetition of the word *I*
and the parallel construction in these sentences help
make Euchner's point? *(The repetition and parallel
construction help emphasize King's connection with the
people, his solidarity with and understanding of their
suffering.)*

> **CRITICAL VOCABULARY**
>
> **revile**: King, like other African Americans, has been
> condemned and insulted.
>
> **ASK STUDENTS** to explain why Euchner suggests
> that King and other African Americans have been
> reviled. *(Segregation and police brutality indicate
> that they have been reviled.)*

Analyze Impact of Word Choice (LINES 228–233)

RI 4

Tell students that Euchner chooses his words carefully to ensure that they convey the meaning he intends. Remind them that he also uses figurative language in his analysis to help make his writing interesting and to help readers see, hear, and feel the intensity of the day.

P **CITE TEXT EVIDENCE** Have students identify the two similes in lines 228–233. *("like an electric shock" in line 229; "like it was a lesson from a great master" in line 233)* Ask students what the similes mean and why Euchner includes them in the text. *("Like an electric shock" means that the words had a powerful effect on Harold. "Like it was a lesson from a great master" means that they listened intently and with reverence. Euchner includes the similes to help readers understand the audience's reaction.)* Have students explain the effect of referring to Harold Bragg as Harold, rather than Mr. Bragg or Bragg. *(It makes him seem more familiar and makes the passage in which he is interviewed seem more like a conversation.)*

CRITICAL VOCABULARY

expanse: Harold's father was shot by a jealous white farmer because his father owned a large area of land.

ASK STUDENTS to explain what exactly would have made the white man jealous that a black man owned an expanse. *(He was jealous that a black man did well enough to own so much land.)*

P Lynn's head to block the sun. For the first part of King's speech, they listen to King "like it was a lesson from a great master."

Now the idea of suffering for redemption surges through Harold's body. He remembers his father telling him about his grandfather—one of the few black landowners in Alabama—sitting on a horse, getting shot by a white farmer who was jealous that a colored man could command such an **expanse**. His father, five years old when this happened back in 1917, saw his father fall dead off the horse.

240   The lesson his father and mother passed on when he told their children that story was: "You return hatred with love."

King's whole speech has told of the hard, violent, brutal, unfair, unjust life of blacks in America. The wrong people have suffered. So many people have been teargassed, beaten, kicked, burned, bombed, shot.

expanse
(ĭk-spăns´) *n.* a large area.

English Language Support

Vocabulary: Affixes Point out that in English, adding affixes, or word parts, to base words is common. Point to the word *unfair* in line 242 and explain that the affix *un-* added to the base word *fair* changes the meaning from "just" to "not just." Point out that adding *-ed* to a verb changes the verb from present tense to past tense, as in the word *bombed* in line 245.

ASK STUDENTS to determine the base word and affix of each of the following words: *unjust* (line 243), *suffered* (line 243), *burned* (line 244). Then ask students to explain how the affix changes the meaning of each word. *(un- changes meaning of just from "fair" to "unfair"; -ed changes tense of suffer and burn from present to past)*

But that suffering—like Christ's suffering on the cross—can bring a better day. That suffering can change people's hearts. That suffering can clear poison from the system.

Then change can come.

250 *Unearned suffering is redemptive.* Believe it, and you will fight on—with Martin. Disbelieve it, and you will be gripped by despair—or the combative, uncompromising, separatist jingoism of Malcolm.[6]

For now, the crowd stands with King. Even the separatists stand with King, now.

For that redemption to happen—to change the world—people need to return to their homes to fight and suffer, still more, for the cause of justice. So:

> Go back to Mississippi,
> go back to Alabama,
> 260 go back to South Carolina,
> go back to Georgia,
> go back to Louisiana,
> go back to the slums and ghettos of our northern
>   cities,
> knowing that somehow this situation can and will be
>   changed. Let us not wallow in the valley of despair,
> I say to you today, my friends.

Just feet from King, Mahalia Jackson[7] calls out. Mahalia is an old family friend of the Kings. She has been a guest in the Kings' 270 house. She was with King in Detroit about a month ago when King talked about a dream.

"Tell them about the dream, Martin!" she shouts. "*Please . . . tell them about the dream!*"

King does not hear her, but he doesn't need to hear her. He already knows he's going to talk about the dream. He shouted out his dream last night, in his hotel room, after everyone else went to bed.

Clarence Jones, sitting about fifteen feet away, sees King grab the podium, lean back, and turn over his prepared text. "These 280 people don't know it," Jones says, "but they are about to go to *church.*"

> So even though we face the difficulties of today and
>   tomorrow, I still have a dream.
> It is a dream deeply rooted in the American Dream . . . .

---

[6] **separatist jingoism of Malcolm:** Malcolm X's belief that African Americans should develop and support their own social institutions and communities.

[7] **Mahalia Jackson:** (1911–1972) a leading African American singer of gospel music who became very active in the civil-rights movement.

WHEN STUDENTS STRUGGLE . . .

Direct students to lines 250–267. Ask students to reread this passage and to discuss how Euchner uses the passage to help readers understand one of the goals of King's speech—what he was trying to accomplish that day. *(Euchner interprets King's lines that begin "Go back..." by suggesting that King urged followers to go back to where they came from and to stand firm in the knowledge that their unearned, unjust suffering will be rewarded with justice.)*

 LEVEL UP TUTORIALS For additional support, assign the following *Level Up* tutorial: **Main Idea and Supporting Details.**

CLOSE READ

Analyze Ideas and Events (LINES 268–277)   RI 3

Remind students that Euchner unfolds his analysis by proceeding through the words of the speech and weaving in interpretation and audience reaction. Point out that he begins the discussion of King's most famous lines from the speech by pivoting the topic to focus on an audience member.

Q CITE TEXT EVIDENCE Have students reread lines 268–277 and explain what they learn about the origin of the "I have a dream" lines. *(King spoke about the ideas in the lines as long as a month before; he shouted them in his hotel room the night before.)* Point out that Euchner had explained that the bad check metaphor was written by someone else. Ask students why Euchner provided these specific details about the "I have a dream" lines in the speech. *(Euchner wants to make the point that the speech's most famous lines were written by King himself.)*

Analyze Impact of Word Choice (LINES 278–284)   RI 4

Point out that in lines 279–281, Euchner notes that Clarence Jones, King's advisor, watched as King turned over his speech and then said, "These people don't know it, but they are about to go to *church.*" Remind students that King was a minister.

R ASK STUDENTS to reread lines 278–284 and explain what Jones may have meant by the statement. *(King has shifted from reading a prepared speech to speaking extemporaneously like the preacher he is. Jones's statement implies that the speech will become more exciting, more passionate, more inspiring.)*

Analyze Ideas and Events   RI 3

(LINES 297–301)

Remind students that Euchner continues to pivot from the speech and interpretation of its language to the reactions of audience members.

S **CITE TEXT EVIDENCE** Have students reread lines 297–301 and explain how Pritchard is different from the other people whose stories and reactions Euchner has featured, namely Harold Bragg and Mahalia Jackson. *(Pritchard is white; the others were African American.)* Ask students why Euchner may have made a point of mentioning people's race. *(He wanted readers to understand that people from all backgrounds listened to King's speech and were moved by it.)* Point out that Euchner relays details about Richard Pritchard, including when and how he arrived at the speech, how he felt when he heard King, and why he attended the March on Washington. Ask students where Euchner likely got such information. *(He either interviewed Pritchard after the event, watched interviews of people during and after the event, or read an interview with Pritchard that was conducted after the event.)*

Analyze Impact of Word   RI 4
Choice   (LINES 302–304)

Tell students to continue to look for examples of figurative language and the use of italics to emphasize specific words.

T **ASK STUDENTS** to reread lines 302–304 and to explain the meaning of "lightning shoots through his body." *(The words wake him up or shock him.)* Then point out in line 303 how Euchner adds the word *feels* in italics and set off by dashes. Discuss why he does this and how the addition of the italicized word changes the meaning of the sentence. *(Euchner adds the word* feel *in italics to emphasize the word. It changes the meaning of the sentence in that Pritchard went beyond remembering his dream—he stepped back into the dream for that moment.)*

> I have a dream that one day this nation will rise up and live out the true meaning of its creed: "We hold these truths to be self-evident: that all men are created equal."
> I have a dream that one day on the red hills of Georgia the sons of former slaves and the sons of former slave owners will be able to sit down together at the table of brotherhood.
> I have a dream that one day even the state of Mississippi, a state sweltering with the heat of injustice, sweltering with the heat of oppression, will be transformed into an oasis of freedom and justice.

290

S Richard Pritchard, a skinny white preacher from Wisconsin who returned to the United States from Africa just last night, sits by the reflecting pool. When his wife told him about the march, he 300 jumped into a car at his family's home in New Jersey. All day he's been jet-lagged and weary from his early morning drive.

But now, lightning shoots through his body as he hears about the dream. He remembers—*feels*—his own dream, which called him to the ministry decades before. **T**

Pritchard became a minister because he believed God saved him as a small child, when he spent three years in the hospital

“ **Talk about the dream transforms time and space.** ”

TO CHALLENGE STUDENTS . . .

Evaluate the Selection Has Euchner succeeded in presenting an analysis of King's speech that is thorough, insightful, and engaging? Have students meet in groups to discuss these aspects of the selection and whether each is or is not effective:

- the use of extensive quotations from the speech
- the inclusion of stories about people who heard the speech
- the analysis of King's style and content
- Euchner's overall style of writing

with tuberculosis. And then, as a young priest, he saw racism in God's own flock. White priests wouldn't take assignments in black churches—and so he decided to become the pastor of a black parish in Kansas City. Later, at a different church, members of his own parish made racist statements. Didn't they understand that God loved blacks as much as whites?

"My dream was to make Christ more realistic," he says. "I used to talk about it—*my dream*. When I was a kid I used to hear how the English talked about the Welsh as savages in the hills, and that's what they were saying about blacks. I could feel how blacks would feel. In Christ there is no Jew or Greek, slave or free, male or female. We are all free in Christ."

So skinny you can see his bones, the Reverend Pritchard dangles his feet in the water. He is being baptized anew. King's dream is his dream. The image almost removes him from the throng, and at the same time connects him even more with the throng.

"It's funny, it hit me with such force."

> I have a dream that my four little children will one
>   day live in a nation where they will not be judged
>   by the color of their skin but by the content of their
>   character.
> I have a dream today.
> I have a dream that one day, down in Alabama, with
>   its vicious racists, with its governor having his
>   lips dripping with the words of interposition and
>   nullification; one day right there in Alabama, little
>   black boys and black girls will be able to join hands
>   with little white boys and white girls as sisters and
>   brothers.
> I have a dream today.
> I have a dream that one day every valley shall be
>   exalted, every hill and mountain shall be made
>   low, the rough places will be made plain, and the
>   crooked places, will be made straight, and the glory
>   of the Lord shall be revealed, and all flesh shall see
>   it together.

Talk about the dream transforms time and space. What might come to pass, later, seems at hand, *now*. With faith, ideals can be more real than the pain or poverty of the here and now.

Sitting on a patch of grass far from the Lincoln Memorial, sipping cold drinks from thermoses, Ruth bat Mordecai and some

CLOSE READ

Analyze Ideas and Events (LINES 313–324)

RI 3

Tell students that in unfolding his analysis of the March on Washington and King's speech, Euchner draws connections between the audience members whose reactions he records and the words of King's speech.

Ⓤ **CITE TEXT EVIDENCE** Have students reread lines 313–324 and explain what central word or idea Euchner uses to connect Pritchard to King's speech. *(the dream, the idea that all people can be equal and free)* Then ask students what the significance is of Euchner's statement "King's dream is his dream." *(It shows that King's words spoke to people, that people identified with what he was saying. It also shows that whites as well as blacks agreed with King.)*

Analyze Impact of Word Choice (LINE 344)

RI 4

Point to line 344 and discuss Euchner's statement "Talk about the dream transforms time and space."

Ⓥ **ASK STUDENTS** what Euchner means by the statement and how it helps readers understand the effect King's words had on people. *(It means that people felt the possibilities of equality as never before, almost as if the changes were being wrought right then.)*

English Language Support

Language: Pronoun Referents Remind students that a **pronoun** is a word used in place of a noun. Point out that common pronouns include *I, me, she, her, he, him, you, it, they, them, who,* and *whom.* Explain that identifying to whom or what a pronoun refers usually involves looking for the noun most recently mentioned. Use a whiteboard to project lines 319–323. Invite volunteers to mark it up. Have them use a different color to highlight each set of pronouns and their corresponding referents.

> So skinny you can see his bones, the Reverend Pritchard
>
> dangles his feet in the water. He is being baptized anew. King's

Analyze Impact of Word Choice on Tone (LINES 351–369)

RI 4

Point out that the **tone** of a work conveys an author's attitude toward his audience and toward the subject matter he is covering. Explain that word choice and sentence structure help convey the tone of a passage. Tone can be formal, humorous, poignant, joyous, or condescending, to name a few.

 ASK STUDENTS what tone Euchner uses in lines 351–369 and which words help create that tone. *(Euchner uses a poignant, joyous tone. He uses words such as* laughing, joy, unutterable beauty, tears, *and* Promised Land *to convey the tone.)*

Tell students that Euchner reproduces dialogue and sometimes dialect, or the way people speak in a particular region, to allow readers to "hear" the conversations and exclamations of people in the audience.

X CITE TEXT EVIDENCE Have students reread lines 361–369 and point to the lines that help them "hear" people's exclamations, the lines that help them feel as if they, too, are witnesses to the event. *(lines 362–366)* Then ask them to explain what print cues best convey the way people spoke. *(Euchner draws out a word in line 365. He uses ellipses to indicate when a voice trails off and italics to indicate when a word is stressed. Exclamation marks indicate shouting.)*

---

kids from a New York–based American Jewish Congress youth
350 group listen to Martin Luther King's dream.

As King gives voice to his dream, Ruth watches some black boys nearby. The boys laugh as King's voice climbs the ladder, higher and higher. They laugh so freely that their bodies shake. Ruth knows the crowd includes cynics, and she resents having her experience of King's dream ruined by *these ones.* How can you openly mock *Dr. King*—at an event like *this*? And nobody seems to care!

"Suddenly," she recalls, "we understand. The black boys are laughing not in mockery but in joy—at the utter preposterousness
360 of what Dr. King promises, and at its unutterable beauty."

Across the Mall, people call out the lines to each other. **X**
"I have a dream," one says,
"That *one* day, little black boys and black girls . . ." says another.
"I have a *dream!*" someone else says.
"*Dowwwn* in Ala*bama* . . ." comes the response.
Strangers shout out: "I have a *dream!*"
Tears fill Harold Bragg's eyes. "It's like being before the pearly gates, as though we had reached the Promised Land," he says, "even though King was laying out what was *to come.*"

370 With this dream, King brings his audience into a separate world, a distant, far-off place, but still so familiar. What is unreal is also very real.

Then King moves to sustain his people for the hard journey ahead. He reminds the crowd that they need faith—stronger than any troubles of the moment—to realize the dream.

> This is our hope. This is the faith that I go back to the
>   South with.
> With this faith we will be able to hew out of the
>   mountain of despair a stone of hope.
380 With this faith we will be able to transform the
>   jangling discords of our nation into a beautiful
>   symphony of brotherhood.
> With this faith we will be able to work together, to pray
>   together, to struggle together, to go to jail together,
>   to stand up for freedom together, knowing that we
>   will be free one day.

King connects simple statements, repeated again and again—"One hundred years later," "Now is the time," "We cannot be satisfied," "Go back," "I have a dream," "With this faith"—to
390 America's true national anthem.

APPLYING ACADEMIC VOCABULARY

enable	reveal

THINK-PAIR-SHARE Have students turn to a partner to discuss the following questions. Guide students to include the academic vocabulary words *enable* and *reveal* in their responses. Ask volunteers to share their responses with the class.

- How does Euchner's use of print cues to reproduce dialogue and dialect **enable** you to "hear" the words people spoke?

- What does Euchner's word choice **reveal** about his attitude toward his subject and his audience?

"This will be the day," he says, "when all of God's children will be able to sing with a new meaning, 'My country, *'tis* of thee, sweet land of *liberty,* of *thee* I sing. Land where my *fathers* died, land of the *pilgrim's* pride, from *every* mountainside, *let freedom ring.*' And if America is to be a great nation this *must* become true."

If . . .

Then, full of the passion of the words of that simple anthem, King imagines freedom ringing—a dreamlike image—and **exhorts** the crowd to make this vision happen. He sings out lines full of
400   sounds and sights—postcards from the American Dream.

> So let freedom ring from the prodigious hilltops of
>   New Hampshire.
> Let freedom ring from the mighty mountains of New
>   York.
> Let freedom ring from the heightening Alleghenies of
>   Pennsylvania!
> Let freedom ring from the snowcapped Rockies of
>   Colorado!
> Let freedom ring from the curvaceous slopes of
410   California!

All of these are Northern places, and their images are ones of pure beauty. But that's not enough, King now **invokes** the sites of repression across the South.

> But not only that.
> Let freedom ring from Stone Mountain of Georgia!
> Let freedom ring from Lookout Mountain of
>   Tennessee!
> Let freedom ring from every hill and molehill of
>   Mississippi!
420   From every mountainside,
>   let freedom ring!

Those lines come from one of King's old friends, a preacher from Chicago named Archibald Carey. In a speech at the 1952 Republican Convention, Carey sang "My Country, 'Tis of Thee" and cried "Let freedom ring!" and issued some of those same postcards.

Finally, dizzy from the view of a nation teeming with freedom, King offers the moment of deliverance.

He sways now. He lifts his whole body with the speech. The
430 people in the crowd follow their King. They sway, they smile, and they laugh with anticipation of every new image.

exhort
(ĭg-zôrt´) *v.* to strongly urge or encourage.

invoke
(ĭn-vōk´) *v.* to refer or call attention to.

WHEN STUDENTS STRUGGLE . . .

Tell students that when they read a nonfiction text aloud, they should use the same print cues they use when they read a fiction text or a speech. Note that punctuation tells them when to pause and when to use intonation to indicate a question or an exclamation.

Ask partners to form pairs to practice fluent reading.

- Divide lines 422–431 into two sections (lines 422–426 and lines 427–431).
- Have one partner read the first section while the other reads the second section. Then have partners switch sections.

CLOSE READ

Analyze Ideas and Events (LINES 401–421)   RI 3

Point out that in analyzing King's speech, Euchner breaks down passages to clarify their meaning.

Y **ASK STUDENTS** to reread 401–421 and explain how Euchner's division of the passage helps clarify the passage's meaning. *(He divides the passage in half, juxtaposing the lines about the North with the lines about the South. In this way, he invites readers to compare and contrast, just as King himself does in the passage.)*

Analyze Impact of Word Choice (LINES 427–431)   RI 4

Explain that Euchner chooses to use **sensory language**—words that appeal to the senses— so that readers can experience what he describes.

Z **CITE TEXT EVIDENCE** Have students reread lines 427–431 and point out words that help them visualize each scene. *(dizzy, sways, lifts, smile, laugh)*

Then, point out this sentence: "The people in the crowd follow their King."

A2 **ASK STUDENTS** what the significance is of referring to King as "their King." *(Euchner is implying that King has the power to sway the people and that they will follow him.)*

CRITICAL VOCABULARY

exhort: King encourages the crowd to help make his dream of freedom come true. **ASK STUDENTS** to explain how King exhorts everyone in the crowd to work toward freedom and justice. *(He repeats the lines "let freedom ring" and names places in both the North and the South.)*

invoke: King calls attention to places in the South that were steeped in repression and racism. **ASK STUDENTS** why it was important for King to invoke the sites of repression in the South. *(It was in those places that King's vision of freedom was most necessary.)*

Analyze Impact of Word Choice (LINES 442–444)   RI 4

Remind students that Euchner uses figurative language to describe events on the day of King's speech.

 CITE TEXT EVIDENCE Have students reread lines 442–444 and cite the use of figurative language. *("blessing the congregation at this great mass")* Ask students to think about King's background as a minister and then ask them what Euchner means by this description. *(The phrase imbues King with the spiritual power of a minister who can lead his congregation as he delivers the last lines of his speech, which invoke God.)*

Analyze Ideas and Events   RI 3
(LINES 445–447)

Point out that Euchner concludes his analysis by quoting the final lines of King's speech.

C2 ASK STUDENTS why Euchner might have concluded with King's words rather than his own. *(King's closing words are powerful and help convey the idea that Euchner has been reiterating in his analysis— that King's speech had a tremendous impact on people.)*

COLLABORATIVE DISCUSSION Direct students to work in pairs to discuss how the writer structures his account of the March on Washington. Tell them to look at how he introduces the topic and how he unfolds his analysis, moving from one point to the next. Remind students to use specific passages and examples to support their conclusions. Have pairs compare their results with the rest of the class.

ASK STUDENTS to share any questions they generated in the course of reading and discussing the selection.

And when this happens,
when we allow freedom to ring,
when we let it *ring* from every village and every
    hamlet,
from *every* state and *every* city,
we will be able to speed up that day when all of God's
    children,
black men and *white* men,
Jews and *Gentiles*,
Protestants and *Catholics*—

    Martin Luther King turns to his right and raises his right arm high, his elbow bent slightly, blessing the congregation at this great mass.
    "—will be able to join hands and sing in the *words* of the old Negro spiritual, "Free at *last*! Free at *last*! Thank God *Almighty*, we are *free at last*!"

COLLABORATIVE DISCUSSION With a partner, discuss how the writer structures his account of the March on Washington. Cite specific details and examples from the text.

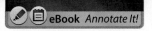
Analyze Ideas and Events

RI 3

To show connections between ideas, authors structure a text so that each sentence and paragraph supports and develops a central idea. In recounting a historical event, authors usually provide readers with details and support for the central idea such as:

- a factual account of the event
- background information
- quotations and anecdotes, or personal stories, from eyewitnesses

Charles Euchner's approach is unusual because he goes beyond what we usually see in a history text to offer his own detailed analysis of the text of Martin Luther King Jr.'s "I Have a Dream" speech. For example, in lines 62–64, Euchner analyzes King's extended metaphor of the bad check.

> And then King introduces Clarence Jones's metaphor of the bad check, so simple and so basic. A bad check represents bad faith, failed promises, broken contracts.

Euchner then goes on to quote from King's speech and includes details of how the audience responds to the metaphor. This structure of support enables Euchner's readers to visualize the actual effect of the speech as it was delivered. This type of idea development throughout the history text shapes and refines the central idea. Think about the other kinds of support Euchner uses in his account. How do the details he includes relate to his analysis of the speech?

Analyzing the Text

RI 1, RI 2, RI 3,
RI 4, RI 5

Cite Text Evidence Support your responses with evidence from the selection.

1. **Analyze** Briefly describe the text structure Euchner uses in his account. How does he organize the text so that each idea is connected and developed? Cite specific examples to support your response.

2. **Analyze** Notice that Euchner uses present-tense verbs in his account. In what verb tense is historical text usually written? What effect does using present-tense verbs create? Cite specific examples to support your response.

3. **Infer** Describe the eyewitness accounts and anecdotes Euchner includes. Why do you think he chose these witnesses? What inference about the crowd can you make based on the witnesses he includes?

4. **Evaluate** Euchner provides background information on historic events and biblical allusions included in "I Have a Dream." Identify one example and explain how it helped you better understand the speech.

Strategies for Annotation

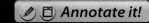 *Annotate it!*

Analyze Ideas and Events

RI 3

Share these strategies for guided or independent analysis:

- Highlight in blue any lines that reflect Euchner's interpretation or analysis of King's speech.
- Highlight in green any examples that support Euchner's interpretation.
- On notes, draw connections between the analysis that Euchner gives and the examples that support his interpretation.

PRACTICE & APPLY

CLOSE READ

Analyze Ideas and Events

RI 3

Point out that authors structure a text so that it makes sense and is easy to follow. Consequently, they usually focus on a central idea and then move from one point to another in support of this idea. Reiterate that Euchner's analysis is unique in that he not only focuses on King's speech, but he also weaves interpretation and audience reaction into the speech. Explain that Euchner's vivid language leaves readers with the feeling that they were there when King delivered his famous words.

Analyzing the Text

RI 1, RI 2, RI 3,
RI 4, RI 5

1. *Euchner organizes his text with an introduction describing how King spoke. He then quotes sections of the speech in order, each one followed by relevant analysis, description, and anecdotes about audience reactions. For example, Euchner quotes from the "I have a dream" passage and then describes how an audience member reacts when others in the audience are laughing.*

2. *Historical text is usually written in the past tense. Using present-tense verbs makes the text seem immediate. The present tense also emphasizes that King's ideas are timeless. For example, in lines 297–301, when Euchner describes Richard Pritchard, it is almost as if the reader knows Pritchard and was there in his New Jersey home when he decided to drive to Washington.*

3. *Euchner describes witnesses who represent a cross-section of society. Euchner probably chose these specific witnesses to lend credibility to his analysis. These were diverse people whose reactions to the speech could also influence the opinion of Euchner's readers. The crowd that was listening was very involved in the speech.*

4. *Answers will vary. One example is the reference to the Tower of Babel and how evil brings catastrophe. This helps illustrate the power behind King's message that African Americans are not willing to wait any longer for change.*

Critical Vocabulary

L 4c

Possible answers:

1. civic; related to community

2. exhort; means to encourage

3. parallel; means similar to

4. expanse; it is a large area

5. revile; means condemn someone you dislike

6. invoke; means to call attention to, or to refer to

7. invocation; it is often used in prayer

8. cadence; music has a cadence or rhythm

Vocabulary Strategy: Words from Greek and Latin

Possible answers:

- **audi:** hear; Her whisper was barely audible.

- **sym:** together with; The mother had sympathy for the sick child.

- **cap:** head; The captain was in charge of the ship at sea.

- **lib:** free; The person was considered liberal because she wanted civil rights reform.

- **rupt:** break; I didn't mean to interrupt, but my message was urgent.

- **poli:** city; New York is a huge metropolis.

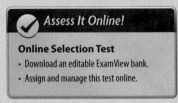

✓ Assess It Online!

Online Selection Test
- Download an editable ExamView bank.
- Assign and manage this test online.

Critical Vocabulary

L 4c

cadence	parallel	invocation	civic
revile	expanse	exhort	invoke

Practice and Apply Explain which Critical Vocabulary word is most closely associated with the underlined word.

1. Which word goes with <u>town</u>? Why?

2. Which word goes with <u>convince</u>? Why?

3. Which word goes with <u>similar</u>? Why?

4. Which word goes with <u>distance</u>? Why?

5. Which word goes with <u>dislike</u>? Why

6. Which word goes with <u>point out</u>? Why?

7. Which word goes with <u>prayer</u>? Why?

8. Which word goes with <u>music</u>? Why?

Vocabulary Strategy: Words from Greek and Latin

Studying the **etymology** of words means that you look at the historical development of words and determine their basic elements. Many words in the English language come from Greek and Latin roots. Knowing the meaning of **roots,** or basic word elements, can help you determine the meaning of unfamiliar words. For example, the Critical Vocabulary word *civic* contains the Latin root *civ-* that means "citizen." Another example is contained in the word *parallel*. This word contains the Greek root *par(a)* that means "beside, near." Knowing the meanings of **civ-** and *par(a)* can help you determine the meanings of other words with the same roots.

Practice and Apply Look up these words from the selection in a dictionary. Write the meaning of the Latin or Greek root word, and then write a sentence using another word with that same root.

Word	Root	Word	Root
audience (line 6)	*audi-*	**liberty** (line 72)	*lib-*
symbolic (line 13)	*sym-*	**bankrupt** (line 81)	*rupt-*
capital (line 65)	*cap-*	**politician** (line 120)	*poli-*

AMERICA The Story of Us: March on Washington

Video by HISTORY®

AS YOU VIEW Identify similarities and differences between the history text and the video. Write down any questions you generate as you watch the video.

COLLABORATIVE DISCUSSION With a partner, discuss the similarities and differences in the history text and the video, supporting your ideas with evidence from both.

ENGLISH LANGUAGE SUPPORT

Comprehension Support Tell students that much of the narration in the video supports the film footage and that the interviews are of famous people explaining the importance of the March on Washington.

- After students have watched the video once, have them watch it again in segments, pausing it to make notes about content.
- Ask them what the music and film footage tell them about the event. *(The music is dramatic and fitting for the topic. The footage shows the crowds and King.)*

Have students discuss the video and text in mixed-language groups.

CLOSE READ

Students can view the video "AMERICA The Story of Us: March on Washington" in their eBooks.

AS YOU VIEW Direct students to use the As You View note to focus their viewing.

Analyze Accounts in Different Mediums   RI 7

Explain that to analyze accounts of a single topic or event in different mediums, students must first look at the broad subject matter featured in each account.

ASK STUDENTS what the video is generally about. *(the March on Washington; what the demonstration sought to accomplish; what it achieved, including the Voting Rights Act and paving the way for an African American president)* Then ask what Euchner's text was generally about. *(a line-by-line analysis of King's speech and reactions from witnesses to the event)*

Tell students that once they have determined the broad subject matter of each account, they should look at the details that are included in each account as well as the details that are left out.

ASK STUDENTS if the views of the crowd in the video gave information that was missing from the text. *(Students may say it was helpful to see the crowds, but that Euchner's descriptions allowed them to visualize the crowd.)* Ask which account gave more information about what King said and how he said it. *(The text gave a line-by-line account of the speech and described how King spoke. The video did not feature the speech.)* Have students explain which account gave more broad information about the civil rights movement. *(The video gave information about segregation and voting rights that the text did not.)* Point out that both accounts featured reaction to and analysis of King's speech. Ask how the accounts differed in this aspect. *(The video showed reaction to and analysis of the speech in general terms and from people explaining its historical significance. The text gave witnesses' personal reactions and offered specific analysis of the speech.)*

COLLABORATIVE DISCUSSION Suggest that pairs consider both the content of each selection and the way it is presented in its medium.

ASK STUDENTS to share any questions they generated in the course of viewing the selection.

PRACTICE & APPLY

ANALYZE

Analyze Accounts in Different Mediums
RI 7

Explain to students that to gain a more complete understanding of a topic, they should seek information presented in a variety of mediums. Point out that while a history text can provide readers with direct quotations from a speech to mull over and decode, as well as an interpretation and explanation about a topic or event, a short documentary video can provide narration, music, and film footage, allowing viewers to actually see and hear what a text can only describe. Point out that no medium can provide a complete account of any event or topic, and that each medium has limits to the information it can provide.

Analyzing Text and Media
RI 1, RI 3, RI 7

1. *The video shows film footage from the day, including footage of King and others marching and of the gathered crowd. It does not focus on his speech or the reaction of the audience, whereas the text does. The video also features perspectives of different people as they look back on the events and its consequences, whereas the text features only Euchner's perspective.*

2. *Possible answer: The inclusion of eyewitness accounts makes the text account very immediate and real. It enhances readers' understanding of what happened that day and what people were thinking.*

3. *Both the text and the video emphasize the impact of the march—the feeling of a momentous occasion, the conviction of the audience that King's speech was expressing their thoughts and feelings, the hope that this march might instigate change in the country.*

Assess It Online!

Online Selection Test
- Download an editable ExamView bank.
- Assign and manage this test online.

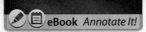 **eBook** *Annotate It!*

Analyze Accounts in Different Mediums
RI 7

Factual information about historic events can be presented in a variety of ways, including written histories and short documentary videos. Each **medium** has particular strengths and weaknesses, and imposes different structures. For example, a short documentary video is under time limitations that require the producer to carefully consider what aspects of the event to include. On the other hand, a video includes images and audio that a written text cannot. To get the most complete picture of a historic event, choose a variety of media sources, and think about the kinds of information that are included, omitted, and emphasized in each account. You might ask yourself these questions about each medium:

- Who is narrating the account?
- What background information is included in the account?
- What details are emphasized in the account?
- What details are missing from the account?

Analyzing Text and Media
RI 1, RI 3, RI 7, W 3

Support your responses with evidence from the selections.

1. **Compare** Describe how the video presents the March on Washington. How does it differ from the history text's account? Cite specific examples from the video and the text.

2. **Analyze** The history text includes eyewitness accounts of the day, while the video uses interviews with people commenting on the significance of the day. How does each type of account affect your understanding of the day?

3. **Evaluate** What ideas are emphasized in both the text and the video? Explain how the video and text together give you a more complete understanding of the March on Washington.

PERFORMANCE TASK

Writing Activity: Account Imagine that you were in the audience for King's speech, and write a one-page first-person account of your experience.

- Gather information and impressions about the event from both the history text and the video.

- Consider how you would respond in that situation, and write a one-page letter or diary entry.

- Be sure to include specific details that convey the atmosphere in the Mall.

- Use the conventions of standard written English.

Assign this performance task.

PERFORMANCE TASK
W 3

Writing Activity: Account Have students work independently to draft their diary entry. Suggest that they review the history text, specifically the passages that feature reaction to King's speech, as well as video of King making his speech, if they can. When students have completed their drafts, have them exchange diary entries with a partner and give each other constructive feedback. Students may share their final drafts in small groups and discuss the elements that make the diary entry especially interesting and realistic.

Write a Narrative

W 3d

TEACH

To complete the second Performance Task, students need to create a vivid and believable fictional narrative about the March on Washington and King's speech. Explain that effective first-person narratives rely on specific details and the narrator's reactions to them. Note that the details do not have to be factual, but they do need to be believable and help readers get an understanding of the day's events.

Suggest that students write their narrative using the following process:

- **Take Notes** Students should reread the texts and view the video again, making notes on specific details and powerful images. These can include quotations from the speech, descriptions and analysis from the history text, or images from the video. They should focus on words, descriptions, or people that students find particularly powerful or interesting.

- **Imagine the Narrator** To construct a believable fictional narrative, students need to identify and know the background and personality of the narrator. They may choose the voice of someone just like themselves—similar age, a student, and so on. Or they might choose the voice of someone unlike themselves—for example, of a different age, sex, or background. Either way, it is important for the writer to know through whose eyes he or she is looking.

- **Focus on Details and Emotional Reactions** To make the narrative vivid and believable, students need to see things and describe them as if they were there. That involves describing details such as a reaction to a particular quotation, a careful description of someone in the crowd, descriptions of the Mall or other surroundings, the way King's voice sounded, and so on.

COLLABORATIVE DISCUSSION

Direct students to work in pairs. Each student should complete the process of taking notes and imagining the narrator. Partners can then share their work and get feedback on ways they might improve their preparation and use the information to write the narrative.

Analyze Ideas and Events

RI 3

RETEACH

Remind students that authors structure nonfiction texts by supporting a central idea with details and examples.

- Have students review the introduction to the history text, lines 1–22. Ask how Euchner introduces his topic. *(He begins by discussing how King speaks. Then he turns to the speech's opening lines and an interpretation of what King said.)*

- Have students look at lines 228–245 and explain what point Euchner is making. *(Euchner shows how the speech spoke to the experiences of a specific audience member.)*

- Ask students what they think the central idea of the text is based on what they have read. *(The central idea is that King was a gifted speaker who effectively used his background and experience to appeal to his audience.)* Then ask how the introduction and lines 228–245 support that central idea. *(The introduction tells King's background and speech patterns, and lines 228–245 show how he affected his audience.)*

 LEVEL UP TUTORIALS Assign the following *Level Up* tutorial: **Point-by-Point Organization**

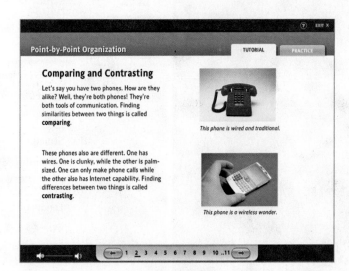

INDEPENDENT READING

Students can apply the skill to an article in a science or history periodical, an encyclopedia article, or a passage in a history book. Have students outline the central idea and highlight supporting details. Ask: Does the writer include enough details to establish a central idea? Does each paragraph support the central idea?

A Eulogy for Dr. Martin Luther King Jr.

For additional background, students can view the video "Class of the 20th Century: 1963–1968" in their eBooks.

Speech by Robert F. Kennedy

Why This Text

Speeches are meant to be heard, not read; sometimes, however, the message is so timely and the messenger so powerful that the meaning comes through even in print. Readers of Kennedy's eulogy, moved as they are by its passion, will nonetheless appreciate its brilliance as a speech, well worthy of the great orator being eulogized. With the help of the close-reading questions, students will examine this speech in terms of its craft and context in order to better understand its place in our shared history.

Background Have students read the background and information about Robert Kennedy, including the circumstances surrounding the eulogy. Kennedy, knowing how unprepared people would be to hear this terrible news, chose his words carefully, as they had to accomplish several things at once—convey a sense of shared grief, pay homage to the great Dr. King, and, importantly, give hope to a people still reeling from the shock of his own brother's murder.

AS YOU READ Ask students to pay attention to the rhetorical devices used to advance the purpose of the speech. How do they help the speaker connect to his audience?

Standards Support

- cite strong and thorough textual evidence
- analyze how an author's ideas are developed
- determine an author's point of view
- analyze how an author uses rhetoric to advance his or her purpose

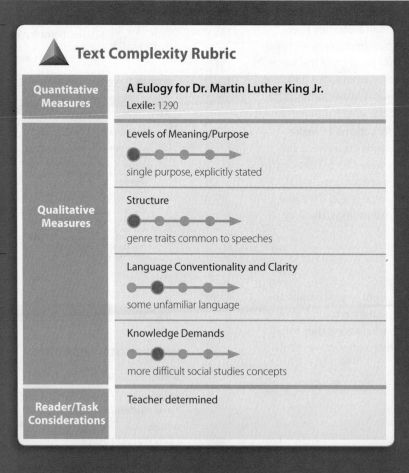

Text Complexity Rubric

	A Eulogy for Dr. Martin Luther King Jr.
Quantitative Measures	Lexile: 1290
Qualitative Measures	**Levels of Meaning/Purpose** single purpose, explicitly stated
	Structure genre traits common to speeches
	Language Conventionality and Clarity some unfamiliar language
	Knowledge Demands more difficult social studies concepts
Reader/Task Considerations	Teacher determined

Strategies for CLOSE READING

Analyze Rhetorical Devices

Students should read this speech carefully all the way through. Close-reading questions at the bottom of the page will help them focus on a thorough analysis of the rhetorical devices the author uses to advance his point of view. As they read, students should jot down comments or questions about the text in the margins.

WHEN STUDENTS STRUGGLE ...

To help students analyze the text of Kennedy's eulogy for Dr. King, have them work in small groups to fill out a chart like the one shown below.

CITE TEXT EVIDENCE For practice in identifying examples of rhetorical devices, ask students to cite text evidence for each feature.

Device	Example
Repetition	"In this difficult day, in this difficult time . . ." "What we need in the United States is not division; what we need in the United States is not hatred . . ."
Parallelism	". . . what kind of nation . . . " ". . . white people amongst white . . ." "We will have difficult times . . . it is not the end of disorder."

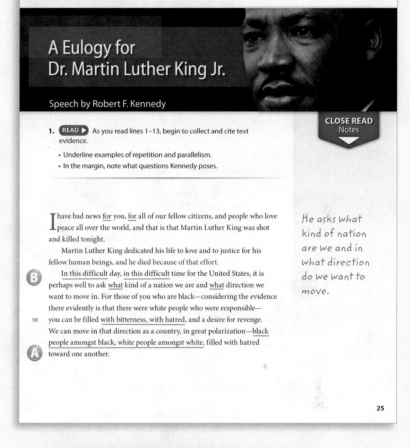

Background *On April 4, 1968, hundreds of African Americans gathered in Indianapolis, Indiana, for what they thought would be an exciting political event. Presidential candidate* **Robert F. Kennedy** *was coming to speak to them. Before he was to deliver his speech, Kennedy was informed that civil rights leader Martin Luther King Jr. had been assassinated earlier that day. Kennedy nevertheless went to the rally, where he found the audience upbeat in anticipation of his appearance. Realizing they were unaware of the tragic events, he began his speech with the following words.*

A Eulogy for Dr. Martin Luther King Jr.

Speech by Robert F. Kennedy

CLOSE READ
Notes

1. **READ ▶** As you read lines 1–13, begin to collect and cite text evidence.
   - Underline examples of repetition and parallelism.
   - In the margin, note what questions Kennedy poses.

I have bad news <u>for</u> you, <u>for</u> all of our fellow citizens, and people who love peace all over the world, and that is that Martin Luther King was shot and killed tonight.

Martin Luther King dedicated his life to love and to justice for his fellow human beings, and he died because of that effort.

B <u>In this difficult</u> day, <u>in this difficult</u> time for the United States, it is perhaps well to ask <u>what</u> kind of a nation we are and <u>what</u> direction we want to move in. For those of you who are black—considering the evidence there evidently is that there were white people who were responsible—
10 you can be filled <u>with bitterness, with hatred</u>, and a desire for revenge. We can move in that direction as a country, in great polarization—<u>black people amongst black, white people amongst white</u>, filled with hatred

A toward one another.

He asks what kind of nation are we and in what direction do we want to move.

25

1. **READ AND CITE TEXT EVIDENCE** Tell students that repetition works to reinforce the speaker's message and create a strong link in the mind of the listener. Here, it may have had another purpose—to create a mood.

A **ASK STUDENTS** to describe the effect this repetition might have had on a roomful of hurt and angry people. Have students cite an example from the text. *Students may cite "In this difficult day, in this difficult time..." (line 6) as an example of the gentle, soothing effect repetition can have on an audience in shock, like a parent comforting a scared child.*

Martin Luther King Jr., leader of the Southern Christian Leadership Council; Attorney General Robert Kennedy; Roy Wilkins, Executive Secretary of the NAACP; and Vice President Lyndon Johnson after a special White House conference on civil rights (June 1963).

> We will have difficult times. We've had difficult times in the past. We will have difficult times in the future.

C Or we can make an effort, as Martin Luther King did, to understand and to comprehend, and to replace that violence, that stain of bloodshed that has spread across our land, with an effort to understand with compassion and love.

D 20 For those of you who are black and are tempted to be filled with hatred and distrust at the injustice of such an act, against all white people, I can only say that I feel in my own heart the same kind of feeling. I had a member of my family killed, but he was killed by a white man. But we have to make an effort in the United States, we have to make an effort to understand, to go beyond these rather difficult times.

My favorite poet was Aeschylus. He wrote, "In our sleep, pain which cannot forget falls drop by drop upon the heart until, in our own despair, against our will, comes wisdom through the awful grace of God."

E What we need in the United States is not division; what we need in the United States is not hatred; what we need in the United States is not violence or lawlessness but love and wisdom, and compassion toward one another, 30 and a feeling of justice towards those who still suffer within our country, whether they be white or they be black.

So I shall ask you tonight to return home, to say a prayer for the family of Martin Luther King, that's true, but more importantly to say a prayer for our own country, which all of us love—a prayer for understanding and that compassion of which I spoke.

We can do well in this country. We will have difficult times. We've had difficult times in the past. We will have difficult times in the future. It is not the end of violence; it is not the end of lawlessness; it is not the end of disorder.

2. ◀ REREAD Reread lines 6–13. How does Kennedy use parallelism to emphasize the potential for American society to become more divided?

Kennedy's use of parallelism emphasizes the unity of the American society in "what kind of nation we are and what direction we want to move" and contrasts that with division in "black people amongst black, white people amongst white."

3. READ ▶ As you read lines 14–26, underline the options Kennedy offers his audience.

4. ◀ REREAD Reread lines 18–23. What is Kennedy referring to when he says he "had a member of my family killed . . ."?

Robert Kennedy's brother John F. Kennedy was assassinated in Dallas while he was President of the United States.

5. READ ▶ As you read lines 27–46, underline the advice that Kennedy gives to his audience.

26

27

2. **REREAD AND CITE TEXT EVIDENCE**

B **ASK STUDENTS** why, in lines 6–13, Kennedy suggested that it was possible that black people would be full of bitterness and hatred and a desire for revenge. *He personally understood the instinct to feel hatred and bitterness, but wanted to show why it would lead to a divided nation.*

3. **READ AND CITE TEXT EVIDENCE**

C **ASK STUDENTS** why Kennedy might have brought in Martin Luther King's ideas at this point in the speech. *He wanted to remind people that King was a man of peace; he wanted them to carry on his legacy and replace violence with compassion.*

FOR ELL STUDENTS The verb *comprehend* is very close to its false Spanish cognate *comprender* (to understand). Point out that *comprehend* goes beyond understanding—it means grasping the importance, nature, or significance of something.

4. **REREAD AND CITE TEXT EVIDENCE**

D **ASK STUDENTS** why Kennedy made reference to the murder of his brother in lines 20–21. *He wanted people to know he had experienced a similar, shocking loss; he was speaking from the heart, as a human being rather than a public figure.*

5. **READ AND CITE TEXT EVIDENCE**

E **ASK STUDENTS** to summarize the advice that Kennedy gives in lines 27–46. *He advises people to act with love rather than hate, and to pray not only for the King family, but for understanding and compassion.*

FOR ELL STUDENTS Encourage students to analyze the double suffix in the word *lawlessness*. Have them work from the base word *law*, and ask volunteers what meaning each of the suffixes (-*less*, -*ness*) adds to the word.

40   But the vast majority of white people and the vast majority of black people in this country want to live together, want to improve the quality of our life, and want justice for all human beings who abide in our land.

    Let us dedicate ourselves to what the Greeks wrote so many years ago: to tame the savageness of man and to make gentle the life of this world.

    Let us dedicate ourselves to that, and say a prayer for our country and for our people.

6. ◀ REREAD AND DISCUSS   With a small group, discuss the central idea Kennedy brings up in his speech. Do you think it's an effective eulogy? Do you think it adequately honored Dr. King?

SHORT RESPONSE

Cite Text Evidence   How does Kennedy's use of rhetoric advance his argument? How does his use of parallelism help speak to a racially divided audience? **Cite evidence** from the text in your reponse.

Kennedy uses repetition—especially of the word "difficult"—to make his argument inclusive; he lets his audience know that he is aware of the problems they all face. The fact that his own brother was also assassinated strengthens his argument, as he can identify with the feelings of those who are angry about Martin Luther King's murder. Kennedy strengthens his argument by appealing to people's better natures, and points out that all people want the same things: quality of life and justice for all human beings.

28

---

6.   REREAD AND DISCUSS USING TEXT EVIDENCE

F   **ASK STUDENTS** to look closely at the themes Kennedy keeps coming back to in his eulogy. Have groups share their responses. *Students may point out that Kennedy effectively defused a potentially inflammatory situation by repeatedly returning to the ideals King stood for and the importance of continuing his work as a way of honoring him.*

SHORT RESPONSE

Cite Text Evidence   Students should:

- determine whether or not they find the eulogy effective.
- give examples of rhetorical devices that further Kennedy's purpose.
- cite text evidence in their response.

TO CHALLENGE STUDENTS . . .

To deepen students' understanding, ask students to search for a video of the eulogy online.

ASK STUDENTS how hearing the eulogy added dimension to the printed word. How important was it to hear the audience reaction? How well did Kennedy handle the situation? Did the speech match, or exceed, their expectations? *The audience reaction gives you a sense of the awesome responsibility Kennedy had. Although visibly shaken himself, he succeeded in offering comfort to a stunned audience. Lines such as "I had a member of my family killed. . . by a white man," although emotionally shocking, were intended to reinforce a sense of unity*

DIG DEEPER

With the class, return to Question 6, Reread and Discuss. Have groups share their responses to the question.

ASK STUDENTS about the way Kennedy handled a very tough situation.

- Have students think about Kennedy's audience. Why had they come to the event? What did they expect to hear? Why do you think Kennedy began his speech the way he did? *The people were supporters of Kennedy's run for the presidency—no one expected this horrible news. Kennedy started his speech in a very blunt, no-nonsense manner. He did not euphemize: he used words like "shot" and killed," possibly with the idea that directness is the most respectful way to present this kind of information.*

- Ask students how the tone of the speech was meant to help people deal with this crisis. *The rhythm and cadence of Kennedy's speech was meant to have a soothing effect and impart a feeling of solemnity.*

- Ask students how Kennedy used King's ideas to help bring people together. *Kennedy knew that people might simply search for revenge; some might blame all white people for the acts of one. Kennedy tried to convey the idea that this was not what King would have wanted; he tried to persuade people that the best way to honor King was to follow the principles he espoused, and for which he died: "to make gentle the life of this world."*

ASK STUDENTS to return to their Short Response answer and revise it based on the class discussion.

from Cairo: My City, Our Revolution

Diary by Ahdaf Soueif

Why This Text?

Reading a diary allows students to analyze events through the point of view of a first-person narrator. This lesson explores how Ahdaf Soueif (äd´äf sū-ĕf´) recounts events and conveys a particular tone toward the subject of the Egyptian Revolution of 2011.

Key Learning Objective: The student will be able to analyze how an author unfolds events in a diary and analyze the impact of word choice on tone.

RI 1	Cite textual evidence.
RI 3	Analyze how the author unfolds events.
RI 4	Analyze the impact of word choice on tone.
W 2b	Develop the topic with well-chosen, relevant, and sufficient facts.
W 2e	Establish and maintain a formal style and objective tone.
W 5	Develop and strengthen writing.
W 7	Conduct short research projects.
W 8	Gather information from multiple sources.
SL 4	Present information, findings, and evidence.
L 1b	Use various types of phrases.
L 4c	Consult reference materials.
L 4d	Verify the preliminary determination of the meaning of a word.
L 6	Acquire and use academic and domain-specific words.

Text Complexity Rubric

Quantitative Measures

Qualitative Measures

Reader/Task Considerations

from Cairo: My City, Our Revolution
Lexile: 990L

Levels of Meaning/Purpose

more than one purpose; implied, easily identified from context

Structure

organization of main ideas and details may be complex, but is clearly stated and generally sequential

Language Conventionality and Clarity

increased unfamiliar language

Knowledge Demands

somewhat complex historical concepts

- Teacher determined
- Vary by individual reader and type of text
- See the Text X-Ray for suggested Reader/Task Considerations.

English Language Support
Before teaching, use the Text X-Ray below for an overview of the text's complexity. The Text X-Ray and the supports and scaffolds in the Teacher's Edition will help you guide students of different skill levels.

Text Complexity: Qualitative Measures

Levels of Meaning/Purpose

more than one purpose; implied, easily identified from context

Help students analyze the impact of word choice on tone.
- Teacher's Edition side notes, pp. 74, 75, 77
- When Students Struggle, p. 75
- Strategies for Annotation, p. 77
- Analyze Impact of Word Choice on Tone, p. 77

Prompt students to discuss inferences drawn from the text.
- Teacher's Edition side notes, pp. 74, 76
- To Challenge Students, p. 76

ZOOM IN ON **ANALYZING TONE** Remind students that **tone** is an author's attitude toward his or her subject. Project lines 49–54.

- Give students time to read the paragraph independently and identify words that convey the author's tone. *("big smile," "sun was shining," "sang and played and joked and chanted")*
- Have students meet with partners to share the words they identified. Have them brainstorm several words that describe the tone.
- Invite pairs to share their ideas with the class. Work together to select the best words to describe the tone. *(Sample answers: happy, proud)*

Structure

organization of main ideas and details may be complex, but is clearly stated and generally sequential

Help students analyze ideas and events.
- Teacher's Edition side notes, pp. 73, 75, 76, 77
- English Language Support, p. 73
- Analyze Ideas and Events, p. 77

To reteach analyzing ideas and events, see
- Analyze Ideas and Events, p. 80a

 Use It! *Level Up* Tutorial: Chronological Order

ZOOM IN ON **ANALYZING TEXT STRUCTURE** Students may think of a **diary** as a record of daily events recorded on the days they occurred. Explain that this diary mentions events that happened both before and after Friday, January 28, 2011. Discuss these points with students:

- The first three paragraphs are written in the **present tense**. This helps draw readers into the experience.
- The next two paragraphs (lines 24–43) continue the same sequence of events but are described in the **past tense**.
- Lines 50–54 describe events that happened a few days later, on February 1, 2011.
- Lines 74–76 refer to events that happened eight months before the date of the diary entry.

Language Conventionality and Clarity

increased unfamiliar language

Teach unfamiliar vocabulary in context.

- Teacher's Edition Critical Vocabulary notes, pp. 73, 75, 76, 79
- Applying Academic Vocabulary, p. 74

Help students analyze imagery.

- Teacher's Edition side note, p. 73

Instruct students in using reference sources to determine word meanings.

- Teacher's Edition side note, p. 79
- Strategies for Annotation, p. 79

Help students understand noun phrases.

- Teacher's Edition side note, p. 80

***ZOOM IN ON* UNPACKING SENTENCES** Tell students that a **noun phrase** consists of a noun and the surrounding words and phrases that modify, or describe, the noun. Explain that one way to identify a noun phrase is to ask whether it can be replaced by a pronoun. For example:

"And that is why we—myself and two beautiful young women— appeared suddenly . . .'"

The underlined noun phrase could be replaced by the pronoun *we*. Work with students to find other noun phrases in lines 24–31, identify the base noun in each, and discuss how the phrases add descriptive detail. *("the Qasr el-Nil underpass," "the Central Security vehicles racing to get out of town," "all the men leaning over the parapet," "the screeching vehicles," "a spot where we could scramble up the bank")*

Knowledge Demands

somewhat complex historical concepts

Support English Learners in understanding the historical context of the diary.

- Teacher's Edition Background note, p. 73

Help students learn more about the topic through research and writing.

- Performance Task, p. 78
- Conduct Research on the Web, p. 80a

 Use It! **Interactive Whiteboard Lesson:** Conducting Research on the Web

***ZOOM IN ON* BUILDING GEOGRAPHICAL KNOWLEDGE** The diary opens with a reference to "the river." Tell students that the Nile River, which runs through Cairo, is the longest river in the world. It flows north through Africa and empties into the Mediterranean Sea. *Qasr el-Nil* means "Palace of the Nile" in Arabic.

Suggested Reader/Task Considerations

You might consider the following before assigning this diary to students.

- Do students have adequate **visualization** skills to imagine events and places described in the text?
- Will the content of the diary entry be of interest to students?

***ZOOM IN ON* SUPPORTING COMPREHENSION**

- Assign each of these passages to a pair of students: lines 1–7, 8–19, 20–31, 32–43, 55–73. Have each pair discuss the **imagery** in the passage and create two pictures depicting key scenes or actions.
- Before students read, tell them that the Arab Spring was fueled in part by social media. Protesters used social media to plan demonstrations and keep each other informed. Suggest that, as students read, they think about how this technology might have been useful to the protesters.

CLOSE READ

Background Have students read the background and information about Ahdaf Soueif (äd´äf sū-ĕf´). Explain that the Arab Spring was a movement marked by mass demonstrations against government corruption, political repression, poverty, and unemployment. Citizens' protests helped end long-standing authoritarian regimes in some countries and helped bring about governmental changes in others. The movement began in Tunisia with an uprising that overthrew the government. The events in this diary took place within days of that occurence. While Egyptian security forces at first responded violently to the protests, the thirty-year Mubarak regime was forced out of power.

AS YOU READ Direct students to use the As You Read statement to focus their reading. Remind students to write down any questions they generate during reading.

Analyze Ideas and Events

RI 3

(LINES 3–13)

Explain that writers use **time-order words** to signal the sequence of events. Point out that Soueif first identifies her current location, then describes her previous one.

ASK STUDENTS to reread lines 3–13. Based on the author's description of her location moments before, ask students to infer why Soueif is traveling in a boat. (*The description of their coughing and choking and the carrier burning where they were moments before suggests that they are in the boat to escape the danger.*)

Analyze Impact of Word Choice (LINES 5–9)

RI 4

Tell students that **imagery** is the use of language that appeals to the senses.

CITE TEXT EVIDENCE Ask what details help readers see and feel what the author experiences. (*Details such as "our coughing and choking subsides" and "a mass of people, all in motion" help readers visualize the scene.*)

> #### CRITICAL VOCABULARY
>
> **opaque**: The air is filled with the tear gas security forces sprayed at protesters.
>
> **ASK STUDENTS** what might make water in a glass look opaque. (*adding baking soda or sugar*)

Background *In 2010, the call for democratic reforms reverberated throughout the Middle East and North Africa in a movement known as the Arab Spring. In Egypt, the unrest forced Hosni Mubarak's long-ruling regime out of power. This excerpt from* **Ahdaf Soueif's** *personal account of the revolution describes the third day of mass protests in Cairo. Soueif (b. 1950) was born in Egypt and resides in both Cairo and London. Her novel* The Map of Love *was a finalist for the Booker Prize for Fiction, and she contributes to the* Guardian *and other English and Arabic news organizations.*

from Cairo: My City, Our Revolution

Diary by Ahdaf Soueif

AS YOU READ Pay attention to details that reveal the author's feelings about Cairo and the revolution.

Friday 28 January, 5.00 p.m.

The river is a still, steely grey, a dull pewter. Small scattered fires burn and fizz in the water. We've pushed out from the shore below the Ramses Hilton and are heading into mid-stream. My two nieces, Salma and Mariam, are on either side of me in the small motor boat. As we get further from the shore our coughing and choking subsides. We can draw breath, even though the breath burns. And we can open our eyes—

10 To see an **opaque** dusk, heavy with tear gas. Up ahead, Qasr el-Nil Bridge is a mass of people, all in motion, but all in place. We look back at where we were just minutes ago, on 6 October Bridge,[1] and see a Central Security Forces personnel carrier on fire, backing off, four young men chasing it, leaping at it, beating at its windscreen. The vehicle is reversing wildly, careering backwards east towards Downtown. Behind us, a ball of fire lands in the river;

opaque
(ō-pāk´) *adj.*
clouded, difficult to see through.

---

[1] **Qasr el–Nil Bridge . . . 6 October Bridge:** two bridges, about two miles apart, that cross the Nile River in central Cairo.

ENGLISH LANGUAGE SUPPORT

Organizational Patterns: Time Sequence Have students use a sequence chart to keep track of the order of events. Encourage them to apply the following strategies:

- Note phrases and clauses that describe the author's actions.
- Identify time-order words that signal when events occurred.

ASK STUDENTS how these events are related.

CLOSE READ

Analyze Ideas and Events

RI 3

(LINES 20–23)

Note that authors often describe events in a way that requires readers to make inferences.

C **ASK STUDENTS** what details Soueif provides about why she decides to return to the site of the protest, and what can students infer about Soueif's reasons based on these details. *(Just before she tells the boatman to change course, Soueif describes, "A great shout goes up from Qasr el-Nil". Readers can infer that the protesters' chants inspire Soueif and her nieces to rejoin the demonstrations.)*

Analyze Impact of Word Choice on Tone (LINES 24–31)

RI 4

Explain to students that the feelings associated with an author's choice of words help the author convey a particular **tone**, or attitude, toward his or her subject.

D **CITE TEXT EVIDENCE** Have students reread lines 24-31. Then ask them to identify words in the paragraph that help Soueif convey an attitude or feeling about the events she describes. *(Words such as suddenly, racing, skittered, screeching, and scramble help convey an attitude or feeling of excitement.)*

---

a bright new pool of flame in the water. The sky too is grey—so different from the airy twilight you normally get on the river at this time of day. The Opera House looms dark on our right and we can barely make out the slender height of the Cairo Tower. We don't know it yet, but the lights of Cairo will not come on tonight.

20 · A great shout goes up from Qasr el-Nil. I look at Salma and Mariam. 'Yes, let's,' they say. I tell the boatman we've changed our minds: we don't want to cross the river to Giza[2] and go home, we want to be dropped off under Qasr el-Nil Bridge.

And that is why we—myself and two beautiful young women—appeared suddenly in the Qasr el-Nil underpass among the Central Security vehicles racing to get out of town and all the men leaning over the parapet[3] above us with stones in their hands stopped in mid-throw and yelled 'Run! Run!' and held off with the stones so they wouldn't hit us as we skittered through the screeching vehicles 30 to a spot where we could scramble up the bank and join the people at the mouth of the bridge. . . .

---

[2] **Giza:** city southwest of Cairo and site of the great pyramids.
[3] **parapet:** a low protective wall along the edge of a raised structure.

74 Collection 2

WHEN STUDENTS STRUGGLE...

To help students understand the impact of word choice on tone, guide students to list in a two-column chart examples from the text that show Soueif's attitude or feelings about the revolution and Cairo. Then have them work with a partner to write a synonym or paraphrase for each example, with the help of a dictionary or thesaurus as needed. Finally, have partners take turns reading aloud each example and synonym/paraphrase. Then have them discuss the differences between each.

LEVEL UP TUTORIALS For additional support, assign the following *Level Up* tutorial: **Paraphrasing.**

Example from Text	Synonym/Paraphrase
"continuous thud of guns" (line 67)	"repetitive sound of firepower"

So we ran through the underpass, scrambled up the bank and found ourselves within, inside, and part of the masses. When we'd seen the crowd from a distance it had seemed like one bulk, solid. Close up like this it was people, individual persons with spaces between them—spaces into which you could fit. We stood on the traffic island in the middle of the road. Behind us was Qasr el-Nil Bridge, in front of us was Tahrir,[4] and we were doing what we Egyptians do best, and what the regime ruling us had tried so hard
40 to destroy: we had come together, as individuals, millions of us, in a great cooperative effort. And this time our project was to save and to **reclaim** our country. We stood on the island in the middle of the road and that was the moment I became part of the revolution. . . .

For twenty years I have shied away from writing about Cairo. It hurt too much. But the city was there, close to me, looking over my shoulder, holding up the **prism** through which I understood the world, inserting herself into everything I wrote. It hurt. And now, miraculously, it doesn't. Because my city is mine again.

'Masr' is Egypt, and 'Masr' is also what Egyptians call Cairo.
50 On Tuesday 1 February, I watched a man surveying the scene in Tahrir with a big smile: the sun was shining and people were everywhere, old and young, rich and poor, they talked and walked and sang and played and joked and chanted. Then he said it out loud: 'Ya Masr, it's been a long time. We have missed you.' . . .

On the traffic island at the Qasr el-Nil entrance to Tahrir you turned 360 degrees and everywhere there were people. I could not tell how many thousands I could see. Close up, people were handing out tissues soaked in vinegar for your nose, Pepsi to bathe your eyes, water to drink. I stumbled and a hand under my elbow
60 steadied me. The way ahead of us was invisible behind the smoke. From time to time there would be a burst of flame. The great hotels: the Semiramis Intercontinental, Shepheard's, the Ramses Hilton, had all darkened their lower floors and locked their doors. On the upper-floor balconies stick figures were watching us. At the other end of the Midan,[5] from the roof of the American University, the snipers were watching us, too. Silently. Everywhere there was a continuous thud of guns and from time to time a loud, **intermittent** rattling sound. We stood. That was our job, the people at the back: we stood and we chanted our declaration of peace: 'Selmeyya!
70 Selmeyya!' while our comrades at the front, unarmed, fought with the security forces. From time to time a great cry would go up and

reclaim
(rĭ-klām´) *v.* to retake possession; reform.

prism
(prĭz´əm) *n.* a transparent, light-refracting object which figuratively refers to an individual's viewpoint.

intermittent
(ĭn´tər-mĭt´nt) *adj.* occurring at erratic or irregular intervals.

---

[4] **Tahrir (te-rər´):** Arabic word for "liberation." Tahrir Square is a large, open area in downtown Cairo.
[5] **Midan (mī́dān):** Arabic word for "Square."

APPLYING ACADEMIC VOCABULARY

reveal	integrate

THINK-PAIR-SHARE Have students turn to a partner to discuss the following questions. Guide students to include the academic vocabulary words *reveal* and *integrate* in their responses. Ask volunteers to share their responses with the class.

- Which words of Soueif's **reveal** her tone?
- How does Soueif **integrate** words with both positive and negative connotations to create shifts in the tone?

CLOSE READ

Analyze Ideas and Events (LINES 44–48)   RI 3

Point out that writers often interrupt the flow of events in narratives to provide background information.

E **ASK STUDENTS** to reread lines 44–48 and summarize how Cairo and the revolution have influenced Soueif as a writer. *(Although it influenced her thinking, Soueif avoided writing about Cairo in the past. Now she wants to write about Cairo because the revolution has made her proud.)*

Analyze Impact of Word Choice on Tone (LINES 61–69)   RI 4

Explain that a writer's **syntax**, or arrangement of words in sentences, can help emphasize ideas and have a cumulative impact on tone.

F **CITE TEXT EVIDENCE** Have students explain how the arrangement of short and long sentences in lines 61–69 has an impact on the meaning and tone. *(The short sentences in lines 66 and 68 help emphasize the ideas in the surrounding sentences and highlight a shift in the tone. "Silently" draws attention to the foreboding, while "We stood" stresses an energized feeling.)*

CRITICAL VOCABULARY

reclaim: The protesters join in a cooperative effort to regain their country from the ruling regime that has repressed their political rights. **ASK STUDENTS** to identify circumstances in which individuals might try to reclaim land or property. *(if something were lost or taken from them)*

prism: Soueif describes how she understands the world through the viewpoint of Cairo, her birthplace. **ASK STUDENTS** to describe how a writer's background may influence the prism through which he or she approaches subjects. *(by relating topics and events to his or her own experiences)*

intermittent: Soueif's description of the noises at the demonstration contribute to a mood of tension. **ASK STUDENTS** to infer what may have caused the intermittent rattling sound that Soueif describes. *(teargas)*

Analyze Ideas and Events

RI 3

(LINES 73–82)

Point out that Soueif interrupts the flow of events again in lines 73–82.

 ASK STUDENTS how the description of the events of eight months ago adds to Soueif's description of the present. (*Informing readers that singing the national anthem was a prosecutable offense provides greater context about the revolution and highlights the significance of the protesters singing at Tahrir [lines 73-77].*)

CRITICAL VOCABULARY

momentous: Soueif describes the significance of the crossroads at which she stands.

ASK STUDENTS to describe why the revolution is a momentous part of Egypt's history. (*It results in an overthrow of the government.*)

COLLABORATIVE DISCUSSION Have student pairs discuss specific textual evidence that suggests why Soueif feels compelled to rejoin the protesters and how she feels empowered and invigorated to become a part of the effort to reclaim her country even though she is risking her life. Then have them share their conclusions with the class as a whole. Accept all reasonable responses.

ASK STUDENTS to share any questions they generated in the course of reading and discussing the selection.

---

we would surge forward: our friends had won us another couple of metres and we followed them and held our ground. We sang the national anthem. Eight months ago some young protestors from the 6 April Group had been arrested in Alexandria for singing the national anthem; it was 'instigatory'[6] the prosecution said. We sang it. On 28 January, standing at that **momentous** crossroads, the Nile behind us, the Arab League building to our left, the old Ministry of Foreign Affairs to our right, seeing nothing up ahead except the gas

80 and smoke and fire that stood between us and our capital, we stood our ground and sang and chanted and placed our lives, with all trust and confidence, in each other's hands.
Some of us died.

momentous
(mō-měn′təs) *adj.* very important; fateful.

COLLABORATIVE DISCUSSION Why does Soueif change her mind about going home? With a partner, discuss how she feels about her decision to become part of the revolution. Cite specific textual evidence from the diary to support your ideas.

---

6 **instigatory:** action that encourages people to rebel.

TO CHALLENGE STUDENTS...

Have advanced learners discuss in small groups how Soueif's description of her decision to join the revolution impacts readers' understanding of the revolution. Discussions should include the following points:

- the dangerousness of the situation
- the risks the protesters assumed

When students have finished, have them share the main points of their discussion with the class.

Analyze Ideas and Events

RI 3

A **diary** is a form of **autobiographical narrative** that includes a daily record of an author's thoughts, experiences, or feelings. Diaries typically recount events in **chronological order;** however, authors often explore relationships between present and past events. For example, Ahdaf Soueif highlights the significance of the protesters singing the Egyptian national anthem by telling readers about protesters who had previously been arrested for doing so. In her diary, Soueif also alludes to events that occur after the entry date of January 28.

When you analyze how an author describes events in a diary, look closely at the order of events and the connections between them. If the author includes information about past and future events, consider how this connects to the current events, helps provide context, and contributes to the overall meaning. Think about why the author chooses to include certain events in a particular order and how this affects your understanding of the text.

Analyze Impact of Word Choice on Tone

RI 4

Tone is an author's attitude toward his or her subject. To create a tone, authors choose words with specific **connotations,** or the attitudes or feelings associated with a word. The connotation of a word or phrase may be positive or negative. For example, the phrase *president's administration* has positive associations, while *president's regime* has negative ones. By noticing an author's choice of words, you can detect and analyze his or her tone.

In "Cairo: My City, Our Revolution," Ahdaf Soueif shifts or changes her tone to reflect the events she is describing. As you analyze the text, think about how specific words impact the tone of particular sentences or whole sections of the text. Use a chart to help you analyze specific words and details.

Word Choice	Tone
"The Opera House looms dark on our right"	*Looms* has a negative connotation and creates a threatening tone in the sentence.

TEACH

CLOSE READ

Analyze Ideas and Events

RI 3

Tell students that they must first identify the sequence of events in order to analyze the connections between them. To illustrate this point, work with students to complete a chart like the one below. Then discuss the cause-effect relationship between the events.

> Soueif flees the protest area by boat.

▼

> Soueif joins the revolution.

Analyze the Impact of Word Choice on Tone

RI 4

To help students analyze the impact of word choice on tone, make sure they understand positive and negative connotations. Read aloud the example in the chart. Then ask students to explain the effects of replacing *looms* with a word that has more positive connotations, such as *appears.* (*The tone would become less threatening.*)

Strategies for Annotation  Annotate it!

Analyze the Impact of Word Choice on Tone

RI 4

Share these strategies for guided or independent analysis:

- Highlight in yellow words and phrases that reveal Soueif's attitude toward her subject.
- On notes, record your descriptions of Soueif's tone for each highlighted area.

> We look back at where we were just minutes ago, on 6 October Bridge, and see a Central Security Forces personnel carrier on fire, backing off, four young men chasing it, leaping at it, beating at its windscreen. The vehicle is reversing wildly, careering backwards east towards Downtown. Behind us, a ball of fire

tone: tense

PRACTICE & APPLY

Analyzing the Text
RI 1, RI 3, RI 4

Possible answers:

1. The description of Cairo as viewed from a distance (lines 8-13) emphasizes the danger and magnitude of the scene. The reader can visualize the throngs of people who look like one big solid mass and the air that's heavy with smoke and tear gas.

2. Phrases and clauses such as "still, steely grey," "small scattered fires burn and fizz," "opaque dusk, heavy with tear gas," "bright new pool of flame," and "the Opera House looms dark" contribute to a serious, forbidding tone.

3. This information makes the scene seem even more threatening and helps the reader understand the seriousness of the situation that the author is about to enter.

4. While the tone is still serious, it becomes more triumphant and empowered. Evidence includes her personification of Egypt, "Ya Masr, it's been a long time" (line 54) and renewed feelings of ownership for her city, "Because my city is mine again" (line 49). The images of the hotels with shuttered ground floors and "stick figures" on the balconies and the sound of the "continuous thud of guns" still add an element of foreboding; however, this is overshadowed by the feelings evoked through the descriptions of the cooperation and solidarity among the protesters, "I stumbled and a hand under my elbow steadied me" (lines 59-60).

5. She describes the city as "looking over [her] shoulder."

6. The scene helps the reader understand the energized mood that the author is describing and the historic significance of the events. The reference to "it's been a long time" helps the reader understand the joy of the people because of the length of their struggle.

7. This creates a more serious tone in contrast to the energized, almost celebratory feel of the previous sentences.

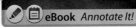

Analyzing the Text
RI 1, RI 3, RI 4,
W 2b, W 7,
W 8, SL 4

Cite Text Evidence Support your responses with evidence from the selection.

1. **Analyze** Soueif first describes Cairo as viewed from the river at a distance, rather than from within the protest. How does this help the reader visualize the scene?

2. **Cite Evidence** Describe the tone of the first two paragraphs. How does Soueif's word choice in the first two paragraphs affect the tone? Give specific examples to support your analysis.

3. **Infer** At the end of the second paragraph Soueif tells readers that "the lights of Cairo will not come on tonight," referring to a government-imposed curfew and shutdown of Internet and phone communications. How does this glimpse into the future contribute to Soueif's description of the present?

4. **Cite Evidence** Once Soueif and her nieces join the protest, there is a distinct shift in the tone. Describe this change, citing specific examples of language that contribute to the tone.

5. **Interpret** Personification is a type of figurative language in which human qualities are given to nonliving things. In lines 45–47, how does Soueif **personify** the city of Cairo?

6. **Infer** In lines 49–54, Soueif provides a description of the scene in Tahrir on February 1. How does this scene help the reader understand how the events are unfolding?

7. **Analyze** Notice how Soueif ends this diary entry with the simple sentence, "Some of us died." How does this sentence contrast with the events she describes in lines 55–58? How does it change the tone of the text?

PERFORMANCE TASK

Research Activity: Informative Oral Report In her diary, Ahdaf Soueif provides her own personal account of the Egyptian revolution of 2011. Explore the topic in greater depth through two brief tasks:

1. Conduct research about a specific event in the revolution. Gather information from multiple sources and remember to cite them following standard format.

2. Write a brief report of your findings and share it with the class. Be sure to include well-chosen, relevant, and sufficient facts in your report.

Assign this performance task.

PERFORMANCE TASK
W 2b, W 7, W 8, SL 4

Research Activity: Informative Oral Report Have students work independently to conduct research and draft their reports. See page 80a for further instruction on using search terms and search-engine qualifiers effectively. Students' reports should synthesize information from multiple sources about a specific event in the revolution.

Critical Vocabulary

opaque   reclaim   prism   intermittent   momentous

Practice and Apply Use the Critical Vocabulary words to answer each question. Then, with a partner, take turns supporting your answers.

1. Which word is an antonym, or a word opposite in meaning, to the word **insignificant**?

2. Which word most closely relates to the word **irregular**?

3. Which word is an antonym to the word **transparent**?

4. Which word most closely relates to the word **reflection**?

5. Which word most closely relates to the word **restore**?

Vocabulary Strategy: Reference Sources

When you read an informational text, looking up words or terms in print and digital **reference sources** such as dictionaries, glossaries or thesauruses can help you better understand the central ideas of the text.

> Read this sentence from Ahdaf Soueif's diary.

> **And this time our project was to save and to <u>reclaim</u> our country.**

In this sentence, you can determine the general meaning of the Critical Vocabulary word *reclaim* by using the context clue "to save." However, if you also look up the word *reclaim* in a dictionary, you gain a further understanding that the people were working to reclaim, or bring back, their country from the ruling regime that had restricted their freedoms.

Practice and Apply The underlined words in these sentences are also used in "Cairo: My City, Our Revolution." Use context clues in each sentence to write a definition for the underlined word. Then look up the words in a dictionary, glossary, or thesaurus. Confirm or revise your definitions with additional information from the reference sources.

1. The protester avoided contact and <u>shied</u> away from the angry crowd.

2. The car went <u>careering</u> toward the barrier at full speed to break it down.

3. The people sent the government a message when they wrote their <u>declaration</u> of freedom.

4. The tall fences could not hold back the crowd as they slowly pushed and <u>surged</u> down the street.

PRACTICE & APPLY

Critical Vocabulary

Answers:

1. *momentous*

2. *intermittent*

3. *opaque*

4. *prism*

5. *reclaim*

Vocabulary Strategy: Reference Sources

Possible answers:

Word	Context Clues	My Guessed Definition	Dictionary Definition
shied	*avoided contact*	*moved*	*avoided contact*
careering	*at full speed*	*speeding*	*rushing at high speed*
declaration	*message*	*letter*	*formal announcement*
surged	*pushed*	*rushed*	*moved or advanced like a wave*

Strategies for Annotation   📝 📖 *Annotate it!*

Reference Sources

Have students reread the diary to clarify the meaning of unfamiliar words or terms. Encourage them to use their eBook annotation tools to do the following:

- Highlight any unfamiliar words in the text.
- Underline context clues that help you infer the word's meaning.
- Use the notes tool to write the word's preliminary definition.
- Use a reference source to check the inferred meaning.

Security vehicles racing to get out of town and all the men leaning over the parapet above us with stones in their hands stopped in mid-throw and yelled 'Run! Run!' and held off with the stones so they wouldn't hit us as we <u>skittered</u> through the screeching vehicles to a spot where we could scramble up the bank and join the people

> inferred meaning: ran quickly

PRACTICE & APPLY

Language and Style: Noun Phrases

L 1b

Point out to students that the graphic organizer provides additional examples of noun phrases from the text. Invite volunteers to suggest other examples of noun phrases that might describe a protest. *(rhythmic chants, billowing flags)*

Possible answers: *Students should follow the conventions of standard English grammar and usage to add noun phrases to their reports. Then they should share and discuss their revisions with a partner.*

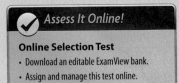

Assess It Online!

Online Selection Test
- Download an editable ExamView bank.
- Assign and manage this test online.

Language and Style: Noun Phrases

L 1b

A **noun phrase** includes a noun and its **modifiers,** or the words that affect the noun's meaning. In "Cairo: My City, Our Revolution," Ahdaf Soueif uses noun phrases to add vivid descriptions of the protests.

Read the following sentence from the diary:

> And we can open our eyes—
> To see <u>an opaque dusk, heavy with tear gas.</u>

By splitting the sentence between the first and second paragraphs, the author emphasizes the underlined noun phrase. The author could have provided the information in this sentence much more simply:

> The tear gas limits our visibility.

Instead, she uses the noun phrase to allow readers to see and feel what the air feels like. Later in the paragraph, the author uses another descriptive noun phrase to contrast this image from the usual appearance and feel of the sky:

> The sky too is grey—so different from the <u>airy twilight</u> you normally get at this time of day.

When you revise your own writing to add descriptive noun phrases, think about the specific meaning you want to convey to your audience. Ask yourself what details need more variety and interest. It may help to jot down ideas in a graphic organizer.

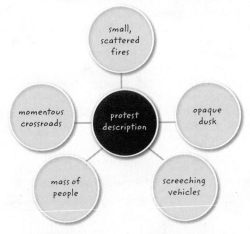

Practice and Apply Look back at the report you created for this selection's Performance Task. Revise the report to add more descriptive noun phrases. Remember to use the conventions of standard English grammar and usage. When you have finished revising, exchange reports with a partner and discuss how you strengthened your writing.

INTERACTIVE WHITEBOARD LESSON
Conduct Research on the Web
W 7

Learn the Skill ▸ Search Strategies

Search Strategies
Review some effective Web search strategies.

Find Information About Countries

Several reputable Web sites offer accurate information about countries of the world.

Examples:
- **CIA World Factbook**
  https://www.cia.gov/library/publications/the-world-factbook/index.html
- **BBC News Country Profiles**
  http://news.bbc.co.uk/2/hi/country_profiles/default.stm

Information About Countries   Primary Sources   Wikis

TEACH

Before students begin research for their Performance Task, review the steps from the whiteboard lesson for doing research:

- **Step 1: Formulate Research Questions** For example: *What events occurred during the Egyptian Revolution? What people or groups were involved in the events?*

- **Step 2: Start Your Search** Determine the best site to begin your search. You might choose to start at a reliable encyclopedia or media site to establish basic facts or use a **keyword search** on a search engine.

- **Step 3: Analyze Your Options** Select the sites that offer the most relevant and reliable information. Remember that commercial sites (.com) and sites such as Wikipedia may not provide accurate or unbiased information. In most cases, government, educational institution, or nonprofit sites (.gov, .edu, .org) are more reliable.

- **Step 4: Refine Your Search** You may need to make your search more specific by using search-engine qualifiers such as AND, OR, or NOT along with search terms to get the information you want.

COLLABORATIVE DISCUSSION

Direct students to work in small groups to complete the first three steps in doing research for the Performance Task. Have them share their results with the group and compare their chosen sources. The group can then work together to provide suggestions for completing the research.

Analyze Ideas and Events
RI 3

RETEACH

Review the following key questions students should ask themselves to analyze ideas and events in an autobiographical narrative:

- What words and phrases show the order of events?

- How does the author reveal his or her ideas about the events?

- For what purposes, if any, does the author interrupt the flow of events?

- How does the order in which points are made affect the readers' understanding of the ideas and events?

- What connections does the author draw between events?

LEVEL UP TUTORIALS Assign the following *Level Up* tutorial: **Chronological Order.**

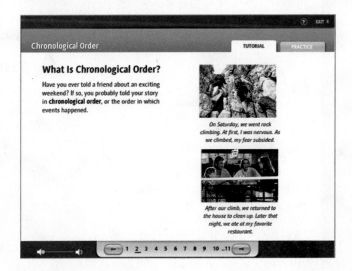

Chronological Order   TUTORIAL   PRACTICE

What Is Chronological Order?

Have you ever told a friend about an exciting weekend? If so, you probably told your story in **chronological order,** or the order in which events happened.

On Saturday, we went rock climbing. At first, I was nervous. As we climbed, my fear subsided.

After our climb, we returned to the house to clean up. Later that night, we ate at my favorite restaurant.

1 2 3 4 5 6 7 8 9 10 ..11

INDEPENDENT READING

Have students apply the skill to another autobiographical narrative they have read and share their analyses in a small group discussion. They should select a passage that uses time-order signal words to show the relationship between events. Students should also note whether the author interrupts the sequence of events to provide additional information about events that happened outside of the main narrative. If so, they should identify and explain how this information changes the readers' understanding of the main narrative.

from Reading Lolita in Tehran

Memoir by Azar Nafisi

from Persepolis 2:
The Story of a Return

Graphic Novel by Marjane Satrapi

Why These Texts?

Students may have some awareness of the way women are treated in Iran from news reports. This lesson explores that subject from the perspective of two Iranian women.

Key Learning Objective: The student will be able to determine author's point of view and analyze accounts in different mediums.

RI 1	Cite textual evidence.
RI 2	Determine a central idea of a text and analyze its development.
RI 6	Determine an author's point of view and analyze how an author uses rhetoric to advance that point of view.
RI 7	Analyze accounts in different mediums.
W 3	Write narratives to develop real or imagined experiences.
W 6	Use technology to produce and publish writing products.
L 3	Apply knowledge of language to make effective choices for meaning or style, and to comprehend more fully when reading.
L 4	Determine the meaning of unknown and multiple-meaning words and phrases.
L 5b	Analyze nuances in the meaning of words with similar denotations.

▲ Text Complexity Rubric

	from **Reading Lolita in Tehran** Lexile: 1150L	*from* **Persepolis 2** Lexile: N/A
Quantitative Measures		
Qualitative Measures	**Levels of Meaning/Purpose** more than one purpose; implied but easy to infer	**Levels of Meaning/Purpose** single purpose, explicitly stated
	Structure organization of main ideas and details is highly complex; not explicit and must be inferred by the reader	**Structure** genre traits more specific to graphic novels
	Language Conventionality and Clarity clear, direct language	**Language Conventionality and Clarity** some familiar language
	Knowledge Demands somewhat complex social studies concepts	**Knowledge Demands** complex civics concepts
Reader/Task Considerations	• Teacher determined • Vary by individual reader and type of text • See the Text X-Ray for suggested Reader/Task Considerations.	

English Language Support
Before teaching, use the Text X-Ray below for an overview of the text's complexity. The Text X-Ray and the supports and scaffolds in the Teacher's Edition will help you guide students of different skill levels.

Meaning Making

Language Development

Effective Expression

Content Knowledge

Foundational Skills

Text Complexity: Qualitative Measures

▲ Levels of Meaning/Purpose

Help students determine an author's point of view.
- Teacher's Edition side notes, pp. 82, 83, 84, 85
- Strategies for Annotation, p. 85
- Determine Author's Point of View, p. 85

Guide students to determine an author's purpose.
- Teacher's Edition side note, p. 81

To help students synthesize information across mediums, see
- Synthesize Information, p. 88a

To reteach determining point of view, see
- Determine Point of View, p. 88a

 Use It! **Interactive Whiteboard Lesson:** Historical and Cultural Contexts

ZOOM IN ON **DETERMINING POINT OF VIEW** Point out that each author describes the effects of the repressive Iranian regime from her own **point of view**. Pose this question: Based on details in the graphic novel, what is Satrapi's view on the main reason the Iranian government enforces such a strict dress code for women?

- Give students time to consider the question independently and take notes.
- Have pairs meet to discuss their ideas and the text details that support them.
- Ask pairs to share their conclusions with the class. *(Sample answer: By forcing women to focus on tiny details of their dress and to live in fear, the government prevents them from opposing other policies that seriously limit their rights.)*

▲ Structure

Help students analyze accounts in different mediums.
- Teacher's Edition side notes, pp. 82, 84, 85
- When Students Struggle, p. 84
- Analyze Accounts in Different Mediums, p. 85

Guide students to rewrite a text account in a different medium.
- Performance Task, p. 86

ZOOM IN ON **SYNTHESIZING ACROSS MEDIUMS** Use these questions to help students **synthesize** ideas from the selections.

- What is the main difference between how the **memoir** and how the **graphic novel** convey ideas? *(The memoir uses text only, while the graphic novel uses both pictures and text.)*
- What ideas do both selections convey about the rules governing Iranian women's dress and appearance? *(The rules are strict, unfair, and hurtful to women.)*
- How do both selections say Iranian women respond to the rules? *(The rules make women fearful, but many women rebel against the rules despite the threat of harsh punishment.)*

▲ Language Conventionality and Clarity

Teach unfamiliar vocabulary in context.

- Teacher's Edition Critical Vocabulary notes, pp. 82, 83, 87
- English Language Support, p. 81
- Applying Academic Vocabulary, p. 83

Help students recognize different verb tenses.

- English Language Support, p. 82

Guide students to analyze and apply the use of rhetorical questions.

- Teacher's Edition side notes, pp. 83, 88

Help students analyze denotations and connotations.

- Teacher's Edition side note, p. 87
- To Challenge Students, p. 87

ZOOM IN ON **USING CONTEXT CLUES** Before students read the graphic novel, display these words and phrases: *revolutionary, discreet, hinged on, subversion, pretext, repression*. Have students record them in a three-column chart with the headings "Word or Phrase," "Definition from Context," and "Dictionary Definition." Have students read the text in pairs, discussing each word or phrase and the **context clues** around it. They should write their best guess as to the word's meaning in the second column. When they have finished reading, have them use a dictionary to check their definitions. They may then record the dictionary definitions in the third column.

▲ Knowledge Demands

Support English Learners in understanding the historical and cultural context of the texts.

- Teacher's Edition Background note, p. 81

ZOOM IN ON **BUILDING HISTORICAL KNOWLEDGE** Have students read the caption in the second panel of the graphic novel. Work with them to clarify the **sequence of events** implied by the caption.

- 1979: The Shah of Iran is overthrown; Ayatollah Khomeini becomes Supreme Leader of the new Islamic Republic.
- 1980–1983: Khomeini's government suppresses opposition to its rule by imprisoning and executing protesters.
- 1990: By the time events in the graphic novel take place, Iranians no longer dare to protest the government openly.

▲ Suggested Reader/Task Considerations

You might consider the following before assigning this memoir and graphic novel to students.

- Might students feel uncomfortable reading or discussing any part of the text?
- Do students have the skills they need to draw **inferences** from details in the text?

ZOOM IN ON **SUPPORTING COMPREHENSION**

- In both texts, the head scarf or hijab is portrayed mainly as a tool for repressing women. Explain that many Muslim women wear the hijab by choice, as a symbol of modesty or privacy. Allow students who wear the hijab to explain, if they would like to, what it means to them.
- Remind students that readers often must **infer** information based on details in the text. Ask them why Sanaz might have to "confront her brother" (line 62) when she gets home. (*Her brother and other men in the family enforce the rules about women's behavior; he may not approve of her book group meetings.*)

TEACH

CLOSE READ

Background Have students read the background and information about the authors. Tell students that in countries with oppressive regimes such as Iran's, openly protesting the government is very dangerous. Both of these selections give an Iranian woman's perspective on living in a country under such a regime.

AS YOU READ Direct students to use the As You Read question to focus their reading.

Determine Author's Purpose
RI 6

Explain that clues to an author's purpose, or reason for writing, can be found in information about their lives. An author usually writes for one or more purposes: to express thoughts or feelings, to explain, to persuade, or to entertain.

Ⓐ ASK STUDENTS to reread the information about Azar Nafisi and Marjane Satrapi. What purpose(s) might these authors have in writing these texts? How might the similarities and differences in their personal histories affect their purpose(s)? Encourage students to provide evidence from the biographies to support their answers and revisit their ideas as they read the texts. *(Both authors are Iranian and their biographies show that they were affected by the changes the revolution brought to Iran. They may have written their texts to inform their readers about life in Iran. However, Marjane Satrapi may also want to share her thoughts and feelings about her difficulties in adolescence, while Azar Nafisi explains how a group of women continued to learn even though the Iranian authorities made it difficult.)*

Background *The Iranian Revolution in the late 1970's resulted in the overthrow of the pro-western Shah of Iran. Iranians established a theocracy, or religious government, based on the rule of Islam. The new government passed laws that segregate men and women and that force women to adhere to an Islamic dress code. Iranian women are required to wear veils that cover their hair and neck and coats that cover their arms and legs. The "morality police" ensure that people comply with the laws. People who do not comply may be taken to the morality police headquarters (called* the Committee *in Persepolis 2) to be questioned, beaten, or jailed.*

from
Reading Lolita in Tehran

Memoir by Azar Nafisi

from **Persepolis 2**

Graphic Novel by Marjane Satrapi
Translated by Anjali Singh

Azar Nafisi (b. 1947), *an Iranian, taught English literature in Tehran from 1979 until 1995. The laws passed after the revolution made Nafisi's job difficult. University faculty scrutinized novels that Nafisi taught, and Nafisi was chastised for not wearing a veil. In 1995, Nafisi left the university and began teaching a small group of women in her home, where they were free to discuss books, like Lolita, that were considered unacceptable by Iranian authorities. In 1997, she left Iran for the United States, where she now teaches.*

Marjane Satrapi (b. 1969) *was born in Iran. After the revolution, Satrapi's parents sent her to Europe to attend school. Later, she studied illustration and learned to create comics.* Persepolis 1 *tells the story of her childhood in Iran, and* Persepolis 2 *tells the story of her adolescence in Europe and Iran and of her struggle to fit in. Both books were made into the animated movie,* Persepolis, *which won many awards. Satrapi has written other graphic novels, including* Chicken with Plums. *She lives in Paris with her husband.*

AS YOU READ Identify points of comparison between the memoir and the graphic novel. Write down any questions you generate as you read.

ENGLISH LANGUAGE SUPPORT

Language: Context Clues Read aloud the background information and the two short biographies while students follow along in the text. When you have finished, invite them to point out words and phrases in each paragraph that are unclear or confusing. Discuss context clues that could help them figure out the meanings. For example, the meaning of the phrase *comply with* in line 7 of the Background paragraph is made clearer by the second use of the word in line 8: "People who do not comply may be taken to the morality police headquarters . . . ." The use of the negative *not* and the consequence makes it clearer that *comply* means "to follow or accept" the laws.

Analyze Accounts in Different Mediums (LINES 4–10) RI 7

Point out to students that although the excerpt from *Reading Lolita in Tehran* doesn't include illustrations, the author does include many details to help readers visualize her account. The author, in fact, directly asks readers to use their imagination.

B **CITE TEXT EVIDENCE** Have students read lines 4–10 and identify the descriptive details the author employs to help readers create a "picture" of Sanaz. *(black robe and scarf, orange shirt and jeans, gold earrings, large bag, lacy black gloves, painted nails)*

Determine Author's Point of View (LINES 12–16) RI 6

Explain that authors use **rhetoric,** or persuasive and effective language, to advance or support their point of view.

C **CITE TEXT EVIDENCE** Have students reread the author's description of Sanaz walking in lines 12–16. What is the author's point of view about how Sanaz must travel? Have them cite details to support their ideas. *(The author is unhappy or angry that Sanaz must change the way she looks and walks to be safe on the street. The author says that "It is in her best interest not to be seen, not be heard or noticed." [lines 13-14] This shows that the author doesn't agree with what Sanaz and all women have to do on the street in Iran.)*

CRITICAL VOCABULARY

segregate: In Iran, women are kept separate from men in public. **ASK STUDENTS** who ensures that women and men are segregated. *(Militia, named the Blood of God, patrol the streets to make sure that women are not in public with men who are not in their family. [lines 17-19])*

allocate: The rear seats of the buses are designated for women. **ASK STUDENTS** to discuss why the seats allocated to women are in the back of the bus and not the front or another location. *(So that the women are not be seen by men. The rear location also indicates that women are second-class citizens.)*

---

from Reading Lolita in Tehran
Memoir by Azar Nafisi

How can I create this other world outside the room? I have no choice but to appeal once again to your imagination. Let's imagine one of the girls, say Sanaz, leaving my house and let us follow her from there to her final destination. She says her good-byes and puts on her black robe and scarf over her orange shirt and jeans, coiling her scarf around her neck to cover her huge gold earrings. She directs wayward strands of hair under the scarf, puts her notes into her large bag, straps it on over her shoulder and walks out into the hall. She pauses a moment on top of the stairs to
10 put on thin lacy black gloves to hide her nail polish.

We follow Sanaz down the stairs, out the door and into the street. You might notice that her gait[1] and her gestures have changed. It is in her best interest not to be seen, not be heard or noticed. She doesn't walk upright, but bends her head towards the ground and doesn't look at passersby. She walks quickly and with a sense of determination. The streets of Tehran and other Iranian cities are patrolled by militia, who ride in white Toyota patrols, four gun-carrying men and women, sometimes followed by a minibus.
20 They are called the Blood of God. They patrol the streets to make sure that women like Sanaz wear their veils properly, do not wear makeup, do not walk in public with men who are not their fathers, brothers or husbands. She will pass slogans on the walls, quotations from Khomeini[2] and a group called the Party of God: MEN WHO WEAR TIES ARE U.S. LACKEYS.[3] VEILING IS A WOMAN'S PROTECTION. Beside the slogan is a charcoal drawing of a woman: her face is featureless and framed by a dark chador.[4] MY SISTER, GUARD YOUR VEIL. MY BROTHER, GUARD YOUR EYES.

If she gets on a bus, the seating is **segregated**. She must enter
30 through the rear door and sit in the back seats, **allocated** to women. Yet in taxis, which accept as many as five passengers, men and women are squeezed together like sardines, as the saying goes, and the same goes with minibuses, where so many of my students complain of being harassed by bearded and God-fearing men.

You might well ask, What is Sanaz thinking as she walks the streets of Tehran? How much does this experience affect her? Most

segregate
(sĕg´rĭ-gāt´) *v.* to cause people to be separated based on gender, race, or other factors.

allocate
(ăl´ə-kāt´) *v.* to assign or designate for.

---

[1] **gait:** manner of walking.
[2] **Khomeini (kō-mā´ nē):** Ruhollah Khomeini (1902–1989), religious and political leader of Iran after the 1979 revolution.
[3] **U.S. lackeys:** people who serve United States policies. The Iranian government is hostile to the U.S. because it supported the former Shah of Iran.
[4] **chador:** a long scarf that covers a Muslim woman's hair, neck, and shoulders.

ENGLISH LANGUAGE SUPPORT

Language: Verb Tenses Review verb forms with students. Invite volunteers to mark up lines 11–29. Underline any progressive forms. Then highlight simple verb forms in yellow and perfect verb forms in blue.

You might notice that her gait and her gestures have changed.

ASK STUDENTS to discuss the effect of the author's use of the simple present tense. *(It conveys a sense of immediacy to Sanaz's journey.)*

probably, she tries to distance her mind as much as possible from her surroundings. Perhaps she is thinking of her brother, or of her distant boyfriend and the time when she will meet him in Turkey.
40 Does she compare her own situation with her mother's when she was the same age? Is she angry that women of her mother's generation could walk the streets freely, enjoy the company of the opposite sex, join the police force, become pilots, live under laws that were among the most progressive in the world regarding women? Does she feel humiliated by the new laws, by the fact that after the revolution, the age of marriage was lowered from eighteen to nine, that stoning became once more the punishment for adultery and prostitution?

   In the course of nearly two decades, the streets have been
50 turned into a war zone, where young women who disobey the rules are hurled into patrol cars, taken to jail, flogged, fined, forced to wash the toilets and humiliated, and as soon as they leave, they go back and do the same thing. Is she aware, Sanaz, of her own power? Does she realize how dangerous she can be when her every stray gesture is a disturbance to public safety? Does she think how vulnerable the Revolutionary Guards are who for over eighteen years have patrolled the streets of Tehran and have had to endure young women like herself, and those of other generations, walking, talking, showing a strand of hair just to remind them that they have
60 not **converted**?

   We have reached Sanaz's house, where we will leave her on her doorstep, perhaps to confront her brother on the other side and to think in her heart of her boyfriend.

   These girls, my girls, had both a real history and a fabricated one. Although they came from very different backgrounds, the regime that ruled them had tried to make their personal identities and histories **irrelevant**. They were never free of the regime's definition of them as Muslim women.

convert
(kən-vûrt′) *v.* to change one's system of beliefs.

irrelevant
(ĭ-rĕl′ə-vənt) *adj.* insignificant, unimportant.

APPLYING ACADEMIC VOCABULARY

enable	reveal

THINK-PAIR-SHARE Have students turn to a partner to discuss the following questions. Guide students to include the academic vocabulary words *enable* and *reveal* in their responses. Ask volunteers to share their responses with the class.

- How does the authors' work **enable** them to help the women of Iran?
- How do the authors use rhetorical techniques to **reveal** the political realities for women in Iran?

CLOSE READ

Determine Author's Point of View (LINES 40–48)   RI 6

Explain that the author conveys her point of view about the regime without literally giving her opinions.

D ASK STUDENTS how lines 40-48 help the author convince readers about her point of view. *(By speculating on Sanaz's thoughts, she educates readers about the changes for women in Iran over the course of one generation. She conveys outrage by contrasting Sanaz's life to that of her mother's at the same age.)*

Language and Style: Rhetorical Questions   L 3
(LINES 41–45)

Remind students that authors often use rhetorical questions to express a viewpoint.

E ASK STUDENTS to reread the rhetorical question in lines 41–45. What viewpoint does the author express in the phrase "live under laws that were among the most progressive in the world regarding women"? *(The author expresses disappointment for Sanaz and for herself. She expresses how much women and society have lost because of the changed laws.)*

> **CRITICAL VOCABULARY**
>
> **converted**: The author points out that women can do small, subtle things to show that they do not share the beliefs of the Revolutionary Guards.
>
> **ASK STUDENTS** why it would be difficult for women to "convert" to the thinking of the Iranian government. *(The government violates women's human rights. Women must submit to the laws, but are not deterred from showing they do not agree.)*
>
> **irrelevant**: The author is emphasizing that the regime's laws regarding women took away their ability to express themselves as individuals.
>
> **ASK STUDENTS** how the regime's laws made personal histories irrelevant. *(By forcing all women to dress the same and not letting them express themselves publicly, the regime made it difficult for women to speak out against it.)*

Determine Author's Point of View (PANEL 1)   RI 6

Explain that in a graphic novel, the author conveys a point of view through both images and words.

F **CITE TEXT EVIDENCE** Have students look at the first panel of the selection. Ask them what aspects of the narrator's physical appearance they notice, and how these details help express the author's point of view when considered along with the text in the panel. (*The text talks about confronting the regime. The woman is wearing traditional Muslim dress. Her arms are crossed in a somewhat defensive gesture. Her face wears an unhappy expression, and her eyebrows are raised, again hinting at defensiveness. These details help convey the author's frustration and sadness that women must confront the regime.*)

COLLABORATIVE DISCUSSION Have student pairs discuss common elements and differences in the memoir and graphic novel. Then have them share their observations with the class as a whole. (*Both text and graphic novel a discuss the difficulties of living in Iran with the Revolutionary Guard (or morality police) harassing women about their dress. Reading Lolita in Tehran takes the reader on a journey with a young women through the streets, while the graphic novel depicts a similar situation from the point of view of a teenage girl. Both texts consider how the repressive laws of Iran have changed the way women live and think. The way the texts speak to the reader is different. Reading Lolita in Tehran asks the reader directly to visualize what the author is describing. The graphic novel tells the "story" from the point of view of the girl, reaching out to the reader in the first person.*)

ASK STUDENTS to share any questions they generated in the course of reading and discussing the selection.

---

from Persepolis 2: The Story of a Return
Graphic Novel by Marjane Satrapi

COLLABORATIVE DISCUSSION With a partner, discuss common elements in the memoir and graphic novel. How is the way the authors communicate with readers similar and different in the texts? Support your ideas with evidence from both.

WHEN STUDENTS STRUGGLE . . .

Draw a Venn diagram or comparison-contrast matrix on the board. Work with students to compare these elements of the two selections.

- Perspective (*In* Reading Lolita in Tehran *readers are invited to "watch" Sanaz. In* Persepolis 2 *the story is told directly to us.*)
- Author's Point of View (*Satrapi is frustrated at the lack of power women have, while Nafisi argues that women still hold power in their small acts of rebellion.*)
- Central Idea (*Both authors focus on and celebrate the fact that all forms of rebellion are valuable when people are fighting repression, but the authors also express disappointment that larger and more effective forms of rebellion are not possible.*)

Determine Author's Point of View
RI 6

Point of view refers to how an author thinks or feels about a subject. In a memoir, an author uses rhetoric, choosing words carefully to advance a point of view. Graphic novelists, however, use both graphics and rhetoric to advance their points of view.

- Azar Nafisi wrote *Reading Lolita in Tehran* after she left Iran to live abroad. Her **perspective** as a woman and a scholar living under an oppressive regime is reflected in the rhetoric she uses. In the excerpt, Nafisi reproduces slogans that scream in uppercase letters: MY SISTER, GUARD YOUR VEIL. MY BROTHER, GUARD YOUR EYES. She constructs phrases such as, "flogged, fined, forced to wash toilets and humiliated," and "when her every stray gesture is a disturbance to public safety" to communicate her point of view.
- Unlike the memoir, *Persepolis 2* tells Marjane Satrapi's story through words and stark black and white images. In this excerpt, the author's perspective as a young woman out of place in a rigid and uncompromising society is reflected in the way the main character's face is drawn. It is also shown in the juxtaposition of panels next to each other. Careful readers must study details in the drawings, as well as read captions and thought bubbles, to understand the author's point of view.

Analyze Accounts in Different Mediums
RI 7

A personal story can be told using different **mediums,** or ways of communicating. Mediums may include memoirs, graphic novels, plays, or films. Each format allows the author to emphasize details that help to tell his or her story. The challenge for the author is determining which medium tells the story in the most compelling way. The challenge for readers or viewers is to determine which details are emphasized and how those details convey the author's message.

Read this sentence from *Reading Lolita in Tehran*:

> They patrol the streets to make sure that women like Sanaz wear their veils properly, do not wear makeup, do not walk in public with men who are not their fathers, brothers or husbands.

Notice how this memoir is a personal account written from memory or first-hand knowledge. The writer uses concrete details and sensory words to help the reader visualize events and people.

In contrast, the middle panel in the second row of *Persepolis 2* provides visuals for the reader to understand a similar situation. Graphic novels show action through images and use words sparingly, through speech bubbles and captions. Readers must pay attention to the visual details in the drawings and to the sequence of the panels to understand the author's message.

TEACH

CLOSE READ

Determine Author's Point of View
RI 6

Ask students to consider how someone with a different point of view might tell *Reading Lolita in Tehran* or *Persepolis 2*. For example, how might the stories be different if told from the point of view of

- an Iranian man who supports women's rights?
- a member of the Iranian police?
- an American woman?

Assign small groups of students one of the above perspectives. Have each group develop a one-page graphic representation telling about the experience of Iranian women from their assigned point of view. As a class, discuss how different points of view changed the way they told the stories.

Analyze Accounts in Different Mediums
RI 7

Help students explore how different mediums offer different opportunities and limitations in telling the same story. Create a list of different mediums, such as text, visual or audio representation, and physical (as in miming) of expression on the board. List the pros and cons of each in conveying a story and important ideas.

Strategies for Annotation
 Annotate it!

Determine Author's Point of View
RI 6

Share these strategies for guided or independent analysis.

- After the first two paragraphs or panels of the selections, make a note about the authors' points of view.
- Underline each visual or rhetorical detail that helps the authors advance their points of view. Reread your underlines, noting the techniques the authors use to advance their points of view.
- At the end of each selection, cite text evidence to show how effective you think each author was in expressing a viewpoint.

cities are patrolled by militia, who ride in white Toyota patrols, four gun-carrying men and women, sometimes followed by a minibus. They are called the Blood of God. They patrol the streets to make sure that women like Sanaz wear their veils properly, do not wear makeup, do not walk in public with men who are not their fathers, brothers or husbands. She will pass slogans on the walls, quotations

Analyzing Text and Media

RI 1, RI 2, RI 6, RI 7

Possible answers:

1. *Details include: Sanaz putting on her black robe over her orange shirt and jeans and coiling her scarf around her neck to cover her earrings. There is a description of how Sanaz walks, with her head bent down, quickly and with determination. The author includes these details to help the reader visualize the "real" Sanaz underneath the dress.*

2. *In "Lolita" the author addresses the reader with phrases like "Let's imagine;" "We follow;" "You might well ask;" which makes us feel more connected to the text. In "Persepolis" the illustrations emphasize the seriousness of the issue and the text conveys the convictions of the author. Both texts effectively communicate the authors' dissatisfaction with the position of women in Iran.*

3. *The author is referring to Sanaz's desire to express herself. Sanaz can be dangerous because she risks disturbing the public order by standing out as an individual. In contrast, the character in "Persepolis" doesn't feel the same empowerment. She talks about how the regime created a society where people were afraid and rebelled in small ways instead of working on solutions to bigger issues.*

4. *In the second panel, graphics portray students, fists raised, protesting. The caption explains that these students were arrested and or killed, and the protests stopped. In the third panel, women are wearing makeup and looking feminine. The caption suggests that these acts were the new form of rebellion: Our struggle was more discreet.*

5. *The regime saw red socks as an act of rebellion, of nonconformity, which they wanted to stomp out.*

6. *The narrator's expression displays unhappiness, worry, and puzzlement. The author points out that women are disturbed by what is happening, but don't know how to make any real changes.*

7. *Both authors emphasize that although the regime forced women to be anonymous, women found ways to rebel and express themselves. The author of "Lolita" expressed that this determination was a threat to the authorities. However, the author of "Persepolis" expresses dismay about the disempowerment of women. Analyzing both works helps the reader understand the complex viewpoints that women in Iran have about their repression.*

 eBook *Annotate It!*

Analyzing Text and Media

RI 1, RI 2, RI 6, RI 7, W 3, W 6

Cite Text Evidence   Support your responses with evidence from the selections.

1. **Interpret** Identify details the author of *Reading Lolita in Tehran* uses to describe Sanaz. Why might the author have included these details?

2. **Critique** How is the rhetoric that both authors use effective in conveying their points of view? Explain with evidence from the texts.

3. **Infer** The author of *Reading Lolita in Tehran* wonders aloud if Sanaz is aware of her own power. What power is the author referring to? Does the main character in *Persepolis* feel that she has a similar power? Explain.

4. **Analyze** Look at the second and third panels in *Persepolis 2*. How does the author use both words and graphics to make a point about how the people's struggle had changed?

5. **Infer** The narrator of *Persepolis 2* says that she spent an entire day at the Committee because of a pair of red socks. What might red socks have **symbolized**, or represented, to the Committee?

6. **Interpret** In *Persepolis 2*, the narrator's facial expression remains the same in each of the panels. How would you describe the narrator's facial expression? How does this consistency help reveal the author's point of view?

7. **Synthesize** What ideas are emphasized in both the text and the graphic novel? Explain how the graphic novel and text together enable readers to have a more complete understanding of the problems women face in Iran.

PERFORMANCE TASK

Media Activity: Graphic Novel Imagine that Nafisi had written her memoir in the form of a graphic novel. How would she have integrated graphics and rhetoric?

- Using a computer or poster board and a pencil, create a series of graphic novel panels that follow Sanaz as she leaves the author's home.

- Add captions and speech and thought bubbles, including details from the memoir that you think advance the story.

- In a small group, compare your graphic representations of Nafisi's memoir. Discuss whether you were able to convey the same ideas and point of view through graphics as Nafisi was able to convey in her memoir. Was your use of rhetoric in your graphic representation as effective as Nafisi's in her memoir?

Assign this performance task.

PERFORMANCE TASK

RI 7, W 3, W 6

Media Activity: Graphic Novel Direct students to reread the selection to identify key visuals and ideas to convey in their graphic novel representations. Have students work in small groups to compare their finished products, and then discuss their observations as a class.

Critical Vocabulary

segregate   allocate   irrelevant   convert

Practice and Apply Use your understanding of the vocabulary words to answer the questions.

1. Are your friends' opinions ever **irrelevant**? Explain.

2. If you were in charge of **allocating** money to each of the clubs or sports teams in school, how would you do it?

3. Why might you **segregate** children according to age?

4. Is someone who believes fiercely in something likely to **convert**? Explain.

Vocabulary Strategy: Denotations and Connotations

A word's **denotation** is its strict dictionary definition. But many words have slight nuances or differences in meaning. These nuances, or **connotations,** have associated meanings and emotions.

Nafisi explains that in Iran, the buses are segregated. The Critical Vocabulary word *segregate* has a similar denotation to the word *separate*. They both mean "to set apart." But the word *segregate* has an altogether different connotation. To segregate suggests separating people or things forcefully, often in an unfair way.

Practice and Apply For each Critical Vocabulary word below, write the word's denotation. Then write the connotation of the word as it appears in the story.

Vocabulary Word	Denotation	Connotation
allocate		
irrelevant		
convert		

Critical Vocabulary

Possible answers:

1. *My friends' opinions about my clothes are irrelevant, because I have my own sense of style.*

2. *If I were in charge of allocating money to clubs or sports teams, I would be fair and allocate the same amount to each group.*

3. *Older children sometimes don't like to play with younger children; their interests are different.*

4. *People who believe fiercely in something are not likely to convert because their commitment to those principles will not permit it.*

Vocabulary Strategy: Denotations and Connotations

Possible answers:

Vocabulary Word	Denotation	Connotation
allocate	to distribute for a particular purpose	to forcibly assign
irrelevant	not related or connected	not important or even valid
convert	to change one's mind, especially about religious beliefs	to change one's mind politically, to be brainwashed by the regime

TO CHALLENGE STUDENTS . . .

Analyze Nuance Have students further explore the expression of connotations and denotations in writing and graphics.

- In newspapers, stories, or other media, have students find an example where one of the vocabulary words is used with a different connotation than it has in *Reading Lolita in Tehran.*

- Then have them write a paragraph using at least two of the selection's vocabulary words to tell a story about life in their community.

- Have students work in pairs to read each other's paragraphs and identify the connotations of some words and phrases. Challenge students to decide how they could represent these nuances in meaning in a graphic format.

Language and Style: Rhetorical Questions   L 3

Discuss with students that writers use rhetorical questions to convey ideas. These types of questions help keep the prose lively and interesting for readers, while also helping the author express a point of view. They are often used to provoke a reader or listener to think about and consider a subject from a different point of view.

Possible answers:

Essays should discuss an injustice, and should employ rhetorical questions correctly and effectively.

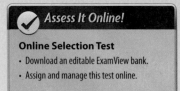

Assess It Online!

Online Selection Test
- Download an editable ExamView bank.
- Assign and manage this test online.

Language and Style: Rhetorical Questions   L 3

Authors strive to make effective choices for meaning or style. In her memoir *Reading Lolita in Tehran*, Azar Nafisi makes repeated use of rhetorical questions to engage the audience and to make a point. **Rhetorical questions** are questions that do not require or expect an answer. Depending on the context, they are often posed for dramatic effect.

Read the following sentence from the memoir.

> **Does she realize how dangerous she can be when her every stray gesture is a disturbance to public safety?**

Nafisi could instead have written the sentence this way:

> **She is dangerous because her every stray gesture is a disturbance to public safety.**

By using a rhetorical question instead of a statement, Nafisi invites the reader to think carefully about the scene described and to agree with her viewpoint. The question does not expect an answer. Instead, it makes a dramatic statement about the way the Iranian regime views women.

Here are some other examples of rhetorical questions in the excerpt from *Reading Lolita in Tehran*.

Rhetorical Question	Meaning
"How can I create this other world outside the room?"	Nafisi uses the rhetorical question as an opener to explain why she creates an imaginary scene involving Sanaz.
"Does she compare her own situation with her mother's when she was the same age?"	The question engages readers and invites them to consider any background knowledge they have about Iran's history.
"Is she aware, Sanaz, of her own power?"	Nafisi uses the rhetorical question to provide dramatic effect and to give the questions that follow meaning.

Practice and Apply Think of an injustice that you have observed or read about. Write a brief paragraph describing and reflecting on the injustice. Use rhetorical questions, as Nafisi does, to convey meaning and for dramatic effect. Remember to check your work for standard English grammar and usage.

Synthesize Information

RI 2

TEACH

Both of these works were written by Iranian women who experienced repression under the Islamic government. The text and graphic novel have similarities and differences. By synthesizing information from multiple sources, students can gain a more complete view of the period and its effects on women. Suggest that students synthesize information by analyzing the development of the central ideas and the tone of the sources to build a more complete view than offered by just one source. Discuss the following:

- **Content** What is the basic content of each source? How are the central ideas of each text developed? How are they similar? How are they different? What information does the first source cover that the second doesn't, and vice versa? How does this additional information contribute to a broader understanding of the content? *(For example, Persepolis introduces the idea that the internal questions created by the fear about the author's appearance crowd out more important questions about the author's rights and freedoms. This idea can be added to the exploration of Sanaz's thoughts in* Reading Lolita in Tehran.*)*

- **Tone** What is the tone of each source? How does each author approach the discomfort of the women involved and the rules concerning their appearance? How does each add to a broader understanding of the period? *(For example,* Reading Lolita in Tehran *refers to the history of the changes and the idea that Iranian women were once treated relatively equally in social, educational, and business situations. The author's tone is one of resentment, anger, and astonishment that the changes could happen so quickly. This adds to the idea that many Iranian women were angry about the changes.)*

COLLABORATIVE DISCUSSION

Have students work in pairs to synthesize information from the two texts. To begin, each can become an "expert" on one of the texts and present information on its central idea(s) and tone. Then students can work together to identify ways the texts are similar and different and how they work together to offer a broader view of the issues and time.

Determine Point of View

RI 6

RETEACH

Review the term *point of view*. Remind students that an author uses rhetoric to advance a point of view. An author's **point of view** is connected to an author's perspective, or the way an author looks at a subject. These works were written from a unique perspective—that of Iranian women who left Iran to live abroad. Ask the following with regard to the texts:

- Are the authors writing for readers in Iran or outside of Iran?
- What details do the authors include for an audience unfamiliar with the culture or place? How does this help the reader understand the authors' points of view?
- What feelings or opinions do the authors convey about their home country? Are they positive, negative, or both?

Lead a discussion about how living away from your country of origin might lead to a change in point of view about political and societal issues occurring in the place that you left.

 If students need further instruction, use this *Interactive Whiteboard*: **Historical and Cultural Contexts.**

INDEPENDENT READING

Students can apply the skill to another memoir. Have them select a passage that conveys the author's point of view then identify the techniques the author uses to convey that point of view to the reader.

The Censors

Short Story by Luisa Valenzuela   Translated by David Unger

Why This Text?

Students regularly encounter texts by authors from a variety of cultural backgrounds. This story vividly reflects the author's cultural background; reading it, students will have an opportunity to analyze the choices she has made to convey her point of view.

▶ **View It!**

Professional Development Podcast:
Text-Dependent Analysis

Key Learning Objective: The student will be able to analyze an author's point of view and cultural background, and also analyze an author's choices about style and structure.

For additional practice:

The Prisoner Who Wore Glasses

Close Reader selection
"The Prisoner Who Wore Glasses"
Short Story by Bessie Head

RL 1 Cite textual evidence.
RL 2 Determine a theme or central idea; provide a summary.
RL 3 Analyze how characters develop, interact, and advance the plot or develop the theme.
RL 4 Determine the meaning of words and phrases.
RL 5 Analyze author's choices.
RL 6 Analyze point of view or cultural experience.
W 7 Conduct research projects.
W 9 Draw evidence from literary texts.
L 1 Demonstrate command of the conventions of standard English.
L 2a–b Use semicolons and colons.
L 4b Identify and use patterns of word changes.

 Text Complexity Rubric

Quantitative Measures	**The Censors** Lexile: 1200L
Qualitative Measures	**Levels of Meaning/Purpose** ●——●——**●**——●——▶ multiple levels of meaning (multiple themes)
	Structure ●——**●**——●——●——▶ few, if any, shifts in point of view
	Language Conventionality and Clarity ●——**●**——●——●——▶ contextual ambiguous language
	Knowledge Demands ●——**●**——●——●——▶ some cultural and literary knowledge useful
Reader/Task Considerations	• Teacher determined • Vary by individual reader and type of text • See the Text X-Ray for suggested Reader/Task Considerations.

English Language Support Before teaching, use the Text X-Ray below for an overview of the text's complexity. The Text X-Ray and the supports and scaffolds in the Teacher's Edition will help you guide students of different skill levels.

Meaning Making
Language Development
Effective Expression
Content Knowledge
Foundational Skills

Text Complexity: Qualitative Measures

Levels of Meaning/Purpose

multiple levels of meaning (multiple themes)

Help students analyze verbal irony.
- Teacher's Edition side note, p. 92
- Analyze Author's Choices, p. 93

Help students summarize text to check comprehension.
- When Students Struggle, p. 90

ZOOM IN ON **ANALYZING VERBAL IRONY** Explain that **verbal irony** occurs when an author says the opposite of what he or she means. Verbal irony can reveal the author's true **point of view**. Help pairs find the verbal irony in each passage below.

- Lines 5–7 (*Valenzuela believes happiness is a feeling that people should value and trust.*)
- Lines 24–28 (*She believes there is nothing noble about censorship or targeting people who might oppose the government.*)
- Lines 70–74 (*She thinks people like Juan who see subversive messages in ordinary communications have lost their instincts and common sense.*)

Structure

few, if any, shifts in point of view

Help students analyze the plot of the short story.
- Teacher's Edition side notes, pp. 89, 90, 91, 92, 93
- Strategies for Annotation, p. 93
- Analyze Author's Choices, p. 93

To reteach analyzing an author's choices, see
- Analyze Author's Choices: Irony, p. 96a

 Use It! **Interactive Whiteboard Lesson:** Irony and Satire

ZOOM IN ON **ANALYZING FORESHADOWING** Tell students that it is easy for a reader to miss examples of **foreshadowing** during a first reading, since they don't know exactly how the story will end. After they have read "The Censors" once, have students review the text to find details that foreshadow the story's ending. Then have students meet with partners to discuss their ideas before sharing their answers with the class. (*Possible answers: "one of fate's dirty tricks" [line 3]; "a fellow worker had his right hand blown off" [lines 51–52]; "his noble mission blurred in his mind" [lines 67–68]; "We don't know if this made him happy" [lines 75–76]; "his darling mother worried, but she couldn't get him back on the right road" [lines 82–83]*)

Language Conventionality and Clarity

contextual ambiguous language

Teach unfamiliar vocabulary in context.
- Teacher's Edition Critical Vocabulary notes, pp. 90, 91, 95
- Applying Academic Vocabulary, p. 91

Help students determine the meanings of idioms.
- Teacher's Edition side note, p. 90
- English Language Support, p. 89

Instruct students in the use of colons and semicolons.
- Teacher's Edition side note, p. 96

ZOOM IN ON **ANALYZING USE OF COLONS AND SEMICOLONS** Work with students to analyze more examples of the author's use of colons and semicolons. Project these sentences and have students tell which purpose from Student Edition page 96 each one represents.

- Lines 29–31: "Well, you've got to . . . stop it." *(colon; introduces a list)*
- Lines 55–57: "After work . . . got promoted." *(semicolon; second idea results from the first)*
- Lines 83–85: "She'd say . . . waiting for you." *(colon; introduces a quotation)*
- Lines 86–88: "But Juan wouldn't . . . nab cheats." *(colon; illustrates what was just stated)*

Knowledge Demands

some cultural and literary knowledge useful

Support English Learners in understanding the historical context of the short story.
- Teacher's Edition Background note, p. 89

Help students analyze the cultural background of the story.
- Teacher's Edition side notes, pp. 89, 91

To support students in learning more about the author's cultural background, see
- Analyze Point of View: Cultural Background, p. 89

ZOOM IN ON **BUILDING CULTURAL KNOWLEDGE** Tell students that this story is set during a period of rule by a dictator in Argentina. Guide them to find key details from the story that describe life under this regime.

- What were the censors used for? *(To examine the contents of correspondence by the government's citizens to prevent any anti-government thoughts or directives)*
- What does Juan fear will happen to Mariana if the censors intercept her letter? *(He's afraid the* Censor's Secret Command *will kidnap Maria and kill her.)*

Suggested Reader/Task Considerations

You might consider the following before assigning this short story to students
- Do students know enough about the topic of censorship to understand this text?
- Will students need support to handle the complexity of this lesson's Performance Task?

ZOOM IN ON **SUPPORTING COMPREHENSION**

- Explain to students that censorship occurs when people in power suppress ideas or images they consider offensive or dangerous. In the United States, free speech is protected by the Constitution. However, dictatorships often practice censorship to protect the state's power.
- To help students brainstorm topics for their letters that might attract a censor's attention, suggest that they reread lines 70–74. Set aside time to meet with students individually if they need help getting started on the task.

CLOSE READ

Background Have students read the background and information about the author. Explain that Argentina's "Dirty War," which began two years after Valenzuela returned to her country and continued until 1983, was a period of brutal military rule during which thousands of people were killed and as many as 30,000 people "disappeared." Some of these victims were activists, but most were ordinary people. Family members of many "disappeared" continue to petition the government for information about their fate, and writers like Luisa Valenzuela continue to remind the world of the injustices.

AS YOU READ Direct students to use the As You Read suggestion to focus their reading. Encourage them to generate questions as they read.

Analyze Author's Choices   RL 5
(LINES 5–11)

Explain that authors sometimes choose not to provide certain details about characters and events.

A ASK STUDENTS why the author chooses not to reveal the contents of Juan's letter to Mariana (lines 9–11). *(We can tell that the relationship is intimate, and private. The fact that Juan wrote the letter is important. Virtually anything in the letter content could be considered suspicious so it isn't necessary for the author to provide specific details.)*

Analyze Point of View: RL 6
Cultural Background (LINES 13–18)

Point out that an author's cultural experience and viewpoint are often revealed through the thoughts and actions of a character.

B ASK STUDENTS what the details in lines 13–18 reveal about the fear and oppression experienced by the people of Argentina. *(The author communicates the repression and harshness of the regime by writing about them through the thoughts of Juan. This shows that the people of Argentina were not free to express themselves; any communication was suspicious. The author's use of the impersonal word "they" conveys the threat of danger.)*

Background *Born in Argentina, Luisa Valenzuela (b. 1938) published her first story at the age of seventeen. After graduating from the University of Buenos Aires, she moved to Paris and traveled abroad for several years. She returned home in 1974 to find political turmoil and oppression: a fascist dictatorship, a system of government in which a leader suppresses opposition through violent means, now ruled Argentina. Despite threats of censorship and physical harm, she began using her writing to document the horrors of life under a dictator.*

The Censors

Short Story by Luisa Valenzuela   Translated by David Unger

AS YOU READ Pay attention to the clues that reveal how Juan's feelings about his work change during the story.

Poor Juan! One day they caught him with his guard down before he could even realize that what he had taken as a stroke of luck was really one of fate's dirty tricks. These things happen the minute you're careless and you let down your guard, as one often does. Juancito let happiness—a feeling you can't trust—get the better of him when he received from a confidential source Mariana's new address in Paris and he knew that she hadn't forgotten him. Without thinking twice, he sat down at his table and wrote her a letter. *The* letter that keeps his mind off his job during the day and
10 won't let him sleep at night (what had he scrawled, what had he put on that sheet of paper he sent to Mariana?).

Juan knows there won't be a problem with the letter's contents, that it's irreproachable, harmless. But what about the rest? He knows that they examine, sniff, feel, and read between the lines of each and every letter, and check its tiniest comma and most accidental stain. He knows that all letters pass from hand to hand and go through all sorts of tests in the huge censorship offices and that, in the end, very few continue on their way. Usually it

The Censors   **89**

ENGLISH LANGUAGE SUPPORT

Vocabulary: Idioms Tell students that the phrase "let down your guard" in line 4 is an example of an idiom. An **idiom** is a familiar expression that signifies something other than the literal meaning of its words. Ask students to speculate on the meaning based on what they have read. *(to relax and stop looking out for danger)* Discuss with students how the idiom contributes to the opening of the story. *(It creates tension.)* Ask them what it suggests about what might happen in the story. *(The character might be hurt.)* Have students look for more idioms as they read, and use context clues to figure out their meaning.

Analyze Language

RL 4

(LINES 21–31)

Explain that **idioms** are familiar expressions that mean something other than the literal meaning of their words. Context can often suggest an idiom's meaning if it is unclear.

C **ASK STUDENTS** to identify the idioms in lines 21–31 and to state their meaning. *("down in the dumps" [sad]; "cashes in" [takes advantage of];"beat them to the punch" [do something first]; "throw sand in its gears" [obstruct]; "get to the bottom of" [solve].)*

Analyze Author's Choices

RL 3, RL 5

(LINES 38–44)

Explain that a character's **motivation**—what he or she wants—drives the **plot,** or sequence of events, forward. Sometimes **foreshadowing** hints at the conflict the character will encounter.

D **CITE TEXT EVIDENCE** What statement does the author include in lines 38–44 that might foreshadow future events? *("Ulterior motives couldn't be overlooked by the Censorship Division" (lines 38–39) suggest that Juan is playing a dangerous game and his employers will watch him carefully in the future. The statement implies that those people with "ulterior motives" will be found and punished.)*

CRITICAL VOCABULARY

staidness: The calmness in the Censorship Division existed because of the serious work that took place there. **ASK STUDENTS** what other buildings might have the same quality of staidness, and what kinds of buildings might have a "festive air." *(Government offices might have the quality of staidness, while a concert hall would seem more festive.)*

negligence: The employer made the claim that the employee was careless because the worker missed a signal that the envelope was sabotaged. **ASK STUDENTS** if they think that Juan believes that his fellow worker lost his hand because of negligence. *(It is possible that there was negligence, although it is likely that anyone working in the explosives section would be very careful.)*

takes months, even years, if there aren't any snags; all this time
20 the freedom, maybe even the life, of both sender and receiver is in
jeopardy. And that's why Juan's so down in the dumps: thinking
that something might happen to Mariana because of his letters.
Of all people, Mariana, who must finally feel safe there where she
always dreamed she'd live. But he knows that the *Censor's Secret
Command* operates all over the world and cashes in on the discount
in air rates; there's nothing to stop them from going as far as that
hidden Paris neighborhood, kidnapping Mariana, and returning to
their cozy homes, certain of having fulfilled their noble mission.

C

Well, you've got to beat them to the punch, do what everyone
30 tries to do: sabotage the machinery, throw sand in its gears, get to
the bottom of the problem so as to stop it.

This was Juan's sound plan when he, like many others, applied
for a censor's job—not because he had a calling or needed a job:
no, he applied simply to intercept his own letter, a consoling but
unoriginal idea. He was hired immediately, for each day more and
more censors are needed and no one would bother to check on his
references.

Ulterior motives couldn't be overlooked by the *Censorship
Division*, but they needn't be too strict with those who applied.
40 They knew how hard it would be for those poor guys to find the
letter they wanted and even if they did, what's a letter or two when
the new censor would snap up so many others? That's how Juan
managed to join the *Post Office's Censorship Division*, with a certain
goal in mind.

D

The building had a festive air on the outside which contrasted
with its inner **staidness**. Little by little, Juan was absorbed by his
job and he felt at peace since he was doing everything he could to
get his letter for Mariana. He didn't even worry when, in his first
month, he was sent to *Section K* where envelopes are very carefully
50 screened for explosives.

It's true that on the third day, a fellow worker had his right
hand blown off by a letter, but the division chief claimed it was
sheer **negligence** on the victim's part. Juan and the other employees
were allowed to go back to their work, albeit feeling less secure.
After work, one of them tried to organize a strike to demand higher
wages for unhealthy work, but Juan didn't join in; after thinking it
over, he reported him to his superiors and thus got promoted.

You don't form a habit by doing something once, he told
himself as he left his boss's office. And when he was transferred to
60 *Section J*, where letters are carefully checked for poison dust, he felt
he had climbed a rung in the ladder.

By working hard, he quickly reached *Section E* where the job
was more interesting, for he could now read and analyze the letters'

staidness
(stād´nĭs) *n.* the quality of being steady, calm, and serious.

negligence
(nĕg´lĭ-jəns) *n.* carelessness or failure to take normal precautions.

WHEN STUDENTS STRUGGLE. . .

To increase students' comprehension, have them work with a partner to reread and then summarize what is happening in lines 32–50. Have students ask each other questions, such as the following: What is Juan's plan? *(to get a job in the Censorship Division so that he can intercept his letter)* What does he do to achieve his goal? *(gets the job)* How does he feel when he begins working at the Censorship Division? *(He becomes involved with his job and doesn't worry about what might happen.)*

> ## "Soon his work became so absorbing to him that his noble mission blurred in his mind."

contents. Here he could even hope to get hold of his letter which, judging by the time that had elapsed, had gone through the other sections and was probably floating around in this one.

Soon his work became so absorbing that his noble mission blurred in his mind. Day after day he crossed out whole paragraphs in red ink, pitilessly chucking many letters into the censored basket.

70 These were horrible days when he was shocked by the subtle and conniving ways employed by people to pass on **subversive** messages; his instincts were so sharp that he found behind a simple 'the weather's unsettled' or 'prices continue to soar' the wavering hand of someone secretly scheming to overthrow the Government.

His zeal brought him swift promotion. We don't know if this made him happy. Very few letters reached him in *Section B*—only a handful passed the other hurdles—so he read them over and over again, passed them under a magnifying glass, searched for microprint with an electronic microscope, and tuned his sense of smell so that he was beat by the time he made it home. He'd

80 barely manage to warm up his soup, eat some fruit, and fall into bed, satisfied with having done his duty. Only his darling mother worried, but she couldn't get him back on the right road. She'd say, though it wasn't always true: Lola called, she's at the bar with the girls, they miss you, they're waiting for you. Or else she'd leave a bottle of red wine on the table. But Juan wouldn't overdo it: any distraction could make him lose his edge and the perfect censor

subversive
(səb-vûr′sĭv) *adj.*
Intended to undermine or overthrow those in power.

The Censors **91**

APPLYING ACADEMIC VOCABULARY

enable	reveal	decline

THINK-PAIR-SHARE Have students turn to a partner to discuss the following questions. Guide students to include the academic vocabulary words *enable* and *reveal* in their responses. Ask volunteers to share their responses with the class.

- Why does Juan think that working in the Censorship Division will **enable** him to intercept his letter to Mariana?

- How does Juan's urgency to find his letter **decline** as he becomes obsessed with his job?

CLOSE READ

Analyze Author's Choices RL 5
(LINES 67–75)

Explain that an author can manipulate time in a story by changing its **pace**—slowing down or speeding up plot events. This can affect the mood of a story.

E **CITE TEXT EVIDENCE** Have students identify words and phrases in lines 67–75 that indicate a change in pace. Ask what type of change in pace is happening. *("Soon" [line 68]; "day after day" (line 68); "zeal" (line 75); "swift promotion" [line 75]. These words indicate a quickening in the pace of events.)*

F **ASK STUDENTS** what mood is created in this section. How does the pacing affect the mood? *(The accelerating pace and description of Juan's days creates a feeling of anxiety, tension, and sadness.)*

Analyze Point of View: Cultural Background RL 6
(LINES 80–86)

Authors often describe aspects of a character's life over a period of time to express a point of view.

G **CITE TEXT EVIDENCE** How does Juan's job change his personal life? What details show this transformation? *(He no longer enjoys eating, feels exhausted, ignores his mother's worrying, and doesn't want to be with friends [lines 80–86].)*

H **ASK STUDENTS** What point of view about Argentinian government is the author expressing in lines 82–83? *(By revealing the mother's concern about Juan and that she isn't able to get him "back on the right road," the author is expressing that the government is also on the wrong track and doing the wrong things.)*

> **CRITICAL VOCABULARY**
>
> **subversive**: Juan believed that many of the letters contained undermining messages, although they seemed to be non-threatening.
>
> **ASK STUDENTS** to explain what the government believed might happen if these subversive messages were not intercepted. *(They might be the first step in overthrowing the government.)*

TEACH

CLOSE READ

Analyze Author's Choices
RL 5

(LINES 88–89)

Tell students that writers sometimes use **verbal irony,** saying the opposite of what is meant.

🄸 **CITE TEXT EVIDENCE** Have students find an example of verbal irony on this page and explain why it is ironic. *(One example is "He had a truly patriotic task" [lines 88–89]. Juan's task is in fact the opposite of patriotic. He may think it is patriotic—demonstrating that he loves his country—but in fact his work causes harm to his fellow citizens.)*

COLLABORATIVE DISCUSSION Have partners discuss Juan's early motivation and his subsequent actions. Students may disagree whether or not the ending of the story is plausible. Have them cite evidence from the story to support their ideas.

ASK STUDENTS to share any questions they generated in the course of reading and discussing the short story.

had to be alert, keen, attentive, and sharp to nab cheats. He had a truly patriotic task, both self-denying and uplifting.

90   His basket for censored letters became the best fed as well as the most cunning basket in the whole *Censorship Division*. He was about to congratulate himself for having finally discovered his true mission, when his letter to Mariana reached his hands. Naturally, he censored it without regret. And just as naturally, he couldn't stop them from executing him the following morning, another victim of his devotion to his work.

COLLABORATIVE DISCUSSION Were you surprised by Juan's change of heart? With a partner, discuss what hints the author provided to make the story's ending plausible. Cite specific evidence from the text to support your ideas.

TO CHALLENGE STUDENTS . . .

Draw Conclusions Have students work independently to write a short description of the art on this page. Encourage them to focus on how the parts of the image represent specific aspects of the text. Tell them to cite line numbers in their description to support their ideas.

ASK STUDENTS how this piece of art supports the author's point of view as it is expressed in the text. *(Possible answer: The piece of art shows the man alone with parts of his life, such as his friend in Paris and his work on letters at the censorship office. In general, the piece represents how the author thinks that the government is so afraid of being overthrown that they are attempting to isolate the people and make it impossible for them to maintain relationships or a sense of community.)*

Analyze Point of View: Cultural Background

RL 6

Luisa Valenzuela's cultural experience as an Argentine writer is reflected in both the content and style of this short story. Valenzuela wrote it upon returning to her native country in 1974 after spending several years abroad. The mood in Buenos Aires, the capital, was one of fear and oppression. Valenzuela once wrote, "Upon returning to my city after a long absence… it wasn't mine any longer. Buenos Aires belonged then to violence and state terrorism." Argentina was rapidly falling under the control of a fascist dictatorship. Working under the threat of censorship, suppression, and violence, Valenzuela believed it was her responsibility as a writer to witness and record the atrocities of the day. Her works, including this short story, explore such difficult topics as censorship, extreme violence, and political repression.

Analyze Author's Choices

RL 5

To communicate their experiences and ideas, writers make specific stylistic and structural choices. You can analyze Valenzuela's choices in this short story by looking at these elements.

Pacing	Foreshadowing	Irony
Pacing is the way in which an author manipulates time. Authors may use techniques to slow the action, thereby creating a mood of tension or mystery. For example, Valenzuela builds tension by devoting the first part of the story to Juan's fear that his letter to Mariana will be found. Conversely, authors may accelerate a story's pace by presenting a series of plot events in rapid succession.	**Foreshadowing** is a writer's use of clues to hint at events that will occur later in the story. Foreshadowing creates suspense, mystery, and surprise, and makes readers eager to find out what will happen next. In this story, the description of a fellow worker's gruesome injury is an example of foreshadowing.	Irony takes place when something happens that is the opposite of what readers would expect. One type is **verbal irony**, when what is said is the opposite of what is meant. The narrator's description of the Censorship Bureau as having "a festive air" is an example of verbal irony. Another type is **situational irony**, in which a character or the reader expects one thing to happen but something else happens instead. Juan's increasing dedication to his job as a censor is an example of situational irony.

The Censors **93**

CLOSE READ

Analyze Point of View: Cultural Background

RL 6

Point out that the threat of censorship—and more extreme punishment—applies equally to the letter-writer, Juan, and the author of this story. Censorship involves not only prohibiting ideas and information from reaching the outside world, but can also threaten the safety of the materials' creators. Discuss with students what Valenzuela is risking to tell this story, and why she might think it is worth taking the risk.

Discuss examples of other texts written by authors from different cultural backgrounds that students have read, and list elements that these various texts and their authors have in common.

Analyze Author's Choices

RL 5

Review the instruction with students, making sure they understand the effects of pacing, foreshadowing, and irony. Have students work in pairs to find and reread these examples in the story and discuss why the author's choice to use these elements was effective.

Strategies for Annotation ✎ 🗐 *Annotate it!*

Analyze Author's Choices

RL 1, RL 5

Share these strategies for guided or independent analysis.

- Highlight in yellow examples of foreshadowing.
- Highlight in blue phrases that indicate changes in pace.
- On notes, indicate passages that are examples of situational irony.

After work, one of them tried to organize a strike to demand higher wages for unhealthy work, but Juan didn't join in; after thinking it over, he reported him to his superiors and thus got promoted.

You don't form a habit by doing something once, he told himself as he left his boss's office. And when he was transferred to

PRACTICE & APPLY

Analyzing the Text

RL 1, RL 2, RL 3, RL 4, RL 5, RL 6

Possible answers:

1. *The tone or attitude toward the character and audience is one of familiarity. The narrator is inviting the audience to share in Juan's experience by using language that is less formal.*

2. *The author increases the pace of events as Juan begins to work at the Censorship Division. The phrase "little by little" shows how Juan is starting to change. As he moves up the Sections, phrases such as "day after day" shows how quickly he is changing.*

3. *The author uses foreshadowing to increase the tension that the reader feels about what might happen to Juan. For example, in line 32, the author writes, "this was Juan's sound plan." This seems to foreshadow that it, in fact, is not a sound plan. Another example is "What's a letter or two when the new censor would snap up so many others?" (lines 41–42). This foreshadows the kind of person Juan will become.*

4. *Juan's goal at the beginning is to find his letter and pass it through so that Mariana receives it and does not suffer any consequences. Over time, Juan's goal becomes to be a perfect censor. The author communicates this change by including details about the incremental steps that lead Juan to change. The author indicates that the work became "so absorbing to him that his noble mission blurred in his mind" (lines 67–68).*

5. *This reveals that Juan is a zealous worker. He censors the most letters, for a variety of obscure reasons.*

6. *Juan has become dedicated to the idea that censorship is necessary and that he is doing his duty. His final action is an example of irony because neither he, nor the reader expected that he would veer from his mission to find the letter and save it from the censors. Valenzuela is suggesting that the government in Argentina retains power by weakening the will of its people to resist, and in some cases, transforms them into the oppressors.*

Analyzing the Text

RL 1, RL 2, RL 3, RL 4, RL 5, RL 6, W 9, L 1

Cite Text Evidence   Support your responses with evidence from the selection.

1. **Infer** The narrator uses many **idioms,** commonly-used expressions that mean something other than the literal meaning of their words. For example, when Juan is "caught . . . with his guard down," the author means that he wasn't being cautious, not that he physically protected himself most of the time. What tone, or attitude toward the character and the audience, do the idioms create?

2. **Analyze** In his career as a censor, Juan moves from *Section K* to *Section B.* Describe the pacing or progression of his advancement. Besides the Section letters, what devices and word choices does the author use to speed up or slow down the pace of the story?

3. **Cite Evidence** How does the author foreshadow, or hint at, the changes that will occur in Juan's personality and his life? Provide examples of foreshadowing from the text, and explain their connection to the story's outcome.

4. **Compare** Compare Juan's work goal or motivation near the beginning of the story with his goal or motivation near the end. How does the author communicate the way this change occurs?

5. **Infer** The narrator calls Juan's basket of letters "the best fed as well as the most cunning basket in the whole *Censorship Division.*" What does this statement reveal about the way Juan performs his job?

6. **Interpret** Why does Juan censor his own letter "without regret"? How is his final action as a censor an example of irony? How does this ending illustrate Valenzuela's point of view about the political situation in Argentina?

PERFORMANCE TASK

Writing Activity: Letter Juan's letter to Mariana is central to this story's plot. Explore that letter through two brief writing tasks. In both pieces of writing, include evidence from the text and use the conventions of standard English.

1. In the character of Juan, write the one-page letter you imagine he wrote to Mariana at the beginning of the story. Then annotate a copy of the letter to identify evidence of anti-government ideas that a censor might find.

2. Write a one-page report in the character of Juan as a *Censorship Division* employee explaining why the letter shows that Juan is a traitor to his country.

Assign this performance task.

PERFORMANCE TASK

RL 1, W 9, L1

Writing Activity: Letter For the first task, have students reread the first paragraph of the story and look for hints about the letter's contents. For the second task, have students look at the details of Juan's work as a censor and cite evidence about the way the censors interpret letters.

Critical Vocabulary

L 4b

staidness   negligence   subversive

Practice and Apply Create a semantic map like the one that follows for each Critical Vocabulary word. Use a dictionary or thesaurus as needed. This example is for a word appearing in line 30 of the story.

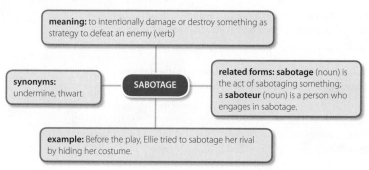

Vocabulary Strategy: Suffixes That Form Nouns

The Critical Vocabulary words *staidness* and *negligence* are formed by adding a noun suffix to an adjective, or describing word. Something that is *staid* shows *staidness*; someone who is *negligent* reveals his *negligence*. Noticing word patterns will help you more quickly develop an accurate definition for any unfamiliar words you encounter in your reading. Here are some common noun suffixes you will see in English words:

Suffixes	Meanings	Examples
–ance, –ence	act or condition of	radiance, excellence
–cy	state or condition of	sufficiency, redundancy
–dom	state, rank, or condition	officialdom, martyrdom
–hood	state or condition of	likelihood, childhood

Practice and Apply For each row of the chart, identify an additional example that uses a suffix shown. With each word you choose, follow these steps:

1. Identify the base—that is, the main word part without the suffix. Note the part of speech (adjective, verb, noun) and meaning of each base word.

2. Write a definition for each word you chose that incorporates the base word meaning and the suffix meaning.

3. Finally, use each word you chose in a sample sentence.

Critical Vocabulary

L 4b

Possible answers:

Staidness—*Synonym:* sedateness**;** *Related form:* staid (*adjective*); Characterized by sedate dignity; Meaning: quality of being stead, calm, and serious (*noun*); Example: The staidness of the party made most people leave early.

Negligence—*Synonym:* careless**;** *Related form:* negligent (*adj.*) inclined to neglect; Meaning: carelessness or failure to take normal precautions (*noun*); Example: The negligence of the food committee meant that there was no pizza at the dance.

Subversive—*Synonym:* Undermining**;** *Related form:* subvert (*verb*) to ruin; Meaning: intended to undermine or overthrow those in power (*adj.*); Example: The subversive people met in a warehouse to plan their revolt.

Vocabulary Strategy: Suffixes That Form Nouns

Possible answers:

reference: *"the act of referring, or directing to a source"* refer (*v.*) *"directing to a source of information"*; The reference book defined terms about government.

leniency: *"the condition of being lenient"* lenient (*adj.*) *"inclined not to be harsh"*; The teacher showed leniency toward the students by giving them more time for the assignment.

freedom: *"the condition of being free from restraint"* free (*adj.*) *"being at liberty"*; Citizens of many countries desire freedom.

motherhood: *"the condition of being a mother"* mother (*n.*) *"a woman who raises a child"*; Most people take motherhood very seriously.

Strategies for Annotation   ✏ 🗎 *Annotate it!*

Suffixes That Form Nouns

L 4b

Give students examples of other common suffixes that form nouns: *-ness* (state, quality, degree); *-ship* (quality, state, or condition); *-ment* (action, process). Encourage them to use their eBook annotation tools to do the following:

- Highlight words with these noun suffixes in the story.
- On a note, identify the base word and identify the part of speech of the base word.

Juancito let happiness—a feeling you can't trust—get the better of him when he received from a confidential source Mariana's new address in Paris and he knew that she hadn't forgotten him.

> base word: happy; part of speech: adjective

Language and Style: Colons and Semicolons

L 2a–b

Tell students that another way a colon can be used is to precede the restatement of an idea. Offer this example:

The dinner was awful: the roast was overdone and the rolls were stale.

Have volunteers suggest other examples for this use of the colon and the three uses of colons shown in the chart.

Possible answers:

Revisions will vary.

Students' revisions should indicate a clear understanding of the use of colons and semicolons. As they share their revisions, have partners note whether semicolons clearly indicate how a second idea results from the first, and if colons are used to provide an example, introduce a question, or introduce a list.

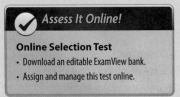

Assess It Online!

Online Selection Test
- Download an editable ExamView bank.
- Assign and manage this test online.

Language and Style: Colons and Semicolons

L 2a–b

An author's use of punctuation not only can help readers understand the message but also can help create meaning and tone. In "The Censors," Luisa Valenzuela uses colons and semicolons to great effect.

Read the following sentence from the story.

And that's why Juan's so down in the dumps: thinking that something might happen to Mariana because of his letter.

The author could instead have written the sentence this way:

Juan's down in the dumps from thinking that something might happen to Mariana because of his letter.

By setting up the sentence as she does, the author involves readers in making meaning. The two-part sentence provides readers with a question (What's bothering Juan?) followed by its answer (Thinking that he's endangered Mariana). Readers naturally pause at the colon to prepare for what comes after it. Here are some other common uses of colons:

Uses of Colons	
Purpose	**Example**
illustrate or provide an example of what was just stated	Argentina has seen much political turmoil: since World War II the nation has endured numerous military coups and dictatorships.
introduce a quotation	Valenzuela is no stranger to censorship: "I wrote . . . thinking that I should write in illegible handwriting so that no one could read over my shoulder."
introduce a list	Valenzuela has lived in many places: Paris, New York, Barcelona, and Buenos Aires.

Now read this sentence from "The Censors":

Usually it takes months, even years, if there aren't any snags; all this time the freedom, maybe even the life, of both sender and receiver is in jeopardy.

Valenzuela could have chosen to create two separate sentences; her use of the semicolon shows that the second idea results from the first.

Practice and Apply Look back at the letter and report you created in response to this selection's Performance Task. Revise each to add at least one colon and one semicolon. Then discuss with a partner how each punctuation mark you added improves your meaning or tone.

Analyze Point of View: Cultural Background

RL 6, W 7

TEACH

Review the background information about the author. Note that many writers draw on their personal experiences or the culture around them as inspiration for their stories. Explain that historical context is the time, place, and social conditions that influence a work of literature. In addition to these factors, a writer's cultural background can include language and various customs and the way he or she perceives events.

Explain that additional research is one way to learn more about how an author's cultural background influenced his or her point of view. To start students thinking about other things they might learn about Argentina, work with students to generate a list of questions that they could answer through further research. Some examples include:

- What circumstances led Argentina toward a fascist dictatorship?
- How did the economic or political climate of Argentina change in the 1960s and 1970s?
- What steps did people take to try to change the government. Were any of these measures successful?

PRACTICE AND APPLY

Have pairs of students research Argentina in the 1970s to better understand the historical and political context of "The Censors." They can use Internet resources and/or print sources. Have them prepare a short oral report on the events and leaders of this period. Both students should speak when delivering the report to the class. Encourage the class to ask questions and identify ways in which "The Censors" reflects the historical and cultural influences of the time.

INTERACTIVE WHITEBOARD LESSON

Analyze Author's Choices: Irony

RL 5

RETEACH

Explain that there are three types of irony: verbal, situational, and dramatic. The story students have read has verbal and situational irony. Explain that **dramatic irony** occurs when the reader, or audience, is aware of something the character doesn't know. One example is Little Red Riding Hood knocking on her grandmother's front door. *We* know the wolf is inside, but *she* doesn't.

Have students follow these steps when analyzing irony in fiction:

Step 1: Read for meaning. What appears to be true, and what is really true?

Step 2: Analyze the effects of irony. Does it create suspense, add humor, or encourage sympathy toward a character?

Step 3: Note how irony affects theme. What is the theme, or message? Does irony make the theme more obvious? If so, how?

INDEPENDENT READING

Form two pairs of students, and assign each pair the same story. Assign another story to two more pairs, and so on. The stories can be the following, or others that include examples of irony.

"The Cask of Amontillado" by Edgar Allen Poe
"The Blue Hotel" by Stephen Crane
"Ransom of Red Chief" by O. Henry
"Story of an Hour" by Kate Chopin

Have students follow the above steps to analyze the stories. Have pairs that read the same story compare their analyses of the story's irony and discuss how the irony affected them as readers.

The Prisoner Who Wore Glasses

Short Story by Bessie Head

Why This Text

Students sometimes read a story without analyzing the cultural background of the author. "The Prisoner Who Wore Glasses" is set in South Africa during apartheid. The story's message is better understood and appreciated when analyzed in the context of the author's historical and cultural background. With the help of the close-reading questions, students will interpret the central message of Head's story. This close reading will lead students to effectively read world literature.

Background Have students read the background and the information about the author. "The Prisoner Who Wore Glasses" is a story set in South Africa that revolves around themes of discrimination, resilience of the human spirit, and the ability of people to bridge racial gaps through cooperation. Introduce the selection by telling students that as the daughter of a white woman and a black man, Head experienced racism in South Africa firsthand.

AS YOU READ Ask students to analyze the cultural experience presented in this story from outside the United States. Which details are clues that the story is not set in the United States?

Standards Support

- cite strong and thorough textual evidence
- analyze how complex characters develop over the course of a text
- analyze an author's choices concerning how to structure a text
- analyze a point of view or cultural experience from outside the United States

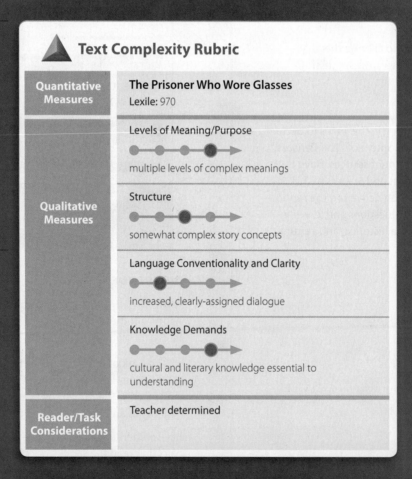

Text Complexity Rubric

Quantitative Measures

The Prisoner Who Wore Glasses
Lexile: 970

Qualitative Measures

Levels of Meaning/Purpose
multiple levels of complex meanings

Structure
somewhat complex story concepts

Language Conventionality and Clarity
increased, clearly-assigned dialogue

Knowledge Demands
cultural and literary knowledge essential to understanding

Reader/Task Considerations

Teacher determined

Analyze Point of View: Cultural Background

Students should read this story carefully all the way through. Close-reading questions at the bottom of the page will help them focus on a thorough analysis of the story. As they read, students should jot down comments or questions about the text in the side margins.

WHEN STUDENTS STRUGGLE . . .

To help students analyze the author's cultural background, have them work in a small group to fill out a chart, such as the one shown below, as they analyze the text.

CITE TEXT EVIDENCE For practice in analyzing a cultural point of view, ask students to cite details from the text that reflect specific cultural context that adds to the plot.

Detail	How It Adds to the Plot
The men in Span One are political prisoners.	They have not committed crimes.
Black warders cannot be in charge of Span One.	The political prisoners must be in favor of black equality.
Brille stands up to the white warder Hannetjie.	Brille is making a symbolic stand against apartheid.
The black prisoners work together with the white warder in cooperation.	The system of apartheid could be overcome by cooperation between the sides.

Background *Apartheid—systematic racial segregation—was initiated in South Africa in 1948 when* **Bessie Head** *was eleven years old. Under apartheid's rigid classification system, she was designated a "colored" person and was denied the full privileges of citizenship in her homeland. Raised from birth by a child welfare agency, she was later placed with foster parents. After training in a missionary school, she worked as a teacher and journalist before emigrating to Botswana, a neighboring country that was then under British rule. Many of her writings explore the tragedies and injustices of South Africa under apartheid rule.*

The Prisoner Who Wore Glasses

Short Story by Bessie Head

CLOSE READ
Notes

1. **READ ▶** As you read lines 1–24, begin to collect and cite text evidence.

   • Underline language that describes the prisoner.
   • Circle text that describes the warder.
   • In the margin, summarize the descriptions.

Scarcely a breath of wind disturbed the stillness of the day and the long rows of cabbages were bright green in the sunlight. Large white clouds drifted slowly across the deep blue sky. Now and then they obscured the sun and caused a chill on the backs of the prisoners who had to work all day long in the cabbage field. This trick the clouds were playing with the sun **(A)** eventually caused one of the prisoners who wore glasses to stop work, straighten up and peer short-sightedly at them. He was a thin little fellow with a hollowed-out chest and comic knobbly knees. He also had a lot of fanciful ideas because he smiled at the clouds.

10   "Perhaps they want me to send a message to the children," he thought, tenderly, noting that the clouds were drifting in the direction of his home **(B)** some hundred miles away. But before he could frame the message, the warder in charge of his work span[1] shouted: "Hey, what do you think you're doing, Brille?"

[1] **work span:** a group or unit of workers.

The prisoner is physically unthreatening. He also has a good imagination.

29

---

1. **READ AND CITE TEXT EVIDENCE** Invite students to begin to analyze the characters of the prisoner and the warder.

(A) ASK STUDENTS to cite evidence to support their summaries of the text that describes the prisoner and the warder. *Students should cite evidence from lines 6–11 and lines 15–16 to support their descriptions of the prisoner, and lines 13–14 and 17–18 to support their descriptions of the warder.*

The warder is cold, brutal, and inhuman.

The prisoner swung round, blinking rapidly, yet at the same time sizing up the enemy. He was a new warder, named Jacobus Stephanus Hannetjie. His eyes were the color of the sky but they were frightening. A simple, primitive, brutal soul gazed out of them. The prisoner bent down quickly and a message was quietly passed down the line: "We're in for trouble this 20 time, comrades."

"Why?" rippled back up the line.

"Because he's not human," the reply rippled down and yet only the crunching of the spades as they turned over the earth disturbed the stillness.

This particular work span was known as Span One. It was composed of ten men and they were all political prisoners. They were grouped together for convenience as it was one of the prison regulations that no black warder should be in charge of a political prisoner lest this prisoner convert him to his view. It never seemed to occur to the authorities that this very reasoning 30 was the strength of Span One and a clue to the strange terror they aroused in the warders. As political prisoners they were unlike the other prisoners in the sense that they felt no guilt nor were they outcasts of society. All guilty men instinctively cower, which was why it was the kind of prison where men got knocked out cold with a blow at the back of the head from an iron bar. Up until the arrival of Warder Hannetjie, no warder had dared beat any member of Span One and no warder had lasted more than a

week with them. The battle was entirely psychological. Span One was assertive and it was beyond the scope of white warders to handle assertive black men. Thus, Span One had got out of control. They were the best 40 thieves and liars in the camp. They lived all day on raw cabbages. They chatted and smoked tobacco. And since they moved, thought, and acted as one, they had perfected every technique of group concealment.

Trouble began that very day between Span One and Warder Hannetjie. It was because of the short-sightedness of Brille. That was the nickname he was given in prison and is the Afrikaans[2] word for someone who wears glasses. Brille could never judge the approach of the prison gates and on several occasions he had munched on cabbages and dropped them almost at the feet of the warder and all previous warders had overlooked this. Not so Warder Hannetjie.

50 "Who dropped that cabbage?" he thundered.

Brille stepped out of line.

"I did," he said meekly.

"All right," said Hannetjie. "The whole Span goes three meals off."

"But I told you I did it," Brille protested.

The blood rushed to Warder Hannetjie's face.

"Look 'ere," he said. "I don't take orders from a kaffir.[3] I don't know

[2] **Afrikaans:** a South African language that developed from Dutch.
[3] **kaffir:** a disparaging term for a black African.

---

2. **◀ REREAD** Reread lines 12–20. State the conflict in your own words.

The prisoner's work span has been taken over by a brutal white warder.

3. **READ ▶** As you read lines 25–42, continue to cite textual evidence.
   • Underline descriptions of Span One.
   • Circle adjectives that describe why Span One is unique.

4. **◀ REREAD** Reread lines 25–42. How does the author foreshadow trouble in the prison? Support your answer with explicit textual evidence.

The author desribes the special treatment given to the prisoners in Span One and explains that "no warder had lasted more than a week with them."

5. **READ ▶** As you read lines 43–102, continue to cite textual evidence.
   • Underline the text that hints at racial conflict.
   • Circle words that show a shift from the present to the past.
   • In the margin of lines 73–94, explain what Brille remembers.

---

2. **REREAD AND CITE TEXT EVIDENCE**

B **ASK STUDENTS** to cite evidence that supports their statement of the story's conflict. *Students should cite text that describes Hannetjie (lines 12–14 and lines 17–18) and text that explains Brille's assessment of Hannetjie (lines 19–20).*

3. **READ AND CITE TEXT EVIDENCE**

C **ASK STUDENTS** to cite text evidence showing that Span One is unique. *Students should cite that Span One was a group of "political" prisoners (line 28). They should cite adjectives such as strange (line 30) and unlike (line 31). The adjective assertive describes how they are unique (line 38). The superlative adjective best (line 39) is another clue that Span One is unique.*

FOR ELL STUDENTS Review that the verb *swung* is the past and past participle of the irregular verb *to swing*, which means "to move vigorously through a wide arc or circle."

4. **REREAD AND CITE TEXT EVIDENCE**

D **ASK STUDENTS** to cite text evidence to support their explanation of how the author foreshadows that there will be trouble in the prison. *Students should cite evidence of Span One getting special treatment (lines 35–36 and lines 40–42) and evidence that they frequently have conflict with warders (lines 36–37).*

5. **READ AND CITE TEXT EVIDENCE**

E **ASK STUDENTS** to cite textual evidence to support their explanation of what Brille remembers. *Students should cite text that describes the violence that occurred in his own home, such as lines 83–85. They should cite evidence that describes the effect this violence had on his life, such as lines 90–91.*

FOR ELL STUDENTS Explain that the expression "blood rushed to (someone's) face" means that the person is embarrassed and her face turns red.

96d Collection 2

what kind of kaffir you think you are. Why don't you say Baas. I'm your Baas, Why don't you say Baas, hey?"

Brille blinked his eyes rapidly but by contrast his voice was strangely

60 calm.

F "I'm twenty years older than you," he said. It was the first thing that came to mind but the comrades seemed to think it a huge joke. A titter swept up the line. The next thing Warder Hannetjie whipped out a knobkerrie and gave Brille several blows about the head. What surprised his comrades was the speed with which Brille had removed his glasses or else they would have been smashed to pieces on the ground. That evening in the cell Brille was very apologetic.

"I'm sorry, comrades," he said. "I've put you into a hell of a mess."

"Never mind, brother," they said. "What happens to one of us, happens

70 to all."

"I'll try to make up for it, comrades," he said. "I'll steal something so that you don't go hungry."

J Privately, Brille was very philosophical about his head wounds. It was the first time an act of violence had been perpetrated against him but he had long been a witness of extreme, almost unbelievable human brutality. He had twelve children and his mind traveled back that evening through the sixteen years of **bedlam** in which he had lived. It had all happened in a small, drab little three-bedroomed house in a small, drab little street in the Eastern Cape, and the children kept coming year after year because neither

80 he nor Martha ever managed the contraceptives the right way, and a teacher's salary never allowed moving to a bigger house, and he was always taking exams to improve his salary only to have it all eaten up by hungry mouths. Everything was pretty horrible, especially the way the children fought. They'd get hold of each other's heads and give them a good bashing against the wall. Martha gave up somewhere along the line so they worked out a thing between them. The bashings, biting and blood were to operate in full swing until he came home. He was to be the bogeyman and when it **E** worked he never failed to have a sense of godhead at the way in which his presence could change savages into fairly reasonable human beings.

90 Yet somehow it was this chaos and mismanagement at the center of his life that drove him into politics. It was really an ordered, beautiful world with just a few basic slogans to learn along with the rights of mankind. At one stage, before things became very bad, there were conferences to attend, all very far away from home.

bedlam:

chaos;
complete
disorder

Brille
remembers
the violence
that occurred
in his own
home. His
chaotic
homelife led
him toward
politics.

"Let's face it," he thought ruefully. "I'm only learning right now what it means to be a politician. All this while I've been running away from Martha and the kids."

100 And the pain in his head brought a hard lump to his throat. That was what the children did to each other daily and Martha wasn't managing and if Warder Hannetjie had not interrupted him that morning he would have sent the following message: "Be good comrades, my children. Cooperate, **G** then life will run smoothly."

The next day Warder Hannetjie, caught this old man of twelve children stealing grapes from the farm shed. They were an enormous quantity of grapes in a ten-gallon tin and for this misdeed the old man spent a week in the isolation cell. In fact, Span One as a whole was in constant trouble. Warder Hannetjie seemed to have eyes at the back of his head. He

110 uncovered the trick about the cabbages, how they were split in two with the spade and immediately covered with earth and then unearthed again and eaten with split-second timing. He found out how tobacco smoke was beaten into the ground and he found out how conversations were whispered down the wind.

For about two weeks Span One lived in acute misery. The cabbages, tobacco, and conversations had been the **pivot** of jail life to them. Then one evening they noticed that their good old comrade who wore the glasses was looking rather pleased with himself. He pulled out a four-ounce packet of

pivot:

central point
on which
something else
depends

6. ◀ **REREAD** Reread the dialogue between Brille and Hannetjie (lines 50–62). From what you know about apartheid, make an inference about why Brille stands up to Hannetjie.

When Brille stands up to the warder, his action is symbolic; it's as if black South Africans are standing up to the white minority and taking back their dignity.

7. **READ** ▶ As you read lines 103–138, continue to cite textual evidence.

• Underline the crimes Hannetjie uncovers.
• Circle the text that describes a turning point of the story.
• Underline text that refers to Brille as a father.

Critical Vocabulary: bedlam (line 77) Ask students to share their definitions of *bedlam*. Ask them to explain how Head's choice of the word *bedlam* impacts meaning in this paragraph. *Answers will vary. Students might say that by choosing a word associated with insanity, Head is commenting on the result of exposure to constant violence.*

FOR ELL STUDENTS Review the meaning of the prefix *mis-*. Point out the word *mismanagement* in line 90. Then ask a volunteer to supply the base word, its meaning, and what meaning the prefix adds to it. *The word* mismanagement *means "supervision of a project done badly or wrongly."*

6. **REREAD AND CITE TEXT EVIDENCE**

F **ASK STUDENTS** to read aloud and discuss their response with a partner. After their discussions, allow students to rewrite their response and add specific textual evidence.

7. **READ AND CITE TEXT EVIDENCE** Point out to students that the development of Hannetjie and Brille's relationship moves the plot forward.

G **ASK STUDENTS** to cite evidence that shows that Hannetjie and Brille have something in common. *Students should point out that they have both been punished for stealing (lines 103–104 and lines 124–126 and 138).*

Critical Vocabulary: pivot (line 114) Ask students to compare definitions of *pivot*. Ask them to determine the meaning of *pivot* as it is used in the story.

tobacco by way of explanation and the comrades fell upon it with great greed. Brille merely smiled. After all, he was the father of many children. But when the last shred had disappeared, it occurred to the comrades that

120 they ought to be puzzled. Someone said: "I say, brother. We're watched like hawks these days. Where did you get the tobacco?"

"Hannetjie gave it to me," said Brille.

There was a long silence. Into it dropped a quiet bombshell.

"I saw Hannetjie in the shed today," and the failing eyesight blinked rapidly. "I caught him in the act of stealing five bags of fertilizer and he bribed me to keep my mouth shut."

There was another long silence.

"Prison is an evil life," Brille continued, apparently discussing some irrelevant matter. "It makes a man contemplate all kinds of evil deeds."

130 He held out his hand and closed it.

"You know, comrades," he said. "I've got Hannetjie. I'll betray him tomorrow."

Everyone began talking at once.

"Forget it, brother. You'll get shot."

Brille laughed.

"I won't," he said. "That is what I mean about evil. I am a father of children and I saw today that Hannetjie is just a child and stupidly truthful. I'm going to punish him severely because we need a good warder."

 The following day, with Brille as witness, Hannetjie confessed to the

140 theft of the fertilizer and was fined a large sum of money. From then on Span One did very much as they pleased while Warder Hannetjie stood by and said nothing. But it was Brille who carried this to extremes. One day, at

---

8. **REREAD** Reread lines 113–138. Why does the author keep mentioning Brille's role as a father? Support your answer with explicit textual evidence.

The author is making the point that the prisoners and the warden all act like children. As Brille plans to punish Hannetjie he says, "I am a father of children and I saw today that Hannetjie is just a child..."

9. **READ** As you read lines 139–183, underline text that describes how life changes for Brille, Hannetjie, and Span One. In the margin, explain how Brille betrays Hannetjie.

34

 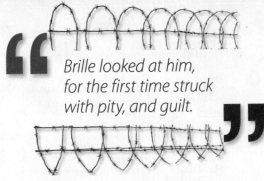

Brille looked at him,
for the first time struck
with pity, and guilt.

the close of work Warder Hannetjie said: "Brille, pick up my jacket and carry it back to the camp."

"But nothing in the regulations says I'm your servant, Hannetjie," Brille replied coolly.

"I've told you not to call me Hannetjie. You must say Baas," but Warder Hannetjie's voice lacked conviction. In turn, Brille squinted up at him.

"I'll tell you something about this Baas business, Hannetjie," he said.

150 "One of these days we are going to run the country. You are going to clean my car. Now, I have a fifteen-year-old son and I'd die of shame if you had to tell him that I ever called you Baas."

Warder Hannetjie went red in the face and picked up his coat.

On another occasion Brille was seen to be walking about the prison yard, openly smoking tobacco. On being taken before the prison commander he claimed to have received the tobacco from Warder Hannetjie. Throughout the tirade from his chief, Warder Hannetjie failed to defend himself but his nerve broke completely. He called Brille to one side.

"Brille," he said. "This thing between you and me must end. You may

160 not know it but I have a wife and children and you're driving me to suicide."

"Why don't you like your own medicine, Hannetjie?" Brille asked quietly.

"I can give you anything you want," Warder Hannetjie said in desperation.

"It's not only me but the whole of Span One," said Brille, cunningly. "The whole of Span One wants something from you."

Warder Hannetjie brightened with relief.

"I think I can manage if it's tobacco you want," he said.

Brille looked at him, for the first time struck with pity, and guilt.

Brille witnesses the warder's theft and gets him in trouble. Brille stands up to Hannetjie and even makes up stories that get him in trouble with his superiors.

35

---

8. **REREAD AND CITE TEXT EVIDENCE**

 ASK STUDENTS to trade their written response with a partner for a peer review. Partners should work together to improve their responses, and then rewrite their answers with specific textual evidence. *Students may cite evidence from line 118 or lines 136–138 to show that Brille has realized that the prisoners and the warder all act like children.*

9. **READ AND CITE TEXT EVIDENCE**

 ASK STUDENTS to cite text evidence to support their description of how life changes for Brille, Hannetjie, and Span One, as well as their explanation of how Brille betrays Hannetjie. *Students should cite evidence from lines 139–142 to show that Span One "did very much as they pleased" after the trial, and lines 149–152 that show how the relationship between the two men changed. Lines 179–181 show that Span One responded to the changes around them by "being the best work span in the camp."*

WHEN STUDENTS STRUGGLE . . .

To help students analyze the developments in the relationship between Brille and Hannetjie, have small groups work together to read aloud lines 139–183 as a script. Assign parts to a narrator, Warder Hannetjie, and Brille.

CITE TEXT EVIDENCE After reading the text aloud, have small groups cite specific lines that show a change in their relationship, such as lines 139–142 (showing that Hannetjie now says nothing when Span One acts out) or lines 147–148 (showing that Hannetjie's voice has lost its conviction). Ask them to explain what the evidence shows.

FOR ELL STUDENTS Point out that the word *tirade* should not be confused with *tired*, though they may sound similar to them. Explain that *tirade* is a long and angry speech.

CLOSE READ
Notes

170 He wondered if he had carried the whole business too far. The man was really a child.

"It's not tobacco we want, but you," he said. "We want you on our side. We want a good warder because without a good warder we won't be able to manage the long stretch ahead."

Warder Hannetjie interpreted this request in his own fashion and <u>his interpretation of what was good and human often left the prisoners of Span One speechless with surprise. He had a way of slipping off his revolver and picking up a spade and digging alongside Span One. He had a way of producing unheard of luxuries like boiled eggs from his farm nearby and</u>

180 <u>things like cigarettes, and Span One responded nobly and got the reputation of being the best work span in the camp.</u> And it wasn't only take from their side. They were awfully good at stealing certain commodities like fertilizer which were needed on the farm of Warder Hannetjie.

10. ◀ **REREAD AND DISCUSS** Reread lines 170–183. With a small group, analyze the parallels between Brille's relationships with his twelve children and his relationships with Hannetjie and Span One. Why did the author choose to include Brille's flashback about life with his wife and children?

SHORT RESPONSE

Cite Text Evidence Head's writing has been described as "having the dimensions of a parable"—a short, simple story illustrating a moral or spiritual truth. What simple truth does Head illustrate in "The Prisoner Who Wore Glasses"? Why is it particularly meaningful given her cultural point of view? **Cite text evidence** from the story.

"Cooperate, then life will run smoothly," is the simple truth transmitted in "The Prisoner Who Wore Glasses." Head illustrates this truth by putting black political prisoners and a brutal white warder at odds. It takes a philosophical father figure with "a lot of fanciful ideas" to bring about cooperation. He sees warder and inmates alike as he sees his children: in need of management and firm discipline. Although the injustice of apartheid is the backdrop of the story, Head's message about cooperation and respect is accessible to everyone.

36

---

10. **REREAD AND DISCUSS USING TEXT EVIDENCE** Refer students to the flashback on page 32, lines 73–102.

J **ASK STUDENTS** to be ready to cite textual evidence to support their analysis of the parallels between Brille's relationships with his twelve children and his relationships with Hannetjie and Span One. *Students should recognize parallels in the violence between his children and Brille's role as disciplinarian.*

SHORT RESPONSE

Cite Text Evidence Student responses will vary, but they should cite evidence from the story to support their responses. Students should:

- state the moral of the story.
- cite text evidence that supports their response.
- analyze Head's cultural point of view.

TO CHALLENGE STUDENTS . . .

For more context, students can research apartheid in South Africa from 1948 through 1991.

ASK STUDENTS to relate how their research helped them analyze Head's cultural experience as it is reflected in "The Prisoner Who Wore Glasses." *Students should explain parallels in South Africa's history and Head's story.*

DIG DEEPER

With the class, return to Question 10, Reread and Discuss. Have students share the results of their discussions.

ASK STUDENTS whether they were satisfied with the outcome of their small-group discussions. Have each group share their conclusions about why Head included Brille's flashback to his time with his wife and children. What textual evidence did students find to support their conclusions?

- Guide each group to share whether they came to a unanimous conclusion about how the flashback worked in the story. If not, have groups share the variety of conclusions that emerged from their discussion.

- Ask groups to share the textual evidence that seemed the most compelling. Did they find explicit textual evidence that showed a parallel between Brille's role with his family and his role within the prison?

- As a class, discuss how Brille's reflections on his family caused him to behave differently with Hannetjie by the end of the story. *Students should realize that his wish for his children to cooperate influenced his decision to stop going "to extremes" (line 142) with Hannetjie.*

ASK STUDENTS to return to their Short Response answer and revise it based on the class discussion.

THE STRUGGLE FOR FREEDOM

The *FYI* site provides links to online articles from a variety of magazines and newspapers. Help students choose a few articles to read to further their exploration of the topic The Struggle for Freedom.

NOVELWISE

Students can unlock the power of novels with this unique resource. Help students read through longer works with these tips:

- Find a Book
- Before You Read
- As You Read
- After You Read

Each book includes introductory material, worksheets, graphic organizers, and discussion guides.

ADDITIONAL TEXTS BY COLLECTION

Suggest students read the following:

- "Beat! Beat! Drums!" by Walt Whitman

Have students read the poem aloud and pay attention to sensory language. After they finish reading, ask them what effect the use of sensory language has on the tone of the poem.

NONFICTION CONNECTIONS

Suggest that students increase their reading of informational texts. The nonfiction connections include

- speeches
- diaries
- true-life accounts
- newspaper articles
- political cartoons

Creating an Independent Reading Program

STUDENTS CHOOSE THEIR OWN BOOKS

Students who choose their own books will be more actively involved in the reading process.

- Discuss with students how they already choose books. Record their responses and post them on a shared class website.
- Discuss with students what topics interest them and why. Then ask them what would make them read something outside their fields of interest.
- Ask students if there are certain authors whose works they like. Give them 5 minutes to review a book, and ask them to use various strategies for determining if they want to read it.
- Explain that some times a book just isn't suitable, and that it's okay to abandon it. Model scenarios where this might be the case.

STRATEGIES FOR SELECTING A BOOK

Work with students to develop strategies to select books in terms of difficulty, content, and interest.

- Have students identify a genre, an author or two, and/or an area of interest they'd like to explore.
- Have them select three books from the classroom or school library.
- Ask students to look at the table of contents. Do the text and illustrations give students an idea of what to expect?
- Ask students to select the most promising book and read the first two pages. How many words did they not know how to define? (If there were more than five, the book is probably too difficult. Three is about right.) At the end of the second page, can students summarize what they've read? ("Yes" is good. "No" means the book is probably too hard for independent reading.)

Write an Argument

Some people argue that freedom is never given; it must be demanded. Choose three texts from this collection, including the anchor text, "I Have a Dream," and identify how each writer addresses the struggle for freedom in his or her society. Then, write an argument in which you cite evidence from all three texts to support your claim.

An effective argument should

- make a claim and develop the claim with valid reasons and relevant evidence from the texts
- anticipate opposing claims and counter them with well-supported reasons and relevant evidence
- establish clear, logical relationships among claims, counterclaims, reasons, and evidence
- include an introduction, a logically structured body linked with transitions, and a conclusion
- follow the conventions of standard written English

W 1a–e Write arguments to support claims.
W 4 Produce clear and coherent writing.
W 5 Develop and strengthen writing.
W 9a–b Draw evidence from literary or informational texts.

PLAN

Analyze the Texts Reread "I Have a Dream" and take notes about how Martin Luther King Jr. addresses the struggle for freedom in American society. Does he believe that freedom is universal or that it must be demanded by the people? Pay attention to specific details as you gather evidence from the text. Then review your two other texts, looking at how the authors address the struggle for freedom.

Gather Evidence Use the annotation tools in your eBook to find evidence about how the authors of your chosen texts address the struggle for freedom. Save each piece of evidence to *my*Notebook, in a folder titled *Collection 2 Performance Task*.

ACADEMIC VOCABULARY

As you share your ideas about freedom, be sure to use these words.

> *decline*
> *enable*
> *impose*
> *integrate*
> *reveal*

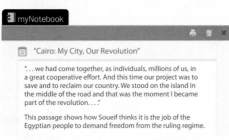

> **myNotebook**
>
> 📄 "Cairo: My City, Our Revolution"
>
> ". . . we had come together, as individuals, millions of us, in a great cooperative effort. And this time our project was to save and to reclaim our country. We stood on the island in the middle of the road and that was the moment I became part of the revolution. . . ."
>
> This passage shows how Soueif thinks it is the job of the Egyptian people to demand freedom from the ruling regime.

WRITE AN ARGUMENT

W 1a-e, W 4, W 5, W 9a-b

Introduce students to the Performance Task by reading the introductory paragraph with them and reviewing the criteria for an effective argument. Clarify that they will need to state an opinion about how to address the struggle for freedom and then support that opinion with persuasive reasons and evidence from "I Have a Dream" and two other texts in the collection. Students may complete this Performance Task in connection with their studies of freedom movements in their social studies classes. Coordinate with other teachers as appropriate.

PLAN

ANALYZE THE TEXTS

As students analyze the texts and take notes, remind them to keep in mind that their goal is to support a claim about how to address the struggle for freedom. Suggest that they decide on their position first and then look for supporting evidence in the texts.

WHEN STUDENTS STRUGGLE

Develop Claims Have students review the collection texts in small groups. As they review each text, have them answer and discuss the following questions:

- How does this writer address the struggle for freedom?
- Do you agree with this writer's point of view? Why or why not?

Remind students to follow turn-taking rules and to offer comments that elaborate on each other's ideas. Students may use their discussions to help them develop their claims and choose which two texts they will analyze in addition to "I Have a Dream."

PERFORMANCE TASK

PLAN

GET ORGANIZED

To help students determine the most effective way to organize their arguments, suggest that partners take turns presenting their claims and evidence and debating opposing viewpoints. Students should consider what went well in the debate and what they might improve as they plan their outlines.

PRODUCE

DRAFT YOUR ESSAY

Remind students that the goal of an argument is to persuade. As they draft their essays, they should keep in mind the language they used to convince their partner to agree with their claim. Emphasize that at this stage they should focus on getting their ideas down and not worry too much about writing perfect sentences.

Mentor Text See how this example from "I Have a Dream" anticipates an opposing claim and counters it.

> " And those who hope that the Negro needed to blow off steam and will now be content will have a rude awakening if the nation returns to business as usual. There will be neither rest nor tranquility in America until the Negro is granted his citizenship rights. "

Interactive Lessons
To help you plan your essay, complete the following lessons:
· Support: Reasons and Evidence
· Building Effective Support

Get Organized Organize your notes in an outline.

- Decide what organizational pattern you will use. Will you present your claim along with all the reasons to support it, and then write about potential opposing claims? Or, will you present one reason to support your claim followed by an opposing claim, and then continue with the next reason and opposing claim?

- Use your organizational pattern to sort the textual evidence you have gathered into a logical order. Will you discuss evidence from each text one by one in different sections of your essay, or will you present evidence from multiple texts in the same section?

- Choose an engaging quotation or detail to introduce your essay.

- Use a closing statement that supports your argument.

PRODUCE

Draft Your Essay Write a draft of your essay, following your outline.

- Introduce your claim. Present your argument in an interesting way that will grab the attention of your readers.

- Present your reasons, evidence, and opposing claims in logically ordered paragraphs.

- Explain how the evidence from the texts supports your ideas about the struggle for freedom in a society.

- Use transitions to clarify the relationships between claims and reasons, between reasons and evidence, and between claims and counterclaims.

- Write a conclusion that follows from and supports your argument.

my WriteSmart

Write your rough draft in *my*WriteSmart. Focus on getting your ideas down rather than perfecting your choice of language.

Interactive Lessons
To help you draft your essay, complete the following lesson:
· Creating a Coherent Argument

ENGLISH LANGUAGE SUPPORT

Understand Text Structure Print out or display the Student Model that accompanies *Interactive Lessons*: Writing Arguments. Ask students to pay attention to the organizational structure of the argument as you read it aloud. Note how the writer uses the words *Those who favor. . . say that* and *While* to introduce and counter an opposing claim. Work with students to list other words and phrases that they might use to develop counterclaims in their own arguments. *(Opponents of this view may argue that _____ . However _____.; Others who disagree often suggest _____. Yet _____.)* Display the list and post an annotated copy of the model for students to refer to as they write their arguments.

Improve Your Draft Have your partner or a group of peers use the questions in the chart to review your draft.

my WriteSmart

Have your partner or a group of peers review your draft in *my*WriteSmart. Ask your reviewers to note any reasons that do not support your claim.

Questions	Tips	Revision Techniques
Does the introduction grab the audience's attention and include a clear claim?	**Underline** the attention-grabbing text. Highlight the claim.	**Revise** the introduction to make it attention-grabbing. Add a claim.
Do valid reasons support the claim? Is each reason supported by evidence?	**Underline** each reason. Highlight each piece of evidence.	**Add** reasons or revise existing ones to make them more valid. Add relevant evidence.
Are opposing claims acknowledged and countered with reasons and evidence?	**Highlight** opposing claims. Underline reasons and evidence that counter them.	**Add** opposing claims. Include reasons and evidence that counter them.
Do transitions clarify relationships between ideas?	**Underline** each transition.	**Add** words, phrases, or clauses to connect related ideas.
Does the conclusion follow logically and support the argument?	**Highlight** the text that supports the argument.	**Add** or revise text to make clear how the conclusion supports the argument.

Interactive Lessons
To help you revise your essay, complete the following lesson:
• What Is a Claim?

Language and Style: Paraphrase or Summarize

To make texts more cohesive, writers often include paraphrases or summaries to refer to an idea provided earlier. Read this passage from "Nobody Turn Me Around: A People's History of the 1963 March on Washington."

> " After recalling the story of Lincoln freeing the slaves, with the simple stroke of a pen in the middle of a bloody war, King laments the inferior position of blacks a century later. "

Euchner summarizes Lincoln's signing of the Emancipation Proclamation, which was discussed earlier, rather than explaining it in detail. This makes the text cohesive. Look for places in your essay where you can paraphrase or summarize ideas explained earlier.

PRESENT

Exchange Essays When your final draft is completed, exchange essays with a partner. Read your partner's essay and point out aspects of the essay that are strong and areas that could be improved.

IMPROVE YOUR DRAFT

Have peer reviewers use the criteria in the chart to evaluate the strengths and weaknesses of their partner's essay. Suggest that they focus their feedback on suggesting revision techniques for improving the parts of the essay that need the most work.

LANGUAGE AND STYLE

Explain that by referencing or recapping previously introduced information, students can emphasize or elaborate on ideas within their arguments or summarize reasons or evidence in their conclusions. Have students reread their drafts to look for places in their essays where referring to previously introduced information will help them achieve these effects.

PRESENT

EXCHANGE ESSAYS

Students will be inspired to do their best work if they have an authentic audience. If possible, arrange to have students post their essays on the school website or blog. They can collaborate on a main page that introduces the topic of freedom and provides links to the essays as well as to other related resources.

TO CHALLENGE STUDENTS...

Moderate an Online Debate Challenge students to moderate an online debate about the struggle for freedom on the school website or blog. Students should pose questions and comment on responses to focus and guide the debate.

PERFORMANCE TASK

USE THE SCORING RUBRIC

Have students use the rubric to score their own arguments. Then have partners evaluate each other's score. Students should use the language of the rubric to provide feedback in each category.

REFLECT ON THE PROCESS

Explain that taking the time to reflect on the writing process in this task will help students apply what they learned and improve their skills. Ask students to think about how well their arguments persuaded the audience. Then have them answer the following questions:

- In what ways could you have made your argument more convincing?
- How well did you anticipate opposing claims?
- What do you think was your most persuasive piece of evidence?

PERFORMANCE TASK RUBRIC
ARGUMENT

	Ideas and Evidence	Organization	Language
4	• The introduction is memorable and persuasive; the claim clearly states a position on a substantive topic. • Valid reasons and relevant evidence from the texts convincingly support the writer's claim. • Opposing claims are anticipated and effectively addressed with counterclaims. • The concluding section effectively summarizes the claim.	• Reasons and textual evidence are organized consistently and logically. • Varied transitions connect reasons and evidence to the writer's claim. • Paraphrases or summaries make the argument more cohesive.	• The writing reflects a formal style and an objective, or controlled, tone. • Sentence beginnings, lengths, and structures vary and have a rhythmic flow. • Spelling, capitalization, and punctuation are correct. If handwritten, the argument is legible. • Grammar and usage are correct.
3	• The introduction could do more to capture the reader's attention; the claim states a position on an issue. • Most reasons and evidence from the texts support the writer's claim, but they could be more convincing. • Opposing claims are anticipated, but the counterclaims need to be developed more. • The concluding section restates the claim.	• The organization of reasons and textual evidence is confusing in a few places. • A few more transitions are needed to connect reasons and evidence to the claim. • Some paraphrases or summaries make the argument cohesive in some places.	• The style is informal in a few places, and the tone is defensive at times. • Sentence beginnings, lengths, and structures vary somewhat. • Several spelling and capitalization mistakes occur, and punctuation is inconsistent. If handwritten, the argument is mostly legible. • Some grammatical and usage errors are repeated in the argument.
2	• The introduction is ordinary; the claim identifies an issue, but the writer's position is not clearly stated. • The reasons and evidence from the texts are not always logical or relevant. • Opposing claims are anticipated but not addressed logically. • The concluding section includes an incomplete summary of the claim.	• The organization of reasons and textual evidence is logical in some places, but it often doesn't follow a pattern. • Many more transitions are needed to connect reasons and evidence to the writer's position. • Paraphrases or summaries are needed to make the argument more cohesive.	• The style becomes informal in many places, and the tone is often dismissive of other viewpoints. • Sentence structures barely vary, and some fragments or run-on sentences are present. • Spelling, capitalization, and punctuation are often incorrect but do not make reading the argument difficult. If handwritten, the argument may be partially illegible. • Grammar and usage are incorrect in many places, but the writer's ideas are still clear.
1	• The introduction is missing. • Significant supporting reasons and evidence from the texts are missing. • Opposing claims are neither anticipated nor addressed. • The concluding section is missing.	• An organizational strategy is not used; reasons and textual evidence are presented randomly. • Transitions are not used, making the argument difficult to understand. • Paraphrases or summaries are not used.	• The style is inappropriate, and the tone is disrespectful. • Repetitive sentence structure, fragments, and run-on sentences make the writing monotonous and hard to follow. • Spelling and capitalization are often incorrect, and punctuation is missing. If handwritten, the argument may be partially or mostly illegible. • Many grammatical and usage errors change the meaning of the writer's ideas.

Image Credits: © Carlos Sánchez Pereyra/Alamy Images

The Bonds Between Us

❝The welfare of each of us is dependent fundamentally
upon the welfare of all of us.❞

—Theodore Roosevelt

101

PLAN

STREAM TO START

Motivate students to read the collection texts, and spark their curiosity about the collection by playing the video in class. After students view the video, ask them to think about two things they hope to learn from reading about how people are linked to family, friends, pets, and community. Call on volunteers to share their responses.

PERFORMANCE TASK PREVIEW

Point out to students that they will complete two performance tasks at the end of the collection. The performance tasks will require them to further analyze the selections in the collections and to synthesize ideas about these analyses. They will present their findings in a variety of products.

ACADEMIC VOCABULARY

Students can acquire facility with the academic vocabulary words through frequent, repeated exposure as they analyze and discuss the selections in the collection. Academic vocabulary can be used in the following instructional contexts. This will enable students to incorporate the academic vocabulary words into their working vocabulary.

- Collaborative Discussion at the end of each selection
- Analyzing the Text questions for each selection
- Selection-level Performance Task
- Vocabulary instruction (for Critical Vocabulary and/or for Vocabulary Strategy)
- Language and Style
- End-of-collection Performance Task for all selections in the collection

ASK STUDENTS to review the Academic Vocabulary word list for this collection. You may wish to pronounce each word aloud, so students hear the correct pronunciation. Then, discuss the definitions and the related forms for each word. Remind students that they will encounter these five academic vocabulary words throughout the collection.

In this collection, you will explore what links us to family, friends, pets, and community.

Stream to Start   hmhfyi.com   Channel One News®

COLLECTION
PERFORMANCE TASK Preview

At the end of this collection, you will have the opportunity to complete two tasks:

- Use narrative techniques in a fictional narrative about interpersonal connections.
- Develop a group multimedia presentation that explores the bonds that people form.

ACADEMIC VOCABULARY

Study the words and their definitions in the chart below. You will use these words as you discuss and write about the texts in this collection.

Word	Definition	Related Forms
capacity (kə-păs´ĭ-tē) *n.*	the ability to contain, hold, produce, or understand something	capacities, incapacitate
confer (kən-fûr´) *v.*	to grant or give to	conferral, conferrable
emerge (ĭ-mûrj´) *v.*	to come forth, out of, or away from	emergence, emergent
generate (jĕn´ə-rāt´) *v.*	to produce or cause something to happen or exist	generative, degenerate
trace (trās) *v.*	to discover or determine the origins or developmental stages of something	traceability, traceable, retrace

102

myNotebook

As students read, analyze, and discuss the texts in this collection, encourage them to use the **my**WordList folder in **my**Notebook to build their own personal word lists.

- **Annotate** Students can highlight vocabulary terms and other unfamiliar words and save each highlighted term to **my**Notebook.
- **Organize** Within **my**Notebook, students can drag each word into the **my**WordList folder.
- **Elaborate** Ask students to add details to the entry for each word, such as a definition, other forms of the word, and a sample sentence.

English Language Support

ENGAGE WITH THE COLLECTION TOPIC

Draw students' attention to the title of the collection: The Bonds Between Us. Clarify that a bond is something that ties or fastens things together; in this case, it refers to the things that connect people, communities, and animals to each other. Explain that the texts in this collection explore the emotional, physical, and intellectual bonds that tie us together.

ACCESS PRIOR KNOWLEDGE Ask students to think about how they relate to the people in their family, their friends, pets, and members of their larger community. Why do they think that connections to the people and animals around them are important? What can be learned from these bonds?

FIVE-WORD SUMMARY

Use this strategy to help students learn how to evaluate text evidence.

- *First,* prior to class, prepare "evidence cards," each of which should contain one point of evidence from a text.
- *Then,* explain that students are going to discuss points of evidence, consider their own opinions, ask questions, and prompt each other for elaboration.
- *Next,* distribute a packet of cards to each student, and gather students into pairs, ensuring that members of each pair hold differing packets.

- *Finally,* have pairs read their evidence cards to each other and then state their current opinions about the topic and the evidence. Remind students to prompt each other for clarification and elaboration as they talk, to ask questions, and to add ideas to propel the discussion forward.

 Collection 3 Digital Resources for English Language Support

INTERACTIVE WHITEBOARD LESSONS

Use the Interactive
Whiteboard Lessons to

LEVEL UP TUTORIALS

Students can access *Level Up* Tutorials from their eBooks to get additional help on analyzing literature, analyzing

Collection 3 Lessons	Media	Teach and Practice
Student Edition | eBook	▶ Video Links H HISTORY A&E Channel One News	**Close Reading and Evidence Tracking**
ANCHOR TEXT Short Story by Jhumpa Lahiri "When Mr. Pirzada Came to Dine"	🔊 **Audio** "When Mr. Pirzada Came to Dine"	**Close Read Screencasts** • Modeled Discussion 1 (lines 34–44) • Modeled Discussion 2 (lines 309–322) • Close Read applicationpdf (lines 392–403) **Strategies for Annotation** • Analyze Character • Analyze Character and Theme • Patterns of Word Changes
CLOSE READER Short Story by Isabel Allende "And of Clay Are We Created"	🔊 **Audio** "And of Clay Are We Created"	
ANCHOR TEXT Science Writing by Frans de Waal "Monkey See, Monkey Do, Monkey Connect"	🔊 **Audio** "Monkey See, Monkey Do, Monkey Connect"	**Close Read Screencasts** • Modeled Discussion 1 (lines 63–72) • Close Read applicationpdf (lines 172–180) **Strategies for Annotation** • Analyze and Evaluate Author's Claims • Words from Greek
CLOSE READER Science Writing by Temple Grandin and Catherine Johnson from *Animals in Translation*	🔊 **Audio** from *Animals in Translation*	
Short Story by Yasunari Kawabata "The Grasshopper and the Bell Cricket"	🔊 **Audio** "The Grasshopper and the Bell Cricket"	**Strategies for Annotation** • Analyze Impact of Word Choice: Tone • Use Context Clues
Informational Text by Dorothy Rowe "With Friends Like These ..."	🔊 **Audio** "With Friends Like These…"	**Strategies for Annotation** • Patterns of Word Change • Adjective and Adverb Phrases
Poem by Natasha Trethewey "At Dusk"	🔊 **Audio** "At Dusk"	**Strategies for Annotation** • Interpret Figurative Language
CLOSE READER Poems About Family "My Ceremony For Taking" by Lara Mann "The Stayer" by Virgil Suárez	🔊 **Audio** "My Ceremony For Taking" 🔊 **Audio** "The Stayer"	
Public Service Announcement from the Corporation for National and Community Service "Count on Us"	▶ **Video** "Count on Us"	
Collection 3 Performance Tasks: A Write a Fictional Narrative B Create a Group Multimedia Presentation	**hmhfyi.com**	**Interactive Lessons** A Writing a Narrative B Using Media in a Presentation

Assess		Extend	Reteach
Performance Task	**✓ Assess It Online!**	**Teacher eBook**	**Teacher eBook**
Writing Activity: Letters	Selection Test	**Support Inferences About a Theme**	**Analyze Character and Theme >** *Level Up* **Tutorial >** Character Traits
Speaking Activity: Debate	Selection Test	**Respond to Diverse Perspectives >** **Interactive Lesson >** Persuasive Planner	**Analyze and Evaluate Author's Claims >** *Level Up* **Tutorial >** Evidence
Writing Activity: Journal Entry or Letter	Selection Test	**Write a Narrative**	**Analyze Impact of Word Choice: Tone >** *Level Up* **Tutorial >** Tone
Speaking Activity: Discussion	Selection Test	**Determine Technical Meanings**	**Analyze Ideas >** *Level Up* **Tutorial >** Reading for Details
Speaking Activity: Poetry Reading	Selection Test	**Analyze Language in Poetry**	**Interpret Figurative Language >** *Level Up* **Tutorial >** Figurative Language
Media Activity: Public Service Announcement	Selection Test	**Evaluate a Speaker's Reasoning >** **Interactive Whiteboard lesson >** Evaluate a Speaker's Reasoning	**Analyze Purpose and Development of Ideas**
A Write a Fictional Narrative **B** Create a Group Multimedia Presentation	Collection Test		

n Assessments
ucting Research
ating Sources

Standards Support and Enrichment

For more instruction and practice in reading literary and informational texts, language, spelling, and speaking and listening, see Teacher Resources > Standards Support and Enrichment.

Collection 3 Lessons	Key Learning Objective	Performance Task
ANCHOR TEXT **Short Story by Jhumpa Lahiri** Lexile 1170L **"When Mr. Pirzada Came to Dine," p. 103A**	**The student will be able to…** cite textual evidence to analyze character and theme in a short story and to support inferences about themes	Writing Activity: Letters
ANCHOR TEXT Lexile 1160L **Science Writing by Frans de Waal** **"Monkey See, Monkey Do, Monkey Connect," p. 123A**	**The student will be able to…** delineate and evaluate an author's claims and determine the technical meanings of words used in the text	Speaking Activity: Debate
Short Story by Yasunari Kawabata Lexile 1060L **"The Grasshopper and the Bell Cricket," p. 133A**	**The student will be able to…** analyze an author's point of view and cultural background and also analyze the impact of word choice on tone	Writing Activity: Journal Entry or Letter
Informational Text by Dorothy Rowe Lexile 1070L **"With Friends Like These . . .," p. 141A**	**The student will be able to…** analyze how an author unfolds a series of ideas in an informational text	Speaking Activity: Discussion
Poem by Natasha Trethewey **"At Dusk," p. 147A**	**The student will be able to…** interpret figurative language	Speaking Activity: Poetry Reading
Public Service Announcement from the Corporation for National and Community Service **"Count on Us," p. 151A**	**The student will be able to…** analyze the purpose and development of ideas in a public service announcement	Media Activity: Public Service Announcement

Collection 3 Performance Tasks:

A Write a Fictional Narrative

B Create a Group Multimedia Presentation

Vocabulary Strategy	Language and Style	Differentiated Instruction	CLOSE READER Selection
Patterns of Word Changes	Adverbial Clauses	**English Language Support:** • Language: Verb Tense • Comprehension: Read Aloud • Culture: American Customs **When Students Struggle:** • Symbolic Meaning • Analyze Character • Comprehension: Character **To Challenge Students:** Write to Convey Mood	Short Story by Isabel Allende "And of Clay Are We Created," p. 122b **Lexile 1220L**
Words from Greek	Colons	**English Language Support:** Language: Suffixes **When Students Struggle:** Claim, Reason, and Evidence **To Challenge Students:** Hold a Discussion	Science Writing by Temple Grandin and Catherine Johnson from *Animals in Translation*, p. 132b **Lexile 950L**
Context Clues	Using Verb Phrases	**English Language Support:** Language: Understand Participles **When Students Struggle:** Inferences Chart **To Challenge Students:** Evaluate Tone	
Patterns of Word Change	Adjective and Adverb Phrases	**English Language Support:** Vocabulary: Phrasal Verbs and Idioms **When Students Struggle:** Trace Development of Ideas	
		English Language Support: Language: Pronoun Referents	Poems About Family "My Ceremony For Taking" by Laura Mann, p. 150c "The Stayer" by Virgil Suárez, p. 150b
		English Language Support: Analyze Purpose and Development of Ideas	
	A Add Details	**A English Language Support:** Understand Narrative Structure **When Students Struggle:** Identify Narrative Techniques **To Challenge Students:** Change the Point of View **B English Language Support:** Plan a Group Multimedia Presentation **When Students Struggle:** Integrate Media Elements **To Challenge Students:** Conduct Field Research	

ANCHOR TEXT When Mr. Pirzada Came to Dine

Short Story by Jhumpa Lahiri

Why This Text?

Students live in a world in which international events and immigration play an important role in everyday life. This lesson explores the choices facing immigrants in resolving cultural conflicts and the growing pains of young people as they grow through personal connections.

Key Learning Objective: The student will be able to cite textual evidence to analyze character and theme in a short story and to support inferences about themes.

For additional practice:

Close Reader selection
"And of Clay Are We Created"
Short Story by Isabel Allende

RL 1   Cite textual evidence.
RL 2   Determine a theme.
RL 3   Analyze how characters develop over the course of a text and develop the theme.
RL 4   Analyze word choices.
RL 5   Analyze an author's choices concerning how to structure a text.
W 3   Write narratives.
L 1b   Use various types of clauses.
L 4b   Identify and correctly use patterns of word changes.

▲ Text Complexity Rubric

Quantitative Measures	**When Mr. Pirzada Came to Dine** Lexile: 1170L
Qualitative Measures	**Levels of Meaning/Purpose** multiple levels of meaning (multiple themes)
	Structure few, if any, shifts in point of view
	Language Conventionality and Clarity increased, clearly assigned dialogue
	Knowledge Demands somewhat unfamiliar experience
Reader/Task Considerations	• Teacher determined • Vary by individual reader and type of text • See the Text X-Ray for suggested Reader/Task Considerations.

English Language Support Before teaching, use the Text X-Ray below for an overview of the text's complexity. The Text X-Ray and the supports and scaffolds in the Teacher's Edition will help you guide students of different skill levels.

Meaning Making

Language Development

Effective Expression

Content Knowledge

Foundational Skills

Text Complexity: Qualitative Measures

Levels of Meaning/Purpose

multiple levels of meaning (multiple themes)

Help students support inferences about theme and character.

- Teacher's Edition side notes, pp. 105, 106, 109, 110, 111, 118, 119
- English Language Support, p. 108
- Support Inferences About Theme, p. 119

Guide students to analyze symbols.

- Teacher's Edition side note, p. 108

To reteach supporting inferences about a theme, see

- Support Inferences About a Theme, p. 122a

 Use It! *Level Up* tutorial: Theme

Interactive Whiteboard Lesson: Theme/Central Idea

***ZOOM IN ON* INFERRING THEME** Discuss how a story's theme, its message about people or life, is conveyed through the plot and characters. Suggest that, as they read, students look for ideas related to growing up. Use these questions to help them make **inferences** about the story's theme:

- What are some of the first things Lilia notices about Mr. Pirzada? (*things that make him seem slightly foreign*)
- Why does Lilia look for a book about Pakistan at the library? (*to understand more about Mr. Pirzada's situation*)
- What does Lilia understand at the end of the story? (*what it feels like to miss someone who is far away*)

Have pairs work together to write a sentence that states a theme about growing up. Ask volunteers to share their sentences with the class.

Structure

few, if any, shifts in point of view

Help students analyze character and theme.

- Teacher's Edition side notes, pp. 103, 104, 106, 107, 108, 110, 112, 113, 115, 116, 117, 118, 119
- Close Read Screencasts, p. 103
- When Students Struggle, pp. 106–107, 113, 115
- Strategies for Annotation, pp. 111, 114, 119
- Analyze Character and Theme, p. 119

To reteach analyzing character and theme, see

- Analyze Character and Theme, p. 122a

 Use It! *Level Up* tutorial: Character Traits

***ZOOM IN ON* ANALYZING CHARACTER AND THEME** The actions of **characters** often help develop a story's **themes**. Help students recognize that ritual actions can form significant themes. Point out the following rituals:

- Mr. Pirzada brings Lilia gifts of candy.
- Lilia stores the candy in a special box and prays for the well-being of Mr. Pirzada's family.

As a class, discuss these related rituals and the messages they send. (*Possible answers: Kindness begets kindness. Treating a person as special can make you special to that person. Children appreciate being treated with respect and kindness.*)

Language Conventionality and Clarity

increased, clearly assigned dialogue

Teach unfamiliar vocabulary in context.

- Teacher's Edition Critical Vocabulary notes, pp. 103, 104, 105, 106, 107, 108, 110, 112, 115, 118, 121
- Applying Academic Vocabulary, pp. 109, 112, 118

Help students recognize and understand verb tenses.

- English Language Support, p. 104

Guide students to analyze adverbial clauses.

- Language and Style: Adverbial Clauses, p. 122

ZOOM IN ON **IDENTIFYING ADVERBIAL CLAUSES** Explain to students that an **adverbial clause** is a subordinate clause that modifies a verb, an adverb, or an adjective. Display the sentence in lines 45–49 and highlight the clause "as I was dropping ice cubes into the water pitcher." Explain that the conjunction *as* indicates two actions taking place at the same time, and have pairs discuss which verb tells what Lilia does as she drops the ice into the pitcher. (*asked*)

Have small groups find other complex sentences in the story and analyze them in the same way. Have each group present their sentences and their analyses of them.

Knowledge Demands

somewhat unfamiliar experience

Support English Learners in understanding the cultural background of the author.

- Teacher's Edition Background note, p. 103
- When Students Struggle, p. 105
- English Language Support, p. 116

ZOOM IN ON **BUILDING BACKGROUND KNOWLEDGE** Tell students that while Jhumpa Lahiri was raised in Rhode Island by Bengali parents, she often visited India as a child and credits both Indian and American cultures for having shaped her perspective on life. Yet, she herself feels neither Indian nor American. Discuss how the author's background is reflected in this story. (*Lilia feels connected to both the United States and India but attends a school that honors only her American heritage.*)

Suggested Reader/Task Considerations

You might consider the following before assigning this short story to students.

- Will students be able to engage with a story that has a much younger protagonist?
- Might readers exposed to the political and cultural content of the text want to learn more about this content?

ZOOM IN ON **SUPPORTING COMPREHENSION**

- Point out that the narrator is reflecting back on her experiences as a 10-year-old. Ask students to think about how their own childhood experiences take on new meaning as they recall them now.
- Ask volunteers familiar with Indian culture to share what they know about it. Have interested students conduct research to find articles that describe the current political situation in Bangladesh, as well as the current political relationship between India and Pakistan.

Background Explain that the author's parents emigrated from India to London, where Lahiri was born. They moved to the United States when she was three years old. Point out that although this short story seems autobiographical, Lahiri was born in 1967 and could not have experienced the events of 1971 as seen through the eyes of the ten-year-old narrator.

AS YOU READ Direct students to use the As You Read statement to help them focus their reading.

Analyze Character and Theme (LINES 1–14)

RL 3

Explain that details about **characters** can help to develop a story's message about life, or **theme**.

A **ASK STUDENTS** to reread lines 1–14, paying attention to the details that describe Mr. Pirzada. Have them explain what the details reveal about Mr. Pirzada's life and about his character. *(Lines 1–3 describe him as a man who maintains hope in the face of the possible loss of his family and the fact that he brings "confections" suggests that he is kind and thoughtful of others, in spite of his own serious troubles. His "three-story home" in Dacca and his lectureship in botany suggest that he is a responsible, successful man; his long marriage and many children suggest that he is a dedicated family man.)* Ask students to speculate about a possible story theme, based on what they know about Mr. Pirzada so far. *(The details suggest themes related to loss or change.)*

> #### CRITICAL VOCABULARY
>
> **autonomy**: The rebellion in East Pakistan was a struggle for independence.
>
> **ASK STUDENTS** to find details in the text to see if autonomy was achieved. *(The text says that Dacca was once a part of Pakistan, but is now the capital of Bangladesh; so, the text reveals that autonomy was indeed achieved.)*

Background *In 2000,* **Jhumpa Lahiri** *(b. 1967) was awarded the Pulitzer Prize for her debut work of fiction, the short-story collection* The Interpreter of Maladies. *This story from the collection is set in 1971, the year in which civil war erupted in Pakistan. At the time, Pakistan had two distinct parts, West Pakistan and East Pakistan. India invaded the region in support of the eastern Pakistani people. The Pakistani army surrendered in the city of Dhaka (Dacca), and East Pakistan became a new nation, Bangladesh.*

When Mr. Pirzada Came to Dine

Short Story by Jhumpa Lahiri

AS YOU READ Pay attention to details that reveal the conflicts faced by the characters during the story. Note any questions as you read.

As you read, save new words to **myWordList**.

In the autumn of 1971 a man used to come to our house, bearing confections in his pocket and hopes of ascertaining the life or death of his family. His name was Mr. Pirzada, and he came from Dacca, now the capital of Bangladesh, but then a part of Pakistan. That year Pakistan was engaged in civil war. The eastern frontier, where Dacca was located, was fighting for **autonomy** from the ruling regime in the west. In March, Dacca had been invaded, torched, and shelled by the Pakistani army. . . . By the end of the summer, three hundred thousand people were said to have died. In
10 Dacca Mr. Pirzada had a three-story home, a lectureship in botany[1] at the university, a wife of twenty years, and seven daughters between the ages of six and sixteen whose names all began with the letter A. "Their mother's idea," he explained one day, producing from his wallet a black-and-white picture of seven girls at a picnic, their braids tied with ribbons, sitting cross-legged in a row, eating

autonomy
(ô-tŏn´ə-mē) *n.*
independent self-governance.

---

[1] **botany** (bŏt´n-ē): the science or study of plants.

Close Read Screencasts ▶ View It!

Modeled Discussions

Have students click the *Close Read* icons in their eBooks to access two screencasts in which readers discuss and annotate the following key passages:

- description of the setting and how the family meets Mr. Pirzada (lines 34–44)
- description of Lilia's interest in Pakistan and lack of teacher support (lines 309–322)

As a class, view and discuss at least one of these videos. Then have students pair up to do an independent close read of an additional passage—Mr. Pirzada's reaction to the TV news of the troubles in Pakistan (lines 392–403).

TEACH

CLOSE READ

Analyze Character and Theme (LINES 31–44)

RL 3

Tell students that they can analyze details about what characters say and do to make inferences about a story's theme.

B **ASK STUDENTS** to reread lines 31–44. What do the details about the narrator's parents reveal about them? What broad theme of the story might be suggested by these details? *(The narrator's parents are from India. They complain about not being able to find the foods they like, and they miss the sense of community that they had in India. They seek out compatriots as a way to find comfort in rekindling memories of their home culture while they try to adjust to a new way of life in America. These details suggest that dealing with change might be a theme of the story.)*

CRITICAL VOCABULARY

compatriots: The narrator's parents were looking for people with whom they could share some social and cultural understanding.

ASK STUDENTS to explain the strategy Lilia's parents use to find compatriots. *(Lilia's parents would search the university directory for listings of people with last names common to India.)*

---

chicken curry off of banana leaves. "How am I to distinguish? Ayesha, Amira, Amina, Aziza, you see the difficulty."

Each week Mr. Pirzada wrote letters to his wife, and sent comic books to each of his seven daughters, but the postal system, along
20 with most everything else in Dacca, had collapsed, and he had not heard a word of them in over six months. Mr. Pirzada, meanwhile, was in America for the year, for he had been awarded a grant from the government of Pakistan to study the foliage of New England. In spring and summer he had gathered data in Vermont and Maine, and in autumn he moved to a university north of Boston, where we lived, to write a short book about his discoveries. The grant was a great honor, but when converted into dollars it was not generous. As a result, Mr. Pirzada lived in a room in a graduate dormitory, and did not own a proper stove or a television set. And so he came
30 to our house to eat dinner and watch the evening news.

At first I knew nothing of the reason for his visits. I was ten years old, and was not surprised that my parents, who were from India, and had a number of Indian acquaintances at the university, should ask Mr. Pirzada to share our meals. It was a small campus, with narrow brick walkways and white pillared buildings, located on the fringes of what seemed to be an even smaller town. The supermarket did not carry mustard oil, doctors did not make house calls, neighbors never dropped by without an invitation, and of these things, every so often, my parents complained. In search of
40 **compatriots**, they used to trail their fingers, at the start of each new semester, through the columns of the university directory, circling surnames familiar to their part of the world. It was in this manner that they discovered Mr. Pirzada, and phoned him, and invited him to our home.

I have no memory of his first visit, or of his second or his third, but by the end of September I had grown so accustomed to Mr. Pirzada's presence in our living room that one evening as I was dropping ice cubes into the water pitcher, I asked my mother to hand me a fourth glass from a cupboard still out of my reach. She
50 was busy at the stove, presiding over a skillet of fried spinach with radishes, and could not hear me because of the drone of the exhaust fan and the fierce scrapes of her spatula. I turned to my father, who was leaning against the refrigerator, eating spiced cashews from a cupped fist.

"What is it, Lilia?"

"A glass for the Indian man."

"Mr. Pirzada won't be coming today. More importantly, Mr. Pirzada is no longer considered Indian," my father announced,

Close Read

compatriot
(kəm-pā′trē-ət) *n.*
a fellow citizen or person from same country.

ENGLISH LANGUAGE SUPPORT

Language: Verb Tense Explain that **past perfect tense** expresses a past action that happened before another past action. It is formed with the helping verb *had* and the past participle form of a verb, such as *collapsed*. Point out the sentence "Each week Mr. Pirzada wrote letters…the postal system…had collapsed" in lines 18–21. Explain that the past perfect *had collapsed* indicates the postal system collapse occurred before Mr. Pirzada wrote the letters.

ASK STUDENTS to reread the next two sentences and ask them which event occurred first in Mr. Pirzada's life:

- Lines 21–23: moved to America / awarded a grant *(awarded a grant)*
- Lines 23–26: gathered data / moved to a university *(gathered data)*

brushing salt from the cashews out of his trim black beard. "Not
60 since Partition.[2] Our country was divided. 1947."

C

When I said I thought that was the date of India's independence
from Britain, my father said, "That too. One moment we were free
and then we were sliced up," he explained, drawing an X with his
finger on the countertop, "like a pie. Hindus here, Muslims there.
Dacca no longer belongs to us." He told me that during Partition
Hindus and Muslims had set fire to each other's homes. For many,
the idea of eating in the other's company was still unthinkable.

It made no sense to me. Mr. Pirzada and my parents spoke the
same language, laughed at the same jokes, looked more or less the
70 same. They ate pickled mangoes with their meals, ate rice every
night for supper with their hands. Like my parents, Mr. Pirzada
took off his shoes before entering a room, chewed fennel seeds after
meals as a digestive, drank no alcohol, for dessert dipped austere
biscuits[3] into successive cups of tea. Nevertheless my father insisted
that I understand the difference, and he led me to a map of the
world taped to the wall over his desk. He seemed concerned that
Mr. Pirzada might take offense if I accidentally referred to him as
an Indian, though I could not really imagine Mr. Pirzada being
offended by much of anything. "Mr. Pirzada is Bengali, but he is
80 a Muslim," my father informed me. "Therefore he lives in East
Pakistan, not India." His finger trailed across the Atlantic, through
Europe, the Mediterranean, the Middle East, and finally to the
sprawling orange diamond that my mother once told me resembled
a woman wearing a sari[4] with her left arm extended. Various
cities had been circled with lines drawn between them to indicate
my parents' travels, and the place of their birth, Calcutta, was
signified by a small silver star. I had been there only once and had
no memory of the trip. "As you see, Lilia, it is a different country,
a different color," my father said. Pakistan was yellow, not orange.
90 I noticed that there were two distinct parts to it, one much larger
than the other, separated by an expanse of Indian territory; it was
as if California and Connecticut **constituted** a nation apart from
the U.S.

My father rapped his knuckles on top of my head. "You are,
of course, aware of the current situation? Aware of East Pakistan's
fight for sovereignty?"[5] I nodded, unaware of the situation.

constitute
(kŏn′stĭ-tōōt′) *v.*
to form or comprise.

---

[2] **Partition:** the division in 1947 of the Indian subcontinent into two
   independent countries, India and Pakistan, after British withdrawal.

[3] **biscuits:** a British term for cookies or crackers.

[4] **sari (sä′rē):** a garment worn mostly by women of Pakistan and India, consisting
   of a length of fabric with one end wrapped around the waist to form a skirt and
   the other end draped over the shoulder or covering the head.

[5] **sovereignty:** complete independence and self-governance.

When Mr. Pirzada Came to Dine **105**

Support Inferences About Theme (LINES 61–89)

RL 1, RL 2

Remind students that key ideas in a text are not
always stated directly. Readers must draw **inferences,**
or logical conclusions based on details in the
text. Guide students to understand the **theme,** or
underlying message, of cultural unity despite political
boundaries—the idea that the characters in the
story are brought together by a common heritage
even though they come from different countries and
observe different religions.

C **CITE TEXT EVIDENCE** Have students reread lines
61–79. Ask them what inferences they can make
about why Mr. Pirzada and Lilia's family are drawn to
each other despite their respective countries' painful
experiences with Partition. (*While Lilia's father stresses
that the differences between Mr. Pirzada and their family
stem from religious differences [lines 61–67] as well
as political ones [lines 74–89], Lilia underscores in her
narrative the commonalities that unite the characters,
including a shared language, an appreciation for the
same type of humor, a common cuisine, and similar
customs [lines 68–74]. Readers can infer that these
shared cultural traits at some level transcend political
boundaries.*)

CRITICAL VOCABULARY

constituted: The narrator uses this comparison
to show that the unwieldy division of Pakistan is
akin to forming a nation that is made up of one
state on the west coast of the United States and
another state on the east coast.

ASK STUDENTS to name the countries that
constitute North America. (*United States, Canada,
Mexico*)

WHEN STUDENTS STRUGGLE…

If students need additional help understanding the references to Partition,
display a map of the Indian subcontinent and briefly explain how the 1947
division of British India into India and Pakistan (which then comprised East
Bengal and West Pakistan) was based on religious demographics. Make
sure students understand that the 1971 civil war referenced in the story led
to East Bengal seceding from Pakistan to form a new nation, Bangladesh.
Then have students reread lines 60–67. Ask them what Lilia's father means
when he says "Dacca no longer belongs to us." (*He uses the word us to refer to
Indians. He means that Dacca used to be part of India, but when the country was
divided by Partition in 1947, Dacca became part of Pakistan.*)

Analyze Character and Theme (LINES 100–116)   RL 1, RL 3

Tell students that **dialogue,** or conversation between characters in a story, reveals what the characters think and feel.

D **CITE TEXT EVIDENCE** Ask: Do Lilia's parents feel she is receiving a good education? Have students cite details to support their answers. *(Lilia's mother, in response to a question posed by Lilia's father, emphasizes that Lilia has "plenty to learn at school" and goes on to contrast it with the stresses Lilia might have faced had she been born and raised back home, including "having to read during power failures by the light of kerosene lamps;" "…the pressures, the tutors, the constant exams." [lines 110–111]. Lilia's father, however, seems to think that there are omissions in Lilia's education. He questions why she has not yet learned anything at school about Partition [line 101]. He responds to his wife's answer by retorting: "But what does she learn about the world? What is she learning?" [lines 115–116])*

Support Inferences About Theme (LINES 132–137)   RL 2

Tell students that authors often use descriptive details to provide clues to a story's theme. Point out the details that describe Mr. Pirzada's appearance in these lines.

E **ASK STUDENTS** to infer a theme based on the image produced by the details of Mr. Pirzada "balancing…two suitcases of equal weight." *(This image suggests a theme of adaptation. Mr. Pirzada is managing the influences of two cultures and doing it well.)*

> ### CRITICAL VOCABULARY
>
> **impeccably**: Mr. Pirzada takes extreme care with his clothing and appearance.
>
> **ASK STUDENTS** to describe what Mr. Pirzada wears in order to be impeccably dressed. *(He wears a suit, a scarf, and a silk tie.)*

We returned to the kitchen, where my mother was draining a pot of boiled rice into a colander. My father opened up the can on the counter and eyed me sharply over the frames of his glasses as he
100 ate some more cashews. "What exactly do they teach you at school? Do you study history? Geography?"

"Lilia has plenty to learn at school," my mother said. "We live here now, she was born here." She seemed genuinely proud of the fact, as if it were a reflection of my character. In her estimation, I knew, I was assured a safe life, an easy life, a fine education, every opportunity. I would never have to eat rationed food, or obey curfews, or watch riots from my rooftop, or hide neighbors in water tanks to prevent them from being shot, as she and my father had. "Imagine having to place her in a decent school. Imagine her
110 having to read during power failures by the light of kerosene lamps. Imagine the pressures, the tutors, the constant exams." She ran a hand through her hair, bobbed to a suitable length for her part-time job as a bank teller. "How can you possibly expect her to know about Partition? Put those nuts away."

"But what does she learn about the world?" My father rattled the cashew can in his hand. "What is she learning?"

We learned American history, of course, and American geography. That year, and every year, it seemed, we began by studying the Revolutionary War. We were taken in school buses
120 on field trips to visit Plymouth Rock,[6] and to walk the Freedom Trail, and to climb to the top of the Bunker Hill Monument.[7] We made dioramas out of colored construction paper depicting George Washington crossing the choppy waters of the Delaware River, and we made puppets of King George wearing white tights and a black bow in his hair. During tests we were given blank maps of the thirteen colonies, and asked to fill in names, dates, capitals. I could do it with my eyes closed.

The next evening Mr. Pirzada arrived, as usual, at six o'clock. Though they were no longer strangers, upon first greeting each
130 other, he and my father maintained the habit of shaking hands.

"Come in, sir. Lilia, Mr. Pirzada's coat, please."

He stepped into the foyer, **impeccably** suited and scarved, with a silk tie knotted at his collar. Each evening he appeared in ensembles of plums, olives, and chocolate browns. He was a compact man, and though his feet were perpetually splayed, and his

impeccably
(ĭm-pĕk ʹə-blē) *adv.*
perfectly.

---

[6] **Plymouth Rock:** a boulder in Plymouth, Massachusetts, said to be the site where the Pilgrims disembarked from the *Mayflower.*

[7] **Freedom Trail . . . Bunker Hill Monument:** historic sites in Boston, which commemorate critical events in the American struggle for independence from Great Britain.

WHEN STUDENTS STRUGGLE . . .

To help students analyze characters, suggest that they begin to fill out a character chart for each of the main characters—Mr. Pirzada, Lilia, and possibly Lilia's father. Model how to begin a chart like the one on the facing page by filling in some preliminary information about Mr. Pirzada. Explain that the final column that assesses what a detail indicates about a character may not be filled out immediately on first reading, but may need further thought or reading before a character's personality becomes clear.

 LEVEL UP TUTORIALS For additional support, assign the following *Level Up* tutorials: **Character Traits.**

belly slightly wide, he nevertheless maintained an efficient posture, as if balancing in either hand two suitcases of equal weight. His ears were insulated by tufts of graying hair that seemed to block out the unpleasant traffic of life. He had thickly lashed eyes shaded with a trace of camphor,[8] a generous mustache that turned up playfully at the ends, and a mole shaped like a flattened raisin in the very center of his left cheek. On his head he wore a black fez[9] made from the wool of Persian lambs, secured by bobby pins, without which I was never to see him. Though my father always offered to fetch him in our car, Mr. Pirzada preferred to walk from his dormitory to our neighborhood, a distance of about twenty minutes on foot, studying trees and shrubs on his way, and when he entered our house his knuckles were pink with the effects of the crisp autumn air.

"Another refugee, I am afraid, on Indian territory."

"They are estimating nine million at the last count," my father said.

Mr. Pirzada handed me his coat, for it was my job to hang it on the rack at the bottom of the stairs. It was made of finely checkered gray-and-blue wool, with a striped lining and horn buttons, and carried in its weave the faint smell of limes. There were no recognizable tags inside, only a hand-stitched label with the phrase "Z. Sayeed, Suitors" embroidered on it in cursive with glossy black thread. On certain days a birch or maple leaf was tucked into a pocket. He unlaced his shoes and lined them against the baseboard; a golden paste clung to the toes and heels, the result of walking through our damp, unraked lawn. Relieved of his trappings, he grazed my throat with his short, restless fingers, the way a person feels for solidity behind a wall before driving in a nail. Then he followed my father to the living room, where the television was tuned to the local news. As soon as they were seated my mother appeared from the kitchen with a plate of mincemeat kebabs with coriander chutney. Mr. Pirzada popped one into his mouth.

"One can only hope," he said, reaching for another, "that Dacca's refugees are as heartily fed. Which reminds me." He reached into his suit pocket and gave me a small plastic egg filled with cinnamon hearts. "For the lady of the house," he said with an almost **imperceptible** splay-footed bow.

"Really, Mr. Pirzada," my mother protested. "Night after night. You spoil her."

"I only spoil children who are incapable of spoiling."

imperceptible
(ĭm′pər-sĕp′tə-bəl)
adj. unnoticeable.

---

[8] **camphor (kăm′fər):** a fragrant compound from an Asian evergreen tree, used in skin-care products.

[9] **fez (fĕz):** a man's felt hat in the shape of a flat-topped cone, worn mainly in the eastern Mediterranean region.

CLOSE READ

Analyze Character and Theme (LINES 149–151) RL 3

Point out that descriptions of what characters do and say can reveal traits that relate to a story's themes. Remind students that Mr. Pirzada is from East Pakistan and that Lilia's father is from India.

F **ASK STUDENTS** to reread lines 149–151 and explain what this short exchange reveals about Mr. Pirzada's character and his connection to his homeland, even though he is thousands of miles away from it. (*Mr. Pirzada likens his showing up at Lilia's family's home to that of his countrymen seeking refuge in India. Lilia's father supports the comment by saying how many refugees have sought shelter in his country. Just as East Pakistanis seek help from neighboring India, Mr. Pirzada, too, seeks comfort from his nearby Indian friends.*)

> **CRITICAL VOCABULARY**
>
> **imperceptible**: Mr. Pirzada makes a bow that is barely noticeable.
>
> **ASK STUDENTS** to explain how Mr. Pirzada's imperceptible bow would be different from a formal one. (*a formal bow would be more noticeable, with a person bending forward or making pronounced gestures*)

Character	Detail	What the detail says about the character
Mr. Pirzada	successful: job, wife, large family	skilled at his work, dedicated to family life
	writes to family each week	cares deeply about family even without regular contact
	eats dinner regularly with Lilia's family	needs Lilia's family for help and enjoys their company

Analyze Character and Theme (LINES 176–183)   RL 3

Note that a character's thoughts, feelings, and observations can help to develop a story's theme.

G **CITE TEXT EVIDENCE** Ask students to reread lines 176–183 and cite specific words that indicate Lilia's changing reactions to Mr. Pirzada. How do Lilia's feelings relate to the story's theme? *(Words such as dread, delight, charmed, flattered, and unsettled all indicate Lilia's reactions to Mr. Pirzada. Lilia's reactions to Mr. Pirzada, and to adults in general, are going through a change. Lilia's description of her feelings helps to develop the theme that growing up can be inspired and assisted by others.)*

Analyze Symbols   RL 3, RL 4
(LINES 215–222)

Tell students that a **symbol** is something that stands for or represents both itself and something else.

H **ASK STUDENTS** to reread lines 215–222 in which Mr. Pirzada goes through the ritual of taking out a pocket watch, winding it, and placing it on his napkin while he eats. Have students explain what the watch symbolizes to Mr. Pirzada. *(his home and his attachment to his family)* In what way is the symbol of a watch appropriate to the theme of the story? *(A watch shows the inevitable progression of time, so it symbolizes the changes that occur over time, such as the changes Lilia experiences as she is growing up.)*

CRITICAL VOCABULARY

succession: Lilia's mother brings out one dish after another.

ASK STUDENTS to suggest a succession of dishes that might be served for a full-course meal in a traditional American restaurant. *(A traditional succession of dishes could be a pair of starters such as soup and salad, followed by a main course paired with potatoes and vegetables, and ending with a dessert accompanied by coffee or tea.)*

G It was an awkward moment for me, one which I awaited in part with dread, in part with delight. I was charmed by the presence of Mr. Pirzada's rotund elegance, and flattered by the faint theatricality of his attentions, yet unsettled by the superb ease of his
180 gestures, which made me feel, for an instant, like a stranger in my own home. It had become our ritual, and for several weeks, before we grew more comfortable with one another, it was the only time he spoke to me directly. I had no response, offered no comment, betrayed no visible reaction to the steady stream of honey-filled lozenges, the raspberry truffles, the slender rolls of sour pastilles. I could not even thank him, for once, when I did, for an especially spectacular peppermint lollipop wrapped in a spray of purple cellophane, he had demanded, "What is this thank-you? The lady at the bank thanks me, the cashier at the shop thanks me, the
190 librarian thanks me when I return an overdue book, the overseas operator thanks me as she tries to connect me to Dacca and fails. If I am buried in this country I will be thanked, no doubt, at my funeral."

It was inappropriate, in my opinion, to consume the candy Mr. Pirzada gave me in a casual manner. I coveted each evening's treasure as I would a jewel, or a coin from a buried kingdom, and I would place it in a small keepsake box made of carved sandalwood beside my bed, in which, long ago in India, my father's mother used to store the ground areca nuts[10] she ate after her morning bath. It
200 was my only memento of a grandmother I had never known, and until Mr. Pirzada came to our lives I could find nothing to put inside it. Every so often before brushing my teeth and laying out my clothes for school the next day, I opened the lid of the box and ate one of his treats.

That night, like every night, we did not eat at the dining table, because it did not provide an unobstructed view of the television set. Instead we huddled around the coffee table, without conversing, our plates perched on the edges of our knees. From the kitchen my mother brought forth the **succession** of dishes: lentils with fried
210 onions, green beans with coconut, fish cooked with raisins in a yogurt sauce. I followed with the water glasses, and the plate of lemon wedges, and the chili peppers, purchased on monthly trips to Chinatown and stored by the pound in the freezer, which they liked to snap open and crush into their food.

succession
(sək-sĕsh´ən) *n.* sequence; ordered arrangement.

H Before eating Mr. Pirzada always did a curious thing. He took out a plain silver watch without a band, which he kept in his breast pocket, held it briefly to one of his tufted ears, and wound it with three swift flicks of his thumb and forefinger. Unlike the watch on

---

[10] **areca (ə-rē´kə) nuts:** seeds of the betel palm, chewed as a stimulant.

ENGLISH LANGUAGE SUPPORT

Comprehension: Read Aloud Read lines 186–193 aloud while students follow along. Use an appropriate tone for Mr. Pirzada's rhetorical question and observations. Point out that the use of the dialogue tag "he demanded" indicates that he views this as an annoying custom. Discuss why he might feel irritated by something Americans consider to be polite and friendly. *(Students might suggest that perhaps appreciation is expressed differently and in a different context in Mr. Pirzada's native country.)*

his wrist, the pocket watch, he had explained to me, was set to the
220 local time in Dacca, eleven hours ahead. For the duration of the
meal the watch rested on his folded napkin on the coffee table. He
never seemed to consult it.

Now that I had learned Mr. Pirzada was not an Indian, I began
to study him with extra care, to try to figure out what made him
different. I decided that the pocket watch was one of those things.
When I saw it that night, as he wound it and arranged it on the
coffee table, an uneasiness possessed me; life, I realized, was being
lived in Dacca first. I imagined Mr. Pirzada's daughters rising from
sleep, tying ribbons in their hair, anticipating breakfast, preparing
230 for school. Our meals, our actions, were only a shadow of what had
already happened there, a lagging ghost of where Mr. Pirzada really
belonged.

At six-thirty, which was when the national news began, my
father raised the volume and adjusted the antennas. Usually I
occupied myself with a book, but that night my father insisted
that I pay attention. On the screen I saw tanks rolling through
dusty streets, and fallen buildings, and forests of unfamiliar trees
into which East Pakistani refugees had fled, seeking safety over

When Mr. Pirzada Came to Dine **109**

CLOSE READ

Support Inferences About Theme (LINES 223–232)
RL 1, RL 2

Explain that because Lilia is the narrator as well as a
character in the story, her description of her thoughts
processes provides important details related to the
theme.

CITE TEXT EVIDENCE Ask students how Lilia's
observations about Mr. Pirzada further develop the
story's theme. *(Lilia studies Mr. Pirzada "with extra care,"
showing that she is consciously trying to understand his
situation more deeply. Her new realization about Mr.
Pirzada and his family in lines 227–228 indicates that
she is beginning to see Mr. Pirzada as living two lives—
the first in Dacca, where his family lives, and where he
ultimately belongs; and the second in the United States,
where he seeks solace and a balm for his homesickness
in the company of Lilia's family and their comforting,
familiar customs.)*

APPLYING ACADEMIC VOCABULARY

capacity	generate

As you discuss "When Mr. Pirzada Came to Dine," incorporate the Collection
3 academic vocabulary words: *capacity* and *generate*. To analyze Lilia's
character, ask students what emotional **capacity** is indicated by her idea
that the candy should not be eaten casually. In considering symbols in the
text, ask students what thoughts are **generated** by Mr. Pirzada's care and
attention to the watch.

Image Credits: (b) ©Loungepark/The Image Bank/Getty Images; (inset) ©Tomas Skopal/Shutterstock

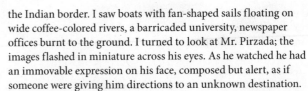

TEACH

CLOSE READ

Analyze Character and Theme (LINES 236–244)

RL 3

Explain that the character of Mr. Pirzada is developed mainly through Lilia's descriptions of him. As they read this passage, point out that Lilia is becoming more and more interested in Mr. Pirzada's thoughts and feelings.

J **CITE TEXT EVIDENCE** Have students cite details that describe Mr. Pirzada's reaction to the disturbing images he sees on TV and explain what the details reveal about his character. *(Mr. Pirzada's "immovable expression" shows he has a stoic attitude and is perhaps holding out hope for his family's survival. The comment that he is "composed but alert," as if he is memorizing "directions to an unknown destination" suggests he is aware that his future may hold sorrow and loss, but he will not go there until it is certain he must.)*

Support Inferences About Theme (LINES 261–282)

RL 1, RL 2

Remind students that valid inferences must be supported by strong textual evidence.

K **CITE TEXT EVIDENCE** Have students reread lines 261–282 to draw conclusions about the changes in Lilia's character. Have them cite evidence about what has inspired the changes. *(In lines 261–263 Lilia says she no longer feels her usual "ceremonious satisfaction" with Mr. Pirzada's candies. Instead, she cannot stop thinking about "the unruly, sweltering world" where his family may be struggling to survive. Because of her new awareness, Lilia takes a new step on her own initiative: she decides to pray for the safety of Mr. Pirzada's family.)*

> #### CRITICAL VOCABULARY
>
> **assailed**: Because of his family's dire situation, Mr. Pirzada could be disturbed by terrible news at any time.
>
> **ASK STUDENTS** to suggest what types of news might assail Mr. Pirzada. *(news about fighting in Pakistan or bad news about his family)*

J **240** the Indian border. I saw boats with fan-shaped sails floating on wide coffee-colored rivers, a barricaded university, newspaper offices burnt to the ground. I turned to look at Mr. Pirzada; the images flashed in miniature across his eyes. As he watched he had an immovable expression on his face, composed but alert, as if someone were giving him directions to an unknown destination.

During the commercial my mother went to the kitchen to get more rice, and my father and Mr. Pirzada deplored the policies of a general named Yahyah Khan. They discussed intrigues I did not know, a catastrophe I could not comprehend. "See, children your age, what they do to survive," my father said as he served me **250** another piece of fish. But I could no longer eat. I could only steal glances at Mr. Pirzada, sitting beside me in his olive green jacket, calmly creating a well in his rice to make room for a second helping of lentils. He was not my notion of a man burdened by such grave concerns. I wondered if the reason he was always so smartly dressed was in preparation to endure with dignity whatever news **assailed** him, perhaps even to attend a funeral at a moment's notice. I wondered, too, what would happen if suddenly his seven daughters were to appear on television, smiling and waving and blowing kisses to Mr. Pirzada from a balcony. I imagined how relieved he **260** would be. But this never happened.

assail
(ə-sāl´) *v.*
attack, disturb.

K That night when I placed the plastic egg filled with cinnamon hearts in the box beside my bed, I did not feel the ceremonious satisfaction I normally did. I tried not to think about Mr. Pirzada, in his lime-scented overcoat, connected to the unruly, sweltering world we had viewed a few hours ago in our bright, carpeted living room. And yet for several moments that was all I could think about. My stomach tightened as I worried whether his wife and seven daughters were now members of the drifting, clamoring crowd that had flashed at intervals on the screen. In an effort to banish the **270** image I looked around my room, at the yellow canopied bed with matching flounced curtains, at framed class pictures mounted on white and violet papered walls, at the penciled inscriptions by the closet door where my father had recorded my height on each of my birthdays. But the more I tried to distract myself, the more I began to convince myself that Mr. Pirzada's family was in all likelihood dead. Eventually I took a square of white chocolate out of the box, and unwrapped it, and then I did something I had never done before. I put the chocolate in my mouth, letting it soften until the last possible moment, and then as I chewed it slowly, I prayed that **280** Mr. Pirzada's family was safe and sound. I had never prayed for anything before, had never been taught or told to, but I decided, given the circumstances, that it was something I should do. That night when I went to the bathroom I only pretended to brush my teeth, for I feared that I would somehow rinse the prayer out as well. I wet the brush and rearranged the tube of paste to prevent my parents from asking any questions, and fell asleep with sugar on my tongue.

No one at school talked about the war followed so faithfully in my living room. We continued to study the American Revolution, and learned about the injustices of taxation without representation, and memorized passages from the Declaration of Independence. During recess the boys would divide in two groups, chasing each other wildly around the swings and seesaws, Redcoats against the colonies. In the classroom our teacher, Mrs. Kenyon, pointed frequently to a map that emerged like a movie screen from the top of the chalkboard, charting the route of the *Mayflower*, or showing us the location of the Liberty Bell. Each week two members of the class gave a report on a particular aspect of the Revolution, and so one day I was sent to the school library with my friend Dora to learn about the surrender at Yorktown. Mrs. Kenyon handed us a slip of paper with the names of three books to look up in the card catalogue. We found them right away, and sat down at a low round table to read and take notes. But I could not concentrate. I returned to the blond-wood shelves, to a section I had noticed labeled "Asia." I saw books about China, India, Indonesia, Korea. Eventually I found a book titled *Pakistan: A Land and Its People*. I sat on a footstool and opened the book. The laminated jacket crackled in my grip. I began turning the pages, filled with photos of rivers and rice fields and men in military uniforms. There was a chapter about Dacca, and I began to read about its rainfall, and its jute[11] production. I was studying a population chart when Dora appeared in the aisle.

"What are you doing back here? Mrs. Kenyon's in the library. She came to check up on us."

I slammed the book shut, too loudly. Mrs. Kenyon emerged, the aroma of her perfume filling up the tiny aisle, and lifted the book by the tip of its spine as if it were a hair clinging to my sweater. She glanced at the cover, then at me.

"Is this book a part of your report, Lilia?"

"No, Mrs. Kenyon."

"Then I see no reason to consult it," she said, replacing it in the slim gap on the shelf. "Do you?"

As weeks passed it grew more and more rare to see any footage from Dacca on the news. The report came after the first

---

[11] **jute:** the fiber from an Asian plant, used for sacking and cording.

Close Read

TEACH

CLOSE READ

Support Inferences About Theme (LINES 305–322)   RL 2

Remind students that Lilia's father had been concerned about the fact that she was not learning about India and Pakistan at school. Now, sent to the school library to research the American Revolution, Lilia seeks out a book about Pakistan.

ASK STUDENTS to read lines 305–322. Ask: What theme is suggested by Lilia's actions in the library? Cite details from the text. *(Lilia's curiosity about the history of Pakistan and her seeking out a book on the subject suggest a theme of connection—both to Mr. Pirzada as well as to her own family's history. Lilia initially goes to the library to research an American history topic, but feels the need to learn more about Pakistan's history instead because the civil war discussed most evenings in her home is never talked about at school.)*

Strategies for Annotation   ✎ ▣ *Annotate it!*

Analyze Character   RL 3

Remind students that writers continue to develop characters throughout a story. Have students use their eBook annotation tools to identify actions or thoughts that help develop the characters of Lilia and Mr. Pirzada in lines 245–288 similar to the example:

- Highlight in yellow lines that are central in developing Lilia's character.
- Highlight in green lines that are central in developing Mr. Pirzada's character.

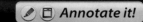

your age, what they do to survive," my father said as he served me another piece of fish. But I could no longer eat. I could only steal glances at Mr. Pirzada, sitting beside me in his olive green jacket, calmly creating a well in his rice to make room for a second helping of lentils. He was not my notion of a man burdened by such grave concerns. I wondered if the reason he was always so smartly dressed

Analyze Character and Theme (LINES 336–343)

RL 1, RL 3

Tell students that when they make inferences about a character, they must draw on their understanding of the character's personality and feelings as well as their own knowledge about people in the real world.

M **CITE TEXT EVIDENCE** Have students reread Lilia's description of what she would prefer to do instead of going to her room to do homework (lines 336–343). Ask them what inferences they can draw about Lilia's emotional growth. Have them support their inferences with textual evidence. *(Lilia's sympathy for Mr. Pirzada motivates her to want to console him, but she shows maturity in her understanding of her limited power to help him. Evidence includes her desire to share in the social atmosphere of the adults and her admission that there is "nothing" she could do beyond eating the candy and praying for the safety of the Pirzada family.)*

CRITICAL VOCABULARY

reiteration: Due to press restrictions, news reports did not offer new information about the civil war. Instead, the reports became restatements of the situation followed by a death toll.

ASK STUDENTS to suggest what the TV newscasters might have said in their reiteration of the situation in East Pakistan. *("Fighting continues in the civil war in East Pakistan with more villages set ablaze. The death toll is now at …")*

---

set of commercials, sometimes the second. The press had been censored, removed, restricted, rerouted. Some days, many days, only a death toll was announced, prefaced by a **reiteration** of the general situation. . . . More villages set ablaze. In spite of it all, night after night, my parents and Mr. Pirzada enjoyed long, leisurely 330 meals. After the television was shut off, and the dishes washed and dried, they joked, and told stories, and dipped biscuits in their tea. When they tired of discussing political matters they discussed, instead, the progress of Mr. Pirzada's book about the deciduous trees[12] of New England, and my father's nomination for tenure, and the peculiar eating habits of my mother's American coworkers at the bank. Eventually I was sent upstairs to do my homework, but through the carpet I heard them as they drank more tea, and listened to cassettes of Kishore Kumar, and played Scrabble on the coffee table, laughing and arguing long into the night about the 340 spellings of English words. I wanted to join them, wanted, above all, to console Mr. Pirzada somehow. But apart from eating a piece of candy for the sake of his family and praying for their safety, there was nothing I could do. They played Scrabble until the eleven o'clock news, and then, sometime around midnight, Mr. Pirzada walked back to his dormitory. For this reason I never saw him leave, but each night as I drifted off to sleep I would hear them, anticipating the birth of a nation on the other side of the world.

One day in October Mr. Pirzada asked upon arrival, "What are these large orange vegetables on people's doorsteps? A type of 350 squash?"

"Pumpkins," my mother replied. "Lilia, remind me to pick one up at the supermarket."

"And the purpose? It indicates what?"

"You make a jack-o'-lantern," I said, grinning ferociously. "Like this. To scare people away."

"I see," Mr. Pirzada said, grinning back. "Very useful."

The next day my mother bought a ten-pound pumpkin, fat and round, and placed it on the dining table. Before supper, while my father and Mr. Pirzada were watching the local news, she told me 360 to decorate it with markers, but I wanted to carve it properly like others I had noticed in the neighborhood.

"Yes, let's carve it," Mr. Pirzada agreed, and rose from the sofa. "Hang the news tonight." Asking no questions, he walked into the kitchen, opened a drawer, and returned, bearing a long serrated knife. He glanced at me for approval. "Shall I?"

---

[12] **deciduous (də-sĭj′ o͞o əs) trees:** trees that shed or lose leaves at the end of the growing season.

reiteration
(rē-ĭt′ə-rā′shən) *n.* restatement or repetition.

APPLYING ACADEMIC VOCABULARY

confer	emerge

As you discuss "When Mr. Pirzada Came to Dine," incorporate the Collection 3 academic vocabulary words: *confer* and *emerge*. To discuss the relationship between Mr. Pirzada and Lilia's parents, ask students to identify a subject about which these characters often **confer.** To discuss events that affect the characters, ask students what events they think will be necessary for a new nation to **emerge** from the war.

I nodded. For the first time we all gathered around the dining table, my mother, my father, Mr. Pirzada, and I. While the television aired unattended we covered the tabletop with newspapers. Mr. Pirzada draped his jacket over the chair behind him, removed a pair of opal cuff links, and rolled up the starched sleeves of his shirt.

"First go around the top, like this," I instructed, demonstrating with my index finger.

He made an initial incision and drew the knife around. When he had come full circle he lifted the cap by the stem; it loosened effortlessly, and Mr. Pirzada leaned over the pumpkin for a moment to inspect and inhale its contents. My mother gave him a long metal spoon with which he gutted the interior until the last bits of string and seeds were gone. My father, meanwhile, separated the seeds from the pulp and set them out to dry on a cookie sheet, so that we could roast them later on. I drew two triangles against the ridged surface for the eyes, which Mr. Pirzada dutifully carved, and crescents for eyebrows, and another triangle for the nose. The mouth was all that remained, and the teeth posed a challenge. I hesitated.

"Smile or frown?" I asked.

"You choose," Mr Pirzada said.

As a compromise I drew a kind of grimace, straight across, neither mournful nor friendly. Mr. Pirzada began carving, without the least bit of intimidation, as if he had been carving jack-o'-lanterns his whole life. He had nearly finished when the national news began. The reporter mentioned Dacca, and we all turned to listen: An Indian official announced that unless the world helped to relieve the burden of East Pakistani refugees, India would have to go to war against Pakistan. The reporter's face dripped with sweat as he relayed the information. He did not wear a tie or jacket, dressed instead as if he himself were about to take part in the battle. He shielded his scorched face as he hollered things to the cameraman. The knife slipped from Mr. Pirzada's hand and made a gash dipping toward the base of the pumpkin.

"Please forgive me." He raised a hand to one side of his face, as if someone had slapped him there. "I am—it is terrible. I will buy another. We will try again."

"Not at all, not at all," my father said. He took the knife from Mr. Pirzada, and carved around the gash, evening it out, dispensing altogether with the teeth I had drawn. What resulted was a disproportionately large hole the size of a lemon, so that our jack-o'-lantern wore an expression of placid astonishment, the eyebrows no longer fierce, floating in frozen surprise above a vacant, geometric gaze.

WHEN STUDENTS STRUGGLE...

Direct students to reread lines 388–400. Point out that Mr. Pirzada's dropping the knife and ruining the jack-o-lantern's mouth is an unfortunate accident in reaction to the dire news from the TV. Ask them why this accident is important in developing Mr. Pirzada's character. *(It is the first time that Mr. Pirzada has shown visible signs of his worry about the war. It shows that he has previously been successful at hiding his concern, but that the deteriorating conditions are affecting him more deeply.)*

CLOSE READ

Analyze Character and Theme (LINES 357–371; 391–403)   RL 3

Point out that this passage shows a new side to the character of Mr. Pirzada.

N **ASK STUDENTS** to reread lines 366–371 and explain what this passage reveals about Mr. Pirzada's personality. What does it indicate about his connection with Lilia? *(Mr. Pirzada has been shown to take great care with his clothing and appearance. However, instead of shying away from a potentially messy operation like carving a pumpkin, he merely removes his expensive cuff links and rolls up his starched shirtsleeves. This shows that he enjoys trying new things. It is also an indication of his desire to please Lilia since Lilia wanted to carve the pumpkin instead of decorating it with markers, as her mother had suggested.)*

Invite students to continue to examine characters' actions and how they help convey an idea about that character's personality.

O **CITE TEXT EVIDENCE** Have students identify the two different reactions Mr. Pirzada displays upon hearing the new reports. *(Mr. Pirzada first drops a knife and makes "a gash dipping toward the base of the pumpkin." He then asks for forgiveness and offers to "buy another.")* Then have students explain what these actions reveal about Mr. Pirzada's personality. *(Mr. Pirzada is obviously affected by the disturbing news, yet he is determined not to become emotional.)*

Remind students that previously Mr. Pirzada always maintained his composure during news reports. During this report, however, he shows visible signs of his worry.

For Halloween I was a witch. Dora, my trick-or-treating partner, was a witch too. We wore black capes fashioned from dyed pillowcases and conical hats with wide cardboard brims. We shaded our faces green with a broken eye shadow that belonged to Dora's mother, and my mother gave us two burlap sacks that had once contained basmati rice, for collecting candy. That year our parents decided that we were old enough to roam the neighborhood unattended. Our plan was to walk from my house to Dora's, from where I was to call to say I had arrived safely, and then

420 Dora's mother would drive me home. My father equipped us with flashlights, and I had to wear my watch and synchronize it with his. We were to return no later than nine o'clock.

When Mr. Pirzada arrived that evening he presented me with a box of chocolate-covered mints.

"In here," I told him, and opened up the burlap sack. "Trick or treat!"

"I understand that you don't really need my contribution this evening," he said, depositing the box. He gazed at my green face, and the hat secured by a string under my chin. Gingerly he lifted

430 the hem of the cape, under which I was wearing a sweater and zipped fleece jacket. "Will you be warm enough?"

114 Collection 3

Analyze Character

RL 3

Explain that one way to analyze characters in literature is to observe and assess changes that occur in characters during the course of the story. These changes may indicate a character's growth or the effects of outside events on the character. Have students use their eBook annotation tools to identify changes in the characters of Lilia and Mr. Pirzada in lines 449–464 similar to the example:

- Highlight in blue lines that indicate a change in Lilia.
- Highlight in pink lines that indicate a change in Mr. Pirzada.

"Perhaps I should accompany them?" Mr. Pirzada suggested. He looked suddenly tired and small, standing there in his splayed, stockinged feet, and his eyes contained a panic I had never seen before. In spite of the cold I began to sweat inside my pillowcase.

"Really, Mr. Pirzada," my mother said, "Lilia will be perfectly safe with her friend."

I nodded, causing the hat to tip to one side.

He set it right. "Perhaps it is best to stand still."

The bottom of our staircase was lined with baskets of miniature candy, and when Mr. Pirzada removed his shoes he did not place them there as he normally did, but inside the closet instead. He began to unbutton his coat, and I waited to take it from him, but Dora called me from the bathroom to say that she needed my help drawing a mole on her chin. When we were finally ready my mother took a
440 picture of us in front of the fireplace, and then I opened the front door to leave. Mr. Pirzada and my father, who had not gone into the living room yet, hovered in the foyer. Outside it was already dark. The air smelled of wet leaves, and our carved jack-o'-lantern flickered impressively against the shrubbery by the door. In the distance came the sounds of scampering feet, and the howls of the older boys who wore no costume at all other than a rubber mask, and the rustling apparel of the youngest children, some so young that they were carried from door to door in the arms of their parents.

"Don't go into any of the houses you don't know," my father
450 warned.

Mr. Pirzada knit his brows together. "Is there any danger?"

"No, no," my mother assured him. "All the children will be out. It's a tradition."

"Perhaps I should accompany them?" Mr. Pirzada suggested. He looked suddenly tired and small, standing there in his splayed, stockinged feet, and his eyes contained a panic I had never seen before. In spite of the cold I began to sweat inside my pillowcase.

"Really, Mr. Pirzada," my mother said, "Lilia will be perfectly safe with her friend."

460 "But if it rains? If they lose their way?"

"Don't worry," I said. It was the first time I had uttered those words to Mr. Pirzada, two simple words I had tried but failed to tell him for weeks, had said only in my prayers. It shamed me now that I had said them for my own sake.

He placed one of his stocky fingers on my cheek, then pressed it to the back of his own hand, leaving a faint green smear. "If the lady insists," he **conceded**, and offered a small bow.

We left, stumbling slightly in our black pointy thrift-store shoes, and when we turned at the end of the driveway to wave
470 good-bye, Mr. Pirzada was standing in the frame of the doorway, a short figure between my parents, waving back.

"Why did that man want to come with us?" Dora asked.

"His daughters are missing." As soon as I said it, I wished I had not. I felt that my saying it made it true, that Mr. Pirzada's daughters really were missing, and that he would never see them again.

concede
(kən-sēd´) v.
to surrender or acknowledge defeat.

When Mr. Pirzada Came to Dine **115**

WHEN STUDENTS STRUGGLE . . .

To ensure student comprehension, direct students to reread lines 461–464. Discuss the reasons that Lilia wants to say "Don't worry" to Mr. Pirzada. (*He is worried about his family in Pakistan because he has not been able to contact them.*)

ASK STUDENTS to explain why Lilia feels shame about using those words for her "own sake" and discuss what this shows about her character. (*She wanted to go with Dora unaccompanied by an adult, so she told Mr. Pirzada not to worry, but then she realizes that Mr. Pirzada's need to be reassured about his family is much more important than what she wants. It shows that she is developing a deeper sense of empathy and understanding.*)

CLOSE READ

Analyze Character and Theme (LINES 451–476) RL 1, RL 3

Explain that characters often change over the course of the story. Changes may be revealed through how the characters look, what they say, and how they act.

P **CITE TEXT EVIDENCE** Direct students to reread lines 451–464 and identify clues that indicate changes in the two main characters. (*Lines 454–457 indicate that Mr. Pirzada looks different than Lilia had ever "seen before" because he looks "tired and small" and his eyes show "panic." In lines 461–464, Lilia is finally able to utter the words she has wanted to say to Mr. Pirzada; however, her new-found self-awareness helps her realize that she has only managed to say "Don't worry" for her own benefit.*)

Point out that writers often create moments in a text when a character makes a realization or reinforces an insight. In this case, Lilia revisits a worry that has been in her mind that she has tried to avoid.

Q **ASK STUDENTS** to reread lines 472–476 and have them explain what Lilia realizes as soon as she tells Dora that Mr. Pirzada's daughters are missing. (*She realizes that it might really be true that his daughters are gone forever.*) Ask students how her realization develops a connection between the themes of growth and loss. (*Lilia's growing maturity is evident when she realizes that she has not fully grasped the extent of the loss Mr. Pirzada faces.*)

CRITICAL VOCABULARY

conceded: Mr. Pirzada reluctantly gives in and does not insist on accompanying Lilia and Dora.

ASK STUDENTS to describe how Mr. Pirzada concedes to Lilia. (*By saying "If the lady insists" and by making a small bow, Mr. Pirzada shows his acceptance of Lilia's assurance.*)

Analyze Author's Choices: Foreshadowing (LINES 496–499) — RL 5

Explain that **foreshadowing** is a technique authors use to create tension in readers by providing a hint as to what will come later.

(R) **ASK STUDENTS** what feeling is created by the sentence "My mother did not seem particularly relieved to hear from me." What is the reason for that feeling? *(The sentence creates a feeling of unease because Lilia's parents and Mr. Pirzada had expressed some concern about her going out alone; they had emphasized the importance of her calling to let them know she was safe at Dora's. The fact that her mother does not seem relieved when Lilia calls suggests that some other issue may have come up.)*

Analyze Character and Theme — RL 3
(LINES 514–517)

Remind students that throughout this story, Lilia has reported that the TV was constantly on at her house, as a connection to news from around the world. Note also that Mr. Pirzada's demeanor has always been depicted as calm and unruffled.

(S) **ASK STUDENTS** what feeling or message is conveyed by the scene of the adults sitting together with the TV turned off and Mr. Pirzada in the uncharacteristic pose of having his head in his hands. What might have happened? *(The quiet TV and Mr. Pirzada's worried, defeated pose indicates that they have received bad news. Perhaps the events in East Pakistan have taken a severe turn for the worse, and they do not want further information about it.)*

"You mean they were kidnapped?" Dora continued. "From a park or something?"

"I didn't mean they were missing. I meant, he misses them.
480 They live in a different country, and he hasn't seen them in a while, that's all."

We went from house to house, walking along pathways and pressing doorbells. Some people had switched off all their lights for effect, or strung rubber bats in their windows. At the McIntyres' a coffin was placed in front of the door, and Mr. McIntyre rose from it in silence, his face covered with chalk, and deposited a fistful of candy corns into our sacks. Several people told me that they had never seen an Indian witch before. Others performed the transaction without comment. As we paved our way with the
490 parallel beams of our flashlights we saw eggs cracked in the middle of the road, and cars covered with shaving cream, and toilet paper garlanding the branches of trees. By the time we reached Dora's house our hands were chapped from carrying our bulging burlap bags, and our feet were sore and swollen. Her mother gave us bandages for our blisters and served us warm cider and caramel popcorn. She reminded me to call my parents to tell them I had arrived safely and when I did I could hear the television in the background. My mother did not seem particularly relieved to hear from me. When I replaced the phone on the receiver it occurred to
500 me that the television wasn't on at Dora's house at all. Her father was lying on the couch, reading a magazine, with a glass of wine on the coffee table, and there was saxophone music playing on the stereo.

After Dora and I had sorted through our plunder, and counted and sampled and traded until we were satisfied, her mother drove me back to my house. I thanked her for the ride, and she waited in the driveway until I made it to the door. In the glare of her headlights I saw that our pumpkin had been shattered, its thick shell strewn in chunks across the grass. I felt the sting of tears in
510 my eyes, and a sudden pain in my throat, as if it had been stuffed with the sharp tiny pebbles that crunched with each step under my aching feet. I opened the door, expecting the three of them to be standing in the foyer, waiting to receive me, and to grieve for our ruined pumpkin, but there was no one. In the living room Mr. Pirzada, my father, and mother were sitting side by side on the sofa. The television was turned off, and Mr. Pirzada had his head in his hands.

What they heard that evening, and for many evenings after that, was that India and Pakistan were drawing closer and closer
520 to war. Troops from both sides lined the border, and Dacca was insisting on nothing short of independence. The war was soon to

ENGLISH LANGUAGE SUPPORT

Culture: American Customs Ask students to review the descriptions of Halloween activities in the story, including carving the jack-o-lantern and Lilia and her friend going trick-or-treating. Ask students to discuss these customs. Explain that Halloween is traditionally seen as a night for relatively harmless mischief, such as throwing eggs, spraying shaving cream, and draping toilet paper on shrubbery. Note that some people go further and destroy property, such as Lilia's jack-o-lantern.

> "Just as I have no memory
> of his first visit,
> I have no memory of his last."

be waged on East Pakistani soil. The United States was siding with West Pakistan, the Soviet Union with India and what was soon to be Bangladesh. War was declared officially on December 4, and twelve days later, the Pakistani army, weakened by having to fight three thousand miles from their source of supplies, surrendered in Dacca. All of these facts I know only now, for they are available to me in any history book, in any library. But then it remained, for the most part, a remote mystery with haphazard clues. What 530 I remember during those twelve days of the war was that my father no longer asked me to watch the news with them, and that Mr. Pirzada stopped bringing me candy, and that my mother refused to serve anything other than boiled eggs with rice for dinner. I remember some nights helping my mother spread a sheet and blankets on the couch so that Mr. Pirzada could sleep there, and high-pitched voices hollering in the middle of the night when my parents called our relatives in Calcutta to learn more details about the situation. Most of all I remember the three of them operating during that time as if they were a single person, sharing a 540 single meal, a single body, a single silence, and a single fear.

In January, Mr. Pirzada flew back to his three-story home in Dacca, to discover what was left of it. We did not see much of him in those final weeks of the year; he was busy finishing his manuscript, and we went to Philadelphia to spend Christmas with friends of my parents. Just as I have no memory of his first visit, I have no memory of his last. My father drove him to the airport one afternoon while I was at school. For a long time we did not hear

When Mr. Pirzada Came to Dine **117**

TO CHALLENGE STUDENTS . . .

Write to Convey Mood Direct students to review lines 529–540 and think about Lilia's memory of the events. Note that these lines represent the narrator's memory at a later date and that her knowledge of the facts at the time was incomplete—"a remote mystery with haphazard clues." Discuss the image of the three adults being so unified in their reaction to the war that they seemed like "a single person." Have students write a third-person description of a meal or another scene in Lilia's house, using vivid descriptions of Lilia's parents and Mr. Pirzada to convey the feeling in the house at the time.

CLOSE READ

Analyze Character   RL 3
(LINES 527–538)

Point out that, just as in real life, unexpected events can cause characters in a story to change their behavior. The way that a character deals with a problem or setback gives insight into a story's theme.

🅣 CITE TEXT EVIDENCE Ask students to explain how each of the adults departs from the normal, hopeful household routines. (*Lilia's father does not ask her to "watch the news"; Mr. Pirzada stops bringing Lilia candy and sometimes sleeps on the couch; and Lilia's mother no longer prepares elaborate meals but only serves "boiled eggs with rice."*) Ask: What does the adults' behavior suggest about the characters' state of mind? (*They have suspended their normal activities in order to process the changes that the war has caused in their lives.*)

Analyze Word Choices: RL 4
Repetition (LINES 538–540)

Tell students that **repetition** is a rhetorical device writers use to focus attention on a particular idea or image.

🅤 ASK STUDENTS to paraphrase the sentence in these lines, using their own words. (*Possible paraphrase: They were all deeply affected by the war, and they all were silent and seemed afraid.*) Compare the paraphrase to the author's sentence and discuss how the author's repetition of the word *single* lends power to her description. Point out that the repetition not only emphasizes the unity of the adults' reactions to the war, but it also develops a theme of connection.

Support Inferences About Theme (LINES 571–579)   RL 1, RL 2

Explain that the closing lines in a story often reinforce one or more of the themes of the story. In some cases, an author may even address the theme specifically.

Ⓥ CITE TEXT EVIDENCE Ask students to identify the lines that address the theme of the story directly. *(lines 575–577)* Then ask them to explain the themes found in these lines. *(Loss: Lilia learns what it is like to "miss someone." Maturity: Lilia understands another person's feelings.)*

CRITICAL VOCABULARY

commemorating: Mr. Pirzada sends a postcard honoring the Muslim New Year.

ASK STUDENTS to describe how commemorating the Muslim New Year might indicate a difference between Mr. Pirzada and Lilia and her parents. *(The date of the Muslim New Year is not the same as the American or Indian New Year that might be celebrated by Lilia and her parents.)*

COLLABORATIVE DISCUSSION Suggest that students create a two-column chart with the columns labeled "Mr. Pirzada" and "Lilia." Have students review the text to list the main conflict each character faces in the story in the respective column. Remind students to note specific details and corresponding page references to support the conflict listed in each column. Accept all reasonable responses.

ASK STUDENTS to share any questions they generated in the course of reading and discussing the selection.

---

from him. Our evenings went on as usual, with dinners in front of the news. The only difference was that Mr. Pirzada and his extra watch were not there to accompany us. According to reports Dacca was repairing itself slowly, with a newly formed parliamentary government. The new leader, Sheikh Mujib Rahman, recently released from prison, asked countries for building materials to replace more than one million houses that had been destroyed in the war. Countless refugees returned from India, greeted, we learned, by unemployment and the threat of famine. Every now and then I studied the map above my father's desk and pictured Mr. Pirzada on that small patch of yellow, perspiring heavily, I imagined, in one of his suits, searching for his family. Of course, the map was outdated by then.

Finally, several months later, we received a card from Mr. Pirzada **commemorating** the Muslim New Year, along with a short letter. He was reunited, he wrote, with his wife and children. All were well, having survived the events of the past year at an estate belonging to his wife's grandparents in the mountains of Shillong. His seven daughters were a bit taller, he wrote, but otherwise they were the same, and he still could not keep their names in order. At the end of the letter he thanked us for our hospitality, adding that although he now understood the meaning of the words "thank you" they still were not adequate to express his gratitude. To celebrate the good news my mother prepared a special dinner that evening, and when we sat down to eat at the coffee table we toasted our water glasses, but I did not feel like celebrating. Though I had not seen him for months, it was only then that I felt Mr. Pirzada's absence. It was only then, raising my water glass in his name, that I knew what it meant to miss someone who was so many miles and hours away, just as he had missed his wife and daughters for so many months. He had no reason to return to us, and my parents predicted, correctly, that we would never see him again. Since January, each night before bed, I had continued to eat, for the sake of Mr. Pirzada's family, a piece of candy I had saved from Halloween. That night there was no need to. Eventually, I threw them away.

commemorate
(kə-mĕm´ə-rāt´) *v.*
to celebrate or honor.

COLLABORATIVE DISCUSSION What conflicts does Mr. Pirzada experience in the story? What conflicts does Lilia face? Who is changed more at the end of the story? Cite textual evidence from the story to support your ideas.

APPLYING ACADEMIC VOCABULARY

capacity	trace

As you discuss "When Mr. Pirzada Came to Dine," incorporate the Collection 3 academic vocabulary words: *capacity* and *trace*. Ask students how Mr. Pirzada's absence increases Lilia's **capacity** to understand how he felt earlier in the story. To develop comprehension, ask students to **trace** the events that caused the map on Lilia's father's wall to become outdated.

Support Inferences About Theme

RL 1, RL 2

A **theme,** or central idea, is an underlying message about life or human nature that emerges from specific details in a story. Authors do not usually state the theme directly; instead, they convey themes with descriptive details, by repeating specific words and images, and through the words and actions of the story's characters. As a reader, you must look for important details and make **inferences,** or logical guesses, about the theme.

In "When Mr. Pirzada Came to Dine," look for clues about theme in the interactions between Mr. Pirzada and Lilia, the 10-year-old narrator of the story. What does Lilia focus on when she describes Mr. Pirzada, his family, and his life in eastern Pakistan? What does Lilia share about her own life? Focus on these key details to make inferences about the theme of the story.

Analyze Character and Theme

RL 3

An author develops **characters** by describing what they do and say, how they interact with other characters, and how they change during the story. Details about the characters often develop the story's themes. The chart provides examples of how to use text evidence to analyze characters and make inferences about theme.

Text Evidence	Examples	Inferences and Questions
Descriptive details about a character's appearance	"He stepped into the foyer, impeccably suited and scarved, with a silk tie knotted at his collar. . . . On his head he wore a black fez made from the wool of Persian lambs, secured by bobby pins. . . ."	This description of Mr. Pirzada shows that he cares about his appearance. What can you infer from his choice of a suit and tie paired with the fez of his homeland?
Character's words and actions	"He reached into his suit pocket and gave me a small plastic egg filled with cinnamon hearts. 'For the lady of the house,' he said . . ."	Mr. Pirzada presents Lilia with gifts throughout the story. What is the meaning behind this special attention?
Character's thoughts and observations	"I began to study him with extra care, to try to figure out what made him different. I decided that the pocket watch was one of those things."	Lilia thinks about Mr. Pirzada's pocket watch. What does she realize about him as she watches him care for his watch?

CLOSE READ

Support Inferences About Theme

RL 1, RL 2

Be sure that students understand the terms related to a story's theme. As a class, discuss the questions posed in this section. Point out that details about Lilia and Mr. Pirzada support the theme of relationships or friendships leading to growth and maturity. Note that stories often have more than one theme. Ask students to use details in the story to make inferences about another theme in the story. *(Another important theme is one of change and how change affects people.)*

Analyze Character and Theme

RL 3

Review the different ways that a writer can develop a character. Invite students to provide additional examples from the story of character development through personal appearance, words and actions, and thoughts and observations. Have students make inferences about the characters based on the examples they provide. *(Lilia's father's questions about the American education system [lines 100–101 and 115–116] suggest that he thinks she is receiving inadequate instruction in history and geography. Readers could infer that he thinks Lilia should be learning more about the world—and where her family originates from—in her history and geography classes.)*

Strategies for Annotation   🖉 🗐 *Annotate it!*

Analyze Character and Theme   RL 3

Share these strategies for guided or independent analysis:

- Highlight in yellow the descriptive details, words, actions, thoughts, and observations related to Lilia.
- Highlight in green the descriptive details, words, actions, thoughts, and observations related to Mr. Pirzada.
- Review your highlighting and make inferences about the characters.
- On a note, record one theme you can infer from the characters' details.

When I saw it that night, as 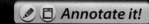he wound it and arranged it on the coffee table, an uneasiness possessed me; life, I realized, was being lived in Dacca first. I imagined Mr. Pirzada's daughters rising from sleep, tying ribbons in their hair, anticipating breakfast, preparing for school. Our meals, our actions, were only a shadow of what had

Analyzing the Text

RL 1, RL 2, RL 3

Possible answers:

1. *He gives her candy, which she treasures and places in a carved box once owned by her grandmother. The gift is special to her because she begins to understand his situation: he wants to make a connection to her because he misses his own children.*

2. *The watch is set eleven hours ahead, to the local time in Dacca, where his family resides. Lilia realizes that Mr. Pirzada's local life is less real to him than his life in Dacca, where he truly belongs. The watch helps him to maintain a connection to his life and family (lines 225–232).*

3. *He feels protective of Lilia and wants to accompany her. He wonders if it's safe (lines 451–460). Lilia knows that his overprotectiveness stems from his fears about his own children and the dangerous world in which they live.*

4. *At first, she knows very little about the conflict. As she learns more and gets to know Mr. Pirzada, she begins to compare her life to the lives of people in the war-torn area (lines 261–276). She realizes how little she and others in her community understand the civil war in Pakistan (lines 288–322). Lilia is developing a broader, more mature outlook on the world and empathy for others.*

5. *The candy represents Mr. Pirzada's attempt to connect to Lilia because he can't reach out to his own daughters. His fez represents his homeland and his "foreignness" in Lilia's world. His pocket watch represents his desire to connect with life in Dacca and his family.*

6. *A possible theme is that growing up means learning to appreciate other people's experiences. As Lilia learns more about Mr. Pirzada's life, especially his worry for his family and the pain of separation that he feels, she becomes less self-centered and wants "above all, to console Mr. Pirzada somehow."*

7. *Earlier in the story, Lilia begins a ritual of eating a piece of candy each night and praying for the safety of Mr. Pirzada's family. At the end of the story, since Lilia knows that Mr. Pirzada's family is safe and he is finally reunited with them, she feels that her ritual is no longer needed.*

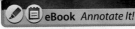 **eBook** *Annotate It!*

Analyzing the Text

RL 1, RL 2, RL 3, W 3

Cite Text Evidence Support your responses with evidence from the selection.

1. **Infer** Describe the gifts that Mr. Pirzada gives Lilia and how Lilia cares for these gifts. Why might she feel she should not eat the candy "in a casual manner"?

2. **Interpret** How is Mr. Pirzada's pocket watch different from the watch he wears on his wrist? What does the pocket watch help Lilia understand about Mr. Pirzada and his situation?

3. **Infer** How does Mr. Pirzada react to the idea of Lilia going out trick-or-treating? What does Lilia mean when she tries to explain it to her friend by saying, "His daughters are missing"?

4. **Analyze** Throughout the story, Lilia listens as her parents and Mr. Pirzada discuss the war between India and Pakistan. Why does she become more interested in the war? What deeper change does this interest represent in Lilia?

5. **Interpret** A **symbol** is something that stands for or represents both itself and something else. The objects associated with characters in a story are often symbols that provide clues about who they are and what they are experiencing. What are at least three objects associated with Mr. Pirzada, and what do they symbolize?

6. **Cite Evidence** What theme about growing up does the story convey? Think about Lilia's experiences and the way she changes during the story.

7. **Draw Conclusions** At the end of the story, why does Lilia feel she can finally throw away her remaining candies from Mr. Pirzada?

PERFORMANCE TASK

Writing Activity: Letters "When Mr. Pirzada Came to Dine" is told from the point of view of 10-year-old Lilia. What might we learn if we could know Mr. Pirzada's point of view? Write two letters from Mr. Pirzada to his family in Dacca. Be sure to base the details in your letters on insights we gain through Lilia's observations in the story.

- In the first letter, have Mr. Pirzada describe Lilia and her family. Have him explain why he enjoys giving Lilia candy and what she does with it.

- In the second letter, have him describe Halloween. Include details about the pumpkin carving and Lilia's trick-or-treating.

Assign this performance task.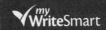

PERFORMANCE TASK

W 3

Writing Activity: Letters Have students think about Mr. Pirzada as he is portrayed in the text before they begin writing. Encourage them to write the letters using speech and thought patterns they think he would use. Have them review the text as needed. Students may share their final drafts in small groups and discuss how the story might be different with Mr. Pirzada as the first-person narrator.

Critical Vocabulary

| autonomy | compatriot | constitute | impeccably | imperceptible |

| succession | assail | reiteration | concede | commemorate |

Practice and Apply With a partner, describe what is similar and different about the words in each pair.

1. autonomy/freedom
2. compatriot/friend
3. constitute/assemble
4. impeccably/neatly
5. imperceptible/slight

6. succession/parade
7. assail/trouble
8. reiteration/emphasis
9. concede/quit
10. commemorate/remember

Vocabulary Strategy: Patterns of Word Changes

Suffixes change a word's meaning and part of speech. For example, the Critical Vocabulary word *succession* is formed by adding the noun suffix *-ion* to a verb, or action word. The verb *succeed*, which means "to follow," becomes the noun *succession*, which means "a series or sequence." Identifying patterns of word changes will help you define unfamiliar words you encounter in your reading. Here are some common English suffixes:

Suffix	Part of Speech	Meaning	Examples
-tion, -ion	noun	act or condition of	revolution, explosion
-ify, -fy	verb	make or become	terrify, specify
-able, -ible	adjective	ability	understandable, approachable

Practice and Apply For each row of the chart, identify another example that uses one of the suffixes shown. With each word you choose, follow these steps:

1. Identify the base, the main word part without the suffix. Note the part of speech (noun, verb, adjective) and meaning of each base word.

2. Write a definition for each word.

3. Use each word in a sample sentence.

Strategies for Annotation 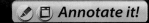 *Annotate it!*

Patterns of Word Changes

Have students use their eBook annotation tools to practice using the patterns of word changes. Have them locate the sentences containing *invitation* (line 38), *education* (line 105), *recognizable* (line 156), *comfortable* (line 182), and *location* (line 297). Then ask students to do the following:

- Highlight in yellow each of the indicated words.
- Use the note feature to identify the base word and its part of speech and then use the word in a sentence.

PRACTICE & APPLY

Critical Vocabulary

Possible answers:

Students should support each answer with evidence from the word's definition or its use in context.

1. *Both mean independence and the ability to decide for oneself;* autonomy *often applies to a country, while* freedom *more often applies to an individual.*

2. *Both imply people who have something in common;* compatriots *come from the same country, while* friends *have a personal relationship regardless of citizenship.*

3. *Both suggest forming a whole;* assembled *has a stronger sense of being made up of individual parts.*

4. *Both suggest attention to detail, but* impeccably *has a stronger connotation of perfection.*

5. *Both mean very small, but* imperceptible *means so small that it cannot be detected, while* slight *is not necessarily that hard to detect.*

6. *A parade of people is one kind of succession, but* succession *can be applied more broadly and abstractly.*

7. *Assail can mean to trouble or bother someone, but it can also have the stronger meaning of "attack violently."*

8. *Reiteration is a form of emphasis because repeating an idea is a way of stressing it.*

9. *To concede means to admit defeat, but to quit means to stop before one is defeated.*

10. *To commemorate means to do something that shows you remember.*

Vocabulary Strategy: Patterns of Word Changes

Possible answers:

Answers will vary. Students should be able to identify a word for each of the suffixes shown. For each word, they need to identify the base word, its parts of speech, and its meaning; write a definition for the word; and use the word in a sentence.

Language and Style: Adverbial Clauses

L 1b

Remind students that using adverbial clauses is a way to clarify meaning and add details to sentences. Suggest that students experiment with their writing by changing simple declarative sentences into sentences with adverbial clauses.

Possible answers:

Answers will vary. When students complete their revisions, they should be able to point to two adverbial clauses.

Assess It Online!

Online Selection Test
- Download an editable ExamView bank.
- Assign and manage this test online.

Language and Style: Adverbial Clauses

L 1b

A **subordinate clause** has a subject and verb but cannot stand alone as a sentence. It is introduced by a subordinating conjunction, such as *how, when, where, why, because,* or *whether*.

An **adverbial clause** is a subordinate clause that functions as an adverb—that is, it modifies a verb, an adjective, or an adverb in a sentence. Authors use adverbial clauses to convey specific meaning and to add variety to their writing.

In the following example from "When Mr. Pirzada Came to Dine," an adverbial clause beginning with the subordinating conjunction *when* modifies the verb *said*:

> When I said I thought that was the date of India's independence from Britain, my father said, "That too."

The adverbial clause makes the connection between the two ideas—what Lilia said and what her father said—clear to readers. Remove the adverbial clause, and the writing becomes choppier and slightly less clear:

> I said I thought that was the date of India's independence from Britain. My father said, "That too."

Now read this sentence:

> He seemed concerned that Mr. Pirzada might take offense if I accidentally referred to him as an Indian, though I could not really imagine Mr. Pirzada being offended by much of anything.

This sentence contains two adverbial clauses. The clause *that Mr. Pirzada might take offense* modifies the verb *concerned*, and the clause *if I accidentally referred to him as an Indian* modifies the verb *take*. These clauses pack a great deal of detail into one complex sentence. Without them, it would not be clear exactly why Lilia's father is concerned:

> He seemed concerned, though I could not really imagine Mr. Pirzada being offended by much of anything.

Practice and Apply Review the letters you created in response to this selection's Performance Task. In both letters, find two places where you can incorporate adverbial clauses into your writing. Have a partner review your work.

Support Inferences About a Theme

RL 2

TEACH

Explain that a **symbol** is a person or thing that represents an idea or quality. Writers use symbols to add deeper levels of meaning to a story. Symbols are often unique to a particular story. A reader must use story clues and his or her own knowledge of the world to interpret or make an **inference** about the meaning of a symbol in a story.

Provide students with the following strategies to help them recognize and interpret symbols:

- Look for people, objects, places, or activities that the author describes in detail or that are mentioned often.
- Notice how characters react to a particular person, object, place, or activity. Why does it seem significant? How does it relate to story events?

Think about how the symbol enhances or deepens the **theme**, or underlying message, of the story.

PRACTICE AND APPLY

Display the following lines on the board or on a device. Ask students to follow the strategies listed above to identify the symbol in each passage and explain how it develops a theme.

- Lines 507–514. *(Symbol: the shattered pumpkin. Theme: The pumpkin represents the friendship that Lilia and Mr. Pirzada have forged. They both learned new things while creating the jack-o-lantern. Like their friendship, it served a purpose but was "shattered" by outside forces. Lilia grieves the loss, as she will later grieve the absence of Mr. Pirzada.)*
- Lines 578–583. *(Symbol: candy. Theme: The candy represents Lilia's concern for Mr. Pirzada and his family; this is indicated by the ritual she has developed around eating just one piece each night while offering a prayer for the Pirzada family. When Mr. Pirzada is reunited with his family, Lilia throws the remaining candy away because her concern is no longer needed.)*

Analyze Character and Theme

RL 3

RETEACH

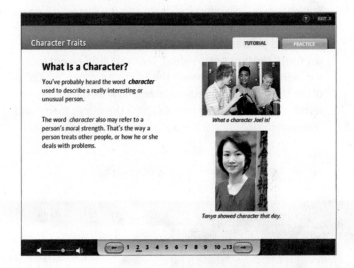

LEVEL UP TUTORIALS Assign the following *Level Up* tutorial: **Character Traits**

Review the ways in which writers reveal character traits and ask students to provide an example of each from the story:

- Appearance *(Possible example: Mr. Pirzada is meticulous about his clothing.)*
- Speech *(Possible example: Mr. Pirzada always speaks respectfully to Lilia.)*
- Actions *(Possible example: Mr. Pirzada carves the pumpkin.)*
- Thoughts *(Possible example: Lilia thinks deeply about Mr. Pirzada's family.)*
- Interactions with others *(Possible example: Lilia's mother does not cook elaborate meals during the war.)*

INDEPENDENT READING

Students can apply the skill by selecting a favorite character from a story, movie, or TV show and determining what they know about the character based on appearance, speech, actions, thoughts, and/or interactions with others. Have them give a basic description of the character's personality and appearance, citing evidence to support their description. Ask: How does the character's appearance and personality relate to the story's theme?

And of Clay Are We Created

Short Story by Isabel Allende

Why This Text

Students may have difficulty identifying the theme of a complex literary text. In this story, a journalist is deeply affected by the plight of a girl trapped by a mudslide. Watching it all from faraway is the narrator, of whom we know little except for her intimate relationship with the journalist. With the help of the close-reading questions, students will explore these relationships to make inferences about the story's theme and draw conclusions about the author's underlying message.

Background Have students read the background and information about Isabel Allende. Point out that Allende's uncle, Salvador Allende, was president of Chile when he was overthrown and assassinated in 1973. As a result of the political turmoil Allende, her husband, and their children fled to Venezuela, where they lived in exile. It was during this period that she began to write her first novel, *The House of the Spirits*, which was based on her own family and the politics of Chile.

AS YOU READ Ask students to pay attention to the way the author uses descriptive details and the interactions of the characters to reveal the story's underlying theme.

Standards Support

- cite strong and thorough textual evidence
- determine a theme or central idea of a text
- analyze how complex characters develop over the course of a text, interact with other characters, and develop the theme

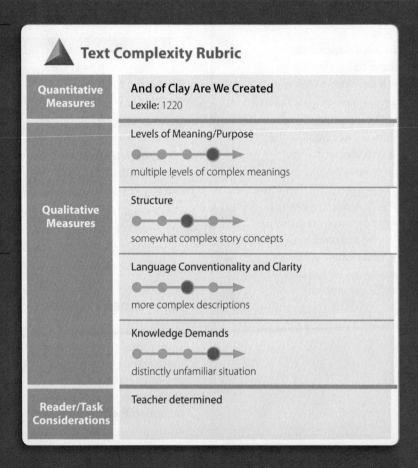

Text Complexity Rubric

Quantitative Measures	And of Clay Are We Created Lexile: 1220
Qualitative Measures	Levels of Meaning/Purpose multiple levels of complex meanings
	Structure somewhat complex story concepts
	Language Conventionality and Clarity more complex descriptions
	Knowledge Demands distinctly unfamiliar situation
Reader/Task Considerations	Teacher determined

Strategies for CLOSE READING

Support Inferences About Theme

Students should read this story carefully all the way through. Close-reading questions at the bottom of the page will help them draw inferences about the story's theme. As they read, students should jot down comments or questions about the text in the margins.

WHEN STUDENTS STRUGGLE . . .

To help students determine the theme in "And of Clay Are We Created," have them work in small groups to fill out a chart like the one shown below.

CITE TEXT EVIDENCE For practice in analyzing how the author uses the characters to reveal the story's theme, ask students to find examples of each detail from the text listed in the chart below.

Details in the Text	Examples
Descriptive details about a character's appearance	"The president of the republic visited the area in his tailored safari jacket to confirm that this was the worst catastrophe of the century . . ." (lines 270–273) "She sank slowly, a flower in the mud." (line 317)
Character's words and actions	"I caught a glimpse of Rolf for a few seconds kneeling beside the mud pit. On the evening news broadcast, he was still in the same position . . ." (lines 286–288) "Rolf assured her that he loved her more than he could ever love anyone . . ." (lines 299–300)
Character's thoughts and observations	"He took excessive risks as an exercise of courage, training by day to conquer the monsters that tormented him by night." (lines 254–256) He was Azucena; he was buried in the clayey mud . . . (lines 257–258)
Symbols used to convey theme	"Your cameras lie forgotten in a closet . . ." (line 322) ". . . how they were freed from the clay, how they rose above the vultures and helicopters, . . . flew above the vast swamp of corruption and laments." (lines 306–308)

Background *On November 13, 1985, the long-dormant Nevado del Ruiz volcano erupted in Colombia, South America. Molten rock and hot gases melted the volcano's thick ice cap and sent deadly mudslides down its slopes. More than 23,000 people died in the disaster—most of them in the town of Armero. The media focused a lot of attention on one thirteen-year-old girl named Omayra Sánchez who was trapped in the mud.* **Isabel Allende** *uses these facts as the basis for this work of fiction. In her story, the trapped girl is named Azucena, and the man who attempts to rescue her is journalist Rolf Carlé.*

And of Clay Are We Created

Short Story by Isabel Allende

CLOSE READ
Notes

1. **READ ▶** As you read lines 1–30, begin to collect and cite evidence from the text.

   • Circle the image that opens the story.
   • In the margin, explain what the author foreshadows will happen to Carlé (lines 1–11).
   • Underline text describing the consequences of the eruption.

They discovered the girl's head protruding from the mud pit, eyes wide open, calling soundlessly. She had a First Communion name, Azucena. Lily. In that vast cemetery where the odor of death was already attracting

A vultures from far away, and where the weeping of orphans and wails of the injured filled the air, the little girl obstinately clinging to life became the symbol of the tragedy. The television cameras transmitted so often the unbearable image of the head budding like a black squash from the clay that

B there was no one who did not recognize her and know her name. And every time we saw her on the screen, right behind her was Rolf Carlé, who had

10 gone there on assignment, never suspecting that he would find a fragment of his past, lost thirty years before.

First a **subterranean** sob rocked the cotton fields, curling them like waves of foam. Geologists had set up their seismographs weeks before and knew that the mountain had awakened again. For some time they had

The author foreshadows that Carlé will find something from his past.

subterranean:
under the surface of the earth

39

---

1. **READ AND CITE TEXT EVIDENCE** Remind students that symbols in a story often provide clues to the story's theme.

A **ASK STUDENTS** to note the frequent references to death in lines 1–11. How does this foreshadow what is to come? *It creates a sense of tragedy.* What do the vultures suggest? (line 4) *Vultures are attracted to the "odor of death"; we know there will be more deaths.*

Critical Vocabulary: subterranean (line 12) Have students share their definitions. Ask them what the phrase *subterranean sob* suggests. *It suggests that some dramatic activity is occurring beneath the earth's surface.*

predicted that the heat of the eruption could detach the eternal ice from the
slopes of the volcano, but no one heeded their warnings; they sounded like
the tales of frightened old women. The towns in the valley went about their
daily life, deaf to the moaning of the earth, until that fateful Wednesday
night in November when a prolonged roar announced the end of the world,
20 and walls of snow broke loose, rolling in an avalanche of clay, stones, and
water that descended on the villages and buried them beneath
unfathomable meters of telluric[1] vomit. As soon as the survivors emerged
from the paralysis of that first awful terror, they could see that houses,
plazas, churches, white cotton plantations, dark coffee forests, cattle
pastures—all had disappeared. Much later, after soldiers and volunteers had
arrived to rescue the living and try to assess the magnitude of the
cataclysm, it was calculated that beneath the mud lay more than twenty
thousand human beings and an indefinite number of animals putrefying in
a viscous soup. Forests and rivers had also been swept away, and there was
30 nothing to be seen but an immense desert of mire.

     When the station called before dawn, Rolf Carlé and I were together. I
crawled out of bed, dazed with sleep, and went to prepare coffee while he
hurriedly dressed. He stuffed his gear in the green canvas backpack he
always carried, and we said goodbye, as we had so many times before. I had
no **presentiments**. I sat in the kitchen, sipping my coffee and planning the
long hours without him, sure that he would be back the next day.

C   He was one of the first to reach the scene, because while other reporters
were fighting their way to the edges of that morass in jeeps, bicycles, or on
foot, each getting there however he could, Rolf Carlé had the advantage of

[1] **telluric:** of or relating to the earth.

cataclysm:
a violent and
destructive
natural event

presentiment:
a feeling that
something is
about to
happen

Armero, Colombia after the eruption of the Nevado del Ruiz volcano.

40 the television helicopter, which flew him over the avalanche. We watched
on our screens the footage captured by his assistant's camera, in which he
was up to his knees in muck, a microphone in his hand, in the midst of a
bedlam of lost children, wounded survivors, corpses, and devastation. The
story came to us in his calm voice. For years he had been a familiar figure
in newscasts, reporting live at the scene of battles and catastrophes with
awesome tenacity. Nothing could stop him, and I was always amazed at his
D   equanimity in the face of danger and suffering; it seemed as if nothing
could shake his fortitude or deter his curiosity. Fear seemed never to touch
him, although he had confessed to me that he was not a courageous man,
50 far from it. I believe that the lens of a camera had a strange effect on him; it
was as if it transported him to a different time from which he could watch
events without actually participating in them. When I knew him better, I
came to realize that this **fictive** distance seemed to protect him from his
own emotions.

equanimity:
calmness,
composure

fictive:
not genuine;
feigned

---

2. ◀ **REREAD** Reread lines 1–11. How does the narrator describe Carlé?
Make an inference about his character based on this and the description
of the devastation in lines 20–30. Cite text evidence in your response.

_The narrator describes Carlé as "right behind" Azucena every time
they saw him. Considering the extreme devastation of the town, you
can infer that Carlé is someone who shows strength and fortitude
amid danger and chaos._

3. **READ ▶** As you read lines 31–65, continue to cite textual evidence.
  • Underline text that describes Carlé's job.
  • Circle the narrator's comments about how using a camera affects Carlé.

4. ◀ **REREAD** Reread lines 31–54. Summarize what you know about the
narrator and her relationship with Carlé. What can you infer about their
emotional connection? Support your answer with textual evidence.

_The narrator is Carlé's wife or girlfriend. She misses him ("long hours
without him"). From her comment about protecting him from his
feelings, we can tell that she knows him intimately. She also indicates
how things between them have changed over time by saying, "When
I knew him better." He seems removed from his emotions, but she
seems to know what he is feeling._

---

2. **REREAD AND CITE TEXT EVIDENCE**

B   ASK STUDENTS to tell what they know about Rolf Carlé so
far. _We know Carlé is a reporter on assignment who will rediscover
his past (lines 8–11)._ What do they know about the narrator? _Lines
8–9 tell us that the narrator is watching Rolf on TV; the narrator
admires him and is proud of him._

3. **READ AND CITE TEXT EVIDENCE**

C   ASK STUDENTS to cite evidence from the text that
indicates Rolf's job. _Lines 37–40 explicitly refer to him as a reporter
in "the television helicopter."_

Critical Vocabulary: cataclysm (line 27) Have students
explain the meaning of _cataclysm_. What kinds of cataclysms
have they seen covered on the news?

Critical Vocabulary: presentiment (line 35) Have students
share their definitions.

4. **REREAD AND CITE TEXT EVIDENCE**   In these lines we learn
more about the narrator's connection to Rolf.

D   ASK STUDENTS to revisit the line "and we said goodbye, as
we had so many times before" (line 34). What does this say about
the couple's relationship? _They had been together for a while; his
leaving to cover a big story was routine; she understood the nature of
his work._

Critical Vocabulary: equanimity (line 47) Have students
explain the meaning of _equanimity_. Who can they think of that
has demonstrated "equanimity in the face of danger"?

Critical Vocabulary: fictive (line 53) Have students explain the
meaning of _fictive_, and ask them how Rolf's "fictive distance"
might help him in his chosen line of work. _It helps him cope with
the horror he regularly witnesses._

Rolf Carlé was in on the story of Azucena from the beginning. He filmed the volunteers who discovered her, and the first persons who tried to reach her; his camera zoomed in on the girl, her dark face, her large desolate eyes, the plastered-down tangle of her hair. The mud was like quicksand around her, and anyone attempting to reach her was in danger of sinking.
60 They threw a rope to her that she made no effort to grasp until they shouted to her to catch it; then she pulled a hand from the mire and tried to move but immediately sank a little deeper. Rolf threw down his knapsack and the rest of his equipment and waded into the quagmire, commenting for his assistant's microphone that it was cold and that one could begin to smell the stench of corpses.

"What's your name?" he asked the girl, and she told him her flower name. "Don't move, Azucena," Rolf Carlé directed, and kept talking to her, without a thought for what he was saying, just to distract her, while slowly he worked his way forward in mud up to his waist. The air around him
70 seemed as murky as the mud.

It was impossible to reach her from the approach he was attempting, so he retreated and circled around where there seemed to be firmer footing. When finally he was close enough, he took the rope and tied it beneath her arms, so they could pull her out. He smiled at her with that smile that crinkles his eyes and makes him look like a little boy; he told her that everything was fine, that he was here with her now, that soon they would have her out. He signaled the others to pull, but as soon as the cord tensed, the girl screamed. They tried again, and her shoulders and arms appeared, but they could move her no farther; she was trapped. Someone suggested
80 that her legs might be caught in the collapsed walls of her house, but she said it was not just rubble, that she was also held by the bodies of her brothers and sisters clinging to her legs.

Carlé is determined to save the girl, but frustrated and heartbroken by his failed attempts.

5. **READ** ▷ As you read lines 66–129, continue to cite textual evidence.
- Underline the actions Carlé undertakes to help Azucena.
- Circle text describing Carlé's attempt to get the pump and what he envisions will happen once it arrives.
- In the margin, make an inference about how Carlé feels as he tries to rescue Azucena (lines 71–82).

E "Don't worry, we'll get you out of here," Rolf promised. Despite the quality of the transmission, I could hear his voice break, and I loved him more than ever. Azucena looked at him but said nothing.

During those first hours Rolf Carlé exhausted all the resources of his **ingenuity** to rescue her. He struggled with poles and ropes, but every tug was an intolerable torture for the imprisoned girl. It occurred to him to use one of the poles as a lever but got no result and had to abandon the idea. He
90 talked a couple of soldiers into working with him for a while, but they had to leave because so many other victims were calling for help. The girl could not move, she barely could breathe, but she did not seem desperate, as if an ancestral resignation allowed her to accept her fate. The reporter, on the other hand, was determined to snatch her from death. Someone brought him a tire, which he placed beneath her arms like a life buoy, and then laid a plank near the hole to hold his weight and allow him to stay closer to her. As it was impossible to remove the rubble blindly, he tried once or twice to dive toward her feet but emerged frustrated, covered with mud, and spitting gravel. He concluded that he would have to have a pump to drain the water,
100 and radioed a request for one but received in return a message that there was no available transport and it could not be sent until the next morning.

"We can't wait that long!" Rolf Carlé shouted, but in the pandemonium no one stopped to **commiserate**. Many more hours would go by before he accepted that time had stagnated and reality had been irreparably distorted.

A military doctor came to examine the girl and observed that her heart was functioning well and that if she did not get too cold she could survive the night.

"Hang on, Azucena, we'll have the pump tomorrow," Rolf Carlé tried to console her.
110 "Don't leave me alone," she begged.

"No, of course I won't leave you."

Someone brought him coffee, and he helped the girl drink it, sip by sip. The warm liquid revived her, and she began telling him about her small life, about her family and her school, about how things were in that little bit of world before the volcano erupted. She was thirteen, and she had never been outside her village. Rolf Carlé, buoyed by a premature optimism, was

F convinced that everything would end well: the pump would arrive, they would drain the water, move the rubble, and Azucena would be transported by helicopter to a hospital where she would recover rapidly and where he
120 could visit her and bring her gifts. He thought, She's already too old for dolls, and I don't know what would please her; maybe a dress. I don't know

ingenuity:
cleverness in discovering, inventing, or planning

commiserate:
to feel or express sorrow or sympathy

42

43

---

5. **READ AND CITE TEXT EVIDENCE** In this section of text the narrator watches Rolf work to save Azucena's life. In lines 84–85 the narrator tells us that she "loved him more than ever."

E **ASK STUDENTS** to explain the narrator's comment. What does Rolf do that affects the narrator so much? *Although his words are encouraging, she can hear his voice break: he is pretending to be strong for the sake of the girl.*

Critical Vocabulary: ingenuity (line 87) Have students explain the meaning of *ingenuity*. Ask them why it took ingenuity to free Azucena. *The rescue workers couldn't pull her out without hurting her; they had to think of other ways to get her free.*

Critical Vocabulary: commiserate (line 103) Have students explain the meaning of *commiserate*. Why did no one stop to commiserate? *The pandemonium prevented people from stopping to react.*

FOR ELL STUDENTS Point to the verb *buoyed* (line 116). Explain, or ask a volunteer to explain, what a buoy is. (Many Spanish speakers might recognize its cognate, *boya*). Then ask another volunteer to guess or explain what the phrase *buoyed by a premature optimism* means. *supported by an unwarranted hopefulness*

much about women, he concluded, amused, reflecting that although he had known many women in his lifetime, none had taught him these details. To pass the hours he began to tell Azucena about his travels and adventures as a news hound, and when he exhausted his memory, he called upon imagination, inventing things he thought might entertain her. From time to time she dozed, but he kept talking in the darkness, to assure her that he was still there and to overcome the menace of uncertainty.

That was a long night.

130　　　Many miles away, I watched Rolf Carlé and the girl on a television screen. I could not bear the wait at home, so I went to National Television, where I often spent entire nights with Rolf editing programs. There, I was near his world, and I could at least get a feeling of what he lived through during those three decisive days. I called all the important people in the city, senators, commanders of the armed forces, the North American ambassador, and the president of National Petroleum, begging them for a pump to remove the silt, but obtained only vague promises. I began to ask for urgent help on radio and television, to see if there wasn't *someone* who could help us. Between calls I would run to the newsroom to monitor the

140　　satellite transmissions that periodically brought new details of the catastrophe. While reporters selected scenes with most impact for the news report, I searched for footage that featured Azucena's mud pit. The screen reduced the disaster to a single plane and accentuated the tremendous distance that separated me from Rolf Carlé; nonetheless, I was there with

6. ◀ REREAD Reread lines 86–129. What do you learn about Rolf and Azucena in these lines? What do the last two sentences suggest about Rolf's character?

Azucena is thirteen and has not traveled outside of her town. She's scared to be alone. The last two sentences suggest that Rolf is protective and strong, with great emotional and physical endurance.

7. READ ▶ As you read lines 130–207, continue to cite textual evidence.

- Underline text explaining how the narrator tries to feel close to Carlé.
- Circle text describing how Carlé tried to help Azucena.
- In the margin, explain what the narrator means when she says Carlé "had completely forgotten the camera" (lines 174–175).

> The child's every suffering hurt me as it did him; I felt his frustration, his impotence.

him. The child's every suffering hurt me as it did him; I felt his frustration, his impotence. Faced with the impossibility of communicating with him, the fantastic idea came to me that if I tried, I could reach him by force of mind and in that way give him encouragement. I concentrated until I was dizzy—a frenzied and futile activity. At times I would be overcome with

150　compassion and burst out crying; at other times, I was so drained I felt as if I were staring through a telescope at the light of a star dead for a million years.

I watched that hell on the first morning broadcast, cadavers of people and animals awash in the current of new rivers formed overnight from the melted snow. Above the mud rose the tops of trees and the bell towers of a church where several people had taken refuge and were patiently awaiting rescue teams. Hundreds of soldiers and volunteers from the civil defense were clawing through rubble searching for survivors, while long rows of ragged specters awaited their turn for a cup of hot broth. Radio networks

160　announced that their phones were jammed with calls from families offering shelter to orphaned children. Drinking water was in scarce supply, along with gasoline and food. Doctors, resigned to amputating arms and legs without anesthesia, pled that at least they be sent serum and painkillers and antibiotics; most of the roads, however, were impassable, and worse were the **bureaucratic** obstacles that stood in the way. To top it all, the clay contaminated by decomposing bodies threatened the living with an outbreak of epidemics.

Azucena was shivering inside the tire that held her above the surface. Immobility and tension had greatly weakened her, but she was conscious

170　and could still be heard when a microphone was held out to her. Her tone was humble, as if apologizing for all the fuss. Rolf Carlé had a growth of beard, and dark circles beneath his eyes; he looked near exhaustion. Even from that enormous distance I could sense the quality of his weariness, so different from the fatigue of other adventures. He had completely forgotten

bureaucratic:
governmental

Ⓖ

6. **REREAD AND CITE TEXT EVIDENCE** In lines 112–129, Rolf sits by Azucena and they talk through the night.

Ⓕ **ASK STUDENTS** what Rolf's optimism conveys about him. *He is thinking positively, and imagining what he will buy for Azucena when she is out. He may be used to things working out the way he wants.*

7. **READ AND CITE TEXT EVIDENCE**

Ⓖ **ASK STUDENTS** to revisit lines 50–54, in which the narrator explains why the camera is so important to Rolf. In light of this, have students consider why his forgetting about it is equally important (lines 174–175). *We know that the camera "protects him from his emotions." Now Rolf is willing to feel emotions he had suppressed.*

Critical Vocabulary: bureaucratic (line 165) Have students share definitions of *bureaucratic*. Why might someone have trouble because of "bureaucratic obstacles" standing in the way? *Students may suggest having trouble reaching a politician on the phone or lodging a complaint against a big company.*

FOR ELL STUDENTS Point to the verb *clawing* (line 158). Explain, or ask a volunteer to explain, what a claw is. Then ask another volunteer to explain what the phrase *clawing through rubble* means. *"scrabbling through the destruction"*

The search for victims and survivors continues in Guayabal, Colombia after the eruption of the Nevado del Ruiz volcano (November 16, 1985).

Carlé is face-to-face with Azucena and not looking at her through his camera.

the camera; he could not look at the girl through a lens any longer. The pictures we were receiving were not his assistant's but those of other reporters who had appropriated Azucena, bestowing on her the pathetic responsibility of embodying the horror of what had happened in that place. With the first light Rolf tried again to dislodge the obstacles that held the girl in her tomb, but he had only his hands to work with; he did not dare use a tool for fear of injuring her. He fed Azucena a cup of the cornmeal mush and bananas the army was distributing, but she immediately vomited it up. A doctor stated that she had a fever but added that there was little he could do: antibiotics were being reserved for cases of gangrene. A priest also passed by and blessed her, hanging a medal of the Virgin around her neck. By evening a gentle, persistent drizzle began to fall.

"The sky is weeping," Azucena murmured, and she, too, began to cry.

"Don't be afraid," Rolf begged. "You have to keep your strength up and be calm. Everything will be fine. I'm with you, and I'll get you out somehow."

Reporters returned to photograph Azucena and ask her the same questions, which she no longer tried to answer. In the meanwhile, more television and movie teams arrived with spools of cable, tapes, film, videos, precision lenses, recorders, sound consoles, lights, reflecting screens, auxiliary motors, cartons of supplies, electricians, sound technicians, and cameramen: Azucena's face was beamed to millions of screens around the world. And all the while Rolf Carlé kept pleading for a pump. The improved technical facilities bore results, and National Television began receiving sharper pictures and clearer sound, the distance seemed suddenly compressed, and I had the horrible sensation that Azucena and Rolf were by my side, separated from me by impenetrable glass. I was able to follow events hour by hour; I knew everything my love did to wrest the girl from her prison and help her endure her suffering; I overheard fragments of what they said to one another and could guess the rest; I was present when she taught Rolf to pray and when he distracted her with the stories I had told him in a thousand and one nights beneath the white mosquito netting of our bed.

When darkness came on the second day, Rolf tried to sing Azucena to sleep with old Austrian folk songs he had learned from his mother, but she was far beyond sleep. They spent most of the night talking, each in a stupor of exhaustion and hunger and shaking with cold. That night, imperceptibly, the unyielding floodgates that had contained Rolf Carlé's past for so many years began to open, and the torrent of all that had lain hidden in the deepest and most secret layers of memory poured out, leveling before it the obstacles that had blocked his consciousness for so long. He could not tell it all to Azucena; she perhaps did not know there was a world beyond the sea or time previous to her own; she was not capable of imagining Europe in

The narrator explains how, through television and other media, she was able to follow Azucena and Carlé, to the point where she felt they "were by my side" but "separated by impenetrable glass."

8. **◀ REREAD** Reread lines 191–207. In the margin, explain what the narrator says about television and intimacy. In what way is it ironic that the improved transmission equipment makes it to the scene while the pump remains unobtainable?

It is ironic that modern equipment is brought in to transmit Azucena's nightmare to the homes and hearts of television viewers, while the simple machine, the pump that would remove the cause of her suffering, is not available.

9. **READ ▶** As you read lines 208–268, continue to cite textual evidence.
- In the margin, explain what you learn about Carlé's past (lines 217–224 and lines 232–248).
- Circle text explaining why Carlé feels he must confront his own fears.
- Underline what Rolf learns about why he takes risks.

8. **REREAD AND CITE TEXT EVIDENCE** In lines 200–201, the narrator tells us that the quality of the technology creates the sense that Rolf and Azucena are right there with her.

H **ASK STUDENTS** how this might affect the narrator emotionally. *She feels the horror more acutely; at the same time she feels she's listening in on a private conversation.*

9. **READ AND CITE TEXT EVIDENCE** Point out that in this section Rolf is suddenly overcome by long-repressed memories.

I **ASK STUDENTS** to explain why Rolf starts thinking about the past. *Rolf sings to Azucena songs his mother sang to him.* What effect does this have on him? *Trying to "mother" the girl in her last hours of life opens up locked memories and a floodgate of emotions.*

He'd had
terrible
experiences
during WW II.

visceral:
felt deeply,
profound

His father was
cruel and
abusive. He
had a "sweet,
retarded"
sister who his
father was
ashamed of.

the years of the war. So he could not tell her of defeat, nor of the afternoon
220 the Russians had led them to the concentration camp to bury prisoners
dead from starvation. Why should he describe to her how the naked bodies
piled like a mountain of firewood resembled fragile china? How could he
tell this dying child about ovens and gallows? Nor did he mention the night
that he had seen his mother naked, shod in stiletto-heeled red boots,
sobbing with humiliation. There was much he did not tell, but in those
hours he relived for the first time all the things his mind had tried to erase.
Azucena had surrendered her fear to him and so, without wishing it, had
obliged Rolf to confront his own. There, beside that hellhole of mud, it was
impossible for Rolf to flee from himself any longer, and the **visceral** terror
230 he had lived as a boy suddenly invaded him. He reverted to the years when
he was the age of Azucena and younger, and, like her, found himself trapped
in a pit without escape, buried in life, his head barely above ground; he saw
before his eyes the boots and legs of his father, who had removed his belt
and was whipping it in the air with the never-forgotten hiss of a viper coiled
to strike. Sorrow flooded through him, intact and precise, as if it had lain
always in his mind, waiting. He was once again in the armoire where his
father locked him to punish him for imagined misbehavior, there where for
eternal hours he had crouched with his eyes closed, not to see the darkness,
with his hands over his ears to shut out the beating of his heart, trembling,
huddled like a cornered animal. Wandering in the mist of his memories he
240 found his sister, Katharina, a sweet, retarded child who spent her life
hiding, with the hope that her father would forget the disgrace of her having
been born. With Katharina, Rolf crawled beneath the dining room table,
and with her hid there under the long white tablecloth, two children forever
embraced, alert to footsteps and voices. Katharina's scent melded with his
own sweat, with aromas of cooking, garlic, soup, freshly baked bread, and
the unexpected odor of putrescent clay. His sister's hand in his, her
frightened breathing, her silk hair against his cheek, the candid gaze of her
eyes. Katharina . . . Katharina materialized before him, floating on the air
like a flag, clothed in the white tablecloth, now a winding sheet, and at last
250 he could weep for her death and for the guilt of having abandoned her. He
understood then that all his exploits as a reporter, the feats that had won
him such recognition and fame, were merely an attempt to keep his most
ancient fears at bay, a stratagem for taking refuge behind a lens to test
whether reality was more tolerable from that perspective. He took excessive
risks as an exercise of courage, training by day to conquer the monsters that
tormented him by night. But he had to come face to face with the moment
of truth; he could not continue to escape his past. He was Azucena; he was
buried in the clayey mud; his terror was not the distant emotion of an
almost forgotten childhood, it was a claw sunk in his throat. In the flush of

260 his tears he saw his mother, dressed in black and clutching her imitation-
crocodile pocketbook to her bosom, just as he had last seen her on the dock
when she had come to put him on the boat to South America. She had not
come to dry his tears, but to tell him to pick up a shovel: the war was over
and now they must bury the dead.

"Don't cry. I don't hurt anymore. I'm fine," Azucena said when dawn
came.

"I'm not crying for you," Rolf Carlé smiled. "I'm crying for myself. I
hurt all over."

The third day in the valley of the cataclysm began with a pale light
270 filtering through storm clouds. The president of the republic visited the area
in his tailored safari jacket to confirm that this was the worst catastrophe of
the century; the country was in mourning; sister nations had offered aid; he
had ordered a state of siege; the armed forces would be merciless; anyone
caught stealing or committing other offenses would be shot on sight. He
added that it was impossible to remove all the corpses or count the
thousands who had disappeared; the entire valley would be declared holy
ground, and bishops would come to celebrate a solemn mass for the souls of
the victims. He went to the army field tents to offer relief in the form of
vague promises to crowds of the rescued, then to the improvised hospital to

10. ◀ REREAD Reread lines 208–268. In what way is Carlé's interaction
with Azucena changing him?

Rolf's interaction with Azucena is making him face painful
memories he has long ago buried. Just as Azucena is buried in mud,
Carlé is buried in the horrors of his traumatic childhood. He realizes
he has pushed himself in his career to keep "his most ancient fears
at bay." He sees now that "he could not continue to escape his past."

11. READ ▶ As you read lines 269–310, continue to cite textual evidence.

• Circle adjectives the narrator uses that indicate her feelings about the
president and his actions.

• Underline text that describes the interactions between Carlé and
Azucena.

Critical Vocabulary: visceral (line 228) Have students share
definitions of *visceral*. What is a visceral understanding? *It's
something that is understood instinctively.*

10. REREAD AND CITE TEXT EVIDENCE

J **ASK STUDENTS** what in Rolf's background makes him
identify so completely with Azucena. How do their situations
mirror each other? *Both have known terror; both have been
forsaken by those who should have been protecting them; like
Azucena, Rolf is "trapped in a pit without escape, buried in life . . ."
(lines 230–231).*

11. READ AND CITE TEXT EVIDENCE

K **ASK STUDENTS** to analyze the president's proposals for
dealing with the crisis. How does his language show he is
removed from the actual situation? *The president talks in
grandiose, bureaucratic, abstract terms: "worst catastrophe of the
century"; "sister nations"; "state of siege"; "armed forces; "all the
corpses" (lines 271–275).*

FOR ELL STUDENTS Explain that a *state of siege* (*estado de sitio*,
in Spanish) is a situation in which police or soldiers take control of
a city or of a whole country.

The town of Armero, Colombia, submerged by floods after the Nevado del Ruiz volcano erupted (November, 18, 1985).

280 offer a word of encouragement to doctors and nurses (worn down) from so many hours of tribulations. Then he asked to be taken to see Azucena, the little girl the whole world had seen. He waved to her with (a limp statesman's) hand, and microphones recorded his emotional voice and paternal tone as he told her that her courage had served as an example to the nation. Rolf Carlé interrupted to ask for a pump, and the president assured him that he personally would attend to the matter. I caught a glimpse of Rolf for a few seconds kneeling beside the mud pit. On the evening news broadcast, he was still in the same position; and I, glued to the screen like a fortune teller to her crystal ball, could tell that something fundamental had changed in

290 him. I knew somehow that during the night his defenses had crumbled and he had given in to grief; finally he was vulnerable. The girl had touched a part of him that he himself had no access to, a part he had never shared with me. Rolf had wanted to console her, but it was Azucena who had given him consolation.

I recognized the precise moment at which Rolf gave up the fight and surrendered to the torture of watching the girl die. I was with them, three days and two nights, spying on them from the other side of life. I was there when she told him that in all her thirteen years no boy had ever loved her and that it was a pity to leave this world without knowing love. Rolf assured

300 her that he loved her more than he could ever love anyone, more than he loved his mother, more than his sister, more than all the women who had slept in his arms, more than he loved me, his life companion, who would have given anything to be trapped in that well in her place, who would have exchanged her life for Azucena's, and I watched as he leaned down to kiss her poor forehead, consumed by a sweet, sad emotion he could not name. I felt how in that instant both were saved from despair, how they were freed from the clay, how they rose above the vultures and helicopters, how together they flew above the vast swamp of corruption and laments. How, finally, they were able to accept death. Rolf Carlé prayed in silence that she

310 would die quickly, because such pain cannot be borne.

By then I had obtained a pump and was in touch with a general who had agreed to ship it the next morning on a military cargo plane. But on the night of that third day, beneath the unblinking focus of quartz lamps and the lens of a hundred cameras, Azucena gave up, her eyes locked with those of the friend who had sustained her to the end. Rolf Carlé removed the life buoy, closed her eyelids, held her to his chest for a few moments, and then let her go. She sank slowly, a flower in the mud.

 You are back with me, but you are not the same man. I often accompany you to the station, and we watch the videos of Azucena again;

---

12. ◄ REREAD   Reread lines 269–286. In the margin, make an inference about how the narrator feels about the president's visit. Support your answer with explicit textual evidence.

13. READ ►   As you read lines 311–326, continue to cite textual evidence.
   • Underline text that describes what happens between Carlé and Azucena.
   • Circle text describing how Carlé is no longer the person he used to be.

50

51

The president's "tailored safari jacket" and "limp statesman's hand" suggest that he is putting on a show rather than providing substantive relief.

---

12.   **REREAD AND CITE TEXT EVIDENCE**

L ASK STUDENTS to describe what the president does when he meets Azucena for the first time. *He "waved to her with a limp statesman's hand" (lines 282–283).* What has Rolf been doing in the meantime? *Rolf "interrupted to ask for a pump" as he is "kneeling beside the mud pit" (lines 284–287).*

13.   **READ AND CITE TEXT EVIDENCE**   Point out that although Rolf is no longer the man he used to be, the narrator is hopeful about their future together.

M ASK STUDENTS to cite evidence showing that the narrator will not abandon Rolf. *She accompanies him to the station and they watch videos of Azucena together; she says she will wait for him to "complete the voyage" into himself and then they will "walk hand in hand, as before" (lines 318–326).*

FOR ELL STUDENTS Explain that *well* is often used as an adverb, but it can also be a noun that means "a deep hole from which water can be removed." In line 303, point out the adjective *that* before *well*. Explain that an adjective is usually followed by a noun, so in this context the meaning of *well* is "a place with water."

320   you study them intently, looking for something you could have done to save
her, something you did not think of in time. Or maybe you study them to
see yourself as if in a mirror, naked. Your cameras lie forgotten in a closet;
you do not write or sing; you sit long hours before the window, staring at
the mountains. Beside you, I wait for you to complete the voyage into
yourself, for the old wounds to heal. I know that when you return from your
nightmares, we shall again walk hand in hand, as before.

14.   **◄ REREAD AND DISCUSS**   Reread lines 318–326. With a small group,
discuss the author's switch to second person point of view in these lines.
Why does she do this, and what effect does it have on you as a reader?

SHORT RESPONSE

Cite Text Evidence   What is a theme of the story? Review your reading
notes and **cite text evidence** to support your answer.

> This selection has several themes. One of the themes is "The
> technology of modern life both brings us together and keeps us
> apart." We are told a story of immense human suffering through the
> eyes of a narrator who views it on television. The media industry is
> portrayed as distancing and isolating but also allowing us to
> participate vicariously in human experience. Through the media we
> can observe a lot, but always at a distance. Another theme is
> "Human connection has the potential for healing lives." The theme is
> supported by the change that occurs within Carlé, who through his
> profound connection with Azucena begins to heal his own long-
> buried wounds.

52

TO CHALLENGE STUDENTS . . .

To give students a real-life context for Allende's story, tell them
that it is based on an actual event: the 1985 eruption of the
Nevado del Ruiz volcano in Colombia, South America, which
caused an estimated 23,000 deaths and destroyed some villages.
The character of Azucena was based on a 13-year-old girl named
Omayra Sánchez. Like the fictional Azucena, Omayra was trapped
beneath the debris of her home for three days while the world
watched. Her death from exposure highlighted the failure of
officials to respond to the disaster by providing much-needed
supplies and equipment.

ASK STUDENTS   to research the real story of Omayra Sánchez.
Have groups collect newspaper and magazine articles about
her death and the public outcry that followed. Each group can
research a different aspect of the story or report on it from a
different point of view.

Students might examine how the government received warnings
from multiple organizations when volcanic activity was first
detected earlier that year; and yet, preparedness measures were
not in place when the eruption took place. Students can compare
Nevado del Ruiz to other well-known volcanoes, for instance, the
eruption of Mount St. Helens in Washington state in 1980 (and
more recently, in 2005).

After students have completed their research, they can do a
point-by-point analysis comparing the fictional and historical
versions of the catastrophe in Colombia. Have them discuss why
Allende might have wanted to change certain details of the story.

---

14.   REREAD AND DISCUSS USING TEXT EVIDENCE   Point out
that for most of the story, the narrator is speaking in the first
person, but in the last paragraph she switches point of view.

N   **ASK STUDENTS**   to analyze the last paragraph. Who is the
"you" the narrator refers to? *The "you" is Rolf.* How does this
change in point of view affect the story? *The narrator is talking
directly to Rolf, almost as if the readers are out of the picture.*

SHORT RESPONSE

Cite Text Evidence   Students' responses should include text
evidence that supports their positions. They should:

- make inferences about the story's theme.
- analyze characters based on their interactions.
- interpret symbols that convey the story's theme.

DIG DEEPER

With the class, return to Question 3, Read. Have students share their responses.

ASK STUDENTS to think about the theme of "fictive distance" in this story.

- Students can provide text evidence showing how technology (i.e., the camera lens, the TV screen) separates people from each other and limits their capacity for empathy.

- Students can explore how the theme of "distance" runs through the story. How is this theme reflected in the relationships between the narrator and Rolf, the narrator and Azucena, and Rolf and Azucena? How does it play out in the actions of the president? How is Rolf's character shaped by his need for distance and his rejection of it?

ASK STUDENTS to return to Question 7, Read. Have students share their responses.

- Have students cite evidence of Rolf's state of mind at the point in the story where he "forgets" about his camera. What do they know about him that might explain his behavior?

- Students may point out Rolf's need to distance himself from his own past. Why might he have needed to create distance?

- Have students think about how well the camera worked for the narrator. How did it serve her interests?

ASK STUDENTS to return to Question 14, Reread and Discuss. Have students discuss their responses.

- Have students cite evidence showing how the author uses character, tone, and point of view to address the theme of "distance."

- Compare the narrator's tone in the last paragraph to the tone of the rest of the story. Which tone is the more distant?

- Have students analyze why the narrator switches from first-person to second-person point of view. What does it say about the narrator's distance from Rolf? What does it say about the author's distance from her subject?

CLOSE READING NOTES

ANCHOR TEXT

Monkey See, Monkey Do, Monkey Connect

Science Writing by Frans de Waal

Why This Text?

Students need to be critical readers of informational texts. This lesson gives students an opportunity to analyze and evaluate a science writer's claims about a topic of high interest.

► **View It!**

Professional Development Podcast:

Teaching Argument

Key Learning Objective: The student will be able to delineate and evaluate an author's claims and determine the technical meanings of words used in the text.

For additional practice:

Close Reader selection
from "Animals in Translation"
Science Writing by Temple Grandin and Catherine Johnson

RI 1 Cite textual evidence.

RI 4 Determine the meaning of words and phrases, including technical meanings; analyze the impact of word choices on tone.

RI 5 Analyze how claims are developed and refined.

RI 8 Delineate and evaluate the argument and claims in a text.

SL 1d Respond to diverse perspectives, summarize points of agreement and disagreement, qualify or justify views and understanding and make new connections.

SL 3 Evaluate a speaker's point of view, reasoning, and use of evidence and rhetoric.

L 2b Use a colon to introduce a list or quotation.

L 4c Consult reference materials.

▲ Text Complexity Rubric

Quantitative Measures	**Monkey See, Monkey Do, Monkey Connect** Lexile: 1160L

Levels of Meaning/Purpose

single level of complex meaning

Structure

organization of main ideas and details complex, but clearly stated and generally sequential

Qualitative Measures

Language Conventionality and Clarity

increased unfamiliar, academic, or domain-specific words

Knowledge Demands

somewhat complex science concepts

Reader/Task Considerations

- Teacher determined
- Vary by individual reader and type of text
- See the Text X-Ray for suggested Reader/Task Considerations.

English Language Support Before teaching, use the Text X-Ray below for an overview of the text's complexity. The Text X-Ray and the supports and scaffolds in the Teacher's Edition will help you guide students of different skill levels.

Meaning Making

Language Development

Effective Expression

Content Knowledge

Foundational Skills

Text Complexity: Qualitative Measures

Levels of Meaning/Purpose

single level of complex meaning

Help students determine technical meanings.

- Teacher's Edition side notes, pp. 123, 124, 125, 126, 127, 128, 129
- English Language Support, p. 124
- Close Read Screencasts, p. 123
- Determine Technical Meanings, p. 129

ZOOM IN ON DETERMINING TECHNICAL MEANINGS Draw students' attention to the **technical** word *pandiculation* in lines 40–41 and the definition the author provides: "stretching and yawning." Then point out the word *pandiculating* in line 43, asking students to explain the sentence in which it appears in their own terms. Guide students to see that *pandiculating* is the verb form of *pandiculation*. (*Soon the whole audience was stretching and yawning.*)

Have pairs use this approach to define *synchrony* (line 124), *empathize* (line 81), and *metamorphose* (line 75). Ask volunteers to share their definitions and reasoning with the class.

Structure

organization of main ideas and details complex, but clearly stated and generally sequential

Help students analyze and evaluate an author's claims.

- Teacher's Edition side notes, pp. 123, 125, 126, 127, 129
- When Students Struggle, p. 126
- Strategies for Annotation, p. 129
- Analyze and Evaluate Author's Claims, p. 129

To reteach analyzing and evaluating author's claims, see

- Analyze and Evaluate Author's Claims, p. 132a

▶ *Use It! Level Up* Tutorial: Citing Textual Evidence

ZOOM IN ON EVALUATING AN AUTHOR'S CLAIMS Clarify that a **claim** is the author's opinion about the topic, and **reasons** are the author's answer to the question *Why do you think so?* Facts, examples, statistics, and quotations from experts may all serve as **evidence** to back up the reasons. As they read, have pairs note reasons and evidence that support the author's claims. As a class, discuss whether the claims are sufficiently supported with reasons and evidence.

Language Conventionality and Clarity

increased unfamiliar, academic, or domain-specific words

Teach unfamiliar vocabulary in context.
- Teacher's Edition Critical Vocabulary notes, pp. 124, 126, 131
- Applying Academic Vocabulary, p. 125

Help students analyze the language used in the text.
- Teacher's Edition side notes, pp. 124, 125

Support students in understanding Greek roots.
- Vocabulary Strategy: Words from Greek, p. 131
- Strategies for Annotation, p. 131

Guide students in using colons in their writing.
- Language and Style: Colons, p. 132

***ZOOM IN ON* USING GREEK ROOTS** Explain that a word's **root** is the central part that carries the meaning and that many English words have roots that are from ancient Greek words. Then divide the words below among small groups. Have each group use a dictionary to identify their word's Greek root(s), and also to list other words with the same root. Ask groups to share their findings with the class.

- *epidemics*, line 3 *(epi, "on, above, around, after"*; dem, *"people"*; epicenter, democracy)*
- *television*, line 9 *(tele, "far"*; telegraph, telescope)*
- *cycle*, line 37 *(cycl, "circle, ring"*; bicycle, recycle, cyclical)*
- *automatically*, line 166 *(auto, "self"*; autoimmune, automobile)*

Knowledge Demands

somewhat complex science concepts

Support English Learners by expanding their knowledge of scientific concepts in this article.
- Teacher's Edition Background note, p. 123

***ZOOM IN ON* BUILDING SCIENTIFIC KNOWLEDGE** Explain that the imitative learning described in this article supports a learning theory called Social Cognitive Theory (SCT), which at its simplest is the belief that people learn by observing others. According to this theory, *identification*, meaning "a strong feeling of connection or similarity," plays an important role in the transfer of knowledge, skills, and behavior. Studies on SCT support the belief that some identification likely precedes imitative behavior.

Suggested Reader/Task Considerations

You might consider the following before assigning this article to students.
- Will the number of technical terms cause students to feel overwhelmed by the text?
- Are students able to make the inferences needed to follow the author's argument?

***ZOOM IN ON* SUPPORTING COMPREHENSION**

- Encourage students to jot down any unfamiliar terms or jargon they come across, such as *laughter contagion, yawn contagion, mood contagion*, and *herd instinct*. Then, as a class, develop definitions for these terms.
- If students are confused by the evidence presented in lines 84–102, have small groups read the passage and discuss these questions: *How does the "ghost box" work? Why can't the chimps watch how it works and learn to repeat the procedure so they can get rewards at any time?* Invite groups to share their responses.

Background Have students read the background note. Explain that chimpanzees share more genetic traits with humans than other primates do. In fact, they share about 98 percent of the same DNA. Researchers have been studying primate behavior for nearly a century; this research has taught us much about human beings as well. The Yerkes National Primate Research Center is one of eight similar institutions in the United States that are funded by the National Institutes of Health.

AS YOU READ Direct students to use the As You Read suggestion to focus their reading.

Determine Technical Meanings (LINES 1–4)

RI 1, RI 4

Remind students that they can use **context clues**—words that are used in a sentence or surrounding sentences in a way that suggest the meaning of another word—to determine the meanings of unknown words, including technical terms.

 CITE TEXT EVIDENCE How does context help you understand the meaning of the word *epidemics* in line 3? Cite specific words and phrases from the text. *(The words "how it spreads" [line 1] and "no one could stop" [lines 3–4] show that an epidemic is a condition that spreads without stopping.)*

Analyze and Evaluate Author's Claims (LINES 1–11)

RI 1, RI 5, RI 8

Explain that, in some informational texts, the writer presents one or more **claims,** or positions, on a specific issue and supports them with **reasons** and **evidence.** Clarify the difference between reasons and evidence. *(Reasons justify claims; evidence supports reasons with facts and examples.)*

B **CITE TEXT EVIDENCE** What claim does the author make in the first paragraph, and what reasons and evidence does he use to support his claim? Cite examples from the text. *(Claim: "It's almost impossible not to laugh when everybody else is" [lines 1–2]. Reason: "we love to laugh and can't resist joining" [lines 7–8]. Evidence: "comedy shows on television have laugh tracks …theater audiences are sometimes sprinkled with 'laugh plants'" [lines 9–10].)*

Frans B.M. de Waal (b. 1948) *was born in the Netherlands. Trained in biology , de Waal analyzes the behaviors and social interactions of primates, an order of mammals that includes monkeys, chimpanzees, gorillas, lemurs, and homo sapiens, or humans. He is the director of The Living Links Center at the Yerkes National Primate Research Center in Lawrenceville, Georgia, and the author of numerous books including* Chimpanzee Politics.

Monkey See, Monkey Do, Monkey Connect

Science Writing by Frans de Waal

AS YOU READ Trace and consider the examples de Waal provides about human and primate behavior. Write down any questions.

B What intrigues me most about laughter is how it spreads. It's almost impossible not to laugh when everybody else is. There have been laughing epidemics, in which no one could stop and some even died in a prolonged fit. There are laughing churches and laugh therapies based on the healing power of laughter. The must-have toy of 1996—Tickle Me Elmo—laughed hysterically after being squeezed three times in a row. All of this because we love to laugh and can't resist joining laughing around us. This is why comedy shows on television have laugh tracks and why theater
10 audiences are sometimes sprinkled with "laugh plants": people paid to produce raucous laughing at any joke that comes along.

The infectiousness of laughter even works across species. Below my office window at the Yerkes Primate Center, I often hear my chimps laugh during rough-and-tumble games, and I cannot suppress a chuckle myself. It's such a happy sound. Tickling and wrestling are the typical laugh triggers for apes, and probably the original ones for humans. The fact that tickling oneself is notoriously ineffective attests to its social significance. And when **A**

Image Credits: (c) ©Toni Angermayer/Photo Researchers/Getty Images; (tr) ©Kuni Takahashi/McClatchy-Tribune/Getty Images

---

Close Read Screencasts   ▶ **View It!**

Modeled Discussions

Have students click the *Close Read* icons in their eBooks to access a screencast in which readers discuss and annotate the following key passage:

- the discussion of the herd instinct (lines 63–72)

As a class, view and discuss this video. Then have students pair up to do an independent close read of an additional passage—the way our bodies and minds connect us in society (lines 172–180).

TEACH

CLOSE READ

Determine Meaning

RI 4

(LINES 21–26)

Explain that an **allusion** is an indirect reference to a well-known person, place, event, or literary work.

C **ASK STUDENTS** how the allusion to Crusoe develops the author's idea that "we're all interconnected" (line 23). *(Readers are expected to know the story of Crusoe surviving on an island, which de Waal compares to the Western idea of individuality. He uses the image of Crusoe as a vivid contrast to his claim that we are, in fact, intimately connected.)*

Determine Technical Meanings (LINES 47–51)

RI 1, RI 4

Tell students they can find the meanings of unknown words by looking at other forms of the word.

D **CITE TEXT EVIDENCE** Review the definition of *synchronization* in line 30. Then read aloud lines 47–51. Ask students to think about the definition of *synchronization* and context clues to understand what *synchrony* means. *("a state where things meet, happen, or exist at the same time"; the context clue is "copying")*

CRITICAL VOCABULARY

empathy: Human beings have the ability to imagine themselves in someone else's situation.
ASK STUDENTS how "running when others run" relates to empathy. *(Moving our bodies in the same way others do is the first stage of empathy, or being able to imagine how they feel.)*

synchronization: Humans and other primates tend to match the actions of other individuals.
ASK STUDENTS how synchronization explains some human and primate behavior. *(We laugh or yawn when others do so.)*

contagion: De Waal describes how yawning can spread from one individual to another.
ASK STUDENTS how de Waal's story about the lecture on yawning illustrates the idea of contagion. *(Just looking at pictures of animals yawning caused people in the room to start yawning.)*

---

young apes put on their play face, their friends join in with the
20 same expression as rapidly and easily as humans do with laughter.

Shared laughter is just one example of our primate sensitivity to others. Instead of being Robinson Crusoes sitting on separate islands,[1] we're all interconnected, both bodily and emotionally. This may be an odd thing to say in the West, with its tradition of individual freedom and liberty, but *Homo sapiens*[2] is remarkably easily swayed in one emotional direction or another by its fellows.

This is precisely where **empathy** and sympathy start—not in the higher regions of imagination, or the ability to consciously reconstruct how we would feel if we were in someone else's
30 situation. It began much more simply, with the **synchronization** of bodies: running when others run, laughing when others laugh, crying when others cry, or yawning when others yawn. Most of us have reached the incredibly advanced stage at which we yawn even at the mere mention of yawning—as you may be doing right now!— but this is only after lots of face-to-face experience.

Yawn **contagion**, too, works across species. Virtually all animals show the peculiar "paroxystic respiratory cycle characterized by a standard cascade of movements over a five- to ten-second period," which is the way the yawn has been defined. I once attended
40 a lecture on involuntary pandiculation (the medical term for stretching and yawning) with slides of horses, lions, and monkeys— and soon the entire audience was pandiculating. Since it so easily triggers a chain reaction, the yawn reflex opens a window onto mood transmission, an essential part of empathy. This makes it all the more intriguing that chimpanzees yawn when they see others do so.

Yawn contagion reflects the power of unconscious synchrony, which is as deeply ingrained in us as in many other animals. Synchrony may be expressed in the copying of small body
50 movements, such as a yawn, but also occurs on a larger scale, involving travel or movement. It is not hard to see its survival value. You're in a flock of birds and one bird suddenly takes off. You have no time to figure out what's going on: You take off at the same instant. Otherwise, you may be lunch.

Or your entire group becomes sleepy and settles down, so you too become sleepy. Mood contagion serves to coordinate activities, which is crucial for any traveling species (as most primates are). If my companions are feeding, I'd better do the same, because once they move off, my chance to forage will be gone. The individual
60 who doesn't stay in tune with what everyone else is doing will lose

empathy
(ĕm´pə-thē) *n.* the ability to understand and identify with another's feelings.

synchronization
(sĭng´krə-nĭ-zā´shən) *n.* coordinated, simultaneous action.

contagion
(kən-tā´jən) *n.* the spreading from one to another.

---

[1] **Robinson Crusoes . . . islands:** Crusoe, the title character of Daniel Defoe's 1719 novel, was stranded alone on a tropical island.

[2] *Homo sapiens* (hō´mō sā´pē-ənz): the species of primates that includes humans.

ENGLISH LANGUAGE SUPPORT

Language: Suffixes Science writing often includes technical vocabulary that can be intimidating to English language learners. Learning the meanings of **suffixes** can help students unpack the meaning of many challenging but ultimately accessible words.

On the board, write the suffixes *-al, -ive, -ous,* and *-tion/-ation.* After each suffix, note its meaning. *(-al: "act or process of"; -ive: "having the nature of"; -ous: "characterized by"; -tion/-ation: "state of being")*

ASK STUDENTS to find words with these suffixes in the selection. *(emotional [line 26]; ineffective [line 18]; various [line 100]; imagination [line 28])* If needed, help students define the base words. Then have students define the words based on their understanding of each base word and suffix.

out like the traveler who doesn't go to the restroom when the bus has stopped.

The herd instinct produces weird phenomena. At one zoo, an entire baboon troop gathered on top of their rock, all staring in exactly the same direction. For an entire week they forgot to eat, mate, and groom. They just kept staring at something in the distance that no one could identify. Local newspapers were carrying pictures of the monkey rock, speculating that perhaps the animals had been frightened by a UFO. But even though this 70 explanation had the unique advantage of combining an account of primate behavior with proof of UFOs, the truth is that no one knew the cause except that the baboons clearly were all of the same mind.

Finding himself in front of the cameras next to his pal President George W. Bush, former British prime minister Tony Blair—known to walk normally at home—would suddenly metamorphose into a distinctly un-English cowboy. He'd swagger with arms hanging loose and chest puffed out. Bush, of course, strutted like this all the time and once explained how, back home in Texas, this is known as "walking." Identification is the hook that draws us in and makes us 80 adopt the situation, emotions, and behavior of those we're close to. They become role models: We empathize with them and emulate[3] them. Thus children often walk like the same-sex parent or mimic their tone of voice when they pick up the phone.

How does one chimp imitate another? Does he identify with the other and absorb its body movements? Or could it be that he doesn't need the other and instead focuses on the problem faced by the other? This can be tested by having a chimpanzee show another how to open a puzzle box with goodies inside. Maybe all that the watching ape needs to understand is how the thing works. He may 90 notice that the door slides to the side or that something needs to be lifted up. The first kind of imitation involves reenactment of observed manipulations; the second merely requires technical know-how.

Thanks to ingenious studies in which chimps were presented with a so-called ghost box, we know which of these two explanations is correct. A ghost box derives its name from the fact that it magically opens and closes by itself so that no actor is needed. If technical know-how were all that mattered, such a box should suffice. But in fact, letting chimps watch a ghost 100 box until they're bored to death—with its various parts moving and producing rewards hundreds of times—doesn't teach them anything.

---

[3] **emulate:** to imitate or behave like.

APPLYING ACADEMIC VOCABULARY

trace	capacity	emerge

As you discuss de Waal's article, incorporate the Collection 3 academic vocabulary words: *trace, capacity,* and *emerge.* Ask students to describe the **capacity** for empathy that the author claims is shared by humans and other primates. What surprising results have **emerged** from primate research? How do scientists use experiments and observation to **trace** the origins of primate and human behavior?

CLOSE READ

Determine Technical Meanings (LINES 63–72)   RI 1, RI 4

Explain that the context for some terms may be several sentences or a lengthy paragraph that describes an example.

E CITE TEXT EVIDENCE The term *herd instinct* is first used in line 63. Ask: How does the context of the paragraph provide clues to the meaning of this term? *(The rest of the paragraph describes a troop of baboons on top of a rock, staring in the same direction for a week. For whatever reason, the "herd," or group, had the "instinct," or impulse, to do the same thing. The last line states that they "clearly were all of the same mind" [line 72].)*

Analyze Impact of Word Choice on Tone (LINES 73–79)   RI 4

Tell students that an author chooses words to create a specific **tone**—to convey his or her attitude toward the subject.

F ASK STUDENTS to read the description of Tony Blair and George W. Bush in lines 73–79. What impact does the use of the words *swagger* and *strutted* have on the tone of the paragraph? *(The tone is humorous, as it creates a picture of exaggerated movement. The author is having a bit of fun in his description of these otherwise very serious men.)*

Analyze and Evaluate Author's Claims (LINES 84–104)   RI 5, RI 8

Explain that a claim may follow from the presentation of evidence.

G ASK STUDENTS to reread lines 84–102 about the "ghost box" and to explain the experiment's conclusion. Based on this evidence, what claim does the author make? *(that apes do need to imitate their fellows in order to learn [lines 103–104])* Has the author provided relevant evidence to support his claim? *(Yes, the description of the experiment with the ghost box is specific and directly related to the claim.)*

TEACH

CLOSE READ

Analyze and Evaluate Author's Claims (LINES 110–123)

RI 1, RI 5, RI 8

Tell students that speakers and writers often include multiple examples to strengthen a claim.

H **CITE TEXT EVIDENCE** Have students identify three examples in the text that show ways in which "bodies insert themselves into everything we perceive or think" (lines 110–111). *(A hill seems very steep to a tired person; a target seems farther away to a person with a heavy backpack; a pianist can identify his own performance by bodily sensation [lines 112–121].)*

Determine Technical Meanings (LINES 126–132)

RI 1, RI 4

Remind students to look for clues in the text that show what a technical term means.

I **CITE TEXT EVIDENCE** Point out the term *body mapping* in line 129. Ask: What context clues suggest the meaning of this term? *("their movements and emotions echo within us" [line 127]; "re-create what we have seen others do" [lines 128–129]; "They can't help but act the way they feel their baby ought to" [line 132])* What does *body mapping* mean? *("using one's body to copy what another person is doing or to show what one wants another person to do")*

CRITICAL VOCABULARY

cognition: De Waal believes the process of learning involves the body as much as the mind.

ASK STUDENTS to explain how "embodied" cognition explains some human and primate behavior. *(We can learn from and connect with others through involuntary imitation.)*

implication: Studying how we learn through our bodies has had an effect on how we view human relationships.

ASK STUDENTS to explain what implications the study of "embodied" cognition might have. *(We will see how important social interactions are to the process of learning.)*

To learn from others, apes need to see actual fellow apes: Imitation requires identification with a body of flesh and blood. We're beginning to realize how much human and animal cognition runs via the body. Instead of our brain being like a little computer that orders the body around, the body-brain relation is a two-way street. The body produces internal sensations and communicates with other bodies, out of which we construct social connections and 110 an appreciation of the surrounding reality. Bodies insert themselves into everything we perceive or think. Did you know, for example, that physical condition colors perception? The same hill is assessed as steeper, just from looking at it, by a tired person than by a well-rested one. An outdoor target is judged as farther away than it really is by a person burdened with a heavy backpack than by one without it.

Or ask a pianist to pick out his own performance from among others he's listening to. Even if this is a new piece that the pianist has performed only once, in silence (on an electronic piano and without headphones on), he will be able to recognize his own play. 120 While listening, he probably re-creates in his head the sort of bodily sensations that accompany an actual performance. He feels the closest match listening to himself, thus recognizing himself through his body as much as through his ears.

The field of "embodied" **cognition** is still very much in its infancy but has profound **implications** for how we look at human relations. We involuntarily enter the bodies of those around us so that their movements and emotions echo within us as if they're our own. This is what allows us, or other primates, to re-create what we have seen others do. Body mapping is mostly hidden and 130 unconscious, but sometimes it "slips out," such as when parents make chewing mouth movements while spoon-feeding their baby. They can't help but act the way they feel their baby ought to. Similarly, parents watching a singing performance of their child often get completely into it, mouthing every word. I myself still remember as a boy standing on the sidelines of soccer games and involuntarily making kicking or jumping moves each time someone I was cheering for got the ball.

The same can be seen in animals, as illustrated in an old black-and-white photograph from Wolfgang Köhler's classic tool-use 140 studies on chimpanzees. One ape, Grande, stands on boxes that she has stacked up to reach bananas hung from the ceiling, while Sultan watches intently. Even though Sultan sits at a distance, he raises his arm in precise synchrony with Grande's grasping movement. Another example comes from a chimpanzee filmed while using a heavy rock as a hammer to crack nuts. The actor is being observed by a younger ape, who swings his own (empty) hand

cognition
(kŏg-nĭsh´ən) *n.* the process or pattern of gaining knowledge.

implication
(ĭm´plĭ-kā´shən) *n.* consequence or effect.

TO CHALLENGE STUDENTS . . .

Hold a Discussion Ask students to think about when they may have experienced empathy, synchrony, and mimicry in relationships with family members or friends. Have them reread lines 133–137. Ask: Have you ever watched a sports event during which you have imitated the actions of a certain player? Have you ever lip-synched (matched lip movements with) favorite songs or speeches? Have students discuss the following question, encouraging them to includes examples from the selection in their answer:

- How do members of social groups benefit by mimicking each other?

Then ask students for personal examples of synchrony or mimicry they feel comfortable sharing to further support their answer to the previous question.

down in sync every time the first one strikes the nut. Body mapping provides a great shortcut to imitation.

150 When I see synchrony and mimicry—whether it concerns yawning, laughing, dancing, or aping—I see social connection and bonding. I see an old herd instinct that has been taken up a notch. It goes beyond the tendency of a mass of individuals galloping in the same direction, crossing the river at the same time. The new level requires that one pay better attention to what others do and absorb how they do it. For example, I knew an old monkey matriarch with a curious drinking style. Instead of the typical slurping with her lips from the surface, she'd dip her entire underarm in the water, then lick the hair on her arm. Her children started doing the same, and then her grandchildren. The entire

160 family was easy to recognize.

There is also the case of a male chimpanzee who had injured his fingers in a fight and hobbled around leaning on a bent wrist instead of his knuckles. Soon all of the young chimpanzees in the colony were walking the same way in single file behind the unlucky male. Like chameleons changing their color to match the environment, primates automatically copy their surroundings.

Monkey See, Monkey Do, Monkey Connect **127**

CLOSE READ

Determine Technical Meanings (LINES 147–152)   RI 4

Tell students that authors often use **synonyms,** or words with similar meanings, to make their writing less repetitive and to express subtle shades of meaning.

J **CITE TEXT EVIDENCE** Have students locate the word *mimicry* in line 149 and identify several terms in the surrounding text that have similar meanings. *(body mapping [line 147], imitation [line 148], synchrony [line 149], herd instinct [line 151].)* Discuss which synonym is closest in meaning to *mimicry.* *(Imitation is the closest synonym; both mean to copy the behavior of another. Body mapping refers more specifically to mimicking physical movements. Synchrony may refer to actions that are mirrored unconsciously. Herd instinct refers to a general tendency to act in accordance with others, rather than to a specific act of mimicry.)*

Analyze and Evaluate Author's Claims (LINES 154–166)   RI 5, RI 8

Toward the end of an essay, an author may support previous claims with more reasons and evidence.

K **ASK STUDENTS** to reread de Waal's statement in lines 154–155: "The new level requires that one pay better attention to what others do and absorb how they do it." What implications do this statement and the subsequent examples suggest? *(Imitation results in social bonding, which is important. Imitation is essential to the survival of the group.)*

WHEN STUDENTS STRUGGLE . . .

To help students understand the difference between reasons and evidence, provide an outline similar to the one given below. Explain that reasons usually answer the question "why;" evidence should answer the question "how."

Claim: It is valuable to study primate behavior.

Reason: It is valuable because we can learn a lot about human behavior, too.

Evidence: Both humans and primates re-create the movements they see others do. In the examples given, parents watching their child sing will mouth the words of a song in accompaniment; one ape observes another's actions, then imitates them.

LEVEL UP TUTORIALS For additional support, assign the following *Level Up* tutorials: **Evidence.**

Determine Technical Meanings (LINES 177–180)

RI 4

Tell students that one way to understand technical vocabulary is to visualize the context.

L ASK STUDENTS to locate the word *nodes* in line 178. Read aloud the sentence in which it appears. Ask students to visualize what the sentence is describing. What does the context suggest that the word means? *(Students might use the words* tight network *and* connects *to visualize a web with many connecting points, or nodes.)*

COLLABORATIVE DISCUSSION Have partners work to create a statement of de Waal's overall claim. *(Like primates, humans are connected through empathy, synchrony, and unconscious imitation. Our actions are influenced by what we see others do.)* Then have them discuss specific reasons and evidence that de Waal uses to support his claim. Have them find at least two examples each of valid reasons and relevant evidence.

ASK STUDENTS to share any questions they generated in the course of reading and discussing the selection.

When I was a boy, my friends in the south of the Netherlands always ridiculed me when I came home from vacations in the north, where I played with boys from Amsterdam. They told me
170 that I talked funny. Unconsciously, I'd return speaking a poor imitation of the harsh northern accent.

The way our bodies—including voice, mood, posture, and so on—are influenced by surrounding bodies is one of the mysteries of human existence, but one that provides the glue that holds entire societies together. It's also one of the most underestimated phenomena, especially in disciplines that view humans as rational decisionmakers. Instead of each individual independently weighing the pros and cons of his or her own actions, we occupy nodes within a tight network that connects all of us in both body and
180 mind.

COLLABORATIVE DISCUSSION What is de Waals's claim about how humans are connected? With a partner, discuss the examples he provides in support of his ideas.

Analyze and Evaluate Author's Claims

RI 5, RI 8

A **claim** is the author's position on a topic or issue. The science article "Monkey See, Monkey Do, Monkey Connect" is an informational text that states a specific claim about the behavior of human beings. Although Frans de Waal is an expert on the topic, it is not enough for him to simply state his claim and expect readers to accept what he is saying. He must **support** his claim throughout the essay with **reasons,** or declarations made to justify an action, decision, or belief, and **evidence** such as facts, details, and examples.

To evaluate de Waal's support for his claim, it is important to delineate, or outline, the reasons and evidence he provides. This will help you evaluate whether he has presented valid reasons and enough support for his claim.

Determine Technical Meanings

RI 4

"Monkey See, Monkey Do, Monkey Connect" contains **technical vocabulary** that may be unfamiliar to you. When you encounter an unfamiliar word, you can use context clues to determine its meaning. The context of a word is made up of the punctuation marks, words, sentences, and paragraphs that surround the word. The chart below shows how a reader might use context clues to define the technical terms *empathy* and *synchronization*.

Technical Words	Context	Meaning of Words
empathy synchronization	"This is precisely where **empathy** and sympathy start—not in the higher regions of imagination, or the ability to consciously reconstruct how we would feel if we were in someone else's situation. It began much more simply, with the **synchronization** of bodies: running when others run, laughing when others laugh, crying when others cry, or yawning when others yawn."	• The word *sympathy* and the phrase "how we would feel if we were in someone else's situation" explains the meaning of *empathy*. • The image of bodies "running when others run, laughing when others laugh, crying when others cry, or yawning when others yawn" helps readers visualize *synchronization*.

CLOSE READ

Analyze and Evaluate Author's Claims

RI 5, RI 8

Review the terms *claim, reasons,* and *evidence* and make sure students can differentiate amongst them. Share this diagram to show the hierarchy of ideas in an argument:

Determine Technical Meanings

RI 4

Tell students that technical vocabulary is used in many fields of study, including medicine, engineering, agriculture, and finance, to name a few. Students might encounter this vocabulary as they read periodicals, websites, blogs, and other sources to find information about various topics.

Discuss with students the value of using context clues to understand the meaning of technical vocabulary. Remind students that context clues can appear immediately before or after the unfamiliar word, a few sentences away, or in a different paragraph.

Strategies for Annotation 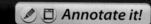 Annotate it!

Analyze and Evaluate Author's Claims

RI 5, RI 8

Share these strategies for guided or independent analysis.

- Highlight in pink a major claim that de Waal makes.
- Highlight in blue the reasons he gives for the claim.
- Use green to highlight evidence that supports each reason.
- On notes, evaluate the quality of the reasons and evidence. Has the author effectively supported the claim?

sensitivity to others. Instead of being Robinson Crusoes sitting on separate islands,[1] we're all interconnected, both bodily and emotionally. This may be an odd thing to say in the West, with its tradition of individual freedom and liberty, but *Homo sapiens*[2] is remarkably easily swayed in one emotional direction or another by its fellows.

PRACTICE & APPLY

Analyzing the Text
RI 1, RI 4, RI 5, RI 8

Possible answers:

1. *The author uses a light, conversational tone throughout the essay. His initial references to laughter establish the tone right away. "It's almost impossible not to laugh when everybody else is" (lines 1–2); "I cannot suppress a chuckle myself" (lines 14–15).*

2. *Humans share "primate sensitivity" that influences a variety of actions (lines 21–26). Support is offered throughout the article in examples from yawning to laughing to speaking and making choices.*

3. *For humans, laughter is contagious. It is easier to laugh when others are also laughing (lines 7–8). Similarly, for apes, play is contagious (lines 15–16). They encourage one another to have fun. This shows that primates are attuned to each other's actions, and it supports the author's claim about human interaction.*

4. *De Waal argues that empathy developed from the way* Homo sapiens *are in tune with each other. In lines 27–83, he gives examples of how people and other primates are keyed to do as others do, such as yawn when others are yawning.*

5. *The "herd instinct" is the tendency to follow what a crowd is doing without really considering why. People look to one another for inspiration and to emulate positive traits. Children follow their parents and look up to them for guidance (lines 81–83). The downside includes following a crowd down a harmful path or making rash decisions based on what others want.*

6. *The box of treats would open and close automatically, without the chimps' needing to learn how to open it (lines 96–98). The chimps actually did not respond to it as well as they responded to being taught by another chimp how to open and close the box. This suggests that interaction is crucial to learning new skills.*

7. *The author believes that interdependence, or the fact that people need one another, is the glue that holds societies together (lines 177–180). Students may cite the anecdote of one world leader imitating the walk of another (lines 73–79) as showing the deep level of connection among individuals and, ultimately, whole societies. Accept all reasonable responses.*

Analyzing the Text
RI 1, RI 4,
RI 5, RI 8,
SL 1d, SL 3, SL 4

Cite Text Evidence   Support your responses with evidence from the selection.

1. **Analyze** An author carefully chooses words and phrases to establish **tone**, or a particular attitude toward his or her subject. For example, some articles use formal language to convey a serious tone while others have a more conversational style. What tone does de Waal establish in the opening paragraphs of his essay? What words and phrases create this tone?

2. **Cite Evidence** What is the primary claim that emerges in this essay? Provide evidence from the text to support your idea.

3. **Interpret** In what ways are the laughing humans described in the first paragraph like the playful chimps de Waal observes? How does this information support his claim?

4. **Identify** In lines 25–26, what does de Waal say developed because ". . . *Homo sapiens* is remarkably easily swayed in one emotional direction or another by its fellows"? Cite evidence from the text in your explanation.

5. **Infer** What is the "herd instinct"? According to de Waal, what is the positive side of people watching and imitating one another? What might be a potential downside to this part of human nature?

6. **Interpret** Explain the significance of the "ghost box." Trace what researchers learned from the ghost box experiment, and how might it relate to the ways in which people learn.

7. **Draw Conclusions** What, according to de Waal, is the "glue that holds entire societies together"? What are the strongest pieces of evidence in the text to support this claim?

PERFORMANCE TASK

Speaking Activity: Argument The author of "Monkey See, Monkey Do, Monkey Connect" presents one view of the ways in which humans relate to one another. Do you agree with his view, or do you believe that people are, or should be, "Robinson Crusoes sitting on separate islands"?

- Form teams of two to three students each, with half arguing the points of the article and half taking the position that humans are, or should be, more "rational decisionmakers."

- Each team should gather evidence to support its position.

- Follow the rules for debating found in the Handbook at the end of this book. Be sure to use appropriate eye contact, adequate volume, and clear pronunciation. Afterward, write a brief evaluation of which side presented a stronger case.

Assign this performance task.

PERFORMANCE TASK
SL 1d, SL 3, SL 4

Speaking Activity: Argument Have students review de Waal's claims about human relations. Teams supporting his claims can gather evidence from the selection. Teams making a contradictory claim should cite evidence from their own knowledge or experience. As students prepare, remind them to present well-supported arguments. Teams should also anticipate the opposing team's claims and compose convincing rebuttals. After the debate, students should cite specific details about each team's presentation to justify their evaluations.

Critical Vocabulary

empathy   chronization   contagion   cognition   implication

Practice and Apply Explain which Critical Vocabulary word listed above is most closely associated with the familiar word shown below.

1. Which vocabulary word is associated with *thinking*?

2. Which vocabulary word is associated with *suggestion*?

3. Which vocabulary word is associated with *sympathy*?

4. Which vocabulary word is associated with *disease*?

5. Which vocabulary word is associated with *coordination*?

Vocabulary Strategy: Words from Greek

A **root** is a word part that contains the core meaning of a word. Many English words contain roots that come from Greek. The Critical Vocabulary word *synchronization* contains the prefix *syn-*, meaning "with or together," combined with the Greek root *chrono*, meaning "time." *Chrono* is the basis of many other words in our everyday vocabulary.

The Greek Root *Chrono*		
chronic	anachronistic	chronometer
chronicle	synchronicity	chronograph

Understanding the meaning of the root *chrono* and using the context clues in the sentences below can help you determine the meaning of the words in the chart.

1. My sister has a *chronic* cough that keeps her awake every night.

2. The book will *chronicle* the history of our town.

3. A computer is *anachronistic* on the set of a play about colonial life.

4. It was *synchronicity* that we bumped into each other without planning to meet.

5. The *chronometer* accurately calculated when it would arrive.

6. We timed ourselves with a *chronograph*.

Practice and Apply The Critical Vocabulary word *empathy* also contains a Greek root, *pathos*. Work with a partner to define the Greek root *pathos*. Then, write about how the meaning of this root,combined with the word's other parts, relates to the meaning of the word *empathy*. Work together to create a chart of other words containing the root *pathos*. Write sentences with the words you identify.

PRACTICE & APPLY

Critical Vocabulary

Answers:

1. *cognition, which means "the process of gaining knowledge"*

2. *implication, because both refer to ideas that follow from other ideas or evidence*

3. *empathy, because to understand another person's feelings is to have empathy*

4. *contagion, because a disease can spread through contagion*

5. *synchronization, which means doing something in a coordinated or organized way*

Vocabulary Strategy: Words from Greek

Possible answers:

The Greek root pathos *refers to feeling or suffering. So, empathy is about understanding someone else's feelings or suffering. Other words containing the root* pathos *include* sympathy, pathological, *and* pathology. *Students should use each of the words they listed correctly in a sentence.*

Strategies for Annotation   ✏ 🖺 **Annotate it!**

Words from Greek

Have students locate the sentences containing *technical* (line 92), *mimicry* (line 149), and *automatically* (line 166). Explain that these words have Greek roots. Share these strategies for guided or independent analysis:

- Highlight the word in yellow. Then look for clues to the word's meaning in the surrounding context. Underline examples, synonyms, or antonyms.
- Identify the word's Greek root and confirm its meaning. On a note, explain how the root tells more about the word's meaning.

instead of his knuckles. Soon all of the young chimpanzees in the colony were walking <u>the same way</u> in single file behind the unlucky male. <u>Like chameleons changing their color</u> to match the environment, primates automatically <u>copy</u> their surroundings.

Language and Style: Colons

L 2b

Review the instruction and examples with students. Then have them locate two additional examples of colons in the selection and identify which usage each one represents.

- *"You have no time to figure out what's going on: You take off at the same instant." (lines 52–54)*
- *"To learn from others, apes need to see actual fellow apes: Imitation requires identification with a body of flesh and blood." (lines 103–104)*

Both are examples of colons used to introduce related independent clauses.

Answers:

Students' paragraphs should demonstrate an understanding of the use of colons for lists and introduce quotations or independent clauses.

 Assess It Online!

Online Selection Test
- Download an editable ExamView bank.
- Assign and manage this test online.

Language and Style: Colons

L 2b

Authors use colons to add clarity to their writing. They also use colons for emphasis in order to draw attention to key ideas. In an essay, colons are commonly used to introduce a list, quotation, or independent clause.

Read this sentence from the essay.

> **This is why comedy shows on television have laugh tracks and why theater audiences are sometimes sprinkled with "laugh plants": people paid to produce raucous laughing at any joke that comes along.**

Notice how de Waal uses the colon to lead into a definition of the term "laugh plants."

In this section of the essay, the colon has a different purpose. It introduces a list.

> **It began much more simply, with the synchronization of bodies: running when others run, laughing when others laugh, crying when others cry, or yawning when others yawn.**

Now read the same sentence without the colon. Consider how the sentence loses clarity without the colon to introduce the list.

> **It began much more simply, with the synchronization of bodies running when others run, laughing when others laugh, crying when others cry, or yawning when others yawn.**

You can also use a colon to introduce a long quotation or a related independent clause.

> **They become role models: We empathize with them and emulate them.**

When an independent clause follows a colon, the clause usually begins with a capital letter.

Practice and Apply Write two paragraphs summarizing key points in the article, "Monkey See, Monkey Do, Monkey Connect." Use colons in at least three places. At least one should introduce a list and one should introduce a quotation or independent clause.

Respond to Diverse Perspectives

SL 1d, SL 3, SL 4

TEACH

To support students as they begin work on the Performance Task, discuss these points:

- Teams supporting de Waal's position on the social nature of learning should review the selection and make notes on the author's key reasons and evidence.

- Teams opposing de Waal's position should conduct research to gather evidence. They might use a search term such as "individual versus social learning" and then review the results for articles written at an appropriate level of complexity.

- Team members should share the results of their research and then work together to develop a clear position statement, or claim.

- Each team should discuss the opposing claims and reasons the other team is likely to present and prepare to respond with strong counterarguments or rebuttals.

- Teams should review the rules for debating and decide who will speak first, who will respond to the other team's argument, and who will summarize the team's claim and strongest reasons at the end of the debate.

 INTERACTIVE LESSON Suggest that students use the *Persuasive Planner* to organize their team's reasons and evidence before the debate.

PRACTICE AND APPLY

Have students conduct their debate. When it is over, help the class evaluate each team's performance by sharing this list of questions:

- Did the team prove that its position on the issue is correct? How thorough was the team's analysis of the issue?
- Were you convinced by the team's argument?
- How effectively did the team present reasons and evidence? Did you understand the reasons? Was the evidence relevant?
- Was the team effective in rebutting arguments made by the other team?
- Did team members behave appropriately by following the rules of the debate and treating everyone with respect?

Analyze and Evaluate Author's Claims

RI 5, RI 8

RETEACH

Review the terms *claim, reasons,* and *evidence.* Then provide the following process and questions students can use to analyze and evaluate an author's claim:

- **Identify the claim.** What position is the author taking on a topic or issue?
- **Find reasons that support the claim.** How does the author justify why he or she has taken this position? Are the reasons valid? That is, are they believable?
- **Find evidence for each reason.** Does the evidence provide enough support for the claim? Are the facts and other details relevant?

Various kinds of evidence include

- **facts:** information that can be proved true
- **statistics:** numbers gathered from research
- **examples:** illustrations of a writer's idea
- **expert opinions:** statements made by authorities on the subject

 LEVEL UP TUTORIALS Assign the following *Level Up* tutorial: **Evidence.**

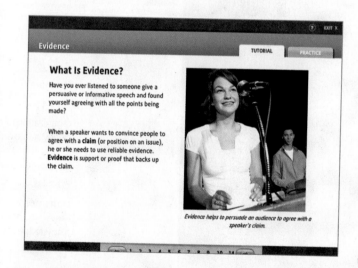

INDEPENDENT READING

Students can apply the skill to another piece of science (or other academic) writing. Suggest that they look for another essay or article on the Yerkes National Primate Research Center website.

from Animals in Translation

Science Writing by Temple Grandin and Catherine Johnson

Why This Text

Students may have difficulty evaluating an argument if they don't understand the author's claims. Arguments such as this one by Temple Grandin and Catherine Johnson may have difficult technical language or complex reasoning that becomes clear only with careful study. With the help of the close-reading questions, students will analyze the development and refinement of the author's claim about the abilities of animals.

Background Have students read the background information about Temple Grandin, an accomplished adult with autism, who is a doctor of animal science, a best-selling author, and a leader in the autism advocacy movement. Introduce the selection by telling students that Grandin believes in the extraordinary ability of animals to perceive the world around them. An expert in animal behavior, one of her recent books—*Animals Make Us Human: Creating the Best Life for Animals*—focuses on the emotional lives of animals.

AS YOU READ Ask students to pay close attention to the reasons Grandin gives to support her claim that animals have "extreme perception." How soon into the selection can students begin to identify her position?

Standards Support

- cite multiple pieces of evidence
- determine the meaning of words and phrases as they are used in a text, including technical meanings
- analyze how an author's ideas and claims are developed and refined
- evaluate the argument and claims in a text, assessing whether the reasoning is valid and the evidence is sufficient

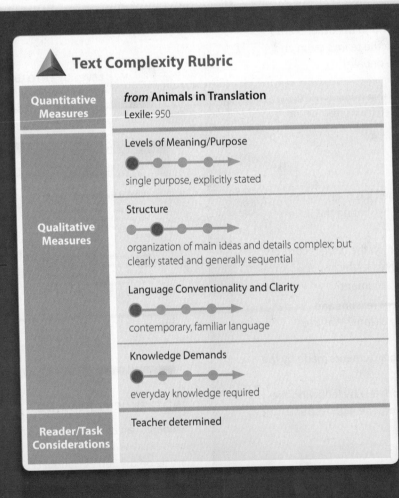

▲ Text Complexity Rubric

Quantitative Measures	*from* Animals in Translation Lexile: 950
Qualitative Measures	**Levels of Meaning/Purpose** single purpose, explicitly stated
	Structure organization of main ideas and details complex; but clearly stated and generally sequential
	Language Conventionality and Clarity contemporary, familiar language
	Knowledge Demands everyday knowledge required
Reader/Task Considerations	Teacher determined

Strategies for CLOSE READING

Analyze an Author's Claims

Students should read this scientific text carefully all the way through. Close-reading questions at the bottom of the page will help them focus on a thorough analysis of the author's claim as well as the counterclaim she cites. As they read, students should record comments or questions about the text in the side margins.

WHEN STUDENTS STRUGGLE . . .

To help students follow the reasons Grandin cites to support her claim, have students work in small groups to fill out a chart, such as the one shown below, as they analyze this scientific text.

CITE TEXT EVIDENCE For practice in analyzing an argument, ask students to cite the evidence that Grandin gives to support her claim.

CLAIM: Animals have astonishing abilities to sense things around them.

SUPPORT:

Reason 1: Compared to humans, animals have "extreme perception."

Reason 2: Animals do not have extrasensory perception (ESP); they have a "supersensitive sensory apparatus."

Reason 3: Jane's cat always knows when Jane is on her way home.

Reason 4: As a "visual thinker," Grandin is able to imagine how Jane's cat uses sound cues to sense Jane's arrival.

Background *One of the world's most accomplished adults with autism,* **Temple Grandin** *is a professor at Colorado State University. She is also the author of several best-selling books, including* Animals In Translation *from which this excerpt is taken. Drawing upon her long career as an animal scientist and her own experiences with autism,* Animals in Translation *provides a unique message about the way animals act, think, and feel.* **Catherine Johnson,** *Grandin's coauthor, specializes in writing about the brain. She is also no stranger to autism—two of her sons are autistic.*

from
Animals in Translation

Science Writing by Temple Grandin and Catherine Johnson

CLOSE READ
Notes

1. **READ ▶** As you read lines 1–8, begin to collect and cite text evidence.

   - Underline the claim Grandin makes about animal perception in the first paragraph, and restate it in the margin.
   - Circle the sentence that explains what most people think about animals.
   - Underline Grandin's claim in the second paragraph.

Extreme Perception: The Mystery of Jane's Cat

Ⓐ Ⓑ Compared to humans, animals have astonishing abilities to perceive things in the world. They have *extreme perception*. Their sensory[1] worlds are so much richer than ours it's almost as if we're deaf and blind. That's probably why a lot of people think animals have ESP.[2] Animals have such incredible abilities to perceive things we can't that the only explanation we can come up with is extrasensory perception. There's even a scientist in England who's written books about animals having ESP. But they don't have ESP, they just have a supersensitive sensory apparatus.

Animals have far greater perception than that of humans.

[1] **sensory:** of or related to any of the five senses.
[2] **ESP:** an abbreviation for extrasensory perception, the act of perceiving or communicating by means other than the five senses.

53

---

1. **READ AND CITE TEXT EVIDENCE** Explain that Grandin opens with a blanket statement in which she claims that "Compared to humans, animals have astonishing abilities to perceive things in the world." This opening serves a dual purpose: it "grabs" the reader's attention and poses the topic this selection will argue.

Ⓐ **ASK STUDENTS** to determine how Grandin begins to address her argument (or claim) by citing specific textual evidence in lines 1–8. *Responses should include references to evidence in lines 1–3 and 8.*

FOR ELL STUDENTS Point out the word *supersensitive* in line 8. Explain that the prefix *super-* means "above" or "beyond," or "to a great degree." Elicit some simple words with this prefix, such as *superhighway* or *supercomputer*, defining each word. Tell students that words with this prefix are often a part of technical vocabulary.

Jane and her husband claim that her cat has ESP because it always knows when Jane comes home, no matter what time.

C
Take the cat who knows when its owner is coming home. My friend
10 Jane, who lives in a city apartment, <u>has a cat who always knows when she's on her way home</u>. Jane's husband works at home, and five minutes before Jane comes home he'll see the cat go to the door, sit down, and wait. Since Jane doesn't come home at the same time every day, the cat isn't going by its sense of time, although animals also have an incredible sense of time. Sigmund Freud[3] used to have his dog with him every time he saw a patient, and he never had to look at his watch to tell when the session was over. The dog always let him know. Parents tell me autistic kids do the same thing. The only explanation Jane and her husband could come up with was ESP. The cat must have been picking up Jane's I'm-coming-home-now thoughts.

20   Jane asked me to figure out how her cat could predict her arrival. Since I've never seen Jane's apartment I used my mother's New York City apartment as a model for solving the mystery. In my imagination I watched my mother's gray Persian cat walk around the apartment and look out the

---

[3] **Sigmund Freud:** Austrian founder of psychoanalysis whose theories significantly influenced modern thought.

2. **◀ REREAD** Reread lines 1–8. In your own words, explain the claim that Grandin makes about animals and ESP. What analogy does she make to get across her point about animals' "abilities to perceive the world"? Support your answer with explicit textual evidence.

Grandin claims that animals have astonishing abilities to sense things around them. She likens the difference in human and animal perceptions to the difference between a deaf and blind person to one with hearing and sight. Rather than having "extra sensory" perception, Grandin claims animals have "super sensory" perception.

3. **READ ▶** As you read lines 9–28, continue to cite textual evidence.
   • Underline text describing the perceptive behavior of Jane's cat.
   • Restate the claim that Jane and her husband make about her cat in the margin (lines 9–19).
   • Circle the claim that Grandin gives to account for the cat's behavior, and restate it in the margin (lines 24–28).

54

> **Jane finally gave me the crucial piece of information that solved the cat mystery . . .**

Grandin thinks that Jane's cat can see her somehow and recognizes her body language.

She uses "videos" in her mind to help her visualize how the cat was getting sound cues.

D
window. Possibly the cat could see Jane walking down the street. Even though he would not be able to see Jane's face from the twelfth floor he would probably be able to recognize her body language. Animals are very sensitive to body language. The cat would probably be able to recognize Jane's walk.

E F
     Next I thought about sound cues. <u>Since I am a visual thinker I used
30 "videos" in my imagination to move the cat around in the apartment to determine how it could be getting sound cues that Jane would be arriving a few minutes later. In my mind's eye I positioned the cat with its ear next to the crack between the door and the door frame.</u> I thought maybe he could hear Jane's voice on the elevator. But as I played a tape of my mother getting onto the elevator in the lobby, I realized that there would be many days when Mother would ride the elevator alone and silent. She would speak on the elevator for only some of the trips—when there were other people in the elevator car with her—but not all of them.

     So I asked Jane, "Is the cat always at the door, or is he at the door only
40 sometimes?"

     She said the cat is always at the door.

     That meant the cat had to be hearing Jane's voice on the elevator every day. After I questioned her some more, Jane finally gave me the crucial piece of information that solved the cat mystery: her building does not have a push-button elevator. The elevator is operated by a person. So when Jane got on the elevator she probably said "Hi" to the operator.

4. **◀ REREAD AND DISCUSS** With a small group, discuss whether you believe Grandin's explanation for the cat's behavior in lines 24–28. Why or why not?

5. **READ ▶** As you read lines 29–58, underline places in the text where Grandin refers to her experiences with autism.

55

---

2. **REREAD AND CITE TEXT EVIDENCE** Grandin counters the claim that assumes that animals possess extrasensory perception (ESP) by proposing that they have "a supersensitive sensory apparatus" instead.

   B **ASK STUDENTS** why many people think animals have ESP. _Students should cite specific textual evidence from lines 1–8._

3. **READ AND CITE TEXT EVIDENCE**

   C **ASK STUDENTS** to read their margin notes to a partner and then write one response that best restates the opposing viewpoint stated by Jane and her husband about Jane's cat. _Students should cite specific evidence from the text in lines 18–19._

4. **REREAD AND DISCUSS USING TEXT EVIDENCE**

   D **ASK STUDENTS** to appoint a reporter for each group to cite specific textual evidence to support whether or not they agree with Grandin's explanation for Jane's cat's behavior. _Students should cite textual evidence from lines 24–28._

5. **READ AND CITE TEXT EVIDENCE** Because Grandin is a "visual thinker," she is able to visualize how Jane's cat is acquiring sound cues to sense Jane's arrival.

   E **ASK STUDENTS** to explain how Grandin uses her experience with autism to create "videos" in her mind to move the cat around Jane's apartment and to play a "tape" of her mother getting into her own elevator. _Grandin was able to visualize the cat in various locations and what it could hear there (lines 30–32). She imagined her mother in a similar situation riding an elevator (lines 34–36 and 48–51)._

CLOSE READ
Notes

She visualizes an elevator operator, and imagines Jane greeting him out loud.

A new image flashed into my head. I created an elevator with an operator for my mother's building. To make the image I used the same method people use in computer graphics. I pulled an image of my mother's
50　elevator out of memory and combined it with an image of the elevator operator I saw one time at the Ritz in Boston. He had white gloves and a black tuxedo. I lifted the brass elevator control panel and its tuxedoed operator from my Ritz memory file and placed them inside my mother's elevator.

That was the answer. The fact that Jane's building had an elevator operator provided the cat with the sound of Jane's voice while Jane was still down on the first floor. That's why the cat went to the door to wait. The cat wasn't predicting Jane's arrival; for the cat Jane was already home.

6. **◀ REREAD** As you reread lines 29–54, note in the margin how Grandin's experiences with autism led her to solve the mystery of Jane's cat.

SHORT RESPONSE

Cite Text Evidence Did Grandin's story about Jane's cat convince you that animals have an amazing ability to perceive their world. Why or why not? Explain, **citing evidence from the text** in your response.

Possible response: It seems clear that animals have an incredible ability to perceive things that humans cannot, displaying a supersensitivity that some people, even scientists, have thought was ESP. Grandin's claim that animals do not have ESP—just a "supersensitive sensory apparatus"—is convincing and is supported by the evidence she offers concerning the behavior of Jane's cat. Although the cat's owners believe it has ESP, Grandin relies on scientific evidence and her own experiences to convince her readers that there is a reason behind animal perceptions, not just a magical sense.

56

6. REREAD AND CITE TEXT EVIDENCE

F **ASK STUDENTS** to discuss the last clue that leads Grandin to solve the mystery of Jane's cat. *Students should recognize that Grandin realizes there is an elevator operator when she uses visual images from her memory. Students should cite evidence from lines 32–36 and 48–51.*

SHORT RESPONSE

Cite Text Evidence Students should:

- explain whether or not Grandin convinced them of her argument.
- give reasons for their point of view.
- cite specific evidence from the text to support their reasons.

TO CHALLENGE STUDENTS . . .

For more context on the behavior of animals and our understanding of it, students can find out more about Temple Grandin's work.

ASK STUDENTS to read other excerpts from *Animals in Translation* or to research Temple Grandin in articles in print or online. Have students report their findings to the class.

- Aside from writing books, what does Grandin do? *She is Professor of Animal Science at Colorado State University. She is an advocate for people with autism, and for animal welfare. She is one of the world's few designers of equipment for handling livestock, and is a consultant to many large livestock companies.*

- What influence has Grandin had on people's understanding of animal behavior? *She has shown that animals experience emotions and pain. Her work improving slaughterhouse systems has resulted in a more humane ending to animals' lives, so much so that she has even received an award from PETA. She is revered by animal rights groups.*

DIG DEEPER

With the class, return to Question 4, Reread and Discuss. Have students share the results of their discussion.

ASK STUDENTS whether they were satisfied with the outcome of their small-group discussions. Have each group share whether or not they agreed with Grandin's explanation for Jane's cat's behavior. What compelling evidence did the groups cite from the selection to support their opinion?

- Encourage students to tell whether there was any convincing text evidence cited by group members holding a minority opinion. If so, why didn't it sway the group?

- Have groups explain how they decided whether or not Grandin's evidence was sufficient to support her findings. Did everyone in the group agree as to what made the evidence sufficient? How did the group resolve any conflicts or disagreements?

- After students have shared the results of their group's discussion, ask whether another group shared any findings they wished they had brought to the table.

ASK STUDENTS to return to their Short Response answer and revise it based on the class discussion.

The Grasshopper and the Bell Cricket

Short Story by Yasunari Kawabata

Why This Text?

Students encounter literary works that reflect the values of other cultures. This lesson explores the ways in which the author's culture can have an influence on the elements of a story.

Key Learning Objective: The student will be able to analyze an author's point of view and cultural background and also analyze the impact of word choice on tone.

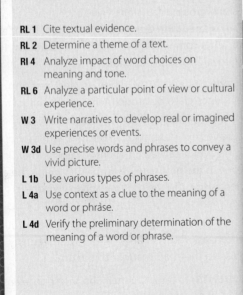

RL 1   Cite textual evidence.

RL 2   Determine a theme of a text.

RI 4   Analyze impact of word choices on meaning and tone.

RL 6   Analyze a particular point of view or cultural experience.

W 3   Write narratives to develop real or imagined experiences or events.

W 3d   Use precise words and phrases to convey a vivid picture.

L 1b   Use various types of phrases.

L 4a   Use context as a clue to the meaning of a word or phrase.

L 4d   Verify the preliminary determination of the meaning of a word or phrase.

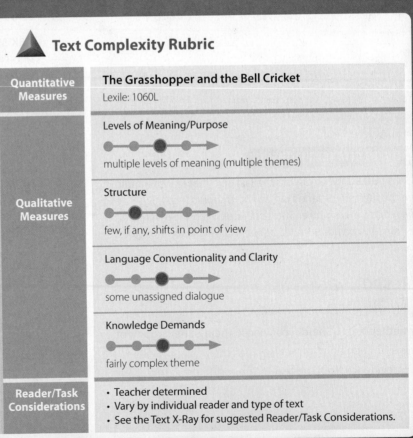

▲ Text Complexity Rubric

Quantitative Measures	**The Grasshopper and the Bell Cricket** Lexile: 1060L
Qualitative Measures	**Levels of Meaning/Purpose** multiple levels of meaning (multiple themes)
	Structure few, if any, shifts in point of view
	Language Conventionality and Clarity some unassigned dialogue
	Knowledge Demands fairly complex theme
Reader/Task Considerations	• Teacher determined • Vary by individual reader and type of text • See the Text X-Ray for suggested Reader/Task Considerations.

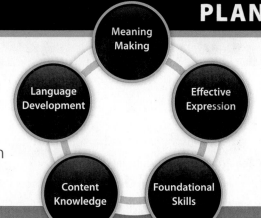

Meaning Making

Language Development

Effective Expression

Content Knowledge

Foundational Skills

TEXT X-RAY

English Language Support Before teaching, use the Text X-Ray below for an overview of the text's complexity. The Text X-Ray and the supports and scaffolds in the Teacher's Edition will help you guide students of different skill levels.

Text Complexity: Qualitative Measures

Levels of Meaning/Purpose

multiple levels of meaning (multiple themes)

Help students recognize the impact of cultural background on an author's point of view.
- Teacher's Edition side notes, pp. 133, 135, 137
- Analyze Point of View: Cultural Background, p. 137

Guide students to support inferences.
- Teacher's Edition side note, p. 135
- When Students Struggle, p. 135

Support students in interpreting a symbol.
- Teacher's Edition side note, p. 136

▶ *Use It!* **Interactive Whiteboard Lesson:** Historical and Cultural Context

ZOOM IN ON **ANALYZING AN AUTHOR'S POINT OF VIEW** Review the information about **point of view** and Japanese culture on page 137. Then have students form pairs. Assign each pair one of the following ideas to look for as they read the story:

- respecting the natural world
- living in harmony with nature
- seeing crickets as a sign of good luck

Have pairs highlight examples in the text. Then have students share their findings in a class discussion. *(Possible responses: respect—handling the cricket carefully in lines 75–79; harmony—following the insect's voice in lines 1–7, inferring a lesson about human life in lines 119–122; crickets as good luck—the children's excitement in lines 80–88)*

Structure

few, if any, shifts in point of view

Help students analyze the impact of word choice and sentence structure on tone.
- Teacher's Edition side notes, pp. 133, 134, 136, 137
- Strategies for Annotation, p. 137
- Analyze Impact of Word Choice: Tone, p. 137

To reteach the impact of word choice on tone, see
- Analyze Impact of Word Choice: Tone, p. 140a

▶ *Use It!* *Level Up* **Tutorial:** Tone

Interactive Whiteboard Lesson: Word Choice and Tone

ZOOM IN ON **ANALYZING SENTENCE STRUCTURE AND TONE** Tell students that tone is an author's attitude toward the subject he or she writes about. A **formal** tone is serious and respectful, while an **informal** tone might be playful or humorous. Read aloud the first two paragraphs of the story, making sure students understand the scene.

Have small groups review the two paragraphs and infer what kind of tone they have. *(formal)* Ask each group to list examples from the paragraphs that support their inference. Then have volunteers from each group share examples.

Language Conventionality and Clarity

some unassigned dialogue

Teach unfamiliar vocabulary in context.

- Teacher's Edition Critical Vocabulary notes, pp. 134, 135, 139
- Applying Academic Vocabulary, p. 134

Help students analyze the language used in the text.

- English Language Support, p. 133

Support students in recognizing various types of context clues.

- Vocabulary Strategy: Context Clues, p. 139
- Strategies for Annotation, p. 139

Guide students in using verb phrases.

- Language and Style: Using Verb Phrases, p. 140

ZOOM IN ON **ANALYZING VERB PHRASES** Review the definition of a **verb phrase** as a combination of one or more helping verbs and a main verb. Point out that "might see" is a **modal** expression; it describes an action that could possibly happen. Then review the story in sections, discussing how verb phrases indicate shifts in time or mood.

- Lines 1–22: Most verbs are in the simple past tense. This is the main narrative.
- Lines 23–43: The past perfect tense introduces a flashback to events that happened before the main narrative.
- Lines 44–107: The main narrative resumes, mostly in the simple past tense.
- Lines 108–128: Using various tenses and modal verbs, the narrator imagines possible future events.

Knowledge Demands

fairly complex theme

Support English Learners in understanding the author's literary and cultural background.

- Teacher's Edition Background note, p. 133

ZOOM IN ON **BUILDING BACKGROUND KNOWLEDGE** Students may be familiar with the Japanese poetic form haiku, which typically has three lines with five, seven, and five syllables, respectively. Point out that haiku often focuses on nature imagery and everyday experiences. Discuss how Kawabata's writing shares some of the characteristics of a haiku style.

Suggested Reader/Task Considerations

You might consider the following before assigning this short story to students.

- Will students be engaged by a story that is more like a poem or a letter than a traditional Western story?
- Do students have the critical thinking skills to interpret the themes expressed at the end of the story?

ZOOM IN ON **SUPPORTING COMPREHENSION**

- Tell students that the plot structure so many Western stories rely upon is only one way to build an engaging narrative. Challenge them to appreciate the vivid imagery of the story by using their visualization skills and to think about the ideas and feelings these scenes evoke.
- As a class, discuss the last three paragraphs of the story. Ask: *What is the narrator's message about dealing with surprises in life? about the value of an individual? about people's ability to sustain happiness?*

CLOSE READ

Yasunari Kawabata Have students read the biographical information about the author. Tell them that although his writing is strongly connected to traditional Japanese literature in its themes, mood of reflective sadness, and form, he was always interested in new literary movements and experimented with several different approaches in the early days of his career. He sought to express feeling in a way that was fresh and powerful. His style is characterized by precise and detailed images that imply meaning rather than explain it.

AS YOU READ Direct students to use the As You Read statement to focus their reading.

Analyze Point of View: Cultural Background
RL 1, RL 6

(LINES 1–10)

Tell students that an author's **cultural background** includes the values, beliefs, and customs of his or her society or family heritage. This cultural background may influence aspects of the author's writing, such as setting, plot, or theme.

A CITE TEXT EVIDENCE Ask students to identify details in lines 1–10 that relate to the Japanese appreciation of nature. *(The narrator mentions "a dusky clump of bushes," "black cherry trees," "an insect's voice," and "orange trees." Additionally, the narrator changes the route of the walk to follow the sound of the insect.)*

Analyze Impact of Word Choice: Tone (LINES 8–10)
RL 4

Explain to students that they can think of tone as the sound of the author's voice. **Tone** shows the attitude that the author wants to communicate to readers about the characters and events in a story. Explain that the author's choice of words develops the tone.

B ASK STUDENTS what tone is suggested by the words in these lines: *exclaimed, surprised, gleaming,* and *hurried. (These words suggest a tone of excitement or anticipation.)*

Yasunari Kawabata (1899–1972) *was born in Osaka, Japan, and became an orphan when he was quite young. This experience may have led to the themes of loneliness and death in much of his writing. He published his first story "Izu Dancer" in 1926, and he became a major author in Japan after his novel* Snow Country *was published in 1948. In 1968, he was awarded the Nobel Prize in Literature "for his narrative mastery, which with great sensibility expresses the essences of the Japanese mind."*

The Grasshopper and the Bell Cricket

Short Story by Yasunari Kawabata   Translated by Lane Dunlop and J. Martin Holman

Image Credits: (t) ©Agence France Presse/Getty Images; (c) ©Daisuke Morita/Photodisc/Getty Images

AS YOU READ Consider the details that show the narrator's feelings throughout the story.

A Walking along the tile-roofed wall of the university, I turned aside and approached the upper school. Behind the white board fence of the school playground, from a dusky clump of bushes under the black cherry trees, an insect's voice could be heard. Walking more slowly and listening to that voice, and feeling reluctant to part with it, I turned right so as not to leave the playground behind. When I turned to the left, the fence gave way to an embankment[1] planted with orange trees. At the corner, I exclaimed with surprise. My eyes gleaming at what they saw up ahead, I hurried forward with short steps. **B**

At the base of the embankment was a bobbing cluster of beautiful varicolored lanterns, such as one might see at a festival in a remote country village. Without going any farther, I knew that it was a group of children on an insect chase among the bushes of the embankment. There were about twenty lanterns. Not only were

---
[1] **embankment:** a man-made elevated area of land used to prevent flooding or to raise a roadway.

The Grasshopper and the Bell Cricket   **133**

ENGLISH LANGUAGE SUPPORT

Language: Understand Participles Explain to students that the *-ing* form of a verb can be used as an adjective. Write this sentence from the story on the board: "My eyes gleaming at what they saw up ahead, I hurried forward with short steps." Point out that the participle *gleaming* modifies or describes the noun *eyes.* Explain that often the participle is found before or after the noun it tells about.

ASK STUDENTS to identify the participle and the noun it modifies in this sentence: "At the base of the embankment was a bobbing cluster of beautiful varicolored lanterns." *(participle: bobbing; noun: cluster)*

CLOSE READ

Analyze Impact of Word Choice: Tone

RL 4

(LINES 44–52)

Tell students that the way in which the author arranges the words in sentences affects the tone.

C **ASK STUDENTS** which words best describe the sentences in this paragraph: *long, short, simple,* or *complex.* Have students give examples to support their response. *(The sentences are complex, or long with many parts. For example, the second and third sentences contain multiple clauses with vivid descriptions of the lanterns.)* Read aloud the paragraph while students listen. Discuss how the sentence structure conveys the narrator's feelings. Ask how the sentence structure helps to communicate this tone. *(The detailed sentences show how interested and fascinated the narrator is in the lanterns.)*

CRITICAL VOCABULARY

lozenge: The narrator describes the openings in the lanterns as diamond-shaped.

ASK STUDENTS to explain the effect of having round, triangular, and lozenge-shaped openings in the lanterns. *(The light from the candle inside would create different patterns as it shone out.)*

loiter: The narrator is fascinated by the children's ingenuity and wants to stay to watch how they approach their insect hunt.

ASK STUDENTS what specific details the author is able to observe as he loiters near the lanterns. *(old-fashioned patterns, flower shapes, the names of children who made the lanterns cut out in squared letters, thick cutout cardboard)*

emanate: The narrator notices that some of the light comes from the lantern windows the children designed and colored themselves.

ASK STUDENTS what feelings might emanate from the narrator at this moment. *(The narrator thinks the lanterns are beautiful and clever. These feelings might emanate in the form of a smile or fixed gaze on the lanterns.)*

---

there crimson, pink, indigo, green, purple, and yellow lanterns, but one lantern glowed with five colors at once. There were even some little red store-bought lanterns. But most of the lanterns were beautiful square ones that the children had made themselves
20   with love and care. The bobbing lanterns, the coming together of children on this lonely slope—surely it was a scene from a fairy tale?

One of the neighborhood children had heard an insect sing on this slope one night. Buying a red lantern, he had come back the next night to find the insect. The night after that, there was another child. This new child could not buy a lantern. Cutting out the back and front of a small carton and papering it, he placed a candle on the bottom and fastened a string to the top. The number of children grew to five, and then to seven. They learned how to color the paper
30   that they stretched over the windows of the cutout cartons, and to draw pictures on it. Then these wise child-artists, cutting out round, three-cornered, and **lozenge** leaf shapes in the cartons, coloring each little window a different color, with circles and diamonds, red and green, made a single and whole decorative pattern. The child with the red lantern discarded it as a tasteless object that could be bought at a store. The child who had made his own lantern threw it away because the design was too simple. The pattern of light that one had had in hand the night before was unsatisfying the morning after. Each day, with cardboard, paper, brush, scissors, penknife, and glue,
40   the children made new lanterns out of their hearts and minds. Look at my lantern! Be the most unusually beautiful! And each night, they had gone out on their insect hunts. These were the twenty children and their beautiful lanterns that I now saw before me.

Wide-eyed, I **loitered** near them. Not only did the square lanterns have old-fashioned patterns and flower shapes, but the names of the children who had made them were cut in squared letters of the syllabary.[2] Different from the painted-over red lanterns, others (made of thick cutout cardboard) had their designs drawn onto the paper windows, so that the candle's light seemed to
50   **emanate** from the form and color of the design itself. The lanterns brought out the shadows of the bushes like dark light. The children crouched eagerly on the slope wherever they heard an insect's voice.

"Does anyone want a grasshopper?" A boy, who had been peering into a bush about thirty feet away from the other children, suddenly straightened up and shouted.

"Yes! Give it to me!" Six or seven children came running up. Crowding behind the boy who had found the grasshopper, they peered into the bush. Brushing away their outstretched hands and

---

lozenge
(lŏz´ĭnj) *n.* a diamond-shaped object.

loiter
(loi´tər) *v.* to stand or wait idly.

emanate
(ĕm´ə-nāt´) *v.* to emit or radiate from.

---

[2] **syllabary:** A set of written characters for a language, with each character representing a syllable.

APPLYING ACADEMIC VOCABULARY

capacity	emerge

In your discussion of "The Grasshopper and the Bell Cricket," incorporate these Collection 3 academic vocabulary words: *capacity* and *emerge.* Discuss what the author means when he says that each day "new lanterns made out of their hearts and minds" **emerged**. Ask students what the children's lanterns reveal about their creative **capacity**.

spreading out his arms, the boy stood as if guarding the bush where
60 the insect was. Waving the lantern in his right hand, he called again
to the other children.

"Does anyone want a grasshopper? A grasshopper!"

"I do! I do!" Four or five more children came running up.
It seemed you could not catch a more precious insect than a
grasshopper. The boy called out a third time.

"Doesn't anyone want a grasshopper?"

Two or three more children came over.

"Yes. I want it."

It was a girl, who just now had come up behind the boy who'd
70 discovered the insect. Lightly turning his body, the boy gracefully
bent forward. Shifting the lantern to his left hand, he reached his
right hand into the bush.

"It's a grasshopper."

"Yes. I'd like to have it."

The boy quickly stood up. As if to say "Here!" he thrust out his
fist that held the insect at the girl. She, slipping her left wrist under
the string of her lantern, enclosed the boy's fist with both hands.
The boy quietly opened his fist. The insect was transferred to
between the girl's thumb and index finger.

80 "Oh! It's not a grasshopper. It's a bell cricket." The girl's eyes
shone as she looked at the small brown insect.

"It's a bell cricket! It's a bell cricket!" The children echoed in an
envious chorus.

"It's a bell cricket. It's a bell cricket."

Glancing with her bright intelligent eyes at the boy who had
given her the cricket, the girl opened the little insect cage hanging
at her side and released the cricket in it.

"It's a bell cricket."

"Oh, it's a bell cricket," the boy who'd captured it muttered.
90 Holding up the insect cage close to his eyes, he looked inside it. By
the light of his beautiful many-colored lantern, also held up at eye
level, he glanced at the girl's face.

Oh, I thought. I felt slightly jealous of the boy, and **sheepish**.
How silly of me not to have understood his actions until now! Then
I caught my breath in surprise. Look! It was something on the girl's
breast that neither the boy who had given her the cricket, nor she
who had accepted it, nor the children who were looking at them
noticed.

In the faint greenish light that fell on the girl's breast, wasn't the
100 name "Fujio" clearly **discernible**? The boy's lantern, which he held
up alongside the girl's insect cage, inscribed his name, cut out in the
green papered aperture, onto her white cotton kimono. The girl's
lantern, which dangled loosely from her wrist, did not project its

sheepish
(shē´pĭsh) *adj.*
showing
embarrassment.

discernible
(dĭ-sûr´nə-bəl) *adj.*
recognizable or
noticeable.

The Grasshopper and the Bell Cricket **135**

WHEN STUDENTS STRUGGLE...

Display an inference chart to increase comprehension of the boy's actions.

What I read	What I know	What I think
The boy asks who wants a grasshopper but doesn't give it away at first. He finally gives it to the girl.	He waited to give the grasshopper to the girl. I realize he wanted to give it to her all along.	The boy likes the girl.

LEVEL UP TUTORIALS For additional support, assign the
following *Level Up* tutorials: **Making Inferences.**

Analyze Point of View: Cultural Background
RL 1, RL 6

(LINES 73–84)

Tell students that the behavior of characters in a short story can reveal the author's values. These values are shaped by his or her culture.

D CITE TEXT EVIDENCE Have students glean from the description of the children's behavior in lines 73–84 what the narrator's feelings are about nature. Ask students to cite specific examples. (*The details reveal and echo the narrator's respect for nature. In lines 78–84, the narrator describes how the boy "quietly opened his fist" and carefully transferred the insect into the girl's hand. He also characterizes the other children's reaction to discovering that the insect is a bell cricket and not a grasshopper as an "envious chorus." These details imply a sense of wonder and respect toward nature.*)

Support Inferences
RL 1

(LINES 85–94)

Review that to make inferences, students should combine details in the text with their own knowledge to make assumptions about what is not stated.

E ASK STUDENTS to reread lines 85–94. What does the narrator's reaction to the boy's actions allow readers to infer? (*The boy wanted all along to give the insect he had found to the girl, so he waited until she came up to him. Readers infer this when in line 92 the boy looks at the girl's face by the light of his lantern.*)

CRITICAL VOCABULARY

sheepish: The narrator feels foolish or embarrassed because he didn't immediately recognize the boy's motivations for his actions. **ASK STUDENTS** how someone who feels sheepish might look. (*A person who feels embarrassed might blush or avoid eye contact.*)

discernible: The narrator sees what the children have not noticed—the boy's name projected onto the girl's kimono. **ASK STUDENTS** why this name might not be discernible to the children. (*They do not observe the interaction as closely as the narrator; they are more interested in observing the bell cricket.*)

Analyze Impact of Word Choice: Tone (LINES 99–114)

RL 1, RL 4

Explain that the sentences and words an author uses can help convey specific feelings about particular characters or events.

F CITE TEXT EVIDENCE Ask students to identify the sentences, phrases, and specific words that convey the narrator's amazement and joy from seeing the children's names projected onto one another. *(the narrator's question [lines 99–100], "alongside," "still one could make out," "trembling patch," "chance interplay," "remembered forever," "accepted," "dreams")*

Determine Meaning

RL 4

(LINES 119–128)

Remind students that a **symbol** is anything that stands for something more than itself. Tell them that authors use symbols to help convey their message. To understand a symbol, students should look at how the object is presented throughout the story and what feelings are associated with it.

G ASK STUDENTS to reread this passage and explain what each insect represents in the story. *(Bell crickets are unique and not as easily found a grasshoppers; "there are not many bell crickets in the world." They represent the people who are special to another person. Grasshoppers are common; "it seems that the world is only full of grasshoppers." They represent the people who do not capture a person's heart)*

COLLABORATIVE DISCUSSION Students should cite specific details from the story that reveal the narrator's feelings. As they revisit the text to answer the questions, encourage them to use cluster diagrams to note the various details that support each of the emotions they identify. Accept all reasonable responses.

ASK STUDENTS to share any questions they generated in the course of reading and discussing the selection.

---

pattern so clearly, but still one could make out, in a trembling patch of red on the boy's waist, the name "Kiyoko." This chance interplay of red and green—if it was chance or play—neither Fujio nor Kiyoko knew about.

Even if they remembered forever that Fujio had given her the cricket and that Kiyoko had accepted it, not even in dreams
110 would Fujio ever know that his name had been written in green on Kiyoko's breast or that Kiyoko's name had been inscribed in red on his waist, nor would Kiyoko ever know that Fujio's name had been inscribed in green on her breast or that her own name had been written in red on Fujio's waist.

Fujio! Even when you have become a young man, laugh with pleasure at a girl's delight when, told that it's a grasshopper, she is given a bell cricket; laugh with affection at a girl's chagrin when, told that it's a bell cricket, she is given a grasshopper.

Even if you have the wit to look by yourself in a bush away from
120 the other children, there are not many bell crickets in the world. Probably you will find a girl like a grasshopper whom you think is a bell cricket.

And finally, to your clouded, wounded heart, even a true bell cricket will seem like a grasshopper. Should that day come, when it seems to you that the world is only full of grasshoppers, I will think it a pity that you have no way to remember tonight's play of light, when your name was written in green by your beautiful lantern on a girl's breast.

COLLABORATIVE DISCUSSION How does the narrator react to the scene on the hill? What does he feel as he watches? With a partner, discuss what details the author provides to show varied emotions. Cite textual evidence to support your ideas.

TO CHALLENGE STUDENTS . . .

Evaluate Tone Have students evaluate how tone contributes to the overall impact of a story on readers. Have pairs rewrite lines 115 to 122 in a casual tone. Encourage them to use colloquialisms, short sentences, and simple vocabulary. Emphasize that rewritten sentences should express the same idea as the original. Provide this version of the last sentence as an example: "Chances are you will find an ugly duckling, but to you, she will be one amazing chick." Have students share their rewritten passages in small groups and compare them with the original lines of the story.

ASK STUDENTS how the difference in tone affects the overall impression they have of the passage, their understanding of the narrator's words, and their feeling about what he is saying. As a group, draw conclusions about the role of tone in a story.

Analyze Point of View: Cultural Background

Point of view involves the perspective from which a story is told. An author's cultural background and experience are part of this perspective, and are often reflected in works of literature. You may need some additional information about the author's cultural background in order to understand what the author is trying to express. "The Grasshopper and the Bell Cricket" was written in the early twentieth century by a Japanese author. Knowing some facts about Japanese culture will help you understand the author's point of view and, as a result, enrich your analysis of this story.

- Traditionally nature is quite important in Japanese culture. The roots of this reverence for nature come from the Shinto religion, which honors all aspects of the natural world: water, rocks, trees, sun, birds, insects.
- Instead of hoping to tame or conquer nature, Japanese aim to live in harmony with it. Japanese culture shows both respect and gratitude for nature.
- In Japan, as in other cultures, crickets are symbols of good luck. The bell cricket is an insect appreciated for its song, not its beauty.

Analyze Impact of Word Choice: Tone

Tone is the writer's attitude toward the subject and characters in a literary work. Authors create tone through the word choices they make. One way to classify tone is as **formal** or **informal**. The chart shows some examples of elements authors use to create a specific tone. You can use this information to help you analyze Kawabata's word choice and evaluate the tone that is created in this short story.

Colloquialisms	Abbreviations and Contractions	Sentence Structure
Colloquialisms are words or phrases used in informal conversation. Consider for example these phrases: *bunch of kids* and *group of children*. The first one is more colloquial and creates a more informal tone.	The use of **abbreviations** and **contractions** tends to make writing more informal. In this story, Kawabata uses some contractions in dialogue, but mostly avoids them.	In addition to word choice, **sentence structure** can contribute to tone. Longer, more complex sentences tend to create a more formal tone, while simpler sentences often create a more informal tone.

CLOSE READ

Analyze Point of View: Cultural Background

RL 6

Point out that knowing an author's perspective enables readers to understand the significance of the ideas in the short story. Organize students into groups. Have them identify all the references to nature that they find in the story; then have them explain how these details illustrate the values of the author's culture.

Analyze Impact of Word Choice: Tone

RL 4

Discuss each boldfaced term, making sure students understand its meaning. Remind students that they use formal and informal elements in their own writing. For example, they would not use the same elements in an email to a potential employer about an afterschool job as they would if they emailed their friend. List these situations on the board and ask students to identify whether they would write their communication in a formal or informal tone.

- a letter to the principal on behalf of the class asking permission for a fundraiser
- a text to your older sibling asking for a ride
- a thank you note to an aunt
- an essay on a midterm exam

Strategies for Annotation   ✎ 🖺 *Annotate it!*

Analyze Impact of Word Choice: Tone

RL 4

Have students use their eBook annotation tools to help them analyze the effect of the author's words on tone. Direct them to do these steps:

- Highlight challenging vocabulary words in yellow.
- Highlight in pink phrases and verb constructions that would not be used in casual conversation.
- Underline complicated sentences.
- Discuss how the tone affects your understanding of the story.

be heard. Walking more slowly and listening to that voice, and feeling reluctant to part with it, I turned right so as not to leave the playground behind. When I turned to the left, the fence gave

PRACTICE & APPLY

Analyzing the Text
RL 1, RL 2, RL 4, RL 6

Possible answers:

1. The first two paragraphs employ a formal tone. "I turned aside and approached" (lines 1–2) is more formal than "I turned and walked toward." The use of the passive "an insect's voice could be heard" (line 4) is more formal than "I heard an insect's voice." Use of the second person ("you might see") can be colloquial, but here the author uses "one might see" (line 12).

2. A reverence toward nature emerges. Examples include attention to the "dusky clump of bushes under the black cherry trees" (lines 3–4), noting of the insect's voice (line 4), children seeking insects (line 14), the leaf and flower shapes on some of the lanterns (lines 29–34), excitement over the grasshopper (lines 56, 63), and the envy at the finding of a bell cricket (lines 82–83).

3. These lines express the idea that people desire things that are not common. The children are "envious" when a bell cricket is found. Understanding the value of bell crickets in Japanese culture allows the reader to appreciate the children's envy.

4. The narrator expresses the underlying message that it is hard to find truly unique individuals. Even though you might be willing to go off the usual path, you are not guaranteed success. You are most likely to find somebody who is not particularly unique but who is special to you.

5. He expresses the idea that all people should be cherished because someone who may be considered "common" to one person may be "special" to another.

6. The tone differs slightly between the beginning and end of the story. The tone remains formal in both places, but at the beginning of the story (lines 20–52), the narrator expresses delight and hope in seeing the children. In the second part of the story (lines 108–128), the tone is darker and more contemplative as the narrator explores the idea of disappointment in life.

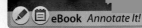

Analyzing the Text
RL 1, RL 2, RL 4, RL 6, W 3d

Cite Text Evidence   Support your responses with evidence from the selection.

1. **Interpret** Examine the first two paragraphs of the story. What is the tone of these paragraphs? Cite words and phrases that contribute to the tone.

2. **Cite Evidence** Remember that nature is important in Japanese culture. What point of view about nature emerges in this selection? Cite details from the story to support your answer.

3. **Analyze** In lines 80–92, what point of view does the narrator express about people? Why is it important to understand the role of bell crickets in Japanese culture in order to understand the narrator's point of view? Explain using details from the story.

4. **Infer** Determine the **theme**, or underlying message, that the narrator expresses in lines 119–122 when he writes, "Even if you have the wit to look by yourself in a bush away from the other children, there are not many bell crickets in the world. Probably you will find a girl like a grasshopper whom you think is a bell cricket".

5. **Draw Conclusions** Think about the narrator's perspective as an older person. What point of view about life is the narrator trying to express in the advice given to Fujio in lines 115–118?

6. **Compare** Is the tone of this story the same at the beginning and at the end? Explain.

PERFORMANCE TASK

Writing Activity: Journal Entry or Letter Think about how specific words can create either an informal or formal tone. In both responses, use key details from the text and standard English.

1. In the character of the girl who receives the bell cricket, use informal language to describe the insect hunts and what happened on this night, as you would in a journal entry.

2. Look at the last three paragraphs. In the character of the narrator, write a personal letter to Fujio. Use a formal tone as you give him your advice.

Assign this performance task.

PERFORMANCE TASK
W 3d

Writing Activity: Journal Entry or Letter Brainstorm with students the attributes of a journal entry. Tell students to use standard English and an informal tone to relate the events that led up to and followed the insect hunt. Before they draft their letters, have students identify the advice they would give Fujio. Tell them that analyzing the word choice and sentence structure in the story will help them emulate the narrator's formal tone in their letters.

Critical Vocabulary

lozenge   loiter   emanate   sheepish   discernible

Practice and Apply Answer the questions to show your understanding of the Critical Vocabulary words. Use a dictionary or thesaurus as needed.

1. Which would you be more likely to do if you are feeling **sheepish**: blush and grin or scowl and shout? Why?

2. If a container **emanates** light, can you see the light or not? Why?

3. Which would be more **discernible,** something written in crayon or in invisible ink? Why?

4. If I **loiter,** do I run away or do I hang around? Why?

5. Which item has a **lozenge** shape: kite or egg? Why?

Vocabulary Strategy: Context Clues

When you read, you can use **context clues** to understand unfamiliar words. **Context** is how a word relates to the overall meaning of a sentence, paragraph, or piece of writing.

Here are some types of context clues you may find in texts:

Synonyms or Definition	Contrast	Examples
The text may provide a definition or synonym.	The text may give an antonym, or contrasting information.	The text may list examples of the word.

Look at this example from the story.

> Then these wise child-artists, cutting out round, three-cornered, and *lozenge* leaf shapes in the cartons . . .

You read that *lozenge* is part of a list of shapes, an example of a shape. You also know from contrasting information that a *lozenge* is not round or three-cornered.

Practice and Apply Locate these words in the story: *discarded* (line 35), *crouched* (line 52), *inscribed* (line 101). Then, use context clues to write definitions for each word. Check your definitions in a dictionary.

PRACTICE & APPLY

Critical Vocabulary

Possible answers:

1. *You'd be more likely to blush and grin because* sheepish *means to be embarrassed by a fault or mistake.*

2. *Yes, you can see it because* emanate *means to emit or give out.*

3. *Crayon would be more discernible because* discernible *means "able to be detected by one of the senses."*

4. *I hang around because* loitered *means to stay in a place without any obvious intent.*

5. *A kite is more lozenge-shaped, because a* lozenge *is a rhombus, or a shape like a diamond.*

Vocabulary Strategy: Context Clues

Possible answers:

- **discarded:** *got rid of something unwanted*
- **crouched:** *stooped or bent down*
- **inscribed:** *marked or written*

Strategies for Annotation   ✏️ 🗐 **Annotate it!**

Use Context Clues

Have students locate the sentences containing *discarded* (line 35), *crouched* (line 52), and *inscribed* (line 101). Encourage them to use their eBook annotation tools to do the following:

- Highlight each word in green.
- Reread the surrounding sentences, looking for clues to the word's meaning. Underline any clues you find, such as examples, synonyms, definitions, or antonyms.
- Review your annotations to determine the word's meaning.

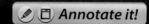

green, made a single and whole decorative pattern. The child with the red lantern discarded it as a tasteless object that could be bought at a store. The child who had made his own lantern threw it away because the design was too simple. The pattern of light

Language and Style: Using Verb Phrases

L 1b

Reinforce these ideas by assigning groups of students one or more paragraphs from the story and having them list the verb phrases they find. Have them discuss how the helping verbs clarify meaning or shifts in time in each phrase.

Possible answers:

When students complete their revisions, ask them to underline at least two new verb phrases they added to their work.

 Assess It Online!

Online Selection Test
- Download an editable ExamView bank.
- Assign and manage this test online.

Language and Style: Using Verb Phrases

L 1b

Verb phrases are a combination of one or more helping verbs and a main verb. In "The Grasshopper and the Bell Cricket," Yasunari Kawabata uses many verb phrases to express shifts in time.

Read this sentence from the story.

At the base of the embankment was a bobbing cluster of beautiful varicolored lanterns such as one <u>might see</u> at a festival in a remote country village.

By using the verb phrase *might see,* the author creates a possibility for a comparison—lanterns on the embankment and lanterns at a festival.

Now, read this sentence from the story.

But most of the lanterns were beautiful square ones which the children <u>had made</u> themselves with love and care.

Here the author uses the verb phrase *had made* to show that the children's action of making the lanterns took place in the past prior to the narrator seeing them.

Note that words might come between the parts of the verb phrase. In this example from the story, *does* and *want* create the verb phrase, and the phrase is interrupted by the subject, a common occurrence in a question.

<u>Does</u> anyone <u>want</u> a grasshopper?

The table shows some common helping verbs. You can use these helping verbs in their different forms in verb phrases.

Common Helping Verbs in Verb Phrases			
	be	can	am
	do	have	may
	might	shall	should
	will	would	could

Practice and Apply With a partner, review your journal entries or letters you created in response to this selection's Performance Task. Note the use of verb phrases in your works. Help each other revise verb phrases to make your writing more effective in showing shifts in time, or work together to create sentences that contain verb phrases. Remember to consider the tense of the verbs when you are revising.

Write a Narrative

W 3

TEACH

Point out to students that their journal entry or letter for the Performance Task will take the form of a **narrative,** as they tell what happened on the insect hunt. Remind them to keep in mind these ideas as they write their narratives:

- Jot down the details to be included before beginning to write. Include the specific stages of the event as well as descriptive words that can help create a mental picture of sights, sounds, smells, and other sensations.
- Put the details in order. Most narratives are told in chronological order from beginning to end. Use transitional words and phrases that help readers understand the order, such as *next, later, afterwards,* and *finally.*
- Create an interesting first sentence that states what the narrative is about and why it is important enough to write about.
- Use first-person point of view. Remember to convey perspective using first-person pronouns, such as *I, me, my, mine, we, us, our,* and *ours.*
- Choose appropriate language. A letter or journal is informal in tone rather than formal. This means that the ideas are expressed in complete sentences that observe standard English, but that contractions, some abbreviations, and colloquialisms, or familiar sayings, are acceptable.
- Write a concluding sentence that sums up the overall impression of the event as well as its significance.

PRACTICE AND APPLY

Have students complete the first draft of their narrative. Then organize them into groups of three or four. Distribute sticky notes or small pieces of paper. Have students take turns reading each other's first drafts. For each reading, have students write one specific way in which the narrative might be improved and write one strength that the narrative contains. Have students circulate their narratives until every person in the group has commented on them. Discuss with students how they can incorporate the suggestions they have received.

Analyze Impact of Word Choice: Tone

RL 4

RETEACH

Review the definition of **tone** as well as the components of the author's style that contribute to it. Project the following excerpt from Martin Luther King Jr.'s speech "I Have a Dream" on the board or a device.

"I have a dream that one day on the red hills of Georgia, sons of former slaves and the sons of former slave owners will be able to sit down together at the table of brotherhood. I have a dream that one day even the state of Mississippi, a state sweltering with the heat of injustice, sweltering with the heat of oppression, will be transformed into an oasis of freedom and justice. I have a dream that my four little children will one day live in a nation where they will not be judged by the color of their skin, but by the content of their character."

Have students identify the tone *(forceful, hopeful)* and elements of the speech that contribute to it. *(The forceful tone comes from repeating "I have a dream," and "sweltering with the heat." King delivers short, powerful words vehemently. The details of his vision contribute to the hopeful tone.)*

 Assign the following *Level Up* tutorial: **Tone.**

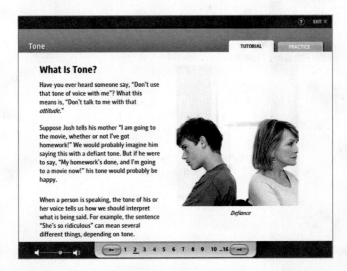

INDEPENDENT READING

Give students a passage from a short story or nonfiction selection that has an informal tone. Have them work in pairs to identify the tone, determine the elements that convey it, and analyze it.

With Friends Like These . . .

Informational Text by Dorothy Rowe

Why This Text?

Friendship is an experience that is particularly relevant to students as they begin forming their identities as young adults through their relationships with peers. This lesson allows students to explore the topic of friendship through the ideas and insights of noted psychologist Dorothy Rowe.

Key Learning Objective: The student will be able to analyze how an author unfolds a series of ideas in an informational text.

RI 1 Cite textual evidence.

RI 3 Analyze how the author unfolds an analysis or series of ideas.

RI 4 Determine technical meanings; analyze the impact of word choices on meaning and tone.

SL 1 Participate effectively in collaborative discussions.

L 1b Use various types of phrases (adjectival, adverbial) to convey specific meanings.

L 4b Identify and correctly use patterns of word changes that indicate different meanings or parts of speech.

▲ Text Complexity Rubric

Quantitative Measures	**With Friends Like These . . .** Lexile: 1070L

Levels of Meaning/Purpose

single topic

Structure

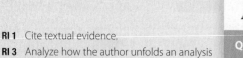

organization of main ideas and details complex, but clearly stated and generally sequential

Language Conventionality and Clarity

some unfamiliar, academic, or domain-specific words

Knowledge Demands

somewhat complex science concepts

Qualitative Measures	(see above)

Reader/Task Considerations	• Teacher determined • Vary by individual reader and type of text • See the Text X-Ray for suggested Reader/Task Considerations.

English Language Support Before teaching, use the Text X-Ray below for an overview of the text's complexity. The Text X-Ray and the supports and scaffolds in the Teacher's Edition will help you guide students of different skill levels.

Meaning Making

Language Development

Effective Expression

Content Knowledge

Foundational Skills

Text Complexity: Qualitative Measures

Levels of Meaning/Purpose

single topic

Help students analyze how an author's language choices affect meaning and tone.
- Teacher's Edition side notes, pp. 141, 142

 Use It! Interactive Whiteboard Lesson: Word Choice and Tone

ZOOM IN ON ANALYZING TONE AND MEANING Point out the selection title. Explain that it refers to the saying "With friends like these, who needs enemies?" The idea is that if your friends treat you badly, they are not true friends. Ask students what **tone**, or attitude, they expect the author to express toward her subject, given the title. *(Possible answer: a humorous or casual tone)* After students read the text, have pairs discuss these questions before sharing their answers with the class:

- Did the text as a whole have the tone that you predicted from the title? Explain.
- Why do you think the author referred to the saying about friends in her title?
- How does the author define true friendship?

Structure

organization of main ideas and details complex, but clearly stated and generally sequential

Help students analyze how ideas are organized in a text.
- Teacher's Edition side notes, pp. 141, 142, 143, 144
- When Students Struggle, p. 143
- Analyze Ideas, p. 144

To reteach analyzing ideas, see
- Analyze Ideas, p. 146aa

 Use It! Level Up Tutorial: Reading for Details

ZOOM IN ON ANALYZING IDEAS Help students recognize some of the **transitions** the author uses to connect ideas. Display lines 1–28. Discuss the **main idea** introduced in the first sentence: Friendships can be difficult. Point out how the last sentence in the paragraph uses the transition *and yet* to express a contrasting idea: We need friendships to enjoy life. The first sentence of the next paragraph starts with the transition *more fundamentally* and adds a new idea: friendships help define who we are. Ask volunteers to identify more examples of transitions in the rest of the passage.

Language Conventionality and Clarity

some unfamiliar, academic, or domain-specific words

Teach unfamiliar vocabulary in context.

- Teacher's Edition Critical Vocabulary notes, pp. 141, 142, 143, 145
- English Language Support, p. 141
- Applying Academic Vocabulary, p. 142

Support students in understanding patterns of word changes.

- Vocabulary Strategy: Patterns of Word Changes, p. 145
- Strategies for Annotation, p. 145

Guide students in using adjective and adverb phrases in their writing.

- Language and Style: Adjective and Adverb Phrases, p. 146
- Strategies for Annotation, p. 146

To teach determining technical meanings, see

- Determine Technical Meanings, p. 146a

ZOOM IN ON **UNPACKING SENTENCES** Tell students that identifying **prepositional phrases** and what they modify can help them understand long sentences. Ask students to list some **prepositions**. *(Sample list: about, above, after, among, before, behind, during, for, in, of, on, toward, until, upon, with)* Then display the sentence in lines 14–18. Work with students to highlight the prepositions, underline the prepositional phrases, and circle the modified words.

> Early in our life our stream of conscious and unconscious constructions create like a real stream, a kind of whirlpool that quickly becomes our most precious possession, that is, our sense of being a person, what we call "I," "me," "myself."

Have pairs apply the same strategy to the sentences in lines 47–49, 69–71, and 85–88.

Knowledge Demands

somewhat complex science concepts

Support English Learners by expanding their knowledge of scientific concepts that contribute to the author's ideas in this text.

ZOOM IN ON **BUILDING SCIENTIFIC BACKGROUND** Dorothy Rowe has been influenced by the Personal Construct Theory developed by psychologist George Kelly. This theory holds that people form their own constructs, or explanations for why certain events typically recur. One's personality is largely made up of the mental constructs through which one views reality. After reading Rowe's text, have students discuss whether it supports Personal Construct Theory.

Suggested Reader/Task Considerations

You might consider the following before assigning this selection to students.

- Will students struggle with vocabulary related to the field of psychology in this text?
- Might some students be too psychologically vulnerable to read about the experiences described?

ZOOM IN ON **SUPPORTING COMPREHENSION**

- Before reading, divide the text among several pairs or groups. Have students scan the text for unfamiliar words, define them using context clues or a dictionary, and then share their findings with the class.
- Allow students to read this article independently, outside of the classroom, where they can react emotionally to the content and then compose themselves.

CLOSE READ

AS YOU READ Instruct students to use the As You Read note to focus their reading.

Analyze Impact of Word Choice on Tone

RI 4

(LINES 1–13)

Inform students that an author's **tone,** or attitude toward a subject, is affected by his or her choices of specific words and details. Tone is usually described using adjectives such as *objective, angry, humorous,* or *sad.*

Ⓐ ASK STUDENTS to reread lines 1–7 and describe Rowe's tone. *(Possible answers: friendly, understanding, knowledgeable, engaging)* Then invite students to identify how Rowe's language and choice of details helps her express that tone. *(The author uses ordinary language and examples that readers can relate to. She also refers to the work of neuroscientists, showing that she takes her topic seriously and is knowledgeable about it.)*

Analyze Ideas

RI 1, RI 3, RI 4

(LINES 14–19)

Explain that authors develop their central ideas by supporting them with details in the form of reasons, facts, or examples. Sometimes they use figurative language to help readers understand the unfamiliar. A **simile** is a figure of speech that compares two unlike things using the word *like* or *as.*

Ⓑ CITE TEXT EVIDENCE Ask students to reread lines 14–19 and identify two examples of similes. *("like a real stream" [line 16]; "Like a whirlpool" [line 18])* Then ask students how these similes help Rowe develop the idea of how the brain works. *(The similes help the reader visualize how the brain's constructions, or ideas about the world, form a sense of self similar to the way a stream creates a whirlpool.)*

CRITICAL VOCABULARY

validated: Rowe says our ideas are validated when events show that our ideas about reality are accurate.

ASK STUDENTS what happens when our ideas about reality are validated. *(We feel secure and confident about who we are.)*

With Friends Like These...

Informational Text by Dorothy Rowe

AS YOU READ Pay attention to the author's ideas about what makes friendship possible between two people. Write down any questions.

We value friends, but the path of friendship, like love, rarely runs smooth. We may feel jealous of a friend's achievements when we want to feel happy for her. We might find it hard to give friends objective advice, unrelated to the person we want them to be. We can be reluctant to allow each other to change, sometimes falling out in a way that is painful for all involved. And yet, friendships are vitally important; central to our enjoyment of life.

More fundamentally, friendships are essential to our sense of who we are. Neuroscientists have shown that our brain does not
10 reveal to us the world as it is, but rather as possible interpretations of what is going on around us, drawn from our past experience. Since no two people ever have exactly the same experience, no two people ever see anything in exactly the same way.

Most of our brain's constructions are unconscious. Early in our life our stream of conscious and unconscious constructions create, like a real stream, a kind of whirlpool that quickly becomes our most precious possession, that is, our sense of being a person, what we call "I," "me," "myself." Like a whirlpool, our sense of being a person cannot exist separately from the stream that created it.
20 Because we cannot see reality directly, all our ideas are guesses about what is going on. Thus our sense of being a person is made up of these guesses. All the time we are creating ideas about who we are, what is happening now, what has happened in our world, and what our future will be. When these ideas are shown by events to be reasonably accurate, that is, our ideas are **validated,** we feel secure in ourselves, but when they are proved wrong, we feel that we are falling apart.

Friends are central to this all-important sense of validation. When a friend confirms to us that the world is as we see it, we feel

validate
(văl´ĭ-dāt´) *v.* to establish the value, truth, or legitimacy of.

With Friends Like These . . . **141**

ENGLISH LANGUAGE SUPPORT

Vocabulary: Phrasal Verbs and Idioms Understanding some of the **phrasal verbs** (verbs that function as a unit with another word) and **idioms** used in the selection may be challenging for some students. Support students' vocabulary development and comprehension by allowing them to read the selection with a native English speaker, focusing on phrases such as these:

- *falling out* (lines 6, 85)
- *falling apart* (lines 27, 54, 55)
- *losing my grip* (line 31)
- *let us down* (line 59)

Analyze Ideas

RI 1, RI 3

(LINES 33–49)

Explain that authors use various techniques to unfold a series of ideas in a text.

- They use subheads to signal transitions to new topics and provide a focus for the text that follows.
- They link sentences or paragraphs by repeating key words and thus create a chain of ideas.

C **CITE TEXT EVIDENCE** Have students reread lines 33–49 and identify words Rowe repeats to link and develop her ideas. *("invalidation" [line 35] and "invalidated" [lines 47, 48]; "assessing" [line 37] and "assessments" [line 38]; "interpretations" [lines 38, 40, 42]; "emotions" [lines 38, 39, 42, 43])* Have students summarize how Rowe develops the idea she expresses at the beginning. *(We develop many ways to prevent feeling invalidated in our sense of self. Emotions help us know whether we feel validated or invalidated.)*

Analyze Language

RI 4

(LINES 50–57)

Explain that **repetition,** or using a word or phrase more than once, is a technique that can emphasize an important idea or show how ideas are related.

D **ASK STUDENTS** to reread lines 50–57 and explain what ideas are conveyed by Rowe's use of repetition. *(Rowe repeats Losing / loss in line 52 to compare her friend's loss of money with her loss of trust in her husband. Both are losses, but she says the loss of trust is worse. In line 54–55, she uses "falling apart" to describe her friend's feelings, but then she turns the phrase around to explain that it is actually her friend's ideas that are falling apart. By fixing the latter problem, her friend will also fix the former.)*

> **CRITICAL VOCABULARY**
>
> **assessing**: Rowe says that we are constantly evaluating how secure we feel in our sense of self.
>
> **ASK STUDENTS** how emotions help us assess how safe we feel in our sense of being a person. *(Positive emotions tell us we feel safe; negative emotions tell us we feel insecure about our sense of self.)*

---

30 safer, reassured. On the other hand, when we say, "I'm shattered," or "I'm losing my grip," we might not be using clichés to describe a bad day but talking about something quite terrifying that we are experiencing: our sense of who we are is being challenged. So terrifying is this experience that we develop many different tactics aimed at warding off invalidation and defending ourselves against being annihilated as a person.

Emotional support

We are constantly **assessing** how safe our sense of being a person is. Our assessments are those interpretations we call emotions. All our emotions relate to the degree of safety or danger our sense of being 40 a person is experiencing. So important are these interpretations to our survival that we do not need to put them into words, although of course we can. Our positive emotions are interpretations to do with safety, while the multitude of negative emotions define the particular kind of danger and its degree. Joy is: "Everything is the way I want it to be"; jealousy is: "How dare that person have something that is rightly mine."

We can be invalidated by events such as the bankruptcy of the firm that employs us, but most frequently we are invalidated by other people.

50 A friend told me how her husband had used her password and pin to drain her bank account and fund his secret gambling habit. Losing her savings was a terrible blow, but far worse was her loss of trust in the person she saw as her best friend.

When she described herself as falling apart, I assured her that what was falling apart were some of her ideas. All she had to do was to endure a period of uncertainty until she could construct ideas that better reflected her situation.

Friendship can be rewarding but, like all relationships, it can also be risky. Other people can let us down, insult or humiliate 60 us, leading us to feel diminished and in danger. Yet we need other people to tell us when we have got our guesses right, and, when we get things wrong, to help us make more accurate assessments. Live completely on your own and your guesses will get further and further away from reality.

The degree of risk we perceive from our friends relates directly to the degree of self-confidence we feel. When confident of ourselves, we feel that we can deal with being invalidated; when lacking self-confidence, we often see danger where no danger need exist. Take jealousy, for example. Feeling self-confident, we can 70 rejoice in our friend's success at a new job; feeling inferior, we see danger and try to defend ourselves with: "It's not fair." We can fail

assess
(ə-sĕs´) *v.* to evaluate.

APPLYING ACADEMIC VOCABULARY

generate	capacity

As you discuss Rowe's informational text, incorporate the Collection 3 academic vocabulary words: *generate* and *capacity*. While exploring the ideas from neuroscience that Rowe presents, ask students to cite evidence of how the brain **generates** ideas about the world. In addition, ask students to cite Rowe's ideas on how friends have the **capacity** to validate or invalidate one another's sense of self.

to see that our friendship should be more important to us than our injured pride.

Our levels of confidence also relate to how ready we are to accept change, and how able we are to allow our friends to change. To feel secure in ourselves, we need to be able to predict events reasonably accurately. We think we know our friends well, and so can predict what they will do. We create a mental image of our friends, and we want to keep them within the bounds of that image. 80 Our need to do this can override our ability to see our friends in the way they see themselves. We do not want them to change because then we would have to change our image of them. Change creates uncertainty, and uncertainty can be frightening.

Falling out

However, an inability to allow change can lead to the end of a friendship. Falling out with a friend shows us that our image of them, from which we **derive** our predictions about that friend, is wrong; and if that is the case, our sense of being a person is threatened.

90 If we lose a friend, we have to change how we see ourselves and our life. Each of us lives in our own individual world of meaning. We need to find friends whose individual world is somewhat similar to our own so that we are able to communicate with one another.

The people who can validate us best are those we can see as equals, and with whom there can be mutual affection, trust, loyalty and acceptance. Such people give us the kind of validation that builds a lasting self-confidence despite the difficulties we encounter.

These are our true friends.

derive
(dĭ-rīv´) *v.* to obtain or extract from.

COLLABORATIVE DISCUSSION Why do certain people become friends while others do not? With a partner, discuss the factors that allow two people to become friends, and the factors that prevent it in other cases. Cite specific textual evidence to support your ideas.

WHEN STUDENTS STRUGGLE . . .

To help students trace the development of ideas in Rowe's text, assign groups a section of the text: lines 1–36, lines 37–83, lines 84–99. Have students read and discuss their assigned section and record the progression of central ideas in a graphic organizer like this one.

> Falling out means image of friend was wrong.

> Losing a friend requires change.

> True friends are similar to us and validate us.

CLOSE READ

Analyze Ideas
RI 1, RI 3

(LINES 84–88)

Explain that another way authors show connections among ideas is through the use of **transitions,** words and phrases that show how ideas relate to one another. For example, *like, as, similarly, in the same way,* and *also* show similarity between ideas; *but, yet, however, unlike, instead,* and *by contrast* show dissimilarity.

E **CITE TEXT EVIDENCE** Ask students to reread lines 84–88 and identify the transition used and explain how it relates the idea in this passage to the idea that came before. *(However [line 84] indicates that Rowe is introducing a contrast. Previously she said that change can be frightening; now she says that "an inability to allow change can lead to the end of a friendship," which might also be frightening.)* Then ask students how Rowe connects fear of change with the fear that comes after losing a friend. *(Rowe says that losing a friend tells us our image of that friend was wrong, and we are afraid for our sense of self when we recognize we were wrong in our ideas and might have to change them.)*

> **CRITICAL VOCABULARY**
>
> **derive**: Rowe says we make predictions about a friend's behavior based on the image we have of him or her.
>
> **ASK STUDENTS** what kinds of predictions they might derive from a relationship with a close friend. *(They might predict accurately how the friend will act in certain situations or what kinds of things the friend will or will not like.)*

COLLABORATIVE DISCUSSION Have students pair up and discuss the factors that allow and prevent the forming of friendships, citing evidence from Rowe's text. Then have them share their conclusions with the whole class. Accept all reasonable responses.

ASK STUDENTS to share any questions they generated in the course of reading and discussing the selection.

PRACTICE & APPLY

Analyze Ideas RI 3

Call on volunteers to read aloud the list of characteristics of an effective informational text. Point out the emphasis on clarity and logical order in presenting central ideas and supporting details.

Then display the first paragraph of Rowe's text on the board or on a device. Call on volunteers to follow the steps for analyzing the text by having them answer these questions:

- What is the central idea of the paragraph? *(Friendships are valuable, although they may be difficult.)*
- How does the author develop and support this idea? *(She presents examples of how friendships can be difficult and then concludes that in spite of difficulties, they are a key to enjoying life.)*
- In what order does the author present her ideas? *(She starts with a general statement, gives some specific examples, and concludes with another general statement.)*

Analyzing the Text RI 1, RI 3, RI 4

Possible answers:

1. *The first-person pronouns create a welcoming, friendly tone and imply that the author and readers share common experiences. By introducing the topic in this way, the author engages readers' interest by showing how it relates to their own experiences.*

2. *She describes how humans construct a sense of self based on guesses about reality that are informed by experience. When these guesses turn out to be correct, people feel validated. In line 28, the author connects the need for validation to friendship: "Friends are central to this all-important sense of validation."*

3. *Lines 74–83 explain that self-confidence is needed to allow friends to change because when a friend changes in an unexpected way, one has to change one's image of both the friend and oneself. This leads directly into the "Falling out" section, which begins with the idea that if one cannot adapt to a friend's changes, the friendship will end. Without the information about self-confidence and change, this idea would not make sense.*

Analyze Ideas RI 3

An informational text presents a series of facts and ideas on a particular topic. The author's challenge is to present his or her ideas in a way that will make sense to readers. An effective informational text

- introduces each idea clearly and in a way that engages readers' interest
- presents ideas in a logical order
- develops ideas with examples and supporting facts
- shows readers the connections between ideas

"With Friends Like These . . ." presents facts and ideas about the important role of friendship in human life. To analyze this text, identify the central idea that the author introduces in each paragraph or section. Think about how the author develops and supports each idea, and how it relates to the ideas presented before and after. Trace the order in which ideas are presented, and consider why the author chose that order. Finally, ask yourself what the author does to engage readers and make them interested in her topic.

Analyzing the Text RI 1, RI 3, RI 4, SL 1, SL 4

Cite Text Evidence Support your responses with evidence from the selection.

1. **Infer** Reread the first paragraph. What **tone**, or attitude, is created by the author's use of the first-person pronouns *we* and *our*? Why do you think she chose to introduce her topic to readers in this way?

2. **Connect** In lines 9–27, the author develops her ideas with information from the fields of neuroscience and psychology. How does she connect this information back to the idea that "friendships are essential to our sense of who we are"?

3. **Analyze** In lines 74–83, the author discusses people's capacity to accept change. Why does she introduce these ideas immediately before the section "Falling out"?

PERFORMANCE TASK

Speaking Activity: Response to Literature Reread lines 94–99 at the end of the selection. Then confer with a partner on the ideas about friendship expressed in these lines.

- Analyze the passage closely by making a list of the specific aspects of true friendship it mentions.
- Discuss each aspect and decide whether you agree that it is essential for a lasting friendship.
- Generate a brief presentation based on your discussion. Include the conclusions you reached and your reasons for them. As you present, use appropriate eye contact, adequate volume, and clear pronunciation.

Assign this performance task.

PERFORMANCE TASK SL 1, SL 4

Speaking Activity: Response to Literature Have students reread the passage and list the specific aspects of friendship mentioned. Have them note whether they agree or disagree with each point and add ideas about things they believe are essential to friendship. Ask them to discuss their ideas with a partner and notice where they agree or disagree. Students' presentations should give conclusions reached in the discussion and the reasons why they reached them.

Critical Vocabulary

L 4b

validate   **assess**   **derive**

Practice and Apply Working with a partner, develop a brief scene that depicts the meaning of each Critical Vocabulary word but does not include the word. Swap your scenes with another pair. Pairs will then analyze each other's scenes and identify the Critical Vocabulary word that is being conveyed in each one.

- an experience that makes a character feel **validated**
- a character **assessing** a situation or another character
- a character who **derives** an idea from something he or she observes

Vocabulary Strategy: Patterns of Word Changes

You have probably noticed that many words can change form to become new words with related meanings. When you learn the common **patterns of word changes,** you can recognize different forms of familiar words and figure out what they mean. Knowing the patterns will also help you spell different forms of a word correctly.

The Critical Vocabulary word *validate* is a verb. By adding affixes, you can change the part of speech and meaning of the word. Adding the suffix *-ion* creates the noun *validation*, which means "the act of establishing the truth or legitimacy of something." Removing *-ate* creates the adjective *valid*, which means "true or legitimate." Adding the prefix *in-* creates the verb *invalidate*, which means "establish that something is not true or legitimate."

This chart shows more words from the selection and their various forms. Note the patterns of spelling changes that occur between verb, noun, and adjective forms.

Verb	Noun	Adjective
relate	relation, relationship	relative
describe	description	descriptive
defend	defense	defensive, indefensible
perceive	perception	perceptive

Practice and Apply For each verb in the chart, identify one new verb that has the same ending (*-ate, -ibe, -end, -ceive*). Then, follow these steps:

1. Create a chart with your words in the first column. Complete the chart with noun and adjective forms of each word.

2. Use a dictionary to check your spelling of the new words.

3. Choose one word from each row of your chart and use it in a sentence.

PRACTICE & APPLY

Critical Vocabulary

L 4b

Possible answers:

Answers will vary. Students should create three scenes. The context of each scene should clearly relate to the definition of each Critical Vocabulary word.

Vocabulary Strategy: Patterns of Word Change

Possible answers:

Verb	Noun	Adjective
operate	operation	operative
prescribe	prescription	prescriptive
offend	offense	offensive
deceive	deception	deceptive

Students should also select four words—one word from each row—and use them correctly in sentences.

Strategies for Annotation 🖊 🗐 **Annotate it!**

Patterns of Word Change

L 4b

Have students locate the sentences containing forms of the Critical Vocabulary words *validate* and *assess* in Rowe's text. Encourage them to use their eBook annotation tools to do the following:

- Underline each form of the vocabulary word.
- Reread the sentences in which the words appear to identify the part of speech.
- Highlight verbs in yellow, nouns in pink, and adjectives in green.

We are constantly <u>assessing</u> how safe our sense of being a person is. Our <u>assessments</u> are those interpretations we call emotions. All our

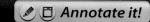

Language and Style: Adjective and Adverb Phrases

L 1b

Tell students that prepositions are words that relate a noun or pronoun (the object of the preposition) to another word in a sentence. Some common prepositions are *at, by, for, from, in, of, on, to,* and *with*. Knowing these facts will help them identify prepositional phrases when they read.

Possible answers:

Answers will vary. Student responses should accurately summarize Dorothy Rowe's ideas about friendship and personal identity. In their revisions, students should use the conventions of standard English grammar to include at least one adjective phrase and one adverb phrase.

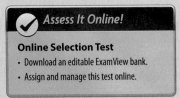

Assess It Online!

Online Selection Test
- Download an editable ExamView bank.
- Assign and manage this test online.

Language and Style: Adjective and Adverb Phrases

L 1b

A **prepositional phrase** is a phrase that consists of a preposition, its object, and any modifiers of the object. Prepositional phrases that modify nouns or pronouns are called **adjective phrases**. Prepositional phrases that modify verbs, adjectives, or adverbs are called **adverb phrases**.

"With Friends Like These . . ." opens with these sentences:

> We value friends, but the path <u>of friendship</u>, like love, rarely runs smooth. We may feel jealous <u>of a friend's achievements</u> when we want to feel happy <u>for her</u>.

The prepositional phrase *of friendship* functions as an adjective modifying *path*. The phrases *of a friend's achievements* and *for her* act as adverbs modifying *jealous* and *happy*. Notice how removing the adverb phrases makes the second sentence much less specific:

> We may feel jealous when we want to feel happy.

This chart shows sentences from the selection that use prepositional phrases as either adjectives or adverbs. Read each sentence carefully and note the relationship between the phrase and the word it modifies. There may be other words between the phrase and the word it modifies.

Adjective Phrase	Adverb Phrase
Each of us lives in our own individual world *of meaning*. (modifies the noun *world*)	More fundamentally, friendships are essential *to our sense of who we are*. (modifies the adjective *essential*)

Practice and Apply Write a summary of the author's ideas about how friendships validate our sense of who we are. Then, revise your paragraph to include at least one of each kind of phrase shown in the chart—a prepositional phrase that functions as an adjective and a prepositional phrase that functions as an adverb.

Strategies for Annotation

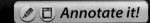 **Annotate it!**

Adjective and Adverb Phrases

L 1b

Have students locate additional passages in the selection that contain examples of adjective and adverb phrases. Encourage them to use their eBook annotation tools to do the following:

- Highlight in blue each adjective phrase.
- Highlight in green each adverb phrase.
- Underline the word(s) that each phrase modifies.

> are, what is happening now, what <u>has happened</u> in our world, and what our future will be. When these ideas <u>are shown</u> by events to be reasonably accurate, that is, our ideas are **validated,** we feel secure

Determine Technical Meanings

RI 4

TEACH

Point out that Rowe's informational text contains a mixture of ordinary language and examples along with technical language that explains ideas about the brain. Using these different types of language allows Rowe to inform readers in a way that is engaging, substantial, and credible. Ask students to look for context clues that help determine the meaning of technical language:

- Look for restatements of the technical term's meaning. You may need to look beyond a sentence or paragraph to find a restatement. The author doesn't define "brain's constructions" when she introduces the phrase. But if you go to the previous paragraph, it's clear the term fits a description: "possible interpretations of what is going on around us, drawn from our experiences."

- Sometimes, a technical term is a familiar word used in an unfamiliar way. For example, *unconscious* (line 14) probably doesn't mean "knocked out" in this context—it doesn't make sense here. Combining what you know of the word's familiar meaning with the context of ordinary brain function, you can infer that *unconscious* here refers to what the brain does in an unaware state.

- Authors can illustrate the meanings of technical terms with examples, analogies, or contrasts. Use all context clues available, but if an unknown terms keeps you from understanding the passage, look it up in a dictionary.

PRACTICE AND APPLY

Have students work with partners to figure out the meanings of the following technical terms from the selection. Students should identify the context clues that led to their definitions:

- **neuroscientist** *(line 10) (definition: scientists who study the nervous system, including the brain; context clues: "have shown that our brain does not reveal to us . . .")*

- **conscious** *(line 15) (definition: self-aware; context clues: "our stream of conscious and unconscious constructions . . .")*

- **overrides** *(line 80) (definition: counteracts; context clues: "our need to [maintain our mental image of our friends]" is contrasted with "our ability to see our friends in the way they see themselves")*

Analyze Ideas

RI 3

RETEACH

Explain that identifying the supporting details used to develop an idea is key to analyzing how an author unfolds a series of ideas in a text. Review these forms of supporting details:

- **Reasons** are statements that explain why. In this sentence, the underlined words are a reason that supports the opinion given (in italics). *Friendships are valuable* <u>because they are central to our sense of who we are.</u>

- **Examples** are used to illustrate an idea. "We may feel jealous of a friend's achievements when we want to feel happy for her" illustrates the idea that friendships are sometimes difficult.

- **Facts** are statements that can be proved or verified. "Neuroscientists have shown that our brain does not reveal to us the world as it is . . ." is a fact that can be verified by checking published articles about the brain.

 LEVEL UP TUTORIALS Assign the following *Level Up* tutorial: **Reading for Details**

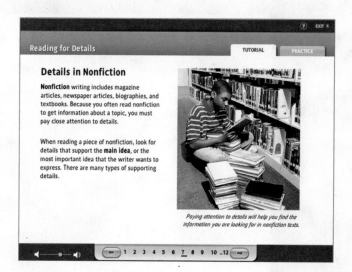

Paying attention to details will help you find the information you are looking for in nonfiction texts.

INDEPENDENT READING

Students can apply the skill to a selection from a textbook or other informational text. Have them work independently to identify the crucial details that help them follow how the ideas evolve throughout the text. Ask students to identify a central idea introduced early in the piece and explain how the author develops the idea by presenting details.

At Dusk

Poem by Natasha Trethewey

Why This Text?

Poetry enriches the lives of those who read it. This lesson looks at how the poet uses words to create vivid images that convey literal and implied meaning.

Key Learning Objective: The student will be able to interpret figurative language.

For additional practice:

Close Read selection
Poems About Family
"My Ceremony For Taking"
by Lara Mann

"The Stayer"
by Virgil Suárez

RL 1 Cite textual evidence.
RL 4 Analyze the impact of word choices on meaning and tone.
L 5a Interpret figures of speech in context.

Text Complexity Rubric

Quantitative Measures	**At Dusk** Lexile: N/A
Qualitative Measures	**Levels of Meaning/Purpose** multiple levels of meaning (multiple themes) **Structure** free verse, no particular patterns **Language Conventionality and Clarity** clear, direct language **Knowledge Demands** everyday knowledge, familiarity with genre conventions required
Reader/Task Considerations	• Teacher determined • Vary by individual reader and type of text • See the Text X-Ray for suggested Reader/Task Considerations.

English Language Support Before teaching, use the Text X-Ray below for an overview of the text's complexity. The Text X-Ray and the supports and scaffolds in the Teacher's Edition will help you guide students of different skill levels.

Meaning Making

Language Development

Effective Expression

Content Knowledge

Foundational Skills

Text Complexity: Qualitative Measures

Levels of Meaning/Purpose

multiple levels of meaning (multiple themes)

Help students analyze imagery and tone.
- Teacher's Edition side notes, pp. 148, 149
- Strategies for Annotation, p. 149
- Interpret Figurative Language, p. 149

To teach students to make inferences about the speaker and poet, see
- Analyze Language in Poetry, p. 150a

To reteach analyzing imagery, see
- Interpret Figurative Language, p. 150a

 Use It! Level Up **Tutorials:** Figurative Language, Imagery

Interactive Whiteboard Lesson: Figurative Language and Imagery

ZOOM IN ON **ANALYZING IMAGERY** Discuss with students different ways a poet can create vivid **images** for the reader. In "At Dusk," the author uses descriptive terms to help readers visualize what is happening. She also uses **figurative language** to compare two things that are very different. Work with students to analyze these examples of figurative language that create images for the reader:

- Lines 3–4: "street lamps just starting to hum / the backdrop of evening" *(Street lamps are compared to singers warming up, creating a sound image.)*
- Line 12: "constellation of fireflies" *(The fireflies are compared to stars, helping readers imagine their number and brilliance.)*

Structure

free verse, no particular patterns

Help students to understand a poem's structure and cohesion.
- English Language Support, p. 147

 Use It! **Interactive Whiteboard Lesson:**
Poetry: Language and Form

ZOOM IN ON **UNDERSTANDING COHESION** Explain to students that in **free verse,** which has no regular patterns, readers must pay attention to the way ideas are presented and connected to understand the **structure** of the poem. Divide students into three groups, assign each a section of the poem, and have them write a short explanation of the focus of that section: lines 1–8 *(the neighbor calling the cat);* lines 9–19 *(the cat's response);* and lines 20–29 *(the author's reflections on the scene).*

Have a member of each group read his or her description. Then discuss as a class how the three sections are connected and why each is important to the structure of the poem.

Language Conventionality and Clarity

clear, direct language

Teach unfamiliar vocabulary in context.

- Applying Academic Vocabulary, p. 148

Guide students in determining pronoun referents.

- English Language Support, p. 147

Prompt students to explore the poem in collaborative discussions.

- Teacher's Edition side note, p. 148

ZOOM IN ON APPLYING ACADEMIC VOCABULARY As students read the poem, have them note any difficult words with which they are unfamiliar, such as *wheedling* (line 5), *luminous* (line 17), or *stitching* (line 27). Have students use context clues to create definitions for the words, and then check their definitions using a dictionary.

Have students replace the difficult words with more familiar synonyms and read their version aloud to a partner. Have pairs discuss how the changes in the words affect the overall tone and mood of the poem.

Knowledge Demands

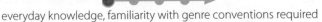

everyday knowledge, familiarity with genre conventions required

Support English Learners in understanding the cultural background of the author.

- Teacher's Edition Background note, p. 147

ZOOM IN ON BUILDING BACKGROUND KNOWLEDGE Share the facts of the poet's background. Help students recognize that the poet experienced a great deal of loss, strife, and grief and that she expresses some of this through her poetry. Encourage them to listen for traces of longing, loss, or missing someone who is gone as they listen to the poem read aloud.

Suggested Reader/Task Considerations

You might consider the following before assigning this poem to students.

- Are all students likely to be engaged by such a quiet, descriptive poem?
- Might students be confused by the unusual diction in the poem's final lines, which convey the poem's central message?

ZOOM IN ON SUPPORTING COMPREHENSION

- Read the poem aloud to students before they start to analyze it. After they have explored its meaning, read it aloud again and encourage students to listen for the musical qualities of the language, as if they are listening to a jazz composition. Discuss how the sound of the poem reinforces and enhances its meaning.
- Explain that "left me to wonder that" in line 25 is unusual phrasing that students would be less likely to see in prose writing. The more common diction would be "left me to wonder whether." The speaker is uncertain whether he or she will ever form a strong bond with another person and be able to call that person home.

Natasha Trethewey Have students read the biographical information about the author. Tell them that Trethewey's father is also a poet and a professor, originally from Canada. Because he is white and her mother was black, they had to go to Ohio to get married because in 1965, marriages between races were still illegal in Mississippi. After her parents' divorce, the young Natasha spent time in Georgia with her mother and in Louisiana with her father. She learned the realities of being a mixed-race child. While with her father, she was treated as if she were white. With her mother, she felt the prejudice still inherent in society.

Trethewey's father encouraged her to start writing at a very young age. After her mother's murder, she turned to poetry to help express her grief. Her poems also explore ideas related to the experiences that shaped her youth, including her identity as both black and white. Along with the personal elements, she incorporates historical context into her writing, often setting her poems in the past.

In addition to her volumes of poetry, she has written a nonfiction book entitled *Beyond Katrina: A Meditation on the Mississippi Gulf Coast.*

AS YOU READ Direct students to use the As You Read statement to focus their reading.

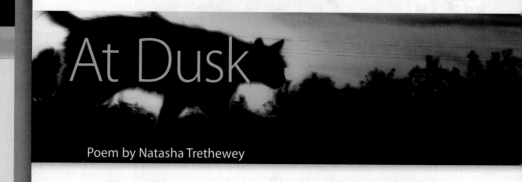

At Dusk

Poem by Natasha Trethewey

Natasha Trethewey *(b. 1966) was named United States Poet Laureate in 2012. She views her responsibility in this role as being someone who has "really got to do the work of bringing poetry to the widest audience possible." A native of Gulfport, Mississippi, Trethewey has published several collections of poetry and is a professor of English and creative writing at Emory University. Her first collection,* Domestic Work *(2000), earned her the Cave Canem Poetry Prize, awarded each year to the best first book by an African American poet. Trethewey has since won many other honors, including the Pulitzer Prize for poetry in 2007 for her book* Native Guard.

AS YOU READ Think about the decision faced by the cat in the poem, and the advantages and disadvantages of each possible course of action. Write down any questions you generate as you read the poem.

ENGLISH LANGUAGE SUPPORT

Language: Pronoun Referents Introduce the poem by clarifying the **pronoun referents.** Read aloud lines 1–8. Point out the phrase "my neighbor" and explain that sometimes the pronoun referent occurs after the pronoun.

- Then read aloud lines 9–19. Ask students what noun is replaced by *she* in these lines. *(the cat)*
- Conclude by reading aloud the last part of the poem. Have students identify the noun to which this use of the pronoun *she* refers. *(the neighbor)*

Write these other pronouns on the board: *they* (line 8); *it* (line 27). Have students work in pairs to identify the noun that each pronoun replaces. *(words; my voice)*

TEACH

CLOSE READ

Interpret Figurative Language (LINES 1–8, 9–19, 20–29)

RL 1, RL 4, L 5a

Read the poem aloud. Remind students that poets create vivid pictures through their choice of words and that these pictures help communicate meaning.

 CITE TEXT EVIDENCE Have students explain the image they see in the first eight lines. *(The speaker's neighbor is leaning out her doorway at dusk, calling her cat.)* What words does the poet use to appeal to readers' sense of hearing in these lines? *(hum, high-pitched wheedling)* Have students discuss how these specific details help them to build a picture of the speaker as well. *(The speaker is observant, perhaps lonely to be so interested in what the neighbor is doing.)*

Have students reread lines 9–19, paying attention to the words and phrases that describe the cat's actions.

B **ASK STUDENTS** why the poet chooses the word *constellation* instead of *group* or *cluster* to describe the fireflies. How does this word choice add to the image created by the phrase? *(A constellation refers to stars. This word shows how bright and magical the fireflies are to the cat.)* In contrast to the "flickering" light of the fireflies, the cat's porch has "a steady circle of light." What does the cat's home represent in this poem? *(safety, security, predictability)*

Remind students that the voice they hear in the poem is the speaker's. The poet may use the speaker to convey an attitude toward a subject.

C **ASK STUDENTS** what the phrase "trails off" suggests about the speaker's feelings when the neighbor stops calling the cat. *(The words suggest disappointment. The speaker may not want the neighbor to feel as lonely as he or she does.)*

COLLABORATIVE DISCUSSION Call on pairs to share their lists with the class. Accept all reasonable responses.

ASK STUDENTS to share any questions they generated in the course of reading and discussing the selection.

At Dusk

A
At first I think she is calling a child,
my neighbor, leaning through her doorway
at dusk, street lamps just starting to hum
the backdrop of evening. Then I hear
5   the high-pitched wheedling we send out
to animals who know only sound, not
the meanings of our words—*here here*—
nor how they sometimes fall short.

B
In another yard, beyond my neighbor's
10 sight, the cat lifts her ears, turns first
toward the voice, then back
to the constellation of fireflies flickering
near her head. It's as if she can't decide
whether to leap over the low hedge,
15 the neat row of flowers, and bound
onto the porch, into the steady circle
of light, or stay where she is: luminous
possibility—all that would keep her
away from home—flitting before her.

C
20 I listen as my neighbor's voice trails off.
She's given up calling for now, left me
to imagine her inside the house waiting,
perhaps in a chair in front of the TV,
or walking around, doing small tasks;
25 left me to wonder that I too might lift
my voice, sure of someone out there,
send it over the lines stitching here
to there, certain the sounds I make
are enough to call someone home.

COLLABORATIVE DISCUSSION Confer with a partner to discuss how the cat's situation is similar to one that a person might face. Generate a list of advantages and disadvantages to returning home versus exploring new possibilities.

APPLYING ACADEMIC VOCABULARY

generate	trace

While discussing "At Dusk," incorporate the following Collection 3 academic vocabulary words: *generate* and *trace*. Ask students what details in the poem **generate** interest in the cat. Then have them **trace** the movements of the neighbor, pointing to the lines in the poem that tell them what she is doing.

Interpret Imagery

A poem captures a moment and often tells a story using compact language. Poets use **imagery,** or descriptive words and phrases that re-create sensory experiences for the reader. They also choose words and phrases carefully to convey a certain **tone**—the attitude an author takes toward a subject; and **mood**—the feeling or atmosphere an author creates for the reader. A poem's tone might be formal or informal, serious or sarcastic. The mood might be dark and brooding,or light and energetic.

Analyzing the word choices Natasha Trethewey makes throughout "At Dusk" will help you see the overall impact that her choices have on the poem's tone, mood, and meaning. This chart can help guide your interpretation of the poem's imagery.

Lines from Poem	Interpretation
"street lamps just starting to hum / the backdrop of evening"	This image establishes the scene. • What does the poet want readers to see and hear? • What mood is created by the darkening sky?
"the cat lifts her ears, turns first / toward the voice, then back / to the constellation of fireflies flickering / near her head. It's as if she can't decide/ whether to leap over the low hedge, / . . .or stay where she is"	The speaker imagines what the cat might be thinking or feeling. • Why might the cat have trouble deciding what to do? • What do you learn about the speaker by the thoughts and feelings she assigns to the cat?
"She's given up calling for now, left me / to imagine her inside the house waiting, / perhaps in a chair in front of the TV"	The speaker watches the neighbor's reaction. • What feeling does the image of someone giving up and settling in front of the TV convey?
"certain the sounds I make / are enough to call someone home"	The poem ends with the speaker's thoughts about what he or she has observed. • What is the mood of the last line of the poem? • Whom might the speaker want to call home?

TEACH

CLOSE READ

Interpret Figurative Language

Display a two-column chart with the headings "Sight" and "Sound." Have students identify the examples of imagery in the poem and indicate which sense the words and phrases appeal to. After completing the chart, discuss how these words and phrases help to build the atmosphere or mood of the poem. Then have students indicate how the examples help them infer the tone of the poem.

Strategies for Annotation 📝 🗒 *Annotate it!*

Interpret Figurative Language

Encourage students to use their eBook annotation tools to do the following:
- Highlight in blue words and phrases that appeal to the sense of sight.
- Highlight in pink words and phrases that appeal to the sense of sound. *(Sample answers: line 5: "high–pitched wheedling"; line 20: "as my neighbor's voice trails off")*

ASK STUDENTS which images stand out in their minds after reading the poem. Why?

near her head. It's as if she can't decide
whether to leap over the low hedge,
the neat row of flowers, and bound
onto the porch, into the steady circle
of light, or stay where she is: luminous

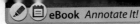
PRACTICE & APPLY

Analyzing the Text

RL 1, RL 4, L 5a

Possible answers:

1. The speaker might be referring to the difficulties that people sometimes have in communicating with each other.

2. The cat's preoccupation with the fireflies in lines 11–14 and 18–19 delays its return. The fireflies represent a "luminous possibility."

3. The speaker seems to be alone. He or she doesn't mention other people, focuses on the neighbor, and yearns "to call someone home" (line 29).

4. The speaker relates to the idea that they both seem to be alone. The speaker imagines the neighbor's response to the unheeded calls and then considers reaching out to someone, too.

5. The images of night ("street lamps just starting to hum the backdrop of evening," "the constellation of fireflies flickering near her head"); loneliness ("I listen as my neighbor's voice trails off... [she's] left me to imagine her inside the house waiting..."); and possibilities ("luminous possibility—all that would keep her away from home—flitting before her") establish a bittersweet tone of longing.

6. Dusk is a time of transition, and the speaker implies that he or she is looking for some kind of change. Because the speaker has a wish to "call someone home," perhaps he or she hopes to reconcile with another person or to end his or her loneliness.

Analyzing the Text

RL 1, RL 4, SL 4, L 5a

Cite Text Evidence   Support your responses with evidence from the selection.

1. **Interpret** The speaker talks about the cat not hearing meanings of our words "nor how they sometimes fall short" (line 8). What might this mean?

2. **Interpret** What might keep the cat from returning home? What might the image of a "constellation of fireflies flickering" represent to the speaker?

3. **Infer** Judging from the speaker's observations, is he or she alone or with people? Support your inference with details from the poem.

4. **Analyze** What connection does the speaker have to the neighbor at this moment? How does the speaker feel when the neighbor gives up on calling the cat?

5. **Analyze** What is the tone of this poem? What words and phrases convey the tone?

6. **Draw Conclusions** Explain the significance of the title "At Dusk."

PERFORMANCE TASK

Speaking Activity: Poetry Reading The language of poetry is meant to be heard as well as read. Get together with a partner or small group to read "At Dusk" aloud.

- Sit across from one another; or, if you are in a small group, sit in a circle facing one another.
- Take turns reading the poem aloud. Practice reading with feeling, emphasizing key words and phrases.

- After your reading, discuss what words and phrase stand out to you when you hear them read aloud.
- Write a brief summary of what you learned by reading the poem aloud.

Assign this performance task.

PERFORMANCE TASK

RL 4, SL 4, L 5a

Speaking Activity: Poetry Reading Encourage students to experiment with pitch, tempo, and volume as they read the poem. As students listen, have them record words and phrases that stand out to them. Explain that their summaries of the reading might state, for example, that the mood of the poem became clearer when they heard it read aloud, or that hearing the poem helped them better appreciate the meaning or beauty of certain phrases.

Analyze Language in Poetry

RL 4

TEACH

Explain to students that a poem's **theme** is the meaning or message about life that the **poet** wants to communicate through both the literal and figurative language he or she uses. In a poem, the **speaker** is the voice that "talks" to the reader, a character similar to a narrator in a short story or novel. The speaker of a poem is not necessarily the poet. For example, in "At Dusk," Natasha Trethewey may or may not have experienced hearing a woman call her cat.

To learn more about the differences between a speaker in a poem and the poet who wrote the poem, a reader can make **inferences,** or logical guesses based on language within the poem. Present these strategies to help students consider the speaker and the poet of "At Dusk."

- In this poem, the speaker is represented by the pronoun "I." Note details about this speaker, such as where he or she is in relation to the action that is being described. Consider the speaker's attitude toward the cat's choices and the neighbor's actions. What language conveys the speaker's attitudes?

- Identify words and phrases that convey the poet's attitude toward the speaker, the characters in the poem, and the reader.

COLLABORATIVE DISCUSSION

Have students work in small groups to apply the strategies and draw some conclusions about the speaker's and the poet's attitudes. Ask: How are they different? In what ways are they alike? Have students list the similarities and differences in their attitudes in a Comparison-Contrast Chart. Have each group share its conclusions with the rest of the class.

Interpret Figurative Language

RL 4, L 5a

RETEACH

Review the term **imagery.** Tell students that imagery is not restricted to poetry. Other writers also use the device to help their readers see, feel, taste, smell, or hear sensations. Have students identify the imagery in this paragraph and the sense to which each example appeals.

The unoiled hinges of the trunk lid shrieked as I slowly lifted it. My heart slammed against my chest wall. Would I find the glittering piles of golden coins that my uncle had promised? Or, would I find yellowed piles of crumbling musty newspapers, as my doubting aunt had predicted? My breath caught in my throat. I gasped. The mystery was solved. (sound: unoiled hinges . . . shrieked, gasped; sight: slowly lifted it, glittering piles of golden coins; touch: heart slammed, breath caught in my throat; sight, touch, and smell: yellow piles of crumbling musty newspapers)

Remind students that imagery contributes to the mood, or atmosphere. Ask them how they feel as they read this passage. *(suspenseful, excited)* Review tone and have students describe the writer's attitude as revealed through words and phrases. *(hopeful)*

 LEVEL UP TUTORIALS Assign the following *Level Up* tutorial: **Figurative Language**

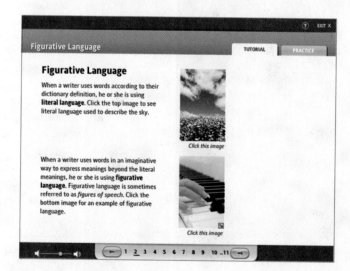

INDEPENDENT READING

Hand out copies of a short poem. Ask students to highlight imagery and discuss in small groups how it brings out key ideas and helps to develop mood and reveal the poem's tone.

Poems About Family

My Ceremony For Taking | ## The Stayer

Poem by Lara Mann | **Poem by Virgil Suárez**

Why These Texts

A poem often presents a lot of information in a small package. The two poems that students will read here are both very short, and the authors have chosen their words carefully to convey mood and meaning. With the help of the close-reading questions, students will analyze these word choices and interpret the figurative language in each poem. This close reading will help students analyze the impact of word choices on each poem's meaning and tone.

Background Have students read the background and discuss the Dylan Thomas quote. Then have them read the biographical information about Lara Mann and Virgil Suárez. Point out that both poets have had to balance the cultures that they have been part of. Ask students to predict what each poem might be about, based on the biographical information and the titles of the poems.

AS YOU READ Ask students to pay attention to the authors' word choices in each poem. In what ways do the words they choose help the author set the tone and mood and deepen the poem's meaning?

Standards Support

- cite strong and thorough textual evidence
- interpret figurative language used in a text
- analyze the cumulative impact of specific word choices on meaning and tone

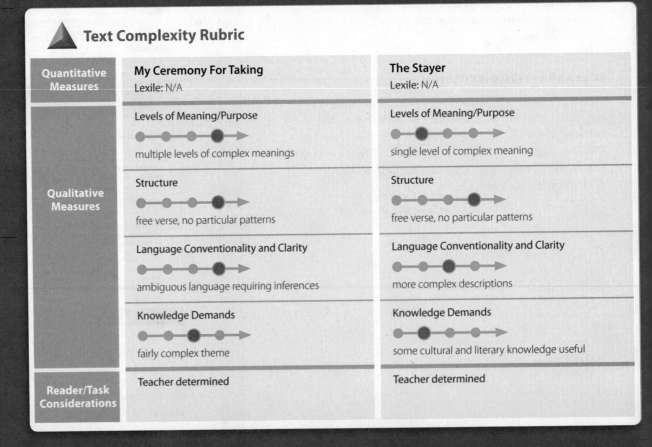

Text Complexity Rubric

	My Ceremony For Taking	The Stayer
Quantitative Measures	Lexile: N/A	Lexile: N/A
Qualitative Measures	**Levels of Meaning/Purpose** — multiple levels of complex meanings	**Levels of Meaning/Purpose** — single level of complex meaning
	Structure — free verse, no particular patterns	**Structure** — free verse, no particular patterns
	Language Conventionality and Clarity — ambiguous language requiring inferences	**Language Conventionality and Clarity** — more complex descriptions
	Knowledge Demands — fairly complex theme	**Knowledge Demands** — some cultural and literary knowledge useful
Reader/Task Considerations	Teacher determined	Teacher determined

Strategies for CLOSE READING

Interpret Figurative Language

Students should read these poems carefully all the way through. Close-reading questions at the bottom of the page will help them analyze the word choices the authors make. As they read, students should jot down comments or questions about the text in the margins.

WHEN STUDENTS STRUGGLE . . .

To help students analyze "My Ceremony For Taking" and "The Stayer," have them work in small groups to fill out a chart like the one shown below.

CITE TEXT EVIDENCE For practice in interpreting figurative language and its effects on a poem's tone, mood, and meaning, ask students to interpret text examples from the poems in the chart.

Words from the Poems	Interpretation
"burned my family's death scaffold"	utterly destroyed the family with finality
"birth dirt"	a small amount of dirt from the place where one was born
"a lock . . . pressed into the dirt I took for payment, to leave part of myself"	the speaker pulls out a lock of her hair and pushes it into the dirt she has taken
"light, the way it darted through holes in the tin roof"	beams of light shine through the holes in the roof
"motes danced in the shaft of white light"	The dust sparkled in the light in the shack.
"the meaning of stay"	Staying is more important than emptiness.

Poems About Family **150c**

Background *Poems about family often give us insights not only into the author's life and upbringing, but also into our own. As you read the two poems selected here, think of these lines written by the poet Dylan Thomas: "You can tear a poem apart to see what makes it tick . . . You're back with the mystery of having been moved by words. The best craftsmanship always leaves holes and gaps . . . so that something that is not in the poem can creep, crawl, flash or thunder in."*

Poems About Family

My Ceremony For Taking	. . . .	Lara Mann
The Stayer	. . . .	Virgil Suárez

Lara Mann *was born in Kansas, and is a member of the Choctaw Nation of Oklahoma. She is of English, Irish, Choctaw, French, German, Scottish, Spanish, Cherokee, Welsh, and Mohawk descent. Common themes in her work include the integration of both Native American and American culture and exposing the inaccurate stereotypes that many Americans assign to Native Americans.*

Virgil Suárez *By the time Virgil Suárez was twelve years old, his family had moved across the ocean twice—first from Cuba to Spain and then from Spain to the United States. These childhood experiences continue to influence the predominant themes of Suárez's works— family ties, immigration, and exile. He draws upon his own memories of people and places for his work, and credits his family for providing him with such an interesting array of characters. He notes, "I write about my life, and my life informs my writing."*

57

1. **READ ▶** As you read lines 1–24, begin to collect and cite text evidence.

   • Underline words and phrases that have similar meanings.
   • Circle examples of figurative language.
   • In the margin, write your interpretation of lines 1–5.

3. **READ ▶** As you read lines 1–34 of "The Stayer," collect and cite text evidence.

   • Circle reasons for Chicho staying in Cuba.
   • In the margin, explain why Chicho is called "crazy."
   • Underline figurative language, or descriptive words, that create tone.

My Ceremony For Taking
Lara Mann

The speaker doesn't know what to do now that her family has been ended by words of hurt.

Ⓐ No one told me how it should be, these steps
for taking. Some things I know without being told.
The words told to me ended my family,
the words I told burned my family's death scaffold;
5 those things we say when we are hurt, to hurt.

I wanted to take pieces of my ancestor's
homes with me, the way some homelands are sacred.
The way some carry their birth dirt for protection.
But these locations are revered, and for me,
10 the taking was blasphemous.

She feels split in half because her family is being torn apart.

Ⓑ My parents split, and I felt
absolutely halved, though what was left of me
was unclear. I needed a ceremony.
It had to require pain,
15 a sacrifice. It had to be missed.

That summer, when we went, my dad and I,
back to Alabama and Mississippi
to try to fix our **fissured** selves.
I pulled out hair many times.
20 Choctaws were known for hair: long, thick, honor-banner, I gave of myself. My hair was my thanks;
parts of me pulled out, white-root waving; a lock,
not just a strand, pressed into the dirt I took
for payment, to leave part of myself.

fissure:
a narrow opening or a crack

2. **◀ REREAD** Reread lines 11–24 of "My Ceremony For Taking." In the margin, explain why the speaker feels "split."

The Stayer
Virgil Suárez

Simply, my uncle Chicho stayed
   back in Cuba, against the family's
advice, because everyone left

   and he chose to stay, and this act
5 of staying marked him as "crazy"
   with most of the men, and he stayed

there in a shack behind my aunt's
   clapboard house, sat in the dark
of most days in the middle

10 of the packed-dirt floor and nodded
Ⓒ at the insistence of light, the way
   it darted through holes in the tin

roof where the rain drummed
   like the gallop of spooked horses.
15 This is where he was born, he chanted

   under his breath to no one, why should
Ⓓ he leave, live in perpetual longing
   within exile? He learned long ago

to count the passing of time
20 in how **motes** danced in the shaft
of white light, the *chicharras*[1] echoed

   their trill against the emptiness
of life, against the wake of resistance
   in this place he knew as a child,

He's called "crazy" because he stayed in Cuba when everyone else left.

motes:
specks of dust

[1] **chicharras:** cicadas, insects that produce a loud buzzing noise.

1. **READ AND CITE TEXT EVIDENCE** Tell students that lines 1–5 of "My Ceremony For Taking" define the situation in the poem.

   Ⓐ **ASK STUDENTS** what the speaker expresses in the first two lines. *She says that she knows what steps she will take, even though nobody told her.* **What has happened?** *She is told that her family is breaking up.*

2. **REREAD AND CITE TEXT EVIDENCE**

   Ⓑ **ASK STUDENTS** to cite text from lines 11–24 that refers to being "split." *Students should cite: "My parents split" (line 11); "I felt absolutely halved" (lines 11–12); "to fix our fissured selves" (line 18); "parts of me pulled out" (line 22).*

   Critical Vocabulary: fissure (line 18) Have students share their definitions of *fissure*. Ask them why the author chose this word. *Fissure means "a narrow opening or a crack," describing the shock the speaker feels.*

3. **READ AND CITE TEXT EVIDENCE** Remind students that figurative language includes similes, metaphors, personification, and imagery.

   Ⓒ **ASK STUDENTS** to describe the tone the figurative language creates in the poem. *Students should note that most of the figurative language involves inanimate objects coming to life. These images highlight the emptiness of life in Cuba. The "motes danced" and the light "darted" describe the stillness of Chicho's life.*

   Critical Vocabulary: motes (line 20) Have students share definitions of *motes*. Point out that the poet chose a short and accurate word rather than a phrase to maintain the rhythm of the line and poem.

   FOR ELL STUDENTS Explain that *clapboard* (line 8) is thin wood that is used to cover the side of a house.

25   as a man, *un hombre*, bend against the idea
           of leaving his country, call him loco.[2]
       What nobody counted on was that answers

           come on to those who sit in the
           quiet of their own countries, tranquil
30   in the **penumbra**, intent on hearing the song

penumbra:
*a place of
partial light*

       of a *tomegüín*[3] as it calls for a mate
           to come nest in the shrubs out there,
       while in here, he witnesses how light

       fills the emptiness with the meaning of stay.

       [2] **loco:** crazy.
       [3] **tomegüín:** a small bird native to Cuba.

4.   ◀ REREAD   Reread "The Stayer." How does the phrase "live in perpetual
       longing within exile" reflect the overall meaning of the poem?

Chicho chooses to stay in Cuba because he was born there and has
history there. However, he lives in exile without his family and
therefore is constantly "longing" for those who left.

SHORT RESPONSE

Cite Text Evidence   In what ways does each poet use figurative language to
communicate a large or complex idea? **Cite evidence from the text.**

In "My Ceremony For Taking," the speaker uses figurative language
to describe how bereft she feels after her parents' split. Using
language such as "The way some carry their birth dirt for
protection" and "My hair was my thanks," she communicates her
longing for a ceremony to mend her broken self. In "The Stayer," the
author uses figurative language to describe the light and sounds
("rain drummed like the gallop of spooked horses") and to evoke the
sense of "longing within exile" that affects both the speaker and his
uncle.

60

4.   **REREAD AND CITE TEXT EVIDENCE**

Ⓓ   ASK STUDENTS to explain in their own words the meaning
of *exile* and *perpetual longing* in lines 17–18. Exile *is living away
from one's own country.* Perpetual longing *is a yearning or desire
that is continuous.*

Critical Vocabulary: penumbra (line 30) Have students share
their definitions of *penumbra*—an area between light and
shadow. You might want to point out that the word has a Latin
root, meaning "almost shadow."

SHORT RESPONSE

Cite Text Evidence   Students' responses should include text
evidence that supports their positions. They should:

• identify the central idea in each poem.
• cite examples of figurative language.
• explain how these examples support each central idea.

TO CHALLENGE STUDENTS . . .

Students have been interpreting figurative language in two
poems. They will now create their own examples of figurative
language.

ASK STUDENTS to work in pairs to write a couplet that includes
original figurative language.

If necessary, you might get them started by having them write
similes, comparisons, metaphors, or imagery to complete the
following:

• as lonely as . . . *possibilities: the last dodo; a king; the moon*
• his heart felt like . . . *possibilities: lightning; a stone; porridge*
• my home is . . . *possibilities: everywhere; the Internet; empty*

DIG DEEPER

With the class, return to the Short Response. Have groups share
their responses to the question.

ASK STUDENTS about the word choices the authors use in their
poems.

• Why did the subject of "My Ceremony For Taking" need a
  ceremony? *She felt "fissured" and wanted to be whole.* Why did
  she leave her hair in the dirt? *She left part of herself in her old
  home and took some ancestral dirt in return.*
• Would the uncle in "The Stayer" have been happier if he had
  left Cuba? *No, he cannot bear the idea of leaving his homeland.*
  How does he keep himself content in his shack? *He wonders at
  the play of the light, the sounds of the rain, insects, and birds, and
  enjoys being at home.*

ASK STUDENTS to return to their Short Response answer and
revise it based on the class discussion.

MEDIA **Count on Us**

Public Service Announcement from the Corporation for National and Community Service

Why This Text?

Students frequently encounter advertisements, including public service announcements, in their daily lives. This lesson examines how to analyze the purpose and development of ideas in a public service announcement about the volunteer activities of the Corporation for National and Community Service.

Key Learning Objective: The student will be able to analyze the purpose and development of ideas in a public service announcement.

RI 1 Cite textual evidence.
RI 2 Determine a central idea and analyze its development.
RI 5 Analyze how ideas are developed.
RI 6 Determine an author's purpose.
W 6 Use technology to produce writing products.
W 7 Conduct research to answer a question or solve a problem.
SL 3 Evaluate point of view, reasoning, and evidence.

▲ Text Complexity Rubric

Quantitative Measures	**Count on Us** Lexile: N/A
Qualitative Measures	**Levels of Meaning/Purpose** more than one purpose; implied, easily identified from context
	Structure implicit problem-solution text structure
	Language Conventionality and Clarity literal, accessible language
	Knowledge Demands everyday knowledge required
Reader/Task Considerations	• Teacher determined • Vary by individual reader and type of text • See the Text X-Ray for suggested Reader/Task Considerations.

English Language Support
Before teaching, use the Text X-Ray below for an overview of the text's complexity. The Text X-Ray and the supports and scaffolds in the Teacher's Edition will help you guide students of different skill levels.

Meaning Making

Language Development

Effective Expression

Content Knowledge

Foundational Skills

Text Complexity: Qualitative Measures

Levels of Meaning/Purpose

more than one purpose; implied, easily identified from context

Help students determine an author's purpose.
- Teacher's Edition side notes, pp. 151, 152
- English Language Support, p. 151
- Analyze Purpose and Development of Ideas, p. 152

To teach evaluating persuasive techniques, see
- Evaluate a Speaker's Reasoning, p. 152a

To reteach analyzing purpose, see
- Analyze Purpose and Development of Ideas, p. 152a

▶ *Use It!* **Interactive Whiteboard Lesson:** Evaluating Arguments

Level Up Tutorial: Persuasive Techniques

ZOOM IN ON **DETERMINING PURPOSE** Remind students that the **purpose** of a PSA is usually to encourage people to take action. After students have watched the video at least once and understand the basic ideas and facts, have pairs complete these sentences:

- The **audience** (the group of people expected to watch the ad) is _____.
- The ad's creators want the audience to learn _____.
- The ad tries to make the audience feel _____.
- The ad's creators hope the audience will take action by _____.

Invite pairs to share their responses in a class discussion of the PSA's purpose.

Structure

implicit problem-solution text structure

Help students analyze development of ideas.
- Teacher's Edition side notes, pp. 151, 152
- English Language Support, p. 151
- Analyze Purpose and Development of Ideas, p. 152

ZOOM IN ON **ANALYZING STRUCTURE** Tell students that the PSA can be described as having a **problem-solution structure:** it tells a story in which people face problems and then find ways to solve them. Divide the class into three groups and assign each group one element to analyze—audio, text, or images. Have groups watch the video, pausing to discuss what they notice about their element. Then reconvene the class to have groups report their findings and discuss how the three elements work together to present problems and solutions.

Language Conventionality and Clarity

literal, accessible language

Teach unfamiliar vocabulary in context.

ZOOM IN ON **PREVIEWING VOCABULARY** Before students view the PSA, tell them that the video includes no spoken words. Then share the following text, which they will see in the PSA:

> During times of crisis, moments of overwhelming destruction and unbearable despair, where there is undeniable need before, during, and after a disaster, National Service is there. The need has never been greater. Count on us.

Make sure students understand the meaning of the sentences. Then have them watch the video, and lead a discussion about how the images and music support the text.

Knowledge Demands

everyday knowledge required

Support English Learners in understanding the history and social reach of this organization.

- Teacher's Edition Background note, p. 151

ZOOM IN ON **BUILDING BACKGROUND KNOWLEDGE** Explain that the Corporation for National and Community Service (CNCS) does more than just help communities recover from disasters. It has six focus areas: disaster services, economic opportunity, education, environmental stewardship, healthy futures, and veterans and military families. It was founded in 1993 for the purpose of helping Americans give back to their communities and to the nation.

Suggested Reader/Task Considerations

You might consider the following before assigning this public service announcement to students.

- Do students live in an area that has experienced a disaster?
- Might this PSA motivate students to want to investigate volunteering opportunities?

ZOOM IN ON **SUPPORTING COMPREHENSION**

- If students have experienced a natural disaster such as one of those shown in the PSA, encourage them to talk about relief efforts their community received and to compare the information presented in the PSA with their own experiences.
- Encourage students to research volunteer organizations that accept participants their age. Discuss potential pros and cons of getting involved in AmeriCorps and/or Teach For America after high school. (These programs have a minimum age requirement of 18.)

CLOSE READ

Background Have students read the background information. Tell them that the Corporation for National and Community Service (CNCS) has been in existence since 1993. Some of its more well-known programs are Senior Corps and AmeriCorps, which train volunteers to provide a variety of services in addition to those shown in this public service announcement, which was produced in 2011.

AS YOU VIEW Direct students to use the As You View directions to focus their viewing.

Determine Author's Purpose and Analyze Development of Ideas

RI 5, RI 6

Tell students that **purpose** is the reason a public service announcement (PSA) is produced. PSAs share the purpose of persuading the audience to do something. A more specific purpose can be inferred by analyzing a PSA's intended audience, message, and call to action.

ASK STUDENTS to identify the audience for this PSA and discuss how it relates to the purpose(s). *(The audience is generally anyone living in the United States; more specifically, it is people who have suffered or might suffer from natural disasters and people who want to help during disasters. The purposes are to reassure people that they can count on the CNCS and to encourage people to volunteer.)*

Explain that the PSA's **structure** is designed to achieve its purpose. A PSA presents the elements of music, text, and visuals in a particular order and combination to achieve the greatest effect.

CITE TEXT EVIDENCE Ask students to review the PSA and explain how shifts in music and visuals demonstrate the structure and contribute to purpose. *(Visuals closely match words. Images of disaster, such as flooding in New Orleans and Iowa, are followed by images of people in need; these are followed by images of volunteers helping people. At the phrase "National Service Is There," the music becomes more upbeat and hopeful.)*

COLLABORATIVE DISCUSSION Have students write down their ideas about other PSAs before meeting with their group to discuss the questions.

ASK STUDENTS to share any questions they generated in the course of viewing the selection.

Background *A public service announcement (PSA) is a message usually produced for television or radio about a topic or issue of interest to the public. The purpose of a PSA is to raise public awareness and encourage the audience to take action. Media and news organizations distribute public service announcements at no charge. This particular announcement is for the Corporation for National and Community Service, a federal agency that provides support to volunteer organizations and to individual volunteers around the country.*

MEDIA ANALYSIS

Count On Us

Public Service Announcement
from the Corporation for National and Community Service

AS YOU VIEW Pay attention to how the visuals, music, and text work together to send a message. Write down any questions you generate during viewing.

Image Credits: (c) ©Jerry McCrea/Star Ledger/Corbis

COLLABORATIVE DISCUSSION In a small group, discuss how this public service announcement compares to others you have seen or heard. What are some common topics or issues that PSAs try to bring to public attention? What kinds of visuals are used to convey ideas?

Count On Us **151**

ENGLISH LANGUAGE SUPPORT

Analyze Purpose and Development of Ideas Because this PSA contains no voiceover, students can focus primarily on what they see. Have students watch the video at least twice to compare the messages they receive from the different elements.

- For the first viewing, have students concentrate on the images and the music. Ask students to explain the message that they received from the PSA based on these two elements.
- For the second viewing, encourage students to pay attention primarily to the words on the screen. Pause or replay the video as needed to allow students to take in the words and clarify understanding. Invite students to share how the words add to their understanding of the purpose of the PSA and the ideas that it conveys.

PRACTICE & APPLY

Analyze Purpose and Development of Ideas

RI 5, RI 6

Discuss the common elements of PSAs. Point out that a PSA uses visuals, music, and text to appeal to logic and emotion. Note that text is part of the logical presentation that conveys the central idea.

Discuss with students the reasons why emotion is such an important part of PSAs. *(because the purpose is to persuade the audience to take action, often to help someone in some way)* Have students explain how other types of advertisements are different from PSAs and tell why they are different. *(Students may say other types of advertisements focus on personal benefits gained from buying something. They appeal to different motivations than PSAs do.)*

Analyzing the Media

RI 2, RI 5, RI 6

Possible answers:

1. *The PSA combines images of people in trouble with music to elicit the viewer's sympathy or empathy. The images help viewers imagine themselves in a similar situation, so they feel inclined to help.*

2. *The visuals, text, and music work together coherently. Each set of images relates to the text that precedes it. "During Times of Crisis" is followed by images of crises, accompanied by dramatic music. Then the focus shifts to images of people helping in disasters. The music is more energetic and the text is bigger and bolder, energizing the viewer.*

3. *The central idea of the PSA is that many people are affected by natural disasters and National Service volunteers are there to help. The purpose is to show the need for volunteers. The "call to action" is to encourage people to volunteer to help. Showing images of volunteers in all age groups includes a broad demographic in the call to action.*

eBook *Annotate It!*

Analyze Purpose and Development of Ideas

RI 5, RI 6

A **public service announcement** (PSA) is a type of advertisement. Advertisements are structured to achieve a purpose. A television commercial, for example, is usually created to encourage people to buy something. A PSA's purpose is to encourage the audience to take action, such as by donating goods and services to victims of a natural disaster. PSAs have these common elements:

clear and concise message	message or central idea is clear even without the audio
logical presentation	visuals, text, and music are arranged logically to support each other in conveying the central idea
emotional hook	visuals and music evoke, or bring forth, particular emotions to engage the audience
critical information	important information is included, such as the name of the organization or important statistics
call to action	viewers understand what the announcement wants them to do

Analyzing the Media

RI 2, RI 5,
RI 6, W 6, SL 4

Cite Text Evidence   Support your responses with evidence from the selection.

1. **Draw Conclusions** How is this public service announcement structured to "hook" the viewer emotionally?

2. **Analyze** Is this PSA organized logically? Do the visuals, text, and music work together to send a coherent message? Cite specific scenes to support your answer.

3. **Identify** Explain the central idea and purpose of this announcement. What "call to action" does it express to viewers?

PERFORMANCE TASK

Media Activity: Informative Announcement Create a public service announcement in which you send a message and call for action.

- Create a PSA to raise awareness of a school issue. Generate a list of possible issues.
- Use video, audio, or a poster format to produce your PSA.

- Remember to give your audience specific details and organize your visuals so that the message and call to action is clear.
- Share your PSA with your class.

Assign this
performance task.

PERFORMANCE TASK

W 6, SL 4

Media Activity: Informative Announcement Begin by brainstorming a list of potential topics. Then organize students into pairs or small groups based on shared interests. Encourage students to consider a format that will effectively convey their message and call to action. See page 152a for suggestions on how to help students select a format and plan the presentation.

Evaluate a Speaker's Reasoning

TEACH

Remind students that the visuals and music in the "Count on Us" PSA persuade viewers to take action by appealing to their emotions. Explain that appeal to emotion is just one of a variety of persuasive techniques used in PSAs and in advertisements.

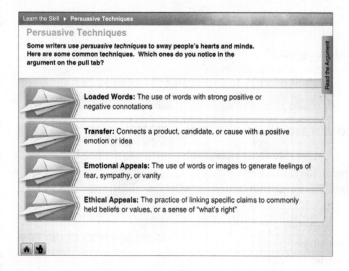

PRACTICE AND APPLY

Choose an advertisement from a print or media source and have students identify its purpose. Then have them analyze the persuasive techniques used to achieve that purpose. Suggest that they consider the following questions about the ad:

- Does it use loaded language?
- Does it appeal to the desire to belong, or fit in?
- Does it appeal to ethics, or doing what is right?

After students analyze the ad, have them discuss whether the persuasive techniques used would be appropriate for a PSA.

Analyze Purpose and Development of Ideas

RETEACH

Remind students that writers usually have one or more of the following purposes for writing: to inform or explain, to persuade, to entertain, or to express thoughts or feelings. The elements that contribute to the structure of a PSA or an ad are carefully chosen to achieve the intended purpose or purposes.

Replay "Count on Us" and guide students to analyze why each of the following elements is included in it:

- Music *(to create two different moods, appeal to emotions)*
- Images of natural disasters *(to show the problem or need)*
- Images of people suffering from natural disasters *(to show the human face of disasters, appeal to emotions)*
- Images of volunteers helping before, during, and after disasters *(to show that volunteers provide help in times of disaster; to create a feeling of hope)*
- Images of people wearing different kinds of T-shirts *(to show that volunteers are drawn from many different groups)*
- Statistics *(to provide evidence and facts that show the concrete effects of volunteer work; to appeal to reason)*
- Repetition of certain words, such as "Count on Us" *(to emphasize the main message: that people can count on the volunteers)*
- The name of the organization and the website *(to let people know who is sponsoring the message and where to find more information)*
- Conclude by asking students to discuss how these elements work together to achieve the specific purposes of the PSA *(to show how volunteers help in the face of natural disasters and to encourage people to volunteer)*

INDEPENDENT READING

Students can practice the skill by working in small groups to analyze an advertisement in print, online, or on television. Encourage them to look at each element and notice how it appeals to reason or emotions and to infer the specific purpose of the advertisement.

THE BONDS BETWEEN US

The FYI site provides links to online articles from a variety of magazines and newspapers. Help students choose a few articles to read to further their exploration of the topic The Bonds Between Us.

ADDITIONAL TEXTS BY COLLECTION

Suggest students read the following:

- "To My Dear and Loving Husband" by Anne Bradstreet
- "Sonnet 18" by William Shakespeare
- "On My First Son" by Ben Jonson
- "Sonnet 43" by Elizabeth Barrett Browning

Have students pick a music style and rewrite one selection in that style. Students can record their performances and post them on a class website.

NOVELWISE

Students can unlock the power of novels with this unique resource. Help students read through longer works with these tips:

- Find a Book
- Before You Read
- As You Read
- After You Read

Each book includes introductory material, worksheets, graphic organizers, and discussion guides.

NONFICTION CONNECTIONS

Suggest that students increase their reading of informational texts. The nonfiction connections include

- speeches
- diaries
- true-life accounts
- newspaper articles
- political cartoons

Creating an Independent Reading Program

DAILY SCHEDULED TIME

Daily scheduled time for independent reading allows students to finish the books they select and helps them develop good independent reading habits.

- Schedule a time when students can read quietly, such as before the bell rings or at the end of class. Try to keep the same time each day.
- Ask students to pick a reasonable length of time to read. Appoint a student to monitor the time.

CLEAR EXPECTATIONS FOR IN-CLASS AND OUTSIDE-OF-CLASS READING

Clear expectations will help students develop good lifelong reading habits.

- Work with students to create and post rules for silent reading time.
- Work with families to establish a homework reading policy. Enlist parents' help in having students read each day. Encourage them to read with their students. Give them a progress report to fill out.
- Hold reading contests throughout the school year. Start with easier tasks. As the year goes on, make the contests more challenging.
- Partner with librarians to help students select books and fill out progress reports.

Write a Fictional Narrative

The texts in this collection focus on our connections to family, friends, pets, and community. Look back at "When Mr. Pirzada Came to Dine" and the other fiction and poetry in this collection. How do these texts use narrative techniques to explore interpersonal connections? Write a narrative that shows how we connect with others.

An effective fictional narrative

- begins by introducing a setting, a narrator, and a main character
- has an engaging plot with a central conflict
- provides a clear sequence of events
- uses a variety of narrative techniques
- includes sensory language and descriptive details
- ends with a logical and satisfying resolution to the conflict

W 3a–e Write narratives.
W 4 Produce clear and coherent writing.
W 5 Develop and strengthen writing.
W 9a–b Draw evidence from literary or informational texts.
SL 1a–d Participate in collaborative discussions.

> **PLAN**

Identify Narrative Techniques Reread your chosen texts, taking notes on narrative techniques. Ask yourself:

- What point of view does each author use to tell the story? Identify the narrator as first person or third person.
- How does the author reveal characters' personalities? Find examples of dialogue or descriptive details.
- How does the author allow important ideas to emerge through the text without stating them directly? For example, what details does the author use to reveal a character's feelings?
- How does the author control pacing? Look for passages with descriptive detail that makes readers slow down. Contrast them with passages in which events take place very quickly.
- How does the author convey themes through the story?

Mentor Text See how this example from "When Mr. Pirzada Came to Dine" reveals that Mr. Pirzada is upset about the news without saying so directly.

> " An Indian official announced that unless the world helped to relieve the burden of East Pakistani refugees, India would have to go to war against Pakistan. . . . The knife slipped from Mr. Pirzada's hand and made a gash dipping toward the base of the pumpkin. "

myNotebook

Use the notebook in your eBook to record examples of narrative techniques in the selections, such as dialogue, pacing, description, and plot lines.

ACADEMIC VOCABULARY

As you discuss narrative techniques with your group, try to use these words.

capacity
confer
emerge
generate
trace

Collection Performance Task A   **153**

Introduce students to the Performance Task by reading the introductory paragraph with them and reviewing the criteria for an effective fictional narrative. Remind students that a fictional narrative tells a made-up story, but its characters must be believable so that readers can relate to them.

> **PLAN**

IDENTIFY NARRATIVE TECHNIQUES

Narrative techniques appear in three selections in this collection: "When Mr. Pirzada Came to Dine," "The Grasshopper and the Bell Cricket" and "At Dusk." Suggest that students recall their favorite parts of each one. If they found the characters or the plot in one selection especially memorable, have them review the text to find out why. The list of questions can help them focus on specific narrative techniques.

View It!

Professional Development Podcast:

Writing Narratives at the Secondary Level

WHEN STUDENTS STRUGGLE . . .

Identify Narrative Techniques As a group, review the Mentor Text example. Ask students why it might be better to show a how a character feels rather than tell the reader directly. (*Possible answer: It makes the narrative more interesting, and it helps the reader identify with the character.*) Review other narrative techniques that students might find in the texts.

Then have students work with a partner to identify at least three examples of each narrative technique in the collection texts. Have them note the technique, title, and page and line numbers for each example. Encourage them to refer to these notes as they write their narratives.

PERFORMANCE TASK A

PLAN

BRAINSTORM

Suggest that as students review their notes, they make connections between ideas that may have started out separately—for example, a character from one story idea and a conflict from a different one. As they narrow down their choices, have them consider which settings and events they can write about in enough detail to be realistic.

PLAN

GET ORGANIZED

When students have completed their outlines or story maps, encourage them to meet with partners to discuss their ideas. Partners should give constructive feedback about the basic structure of the plot, such as whether the sequence of events is clear and whether the conflict is resolved in a logical way.

PRODUCE

DRAFT YOUR NARRATIVE

Suggest that, as they draft, students imagine they are telling their story to a friend. While using their outlines or story maps for reference, they should let the narrative unfold naturally. They may find themselves adding an extra scene or two in order to clarify connections between characters and events.

Have a Group Discussion Discuss your analysis of narrative techniques in a group with two other classmates. Each classmate will present his or her reflections on one text.

- Take turns presenting your analyses.
- Take notes on the points your classmates raise and questions you might ask. Answer questions from your classmates respectfully.
- After all three texts have been presented, evaluate the narrative techniques used in each text. Which techniques were effective?
- Decide which narrative techniques to use in your own story.

Interactive Lessons
To help you plan your narrative, complete the following lesson:
· Narrative Techniques

Brainstorm Use a web diagram or other graphic organizer to generate ideas for your narrative. Think about things that connect people to one another, such as interests, goals, ethnicity, nationality, neighborhood, or school. Building on one of these connections, write down ideas for characters, setting, plot, conflict, and theme.

Get Organized Create an outline or use a story map to clarify the structure of your narrative. Refer to your notes and the texts to help you. Ask yourself:

- How can the beginning of my story engage readers?
- What is the story's plot? What is the central conflict?
- What is the sequence of events? How do they lead to a climax—a turning point or moment of greatest intensity?
- How does the story end? Is the conflict resolved? How?
- Which point of view will you use in your narrative? Take notes on other narrative techniques you plan to use.
- What will readers want to know about your characters and setting? Describe your characters' appearance, personality, and other unique characteristics. Give details about the setting.
- What details convey a theme about personal connections?

PRODUCE

Draft Your Narrative Write a draft of your narrative, following your notes, outline, and graphic organizers.

- Begin by introducing the setting, the main character(s), and an experience or conflict that will be central to the plot.
- Describe a sequence of events surrounding the conflict.
- Use descriptive details, sensory language, and narrative techniques such as dialogue.
- Provide a satisfying ending that resolves the central conflict.

WriteSmart

Write your rough draft in *my*WriteSmart. Focus on getting your ideas down, rather than perfecting your choice of language.

Interactive Lessons
To help you draft your narrative, complete the following lesson:
· Narrative Structures

ENGLISH LANGUAGE SUPPORT

Understand Narrative Structure Display the Student Model that accompanies the *Interactive Lessons:* Writing Narratives. Read the narrative aloud with students following along. Discuss that a narrative has a beginning, middle, and end. The beginning, or exposition, introduces the setting and the characters. Point out details about setting in the first three paragraphs of the Student Model (*"two years ago," "Saturday morning," "spring day," "Lewiston"*). Tell students that the middle, or rising action, describes the character's conflict. Ask students to summarize the conflict in the Student Model. *(The character finds her community uninteresting.)* Then explain that the climax is the turning point in the story. Have students reread paragraphs eight through ten chorally to examine the climax. Finally, a narrative will have falling action, where the character begins to resolve the conflict, and the resolution, or end. Discuss how the character in the Student Model sees her community differently after helping to save it.

Language and Style: Add Details

Adverbs, adverb phrases, and prepositional phrases can add detail to descriptions by telling about the time, place, manner, or cause of an action. Read the following passage from "When Mr. Pirzada Came to Dine."

> " I nodded. For the first time we all gathered around the dining table, my mother, my father, Mr. Pirzada, and I. While the television aired unattended we covered the tabletop with newspapers. "

Note that details about the characters' actions are revealed through the phrases "for the first time" and "while the television aired unattended." Look for places in your own narrative where you can improve your descriptions by adding details like these.

REVISE

Review Your Draft Have your partner or group of peers review your draft. Use the following chart to revise your draft.

Have your partner or a group of peers review your draft in *my*WriteSmart. Ask your reviewers to note any places where the plot could be better developed.

Questions	Tips	Revision Techniques
Does the beginning of the story introduce the setting, the main characters, and the conflict?	**Underline** details that reveal the setting. **Highlight** the names of the main characters. **Note** the main conflict in the story.	**Add** information about the setting, characters, and conflict, if needed.
Is the narrative told from a consistent point of view?	**Note** any instances where the point of view changes.	**Change** any pronouns to make the point of view consistent.
Is the sequence of events clear?	**Number** the sequence of events as they appear in the narrative.	**Reorder** events in chronological order, if needed.
Are narrative techniques such as dialogue, pacing, and description included?	**Note** at least one example of each narrative technique in your story.	**Elaborate** by adding more narrative techniques as needed.
Does the conclusion include a logical and satisfying resolution to the main conflict?	**Underline** details that reveal the resolution to the conflict.	**Add** details that tell how the conflict is resolved.

PRESENT

Create a Finished Copy Choose a way to share your fictional narrative. You might post it to a class blog or read it out loud to a group of classmates. Be prepared to answer questions or respond to comments from the people you share it with.

ENGLISH LANGUAGE SUPPORT

Add Details Have pairs or small groups share short excerpts from their narratives. For each excerpt, have the group suggest places where adverbs, adverb phrases, and prepositional phrases could be added to make text more interesting. However, remind students to keep in mind how details affect the pace of the narrative. Have students read aloud the versions before and after adding details and compare the versions' impacts.

PERFORMANCE TASK A

PRODUCE

LANGUAGE AND STYLE

Tell students that when they add details to their narratives, they may want to read the text and ask themselves questions. For example, if they cannot answer such questions as *When did this happen?* or *Why did my character do that?*, they should consider adding more details with adverbs, adverb phrases, or prepositional phrases.

REVISE

REVIEW YOUR DRAFT

As students use the chart to review their drafts, encourage them to examine dialogue and theme more closely.

To check whether their dialogue sounds natural, suggest that students read it aloud. Point out that characters will not all speak in the same way but that each character's speech patterns should be consistent throughout the story. Also remind students to make sure their narrative conveys a theme about personal connections. If the theme is not clear at the end of the story, they should revise accordingly.

PRESENT

CREATE A FINISHED COPY

Encourage students who will read their narratives aloud to practice before they present to the group. Some students may choose to make audio or video podcasts of their readings, including the question-and-answer sessions. Post these podcasts on the school website, if possible, along with the text of the narratives.

PERFORMANCE TASK A

USE THE SCORING RUBRIC

Have partners use the rubric to assess each other's narratives. Remind them that a fictional narrative should tell a good story, one that makes readers eager to hear what happens. Therefore, each narrative needs a memorable beginning, realistic dialogue, and a plot with a clear sequence of events. In addition, students should pay attention to spelling, grammar, and usage, because errors can distract readers from the narrative. Suggest that students read their narratives to each other in sections and give feedback about which parts of the text to adjust to achieve the best results.

REFLECT ON THE PROCESS

Remind students that reflecting on their work will help them be even more successful on future performance tasks. Ask each student to think about how effectively his or her narrative showed a connection to others. Then have groups answer and discuss the following questions.

- How did looking back at the fiction and poetry in the collection help you understand narrative techniques?

- What part of the narrative did you find most challenging to write? What processes did you learn that might help you write another narrative?

- How did writing this fictional narrative help you understand interpersonal connections in a new or different way?

PERFORMANCE TASK A RUBRIC
FICTIONAL NARRATIVE

	Ideas and Evidence	Organization	Language
4	• The story begins memorably; the exposition clearly introduces the setting and a main character and establishes the conflict in a unique way. • The writer uses precise description and realistic dialogue to develop characters and events. • The plot is thoroughly developed; the story reveals a significant theme. • The story ends by resolving the conflict and tying up loose ends.	• The sequence of events is effective, clear, and logical. • The pace and organization keep the reader curious about the next plot event.	• The point of view is effective and consistent throughout the story. • Vivid sensory details reveal the setting and characters. • Sentence beginnings, lengths, and structures vary and have a rhythmic flow. • Spelling, capitalization, and punctuation are correct. If handwritten, the narrative is legible. • Grammar and usage are correct.
3	• The exposition introduces the setting, a main character, and a conflict, but it could be more engaging. • The writer often uses description and dialogue to develop characters and events. • The plot is adequately developed; the story suggests a theme. • The story resolves the conflict, but more details are needed to bring the plot to a satisfying conclusion.	• The sequence of events is mostly clear and logical. • The pace could move along more quickly to hold the reader's interest.	• The point of view is mostly consistent. • A few more sensory details are needed to describe the setting and characters. • Sentence beginnings, lengths, and structures mostly vary. • Several spelling, capitalization, and punctuation mistakes occur. If handwritten, the narrative is mostly legible. • Some grammatical and usage errors are repeated in the story.
2	• The story opening is uneventful; the exposition identifies a setting and a main character but only hints at a conflict. • The writer occasionally uses description and dialogue to develop characters and events. • The plot development is uneven in a few places; a theme is only hinted at. • The story resolves some parts of the conflict.	• The sequence of events is confusing in a few places. • The pace often lags.	• The point of view shifts in a few places. • The sensory details are ordinary or not used regularly enough. • Sentence structures vary somewhat. • Spelling, capitalization, and punctuation are often incorrect but do not make comprehending the story difficult. If handwritten, the narrative may be partially illegible. • Grammar and usage are incorrect in many places, but the writer's ideas are still clear.
1	• The exposition is missing critical information about the setting and main character and does not set up a conflict. • The writer does not use description and dialogue to develop characters and events. • The plot is barely developed and lacks a theme. • The story lacks a clear resolution.	• There is no clear sequence of events, making it easy for the reader to lose interest in the plot. • The pace is ineffective.	• The story lacks a clear point of view. • Sensory details are rarely or never used to describe the setting and characters. • A repetitive sentence structure makes the writing monotonous. • Spelling, capitalization, and punctuation are incorrect throughout. If handwritten, the narrative may be partially or mostly illegible. • Many grammatical and usage errors change the meaning of the writer's ideas.

TO CHALLENGE STUDENTS . . .

Change the Point of View Challenge students to rewrite all or part of their fictional narratives from a different point of view. Remind them to consider how the beginning, the plot, the details, and the conclusion might change if looked at from a different perspective. After they finish, have them present and discuss their work in a small group. Encourage students to think about why it is important to consider different points of view when exploring interpersonal connections.

Create a Group Multimedia Presentation

This collection focuses on the connections we form with others. Look back at the anchor text, "Monkey See, Monkey Do, Monkey Connect," and at the other texts in the collection. Then collaborate on a multimedia presentation about the way people form bonds with others.

W 6 Use technology to produce, publish, and update writing products.
SL 1a–d Participate effectively in collaborative discussions.
SL 2 Integrate multiple sources of information in media or formats.
SL 4 Present information, findings, and supporting evidence.
SL 5 Make strategic use of digital media in presentations.
SL 6 Adapt speech to a variety of contexts and tasks.

An effective multimedia presentation	Participants in an effective collaboration
• uses technology to share information through text, graphics, images, and sound	• prepare in advance by reading and analyzing the chosen texts
• integrates information from a variety of sources and media	• work with group members to decide on the goals and deadlines of the project and to assign individual roles
• presents information and evidence from the texts clearly, concisely, and logically	• encourage participation from all group members
• uses language and structures appropriate for a presentation	• allow for different perspectives and seek to achieve consensus

PLAN

Analyze the Texts Reread "Monkey See, Monkey Do, Monkey Connect" and two other texts from the collection. Use the annotation tools in your eBook to find examples, details, and quotations about how bonds are formed. Save each idea to *my*Notebook, in a folder called *Collection 3 Performance Task B*.

ACADEMIC VOCABULARY

As you share ideas for your multimedia presentation, try to use these words.

capacity
confer
emerge
generate
trace

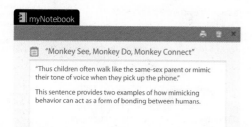

ENGLISH LANGUAGE SUPPORT

Plan a Group Multimedia Presentation Make sure students understand that their presentations will focus on the bonds that humans form with one another. Explain that students will contribute to the planning process by sharing ideas from their analyses of the texts. Provide the following sentence frames to help group members discuss the information they found in each text.

- One type of human bonding in this text is _____.
- Text details that help explain this bond include _____.

CREATE A GROUP MULTIMEDIA PRESENTATION

Point out to students that there are two aspects to this Performance Task: creating a multimedia presentation and collaborating with a group to complete it. Ask a volunteer to read aloud the introductory paragraph and then review the two lists of criteria. Discuss how completing this task with a group will be different from working on it independently. Which parts might be easier or more difficult with a group?

PLAN

ANALYZE THE TEXTS

Suggest that students review any notes they made while reading the texts, as well as their answers to the Analyzing the Text questions for each selection. Remind them that they will be discussing their ideas with their group, so they should take notes in a format that allows for easy reference during the discussion. For example, they might use the highlighting tool in their eBooks to mark the most relevant details in the text.

- I think this type of bonding is interesting because _____.
- To present this information to our audience, we could show _____.
- I see your point about _____, but I also think _____.

PERFORMANCE TASK B

PLAN

ASSIGN PARTS OF THE PRESENTATION

Point out that it makes sense to assign each group member a role about which he or she feels confident. However, encourage students to stretch themselves and volunteer to explore challenging selections and use technology that is less familiar to them. That way the task will be a better learning experience. They can always ask for help as needed.

PRODUCE

STORYBOARD THE PARTS

As students work together to create their storyboards, suggest that they create a separate index card for each part of the presentation. They can then move the cards around as they discuss the best order for presenting the multimedia segments.

Get Organized Join a small group to prepare for the presentation.

- Select an effective leader and a reliable recorder.
- Determine rules for discussions, including how participants will take turns, make decisions, and resolve disagreements.
- Remind all participants to contribute relevant information, listen attentively, ask pertinent questions, and clarify ideas.

Assign Parts of the Presentation Select an element of the presentation for each group member to produce.

- Discuss the texts, and generate ideas for the main points of the presentation. The recorder should write down final decisions.
- Find out what types of software and technology are available to you. Your school may have an authoring program that will allow you to combine word processing with different types of media.
- Decide which type of media (video, audio, slide show, and so on) you will use to present each main point.
- Assign a group member to write and produce a specific part of the presentation. For example, each group member might focus on a unique way that human beings form bonds or on a particular chosen text.

PRODUCE

Write and Produce Your Part Use your notes and the available technology to create your part of the presentation.

- Write down a clear statement of the main point you will convey.
- Use the type of media your group selected to illustrate your main idea. Try to use the technology to its full capacity. For example, don't use a video clip to show a still image; instead, use it to show a scene with action and movement.
- Trace your main points back to evidence from the texts.

Storyboard the Parts Join your group and combine individual parts of the presentation to form a logically ordered, cohesive whole.

- Have each group member share his or her part.
- Determine a logical order in which you will present the parts.
- Create a storyboard to show exactly what your audience will see and hear in each part of the presentation. Remember that a storyboard is a series of sketches that presents scenes in sequential order.

Interactive Lessons
To help you plan your presentation, complete the following lessons:
· Participating in Collaborative Discussions: Establishing and Following Procedure
· Using Media in a Presentation: Types of Media: Audio, Video, and Images

✓ my WriteSmart

Produce a rough draft of your presentation using the authoring software of your choice. Then upload your draft to *my*WriteSmart for a peer and teacher review.

Interactive Lessons
To help you draft your presentation, complete the following lesson:
· Using Media in a Presentation: Using Presentation Software

WHEN STUDENTS STRUGGLE...

Integrate Media Elements Suggest that students organize each part of the presentation around a main point and supporting evidence. Provide students with an idea-and-details graphic organizer for planning their parts. Then have them jot down ideas about how they might use media elements to present each piece of information. Finally, have group members discuss their ideas to choose the most effective way to integrate media elements. Provide the following questions to help them:

- What media elements will help make my part interesting to the audience?
- Which media elements will improve the presentation? Will any elements distract the audience?
- What other strategies can I use to help the audience understand my ideas?

REVISE

PRACTICE YOUR PRESENTATION

Emphasize that students should review the criteria listed in the Performance Task B Rubric. Working with their group, they can use the criteria as a guide for determining which aspects of their presentation to revise.

PRESENT

SHARE YOUR PRESENTATION

Have the whole class discuss similarities and differences among groups' presentations, noting both strengths and weaknesses. If a group posts a video of the presentation on the class or school website, have members create a comments section for their audience to ask questions and provide feedback. Group members can take turns responding to comments online.

REVISE

Practice Your Presentation Your group should now have a rough version of your final presentation. Following your storyboard, practice delivering the presentation. As you observe how it unfolds, keep these questions in mind:

- Does the opening to each part of the presentation grab the audience's attention? If not, consider starting with an intriguing question or an interesting video clip.
- Are the transitions between ideas and between types of media smooth? If not, can pieces of the presentation be rearranged or reworked?
- Are there any problems with the technology that need to be solved? For example, will the audience have trouble seeing or hearing anything? Is it possible to start audio and video clips at exactly the right time?

Make Sense of Things Now that you've practiced, it's time to revise your presentation. Refer to the chart on the following page for the characteristics of a well-planned multimedia presentation. With your group, make any adjustments necessary to ensure that

- your presentation begins in a way that engages the audience
- your audience will easily understand your main points and the evidence you present for each point
- the presentation integrates a variety of media in an effective way
- each part of the presentation takes full advantage of the type of technology used
- the presentation ends with a satisfying conclusion
- the entire presentation demonstrates an appropriate use of standard English

myWriteSmart

Have your group of peers review your draft in *my*WriteSmart. Ask your reviewers to note any main points that are not adequately supported with evidence.

Interactive Lessons
To help you revise your presentation, complete the following lesson:
- Using Media in a Presentation: Practicing Your Presentation

PRESENT

Share Your Presentation Discuss with your group how to deliver your presentation to the rest of your classmates. The way you present will depend on the types of technology used. You may be able to have small groups explore your project independently, or you may need to present to the whole class. In either situation, allow your audience to comment, ask questions, and provide feedback.

- Find out what aspects of your presentation were strong.
- Ask how your presentation could be improved.

TO CHALLENGE STUDENTS...

Conduct Field Research Challenge students to conduct field research on an aspect of human bonding mentioned in the collection texts. Students may report on direct observations or conduct surveys or interviews. Encourage them to incorporate their research results into their presentations.

PERFORMANCE TASK B

USE THE SCORING RUBRIC

Have groups of three score each other's presentations, with each member focusing on just one of the three rubric categories. Ask students to write brief explanations of each score they've given.

REFLECT ON THE PROCESS

Explain that taking the time to reflect on their planning and presentation processes will help students apply what they learned and improve their skills. Ask students to think about how well their presentations engaged and informed their audience. Have them answer and discuss the following questions:

- How well did the group work together to plan and organize the project? What would you do differently in a future project?
- What were the most effective media elements in your presentation? How smoothly did you transition between different media types?
- What aspects of the presentation do you think your audience found most engaging?

PERFORMANCE TASK B RUBRIC
MULTIMEDIA PRESENTATION

	Ideas and Evidence	Organization	Language
4	• The presentation begins memorably and engages the audience's attention. • Information and supporting evidence are presented clearly, concisely, and logically. • The presentation uses digital media strategically to enhance the audience's understanding and to add interest.	• The topic is clearly introduced at the start of the presentation. • The presentation maintains a consistent focus on the topic. • The presentation ends with a satisfying and thought-provoking conclusion.	• The presentation maintains a consistent and appropriately formal tone through the use of standard English. • The presentation uses specialized and technical vocabulary as appropriate, clearly defining these terms for the audience. • Narration flows smoothly with the use of transitions and varied sentence structures.
3	• The presentation starts in a way that engages the audience. • Information and supporting evidence are presented clearly and logically, although some unnecessary information is included. • The presentation uses digital media in a way that helps the audience understand the topic.	• The topic is introduced at the start of the presentation. • The presentation stays focused on the topic, with a few minor lapses. • The presentation ends with an appropriate conclusion.	• The presentation mostly maintains a formal tone through the use of standard English. • The presentation uses some specialized and technical vocabulary and defines these terms for the audience. • Narration mostly flows smoothly with the use of transitions and varied sentence structures.
2	• The presentation has a somewhat bland opening that may not engage the audience. • Most information and supporting evidence are presented clearly, but there is some unnecessary information and some gaps in logic. • The use of digital media does not work to enhance the audience's understanding.	• The topic is hinted at but not made clear at the start of the presentation. • The presentation strays from the topic in several places. • The presentation ends with a brief concluding statement but leaves some ideas unresolved.	• The presentation has an inconsistent tone, sometimes using nonstandard or very informal English. • The presentation uses few specialized or technical vocabulary words and fails to define these terms for the audience. • Narration needs more transitions to clarify links between ideas and uses monotonous sentence structures.
1	• The presentation opens in a way that does not engage the audience. • Information is not presented clearly and logically and supporting evidence is lacking. • The presentation uses digital media ineffectively, causing confusion for the audience.	• No clear topic is introduced at the start of the presentation. • The presentation lacks focus throughout. • The presentation ends abruptly.	• The presentation has an overly informal tone, using nonstandard English and/or slang. • The presentation uses vague language and no specialized terms. • Narration lacks transitions to clarify links between ideas and uses choppy simple sentences.

Image Credit: ©Sandy MacKenzie/Shutterstock

Sweet Sorrow

"Love is the great intangible."

—Diane Ackerman

161

STREAM TO START

Motivate students to read the collection texts and spark their curiosity about the collection by playing the video and watching it in class. After students watch the video, ask them to think about two things they hope to learn from reading about the challenging aspects of human relationships. Call on volunteers to share their responses.

PERFORMANCE TASK PREVIEW

Point out to students that they will complete a performance task at the end of the collection. The performance task will require them to further analyze the selections in the collection and to synthesize ideas about these analyses. They will present their findings in a variety of products.

ACADEMIC VOCABULARY

View It!

Professional Development Podcast:

Academic Vocabulary

Students can acquire facility with the academic vocabulary words through frequent, repeated exposure as they analyze and discuss the selections in the collection. Academic vocabulary can be used in the following instructional contexts. This will enable students to incorporate the academic vocabulary words into their working vocabulary.

- Collaborative Discussion at the end of each selection
- Analyzing the Text questions for each selection
- Selection-level Performance Task
- Vocabulary instruction (for Critical Vocabulary and/or for Vocabulary Strategy)
- Language and Style
- End-of-collection Performance Task for all selections in the collection

ASK STUDENTS to review the Academic Vocabulary word list for this collection. You may wish to pronounce each word aloud, so students hear the correct pronunciation. Then, discuss the definitions and the related forms for each word. Remind students that they will encounter these five academic vocabulary words throughout the collection.

COLLECTION **4**

Sweet Sorrow

This collection explores the nature of love and the conflicts surrounding it.

Stream to Start

fyi
hmhfyi.com

Channel One News®

COLLECTION

PERFORMANCE TASK Preview

At the end of this collection, you will have the opportunity to complete a task:

- Write an analytical essay exploring an aspect of love.

ACADEMIC VOCABULARY

Study the words and their definitions in the chart below. You will use these words as you discuss and write about the texts in this collection.

Word	Definition	Related Forms
attribute (ăt′rə-byōōt′) *n.*	a characteristic, quality, or trait	attributable, attributed
commit (kə-mĭt′) *v.*	to carry out, engage in, or perform	commitment, recommit
expose (ĭk-spōz′) *v.*	to make visible or reveal	exposure, exposition
initiate (ĭ-nĭsh′ē-āt′) *v.*	to start or cause to begin	initiative, initiator
underlie (ŭn′dər-lī′) *v.*	to be the cause or support of	underlying, underlay

---

 myNotebook

As students read, analyze, and discuss the texts in this collection, encourage them to use the *my*WordList folder in *my*Notebook to build their own personal word lists.

- **Annotate** Students can highlight vocabulary terms and other unfamiliar words and save each highlighted term to *my*Notebook.
- **Organize** Within *my*Notebook, students can drag each word into the *my*WordList folder.
- **Elaborate** Ask students to add details to the entry for each word, such as a definition, other forms of the word, and a sample sentence.

English Language Support

ENGAGE WITH THE COLLECTION TOPIC

Draw students' attention to the title of the collection: Sweet Sorrow. Tell students that this collection presents ideas and information about how love is and has been viewed and experienced in various contexts. Explain that a large part of this collection explores the concept of love through the lens of *Romeo and Juliet*, a play by William Shakespeare.

ACCESS PRIOR KNOWLEDGE Ask students to think about what they know about love. Discuss a definition or description of what they feel for a person they care about. How is it possible that love can be both a wonderful and a sorrowful emotion?

TAKING NOTES

Use this strategy to help students learn how to take notes as they read or discuss a text. Explain that taking good notes will help them better understand a complex text.

- **First,** before reading, provide a graphic organizer students can use for notetaking, such as a story map, timeline, or character chart. Explain the purposes of each section of the organizer.
- **Then,** display a passage from a text, and ask students to take notes in the graphic organizer, reminding them to write down important and memorable ideas and details.
- **Next,** have small groups of students present and explain each point listed on their graphic organizer, along with

reasons for having included each one. Tell groups that their task is to come to agreement about which notes are accurate and significant and most likely to be useful.
- **Finally,** distribute a single, blank copy of the graphic organizer to each group; have the groups complete it together, according to the conclusions they reached in discussion. Have representatives from each group present their graphic organizer to the class for discussion.

> Collection 4 Digital Resources for English Language Support

INTERACTIVE WHITEBOARD LESSONS

Use the Interactive Whiteboard Lessons to provide additional support on

- character development and motivation
- plot and conflict
- word choice and tone

LEVEL UP TUTORIALS

Students can access *Level Up* Tutorials from their eBooks to get additional help with analyzing literature, analyzing informational text, reading skills, vocabulary skills, and language conventions.

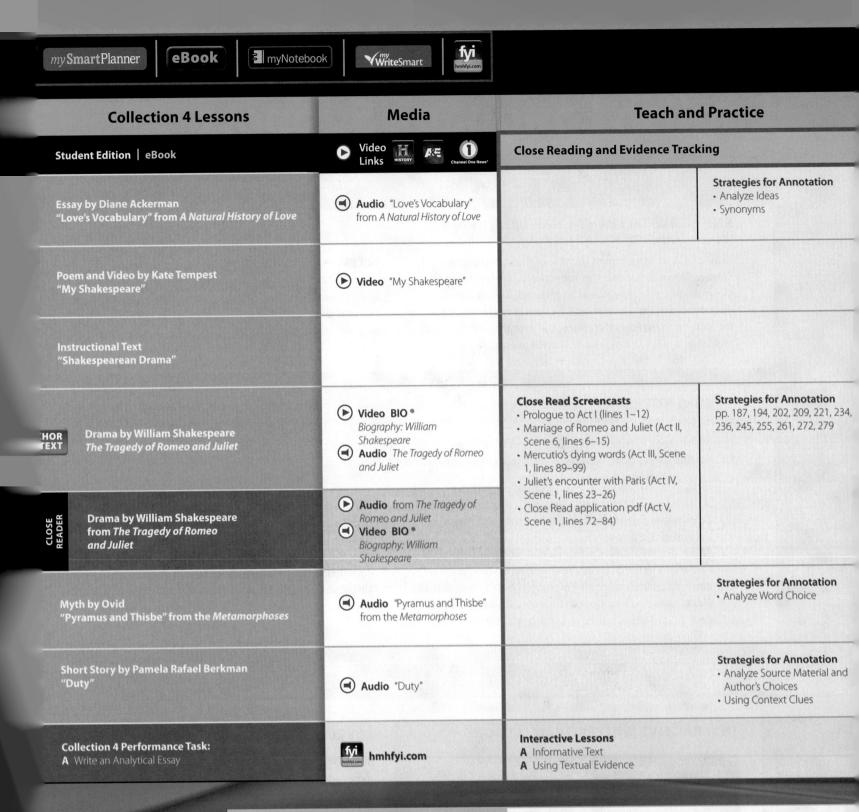

Collection 4 Lessons	Media	Teach and Practice	
Student Edition | eBook	▶ Video Links HISTORY A&E Channel One News®	**Close Reading and Evidence Tracking**	
Essay by Diane Ackerman "Love's Vocabulary" from *A Natural History of Love*	🔊 **Audio** "Love's Vocabulary" from *A Natural History of Love*		**Strategies for Annotation** • Analyze Ideas • Synonyms
Poem and Video by Kate Tempest "My Shakespeare"	▶ **Video** "My Shakespeare"		
Instructional Text "Shakespearean Drama"			
ANCHOR TEXT **Drama by William Shakespeare** *The Tragedy of Romeo and Juliet*	▶ **Video BIO ®** *Biography: William Shakespeare* 🔊 **Audio** *The Tragedy of Romeo and Juliet*	**Close Read Screencasts** • Prologue to Act I (lines 1–12) • Marriage of Romeo and Juliet (Act II, Scene 6, lines 6–15) • Mercutio's dying words (Act III, Scene 1, lines 89–99) • Juliet's encounter with Paris (Act IV, Scene 1, lines 23–26) • Close Read application pdf (Act V, Scene 1, lines 72–84)	**Strategies for Annotation** pp. 187, 194, 202, 209, 221, 234, 236, 245, 255, 261, 272, 279
CLOSE READER **Drama by William Shakespeare** from *The Tragedy of Romeo and Juliet*	▶ **Audio** from *The Tragedy of Romeo and Juliet* 🔊 **Video BIO ®** *Biography: William Shakespeare*		
Myth by Ovid "Pyramus and Thisbe" from the *Metamorphoses*	🔊 **Audio** "Pyramus and Thisbe" from the *Metamorphoses*		**Strategies for Annotation** • Analyze Word Choice
Short Story by Pamela Rafael Berkman "Duty"	🔊 **Audio** "Duty"		**Strategies for Annotation** • Analyze Source Material and Author's Choices • Using Context Clues
Collection 4 Performance Task: **A** Write an Analytical Essay	fyi **hmhfyi.com**	**Interactive Lessons** **A** Informative Text **A** Using Textual Evidence	

For Systematic Coverage of Writing and Speaking & Listening Standards	**Interactive Lessons** Using Textual Evidence Using Media in Presentation

Assess		Extend	Reteach
Performance Task	**✓ Assess It Online!**	**Teacher eBook**	**Teacher eBook**
Speaking Activity: Discussion	Selection Test	**Analyze Ideas: Participate in Collaborative Discussion > Interactive Whiteboard Lessons >** Text Structure and Meaning	**Analyze Ideas >** *Level Up* **Tutorial >** Reading for Details
Media Activity: Reflection	Selection Test	**Analyze Language**	**Analyze Source Material >** *Level Up* **Tutorial >** Universal and Recurring Themes
Act I: Speaking Activity: Discussion Act II: Speaking Activity: Debate Act III: Writing Activity: Journal Entries Act IV: Speaking and Writing Activity: Dramatic Reading and Letter Act V: Writing Activity: Eulogy	Selection Tests, Acts I–V	**Analyze Character**	**Analyze Author's Choices: Parallel Plots >** *Level Up* **Tutorial >** Plot: Sequence of Events
Writing Activity: Essay	Selection Test	**Write an Analytical Essay**	**Analyze Source Material**
Writing Activity: Journal Entries	Selection Test	**Analyze Representations in Different Mediums**	**Author's Choices: Point of View >** *Level Up* **Tutorial >** Point of View
A Write an Analytical Essay	Collection Test		

Lesson Assessments Using Textual Evidence Using Media in Presentation	**Standards Support and Enrichment**	For more instruction and practice in reading literary and informational texts, language, spelling, and speaking and listening, see Teacher Resources > Standards Support and Enrichment.

Collection 4 Lessons	Key Learning Objective	Performance Task
Essay by Diane Ackerman **"Love's Vocabulary" from** *A Natural History of Love*, **p. 163A** — Lexile 1020L	**The student will be able to…** analyze ideas presented in an essay and determine word meanings	Speaking Activity: Discussion
Poem and Video by Kate Tempest **"My Shakespeare," p. 173A**	**The student will be able to…** analyze how a modern artist draws on and transforms source material for a new artistic expression	Media Activity: Reflection
Instructional Text **"Shakespearean Drama," p. 177A**		
ANCHOR TEXT **Drama by William Shakespeare** *The Tragedy of Romeo and Juliet*, **p. 177A**	**The student will be able to…** analyze character motivations and parallel plots	Act I: Speaking Activity: Discussion Act II: Speaking Activity: Debate Act III: Writing Activity: Journal Entries Act IV: Speaking and Writing Activity: Dramatic Reading and Letter Act V: Writing Activity: Eulogy
EXEMPLAR **Myth Retold by Ovid** **"Pyramus and Thisbe" from the** *Metamorphoses*, **p. 283A**	**The student will be able to…** analyze source material	Writing Activity: Essay
Short Story by Pamela Rafael Berkman **"Duty," p. 289A** — Lexile 940L	**The student will be able to…** analyze how an author draws on and transforms source material and how an author's choice of point of view creates desired effects	Writing Activity: Journal Entries

Collection 4 Performance Task:

Write an Analytical Essay

Vocabulary Strategy	Language and Style	Differentiated Instruction	CLOSE READER Selection
Synonyms	Participial Phrases	**English Language Support:** Language: Punctuation **When Students Struggle:** Comprehension Support **To Challenge Students:** • Write a Poem • Explore an Allusion	
		English Language Support: Vocabulary: Figurative Language **When Students Struggle:** Develop Reading Fluency	
		English Language Support: Language: Allusions **When Students Struggle:** • Identify Protagonist and Antagonist • Paraphrase Difficult Lines **To Challenge Students:** Sketch and Analyze the Globe Theater	
Puns	Parallel Structure	**English Language Support:** pp. 184, 186, 188, 189, 197, 200, 208, 212, 213, 214, 218, 223, 229, 235, 239, 241, 246, 248, 260, 267, 271, 281 **When Students Struggle:** pp. 185, 191, 192–193, 195, 196, 201, 204, 210, 216–217, 222, 224–225, 230–231, 233, 242–243, 244, 247, 250, 256–257, 263, 268–269, 270, 277 **To Challenge Students:** pp. 199, 203, 205, 219, 226, 232, 240, 251, 254, 262, 274, 278	Drama by William Shakespeare from *The Tragedy of Romeo and Juliet*, p. 282b
		English Language Support: • Language: Punctuation • Vocabulary: Denotation/Connotation **When Students Struggle:** • Develop Reading Fluency • Comprehension: Cause and Effect	
Context Clues	Independent and Dependent Clauses	**English Language Support:** • Vocabulary: Figurative Language • Analyze Cause-and-Effect Organization • Language: Personal Pronoun Referents **When Students Struggle:** • Develop Reading Fluency • Examine Character Traits **To Challenge Students:** Innovate on Story Ideas	
	Precise Vocabulary	**English Language Support:** Use Precise Language **When Students Struggle:** Analyze the Texts **To Challenge Students:** Create a Performance	

from Love's Vocabulary

Essay by Diane Ackerman

Why This Text?

At one point or another, every student will ponder the word *love*. In this lesson, students will analyze a gifted writer's insightful, informative, and often humorous observations about the vocabulary of love.

Key Learning Objective: Students will learn to analyze ideas presented in an essay and determine word meanings.

RI 1 Cite textual evidence to support analysis.

RI 2 Determine a central idea; provide an objective summary.

RI 3 Analyze ideas.

RI 4 Determine the meaning of words and phrases; analyze the cumulative impact of word choices on meaning and tone.

RI 5 Analyze how ideas are developed and refined.

W 10 Write routinely over extended and shorter time frames.

SL 1 Participate in collaborative discussions.

L 1b Use various types of phrases.

L 4a Use context as a clue to the meaning of a word or phrase.

L 4c Consult reference materials.

L 4d Verify the meaning of a word or phrase.

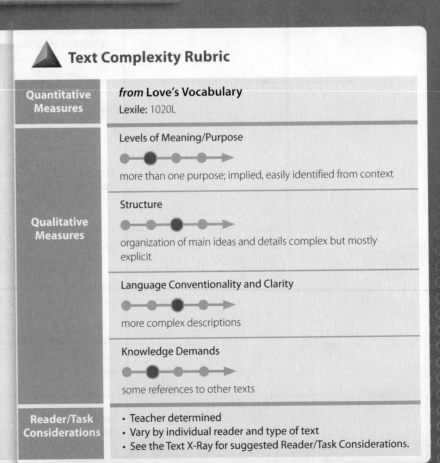

▲ Text Complexity Rubric

Quantitative Measures	*from* Love's Vocabulary Lexile: 1020L
Qualitative Measures	**Levels of Meaning/Purpose** more than one purpose; implied, easily identified from context
	Structure organization of main ideas and details complex but mostly explicit
	Language Conventionality and Clarity more complex descriptions
	Knowledge Demands some references to other texts
Reader/Task Considerations	• Teacher determined • Vary by individual reader and type of text • See the Text X-Ray for suggested Reader/Task Considerations.

English Language Support Before teaching, use the Text X-Ray below for an overview of the text's complexity. The Text X-Ray and supports and scaffolds in the Teacher's Edition will help you guide students of different skill levels.

Meaning Making · Language Development · Effective Expression · Content Knowledge · Foundational Skills

Text Complexity: Qualitative Measures

Levels of Meaning/Purpose

more than one purpose; implied, easily identified from context

Help students analyze how an author's language choices affect meaning.

- Teacher's Edition side notes, pp. 163, 164, 165, 167, 169
- Determine Word Meanings, p. 169

ZOOM IN ON ANALYZING MEANING Explain to students that **figurative language** compares two things in a creative way that is not meant to be taken literally. Define and point out examples of **personification** (lines 8–9), **metaphor** (lines 2–4), and **simile** (lines 10–11). Then divide the selection's ten paragraphs among pairs of students. Have each pair read their section, noting examples of figurative language as well as any other language that is interesting or confusing. Call on pairs to share their findings in a class discussion. As they share their examples, point out any words or expressions that have particular **connotations**, or associated feelings, that help convey the author's **tone** or attitude toward her subject.

Structure

organization of main ideas and details complex but mostly explicit

Help students analyze how an author organizes and presents ideas.

- Teacher's Edition side notes, pp. 163, 164, 165, 166, 168, 169
- When Students Struggle, p. 164
- Strategies for Annotation, p. 169
- Analyze Ideas, p. 169

To reteach analyzing main ideas and supporting details, see

- Analyze Ideas, p. 172a

 **Use It!** *Level Up* Tutorial: Reading for Details

ZOOM IN ON ANALYZING IDEAS Point out that the meaning of the word *love* is the **central idea** of the essay. The author expands on its meaning in each paragraph. So, looking for the word *love* may help students spot the main idea of each paragraph, which gives a new perspective on love. Display the second paragraph (lines 12–27) on the board and work with students to identify the sentences that state its main idea. *("Love is the white light. . . . one simple word.")* Discuss how the details about the prism in lines 12–15 help support this idea. *(The author uses light and a prism as a metaphor for love and art. Just as white light is broken into many colors by a prism, art shows the many different aspects of love.)* Suggest that students read each paragraph once to get an overview of all the details and examples and then a second time to identify the main idea.

Language Conventionality and Clarity

more complex descriptions

Teach unfamiliar vocabulary in context.

- Teacher's Edition Critical Vocabulary notes, pp. 163, 164, 165, 166, 171
- Applying Academic Vocabulary, p. 165
- Vocabulary Strategy: Synonyms, p. 171
- Strategies for Annotation, p. 171

Help students understand the role of quotation marks in an essay.

- English Language Support, p. 163

Guide students in using participial phrases in their writing.

- Language and Style: Participial Phrases, p. 172

To teach students how to participate in a collaborative discussion, see

- Analyze Ideas: Participate in a Collaborative Discussion, p. 172a

 Use It! **Interactive Whiteboard Lesson:** Text Structure and Meaning

ZOOM IN ON **USING SYNONYMS** Students may struggle to identify **synonyms** in context if both words are unfamiliar. Allow them to use a dictionary or thesaurus to complete the Practice and Apply activity for Vocabulary Strategy: Synonyms on page 171. Suggest that they first try to think of a word in their first language that means the same as the target word. Then they can use the reference source to check their answer. Pair students with native English speakers to discuss connotations (associated feelings) or shades of meaning that differentiate the synonyms. Students may use the *my*WordList folder in *my*Notebook to record their new words with definitions, synonyms, and connotations.

Knowledge Demands

some references to other texts

Support English Learners by helping them learn more about the author.

- Teacher's Edition Background note, p. 163

ZOOM IN ON **BUILDING KNOWLEDGE** Help students understand Ackerman's mention of Cupid in the concluding parts of the essay. Explain that in the ancient Roman mythology, Cupid is the god of love. He is usually depicted as a little boy who can fly and is equipped with a bow and arrows. Whoever is struck by Cupid's arrow falls uncontrollably in love. Ackerman uses this reference to Cupid to illustrate the often unexpected and helpless condition of romantic love.

Suggested Reader/Task Considerations

You might consider the following before assigning this essay to students.

- Will students understand their **purpose** for reading the essay, which is an extended discussion of the meaning of a single word?
- Do students have the language skills necessary to decode the **figurative language** in the essay?

ZOOM IN ON **SUPPORTING COMPREHENSION**

- Use lines 62–66 to introduce the essay's **central idea** and **purpose**. English learners will be able to relate to the confusion that results when one word is used to mean so many different things. Tell them that the author also believes *love* is a tricky word, and that they should read to learn more about its various meanings.
- If students stumble over the **figurative language**, pair them with native English speakers who can help them understand when **similes**, **metaphors**, and **personification** are being used and what those figures of speech are intended to convey.

TEACH

CLOSE READ

Diane Ackerman Have students read the information about the author. Tell students that Ackerman's deep interest in natural history is evident in all of her work. Note that in addition to writing nonfiction, Ackerman is also an award-winning poet.

AS YOU READ Direct students to use the As You Read suggestion to focus their reading.

Determine Word Meanings (LINES 2–4)   RI 4

Explain that the author uses **figurative language** throughout the essay. **Metaphors** are figures of speech that directly compare two unlike things. Ackerman uses words that have positive or negative **connotations**, or shades of meaning, which have a cumulative effect.

Ⓐ **ASK STUDENTS** what is being compared in lines 2–4. What connotations do the words have? What is their cumulative effect? (*Hate is compared to a vicious predator; fear to a bat in a confined space; jealousy to a spider. The words* stalks, dripping fangs, leather wings, *and* sticky webs *have negative connotations. The cumulative effect is to conjure up images of the nightmarish "beasts" that Ackerman describes.*)

Analyze Ideas (LINES 1–11)   RI 3

Tell students that the **central idea** is the author's main point about the topic. As they read the essay, have them look for other ideas that develop the central idea.

Ⓑ **CITE TEXT EVIDENCE** Have students identify the central idea Ackerman presents at the very beginning of the essay. (*"Love is the great intangible" [line 1].*) How does she support this idea? (*She calls love a "dream state" and in lines 7-8 uses contradictory adjectives to describe love's moods, showing it is not easily defined: "Frantic and serene, vigilant and calm, wrung-out and fortified, explosive and sedate."*)

CRITICAL VOCABULARY

intangible: To Ackerman, love is difficult to touch or understand. **ASK STUDENTS** to suggest other intangible qualities. (*Possible answers: leadership, intelligence, loyalty*)

Diane Ackerman (b. 1948), *author of* A Natural History of the Senses, An Alchemy of Mind, *and* The Zookeeper's Wife, *weaves her love of science and natural history into her poetry, fiction, and nonfiction. Her memoir,* One Hundred Names for Love, *chronicles her husband's struggle to reclaim language after a stroke. In describing that time, Ackerman said, "I've always transcended best by pretending that I'm Margaret Mead viewing a scene for the first time or an alien from another planet regarding the spectacle of life on Earth and discovering how spectacular, unexpected, and beautiful it is."*

from Love's Vocabulary

Essay by Diane Ackerman

AS YOU READ Pay attention to the many creative descriptions of love throughout the essay. Write down any questions you generate during reading.

🔲 myNotebook

As you read, save new words to *myWordList*.

Love is the great **intangible**. In our nightmares, we can create beasts out of pure emotion. Hate stalks the streets with dripping fangs, fear flies down narrow alleyways on leather wings, and jealousy spins sticky webs across the sky. In daydreams, we can maneuver with poise, foiling an opponent, scoring high on fields of glory while crowds cheer, cutting fast to the heart of an adventure. But what dream state is love? Frantic and serene, vigilant and calm, wrung-out and fortified, explosive and sedate—love commands a vast army of moods. Hoping for victory, limping from the latest
10 skirmish, lovers enter the arena once again. Sitting still, we are as daring as gladiators.

When I set a glass prism on a windowsill and allow the sun to flood through it, a spectrum of colors dances on the floor. What we call "white" is a rainbow of colored rays packed into a small space. The prism sets them free. Love is the white light of emotion. It includes many feelings which, out of laziness and confusion, we crowd into one simple word. Art is the prism that sets them free,

intangible
(ĭn-tăn´jə-bəl) *n.* something that is difficult to grasp or explain.

Love's Vocabulary   **163**

ENGLISH LANGUAGE SUPPORT

Language: Punctuation Draw students' attention to the text in quotation marks on lines 22–23. Point out that the marks set off a direct quotation. Explain that quotation marks have many purposes; in this essay, they are used to call attention to: statements made by the author or another person; statements suggesting common understandings; definitions of words; and the titles of poems and other works.

ASK STUDENTS to find examples of the above (*e.g., lines 14, 36, 44, 63–73, 99*) and use context clues to determine how they contribute to meaning. Next, have students explain to each other what the quotations signify and why the author uses them.

Determine Word Meanings (LINES 37–38)

RI 4

Tell students that **similes** are figures of speech that make comparisons, often using the words *like* or *as*. The words authors use in figurative language such as similes can have **connotations** that are positive or negative.

C **ASK STUDENTS** to reread lines 28–40 and identify the simile. Then have them explain whether it has a positive or negative connotation. *(Simile: "heavy as a heartbeat" [lines 37–38]. The word heavy suggests both a feeling of grief and a physical condition of weariness; the connotation is negative.)*

Analyze Ideas (LINES 41–52)

RI 3, RI 5

Explain that authors develop and refine their ideas by supporting them with reasons, facts, and examples.

D **CITE TEXT EVIDENCE** What are some facts, reasons, and examples that Ackerman uses to support her idea that love "can mean almost nothing or absolutely everything" (lines 41–42)? Cite examples from the essay. *(Love is the first word conjugated by students of Latin [lines 42–43]; it is a "universally understood motive for crime" [lines 43–44]; it "seeps into the machinery of life to keep generation after generation in motion" [lines 49–50]; and it is a "positive force" that "ennobles the one feeling it" [lines 51–52].)*

CRITICAL VOCABULARY

guise: Ackerman says that the form in which love appears depends on many factors.

ASK STUDENTS to explain what factors might influence the guise in which love comes. *(The guises of love are influenced, among other things, by culture, background, and beliefs.)*

---

then follows the gyrations[1] of one or a few. When art separates this thick tangle of feelings, love bares its bones. But it cannot
20 be measured or mapped. Everyone admits that love is wonderful and necessary, yet no one can agree on what it is. I once heard a sportscaster say of a basketball player, "He does all the intangibles. Just watch him do his dance." As lofty as the idea of love can be, no image is too profane to help explain it. Years ago, I fell in love with someone who was both a sport and a pastime. At the end, he made fade-away jump shots in my life. But, for a while, love did all the intangibles. It lets us do our finest dance.

Love. What a small word we use for an idea so immense and powerful it has altered the flow of history, calmed monsters, kindled
30 works of art, cheered the forlorn, turned tough guys to mush, consoled the enslaved, driven strong women mad, glorified the humble, fueled national scandals, bankrupted robber barons, and made mincemeat of kings. How can love's spaciousness be conveyed in the narrow confines of one syllable? If we search for the source of the word, we find a history vague and confusing, stretching back to the Sanskrit *lubhyati* ("he desires"). I'm sure the etymology rambles back much farther than that, to a one-syllable word heavy as a heartbeat. Love is an ancient delirium, a desire older than civilization, with taproots[2] stretching deep into dark and mysterious
40 days.

C

We use the word *love* in such a sloppy way that it can mean almost nothing or absolutely everything. It is the first conjugation[3] students of Latin learn. It is a universally understood motive for crime. "Ah, he was in love," we sigh, "well, that explains it." In fact, in some European and South American countries, even murder is forgivable if it was "a crime of passion." Love, like truth, is the unassailable defense. Whoever first said "love makes the world go round" (it was an anonymous Frenchman) probably was not thinking about celestial mechanics, but the way love seeps into the
50 machinery of life to keep generation after generation in motion. We think of love as a positive force that somehow ennobles the one feeling it. When a friend confesses that he's in love, we congratulate him.

D

In folk stories, unsuspecting lads and lasses ingest a love potion and quickly lose their hearts. As with all intoxicants, love comes in many **guises** and strengths. It has a mixed bouquet, and may include some piquant ingredients.[4] One's taste in love will have a

guise
(gīz) *n.* form or outward appearance; outfit.

---

[1] **gyrations:** spiral or circular movements.
[2] **taproots:** the main roots of a tree or plant from which other roots grow.
[3] **conjugation:** in grammar, the various forms of a verb.
[4] **piquant (pē´kənt) ingredients:** components that make something pleasantly spicy.

WHEN STUDENTS STRUGGLE...

Comprehension Support Give students a strategy they can use to understand ideas as they unfold in the essay and to identify supporting facts, reasons, and examples. Have students work with a partner to complete a Main Idea and Details chart for lines 28–40. Encourage students to create similar charts for other important ideas in the essay.

Main Idea	Details
Love is a small word for a big idea.	It has altered history. It has kindled art. It has fueled scandals.

"We use the word love in such a sloppy way that it can mean almost nothing or absolutely everything."

lot to do with one's culture, upbringing, generation, religion, era, gender, and so on. Ironically, although we sometimes think of it
60 as the ultimate Oneness, love isn't monotone or uniform. Like a batik[5] created from many emotional colors, it is a fabric whose pattern and brightness may vary. What is my goddaughter to think when she hears her mother say: "I love Ben & Jerry's Cherry Garcia ice cream"; "I really loved my high school boyfriend"; "Don't you just love this sweater?" "I'd love to go to the lake for a week this summer"; "Mommy loves you." Since all we have is one word, we talk about love in **increments** or unwieldy ratios. "How much do you love me?" a child asks. Because the parent can't answer *I* (verb that means unconditional parental love) *you,* she may fling her
70 arms wide, as if welcoming the sun and sky, stretching her body to its limit, spreading her fingers to encompass all of Creation, and say: "This much!" Or: "Think of the biggest thing you can imagine. Now double it. I love you a hundred times that much!"

When Elizabeth Barrett Browning wrote her famous sonnet "How do I love thee?" she didn't "count the ways" because she had an arithmetical turn of mind, but because English poets have always had to search hard for personal signals of their love. As a society, we are embarrassed by love. We treat it as if it were an obscenity. We reluctantly admit it. Even saying the word makes
80 us stumble and blush. Why should we be ashamed of an emotion so beautiful and natural? In teaching writing students, I've sometimes given them the assignment of writing a love poem. "Be precise, be

increment
(ĭn´krə-mənt) *n.* an addition or increase by a standard measure of growth.

---
[5] **batik** (bə-tēk´): colorful design created by applying different dyes and wax to fabric.

APPLYING ACADEMIC VOCABULARY

underlie	expose

As you discuss Ackerman's essay, incorporate the following Collection 4 academic vocabulary words: *underlie* and *expose.* Discuss how love **underlies** so many human actions, even though the exact meaning of the word eludes us. Have students explain why people are embarrassed to **expose** their feelings and their thoughts about love.

CLOSE READ

Determine Word Meanings (LINES 66–73)   RI 4

Tell students that **tone**, the author's attitude toward the subject or the reader, is conveyed through word choice and the feelings or images that these words create.

E **CITE TEXT EVIDENCE** Read aloud the passage beginning with the statement, "Since all we have is one word" *(line 66)* and concluding with "a hundred times that much!" *(line 73).* What is the author's tone in this passage? Explain how the author's choice of words creates this tone. *(The author creates a light, engaging, and affectionate tone by choosing words and phrases that have warm, comforting connotations, such as "arms wide," "welcoming the sun and sky," and "encompass.")*

Analyze Ideas (LINES 74–77)   RI 4

Tell students that an author often provides examples that support an idea introduced in an earlier passage. Read aloud the following passage from lines 15–18 of the essay: "Love is the white light of emotion. It includes many feelings which, out of laziness and confusion, we crowd into one simple word. Art is the prism that sets them [feelings] free."

F **ASK STUDENTS** how Ackerman's description of Elizabeth Barrett Browning *(lines 74–77)* relates to this earlier statement. *(Ackerman suggests that Browning's poems are an attempt to "get at" the meaning of love.)*

CRITICAL VOCABULARY

increment: According to Ackerman, we try to express the depth and extent of our love by asserting it little by little, over time.

ASK STUDENTS to give an example of something that might increase in increments. *(Possible answers: wages, costs, fares, voltage, taxes)*

Analyze Ideas (LINES 85–122)   RI 1, RI 3

Explain that authors use examples to create bridges between ideas.

G **CITE TEXT EVIDENCE** Have students reread lines 85–93 and lines 111–122. Ask: How does the example of the ancient Egyptian woman in the Detroit automobile factory create a bridge between ideas? What are those ideas? In what way is their order significant? Cite examples from the text to support your conclusions. (*The first idea, in lines 85–93, is that our vocabulary for speaking about love is so limited that we have difficulty talking about it. The second idea, in lines 111–122, is that people do not really need language to recognize and understand love. The Egyptian woman is in a strange environment that she does not understand, yet the sight of two lovers kissing [lines 117–121] is immediately understandable to her. The order of the ideas suggests that the author's views are becoming more positive: both ideas show that love is intangible, but in the second case, love is pleasant, rather than a source of anxiety.*)

CRITICAL VOCABULARY

supple: Ackerman says that a flexible vocabulary is required to describe a complicated emotion such as love.

ASK STUDENTS to explain what a supple vocabulary of love would include. (*It would include words to describe the many moods and emotions related to love.*)

gradation: Ackerman says that there are many verbs to express the subtle degrees of hate.

ASK STUDENTS to name some words that describe gradations of hate. (*Verbs that express the subtle gradations of hate might include* abhor, abominate, despise, loathe, *and* repulse.)

---

individual, and be descriptive. But don't use any clichés," I caution them, "or any curse words." Part of the reason for this assignment is that it helps them understand how inhibited we are about love. Love is the most important thing in our lives, a passion for which we would fight or die, and yet we're reluctant to linger over its name. Without a **supple** vocabulary, we can't even talk or think about it directly. On the other hand, we have many sharp verbs for the ways

90   in which human beings can hurt one another, dozens of verbs for the subtle **gradations** of hate. But there are pitifully few synonyms for love. Our vocabulary of love and lovemaking is so paltry that a poet has to choose among clichés, profanities, or euphemisms. Fortunately, this has led to some richly imagined works of art. It has inspired poets to create their own private vocabularies. Mrs. Browning sent her husband a poetic abacus[6] of love, which in a roundabout way expressed the sum of her feelings. Other lovers have tried to calibrate their love in equally ingenious ways. In "The Flea," John Donne watches a flea suck blood from his arm

100   and his beloved's, and rejoices that their blood marries in the flea's stomach.

Yes, lovers are most often reduced to comparatives and quantities. "Do you love me more than her?" we ask. "Will you love me less if I don't do what you say?" We are afraid to face love head-on. We think of it as a sort of traffic accident of the heart. It is an emotion that scares us more than cruelty, more than violence, more than hatred. We allow ourselves to be foiled by the vagueness of the word. After all, love requires the utmost vulnerability. We equip someone with freshly sharpened knives; strip naked; then invite

110   him to stand close. What could be scarier?

If you took a woman from ancient Egypt and put her in an automobile factory in Detroit, she would be understandably disoriented. Everything would be new, especially her ability to stroke the wall and make light flood the room, touch the wall elsewhere and fill the room with summer's warm breezes or winter's blast. She'd be astonished by telephones, computers, fashions, language, and customs. But if she saw a man and woman stealing a kiss in a quiet corner, she would smile. People everywhere and everywhen understand the phenomenon of love, just as they

120   understand the appeal of music, finding it deeply meaningful even if they cannot explain exactly what that meaning is, or why they respond viscerally to one composer and not another. Our Egyptian woman, who prefers the birdlike twittering of a sistrum,[7] and a twentieth-century man, who prefers the clashing jaws of heavy

---

[6] **abacus:** a device for performing calculations by manipulating beads strung on wires in a rectangular frame.

[7] **sistrum:** an ancient percussion instrument that sounds like a metal rattle.

supple
(sŭp´əl) *adj.* flexible or easily adaptable.

gradation
(grā-dā´shən) *n.* a slight, successive change in color, degree or tone.

TO CHALLENGE STUDENTS . . .

Write a Poem What is a good love poem? Have students complete the assignment Ackerman gives her own students: Write a love poem that is precise, individual, and descriptive, but that does not contain clichés or curse words. Have students who feel comfortable doing so share their poems with the class. Discuss whether or not poems presented meet the above criteria, keeping this as a fun activity, without offering any suggestions about what is right or wrong.

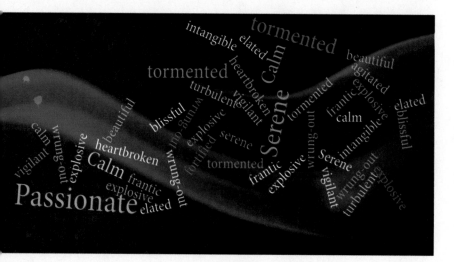

metal, share a passion for music that both would understand. So it is with love. Values, customs, and protocols may vary from ancient days to the present, but not the majesty of love. People are unique in the way they walk, dress, and gesture, yet we're able to look at two people—one wearing a business suit, the other a sarong[8]—
130 and recognize that both of them are clothed. Love also has many fashions, some bizarre and (to our taste) shocking, others more familiar, but all are part of a phantasmagoria[9] we know. In the Serengeti[10] of the heart, time and nation are irrelevant. On that plain, all fires are the same fire.

   Remember the feeling of an elevator falling in your chest when you said good-bye to a loved one? Parting is more than sweet sorrow, it pulls you apart when you are glued together. It feels like hunger pains, and we use the same word, *pang*. Perhaps this is why Cupid is depicted with a quiver of arrows, because at times love feels like
140 being pierced in the chest. It is a wholesome violence. Common as child birth, love seems rare nonetheless, always catches one by surprise, and cannot be taught. Each child rediscovers it, each couple redefines it, each parent reinvents it. People search for love as if it were a city lost beneath the desert dunes, where pleasure is the law, the streets are lined with brocade cushions, and the sun never sets.

---

[8] **sarong:** a traditional Southeast Asian women's garment made from a long piece of fabric that is wrapped around the body.

[9] **phantasmagoria (făn-tăz´mə-gôr´ē-ə):** a dreamlike sequence of surreal images or events.

[10] **Serengeti:** a vast plain in Tanzania known for its migratory animals.

TO CHALLENGE STUDENTS . . .

Explore an Allusion Why would a lover say that "parting [is] more than sweet sorrow"? Point out this phrase in line 136. Explain that it is an **allusion**, or a reference to another work of literature. Ask students if they can identify the allusion, and if the phrasing is the same as in the original work *(Romeo and Juliet; "parting is such sweet sorrow")*. Provide copies of the scene in the play where this sentence is found (Act II, Scene 2) and ask volunteers to read it aloud. Then have small groups discuss the ways in which Romeo and Juliet attempt to express their love. Encourage interested students to read or watch a film version of the entire play.

CLOSE READ

Determine Word Meanings (LINES 138–145) — RI 4

Remind students that a **simile** is a form of figurative language that makes an imaginative comparison between unlike things.

H **ASK STUDENTS** to reread lines 138–140. Have them explain the simile in these lines. What comparison is made? What does it say about love? *(The simile compares love to being pierced in the chest by an arrow. It is saying that love can cause people to feel intense emotional pain.)*

Explain that **tone** is the author's attitude toward the subject or the reader of the work. Tone can be determined by analyzing a writer's word choice.

I **CITE TEXT EVIDENCE** Ask students to reread this sentence in lines 143–145: "People search for love as if it were a city lost beneath the desert dunes, where pleasure is the law, the streets are lined with brocade cushions, and the sun never sets." Have them explain the tone of the description, and ask them to cite the word choices that create that tone. *(The tone is expansive, romantic, and mysterious. Words and phrases such as "a city lost," "pleasure," "brocade cushions," and "sun never sets" have positive connotations and create images of an appealing, lush place.)*

Analyze Ideas (LINES 155–156)   RI 1, RI 3

Tell students that authors sometimes repeat ideas in order to reinforce them. Read aloud lines 126–127: *"Values, customs, and protocols may vary from ancient days to the present, but not the majesty of love."*

J **CITE TEXT EVIDENCE** Ask students to reread the last paragraph of the essay (lines 134–145). Which sentence in the final paragraph repeats the idea expressed in lines 126–127? How does the second statement expand on the first statement? *(The sentence in lines 155–156 echoes the one in lines 126–127: "Custom, culture, and tastes vary, but not love itself, not the essence of the emotion." The second statement suggests that although many things change throughout history, the essence of love never changes.)*

COLLABORATIVE DISCUSSION Have students pair up and discuss how the ideas Ackerman describes throughout the essay attempt to answer the question. Ask them to identify the descriptions they think are best and have them work separately or together to gather evidence to support their ideas.

ASK STUDENTS to share any questions they generated in the course of reading and discussing the selection.

If it's so obvious and popular, then what is love? I began researching this book because I had many questions, not because I knew at the outset what answers I might find. Like most people, I believed what I had been told: that the idea of love was invented by
150 the Greeks, and romantic love began in the Middle Ages. I know now how misguided such hearsay is. We can find romantic love in the earliest writings of our kind. Much of the vocabulary of love, and the imagery lovers use, has not changed for thousands of years. Why do the same images come to mind when people describe their romantic feelings? Custom, culture, and tastes vary, but not love itself, not the essence of the emotion. **J**

COLLABORATIVE DISCUSSION Does the author answer the question "What is love?" With a partner, discuss how love is described in the essay. Select the description you think is best and support your choice with evidence from the text.

Analyze Ideas

RI 3

In her essay, Diane Ackerman explores the concept of love in all of its mystery and complexity. Calling love "the great intangible" that no one can adequately define, she unfolds a series of ideas about love, from across time and place, and she supports each idea by providing facts, details, and examples. Throughout the essay, Ackerman makes connections to her central point about the language we use to describe love.

In analyzing the ideas presented in the essay, consider these questions:

- What is the significance of the order in which Ackerman introduces her ideas or makes her points?
- How does the author introduce, develop, and support each idea?
- How does the author make connections between her many ideas on love? Does she repeat any of these ideas?

Determine Word Meanings

RI 4

Nonfiction writers often use literary techniques and elements such as figures of speech and allusions to convey ideas and to set a tone. Analyze Ackerman's use of literary techniques in this essay by looking at the elements in the chart.

Figurative Language	Connotation	Tone
Authors use **figurative language**—such as similes, metaphors, and personification—to help readers make connections to their own experiences. **Personification,** for example, attributes human qualities or abilities to an object, animal, or idea. In the first paragraph, how does the author personify the emotions of hate, fear, and jealousy? What does this personification imply about the power of emotions?	To influence how readers respond to their ideas, authors choose words and phrases that have **connotations,** or shades of associated meaning. For example, consider the underlying message the author conveys by using words and phrases such as "fields of glory," "love commands," "victory," and "daring as gladiators." What is the cumulative effect of employing so many figurative words?	**Tone** is the writer's attitude toward the subject or toward the reader of a work. To analyze tone, consider the writer's word choices. Are the connotations mostly positive or mostly negative? What kind of images do figures of speech present? How does Ackerman's use of an invented word ("People everywhere and *everywhen* . . .") convey her tone?

CLOSE READ

Analyze Ideas

RI 3

Have students work in small groups to discuss the bulleted questions. Before they begin, have them reread the essay and record the central ideas that Ackerman unfolds during the course of the essay. Then ask volunteers to read aloud the questions to consider as they analyze the ideas in the essay. Have students make connections between the ideas in the essay and the author's central point.

Determine Word Meanings

RI 4

Review the literary techniques and elements in the chart. Then have partners answer each question, referring explicitly to the criteria in the text.

Strategies for Annotation 📝 📄 *Annotate it!*

Analyze Ideas

RI 1, RI 3

Encourage students to use their eBook annotation tools to do the following:

- Highlight in yellow an idea that Ackerman states.
- Highlight in blue the details and examples she uses to support her idea.
- On a note, describe how this idea relates to the central point of the essay.

stealing a kiss in a quiet corner, she would smile. People everywhere and everywhen understand the phenomenon of love, just as they understand the appeal of music, finding it deeply meaningful even if they cannot explain exactly what that meaning is, why they respond viscerally to one composer and not another.

PRACTICE & APPLY

Analyzing the Text

RI 1, RI 2, RI 3, RI 4, RI 5

Possible answers:

1. *Ackerman is saying that love is an emotion that cannot be easily understood; it is ethereal. She develops this idea by comparing love to a dream state that has aspects of both nightmare and daydream, yet it is neither. Ackerman describes contrasting images and conflicting emotions to convey the ambiguous, paradoxical nature of love. For example, she describes love as "frantic and serene, vigilant and calm, wrung-out and fortified, explosive and sedate."*

2. *Ackerman presents love as being heroic, artistic, healing, calming, compassionate, annoying, uplifting, and corrupting. Her tone is informal; she exaggerates for humorous effect, using colloquial language such as "turned tough guys to mush," and "made mincemeat of kings."*

3. *Ackerman uses a metaphor to compare love to "a fabric whose pattern and brightness may vary." She also provides a series of quotations that exemplify the many different contexts for love, ranging from love of food to love of a child.*

4. *Ackerman includes references to the poems to support her idea that our vocabulary for speaking about love is so limited that people are forced to be very creative in order to express their feelings. Elizabeth Barrett Browning comes up with the conceit of counting the many ways she loves, and John Donne uses the extraordinary image of lovers' blood mingling in the stomach of a flea.*

5. *In the metaphor comparing love to a "traffic accident of the heart," Ackerman conveys the idea that people think of love as dangerous because it they have little control over it and it can hurt them.*

6. *The statement means that love is a constant in human history. Ackerman supports this idea with the example of seeing two people wearing very different clothing, yet recognizing that what they have in common is that they are both clothed.*

7. *Students' responses may vary but should be supported by text evidence. Students may suggest that Ackerman's tone is informal, inquisitive, enthusiastic, playful, or whimsical.*

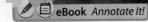

Analyzing the Text

RI 1, RI 2, RI 3, RI 4, RI 5, W 10, SL 1, SL 4

Cite Text Evidence Support your responses with evidence from the selection.

1. **Infer** Ackerman begins by stating that "Love is the great intangible." What does she mean by this statement? What details and examples in the first two paragraphs help to support this idea?

2. **Evaluate** In lines 28–33, what human qualities does Ackerman attribute to love? Describe the tone she creates by this use of personification.

3. **Cite Evidence** In lines 60–62, how does Ackerman use figurative language to support her idea that love "isn't monotone or uniform"? What additional evidence does she provide to support this point?

4. **Analyze** Why does Ackerman include references to Elizabeth Barrett Browning's poem "How Do I Love Thee?" and John Donne's poem "The Flea"? What point is she trying to make by citing these literary works?

5. **Infer** In line 105, Ackerman calls love "a sort of traffic accident of the heart." What idea about love is she conveying?

6. **Interpret** In lines 126–127, Ackerman writes, "Values, customs, and protocols may vary from ancient days to the present, but not the majesty of love." What does she mean by this statement? What example does she use to develop this idea?

7. **Evaluate** What is Ackerman's tone throughout the essay? Cite specific words and phrases she uses to create the tone.

PERFORMANCE TASK

Speaking Activity: Informative Presentation With a group, prepare a presentation on Ackerman's view that, as a nation, "we are embarrassed by love."

1. As the basis of your presentation, ask yourself these questions:

   - Why does Ackerman say we are embarrassed by love or inhibited about it? What evidence does she cite?
   - Does Ackerman herself find love embarrassing? Cite examples from the text.

2. Give a presentation based on your findings. Be sure to include specific examples from the text. Use appropriate eye contact and adequate volume to emphasize important ideas. As you speak, remember to use the conventions of standard English and to pronounce every word clearly and correctly.

Assign this performance task.

PERFORMANCE TASK

W 10, SL 1

Speaking Activity: Informative Presentation Have students reread the essay to cite evidence for the idea that we are "embarrassed by love." Encourage students to review the text and take notes about the evidence they find to help them answer the questions in their books. Remind students that their presentations should include examples from the text that support each idea. Have students do their presentations in a small group and then discuss their ideas. See page 172a for further instruction on participating in a collaborative discussion.

Critical Vocabulary

L 4a, L 4c, L 4d

intangible　　guise　　increment　　supple　　gradation

Practice and Apply　Create a semantic map like the one shown for the remaining Critical Vocabulary words. Use a dictionary or thesaurus as needed.

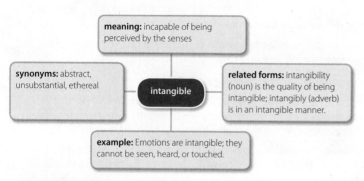

meaning: incapable of being perceived by the senses

synonyms: abstract, unsubstantial, ethereal

intangible

related forms: intangibility (noun) is the quality of being intangible; intangibly (adverb) is in an intangible manner.

example: Emotions are intangible; they cannot be seen, heard, or touched.

Vocabulary Strategy: Synonyms

When you encounter an unfamiliar word in an essay, you can often determine its meaning by substituting a **synonym**—a word with a similar meaning—for the unfamiliar word. For example, in the first line of the essay, Ackerman uses the Critical Vocabulary word *intangible*. The context clue "dream state" later in the paragraph indicates something unsubstantial. The synonym *unsubstantial* makes sense in the sentence.

Practice and Apply　Work with a partner to locate these words in the essay: *immense* (line 28), *ennobles* (line 51), *monotone* (line 60), *inhibited* (line 85). Follow these steps:

1. Look for a synonym in the sentence or paragraph where the unfamiliar word occurs.

2. Use context clues to determine meaning and think of a synonym that fits.

3. Substitute your synonym for the unfamiliar word to see if it makes sense.

4. Consult a dictionary or a thesaurus to confirm the meaning.

PRACTICE & APPLY

Critical Vocabulary

L 4a, L 4c, L 4d

Possible answers:

guise

meaning: form, outward appearance
related forms: disguise
example: Sherlock went undercover in the guise of a street peddler.
synonym: role

increment

meaning: gradual growth
related forms: incremental
example: Her salary has increased in increments of five percent per year.
synonym: addition

supple

meaning: flexible
related forms: suppleness
example: The supple gymnast gave an amazing performance.
synonym: adaptable

gradation

meaning: slight change
related forms: gradational, gradationally
example: The painting shows a smooth gradation of colors from deep blue to pale blue.
synonym: distinction, shade

Vocabulary Strategy: Synonyms

Possible answers:

immense: huge
ennobles: enriches
monotone: uniformity
inhibited: reluctant

Strategies for Annotation　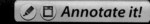 *Annotate it!*

Synonyms

L 4a, L 4c, L 4d

Have students locate *sedate* (line 8), *confines* (line 34), *ingest* (line 54), and *calibrate* (line 98) and look for context clues that suggest synonyms.

- Highlight the word in pink.
- Look for context clues. Highlight these in green.
- Determine a synonym for the word, and confirm the meaning by consulting a dictionary or thesaurus.
- On a note, insert the synonym in place of the word and see if it makes sense.

> In folk stories, unsuspecting lads and lasses ingest a love potion and quickly lose their hearts. As with all intoxicants, love comes in many guides and strengths. It has a mixed bouquet, and may include some piquant ingredients. One's taste in love will have a

PRACTICE & APPLY

Language and Style: Participial Phrases

Review the instruction and verify that students understand participial phrases. Read aloud the two examples, emphasizing the choppy, boring rhythm of the example that does not use a participial phrase. Discuss how the addition of participial phrases makes the images and ideas more vivid and interesting. Invite volunteers to find examples in the essay to illustrate the bulleted rules.

Possible answers:

Students' revisions should add meaning and details to their summaries.

Assess It Online!

Online Selection Test
- Download an editable ExamView bank.
- Assign and manage this test online.

Language and Style: Participial Phrases

A **participle** is a verb form that functions as an adjective. Like adjectives, they modify nouns and pronouns. Most participles are present-participle forms, ending in *–ing*, or past-participle forms, ending in *–ed* or *–en*. A **participial phrase** is a group of words that consists of either the present or past participle form of a verb and its modifiers. For example, the participial phrase in this sentence from "Love's Vocabulary" consists of a present participle (sitting) and an adverb (still):

> <u>Sitting still</u>, we are as daring as gladiators.

The phrase *sitting still* modifies the pronoun *we*. The author could have conveyed the same information this way:

> We are sitting still. We are as daring as gladiators.

However, the rhythm of these two sentences is choppy and uninteresting. Reread Ackerman's sentence and notice how her use of a participial phrase to combine the ideas adds variety and interest to her writing.

Several participial phrases may be used in one sentence to show different actions. Ackerman creates a sense of drama and builds interest by using participial phrases in combination to show several actions:

> <u>Hoping for victory</u>, <u>limping from the latest skirmish</u>, lovers enter the arena once again.

Here, two participial phrases, separated by commas, modify the noun *lovers*. Ackerman could have written simply, "Lovers enter the arena once again." However, she includes participial phrases to tell us more about the lovers. She adds meaning by describing the lovers' states of mind and by presenting a dramatic visual image.

Participial phrases may be placed at the beginning, the middle, or the end of a sentence. When using participial phrases in your own writing, it is important to place them carefully and to use punctuation correctly for clarity.

- A participial phrase should be placed close to the word it modifies, to avoid confusing the reader.
- A participial phrase that begins a sentence is followed by a comma.
- A participial phrase that is at the end of a sentence is preceded by a comma.
- A participial phrase that occurs in the middle of a sentence is set off by two commas, unless it is essential to the meaning of the sentence. If the sentence would not make sense without the phrase, omit the commas.

Practice and Apply Look back at the summary of the discussion about love and embarrassment you created in this selection's Performance Task. In your same group, revise the summary to add at least three participial phrases. Then discuss how the participial phrases improve the meaning or tone of the summary.

INTERACTIVE WHITEBOARD LESSON

Analyze Ideas: Participate in a Collaborative Discussion

RI 3, SL 1

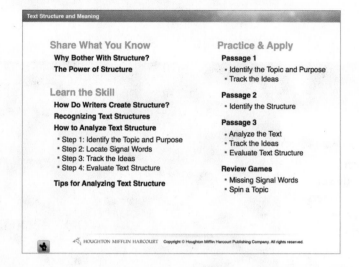

TEACH

Before students work on the Performance Task, review with them the requirements for successful participation in a **collaborative discussion:**

- Come to discussions prepared. During the discussion, refer to evidence to stimulate a thoughtful, well-reasoned exchange of ideas.
- Work with peers to set rules for discussions and decision-making.
- Ask and respond to questions.
- Actively incorporate others into the discussion.
- Clarify, verify, or challenge ideas and conclusions.
- Respond thoughtfully to different perspectives.
- Summarize points of agreement and disagreement.
- Make new connections in light of the evidence and reasoning presented.

COLLABORATIVE DISCUSSION

Direct students to complete the Performance Task, referring to what they have learned in this lesson.

Analyze Ideas

RI 3

RETEACH

Review what students have learned about finding supporting reasons, examples, and details in a text.

- **Reasons** are statements that support a claim or an idea.
- **Examples** are used to illustrate an idea.
- **Facts** are statements that can be proved or verified.

Tell students that they can apply this skill in reverse—that is, they can examine reasons, examples, and facts to infer the key idea. For example, Ackerman presents the example of the ancient Egyptian woman's reaction to modern life (lines 13–17) and then describes her reaction to seeing lovers kissing (lines 17–18) to suggest the idea that the woman has more in common with modern people than one would think.

LEVEL UP TUTORIALS Assign the following *Level Up* tutorial: **Reading for Details.**

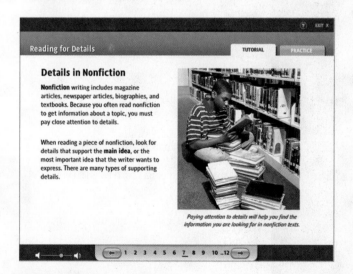

INDEPENDENT READING

Students can apply the skill to a selection from a textbook or other informational text. Have them work independently to infer the key ideas from the details in the text.

my Smart Planner — Create lesson plans and access resources online.

MEDIA My Shakespeare

Poem by Kate Tempest

Why This Text?

Students should realize there are clear links between classic myths, legends, plays, and modern artistic creations. This poem and a video of its performance illustrate this connection between the words, characters, and themes of Shakespeare and the creative artists who followed—including those who are leading the way to new forms of expression in the 21st century.

Key Learning Objective: The student will be able to analyze how a modern artist draws on and transforms source material for a new artistic expression.

RL 1 Cite textual evidence.
RL 2 Determine theme.
RL 4 Analyze the impact of word choices on meaning and tone.
RL 7 Analyze representations in two different mediums.
RL 9 Analyze source material.
L 3 Understand how language functions in different contexts.

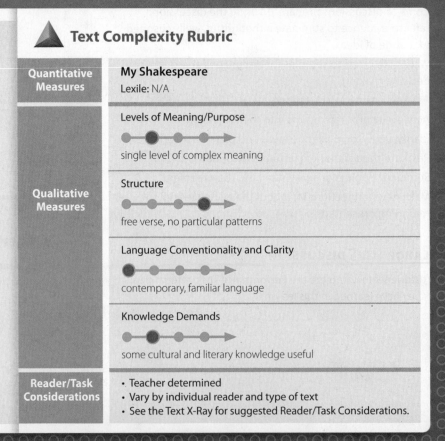

▲ Text Complexity Rubric

Quantitative Measures

My Shakespeare
Lexile: N/A

Qualitative Measures

Levels of Meaning/Purpose

single level of complex meaning

Structure

free verse, no particular patterns

Language Conventionality and Clarity

contemporary, familiar language

Knowledge Demands

some cultural and literary knowledge useful

Reader/Task Considerations
• Teacher determined
• Vary by individual reader and type of text
• See the Text X-Ray for suggested Reader/Task Considerations.

Meaning Making

Language Development

Effective Expression

Content Knowledge

Foundational Skills

English Language Support Before teaching, use the Text X-Ray below for an overview of the text's complexity. The Text X-Ray and supports and scaffolds in the Teacher's Edition will help you guide students of different skill levels

Text Complexity: Qualitative Measures

Levels of Meaning/Purpose

single level of complex meaning

Help students analyze meaning in a poem and performance inspired by Shakespeare.

- Teacher's Edition side notes, pp. 173, 174, 175, 176
- When Students Struggle, p. 174
- Analyze Source Material: Interpretations of Shakespeare, p. 176

To reteach analyzing source material and themes, see.

- Analyze Source Material, p. 176a

 Use It! Level Up **Tutorial:** Universal and Recurring Themes

ZOOM IN ON **ANALYZING INTERPRETATIONS** Have students read the poem to themselves before they watch Tempest's performance of it. Then have small groups compare their understanding of the poem before and after they saw it performed. Provide these sentence frames:

- One idea from the poem that the video supports is ___.
- When Tempest says, "He's my Shakespeare," she means ___.
- Tempest's gestures, or body movements, add to the poem's meaning by ___.
- The style of the video helps viewers understand that Shakespeare is ___.

Have groups share their ideas in a class discussion.

Structure

free verse, no particular patterns

Help students analyze the structure of a free-verse poem.

- Teacher's Edition side note, p. 174
- Analyze Source Material: Interpretations of Shakespeare, p. 176

ZOOM IN ON **ANALYZING CHARACTER AND THEME** Tell students that while **free verse** does not have a prescribed structure, **sound devices** such as **alliteration** ("father with a favorite") and **rhyme** ("rest" and "chest") help make connections between words and across lines. Have students work with a partner to identify other examples of sound devices within the poem. As they listen to the performance, have students follow along with the text, noting examples of sound devices.

Language Conventionality and Clarity

contemporary, familiar language

Teach unfamiliar vocabulary in context.

- Applying Academic Vocabulary, p. 175
- Teacher's Edition side note, p. 175
- English Language Support, p. 173

Prompt students to discuss the impact of the video performance.

- Teacher's Edition side note, p. 175

To teach analyzing allusions, see

- Analyze Language, p. 176a

 Use It! **Interactive Whiteboard Lessons:** Figurative Language and Imagery, Sound Devices in Poetry

ZOOM IN ON **PREVIEWING IDIOMS** Explain that many phrases from Shakespeare's writing have become **idioms** in modern English—expressions that mean something different from the literal or exact meaning of the words. Before students watch or read Tempest's work, discuss some of the idioms she cites in lines 18–28.

- "set your teeth on edge" ("make you feel annoyed")
- "method in our madness" (*"plan that explains odd behavior"*)
- "hair standing on end" (*"feeling afraid"*)
- "our hearts were upon our sleeves" (*"we showed our feelings openly"*)
- "break the ice" (*"make people feel more relaxed"*)
- "green eyed monster" (*"envy"*)
- "in a pickle" (*"in trouble"*)

Knowledge Demands

some cultural and literary knowledge useful

Help students identify with and know the poet better by sharing some additional facts about her background.

- Teacher's Edition Background note, p. 173

ZOOM IN ON **BUILDING KNOWLEDGE** Kate Tempest (born Kate Calvert in 1985) is a great role model for students who may feel like they don't "fit in." She describes herself as having been detached, alienated, angry, and disruptive during secondary school. Even in college, she found that she was very different from her classmates. Her discovery of hip-hop and rapping changed her life by giving her a way to express herself and a community.

Suggested Reader/Task Considerations

You might consider the following before assigning this poem and performance to students.

- Do students have adequate familiarity with British pronunciations to comprehend Tempest's rapid-fire delivery of her poem?
- Do students have enough knowledge of vocabulary to recognize the **idioms** and **allusions** in the text?

ZOOM IN ON **SUPPORTING COMPREHENSION**

- Suggest that students pause the video as needed to check the text; then they can replay the sections they missed. Also encourage them to pay attention to Tempest's gestures. For example, at one point she counts off on her fingers the points she is making, which shows she is listing examples or evidence.
- Pair English learners with native English speakers who can help them recognize and decode idioms and allusions. This may also benefit native speakers who are so used to hearing the idioms that they might otherwise fail to notice them.

CLOSE READ

Kate Tempest Have students read the information about the author and the 2012 World Shakespeare Festival. Explain that like modern rappers, Shakespeare provided popular entertainment for all classes of people while serving to explore and illuminate themes that have fascinated people for centuries.

Kate Tempest's poem, along with the work of hundreds of others in the World Shakespeare Festival, show that the bard's works remain as inspirational and moving for young people today as they have for centuries. Tempest's performance demonstrates her emotional involvement with Shakespeare's language and characters, and she makes her connection clearly personal through the title and the last lines of the poem.

Suggest that if Shakespeare can inspire such emotion in a young, popular rapper and poet like Kate Tempest, then Shakespeare's works might deserve close attention. Although the words and characters are old, the ideas, conflicts, and themes are as new as tomorrow's dawn.

AS YOU VIEW AND READ Direct students to use the As You View and Read note to focus their reading and viewing.

Analyze Source Material   RL 7, RL 9
(VIDEO)

In addition to thinking about Kate Tempest's delivery, ask students to note style elements of the video itself, such as its shot composition, industrial setting, rapid-fire cuts, brief flashes of color and text insertions, etc.

Ⓐ **ASK STUDENTS** to explain how these stylistic features contribute to the video's overall tone and meaning. Suggest that they consider how the viewing experience might differ if the video were developed in a different style, such as using steady shots and smooth dissolves within a pastoral setting. Would this influence their understanding of the text? *(Answers will vary. Students should show that they have considered how the stylistic features affected the way they understood the ideas in the video. For example, students may mention the text insertions as helpful or perhaps disruptive.)*

Background Kate Tempest *is a London-born poet, playwright, and rapper. She began performing at age 16 and has performed all over the world, winning acclaim and awards at music festivals and poetry slams. Her first collection of poetry,* Everything Speaks in its Own Way, *was published in 2012 and includes a CD and a DVD along with the text. The Royal Shakespeare Company commissioned Kate to write and perform "My Shakespeare" for the World Shakespeare Festival in 2012. Thousands of artists from around the world participated in this festival throughout Britain as well as online.*

MEDIA ANALYSIS

My Shakespeare

Poem by Kate Tempest

AS YOU VIEW AND READ Think about what Kate Tempest's delivery—her voice and gestures—add to the poem. Write down any questions you generate during both viewing and reading.

Image Credits: ©Royal Shakespeare Company

My Shakespeare   **173**

ENGLISH LANGUAGE SUPPORT

Vocabulary: Figurative Language Explain that lines 18–28 contain some of Shakespeare's figurative phrases that have become commonly used in modern speech.

ASK STUDENTS to review the lines listed below. As necessary, help them understand the idiomatic meaning of each phrase.

- Lines 18–19, "set your teeth on edge" *(create discomfort or distaste)*
- Line 20, "method in our madness" *(a reason behind surprising actions)*
- Lines 22–23, "hearts were upon our sleeves" *(emotions were obvious)*
- Line 25, "the pen is mightier than the sword" *(words and thoughts can be more powerful than physical force)*

Analyze Theme (LINES 1–17)   RL 2

Remind students that a **theme** is the dominating or central idea of a literary work. Have students think about Tempest's main idea as they read and reread the poem.

 ASK STUDENTS to summarize the general idea of the first three stanzas. Make sure that they first connect the possessive pronoun that begins each stanza with the poem's title. *(Shakespeare is present in a broad variety of human situations, possibly through the omnipresence of the many archetypical characters he created. Tempest is speaking about Shakespeare's ubiquity, not only in contemporary language and theater, but also in our lives.)*

Analyze Word Choice   RL 4

(LINES 1–7)

Explain to students that **alliteration** is the repetition of the initial sound of two or more words in a line, as in "same sound." **Rhyme** is the repetition of the same or similar sound created by vowels and consonants the ends of words, as in "found sound." Both are examples of **sound devices.**

 CITE TEXT EVIDENCE Ask students to identify the sound devices that Tempest employs in the first stanza. *(alliteration: whispered word, father with a favorite; rhyme: rest and chest)* Once students locate the examples, have them cite additional examples of alliteration and rhyme throughout the poem. Point out that although "My Shakespeare" is an example of free verse, without regular meter or rhyme pattern, these poetic conventions add a surprising emphasis to lines.

My Shakespeare

Performance by Kate Tempest

He's in every lover who ever stood alone beneath a window,
In every jealous whispered word,
in every ghost that will not rest.
He's in every father with a favorite,
5   Every eye that stops to linger
On what someone else has got, and feels the tightening in their
    chest.

He's in every young man growing boastful,
Every worn out elder, drunk all day;
muttering false prophecies and squandering their lot.
10 He's there—in every mix-up that spirals far out of control—and
    never seems to end,
even when its beginnings are forgot.

He's in every girl who ever used her wits. Who ever did her best.
In every vain admirer,
Every passionate, ambitious social climber,
15 And in every misheard word that ever led to tempers fraying,
Every pawn that moves exactly as the player wants it to,
And still remains convinced that it's not playing.

He's in every star crossed lover, in every thought that ever set your
teeth on edge, in every breathless hero, stepping closer to the ledge,
20 his is the method in our madness, as pure as the driven snow—his is
the hair standing on end, he saw that all that glittered was not gold.
He knew we hadn't slept a wink, and that our hearts were upon our
sleeves, and that the beast with two backs had us all upon our knees
as we fought fire with fire, he knew that too much of a good thing,
25 can leave you up in arms, the pen is mightier than the sword, still
his words seem to sing our names as they strike, and his is the milk
of human kindness, warm enough to break the ice—his, the green
eyed monster, in a pickle, still, discretion is the better part of valor,
his letters with their arms around each others shoulders, swagger
30 towards the ends of their sentences, pleased with what they've done,
his words are the setting for our stories—he has become a poet who
poetics have embedded themselves deep within the fabric of our
language, he's in our mouths, his words have tangled round our own
and given rise to expressions so effective in expressing how we feel,
35 we can't imagine how we'd feel without them.

WHEN STUDENTS STRUGGLE...

To develop reading fluency, divide students into groups of three. Have them alternate reading one of the first three stanzas of the poem out loud. Emphasize that people often read poems aloud, using different pacing and emphasis, in order to explore and discover meaning. Students study the video performance before beginning their own readings, but they should attempt to develop their own style and emphasis rather than mimic Tempest's performance

After each student has read each stanza aloud once (three readings of the stanzas), ask volunteer groups to present their readings to the class. Discuss how different voices and different presentations can change the impact of a poem.

See—he's less the tights and garters—more the sons demanding **E**
  answers from the absence of their fathers.
The hot darkness of your last embrace.
He's in the laughter of the night before, the tightened jaw of the
  morning after,
He's in us. Part and parcel of our Royals and our rascals.
40 He's more than something taught in classrooms, in language that's
  hard to understand,
he's more than a feeling of inadequacy when we sit for our exams,
He's in every wise woman, every pitiful villain,
Every great king, every sore loser, every fake tear.
His legacy exists in the life that lives in everything he's written,
45 And me, I see him everywhere, he's my Shakespeare.

COLLABORATIVE DISCUSSION With a partner, discuss the overall effect of the video. Cite words and phrases in the video that depart from the text of the poem and consider whether these variations affect your response.

APPLYING ACADEMIC VOCABULARY

attribute	underlie

As you discuss the video performance of the poem, incorporate the Collection 4 academic vocabulary words: *attribute* and *underlie*. Ask students to identify **attributes** of Tempest's character that make her performance so powerful. Discuss what beliefs, motivations, and passions **underlie** her ability to write and perform such a moving poem.

CLOSE READ

Determine Figurative Meanings (LINES 18–28; 36–37)

RL 1, RL 4, RL 9, L 5a

Explain that an **adage** is a concise, memorable statement of an idea; a **cliché** is a commonly overused phrase that describes an idea or situation; and an **idiom** is a group of words that mean something other than their original meaning. Note that the fourth stanza has several examples of figures of speech that originated in Shakespeare's work.

D **CITE TEXT EVIDENCE** Have students reread lines 18–28. Have them identify any adages, clichés, or idioms with which they are familiar. Have them list and categorize these phrases and paraphrase their meanings. Then ask them to consider Tempest's purpose for including them in her poem. *(Sample answers: adages—all that glittered was not gold, pen is mightier than the sword; clichés—star crossed lover, fought fire with fire, pure as driven snow; idioms—set your teeth on edge, method in our madness. She wants to demonstrate the extent to which Shakespeare's language has permeated our everyday language.)*

E **ASK STUDENTS** to identify, paraphrase, and explain the figurative language in lines 36 and 37. *(Tempest compares two metaphors to show that Shakespeare is more relevant to modern social issues [i.e., single-parent families] than to the distant past [Elizabethan fashion].)*

Analyze Theme (LINES 36–45)

RL 2

Explain that poets can convey their themes inferentially or they can state them explicitly.

F **ASK STUDENTS** to summarize the central idea of the final stanza. *(Shakespeare is important and very much present in contemporary life.)* Have them locate in the stanza the poem's overall theme *(lines 44–45)*.

COLLABORATIVE DISCUSSION Call on pairs to share their interpretations of the video with the class. Accept all reasonable responses. Discuss areas of consensus or disagreement with the whole class.

ASK STUDENTS to share any questions they generated in the course of viewing, reading, and discussing the selection.

Analyze Source Material: Interpretations of Shakespeare

RL 9

Have students discuss their own encounters with Shakespeare's work in any media. Ask students to consider the different yet related experiences of viewing a performance, reading it silently, and reading it aloud. Have them identify any particular strengths and weaknesses of each presentation.

Analyzing Text and Video

RL 1, RL 2, RL 9, W 6

Possible answers:

1. *The repetition signals that what follows is another allusion to one of Shakespeare's characters or themes. Tempest is conveying the message that Shakespeare's characters and themes connect to human emotions and experiences that are so universal and timeless that we can recognize the same forces at work in ourselves and in the people around us.*

2. *Tempest is referring to the fact that many colorful phrases from Shakespeare's plays have become such an accepted part of our everyday language that we use them without even realizing that Shakespeare coined them. As evidence, Tempest provides a long list of phrases, from "star crossed lover" to "the green eyed monster," to "the better part of valor."*

3. *The text emphasizes that what Shakespeare is really about is life—human emotions with which we can all connect. Tempest's passion and sincerity, combined with the contemporary style of her performance, drive home the idea of Shakespeare's relevance.*

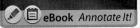 eBook *Annotate It!*

Analyze Source Material: Interpretations of Shakespeare

RL 9

Kate Tempest's passionate performance of her poem demonstrates the great appeal Shakespeare has for today's youth. Shakespeare's work has been translated into more than 80 languages; it has been adapted, televised, filmed, recorded, and digitized. Shakespeare's significant presence on the Internet attests to the fact that his work has inspired—and is still inspiring—the work of countless artists.

Authors often draw on historical, literary, and cultural sources for themes or topics, using their own imagination to transform the source material into their own original works of art. Just as Shakespeare drew inspiration from earlier sources, Kate Tempest attributes her inspiration for "My Shakespeare" to the works of Shakespeare himself. In the first three stanzas, she makes allusions to the characters, themes, and scenarios exposed in Shakespeare's well-known plays. The fourth stanza comprises phrases coined by Shakespeare that are still in use today. In the last stanza, Tempest gets at the heart of Shakespeare's continued relevance.

Analyzing Text and Video

RL 1, RL 2, RL 9, W 6

Cite Text Evidence Support your responses with evidence from the selection.

1. **Infer** "He's in every lover . . . beneath a window" is an allusion to Romeo that is recognizable even to readers who have not read *Romeo and Juliet*. What does the repetition of the words "in every" throughout the poem signal to readers? What message does Tempest convey through these words?

2. **Cite Evidence** Explain the statement that Shakespeare is "in our mouths, his words have tangled round our own." What evidence does the author provide to support this idea?

3. **Analyze** In the last stanza, Tempest acknowledges the negative ideas that today's young people might have about Shakespeare. How do the text and the video work together to refute these ideas?

PERFORMANCE TASK

Media Activity: Reflection Can Kate Tempest's Shakespeare be *your* Shakespeare?

- Create a blog that features Kate Tempest's performance of "My Shakespeare."
- Write an introduction or make your own video to introduce Kate Tempest's performance.

- Explain how you responded to the poem, citing specific examples from the text and the video.
- Use conventions of standard written English.

Assign this performance task.

PERFORMANCE TASK

RL 9

Media Activity: Reflection Remind students to consider the visual aspects of Kate Tempest's video and to discuss how these elements influence the overall impact of her performance. Encourage interested students to incorporate images and multimedia elements into their blogs.

Analyze Language

RL 4

TEACH

Remind students that an **allusion** is a figure of speech that indirectly refers to a literary or historical person, place, event, or to another literary or artistic work. Writers use allusions to add evocative connotations, greater depth, and deeper meaning to a text. However, in order for an allusion to function effectively, the reader must be able to recognize the reference and understand its meaning.

For example, when Mercutio, a character in *The Tragedy of Romeo and Juliet,* says, "O, then I see Queen Mab hath been with you," he is alluding to Mab, a fairy queen. Everyone in Shakespeare's audience would have easily recognized the allusion to a character in popular folk tales.

PRACTICE AND APPLY

Point out that, given the title and context of "My Shakespeare," readers should expect to encounter allusions to Shakespeare's plays. Even Kate Tempest's name combines an allusion to Kate from *The Taming of the Shrew* and the title of *The Tempest.* Ask volunteers to cite and explain any allusions that they may have noticed.

Then have students reread the first three stanzas of the poem. Explain that all the descriptions of people in these lines, from the lover to the pawn, are allusions to characters in Shakespeare's plays.

Divide the class into small groups. Assign one stanza to each group, and ask them to identify to which characters or plays their stanza refers. Students will likely need to conduct research to complete the task. Then have each group share their findings with the class.

- Possible allusions in lines 1–17 include the following: First stanza: Romeo, Othello, Hamlet, Macbeth, Lear, Iago
- Second stanza: *The Merry Wives of Windsor,* Falstaff, *A Midsummer Night's Dream*
- Third stanza: Rosalind, *Much Ado About Nothing,* Lady Macbeth, Rosencrantz and Guildenstern

Analyze Source Material

RL 9

RETEACH

Review the concept of authors and artists incorporating the plots and themes of other works, particularly from classic texts of the past. Explain that Greek myths provided source materials for Roman poets, Roman works served as sources for Shakespearean plays, and Shakespeare inspired *Star Wars*, as well as many other modern artists.

One explanation for such a continuum of content is that these sources all express **universal themes**, common experiences and ideas about human life that have persisted in our culture for millennia. These themes—of love, hate, envy, sacrifice, revenge—and the archetypal heroes and villains who embody them, resurface and reappear in a variety of related sources.

 LEVEL UP TUTORIALS Assign the following *Level Up* tutorial: **Universal and Recurring Themes**

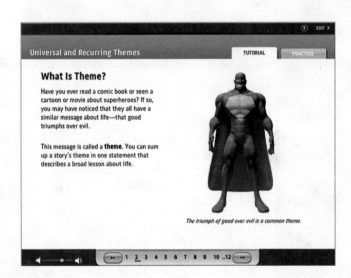

INDEPENDENT READING

Students can apply the skill to other pieces of literature. Ask them to identify examples of sources on which other texts, movies, or other performances have been based. Students can share their ideas and interpretations in pairs or small groups.

ANCHOR TEXT

The Tragedy of Romeo and Juliet

Drama by William Shakespeare

Why This Text?

Variations on the story of Romeo and Juliet abound, epitomizing as it does the passionate intensity of young love. In this lesson, students are introduced to the beauty of the language, the timelessness of the characters and theme, and the complexities of the plot in Shakespeare's enduring classic.

▶ **View It!**

Professional Development Podcast:

Text-Dependent Analysis

Key Learning Objective: The student will be able analyze character motivations and parallel plots.

For additional practice:

Close Reader selection
from The Tragedy of Romeo and Juliet, Prologue and Act 2, Scene 2
Drama by William Shakespeare

RL 1 Cite textual evidence.

RL 2 Determine a theme and analyze its development.

RL 3 Analyze how complex characters develop over the course of the text.

RL 4 Determine the meaning of words and phrases as they are used in a text.

RL 5 Analyze an author's choices concerning how to structure a text, order events (parallel plots), and manipulate time.

W 3 Write narratives to develop real or imagined experiences.

W 10 Write routinely over extended time frames and shorter time frames.

SL 1 Initiate and participate effectively in a range of collaborative discussions.

L 1a Use parallel structure.

L 5a Interpret figures of speech in context.

▲ Text Complexity Rubric

Quantitative Measures	**The Tragedy of Romeo and Juliet** Lexile: N/A
Qualitative Measures	**Levels of Meaning/Purpose** ●─●─●─●─► multiple levels of meaning (multiple themes)
	Structure ●─●─●─●─► complex structures
	Language Conventionality and Clarity ●─●─●─●─► archaic, unfamiliar language
	Knowledge Demands ●─●─●─●─► cultural and literary knowledge essential to understanding
Reader/Task Considerations	• Teacher determined • Vary by individual reader and type of text • See the Text X-Ray for suggested Reader/Task Considerations.

Meaning Making

Language Development

Effective Expression

Content Knowledge

Foundational Skills

English Language Support Before teaching, use the Text X-Ray below for an overview of the text's complexity. The Text X-Ray and supports and scaffolds in the Teacher's Edition will help you guide students of different skill levels.

Text Complexity: Qualitative Measures

Levels of Meaning/Purpose

multiple levels of meaning (multiple themes)

Guide students to analyze and support inferences about characters.

- Teacher's Edition side notes, pp. 177, 182–205, 207–226, 228–251, 253–264, 266–278, 279
- When Students Struggle, pp. 177, 185, 195, 196, 224–225, 250
- Strategies for Annotation, pp. 187, 194, 221, 255, 272, 279
- Analyze Character: Motivations, p. 279

Support students' comprehension of the text.

- Close Read Screencasts, pp. 183, 207, 228, 253
- English Language Support, pp. 184, 218, 271
- When Students Struggle, pp. 179, 192–193, 210, 230–231, 242–243, 247, 263, 270, 277

Help students determine the play's themes.

- Teacher's Edition side notes, pp. 214, 226, 278

ZOOM IN ON **ANALYZING CHARACTER MOTIVATION** Explain to students that a **motivation** is a reason why a **character** does something. As students read the play, have pairs meet at the end of each act to discuss the five factors listed on page 279. Which factors motivated which characters during the act? Give them the following list of questions to consider, and then have them share their answers in small groups.

- Who did something to please his or her family?
- Who acted because of love or passion?
- What did a character do because he or she felt afraid?
- Did a misunderstanding or mistake cause a character to do something?
- Did anyone take action because he or she felt hopeless or sad?

Structure

complex structures

Teach students to analyze plot, including parallel plots.

- Teacher's Edition side notes, pp. 182–205, 207–226, 228–251, 253–264, 266–278, 279
- When Students Struggle, pp. 216–217, 222, 233, 244, 256–257, 268–269
- Strategies for Annotation, pp. 202, 279
- Analyze Author's Choices: Parallel Plots, p. 279

Guide students to analyze text structure.

- Teacher's Edition side notes, pp. 177, 179, 183, 207, 256

To reteach analyzing parallel plots, see

- Analyze Author's Choices: Parallel Plots, p. 282a

ZOOM IN ON **ANALYZING PARALLEL PLOTS** Have pairs focus on the play's two main **parallel plots**—the story of the feud between the Montague and Capulet families, and the love story between Romeo and Juliet. Partners should each fill out a story map for one of the plots, noting the **characters**, central **conflict**, and major **events**. Have pairs work on their story maps as they finish reading each act. After pairs have filled in their maps for each act, convene the class to discuss how the two plots interact. Ask: *How are the events in one story affecting the other story? How do the plots contrast with each other?*

Language Conventionality and Clarity

archaic, unfamiliar language

Teach unfamiliar vocabulary in context.

- Applying Academic Vocabulary, p. 182, 211, 237, 258, 275

Guide students to understand the language of Shakespeare, including archaic and figurative language, blank verse, allusions, and word play.

- Teacher's Edition side notes, pp. 178, 179, 181, 182–205, 207–226, 228–251, 253–264, 266–278
- English Language Support, pp. 178, 186, 188, 189, 197, 200, 212, 213, 223, 229, 235, 239, 248, 281
- When Students Struggle, pp. 179, 201
- Strategies for Annotation, pp. 209, 234, 236, 245, 261
- Vocabulary Strategy: Puns, p. 281

Help students understand multiple-meaning words.

- English Language Support, p. 241

Help students understand parallel structure.

- Language and Style: Parallel Structure, p. 282

ZOOM IN ON **RECOGNIZING PUNS** Help students grasp that many English words have more than one meaning. Explain that a **pun** is a kind of **word play**, and describe these two kinds:

- Two or more meanings of the same word make sense in the sentence.
- Two different words that sound the same appear close together.

Display lines 11–22 in Act I, Scene 4. Together, identify the puns in this passage and decide which kind each one is. *("Being but heavy, I will bear the light"; "You have . . . nimble soles; I have a soul of lead"; "I am too sore enpierced . . . To soar with his light feathers"; "so bound / I cannot bound")* Tell students that they should be alert to such word play as they read, but they do not need to analyze every pun to enjoy the play.

Knowledge Demands

cultural and literary knowledge essential to understanding

Support English Learners in understanding the play's historical and cultural context.

- Teacher's Edition side notes, pp. 180, 181, 182
- English Language Support, pp. 214, 246, 267
- When Students Struggle, p. 191

 For more context and historical background, students can view the video "Biography: William Shakespeare" in their eBooks.

ZOOM IN ON **BUILDING CULTURAL KNOWLEDGE** Shakespeare presents the couple as "star-crossed lovers," doomed to disaster by fate. To understand what star-crossed means, you have to realize that most people of Shakespeare's time believed in astrology. They believed that the course of their lives was partly determined by the hour, day, month, and year of their birth-hence "the stars" under which they were born.

Suggested Reader/Task Considerations

You might consider the following before assigning this essay to students.

- Will the language and style of this play be off-putting to some students?
- Do students possess the necessary attention to read and comprehend the text?

ZOOM IN ON **SUPPORTING COMPREHENSION**

- Teach Kate Tempest's poem and performance before the play to help students recognize the poet's relevance despite the foreign-sounding language.
- Suggest that students work in small groups to take on the roles of the characters in each act.

Characteristics of Shakespearean Tragedy

Characters

Remind students that drama develops understanding of character and plot through dialogue and action. Through what they say and do, characters reveal their traits, motivations, thoughts, and feelings. Point out that the conflict, or struggle, between the antagonist and the protagonist, or hero, drives the action as the characters try to solve the complications resulting from it. Explain also that Shakespeare's plays are populated with many minor characters. Often a foil is a minor character.

Dramatic Conventions

To familiarize students with the dramatic conventions in the chart, use this activity:

- Have volunteers improvise dialogue for a soliloquy and an aside. Prompt them by suggesting that their character feels discouraged about a test grade or hopeful about being nominated for a class officer position.
- Have students give examples of comic relief or dramatic irony from television shows or films.
- As a class, discuss what each dramatic convention adds to the drama.

Shakespearean Drama

Shakespeare's 38 plays may be more popular today than they were in Elizabethan times. While Shakespeare's comedies and histories remain crowd-pleasing classics, his tragedies are perhaps his most powerful works. One of the most famous, **The Tragedy of Romeo and Juliet,** *relates the tale of two love-struck teens caught between the tension of their feuding families.*

Characteristics of Shakespearean Tragedy

A **tragedy** is a drama that results in a catastrophe—most often death—for the main characters. Shakespearean tragedies, however, offer us more than just despair; they provide comic moments that counter the underlying tension of the serious plot. Before you begin *The Tragedy of Romeo and Juliet,* familiarize yourself with some of the character types and dramatic conventions of Shakespearean tragedy.

Characters	Dramatic Conventions
Tragic Hero • the protagonist, or central character • usually fails or dies because of a character flaw or a cruel twist of fate	**Soliloquy** • a speech given by a character alone • exposes a character's thoughts and feelings to the audience
Antagonist • the adversary or hostile force opposing the protagonist • can be a character, a group of characters, or a nonhuman entity	**Aside** • a character's remark that others on stage do not hear • reveals the character's private thoughts
Foil • a character whose personality and attitude contrast sharply with those of another character • emphasizes another character's attributes and traits, such as a timid, introverted character making a talkative one seem even chattier	**Dramatic Irony** • when the audience knows more than the characters • helps build suspense
	Comic Relief • a humorous scene or speech intended to relieve tension • heightens the seriousness of the main action by contrast

WHEN STUDENTS STRUGGLE . . .

Write the terms *tragic hero (protagonist), antagonist,* and *foil* on the board. Then list the characters from a familiar story or movie. Have students work in pairs to identify the tragic hero/protagonist, the antagonist, and a foil for the protagonist.

ASK STUDENTS to explain the role of each character in the story or film. Then have them discuss how the conflict between the protagonist and the antagonist leads to the action of the story.

The Language of Shakespeare

Blank Verse

To help students hear the stressed and unstressed syllables, read these two lines of iambic pentameter from the play aloud:
Yet tell me not, for I have heard it all. Here's much to do with hate but more with love.

Read them a second time, tapping a ruler or pencil at every stressed syllable. Have students count the number of stresses in each line.

Allusion and Word Play

Clarify the concept of an allusion by pointing out that Romeo himself has become an allusion. Tell students that a male in love or pining away for a woman is referred to as a Romeo. Make sure that students are aware of the difference between *allusion* and *illusion* both in spelling and meaning. An illusion is a false perception.

To illustrate the concept of a pun, write this example on the board:

Time flies like an arrow. Fruit flies like a banana.

Have students point out the two words that have dual meanings and thus create the humor. *(flies, like)*

Elizabethan Words to Know

Read each word aloud for students. Have them repeat the words. Then write this sentence on the board:

If anything should happen before the morning, then please hurry to send a message right away from here.

Have students identify which words can be replaced with entries from the glossary. Rewrite the sentence with their suggestions. *(An aught should happen ere the morrow, prithee hie to send a message anon hence.)*

The Language of Shakespeare

Blank Verse Shakespeare wrote his plays primarily in blank verse, unrhymed lines of **iambic pentameter**, a meter that contains five unstressed syllables (˘), each followed by a stressed syllable (´). Read the following lines aloud, making sure to emphasize each stressed syllable:

> *Here's much to do with hate but more with love.*

While this pattern forms the general rule, variations in the rhythm prevent the play from sounding monotonous. As you read, pay close attention to places where characters speak in rhyming poetry instead of unrhymed verse.

Allusion and Word Play An **allusion** is a reference to a literary or historical person or event that the audience is expected to know. Shakespeare's audience was familiar with Greek and Roman mythology and the Bible, so his plays include many references to these works.

Shakespeare also includes many **puns,** humor resulting from words with similar sounds and different meanings. For example, a depressed Romeo utters a pun using the word *light* when he offers to carry a torch: "Being but heavy, I will bear the light."

Elizabethan Words to Know

'a: he.

an, and: if.

anon: soon; right away.

aught: anything.

coz: short for cousin; used to refer to relatives or close friends.

ere: before.

e'er: ever.

god-den: good evening.

God gi' go-den: God give you a good evening.

hence: from here.

hie: hurry.

hither: here.

marry: a short form of "by the Virgin Mary" and so a mild exclamation.

morrow: morning.

naught: nothing.

o'er: over.

prithee: pray thee, or please.

sirrah: a term used to address a servant.

soft: be still; quiet; wait a minute.

thither: there.

whence: where.

wherefore: why.

wot: know.

yond, yonder: over there.

ENGLISH LANGUAGE SUPPORT

Language: Allusions Review the definition of allusions with students, reminding them that they may have encountered this device in other literary works. Explain that by using allusions, Shakespeare conveys meaning without having to explain it. Tell them that often they can identify allusions by looking for capitalized names that do not refer to characters and by checking the marginal notes, which sometimes explain the reference. Write this line on the board: "She'll not be hit with Cupid's arrow." Tell students that Cupid is the god of love. Being hit by Cupid's arrow means that the person falls in love.

Reading Shakespearean Drama

Use the following tips to help you better understand *Romeo and Juliet*:

Reading Drama

- Study the opening cast of characters to see who's in the play.

- Read the stage directions to find out where a scene takes place as well as who's on stage and what they're doing. Stage directions in *Romeo and Juliet* are minimal, so you'll sometimes have to infer what's happening from the dialogue.

- Visualize the setting and the action by noting key details in the stage directions.

Reading Shakespearean Tragedy

- Keep track of the relationships between characters—are they friends, relatives, or enemies? Also, consider a character's dramatic function—tragic hero, antagonist, foil, or comic relief—which will help you interpret his or her words and actions.

- Note important character traits revealed through dialogue, soliloquies, and asides, as well as the through the action. Do the characters exhibit any flaws or weaknesses?

- Look for cause-and-effect relationships between events, especially those events that lead to the tragic outcome. You can keep track of them by using a graphic like this flowchart.

Cause
To cheer up Romeo, Benvolio and some other Montagues lead him to a party that the Capulets are giving.

Effect
At the party, Romeo sees Juliet for the first time, and he falls madly in love with her.

Reading Shakespeare's Language

- Use the marginal notes to figure out word meanings and unusual sentence structures. Record difficult lines and then rephrase them in modern speech.

- Paraphrase passages to help clarify their meaning and to summarize events, ideas, and themes. Use your own words without including your own opinions.

- Just as when you read poetry, don't automatically stop reading when you come to the end of a line. Look carefully at each line's punctuation and consider the meaning of the complete sentence or phrase.

WHEN STUDENTS STRUGGLE . . .

Tell students that paraphrasing difficult lines of the text will improve their understanding of character and plot. Project lines 89–96 from Scene 1 in Act I on the whiteboard. Paraphrase the first two lines, modeling for students how to use marginal notes and the context. *(Sample: If there is any more fighting, you will be executed.)*

Have students work in pairs to complete the paraphrase. Ask them to volunteer what they have written. Write the sentences on the board and read them aloud. Discuss how paraphrasing increases their understanding of this part of the text.

Reading Shakespearean Drama

Reading Drama

Make sure students understand the terms *cast, stage directions, dialogue,* and *setting.* Project on the whiteboard or have students turn to pages 182 and 183. Point out the cast of characters on page 182; then have students identify examples of stage directions and dialogue on page 183. Ask them where the first scene takes place. *(a public square in Verona)* Tell them that stage directions often contain important information about the elements of the drama, such as a character's appearance, actions, and speech, and where and when the action takes place. Elicit from students examples of other plays that they have read that have included stage directions.

Reading Shakespearean Tragedy

Tell students that Shakespeare's plays are divided into five acts. Briefly review these ideas about the plot: Act I: exposition, conflict; Act II: rising action, complications; Act III: turning point (which determines play's direction); Act IV: falling action; Act V: climax, conclusion. Have students keep this organization in mind as they read each act. Also explain that each act is divided into scenes. Encourage students to summarize key ideas they learn about character and plot after each scene.

Reading Shakespeare's Language

Return to page 183 on the whiteboard. Call on volunteers to correlate marginal notes to lines in the play. Suggest that they read these notes before reading each page.

Explain that they should read each passage completely first before paraphrasing it in order to get help from the context. Remind them that they can paraphrase aloud or mentally—not all paraphrasing has to be written down.

Elizabethan Theater

A Wide Audience

Ask a volunteer to read this section aloud. Have students identify comparable entertainment in modern society to the plays in the Elizabethan age. *(movies, concerts, shows)* Discuss the pressure that a playwright would have to appeal to such a diverse audience. Tell students that *Romeo and Juliet* has something for everyone: romance, violence, tragedy, humor.

The Globe

Have students read the description of the Globe Theater. If possible, display for them sketches of the original or photographs of the rebuilt Globe, to help them visualize its structure. Explain that members of the audience in the courtyard had to stand throughout the play; that enabled more spectators to crowd in. It also meant that the rowdiest audience members were very close to the actors, an incentive for the actors to do their best.

Staging

As a class, define these terms: *scenery, props, costumes*. Have students explain how these elements of staging were used in the Elizabethan theater.

Clarify for students that Shakespeare belonged to a theater company. The members of this company were the actors for each of the plays they put on. That is one of the reasons that Shakespeare's plays have many characters; he wrote a part for each of his fellow actors.

Elizabethan Theater

A Wide Audience

Though acting companies toured throughout England, London was the center of the Elizabethan stage. One reason that London's theaters did so well was that they attracted an avid audience of rich and poor alike. In fact, Elizabethan theaters were among the few forms of entertainment available to working-class people, and one of the only places where people of all classes could mix. Shakespeare appealed to English audience members of all classes because he always included variety in his plays. He presented poetic speeches, exciting action scenes, fast-paced humor, and wise observations about human nature. His characters performed acts of bravery and kindness and committed heinous crimes. As a result, his work was respected by the educated and powerful people of the day, and the common people loved him too.

The Globe

In 1599, Shakespeare and other shareholders of The Lord Chamberlain's Men built the Globe Theater, a three-story wooden structure with an open courtyard at its center where the actors performed on an elevated platform. The theater held 3,000 people, with most of them standing near the courtyard stage in an area known as the pit. The pit audience paid the lowest admission fee—usually just one penny. Theatergoers willing and able to pay more sat in the covered inner balconies that surrounded the courtyard.

The audiences became emotionally involved in the performances and openly displayed their pleasure or disapproval. They cheered, booed and hissed, and even threw rotten vegetables. They roared their approval at battle scenes and swordfights, the cheers competing with such dramatic sound effects as trumpet blares, drum rolls, and thunder claps.

Staging

Elizabethan theater relied heavily on an audience's imagination. Most theaters had no curtains, no lighting, and very little scenery. Instead, props, sound effects, and certain lines of dialogue defined the setting of a scene. While the staging was simple, the scenes were hardly dull. Flashing swords, brightly colored banners, and elegant costumes contributed to the spectacle.

The costumes also helped audience members imagine that women appeared in the female roles, which were actually performed by young men. In Shakespeare's time, women could not belong to theater companies in England—Elizabethan society considered it highly improper for a woman to appear on stage. As a result, boys underwent a rigorous initiation into the dramatic techniques, dance routines, and vocal qualities necessary to perform the female parts.

TO CHALLENGE STUDENTS . . .

Sketch and Analyze the Globe Theater What was it like to see a play in Shakespeare's day? Have students work in small groups to create a sketch o Globe Theater as it might have appeared at the time. Suggest they do a cut view to allow them to show the inside of the theater. Encourage them to us details of the structure included on this page as well as additional sources, reliable Web sites. Have them label these and other parts of their sketch: st courtyard, covered balcony seating.

ASK STUDENTS to present their sketches to the class. Have them explain th impact of the three-sided stage on the staging of plays, citing both pros an

CLOSE READ

For more context and historical background, students can view the video "Biography: William Shakespeare" in their eBooks.

William Shakespeare Have students read the biographical information on William Shakespeare. Explain to them that even though Shakespeare only attended grammar school, his education would have exposed him to the classics and enabled him to draw plot ideas from ancient stories as well as make literary allusions. He most likely studied Latin grammar, Latin literature, and rhetoric.

Language Tell students that Shakespeare contributed more words, phrases, and expressions to the English language than any other writer. Some words were his own invention, for example, *assassination, bump,* and *lonely*. Others may have been part of the Elizabethan vernacular; by incorporating them into his plays, he made them a permanent part of the English language.

Explain that many of his expressions have become "household words"—a term first used in Shakespeare's play *Henry V*. For example, the sayings "dead as a doornail" (*Henry VI, Part 2*); "laughingstock" (*The Merry Wives of Windsor*); and "for goodness' sake" (*Henry VIII*) are actually quotations from Shakespeare's plays.

Language: Inverted Word Order Explain that Shakespeare occasionally uses inverted word order in his sentences, putting the verb before the subject. Tell students that rearranging the subject and verb will help them understand a line more easily. Preview some of the text in the play with students. For example, write Juliet's comment from Act I, Scene 3 (lines 99–100) on the board: "But no more deep will I endart mine eye / Than your consent gives strength to make it fly." Rewrite the lines as it might be more commonly expressed: "I will endart mine eye no more deep...."

Analyze Accounts in Different Mediums   RI 7

After students have read the biography of Shakespeare on this page, have them view the A&E video biography accessible through their eBooks. Ask students to discuss which details and ideas about Shakespeare's life are emphasized in each biography. Follow up by asking students how the nature of each medium might emphasize different aspects of Shakespeare's life.

The Tragedy of Romeo and Juliet

Drama by William Shakespeare

William Shakespeare *has long been considered the greatest writer in the English language—and perhaps the greatest playwright of all time. Four hundred years after their premier performances, his plays remain more popular than ever, and they have been produced more often and in more countries than those of any other author. However, despite Shakespeare's renown we have relatively few details about his life and career as an actor, poet, and playwright.*

Shakespeare came from Stratford-upon-Avon, a small village about 90 miles northwest of London, and was probably born in 1564. Though no records exist, we assume that he attended the local grammar school. In 1582 he married Anne Hathaway, daughter of a farmer. The couple's first child arrived in 1583, and twins, a boy and a girl, followed two years later.

We know nothing about the next seven years of Shakespeare's life, but he likely left his family behind and joined a traveling theater troupe. His trail resurfaces in London, where he had become a successful poet and playwright. He wrote for and acted with The Lord Chamberlain's Men, a popular theater troupe. By 1597, the year that The Tragedy of Romeo and Juliet *was published, he had become a shareholder of the theater company. As his popularity grew, Shakespeare also became part owner of London's Globe Theater. In 1603 King James I became a patron of the Globe Theater, and the theater troupe became known as The King's Men.*

In 1609 Shakespeare published his sonnets, a series of poems that received wide popular acclaim. Shakespeare then began to take advantage of his wealth and fame, spending more time in Stratford-upon-Avon and retiring there permanently around 1612. He would write no more plays after that year. No records confirm the cause or date of his death; a monument marking his gravesite indicates that he passed away on April 23, 1616. Although we have little data documenting his life, more pages have been written about Shakespeare than about any author in the history of Western civilization.

Image Credits: (tl) ©Madlen/Shutterstock; (tcl) ©AKaiser/Shutterstock; (tc) ©Morphart Creations Inc./Shutterstock; (tcr) ©Olemac/Shutterstock; (tr) ©Shutterstock; (c) ©Leemage/Universal Images Group/Getty Images

TEACH

CLOSE READ

Cast

Read each name aloud, pausing to allow students to repeat it. Draw their attention to the phonetic pronunciations given for the more difficult names. Point out the details about how the characters are related to each other.

Then provide this additional information to students:

- Verona was a city-state; in other words, it had its own government. Prince Escalus is the head of this government.
- An apothecary is a pharmacist. In the 1300s, apothecaries did not need special licenses or certification, just access to the kinds of herbs and drugs that were used by doctors in those days.
- The watchman provides security for the cemetery.
- The chorus has a role similar to that of a narrator, providing information to the audience that would not otherwise be known.

THE TIME: The 14th century

THE PLACE: Verona (və-rō´nə) and Mantua (măn´chōō-ə) in northern Italy

CAST

The Montagues

Lord Montague (mŏn´tə-gyōō´)
Lady Montague
Romeo, son of Montague
Benvolio (bĕn-vō´lē-ō), nephew of Montague and friend of Romeo
Balthasar (băl´thə-sär´), servant to Romeo
Abram, servant to Montague

The Capulets

Lord Capulet (kăp´yōō-lĕt´)
Lady Capulet
Juliet, daughter of Capulet
Tybalt (tĭb´əlt), nephew of Lady Capulet
Nurse to Juliet
Peter, servant to Juliet's nurse
Sampson, servant to Capulet
Gregory, servant to Capulet
An Old Man of the Capulet family

Others

Prince Escalus (ĕs´kə-ləs), ruler of Verona
Mercutio (mĕr-kyōō´shē-ō), kinsman of the prince and friend of Romeo
Friar Laurence, a Franciscan priest
Friar John, another Franciscan priest
Count Paris, a young nobleman, kinsman of the prince
Apothecary (ə-pŏth´ĭ-kĕr´ē)
Page to Paris
Chief Watchman
Three Musicians
An Officer
Chorus
Citizens of Verona, **Gentlemen** and **Gentlewomen** of both houses, **Maskers, Torchbearers, Pages, Guards, Watchmen, Servants,** and **Attendants**

APPLYING ACADEMIC VOCABULARY

expose	underlie

As you discuss the opening scene of the play, incorporate the Collection 4 academic vocabulary words: *expose* and *underlie*. Have students probe the extent of the feud by explaining what the conversation between Sampson and Gregory **exposes** about the servants' involvement. As a class, speculate on the causes that **underlie** this animosity between the families.

AS YOU READ Look for clues that reveal the personalities of Romeo and Juliet. Write down any questions you generate during reading.

Prologue

[*Enter* Chorus.]

A

Chorus. Two households, both alike in dignity,
In fair Verona, where we lay our scene,
From ancient grudge break to new mutiny,
Where civil blood makes civil hands unclean.
5 From forth the fatal loins of these two foes,
A pair of star-crossed lovers take their life,
Whose misadventured piteous overthrows
Doth with their death bury their parents' strife.
The fearful passage of their death-marked love,
10 And the continuance of their parents' rage,
Which, but their children's end, naught could remove,
Is now the two hours' traffic of our stage,
The which if you with patient ears attend,
What here shall miss, our toil shall strive to mend.

[*Exit.*]

ACT I

Scene 1 *A public square in Verona.*

[*Enter* Sampson *and* Gregory, *servants of the house of Capulet, armed with swords and bucklers (shields).*]

B

Sampson. Gregory, on my word, we'll not carry coals.

Gregory. No, for then we should be colliers.

Sampson. I mean, an we be in choler, we'll draw.

Gregory. Ay, while you live, draw your neck out of collar.

5 **Sampson.** I strike quickly, being moved.

Gregory. But thou art not quickly moved to strike.

Sampson. A dog of that house of Montague moves me.

Gregory. To move is to stir, and to be valiant is to stand. Therefore, if thou art moved, thou runnest away.

10 **Sampson.** A dog of that house shall move me to stand. I will take the wall of any man or maid of Montague's.

Gregory. That shows thee a weak slave, for the weakest goes to the wall.

3–4 ancient... unclean: A new outbreak of fighting (**mutiny**) between families has caused the citizens of Verona to have one another's blood on their hands.

6 star-crossed: doomed. The position of the stars when the lovers were born was not favorable. In Shakespeare's day, people took astrology very seriously.

7 misadventured: unlucky.

11 but: except for; **naught:** nothing.

14 what... mend: The play will fill in the details not mentioned in the prologue.

1–2 we'll not carry coals: we won't stand to be insulted; **colliers:** those involved in the dirty work of hauling coal, who were often the butt of jokes.

3–4 in choler: angry; **collar:** a hangman's noose.

11 take the wall: walk. People of higher rank had the privilege of walking closer to the wall, to avoid any water or garbage in the street.

The Tragedy of Romeo and Juliet: Act I, Scene 1 **183**

---

ose Read Screencasts

odeled Discussions

ve students click the *Close Read* icons in their eBooks to access the screencast in nich readers discuss and annotate the following key passage:

- Prologue to Act I (lines 1–12)

a class, view and discuss the video.

CLOSE READ

AS YOU READ Direct students to use the As You Read note to focus their reading.

Analyze Author's Choices: Text Structure (LINES 1–14)

RL 5

Remind students that the chorus fulfills the role of the narrator. Point out that this speech, which is spoken before the play's action begins, identifies the setting and provides an overview of the plot.

A **ASK STUDENTS** what they learn about the two families from the phrase "both alike in dignity." *(They occupy a similar status in society.)* Have students discuss the effect on the audience of knowing the events that will occur before the play begins. *(Knowing the outcome decreases the suspense in one way, but it adds tension in another as the audience is not clear when or where or how the demise of the lovers will occur.)* According to lines 3-4, what is the relationship like between the two families? *(They have been feuding for a long time.)* According to line 6, what does the Prologue say has happened to Romeo and Juliet? *(They killed themselves.)*

Determine Figurative Meanings: Puns

RL 4, L 5a

(Sc. 1, LINES 1–13)

The play opens with two Capulet servants insulting each other through the use of **puns,** or plays on the multiple meanings of words. Project lines 5–11 on the board. Ask volunteers to underline instances of the word *move.* Remind students to use context clues to figure out different meanings of *move* used here.

B **ASK STUDENTS** to explain the characters' play on the word *move* by discussing which definition each speaker uses. *(Sampson says he would attack if he were "moved," in the sense of being made angry. Gregory says he is not quick at swordplay—he does not move quickly. Sampson retorts that seeing a Montague would move him, or make him angry. Gregory says he would move all right, but only to run away. Sampson says he would be moved, or inclined to stay and fight if it were a Montague.)* Have students discuss how their dialogue affects the mood of this scene. *(Their puns and insults make this part of Scene I humorous.)*

The Tragedy of Romeo and Juliet: Act I, Scene 1 **183**

Analyze Author's Choices: Parallel Plots

RL 5

(Sc. 1, LINES 27–48)

Tell students that in a full-length, complex drama, such as this one, there is often more than one story line. These plots develop simultaneously along with the major plot—in this play, the love story of Romeo and Juliet. Explain that these **parallel plots** often complicate the characters' lives and hinder their efforts to resolve the central conflict, or problem. Clarify for students that the feud between the Montagues and the Capulets is an important parallel plot.

C ASK STUDENTS to reread the lines and the marginal notes. What does Sampson do when he sees the Montague servants? Why? (*In line 30 he pulls out his sword in anticipation of a fight. He bites his thumb at them [line 36], which is an insult. He wants to provoke them to fight.*) Why does he take back his gesture? (*He realizes that he could get into trouble if he is the first one to start the fight.*) What do the servants' actions reveal about the conflict between the two families? (*It is serious and may include bloodshed; it is a matter of pride; it involves everyone with a connection to the families.*)

Sampson. 'Tis true; and therefore women, being the weaker
15 vessels, are ever thrust to the wall. Therefore push I will
Montague's men from the wall and thrust his maids to the wall.

Gregory. The quarrel is between our masters and us their men.

Sampson. 'Tis all one. I will show myself a tyrant. When I have
fought with the men, I will be cruel with the maids: I will cut
20 off their heads.

Gregory. The heads of the maids?

Sampson. Ay, the heads of the maids, or their maidenheads.
Take it in what sense thou wilt.

Gregory. They must take it in sense that feel it.

25 **Sampson.** Me they shall feel while I am able to stand;
and 'tis known I am a pretty piece of flesh.

Gregory. 'Tis well thou art not fish; if thou hadst, thou hadst
been poor-John. Draw thy tool! Here comes two of the house
of Montagues.

[*Enter* Abram *and* Balthasar, *servants to the Montagues.*]

30 **Sampson.** My naked weapon is out. Quarrel! I will back thee.

Gregory. How? turn thy back and run?

Sampson. Fear me not.

Gregory. No, marry. I fear thee!

Sampson. Let us take the law of our sides; let them begin.

35 **Gregory.** I will frown as I pass by, and let them take it as they list.

Sampson. Nay, as they dare. I will bite my thumb at them;
which is disgrace to them, if they bear it.

Abram. Do you bite your thumb at us, sir?

Sampson. I do bite my thumb, sir.

40 **Abram.** Do you bite your thumb at us, sir?

Sampson [*aside to* Gregory]. Is the law of our side if I say ay?

Gregory [*aside to* Sampson]. No.

Sampson. No, sir, I do not bite my thumb at you, sir; but I bite
my thumb, sir.

45 **Gregory.** Do you quarrel, sir?

Abram. Quarrel, sir? No, sir.

Sampson. But if you do, sir, I am for you. I serve as good a man
as you.

14–24 Sampson's tough talk includes boasts about his ability to overpower women.

28 poor-John: a salted fish, considered fit only for poor people to eat.

33 marry: a short form of "by the Virgin Mary" and so a mild exclamation.

34–44 Gregory and Sampson decide to pick a fight by insulting the Montague servants with a rude gesture (**bite my thumb**).

ENGLISH LANGUAGE SUPPORT

Comprehension Support Display a two-column chart on the board. In each row of the left column, write one of the sentences from this brief summary of lines 30–65.

Gregory and Sampson start a fight by insulting Abram.
Benvolio stops the fight.
Tybalt arrives and fights with Benvolio.

ASK STUDENTS to work in mixed-ability language groups and match the sentence of the summary to the lines in the play that show each event taking place. Have them identify the words in the original text that helped them make their match.

Abram. No better.

50 **Sampson.** Well, sir.

[*Enter Benvolio, nephew of Montague and first cousin of Romeo.*]

Gregory [*aside to Sampson*]. Say "better." Here comes one of my master's kinsmen.

Sampson. Yes, better, sir.

Abram. You lie.

55 **Sampson.** Draw, if you be men. Gregory, remember thy swashing blow.

[*They fight.*]

Benvolio. Part, fools!   [*beats down their swords*]
Put up your swords. You know not what you do.

[*Enter Tybalt, hot-headed nephew of Lady Capulet and first cousin of Juliet.*]

Tybalt. What, art thou drawn among these heartless hinds?
60 Turn thee, Benvolio! look upon thy death.

59 heartless hinds: cowardly servants.

Benvolio. I do but keep the peace. Put up thy sword,
Or manage it to part these men with me.

Tybalt. What, drawn, and talk of peace? I hate the word
As I hate hell, all Montagues, and thee.
65 Have at thee, coward!

63 drawn: with your sword out.

65 Have at thee: Defend yourself.

[*They fight.*]

[*Enter several of both houses, who join the fray; then enter Citizens and Peace Officers, with clubs.*]

Officer. Clubs, bills, and partisans! Strike! beat them down!

66 bills, and partisans: spears.

Citizens. Down with the Capulets! Down with the Montagues!

[*Enter old Capulet and Lady Capulet.*]

Capulet. What noise is this? Give me my long sword, ho!

Lady Capulet. A crutch, a crutch! Why call you for a sword?

69 A crutch ... sword: You need a crutch more than a sword.

70 **Capulet.** My sword, I say! Old Montague is come
And flourishes his blade in spite of me.

[*Enter old Montague and Lady Montague.*]

Montague. Thou villain Capulet!—Hold me not, let me go.

Lady Montague. Thou shalt not stir one foot to seek a foe.

[*Enter Prince Escalus, with attendants. At first no one hears him.*]

WHEN STUDENTS STRUGGLE...

To increase students' understanding of what happens in this scene, ask for volunteers to represent the four servants, Benvolio, and Tybalt. Begin with the four servants "on the stage." Then have them read their lines aloud beginning with line 30. Pause after line 50 to move Benvolio onto the stage and Tybalt just offstage, and have them read their lines as well. Pause after line 58 to move Tybalt onto the stage before completing the scene.

ASK STUDENTS to work in pairs to write a brief summary of what happens in this scene. Have them explain how this scene helps them to understand more about the feud between the two families.

CLOSE READ

Analyze Character: Motivations (Sc. 1, LINES 51–65)   RL 3

Tell students that a **character's motivation** refers to the emotion or condition that prompts him or her to do something.

D ASK STUDENTS why Gregory's attitude toward fighting changes. *(When he sees Tybalt approaching, he wants to fight. He may think that Tybalt will back him up; he may want praise from Tybalt for engaging the "enemy.")*

Remind students that playwrights often use contrast to illustrate the traits and motivations of characters more clearly.

E ASK STUDENTS to explain how Tybalt's actions contrast with Benvolio's. *(Benvolio tries to break up the fight; Tybalt continues it.)* What characteristic of Benvolio's is brought out through this contrast? What characteristic of Tybalt's? *(Benvolio is shown to be a peacemaker, while stage directions and his actions show that Tybalt is "hot-headed" and looking to fight.)*

Support Inferences   RL 1
(Sc. 1, LINES 68–73)

Tell students that they can make logical assumptions based on what characters say and do.

F CITE TEXT EVIDENCE Have students support the inference that Lady Montague and Lady Capulet are more sensible than their husbands. *(Lady Capulet says that her husband needs a crutch more than a sword [line 69]; Lady Montague holds her husband back and won't let him fight with Lord Capulet [lines 72–73].)*

CLOSE READ

Analyze Author's Choices: Parallel Plots (Sc. 1, LINES 74–96)

RL 5

Reread the Prince's speech aloud with students to help ensure comprehension.

(G) CITE TEXT EVIDENCE Have students summarize the Prince's warning to the two families about their feud, citing evidence from the text to support their statements. *(He calls the families "enemies of peace" [line 74] and points out that someone could be seriously hurt in their brawls, saying, "you beasts, / That quench the fire of your pernicious rage / With purple fountains issuing from your veins!" [lines 76–78]. He notes that the two families have already disturbed the peace with three previous brawls [lines 82–84]. He also says in lines 89–90 that if there is another brawl, Lord Montague and Lord Capulet will pay with their lives.)*

Interpret Figurative Language (Sc. 1, LINES 109–116)

RL 4, L 5a

Explain to students that because there were few special effects and little scenery, Shakespeare's language had to supply the audience with vivid images to draw them into the action and help them visualize setting. Tell students that to do this, he often uses **metaphors,** comparisons between two unlike things in which one is said to be the other.

(H) ASK STUDENTS to identify the metaphor in Benvolio's response to Lady Montague. What image does this metaphor create? What practical information does it also convey? *(Benvolio says that the sun "peered forth the golden window of the East." This metaphor creates the image of a brilliant sunrise with the golden sun flooding the sky. It tells Lady Montague just before dawn, Romeo was out walking alone in a sycamore grove.)*

Prince. Rebellious subjects, enemies to peace,
75 Profaners of this neighbor-stained steel—
   Will they not hear? What, ho! you men, you beasts,
   That quench the fire of your pernicious rage
   With purple fountains issuing from your veins!
   On pain of torture, from those bloody hands
80 Throw your mistempered weapons to the ground
   And hear the sentence of your moved prince.
   Three civil brawls, bred of an airy word
   By thee, old Capulet, and Montague,
   Have thrice disturbed the quiet of our streets
85 And made Verona's ancient citizens
   Cast by their grave beseeming ornaments
   To wield old partisans, in hands as old,
   Cankered with peace, to part your cankered hate.
   If ever you disturb our streets again,
90 Your lives shall pay the forfeit of the peace.
   For this time all the rest depart away.
   You, Capulet, shall go along with me;
   And, Montague, come you this afternoon,
   To know our farther pleasure in this case,
95 To old Freetown, our common judgment place.
   Once more, on pain of death, all men depart.

   [*Exeunt all but* Montague, Lady Montague, *and* Benvolio.]

   Montague. Who set this ancient quarrel new abroach?
   Speak, nephew, were you by when it began?

   Benvolio. Here were the servants of your adversary
100 And yours, close fighting ere I did approach.
   I drew to part them. In the instant came
   The fiery Tybalt, with his sword prepared;
   Which, as he breathed defiance to my ears,
   He swung about his head and cut the winds,
105 Who, nothing hurt withal, hissed him in scorn.
   While we were interchanging thrusts and blows,
   Came more and more, and fought on part and part,
   Till the Prince came, who parted either part.

   Lady Montague. O, where is Romeo? Saw you him today?
110 Right glad I am he was not at this fray.

   Benvolio. Madam, an hour before the worshiped sun
   Peered forth the golden window of the East,
   A troubled mind drave me to walk abroad,
   Where, underneath the grove of sycamore
115 That westward rooteth from the city's side,
   So early walking did I see your son.

74–81 The prince is furious about the street fighting caused by the feud. He orders the men to drop their weapons and pay attention.

77 pernicious: destructive.

82–90 Three . . . peace: The prince holds Capulet and Montague responsible for three recent street fights, each probably started by an offhand remark or insult (**airy word**). He warns that they will be put to death if any more fights occur.

Exeunt: the plural form of *exit,* indicating that more than one person is leaving the stage.

97 Who . . . abroach: Who reopened this old argument?

99 adversary: enemy.

100 ere: before.

107 on part and part: some on one side, some on the other.

110 fray: fight.

113 drave: drove.

115 rooteth: grows.

ENGLISH LANGUAGE SUPPORT

Vocabulary: Figurative Language Remind students that they can sometimes use the context of a figurative phrase to help define it. Point out "neighbor-stained steel" in line 75. Explain that since a fight has just occurred between citizens of Verona, this phrase can be interpreted to mean "swords stained with the blood of fellow citizens, or neighbors."

ASK STUDENTS to work in pairs to define these additional phrases using context clues: "quench the fire" in line 77 *(show your anger);* "purple fountains" in line 78 *(spurts of blood);* "mistempered weapons" in line 80 *(swords used in anger);* "cankered hate" in line 88 *(feud, diseased hate).* Encourage them to use the same strategy to determine the meanings of other figurative expressions as they continue reading.

Towards him I made, but he was ware of me
And stole into the covert of the wood.
I—measuring his affections by my own,
120 Which then most sought where most might not be found,
Being one too many by my weary self—
Pursued my humor, not pursuing his,
And gladly shunned who gladly fled from me.

Montague. Many a morning hath he there been seen,
125 With tears augmenting the fresh morning's dew,
Adding to clouds more clouds with his deep sighs;
But all so soon as the all-cheering sun
Should in the farthest East begin to draw
The shady curtains from Aurora's bed,
130 Away from light steals home my heavy son
And private in his chamber pens himself,
Shuts up his windows, locks fair daylight out,
And makes himself an artificial night.
Black and portentous must this humor prove
135 Unless good counsel may the cause remove.

Benvolio. My noble uncle, do you know the cause?

Montague. I neither know it nor can learn of him.

Benvolio. Have you importuned him by any means?

Montague. Both by myself and many other friends;
140 But he, his own affections' counselor,
Is to himself—I will not say how true—
But to himself so secret and so close,
So far from sounding and discovery,
As is the bud bit with an envious worm
145 Ere he can spread his sweet leaves to the air
Or dedicate his beauty to the sun.
Could we but learn from whence his sorrows grow,
We would as willingly give cure as know.

[*Enter* Romeo *lost in thought.*]

Benvolio. See, where he comes. So please you step aside,
150 I'll know his grievance, or be much denied.

Montague. I would thou wert so happy by thy stay
To hear true shrift. Come, madam, let's away.

[*Exeunt* Montague *and* Lady.]

Benvolio. Good morrow, cousin.

Romeo.   Is the day so young?

Benvolio. But new struck nine.

117–123 made: moved; **covert:** covering. Romeo saw Benvolio coming and hid in the woods. Benvolio himself was seeking solitude and did not go after him.

124–135 Romeo has been seen wandering through the woods at night, crying. At dawn he returns home and locks himself in his room. Montague feels that his son needs guidance.

129 Aurora's bed: Aurora was the goddess of the dawn.

134 portentous: indicating evil to come; threatening.

138 importuned: asked in an urgent way.

140 his own affections' counselor: Romeo keeps to himself.

143–148 so far from . . . know: Finding out what Romeo is thinking is almost impossible. Montague compares his son to a young bud destroyed by the bite of a worm before it has a chance to open its leaves. Montague wants to find out what is bothering Romeo so he can help him.

152 shrift: confession.

153 cousin: any relative or close friend. The informal version is *coz*.

CLOSE READ

Analyze Character: Motivations (Sc. 1, LINES 117–123; 149–150)

RL 3

Tell students that often **characters' motivations,** or the reasons for their actions, are not explicitly stated. Readers must make inferences based on the characters' actions and words as well as what others say about them.

I **ASK STUDENTS** to reread lines 117–123. Then have them explain what Benvolio was doing when he saw Romeo, and why. *(Benvolio had a troubled mind so was out walking very early. He couldn't sleep.)* What does this information about Benvolio suggest about Romeo? *(Romeo must also have a troubled mind since he too is walking out early alone.)* What is Lord Montague's feeling about his son? *(He thinks something is wrong. He is concerned about Romeo.)*

Explain to students that as a friend and relative of Romeo's, Benvolio plays an important part.

J **ASK STUDENTS** to reread lines 149–150. What can they infer about why Benvolio makes this offer to Lord Montague? *(Benvolio has already been shown to be sensitive and caring; his offer to find out what is wrong with Romeo is motivated by his concern for his cousin and for Lord and Lady Montague, who are very worried about their son.)*

Strategies for Annotation

Annotate it!

Analyze Character: Motivations

RL 3

Have students use their eBook annotation tools to analyze Romeo's behavior as revealed in lines 117–150:

- Highlight in pink what Benvolio says about Romeo.
- Highlight in blue the description that Lord Montague gives of his son Romeo.
- On a note, paraphrase these lines.
- Use the paraphrases to infer possible motives for Romeo's behavior.

But all so soon as the all-cheering sun
Should in the farthest East begin to draw
The shady curtains from Aurora's bed,
Away from light steals home my heavy son
And private in his chamber pens himself,
Shuts up his windows, locks fair daylight out,

Analyze Character: Motivations

RL 3

(Sc. 1, LINES 155–167)

Remind students that audience members often know information that characters do not.

K **ASK STUDENTS** to reread Benvolio's comments to Romeo. What is Benvolio's purpose in this conversation? *(He is trying to find out what is wrong with Romeo.)* Does Romeo suspect his intention? Why or why not? *(Romeo suspects nothing because he is so preoccupied with his own problems. It takes him a long time to even notice that there was a big fight in the square [line 166].)*

Romeo.   Ay me! sad hours seem long.
155 Was that my father that went hence so fast?

Benvolio. It was. What sadness lengthens Romeo's hours?

Romeo. Not having that which having makes them short.

Benvolio. In love?

Romeo. Out—

160 **Benvolio.** Of love?

Romeo. Out of her favor where I am in love.

Benvolio. Alas that love, so gentle in his view,
Should be so tyrannous and rough in proof!

Romeo. Alas that love, whose view is muffled still,
165 Should without eyes see pathways to his will!
Where shall we dine?—O me! What fray was here?—
Yet tell me not, for I have heard it all.

162–165 love: references to Cupid, the god of love, typically pictured as a blind boy with wings and a bow and arrow. Anyone hit by one of his arrows falls in love instantly.

188 Collection 4

ENGLISH LANGUAGE SUPPORT

Language: Patterns of Conversational Speech Using a whiteboard, project lines 155–167. Explain to students that in a conversation between friends, the speakers may not use complete sentences and may interrupt each other or themselves. Read this passage aloud. Then invite volunteers to mark up the lines:

- Highlight incomplete sentences in pink.
- Highlight dashes in green.

ASK STUDENTS to identify the function of the dashes based on their use in this passage. *(to indicate an interruption)* Then ask them how the incomplete sentences affect the sound of the dialogue.

Romeo. Not having that which having makes them short.

Benvolio. In love?

Romeo. Out—

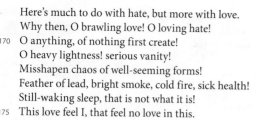

Here's much to do with hate, but more with love.
Why then, O brawling love! O loving hate!
170 O anything, of nothing first create!
O heavy lightness! serious vanity!
Misshapen chaos of well-seeming forms!
Feather of lead, bright smoke, cold fire, sick health!
Still-waking sleep, that is not what it is!
175 This love feel I, that feel no love in this.
Dost thou not laugh?

Benvolio.   No, coz, I rather weep.

Romeo. Good heart, at what?

Benvolio.   At thy good heart's oppression.

Romeo. Why, such is love's transgression.
Griefs of mine own lie heavy in my breast,
180 Which thou wilt propagate, to have it prest
With more of thine. This love that thou hast shown
Doth add more grief to too much of mine own.
Love is a smoke raised with the fume of sighs;
Being purged, a fire sparkling in lovers' eyes;
185 Being vexed, a sea nourished with lovers' tears.
What is it else? A madness most discreet,
A choking gall, and a preserving sweet.
Farewell, my coz.

Benvolio.   Soft! I will go along.
An if you leave me so, you do me wrong.

190 **Romeo.** Tut! I have lost myself; I am not here:
This is not Romeo, he's some other where.

Benvolio. Tell me in sadness, who is that you love?

Romeo. What, shall I groan and tell thee?

Benvolio.   Groan? Why, no;
But sadly tell me who.

195 **Romeo.** Bid a sick man in sadness make his will.
Ah, word ill urged to one that is so ill!
In sadness, cousin, I do love a woman.

Benvolio. I aimed so near when I supposed you loved.

Romeo. A right good markman! And she's fair I love.

200 **Benvolio.** A right fair mark, fair coz, is soonest hit.

Romeo. Well, in that hit you miss. She'll not be hit
With Cupid's arrow. She hath Dian's wit,
And, in strong proof of chastity well armed,

168–176 Romeo, confused and upset, tries to describe his feelings about love. He uses phrases like "loving hate" and other contradictory expressions.

176–182 Benvolio expresses his sympathy for Romeo. Romeo replies that this is one more problem caused by love. He now feels worse than before because he must carry the weight of Benvolio's sympathy along with his own grief.

184 purged: cleansed (of the smoke).

185 vexed: troubled.

187 gall: something causing bitterness or hate.

188 Soft: Wait a minute.

192 sadness: seriousness.

201–204 She'll . . . unharmed: The girl isn't interested in falling in love. She is like Diana, the goddess of chastity.

The Tragedy of Romeo and Juliet: Act I, Scene 1   **189**

TEACH

CLOSE READ

Support Inferences   RL 1
(Sc. 1, LINES 169–175)

Tell students that the kind of language a character uses can help to reveal ideas about his or her mood or situation.

L **ASK STUDENTS** to describe the language Romeo uses in this speech to express his feelings about love. *(contradictory, or opposing, terms such as "heavy lightness")* What do these contradictory terms reveal about his feelings about love? *(Romeo is confused because love is supposed to make people feel happy, but it makes him feel frustrated and sad. "This love feel I, that feel no love in this.")*

Analyze Author's Choices: RL 5
Parallel Plots
(Sc. 1, LINES 190–204)

Tell students that another parallel plot is developed through Romeo's conversation with Benvolio. Direct them to look for details that explain the **conflict,** or problem, as well as the characters involved.

M **ASK STUDENTS** to summarize what they learn about this plot. *(Romeo is in love with a woman who does not return his love. He says that "She'll not be hit with Cupid's arrow." In other words, she is immune to Romeo's charms.)*

ENGLISH LANGUAGE SUPPORT

Language: Paradoxical Statements Have students reread the margin notes for lines 168–176. Emphasize that speaking in opposites shows Romeo's confusion over the fact that love, which should make him happy, has made him miserable. Point to the phrase "heavy lightness" in line 171 and explain that it can be restated as "what should feel light feels heavy."

ASK STUDENTS to work in pairs to restate the meaning of each of these opposites in lines 171–173: "serious vanity" *(What should be unimportant is serious)*; "feather of lead" *(A lightweight feather feels as heavy as lead)*; "bright smoke" *(Dark smoke is actually bright)*; "cold fire" *(Fire, which should be hot, is now cold)*.

The Tragedy of Romeo and Juliet: Act I, Scene 1   **189**

Analyze Author's Choices: Parallel Plots

RL 5

(Sc. 1, LINES 201–231)

Read these lines aloud to students to help them discover what additional details they can learn about this particular story line.

 CITE TEXT EVIDENCE Have students explain why the woman does not return Romeo's love. (*"She'll not be hit / With Cupid's arrow" [lines 201–202] and has "sworn that she will still live chaste."*) Ask students how they would describe Romeo's reaction to his problem. What inferences about his character can they make from his behavior and words? (*Romeo reacts by plunging into depression. He appears to be intense and emotional.*) How does Benvolio vow to help Romeo resolve this conflict? (*Benvolio says that he will find someone that will make Romeo forget this woman [lines 218–221].*)

From Love's weak childish bow she lives unharmed.
205 She will not stay the siege of loving terms,
Nor bide the encounter of assailing eyes,
Nor ope her lap to saint-seducing gold.
O, she is rich in beauty; only poor
That, when she dies, with beauty dies her store.

210 **Benvolio.** Then she hath sworn that she will still live chaste?

Romeo. She hath, and in that sparing makes huge waste;
For beauty, starved with her severity,
Cuts beauty off from all posterity.
She is too fair, too wise, wisely too fair,
215 To merit bliss by making me despair.
She hath forsworn to love, and in that vow
Do I live dead that live to tell it now.

Benvolio. Be ruled by me: forget to think of her.

Romeo. O, teach me how I should forget to think!

220 **Benvolio.** By giving liberty unto thine eyes:
Examine other beauties.

Romeo.   'Tis the way
To call hers (exquisite) in question more.
These happy masks that kiss fair ladies' brows,
Being black, puts us in mind they hide the fair.
225 He that is strucken blind cannot forget
The precious treasure of his eyesight lost.
Show me a mistress that is passing fair,
What doth her beauty serve but as a note
Where I may read who passed that passing fair?
230 Farewell. Thou canst not teach me to forget.

Benvolio. I'll pay that doctrine, or else die in debt.

[*Exeunt.*]

Scene 2 *A street near the Capulet house.*

[*Enter* Capulet *with* Paris, *a kinsman of the Prince, and* Servant.]

Capulet. But Montague is bound as well as I,
In penalty alike; and 'tis not hard, I think,
For men so old as we to keep the peace.

Paris. Of honorable reckoning are you both,
5 And pity 'tis you lived at odds so long.
But now, my lord, what say you to my suit?

Capulet. But saying o'er what I have said before:
My child is yet a stranger in the world,

205–207 She will not ... gold: She is not swayed by Romeo's love or his wealth.

212–213 For beauty ... posterity: She wastes her beauty, which will not be passed on to future generations.

215–216 To merit ... despair: The girl will reach heaven (**bliss**) by being so virtuous, which causes Romeo to feel despair; **forsworn to:** sworn not to.

221–222 'Tis ... more: That would only make me appreciate my own love's beauty more.

223 Masks were worn by Elizabethan women to protect their faces from the sun.

227–229 Show me ... fair: A woman who is exceedingly (**passing**) beautiful will only remind me of my love, who is even prettier.

231 I'll pay ... debt: I'll convince you you're wrong, or die trying.

1 bound: obligated.

4 reckoning: reputation.

6 what say ... suit: Paris is asking for Capulet's response to his proposal to marry Juliet.

She hath not seen the change of fourteen years;
10 Let two more summers wither in their pride
Ere we may think her ripe to be a bride.

Paris. Younger than she are happy mothers made.

Capulet. And too soon marred are those so early made.
The earth hath swallowed all my hopes but she;
15 She is the hopeful lady of my earth.
But woo her, gentle Paris, get her heart;
My will to her consent is but a part.
An she agree, within her scope of choice
Lies my consent and fair according voice.
20 This night I hold an old accustomed feast,
Whereto I have invited many a guest,
Such as I love, and you among the store,
One more, most welcome, makes my number more.
At my poor house look to behold this night
25 Earth-treading stars that make dark heaven light.
Such comfort as do lusty young men feel
When well-appareled April on the heel
Of limping Winter treads, even such delight
Among fresh female buds shall you this night
30 Inherit at my house. Hear all, all see,
And like her most whose merit most shall be;
Which, on more view of many, mine, being one,
May stand in number, though in reck'ning none.
Come, go with me.　　　　[*to* Servant, *giving him a paper*]
　　　　　　Go, sirrah, trudge about
35 Through fair Verona; find those persons out
Whose names are written there, and to them say,
My house and welcome on their pleasure stay.

[*Exeunt* Capulet *and* Paris.]

Servant. Find them out whose names are written here! It is
written that the shoemaker should meddle with his yard and the
40 tailor with his last, the fisher with his pencil and the painter
with his nets; but I am sent to find those persons whose names
are here writ, and can never find what names the writing person
hath here writ. I must to the learned. In good time!

[*Enter* Benvolio *and* Romeo.]

Benvolio. Tut, man, one fire burns out another's burning;
45 One pain is lessened by another's anguish;
Turn giddy, and be help by backward turning;
One desperate grief cures with another's languish.

10 Let two more
summers . . . pride: let
two more years pass.

14 The earth . . . she:
All my children are dead
except Juliet.

16 woo her: try to win
her heart.

18–19 An . . . voice: I
will give my approval to
the one she chooses.

20 old accustomed
feast: a traditional or
annual party.

29–33 Among . . . none:
Tonight at the party you
will see the loveliest
girls in Verona, including
Juliet. When you see all
of them together, your
opinion of Juliet may
change.

34 sirrah: a term used
to address a servant.

38–43 The servant
cannot read. He
confuses the craftsmen
and their tools, tapping
a typical source of
humor for Elizabethan
comic characters.

44–49 Tut, man . . . die:
Benvolio says Romeo
should find a new love—
that a "new infection"
will cure the old one.

CLOSE READ

Analyze Author's Choices: Parallel Plots (Sc. 2, LINES 9–19)　　RL 5

Point out that in this scene a third parallel plot is introduced. Tell students that the events in this plot will have an impact on the major story line later in the play.

Ⓞ **ASK STUDENTS** to explain Paris's purpose in visiting Lord Capulet. *(He wants to marry Juliet.)* Why does Lord Capulet appear somewhat reluctant to immediately give his consent? *(He feels Juliet is still too young [lines 9–11], and he thinks women who are mothers too young are marred [line 13]. She is the only living child he has left [line 14].)*

WHEN STUDENTS STRUGGLE . . .

Culture: Historical Context Provide the following background information to help students analyze the exchange between Paris and Lord Capulet.

- Because the life span was shorter, girls usually married in their early teens.
- The marriages of girls of wealthy or noble parents were arranged, often before they were even of marriageable age. Marrying a daughter into another influential family created powerful alliances and brought political and material advantages.
- The family of the girl provided a dowry, a gift of money or property, which became the groom's possession.

Analyze Author's Choices: Parallel Plots

RL 5

(Sc. 2, LINES 56–81)

Remind students that the Capulets are the enemies of Romeo's family.

P CITE TEXT EVIDENCE Have students read the passage aloud, then summarize what happens. *(One of Capulet's servants asks Romeo to read a document which turns out to be an invitation to guests to attend a party at the Capulets. The servant, unaware of Romeo's identity as a Montague, invites him to the party as long as he is not a Montague.)* Have students explain why they think Romeo will take the chance of attending the party at the Capulet house. *(The woman he loves, Rosaline, is invited [line 69].)* Have students discuss what could possibly happen if Romeo does attend. *(There could be problems if his identity is discovered.)*

Take thou some new infection to thy eye,
And the rank poison of the old will die.

50 **Romeo.** Your plantain leaf is excellent for that.

Benvolio. For what, I pray thee?

Romeo.   For your broken shin.

Benvolio. Why, Romeo, art thou mad?

Romeo. Not mad, but bound more than a madman is;
Shut up in prison, kept without my food,
55 Whipped and tormented and—God-den, good fellow.

Servant. God gi' go-den. I pray, sir, can you read?

Romeo. Ay, mine own fortune in my misery.

Servant. Perhaps you have learned it without book. But
I pray, can you read anything you see?

60 **Romeo.** Ay, if I know the letters and the language.

Servant. Ye say honestly. Rest you merry!

[Romeo's joking goes over the clown's head. He concludes that Romeo cannot read and prepares to seek someone who can.]

Romeo. Stay, fellow; I can read.   [He reads.]
"Signior Martino and his wife and daughters;
County Anselmo and his beauteous sisters;
65 The lady widow of Vitruvio;
Signior Placentio and his lovely nieces;
Mercutio and his brother Valentine;
Mine uncle Capulet, his wife, and daughters;
My fair niece Rosaline and Livia;
70 Signior Valentio and his cousin Tybalt;
Lucio and the lively Helena."
[gives back the paper]
A fair assembly. Whither should they come?

Servant. Up.

Romeo. Whither?

75 **Servant.** To supper, to our house.

Romeo. Whose house?

Servant. My master's.

Romeo. Indeed I should have asked you that before.

Servant. Now I'll tell you without asking. My master is the great
80 rich Capulet; and if you be not of the house of Montagues, I
pray come and crush a cup of wine. Rest you merry!

55 God-den: good evening. Romeo interrupts his lament to talk to the servant.

56 God gi' go-den: God give you a good evening.

69 Rosaline: This is the woman that Romeo is in love with. Mercutio, a friend of both Romeo and the Capulets, is also invited to the party.

72 whither: where.

81 crush a cup of wine: slang for "drink some wine."

WHEN STUDENTS STRUGGLE...

To guide students' comprehension of the cause-and-effect relationship that drives the action of this part of the plot, have them work together to complete a chart similar to the one shown. Prompt students by filling in one or more of the boxes. Then have them review from line 176 in Scene 1 to line 101 in Scene 2 to complete the chart. Have students add to the chart as they read further.

[*Exit.*]

Benvolio. At this same ancient feast of Capulet's
Sups the fair Rosaline whom thou so lovest,
With all the admired beauties of Verona.
85 Go thither, and with unattainted eye
Compare her face with some that I shall show,
And I will make thee think thy swan a crow.

85 unattainted:
unbiased; unprejudiced.

Romeo. When the devout religion of mine eye
Maintains such falsehood, then turn tears to fires;
90 And these, who, often drowned, could never die,
Transparent heretics, be burnt for liars!
One fairer than my love? The all-seeing sun
Ne'er saw her match since first the world begun.

88–91 When . . . liars:
If the love I have for
Rosaline, which is like
a religion, changes
because of such a lie
(that others may be
more beautiful), let my
tears be turned to fire
and my eyes be burned.

Benvolio. Tut! you saw her fair, none else being by,
95 Herself poised with herself in either eye;
But in that crystal scales let there be weighed
Your lady's love against some other maid
That I will show you shining at this feast,
And she shall scant show well that now shows best.

94–99 Tut . . . best:
You've seen Rosaline
alone; now compare
her with some other
women.

100 **Romeo.** I'll go along, no such sight to be shown,
But to rejoice in splendor of mine own.

100–101 Romeo agrees
to go to the party, but
only to see Rosaline.

[*Exeunt.*]

Scene 3 *Capulet's house.*

[*Enter* Lady Capulet *and* Nurse.]

Lady Capulet. Nurse, where's my daughter? Call her forth to me.

Nurse. Now, by my maidenhead at twelve year old,
I bade her come. What, lamb! what, ladybird!
God forbid! Where's this girl? What, Juliet!

[*Enter* Juliet.]

5 **Juliet.** How now? Who calls?

Nurse. Your mother.

Juliet. Madam, I am here. What is your will?

Lady Capulet. This is the matter—Nurse, give leave awhile,
We must talk in secret. Nurse, come back again;
10 I have remembered me, thou's hear our counsel.
Thou knowest my daughter's of a pretty age.

**8–11 give leave . . .
counsel:** Lady Capulet
seems nervous, not sure
whether she wants the
nurse to stay or leave;
of a pretty age: of an
attractive age, ready for
marriage.

Nurse. Faith, I can tell her age unto an hour.

Lady Capulet. She's not fourteen.

The Tragedy of Romeo and Juliet: Act I, Scene 3 **193**

Analyze Character: Motivations (Sc. 2, LINES 82–102)   RL 3

Have students recall Benvolio's pledge to Romeo at the end of Scene 1 that he would make Romeo forget Rosaline "or else die in debt."

Q ASK STUDENTS what Benvolio means when he says "Compare her face with some that I shall show, / And I will make thee think thy swan a crow" in lines 86–87. (*He will find someone so beautiful that Rosaline will look unattractive in comparison.*) Why is Benvolio so confident that he can make Romeo get over Rosaline? (*He thinks that Romeo loves Rosaline because there is no one else to compare her to [line 94].*)

Analyze Author's Choices: Parallel Plots (Sc. 3, LINES 1-19)   RL 5

Remind students that they may need to synthesize information about a character from clues provided by other characters in the play.

R CITE TEXT EVIDENCE At this point in the play, how old is Juliet? (*She is 13 years old [lines 13 and 15].*) When is her next birthday, and how old will she be? (*In two weeks "and odd days," at Lammas Eve, she will turn 14 [line 18].*)

Cause:	Effect/Cause:	Effect/Cause:	Effect/Cause:
Romeo loves a woman who does not return his love.	*Romeo is depressed.*	*Benvolio vows to cheer him up by taking him to the party.*	*Romeo will see Rosaline and meet Juliet.*

Analyze Character   RL 3

(Sc. 3, LINES 17–49)

Tell students that although it seems rambling, the nurse's speech serves several purposes. It reveals character traits of the nurse as well as her relationship to Juliet. Explain that the nurse is another minor character who plays an important role. Read the nurse's long speech carefully with your students, stopping frequently to make sure that students understand what the nurse says.

S **CITE TEXT EVIDENCE** Have students describe how the nurse feels about Juliet. Ask students to cite evidence in support of their inference. *(The nurse thinks of Juliet as her own child. This is shown by the detailed memories she has of important events in Juliet's childhood [lines 24–34] and the obvious fondness with which she speaks of her.)* Ask students what they can infer about the nurse's character from what she says and how she says it. *(The nurse is very down-to-earth and coarse. She has no trouble talking about personal details. She has a good sense of humor, shown when she laughs at the recollection of Juliet falling for her husband's joke [lines 36–49]. She is devoted to Juliet.)*

Nurse.   I'll lay fourteen of my teeth—
And yet, to my teen be it spoken, I have but four—
15   She's not fourteen. How long is it now
To Lammastide?

Lady Capulet.   A fortnight and odd days.

Nurse. Even or odd, of all days in the year,
Come Lammas Eve at night shall she be fourteen.
Susan and she (God rest all Christian souls!)
20   Were of an age. Well, Susan is with God;
She was too good for me. But, as I said,
On Lammas Eve at night shall she be fourteen;
That shall she, marry; I remember it well.
'Tis since the earthquake now eleven years;
25   And she was weaned (I never shall forget it),
Of all the days of the year, upon that day.
For I had then laid wormwood to my dug,
Sitting in the sun under the dovehouse wall.
My lord and you were then at Mantua—
30   Nay, I do bear a brain—But, as I said,
When it did taste the wormwood on the nipple
Of my dug and felt it bitter, pretty fool,
To see it tetchy and fall out with the dug!
Shake, quoth the dovehouse! 'Twas no need, I trow,
35   To bid me trudge.
And since that time it is eleven years,
For then she could stand alone; nay, by the rood,
She could have run and waddled all about;
For even the day before, she broke her brow;
40   And then my husband (God be with his soul!
'A was a merry man) took up the child.
"Yea," quoth he, "dost thou fall upon thy face?
Thou wilt fall backward when thou has more wit,
Wilt thou not, Jule?" And, by my holidam,
45   The pretty wretch left crying, and said "Ay."
To see now how a jest shall come about!
I warrant, an I should live a thousand years,
I never should forget it. "Wilt thou not, Jule?" quoth he,
And, pretty fool, it stinted, and said "Ay."

50   **Lady Capulet.** Enough of this. I pray thee hold thy peace.

Nurse. Yes, madam. Yet I cannot choose but laugh
To think it should leave crying and say "Ay."
And yet, I warrant, it had upon its brow
A bump as big as a young cock'rel's stone;
55   A perilous knock; and it cried bitterly.

14 **teen:** sorrow.

16 **Lammastide:** August 1, a religious feast day. It is two weeks (**a fortnight**) away.

17–49 The nurse babbles about Juliet's childhood. Her own daughter, Susan, was the same age as Juliet, and died in infancy, leaving the nurse available to become a wet nurse to (that is, breastfeed) Juliet. An earthquake happened on the day she stopped breastfeeding Juliet (**she was weaned**).

27 **laid wormwood to my dug:** applied a plant with a bitter taste to her breast to discourage the child from breastfeeding.

33 **tetchy:** cranky.

34–35 **Shake … trudge:** When the dove house shook, I knew enough to leave.

37 **by the rood:** by the cross of Christ (a mild oath).

39 **broke her brow:** cut her forehead.

42–49 "Yea,"…"Ay": The nurse's husband made a crude joke, asking the baby whether she'd fall the other way (on her back) when she was older. Although Juliet didn't understand the question, she stopped crying (**stinted**) and answered "Yes." The nurse finds the story so funny that she can't stop retelling it.

Strategies for Annotation   ✎ 🗐 *Annotate it!*

Analyze Character   RL 3

Have students use their eBook annotation tools to help them analyze the nurse's character:

- Highlight in yellow the details that the nurse remembers about Juliet's childhood.
- Highlight in blue the idiosyncrasies of her speech, such as parenthetical comments.
- Review what is highlighted to develop a picture of the kind of person who would talk in this way and say these things.

On Lammas Eve at night shall she be fourteen;

That shall she, marry; I remember it well.

'Tis since the earthquake now eleven years;

And she was weaned 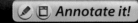(I never shall forget it),

"Yea," quoth my husband, "fallst upon thy face?
Thou wilt fall backward when thou comest to age,
Wilt thou not, Jule?" It stinted, and said "Ay."

Juliet. And stint thou too, I pray thee, nurse, say I.

60 **Nurse.** Peace, I have done. God mark thee to his grace!
Thou wast the prettiest babe that e'er I nursed.
An I might live to see thee married once,
I have my wish.

Lady Capulet. Marry, that "marry" is the very theme
65 I came to talk of. Tell me, daughter Juliet,
How stands your disposition to be married?

Juliet. It is an honor that I dream not of.

Nurse. An honor? Were not I thine only nurse,
I would say thou hadst sucked wisdom from thy teat.

70 **Lady Capulet.** Well, think of marriage now. Younger than you,
Here in Verona, ladies of esteem,
Are made already mothers. By my count,
I was your mother much upon these years
That you are now a maid. Thus then in brief:
75 The valiant Paris seeks you for his love.

Nurse. A man, young lady! lady, such a man
As all the world—why he's a man of wax.

Lady Capulet. Verona's summer hath not such a flower.

64 Marry ... "marry":
two different usages of
the same word—the first
meaning "by the Virgin
Mary" and the second
meaning "to wed."

73–74 I was ... maid:
I was your mother at
about your age, yet you
are still unmarried.

77 a man of wax: a man
so perfect he could be a
wax statue, of the type
sculptors once used as
models for their works.

CLOSE READ

Support Inferences
RL 1

(Sc. 3, LINES 59–75)

Tell students that characters' interactions with each other can be used to support inferences about their relationships.

T **CITE TEXT EVIDENCE** Have students make inferences about Juliet's feeling toward the nurse. *(Juliet appears very fond of the nurse. She tells her to stop talking but in a tone that is gentle and kind.)* Ask students how they would describe Juliet's attitude toward her mother. *(She is respectful as shown in her response to her mother's question about marriage.)*

WHEN STUDENTS STRUGGLE ...

Have students study the image from the 1968 film version of the play. Then ask them to work in pairs to answer these questions:

- What idea about the relationship between Juliet and the nurse is brought out here? Explain.
- How would you describe Juliet's attitude toward her mother in this image? Why?
- What does the appearance of each character suggest about her personality? Note posture and expression.

Have students share their answers to the questions. As a class, return to the text to find the lines that support the inferences they have made about character.

Interpret Figurative Language

RL 4, L 5a

(Sc. 3, LINES 80–95)

Direct students to read this speech carefully, noting the **extended metaphor** that Lady Capulet uses to achieve her purpose. An extended metaphor is an extended comparison between two unlike things.

Ⓤ CITE TEXT EVIDENCE Have students identify the comparison in the extended metaphor. *(Lady Capulet compares Paris to a book).* Then have them explain the features of Paris that Lady Capulet emphasizes in her comparison. *(She says that he is good-looking: "find delight writ there with beauty's pen" [line 83] and that every one of his features "lends content" [line 85]. She suggests that Paris has more substance or personality than it first appears: "And what obscured in this fair volume lies / Find written in the margent of his eyes.")* What attribute is suggested in line 94, "So shall you share all that he doth possess"? *(She implies that he is also wealthy.)*

Support Inferences

RL 1

(Sc. 3, LINES 98–100)

Remind students that they are building up an idea of Juliet's character from what she says and does in this scene.

Ⓥ ASK STUDENTS to explain Juliet's reply. *(She will look Paris over at the party, but she will wait upon her mother's approval before she allows herself to become attached to him.)* What do Juliet's words reveal about her character? *(She is an obedient daughter, who tries to please her parents.)*

Nurse. Nay, he's a flower, in faith—a very flower.

80 **Lady Capulet.** What say you? Can you love the gentleman?
This night you shall behold him at our feast.
Read o'er the volume of young Paris' face,
And find delight writ there with beauty's pen;
Examine every several lineament,
85 And see how one another lends content;
And what obscured in this fair volume lies
Find written in the margent of his eyes.
This precious book of love, this unbound lover,
To beautify him only lacks a cover.
90 The fish lives in the sea, and 'tis much pride
For fair without the fair within to hide.
That book in many's eyes doth share the glory,
That in gold clasps locks in the golden story;
So shall you share all that he doth possess,
95 By having him making yourself no less.

Nurse. No less? Nay, bigger! Women grow by men.

Lady Capulet. Speak briefly, can you like of Paris' love?

Juliet. I'll look to like, if looking liking move;
But no more deep will I endart mine eye
100 Than your consent gives strength to make it fly.

[*Enter a* Servingman.]

Servingman. Madam, the guests are come, supper served up, you called, my young lady asked for, the nurse cursed in the pantry, and everything in extremity. I must hence to wait. I beseech you follow straight.

105 **Lady Capulet.** We follow thee. [*Exit* Servingman.] Juliet, the County stays.

Nurse. Go, girl, seek happy nights to happy days.

[*Exeunt.*]

Scene 4 *A street near the Capulet house.*

[*Enter* Romeo, Mercutio, Benvolio, *with five or six other* Maskers; Torchbearers.]

Romeo. What, shall this speech be spoke for our excuse?
Or shall we on without apology?

Benvolio. The date is out of such prolixity.
We'll have no Cupid hoodwinked with a scarf,
5 Bearing a Tartar's painted bow of lath,
Scaring the ladies like a crowkeeper;
Nor no without-book prologue, faintly spoke

82–89 Read . . . cover: Lady Capulet uses an extended metaphor that compares Paris to a book that Juliet should read.

84 every several lineament: each separate feature (of Paris' face).

87 margent . . . eyes: She compares Paris' eyes to the margin of a page, where notes are written to explain the content.

88–91 This . . . hide: This beautiful book (Paris) needs only a cover (wife) to become even better. He may be hiding even more wonderful qualities inside.

96 Women get bigger (pregnant) when they marry.

98–100 I'll look . . . fly: I'll look at him with the intention of liking him, if simply looking can make me like him; **endart:** look deeply, as if penetrating with a dart.

103–104 extremity: great confusion; **straight:** immediately.

105 the County stays: Count Paris is waiting for you.

1–10 What, shall this . . . be gone: Romeo asks whether they should send a messenger announcing their arrival at the party. Benvolio says that they'll dance one dance (**measure them a measure**) and then leave.

WHEN STUDENTS STRUGGLE . . .

Display a Venn diagram on the board. Then ask students to reread Lord Capulet's comments to Paris in lines 13–33 as well as what Lady Capulet says in lines 80–95. Have them work together to identify ways in which Lord and Lady Capulet's attitudes about Juliet's marriage to Paris are the same and different. *(Lord Capulet: does not want Juliet to marry too early; believes early mothers are marred. Both: wish for Juliet's happiness; hope that she will be agreeable to the plan. Lady Capulet: feels it is time Juliet is married; thinks Paris is a good husband for Juliet.)*

After the prompter, for our entrance;
But let them measure us by what they will,
10　We'll measure them a measure, and be gone.

Romeo. Give me a torch. I am not for this ambling;
Being but heavy, I will bear the light.

Mercutio. Nay, gentle Romeo, we must have you dance.

Romeo. Not I, believe me. You have dancing shoes
15　With nimble soles; I have a soul of lead
So stakes me to the ground I cannot move.

Mercutio. You are a lover. Borrow Cupid's wings
And soar with them above a common bound.

Romeo. I am too sore enpiercèd with his shaft
20　To soar with his light feathers, and so bound
I cannot bound a pitch above dull woe.
Under love's heavy burden do I sink.

Mercutio. And, to sink in it, should you burden love—
Too great oppression for a tender thing.

25　**Romeo.** Is love a tender thing? It is too rough,
Too rude, too boist'rous, and it pricks like thorn.

Mercutio. If love be rough with you, be rough with love.
Prick love for pricking, and you beat love down.
Give me a case to put my visage in.
30　A visor for a visor! What care I
What curious eye doth quote deformities?
Here are the beetle brows shall blush for me.

Benvolio. Come, knock and enter, and no sooner in
But every man betake him to his legs.

35　**Romeo.** A torch for me! Let wantons light of heart
Tickle the senseless rushes with their heels;
For I am proverbed with a grandsire phrase,
I'll be a candle-holder and look on;
The game was ne'er so fair, and I am done.

40　**Mercutio.** Tut, dun's the mouse, the constable's own word!
If thou art Dun, we'll draw thee from the mire
Of, save your reverence, love, wherein thou stickst
Up to the ears. Come, we burn daylight, ho!

Romeo. Nay, that's not so.

Mercutio.　　　　　　I mean, sir, in delay
45　We waste our lights in vain, like lamps by day.

12 heavy: sad. Romeo makes a joke based on the meanings of *heavy* and *light*.

14–32 Romeo continues to talk about his sadness, while Mercutio jokingly makes fun of him to try to cheer him up.

29–32 Give . . . for me: Give me a mask for an ugly face. I don't care if people notice my appearance. Here, look at my bushy eyebrows.

34 betake . . . legs: dance.

35–38 Let . . . look on: Let playful people tickle the grass (**rushes**) on the floor with their dancing. I'll follow the old saying (**grandsire phrase**) and just be a spectator.

40–43 Tut . . . daylight: Mercutio jokes, using various meanings of the word *dun*, which sounds like Romeo's last word, *done*. He concludes by saying they should not waste time (**burn daylight**).

The Tragedy of Romeo and Juliet: Act I, Scene 4　**197**

ENGLISH LANGUAGE SUPPORT

Language: Inverted Word Order Explain that Shakespeare occasionally uses inverted word order in his sentences, putting the verb before the subject. Tell students that rearranging the subject and verb will help them understand the line more easily. Write Juliet's comment in lines 99–100 on the board: "But no more deep will I endart mine eye / Than your consent gives strength to make it fly." Rewrite this as it might be more commonly expressed: "I will endart mine eye no more deep. . . ."

ASK STUDENTS to restate these lines, putting the subject first: Scene 3, line 94: "So shall you share all that he doth possess." (*You shall share all that he doth possess.*); Scene 4, line 22: "Under love's heavy burden do I sink." (*Under love's heavy burden I do sink.*) Encourage them to rearrange the word order when they see other inverted sentences.

CLOSE READ

Interpret Figurative Language: Puns　RL 4, L 5a

(Sc. 4, LINES 11–22)

Have students volunteer to read this dialogue aloud, noting what is revealed about Romeo by the play on words. Remind students to look for individual words that have multiple meanings or pairs of words that sound similar but are spelled differently from each other.

Ⓦ **CITE TEXT EVIDENCE** Have students identify the puns in these lines. What do they reveal about Romeo's mood? (*In line 12, Romeo makes a pun by using the word* heavy *to mean both "sad" and "of great weight" and the word* light *to mean "luminous" and "of little weight." In line 15, Romeo's pun comes from pairing the words* soul *and* soles *when explaining his unhappiness. In lines 19–20, Romeo puns on the words* sore *["in pain"] and* soar *["fly"]. These puns show that Romeo remains depressed but is attempting to make light of his misery.*)

Analyze Character　RL 3

(Sc. 4, LINES 23–43)

Point out that Mercutio makes his appearance for the first time in this scene. Remind students that the dialogue between characters often provides clues as to their traits and relationships. Recruit student volunteers to read this dialogue aloud.

Ⓧ **ASK STUDENTS** how they would describe Romeo's conversation with Mercutio. What kind of friend is Mercutio to Romeo? (*Their exchange of comments suggests that Mercutio is funny and quick-witted. He also does not seem to have a lot of patience with Romeo's lovesickness. "If love be rough with you, be rough with love." He tries to lift Romeo's spirits by jollying him out of his depression by making jokes.*)

Support Inferences

RL 1, RL 7

(PHOTOGRAPH)

Remind students that each production of *Romeo and Juliet* suggests the director's own vision of the characters, setting, and action.

Y **ASK STUDENTS** what mood is created by the scene in the photograph. Why? *(The party-goers seem startled by something. The lighting throws shadows, creating a gloomy mood, not one that is festive.)*

Image Credits: (t) ©Mary Evans/BHE Films/Dino De Laurentiis Cinematografica/Verona Prod/Ronald Grant/Everett Collection, Inc.; (tr) ©vectorkat/Shutterstock

Take our good meaning, for our judgment sits
Five times in that ere once in our five wits.

Romeo. And we mean well in going to this masque;
But 'tis no wit to go.

Mercutio.   Why, may one ask?

50 **Romeo.** I dreamt a dream tonight.

Mercutio.   And so did I.

Romeo. Well, what was yours?

Mercutio.   That dreamers often lie.

Romeo. In bed asleep, while they do dream things true.

Mercutio. O, then I see Queen Mab hath been with you.
She is the fairies' midwife, and she comes
55 In shape no bigger than an agate stone
On the forefinger of an alderman,

53–95 Mercutio talks of Mab, queen of the fairies, a folktale character well-known to Shakespeare's audience. His language includes vivid descriptions, puns, and satires of people; and ultimately he gets caught up in his own wild imaginings.

55 agate stone: jewel for a ring.

Drawn with a team of little atomies
Athwart men's noses as they lie asleep;
Her wagon spokes made of long spinners' legs,
60   The cover, of the wings of grasshoppers;
Her traces, of the smallest spider's web;
Her collars, of the moonshine's wat'ry beams;
Her whip, of cricket's bone; the lash, of film;
Her wagoner, a small grey-coated gnat,
65   Not half so big as a round little worm
Pricked from the lazy finger of a maid;
Her chariot is an empty hazelnut,
Made by the joiner squirrel or old grub,
Time out o' mind the fairies' coachmakers.
70   And in this state she gallops night by night
Through lovers' brains, and then they dream of love;
O'er courtiers' knees, that dream on curtsies straight;
O'er lawyers' fingers, who straight dream on fees;
O'er ladies' lips, who straight on kisses dream,
75   Which oft the angry Mab with blisters plagues,
Because their breaths with sweetmeats tainted are.
Sometime she gallops o'er a courtier's nose,
And then dreams he of smelling out a suit,
And sometime comes she with a tithe-pig's tail
80   Tickling a parson's nose as 'a lies asleep,
Then dreams he of another benefice.
Sometime she driveth o'er a soldier's neck,
And then dreams he of cutting foreign throats,
Of breaches, ambuscadoes, Spanish blades,
85   Of healths five fathom deep; and then anon
Drums in his ear, at which he starts and wakes,
And being thus frighted, swears a prayer or two
And sleeps again. This is that very Mab
That plaits the manes of horses in the night
90   And bakes the elflocks in foul sluttish hairs,
Which once untangled much misfortune bodes.
This is the hag, when maids lie on their backs,
That presses them and learns them first to bear,
Making them women of good carriage.
95   This is she—

Romeo.   Peace, peace, Mercutio, peace!
Thou talkst of nothing.

Mercutio.   True, I talk of dreams;
Which are the children of an idle brain,
Begot of nothing but vain fantasy;
Which is as thin of substance as the air,

57 atomies: tiny creatures.

59 spinners' legs: spiders' legs.

61 traces: harness.

68 joiner: carpenter.

77–78 Sometimes she ... suit: Sometimes Mab makes a member of the king's court dream of receiving special favors.

81 benefice: a well-paying position for a clergyman.

84 ambuscadoes: ambushes; **Spanish blades:** high-quality Spanish swords.

89 plaits: braids.

96–103 True ... South: Mercutio is trying to keep Romeo from taking his dreams too seriously.

TEACH

CLOSE READ

Analyze Character: Motivations (Sc. 4, LINES 53–95)
RL 3

Remind students that just before Mercutio launches into this speech, Romeo tells him about a dream he had.

(Z) CITE TEXT EVIDENCE Have students explain where dreams come from according to Mercutio. *(They come from Queen Mab, queen of the fairies who visits people while they are sleeping, riding her wagon made from "an empty hazelnut" [line 67]. What they dream about depends on where she gallops.)*

TO CHALLENGE STUDENTS ...

Discuss the Function of a Scene Have students review Scene 4. Point out that this scene does not seem to advance the plot. Ask students: Is Scene 4 merely an amusing digression or does it fulfill a greater purpose? Organize students into small groups and ask them to discuss this question. Have them consider whether this scene

- contributes to essential understanding of character
- expresses important themes through the speeches and interactions of the characters
- affects the pacing of the play
- conveys mood

ASK STUDENTS to share their conclusions about the function of the scene with the class. Encourage them to offer details in support.

Analyze Author's Choices: Parallel Plots

RL 5

(Sc. 4, LINES 106–113)

A2 ASK STUDENTS whether Mercutio's efforts to minimize the importance of Romeo's dream worked. Why or why not? *(They did not work. Romeo is still fearful that something bad will happen in the future.)* What do lines 112–113 suggest about the reason Romeo goes to the party in spite of his feelings? *(He feels he is in the hands of fate.)*

Analyze Word Choice

RL 4

(Sc. 5, LINES 1–13)

Direct students to read this short scene paying attention to the language used by the servants.

B2 ASK STUDENTS what the purpose of this scene is. *(It breaks the mood of foreboding set by Romeo's speech, using puns that provide light relief. It creates the party atmosphere by showing the hustle and bustle of preparation.)*

---

100 And more inconstant than the wind, who woos
Even now the frozen bosom of the North
And, being angered, puffs away from thence,
Turning his face to the dew-dropping South.

Benvolio. This wind you talk of blows us from ourselves.
105 Supper is done, and we shall come too late.

A2

Romeo. I fear, too early; for my mind misgives
Some consequence, yet hanging in the stars,
Shall bitterly begin his fearful date
With this night's revels and expire the term
110 Of a despised life, closed in my breast,
By some vile forfeit of untimely death.
But he that hath the steerage of my course
Direct my sail! On, lusty gentlemen!

Benvolio. Strike, drum.

[*Exeunt.*]

Scene 5 *A hall in Capulet's house; the scene of the party.*

[Servingmen *come forth with napkins.*]

B2

First Servingman. Where's Potpan, that he helps not to take away? He shift a trencher! he scrape a trencher!

Second Servingman. When good manners shall lie all in one or two men's hands, and they unwashed too, 'tis a foul thing.

5 **First Servingman.** Away with the joint-stools, remove the court-cupboard, look to the plate. Good thou, save me a piece of marchpane and, as thou lovest me, let the porter let in Susan Grindstone and Nell. Anthony, and Potpan!

Second Servingman. Ay, boy, ready.

10 **First Servingman.** You are looked for and called for, asked for and sought for, in the great chamber.

Third Servingman. We cannot be here and there too. Cheerly, boys! Be brisk awhile, and the longer liver take all.

[*Exeunt.*]

[Maskers *appear with* Capulet, Lady Capulet, Juliet, *all the* Guests, *and* Servants.]

Capulet. Welcome, gentlemen! Ladies that have their toes
15 Unplagued with corns will have a bout with you.
Ah ha, my mistresses! which of you all
Will now deny to dance? She that makes dainty,
She I'll swear hath corns. Am I come near ye now?
Welcome, gentlemen! I have seen the day

106–111 Romeo, still depressed, fears that some terrible event caused by the stars will begin at the party. Remember the phrase "star-crossed lovers" from the prologue.

1–13 These opening lines are a comic conversation among three servants as they work.

2 trencher: wooden plate.

6–7 plate: silverware and silver plates; **marchpane:** marzipan, a sweet made from almond paste.

14–27 Capulet welcomes his guests and invites them all to dance. He alternates talking with his guests and telling the servants what to do.

17–18 She that . . . corns: Any woman too shy to dance will be assumed to have corns, ugly and painful growths on the toes.

ENGLISH LANGUAGE SUPPORT

Language: Dialogue Project lines 14–32 on the board. Invite volunteers to mark up the text as directed:

- Highlight the lines Lord Capulet speaks to his guests in green.
- Highlight the lines he directs to the servants and musicians in blue.
- Highlight the lines he speaks to his cousin in pink.

ASK STUDENTS how the actor playing this part would show to whom he was speaking. Point out that in the written text, cues such as "gentlemen" help to identify the person being spoken to.

More light, you knaves! and turn the tables up,

And quench the fire, the room is grown too hot.

Ah, sirrah, this unlooked-for sport comes well.

You are welcome, gentlemen! Come, musicians, play.

A hall, a hall! give room! and foot it, girls. . . .

20 That I have worn a visor and could tell   **20 visor:** mask.
    A whispering tale in a fair lady's ear,
    Such as would please. 'Tis gone, 'tis gone, 'tis gone!
    You are welcome, gentlemen! Come, musicians, play.
    A hall, a hall! give room! and foot it, girls.

    [Music plays and they dance.]

25 More light, you knaves! and turn the tables up,
    And quench the fire, the room is grown too hot.
    Ah, sirrah, this unlooked-for sport comes well.   **28–38** Capulet and
    Nay, sit, nay, sit, good cousin Capulet,   his relative watch the
    For you and I are past our dancing days.   dancing as they talk of
                                                          days gone by.
30 How long is't now since last yourself and I
    Were in a mask?

    Second Capulet. By'r Lady, thirty years.

    Capulet. What, man? 'Tis not so much, 'tis not so much!
    'Tis since the nuptial of Lucentio,   **33 nuptial:** marriage.
    Come Pentecost as quickly as it will,
35 Some five-and-twenty years, and then we masked.

    Second Capulet. 'Tis more, 'tis more! His son is elder, sir;
    His son is thirty.

    Capulet.   Will you tell me that?
    His son was but a ward two years ago.

    Romeo [*to a* Servingman]. What lady's that, which doth enrich
        the hand
40 Of yonder knight?

    Servant. I know not, sir.

    Romeo. O, she doth teach the torches to burn bright!
    It seems she hangs upon the cheek of night
    Like a rich jewel in an Ethiop's ear—   **44–45 Ethiop's ear:**
                                                          the ear of an Ethiopian
45 Beauty too rich for use, for earth too dear!   (African); **for earth too**
    So shows a snowy dove trooping with crows   **dear:** too precious for
    As yonder lady o'er her fellows shows.   this world.
    The measure done, I'll watch her place of stand
    And, touching hers, make blessed my rude hand.
50 Did my heart love till now? Forswear it, sight!
    For I ne'er saw true beauty till this night.

    Tybalt. This, by his voice, should be a Montague.   **52–57** Tybalt
    Fetch me my rapier, boy. What, dares the slave   recognizes Romeo's
    Come hither, covered with an antic face,   voice and tells his
                                                           servant to get his sword
55 To fleer and scorn at our solemnity?   (**rapier**). He thinks
    Now, by the stock and honor of my kin,   Romeo has come to
    To strike him dead I hold it not a sin.   make fun of (**fleer**) their
                                                           party.

TEACH

CLOSE READ

Determine Figurative   RL 4
Meanings (Sc. 5, LINES 42–51)

Tell students that this speech uttered by Romeo is memorable both for its importance to the plot and for its beauty. Have students note how Shakespeare uses **hyperbole** (exaggeration) and **similes** (comparisons between two unlike things using *as* or *like*) to show Romeo's feelings.

C2 **ASK STUDENTS** to explain what has happened to Romeo. *(He has fallen in love with a woman he sees.)* Ask students to identify the hyperbole in this speech. What effect does it have on the audience's realization of his feelings? *(Romeo says that she teaches "the torches to burn bright!" This exaggeration shows how intense his feelings are.)* How does he use similes to convey her beauty in his eyes? *(He says that she stands out against "the cheek of night / Like a rich jewel in an Ethiop's ear." He says that she is a dove amongst black crows.)*

Analyze Author's Choices: RL 5
Parallel Plots (Sc. 5, LINES 52–57)

Remind students that Romeo is actually in the house of his sworn enemies, the Capulets.

D2 **ASK STUDENTS** to identify Tybalt *(He is Juliet's cousin, and thus a Capulet.)* and to explain Tybalt's reaction when he hears Romeo's voice. What does he want to do? *(Tybalt is furious that a Montague would crash the party. He may also be suspicious of Romeo's motives. He wants to kill Romeo.)*

WHEN STUDENTS STRUGGLE . . .

Explain that reading poetry aloud conveys the meaning more clearly. Tell students that when they read a passage of poetry aloud, they should keep in mind these guidelines:

- Do not stop at the end of a line unless there is punctuation. Pause when you see commas or semicolons. Stop when you see periods and other end marks.
- Vary your volume, rate, and pitch to express emotions and emphasize ideas.
- Pronounce your words clearly and completely.

Model how to read lines 42–51 aloud as students follow along. Then have partners take turns reading the passage to each other.

Support Inferences   RL 1

(Sc. 5, LINES 63–71)

Point out to students that a character's motivations can often be inferred from details in the text.

E2 ASK STUDENTS how Lord Capulet reacts to Romeo's presence at the ball. Why? *(Surprisingly, Lord Capulet is content to have Romeo stay. He does not anticipate that Romeo will cause any trouble. He also does not want Tybalt to be responsible for harm coming to Romeo on Capulet's own property after the Prince's warning to avoid conflict with the Montagues.)*

Capulet. Why, how now, kinsman? Wherefore storm you so?

Tybalt. Uncle, this is a Montague, our foe;
60 A villain, that is hither come in spite
To scorn at our solemnity this night.

Capulet. Young Romeo is it?

Tybalt.   'Tis he, that villain Romeo.

Capulet. Content thee, gentle coz, let him alone.
'A bears him like a portly gentleman,
65 And, to say truth, Verona brags of him
To be a virtuous and well-governed youth.
I would not for the wealth of all this town
Here in my house do him disparagement.
Therefore be patient, take no note of him.
70 It is my will; the which if thou respect,
Show a fair presence and put off these frowns,
An ill-beseeming semblance for a feast.

64 portly: dignified.

68 do him disparagement: speak critically or insultingly to him.

72 semblance: outward appearance.

Image Credits: (t) ©Everett Collection, Inc.; (tc) ©AKaiser/Shutterstock

202   Collection 4

Strategies for Annotation    Annotate it!

Analyze Author's Choices: RL 5
Parallel Plots

Have students use their eBook annotation tools to analyze how lines 63–90 advance the plot:

- Highlight in blue the reasons that Capulet wants Romeo left alone.
- On a note, summarize the consequences he fears if something were to happen to Romeo in his house.
- Highlight in green the lines that show Tybalt's anger.
- On a note, explain Tybalt's internal and external conflicts and how he may try to resolve them.

Tybalt. It fits when such a villain is a guest.

I'll not endure him.

Capulet. He shall be endured.

What, goodman boy? I say he shall. Go to!…

You'll make a mutiny among my guests!

You will set cock-a-hoop! You'll be the man.

Tybalt. It fits when such a villain is a guest.
I'll not endure him.

Capulet.   He shall be endured.
75 What, goodman boy? I say he shall. Go to!
Am I the master here, or you? Go to!
You'll not endure him? God shall mend my soul!
You'll make a mutiny among my guests!
You will set cock-a-hoop! You'll be the man.

80 **Tybalt.** Why, uncle, 'tis a shame.

Capulet.   Go to, go to!
You are a saucy boy. Is't so, indeed?
This trick may chance to scathe you. I know what.
You must contrary me! Marry, 'tis time.—
Well said, my hearts!—You are a princox—go!
85 Be quiet, or—More light, more light!—For shame!
I'll make you quiet; what!—Cheerly, my hearts!

Tybalt. Patience perforce with willful choler meeting
Makes my flesh tremble in their different greeting.
I will withdraw; but this intrusion shall,
90 Now seeming sweet, convert to bitter gall.

[*Exit.*]

Romeo. If I profane with my unworthiest hand
This holy shrine, the gentle fine is this:
My lips, two blushing pilgrims, ready stand
To smooth that rough touch with a tender kiss.

95 **Juliet.** Good pilgrim, you do wrong your hand too much,
Which mannerly devotion shows in this;
For saints have hands that pilgrims' hands do touch,
And palm to palm is holy palmers' kiss.

Romeo. Have not saints lips, and holy palmers too?

100 **Juliet.** Ay, pilgrim, lips that they must use in prayer.

Romeo. O, then, dear saint, let lips do what hands do!
They pray; grant thou, lest faith turn to despair.

Juliet. Saints do not move, though grant for prayers' sake.

Romeo. Then move not while my prayer's effect I take.
105 Thus from my lips, by thine my sin is purged.

[*kisses her*]

Juliet. Then have my lips the sin that they have took.

Romeo. Sin from my lips? O trespass sweetly urged!
Give me my sin again.

The Tragedy of Romeo and Juliet: Act I, Scene 5 **203**

---

75 goodman boy: a term used to address an inferior; **Go to:** Stop, that's enough!

79 set cock-a-hoop: cause everything to be upset.

82–83 scathe: harm; **I know . . . contrary me:** I know what I'm doing! Don't you dare challenge my authority.

84–86 Capulet intersperses his angry speech to Tybalt with comments to his guests and servants.

87–90 Patience . . . gall: Tybalt says he will restrain himself, but his suppressed anger (**choler**) makes his body shake.

91–108 Romeo and Juliet are in the middle of the dance floor, with eyes only for each other. They touch the palms of their hands. Their conversation revolves around Romeo's comparison of his lips to pilgrims who have traveled to a holy shrine. Juliet goes along with the comparison.

105 purged: washed away.

Analyze Author's Choices: Parallel Plots (Sc. 5, LINES 80–90) RL 5

Remind students that a playwright may use **foreshadowing,** or hinting what may happen in the future, to maintain the audience's interest in his or her plot.

F2 **ASK STUDENTS** what is foreshadowed by Tybalt's reaction to his uncle's command to leave Romeo alone. Have them cite details in support. (*Tybalt is very angry that his uncle has forbidden him to harm Romeo. He says "I will withdraw; but this intrusion shall, / Now seeming sweet, convert to bitter gall." These lines indicate that he will do as his uncle says for the moment, but wait for a later opportunity to hurt Romeo. They foreshadow that there will be problems between the two in the future.*)

Determine Figurative Meanings (Sc. 5, LINES 91–105) RL 4

Tell students that the dialogue in this first meeting between Romeo and Juliet develops an elaborate extended metaphor. Provide students with background regarding shrines and pilgrimages. Have the class pay attention to the details that each character contributes to the extended metaphor as student volunteers read the dialogue aloud.

G2 **ASK STUDENTS** to explain to what Romeo compares Juliet in line 92 and 101. (*He compares her first to the holy shrine of a saint, then to the saint herself.*) How do the other references in these lines develop this comparison? (*He calls his lips "blushing pilgrims" that would like to smooth the roughness of his hand on the holy shrine. She calls Romeo a pilgrim, or palmer, referring to the palms of their hands together as well as a pilgrim who carries palms. They both compare kissing to praying.*) Have students explain what idea about their relationship this metaphor conveys. (*They idolize each other. It shows the intensity of their instant devotion.*)

Analyze Author's Choices: Parallel Plots

RL 5

(Sc. 5, LINES 111–117)

Remind students that as the play progresses, the plots will begin to intersect.

H2 **ASK STUDENTS** what Romeo's remark in line 117 shows that he realizes. (*He will not be able to pursue this relationship openly because he and Juliet come from warring families.*) Have students discuss what else the audience knows that Romeo does not about a circumstance that will affect their relationship. (*Juliet is meant to marry Paris.*)

Determine Figurative Meanings

RL 4

(Sc. 5, LINES 136–139)

Tell students that language can be a unifying element in a literary work of this length.

12 **ASK STUDENTS** how Juliet's language in this speech relates back to Romeo's in lines 169–176 of Scene 1. (*She expresses her conflicting feelings in paradoxical language: "My grave is like to be my wedding bed"; "My only love, sprung from my only hate!" Romeo also used contradictions when expressing his anguish over Rosaline's lack of interest.*) Have students explain what idea about love this literary device conveys. (*This language supports the idea that love is both sublime and awful. It can take someone to heights, then send them crashing down.*)

[*kisses her*]

Juliet. You kiss by the book.

Nurse. Madam, your mother craves a word with you.

110 **Romeo.** What is her mother?

Nurse. Marry, bachelor,
Her mother is the lady of the house.
And a good lady, and a wise and virtuous.
I nursed her daughter that you talked withal.
I tell you, he that can lay hold of her
115 Shall have the chinks.

Romeo. Is she a Capulet?
O dear account! my life is my foe's debt.

Benvolio. Away, be gone, the sport is at the best.

Romeo. Ay, so I fear; the more is my unrest.

Capulet. Nay, gentlemen, prepare not to be gone;
120 We have a trifling foolish banquet towards.

[*They whisper in his ear.*]
Is it e'en so? Why then, I thank you all.
I thank you, honest gentlemen. Good night.
More torches here! [*Exeunt* Maskers.] Come on then, let's to bed.
Ah, sirrah, by my fay, it waxes late;
125 I'll to my rest.

[*Exeunt all but* Juliet *and Nurse.*]

Juliet. Come hither, nurse. What is yond gentleman?

Nurse. The son and heir of old Tiberio.

Juliet. What's he that now is going out of door?

Nurse. Marry, that, I think, be young Petruchio.

130 **Juliet.** What's he that follows there, that would not dance?

Nurse. I know not.

Juliet. Go ask his name.—If he be married,
My grave is like to be my wedding bed.

Nurse. His name is Romeo, and a Montague,
135 The only son of your great enemy.

Juliet. My only love, sprung from my only hate!
Too early seen unknown, and known too late!
Prodigious birth of love it is to me
That I must love a loathed enemy.

140 **Nurse.** What's this? what's this?

108 kiss by the book: Juliet could mean "You kiss like someone who has practiced." Or she could be teasing Romeo, meaning "You kiss coldly, as though you had learned how by reading a book."

109 At the nurse's message, Juliet walks to her mother.

115 shall have the chinks: shall become rich.

116 my life . . . debt: my life belongs to my enemy.

120 towards: coming up.

137–138 Too early . . . too late: I fell in love with him before I learned who he is; **prodigious:** abnormal; unlucky.

WHEN STUDENTS STRUGGLE . . .

Remind students that dramatic irony occurs when the audience knows something that the characters do not. Explain that Shakespeare uses dramatic irony to add suspense; what the characters do not know usually leads to problems for them, which the audience can anticipate. List these examples of dramatic irony from Act I on the board:

- Romeo meets and falls in love with Juliet, who is a Capulet.
- Juliet loves Romeo.
- Juliet's parents have arranged for her to marry Paris.

ASK STUDENTS who is unaware of each circumstance and when or if that character finds out. Then discuss why each situation is a problem.

Juliet.   A rhyme I learnt even now
Of one I danced withal.

[*One calls within, "Juliet."*]

Nurse.   Anon, anon!
Come, let's away; the strangers all are gone.

[*Exeunt.*]

COLLABORATIVE DISCUSSION With a partner, discuss your first impressions of Romeo and Juliet. What are they like? What actions or lines of dialogue reveal their personalities?

Analyze Character: Motivations (Sc. 5, LINES 141–142)

RL 3

Explain to students that both Romeo and Juliet are complex characters. A **complex character** is capable of change.

 ASK STUDENTS why Juliet responds to the nurse's question as she does. *(She does not want to tell the nurse what has happened.)* What quality does her response show that was not apparent previously? *(She shows a desire to act independently, rather than be agreeable or obedient.)*

COLLABORATIVE DISCUSSION Encourage students to review Act I and note specific lines from which they can draw inferences about the characters of Romeo and Juliet. Have students combine their lists with their partner's and share them with the class. Accept all reasonable responses.

ASK STUDENTS to share any questions they generated in the course of reading and discussing the selection.

TO CHALLENGE STUDENTS . . .

Analyze Paradox Explain to students that apparent contradictions that make sense are a literary device called paradox. Point out that Shakespeare uses paradox to great effect to convey characters' conflict and the dual nature of some of the situations in which they find themselves.

- Ask students to work together to identify the paradoxes in lines 116–144. *(Examples: "My grave is like to be my wedding bed"; "My only love sprung from my only hate.")*
- Have them explain the truth of each apparent contradiction.
- Then ask students what ideas about theme and future plot developments are brought out through these paradoxes.

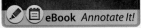

PRACTICE & APPLY

Analyzing the Text

RL 2, RL 3, RL 4, RL 5

Possible answers:

1. The Prologue tells of two households, "both alike in dignity…from ancient grudge break to new mutiny, where civil blood makes civil hands unclean." It then alludes to the fate of Romeo and Juliet, "a pair of star-crossed lovers" born to these households and who have killed themselves. This sets the stage for the tragedy.

2. Tybalt is inclined to feel hatred and want to fight, and he is not interested in talking of peace. He acts before thinking. He will likely spur the conflict in the play.

3. Tybalt and Benvolio are foils. Tybalt is brash and combative; Benvolio is reserved and contemplative. Romeo and Mercutio can also be seen as foils. Romeo is an impulsive romantic, and Mercutio, who is realistic and values common sense, often ridicules Romeo's dreamy romanticism.

4. Act I offers humorous interactions between Mercutio and Romeo (i.e., Scene 4, lines 35–43), as well as between Nurse and Juliet (Scene 3, lines 42–59). Mercutio mocks Romeo's romantic nature, and there is humor in Nurse's manner of speaking.

5. In Scene 4, Romeo fears a terrible event will begin at the party. He speaks of untimely death and of a consequence "hanging in the stars." This echoes the gloomy predictions of the Prologue. The statement in Scene 5 foreshadows Juliet's tragic end, also alluded to in the Prologue.

6. The continued, heated fights between the Capulets and the Montagues will likely influence future events. Juliet's family's wish for her to marry Paris and her rebellion against this idea is a key conflict. Romeo and Juliet's meeting and falling in love is likely to have dire consequences, given the strife between their families.

 eBook Annotate It!

Analyzing the Text

RL 2, RL 3,
RL 4, RL 5, SL 1

Cite Text Evidence   Support your responses with evidence from the selection.

1. **Interpret** An important **theme,** or message, in *Romeo and Juliet* is the struggle against fate, or forces that determine how a person's life will turn out. Explain how Act I's Prologue establishes the fate of the main characters and introduces the struggles they will face.

2. **Infer** In Scene 1, Tybalt says, "What, drawn, and talk of peace? I hate the word / As I hate hell, all Montagues, and thee. / Have at thee, coward!" (lines 63–65). What can you infer about Tybalt's personality and his role in the play, based on these words?

3. **Analyze** A **foil** is a character who highlights, through sharp contrast, the qualities of another character. Which two sets of characters in Act I are foils for each other? What do you learn about the characters by seeing them in contrast to one another?

4. **Identify** *Romeo and Juliet* is a play that deals with serious and tragic events, yet Shakespeare does weave jokes and comical situations into Act I. One example is the conversation among the servants at the beginning of Scene 5. Identify other examples of humor in the first act.

5. **Interpret** Foreshadowing is the use of hints or clues to suggest events that will happen later in the story. Explain the **foreshadowing** in these lines from Act I:
   - Scene 4, lines 106–111
   - Scene 5, line 133

6. **Predict** Which events in Act I seem key to setting up the conflicts that will move the action of the rest of the play forward? Explain your response.

PERFORMANCE TASK

 WriteSmart

Speaking Activity: Discussion In *Romeo and Juliet*, characters are motivated by passion and strong emotions.

- Notice that throughout Act I, Shakespeare contrasts themes of love and hate through characters' words and actions.
- Work with a partner to identify passages that express love or hate. Read the passages aloud with your partner. Read with feeling to express the emotions that underlie the words.

- Discuss what dramatic effect Shakespeare creates by pairing these two emotions in the first act of the play.
- Write a summary that outlines the main points of your discussion.

Assign this performance task.   WriteSmart

PERFORMANCE TASK

SL 1

Speaking Activity: Discussion After students have chosen their passages, ask volunteers to read them aloud for the class. Then have pairs work independently on their analyses of the dramatic effect. Remind them that their summaries should contain only the most important points of their discussion.

CLOSE READ

AS YOU READ Direct students to use the As You Read note to focus their reading. Remind them to write down questions they generate as they read.

Analyze Author's Choices: Text Structure (LINES 1–14)
RL 5

Point out that the chorus has the dual function of summarizing the action from the previous act and giving an overview of what is to come.

 ASK STUDENTS to reread line 5, "Now Romeo is beloved, and loves again." Ask them what this line identifies as the difference between the situation with Rosaline and the one with Juliet. *(Juliet loves him in return.)* Have students discuss the conflict Romeo and Juliet will encounter in the pursuit of their love. *(As enemies, they will not be easily able to see each other.)* What lines support the idea that love will find a way? *("But passion lends them power, time means, to meet, / Temp'ring extremities with extreme sweet.")*

Interpret Figurative Language (Sc. 1, LINES 1–2)
RL 4, L 5a

Remind students to look for figurative language as they read the dialogue between Romeo and Juliet. Explain that Shakespeare uses the language of poetry, such as metaphor, to help communicate the intensity of his characters' emotions.

B **ASK STUDENTS** to explain the metaphor Romeo uses to describe his relationship with Juliet. What does this metaphor express about his feelings for her? *(Romeo says that Juliet is his heart; he calls himself the earth and says that she is the center of the earth. He is saying that he feels incomplete without her; he cannot bear to leave the essential part of him.)*

AS YOU READ Look for words and phrases that reveal the developing relationship between Romeo and Juliet and the intensity of their feelings for each other. Write down any questions you generate during reading.

Prologue

[*Enter* Chorus.]

 Chorus. Now old desire doth in his deathbed lie,
And young affection gapes to be his heir.
That fair for which love groaned for and would die,
With tender Juliet matched, is now not fair.
5 Now Romeo is beloved, and loves again,
Alike bewitched by the charm of looks;
But to his foe supposed he must complain,
And she steal love's sweet bait from fearful hooks.
Being held a foe, he may not have access
10 To breathe such vows as lovers use to swear,
And she as much in love, her means much less
To meet her new beloved anywhere;
But passion lends them power, time means, to meet,
Temp'ring extremities with extreme sweet.

[*Exit.*]

1–4 Now . . . fair: Romeo's love for Rosaline (**old desire**) is now dead. His new love for Juliet (**young affection**) replaces the old.

7 but . . . complain: Juliet, a Capulet, is Romeo's supposed enemy, yet she is the one to whom he must plead (**complain**) his love.

14 Temp'ring . . . sweet: moderating great difficulties with extreme delights.

ACT II

Scene 1 *A lane by the wall of Capulet's orchard.*

[*Enter* Romeo *alone.*]

B **Romeo.** Can I go forward when my heart is here?
Turn back, dull earth, and find thy center out.

[*climbs the wall and leaps down within it*]

[*Enter* Benvolio *with* Mercutio.]

Benvolio. Romeo! my cousin Romeo! Romeo!

Mercutio. He is wise,
And, on my life, hath stol'n him home to bed.

5 **Benvolio.** He ran this way, and leapt this orchard wall.
Call, good Mercutio.

Mercutio. Nay, I'll conjure too.
Romeo! humors! madman! passion! lover!
Appear thou in the likeness of a sigh;
Speak but one rhyme, and I am satisfied!
10 Cry but "Ay me!" pronounce but "love" and "dove";
Speak to my gossip Venus one fair word,
One nickname for her purblind son and heir,
Young Adam Cupid, he that shot so trim

1–2 Can . . . out: How can I leave when Juliet is still here? My body (**dull earth**) has to find its heart (**center**).

6 conjure: use magic to call him.

8–21 Appear . . . us: Mercutio jokes about Romeo's lovesickness.

The Tragedy of Romeo and Juliet: Act II, Scene 1 **207**

Close Read Screencasts ▶ View It!

Modeled Discussions

Have students click the *Close Read* icons in their eBooks to access the screencast in which readers discuss and annotate the following key passage:

- marriage of Romeo and Juliet (Act II, Scene 6, lines 6–15)

As a class, view and discuss the video.

Analyze Author's Choices: Parallel Plots

RL 5

(Sc. 1, LINES 17–32)

Review the definition of **dramatic irony** with students. Point out that knowing what the characters do not know adds interest to the drama.

C CITE TEXT EVIDENCE Have students explain the dramatic irony in this part of the scene. Have them cite details that support their explanation. *(Mercutio and Benvolio still believe that Romeo loves Rosaline and is mourning over her. Mercutio says "I conjure thee by Rosaline's bright eyes." Benvolio says that Romeo "hath hid himself among these trees." [line 30])* Why might his friends be concerned over Romeo's actions here? *(He seems to have deliberately put himself in harm's way by trespassing on the Capulet grounds.)*

Analyze Character

RL 3

(Sc. 1, LINES 33–41)

Draw students' attention to Mercutio's lengthy speeches in this scene. Discuss with students how even though his character was not introduced until late in Act I, he has become a highly visible presence in the play.

D ASK STUDENTS how Mercutio's dialogue in this scene adds to their impression of his character. *(He is very high-spirited. He makes fun of Romeo's lovesickness. He pushes the boundaries with his crude humor and outrageous puns.)*

When King Cophetua loved the beggar maid!
15 He heareth not, he stirreth not, he moveth not;
The ape is dead, and I must conjure him.
I conjure thee by Rosaline's bright eyes,
By her high forehead and her scarlet lip,
By her fine foot, straight leg, and quivering thigh,
20 And the demesnes that there adjacent lie,
That in thy likeness thou appear to us!

Benvolio. An if he hear thee, thou wilt anger him.

Mercutio. This cannot anger him. 'Twould anger him
To raise a spirit in his mistress' circle
25 Of some strange nature, letting it there stand
Till she had laid it and conjured it down.
That were some spite; my invocation
Is fair and honest and in his mistress' name
I conjure only but to raise up him.

30 **Benvolio.** Come, he hath hid himself among these trees
To be consorted with the humorous night.
Blind is his love, and best befits the dark.

Mercutio. If love be blind, love cannot hit the mark.
Now will he sit under a medlar tree
35 And wish his mistress were that kind of fruit
As maids call medlars when they laugh alone.
Oh, Romeo, that she were, O, that she were
An open et cetera, thou a pop'rin pear!
Romeo, good night. I'll to my truckle bed;
40 This field-bed is too cold for me to sleep.
Come, shall we go?

Benvolio.   Go then, for 'tis in vain
To seek him here that means not to be found.

[*Exeunt.*]

Scene 2 *Capulet's orchard.*

[*Enter Romeo.*]

Romeo. He jests at scars that never felt a wound.

[*Enter Juliet above at a window.*]

But soft! What light through yonder window breaks?
It is the East, and Juliet is the sun!
Arise, fair sun, and kill the envious moon,
5 Who is already sick and pale with grief
That thou her maid art far more fair than she.
Be not her maid, since she is envious;

20 demesnes: areas; **adjacent:** next to.

23–29 'Twould . . . raise up him: It would anger him if I called a stranger to join his beloved (**mistress**), but I'm only calling Romeo to join her.

31 To be . . . night: to keep company with the night, which is as gloomy as Romeo is.

34 medlar: a fruit that looks like a small brown apple.

39 truckle bed: trundle bed, a small bed that fits in beneath a bigger one.

1 He jests . . . wound: Romeo has overheard Mercutio and comments that Mercutio makes fun of love because he has never been wounded by it.

ENGLISH LANGUAGE SUPPORT

Language: Pronoun Referents Display this chart of pronouns and their referents from the Prologue.

his (lines 1, 2)	*old desire (Rosaline)*
his / he (lines 7, 9)	*Romeo*
she / her (lines 8, 11, 12)	*Juliet*
them (line 13)	*Romeo and Juliet*

Then project the prologue on the board. Point to each pronoun and have students name the referent. Invite volunteers to underline the referents in the text.

Her vestal livery is but sick and green,
And none but fools do wear it; cast it off.
10 It is my lady; O, it is my love!
O that she knew she were!
She speaks, yet she says nothing. What of that?
Her eye discourses; I will answer it.
I am too bold; 'tis not to me she speaks.
15 Two of the fairest stars in all the heaven,
Having some business, do entreat her eyes
To twinkle in their spheres till they return.
What if her eyes were there, they in her head?
The brightness of her cheek would shame those stars
20 As daylight doth a lamp; her eyes in heaven
Would through the airy region stream so bright
That birds would sing and think it were not night.
See how she leans her cheek upon her hand!
O that I were a glove upon that hand,
25 That I might touch that cheek!

Juliet.   Ay me!

Romeo.   She speaks.
O, speak again, bright angel! for thou art
As glorious to this night, being o'er my head,

**13–14 Her eye . . .
speaks:** Romeo shifts
back and forth between
wanting to speak to
Juliet and being afraid.

**15–22 Two of . . . not
night:** Romeo compares
Juliet's eyes to stars in
the sky.

25 Juliet begins to
speak, not knowing that
Romeo is nearby.

**26–32 thou art . . . of
the air:** He compares
Juliet to an angel
(**winged messenger of
heaven**) who stands on
(**bestrides**) the clouds.

CLOSE READ

Analyze Character:
Motivations (Sc. 2, LINES 1–25)   RL 3

Explain that Shakespeare often makes use of the
dramatic form of speech called a **soliloquy**. In a
soliloquy, the character is alone and, unrestrained by
the presence of others, speaks his or her innermost
thoughts. Ask a student volunteer to read the
soliloquy aloud.

Ⓔ ASK STUDENTS what provokes Romeo to speak
aloud. *(He thinks he sees Juliet in the window and
cannot restrain his emotion.)* To what does he compare
Juliet in the speech? *(He compares her to the sun and
her eyes to the brightest stars in the heavens. [lines
15-17])* What does this soliloquy reveal about his
thoughts? *(It shows that he is enraptured by Juliet's
beauty, that he idealizes her, that he is uncertain about
how to communicate with her, and that he wants to
touch her.)*

Strategies for Annotation   ✏️ 🗒️ *Annotate it!*

Analyze Figurative Language   RL 4

Have students use their eBook annotation tools to analyze the
figurative language in Romeo's soliloquy. Tell them to do the following:

- Highlight each metaphor in blue. On a note, explain what is
  being compared.
- Highlight each simile in yellow and explain the comparison on a
  note.
- In small groups, discuss how Shakespeare's language makes this
  speech memorable.

The brightness of her cheek would shame those stars

As daylight doth a lamp; her eyes in heaven

Would through the airy region stream so bright

That birds would sing and think it were not night.

Support Inferences

RL 1

(Sc. 2, LINES 33–53)

Direct students' attention to the thoughts that Juliet speaks aloud believing that she is alone. Have them consider what her words reveal about her character. Ask a student volunteer to read Juliet's lines aloud. Review the lines with students to ensure that they comprehend them.

F CITE TEXT EVIDENCE What does Juliet say that shows the strength of her feeling for Romeo? *(She says that if he would swear to love her, she will forsake her name. [lines 35-36])* Discuss with students how Juliet is naturally startled to think someone is in the garden. Why might she also be fearful, given what she has just said? *(It could be one of her relatives who has overheard her, in which case Romeo could be in danger.)* How have Juliet's priorities changed since Act I? *(In Act I, pleasing her family was her priority. In this scene, she shows that she is willing to lay family loyalty aside in order to be with Romeo.)*

Analyze Author's Choices: Parallel Plots

RL 5

(Sc. 2, LINES 54–65)

Point out that playwrights use dialogue to develop the unity of their play by referring to past events and other story lines.

G ASK STUDENTS how Romeo addresses Juliet. Why? *(He calls her "dear saint" [line 55] because that is what he called her at the party. She cannot see him yet, so he is giving her a clue to his identity.)* Ask students what warning Juliet gives to Romeo. What is the impact of this reminder on the audience? *(In lines 63-65, she warns Romeo that if her family finds him on the grounds, he could be killed. This reminds the audience of the conflict between the two families that places the relationship between Romeo and Juliet in jeopardy.)*

Unto the white-upturned wond'ring eyes
30   Of mortals that fall back to gaze on him
    When he bestrides the lazy-pacing clouds
    And sails upon the bosom of the air.

Juliet. O Romeo, Romeo! wherefore art thou Romeo?
    Deny thy father and refuse thy name!
35   Or, if thou wilt not, be but sworn my love,
    And I'll no longer be a Capulet.

33 wherefore: why. Juliet asks why Romeo is who he is—someone from her enemy's family.

Romeo [*aside*]. Shall I hear more, or shall I speak at this?

Juliet. 'Tis but thy name that is my enemy.
    Thou art thyself, though not a Montague.
40   What's Montague? It is nor hand, nor foot,
    Nor arm, nor face, nor any other part
    Belonging to a man. O, be some other name!
    What's in a name? That which we call a rose
    By any other name would smell as sweet.
45   So Romeo would, were he not Romeo called,
    Retain that dear perfection which he owes
    Without that title. Romeo, doff thy name;
    And for that name, which is no part of thee,
    Take all myself.

43–47 Juliet tries to convince herself that a name is just a meaningless word that has nothing to do with the person. She asks Romeo to get rid of (**doff**) his name.

Romeo.   I take thee at thy word.
50   Call me but love, and I'll be new baptized;
    Henceforth I never will be Romeo.

Juliet. What man art thou that, thus bescreened in night,
    So stumblest on my counsel?

52–53 Juliet is startled that someone hiding (**bescreened**) nearby hears her private thoughts (**counsel**).

Romeo.   By a name
    I know not how to tell thee who I am.
55   My name, dear saint, is hateful to myself,
    Because it is an enemy to thee.
    Had I it written, I would tear the word.

Juliet. My ears have yet not drunk a hundred words
    Of that tongue's utterance, yet I know the sound.
60   Art thou not Romeo, and a Montague?

Romeo. Neither, fair saint, if either thee dislike.

Juliet. How camest thou hither, tell me, and wherefore?
    The orchard walls are high and hard to climb,
    And the place death, considering who thou art,
65   If any of my kinsmen find thee here.

66–69 With...me: Love helped me climb (**o'erperch**) the walls. Neither walls nor your relatives are a hindrance (**let**) to me.

Romeo. With love's light wings did I o'erperch these walls;
    For stony limits cannot hold love out,

WHEN STUDENTS STRUGGLE...

Review the basic conflict that stands in the way of Romeo and Juliet's relationship, eliciting from students that it is their families' feud with each other. Explain that in lines 38–49, Juliet considers the implications of Romeo being a Montague, her family's enemy.

Organize students into pairs and have them paraphrase one of the complete thoughts in the passage. Call on pairs to write their paraphrases on the board in order. Read them together as a class.

ASK STUDENTS to express Juliet's main idea in this speech. *(that a name does not hold the essence of a person; it is just a superficial formality)*

And what love can do, that dares love attempt.
Therefore thy kinsmen are no let to me.

70 **Juliet.** If they do see thee, they will murder thee.

Romeo. Alack, there lies more peril in thine eye
Than twenty of their swords! Look thou but sweet,
And I am proof against their enmity.

Juliet. I would not for the world they saw thee here.

75 **Romeo.** I have night's cloak to hide me from their sight;
And but thou love me, let them find me here.
My life were better ended by their hate
Than death prorogued, wanting of thy love.

Juliet. By whose direction foundst thou out this place?

80 **Romeo.** By love, that first did prompt me to enquire.
He lent me counsel, and I lent him eyes.
I am no pilot, yet, wert thou as far
As that vast shore washed with the farthest sea,
I would adventure for such merchandise.

85 **Juliet.** Thou knowest the mask of night is on my face;
Else would a maiden blush bepaint my cheek
For that which thou hast heard me speak tonight.
Fain would I dwell on form—fain, fain deny
What I have spoke; but farewell compliment!

90 Dost thou love me? I know thou wilt say "Ay";
And I will take thy word. Yet, if thou swearst,
Thou mayst prove false. At lovers' perjuries,
They say Jove laughs. O gentle Romeo,
If thou dost love, pronounce it faithfully.

95 Or if thou thinkst I am too quickly won,
I'll frown, and be perverse, and say thee nay,
So thou wilt woo; but else, not for the world.
In truth, fair Montague, I am too fond,
And therefore thou mayst think my 'havior light;

100 But trust me, gentleman, I'll prove more true
Than those that have more cunning to be strange.
I should have been more strange, I must confess,
But that thou overheardst, ere I was ware,
My true love's passion. Therefore pardon me,

105 And not impute this yielding to light love,
Which the dark night hath so discovered.

Romeo. Lady, by yonder blessed moon I swear,
That tips with silver all these fruit-tree tops—

72–73 Look . . . enmity: Smile on me, and I will be defended against my enemies' hatred (**enmity**).

78 than death . . . love: than my death postponed (**prorogued**) if you don't love me.

85–89 Thou . . . compliment: Had I known you were listening, I would have gladly (**fain**) behaved more properly, but now it's too late for good manners (**farewell compliment**).

92–93 At . . . laughs: Jove, the king of the gods, laughs at lovers who lie to each other.

95–101 Or if . . . strange: You might think I've fallen in love too easily and that I'm too outspoken. But I'll be truer to you than those who play games to hide their real feelings (**be strange**).

The Tragedy of Romeo and Juliet: Act II, Scene 2   **211**

APPLYING ACADEMIC VOCABULARY

commit	initiate

As you discuss Act II, incorporate the Collection 4 academic vocabulary words: *commit* and *initiate*. Have students discuss how Shakespeare uses the device of having each overhear the other to **initiate** their relationship. Ask them how Romeo must then show that he is willing to **commit** to Juliet.

CLOSE READ

Analyze Character: RL 3
Motivations (Sc. 2, LINES 75–79)

Point out that throughout the play, the idea of death being preferable to separation recurs. Note that Romeo and Juliet also frequently use **hyperbole**, or exaggerated language, to express their love.

Ⓗ ASK STUDENTS whether they think Romeo is serious in his declaration. Why or why not? (*Possible answers include that Romeo is intense in his passions just as he was with Rosaline, which suggests this new attraction may vanish just as fast. Romeo's passionate words could also show that he is deeply serious about his love for Juliet.*)

Analyze Author's Choices: RL 5
Plot (Sc. 2, LINES 85–106)

Tell students that with this balcony scene the major **plot,** the story of Romeo and Juliet's relationship, advances quickly. Review these lines with students to ensure that they understand what takes place here.

Ⓘ ASK STUDENTS why Juliet tells Romeo that she feels embarrassed. What does she say he would see if it were not so dark? (*She feels embarrassed because he heard her say that she loved him. He would see her blush if it were not so dark [lines 86-87].*) Have students explain what she means in lines 102-104 when she says "I should have been more strange, I must confess, / But that thou overheardst, ere I was ware, / My true love's passion." (*As befitting a lady, she should not have let him know her true feelings so soon, but she had no idea that he could overhear her as she was declaring her love for him.*) Have students explain how Juliet's candor might affect the progress of their relationship. (*Because she is so open with her feelings, she accelerates the rate at which their courtship progresses.*)

Analyze Figurative Language

RL 4

(Sc. 2, LINES 109–141)

Tell students that while the dialogue between characters advances plot, it also includes figurative language that provides insight into the characters and their relationships.

 CITE TEXT EVIDENCE Ask students why Juliet does not want Romeo to swear his love to her by the moon. *(The moon changes daily, diminishing and then increasing. Juliet wants something more constant or dependable.)* Why does Juliet compare their love to lightning in lines 118–120? What does this comparison reveal about her feelings? *(Lightning is fast and violent, over with before one has time to even know it is there. She doesn't want their love to be the same. She worries because everything is happening so quickly and may disappear just as quickly.)* Ask students what Romeo says that conveys a similar idea. *("I am afeard…all this is but a dream." [lines 139–140])* Both characters express their sense that the relationship may be moving too fast.

Juliet. O, swear not by the moon, the inconstant moon,
110 That monthly changes in her circled orb,
Lest that thy love prove likewise variable.

Romeo. What shall I swear by?

Juliet.   Do not swear at all;
Or if thou wilt, swear by thy gracious self,
Which is the god of my idolatry,
115 And I'll believe thee.

Romeo.   If my heart's dear love—

Juliet. Well, do not swear. Although I joy in thee,
I have no joy of this contract tonight.
It is too rash, too unadvised, too sudden;
Too like the lightning, which doth cease to be
120 Ere one can say "It lightens." Sweet, good night!
This bud of love, by summer's ripening breath,
May prove a beauteous flow'r when next we meet.
Good night, good night! As sweet repose and rest
Come to thy heart as that within my breast!

125 **Romeo.** O, wilt thou leave me so unsatisfied?

Juliet. What satisfaction canst thou have tonight?

Romeo. The exchange of thy love's faithful vow for mine.

Juliet. I gave thee mine before thou didst request it;
And yet I would it were to give again.

130 **Romeo.** Wouldst thou withdraw it? For what purpose, love?

Juliet. But to be frank and give it thee again.
And yet I wish but for the thing I have.
My bounty is as boundless as the sea,
My love as deep; the more I give to thee,
135 The more I have, for both are infinite.
I hear some noise within. Dear love, adieu!

[Nurse *calls within.*]

Anon, good nurse! Sweet Montague, be true.
Stay but a little, I will come again.

[*Exit.*]

Romeo. O blessed, blessed night! I am afeard,
140 Being in night, all this is but a dream,
Too flattering-sweet to be substantial.

[*Re-enter* Juliet, *above.*]

Juliet. Three words, dear Romeo, and good night indeed.
If that thy bent of love be honorable,

117 I have … contract: I am concerned about this declaration of love (**contract**).

ENGLISH LANGUAGE SUPPORT

Vocabulary: Multiple-Meaning Words Remind students that many words in English have different meanings depending on how they are used. Point out *swear* in lines 112, 113, 114, 117. Explain that students may be more familiar with its meaning "to use profanity or curse." In these lines, its meaning is "to make a pledge or vow." Tell students that the context clue "faithful vow" in line 127 confirms this meaning of *swear*.

ASK STUDENTS to work in pairs to determine the contextual meanings of *rash* ("impulsive, thoughtless") in line 118, and *bent* ("inclination, desire") in line 143.

Thy purpose marriage, send me word tomorrow,
145   By one that I'll procure to come to thee,
Where and what time thou wilt perform the rite;
And all my fortunes at thy foot I'll lay
And follow thee my lord throughout the world.

Nurse [*within*]. Madam!

150   **Juliet.** I come, anon.—But if thou meanst not well,
I do beseech thee—

Nurse [*within*].   Madam!

Juliet.   By-and-by I come.—
To cease thy suit and leave me to my grief.
Tomorrow will I send.

Romeo.   So thrive my soul—

Juliet. A thousand times good night! [*Exit.*]

155   **Romeo.** A thousand times the worse, to want thy light!
Love goes toward love as schoolboys from their books;
But love from love, towards school with heavy looks.

[*Enter* Juliet *again, above.*]

Juliet. Hist! Romeo, hist! O for a falc'ner's voice
To lure this tassel-gentle back again!
160   Bondage is hoarse and may not speak aloud;
Else would I tear the cave where Echo lies,
And make her airy tongue more hoarse than mine
With repetition of my Romeo's name.
Romeo!

165   **Romeo.** It is my soul that calls upon my name.
How silver-sweet sound lovers' tongues by night,
Like softest music to attending ears!

Juliet. Romeo!

Romeo.   My sweet?

Juliet.   What o'clock tomorrow
Shall I send to thee?

Romeo.   By the hour of nine.

170   **Juliet.** I will not fail. 'Tis twenty years till then.
I have forgot why I did call thee back.

Romeo. Let me stand here till thou remember it.

Juliet. I shall forget, to have thee still stand there,
Rememb'ring how I love thy company.

150–151 But if . . . thee:
Juliet is still worried that
Romeo is not serious.

**156–157 Love . . .
looks:** The simile means
that lovers meet as
eagerly as schoolboys
leave their books;
lovers separate with the
sadness of boys going to
school.

158–163 Hist . . . name:
I wish I could speak
your name as loudly
as a falconer calls his
falcon (**tassel-gentle**),
but because of my
parents I must whisper.
Echo was a nymph in
Greek mythology whose
unreturned love for
Narcissus caused her to
waste away till only her
voice was left.

CLOSE READ

Analyze Character: RL 3
Motivations (Sc. 2, LINES 142–149)

Remind students that, like people in real life,
Shakespeare's characters act and speak from a variety
of motivations.

Ⓚ ASK STUDENTS what Juliet demands from
Romeo. (*She wants him to arrange their marriage.*)
Have students discuss what motivates this request
on Juliet's part. (*She is afraid their families will find
out and stop them from seeing each other. She wants
Romeo's total commitment to a long-term union, not to a
relationship that burns brightly, but only for a short time.*)

ENGLISH LANGUAGE SUPPORT

Language: Contractions Tell students that apostrophes often indicate
that one or more letters have been left out of a word or words. In poetic
verse, most often contractions are used to enable the poet to sustain
verbal rhythm. Point out that the dialogue in this passage includes
standard verb contractions, such as *I'll* ("I will"), as well as contractions
created for the purpose of the meter, such as *falc'ner* instead of *falconer* in
line 158.

ASK STUDENTS to identify the letters missing from the contraction *'Tis* in
line 170 and *Rememb'ring* from line 174.

Analyze Character: Motivations

RL 3

(Sc. 2, LINES 187–190)

L **ASK STUDENTS** why Romeo is going to see Friar Laurence. Have them explain what is revealed by his action. (*Romeo is going to arrange the marriage with Juliet. This haste shows that he is sincere.*)

Determine Theme

RL 2

(Sc. 3, LINES 1–22)

Tell students that Friar Laurence is another minor character who, like Benvolio, Mercutio, and Nurse, plays a significant role in the plot. Carefully reread this speech with students to clarify the friar's insights about life and human nature and how these insights shed light on Romeo and Juliet's relationship.

M **ASK STUDENTS** to reread lines 9-20 in the friar's speech: "That earth that's nature's mother is her tomb, / What is her burying grave, that is her womb." What idea does the Friar convey with these contradictory statements? (*He is describing the duality of nature and human nature in that both hold life-giving and life-destroying potential.*) What earlier statements in the play do Friar Laurence's contradictions echo? (*Romeo and Juliet's many contradictory descriptions of love.*)

M **ASK STUDENTS** what warning the friar gives about the qualities of both people and plants. (*He says that good can lead to evil if turned from its true purpose. Evil can sometimes lead to good.*) How might this warning function as foreshadowing? (*Even though the love of Romeo and Juliet seems a good thing, it might have negative consequences.*)

---

175 **Romeo.** And I'll still stay, to have thee still forget,
Forgetting any other home but this.

Juliet. 'Tis almost morning. I would have thee gone—
And yet no farther than a wanton's bird,
That lets it hop a little from her hand,
180 Like a poor prisoner in his twisted gyves,
And with a silk thread plucks it back again,
So loving-jealous of his liberty.

Romeo. I would I were thy bird.

Juliet.   Sweet, so would I.
Yet I should kill thee with much cherishing.
185 Good night, good night! Parting is such sweet sorrow,
That I shall say good night till it be morrow.

[*Exit.*]

Romeo. Sleep dwell upon thine eyes, peace in thy breast!
Would I were sleep and peace, so sweet to rest!
Hence will I to my ghostly father's cell,
190 His help to crave and my dear hap to tell.

[*Exit.*]

Scene 3 *Friar Laurence's cell in the monastery.*

[*Enter* Friar Laurence *alone, with a basket.*]

Friar Laurence. The grey-eyed morn smiles on the frowning night,
Chequ'ring the Eastern clouds with streaks of light;
And flecked darkness like a drunkard reels
From forth day's path and Titan's fiery wheels.
5 Now, ere the sun advance his burning eye
The day to cheer and night's dank dew to dry,
I must upfill this osier cage of ours
With baleful weeds and precious-juiced flowers.
The earth that's nature's mother is her tomb,
10 What is her burying grave, that is her womb;
And from her womb children of divers kind
We sucking on her natural bosom find;
Many for many virtues excellent,
None but for some, and yet all different.
15 O, mickle is the powerful grace that lies
In plants, herbs, stones, and their true qualities;
For naught so vile that on the earth doth live
But to the earth some special good doth give;
Nor aught so good but, strained from that fair use,
20 Revolts from true birth, stumbling on abuse.

177–182 I would . . . liberty: I know you must go, but I want you close to me like a pet bird that a thoughtless child (**wanton**) keeps on a string.

189–190 ghostly father: spiritual adviser or priest; **dear hap:** good fortune.

4 Titan is the god whose chariot pulls the sun into the sky each morning.

7 osier cage: willow basket.

9–12 The earth . . . find: The same earth that acts as a tomb is also the womb, or birthplace, of various useful plants that people can harvest.

15–18 mickle: great. The friar says that nothing from the earth is so evil that it doesn't do some good.

ENGLISH LANGUAGE SUPPORT

Culture: Historical Context To help students understand the role of Friar Laurence in both Romeo's and Juliet's lives, provide this information:

- Friar Laurence is a member of a religious order founded by St. Francis of Assisi in 1209. Friars typically renounced material possessions, lived in simple rooms, or cells, in monasteries, and grew their food.

- The play is set in Italy in the 1300s, in a predominantly Roman Catholic country. Friar Laurence serves as the priest for the Montague and Capulet families, hearing their confessions, performing marriages, and conducting funerals. By the late 1500s in England, Catholicism could not be practiced openly, making Friar Laurence a rather controversial figure in the play.

Virtue itself turns vice, being misapplied,
And vice sometime's by action dignified.
Within the infant rind of this small flower
Poison hath residence, and medicine power;
25 For this, being smelt, with that part cheers each part;
Being tasted, slays all senses with the heart.
Two such opposed kings encamp them still
In man as well as herbs—grace and rude will;
And where the worser is predominant,
30 Full soon the canker death eats up that plant.

[*Enter* Romeo.]

Romeo. Good morrow, father.

Friar Laurence.   Benedicite!
What early tongue so sweet saluteth me?
Young son, it argues a distempered head
So soon to bid good morrow to thy bed.
35 Care keeps his watch in every old man's eye,
And where care lodges sleep will never lie;
But where unbruised youth with unstuffed brain
Doth couch his limbs, there golden sleep doth reign.
Therefore thy earliness doth me assure
40 Thou art uproused with some distemp'rature;

28 grace and rude will: good and evil. Both exist in people as well as in plants.

31 Benedicite (bĕ´nĕ-dī´sĭ-tē´): God bless you.

33–42 it argues . . . tonight: Only a disturbed (**distempered**) mind could make you get up so early. Old people may have trouble sleeping, but it is not normal for someone as young as you. Or were you up all night?

The Tragedy of Romeo and Juliet: Act II, Scene 3 **215**

Support Inferences (PHOTOGRAPH)   RL 1, RL 7

Have students examine the image from the 1968 film version of *Romeo and Juliet*.

Ⓝ ASK STUDENTS what ideas about the relationship between the friar and Romeo can be inferred from this photograph. Explain. (*Their laughter and obvious ease with each other suggest that they are good friends. The friar is someone with whom Romeo feels comfortable.*)

Analyze Character: Motivations (Sc. 3, LINES 31–40)   RL 3

Point out that people do not always know the motives behind someone's actions. Similarly, in drama, the playwright can use devices such as **dramatic irony** to enable the audience to be aware of circumstances influencing a character's actions while keeping the other characters in ignorance.

Ⓞ ASK STUDENTS to explain the dramatic irony the friar expresses in lines 39–40. (*He fears that something is wrong with Romeo, but the audience knows that Romeo is there because he wants to arrange his marriage to Juliet.*)

Analyze Author's Choices: Parallel Plots

RL 5

(Sc. 3, LINES 43–46)

Use these lines to review with students how the subplot of Rosaline and Romeo has affected the main events of the play.

P **ASK STUDENTS** how Romeo reacts to the name of Rosaline. Why? *(He has completely forgotten about her because he is so absorbed in his new love for Juliet.)*

Analyze Word Choice

RL 4

(Sc. 3, LINES 48–70)

Explain to students that language can be used to muddle meaning as well as clarify it.

Q **CITE TEXT EVIDENCE** Have students explain why the friar tells Romeo to speak more plainly (lines 55-56). *(To the friar, Romeo is talking in riddles by saying that he has been "feasting with mine enemy" who has wounded him "[t]hat's by me wounded.")* Why is this language particularly confusing to the friar? *(He has no idea that Romeo has fallen in love with Juliet.)*

Direct students to note the contrast in Romeo's language in this part of the dialogue and consider what this change reveals.

R **ASK STUDENTS** to describe the style of Romeo's speech in lines 57–70. How has it changed? *(Romeo is clear, concise, and factual. The change in his style of speaking shows his seriousness about wanting the friar to understand the situation and to marry them.)* Ask students what shows the friar's strong reaction. Why does he feel this way? *(The friar is astonished as shown by his exclamations to Saint Francis and Jesu Maria. He is surprised because he witnessed Romeo's supposed devotion to Rosaline and his extreme despair over her lack of interest.)*

Or if not so, then here I hit it right—
Our Romeo hath not been in bed tonight.

Romeo. That last is true, the sweeter rest was mine.

Friar Laurence. God pardon sin! Wast thou with Rosaline?

P 45 **Romeo.** With Rosaline, my ghostly father? No.
I have forgot that name, and that name's woe.

Friar Laurence. That's my good son! But where hast thou been then?

Q **Romeo.** I'll tell thee ere thou ask it me again.
I have been feasting with mine enemy,
50 Where on a sudden one hath wounded me
That's by me wounded. Both our remedies
Within thy help and holy physic lies.
I bear no hatred, blessed man, for, lo,
My intercession likewise steads my foe.

55 **Friar Laurence.** Be plain, good son, and homely in thy drift.
Riddling confession finds but riddling shrift.

R **Romeo.** Then plainly know my heart's dear love is set
On the fair daughter of rich Capulet;
As mine on hers, so hers is set on mine,
60 And all combined, save what thou must combine
By holy marriage. When, and where, and how
We met, we wooed, and made exchange of vow,
I'll tell thee as we pass; but this I pray,
That thou consent to marry us today.

65 **Friar Laurence.** Holy Saint Francis! What a change is here!
Is Rosaline, that thou didst love so dear,
So soon forsaken? Young men's love then lies
Not truly in their hearts, but in their eyes.
Jesu Maria! What a deal of brine
70 Hath washed thy sallow cheeks for Rosaline!
How much salt water thrown away in waste,
To season love, that of it doth not taste!
The sun not yet thy sighs from heaven clears,
Thy old groans ring yet in mine ancient ears.
75 Lo, here upon thy cheek the stain doth sit
Of an old tear that is not washed off yet.
If e'er thou wast thyself, and these woes thine,
Thou and these woes were all for Rosaline.
And art thou changed? Pronounce this sentence then:
80 Women may fall when there's no strength in men.

Romeo. Thou chidst me oft for loving Rosaline.

49–56 Romeo tries to explain the situation, asking for help both for himself and his "foe" (Juliet). The friar does not understand Romeo's convoluted language and asks him to speak clearly so that he can help.

69 brine: salt water—that is, the tears that Romeo has been shedding for Rosaline.

80 Women...men: If men are so weak, women may be forgiven for sinning.

81–82 chidst: scolded. The friar replies that he scolded Romeo for being lovesick, not for loving.

WHEN STUDENTS STRUGGLE...

To guide students' comprehension of plot, have them work in pairs to create a timeline charting the events that have happened since the Capulets' party. Have them identify approximately when each of these events takes place to help them see how compressed this part of the plot is.

After students have completed their timelines, ask them to present them to the class. Clarify differences between individual timelines and create a class version to display and add to during the rest of Act II.

 LEVEL UP TUTORIALS For additional support, assign the following *Level Up* tutorial: **Plot: Sequence of Events.**

Friar Laurence. For doting, not for loving, pupil mine.

Romeo. And badest me bury love.

Friar Laurence.   Not in a grave
To lay one in, another ought to have.

85 **Romeo.** I pray thee chide not. She whom I love now
Doth grace for grace and love for love allow.
The other did not so.

Friar Laurence.   O, she knew well
Thy love did read by rote, that could not spell.
But come, young waverer, come go with me.
90 In one respect I'll thy assistant be;
For this alliance may so happy prove
To turn your households' rancor to pure love.

Romeo. O, let us hence! I stand on sudden haste.

Friar Laurence. Wisely, and slow. They stumble that run fast.

[*Exeunt.*]

Scene 4 *A street.*

[*Enter* Benvolio *and* Mercutio.]

Mercutio. Where the devil should this Romeo be?
Came he not home tonight?

Benvolio. Not to his father's. I spoke with his man.

Mercutio. Why, that same pale hard-hearted wench, that
     Rosaline,
5 Torments him so that he will sure run mad.

Benvolio. Tybalt, the kinsman to old Capulet,
Hath sent a letter to his father's house.

Mercutio. A challenge, on my life.

Benvolio. Romeo will answer it.

10 **Mercutio.** Any man that can write may answer a letter.

Benvolio. Nay, he will answer the letter's master, how he dares,
being dared.

Mercutio. Alas, poor Romeo, he is already dead! stabbed with a
white wench's black eye; shot through the ear with a love song;
15 the very pin of his heart cleft with the blind bow-boy's butt-shaft;
and is he a man to encounter Tybalt?

Benvolio. Why, what is Tybalt?

85–88 She whom . . . spell: Romeo says that the woman he loves feels the same way about him. That wasn't true of Rosaline. The friar replies that Rosaline knew that he didn't know what real love is.

91–92 For this . . . prove: this marriage may work out so well; **rancor:** bitter hate.

3 man: servant.

6–12 Tybalt . . . dared: Tybalt, still angry with Romeo, has sent a letter challenging Romeo to a duel. Benvolio says that Romeo will accept Tybalt's challenge and fight him.

15 blind bow-boy's butt-shaft: Cupid's dull practice arrow. Mercutio suggests that Romeo fell in love with very little work on Cupid's part.

Analyze Character: Motivations (Sc. 3, LINES 81–94)   RL 3

Remind students of the friar's opening speech. Have them consider how having good intentions does not always guarantee a happy or positive outcome.

(S) **CITE TEXT EVIDENCE** Have students identify the lines that explain why the friar agrees to marry Romeo and Juliet. (*"In one respect I'll thy assistant be; / For this alliance may so happy prove / To turn your households' rancor to pure love."*) Have students infer other reasons for the friar's cooperation. (*He is fond of Romeo so wants to help him; he may fear what Romeo would do if he is not able to marry Juliet.*)

Analyze Author's Choices: Parallel Plots (Sc. 4, LINES 1–17)   RL 5

Tell students that the action of the drama rises, complicated by each new event or crisis, throughout the second act, creating tension and suspense. Review with students Tybalt's role up to this point in the play (he was angered by Romeo's appearance at the Capulets' feast and wants to fight Romeo).

(T) **ASK STUDENTS** to infer how Benvolio and Mercutio feel. Why? (*They are concerned for Romeo. They are worried that if he does go to meet Tybalt, he will not fare well in the fight.*) How does this new event add a complication to the plot? (*A fight between Tybalt and Romeo could lead to the death of one of them or of others who may become involved.*)

Romeo meets Juliet for the first time	→	night of the party
Romeo sneaks into the Capulet garden	→	right after party
Romeo arranges wedding with the friar	→	morning after party

Analyze Word Choice RL 4

(Sc. 4, LINES 18–24; 34–41)

Read aloud lines 18–24. Ask students to reread the lines silently, consulting the margin notes. Remind students that Mercutio uses his language to playfully express some important ideas.

U **ASK STUDENTS** what Mercutio is saying in lines 18–24 through this comparison of Tybalt to his namesake, the cat. *(He is saying that Tybalt is a clever and skillful duelist who knows all the moves.)*

Make sure students understand the numerous allusions that Mercutio uses in this speech (lines 34–41) to joke about the depth of Romeo's love for Rosaline.

V **ASK STUDENTS** to describe Mercutio's attitude toward Romeo's feelings based on his choice of words. *(Mercutio makes fun of Romeo's lovesickness.)* Apart from making fun of Romeo, why is Mercutio so aware of Romeo's lovesick state? *(He is fearful that it will distract him if he ends up fighting Tybalt.)* What is the dramatic irony of Mercutio's speech? *(The audience knows that Romeo now appears to be intensely in love with Juliet. These comparisons still describe him, but his feelings are directed toward someone else.)*

Mercutio. More than Prince of Cats, I can tell you. O, he's the courageous captain of compliments. He fights as you sing
20 pricksong—keeps time, distance, and proportion; rests me his minim rest, one, two, and the third in your bosom! the very butcher of a silk button, a duelist, a duelist! a gentleman of the very first house, of the first and second cause. Ah, the immortal *passado!* the *punto reverso!* the *hay!*

25 **Benvolio.** The what?

Mercutio. The pox of such antic, lisping, affecting fantasticoes—these new tuners of accent! "By Jesu, a very good blade! a very tall man! a very good whore!" Why, is not this a lamentable thing, grandsire, that we should be thus afflicted with these strange flies,
30 these fashion-mongers, these perdona-mi's, who stand so much on the new form that they cannot sit at ease on the old bench? O, their bones, their bones!

[*Enter* Romeo, *no longer moody.*]

Benvolio. Here comes Romeo! here comes Romeo!

Mercutio. Without his roe, like a dried herring. O, flesh, flesh,
35 how art thou fishified! Now is he for the numbers that Petrarch flowed in. Laura, to his lady, was but a kitchen wench (marry, she had a better love to berhyme her), Dido a dowdy, Cleopatra a gypsy, Helen and Hero hildings and harlots, Thisbe a grey eye or so, but not to the purpose. Signior Romeo, *bon jour!* There's
40 a French salutation to your French slop. You gave us the counterfeit fairly last night.

Romeo. Good morrow to you both. What counterfeit did I give you?

Mercutio. The slip, sir, the slip. Can you not conceive?

45 **Romeo.** Pardon, good Mercutio. My business was great, and in such a case as mine a man may strain courtesy.

Mercutio. That's as much as to say, such a case as yours constrains a man to bow in the hams.

Romeo. Meaning, to curtsy.

50 **Mercutio.** Thou hast most kindly hit it.

Romeo. A most courteous exposition.

Mercutio. Nay, I am the very pink of courtesy.

Romeo. Pink for flower.

Mercutio. Right.

55 **Romeo.** Why, then is my pump well-flowered.

18–24 More than ... hay: Prince of Cats refers to a cat in a fable, named Tybalt. Mercutio makes fun of Tybalt's new style of dueling, comparing it to singing (**pricksong**). *Passado, punto reverso,* and **hay** were terms used in the new dueling style.

26–32 The pox ... their bones: Mercutio continues to make fun of people who embrace new styles and new manners of speaking.

34–39 without his roe: only part of himself (Mercutio makes fun of Romeo's name and his lovesickness; **numbers:** verses. Petrarch wrote sonnets to his love, Laura. According to Mercutio, Romeo's feelings for Rosaline are so intense that great loves in literature could never measure up.

39–44 *bon jour:* "Good day" in French; **There's ... last night:** Here's a greeting to match your fancy French trousers (**slop**). You did a good job of getting away from us last night. (A piece of counterfeit money was called a **slip**.)

55 pump: shoe; **well-flowered:** Shoes with flowerlike designs.

ENGLISH LANGUAGE SUPPORT

Comprehension: Foreshadowing Project lines 1–24 on the whiteboard. To help students understand foreshadowing, ask for volunteers to mark up the text.

- Highlight in pink lines that refer to Tybalt challenging Romeo to fight a duel. *(lines 6–12)*
- Highlight in yellow lines that refer to Tybalt's ability with the sword.

Have students restate what the lines say. Discuss what event these ideas hint at.

minim rest, one, two, and the third in your bosom! the very butcher of a silk button, a duelist, a duelist! a gentleman of the very first house, of the first and second cause. Ah, the immortal *passado! the punto reverso!*

Mercutio. Well said! Follow me this jest now till thou hast worn out thy pump, that, when the single sole of it is worn, the jest may remain, after the wearing, solely singular.

Romeo. Oh, single-soled jest, solely singular for the singleness!

60 **Mercutio.** Come between us, good Benvolio! My wits faint.

Romeo. Switch and spurs, switch and spurs! or I'll cry a match.

Mercutio. Nay, if our wits run the wild-goose chase, I am done; for thou hast more of the wild goose in one of thy wits than, I am sure, I have in my whole five. Was I with you there for the
65 goose?

Romeo. Thou wast never with me for anything when thou wast not there for the goose.

Mercutio. I will bite thee by the ear for that jest.

Romeo. Nay, good goose, bite not!

70 **Mercutio.** Thy wit is a very bitter sweeting; it is a most sharp sauce.

Romeo. And is it not, then, well served in to a sweet goose?

61 Switch . . . match: Keep going, or I'll claim victory.

64–65 Was . . . goose: Have I proved that you are a foolish person?

TEACH

CLOSE READ

Support Inferences (PHOTOGRAPH)   RL 1, RL 7

Remind students that the subject of a photograph as well as the lighting and other elements can convey a particular mood or feeling.

W **CITE TEXT EVIDENCE** Ask students why this photograph creates an ominous mood. *(The figures are unseen; only their shadows are visible. These shadows and the subdued lighting suggest an ominous mood.)*

Analyze Character   RL 3

(Sc. 4, LINES 56–72)

Have students review the first dialogue between Romeo and Mercutio in Scene 4 of Act I (lines 11–26) before reading these lines.

X **ASK STUDENTS** what they notice about Romeo's responses in this exchange with Mercutio as compared to their conversation in Act I. *(Romeo is quick with his replies; he makes no reference to his feelings but responds only to the actual jest that Mercutio is making. In Act I, he turned every reply into a reference to his depressed spirits.)*

TO CHALLENGE STUDENTS . . .

Analyze Wordplay What's in a pun? Invite students to work in pairs to analyze the play on the word *goose* in lines 60–76. Before they begin, tell them that it refers both to someone who is a silly fool and to the water bird. In Shakespeare's time, a goose was a staple meat dish. Alive, geese can be aggressive, hissing and biting at people who trespass near their nests.

Have pairs explain their analysis of the pun. Then ask them how this play on words builds their understanding of the character of Mercutio and shows Romeo when he is not burdened by unrequited love.

Support Inferences RL 1

(Sc. 4, LINES 77–81)

Y **ASK STUDENTS** what Mercutio thinks that he has accomplished through his humor. *(He believes that he has cheered Romeo up.)* What is his opinion about people that brood over love? Ask students to infer why Mercutio may feel this way. *(He believes that "driveling love" is ridiculous and irritating. He may feel this way because he has never experienced this kind of emotion firsthand.)*

Analyze Author's Choices: RL 5
Parallel Plots (Sc. 4, LINES 89–108)

Remind students that this scene began with Tybalt's challenge to Romeo.

Z **ASK STUDENTS** how this encounter with the nurse presents a contrast to the threat hanging over Romeo's head. *(The nurse's mannerisms as well as the characters' baiting of her are humorous.)* Why does Shakespeare structure his play in this way? *(He is showing the youthful liveliness of the characters and their capacity for joy in order to intensify the tragedy of what happens later.)*

Mercutio. O, here's a wit of cheveril, that stretches from an inch narrow to an ell broad!

75 **Romeo.** I stretch it out for that word "broad," which, added to the goose, proves thee far and wide a broad goose.

Mercutio. Why, is not this better now than groaning for love? Now art thou sociable, now art thou Romeo; now art thou what thou art, by art as well as by nature. For this driveling love is like

80 a great natural that runs lolling up and down to hide his bauble in a hole.

Benvolio. Stop there, stop there!

Mercutio. Thou desirest me to stop in my tale against the hair.

Benvolio. Thou wouldst else have made thy tale large.

85 **Mercutio.** O, thou art deceived! I would have made it short; for I was come to the whole depth of my tale, and meant indeed to occupy the argument no longer.

[*Enter* Nurse *and* Peter, *her servant. He is carrying a large fan.*]

Romeo. Here's goodly gear!

Mercutio. A sail, a sail!

90 **Benvolio.** Two, two! a shirt and a smock.

Nurse. Peter!

Peter. Anon.

Nurse. My fan, Peter.

Mercutio. Good Peter, to hide her face; for her fan's the fairer of

95 the two.

Nurse. God ye good morrow, gentlemen.

Mercutio. God ye good-den, fair gentlewoman.

Nurse. Is it good-den?

Mercutio. 'Tis no less, I tell ye, for the bawdy hand of the dial is

100 now upon the prick of noon.

Nurse. Out upon you! What a man are you!

Romeo. One, gentlewoman, that God hath made himself to mar.

Nurse. By my troth, it is well said. "For himself to mar," quoth'a? Gentlemen, can any of you tell me where I may find the young

105 Romeo?

Romeo. I can tell you; but young Romeo will be older when you have found him than he was when you sought him. I am the youngest of that name, for fault of a worse.

73 cheveril: kidskin, which is flexible. Mercutio means that a little wit stretches a long way.

80–81 great natural: an idiot, like a jester or clown who carries a fool's stick (**bauble**).

88–89 goodly gear: something fine to joke about; **a sail:** Mercutio likens the nurse in all her petticoats to a huge ship coming toward them.

93 Fans were usually carried only by fine ladies. The nurse is trying to pretend that she is more than a servant.

Nurse. You say well.

A2

110 **Mercutio.** Yea, is the worst well? Very well took, i' faith! wisely, wisely.

Nurse. If you be he, sir, I desire some confidence with you.

Benvolio. She will endite him to some supper.

Mercutio. A bawd, a bawd, a bawd! So ho!

115 **Romeo.** What hast thou found?

Mercutio. No hare, sir; unless a hare, sir, in a lenten pie, that is something stale and hoar ere it be spent.

[*sings*]

> "An old hare hoar,
> And an old hare hoar,
120 > Is very good meat in Lent.
> But a hare that is hoar,
> Is too much for a score
> When it hoars ere it be spent."

Romeo, will you come to your father's? We'll to dinner thither.

125 **Romeo.** I will follow you.

Mercutio. Farewell, ancient lady. Farewell, [*sings*] lady, lady, lady.

[*Exeunt* Mercutio *and* Benvolio.]

Nurse. Marry, farewell! I pray you, sir, what saucy merchant was this that was so full of his ropery?

Romeo. A gentleman, nurse, that loves to hear himself talk and
130 will speak more in a minute than he will stand to in a month.

B2

Nurse. An 'a speak anything against me, I'll take him down, an 'a were lustier than he is, and twenty such Jacks; and if I cannot, I'll find those that shall. Scurvy knave! I am none of his flirt-gills; I am none of his skainsmates. [*turning to* Peter] And thou must
135 stand by too, and suffer every knave to use me at his pleasure?

Peter. I saw no man use you at his pleasure. If I had, my weapon should quickly have been out, I warrant you. I dare draw as soon as another man, if I see occasion in a good quarrel, and the law on my side.

140 **Nurse.** Now, afore God, I am so vexed that every part about me quivers. Scurvy knave! Pray you, sir, a word; and as I told you, my young lady bade me enquire you out. What she bid me say, I will keep to myself; but first let me tell ye, if ye should lead her into a fool's paradise, as they say, it were a very gross kind of
145 behavior, as they say; for the gentlewoman is young; and

112–113 confidence:
The nurse means *conference;* she uses big words without understanding their meaning; **endite:** Benvolio makes fun of the nurse by using this word rather than *invite.*

114–124 Mercutio calls the nurse a **bawd,** or woman who runs a house of prostitution. His song uses the insulting puns **hare,** a rabbit or prostitute, and **hoar,** old.

128 ropery: roguery, or jokes.

133–134 The nurse is angry that Mercutio treated her like one of his loose women (**flirt-gills**) or his gangsterlike friends (**skainsmates**).

142–147 The nurse warns Romeo that he'd better mean what he said about marrying Juliet.

TEACH

CLOSE READ

Support Inferences   RL 5

(Sc. 4, LINES 110–126)

A2 ASK STUDENTS how Mercutio and Benvolio treat the nurse. (*They are unkind and ridicule the nurse for mispronouncing words.*) What do their actions tell you about their characters? (*Mercutio's and Benvolio's behavior shows that they are playful. It also reveals that they are class conscious, for they ridicule the low standing of the nurse.*)

Analyze Author's Choices: RL 5
Parallel Plots (Sc. 4, LINES 127–139)

B2 ASK STUDENTS what they know about the nurse's purpose that Benvolio and Mercutio are unaware of. (*She is there on Juliet's behalf to see what arrangements Romeo has made.*)

Strategies for Annotation   ✏️ 🖥️ **Annotate it!**

Analyze Character   RL 3

Have students use their eBook annotation tools to analyze how character adds humor in lines 131–139.

- Highlight in green what the nurse says she will do to Mercutio if he ever insults her again. Paraphrase her meaning on a note.
- Highlight in blue what she says to Peter. On a note, explain what the words could mean and what she means.
- Restate Peter's defense on a note.
- Discuss why the exchange between the nurse and Peter is funny.

Nurse. An 'a speak anything against me, I'll take him down, an 'a were lustier than he is, and twenty such Jacks; and if I cannot, I'll find those that shall. Scurvy knave! I am none of his flirt-gills; I am none of his skainsmates. [*turning* to Peter] And thou must stand by too, and suffer every knave to use me at his pleasure?

Analyze Character: Motivations

RL 3

(Sc. 4, LINES 140–168)

To help students understand how scattered the nurse's thoughts are, read this passage of dialogue aloud with the appropriate emphasis.

 CITE TEXT EVIDENCE Ask students how the nurse's love for Juliet is shown in her comments. *(She refuses to divulge any information about Juliet until she ascertains whether Romeo's intentions are true. She warns him that if he is toying with Juliet's affections, he will be guilty of a "very gross kind of behavior.")* What does she say that she is going to tell Juliet? Why does Romeo question her? *(She says that she is going to tell Juliet that Romeo protests. Since that is meaningless, Romeo stops her to give her the real message.)*

Point out that by taking Romeo's coins the nurse becomes an accomplice to the plan.

 ASK STUDENTS to recall what the nurse said about Paris. *(She called him a man of wax, meaning that he was so handsome and a good husband for her Juliet [Act I, Scene 3, line 77].)* Why does she agree to help Romeo in his plan to marry Juliet? *(She is easily influenced by the person who has her ear at the moment; she thinks it is romantic; she wants her Juliet to be happy.)*

---

therefore, if you should deal double with her, truly it were an ill thing to be offered to any gentlewoman, and very weak dealing.

Romeo. Nurse, commend me to thy lady and mistress. I protest unto thee—

150 **Nurse.** Good heart, and i' faith I will tell her as much. Lord, Lord! she will be a joyful woman.

Romeo. What wilt thou tell her, nurse? Thou dost not mark me.

Nurse. I will tell her, sir, that you do protest, which, as I take it, is a gentlemanlike offer.

155 **Romeo.** Bid her devise
Some means to come to shrift this afternoon;
And there she shall at Friar Laurence' cell
Be shrived and married. Here is for thy pains.

Nurse. No, truly, sir; not a penny.

160 **Romeo.** Go to! I say you shall.

Nurse. This afternoon, sir? Well, she shall be there.

Romeo. And stay, good nurse, behind the abbey wall.
Within this hour my man shall be with thee
And bring thee cords made like a tackled stair,
165 Which to the high topgallant of my joy
Must be my convoy in the secret night.
Farewell. Be trusty, and I'll quit thy pains.
Farewell. Commend me to thy mistress.

Nurse. Now God in heaven bless thee! Hark you, sir.

170 **Romeo.** What sayst thou, my dear nurse?

Nurse. Is your man secret? Did you ne'er hear say,
Two may keep counsel, putting one away?

Romeo. I warrant thee my man's as true as steel.

Nurse. Well, sir, my mistress is the sweetest lady. Lord, Lord!
175 when 'twas a little prating thing—O, there is a nobleman in town, one Paris, that would fain lay knife aboard; but she, good soul, had as lief see a toad, a very toad, as see him. I anger her sometimes, and tell her that Paris is the properer man; but I'll warrant you, when I say so, she looks as pale as any clout in the
180 versal world. Doth not rosemary and Romeo begin both with a letter?

Romeo. Ay, nurse, what of that? Both with an R.

Nurse. Ah, mocker! that's the dog's name. R is for the—No; I know it begins with some other letter; and she hath the prettiest

148 commend me: give my respectful greetings.

155–159 Romeo tells the nurse to have Juliet come to Friar Laurence's cell this afternoon, using the excuse that she is going to confess her sins (**shrift**). There she will receive forgiveness for her sins (**be shrived**) and be married.

164–165 tackled stair: rope ladder; **topgallant:** highest point.

167 quit thy pains: reward you.

174–177 The nurse begins to babble about Paris' proposal but says that Juliet would rather look at a toad than at Paris.

179–186 clout: old cloth; **the versal world:** the entire world; **Doth not . . . hear it:** The nurse tries to recall a clever saying that Juliet made up about Romeo and rosemary, the herb, but cannot remember it. She is sure that the two words couldn't begin with *R* because this letter sounds like a snarling dog; **sententious:** The nurse means *sentences*.

WHEN STUDENTS STRUGGLE . . .

Make sure students understand the instructions given to the nurse by Romeo by having them reread lines 155–168 and complete this outline:

1. Immediately, the nurse must tell Juliet to…*(go to Friar Laurence's cell in the afternoon to meet Romeo)*

2. In one hour, the nurse must meet a man behind the abbey to…*(get a rope ladder)*

3. Later that night, Romeo will use…*(the rope ladder to get to Juliet's room)*

Suggest that students add these events to their timelines to gain a more complete picture of what takes place within the twenty-four hours.

185   sententious of it, of you and rosemary, that it would do you good
to hear it.

Romeo. Commend me to thy lady.

Nurse. Ay, a thousand times. [*Exit* Romeo.] Peter!

Peter. Anon.

190   **Nurse.** Peter, take my fan, and go before, and apace.

[*Exeunt.*]

190 apace: quickly.

Scene 5 *Capulet's orchard.*

[*Enter* Juliet.]

Juliet. The clock struck nine when I did send the nurse;
In half an hour she promised to return.
Perchance she cannot meet him. That's not so.
O, she is lame! Love's heralds should be thoughts,
5   Which ten times faster glide than the sun's beams
Driving back shadows over lowering hills.
Therefore do nimble-pinioned doves draw Love,
And therefore hath the wind-swift Cupid wings.
Now is the sun upon the highmost hill
10 Of this day's journey, and from nine till twelve
Is three long hours; yet she is not come.
Had she affections and warm youthful blood,
She would be as swift in motion as a ball;
My words would bandy her to my sweet love,
15 And his to me.
But old folks, many feign as they were dead—
Unwieldy, slow, heavy, and pale as lead.
[*Enter* Nurse *and* Peter.] O God, she comes! O honey nurse,
    what news?
Hast thou met with him? Send thy man away.

20 **Nurse.** Peter, stay at the gate.

[*Exit* Peter.]

Juliet. Now, good sweet nurse—O Lord, why lookst thou sad?
Though news be sad, yet tell them merrily;
If good, thou shamest the music of sweet news
By playing it to me with so sour a face.

25 **Nurse.** I am aweary, give me leave awhile.
Fie, how my bones ache! What a jaunce have I had!

Juliet. I would thou hadst my bones, and I thy news.
Nay, come, I pray thee speak. Good, good nurse, speak.

4–6 Love's . . . hills:
Love's messengers
should be thoughts,
which travel ten times
faster than sunbeams.

**7 nimble-pinioned
. . . Love:** Swift-winged
doves pull the chariot of
Venus, goddess of love.

14 bandy: toss.

16 feign as: act as if.

21–22 The nurse teases
Juliet by putting on a
sad face as if the news
were bad.

**25–26 give me . . . I
had:** Leave me alone for
a while. I ache all over
because of the running
back and forth I've been
doing.

CLOSE READ

> ### Analyze Word Choice   RL 4
> (Sc. 5, LINES 1–17)
>
> Draw students' attention to the allusions explained in
> the margin notes.
>
> **E2 ASK STUDENTS** what Juliet's allusions to
> Venus and to Cupid emphasize about her state of
> mind as she waits for the nurse to return. (*These
> allusions emphasize her focus on Romeo, her poetic,
> idealized view of love, and her nervousness as she
> waits for the nurse to return.*) How does
> Juliet's description of the nurse contrast with her
> characterization of love as having "wind-swift" wings?
> (*She calls the nurse and "old folks" "unwieldy, slow,
> heavy, and pale as lead," thus inferior to young people
> energized by love.*)

ENGLISH LANGUAGE SUPPORT

Language: Ellipsis Explain to students that some of Shakespeare's lines
have words left out in order to create a certain rhythm. They can figure
out the missing words by looking before and after the line. Point out that
in line 188 of Scene 4, the nurse says, "Ay, a thousand times" rather than
"Ay, I will commend you a thousand times."

ASK STUDENTS to work together to fill in the missing words for these
lines: Scene 4, line 190, "go before, and apace"; in Scene 5, line 23, "If
good"; Scene 5, line 27, "I thy news." (*go before* **me**, *and apace; if* **the news
be** *good; I* **had** *thy news*)

Analyze Character   RL 3

(Sc. 5, LINES 29–66)

Explain to students that the nurse is not a **complex character,** that is, she will not change. She has some obvious traits that define her and that remain the same throughout the play. Ask student volunteers to read this scene aloud, with appropriate emphasis and emotion.

(F2) ASK STUDENTS to reread the nurse's responses to Juliet's questions. Why do they create humor? *(She digresses to such an extent, she fails to answer Juliet's questions.)* Are the nurse's actions deliberate? Why or why not? *(No. That is her major trait. She is not able to stay focused.)* What is the effect of the nurse's responses on Juliet? Would the effect be the same or different for the audience? *(Juliet grows more and more impatient and possibly worried as well. The audience knows what Romeo has said so is not kept in suspense. Audience members would derive humor from this scene.)*

Nurse. Jesu, what haste! Can you not stay awhile?
30   Do you not see that I am out of breath?

Juliet. How art thou out of breath when thou hast breath
To say to me that thou art out of breath?
The excuse that thou dost make in this delay
Is longer than the tale thou dost excuse.
35   Is thy news good or bad? Answer to that.
Say either, and I'll stay the circumstance.
Let me be satisfied, is't good or bad?

> **36 I'll . . . circumstance:** I'll wait for the details.

(F2)   **Nurse.** Well, you have made a simple choice; you know not how
to choose a man. Romeo? No, not he. Though his face be better
40   than any man's, yet his leg excels all men's; and for a hand and a
foot, and a body, though they be not to be talked on, yet they are
past compare. He is not the flower of courtesy, but, I'll warrant
him, as gentle as a lamb. Go thy ways, wench; serve God. What,
have you dined at home?

> **38 simple:** foolish.

45   **Juliet.** No, no. But all this did I know before.
What say he of our marriage? What of that?

Nurse. Lord, how my head aches! What a head have I!
It beats as it would fall in twenty pieces.
My back o' t'other side—ah, my back, my back!
50   Beshrew your heart for sending me about
To catch my death with jauncing up and down!

> **50–51 Beshrew . . . down:** Curse you for making me endanger my health by running around.

Juliet. I' faith, I am sorry that thou art not well.
Sweet, sweet, sweet nurse, tell me, what says my love?

Nurse. Your love says, like an honest gentleman, and a
courteous,
55   and a kind, and a handsome, and, I warrant, a virtuous—Where
is your mother?

Juliet. Where is my mother? Why, she is within.
Where should she be? How oddly thou repliest!
"Your love says, like an honest gentleman,
60   'Where is your mother?'"

Nurse.   O God's Lady dear!
Are you so hot? Marry come up, I trow.
Is this the poultice for my aching bones?
Hence forward do your messages yourself.

> **61–62 Marry . . . bones:** Control yourself! Is this the treatment I get for my pain?

Juliet. Here's such a coil! Come, what says Romeo?

> **64 coil:** fuss.

65   **Nurse.** Have you got leave to go to shrift today?

Juliet. I have.

WHEN STUDENTS STRUGGLE . . .

Discuss with students how both Friar Laurence and the nurse facilitate the marriage of Romeo and Juliet. To help students see how Friar Laurence and the nurse are the same and different, have them complete a Venn diagram similar to the one on page 225.

Encourage students to refer to Scene 3, Scene 5, and Scene 6 for details to include in their diagrams.

Nurse. Then hie you hence to Friar Laurence' cell;
There stays a husband to make you a wife.
Now comes the wanton blood up in your cheeks:

70 They'll be in scarlet straight at any news.
Hie you to church; I must another way,
To fetch a ladder, by the which your love
Must climb a bird's nest soon when it is dark.
I am the drudge, and toil in your delight;

75 But you shall bear the burden soon at night.
Go; I'll to dinner; hie you to the cell.

Juliet. Hie to high fortune! Honest nurse, farewell.

[*Exeunt.*]

Scene 6 *Friar Laurence's cell.*

[*Enter* Friar Laurence *and* Romeo.]

Friar Laurence. So smile the heavens upon this holy act
That after-hours with sorrow chide us not!

Romeo. Amen, amen! But come what sorrow can,
It cannot countervail the exchange of joy

5 That one short minute gives me in her sight.

71–73 The nurse will get the ladder that Romeo will use to climb to Juliet's room after they are married.

1–2 So smile . . . us not: May heaven so bless this act that we won't regret it in the future (**after-hours**).

4 countervail: outweigh.

Image Credits: (t) ©Paramount/Photofest; (tc) ©vectorkat/Shutterstock

---

CLOSE READ

Support Inferences (PHOTOGRAPH) RL 1, RL 7

Have students look closely at the actors chosen to play Romeo and Juliet in the 1968 film version.

G2 ASK STUDENTS why the director may have chosen the actress who plays Juliet. (*She is young and beautiful; she has an air of innocence.*)

Analyze Author's Choices: Parallel Plots (Sc. 6, LINES 3–8) RL 5

Remind students that a playwright may use **foreshadowing,** or hint what may happen in the future, to maintain the audience's interest in the plot.

H2 CITE TEXT EVIDENCE Ask students which words or phrases in Romeo's speech suggest a tragic future. (*The words* sorrow, one short minute, *and* love-devouring death *hint at a tragic turn in events.*)

Friar Laurence
• is wise, thoughtful, and sensible
• will marry Romeo and Juliet in hopes of ending the feud
• is concerned about the consequences of their intense passion

Both
• offer practical help with the arrangements
• care about Romeo and Juliet

Nurse
• is somewhat foolish, bawdy, and coarse
• offers to help the cause of young love, has no understanding of possible consequences

TEACH

CLOSE READ

Determine Theme
RL 2

(Sc. 6, LINES 9–15)

Have students recall Friar Laurence's previous advice to Romeo about love (Act II, Scene 4, lines 81–84).

 ASK STUDENTS to reread Friar Laurence's caution to Romeo. Based on Romeo's past romantic history, what is Friar Laurence fearful of here? *(He is worried that Romeo's love will burn out as quickly as it came. He fears that overly intense love cannot sustain itself.)*

Analyze Character: Motivations
RL 3

(Sc. 6, LINES 21–37)

Point out that each of the three characters speaks in this passage. Have students examine what they say and how they say it for clues to their feelings.

ASK STUDENTS to contrast Romeo's speech with Juliet's. What does this difference reveal about their two characters? *(Romeo's speech is characteristically extravagant and hyperbolic. He attempts to express his great joy and his great love for Juliet. Juliet, on the other hand, says that words are inadequate to express what she feels. She shows herself in many ways to be the more sensible and down-to-earth one.)* What is Friar Laurence's tone? Explain. *(Friar Laurence may be gently teasing but also quite serious that he will safeguard their virtue until they are married.)*

COLLABORATIVE DISCUSSION Encourage students to review the events that have occurred since Romeo and Juliet met at the party. Ask them to consider whether decisions made in haste are always good ones. Have them also think about what is driving the characters' actions. Are Romeo and Juliet really in love, or are they simply carried away by passion? After pairs have discussed their ideas, have them share their conclusions with the class as a whole. Accept all reasonable responses.

ASK STUDENTS to share any questions they generated in the course of reading and discussing the selection.

Close Read

Do thou but close our hands with holy words,
Then love-devouring death do what he dare—
It is enough I may but call her mine.

Friar Laurence. These violent delights have violent ends
10 And in their triumph die, like fire and powder,
Which, as they kiss, consume. The sweetest honey
Is loathsome in his own deliciousness
And in the taste confounds the appetite.
Therefore love moderately: long love doth so;
15 Too swift arrives as tardy as too slow.

[*Enter Juliet.*]

Here comes the lady. O, so light a foot
Will ne'er wear out the everlasting flint.
A lover may bestride the gossamer
That idles in the wanton summer air,
20 And yet not fall; so light is vanity.

Juliet. Good even to my ghostly confessor.

Friar Laurence. Romeo shall thank thee, daughter, for us both.

Juliet. As much to him, else is his thanks too much.

Romeo. Ah, Juliet, if the measure of thy joy
25 Be heaped like mine, and that thy skill be more
To blazon it, then sweeten with thy breath
This neighbor air, and let rich music's tongue
Unfold the imagined happiness that both
Receive in either by this dear encounter.

30 **Juliet.** Conceit, more rich in matter than in words,
Brags of his substance, not of ornament.
They are but beggars that can count their worth;
But my true love is grown to such excess
I cannot sum up sum of half my wealth.

35 **Friar Laurence.** Come, come with me, and we will make short work;
For, by your leaves, you shall not stay alone
Till Holy Church incorporate two in one.

[*Exeunt.*]

9–15 These...slow: The friar compares Romeo's passion to gunpowder and the fire that ignites it—both are destroyed—then to honey, whose sweetness can destroy the appetite. He reminds Romeo to practice moderation in love.

23 as much to him: I give the same greeting to Romeo that he offers to me.

24–29 if the measure ...encounter: If you are as happy as I am and have more skill to proclaim it, then sweeten the air by singing of our happiness to the world.

30–31 Conceit ...ornament: True understanding (**conceit**) needs no words.

COLLABORATIVE DISCUSSION Romeo and Juliet fall in love and make life-changing decisions in a matter of days. Meet with a partner to discuss how this speed and intensity creates tension for the audience and affects the characters' actions.

TO CHALLENGE STUDENTS...

Analyze a Character's Decision How wise is Friar Laurence? Have students organize small groups to discuss Friar Laurence's decision to marry Romeo and Juliet. In preparation, have students develop a cause-and-effect chart that looks at all the options he had and the possible consequences of each choice. Then have students discuss whether he made the right decision based on what he foresaw as the outcome. Have them summarize their conclusions and present them to the class. As a class, come to a consensus on the wisdom of Friar Laurence's actions.

Analyzing the Text

RL 1, RL 2,
RL 3, RL 4,
RL 5, SL 1

Cite Text Evidence   Support your responses with evidence from the selection.

1. **Interpret** In literature, a **motif** is a repeated image, idea, or theme. Explain the light/dark or day/night motif in Romeo's speech at the beginning of Act II, Scene 2. What does he mean when he refers to Juliet as "the sun"? Where else in Act II does this motif appear?

2. **Analyze** In Act II, Scene 2, Juliet says, "What's in a name? That which we call a rose / By any other name would smell as sweet" (lines 43–44). What does she mean? How does this comparison relate to one of the conflicts in her life?

3. **Infer** After declaring their love for one another, why do Romeo and Juliet want to commit themselves right away to marriage? Support your inference with evidence from the text.

4. **Cite Evidence** In Scene 3, why is Friar Laurence suspicious of Romeo's declaration of love for Juliet? What is his motivation for agreeing to marry Romeo and Juliet, despite his reservations?

5. **Analyze** Explain Juliet's relationship with her nurse. What is the Nurse's primary motivation in helping Juliet to be with Romeo?

6. **Predict** In Scene 6, Friar Laurence urges Romeo to be cautious. Given what you know about Romeo, and about the fates guiding the "star-crossed lovers," do you think Romeo will take his advice? Explain.

PERFORMANCE TASK

Speaking Activity: Debate Both Friar Laurence and Mercutio have personal attributes that put them at odds with Romeo's passion. Analyze their differences and hold a debate in which each character presents his point of view.

- Working with two other students, discuss the characteristics and motivations of Friar Laurence, Mercutio, and Romeo. What differences do these three demonstrate in Act II?

- With each person in your group taking the point of view of one of these characters, debate Romeo's plan to marry Juliet.
- Work together to write a summary of your debate.

PRACTICE & APPLY

Analyzing the Text

RL 1, RL 2, RL 3,
RL 4, RL 5

Possible answers:

1. The sun functions as a central force around which earth orbits and draws energy, light, and warmth. Romeo feels that his relationship with Juliet is a microcosm of this phenomenon (Scene 2, lines 2–25). He depends on Juliet as a life-affirming source just as the earth does the sun. The light/dark motif also appears when Romeo compares her eyes to stars that shine so brightly in the night, birds sing, thinking it is day.

2. She does not feel her love for Romeo should be forbidden, just because he happens to be a Montague. His name matters little to her—it is the person she loves. He is the same person whether he is a Montague or has a different name.

3. They feel a sense of urgency because of their families. They feel people will try to break their bond. Juliet also has to fear the marriage being arranged between her and Paris. (Scene 2, lines 94–105)

4. He feels Romeo is impulsive and hopelessly romantic. He knows Romeo just had the same feelings for Rosaline, who rejected him (lines 65–80). He ultimately decides to support them because he believes it could bring peace between their families (Scene 3, lines 90–92).

5. Juliet has a close relationship with her nurse. In many ways she is closer to her nurse than she is to her mother. The Nurse's primary motivation in helping Romeo and Juliet is seeing Juliet happy (Scene 5, line 74).

6. Romeo is guided by his emotions and is not likely to act cautiously. His mind, at this point, is focused only on Juliet. Given the intensity of his feelings for her, he is unlikely to take Friar Laurence's advice.

Assign this
performance task.

PERFORMANCE TASK

SL 1

Speaking Activity: Debate Remind students to keep in mind the essential characteristics of both Friar Laurence and Mercutio as revealed through their speech. Encourage them to draw from what each character says to support their view in the debate.

AS YOU READ Direct students to use the As You Read note to focus their reading.

Analyze Character: RL 3
Motivations (Sc. 1, LINES 1–28)

Tell students that by developing characters who show opposite traits the playwright can more clearly illustrate the personalities of each.

 CITE TEXT EVIDENCE Ask students how the words and tone of their speech illustrate the differences between Benvolio and Mercutio. *(Benvolio is worried and wants to avoid a brawl. He urges Mercutio to go home so that they won't encounter any Capulets. Mercutio, on the other hand, appears eager for a fight and full of his usual energy.)*

Analyze Author's Choices: RL 5
Parallel Plots (Sc. 1, LINES 30–32)

Have students recall Tybalt's and Romeo's relationship up to this point in the play.

B **ASK STUDENTS** what is foreshadowed by the appearance of Tybalt. What is the effect of his appearance on Benvolio, Mercutio, and the audience? *(Tybalt's appearance means that there will be a fight. Benvolio is stricken; Mercutio is defiant; the audience feels suspense.)*

AS YOU READ Notice how events begin to shift in a more ominous or dangerous direction in this act. Write down any questions you generate during reading.

ACT III

Scene 1 *A public place.*

[*Enter* Mercutio, Benvolio, Page, *and* Servants.]

A

Benvolio. I pray thee, good Mercutio, let's retire.
The day is hot, the Capulets abroad,
And if we meet, we shall not scape a brawl,
For now, these hot days, is the mad blood stirring.

5   **Mercutio.** Thou art like one of those fellows that, when he enters the confines of a tavern, claps me his sword upon the table and says "God send me no need of thee!" and by the operation of the second cup draws him on the drawer, when indeed there is no need.

10   **Benvolio.** Am I like such a fellow?

Mercutio. Come, come, thou art as hot a Jack in thy mood as any in Italy; and as soon moved to be moody, and as soon moody to be moved.

Benvolio. And what to?

15   **Mercutio.** Nay an there were two such, we should have none shortly, for one would kill the other. Thou! why, thou wilt quarrel with a man that hath a hair more or a hair less in his beard than thou hast. Thou wilt quarrel with a man for cracking nuts, having no other reason but because thou hast hazel eyes.
20   What eye but such an eye would spy out such a quarrel? Thy head is as full of quarrels as an egg is full of meat; and yet thy head hath been beaten as addle as an egg for quarreling. Thou hast quarreled with a man for coughing in the street, because he hath wakened thy dog that hath lain asleep in the sun. Didst
25   thou not fall out with a tailor for wearing his new doublet before Easter? with another for tying his new shoes with old riband? And yet thou wilt tutor me from quarreling!

Benvolio. An I were so apt to quarrel as thou art, any man should buy the fee simple of my life for an hour and a quarter.

30   **Mercutio.** The fee simple? O simple!

[*Enter* Tybalt *and others.*]

B

Benvolio. By my head, here come the Capulets.

Mercutio. By my heel, I care not.

3–4 we shall ... stirring: We shall not avoid a fight, since the heat makes people ill-tempered.

7–8 by the ... drawer: feeling the effects of a second drink, is ready to fight (**draw on**) the waiter who's pouring the drinks (**drawer**).

12–13 as soon moved ... to be moved: as likely to get angry and start a fight.

15–27 Mercutio teases his friend by insisting that Benvolio is quick to pick a fight, though everyone knows that Benvolio is gentle and peace loving.

25 doublet: jacket.

26 riband: ribbon or laces.

28–29 An I ... quarter: If I picked fights as quickly as you do, anybody could own me for the smallest amount of money.

Close Read Screencasts   View It!

Modeled Discussions

Have students click the *Close Read* icons in their eBooks to access a screencast in which readers discuss and annotate the following passage:

- Mercutio's dying words (Act III, Scene 1, lines 89–99)

As a class, view and discuss the video.

Tybalt. Follow me close, for I will speak to them. Gentlemen, good den. A word with one of you.

35 **Mercutio.** And but one word with one of us? Couple it with something; make it a word and a blow.

Tybalt. You shall find me apt enough to that, sir, an you will give me occasion.

Mercutio. Could you not take some occasion without giving?

40 **Tybalt.** Mercutio, thou consortest with Romeo.

Mercutio. Consort? What, dost thou make us minstrels? An thou make minstrels of us, look to hear nothing but discords. Here's my fiddlestick; here's that shall make you dance. Zounds, consort!

45 **Benvolio.** We talk here in the public haunt of men.
Either withdraw unto some private place
And reason coldly of your grievances,
Or else depart. Here all eyes gaze on us.

Mercutio. Men's eyes were made to look, and let them gaze.
50 I will not budge for no man's pleasure, I.

[*Enter* Romeo.]

Tybalt. Well, peace be with you, sir. Here comes my man.

Mercutio. But I'll be hanged, sir, if he wear your livery.
Marry, go before to field, he'll be your follower!
Your worship in that sense may call him man.

55 **Tybalt.** Romeo, the love I bear thee can afford
No better term than this: thou art a villain.

Romeo. Tybalt, the reason that I have to love thee
Doth much excuse the appertaining rage
To such a greeting. Villain am I none.
60 Therefore farewell. I see thou knowst me not.

Tybalt. Boy, this shall not excuse the injuries
That thou hast done me; therefore turn and draw. **D**

Romeo. I do protest I never injured thee,
But love thee better than thou canst devise
65 Till thou shalt know the reason of my love;
And so, good Capulet, which name I tender
As dearly as mine own, be satisfied.

Mercutio. O calm, dishonorable, vile submission!
Alla stoccata carries it away.

40–44 consortest: friends with; Mercutio pretends to misunderstand him, assuming that Tybalt is insulting him by calling Romeo and him a **consort,** a group of traveling musicians. He then refers to his sword as his **fiddlestick,** the bow for a fiddle.

51–54 Mercutio again pretends to misunderstand Tybalt. By **my man,** Tybalt means "the man I'm looking for." Mercutio takes it to mean "my servant." (**Livery** is a servant's uniform.)

57–59 I forgive your anger because I have reason to love you.

61 Boy: an insulting term of address.

66 tender: cherish.

68–70 Mercutio assumes that Romeo is afraid to fight. **Alla stoccata** is a move used in sword fighting.

The Tragedy of Romeo and Juliet: Act III, Scene 1 **229**

ENGLISH LANGUAGE SUPPORT

Language: Inverted Word Order Tell students that in some lines, Shakespeare places the negative word at or near the end of the sentence. Point out Mercutio's comment in line 32: "By my heel, I care not." Explain that this placement emphasizes the word "not" and maintains the rhythm of the passage. Ordinarily, the sentence would be phrased as "By my heel, I do not care."

- **ASK STUDENTS** to find another line in which the negative word appears at or near the end. Then have them work together to restate the line in a way that eliminates the inverted order. *(line 59: I am no villain; line 60: I see you do not know me.)*

CLOSE READ

Analyze Author's Choices: RL 5
Parallel Plots (Sc. 1, LINES 33–69)

Review the parallel plots in the play with students. Tell them that as they read this act they should look for the ways in which these plots come together.

C **CITE TEXT EVIDENCE** Ask student volunteers to take different parts and read this section aloud. Have students think about the mounting conflict. Ask: Who is responsible for starting this fight? *(Tybalt is responsible. He makes the initial challenge and calls Romeo a "villain" in line 56. But Mercutio is not without blame. He repeatedly goads Tybalt to fight. "Couple it with something. Make it a word and a blow." [lines 35-36]; "Here's my fiddlestick. Here's that shall make you dance." [lines 42-43])*

Analyze Character: RL 3
Motivations (Sc. 1, LINES 57–69)

Remind students of the importance of **dramatic irony** in a tragedy. Because the characters do not know the complete story, they often make mistakes that lead to tragic consequences.

D2 **ASK STUDENTS** what each character in the scene knows about Romeo's love of Juliet at this point. *(Mercutio, Benvolio, and Tybalt are all ignorant of it.)* What is Romeo's motive for not wanting to fight Tybalt? *(He is now related to Tybalt through his marriage to Juliet.)* What is the effect of Romeo's words on Mercutio? Why? *(Mercutio is angered on Romeo's behalf because he thinks Romeo is a coward. He will fight in his stead. He has no idea of the true meaning behind Romeo's words.)*

Analyze Character: Motivations (Sc. 1, LINES 70–79)

RL 3

Tell students that characters' actions must be consistent with the traits that have been developed throughout.

Ⓔ ASK STUDENTS whether Mercutio's actions here fit the ideas about his personality as conveyed in previous scenes. Why or why not? *(Mercutio is loyal to his friends as shown in his attempts to lift Romeo's depression; headstrong and fiery, he pushes the limits with his words and actions. So his defense of Romeo's honor is in character with what has been established about him previously.)*

[*draws*]

70   Tybalt, you ratcatcher, will you walk?

Tybalt. What wouldst thou have with me?

Mercutio. Good King of Cats, nothing but one of your nine lives. That I mean to make bold withal, and, as you shall use me hereafter, dry-beat the rest of the eight. Will you pluck your
75   sword out of his pilcher by the ears? Make haste, lest mine be about your ears ere it be out.

Tybalt. I am for you.

[*draws*]

Romeo. Gentle Mercutio, put thy rapier up.

Mercutio. Come, sir, your *passado!*

[*They fight.*]

80   **Romeo.** Draw, Benvolio; beat down their weapons.
Gentlemen, for shame! forbear this outrage!
Tybalt, Mercutio, the Prince expressly hath

72–74 nothing but . . . eight: I intend to take one of your nine lives (as a cat supposedly has) and give a beating to the other eight.

79 *passado:* a sword-fighting maneuver.

80–84 Romeo wants Benvolio to help him stop the fight. They are able to hold back Mercutio.

Image Credits: ©Everett Collection, Inc.

WHEN STUDENTS STRUGGLE . . .

Explain that, in this scene, events occur that will determine whether the ending of the play is happy or tragic. To help students see the relationships between characters' actions and their outcomes, list these events on the board in random order:

Tybalt challenges Romeo.
Mercutio fights Tybalt.
Romeo holds Mercutio back.
Tybalt kills Mercutio.
Romeo seeks revenge on Tybalt.

ASK STUDENTS to create cause-and-effect diagrams that show how one event in the list leads to another. Tell them that one event is both a cause and an effect.

Forbid this bandying in Verona streets.
Hold, Tybalt! Good Mercutio!

[Tybalt, *under* Romeo's *arm, thrusts* Mercutio *in, and flies with his* Men.]

Mercutio.   I am hurt.
85 A plague o' both your houses! I am sped.
Is he gone and hath nothing?

Benvolio.   What, art thou hurt?

Mercutio. Ay, ay, a scratch, a scratch. Marry, 'tis enough.
Where is my page? Go, villain, fetch a surgeon.

[*Exit* Page.]

Romeo. Courage, man. The hurt cannot be much.

90 **Mercutio.** No, 'tis not so deep as a well, nor so wide as a church
door; but 'tis enough, 'twill serve. Ask for me tomorrow, and you
shall find me a grave man. I am peppered, I warrant, for this
world. A plague o' both your houses! Zounds, a dog, a rat, a
mouse, a cat, to scratch a man to death! A braggart, a rogue, a
95 villain, that fights by the book of arithmetic! Why the devil
came you between us? I was hurt under your arm.

Romeo. I thought all for the best.

Mercutio. Help me into some house, Benvolio,
Or I shall faint. A plague o' both your houses!
100 They have made worms' meat of me. I have it,
And soundly too. Your houses!

[*Exit, supported by* Benvolio.]

Romeo. This gentleman, the Prince's near ally,
My very friend, hath got this mortal hurt
In my behalf—my reputation stained
105 With Tybalt's slander—Tybalt, that an hour
Hath been my kinsman, O sweet Juliet,
Thy beauty hath made me effeminate
And in my temper softened valor's steel!

[*Reenter* Benvolio.]

Benvolio. O Romeo, Romeo, brave Mercutio's dead!
110 That gallant spirit hath aspired the clouds,
Which too untimely here did scorn the earth.

Romeo. This day's black fate on mo days doth depend;
This but begins the woe others must end.

[*Reenter* Tybalt.]

83 bandying: fighting.

85 A plague . . . sped: I curse both the Montagues and the Capulets. I am destroyed.

102–108 This gentleman . . . valor's steel: My friend has died protecting my reputation against a man who has been my relative for only an hour. My love for Juliet has made me less manly and brave.

110 aspired: soared to.

112–113 This day's . . . must end: This awful day will be followed by more of the same.

TEACH

CLOSE READ

Analyze Word Choice   RL 4
(Sc. 1, LINES 90–96)

Remind students that a **pun** is a joke or humor resulting from words with similar sounds that have different meanings.

F **ASK STUDENTS** to reread lines 90–96 and focus on a wounded Mercutio's words to Romeo. Have them find the pun in his lines. (*"Ask for me tomorrow, and you shall find me a grave man."*) Ask what is implied by his choice of words. (*The word* grave *here is used as an adjective—meaning "serious" or somber"—but when used as a noun, the word means "burial site." Mercurio intends the pun to mean that the next day, he will be a somber man because he will be dead.*)

Analyze Character: RL 3
Motivations (Sc. 1, LINES 102–113)

Have students review the events leading to Mercutio's death.

G **CITE TEXT EVIDENCE** Have students predict what Romeo will do in reaction to Mercutio's death. Have them cite details to support their response. (*Romeo will seek out Tybalt and get revenge. The lines "Thy beauty hath made me effeminate / And in my temper softened valor's steel" as well as "This but begins the woe others must end" all foreshadow that Romeo will take action.*)

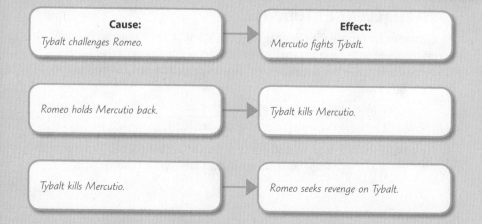

Cause:	Effect:
Tybalt challenges Romeo.	Mercutio fights Tybalt.
Romeo holds Mercutio back.	Tybalt kills Mercutio.
Tybalt kills Mercutio.	Romeo seeks revenge on Tybalt.

Analyze Author's Choices: Parallel Plots (Sc. 1, LINES 115–128)

RL 5

Review the structure of a Shakespearean drama with students. Explain that in Act III, the **turning point** occurs. This is an event that determines how the rest of the play will unfold.

 ASK STUDENTS why Tybalt's death is the play's turning point. Have them consider all of the implications of this event. (*By killing Tybalt, Romeo will now have to face the civil punishment handed out by Prince Escalus, possibly death. Additionally, he has killed Juliet's relative. This event makes the possibility of a happy ending unlikely.*)

Benvolio. Here comes the furious Tybalt back again.

115 **Romeo.** Alive in triumph, and Mercutio slain?
Away to heaven respective lenity,
And fire-eyed fury be my conduct now!
Now, Tybalt, take the "villain" back again
That late thou gavest me, for Mercutio's soul
120 Is but a little way above our heads,
Staying for thine to keep him company.
Either thou or I, or both, must go with him.

Tybalt. Thou, wretched boy, that didst consort him here,
Shalt with him hence.

Romeo.   This shall determine that.
[*They fight.* Tybalt *falls.*]

125 **Benvolio.** Romeo, away, be gone!
The citizens are up, and Tybalt slain.
Stand not amazed. The Prince will doom thee death
If thou art taken. Hence, be gone, away!

Romeo. O, I am fortune's fool!

Benvolio.   Why dost thou stay?
[*Exit* Romeo.]
[*Enter* Citizens.]

130 **Citizen.** Which way ran he that killed Mercutio?
Tybalt, that murderer, which way ran he?

Benvolio. There lies that Tybalt.

Citizen.   Up, sir, go with me.
I charge thee in the Prince's name obey.
[*Enter* Prince *with his* Attendants, Montague, Capulet, *their* Wives,
and others.]

Prince. Where are the vile beginners of this fray?

135 **Benvolio.** O noble Prince, I can discover all
The unlucky manage of this fatal brawl.
There lies the man, slain by young Romeo,
That slew thy kinsman, brave Mercutio.

Lady Capulet. Tybalt, my cousin! O my brother's child!
140 O Prince! O cousin! O husband! O, the blood is spilled
Of my dear kinsman! Prince, as thou art true,
For blood of ours shed blood of Montague.
O cousin, cousin!

Prince. Benvolio, who began this bloody fray?

116 respective lenity: considerate mildness.

124 The sword fight probably goes on for several minutes, till Romeo runs his sword through Tybalt.

129 I am fortune's fool: Fate has made a fool of me.

135–136 Benvolio says he can tell (**discover**) what happened.

141–142 as thou … Montague: If your word is good, you will sentence Romeo to death for killing a Capulet.

232 Collection 4

TO CHALLENGE STUDENTS . . .

Consider Alternate Plot Events Ask: Did Mercutio's ignorance of Romeo's involvement with Juliet lead to his death? Point out to students that Mercutio dies without knowing of Romeo's marriage to Juliet. Ask students to consider these questions:

- Would Mercutio's actions or attitude have been different if he had known?
- Might he have avoided the duel that killed him?

Have students write a paragraph or two in response, citing details to support their position. Invite students to compare their analyses in small groups.

145 **Benvolio.** Tybalt, here slain, whom Romeo's hand did slay.
Romeo, that spoke him fair, bid him bethink
How nice the quarrel was, and urged withal
Your high displeasure. All this—uttered
With gentle breath, calm look, knees humbly bowed—
150 Could not take truce with the unruly spleen
Of Tybalt deaf to peace, but that he tilts
With piercing steel at bold Mercutio's breast;
Who, all as hot, turns deadly point to point,
And, with a martial scorn, with one hand beats
155 Cold death aside and with the other sends
It back to Tybalt, whose dexterity
Retorts it. Romeo he cries aloud,
"Hold, friends! friends, part!" and swifter than his tongue,
His agile arm beats down their fatal points,
160 And 'twixt them rushes; underneath whose arm
An envious thrust from Tybalt hit the life
Of stout Mercutio, and then Tybalt fled,
But by-and-by comes back to Romeo,
Who had but newly entertained revenge,
165 And to't they go like lightning; for, ere I
Could draw to part them, was stout Tybalt slain;
And, as he fell, did Romeo turn and fly.
This is the truth, or let Benvolio die.

Lady Capulet. He is a kinsman to the Montague;
170 Affection makes him false, he speaks not true.
Some twenty of them fought in this black strife,
And all those twenty could but kill one life.
I beg for justice, which thou, Prince, must give.
Romeo slew Tybalt; Romeo must not live.

175 **Prince.** Romeo slew him; he slew Mercutio.
Who now the price of his dear blood doth owe?

Montague. Not Romeo, Prince; he was Mercutio's friend;
His fault concludes but what the law should end,
The life of Tybalt.

Prince.   And for that offense
180 Immediately we do exile him hence.
I have an interest in your hate's proceeding,
My blood for your rude brawls doth lie a-bleeding;
But I'll amerce you with so strong a fine
That you shall all repent the loss of mine.
185 I will be deaf to pleading and excuses;
Nor tears nor prayers shall purchase out abuses.
Therefore use none. Let Romeo hence in haste,

146–147 Romeo, that . . . was: Romeo talked calmly (**fair**) and told Tybalt to think how trivial (**nice**) the argument was.

150–151 could . . . peace: could not quiet the anger of Tybalt, who would not listen to pleas for peace.

156–157 whose dexterity retorts it: whose skill returns it.

159–160 his agile . . . rushes: He rushed between them and pushed down their swords.

164 entertained: thought of.

178–179 Romeo is guilty only of avenging Mercutio's death, which the law would have done anyway.

179–190 The prince banishes Romeo from Verona. He angrily points out that one of his own relatives is dead because of the feud and declares that Romeo will be put to death unless he flees immediately.

WHEN STUDENTS STRUGGLE . . .

To ensure students understand that Tybalt's death is a turning point, draw a simple plot diagram resembling this one on the board. Place Tybalt's death at the peak.

ASK STUDENTS what direction the action takes after Tybalt's death. (*Romeo and Juliet's situation becomes more desperate because Romeo is banished. They start reacting in hasty ways that lead to their downfall.*)

CLOSE READ

Analyze Character: Motivations (Sc. 1, LINES 145–179)   RL 3

Tell students to compare Benvolio's version of events with what actually occurred

I **ASK STUDENTS** to reread lines 145–152. In what way does Benvolio's story differ from the actual sequence of events? Why? (*He does not explain that Mercutio taunted Tybalt or that he drew first. He wants the Prince to know that Tybalt started the fight.*) How does Benvolio's description of Romeo's actions and Mercutio's death reveal his motivation? (*He wants to try to keep Romeo out of trouble.*)

Point out that this is an emotionally charged scene. The fight has claimed the life of two young men and put the fate of a third in jeopardy. The characters speak out of their grief and fear.

J **ASK STUDENTS** why Lady Capulet thinks Benvolio is lying. What does she say happened? (*Lady Capulet thinks that Benvolio is lying because she cannot imagine that one Montague would endanger another by telling the truth. She believes that twenty men overcame Tybalt so that Romeo could kill him in cold blood.*) What does she want the Prince to do? (*She wants the Prince to execute Romeo.*) What is Lord Montague's argument? (*Tybalt would have been executed for killing Mercutio; therefore, Romeo just finished what the law would have done.*)

Analyze Author's Choices: Parallel Plots (Sc. 1, LINES 179–187)   RL 5

Read the Prince's decision aloud.

K **ASK STUDENTS** what the Prince decides. (*banishment for Romeo*) Why does he make this decision? (*He recognizes that, indeed, Romeo cannot be held responsible for the fight, but he did kill Tybalt. Additionally, the Prince's own relative Mercutio, a member of the Montagues, is dead because of this feud.*)

Analyze Author's Choices: Parallel Plots (Sc. 2, LINES 1–31)

RL 5

Point out that this scene opens with Juliet uttering a **soliloquy,** or a speech given by a character alone onstage which reveals the character's thinking or feelings. Read the soliloquy aloud with appropriate emphasis and emotion.

L **ASK STUDENTS** to summarize what Juliet expresses in her soliloquy. *(She is eager to see Romeo for their wedding night. Time cannot pass quickly enough.)* What does the audience know that Juliet does not? What is the effect of this knowledge? *(The audience knows that Mercutio and Tybalt are dead and that Romeo is banished. This knowledge makes them feel sorry for Juliet, who is completely unaware of this tragedy about to change her world.)* Have students summarize what Juliet expresses in this speech.

ASK STUDENTS what effect Juliet's mention of death in lines 21–25 has on the audience. *(Juliet is anxiously awaiting her wedding night. She is filled with anticipation and joy. However, her mention of death is chilling to the audience, who knows that the lovers will ultimately die tragically. It increases our pity for Juliet.)*

Else, when he is found, that hour is his last.
Bear hence this body, and attend our will.
190   Mercy but murders, pardoning those that kill.

[*Exeunt.*]

Scene 2   *Capulet's orchard.*

[*Enter* Juliet *alone.*]

L

Juliet. Gallop apace, you fiery-footed steeds,
Toward Phoebus' lodging! Such a wagoner
As Phaëton would whip you to the West,
And bring in cloudy night immediately.
5   Spread thy close curtain, love-performing night,
That runaways' eyes may wink, and Romeo
Leap to these arms, untalked of and unseen.
Lovers can see to do their amorous rites
By their own beauties; or, if love be blind,
10   It best agrees with night. Come, civil night,
Thou sober-suited matron, all in black,
And learn me how to lose a winning match,
Played for a pair of stainless maidenhoods.
Hood my unmanned blood bating in my cheeks
15   With thy black mantle; till strange love, grown bold,
Think true love acted simple modesty.
Come, night; come, Romeo, come; thou day in night;
For thou wilt lie upon the wings of night
Whiter than new snow on a raven's back.
20   Come, gentle night; come, loving, black-browed night;
Give me my Romeo; and, when he shall die,
Take him and cut him out in little stars,
And he will make the face of heaven so fine
That all the world will be in love with night
25   And pay no worship to the garish sun.
O, I have bought the mansion of a love,
But not possessed it; and though I am sold,
Not yet enjoyed. So tedious is this day
As is the night before some festival
30   To an impatient child that hath new robes
And may not wear them. Oh, here comes my nurse,

[*Enter* Nurse, *wringing her hands, with the ladder of cords in her lap.*]

And she brings news; and every tongue that speaks
But Romeo's name speaks heavenly eloquence.
Now, nurse, what news? What hast thou there? the cords
35   That Romeo bid thee fetch?

2–3 Phoebus: Apollo, the god of the sun; **Phaëton:** a mortal who lost control of the sun's chariot when he drove it too fast.

14–16 Hood . . . modesty: Juliet asks that the darkness hide her blushing cheeks on her wedding night.

26–27 I have . . . possessed it: Juliet protests that she has gone through the wedding ceremony (**bought the mansion**) but is still waiting to enjoy the rewards of marriage.

34 the cords: the rope ladder.

Strategies for Annotation   ✎ 🗐 Annotate it!

Analyze Word Choice

RL 4

Have students use their eBook tools to help them analyze and appreciate the poetic language in Juliet's soliloquy:

- Highlight in yellow examples of similes.
- Highlight in green examples of metaphor.
- In a small group, compare annotations. Discuss how the use of these devices conveys Juliet's emotion to the audience more effectively than literal prose.

O, I have bought the mansion of a love,

But not possessed it; and though I am sold,

Not yet enjoyed. So tedious is this day

As is the night before some festival

To an impatient child that hath new robes

Nurse. Ay, ay, the cords.

Juliet. Ay me! what news? Why dost thou wring thy hands?

Nurse. Ah, well-a-day! he's dead, he's dead, he's dead!
We are undone, lady, we are undone!
Alack the day! he's gone, he's killed, he's dead!

40 **Juliet.** Can heaven be so envious?

Nurse. Romeo can,
Though heaven cannot. O Romeo, Romeo!
Who ever would have thought it? Romeo!

Juliet. What devil art thou that dost torment me thus?
This torture should be roared in dismal hell.
45 Hath Romeo slain himself? Say thou but "I,"
And that bare vowel "I" shall poison more
Than the death-darting eye of a cockatrice.
I am not I, if there be such an "I,"
Or those eyes shut, that make thee answer "I."
50 If he be slain, say "I," or if not, "no."
Brief sounds determine of my weal or woe.

Nurse. I saw the wound, I saw it with mine eyes,
(God save the mark!) here on his manly breast.
A piteous corse, a bloody piteous corse;
55 Pale, pale as ashes, all bedaubed in blood,
All in gore blood. I swounded at the sight.

Juliet. O, break, my heart! poor bankrout, break at once!
To prison, eyes; ne'er look on liberty!
Vile earth, to earth resign; end motion here,
60 And thou and Romeo press one heavy bier!

Nurse. O Tybalt, Tybalt, the best friend I had!
O courteous Tybalt! honest gentleman!
That ever I should live to see thee dead!

Juliet. What storm is this that blows so contrary?
65 Is Romeo slaughtered, and is Tybalt dead?
My dear-loved cousin, and my dearer lord?
Then, dreadful trumpet, sound the general doom!
For who is living, if those two are gone?

Nurse. Tybalt is gone, and Romeo banished;
70 Romeo that killed him, he is banished.

Juliet. O God! Did Romeo's hand shed Tybalt's blood?

Nurse. It did! it did! alas the day, it did!

37–42 well-a-day: an expression used when someone has bad news. The nurse wails and moans without clearly explaining what has happened, leading Juliet to assume that Romeo is dead.

45–50 Juliet's "I" means "aye," or "yes." A **cockatrice** is a mythological beast whose glance kills its victims.

51 my weal or woe: my happiness or sorrow.

53–56 God . . . mark: an expression meant to scare off evil powers, similar to "Knock on wood"; **corse:** corpse; **swounded:** fainted.

57–60 Juliet say her heart is broken and bankrupt (**bankrout**). She wants to be buried with Romeo, sharing his burial platform (**bier**).

CLOSE READ

Analyze Author's Choices: RL 5
Parallel Plots (Sc. 2, LINES 36–60)

Remind students that the nurse's dominant trait is the inability to speak directly and concisely. Have them think about the way in which she affects this scene with her delivery of the news.

Ⓜ **CITE TEXT EVIDENCE** Have students discuss the dramatic irony of this scene. (*Juliet believes that Romeo is dead. He is not dead but will be by the end of the play.*) How does the nurse's delivery of the news compound the confusion? Of whom is she actually speaking? (*She uses no names, just pronouns that could refer to anyone. She is actually saying that Tybalt is dead and that Romeo killed him.*)

ENGLISH LANGUAGE SUPPORT

Vocabulary: Homophones Project lines 45–50 on the whiteboard. Point out that in these lines, Shakespeare uses homophones, or words that sound alike: the pronoun *I*, the word *eye*, and the implied word *ay*, meaning "yes." Explain that some of the pronouns should, in fact, be *ay*. Invite volunteers to mark up the text:

- Circle the homophones.

- Highlight the *I*s that should be replaced with *ay*.

After volunteers have marked up the text, read each line with the correct homophone as students follow along. Discuss how the replacement of *I* with *ay* changes the meaning of the line.

CLOSE READ

Analyze Character: Motivations (Sc. 2, LINES 73–101)

RL 3

Direct students' attention to the range of emotions that Juliet experiences in this scene.

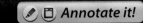 **ASK STUDENTS** to describe Juliet's first reaction once she understands what has happened. Why does she feel this way? *(She is furious at Romeo and calls him a "beautiful tyrant" and "fiend angelical." She is grief-stricken over Tybalt and cannot believe that Romeo could do such a thing.)* In contrast, what does she say to the nurse? Why? *(She defends Romeo in the face of the nurse's criticism, saying "blistered be thy tongue." Hearing Romeo criticized aloud awakens her loyalty to her husband.)* What realization does she come to as shown in lines 100–101? *(She realizes that Tybalt would have killed Romeo if Romeo had not killed him first.)*

Juliet. O serpent heart, hid with a flow'ring face!
Did ever dragon keep so fair a cave?
75   Beautiful tyrant! fiend angelical!
Dove-feathered raven! wolvish-ravening lamb!
Despised substance of divinest show!
Just opposite to what thou justly seemst,
A damned saint, an honorable villain!
80   O nature, what hadst thou to do in hell
When thou didst bower the spirit of a fiend
In mortal paradise of such sweet flesh?
Was ever book containing such vile matter
So fairly bound? O, that deceit should dwell
85   In such a gorgeous palace!

Nurse.   There's no trust,
No faith, no honesty in men; all perjured,
All forsworn, all naught, all dissemblers.
Ah, where's my man? Give me some aqua vitae.
These griefs, these woes, these sorrows make me old.
90   Shame come to Romeo!

Juliet.   Blistered be thy tongue
For such a wish! He was not born to shame.
Upon his brow shame is ashamed to sit;
For 'tis a throne where honor may be crowned
Sole monarch of the universal earth.
95   O, what a beast was I to chide at him!

Nurse. Will you speak well of him that killed your cousin?

Juliet. Shall I speak ill of him that is my husband?
Ah, poor my lord, what tongue shall smooth thy name
When I, thy three-hours' wife, have mangled it?
100 But wherefore, villain, didst thou kill my cousin?
That villain cousin would have killed my husband.
Back, foolish tears, back to your native spring!
Your tributary drops belong to woe,
Which you, mistaking, offer up to joy.
105 My husband lives, that Tybalt would have slain;
And Tybalt's dead, that would have slain my husband.
All this is comfort; wherefore weep I then?
Some word there was, worser than Tybalt's death,
That murdered me. I would forget it fain;
110 But O, it presses to my memory
Like damned guilty deeds to sinners' minds!
"Tybalt is dead, and Romeo—banished."
That "banished," that one word "banished,"
Hath slain ten thousand Tybalts. Tybalt's death

81 bower . . . fiend: give a home to the spirit of a demon.

87 all . . . dissemblers: All are liars and pretenders.

88 aqua vitae: brandy.

102–106 Juliet is uncertain whether her tears should be of joy or of sorrow.

Strategies for Annotation   🖊 📖 *Annotate it!*

Interpret Figurative Language

RL 4, L 5a

Have students use their eBook tools to help them analyze how the paradoxical language in lines 73–85 reveals Juliet's emotions:

- Highlight in pink each oxymoron, or phrase which features contradictory words.
- On a note, explain what each means.
- In small groups, discuss each oxymoron and how it makes sense in this context. Then explain how Shakespeare's use of oxymorons affects the audience's understanding of Juliet's emotions.

A damned saint, an honorable villain!

O nature, what hadst thou to do in hell

When thou didst bower the spirit of a fiend

In mortal paradise of such sweet flesh?

115 Was woe enough, if it had ended there;
Or, if sour woe delights in fellowship
And needly will be ranked with other griefs,
Why followed not, when she said "Tybalt's dead,"
Thy father, or thy mother, nay, or both,
120 Which modern lamentation might have moved?
But with a rearward following Tybalt's death,
"Romeo is banished"—to speak that word
Is father, mother, Tybalt, Romeo, Juliet,
All slain, all dead. "Romeo is banished"—
125 There is no end, no limit, measure, bound,
In that word's death; no words can that woe sound.
Where is my father and my mother, nurse?

Nurse. Weeping and wailing over Tybalt's corse.
Will you go to them? I will bring you thither.

130 **Juliet.** Wash they his wounds with tears? Mine shall be spent,
When theirs are dry, for Romeo's banishment.
Take up those cords. Poor ropes, you are beguiled,
Both you and I, for Romeo is exiled.
He made you for a highway to my bed;
135 But I, a maid, die maiden-widowed.
Come, cords; come, nurse. I'll to my wedding bed;
And death, not Romeo, take my maidenhead!

114–127 If the news of Tybalt's death had been followed by the news of her parents' deaths, Juliet would have felt grief. To follow the story of Tybalt's death with the news of Romeo's banishment creates a sorrow so deep it cannot be expressed in words.

132 beguiled: cheated.

135–137 I . . . maidenhead: I will die a widow without ever really having been a wife. Death, not Romeo, will be my husband.

The Tragedy of Romeo and Juliet: Act III, Scene 2 **237**

Image Credits: (t) ©Everett Collection, Inc.; (tc) ©vectorkat/Shutterstock

Analyze Character: RL 3
Motivations (Sc. 2, LINES 125–131)

Discuss with students how Juliet's house is mourning Tybalt and what that means for her.

Ⓐ **ASK STUDENTS** how Juliet will have to act in this situation. Why? *(Juliet will have to show grief for Tybalt yet conceal her grief about Romeo's banishment from her family.)*

APPLYING ACADEMIC VOCABULARY

attribute	underlie

As you discuss the events in this act, incorporate the Collection 4 academic vocabulary words: *attribute* and *underlie*. To examine Mercutio's motivation in fighting Tybalt, ask students to describe his **attributes** as a friend. Then have them explain what idea **underlies** Juliet's words in lines 130–137 in Scene 2.

CLOSE READ

Analyze Character:
Motivations (Sc. 2, LINES 138–143)   RL 3

 ASK STUDENTS why the nurse offers to find Romeo. What did Juliet say that prompts her action? *(Juliet's earlier words about wishing to die [lines 136–137] worry the nurse. She thinks that seeing Romeo will help her Juliet recover her spirits.)* Why does Juliet send her ring to Romeo? *(to show that she remains loyal to him)*

Analyze Author's Choices:
Parallel Plots (Sc. 3, LINES 10–28)   RL 5

Q **CITE TEXT EVIDENCE** Ask students how this scene parallels Scene 2. Remind students to include specific details and examples from the text. *(Romeo experiences a similar gamut of emotions as Juliet and must be comforted by Friar Laurence, just as the nurse attempted to comfort Juliet. Romeo, like Juliet, speaks with intensity of preferring death to separation from his beloved.)*

ASK STUDENTS how Romeo reacts to the Prince's edict that he is banished. Why? *(He is stricken because it means that he will be separated from Juliet.)* What suggests that the friar is angry at Romeo's lack of gratitude for this more merciful punishment? *(He says, "rude unthankfulness!…This is dear mercy, and thou seest it not.")*

Nurse. Hie to your chamber. I'll find Romeo
To comfort you. I wot well where he is.

140   Hark ye, your Romeo will be here at night.
I'll to him; he is hid at Laurence' cell.

     139 **wot:** know.

Juliet. O, find him! give this ring to my true knight
And bid him come to take his last farewell.

[*Exeunt.*]

Scene 3 *Friar Laurence's cell.*

[*Enter* Friar Laurence.]

Friar Laurence. Romeo, come forth; come forth, thou fearful man.
Affliction is enamored of thy parts,
And thou art wedded to calamity.

     2 **affliction . . . parts:** Trouble loves you.

[*Enter* Romeo.]

Romeo. Father, what news? What is the Prince's doom?
5   What sorrow craves acquaintance at my hand
That I yet know not?

     4 **doom:** sentence.

Friar Laurence.   Too familiar
Is my dear son with such sour company.
I bring thee tidings of the Prince's doom.

Romeo. What less than doomsday is the Prince's doom?

     9 **doomsday:** death.

10   **Friar Laurence.** A gentler judgment vanished from his lips—
Not body's death, but body's banishment.

     10 **vanished:** came.

Romeo. Ha, banishment? Be merciful, say "death";
For exile hath more terror in his look,
Much more than death. Do not say "banishment."

15   **Friar Laurence.** Hence from Verona art thou banished.
Be patient, for the world is broad and wide.

Romeo. There is no world without Verona walls,
But purgatory, torture, hell itself.
Hence banished is banish'd from the world,
20   And world's exile is death. Then "banishment,"
Is death misterm'd. Calling death "banishment,"
Thou cuttst my head off with a golden axe
And smilest upon the stroke that murders me.

     17–23 **There is . . . murders me:** Being exiled outside Verona's walls is as bad as being dead. And yet you smile at my misfortune.

Friar Laurence. O deadly sin! O rude unthankfulness!
25   Thy fault our law calls death; but the kind Prince,
Taking thy part, hath rushed aside the law,
And turned that black word death to banishment.
This is dear mercy, and thou seest it not.

Romeo. 'Tis torture, and not mercy. Heaven is here,
30 Where Juliet lives; and every cat and dog
And little mouse, every unworthy thing,
Live here in heaven and may look on her;
But Romeo may not. More validity,
More honorable state, more courtship lives
35 In carrion flies than Romeo. They may seize
On the white wonder of dear Juliet's hand
And steal immortal blessing from her lips,
Who, even in pure and vestal modesty,
Still blush, as thinking their own kisses sin;
40 But Romeo may not—he is banished.
This may flies do, when I from this must fly;
They are free men, but I am banished.
And sayst thou yet that exile is not death?
Hadst thou no poison mixed, no sharp-ground knife,
45 No sudden mean of death, though ne'er so mean,
But "banished" to kill me—"banished"?
O friar, the damned use that word in hell;
Howling attends it! How hast thou the heart,
Being a divine, a ghostly confessor,
50 A sin-absolver, and my friend professed,
To mangle me with that word "banished"?

Friar Laurence. Thou fond mad man, hear me a little speak.

Romeo. O, thou wilt speak again of banishment.

Friar Laurence. I'll give thee armor to keep off that word;
55 Adversity's sweet milk, philosophy,
To comfort thee, though thou art banished.

Romeo. Yet "banished"? Hang up philosophy!
Unless philosophy can make a Juliet,
Displant a town, reverse a prince's doom,
60 It helps not, it prevails not. Talk no more.

Friar Laurence. O, then I see that madmen have no ears.

Romeo. How should they, when that wise men have no eyes?

Friar Laurence. Let me dispute with thee of thy estate.

Romeo. Thou canst not speak of that thou dost not feel.
65 Wert thou as young as I, Juliet thy love,
An hour but married, Tybalt murdered,
Doting like me, and like me banished,
Then mightst thou speak, then mightst thou tear thy hair,
And fall upon the ground, as I do now,
70 Taking the measure of an unmade grave.

33–35 More validity . . . than Romeo: Even flies that live off the dead (**carrion**) will be able to get closer to Juliet than Romeo will.

44–46 Hadst . . . to kill me: Couldn't you have killed me with poison or a knife instead of with that awful word *banished*?

52 fond: foolish.

54–56 The friar offers philosophical comfort and counseling (**adversity's sweet milk**) as a way to overcome hardship.

63 dispute: discuss; **estate:** situation.

TEACH

CLOSE READ

Analyze Character   RL 3
(Sc. 3, LINES 29–51)

Have students recall Romeo's early appearances in the play and consider what they learned about his character previously.

(R) ASK STUDENTS why Romeo views death as more desirable than banishment. *(Knowing that Juliet is in Verona but that he can't see her is worse than being dead for him.)* Have students discuss whether the portrayal of Romeo here is consistent with what they already know about him. Why or why not? *(Romeo's character has always been emotional and dramatic; he uses language extravagantly to express his feelings. He does the same here, reacting with his heart rather than his head.)*

Support Inferences   RL 1
(Sc. 3, LINES 54–70)

Direct students' attention to the few lines that the friar speaks here. Remind them that they can make inferences about character and motivation from what they read.

(S) CITE TEXT EVIDENCE Have students explain whether Romeo believes Friar Laurence is consoling him effectively. *(Romeo finds Friar Laurence's attempts to console him ineffective. In line 64, he basically dismisses him, saying "Thou canst not speak of that thou dost not feel.")*

ENGLISH LANGUAGE SUPPORT

Vocabulary: Word Play Project lines 29–41 on a whiteboard. Explain that in this part, Romeo refers to two meanings of "fly": the insect and the action of leaving somewhere quickly. Invite a volunteer to mark up the text:

- Highlight forms of the word that refer to the insect in yellow.
- Highlight forms of the word that refer to the action in green.

ASK STUDENTS how Romeo feels toward the flies that are able to touch Juliet. What does he mean when he says he must fly?

This may flies do, when I from this must fly;

Analyze Author's Choices: Parallel Plots (Sc. 3, LINES 93–102)

RL 5

Review the definitions of internal and external conflict with students. Remind them that the plot is driven by the main character's conflicts and efforts to resolve them.

T **ASK STUDENTS** what conflicts Romeo is experiencing. *(He is banished from Verona, which is an external conflict—character versus society. He will be separated from Juliet, which is creating internal conflict for him. He also reveals in this speech another internal conflict, which is that he fears Juliet blames him for Tybalt's death.)*

[Nurse *knocks within*.]

Friar Laurence. Arise; one knocks. Good Romeo, hide thyself.

Romeo. Not I; unless the breath of heartsick groans
Mist-like infold me from the search of eyes.

72–73 Romeo will hide only if his sighs create a mist and shield him from sight.

[*knock*]

Friar Laurence. Hark, how they knock! Who's there? Romeo, arise;
75   Thou wilt be taken.—Stay awhile!—Stand up;

[*knock*]

Run to my study.—By-and-by!—God's will,
What simpleness is this.—I come, I come!

[*knock*]

Who knocks so hard? Whence come you? What's your will?

Nurse [*within*]. Let me come in, and you shall know my errand.
80   I come from Lady Juliet.

Friar Laurence.   Welcome then.

[*Enter Nurse.*]

Nurse. O holy friar, O, tell me, holy friar,
Where is my lady's lord, where's Romeo?

Friar Laurence. There on the ground, with his own tears made drunk.

Nurse. O, he is even in my mistress' case,
85   Just in her case! O woeful sympathy!
Piteous predicament! Even so lies she,
Blubb'ring and weeping, weeping and blubbering.
Stand up, stand up! Stand, an you be a man.
For Juliet's sake, for her sake, rise and stand!
90   Why should you fall into so deep an O?

84–85 he is even . . . her case: He is acting the same way that Juliet is.

90 into so deep an O: into such deep grief.

Romeo [*rises*]. Nurse—

Nurse. Ah sir! ah sir! Well, death's the end of all.

Romeo. Spakest thou of Juliet? How is it with her?
Doth not she think me an old murderer,
95   Now I have stained the childhood of our joy
With blood removed but little from her own?
Where is she? and how doth she? and what says
My concealed lady to our canceled love?

96 blood . . . from her own: the blood of a close relative of hers.

98 concealed lady: secret bride.

Nurse. O, she says nothing, sir, but weeps and weeps;
100   And now falls on her bed, and then starts up,
And Tybalt calls; and then on Romeo cries,
And then down falls again.

TO CHALLENGE STUDENTS . . .

Analyze Dialogue Remind students that in previous scenes, the nurse's speeches have been written in prose. In lines 84–90, however, she speaks in blank verse. Have students evaluate her lines. Ask them to discuss in small groups these points:

- why Shakespeare might have changed her speech pattern
- whether Shakespeare is being inconsistent in portraying her character

Have groups offer a summary of the main ideas they bring out in their discussion.

Romeo.   As if that name,
Shot from the deadly level of a gun,
Did murder her; as that name's cursed hand

105 Murdered her kinsman. O tell me, friar, tell me,
In what vile part of this anatomy
Doth my name lodge? Tell me, that I may sack
The hateful mansion.

[*draws his dagger*]

Friar Laurence.   Hold thy desperate hand.
Art thou a man? Thy form cries out thou art;

110 Thy tears are womanish, thy wild acts denote
The unreasonable fury of a beast.
Unseemly woman in a seeming man!
Or ill-beseeming beast in seeming both!
Thou hast amazed me. By my holy order,

115 I thought thy disposition better tempered.
Hast thou slain Tybalt? Wilt thou slay thyself?
And slay thy lady too that lives in thee,
By doing damned hate upon thyself?
Why railst thou on thy birth, the heaven, and earth?

120 Since birth and heaven and earth, all three do meet
In thee at once; which thou at once wouldst lose.
Fie, fie, thou shamest thy shape, thy love, thy wit,
Which, like a usurer, aboundst in all,
And usest none in that true use indeed

125 Which should bedeck thy shape, thy love, thy wit.
Thy noble shape is but a form of wax,
Digressing from the valor of a man;
Thy dear love sworn but hollow perjury,
Killing that love which thou hast vowed to cherish;

130 Thy wit, that ornament to shape and love,
Misshapen in the conduct of them both,
Like powder in a skilless soldier's flask,
Is set afire by thine own ignorance,
And thou dismembered with thine own defense.

135 What, rouse thee, man! Thy Juliet is alive,
For whose dear sake thou wast but lately dead.
There art thou happy. Tybalt would kill thee,
But thou slewest Tybalt. There art thou happy.
The law, that threatened death, becomes thy friend

140 And turns it to exile. There art thou happy.
A pack of blessings light upon thy back;
Happiness courts thee in her best array;
But, like a misbehaved and sullen wench,
Thou poutst upon thy fortune and thy love.

102 that name: the name Romeo.

106–108 in what vile part . . . mansion: Romeo asks where in his body (**anatomy**) his name can be found so that he can cut the name out.

108–125 Hold thy . . . bedeck thy shape, thy love, thy wit: You're not acting like a man. Would you send your soul to hell by committing suicide (**doing damned hate upon thyself**)? Why do you curse your birth, heaven, and earth? You are refusing to make good use of your advantages, just as a miser refuses to spend his money.

126–134 The friar explains how by acting as he is, Romeo is misusing his shape (his outer form or body), his love, and his wit (his mind or intellect).

CLOSE READ

Analyze Character: Motivations   (Sc. 3, LINES 108–144)   RL 3

Remind students that Friar Laurence, unlike the nurse, is educated and wise and able to express himself eloquently. Have them read this speech carefully to determine what he says to Romeo in an effort to bring him to his senses.

Ⓤ CITE TEXT EVIDENCE Have students explain Friar Laurence's attitude toward Romeo in the first part of the speech. What words and phrases convey this tone? *(In lines 109-113, the friar's tone is disgusted and angry. He tells Romeo that his tears are womanish and that he is acting like a beast, not a man.)* What is the friar's motive in beginning his speech in this way? *(He is trying to shame Romeo into summoning his inner strength.)* How does he reinforce this purpose in lines 143–145? *(He returns to his original tone telling Romeo he is acting like a "misbehaved and sullen wench.")*

ENGLISH LANGUAGE SUPPORT

Vocabulary: Multiple-Meaning Words Explain that many words in English can have different meanings depending on the context in which they appear. An example is *wit* (line 125), which can mean "humor" but here means "intellect or mind."

ASK STUDENTS to look up these words in a dictionary and determine the correct meanings for the selection context: *lodge* (line 107), *sack* (line 107), *fortune* (line 144).

Analyze Author's Choices: Parallel Plots (Sc. 3, LINES 146–172)

RL 5

V ASK STUDENTS to explain why Romeo must leave for Mantua before daybreak. *(If he is found in Verona, he will be executed.)* Have them discuss the friar's plan and consider whether it sounds feasible. Why or why not? *(The plan appears straightforward and appears as if it might work. Romeo must stay in Mantua until such a time that he may be pardoned, and is able to return.)*

---

145 Take heed, take heed, for such die miserable.
Go get thee to thy love, as was decreed,
Ascend her chamber, hence and comfort her.
But look thou stay not till the watch be set,
For then thou canst not pass to Mantua,
150 Where thou shalt live till we can find a time
To blaze your marriage, reconcile your friends,
Beg pardon of the Prince, and call thee back
With twenty hundred thousand times more joy
Than thou wentst forth in lamentation.
155 Go before, nurse. Commend me to thy lady,
And bid her hasten all the house to bed,
Which heavy sorrow makes them apt unto.
Romeo is coming.

Nurse. O Lord, I could have stayed here all the night
160 To hear good counsel. O, what learning is!
My lord, I'll tell my lady you will come.

Romeo. Do so, and bid my sweet prepare to chide.

[Nurse *offers to go and turns again.*]

Nurse. Here is a ring she bid me give you, sir.
Hie you, make haste, for it grows very late.

[*Exit.*]

165 **Romeo.** How well my comfort is revived by this!

Friar Laurence. Go hence; good night; and here stands all your
state:
Either be gone before the watch be set,
Or by the break of day disguised from hence.
Sojourn in Mantua. I'll find out your man,
170 And he shall signify from time to time
Every good hap to you that chances here.
Give me thy hand. 'Tis late. Farewell; good night.

Romeo. But that a joy past joy calls out on me,
It were a grief so brief to part with thee.
175 Farewell.

[*Exeunt.*]

Scene 4 *Capulet's house.*

[*Enter* Capulet, Lady Capulet, *and* Paris.]

Capulet. Things have fall'n out, sir, so unluckily
That we have had no time to move our daughter.
Look you, she loved her kinsman Tybalt dearly,
And so did I. Well, we were born to die.

148–149 look . . . Mantua: Leave before the guards take their places at the city gates; otherwise you will not be able to escape.

151 blaze . . . friends: announce your marriage and get the families (**friends**) to stop feuding.

162 bid . . . chide: Tell Juliet to get ready to scold me for the way I've behaved.

166–171 and here . . . here: Either leave before the night watchmen go on duty, or get out at dawn in a disguise. Stay awhile in Mantua. I'll find your servant and send messages to you about what good things are happening here.

1–2 Things have . . . our daughter: Such terrible things have happened that we haven't had time to persuade (**move**) Juliet to think about your marriage proposal.

242 Collection 4

WHEN STUDENTS STRUGGLE . . .

To ensure that students understand the responsibilities of both Romeo and Friar Laurence in the plan that the friar proposes, have them complete a chart that explains what each must do. Ask students to insert the line numbers of the details they include. Use the chart shown as a model. After students have finished their charts, discuss the ideas they have included.

ASK STUDENTS to explain why this plan should work. Keeping in mind that this is a tragedy, have them predict what might possibly go wrong.

5 'Tis very late; she'll not come down tonight.
I promise you, but for your company,
I would have been abed an hour ago.

Paris. These times of woe afford no time to woo.
Madam, good night. Commend me to your daughter.

10 **Lady Capulet.** I will, and know her mind early tomorrow;
Tonight she's mewed up to her heaviness.

[Paris *offers to go and* Capulet *calls him again.*]

Capulet. Sir Paris, I will make a desperate tender
Of my child's love. I think she will be ruled
In all respects by me; nay more, I doubt it not.
15 Wife, go you to her ere you go to bed;
Acquaint her here of my son Paris' love
And bid her (mark you me?) on Wednesday next—
But, soft! what day is this?

Paris.   Monday, my lord.

Capulet. Monday! ha, ha! Well, Wednesday is too soon.
20 A Thursday let it be—a Thursday, tell her,
She shall be married to this noble earl.

8 Sad times are not good times for talking of marriage.

11 Tonight she is locked up with her sorrow.

12 desperate tender: bold offer.

The Tragedy of Romeo and Juliet: Act III, Scene 4   **243**

Image Credits: (t) ©Paramount/Photofest; (c) ©vectorkat/Shutterstock

CLOSE READ

Analyze Author's Choices: Parallel Plots (Sc. 4, LINES 5–21)   RL 5

Point out that as this scene unfolds, the audience is aware of intense dramatic irony.

W **ASK STUDENTS** to explain what the Capulets believe is the reason for Juliet's "heaviness." What is the real reason known by the audience? (*Her parents think Juliet is sad over Tybalt's death. The audience knows that she is grieving Romeo's banishment.*) What is Lord Capulet's plan for Juliet and how does it complicate the plot? (*Lord Capulet will order Juliet to marry Paris within days. Since she is already married to Romeo, marrying Paris will be impossible for her to do, both legally and emotionally.*)

Romeo's responsibilities	Friar Laurence's jobs
comfort Juliet (lines 146–147)	announce the marriage and reconcile the families (lines 150–151)
go to Mantua (lines 148–150 and 167–169)	try to get Prince Escalus to pardon Romeo (lines 152–154)
await messages from Friar Laurence (lines 148–150 and 167–169) and the call to return to Verona (lines 152–154)	keep Romeo informed and eventually bring him back to Verona (lines 150–152 and 169–171)

Analyze Author's Choices:

RL 5

Plot (Sc. 5, LINES 1–23)

Remind students that the setting changes with each new scene.

X **ASK STUDENTS** to note where Romeo and Juliet are and when this action is taking place. Have them explain the conflict that is revealed by their dialogue. *(It is the morning on Juliet's balcony. They have spent their wedding night together and now Romeo must leave to avoid execution. Juliet is trying to convince him to stay.)* How does line 23 sum up Romeo's conflict? *(He says he "has more care to stay than will to go." In other words, he would rather stay and face possible consequences than leave his wife.)*

Will you be ready? Do you like this haste?
We'll keep no great ado—a friend or two;
For hark you, Tybalt being slain so late,
25 It may be thought we held him carelessly,
Being our kinsman, if we revel much.
Therefore we'll have some half a dozen friends,
And there an end. But what say you to Thursday?

23 no great ado: no big festivity.

    Paris. My lord, I would that Thursday were tomorrow.

30 **Capulet.** Well, get you gone. A Thursday be it then.
Go you to Juliet ere you go to bed;
Prepare her, wife, against this wedding day.
Farewell, my lord.—Light to my chamber, ho!
Afore me, it is so very very late
35 That we may call it early by-and-by.
Good night.

34–35 it is . . . by-and-by: It's so late at night that soon we'll be calling it early in the morning.

    [*Exeunt.*]

Scene 5 *Capulet's orchard.*

[*Enter* Romeo *and* Juliet *above, at the window.*]

X **Juliet.** Wilt thou be gone? It is not yet near day.
It was the nightingale, and not the lark,
That pierced the fearful hollow of thine ear.
Nightly she sings on yond pomegranate tree.
5 Believe me, love, it was the nightingale.

2 It was . . . lark: The nightingale sings at night; the lark sings in the morning.

    Romeo. It was the lark, the herald of the morn;
No nightingale. Look, love, what envious streaks
Do lace the severing clouds in yonder East.
Night's candles are burnt out, and jocund day
10 Stands tiptoe on the misty mountain tops.
I must be gone and live, or stay and die.

9 Night's candles: stars.

    Juliet. Yond light is not daylight; I know it, I.
It is some meteor that the sun exhales
To be to thee this night a torchbearer
15 And light thee on thy way to Mantua.
Therefore stay yet; thou needst not to be gone.

12–25 Juliet continues to pretend it is night to keep Romeo from leaving. Romeo says he'll stay if Juliet wishes it, even if it means death.

    Romeo. Let me be ta'en, let me be put to death.
I am content, so thou wilt have it so.
I'll say yon grey is not the morning's eye,
20 'Tis but the pale reflex of Cynthia's brow;
Nor that is not the lark whose notes do beat
The vaulty heaven so high above our heads.
I have more care to stay than will to go.

20 Cynthia's brow: Cynthia is another name for Diana, the Roman goddess of the moon. She was often pictured with a crescent moon on her forehead.

WHEN STUDENTS STRUGGLE . . .

Have students create a timeline showing the chronology of events in this act.

- Review their timelines from Act II. They should begin with the party and end with Romeo and Juliet's wedding the next afternoon, less than a day later.
- Together, identify the key events to place on their timelines for Act III. *(deaths of Mercutio and Tybalt, the announcement of Romeo's exile, Romeo and Juliet's wedding night, Romeo's departure for Mantua, planned wedding of Juliet to Paris)*
- Discuss the timeframe in which these events take place. *(Monday and Monday night, Tuesday morning, Thursday for planned wedding)*

ASK STUDENTS to compare their timelines in small groups.

Come, death, and welcome! Juliet wills it so.
25 How is't, my soul? Let's talk; it is not day.

Juliet. It is, it is! Hie hence, be gone, away!
It is the lark that sings so out of tune,
Straining harsh discords and unpleasing sharps.
Some say the lark makes sweet division;
30 This doth not so, for she divideth us.
Some say the lark and loathed toad changed eyes;
O, now I would they had changed voices too,
Since arm from arm that voice doth us affray,
Hunting thee hence with hunt's-up to the day!
35 O, now be gone! More light and light it grows.

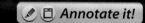

Romeo. More light and light—more dark and dark our woes!

[*Enter Nurse, hastily.*]

Nurse. Madam!

Juliet. Nurse?

Nurse. Your lady mother is coming to your chamber.
40 The day is broke; be wary, look about.

[*Exit.*]

Juliet. Then, window, let day in, and let life out.

Romeo. Farewell, farewell! One kiss, and I'll descend.

[*He starts down the ladder.*]

26 Romeo's mention of death frightens Juliet, and she urges him to leave quickly.

29 division: melody.

31–34 I wish the lark had the voice of the hated (**loathed**) toad, since its voice is frightening us apart and acting as a morning song for hunters (**hunt's-up**).

Image Credits: ©Paramount/Photofest

CLOSE READ

Support Inferences   RL 1, RL 7

(PHOTOGRAPH)

Y **ASK STUDENTS** to reconstruct what is happening from the posture and expressions of the actors in the photograph. (*Romeo is looking away as if the nurse has just come in to warn them that Juliet's mother is on her way or as if he is contemplating his impending exile. Juliet is clinging to Romeo, showing her reluctance to let him go.*)

Interpret Figurative Language (LINE 36)   RL 4, L 5a

Have students analyze how Romeo's use of figurative language in line 36 reveals his feelings.

Z **ASK STUDENTS** how Romeo's words reveal his feelings about the situation in which he and Juliet find themselves. (*By saying "More light and light—more dark and dark are woes," Romeo means that as the day breaks and light grows, the couple's troubles grow darker, or become more serious. Romeo is conveying his distress about their situation.*)

Strategies for Annotation   🖉 📋 Annotate it!

Analyze Word Choice   RL 4

Have students use their eBook tools to trace the images of light and dark in lines 1–36:

- Highlight each reference to light or day in blue. On a note, explain what light/day represents in this dialogue.
- Highlight each reference to night or dark in yellow. Explain on a note what night/dark represents.
- Review your annotations and discuss how these images of light and dark relate to the characters' conflict.

Juliet. Nightly she sings on yond pomegranate tree.

Believe me, love, it was the nightingale.

Romeo. It was the lark, the herald of the morn;

No nightingale. Look, love, what envious streaks

Do lace the severing clouds in yonder East.

Analyze Author's Choices:
Plot (Sc. 5, LINES 51–59)   RL 5

Tell students that this farewell scene presents multiple contrasts that add to its emotional impact on the audience. Have students reread Romeo and Juliet's first farewell in Act II, Scene 2.

A2 **ASK STUDENTS** how this parting is different from Romeo and Juliet's first farewell in Scene 2 of Act II. *(The first scene promised future happiness. They were optimistic in their young love for each other. As they say goodbye here, they face the uncertainty of knowing whether they will ever see each other again.)* What is the effect of this later farewell scene on the audience? Why? *(This scene is particularly sad because the audience knows that it is the last time that Romeo and Juliet will see each other.)*

Analyze Character:
Motivations (Sc. 5, LINES 69–74)   RL 3

Remind students of what they know about Lady Capulet's purpose in coming to Juliet's room.

B2 **ASK STUDENTS** why Lady Capulet tells Juliet that "much of grief shows still some want of wit." What is her primary concern right now? *(She wants Juliet to snap out of her grief. Lady Capulet's concern is that the wedding between Juliet and Paris take place.)*

Juliet. Art thou gone so, my lord, my love, my friend?
I must hear from thee every day in the hour,
45 For in a minute there are many days.
O, by this count I shall be much in years
Ere I again behold my Romeo!

Romeo. Farewell!
I will omit no opportunity
50 That may convey my greetings, love, to thee.

A2 **Juliet.** O, thinkst thou we shall ever meet again?

Romeo. I doubt it not; and all these woes shall serve
For sweet discourses in our time to come.

Juliet. O God, I have an ill-divining soul!
55 Methinks I see thee, now thou art below,
As one dead in the bottom of a tomb.
Either my eyesight fails, or thou lookst pale.

Romeo. And trust me, love, in my eye so do you.
Dry sorrow drinks our blood. Adieu! adieu!

[*Exit.*]

60 **Juliet.** O Fortune, Fortune! all men call thee fickle.
If thou art fickle, what dost thou with him
That is renowned for faith? Be fickle, Fortune,
For then I hope thou wilt not keep him long
But send him back.

Lady Capulet [*within*]. Ho, daughter! are you up?

65 **Juliet.** Who is't that calls? It is my lady mother.
Is she not down so late, or up so early?
What unaccustomed cause procures her hither?

[*Enter Lady Capulet.*]

Lady Capulet. Why, how now, Juliet?

Juliet.   Madam, I am not well.

B2 **Lady Capulet.** Evermore weeping for your cousin's death?
70 What, wilt thou wash him from his grave with tears?
An if thou couldst, thou couldst not make him live.
Therefore have done. Some grief shows much of love;
But much of grief shows still some want of wit.

Juliet. Yet let me weep for such a feeling loss.

75 **Lady Capulet.** So shall you feel the loss, but not the friend
Which you weep for.

Juliet.   Feeling so the loss,
I cannot choose but ever weep the friend.

46 much in years: very old.

54–56 I have . . . tomb: Juliet sees an evil vision of the future.

59 Dry . . . blood: People believed that sorrow drained the blood from the heart, causing a sad person to look pale.

60–62 fickle: changeable in loyalty or affection. Juliet asks fickle Fortune why it has anything to do with Romeo, who is the opposite of fickle.

67 What . . . hither: What unusual reason brings her here?

72–73 have . . . wit: Stop crying (**have done**). A little grief is evidence of love, while too much grief shows a lack of good sense (**want of wit**).

ENGLISH LANGUAGE SUPPORT

Culture: Historical Background Provide students with background information to help them understand the events more clearly:

- "Fortune" refers to the idea of a cosmic force that affected the lives of individuals, a belief held by Elizabethans. Juliet hopes that although Fortune has cast them so low, it will raise them up again soon.

- Contemporary readers might wonder why Juliet does not go with Romeo to Mantua. However, the culture of the age in which the play was written saw young girls as the "property" of their parents. Although they could marry, they had no independence and did not even go outdoors unaccompanied, so the thought would not have crossed their minds.

Lady Capulet. Well, girl, thou weepst not so much for his death
As that the villain lives which slaughtered him.

80 **Juliet.** What villain, madam?

Lady Capulet.   That same villain Romeo.

Juliet [*aside*]. Villain and he be many miles asunder.—
God pardon him! I do, with all my heart;
And yet no man like he doth grieve my heart.

Lady Capulet. That is because the traitor murderer lives.

85 **Juliet.** Ay, madam, from the reach of these my hands.
Would none but I might venge my cousin's death!

Lady Capulet. We will have vengeance for it, fear thou not.
Then weep no more. I'll send to one in Mantua,
Where that same banished runagate doth live,
90 Shall give him such an unaccustomed dram
That he shall soon keep Tybalt company;
And then I hope thou wilt be satisfied.

Juliet. Indeed I never shall be satisfied
With Romeo till I behold him—dead—
95 Is my poor heart so for a kinsman vexed.
Madam, if you could find out but a man
To bear a poison, I would temper it;
That Romeo should, upon receipt thereof,
Soon sleep in quiet. O, how my heart abhors
100 To hear him named and cannot come to him,
To wreak the love I bore my cousin Tybalt
Upon his body that hath slaughtered him!

Lady Capulet. Find thou the means, and I'll find such a man.
But now I'll tell thee joyful tidings, girl.

105 **Juliet.** And joy comes well in such a needy time.
What are they, I beseech your ladyship?

Lady Capulet. Well, well, thou hast a careful father, child;
One who, to put thee from thy heaviness,
Hath sorted out a sudden day of joy
110 That thou expects not nor I looked not for.

Juliet. Madam, in happy time! What day is that?

Lady Capulet. Marry, my child, early next Thursday morn
The gallant, young, and noble gentleman,
The County Paris, at Saint Peter's Church,
115 Shall happily make thee there a joyful bride.

81–102 In these lines Juliet's words have double meanings. To avoid lying to her mother, she chooses her words carefully. They can mean what her mother wants to hear—or what Juliet really has on her mind.

89 runagate: runaway.
90 unaccustomed dram: poison.

93–102 Dead could refer either to Romeo or to Juliet's heart. Juliet says that if her mother could find someone to carry a poison to Romeo, she would mix (**temper**) it herself.

CLOSE READ

Analyze Word Choice   RL 4

(Sc. 5, LINES 87–102)

Point out that the dramatic irony of this part of the scene enables the audience to appreciate Juliet's skill in maintaining her loyalty to Romeo while saying the right sentiments to her mother. Emphasize the importance of the punctuation and line breaks in helping to disguise her meaning.

⊂2 ASK STUDENTS what Juliet is really saying in lines 93–95 versus her mother's interpretation of these lines. *(Juliet is saying that she shall never be happy until she sees Romeo. Her heart is dead at the thought of her kinsman [Romeo] suffering. Her mother believes that she is saying she wants Romeo dead because of what he did to Tybalt.)* What is Juliet actually saying in lines 96–99 when she mentions the kind of poison she would send to Romeo? What does her mother hear instead? *(Juliet would send him a sleeping potion that would give him rest and peace, but her mother thinks Juliet is saying she wants to kill Romeo with poison.)*

⊂2 CITE TEXT EVIDENCE How do Juliet's last lines convince her mother of the strength of her feelings about Romeo while at the same time expressing her true feelings? *(Her mother hears that Juliet would take out her love for Tybalt and misery at his death upon Romeo. In reality Juliet is saying that she hates being separated from Romeo and would "wreak the love I bore my cousin" upon Romeo's body. In other words, she would love him, not hate him.)*

WHEN STUDENTS STRUGGLE . . .

Tell students that the key to the meaning of Juliet's speech in lines 93–102 is the timing and expression in which the lines are read. Draw students' attention to the punctuation that clarifies when to stop and what words to group together.

- Model how to read the speech. Have students echo-read each set of lines with you.
- Have students form pairs. Have each partner read the speech aloud.
- Have the other partner listen to how the reader uses the punctuation, timing, and voice expression to convey Juliet's meaning.
- Have partners switch roles.

TEACH

CLOSE READ

Analyze Character: Motivations (Sc. 5, LINES 116–123; 139–157)

RL 3

 ASK STUDENTS what Juliet's purpose is in this speech. What argument does she use to try to achieve her purpose? Why? *(Juliet must somehow convince her parents to postpone the wedding. She needs more time to figure out a plan. Therefore, she expresses surprise at the haste, suggesting that perhaps it is unseemly.)*

Explain that characters, like people in real life, react to stress in different ways.

E2 **ASK STUDENTS** how her response to their news affects her parents. Why? *(They are enraged that their daughter refuses to obey them. She has always been respectful and cooperative, so this defiance surprises them as well.)* Have students discuss what other emotions might be motivating their outburst at Juliet. Remind them that the Capulets have just seen their nephew killed. *(The Capulets may want to see Juliet safe and settled before anything else happens. They also view her as their possession, so do not think that she has a say in her own destiny.)*

Juliet. Now by Saint Peter's Church, and Peter too,
He shall not make me there a joyful bride!
I wonder at this haste, that I must wed
Ere he that should be husband comes to woo.
120 I pray you tell my lord and father, madam,
I will not marry yet; and when I do, I swear
It shall be Romeo, whom you know I hate,
Rather than Paris. These are news indeed!

Lady Capulet. Here comes your father. Tell him so yourself,
125 And see how he will take it at your hands.

[*Enter* Capulet *and* Nurse.]

Capulet. When the sun sets the air doth drizzle dew,
But for the sunset of my brother's son
It rains downright.
How now? a conduit, girl? What, still in tears?
130 Evermore show'ring? In one little body
Thou counterfeitst a bark, a sea, a wind:
For still thy eyes, which I may call the sea,
Do ebb and flow with tears; the bark thy body is,
Sailing in this salt flood; the winds, thy sighs,
135 Who, raging with thy tears and they with them,
Without a sudden calm will overset
Thy tempest-tossed body. How now, wife?
Have you delivered to her our decree?

Lady Capulet. Ay, sir; but she will none, she gives you thanks.
140 I would the fool were married to her grave!

Capulet. Soft! take me with you, take me with you, wife.
How? Will she none? Doth she not give us thanks?
Is she not proud? Doth she not count her blest,
Unworthy as she is, that we have wrought
145 So worthy a gentleman to be her bridegroom?

Juliet. Not proud you have, but thankful that you have.
Proud can I never be of what I hate,
But thankful even for hate that is meant love.

Capulet. How, how, how, how, choplogic? What is this?
150 "Proud"—and "I thank you"—and "I thank you not"—
And yet "not proud"? Mistress minion you,
Thank me no thankings, nor proud me no prouds,
But fettle your fine joints 'gainst Thursday next
To go with Paris to Saint Peter's Church,
155 Or I will drag thee on a hurdle thither.
Out, you green-sickness carrion! out, you baggage!
You tallow-face!

127 the sunset . . . son: the death of Tybalt.

129–137 conduit: fountain. Capulet compares Juliet to a boat (**bark**), an ocean, and the wind because of her excessive crying.

141 take me with you: let me understand you.

146–148 Not proud . . . meant love: I'm not pleased, but I am grateful for your intentions.

149–157 Capulet calls Juliet a person who argues over fine points (**choplogic**) and a spoiled child (**minion**). He tells her to prepare herself (**fettle your fine joints**) for the wedding or he'll haul her there in a cart for criminals (**hurdle**). He calls her a piece of dead flesh (**green-sickness carrion**) and a coward (**tallow-face**).

248 Collection 4

ENGLISH LANGUAGE SUPPORT

Vocabulary: Idiomatic Expressions Tell students that idiomatic expressions are those that mean something different from the literal meaning of the words. Point out "take it at your hands" in line 125. Work with students to use the context in which the phrase occurs to define it. *(see how he will react to hearing the news from you)*

ASK STUDENTS to work in pairs to define these other expressions using context clues: "You are too hot" (line 176); "lay hand on heart" (line 191).

Lady Capulet. Fie, fie; what, are you mad?

Juliet. Good father, I beseech you on my knees,

[*She kneels down.*]

Hear me with patience but to speak a word.

160 **Capulet.** Hang thee, young baggage! disobedient wretch!
I tell thee what—get thee to church a Thursday
Or never after look me in the face.
Speak not, reply not, do not answer me!
My fingers itch. Wife, we scarce thought us blest
165 That God had lent us but this only child;
But now I see this one is one too much,
And that we have a curse in having her.
Out on her, hilding!

Nurse. God in heaven bless her!
You are to blame, my lord, to rate her so.

170 **Capulet.** And why, my Lady Wisdom? Hold your tongue,
Good Prudence. Smatter with your gossips, go!

Nurse. I speak no treason.

Capulet. O, God-i-god-en!

Nurse. May not one speak?

Capulet. Peace, you mumbling fool!
Utter your gravity o'er a gossip's bowl,
175 For here we need it not.

Lady Capulet. You are too hot.

Capulet. God's bread! it makes me mad. Day, night, late, early,
At home, abroad, alone, in company,
Waking or sleeping, still my care hath been
To have her matched; and having now provided
180 A gentleman of princely parentage,
Of fair demesnes, youthful, and nobly trained,
Stuffed, as they say, with honorable parts,
Proportioned as one's thought would wish a man—
And then to have a wretched puling fool,
185 A whining mammet, in her fortunes tender,
To answer "I'll not wed, I cannot love;
I am too young, I pray you pardon me"!
But, an you will not wed, I'll pardon you.
Graze where you will, you shall not house with me.
190 Look to't, think on't; I do not use to jest.
Thursday is near; lay hand on heart, advise:
An you be mine, I'll give you to my friend;

164 My fingers itch: I feel like hitting you.

168 hilding: a good-for-nothing person.

171 smatter: chatter.

174 Utter . . . bowl: Save your words of wisdom for a gathering of gossips.

179 matched: married.

184 puling: crying.
185 mammet: doll.

189–195 Capulet swears that he'll kick Juliet out and cut her off financially if she refuses to marry.

CLOSE READ

Analyze Author's Choices: Parallel Plots (Sc. 5, LINES 160–168)   RL 5

Remind students that **complications** are problems that arise that prevent characters from resolving the major conflict.

🄕🄖 **ASK STUDENTS** how Lord Capulet's decision complicates the plot. *(He says that if Juliet does not marry Paris on Thursday, he will disown her.)*

Analyze Character: Motivations (Sc. 5, LINES 168–175)   RL 3

Point out that in Capulet's eyes, the nurse has no right to join the conversation he is having with his family. She is his employee and belongs to a much lower social class. Therefore, it is courageous for the nurse to contradict him.

🄖 **ASK STUDENTS** what motivates the nurse to speak up. *(She is protective of Juliet; she feels that her parents are being unjust toward her. She knows the real situation that Juliet faces.)*

Analyze Character

RL 3

(Sc. 5, LINES 203–204)

 ASK STUDENTS what Lady Capulet's last words to Juliet show about her loyalties. *(She will side with her husband on this issue, and is "done" with her daughter.)* Ask students whether her reaction is realistic. Why or why not? *(Yes. She has no idea why Juliet does not want to marry Paris and sees it as being disobedient. She was married at a younger age than Juliet is now.)*

An you be not, hang, beg, starve, die in the streets,
For, by my soul, I'll ne'er acknowledge thee,
195   Nor what is mine shall never do thee good.
Trust to't. Bethink you. I'll not be forsworn.

[*Exit.*]

Juliet. Is there no pity sitting in the clouds
That sees into the bottom of my grief?
O sweet my mother, cast me not away!
200   Delay this marriage for a month, a week;
Or if you do not, make the bridal bed
In that dim monument where Tybalt lies.

Lady Capulet. Talk not to me, for I'll not speak a word.
Do as thou wilt, for I have done with thee.

[*Exit.*]

205   **Juliet.** O God!—O nurse, how shall this be prevented?
My husband is on earth, my faith in heaven.
How shall that faith return again to earth
Unless that husband send it me from heaven
By leaving earth? Comfort me, counsel me.
210   Alack, alack, that heaven should practice stratagems
Upon so soft a subject as myself!
What sayst thou? Hast thou not a word of joy?
Some comfort, nurse.

196 I'll not be forsworn: I will not break my promise to Paris.

207–211 Juliet is worried about the sin of being married to two men. She asks how heaven can play such tricks (**practice stratagems**) on her.

Image Credits: ©Flickr Select/foxline.com.ua/Getty Images

WHEN STUDENTS STRUGGLE . . .

By the end of this act, everyone who has come into contact with Juliet has turned against her. Explain that Shakespeare created complex characters who often act from more than one motivation. Write these possible motivations on the board: family obligation, anger, fear, misunderstanding, anxiety, control, despair.

ASK STUDENTS to work in pairs to match the nurse, Lord Capulet, and Lady Capulet with one or more of the motives on the board or another of their choosing to explain why that character acts as he or she does in this scene. Have them explain how the force drives the behavior of the character.

Nurse.   Faith, here it is.
Romeo is banish'd; and all the world to nothing
215   That he dares ne'er come back to challenge you;
Or if he do, it needs must be by stealth.
Then, since the case so stands as now it doth,
I think it best you married with the County.
O, he's a lovely gentleman!
220   Romeo's a dishclout to him. An eagle, madam,
Hath not so green, so quick, so fair an eye
As Paris hath. Beshrew my very heart,
I think you are happy in this second match,
For it excels your first; or if it did not,
225   Your first is dead—or 'twere as good he were
As living here and you no use of him.

Juliet. Speak'st thou this from thy heart?

Nurse. And from my soul too; else beshrew them both.

Juliet. Amen!

230   **Nurse.** What?

Juliet. Well, thou hast comforted me marvelous much.
Go in; and tell my lady I am gone,
Having displeased my father, to Laurence' cell,
To make confession and to be absolved.

235   **Nurse.** Marry, I will; and this is wisely done.

[*Exit.*]

Juliet. Ancient damnation! O most wicked fiend!
Is it more sin to wish me thus forsworn,
Or to dispraise my lord with that same tongue
Which she hath praised him with above compare
240   So many thousand times? Go, counselor!
Thou and my bosom henceforth shall be twain.
I'll to the friar to know his remedy.
If all else fail, myself have power to die.

[*Exit.*]

---

222 beshrew: curse.

223–225 This new marriage will be better than the first, which is as good as over.

229 Amen: I agree— that is, curse your heart and soul.

236–238 Ancient damnation: old devil; **dispraise:** criticize.

241 Thou . . . twain: I'll no longer tell you my secrets.

COLLABORATIVE DISCUSSION Discuss with a partner the chain of events that begins to turn the story of Romeo and Juliet into a tragedy. Do you believe the main characters are making mistakes that will lead them down a tragic path? Cite textual evidence to support your ideas.

TO CHALLENGE STUDENTS . . .

Deliver a Soliloquy Poetry is most appreciated when it is heard. Have students choose a soliloquy or major speech in this act and do the following:

- Prepare a speaking copy of the speech. Highlight or underline punctuation, words to be emphasized, and places to look at the audience or show a particular expression.

- Practice reading your speech to a partner. Partners should offer constructive feedback on strengths and weaknesses of the delivery.

- Deliver your speech to the class. After the speeches have been presented, discuss how hearing them read aloud contributed to their meaning.

CLOSE READ

Analyze Character   RL 3

(Sc. 5, LINES 213–243)

Draw students' attention to the nurse's speech in lines 213–243.

⑫ ASK STUDENTS what the nurse advises Juliet to do. *(The nurse advises that now that Romeo is gone, he is as good as dead anyway. Juliet needs to make the best of the situation and marry Paris.)* What does this confirm about the nurse's character? *(Always prone to being flighty, the Nurse suddenly changes course from being romantic to strategic and practical. Her intentions are likely good, but she now appears untrustworthy.)*

Tell students that characters' relationships reflect those in real life. Circumstances may alter the way the characters feel about each other.

⑫ CITE TEXT EVIDENCE Have students explain the effect of the nurse's advice on Juliet. In what way does their relationship change? Cite details that support this view. *(Juliet cuts the nurse off. She will no longer tell her what she is thinking. Juliet expresses this change in their relationship with the lines, "Go, counselor! Thou and my bosom henceforth shall be twain.")* What does Juliet's new resolution reveal about her character? *(She is becoming more independent.)*

COLLABORATIVE DISCUSSION Have students pair up and trace all of the events that have occurred in this act, identifying causes that may have contributed to each. Have them discuss whether they think the characters could have acted otherwise. Have them share their conclusions with the class as a whole. Accept all reasonable responses.

ASK STUDENTS to share any questions they generated in the course of reading and discussing the selection.

PRACTICE & APPLY

Analyzing the Text

RL 1, RL 2, RL 3, RL 4, RL 5

Possible answers:

1. The "houses" are those of the Capulet and Montague families, whose rivalry led to his death. Mercutio's remark foreshadows the grief that will come to both families through Romeo and Juliet's tragedy.

2. Romeo is motivated by rage when Tybalt kills Mercutio. Romeo loses control, and while his anger and grief are justifiable, it was probably unwise to kill a member of the Capulet family. This action will only cause more violence and possibly create even more problems for him and for Juliet.

3. Since they both behave emotionally and irrationally, they need older and wiser people to guide them and help them to solve problems. For example, in Scene 3, lines 110–111, Friar Laurence says, "thy wild acts denote/ The unreasonable fury of a beast."

4. He is thinking only of himself and not acting in a rational, open-minded manner. A likely consequence is driving his daughter away or somehow putting her in danger.

5. As Romeo alluded to earlier, darkness provides a place for them to hide and be safe. Juliet also knows that Romeo must leave when it's daylight.

6. The nurse, purely out of concern, tells Juliet she should forget Romeo and marry Paris (Scene 5, lines 214–226). In saying this, she loses Juliet's trust (lines 240–241).

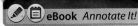

Analyzing the Text

Cite Text Evidence Support your responses with evidence from the selection.

1. **Interpret** What is the meaning of Mercutio's repeated curse, "A plague o' both your houses!" (Scene 1, lines 85, 93)? What might this curse foreshadow?

2. **Evaluate** What is Romeo's motivation for killing Tybalt? Is his action justified or a mistake? Explain your response.

3. **Cite Evidence** In what ways do Romeo and Juliet need the help of Friar Laurence and the Nurse in order to save their love and move forward? Support your response with evidence from the text.

4. **Analyze** In Scene 5, Lord Capulet becomes enraged when Juliet says she will not marry Paris. In what way are his words and actions in this scene like those of Romeo and Juliet? What are the likely consequences of his actions?

5. **Interpret** Explore how Shakespeare continues to use the light/dark or day/night motif in Scene 5, lines 1–35. Why does Juliet want the darkness to continue?

6. **Analyze** How and why does Juliet's relationship with her nurse change? Do you believe Juliet is justified in her feelings toward the nurse? Explain, citing details from the text.

PERFORMANCE TASK

Writing Activity: Journal Entries Use two brief writing tasks to explore the parallel feelings of despair Romeo and Juliet feel in Act III.

1. Write a one-page journal entry from the point of view of Juliet when she learns of the death of Tybalt.

2. Write a one-page journal entry from the point of view of Romeo when he is at the Friar's cell awaiting exile.

Base both pieces of writing on evidence from the text.

Assign this performance task.

PERFORMANCE TASK

W 10

Writing Activity: Journal Entries Have students review each scene, jotting down details of dialogue that reveal each character's feelings. Remind them that the journal entry will be written from the first-person point of view. Suggest that they share their entries in small groups to compare perspectives.

AS YOU READ Direct students to use the As You Read note to focus their reading.

Analyze Character: Motivations (Sc. 1, LINES 1–15)   RL 3

Remind students that the events in this act will move the plot closer to its tragic conclusion.

(A) ASK STUDENTS what the friar's motive is for wanting to slow down the marriage preparations for Paris and Juliet. *(He knows that Juliet is already married because he performed the wedding. He needs time to figure out what to do.)* What does Paris say is Lord Capulet's motive for hurrying the wedding along? *(Lord Capulet thinks getting married will help Juliet get over her grief about Tybalt.)*

Analyze Word Choice   RL 4

(Sc. 1, LINES 18–25)

Point out that just as Juliet manipulatd her words to sound convincing to her mother while defending Romeo, she tries to manage the same performance here with Paris.

(B) CITE TEXT EVIDENCE Have students explain the double meanings in Juliet's exchange with Paris by citing text evidence. *(She says she will be happy when she can be not "your wife," but "a wife," meaning a wife to Romeo. When Paris reminds her of their upcoming wedding, she says, "What must be shall be," meaning that the wedding will not happen. She tells Paris: "I will confess to you that I love him," meaning Romeo. Paris mistakenly thinks she is talking about Paris.)*

AS YOU READ Note the details of the plan Juliet and Friar Laurence initiate in this act. Pay attention to the reactions of other characters as the plan unfolds. Write down any questions you generate during reading.

ACT IV

Scene 1 *Friar Laurence's cell.*

[*Enter* Friar Laurence *and* Paris.]

(A) **Friar Laurence.** On Thursday, sir? The time is very short.

Paris. My father Capulet will have it so,
And I am nothing slow to slack his haste.

Friar Laurence. You say you do not know the lady's mind.
5   Uneven is the course; I like it not.

Paris. Immoderately she weeps for Tybalt's death,
And therefore have I little talked of love;
For Venus smiles not in a house of tears.
Now, sir, her father counts it dangerous
10   That she do give her sorrow so much sway,
And in his wisdom hastes our marriage
To stop the inundation of her tears,
Which, too much minded by herself alone,
May be put from her by society.
15   Now do you know the reason of this haste.

Friar Laurence [*aside*]. I would I knew not why it should be
    slowed.—
Look, sir, here comes the lady toward my cell.

[*Enter* Juliet.]

Paris. Happily met, my lady and my wife!

(B) **Juliet.** That may be, sir, when I may be a wife.

20   **Paris.** That may be must be, love, on Thursday next.

Juliet. What must be shall be.

Friar Laurence.   That's a certain text.

Paris. Come you to make confession to this father?

Juliet. To answer that, I should confess to you.

Paris. Do not deny to him that you love me.

25   **Juliet.** I will confess to you that I love him.

Paris. So will ye, I am sure, that you love me.

Juliet. If I do so, it will be of more price,
Being spoke behind your back, than to your face.

2–3 My … haste: Capulet is eager to have the wedding on Thursday and so am I.

4–5 You … course: You don't know how Juliet feels about this. It's a very uncertain (**uneven**) plan.

13–14 Which … society: which, thought about too much by her in privacy, may be put from her mind if she is forced to be with others.

Close Read Screencasts   View It!

Modeled Discussions

Have students click the Close Read icons in their eBooks to access a screencast in which readers discuss and annotate the following passage:

- Juliet's exchange with Paris in Friar Laurence's cell. (Act IV, Scene 1, lines 22–36) As a class, view and discuss the video.

Analyze Character: Motivations

RL 3

(Sc. 1, LINES 44–69)

Tell students that sometimes external circumstances motivate characters to act; sometimes inner convictions are the reasons for their actions. Ask student volunteers to read this dialogue aloud as the rest of the class reads along silently.

C ASK STUDENTS what details suggest that the friar views the situation as seriously as Juliet does. *(He says in lines 46–47 that "it strains me past the compass of my wits." This inspires him to hatch a desperate plan.)* Infer why Friar Laurence is motivated to help Juliet any way that he can. Have students consider what they know about Friar Laurence's vocation. *(He is a priest; it would be wrong (sinful) for him to perform a second wedding knowing about the first; he cares about Romeo and hopes that his marriage to Juliet may still bring an end to the strife between their families.)*

As students read Juliet's speech, have them also recall Romeo's similar threats in Scene 3 of the previous act.

D CITE TEXT EVIDENCE How does Juliet view her marriage bond to Romeo? Explain. *(In lines 55–59, Juliet says that God joined her heart and Romeo's, the friar joined their hands, and rather than dishonor that bond, she will kill herself.)* How is it similar to Romeo's reaction in Act III? *(Juliet is being forced to do something that is wrong because of her marriage to Romeo. She cannot tell her parents; she cannot dishonor her vows. As a result, she considers killing herself.)*

Paris. Poor soul, thy face is much abused with tears.

30 **Juliet.** The tears have got small victory by that,
For it was bad enough before their spite.

Paris. Thou wrongst it more than tears with that report.

Juliet. That is no slander, sir, which is a truth;
And what I spake, I spake it to my face.

35 **Paris.** Thy face is mine, and thou hast slandered it.

Juliet. It may be so, for it is not mine own.
Are you at leisure, holy father, now,
Or shall I come to you at evening mass?

Friar Laurence. My leisure serves me, pensive daughter, now.
40 My lord, we must entreat the time alone.

Paris. God shield I should disturb devotion!
Juliet, on Thursday early will I rouse ye.
Till then, adieu, and keep this holy kiss.

[*Exit.*]

Juliet. O, shut the door! and when thou hast done so,
45 Come weep with me—past hope, past cure, past help!

Friar Laurence. Ah, Juliet, I already know thy grief;
It strains me past the compass of my wits.
I hear thou must, and nothing may prorogue it,
On Thursday next be married to this County.

50 **Juliet.** Tell me not, friar, that thou hearst of this,
Unless thou tell me how I may prevent it.
If in thy wisdom thou canst give no help,
Do thou but call my resolution wise
And with this knife I'll help it presently.
55 God joined my heart and Romeo's, thou our hands;
And ere this hand, by thee to Romeo's sealed,
Shall be the label to another deed,
Or my true heart with treacherous revolt
Turn to another, this shall slay them both.
60 Therefore, out of thy long-experienced time,
Give me some present counsel; or, behold,
'Twixt my extremes and me this bloody knife
Shall play the umpire, arbitrating that
Which the commission of thy years and art
65 Could to no issue of true honor bring.
Be not so long to speak. I long to die
If what thou speakst speak not of remedy.

Friar Laurence. Hold, daughter, I do spy a kind of hope,
Which craves as desperate an execution

30–31 The tears ... spite: The tears haven't ruined my face; it wasn't all that beautiful before they did their damage.

35 Paris says he owns Juliet's face (since she will soon marry him). Insulting her face, he says, insults him, its owner.

47–48 compass: limit; **prorogue:** postpone.

52–53 If in ... wise: If you can't find a way to help me, at least agree that my plan is wise.

56–67 And ere this hand ... of remedy: Before I sign another wedding agreement (**deed**), I will use this knife to kill myself. If you, with your years of experience (**long-experienced time**), can't help me, I'll end my sufferings (**extremes**) and solve the problem myself.

TO CHALLENGE STUDENTS...

Compare Two Relationships How is the chemistry between Juliet and Paris? Point out that, as far as the audience knows, this meeting between Juliet and Paris is the first time they have exchanged words. Ask students to compare this encounter with Romeo and Juliet's meeting at the party in Act I.

- Have students organize their comparison in a graphic organizer.
- Ask them to examine tone, figures of speech, and ideas.
- Have them draw conclusions about the character of Paris based on their comparison.
- Ask them to share their comparisons and conclusions in small groups.

70 As that is desperate which we would prevent.
   If, rather than to marry County Paris,
   Thou hast the strength of will to slay thyself,
   Then is it likely thou wilt undertake
   A thing like death to chide away this shame,
75 That copest with death himself to scape from it;
   And, if thou darest, I'll give thee remedy.

   Juliet. O, bid me leap, rather than marry Paris,
   From off the battlements of yonder tower,
   Or walk in thievish ways, or bid me lurk
80 Where serpents are; chain me with roaring bears,
   Or shut me nightly in a charnel house,
   O'ercovered quite with dead men's rattling bones,
   With reeky shanks and yellow chapless skulls;
   Or bid me go into a new-made grave
85 And hide me with a dead man in his shroud—
   Things that, to hear them told, have made me tremble—
   And I will do it without fear or doubt,
   To live an unstained wife to my sweet love.

   Friar Laurence. Hold, then. Go home, be merry, give consent
90 To marry Paris. Wednesday is tomorrow.
   Tomorrow night look that thou lie alone:
   Let not the nurse lie with thee in thy chamber.
   Take thou this vial, being then in bed,
   And this distilled liquor drink thou off;
95 When presently through all thy veins shall run
   A cold and drowsy humor; for no pulse
   Shall keep his native progress, but surcease;
   No warmth, no breath, shall testify thou livest;
   The roses in thy lips and cheeks shall fade
100 To paly ashes, thy eyes' windows fall
   Like death when he shuts up the day of life;
   Each part, deprived of supple government,
   Shall, stiff and stark and cold, appear like death;
   And in this borrowed likeness of shrunk death
105 Thou shalt continue two-and-forty hours,
   And then awake as from a pleasant sleep.
   Now, when the bridegroom in the morning comes
   To rouse thee from thy bed, there art thou dead.
   Then, as the manner of our country is,
110 In thy best robes uncovered on the bier
   Thou shalt be borne to that same ancient vault
   Where all the kindred of the Capulets lie.
   In the meantime, against thou shalt awake,
   Shall Romeo by my letters know our drift;

71–76 If, rather than . . . remedy: If you are desperate enough to kill yourself, then you'll be daring enough to try the deathlike solution that I propose.

77–88 Juliet lists the things she would do rather than marry Paris. **charnel house:** a storehouse for bones; **reeky shanks:** stinking bones; **chapless:** without jaws.

93 vial: small bottle.

96–106 humor: liquid; **no pulse . . . pleasant sleep:** Your pulse will stop (**surcease**), and you will turn cold, pale, and stiff, as if you were dead; this condition will last for 42 hours.

111–112 same ancient vault . . . lie: same ancient tomb where all members of the Capulet family are buried.

114 drift: plan.

The Tragedy of Romeo and Juliet: Act IV, Scene 1   **255**

TEACH

CLOSE READ

Analyze Character: Motivations (Sc. 1, LINES 71–88)   RL 3

E ASK STUDENTS to consider how calmly Friar Laurence listens to Juliet threaten to kill herself in lines 50–67. How does that speech motivate him to share his plan with her? *(Her apparent sincerity in wishing to die rather than marry Paris convinces the friar that she will be willing to undertake this tricky and potentially dangerous plan.)* Have students discuss whether Juliet dislikes Paris so intensely that she is willing to go to these lengths to avoid marrying him. *(At the end of her speech, Juliet says that she will do all this to "live an unstained wife to my sweet love." These words suggest that it is her desire to remain true to Romeo more than any feeling toward Paris that motivates her.)*

Analyze Author's Choices: Plot (Sc. 1, LINES 89–114)   RL 3, RL 5

Ask students to reread the friar's plan, then to summarize the steps in the plan in the correct order.

F ASK STUDENTS how the elements of the friar's plan were foreshadowed when the friar first appeared in the play. *(He was working with plants that had medicinal purposes.)* Why is the timing of the friar's plan critical? *(The potion will only last for forty-two hours.)*

Strategies for Annotation   *Annotate it!*

Analyze Character: Motivations   RL 3

Have students use their eBook annotation tools to analyze lines 77–88. Have them do the following:

- Highlight each action in green that would cause Juliet to die before marrying Paris.
- Highlight each action in blue that would lead to a result that would cause Paris to reject her.
- Review your annotations and discuss why Shakespeare included such specific details in this speech.

Or walk in thievish ways, or bid me lurk Where serpents are; chain me with roaring bears, Or shut me nightly in a charnel house, O'ercovered quite with dead men's rattling bones, With reeky shanks and yellow chapless skulls;

The Tragedy of Romeo and Juliet: Act IV, Scene 1   **255**

Analyze Author's Choices: Plot (Sc. 1, LINES 115–126)

RL 5, RL 3

Review the steps in Friar Laurence's plan with students.

G **ASK STUDENTS** to explain what the risks of Friar Laurence's plan might be. *(Friar Laurence has said more than once that valor is needed to carry it out. The danger might be that the dose will be too great and Juliet won't wake up, or she will wake up too soon.)* What is an essential component of the plan? *(that Romeo get word of the plan and be there when she wakes up)*

Analyze Author's Choices: Text Structure (Sc. 2, LINES 1–8)

RL 5

Direct students' attention to the conversation among the servants. Have them look for elements of humor in what they say.

H **ASK STUDENTS** to think about the purpose that comic relief serves. Why might Shakespeare have chosen to begin this scene with a light, humorous conversation? *(This scene provides a welcome contrast to the heavy, dark conversation of Scene 1. It shows that no matter what personal crisis someone is going through, life goes on around them. Since the focus of the scene is the wedding, this conversation is appropriate.)*

G

115 And hither shall he come; and he and I
Will watch thy waking, and that very night
Shall Romeo bear thee hence to Mantua.
And this shall free thee from this present shame,
If no inconstant toy nor womanish fear
120 Abate thy valor in the acting it.

119–120 **inconstant toy:** foolish whim; **abate thy valor:** weaken your courage.

Juliet. Give me, give me! O, tell me not of fear!

Friar Laurence. Hold! Get you gone, be strong and prosperous
In this resolve. I'll send a friar with speed
To Mantua, with my letters to thy lord.

125 **Juliet.** Love give me strength! and strength shall help afford.
Farewell, dear father.

[*Exeunt.*]

Scene 2 *Capulet's house.*

[*Enter* Capulet, Lady Capulet, Nurse, *and* Servingmen.]

H

Capulet. So many guests invite as here are writ.

[*Exit a* Servingman.]

Sirrah, go hire me twenty cunning cooks.

Servingman. You shall have none ill, sir; for I'll try if they can lick their fingers.

1–8 Capulet is having a cheerful conversation with his servants about the wedding preparations. One servant assures him that he will test (**try**) the cooks he hires by making them taste their own food (**lick their fingers**).

5 **Capulet.** How canst thou try them so?

Servingman. Marry, sir, 'tis an ill cook that cannot lick his own fingers. Therefore he that cannot lick his fingers goes not with me.

Capulet. Go, begone.

[*Exit* Servingman.]

10 We shall be much unfurnished for this time.
What, is my daughter gone to Friar Laurence?

10 **unfurnished:** unprepared.

Nurse. Ay, forsooth.

Capulet. Well, he may chance to do some good on her.
A peevish self-willed harlotry it is.

14 A silly, stubborn girl she is.

[*Enter* Juliet.]

15 **Nurse.** See where she comes from shrift with merry look.

Capulet. How now, my headstrong? Where have you been gadding?

Juliet. Where I have learnt me to repent the sin
Of disobedient opposition
To you and your behests, and am enjoined

19 **behests:** orders; **enjoined:** commanded.

WHEN STUDENTS STRUGGLE...

Tell students that Friar Laurence's plan is central to the action of the remaining scenes of the play. To ensure that they understand the plan, ask them to organize those steps according to who must perform them and when in a chart similar to the one on page 257. Remind them to reread lines 89–120 before they begin.

ASK STUDENTS to contribute their ideas to a class chart. As a class, discuss the potential problems that might arise with this plan.

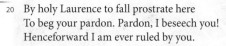

20 By holy Laurence to fall prostrate here
To beg your pardon. Pardon, I beseech you!
Henceforward I am ever ruled by you.

Capulet. Send for the County. Go tell him of this.
I'll have this knot knit up tomorrow morning.

25 **Juliet.** I met the youthful lord at Laurence' cell
And gave him what becomed love I might,
Not stepping o'er the bounds of modesty.

Capulet. Why, I am glad on't. This is well. Stand up.
This is as't should be. Let me see the County.
30 Ay, marry, go, I say, and fetch him hither.
Now, afore God, this reverend holy friar,
All our whole city is much bound to him.

Juliet. Nurse, will you go with me into my closet
To help me sort such needful ornaments
35 As you think fit to furnish me tomorrow?

Lady Capulet. No, not till Thursday. There is time enough.

Capulet. Go, nurse, go with her. We'll to church tomorrow.

[*Exeunt* Juliet *and* Nurse.]

Lady Capulet. We shall be short in our provision.
'Tis now near night.

Capulet.   Tush, I will stir about,
40 And all things shall be well, I warrant thee, wife.
Go thou to Juliet, help to deck up her.
I'll not to bed tonight; let me alone.
I'll play the housewife for this once. What, ho!
They are all forth; well, I will walk myself
45 To County Paris, to prepare him up
Against tomorrow. My heart is wondrous light,
Since this same wayward girl is so reclaimed.

[*Exeunt.*]

Scene 3 *Juliet's bedroom.*

[*Enter* Juliet *and* Nurse.]

Juliet. Ay, those attires are best; but, gentle nurse,
I pray thee leave me to myself tonight;
For I have need of many orisons
To move the heavens to smile upon my state,
5 Which, well thou knowest, is cross and full of sin.

[*Enter* Lady Capulet.]

Lady Capulet. What, are you busy, ho? Need you my help?

24 I'll have this wedding scheduled for tomorrow morning.

36–39 Lady Capulet urges her husband to wait until Thursday as originally planned. She needs time to get food (**provision**) ready for the wedding party.

39–46 Capulet is so set on Wednesday that he promises to make the arrangements himself.

3 orisons: prayers.

The Tragedy of Romeo and Juliet: Act IV, Scene 3 **257**

CLOSE READ

Analyze Author's Choices: RL 5
Irony (Sc. 2, LINES 17–37)

Tell students that, in addition to dramatic irony, playwrights sometimes incorporate situational irony into their plays. **Situational irony** is the contrast between what a character expects to happen and what actually does.

ⓘ ASK STUDENTS what is ironic about Capulet's reaction to Juliet's change of heart. (*He moves the wedding up a day, so that she will be married on Wednesday rather than Thursday.*) Have students discuss the additional irony of Capulet's comments that "afore God, this reverend holy friar, / Our whole city is much bound to him." (*If Capulet knew the friar's many secret actions, he would not be praising him. The friar has married Juliet to Romeo, is scheming to overturn Romeo's sentence of banishment, and is conspiring with Juliet to trick her father into believing she is dead.*)

Analyze Author's Choices: RL 5
Plot (Sc. 2, LINES 45–47)

Ⓙ ASK STUDENTS what moving the wedding up one day does to Friar Laurence's plan. (*It means that Juliet must take the potion Tuesday night rather than Wednesday giving the friar one less day to get in touch with Romeo and Romeo one less day to get to Verona.*)

Juliet

| Returns home and agrees to marry Paris. | → | Drinks the potion on Wednesday night, which will make her appear dead. | → | Wakes up 42 hours later in the burial vault. |

Friar Laurence

| Sends a message to Romeo. | → | Presides over the funeral of Juliet. | → | Meets Romeo and takes him to the vault to await Juliet's awakening. | → | Helps them get to Mantua. |

Analyze Character: Motivations

RL 3

(Sc. 3, LINES 14–29)

Tell students that this soliloquy gives the audience insight into Juliet's feelings as she prepares to drink the potion that will decide her fate.

K ASK STUDENTS what the first six lines of the speech reveal about Juliet's conflict. *(She knows that it is unlikely that she will see her nurse or her mother again for a long while. She expresses her fears about drinking the potion.)* Have students discuss Juliet's questioning of Friar Laurence's motives in giving her the potion. Does evidence suggest she is serious about her fears? *(She wonders if the friar has really given her a potion to kill her since he would be dishonored if his role in the plot came to light. She dismisses this suspicion, however, saying "he hath still been tried a holy man.")*

Juliet. No madam; we have culled such necessaries
As are behooveful for our state tomorrow.
So please you, let me now be left alone,
10 And let the nurse this night sit up with you;
For I am sure you have your hands full all
In this so sudden business.

Lady Capulet.   Good night.
Get thee to bed and rest, for thou hast need.

[*Exeunt* Lady Capulet *and* Nurse.]

Juliet. Farewell! God knows when we shall meet again.
15 I have a faint cold fear thrills through my veins
That almost freezes up the heat of life.
I'll call them back again to comfort me.
Nurse!—What should she do here?
My dismal scene I needs must act alone.
20 Come, vial.
What if this mixture do not work at all?
Shall I be married then tomorrow morning?
No, no! This shall forbid it. Lie thou there.

[*lays down a dagger*]

What if it be a poison which the friar
25 Subtly hath ministered to have me dead,
Lest in this marriage he should be dishonored
Because he married me before to Romeo?
I fear it is; and yet methinks it should not,
For he hath still been tried a holy man.

7–8 we have . . . tomorrow: We have picked out (**culled**) everything appropriate for the wedding tomorrow.

23 This shall forbid it: A dagger will be her alternative means of keeping from marrying Paris.

24–58 Juliet lists her various doubts and fears about what she is about to do.

Image Credits: (t) ©Everett Collection, Inc.; (tc) ©AKaiser/Shutterstock

258 Collection 4

APPLYING ACADEMIC VOCABULARY

commit	initiate

As you discuss the events in this act, incorporate the Collection 4 academic vocabulary words: *commit* and *initiate*. Ask students to explain the lengths to which Juliet is willing to go to **commit** herself to Romeo. Then ask students what events they predict her action of taking the potion will **initiate.**

30 How if, when I am laid into the tomb,
   I wake before the time that Romeo
   Come to redeem me? There's a fearful point!
   Shall I not then be stifled in the vault,
   To whose foul mouth no healthsome air breathes in,
35 And there die strangled ere my Romeo comes?
   Or, if I live, is it not very like
   The horrible conceit of death and night,
   Together with the terror of the place—
   As in a vault, an ancient receptacle
40 Where for this many hundred years the bones
   Of all my buried ancestors are packed;
   Where bloody Tybalt, yet but green in earth,
   Lies fest'ring in his shroud; where, as they say,
   At some hours in the night spirits resort—
45 Alack, alack, is it not like that I,
   So early waking—what with loathsome smells,
   And shrieks like mandrakes torn out of the earth,
   That living mortals, hearing them, run mad—
   O, if I wake, shall I not be distraught,
50 Environed with all these hideous fears,
   And madly play with my forefathers' joints,
   And pluck the mangled Tybalt from his shroud,
   And, in this rage, with some great kinsman's bone
   As with a club dash out my desp'rate brains?
55 O, look! methinks I see my cousin's ghost
   Seeking out Romeo, that did spit his body
   Upon a rapier's point. Stay, Tybalt, stay!
   Romeo, I come! this do I drink to thee.

[*She drinks and falls upon her bed within the curtains.*]

Scene 4 *Capulet's house.*

[*Enter* Lady Capulet *and* Nurse.]

Lady Capulet. Hold, take these keys and fetch more spices, nurse.

Nurse. They call for dates and quinces in the pastry.

[*Enter* Capulet.]

Capulet. Come, stir, stir, stir! The second cock hath crowed,
   The curfew bell hath rung, 'tis three o'clock.
5 Look to the baked meats, good Angelica;
   Spare not for cost.

Nurse.   Go, you cot-quean, go,
   Get you to bed! Faith, you'll be sick tomorrow
   For this night's watching.

36–43 Juliet fears the vision (**conceit**) she might have on waking in the family tomb and seeing the rotting body of Tybalt.

45–54 She fears that the smells together with the sounds of ghosts screaming might make her lose her mind and commit bizarre acts. Mandrake root was thought to look like the human form and to scream when pulled from the ground.

57 stay: stop.

2 pastry: the room where baking is done.

5 Angelica: In his happy mood, Capulet calls the nurse by her name.

6 cot-quean: a "cottage quean," or housewife. This is a joke about Capulet doing women's work (arranging the party).

CLOSE READ

Analyze Character: Motivations (Sc. 3, LINES 30–58)   RL 3

Tell students that knowing a character's motivations helps the audience make inferences about his or her inner traits.

ASK STUDENTS what Juliet lists in her speech. *(her worst fears)* What image motivates her to drink the potion in spite of her imaginings? Why? *(She sees Tybalt trying to seek revenge on Romeo from the grave. She hurries to drink the potion thinking that she might prevent Tybalt from doing harm to Romeo by joining him.)*

Analyze Author's Choices: Parallel Plots

RL 5

(Sc. 4, LINES 9–28)

Point out that the structure of a play enables audiences to follow two separate story lines that are taking place at the same time.

(M) ASK STUDENTS how this scene increases the emotional impact of Juliet's actions in the previous scene. *(The audience sees the lightheartedness of Juliet's family and feels even sorrier for her that she has to make such a difficult decision by herself. This happiness also intensifies the audience's realization of the sadness these same characters will feel when they find Juliet apparently dead.)*

Capulet. No, not a whit. What, I have watched ere now
10 All night for lesser cause, and ne'er been sick.

Lady Capulet. Ay, you have been a mouse-hunt in your time;
But I will watch you from such watching now.

[*Exeunt* Lady Capulet *and* Nurse.]

Capulet. A jealous hood, a jealous hood!

[*Enter three or four* Servants, *with spits and logs and baskets.*]
                                        Now, fellow,
What is there?

15 **First Servant.** Things for the cook, sir; but I know not what.

Capulet. Make haste, make haste. [*Exit* Servant.] Sirrah, fetch
    drier logs.
Call Peter; he will show thee where they are.

Second Servant. I have a head, sir, that will find out logs
And never trouble Peter for the matter.

20 **Capulet.** Mass, and well said, merry whoreson, ha!
Thou shalt be loggerhead. [*Exit* Servant.] Good faith, 'tis day.
The County will be here with music straight,
For so he said he would. [*music within*] I hear him near.
Nurse! Wife! What, ho! What, nurse, I say!

[*Reenter* Nurse.]

25 Go waken Juliet; go and trim her up.
I'll go and chat with Paris. Hie, make haste,
Make haste! The bridegroom he is come already:
Make haste, I say.

[*Exeunt.*]

Scene 5 *Juliet's bedroom.*

[*Enter* Nurse.]

Nurse. Mistress! what, mistress! Juliet! Fast, I warrant her, she.
Why, lamb! why, lady! Fie, you slugabed!
Why, love, I say! madam! sweetheart! Why, bride!
What, not a word? You take your pennyworths now,
5 Sleep for a week; for the next night, I warrant,
The County Paris hath set up his rest
That you shall rest but little. God forgive me,
Marry and amen, how sound is she asleep!
I needs must wake her. Madam, madam, madam!
10 Aye, let the County take you in your bed,
He'll fright you up, i' faith. Will it not be?

[*opens the curtains*]

11–13 Lord and Lady Capulet joke about his being a woman chaser (**mouse-hunt**) as a young man. He makes fun of her jealousy (**jealous hood**).

20–23 The joking between Capulet and his servants includes the mild oath **Mass,** short for "by the Mass," and **loggerhead,** a word for a stupid person as well as a pun, since the servant is searching for drier logs. **straight:** right away.

1–11 The nurse chatters as she bustles around the room. She calls Juliet a **slugabed,** or sleepyhead, who is trying to get her **pennyworths,** or small portions, of rest now, since after the wedding Paris won't let her get much sleep.

ENGLISH LANGUAGE SUPPORT

Comprehension Support Point out that dramatic irony is an important device throughout this play and especially in the last acts. Review the definition of dramatic irony. *(The audience knows something the characters do not.)* Then display a two-column chart on the board with the headings "What the Characters Know" and "What the Audience Knows." In the first column, write these two examples: (row 1) Juliet is in her bedroom asleep. (row 2) Juliet will not marry Paris on Wednesday.

ASK STUDENTS to work together to explain what the audience knows about each of these situations. Guide students to see that their extra knowledge is the dramatic irony.

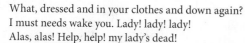

What, dressed and in your clothes and down again?
I must needs wake you. Lady! lady! lady!
Alas, alas! Help, help! my lady's dead!
15 O well-a-day that ever I was born!
Some aqua vitae, ho! My lord! my lady!

[*Enter* Lady Capulet.]

Lady Capulet. What noise is here?

Nurse.   O lamentable day!

Lady Capulet. What is the matter?

Nurse.   Look, look! O heavy day!

Lady Capulet. O me, O me! My child, my only life!
20 Revive, look up, or I will die with thee!
Help! help! Call help.

[*Enter* Capulet.]

Capulet. For shame, bring Juliet forth; her lord is come.

Nurse. She's dead, deceased; she's dead! Alack the day!

Lady Capulet. Alack the day, she's dead, she's dead, she's dead!

25 **Capulet.** Ha! let me see her. Out alas! she's cold,
Her blood is settled, and her joints are stiff;
Life and these lips have long been separated.
Death lies on her like an untimely frost
Upon the sweetest flower of all the field.

30 **Nurse.** O lamentable day!

Lady Capulet.   O woeful time!

Capulet. Death, that hath ta'en her hence to make me wail,
Ties up my tongue and will not let me speak.

[*Enter* Friar Laurence *and* Paris, *with* Musicians.]

Friar Laurence. Come, is the bride ready to go to church?

Capulet. Ready to go, but never to return.
35 O son, the night before thy wedding day
Hath death lain with thy wife. See, there she lies,
Flower as she was, deflowered by him.
Death is my son-in-law, Death is my heir;
My daughter he hath wedded. I will die
40 And leave him all. Life, living, all is Death's.

Paris. Have I thought long to see this morning's face,
And doth it give me such a sight as this?

Lady Capulet. Accursed, unhappy, wretched, hateful day!
Most miserable hour that e'er time saw

17 lamentable: filled with grief.

40 Life ... Death's: My life, my possessions, and everything else of mine belongs to Death.

TEACH

CLOSE READ

Interpret Figurative Language (Sc. 5, LINES 12–29)   RL 4

Remind students that figurative language is a powerful way to express emotions and ideas without wordy explanations.

N ASK STUDENTS what ideas and feelings Lord Capulet conveys in the simile in lines 28–29. (*He compares Juliet to a flower that has been killed by an untimely frost. In other words, she died before her time.*)

Analyze Author's Choices   RL 5
(Sc. 5, LINES 32–42)

Remind students that dramatic irony occurs when the audience knows something that the characters do not.

O CITE TEXT EVIDENCE How is Capulet's description of Death an example of dramatic irony in this situation? (*Capulet refers to Death as Juliet's husband and his son-in-law in lines 35–39. Capulet does not realize that Juliet is already married to Romeo, and that she and Romeo will be dead by the end of the play, knowledge the audience already has.*)

Strategies for Annotation   🖉 🗐 *Annotate it!*

Interpret Figurative Language   RL 4

Explain that personification is a figure of speech that gives inanimate objects or abstract concepts human characteristics. Encourage students to use their eBook annotation tools to analyze the use of personification in lines 34–40:

- Highlight the phrases that personify Death.
- On a note, explain what Death is compared to.
- Discuss in a small group how the use of personification reveals Lord Capulet's feelings and adds to the emotional impact of the scene.

O son, the night before thy wedding day

Hath death lain with thy wife. See, there she lies,

Flower as she was, deflowered by him.

Death is my son-in-law, Death is my heir;

Analyze Character: Motivations

RL 3

(Sc. 5, LINES 65–83)

Ask a student volunteer to read these lines aloud. Direct students to focus on the friar's purpose in this speech as well as the challenges that he faces in delivering it.

P **CITE TEXT EVIDENCE** Ask students what the friar's first lines reveal about the setting and his initial purpose. *(Juliet's bedroom is a scene of chaos. He says, "Peace, ho, for shame! Confusion's cure lives not / In these confusions." His initial purpose is to restore order.)* According to Friar Laurence, what is the highest form of human achievement? *(In lines 70-75, he says it is to live in heaven.)* Why does he tell them this? *(So that they will be happy for Juliet.)* Why does he urge them to get Juliet to the church for her funeral in the last lines of his speech? *(The friar knows that the potion will last only for a certain amount of time.)*

---

45 In lasting labor of his pilgrimage!
    But one, poor one, one poor and loving child,
    But one thing to rejoice and solace in,
    And cruel Death hath catched it from my sight!

    Nurse. O woe! O woeful, woeful, woeful day!
50 Most lamentable day, most woeful day
    That ever, ever I did yet behold!
    O day! O day! O day! O hateful day!
    Never was seen so black a day as this.
    O woeful day! O woeful day!

55 **Paris.** Beguiled, divorced, wronged, spited, slain!
    Most detestable Death, by thee beguiled,
    By cruel, cruel thee quite overthrown!
    O love! O life! not life, but love in death!

    Capulet. Despised, distressed, hated, martyred, killed!
60 Uncomfortable time, why camest thou now
    To murder, murder our solemnity?
    O child! O child! my soul, and not my child!
    Dead art thou, dead! alack, my child is dead,
    And with my child my joys are buried!

65 **Friar Laurence.** Peace, ho, for shame! Confusion's cure lives not
    In these confusions. Heaven and yourself
    Had part in this fair maid! now heaven hath all,
    And all the better is it for the maid.
    Your part in her you could not keep from death,
70 But heaven keeps his part in eternal life.
    The most you sought was her promotion,
    For 'twas your heaven she should be advanced;
    And weep ye now, seeing she is advanced
    Above the clouds, as high as heaven itself?
75 O, in this love, you love your child so ill
    That you run mad, seeing that she is well.
    She's not well married that lives married long,
    But she's best married that dies married young.
    Dry up your tears and stick your rosemary
80 On this fair corse, and, as the custom is,
    In all her best array bear her to church;
    For though fond nature bids us all lament,
    Yet nature's tears are reason's merriment.

    Capulet. All things that we ordained festival
85 Turn from their office to black funeral—
    Our instruments to melancholy bells,
    Our wedding cheer to a sad burial feast;

46–48 But one . . . my sight: I had only one child to make me happy, and Death has taken (**catched**) her from me.

55 Beguiled: tricked

60–61 why . . . solemnity: Why did Death have to come to murder our celebration?

65–78 The friar says that the cure for disaster (**confusion**) cannot be found in cries of grief. Juliet's family and heaven once shared her; now heaven has all of her. All the family ever wanted was the best for her; now she's in heaven—what could be better than that? It is best to die young, when the soul is still pure, without sin.

79–80 stick . . . corse: Put rosemary, an herb, on her corpse.

82–83 though . . . merriment: Though it's natural to cry, common sense tells us we should rejoice for the dead.

84 ordained festival: intended for the wedding.

TO CHALLENGE STUDENTS . . .

Analyze Shakespeare's Syntax Discuss with students how Shakespeare inverts word order for effect, for emphasis, and to better fit with his poetic meter.

ASK STUDENTS to examine lines 56, 60, 63, 65, and 73. Have them explain Shakespeare's reason in each line for the inversion. *(The inversions in lines 56 and 65 conform to meter. The inversion in line 60 creates a dramatic effect. The inversion in line 63 creates emphasis [on* dead*]. The inversion in line 73 creates emphasis [on* weep *and* now*].)*

Our solemn hymns to sullen dirges change;
Our bridal flowers serve for a buried corse;
90 And all things change them to the contrary.

Friar Laurence. Sir, go you in; and, madam, go with him;
And go, Sir Paris. Every one prepare
To follow this fair corse unto her grave.
The heavens do lower upon you for some ill;
95 Move them no more by crossing their high will.

[*Exeunt* Capulet, Lady Capulet, Paris, *and* Friar.]

First Musician. Faith, we may put up our pipes, and be gone.

Nurse. Honest good fellows, ah, put up, put up,
For well you know this is a pitiful case.

[*Exit.*]

Second Musician. Aye, by my troth, the case may be amended.

[*Enter* Peter.]

100 **Peter.** Musicians, oh, musicians, "Heart's ease, heart's ease." Oh,
an you will have me live, play "Heart's ease."

First Musician. Why "Heart's ease"?

Peter. Oh, musicians, because my heart itself plays "My heart is
full of woe." Oh, play me some merry dump, to comfort me.

105 **First Musician.** Not a dump we, 'tis no time to play now.

Peter. You will not, then?

First Musician. No.

Peter. I will then give it you soundly.

First Musician. What will you give us?

88 sullen dirges: sad, mournful tunes.

94–95 The heavens ... will: The fates (**heavens**) frown on you for some wrong you have done. Don't tempt them by refusing to accept their will (Juliet's death).

Image Credits: (t) ©Artem Furman/Shutterstock; (tl) ©AKaiser/Shutterstock

The Tragedy of Romeo and Juliet: Act IV, Scene 5 **263**

CLOSE READ

Analyze Language: Puns RL 4
(Sc. 5, LINES 96–99)

Point out that once again a comic scene follows a scene of high emotion.

Q ASK STUDENTS to note that the musician is talking about the case for his instrument. What "case" is the nurse referring to? (*The case is the situation of Juliet's apparent death.*)

WHEN STUDENTS STRUGGLE...

Remind students that paraphrasing the words of a character can help them better understand the meaning. Have students work in pairs to restate what Friar Laurence says in lines 77–83 and 94–95. Tell them to consult the margin notes for explanations of difficult lines.

ASK STUDENTS to share their paraphrases. Discuss with them the challenges of Friar Laurence's role in this scene with the family.

Analyze Author's Choices

RL 5

(Sc. 5, LINES 110–124)

As students read this scene, tell them that Peter, who is usually accompanying the nurse and being bossed around by her, is the one bossing around the musicians, enjoying his chance to be in charge. Remind students that this comic scene serves a variety of purposes.

(R) ASK STUDENTS what the lightheartedness of this scene would suggest to the audience who knows the truth of Juliet's apparent death. *(The audience might believe, at least temporarily, that there is hope for a happy ending.)*

COLLABORATIVE DISCUSSION Have students consider how it is possible for the audience to have a sense of hope about Romeo and Juliet's situation even when they know the play ends tragically. Accept all reasonable responses.

ASK STUDENTS to share any questions they generated in the course of reading and discussing the selection.

110 **Peter.** No money, on my faith, but the gleek. I will give you the minstrel.

First Musician. Then will I give you the serving creature.

Peter. Then will I lay the serving creature's dagger on your pate. I will carry no crotchets. I'll re you, I'll fa you, do you note me?

113 pate: top of the head.

115 **First Musician.** An you re us and fa us, you note us.

Second Musician. Pray you put up your dagger, and put out your wit.

Peter. Then have at you with my wit! I will drybeat you with an iron wit, and put up my iron dagger. Answer me like men:

120
    "When griping grief the heart doth wound
    And doleful dumps the mind oppress,
    Then music with her " "He ask—"
Why "silver sound"? Why "music with her silver sound"?—What say you, Simon Catling?

125 **First Musician.** Marry, sir, because silver hath a sweet sound.

Peter. Pretty! What say you, Hugh Rebeck?

Second Musician. I say "silver sound" because musicians sound for silver.

Peter. Pretty too! What say you, James Soundpost?

130 **Third Musician.** Faith, I know not what to say.

Peter. Oh, I cry you mercy, you are the singer. I will say for you. It is "music with her silver sound" because musicians have no gold for sounding.
    "Then music with her silver sound
135   With speedy help doth lend redress."

[*Exit.*]

First Musician. What a pestilent knave is this same!

136 pestilent: bothersome; irritating.

Second Musician. Hang him, Jack! Come, we'll in here. Tarry for the mourners, and stay dinner.

[*Exeunt.*]

COLLABORATIVE DISCUSSION With a partner, discuss the measures taken by Juliet and Friar Laurence to fool Juliet's family. Do you agree with their plan and think there were no other options, or do you think the plan was selfish or unwise? Support your ideas with details from the play.

264 Collection 4

Analyzing the Text

RL 2, RL 3,
RL 4, RL 5, W 10, SL 4

Cite Text Evidence   Support your responses with evidence from the selection.

1. **Analyze** Review Juliet's dialogue with Paris in Scene 1. If Juliet had never met Romeo, might she have fallen in love with Paris? Explain your response.

2. **Identify** Shakespeare often employs a literary technique known as dramatic irony. **Dramatic irony** exists when the reader or viewer knows something that one or more of the characters do not. For example, when Paris asks Juliet to confess to Friar Laurence that she loves him, she carefully avoids denying it. We know that Juliet loves Romeo, not Paris. Identify two other examples of dramatic irony in Act IV. Explain how these ironic moments contribute to the building tension in the play.

3. **Analyze** In Scene 2, how does Shakespeare increase the pace of the plot even further? What effect is this likely to have on the audience?

4. **Interpret** What fears does Juliet have before going through with Friar Laurence's plan? What do her fears reveal about her state of mind?

5. **Compare** Juliet drinks the sleeping potion, despite her fears. What does this reveal about her character? Has she changed from the beginning of the play, before she met Romeo? Explain your response.

6. **Analyze** Shakespeare includes a humorous exchange between Peter and the musicians at the end of Act IV, right after Juliet's family discovers her body. What is the impact of this choice on the audience? What message is conveyed by having a humorous scene immediately follow a tragic one?

PERFORMANCE TASK

Speaking and Writing Activity: Dramatic Reading With a small group, prepare a dramatic reading of Scene 4 and Scene 5 (lines 1–21).

1. Assign roles to each member of the group.

2. Read over your role and memorize your lines. Notice the excitement expressed by the characters in Scene 4 and the grief they express in Scene 5.

3. Make notes on how you will convey the emotion of the words on the page in your reading. Think about when you might change your tone, adjust your voice, or read more quickly or slowly.

4. Give your dramatic reading. Try to capture the emotion of the words on the page as Shakespeare wrote them.

PERFORMANCE TASK

W 10

Speaking and Writing Activity: Dramatic Reading Assign characters from Scenes 4 and 5. Have group members perform staged readings of the dialogue. Model reading excerpts with tones of excitement (Scene 4, lines 1–4) and grief (Scene 5, lines 19–21). Suggest that students think back and make notes about situations in their own lives when they were excited or sad in order to understand the tone or vocal level that would be appropriate in their dramatic reading.

PRACTICE & APPLY

Analyzing the Text

RL 2, RL 3, RL 4, RL 5

Possible answers:

1. *Based on the dialogue, they do not seem like a good match. Juliet is clever with words, responding to Paris's remarks in ways that either confuse him or change the subject without revealing what she is truly thinking. Paris cannot match her wordplay, nor can he understand that she does not love him. The spoiled son of a rich man who is used to getting everything he wants, he cannot realize why Juliet might take offense at a comment like "Thy face is mine, and thou hast slandered it" (line 35).*

2. *Examples include Paris's comment that Juliet's excessive weeping is because of Tybalt's death (Scene 1, line 6), when the audience knows she cries over Romeo's exile and her impending marriage to Paris. Also, Capulet praises Friar Laurence—"this reverend holy friar, / All our whole city is much bound to him" (Scene 2, lines 31–32)—not realizing that the Friar is plotting to undermine the wedding.*

3. *Capulet is so pleased that Juliet has agreed to marry Paris that he moves the date from Thursday back to Wednesday (lines 23–26). This increases the pace and the tension for the audience because events have already been unfolding very quickly, and the dangerous plan that Juliet and the friar have devised may fail now that there is less time for all of its elements to fall into place.*

4. *She wonders if perhaps she can't trust Friar Laurence after all—that maybe he is not truly on her side. Then she talks about her fear of waking up in a tomb surrounded by dead members of her family. Her fears show that the haste with which she has made important decisions has contributed to her mental state of confusion and anxiety.*

5. *She is taking control of her own destiny and facing her fears. At the beginning of the play she is sheltered and doesn't have to do much for herself or openly challenge her parents. Now she is deciding to take matters into her own hands and is showing determination.*

6. *Shakespeare uses humor to provide the audience with some comic relief after an intense, tragic scene. The exchange relieves some of the tension and grief, and it conveys the message that life still goes on in the midst of tragedy.*

TEACH

CLOSE READ

AS YOU READ Direct students to use the As You Read note to focus their reading.

Analyze Author's Choices: Parallel Plots (Sc. 1, LINES 1–32)   RL 5

Review with students the events of Act IV. Remind them that Romeo is unaware of these events at the time that the scene opens.

A **ASK STUDENTS** why Shakespeare opens this scene with Romeo in a joyful mood. *(His joy heightens the tragedy of the news he receives.)*

Discuss with students how the historical context of the play affects the action. Without forms of modern communication, Romeo is totally dependent upon messengers to bring him information.

B **ASK STUDENTS** why Romeo must repeat his request for news of Juliet twice. What does Balthasar's response suggest that he is doing? *(Balthasar is trying to avoid giving him the news that Juliet is dead.)* Ask students how Balthasar came by this news. *(He saw the procession take Juliet to the vault and hastened to tell Romeo.)* Have students note the description of Romeo as "pale and wild." What might be foreshadowed by these details? *(Romeo will do something rash once he gets back to Verona.)*

AS YOU READ Notice the unexpected events, misunderstandings, and examples of poor timing that finally bring the play to its tragic end. Write down any questions you generate during reading.

ACT V

Scene 1 *A street in Mantua.*

[Enter Romeo.]

A
Romeo. If I may trust the flattering truth of sleep,
My dreams presage some joyful news at hand.
My bosom's lord sits lightly in his throne,
And all this day an unaccustomed spirit
5 Lifts me above the ground with cheerful thoughts.
I dreamt my lady came and found me dead
(Strange dream that gives a dead man leave to think!)
And breathed such life with kisses in my lips
That I revived and was an emperor.
10 Ah me! how sweet is love itself possessed,
When but love's shadows are so rich in joy!

[Enter Romeo's servant, Balthasar, *booted.]*

B
News from Verona! How now, Balthasar?
Dost thou not bring me letters from the friar?
How doth my lady? Is my father well?
15 How fares my Juliet? That I ask again,
For nothing can be ill if she be well.

Balthasar. Then she is well, and nothing can be ill.
Her body sleeps in Capels' monument,
And her immortal part with angels lives.
20 I saw her laid low in her kindred's vault
And presently took post to tell it you.
O, pardon me for bringing these ill news,
Since you did leave it for my office, sir.

Romeo. Is it e'en so? Then I defy you, stars!
25 Thou knowst my lodging. Get me ink and paper
And hire posthorses. I will hence tonight.

Balthasar. I do beseech you, sir, have patience.
Your looks are pale and wild and do import
Some misadventure.

Romeo.   Tush, thou art deceived.
30 Leave me and do the thing I bid thee do.
Hast thou no letters to me from the friar?

Balthasar. No, my good lord.

17–19 Balthasar replies that Juliet is well, since although her body lies in the Capulets' (**Capels'**) burial vault, her soul (**her immortal part**) is with the angels.

21 presently took post: immediately rode (to Mantua).

23 you did . . . office: you gave me the duty of reporting important news to you.

24 I . . . stars: Romeo angrily challenges fate, which has caused him so much grief.

28–29 import some misadventure: suggest that something bad will happen.

Close Read Screencasts   View It!

Modeled Discussions

Have students pair up and do an independent close read of the following passage—Romeo's purchase of poison (Act V, Scene 1, lines 72–84).

As a class, discuss the passage.

Romeo.   No matter. Get thee gone
And hire those horses. I'll be with thee straight.

[*Exit* Balthasar.]

Well, Juliet, I will lie with thee tonight.

35   Let's see for means. O mischief, thou art swift
To enter in the thoughts of desperate men!
I do remember an apothecary,
And hereabouts he dwells, which late I noted
In tattered weeds, with overwhelming brows,

40   Culling of simples. Meager were his looks,
Sharp misery had worn him to the bones;
And in his needy shop a tortoise hung,
An alligator stuffed, and other skins
Of ill-shaped fishes; and about his shelves

45   A beggarly account of empty boxes,
Green earthen pots, bladders, and musty seeds,
Remnants of packthread, and old cakes of roses
Were thinly scattered, to make up a show.
Noting this penury, to myself I said,

50   "An if a man did need a poison now
Whose sale is present death in Mantua,
Here lives a caitiff wretch would sell it him."
O, this same thought did but forerun my need,
And this same needy man must sell it me.

55   As I remember, this should be the house.
Being holiday, the beggar's shop is shut.
What, ho! apothecary!

[*Enter* Apothecary.]

Apothecary.   Who calls so loud?

Romeo. Come hither, man. I see that thou art poor.
Hold, there is forty ducats. Let me have

60   A dram of poison, such soon-speeding gear
As will disperse itself through all the veins
That the life-weary taker may fall dead,
And that the trunk may be discharged of breath
As violently as hasty powder fired

65   Doth hurry from the fatal cannon's womb.

Apothecary. Such mortal drugs I have; but Mantua's law
Is death to any he that utters them.

Romeo. Art thou so bare and full of wretchedness
And fearest to die? Famine is in thy cheeks,

70   Need and oppression starveth in thine eyes,
Contempt and beggary hangs upon thy back:

**35–40 Let's . . .
means:** Let me find a
way (to join Juliet in
death); **apothecary:**
pharmacist; **tattered
weeds:** ragged clothes;
culling of simples:
selecting herbs.

47 cakes of roses: rose
petals pressed together
to create a perfume.

49 penury: poverty.

**50–52 "An if a man . . .
sell it him":** Though it is
a crime to sell poison in
Mantua, the apothecary
is such a miserable
(**caitiff**) wretch that he
would probably do it for
the money.

59 ducats: gold coins.

60–65 Romeo wants
fast-acting (**soon-
speeding**) poison that
will work as quickly as
gunpowder exploding in
a cannon.

67 any . . . them: any
person who dispenses or
sells them.

ENGLISH LANGUAGE SUPPORT

Culture: Historical Background Provide students with these facts:

- Apothecaries were similar to pharmacists. In Shakespeare's time, however, they were the lowest level of medical practitioner, below physicians and surgeons.

- They prepared and sold the drugs prescribed by a physician.

- Many apothecaries were dishonest, selling fake prescriptions to those unable to afford them. This apothecary is very poor, but he appears honest, since he hesitates to sell Romeo what he needs.

ASK STUDENTS to reread the description of the apothecary. Help them identify phrases that show his poverty.

CLOSE READ

Analyze Character: Motivations (Sc. 1, LINES 34–57)   RL 3

Have students consider what they know of Romeo's character. As they read this passage, have them think about how those traits are or are not illustrated in the decisions that he makes.

C **ASK STUDENTS** to explain what Romeo means in line 34. (*Romeo intends to kill himself so that he can be with Juliet in death.*) Have them discuss whether he considers his options or plunges immediately into action. Is his approach consistent with the way he has acted in the past? Explain. (*As he has in the past, Romeo plunges into action without thinking of possible options, such as consulting Friar Laurence, or consequences, such as what will happen when he returns to Verona.*) What does Romeo want from the apothecary? Have students explain what Romeo thinks will motivate the apothecary to help him. (*Romeo wants poison from the apothecary. He believes that the extreme poverty of the apothecary will make him happy to sell it to Romeo.*)

Analyze Author's Choices: Irony (Sc. 1, LINES 66–71)   RL 5

Remind students that irony is a tool used by dramatists to bring out ideas.

D **CITE TEXT EVIDENCE** Have students explain how Romeo uses irony to persuade the apothecary to sell him what he needs. (*The apothecary originally protests that if he sells poison to Romeo and is caught, he will be put to death. Romeo points out the irony of his fear—since the apothecary is poor, he is living an existence more miserable than death.*)

TEACH

CLOSE READ

Analyze Word Choice

RL 4

(Sc. 1, LINES 75–86)

Remind students that the language of Shakespeare's play conveys more than its literal meaning. Direct students to the definition of *cordial* in the side margin.

E ASK STUDENTS why Romeo refers to the poison as a "cordial." *(Like a cordial, or a medicinal drink, the poison will restore Juliet to him when he joins her in death.)*

Analyze Author's Choices: Parallel Plots

RL 5

(Sc. 2, LINES 1–20)

Explain that students can expect the action to move quickly because this is the last act of the play. Review the significance of Friar Laurence's letter to Romeo and how he plans to deliver it.

F ASK STUDENTS why Friar John failed to deliver the letter. *(He was detained while quarantined for possibly carrying a plague. Believing the letter to be infected as well, messengers refused to carry it further.)* How does Friar John's news affect Friar Laurence? Why? *(Friar Laurence realizes that Romeo did not get his message. This could have grave consequences.)z*

The world is not thy friend, nor the world's law;
The world affords no law to make thee rich;
Then be not poor, but break it and take this.

75 **Apothecary.** My poverty but not my will consents.

E **Romeo.** I pay thy poverty and not thy will.

Apothecary. Put this in any liquid thing you will
And drink it off, and if you had the strength
Of twenty men, it would dispatch you straight.

80 **Romeo.** There is thy gold—worse poison to men's souls,
Doing more murder in this loathsome world,
Than these poor compounds that thou mayst not sell.
I sell thee poison; thou hast sold me none.
Farewell. Buy food and get thyself in flesh.

85 Come, cordial and not poison, go with me
To Juliet's grave; for there must I use thee.

[*Exeunt.*]

Scene 2 *Friar Laurence's cell in Verona.*

[*Enter* Friar John.]

Friar John. Holy Franciscan friar, brother, ho!

[*Enter* Friar Laurence.]

F **Friar Laurence.** This same should be the voice of Friar John.
Welcome from Mantua. What says Romeo?
Or, if his mind be writ, give me his letter.

5 **Friar John.** Going to find a barefoot brother out,
One of our order to associate me,
Here in this city visiting the sick,
And finding him, the searchers of the town,
Suspecting that we both were in a house

10 Where the infectious pestilence did reign,
Sealed up the doors, and would not let us forth,
So that my speed to Mantua there was stayed.

Friar Laurence. Who bare my letter, then, to Romeo?

Friar John. I could not send it—here it is again—

15 Nor get a messenger to bring it thee,
So fearful were they of infection.

Friar Laurence. Unhappy fortune! By my brotherhood,
The letter was not nice, but full of charge,
Of dear import, and the neglecting it

20 May do much danger. Friar John, go hence,

72–74 Romeo urges the apothecary to improve his situation by breaking the law and selling him the poison.

75 I'm doing this for the money, not because I think it's right.

79 dispatch you straight: kill you instantly.

85 Romeo refers to the poison as a **cordial**, a drink believed to be good for the heart.

5–12 Friar John asked another friar (**barefoot brother**) to go with him to Mantua. The health officials of the town, believing that the friars had come into contact with a deadly plague (**infectious pestilence**), locked them up to keep them from infecting others.

13 bare: carried (bore).

18–20 The letter wasn't trivial (**nice**) but contained a message of great importance (**dear import**). The fact that it wasn't sent (**neglecting it**) may cause great harm.

WHEN STUDENTS STRUGGLE . . .

Point out that the failure of Friar John to deliver Friar Laurence's letter is another complication in the plot. This event is the cause of other events, some of which have already occurred and some of which might occur. Have students identify the effects that they know of already as well as those that they can predict. Have them organize their cause and effects in a chart similar to the one shown.

ASK STUDENTS to complete their charts and share them in a small group. Have them explain what must happen in order for the characters to avoid tragedy.

Get me an iron crow and bring it straight
Unto my cell.

Friar John. Brother, I'll go and bring it thee.

[*Exit.*]

Friar Laurence. Now must I to the monument alone.
Within this three hours will fair Juliet wake.
25 She will beshrew me much that Romeo
Hath had no notice of these accidents;
But I will write again to Mantua,
And keep her at my cell till Romeo come—
Poor living corse, closed in a dead man's tomb!

[*Exit.*]

Scene 3 *The cemetery that contains the Capulets' tomb.*

[*Enter* Paris *and his* Page *with flowers and a torch.*]

Paris. Give me thy torch, boy. Hence, and stand aloof.
Yet put it out, for I would not be seen.
Under yond yew tree lay thee all along,
Holding thine ear close to the hollow ground.
5 So shall no foot upon the churchyard tread
(Being loose, unfirm, with digging up of graves)
But thou shalt hear it. Whistle then to me,
As signal that thou hearst something approach.
Give me those flowers. Do as I bid thee, go.

10 **Page** [*aside*]. I am almost afraid to stand alone
Here in the churchyard; yet I will adventure.

[*withdraws*]

21 iron crow: crowbar.

25–26 She . . . accidents: She will be furious with me when she learns that Romeo doesn't know what has happened.

1 aloof: some distance away.

The Tragedy of Romeo and Juliet: Act V, Scene 3 **269**

Image Credits: (t) ©Everett Collection, Inc.; (tr) ©AKaiser/Shutterstock

CLOSE READ

Analyze Author's Choices   RL 5
(Sc. 2, LINES 23–29)

G **ASK STUDENTS** to explain the irony of Friar Laurence's fear of what might happen as a result of Friar John's news. *(He thinks the worst that could happen is that Juliet will awaken and Romeo won't be there. The irony is that far greater tragedy will result from the letter not being delivered.)*

Analyze Character: RL 3
Motivations (Sc. 3, LINES 1–11)

Remind students that the appearances of Paris in the play have not revealed much about his character. As they read Scene 3, have them note details that reveal more about his traits.

H **ASK STUDENTS** what they can infer about the reason that Paris is in the graveyard. What does this motive reveal about his character? *(He has flowers, suggesting that he has come to leave them for Juliet. This implies that he did have affection for her.)*

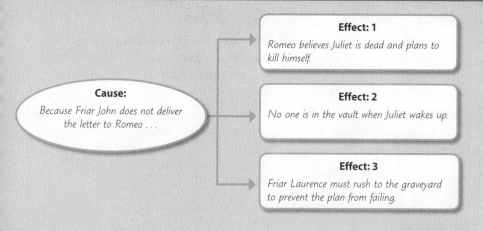

Effect: 1
Romeo believes Juliet is dead and plans to kill himself.

Cause:
Because Friar John does not deliver the letter to Romeo . . .

Effect: 2
No one is in the vault when Juliet wakes up.

Effect: 3
Friar Laurence must rush to the graveyard to prevent the plan from failing.

TEACH

CLOSE READ

Analyze Character: Motivations (Sc. 3, LINES 22–39)

RL 3

Point out that in this speech to Balthasar, Romeo explains why he must enter the vault. Remind students to consider what they know about his true intentions.

Ⓘ CITE TEXT EVIDENCE Have students explain the two reasons that Romeo states for entering the tomb. What is the third reason that he implies? *(In lines 28–32, he tells Balthasar that he wants to see Juliet's face one last time and take a ring from her finger. In lines 34 and 37, he hints that his third reason is to do violence, likely to himself.)* Ask students whether Balthasar is convinced by Romeo's explanation. Why or why not? *(He is not convinced. He says: "I'll hide me hereabout. / His looks I fear, and his intents I doubt.")*

Paris. Sweet flower, with flowers thy bridal bed I strew

[*He strews the tomb with flowers.*]

(O woe! thy canopy is dust and stones)
Which with sweet water nightly I will dew;
15   Or, wanting that, with tears distilled by moans.
The obsequies that I for thee will keep
Nightly shall be to strew thy grave and weep.

[*The* Page *whistles.*]

The boy gives warning something doth approach.
What cursed foot wanders this way tonight
20   To cross my obsequies and true love's rite?
What, with a torch? Muffle me, night, awhile.

[*withdraws*]

[*Enter* Romeo *and* Balthasar *with a torch, a mattock, and a crow of iron.*]

Romeo. Give me that mattock and the wrenching iron.
Hold, take this letter. Early in the morning
See thou deliver it to my lord and father.
25   Give me the light. Upon thy life I charge thee,
Whate'er thou hearest or seest, stand all aloof
And do not interrupt me in my course.
Why I descend into this bed of death
Is partly to behold my lady's face,
30   But chiefly to take thence from her dead finger
A precious ring—a ring that I must use
In dear employment. Therefore hence, be gone.
But if thou, jealous, dost return to pry
In what I farther shall intend to do,
35   By heaven, I will tear thee joint by joint
And strew this hungry churchyard with thy limbs.
The time and my intents are savage-wild,
More fierce and more inexorable far
Than empty tigers or the roaring sea.

40   **Balthasar.** I will be gone, sir, and not trouble you.

Romeo. So shalt thou show me friendship. Take thou that.
Live, and be prosperous; and farewell, good fellow.

Balthasar [*aside*]. For all this same, I'll hide me hereabout.
His looks I fear, and his intents I doubt.

[*withdraws*]

45   **Romeo.** Thou detestable maw, thou womb of death,
Gorged with the dearest morsel of the earth,

12–17 Paris promises to decorate Juliet's grave with flowers and sprinkle it with either perfume (**sweet water**) or his tears. He will perform these honoring rites (**obsequies**) every night.

20 cross: interfere with.

21 muffle: hide.

mattock . . . iron: an ax and a crowbar.

32 in dear employment: for an important purpose.

33 jealous: curious.

37–39 Romeo's intention is more unstoppable (**inexorable**) than hungry (**empty**) tigers or the waves of an ocean.

45–48 Romeo addresses the tomb as though it were devouring people. He calls it a hateful stomach (**detestable maw**) that is filled (**gorged**) with Juliet, the **dearest morsel of the earth**.

270   Collection 4

WHEN STUDENTS STRUGGLE . . .

To guide students' comprehension of this scene, display a sketch of the graveyard on the board with the Capulet mausoleum marked. Write these characters' names on the board: Page, Paris, Romeo, Balthasar. Have students reread these lines: 1–11, 25–27, 40–44.

ASK STUDENTS to explain where each of the characters is in relationship to the vault. Ask them why the locations of the page and Balthasar might be important later.

Thus I enforce thy rotten jaws to open,
And in despite I'll cram thee with more food.

[Romeo *opens the tomb.*]

Paris. This is that banish'd haughty Montague
50 That murdered my love's cousin—with which grief
It is supposed the fair creature died—
And here is come to do some villainous shame
To the dead bodies. I will apprehend him.
Stop thy unhallowed toil, vile Montague!
55 Can vengeance be pursued further than death?
Condemnéd villain, I do apprehend thee.
Obey, and go with me; for thou must die.

Romeo. I must indeed; and therefore came I hither.
Good gentle youth, tempt not a desp'rate man.
60 Fly hence and leave me. Think upon these gone;
Let them affright thee. I beseech thee, youth,
Put not another sin upon my head
By urging me to fury. O, be gone!
By heaven, I love thee better than myself.
65 For I come hither armed against myself.
Stay not, be gone. Live, and hereafter say
A madman's mercy bid thee run away.

Paris. I do defy thy conjuration
And apprehend thee for a felon here.

70 **Romeo.** Wilt thou provoke me? Then have at thee, boy!

[*They fight.*]

Page. O Lord, they fight! I will go call the watch.

[*Exit.*]

Paris. O, I am slain! [*falls*] If thou be merciful,
Open the tomb, lay me with Juliet.

[*dies*]

Romeo. In faith, I will. Let me peruse this face.
75 Mercutio's kinsman, noble County Paris!
What said my man when my betosséd soul
Did not attend him as we rode? I think
He told me Paris should have married Juliet.
Said he not so? or did I dream it so?
80 Or am I mad, hearing him talk of Juliet,
To think it was so? O, give me thy hand,
One writ with me in sour misfortune's book!
I'll bury thee in a triumphant grave.
A grave? O, no, a lantern, slaughtered youth,

49–53 Recognizing Romeo, Paris speaks these first few lines to himself. He is angry with Romeo, believing that Romeo's killing Tybalt caused Juliet to die of grief.

68 I reject your appeal.

82 Romeo notes that, like himself, Paris has been a victim of bad luck.

84–87 Romeo will bury Paris with Juliet, whose beauty fills the tomb with light. Paris' corpse (**Death**) is being buried (**interred**) by a dead man in that Romeo expects to be dead soon.

Analyze Character: Motivations (Sc. 3, LINES 49–70)   RL 3

Remind students that misunderstanding is a major reason why tragic events occur.

J ASK STUDENTS to explain Paris's perception of Romeo and his presence at the graveyard. For what does Paris blame Romeo? *(Paris thinks that Romeo is the enemy, since he is a Montague. He thinks that he has come to do harm to the graves [lines 52–52]. He also thinks that Romeo is the cause of Juliet's death, since it is believed that Juliet died of grief over Tybalt's death.)*

Tell students that, like people in real life, sometimes characters rise to the occasion and show their best side when under pressure.

K ASK STUDENTS what Romeo means in lines 61–63 when he says, "I beseech thee, youth, / Put not another sin upon my head / By urging me to fury." What qualities do his words in this speech show? *(Romeo begs Paris to leave and not to engage him in a fight. He doesn't want another death on his conscience, nor does he want to be distracted from his plan to be with Juliet.)*

ENGLISH LANGUAGE SUPPORT

Comprehension Support To help students understand Paris's role in this final scene, project lines 49–56 on a whiteboard. Invite volunteers to mark up the text. Remind students that they may reorder the sentences to help understand them:

- Highlight in yellow what Paris accuses Romeo of having done and the effect of that action.
- Highlight in blue what Paris suspects Romeo is doing in the graveyard.

ASK STUDENTS to explain what Paris is feeling when he sees Romeo and why he confronts him.

That murdered my love's cousin—with which grief

It is supposed the fair creature died—

And here is come to do some villainous shame

To the dead bodies. I will apprehend him

Analyze Author's Choices RL 5

(Sc. 3, LINES 88–120)

Ask a student volunteer to read Romeo's final soliloquy aloud. Discuss the actions he might be taking as he speaks these words.

L CITE TEXT EVIDENCE Have students identify the part of the speech that reminds the audience what they know about Juliet's death. *(In lines 91–96, Romeo comments on how alive Juliet looks, even though she has been dead for almost two days. He says that death "Hath had no power yet upon thy beauty" and "Beauty's ensign yet is crimson in thy lips and in thy cheeks." [lines 93–95] These lines remind the audience that Juliet indeed is alive.)* Have students recall the specifications that Romeo gave the apothecary for what kind of poison he wanted. What is the irony of Romeo having received what he requested? *(He dies just before Friar Laurence arrives. A slower poison might have allowed Friar Laurence to revive him.)* Why are Romeo's last words ("Thus with a kiss I die.") also ironic? *(They merge love and death, two forces the couple would have been better off keeping separate.)*

85 For here lies Juliet, and her beauty makes
This vault a feasting presence full of light.
Death, lie thou there, by a dead man interred.

[*lays* Paris *in the tomb*]

How oft when men are at the point of death
Have they been merry! which their keepers call
90 A lightning before death. O, how may I
Call this a lightning? O my love! my wife!
Death, that hath sucked the honey of thy breath,
Hath had no power yet upon thy beauty.
Thou art not conquered. Beauty's ensign yet
95 Is crimson in thy lips and in thy cheeks,
And death's pale flag is not advanced there.
Tybalt, liest thou there in thy bloody sheet?
O, what more favor can I do to thee
Than with that hand that cut thy youth in twain
100 To sunder his that was thine enemy?
Forgive me, cousin! Ah, dear Juliet,
Why art thou yet so fair? Shall I believe
That unsubstantial Death is amorous,
And that the lean abhorred monster keeps
105 Thee here in dark to be his paramour?
For fear of that I still will stay with thee
And never from this palace of dim night
Depart again. Here, here will I remain
With worms that are thy chambermaids. O, here
110 Will I set up my everlasting rest
And shake the yoke of inauspicious stars
From this world-wearied flesh. Eyes, look your last!
Arms, take your last embrace! and, lips, O you
The doors of breath, seal with a righteous kiss
115 A dateless bargain to engrossing death!
Come, bitter conduct; come, unsavory guide!
Thou desperate pilot, now at once run on
The dashing rocks thy seasick weary bark!
Here's to my love! [*drinks*] O true apothecary!
120 Thy drugs are quick. Thus with a kiss I die.

[*falls*]

[*Enter* Friar Laurence, *with lantern, crow, and spade.*]

Friar Laurence. Saint Francis be my speed! how oft tonight
Have my old feet stumbled at graves! Who's there?

Balthasar. Here's one, a friend, and one that knows you well.

94 **ensign:** sign.

98–100 **O, what . . . enemy:** I can best repay you (Tybalt) by killing your enemy (myself) with the same hand that cut your youth in two (**twain**).

102–105 Romeo can't get over how beautiful Juliet still looks. He asks whether Death is loving (**amorous**) and whether it has taken Juliet as its lover (**paramour**).

111–112 **shake . . . flesh:** rid myself of the burden of an unhappy fate (**inauspicious stars**).

115 **dateless:** eternal; never-ending. Romeo means that what he is about to do can never be undone.

117–118 Romeo compares himself to the pilot of a ship (**bark**) who is going to crash on the rocks because he is so weary and sick.

Strategies for Annotation ✏ 📄 **Annotate it!**

Analyze Character RL 3

Have students use their eBook annotation tools to analyze Romeo's soliloquy in lines 75–120 by performing these steps:

- Highlight in blue the lines that tell how Romeo feels upon seeing that it is Paris he has killed.
- Highlight in yellow the lines that personify death and its effects upon Juliet.
- Highlight in green lines that show Romeo's reaction to Tybalt's body.
- With a group, discuss the function of this soliloquy in the plot.

To sunder his that was thine enemy?

Forgive me, cousin! Ah, dear Juliet,

Why art thou yet so fair? Shall I believe

That unsubstantial Death is amorous,

And that the lean abhorred monster keeps

Thee here in dark to be his paramour?

Friar Laurence. Bliss be upon you! Tell me, good my friend,
125   What torch is yond that vainly lends his light
To grubs and eyeless skulls? As I discern,
It burneth in the Capels' monument.

Balthasar. It doth so, holy sir; and there's my master,
One that you love.

Friar Laurence.   Who is it?

Balthasar.   Romeo.

130   **Friar Laurence.** How long hath he been there?

Balthasar.   Full half an hour.

Friar Laurence. Go with me to the vault.

Balthasar.   I dare not, sir.
My master knows not but I am gone hence,
And fearfully did menace me with death
If I did stay to look on his intents.

135   **Friar Laurence.** Stay then; I'll go alone. Fear comes upon me.
O, much I fear some ill unthrifty thing.

Balthasar. As I did sleep under this yew tree here,
I dreamt my master and another fought,
And that my master slew him.

Friar Laurence.   Romeo!

[stoops and looks on the blood and weapons]

140   Alack, alack, what blood is this which stains
The stony entrance of this sepulcher?
What mean these masterless and gory swords
To lie discolored by this place of peace?

[enters the tomb]

Romeo! O, pale! Who else? What, Paris too?
145   And steeped in blood? Ah, what an unkind hour
Is guilty of this lamentable chance!
The lady stirs.

[Juliet rises.]

Juliet. O comfortable friar! where is my lord?
I do remember well where I should be,
150   And there I am. Where is my Romeo?

Friar Laurence. I hear some noise. Lady, come from that nest
Of death, contagion, and unnatural sleep.
A greater power than we can contradict
Hath thwarted our intents. Come, come away.

132–134 My master ...intents: My master told me to go away and threatened me with death if I watched what he did.

136 unthrifty: unlucky.

140–143 Alack ... place of peace? Why are these bloody swords lying here at the tomb (**sepulcher**), a place that should be peaceful? (The swords are also **masterless,** or without their owners.)

148 comfortable: comforting.

153–154 A greater ...intents: A greater force than we can fight (**contradict**) has ruined our plans (**thwarted our intents**).

The Tragedy of Romeo and Juliet: Act V, Scene 3   **273**

CLOSE READ

Support Inferences   RL 1
(Sc. 3, LINES 128–136)

Remind students that they must often use clues in the dialogue to infer characters' emotions.

M   CITE TEXT EVIDENCE Have students infer Friar Laurence's feelings as he approaches the vault. Ask them to cite details in support of their inference. *(He is very worried when he hears that Romeo is already in there. He says that he fears "some ill unthrifty thing.")*

Analyze Character: Motivations   RL 3
(Sc. 3, LINES 148–154)

Have students note what the friar finds when he enters the vault.

N   ASK STUDENTS what the friar wants Juliet to do and why. *(He urges her to hurry away with him; he wants to spare her as much anguish as he can by not allowing her to linger in the tomb tomb near Romeo's corpse.)*

Analyze Character: Motivations (Sc. 3, LINES 155–159)

RL 3

Direct students' attention back to line 151 to help them infer the friar's motivations.

◯ ASK STUDENTS why the friar is so anxious to leave the vault. *(He hears a noise and realizes that the watch is coming. He is fearful of the consequences that await him if it is discovered what he has done to help Romeo and Juliet and how his actions have led to this tragedy with Paris and Romeo both dead.)* Have students discuss how his hasty departure might reflect his state of mind. *(Leaving Juliet in the tomb is not consistent with his character. It shows how upset and flustered he is. He may also be in shock.)*

155 Thy husband in thy bosom there lies dead;
And Paris too. Come, I'll dispose of thee
Among a sisterhood of holy nuns.
Stay not to question, for the watch is coming.
Come, go, good Juliet. I dare no longer stay.

160 **Juliet.** Go, get thee hence, for I will not away.

[*Exit* Friar Laurence.]

What's here? A cup, closed in my true love's hand?
Poison, I see, hath been his timeless end.
O churl! drunk all, and left no friendly drop
To help me after? I will kiss thy lips.
165 Haply some poison yet doth hang on them
To make me die with a restorative.

[*kisses him*]

Thy lips are warm!

Chief Watchman [*within*]. Lead, boy. Which way?

Juliet. Yea, noise? Then I'll be brief. O happy dagger!

[*snatches Romeo's dagger*]

170 This is thy sheath; there rust, and let me die.

[*She stabs herself and falls.*]

[*Enter* Watchmen *with the* Page *of Paris.*]

Page. This is the place. There, where the torch doth burn.

Chief Watchman. The ground is bloody. Search about the churchyard.
Go, some of you; whoe'er you find attach.

156–157 I'll dispose . . . nuns: I'll find a place for you in a convent of nuns.

162 timeless: happening before its proper time.

163 churl: miser.

165 Haply: perhaps.

173 attach: arrest.

Image Credits: (t) ©Everett Collection, Inc.; (tr) ©AKaiser/Shutterstock

TO CHALLENGE STUDENTS . . .

Analyze a Character's Behavior Why does Friar Laurence leave Juliet alone with her broken heart and a dagger? Discuss with students their reactions upon realizing that the friar leaves the vault with Juliet still alive in it. Have them form small groups. Ask them to formulate at least three possible explanations for the friar's behavior, then decide which one they find most convincing.

Have groups review the details throughout the play and come to a conclusion that they can support with evidence from the play. Ask them to defend their explanation to the class, presenting evidence in support.

[*Exeunt some of the* Watch.]

P 175 Pitiful sight! here lies the County slain;
And Juliet bleeding, warm, and newly dead,
Who here hath lain this two days buried.
Go, tell the Prince; run to the Capulets;
Raise up the Montagues; some others search.

178 Raise up: awaken.

[*Exeunt others of the* Watch.]

We see the ground whereon these woes do lie,
180 But the true ground of all these piteous woes
We cannot without circumstance descry.

179–181 We see . . . descry: We see the earth (**ground**) these bodies lie on. But the real cause (**true ground**) of these deaths is yet for us to discover (**descry**).

[*Reenter some of the* Watch, *with* Balthasar.]

Second Watchman. Here's Romeo's man. We found him in the churchyard.

Chief Watchman. Hold him in safety till the Prince come hither.

182–187 The guards arrest Balthasar and Friar Laurence as suspicious characters.

[*Reenter* Friar Laurence *and another* Watchman.]

Third Watchman. Here is a friar that trembles, sighs, and weeps.
185 We took this mattock and this spade from him
As he was coming from this churchyard side.

Chief Watchman. A great suspicion! Stay the friar too.

[*Enter the* Prince *and* Attendants.]

Prince. What misadventure is so early up,
That calls our person from our morning rest?

[*Enter* Capulet, Lady Capulet, *and others*.]

190 **Capulet.** What should it be, that they so shriek abroad?

Lady Capulet. The people in the street cry "Romeo,"
Some "Juliet," and some "Paris"; and all run,
With open outcry, toward our monument.

Prince. What fear is this which startles in our ears?

194 startles: causes alarm.

195 **Chief Watchman.** Sovereign, here lies the County Paris slain;
And Romeo dead, and Juliet, dead before,
Warm and new killed.

Prince. Search, seek, and know how this foul murder comes.

Chief Watchman. Here is a friar, and slaughtered Romeo's man,
200 With instruments upon them fit to open
These dead men's tombs.

Capulet. O heavens! O wife, look how our daughter bleeds!
This dagger hath mista'en, for, lo, his house
Is empty on the back of Montague,
205 And it missheathed in my daughter's bosom!

203–205 This dagger . . . in my daughter's bosom: This dagger has missed its target. It should rest in the sheath (**house**) that Romeo wears. Instead it is in Juliet's chest.

Analyze Author's Choices: Parallel Plots (Sc. 3, LINES 174–205)

RL 5

Tell students that the threads of various plots that have run through the play are tied up in this final scene.

P ASK STUDENTS to summarize how the feud between the two families determined the outcome of the relationship between Romeo and Juliet. Who else suffered as a result of this hostility between the families? *(The feud between the families meant that Romeo and Juliet could not marry openly. Their secret marriage and Romeo's banishment consequently led to their deaths. Mercutio, Tybalt, and Paris have also been sacrificed to the feud.)*

Point out that Prince Escalus refers to "this foul murder" and the Chief Watchman to "slaughtered" Romeo.

Q ASK STUDENTS to note that the onlookers describe this scene as one of hate. In what ironic sense is it a scene of love? *(Romeo has killed himself for love. Paris was killed because of his desire to protect his love. Juliet killed herself because Romeo, her love, was dead.)*

APPLYING ACADEMIC VOCABULARY

expose	underlie

As you discuss the final act of *Romeo and Juliet,* incorporate the Collection 4 academic vocabulary words: *expose* and *underlie*. Ask students what important themes the events in this act **expose**. Have them support their interpretation of the meaning that **underlies** these events with details from the text.

Analyze Character:
Motivations (Sc. 3, LINES 210–227)

RL 3

Have students note that the friar steps forward to explain the deaths.

R **ASK STUDENTS** why the friar does this. *(He has been very involved in the plot. He is neither a Montague nor a Capulet and is a priest so he might be counted on to narrate the events objectively. He also wishes to confess and be pardoned for his involvement at the same time ["And here I stand, both to impeach and purge / Myself impeached and myself excused."])*

Lady Capulet. O me! this sight of death is as a bell
That warns my old age to a sepulcher.

[*Enter* Montague *and others.*]

Prince. Come, Montague; for thou art early up
To see thy son and heir now early down.

210   **Montague.** Alas, my liege, my wife is dead tonight!
Grief of my son's exile hath stopped her breath.
What further woe conspires against mine age?

Prince. Look, and thou shalt see.

Montague. O thou untaught! what manners is in this,
215   To press before thy father to a grave?

Prince. Seal up the mouth of outrage for a while,
Till we can clear these ambiguities
And know their spring, their head, their true descent;
And then will I be general of your woes
220   And lead you even to death. Meantime forbear,
And let mischance be slave to patience.
Bring forth the parties of suspicion.

Friar Laurence. I am the greatest, able to do least,
Yet most suspected, as the time and place
225   Doth make against me, of this direful murder;
And here I stand, both to impeach and purge
Myself condemned and myself excused.

Prince. Then say at once what thou dost know in this.

Friar Laurence. I will be brief, for my short date of breath
230   Is not so long as is a tedious tale.
Romeo, there dead, was husband to that Juliet;
And she, there dead, that Romeo's faithful wife.
I married them; and their stol'n marriage day
Was Tybalt's doomsday, whose untimely death
235   Banish'd the new-made bridegroom from this city;
For whom, and not for Tybalt, Juliet pined.
You, to remove that siege of grief from her,
Betrothed and would have married her perforce
To County Paris. Then comes she to me
240   And with wild looks bid me devise some mean
To rid her from this second marriage,
Or in my cell there would she kill herself.
Then gave I her (so tutored by my art)
A sleeping potion; which so took effect
245   As I intended, for it wrought on her
The form of death. Meantime I writ to Romeo

210 liege: lord.

214–215 what manners . . . grave: What kind of behavior is this, for a son to die before his father?

216–221 Seal . . . patience: Stop your emotional outbursts until we can find out the source (**spring**) of these confusing events (**ambiguities**). Wait (**forbear**) and be patient, and let's find out what happened.

223–227 Friar Laurence confesses that he is most responsible for these events. He will both accuse (**impeach**) himself and clear (**purge**) himself of guilt.

236 It was Romeo's banishment, not Tybalt's death, that made Juliet so sad.

WHEN STUDENTS STRUGGLE . . .

To help students identify and organize the important events that take place in this act, ha
them complete a sequence chain resembling the one shown. Remind them to record the
details in chronological order.

ASK STUDENTS to review their chains and summarize these events in one or two senten

 LEVEL UP TUTORIALS For additional support, assign the
following *Level Up* tutorial: **Plot: Sequence of Events.**

That he should hither come as this dire night
To help to take her from her borrowed grave,
Being the time the potion's force should cease.

248 borrowed: temporary.

250 But he which bore my letter, Friar John,
Was stayed by accident, and yesternight
Returned my letter back. Then all alone
At the prefixed hour of her waking
Came I to take her from her kindred's vault;

254 kindred's: family's.

255 Meaning to keep her closely at my cell
Till I conveniently could send to Romeo.
But when I came, some minute ere the time
Of her awaking, here untimely lay
The noble Paris and true Romeo dead.

260 She wakes; and I entreated her come forth
And bear this work of heaven with patience;
But then a noise did scare me from the tomb,
And she, too desperate, would not go with me,
But, as it seems, did violence on herself.

265 All this I know, and to the marriage
Her nurse is privy; and if aught in this
Miscarried by my fault, let my old life
Be sacrificed, some hour before his time,
Unto the rigor of severest law.

265–269 and to . . . law: Her nurse can bear witness to this secret marriage. If I am responsible for any of this, let the law punish me with death.

270 **Prince.** We still have known thee for a holy man.
Where's Romeo's man? What can he say in this?

Balthasar. I brought my master news of Juliet's death;
And then in post he came from Mantua
To this same place, to this same monument.

273 in post: at full speed.

275 This letter he early bid me give his father,
And threatened me with death, going in the vault,
If I departed not and left him there.

Prince. Give me the letter. I will look on it.
Where is the County's page that raised the watch?
280 Sirrah, what made your master in this place?

279–280 The Prince asks for Paris' servant, who notified the guards (**raised the watch**). Then he asks the servant why Paris was at the cemetery.

Page. He came with flowers to strew his lady's grave;
And bid me stand aloof, and so I did.
Anon comes one with light to ope the tomb;
And by-and-by my master drew on him;
285 And then I ran away to call the watch.

283–285 Anon . . . call the watch: Soon (**anon**) someone with a light came and opened the tomb. Paris drew his sword, and I ran to call the guards.

Prince. This letter doth make good the friar's words,
Their course of love, the tidings of her death;
And here he writes that he did buy a poison
Of a poor 'pothecary, and therewithal

The Tragedy of Romeo and Juliet: Act V, Scene 3 **277**

CLOSE READ

Analyze Character: Motivations (Sc. 3, LINES 265–272)

RL 3

Have students note how the prince responds to the friar's words.

S **CITE TEXT EVIDENCE** Ask students how the friar redeems himself at the end of his speech. What does Prince Escalus say that shows his reaction to the friar's words? (*The friar accepts the blame for what has happened. He says, "let my old life / Be sacrificed, some hour before his time, / Unto the rigor of severest law." Prince Escalus shows him mercy. He says, "We still have known thee for a holy man."*)

| Paris brings flowers to Juliet's grave. | Romeo arrives at the cemetery. | Romeo fights with and kills Paris. | Romeo enters the vault and kills himself. | | |

CLOSE READ

Determine Theme RL 2

(Sc. 3, LINES 291–304)

Have students read these lines carefully to determine what important ideas Prince Escalus brings out.

Ⓤ **CITE TEXT EVIDENCE** Ask students how the outcome of the play relates to the friar's earlier observations about nature. Have them cite text evidence from the friar's speech in Act II to support their response. *(Friar Laurence refers to the cycle of life and death in which opposites are intertwined: "The earth that's nature's mother is her tomb, / What is her burying grave, that is her womb..." [Scene 3, lines 9–10]. Similarly, the love of Romeo and Juliet, although a virtue, led to death. Their deaths, although an evil, may lead to virtue through the unifying of their families and the ending of the feud.)*

COLLABORATIVE DISCUSSION Have students pair up and discuss specific reasons that the play still appeals to today's audiences and why directors continue to make new versions of it. Then have them share their conclusions with the class as a whole. Accept all reasonable responses.

ASK STUDENTS to share any questions they generated in the course of reading and discussing the selection.

Ⓣ

290 Came to this vault to die and lie with Juliet.
Where be these enemies? Capulet, Montague,
See what a scourge is laid upon your hate,
That heaven finds means to kill your joys with love!
And I, for winking at your discords too,
295 Have lost a brace of kinsmen. All are punished.

Capulet. O brother Montague, give me thy hand.
This is my daughter's jointure, for no more
Can I demand.

Ⓤ

Montague. But I can give thee more;
For I will raise her statue in pure gold,
300 That whiles Verona by that name is known,
There shall no figure at such rate be set
As that of true and faithful Juliet.

Capulet. As rich shall Romeo's by his lady's lie—
Poor sacrifices of our enmity!

305 **Prince.** A glooming peace this morning with it brings.
The sun for sorrow will not show his head.
Go hence, to have more talk of these sad things;
Some shall be pardoned, and some punished;
For never was a story of more woe
310 Than this of Juliet and her Romeo.

[*Exeunt.*]

COLLABORATIVE DISCUSSION Working in a small group, review the events that lead to the tragic ending. Then discuss what makes *The Tragedy of Romeo and Juliet* still popular with today's audiences.

292–295 See what ... punished: Look at the punishment your hatred has brought on you. Heaven has killed your children (**joys**) with love. For shutting my eyes to your arguments (**discords**), I have lost two relatives. We have all been punished.

297–298 jointure: dowry, the payment a bride's father traditionally made to the groom. Capulet means that no one could demand more of a bride's father than he has already paid.

301 at such rate be set: be valued so highly.

303–304 Capulet promises to do for Romeo what Montague will do for Juliet. Their children have become sacrifices to their hatred (**enmity**).

TO CHALLENGE STUDENTS...

Reimagine a Scene Who is missing from this scene? Point out to students that the nurse and Benvolio are not present in this last scene. Discuss how this omission is particularly striking since the nurse is the person closest to Juliet and Benvolio is Romeo's best friend.

Have students collaborate with a partner to decide how the two might have been incorporated into the scene and what they might have said.

ASK STUDENTS to share their ideas with the class. Then invite students to explain their thoughts on why Shakespeare might have chosen to exclude the two from the scene.

Analyze Character: Motivations

Characters in a literary work, like real people, have **motivations,** or reasons, for their actions. A character can be motivated by a variety of factors: by a goal, by loyalty to a group or cause, or by an emotion such as love, anger, or jealousy. A **complex character** is one who is driven by multiple, and sometimes conflicting, motivations at the same time.

In *Romeo and Juliet*, the character of Tybalt is an example of a character who is not particularly complex. What is Tybalt's single motivation before he meets his demise? The characters of Romeo and Juliet, on the other hand, are complex characters tormented throughout the play by conflicting motivations. Their struggles form the basis of the action in the play—and time after time prevent them from being able to live happily ever after. Think about the following factors:

- **Family obligation** In what ways do their families create conflict in their lives?
- **Love and passion** How does their love motivate them to meet new challenges?
- **Fear** How does fear shape their actions and prevent them from living and loving each other freely?
- **Misunderstanding** What twists and turns in the plot, as well as miscommunication, create conflict and drive them to make bad choices?
- **Despair** What actions by Romeo and Juliet are driven by extreme feelings of hopelessness?

Analyze Author's Choices: Parallel Plots

Romeo and Juliet is not a simple love story. It is a complex drama featuring **parallel plots**—separate story lines happening at the same time and linked by common characters and themes. The chart can help you identify and understand parallel plots in the play.

Plot	Purpose
The feud between the Capulets and the Montagues	How does this plot contribute to the drama of the play?
Romeo's unrequited love for Rosaline	What do we learn about Romeo through this experience?
Juliet's marriage proposal from Paris	What do we learn about Juliet and her relationship with her family?

Shakespeare also carefully structures his drama in a meaningful way. Recall that Acts I and II are comedic, featuring jokes and young love, while Act III leads to the final tragedy. What is the effect of this contrast?

CLOSE READ

Analyze Character: Motivations

Make sure that students understand that complex characters show change and have many dimensions in addition to acting on various motivations.

To help students comprehend the motivations of Romeo and Juliet more clearly, organize them into five groups. Assign each group an act. Have students review their act to find instances in which the main characters are driven to take action. Tell them to identify the emotion or condition that led the characters to take this action.

Analyze Author's Choices: Parallel Plots

As a class, list all of the separate story lines on the board. Discuss how each one affects the major plot involving Romeo and Juliet.

Strategies for Annotation   *Annotate it!*

Analyze Character: Motivations   RL 3

Have students use their eBook annotation tools to identify the motivations behind the main characters' actions. Suggest that they take the following steps:

- Skim the act to identify actions that Romeo and Juliet take.
- Highlight each significant action.
- On a note, identify what drives them to take that action.

O, look! methinks I see my cousin's ghost

Seeking out Romeo, that did spit his body

Upon a rapier's point. Stay, Tybalt, stay!

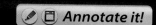 Romeo, I come! this do I drink to thee.

PRACTICE & APPLY

Analyzing the Text

RL 1, RL 2, RL 3, RL 5

Possible answers:

1. *Romeo dreams of Juliet finding him dead and then reviving him with kisses. The former part of the dream foreshadows events in Act V, Scene 3.*

2. *He says, "Juliet, I will lie with thee tonight." He immediately plots his own death without considering other options or verifying whether or not the news of her death is true. His response reveals his passionate, impulsive nature.*

3. *Friar Laurence fears what Romeo will do if he believes Juliet is dead. Here their elaborate plans begin to go tragically awry.*

4. *He is motivated by a desire to explain the events that led to the deaths, events that only he knows about. He also wants to confess his own responsibility for what happened and to gain forgiveness from the Prince and the others. He hints that the Capulets (lines 237–239) caused Juliet to feel so desperate that he had no choice but to step in, and he mentions that the nurse also knew about the secret marriage (lines 265–266).*

5. *He blames himself for not resolving the feud between the families. He says, "I, for winking at your discords too, / have lost a brace of kinsmen. All are punished " (lines 294–295).*

6. *Juliet wants to please her mother by considering Paris, suggesting she is obedient and trustful of her parents' judgment. Romeo, by contrast, is wildly romantic in his despair over Rosaline—which immediately dissipates when he lays eyes on Juliet. Juliet, transformed by the love she feels from their first meeting, becomes more like Romeo: passionate and willing to do anything to be with the person she loves.*

7. *Answers will vary, but students should support their ideas with details in the text. The tragic chain of events is also attributable to human factors. Students can point to the feuding families, as well as to Juliet's impending forced marriage to Paris. They can also point to Romeo's impulsivity and to Friar Laurence's desire to help, which perhaps went too far.*

8. *Students might say that Romeo's tragic flaw is that he is too impulsive and fails to think things through, qualities that often lead him astray. Juliet's tragic flaws might include her naïveté and her willingness to go along with Romeo.*

Analyzing the Text

RL 1, RL 2,
RL 3, RL 5, W 3

Cite Text Evidence   Support your responses with evidence from the selection.

1. **Interpret** What dream does Romeo describe at the beginning of Act V, Scene 1? What part of his dream foreshadows events to come?

2. **Analyze** What plan does Romeo immediately formulate when he learns of Juliet's death? What does his response to her death expose about his character?

3. **Infer** In Scene 2, why is Friar Laurence in a panic when he finds out that his letter was not delivered to Romeo? Why is this a key turning point in the plot?

4. **Analyze** Reread Friar Laurence's speech in Scene 3, lines 223–269. What various and possibly conflicting motivations does he have for making these remarks?

5. **Interpret** Whom does Prince Escalus blame for the tragic events? Support your answer with details from his words in the last scene of the play.

6. **Connect** Recall Juliet's response when her mother suggests the idea of marrying Paris (Act I, Scene 3, lines 98–100). What does this reveal about Juliet's character before she meets Romeo? How does this contrast with Romeo's character in the parallel plot involving Rosaline? By Act V, how has Juliet changed?

7. **Analyze** Fate, or forces over which people have no control, is an important theme in this tragedy. Many events are blamed upon fate, starting with Shakespeare's description of Romeo and Juliet as "star-crossed lovers" in the Prologue. However, many events can also be blamed on the actions of characters. Do you believe fate or free will caused this tragic ending? Explain.

8. **Analyze** In a tragedy, a hero or heroine's character flaw is usually the cause of his or her downfall. Do you believe Romeo or Juliet had a character flaw that led to his or her death? Support your idea with evidence from the play.

PERFORMANCE TASK

Writing Activity: Eulogy Use your knowledge of Romeo and Juliet to write a eulogy, a tribute to someone who has died, for both of them.

1. With a partner, brainstorm important details about their lives and their relationship. Think about their motivations, how they fell in love, the challenges they faced, and how they changed each other.

2. With your partner, craft your eulogy, highlighting key details about the characters of the two young people. Be sure your ideas are grounded in details from the play.

In both pieces of writing, include evidence from the text and use the conventions of standard English.

Assign this performance task.

PERFORMANCE TASK   W 3

Writing Activity: Eulogy Explain that a eulogy is a formal speech often delivered at a funeral service. It is usually given by a friend or family member of the deceased, and its purpose is to extoll the subject's positive qualities and to explain the mourner's grief. Have partners create a list of Romeo's and Juliet's positive attributes and then locate episodes from the play where they exhibit them. The resulting anecdotes will provide content for their eulogies. Encourage students to decide on a pattern of organization before beginning to write.

Vocabulary Strategy: Puns

Shakespeare was a master of clever word play, including the use of puns. A **pun** is a joke built upon multiple meanings of a word or upon two words that sound similar but have different meanings. Near the end of Act IV, Peter challenges the musicians to help him develop a pun based on a verse.

> **Peter.** "When griping grief the heart doth wound
> And doleful dumps the mind oppress,
> Then music with her silver sound—"
>
> Why "silver sound"? Why "music with her silver sound"?—What say you, Simon Catling?
>
> **First Musician.** Marry, sir, because silver hath a sweet sound.
>
> **Peter.** Pretty! What say you, Hugh Rebeck?
>
> **Second Musician.** I say "silver sound" because musicians sound for silver.
>
> **Peter.** Pretty too! What say you, James Soundpost?
>
> **Third Musician.** Faith, I know not what to say.
>
> **Peter.** Oh, I cry you mercy, you are the singer. I will say for you. It is "music with her silver sound" because musicians have no gold for sounding.

Notice the multiple meanings for the phrase *silver sound*. The first musician uses *sound* as a noun. The adjective *silver* has a pleasant connotation, making the phrase mean "a sweet or beautiful sound." The second musician and Peter use *sound* as a verb. They use the word *silver* as a reference to money and to a metal that has a lesser value than gold. To the second musician and Peter, the phrase *silver sound* means "to make music for money, silver money, though, not gold."

Practice and Apply With a partner, locate and explain these puns from the play. Then brainstorm a few multiple-meaning words and words that sound similar but have different meanings that you could use in original puns. Write a brief dialogue like the one between Peter and the musicians that uses your puns.

1. "You have dancing shoes / With nimble soles; I have a soul of lead / So stakes me to the ground I cannot move." (Act I, Scene 4, lines 14–16)

2. "Ask for me tomorrow, and you shall find me a grave man." (Act III, Scene 1, lines 91–92)

CLOSE READ

Vocabulary Strategy: Puns

Find additional examples throughout the play if students need more help understanding the play on words. Before they begin their original puns, brainstorm possible words as a class, listing them on the board for students to refer to.

Possible answers:

1. *This pun uses homophones,* sole *and* soul, *to make a contrast between the lightness of spirit implied by dancing and the heaviness that Romeo feels in his heart.*

2. *The pun is on the word* grave, *which can mean "somber" as well as "a burial site."*

ENGLISH LANGUAGE SUPPORT

Vocabulary: Puns Students may find it difficult to understand puns. Tell students that puns depend on words having more than one meaning that could possibly make sense in the context of the sentence. Use the second example in the exercise to illustrate. Explain that the character Mercutio is badly hurt. He says to Romeo, "Ask for me tomorrow, and you shall find me a grave man."

Write the line on the board and underline the word *grave*. Have students identify possible meanings for *grave* using prior knowledge or a dictionary. Then have them explain the two meanings that Mercutio is referring to in his word play. Make sure they see that he will be a serious man the next day because he will be dead, or in his grave.

Language and Style: Parallel Structure

L 1a

Review the instruction and the examples with students. Point out that repetition and parallelism are closely related, and that parallelism often involves the repetition of certain words. They key to parallelism is the repetition of a grammatical structure, however. Repeating the words *but* and *for* in the first two examples does not create much of an effect by itself; it is the fact that the words are used the same way in adjacent phrases or clauses that creates a meaningful effect.

Possible answers:

Elicit sentences from students that they have included in the eulogies. As a class, rewrite them to include parallel structures. Contrast the before-and-after versions to help students understand the impact of parallelism in their own writing.

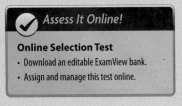

Assess It Online!

Online Selection Test
- Download an editable ExamView bank.
- Assign and manage this test online.

Language and Style: Parallel Structure

L 1a

Parallel structure is the repetition of words, phrases, or grammatical structures in order to add emphasis or to improve the sound and rhythm of a piece of writing. Shakespeare regularly makes use of parallel structure to create cadence, or a balanced, rhythmic flow of words. Here is an example from Act II, Scene 1, lines 8–11:

> Appear thou in the likeness of a sigh;
> Speak but one rhyme, and I am satisfied!
> Cry but "Ay me!" pronounce but "love" and "dove";
> Speak to my gossip Venus one fair word . . .

Shakespeare repeats the phrasing of a verb followed by *but*: "Speak but . . . Cry but . . . pronounce but. . . ." The parallel grammatical structures give equal weight to each phrase. Any one of these three tiny gestures from Rosaline, Mercutio jokes, would cause lovesick Romeo to rejoice. Read the passage aloud and you will hear the cadence that the parallel structures lend to the verse.

This example from Act I, Scene 5, lines 10–11 contains a series of four past-tense verbs, each followed by the word *for*:

> You are looked for and called for, asked for and sought for, in the great chamber.

In this case, the speaker (a servant) sounds rather ridiculous, as if he is trying to use flowery language to deliver a simple message.

In the next example, from Act IV Scene 1, lines 102–103, Shakespeare repeats three parallel adjectives:

> Each part, deprived of supple government,
> Shall, stiff and stark and cold, appear like death;

Friar Laurence uses these grim adjectives to describe what Juliet's body will be like once she drinks the potion. The repetition gives his speech a somber rhythm, like a funeral march.

Practice and Apply Revise the eulogy you wrote in this selection's Performance Task to include at least two examples of parallel structures. Share your revised work with a partner and discuss how the parallel structures increase the power and clarity of your language.

Analyze Character

RL 3

TEACH

To help students answer Analyzing the Text question #8, discuss these ideas about **character flaws.**

- In most Shakespearean dramas, the hero, or protagonist, is brought to disaster because of a characteristic that is a flaw, or weakness. Tell them that this quality may start out as a strength that helps the hero to achieve greatness. For example, the tragic hero Macbeth is ambitious. Ambition can be a good quality if controlled. Macbeth's ambition becomes excessive, however; his quest for more power drives his decision making. These bad decisions eventually lead to his downfall.

- Point out that neither Romeo nor Juliet achieves greatness. In this play, Shakespeare chose to focus on two ordinary people who meet tragic ends. Tell students that in that sense, they are not tragic heroes. Some of their misfortune is caused by mistiming, misunderstanding, and circumstances beyond their control. But the choices they make also affect their destinies. Tell students that they can determine whether these decisions are the result of a character flaw by answering these questions:

- *What are the character's predominant traits or qualities?*

- *Which of these traits has the greatest influence on the character's decision-making?*

- *What is the outcome of those decisions? Are they good or bad?*

COLLABORATIVE DISCUSSION

Direct students to work with a partner to answer each question about the characters Romeo and Juliet. Encourage them to take notes reflecting what they conclude in response to whether the character has a flaw that led to his or her death. Invite pairs to share their conclusions with the class.

Analyze Author's Choices: Parallel Plots

RL 5

RETEACH

Remind students that **parallel plots** develop at the same time as the major plot. As students know from reading *The Tragedy of Romeo and Juliet*, these subplots intersect or converge with the main plot at some point in the play, affecting the course of the action. Tell students that although parallel plots appear in longer works, shorter selections may have more than one plot as well.

- Choose a selection or movie with which students are familiar, for example, "When Mr. Pirzada Came to Dine." Have students identify the major story line or plot. *(The major plot involves the experiences that help Lilia to grow up.)* Ask students to identify a parallel plot in the work under discussion. *(What is happening to Mr. Pirzada's family in Pakistan is a parallel plot.)*

- Have students explain how the parallel plot affects the major plot. *(Mr. Pirzada becomes increasingly concerned about the plight of his family; this leads Lilia to be concerned about them too and thus mature as she begins to care about other people.)*

 LEVEL UP TUTORIALS Assign the following *Level Up* tutorial: **Plot: Sequence of Events**

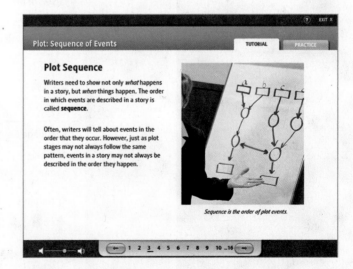

INDEPENDENT READING

Have students work independently to identify the parallel plots of another work they have read. Ask: What are the parallel plots? How do they affect the main plot?

from The Tragedy of Romeo and Juliet

Drama by William Shakespeare

For more context and historical background, students can view the video "Biography: William Shakespeare" in their eBooks.

Why This Text

Students often have difficulty relating to Shakespeare's characters, who speak ornate sixteenth-century language, although people today experience many of the same emotions and longings. With the help of the close-reading questions, students will analyze the main characters and their motivations and desires. This close reading will lead students to an understanding of how characters' behavior and words can reveal their motivations.

Background Have students read the background about *Romeo and Juliet* and its author, William Shakespeare. They can also view the biography of Shakespeare in their eBooks. Tell students that Shakespeare is considered the finest playwright in the English language. Point out that many modern plays, stories, and even films are loosely based on his works.

AS YOU READ Remind students that a drama depends on dialogue to reveal characters' motivations. At what points in the play do Romeo and Juliet show what emotions move them to action?

Standards Support

- cite strong and thorough textual evidence
- analyze how complex characters develop over the course of a text and advance the plot
- analyze the impact of specific word choices on tone
- analyze an author's choices concerning how to structure a text and order events within it

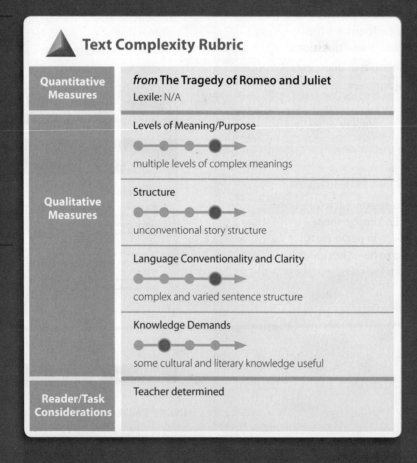

Text Complexity Rubric

Quantitative Measures

from The Tragedy of Romeo and Juliet
Lexile: N/A

Qualitative Measures

Levels of Meaning/Purpose
multiple levels of complex meanings

Structure
unconventional story structure

Language Conventionality and Clarity
complex and varied sentence structure

Knowledge Demands
some cultural and literary knowledge useful

Reader/Task Considerations
Teacher determined

Strategies for CLOSE READING

Analyze Character: Motivations

Students should read this excerpt from *Romeo and Juliet* carefully all the way through. Close-reading questions at the bottom of the page will help them understand how the characters' words reveal conflicting feelings and motivations. As they read, students should jot down comments or questions about the text in the margins.

WHEN STUDENTS STRUGGLE . . .

To help students analyze character's motivations, have them work in small groups to fill out a chart like the one shown below.

CITE TEXT EVIDENCE For practice in determining a character's motivations, ask students to give text examples and identify the speaker's motivation for each speech.

Character's Action or Words	Motivation
Romeo "By a name I know not how to tell thee who I am. My name, dear saint, is hateful to myself, Because it is an enemy to thee." (Act II, Scene 2, lines 53–56)	Romeo wants to be honest about his identity as a member of an enemy family, but he also wants to be someone who is pleasing to Juliet.
Juliet "If thou dost love, pronounce it faithfully. Or if thou thinkst I am too quickly won, I'll frown, and be perverse, and say thee nay." (Act II, Scene 2, lines 94–96)	Juliet wants Romeo to declare his love, but then she worries that he might think that she's throwing herself at him.

Background *It sounds like a love story ripped from the tabloids. Two teenagers fall in love. Then they learn that their parents hate one another. Murder and suffering follow, and by the end, a whole town is mourning. What love can—and cannot—overcome is at the core of Romeo and Juliet, considered by many to be the greatest love story of all time. This play by* **William Shakespeare (1564–1616)** *was one of his earlier works. It was probably first performed in the mid-1590s, when he would have been about thirty years old. As was the custom at that time, Shakespeare based his play on a story that already existed.*

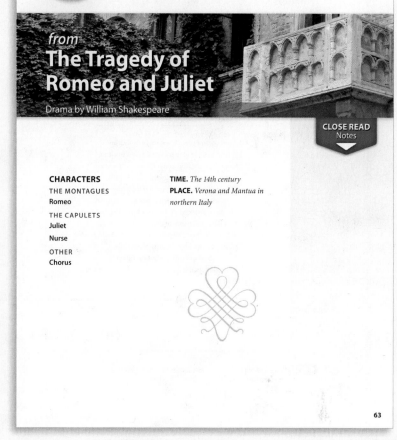

from
The Tragedy of Romeo and Juliet

Drama by William Shakespeare

CLOSE READ
Notes

CHARACTERS
THE MONTAGUES
Romeo
THE CAPULETS
Juliet
Nurse
OTHER
Chorus

TIME. *The 14th century*
PLACE. *Verona and Mantua in northern Italy*

63

1. READ ▶ As you read the Prologue, begin to cite text evidence.

- Circle text that describes the similar backgrounds of Romeo and Juliet.
- Underline clues that tell what will happen to the title characters.
- In the margin, explain how Shakespeare sets out one of the play's major themes—the conflict between love and hate.

The Chorus is an individual actor who serves as a narrator. He enters from the back of the stage to introduce and explain the theme of the play. His job is to "hook" the audience's interest by telling them just enough to quiet them down and make them eager for more. In this prologue, the Chorus explains the age-old feud between two prominent families of the Italian city of Verona.

PROLOGUE

[*Enter Chorus.*]
Chorus. Two households, both alike in dignity,
In fair Verona, where we lay our scene,

A From ancient grudge break to new **mutiny**,
Where civil blood makes civil hands unclean.

5 From forth the fatal loins¹ of these two foes,
A pair of star-crossed¹ lovers take their life,²
Whose misadventured³ piteous overthrows

B Doth with their death bury their parents' strife.
The fearful passage of their death-marked love,

10 And the continuance of their parents' rage,
Which, but their children's end, naught could remove,
Is now the two hours' traffic of our stage,
The which if you with patient ears attend,
What here shall miss, our toil shall strive to mend.
[*Exit.*]

mutiny:
rebellion

----
¹ **star-crossed:** doomed. The position of the stars when the lovers were born was not favorable. In Shakespeare's day, people took astrology very seriously.
² **take their life:** are born, begin their lives.
³ **misadventured:** unlucky.

Shakespeare says that two people whose families have been feuding for years will fall in love.

2. ◀ REREAD Reread lines 6–10. What effect does the Chorus say that death will have on the remaining characters?

Death will end the feud between the families.

64

3. READ ▶ As you read lines 1–25 of Act II, Scene 2, continue to cite text evidence.

- Underline a metaphor that Romeo uses to describe Juliet.
- In the margin, explain Romeo's conflicting motivations (lines 13–14).

Prior to this scene, Romeo, a Montague, and his friends snuck into a masquerade ball given by the Capulet family. There, Romeo and Juliet, who is a Capulet, fall in love at first sight. Only after they talk and kiss do they discover they have fallen in love with the enemy. After the ball, Romeo hides in Lord Capulet's orchard, hoping for a chance to see Juliet on her balcony.

Act II

Scene 2 • Capulet's orchard.

[*Enter Romeo.*]
Romeo. He jests at scars that never felt a wound.¹
[*Enter Juliet above at a window.*]
But soft! What light through yonder window breaks?
It is the East, and Juliet is the sun!
Arise, fair sun, and kill the envious moon,

5 Who is already sick and pale with grief
That thou her maid art far more fair than she.
Be not her maid, since she is envious;
Her vestal livery is but sick and green,
And none but fools do wear it; cast it off.

10 It is my lady; O, it is my love!
O that she knew she were!
She speaks, yet she says nothing. What of that?

C Her eye discourses; I will answer it.
I am too bold; 'tis not to me she speaks.

15 Two of the fairest stars in all the heaven,
Having some business, do entreat² her eyes
To twinkle in their spheres till they return.
What if her eyes were there, they in her head?
The brightness of her cheek would shame those stars

Romeo both wants to speak to Juliet and is afraid of speaking to her.

----
¹ **He jests at scars that never felt a wound:** Earlier, Romeo's friend Mercutio makes fun of love. Here, Romeo says he makes fun of it because he has never been wounded by it.
² **entreat:** beg, urge.

65

---

1. READ AND CITE TEXT EVIDENCE

A **ASK STUDENTS** to cite evidence in lines 1–14 showing that the families have been feuding. *The families have an "ancient grudge" but also get into new quarrels ("mutiny"), and blood has probably been spilt in this feud ("Where civil blood makes civil hands unclean."). The parents feel "rage" that is ongoing.*

2. REREAD AND CITE TEXT EVIDENCE

B **ASK STUDENTS** what other characters besides the two "star-crossed lovers" are mentioned in lines 6–10. What happens to them? *Students should identify the parents of the two lovers. The death of the lovers buries "their parents' strife." The parents' rage is ended only by the death of their children.*

Critical Vocabulary: mutiny (line 3) Have students share their definitions of *mutiny*. Point out that in this context, *mutiny* also means "fighting."

3. READ AND CITE TEXT EVIDENCE Point out to students that Romeo's dialogue is in the form of a soliloquy—he is speaking aloud to himself (and of course to the audience). Juliet cannot hear him and indeed doesn't know he is there.

C **ASK STUDENTS** to look at lines 10–14. How do these lines show that Romeo has two impulses that pull him in opposite directions? *Students may say that Romeo wishes that Juliet could know that he loves her. He wants to say something ("Her eye discourses; I will answer it.") but then feels that this would be too bold.*

FOR ELL STUDENTS Point out that *art* (line 6), in this context, is not the noun, but an old form of *are*, of the verb *to be*.

D 20 As daylight doth a lamp; her eyes in heaven
Would through the airy region stream so bright
That birds would sing and think it were not night.
See how she leans her cheek upon her hand!
O that I were a glove upon that hand,
25 That I might touch that cheek!
Juliet.   Ay me!
Romeo.   She speaks.
O, speak again, bright angel! for thou art
As glorious to this night, being o'er my head,
As is a winged messenger of heaven
Unto the white-upturned wond'ring eyes
30 Of mortals that fall back to gaze on him
When he bestrides³ the lazy-pacing clouds
And sails upon the bosom of the air.

E **Juliet.** O Romeo, Romeo! Wherefore⁴ art thou Romeo?
Deny thy father and refuse thy name!
35 Or, if thou wilt not, be but sworn my love,
And I'll no longer be a Capulet.
Romeo [*aside*]. Shall I hear more, or shall I speak at this?

F **Juliet.** 'Tis but thy name that is my enemy.
Thou art thyself, though not⁵ a Montague.
40 What's Montague? It is nor hand, nor foot,
Nor arm, nor face, nor any other part
Belonging to a man. O, be some other name!
What's in a name? That which we call a rose
By any other name would smell as sweet.

---

³ **bestrides:** stands on.
⁴ **wherefore:** why.
⁵ **though not:** if you were not.

Juliet wants Romeo to deny his father's name. If he will not, she promises to give up her name if he swears his love to her.

4. ◀ **REREAD AND DISCUSS** Reread lines 1–25 of Act II, Scene 2. In a small group, discuss how Romeo expresses his love for Juliet. To what does he compare her eyes?

5. **READ** ▶ As you read lines 26–53, continue to cite evidence.
- In the margin, explain what Juliet wants from Romeo (lines 33–36).
- Underline the first lines where one character knowingly addresses the other directly.
- Circle the lines where Juliet realizes she has been overheard.

45 So Romeo would, were he not Romeo called,
Retain that dear perfection which he owes⁶
Without that title. Romeo, doff⁷ thy name;
And for that name, which is no part of thee,
Take all myself.
Romeo.   I take thee at thy word.
50 Call me but love, and I'll be new baptized;
Henceforth⁸ I never will be Romeo.
Juliet. What man art thou that, thus bescreened⁹ in night,
So stumblest on my counsel?¹⁰
Romeo.   By a name
I know not how to tell thee who I am.
55 My name, dear saint, is hateful to myself,
Because it is an enemy to thee.
Had I it written, I would tear the word.
G **Juliet.** My ears have yet not drunk a hundred words
Of that tongue's utterance,¹¹ yet I know the sound.
60 Art thou not Romeo, and a Montague?
Romeo. Neither, fair saint, if either thee dislike.
H **Juliet.** How camest thou hither, tell me, and wherefore?
The orchard walls are high and hard to climb,
And the place death, considering who thou art,
65 If any of my kinsmen find thee here.

---

⁶ **owes:** owns, possesses.
⁷ **doff:** get rid of.
⁸ **henceforth:** from now on.
⁹ **bescreened:** hidden.
¹⁰ **counsel:** thoughts.
¹¹ **utterance:** speech.

6. ◀ **REREAD** Reread lines 38–49. What is Juliet saying about names here?

She thinks a name is unimportant. Just as a rose would still smell sweet if it weren't called a rose, so Juliet would still love Romeo if he weren't a Montague.

7. **READ** ▶ As you read lines 54–79, continue to cite textual evidence.
- Underline the text where Juliet worries about what will happen if her family finds Romeo on Capulet property.
- In the margin, explain what would distress Romeo more than facing death (lines 75–78).

---

4. **REREAD AND DISCUSS USING TEXT EVIDENCE**

D **ASK STUDENTS** what image Romeo uses to describe Juliet in lines 20–25. What does this image have in common with the other images that he has already used to describe her? *All of Romeo's images so far have to do with light: he says that "Juliet is the sun" (line 3); he compares her eyes to stars (lines 15–19), and in lines 20–25, he says that if her eyes were in the night sky, birds would think it was daylight.*

5. **READ AND CITE TEXT EVIDENCE**

E **ASK STUDENTS** what lines 33–36 reveal about Juliet's feelings for Romeo. *Students should understand that Juliet is declaring her love for Romeo even though she knows he is a Montague, her family's enemy.*

6. **REREAD AND CITE TEXT EVIDENCE** Nearly all the characters are allied with one side or another in the Capulet-Montague feud.

F **ASK STUDENTS** to reread lines 40–42 and then restate Juliet's lines in their own words. *Possible response: What does the name Montague mean? It's not a hand, foot, arm, face, or any physical thing that makes a man.*

7. **READ AND CITE TEXT EVIDENCE**

G **ASK STUDENTS** to look at lines 58–74. How do Juliet's statements about what the Capulets will do to Romeo reflect back to the Prologue? *They remind us that the Prologue has said that the conflict between the families is bloody and serious, and that a pair of lovers from the warring families will die.*

FOR ELL STUDENTS Challenge your ELL students to guess the meaning of *thee* ("you," object pronoun), *thy* ("your"), and *thou* ("you," subject pronoun).

from The Tragedy of Romeo and Juliet **282e**

Romeo. With love's light wings did I o'erperch these walls;
For stony limits cannot hold love out,
And what love can do, that dares love attempt.
Therefore thy kinsmen are no let[12] to me.

70 **Juliet.** If they do see thee, they will murder thee.
Romeo. Alack, there lies more peril in thine eye
Than twenty of their swords! Look thou but sweet,
And I am proof against their enmity.
Juliet. I would not for the world they saw thee here.

75 **Romeo.** I have night's cloak to hide me from their sight;
And but thou love me, let them find me here.
My life were better ended by their hate
Than death prorogued,[13] wanting of thy love.
Juliet. By whose direction foundst thou out this place?

80 **Romeo.** By love, that first did prompt me to enquire.
He lent me counsel, and I lent him eyes.
I am no pilot, yet, wert thou as far
As that vast shore washed with the farthest sea,
I would adventure for such merchandise.

85 **Juliet.** Thou knowest the mask of night is on my face;
Else would a maiden blush bepaint my cheek
For that which thou hast heard me speak tonight.

---
[12] **let:** hindrance, obstacle.
[13] **prorogued:** postponed.

Romeo says he'd rather die than not have Juliet's love.

8. **◄ REREAD** Reread lines 62–79. Juliet has not spoken directly to Romeo of her feelings for him. What might be holding her back? What clues do you have about her emotions from her words here and earlier in Scene 2?

She has feelings for him because of the way she spoke before she knew he was listening, but now she seems mostly afraid that her relatives will come after him.

9. **READ ►** As you read lines 80–106, continue to cite textual evidence.
- In the margin, explain how Juliet feels about being overheard by Romeo (lines 85–89).
- Underline lines that show Juliet is worried that she will make a bad impression on Romeo by falling for him too easily.

68

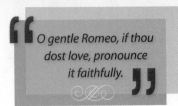

> *O gentle Romeo, if thou dost love, pronounce it faithfully.*

Fain[14] would I dwell on form—fain, fain deny
What I have spoke; but farewell compliment!

90 Dost thou love me? I know thou wilt say "Ay";
And I will take thy word. Yet, if thou swearst,
Thou mayst prove false. At lovers' perjuries,
They say Jove[15] laughs. O gentle Romeo,
If thou dost love, pronounce it faithfully.

95 Or if thou thinkst I am too quickly won,
I'll frown, and be perverse, and say thee nay,
So thou wilt woo; but else, not for the world.
In truth, fair Montague, I am too fond,
And therefore thou mayst think my 'havior light;

100 But trust me, gentleman, I'll prove more true
Than those that have more cunning to be strange.[16]
I should have been more strange, I must confess,
But that thou overheardst, ere I was ware,[17]
My true love's passion. Therefore pardon me,

105 And not impute this yielding to light love,
Which the dark night hath so discovered.

---
[14] **fain:** willingly.
[15] **Jove:** another name for the Roman god Jupiter, king of the gods.
[16] **strange:** aloof, cold.
[17] **ware:** aware.

Juliet is embarrassed that Romeo has overheard her. She'd like to deny what she said.

10. **◄ REREAD** Reread lines 85–106. Explain the shifts in emotions Juliet experiences in this soliloquy.

At first Juliet is embarrassed, then she becomes frank, pleading, then shifting to anxiety, and doubt. She's afraid Romeo will lie about loving her, and then chides herself for loving him too quickly.

69

---

8. **REREAD AND CITE TEXT EVIDENCE** Point out that Juliet has already declared her longing for Romeo—but not directly to him, because she didn't know he was listening.

H **ASK STUDENTS** to look at lines 62–74 and compare what Juliet says to Romeo directly with what she said earlier. *Before, she spoke of him lovingly. Now, she doesn't speak of her love but worries that he will be killed if her family finds him there.*

9. **READ AND CITE TEXT EVIDENCE**

I **ASK STUDENTS** to read lines 85–89 and 93–99 and think about Juliet as if she were a real or fictional girl of today. How does she react when she realizes that she has been noticed by a boy she has feelings for? *She admits embarrassment by saying that she is blushing. She would love to take back what she said and worries that Romeo will think that she's too forward.*

10. **REREAD AND CITE TEXT EVIDENCE**

J **ASK STUDENTS** to read lines 90–106 and think about how Shakespeare treats the conflicting feelings of trust and doubt. What words does Juliet use to show that she wants to trust Romeo and to be trusted herself? *Juliet says "I will take thy word" (line 91), but then expresses doubt, "Thou mayst prove false" (line 92). She later asks Romeo to trust her, because she isn't like "those that have more cunning" (line 101).*

(K) Romeo. Lady, by yonder blessed moon I swear,
That tips with silver all these fruit-tree tops—
Juliet. O, swear not by the moon, the inconstant moon,
110 That monthly changes in her circled orb,
Lest that thy love prove likewise variable.
Romeo. What shall I swear by?
Juliet. Do not swear at all;
Or if thou wilt, swear by thy gracious self,
Which is the god of my idolatry,
115 And I'll believe thee.
Romeo. If my heart's dear love—
Juliet. Well, do not swear. Although I joy in thee,
I have no joy of this contract[18] tonight.
It is too rash, too unadvised, too sudden;
Too like the lightning, which doth cease to be
120 Ere one can say "It lightens." Sweet, good night!
This bud of love, by summer's ripening breath,
May prove a beauteous flow'r when next we meet.
Good night, good night! As sweet repose and rest
Come to thy heart as that within my breast!
125 **Romeo.** O, wilt thou leave me so unsatisfied?
Juliet. What satisfaction canst thou have tonight?
Romeo. The exchange of thy love's faithful vow for mine.
Juliet. I gave thee mine before thou didst request it;
And yet I would it were to give again.
130 **Romeo.** Wouldst thou withdraw it? For what purpose, love?
Juliet. But to be frank and give it thee again.
And yet I wish but for the thing I have.
My bounty is as boundless as the sea,
My love as deep; the more I give to thee,
135 The more I have, for both are infinite.
(L) I hear some noise within. Dear love, adieu!

[18]**contract:** declaration of love.

Juliet is uneasy about her relationship with Romeo. She's afraid everything is happening too quickly.

11. **READ ▶** As you read lines 107–141, continue to cite textual evidence.
   • Underline the line in which Romeo states what he wants of Juliet.
   • Circle each time a character "swears" or promises something.
   • In the margin, explain what Juliet is feeling.

70

[*Nurse calls within.*]
Anon[19], good nurse! Sweet Montague, be true.
Stay but a little, I will come again.
[*Exit.*]
Romeo. O blessed, blessed night! I am afeard,
140 Being in night, all this is but a dream,
Too flattering-sweet to be substantial.
(N) [*Re-enter Juliet, above.*]
(M) Juliet. Three words, dear Romeo, and good night indeed.
If that thy bent of love be honorable,
Thy purpose marriage, send me word tomorrow,
145 By one that I'll procure to come to thee,
Where and what time thou wilt perform the rite;
And all my fortunes at thy foot I'll lay
And follow thee my lord throughout the world.
Nurse [*within*]. Madam!
150 **Juliet.** I come, anon.—But if thou meanst not well,
I do beseech thee—
Nurse [*within*]. Madam!
Juliet. By-and-by I come.
—To cease thy suit and leave me to my grief.
Tomorrow will I send.

[19]**anon:** right away.

Juliet and Romeo plan to get married tomorrow. Romeo will send a message to Juliet. The audience already knows that they will die.

12. **◀ REREAD** Reread lines 136–138. What happens in these lines? What other character is introduced here?

Juliet hears her nurse calling her and tells her she will be right there. She leaves and says she will come back to see Romeo one more time. The new character is Juliet's nurse.

13. **READ ▶** As you read lines 142–169, continue to cite textual evidence.
   • Underline the lines in which Juliet tells Romeo what she wants him to do.
   • In the margin, explain the plans the couple makes. What does the audience already know from the prologue?

71

---

11. READ AND CITE TEXT EVIDENCE

(K) ASK STUDENTS to reread the exchange in lines 107–115, where Romeo is trying to make a vow of love to Juliet. Why does Juliet reject his first attempt to make this promise? *Romeo tries to swear by the moon, but Juliet worries that because the moon is so changeable in its appearance ("inconstant"), such a vow can't be trusted.*

FOR ELL STUDENTS Explain that the apostrophe in *flow'r* is used to shorten a noun—*flower*—so that it is one syllable. The apostrophe takes the place of the eliminated letter.

12. REREAD AND CITE TEXT EVIDENCE

(L) ASK STUDENTS how Shakespeare shows that another character is in the scene and identifies this character without having her appear. *The play doesn't show the nurse's response. She is identified only when Juliet addresses her as "good nurse."*

13. READ AND CITE TEXT EVIDENCE

(M) ASK STUDENTS to look back at the Prologue and review the words of the Chorus. Then ask them to reread lines 143–148. What do Romeo and Juliet look forward to in their future? What has Shakespeare said about their future? *They are beginning to speak of marriage. Juliet promises to "follow thee my lord throughout the world." However, the Chorus has said that they will die.*

Romeo.   So thrive my soul—

Juliet. A thousand times good night! [*Exit*.]

155 **Romeo.** A thousand times the worse, to want thy light!

Love goes toward love as schoolboys from their books;

But love from love, towards school with heavy looks.

[*Enter* Juliet *again, above*.]

Juliet. Hist![20] Romeo, hist! O for a falc'ner's voice

To lure this tassel-gentle[21] back again!

160 Bondage is hoarse and may not speak aloud;

Else would I tear the cave where Echo lies,

And make her airy tongue more hoarse than mine

With repetition of my Romeo's name.

Romeo!

165 **Romeo.** It is my soul that calls upon my name.

How silver-sweet sound lovers' tongues by night,

Like softest music to attending ears!

Juliet. Romeo!

Romeo.   My sweet?

Juliet.   What o'clock tomorrow

Shall I send to thee?

Romeo.   By the hour of nine.

---

[20]**hist:** listen.

[21]**a falc'ner's voice, to lure this tassel-gentle:** A falconer trains and cares for tame falcons
used for hunting; a tassel-gentle (or tiercel-gentle) is a variety of falcon.

14. ◀ **REREAD** Reread lines 142–169. How does Shakespeare use Juliet's
leaving and returning to reveal more about Juliet's feelings?

*Juliet keeps coming back to talk with Romeo. This shows that she is
in love with him. She can't bear to part with him, so she keeps
returning.*

72

---

170 **Juliet.** I will not fail. 'Tis twenty years till then.

I have forgot why I did call thee back.

Romeo. Let me stand here till thou remember it.

Juliet. I shall forget, to have thee still stand there,

Rememb'ring how I love thy company.

175 **Romeo.** And I'll still stay, to have thee still forget,

Forgetting any other home but this.

Juliet. 'Tis almost morning. I would have thee gone—

And yet no farther than a wanton's[22] bird,

That lets it hop a little from her hand,

180 Like a poor prisoner in his twisted gyves,[23]

And with a silk thread plucks it back again,

So loving-jealous of his liberty.

Romeo. I would I were thy bird.

Juliet.   Sweet, so would I.

Yet I should kill thee with much cherishing.

---

[22]**wanton:** spoiled young girl.

[23]**twisted gyves:** shackles.

*Juliet wants to
let him go
because it's
morning, but
also wants to
keep him by
her side.*

15. **READ** ▶ As you read lines 170–190, continue to cite textual evidence.

• Underline the promises Romeo and Juliet make to each other.

• In the margin, explain in your own words the meaning of Juliet's words to
Romeo (lines 177–182).

16. ◀ **REREAD** Reread lines 177–186. Note some examples of
contradictions—saying opposite things—that Juliet says here. What
does this tell you about Juliet's motivations?

*Juliet tells Romeo that she wants him to go because it's almost
morning, but she wants to keep him close. She says that she might kill
him with "much cherishing." She also refers to parting as "sweet
sorrow." These contradictions convey the idea that strong positive
and negative emotions can often be very close together.*

73

---

14. **REREAD AND CITE TEXT EVIDENCE** Remind students that
sometimes playwrights use stage directions as a tool to reveal
characters' motivations and actions.

(N) **ASK STUDENTS** to reread the stage directions in these
lines. What is Juliet doing throughout this section? What kinds of
emotions would compel someone to keep coming back to
continue a conversation? *She keeps coming back out to talk with
Romeo. Students might suggest that she is overwhelmed and
confused by her emotions, so she wants to continue speaking.*

15. **READ AND CITE TEXT EVIDENCE** The image in lines 177–182
may be challenging because of its archaic wording. Encourage
students to use footnotes as they read these lines.

(O) **ASK STUDENTS** to read lines 177–182, along with the
footnotes. What are the figures in Juliet's image? *Encourage
students to visualize and identify a young girl holding a length of silk
cord attached to the leg of a tamed bird, the way a prisoner in leg
chains is tethered, so she can control its movement.*

16. **REREAD AND CITE TEXT EVIDENCE**

(P) **ASK STUDENTS** to reread line 184. Explain that the word
should here means "would," not "ought to." What is the effect of
the contradiction in this line? *The destructive word* kill *and the
loving word* cherishing, *when combined, are jarring. They show
Juliet's heightened and confused emotions.*

185   Good night, good night! Parting is such sweet sorrow,
      That I shall say good night till it be morrow.
      [*Exit.*]
      Romeo. Sleep dwell upon thine eyes, peace in thy breast!
      Would I were sleep and peace, so sweet to rest!
      Hence will I to my ghostly father's[24] cell,
190   His help to crave and my dear hap[25] to tell.
      [*Exit.*]

      ---
      [24]**ghostly father:** priest, spiritual advisor.
      [25]**dear hap:** good fortune.

SHORT RESPONSE

Cite Text Evidence   Compare the tone of the Prologue to that of Act II, Scene 2. How might knowing the statements in the Prologue color an audience's view of the later scene between Romeo and Juliet? **Cite examples from the text** of the Prologue and Act II, Scene 2 as evidence.

The Prologue is tragic in tone. The chorus introduces the "ancient grudge" of the two families, and it announces that the love of the two main characters is doomed to end in death, using words such as "death," "blood," "rage," and "death-marked love" to create a feeling of disaster. The balcony scene is lyrical and hopeful in tone, as Romeo and Juliet declare their love for each other both in soliloquies and in dialogue. Shakespeare uses images of all kinds of light, including a comparison of Juliet to the sun and her eyes to stars. He also compares Juliet to an angel—a "winged messenger of heaven." Knowing that the love between Romeo and Juliet will end in their death gives the balcony scene an edge of tension. This tension is heightened by the dialogue from both characters about the difficulty of being from feuding families.

74

SHORT RESPONSE

Cite Text Evidence   Students' responses should include text evidence that supports their positions. They should:

- identify the tone of the Prologue, and give examples of wording that creates that tone.
- identify the tone of Act II, Scene 2, and give examples of wording that creates that tone.
- Explain the effect that the Prologue has on Act II, Scene 2.

TO CHALLENGE STUDENTS . . .

Shakespeare created many memorable heroines in addition to Juliet, and not all his heroines faced tragic endings. Some famous Shakespearean women who experienced happy endings include Viola in *Twelfth Night*, Portia in *The Merchant of Venice*, Titania in *A Midsummer Night's Dream*, and Rosalind in *As You Like It*.

ASK STUDENTS to research another Shakespearean heroine from his comedies. Students might make their choices from the ones mentioned above or choose other heroines. Have students read a synopsis of the comedy that stars the heroine they chose and then write a paragraph or two using their research, telling about their heroine's motivation. Have students compare their findings with those of other students.

DIG DEEPER

With the class, return to Question 10, Reread, on page 69. Have students share their responses.

ASK STUDENTS to cite the text evidence that led to their description of Juliet's shifting emotions.

- Have students identify Juliet's reaction that begins with line 85. What physical reaction does she describe to convey her feelings? *She is embarrassed. She says that she is blushing.*
- Ask what she says that she wishes she could do now that she knows that Romeo has heard her. *She would love to deny what she has said.*
- Ask what two conflicting feelings she displays in lines 90–99. *She says she'll trust Romeo if he says he loves her, but then she worries that he will prove false. Then she begs him to tell the truth. After that she worries that he will think she is too easily won and thinks she would have been more "strange" (aloof) if she had realized he could hear.*
- Have students explain what lines 100–106 show about her deepest feelings for Romeo. *She is honest about the fact that what she declared earlier were her true feelings ("my true love's passion") for Romeo.*
- Have students tell what effect they think such honesty ought to have on Romeo.

ASK STUDENTS to return to their answer and revise it based on the class discussion.

my **Smart**Planner Create lesson plans and access resources online.

EXEMPLAR **Pyramus and Thisbe**

Myth Retold by Ovid Translated by Allen Mandelbaum

Why This Text?

Students often encounter a literary work that draws on great stories or poems that came before it. This lesson explores the poem "Pyramus and Thisbe," a myth retold by Ovid that inspired Shakespeare's tragedy *Romeo and Juliet*.

View It!

Professional Development Podcast:

Text Complexity

Key Learning Objective: The student will be able to analyze source material.

RL 1 Cite textual evidence.

RL 2 Determine a theme.

RL 3 Analyze how complex characters advance the plot or develop the theme.

RL 4 Determine the meaning of words and phrases as they are used in the text, including figurative and connotative meanings.

RL 5 Analyze how an author's choices concerning how to structure a text create such effects as mystery, tension, or surprise.

RL 9 Analyze how an author draws on and transforms source material in a specific work.

W 2 Write texts to examine complex ideas clearly and accurately through effective organization and analysis.

W 9 Draw evidence from literary or informational texts to support analysis, reflection, and research.

▲ Text Complexity Rubric

Quantitative Measures	**Pyramus and Thisbe** Lexile: N/A
Qualitative Measures	**Levels of Meaning/Purpose** single level of complex meaning
	Structure narrrative, little structural complexity
	Language Conventionality and Clarity more complex sentence structure
	Knowledge Demands moderately complex theme
Reader/Task Considerations	• Teacher determined • Vary by individual reader and type of text • See the Text X-Ray for suggested Reader/Task Considerations.

English Language Support

Before teaching, use the Text X-Ray below for an overview of the text's complexity. The Text X-Ray and supports and scaffolds in the Teacher's Edition will help you guide students of different skill levels.

Meaning Making · Language Development · Effective Expression · Content Knowledge · Foundational Skills

Text Complexity: Qualitative Measures

Levels of Meaning/Purpose

single level of complex meaning

Help students analyze source material that inspired another author's work.

- Teacher's Edition side notes, pp. 283, 284, 285, 286, 287, 288
- Performance Task, p. 288
- Strategies for Annotation, p. 288
- Analyze Source Material, p. 288

Guide students to determine themes.

- Teacher's Edition side notes, pp. 284, 287

To reteach analyzing source material, see

- Analyze Source Material, p. 288a

 Use It! Interactive Whiteboard Lesson: Theme/Central Idea, Comparing Texts

ZOOM IN ON ANALYZING THEME Read aloud the poem's first stanza. Then display lines 7–16. Clarify any vocabulary that is unfamiliar to students. Explain that line 16 is a **proverb**—a brief saying that expresses an idea or belief that many people would agree with. Then discuss these questions:

- What does the word *fire* in the proverb really mean? *(love or passion, as in "the flame of love" in line 13)*
- How can the proverb be restated to show what it says about love? *(When people are forced to hide their love, it grows stronger.)*
- A **theme** is a message about life or human nature conveyed through a poem or story. Could the proverb be a theme of this poem? *(yes)*

As students read the poem, have them think about how this theme is developed through the characters and events.

Structure

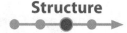

narrative, little structural complexity

Help students analyze plot elements in a narrative poem.

- Teacher's Edition side notes, pp. 284, 285, 286

Guide students in comprehending cause and effect.

- When Students Struggle, p. 287

ZOOM IN ON ANALYZING PLOT STRUCTURE Have students work in pairs to summarize "Pyramus and Thisbe." First, point out that Ovid's work is a **narrative poem**—it has a plot, or a series of events in which characters try to solve a problem, just like a play or a short story. Have each pair list the major events in "Pyramus and Thisbe." Suggest that they pause after each of the following sections to write a sentence summarizing what has happened: 1–16, 17–35, 36–55, 55–61, 62–69, 69–73, 73–84, 84–98, 98–106, 106–126, 127–129, 129–151, 151–152. Invite pairs to share their work in a class discussion.

Language Conventionality and Clarity

more complex sentence structure

Teach unfamiliar vocabulary in context.

- Applying Academic Vocabulary, p. 286

Guide students to analyze the language used in a poem.

- Teacher's Edition side notes, pp. 284, 286
- English Language Support, p. 283, 285

Help students develop reading fluency.

- When Students Struggle, p. 284

ZOOM IN ON ANALYZING IMAGERY Display lines 58–73 and ask volunteers to identify words and phrases that create vivid **imagery** that appeals to readers' senses. *("amid the dark," "face is veiled," "a lioness / just done with killing," "blood dripped down / her jaws, her mouth was frothing," "cool spring," "moonlight," "trembling feet," "shadowed cave," "shawl slips from her shoulders," "with her bloodstained jaws, / tears it to tatters")* Then have students work independently or in pairs to review the poem for other examples of imagery. Ask them to note the senses to which each image appeals and the feeling it creates. Students may also choose to sketch some of the visual images. Have students share their findings in small groups.

Knowledge Demands

moderately complex theme

Support English Learners by providing more information about the poet and his work.

- Teacher's Edition Background note, p. 283

ZOOM IN ON BUILDING BACKGROUND KNOWLEDGE Share with students a key similarity to *Romeo and Juliet* that is not obvious from this translation of Ovid's poem: the parents of Pyramus and Thisbe prohibit their children from marrying because of a long-standing feud between their families. Also help students understand why Ovid might have chosen to have the lovers meet at a tomb. In ancient Roman cities, tombs were usually placed on the outskirts of towns and along the main roads that led into the towns. So, the major landmark farthest from a town's center would likely have been a tomb.

Suggested Reader/Task Considerations

You might consider the following before assigning this essay to students.

- Is it possible to link the content of this poem to students' social studies classwork, such as their studies of ancient Mesopotamia?
- Will the content of the poem engage and interest students, since they are already familiar with the story from *Romeo and Juliet*?

ZOOM IN ON SUPPORTING COMPREHENSION

- Explain that Babylon is the most famous city from ancient Mesopotamia. Then encourage students to share what they may have learned about Mesopotamian culture, society, and cities from their social studies classes.
- Have students keep in mind that a single story can be interpreted and presented in many ways. As they compare Ovid's and Shakespeare's versions, have them think about how they could tell the story in a modern setting, perhaps as a film or a graphic novel.

CLOSE READ

Publius Ovidius Naso (Ovid) Have students read the biographical information about Ovid. Explain that Ovid's *Metamorphoses* was a fifteen-book poem. Ovid's influence on literature became so great in the twelfth and thirteenth centuries that this time period is sometimes known as the "Age of Ovid." Explain that Ovid's works continued to influence writers into the seventeenth century, including, of course, William Shakespeare.

AS YOU READ Direct students to use the As You Read note to focus their reading.

Analyze Source Material
RL 9

(LINES 1–11)

Tell students that just as Ovid borrowed from myths that were passed down through the generations, so, too, Shakespeare borrowed from Ovid.

Ⓐ ASK STUDENTS how the poem resembles the story of Romeo and Juliet so far. *(It is the story of young lovers who live in the same city but are forbidden to marry.)* Then ask students what element of Romeo and Juliet's relationship differs from the story of Pyramus and Thisbe. Have them cite text evidence to support their answer. *(Romeo and Juliet met at a party and fell instantly in love, but Ovid does not describe the first meeting of Pyramus and Thisbe. He says only that "they owed / their first encounters to their living close / beside each other." Unlike Romeo and Juliet, Pyramus and Thisbe did not fall in love instantly; instead, their love grew as they came to know each other.)*

Publius Ovidius Naso (Ovid) (43 BC–AD 17) *is considered one of the greatest Roman poets. His family expected him to become a government official. However, his overriding interest in writing poetry initiated a change in career. His first published work,* Amores *(The Loves), a series of short poems about a love affair, was a success. After becoming popular through his early poems about love and intrigue, he started an ambitious narrative poem called* Metamorphoses. *This work retells important myths from ancient Greece and Rome , including "Pyramus and Thisbe."*

Pyramus and Thisbe

Myth Retold by Ovid   Translated by Allen Mandelbaum

AS YOU READ Pay attention to the similarities between the plot of this myth and other stories you have read or movies that you have seen. Write down any questions you generate during reading.

> The house of Pyramus[1] and that of Thisbe[2]
> stood side by side within the mighty city
> ringed by the tall brick walls Semíramis
> had built[3]—so we are told. If you searched all
> 5 the East, you'd find no girl with greater charm
> than Thisbe; and no boy in Babylon
> was handsomer than Pyramus. They owed
> their first encounters to their living close
> beside each other—but with time, love grows.
> 10 Theirs did—indeed they wanted to be wed,
> but marriage was forbidden by their parents:
> yet there's one thing that parents can't prevent:

---

[1] **Pyramus** (pĭr´ə-məs).

[2] **Thisbe** (thĭz´be).

[3] **the mighty city . . . had built:** the walled city of Babylon (băb´ə-lən), the ruins of which are south of Baghdad, Iraq. In Greek mythology, it was founded by Semíramis (sə-mĭr´ə-məs), a powerful Assyrian queen.

Image Credits: ©Saul Landell/mex/Flickr/Getty Images

Pyramus and Thisbe **283**

ENGLISH LANGUAGE SUPPORT

Language: Punctuation Explain that an **em dash** is used to set off a clause or a part of a sentence and that it is used for dramatic effect. Point out the em dash in line 4 and ask students how it helps to call attention to the clause "so we are told." Then point out the **colons** used in lines 11 and 12. Explain that colons between sentences signal that the second sentence is defining or explaining the first.

ASK STUDENTS how the sentence in line 13 helps explain the sentence in line 12. *(Line 13 explains the one thing that parents can't prevent.)*

TEACH

CLOSE READ

Analyze Language

RL 4

(LINES 12–16)

Explain that a **proverb** is a short saying that expresses commonly held ideas. Point out the proverb in line 16.

B **ASK STUDENTS** to explain the meaning of this proverb. *(When something is suppressed, it becomes more powerful.)* Ask: How does the proverb relate to Pyramus and Thisbe? *(Pyramus and Thisbe were not allowed to express their love openly. Because it was hidden, it became more powerful.)*

Analyze Source Material

RL 9

(LINES 23–51)

Point out that "Pyramus and Thisbe" is a narrative poem and *Romeo and Juliet* a dramatic play. Explain that while Shakespeare gained inspiration from Ovid's poem, he transformed elements of the story to suit the dramatic genre.

C **ASK STUDENTS** to reread lines 23–35 and explain how Pyramus and Thisbe manage to communicate with each other. How does their situation differ from that of Romeo and Juliet? *(Pyramus and Thisbe rely on the fissure in the wall to communicate messages to each other. Romeo and Juliet passed messages to each other through Juliet's nurse.)*

D **CITE TEXT EVIDENCE** Have students reread lines 43–51 ("Then, in low…in darkness;"). Ask them to cite examples of plot elements that inspired Shakespeare and examples of plot elements that Shakespeare modified. *(In lines 44–50, Pyramus and Thisbe devise a plan to evade their guardians and meet at a tomb. In the play, Juliet devises a plan to escape her family so she can be with Romeo in a nearby city. They also plan to meet at a tomb. Unlike Pyramus and Thisbe, Romeo and Juliet have accomplices.)*

B the flame of love that burned in both of them.
They had no confidant—and so used signs:
15   with these each lover read the other's mind:
when covered, fire acquires still more force.

The wall their houses shared had one thin crack,
which formed when they were built and then was left;
in all these years, no one had seen that cleft;
20   but lovers will discover every thing:
you were the first to find it, and you made
that cleft a passageway which speech could take.
For there the least of whispers was kept safe:
it crossed that cleft with words of tenderness. **C**
25   And Pyramus and Thisbe often stood,
he on this side and she on that; and when
each heard the other sigh, the lovers said:
"O jealous wall, why do you block our path?
Oh wouldn't it be better if you let
30   our bodies join each other fully or,
if that is asking for too much, just stretched
your fissure wide enough to let us kiss!
And we are not ungrateful: we admit
our words reach loving ears." And having talked
35   in vain, the lovers still remained apart.
Just so, one night, they wished each other well,
and each delivered kisses to the wall—
although those kisses could not reach their goal.
But on the morning after, when firstlight
40   had banished night's bright star-fires from the sky
and sun had left the brine-soaked[4] meadows dry,
again they took their places at the cleft.
Then, in low whispers—after their laments—
those two devised this plan: they'd circumvent **D**
45   their guardians' watchful eyes[5] and, cloaked by night,
in silence, slip out from their homes and reach
a site outside the city. Lest each lose
the other as they wandered separately
across the open fields, they were to meet
50   at Ninus' tomb[6] and hide beneath a tree
in darkness; for beside that tomb there stood

---

[4] **brine-soaked:** dew-covered.
[5] **they'd circumvent . . . eyes:** They would sneak past their parents.
[6] **Ninus** (nīʹnəs) **tomb:** According to Greek legend, King Ninus was Semíramis' husband. When he died, she marked his burial place with a tall monument outside the walls of Babylon.

WHEN STUDENTS STRUGGLE...

Develop Reading Fluency Use the passage in which Pyramus and Thisbe speak through the cleft in the wall to give students practice in reading poetry. Remind them that fluent readers read poetry with expression. Advise them to use punctuation marks rather than line breaks to determine when to pause or what to emphasize. Point out that words in quotation marks should be spoken as dialogue, with expression.

First, model for students an effective reading of the passage (lines 17–38). Then have students echo read, as you slightly exaggerate the pauses indicated by punctuation. To conclude the activity, ask students how reading poetry aloud differs from reading nonfiction.

a tall mulberry⁷ close to a cool spring,
a tree well weighted down with snow-white berries.
Delighted with their plan—impatiently—
55   they waited for the close of day. At last
the sun plunged down into the waves, and night
emerged from those same waves.

Now Thisbe takes
great care, that none detect her as she makes
her way out from the house amid the dark;
60   her face is veiled; she finds the tomb; she sits
beneath the tree they'd chosen for their tryst.
Love made her bold. But now a lioness
just done with killing oxen—blood dripped down
her jaws, her mouth was frothing—comes to slake
65   her thirst at a cool spring close to the tree.
By moonlight, Thisbe sees the savage beast;
with trembling feet, the girl is quick to seek
a shadowed cave; but even as she flees,
her shawl slips from her shoulders. Thirst appeased,
70   the lioness is heading for the woods
when she, by chance, spies the abandoned shawl
upon the ground and, with her bloodstained jaws,
tears it to tatters.

Pyramus had left
a little later than his Thisbe had,
75   and he could see what surely were the tracks
of a wild beast left clearly on deep dust.
His face grew ashen. And when he had found
the bloodstained shawl, he cried: "Now this same night
will see two lovers lose their lives: she was
80   the one more worthy of long life: it's I
who bear the guilt for this. O my poor girl,
it's I who led you to your death; I said
you were to reach this fearful place by night;
I let you be the first who would arrive.
85   O all you lions with your lairs beneath
this cliff, come now, and with your fierce jaws feast
upon my wretched guts! But cowards talk
as I do—longing for their death but not
prepared to act." At this he gathered up
90   the bloody tatters of his Thisbe's shawl

---

⁷ **mulberry:** a type of tree that produces small, sweet berries, which are usually deep red or purple in color.

Pyramus and Thisbe   **285**

ENGLISH LANGUAGE SUPPORT

Vocabulary: Denotation/Connotation Explain to students that some words have **connotations,** or suggested meanings that are slightly different from the word's literal meaning, or **denotation.** Point out the word *shadowed* in line 68 and ask students what image comes to mind when they read the word. *(something dark and scary)* Then explain that poets choose their words carefully so that each word has maximum emotional impact. Have students work in mixed groups to note other words in lines 58–89 that have strong connotations. *("tryst" [line 61]; "frothing" [line 64]; "savage" [line 66]; "tatters [line 73]; "wretched" [line 87])*

CLOSE READ

Analyze Source Material   RL 9

(LINES 51–53)

Tell students that people used myths to explain natural phenomena, such as why thunder occurs.

E   ASK STUDENTS why Ovid describes the mulberry tree in the story as having white berries, while the footnote says that mulberries are red or purple. *(The myth will likely explain why the berries' color changes.)*

Analyze Author's Choices   RL 5

(LINES 52–53, 69–73)

Explain that **foreshadowing** is a technique in which authors hint at upcoming events. Point out that foreshadowing adds mystery and tension to a story.

F   ASK STUDENTS how the snow-white berries might be a kind of foreshadowing that adds tension to the story. *(The reader knows the color of the berries will change to red or purple, so the mention of the white berries signals that some event, perhaps a bloody event, will make the berries change color.)* Then direct students to lines 69–73: "her shawl slips from her shoulders…the lioness…tears it to tatters." Have students explain how these lines might foreshadow future events. *(The shawl, torn to tatters by bloodstained jaws, hints at a violent death.)*

Analyze Source Material   RL 9

(LINES 73–89)

Ask students to continue looking for plot elements in Ovid's poem that were adapted in *Romeo and Juliet.*

G   CITE TEXT EVIDENCE Have students reread lines 73–89 of the poem and compare them to lines 77–80 in Act V, Scene 1 of Shakespeare's *Romeo and Juliet,* in which Romeo learns that Juliet is dead. Ask: How is Shakespeare's version of events similar to and different from events in the poem? *(Romeo assumes Juliet is dead, just as Pyramus assumes that Thisbe is dead. But Pyramus jumps to conclusions when he sees Thisbe's blood-stained shawl, whereas Romeo is told of Juliet's death by a confidant.)*

Analyze Source Material   RL 9

(LINES 92–106)

Remind students that Shakespeare was inspired by some of the major plot elements of "Pyramus and Thisbe." Then have students recall the dramatic scene in Act V, Scene 3 of *Romeo and Juliet* in which Romeo commits suicide.

Ⓗ CITE TEXT EVIDENCE Have students reread lines 92–106 and ask them what plot elements Shakespeare borrowed from the poem. *(Both men were mistaken in thinking their beloved was dead; both committed suicide and died pointlessly.)* In what way are the death scenes of Pyramus and Romeo similar? *(Both weep and cry over the death of their beloved. Both give long speeches and then die quickly.)* What element of the death scene did Shakespeare choose not to borrow? *(He did not have Romeo kill himself with a dagger. Instead, Romeo used poison.)*

Analyze Language   RL 4

(LINES 113–129)

Explain that **imagery** is vivid descriptive language that appeals to one or more of the senses (sight, hearing, smell, touch, and taste). Imagery makes writing vivid and helps readers visualize what they read.

Ⓘ CITE TEXT EVIDENCE Have students reread lines 113–129 and ask them to identify examples of imagery, or vivid descriptions that add to the intensity of emotion in the story. *(Lines 114–117 contain the images of Thisbe discovering "the writhing body," "the bloody limbs," and Thisbe, "paler than boxwood," trembling "as the sea / when light wind stirs its surface." In lines 120–122, Thisbe "tears her hair," and "fills his wounds with tears / that mingle with his blood." In lines 127–129, Pyramus lifts up "his eyes / weighed down by death.")*

Ⓗ
and set them underneath the shady tree
where he and she had planned to meet. He wept
and cried out as he held that dear shawl fast:
"Now drink from my blood, too!" And then he drew
95   his dagger from his belt and thrust it hard
into his guts. And as he died, he wrenched
the dagger from his gushing wound. He fell,
supine, along the ground. The blood leaped high;
it spouted like a broken leaden pipe
100   that, through a slender hole where it is worn,
sends out a long and hissing stream as jets
of water cleave the air. And that tree's fruits,
snow-white before, are bloodstained now; the roots
are also drenched with Pyramus' dark blood,
105   and from those roots the hanging berries draw
a darker, purple color.

    Now the girl
again seeks out the tree: though trembling still,
she would not fail his tryst;[8] with eyes and soul
she looks for Pyramus; she wants to tell
110   her lover how she had escaped such perils.
She finds the place—the tree's familiar shape;
but seeing all the berries' color changed,
she is not sure. And as she hesitates,
she sights the writhing body on the ground—
Ⓘ 115   the bloody limbs—and, paler than boxwood,[9]
retreats; she trembles—even as the sea
when light wind stirs its surface. She is quick
to recognize her lover; with loud blows
she beats her arms—though they do not deserve
120   such punishment. She tears her hair, enfolds
her love's dear form; she fills his wounds with tears
that mingle with his blood; and while she plants
her kisses on his cold face, she laments:
"What struck you, Pyramus? Why have I lost
125   my love? It is your Thisbe—I—who call
your name! Respond! Lift up your fallen head!"
He heard her name; and lifting up his eyes
weighed down by death, he saw her face—and then
he closed his eyes again.

---

8   **fail his tryst:** neglect to meet him.
9   **boxwood:** a white or light yellow type of wood.

APPLYING ACADEMIC VOCABULARY

commit	underlie

As you discuss the ways in which Shakespeare adapted plot elements and themes from Ovid's poem "Pyramus and Thisbe," incorporate the Collection 4 academic vocabulary words: *commit* and *underlie*. Ask students if the theme of the impulsive nature of love, which **underlies** the play, is developed in the poem. Then ask students how the fact that the main characters in both the play and the poem **commit** suicide supports the theme of impulsive love.

                                            She recognized
130 her own shawl and his dagger's ivory sheath.
     She cried: "Dear boy, you died by your own hand:
     your love has killed you. But I, too, command
     the force to face at least this task: I can
     claim love, and it will give me strength enough
135 to strike myself. I'll follow you in death;
     and men will say that I—unfortunate—
     was both the cause and comrade of your fate.
     Nothing but death could sever you from me;
     but now death has no power to prevent
140 my joining you. I call upon his parents
     and mine; I plead for him and me—do not
     deny to us—united by true love,
     who share this fatal moment—one same tomb.
     And may you, mulberry, whose boughs now shade
145 one wretched body and will soon shade two,
     forever bear these darkly colored fruits
     as signs of our sad end, that men remember
     the death we met together." With these words,
     she placed the dagger's point beneath her breast,
150 then leaned against the blade still warm with her
     dear lover's blood. The gods and parents heard
     her prayer, and they were stirred. Her wish was granted.

COLLABORATIVE DISCUSSION With a partner, discuss the underlying
story of this myth. How is it similar to other stories you have read or
movies you have seen? Cite details from the myth as you compare it with
other stories.

WHEN STUDENTS STRUGGLE . . .

Comprehension: Cause and Effect Tell students that some stories have a
cause-effect structure. A **cause** is why something happens and the **effect**
is what happens as a result of the cause. Point out that each effect can in
turn be a cause for another effect. Display the Interactive Graphic Organizer:
Cause-and-Effect Chain. Ask students to work with a partner to complete the
chain of events and then discuss how each event causes the next.

Cause	**Effect/Cause**	**Effect/Cause**
Thisbe drops her shawl when she hides from the lion	*The lion rips the shawl, bloodying it.*	

TEACH

CLOSE READ

Determine Themes   RL 2
(LINES 129–137)

Remind students that a story's **theme** is its underlying
message, or recurring idea. Note that a story may
have more than one theme.

Ⓙ ASK STUDENTS to reread lines 129–137. What
overarching theme relates to Thisbe's exclamation,
"your love has killed you"? *(The line emphasizes the
power of love, which is one of the poem's themes.)* How
do lines 136–137 ["I—unfortunate— / was both
the cause and comrade of your fate"] help illustrate
another theme that is also developed in Shakespeare?
*(This notion of fate or luck is a theme in both the poem
and the play.)*

Analyze Source Material   RL 9
(LINES 144–152)

Ask students to continue to note plot elements in the
poem that are reflected in Shakespeare's play.

Ⓚ CITE TEXT EVIDENCE Have students reread the
ending of the poem, lines 144–152, and explain how
Thisbe's death inspired Juliet's death in the play. Have
students cite details to support their answers. *(In
lines 148–151, Thisbe takes Pyramus's dagger and falls
on it, killing herself, just as Juliet takes Romeo's dagger
and stabs herself. They both die near the body of their
beloved.)*

COLLABORATIVE DISCUSSION Have students pair
up to discuss the central story of the myth. Remind
them that the central story was not only adapted by
Shakespeare, but by many authors and movie makers.
Have them share their conclusions with the class.

ASK STUDENTS to share any questions they generated
in the course of reading and discussing the selection.

Analyze Source Material   RL 9

Explain that to analyze source material for a work, students must determine what an author borrowed from the original source and what themes the texts share. Discuss how reading an original text adds to the understanding of a text drawn from it.

Analyzing the Text   RL 1, RL 2, RL 3, RL 5, W 9

1. *In* Romeo and Juliet, *the lovers' parents are enemies; in "Pyramus and Thisbe," the parents do not want them to marry, but they are not enemies. Shakespeare adapts the idea of star-crossed lovers by adding characters and information about the families.*

2. *In this scene, Thisbe speaks to a dying Pyramus and commits suicide to be with him in eternity after beseeching the gods and her parents to recognize their love. Romeo, assuming Juliet is dead, expresses his love for her before killing himself. Both Thisbe and Romeo feel guilt for their lovers' deaths and both feel compelled to follow their beloveds into death. But Romeo does not expect the gods or the parents to understand. He is more alone and perhaps more self-absorbed than Thisbe.*

3. *One theme might be the power of love and fate. Thisbe calls herself the "cause and comrade" of Pyramus's fate. Juliet kills herself when she realizes she has played a role in Romeo's death. The couples are fated to be together, if not in life, then in death. This theme is still popular today in a variety of media.*

---

eBook *Annotate It!*

Analyze Source Material   RL 9

Authors often gain inspiration from the works of other writers. For example, in his retelling of "Pyramus and Thisbe," Ovid was influenced by an ancient myth, passed down orally and in writing for generations. Ovid transformed the story of the unlucky Pyramus and Thisbe into a narrative poem by approaching the themes and topic from a fresh perspective, adjusting the character development, and strengthening the structure of the earlier myth. In the same manner, Shakespeare was influenced by and drew upon the works of Ovid as he wrote *The Tragedy of Romeo and Juliet*. Consider these points as you analyze how an author draws upon and transforms ideas from a specific text.

- What elements does the writer borrow from the source text?
- Do the texts share a topic or theme—that is, an enduring message?
- How does the writer transform elements from the original text?

Analyzing the Text   RL 1, RL 2, RL 3, RL 5, W 9a

Cite Text Evidence   Support your responses with evidence from the selection.

1. **Connect** In the Prologue to *Romeo and Juliet*, the play is summarized in this manner, "A pair of star-crossed lovers take their life, / Whose misadventured piteous overthrows / Doth with their death bury their parents' strife." What changes did Shakespeare make to the central ideas of "Pyramus and Thisbe"?

2. **Compare** Reread lines 107–152 in the poem. How does this scene compare to Act V, Scene 3, lines 74–120, of *Romeo and Juliet*?

3. **Connect** What common **theme,** or message, can be attributed to both "Pyramus and Thisbe" and *Romeo and Juliet*? Is this theme still relevant to audiences today? Cite evidence from both sources.

PERFORMANCE TASK

Writing Activity: Essay Write a comparison of "Pyramus and Thisbe" and *Romeo and Juliet*.

- Consider the fact that *Romeo and Juliet* is a play, while "Pyramus and Thisbe" is a narrative poem.
- Compare and contrast the play and the narrative poem in terms of plot, conflict, and characters.

- In your essay, consider how the genre of each text affects these elements.
- Review your essay with a partner and revise for standard English grammar and usage.

Strategies for Annotation   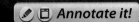 *Annotate it!*

Analyze Source Material   RL 9

Share these strategies for guided or independent analysis:

- Highlight in green the plot elements that Shakespeare borrowed from the poem.
- Highlight in yellow the plot elements that Shakespeare modified in his play.
- On a note, explain how Shakespeare adapted specific plot elements in his play.

> than This be; and no boy in Babylon
>
> was handsomer than Pyramus. They owed
>
> their first encounters to their living close
>
> beside each other—but with time, love grows.
>
> Theirs did—indeed they wanted to be wed,
>
> but marriage was forbidden by their parents:

Write an Analytical Essay

W 2

TEACH

Explain to students that an analytical comparison describes the similarities and differences between two or more works and also explains the significance of the comparison. Before students begin the Performance Task, review the steps for writing a comparison essay.

- **Step 1: Review the Material and Take Notes** Skim each work, making notes about similarities and differences in terms of plot, conflict, and characters.
- **Step 2: Create an Outline** Determine how the essay will be organized. For example, will you address the elements of plot, conflict, and characters in the poem and then address the same elements in the play, noting where they are similar or different? Or will you compare and contrast plot, then conflict, and then characters? After you determine the organization, create an outline that includes the notes you took when you reviewed the material.
- **Step 3: Write a Thesis Statement** Remember, a thesis statement summarizes the purpose of your essay. Writing it before you begin your essay helps you focus your writing. The thesis statement should include the works you are comparing ("Pyramus and Thisbe" and *The Tragedy of Romeo and Juliet*), the grounds for comparison (plot, conflict, and character), and the purpose of the comparison (What do you want to say about the comparison?).
- **Step 4: Write a Draft** Use the outline and the thesis statement to write a first draft of the paper.
- **Step 5: Revise** Review your essay for clarity and style. Read critically: Have you used transitions to move from one topic to the next? Have you kept your topic focused, as much as possible, on the thesis statement? Is the topic of each paragraph clear and obvious? Do you have introductory and concluding paragraphs?
- **Step 6: Edit** Check your essay for spelling, punctuation, and grammatical errors. If you have used quotations from the poem or play, check that they have been accurately recorded and punctuated.

Analyze Source Material

RL 9

RETEACH

Remind students that authors are inspired by existing stories or literary works and that they may borrow lightly from another work, using a character, a setting, or even a quotation from an existing work. They may also borrow extensively, adapting some of the central plot elements and themes and reworking them so that they speak to a contemporary audience. Then ask students if they can think of a play, movie, book, or song that may have been inspired by *Romeo and Juliet*.

- If students have trouble naming a work that was inspired by *Romeo and Juliet*, point out that the play (and movie) *West Side Story*, the book *Julio and Romiette,* the *Twilight* series, the movie *Titanic*, and the song "Love Story" all drew on and transformed some elements of *Romeo and Juliet*.
- Ask students which elements in the work they cited were borrowed from *Romeo and Juliet*. *(Sample answer: The* Twilight *series features forbidden love, which is a theme borrowed from the play.)*
- Then ask students which elements were adapted or modified from *Romeo and Juliet*. *(Sample answer: The movie* Titanic *features young lovers whose fate is to be separated by death. But unlike Romeo and Juliet, who both die, Jack dies and Rose survives when the ship sinks.)*

INDEPENDENT READING

Students can apply the skill by viewing the movie *West Side Story* or by reading the book *Julio and Romiette.* After they have read or viewed their selection, have them work independently to look back at *Romeo and Juliet*, noting which elements of conflict, characterization, and theme from Shakespeare are reflected in their selection. Ask students to list their findings in chart form and then have them discuss their analysis in small groups.

Duty

Short Story by Pamela Rafael Berkman

Why This Text?

To get the most from what they read in literature and in media, students can analyze the relationship of one work to another work that may have served as a source of inspiration for the text. They can also analyze how the author's choice of a point of view affects the story. This lesson provides a vivid example of how a modern author has drawn on Shakespeare's work and used a different point of view to create a new and unique work.

Key Learning Objective: The student will be able to analyze how an author draws on and transforms source material and how an author's choice of point of view creates desired effects.

RL 2 Determine theme.
RL 3 Analyze complex characters.
RL 4 Determine figurative meanings.
RL 5 Analyze author's choices.
RL 7 Analyze representation in different mediums.
RL 9 Analyze source material.
W 3 Write a narrative.
L 1b Use various types of clauses.
L 3 Understand how language functions in different contexts.
L 4a Use context as a clue to the meaning of a word.
L 4d Verify the meaning of a word or phrase.

▲ Text Complexity Rubric

Quantitative Measures	**Duty** **Lexile:** 940L
	Levels of Meaning/Purpose  single level of complex meaning
Qualitative Measures	**Structure**  some unconventional story structure elements
	Language Conventionality and Clarity  more complex sentence structure
	Knowledge Demands many references or allusions to other texts
Reader/Task Considerations	• Teacher determined • Vary by individual reader and type of text • See the Text X-Ray for suggested Reader/Task Considerations.

English Language Support Before teaching, use the Text X-Ray below for an overview of the text's complexity. The Text X-Ray and supports and scaffolds in the Teacher's Edition will help you guide students of different skill levels.

Meaning Making

Language Development

Effective Expression

Content Knowledge

Foundational Skills

Text Complexity: Qualitative Measures

Levels of Meaning/Purpose

single level of complex meaning

Help students analyze a contemporary interpretation of Shakespeare.
- Teacher's Edition side notes, pp. 289, 290, 292, 293, 296, 297
- Strategies for Annotation, p. 297
- Analyze Source Material: Interpretations of Shakespeare, p. 297

Guide students in determining theme.
- Teacher's Edition side note, p. 295

Help students analyze complex characters.
- Teacher's Edition side notes, pp. 291, 294, 296
- When Students Struggle, p. 294

To teach comparing literary and film interpretations of source material, see
- Analyze Representations in Different Mediums, p. 300a

 Use It! **Interactive Whiteboard Lesson:** Theme/Central Idea

ZOOM IN ON **ANALYZING AN INTERPRETATION** After students have read the story once, divide sections of the text among pairs or small groups. Each group should review their section and note all the details that directly relate to Shakespeare's text. If time allows, have them return to *Romeo and Juliet* to find specific lines that inspired the details in Berkman's text. Ask students to share their findings in a class discussion. Then ask them to identify details that Berkman invented for her story. List these on the board. End the discussion by asking students why they think the author may have chosen to explore Lady Capulet's character in this kind of story. *(Possible responses: to create a surprising new twist on a familiar character; to suggest motivations for her behavior that were missing from the play)*

Structure

some unconventional story structure elements

Help students analyze how point of view affects a story.
- Teacher's Edition side notes, pp. 289, 292, 293, 295, 296, 297
- Performance Task, p. 298
- Strategies for Annotation, p. 297
- Author's Choices: Point of View, p. 297

Help students analyze cause-and-effect organization.
- English Language Support, p. 293

To reteach analyzing point of view, see
- Author's Choices: Point of View, p. 300a

 Use It! *Level Up* **Tutorial:** Point of View
Interactive Whiteboard Lesson: Point of View

ZOOM IN ON **ANALYZING POINT OF VIEW** Display the first paragraph of the story and read it aloud. Ask students to identify details that provide clues about the **narrator,** or the person telling the story. *(Possible responses: first-person pronouns "we" and "I"; references to "Juliet," "our daughter," and "my husband"; fact that the narrator is "summoned . . . [by] the prince . . . to the opening of our tomb")* Lead them to conclude that the narrator is Lady Capulet, Juliet's mother. After students have read the story, have pairs answer these questions, finding evidence in the text: *What opinions about people and events does Lady Capulet express? What feelings does she reveal? At the beginning of the story, what events from the play does she know about and not know about? What ideas about life does Lady Capulet express?*

Language Conventionality and Clarity

more complex sentence structure

Teach unfamiliar vocabulary in context.

- Teacher's Edition Critical Vocabulary notes, pp. 290, 292, 293, 299
- Applying Academic Vocabulary, pp. 290, 295
- English Language Support, p. 289
- Vocabulary Strategy: Context Clues, p. 299
- Strategies for Annotation, p. 299

Help students develop reading fluency.

- When Students Struggle, p. 291

Support students in understanding personal pronoun referents.

- English Language Support, p. 296

Guide students in using independent and dependent clauses.

- Language and Style: Independent and Dependent Clauses, p. 300

ZOOM IN ON **UNPACKING SENTENCES** Review the definitions of **independent** and **dependent clauses** on page 300, and tell students that identifying these clauses can help them understand long, complex sentences in the text. Display lines 47–52 and work with students to identify the independent clause *("He does not bleed")* and the three conjunctions that introduce dependent clauses *("though," "as though," "before")*. Discuss how the dependent clauses add descriptive details that help readers imagine exactly what Romeo looks like and how he must have died. Have pairs analyze the sentence in lines 62–67 in a similar way as you circulate to provide assistance.

Knowledge Demands

many references or allusions to other texts

Support English Learners by expanding their knowledge of the story's setting.

ZOOM IN ON **BUILDING HISTORICAL KNOWLEDGE** "Duty" is set in a mausoleum, an above-ground burial site in which the dead are laid out as if asleep on beds of stone. The characters Romeo and Juliet are fictional, but Shakespeare's story is so powerful that by the early 1800s, people had begun to identify an empty sarcophagus in a Franciscan convent outside Verona, Italy, as "Juliet's tomb." In the 1930s, hoping to capitalize on a Hollywood movie version of *Romeo and Juliet,* the city transformed it into a tourist attraction. Today, people come from around the world to be married at the site or just to view the tomb.

Suggested Reader/Task Considerations

You might consider the following before assigning this short story to students.

- Do readers have the maturity and insight needed to understand the narrator's attitudes and behavior?
- Might some readers of this story be inspired to utilize similar source material for their own writing?

ZOOM IN ON **SUPPORTING COMPREHENSION**

- Point out that in "Duty," Lady Capulet is just 27 years old and married to an old man she does not love. Ask students to imagine the bitterness they might feel if they had given up hope of romantic love because their family demanded it. In this situation, how would Juliet's behavior appear to them?
- Encourage students to seek out Ovid's *Metamorphoses* or other "classics" to use as sources for their own stories. Point out that **parody**—a humorous imitation of another work—is a fun and acceptable way to use the material of others.

AS YOU READ Direct students to use the As You Read note to focus their reading.

Analyze Source Material   RL 9

(LINES 1–15)

Tell students that authors who use source material from other works may borrow some material directly from the source. This may include a plot, setting, characters, and possibly themes. However, to make their story distinct from the source material, they must transform other parts of the story to vary from the original.

A **CITE TEXT EVIDENCE** Have students reread lines 1–15. Have them identify the lines that borrow events, setting, characters, and plot directly from *Romeo and Juliet*. *(Lines 1–2 use the image of people running in the streets. Lines 6–7 use the events and characters of the Capulet family being called to the tomb. Line 9 uses the image of the stone rolled away from the opening of the tomb. Lines 13–15 recall the events of the deaths of both Romeo and Juliet and the "pretense" of her earlier death.)*

Have students reread lines 13–14. Explain that in some cases, a writer may quote directly from the source material or make a direct allusion to it.

B **ASK STUDENTS** to recall an image from *Romeo and Juliet* that is echoed here. *(In Act V, Scene 3 of* Romeo and Juliet, *lines 203–205, Lord Capulet uses the image of a dagger that has "missheathed in my daughter's bosom." This is echoed by Lady Capulet saying that Juliet made a "dagger's sheath of her breasts," in lines 13–14 of the story.)*

Author's Choices: Point of View   RL 4, RL 5

(LINES 16–21)

Explain that the **first-person narrator** of this story is very different from the third-person perspective of *Romeo and Juliet*. She provides a first-person description of the setting and characters, often using figurative language, and describes characters according to her own perspective.

C **CITE TEXT EVIDENCE** Direct students to reread lines 16–21. Have them identify instances of figurative language used by the first-person narrator that indicate her perspective. *(She describes Tybalt's body as "green and stinking" and refers to Paris as a "fool".)*

Duty

Short Story by Pamela Rafael Berkman

AS YOU READ Notice who is telling the story and think about what you already know about the play *The Tragedy of Romeo and Juliet.* Write down any questions you generate during reading.

W e heard the running in the streets, we heard the name "Romeo!" called out, but not "Juliet." We had no reason to think Juliet. We knew nothing of what had happened, we thought our daughter already dead. But then we found ourselves summoned, not by servants but by armed men, come from the prince. We were sent for, my husband and I, to come to the opening of our tomb, the tomb of our family, the great yawning maw[1] of death. It had been newly fed.

When we came we found the stone rolled away, like that which 10 covered Our Savior's grave.[2] Now I stand over the bodies of my girl and my enemy's boy, here in the dusty crypt. They are coiled like pale snakes, young serpents of death, he contorted more awfully, by cause of the poison. She stabbed herself instead, made a dagger's sheath of her breasts. And her earlier death was a pretense, to get her to this place and away from us.

The chamber is lined with gloomy stones, the skeletons are faded, gray, common in the sickly light of day that feebly shines—if "shine" is the word could be used for it—through the opening. My nephew Tybalt is over there, a few feet off, green and stinking on his 20 bier,[3] dead three days ago. Crumpled beside him is that fool Paris, who no less than Romeo died for love of my daughter. And I stand and look across the children, across all these pallets of the dead, adorned with jewels, flowers still fresh around Juliet, kept so in

---

[1] **yawning maw:** jaws opened wide.
[2] **the stone . . . Our Savior's grave:** three women who visited the burial site of Jesus discovered that the stone sealing the tomb had been moved and that his body was gone.
[3] **bier (bîr):** a platform that holds a body or a coffin before it is buried.

ENGLISH LANGUAGE SUPPORT

Vocabulary: Figurative Language Like Shakespeare, Berkman uses figurative language to establish a mood and make the narrative vivid. Help students review the following lines, identify the figurative language used, and explain why it is effective.

- Lines 6–8 "…the great yawning maw of death. It had been newly fed." *(a metaphor that makes the tomb a large mouth that can be "fed" or devour people)*
- Lines 11–13 "…coiled like pale snakes, young serpents of death" *(a simile that creates a feeling of dread, since most people are not comfortable with snakes or dead bodies that look like "serpents")*
- Lines 16–18 "…sickly light of day…if 'shine' is the word could be used for it…" *(vivid language that increases the discomfort at a "gloomy" and "sickly" scene)*

TEACH

CLOSE READ

Analyze Source Material RL 9

(LINES 42–52)

Review the idea that an author may pick up the basic plot of a work of literature but then transform it through the eyes of a different narrator.

D **ASK STUDENTS** to reread lines 42–52. Ask them to describe how these lines use the basic plot of *Romeo and Juliet* but transform it through the use of a first-person narrator. (*This paragraph uses the plot of* Romeo and Juliet *that involves Juliet stabbing herself and Romeo poisoning himself. However, the first-person narrator here makes the images much more vivid and horrible by describing the color of Juliet's dead body and the posture of Romeo in the throes of poison, a specific description the play does not include.*)

> #### CRITICAL VOCABULARY
>
> **bereaved**: Note that Berkman's descriptions of Lady Capulet's thoughts indicate that she is grieving in an unorthodox way.
>
> **ASK STUDENTS** to suggest ways they might expect Lady Capulet to act or think as a bereaved parent. (*She might be crying or shocked in disbelief; she might be searching for the cause of her daughter's death.*)
>
> **afflicted**: Note that Lady Capulet uses this word twice in the paragraph—lines 36 and 38—and through this description begins to reveal her character.
>
> **ASK STUDENTS** what Lady Capulet's attitude is towards those who are afflicted with "greensickness." (*She is not sympathetic and sees their affliction as a "weakness."*)
>
> **succumb**: This description also helps show Lady Capulet's steely character.
>
> **ASK STUDENTS** to describe what they interpret about Lady Capulet's character because she does not succumb to "the female weakness." (*She is a strong woman who does not see other women as generally strong.*)

---

the cool of this underground place. I stare across them at Romeo's father, Montague.

'Tis not only ourselves, the **bereaved** parents, my husband and I and *his* father and mother, about the tomb now. The county Paris's page, the wretched boy Romeo's attendant Balthasar, the old friar, the prince, Nurse—all are clustered here. And outside the entrance,
30 so short a time ago closed off by the great stone, there gather peasants, working men, merchants, beggars in rags, courtesans, and prostitutes, all the city. The day will not be bright, we feel that even now, the dawn so gray and stale, not fresh and cool as a dawn should be. No breezy wind and yet no heat. A still, dead dawn.

My daughter is pale. When she was alive I wondered if she was **afflicted** with the greensickness, that odd anemic draining of the blood from the face that makes girls her age often so white, with no roses in their skins. I was not so afflicted myself, though many of my sisters and cousins were so. I was, I fear, not sympathetic to
40 their weakness, flushed and strong as I always was, their faces white as tallow.[4]

Now I know she could not have been ill in that kind. I had not seen pale until I saw this face before me; in life she was a red rose compared with this creature drained of blood, all the blood of her body warm on these disgusting stones, running in rivulets[5] between them, dyeing the mortar, the source of the river the sharp little dagger still in her left breast. *He* does not bleed, though he is twisted about horribly, his face an ugly contortion of death, one side of his mouth high in a kind of crooked smile, his fingers held
50 up, bent backward and stiff before his eyes, as though he wished to obscure those orbs[6] from our sight but could not succeed before the last convulsion seized him.

Mistress Montague—I do beg pardon, *Lady* Montague—is about to faint. Not I. I do not **succumb** to the female weakness of fear of blood, or of the dead. But she cries out to her husband, who stands, it seems, amazed, without comprehension or action. Clouds pass over the faint sun outside, and the light is for a moment yet more gray.

And it is very strange, to be watching so closely the clouds
60 and the light outside the tomb at this moment, and I am sure if I were more foolish I would wonder if I were heartless. Perhaps I do wonder yet. How strange, to watch myself watch the clouds and the light, to feel so very much abroad from here where I am, so removed that I watch myself *watching myself* watch the clouds and the light

---

[4] **tallow:** hard fat derived from animals, used to make candles and soap.

[5] **rivulets:** small streams.

[6] **orbs:** globes or spheres; here it is referring to Romeo's eyes.

bereaved
(bĭ-rēvd´) *adj.* having suffered the loss of a loved one; grieving.

afflict
(ə-flĭkt´) *v.* to cause pain to; to trouble.

succumb
(sə-kŭm´) *v.* to surrender or fall victim to.

APPLYING ACADEMIC VOCABULARY

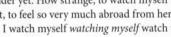

| expose | attribute |

As you discuss the opening pages, incorporate the Collection 4 academic vocabulary words: *expose* and *attribute*. Ask students to identify specific lines that **expose** the character of Lady Capulet. Ask them to discuss the **attributes** of her character that they find surprising and that may be developed further in the story.

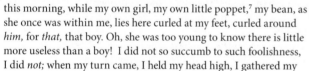

this morning, while my own girl, my own little poppet,[7] my bean, as
she once was within me, lies here curled at my feet, curled around
him, for *that,* that boy. Oh, she was too young to know there is little
more useless than a boy! I did not so succumb to such foolishness,
I did *not;* when my turn came, I held my head high, I gathered my

---

[7] **poppet:** a cute, darling child.

CLOSE READ

Analyze Complex Characters (LINES 59–68) RL 3

Explain that good literature involves **complex characters.** Complex characters are not stereotypes who can be easily classified as good or bad. They instead tend to have a mixture of intriguing and often conflicting character traits.

E CITE TEXT EVIDENCE Have students reread lines 59–68. Have them identify the lines that indicate important character traits about the narrator, Lady Capulet. *(Lines 59–62 indicate that Lady Capulet is aware of her own thoughts and others' perceptions of her. Lines 65–67 show that Lady Capulet has tender feelings as a mother toward Juliet. Lines 66–68 illustrate her bitterness toward Romeo, who she believes was no more than a "useless boy.")*

WHEN STUDENTS STRUGGLE . . .

To develop reading fluency, have pairs read lines 36–52 aloud. Have them alternate paragraphs and, after a first reading, switch the order of reading. Before they begin reading, they should discuss Lady Capulet's character and how they think she might sound if she were saying these lines aloud.

Direct students' attention to the author's use of italics in line 47 for *He* and discuss how this might be emphasized in oral reading. They should also consider powerful, descriptive words such as *sympathetic* (line 39), *weakness* (line 40), *creature* (line 44), *disgusting* (line 45), and *horribly* (line 48) and decide on how these might be treated in oral reading. Emphasize that students should use appropriate intonation and pacing.

Analyze Source Material   RL 9

(LINES 72–80)

Review the idea that an author can use source material for the basic plot, and then transform the material by giving it a different focus or description.

 CITE TEXT EVIDENCE Ask students to reread lines 72–80 and identify lines that support the plot taken from *Romeo and Juliet* and other lines that transform the ideas from the source material through new information added by the first-person narrator. *(Berkman conforms to the plot of* Romeo and Juliet *in lines 72–74 by suggesting that Romeo wrenched the stone away from the door. The first-person narrator adds new information in her description of her age and the ages of Montague and her husband in lines 75–80.)*

Author's Choices: Point of   RL 5
View (LINES 102–106)

Discuss the idea that a first-person narrator can provide an alternate view of characters or actions in the source material. Note that different people often judge a person or actions differently.

G **ASK STUDENTS** to reread lines 102–106 and describe how Lady Capulet's judgment of Friar Lawrence differs from the general judgment of him in *Romeo and Juliet*. *(Lady Capulet judges the Friar's attempts at helping the lovers as a mistake that helped bring about their death. In the play, the final word on the friar is the Prince's statement that he is known as a "holy man.")*

CRITICAL VOCABULARY

deludes: Explain that this usage usually carries a negative connotation: it implies that people are not capable of looking at the truth.

ASK STUDENTS to identify what Lady Capulet sees as the truth that the friar is not admitting by deluding himself. *(There can be no rational or sensible explanation for the deaths of four young people.)*

---

70   strength, I performed the duty required of me, the duty that was best for all, for me, even now. I know this.

How was the stone at the door of the tomb rolled away? I suppose that boy wrenched it aside with the strength of his doomed love. Boys. No boy ever did any such thing for me, despite my beauty. I am still beautiful. I am twenty-seven. I was only a year older than she is—was—now when my old husband, Capulet, and I conceived her. The boy's father, Montague, is yet only thirty. He may have another son, if he has none already. He is not old. Not gray and cantankerous,[8] like my husband. Who smells of decay.
80   Like this tomb.

She has no age now, I suppose, my daughter. My bean.

We have been waiting for the prince to speak first. He carries in his hand a letter, the red seal of which he breaks, and then begins.

"Here he writes that he did buy poison of a poor apothecary, and therewithal came to this vault to die and lie with Juliet."

We know it all. We heard it shouted among the crowd in the streets as we came, despite the rhythmic metal steps of our escorts. "Romeo is dead!" "Juliet did love him!" "They lie now in each other's arms in the tomb in the churchyard!" "She was not truly
90   dead yesterday! Did you hear?" "They were married and none knew!" How do such things creep so quickly, like the plague, into the common knowledge of the city?

Yet the prince would have none but himself give the story authority. He would officiate at it. He further reads the note, the confession of the mortal sin of suicide, left by that boy to his father confessor, Friar Lawrence. The friar nods sagely, as though he knows something, as though he can build for us from this fleshy, deadly crypt some sense and order. But he cannot. Who could build such things, with three boys and a girl slimy with death arranged
100   about us? Order? Cause? Effect? He **deludes** himself with his own importance.

The friar speaks. "Romeo, there, was husband to that Juliet, and she, there dead, that Romeo's faithful wife. I married them."

Why? How dare he marry children against what he knew would be the wishes of their parents! He's to blame, *I* know, however history may hold it, however gently the prince looks on him now.

"How came your master here?" His Grace requests of poor Paris's page. "To duel with Romeo Montague and die, before this pair then took their own lives?"
110   The servant stutters, a simpleton, addressed by so great a personage, then manages, "He came with flowers to strew his lady's grave, and bid me stand aloof, and so I did."

delude
(dĭ-lōōd´) *v.* to deceive or instill a false belief in.

---

[8] **cantankerous:** grouchy.

TO CHALLENGE STUDENTS . . .

Innovate on Story Ideas Have student pairs discuss how Berkman used Shakespeare's play as an inspiration for her short story and built upon it to create a unique, new story. Then have them choose a well-known tale and write a new story using elements of the plot, setting, characters, and themes of the original story. Have them present their story from a unique point of view and include the following points:

- Events in the plot that are essentially the same in both stories and ones that are clearly different in both stories.

- Dialogue or description taken directly from the original text, but surrounded by material that is unique to the narrator students have chosen for their story.

Have pairs share copies of their completed stories with other interested students.

Oh, Paris. Milksop.[9] Even as she rejected him in death, he was slave to my daughter's beauty, which was not fine or perfect but simply youthful. Paris, you tadpole, you eunuch.[10]

Nurse is babbling, telling all, hysterical. "You were too hot!" she screams at my husband, as I did when Juliet refused to marry the county Paris, only the day before yesterday—though I was enraged with my daughter, no less than my husband was. How was I to
120 know the fool had already surrendered the prize to this callow boy, this stepped-upon worm at my feet? Yet my lord threatened to turn her from the house, and that I would have no woman suffer. Now with Nurse and all the company, I turn accusing upon my husband, old Lord Capulet. His nose so long, his hair so thin and falling about his ears. He had no time to dress, his doublet is on over his nightshirt, his legs are scrawny and goatlike, though his stomach bulges. Tears quiver over the end of his nose. Regret. Can it be that my hot-blooded lord and master feels regret? I have no mercy on him. There, do you see? I say with my accusing eyes. 'Twas his
130 doing, all his and his men's fancies and prides.

But Nurse turns on me. She nursed me, too, when she was a girl and I but three weeks old, and yet she turns on me. "God in heaven bless her!" she cries, spittle on her purple face, waving her arms above my blood-drained daughter. Her own daughter dead, she poured all herself into mine. What a creature. "You were to blame, my lady, to rate her so!" Well.

She turns to the prince. "I tried, Your Grace, to defend her from the second marriage, unholy as it was." Liar. "And my lady told her, 'Talk not to me, for I'll not speak a word. Do as thou wilt, for I have
140 done with thee.' Oh, how could a mother?"

I see the **repulsed** stares turn toward me. Simperers. It is unexpected in a mother? But yet not in a father? I did what must be done. What else was I to do? 'Twas her father's word was law, not mine.

Yet Nurse babbles on. "Cold, cold mother. My lamb, she was a faithful wife!" she screams, and throws herself upon her. The prince's men drag her away as she screams, and there is an awkward moment as they push her through the narrow opening, out into the street and the crowd. We hear her screams continue, though
150 they fade, and are finally drowned by the steps, the clinks, of her guardians.

Friar Lawrence, now, must have his say. He whirls upon me and my husband. "You!"

repulsed
(rĭ-pŭlsd´) *adj.*
disgusted.

---
[9] **Milksop:** a weak, cowardly man.
[10] **eunuch:** a person who lacks "masculinity"; one who has been castrated.

ENGLISH LANGUAGE SUPPORT

Analyze Cause-and-Effect Organization Direct students to lines 116–151. Explain that Nurse's actions create several effects. Then have students complete two cause-effect diagrams related to Nurse's words. Discuss within a small group how the cause-and-effect organization helps the reader understand the events.

CLOSE READ

Analyze Source Material   RL 9
(LINES 116–136)

Explain that authors may take characters from a source and have them behave differently or appear in different places in the new story.

H **ASK STUDENTS** to reread lines 116–136. Have them identify how this description differs from the play and how Berkman transforms the source material to add new information. *(Nurse is not present in the play's final scene and speaks no lines. Berkman adds new information through Nurse's accusations against Lord and Lady Capulet and in Lady Capulet's thoughts about her husband's guilt and her attitude towards him.)*

Author's Choices: Point of   RL 5
View (LINES 134–135)

Discuss the idea that a first-person narrator can analyze a character in a way a third-person narrator cannot and can also have biases that color the judgments and descriptions of other characters.

I **ASK STUDENTS** to reread lines 134–135 and describe how Lady Capulet's judgment of Nurse's motivations may be faulty or accurate. *(She suggests that Nurse's interest in Juliet is somehow unhealthy because her own child died. Her description of Nurse's motivations may be accurate, but Nurse's assessment of Lord and Lady Capulet's actions may also be accurate.)*

CRITICAL VOCABULARY

repulsed: Explain that this adjectives carries a strong negative connotation that makes it a stronger word than its synonym *disgusted* and more synonymous with *sickened* or *revolted.*

ASK STUDENTS to explain Lady Capulet's reactions to the people who give her repulsed stares and why the people are repulsed by her actions. *(She is disdainful of those who judge her turning away Juliet's plea for help as a repulsive act.)*

Cause:		Effect:		Cause:		Cause / Effect:		Effect:
Nurse accuses Lord Capulet	▷	Lord Capulet weeps	▷	Nurse accuses Lady Capulet	▷	Lady Capulet does not respond	▷	Nurse throws herself on Juliet's body

Analyze Complex Characters (LINES 155–164)

RL 3

In writing that transforms source material, authors may develop characters by having them interact with other characters in new or unexpected ways. Remind students that there is no exchange between Friar Lawrence and Lady Capulet in the final scene of *Romeo and Juliet*.

J **ASK STUDENTS** to reread lines 155–164. Have them paraphrase the friar's charges against the Capulets and describe Lady Capulet's thoughts in response. *(Friar Lawrence charges that the Capulets treated Juliet poorly by attempting to force her marriage to Paris. He also charges Lady Capulet with encouraging the death of Romeo because he had killed Tybalt. Lady Capulet responds with scornful thoughts, thinking that the friar had no right judge her actions as a mother and that other women throughout history have been very fierce and bloodthirsty.)*

"Are you content, bloodthirsty woman? *Are* you a woman? Unnatural creature!"

"Good Father?" I answer. I am calm. I answer with dignity.

"You betrothed and would have married her perforce to county Paris! Then she comes to me." He gulps air and turns to the little group about us, his hand outstretched to point me out. "And you called for the death of Romeo when he killed your hot-blooded kinsman! Are you content, bloodthirsty woman? *Are* you a woman?
160 Unnatural creature!"

A man, a *eunuch*, to judge a mother! How dare he! When in old Sparta a prisoner of war was to be executed, was it not to their women that he was handed? Was it not their women who tore him to bits? "Unnatural creature," indeed!

And cold, am I? "Do as thou wilt, for I have done with thee." So I did say. And had her father not already spoken? I was merciful, quick, as I hear are the mothers in that far-off savage land of

WHEN STUDENTS STRUGGLE...

To help students understand lines 165–169, discuss Lady Capulet's words. Ask why others might think her "cold" and why she mentions that Juliet's father had already spoken. *(She reminds readers that Lord Capulet had threatened to throw Juliet out if she refused to marry Paris even if Lady Capulet didn't agree. Lady Capulet expresses she isn't cold in echoing her husband's threat because ultimately her words don't carry any weight.)*

Then discuss the custom of "the mothers in that far-off savage land of legend Tchin." *(China)*. Explain that is a reference to a once-accepted expectation that mothers break their young daughters' feet to keep them small. Ask why Lady Capulet sees herself as "merciful" as some Chinese mothers. *(She believes that her threat was an unpleasant but necessary job that, if performed quickly, would be less painful for Juliet.)*

legend, Tchin, where they must by law break their daughter's feet, to keep them small as a child's forever. Best for young Juliet to
170 close her eyes and get it done with, the thing accomplished, go to the wedding as though one were a guest, get to the church, only go, no need to think, allow yourself to be dressed by your maids beforehand as though only for a feast, as I did when I was married to this old man. It is like saying one's rosary; simply making the mouth and body move, no need to hold the thoughts in your mind as you do what you do. The things you need do are most often simple enough. So I would have told her on her wedding morning, had I been given the chance. I knew that in the end such a course would be easiest for her.

180   I did not know, of course, about *his* son. Montague's. I confess I see why my daughter had a preference. Paris is—was—milk toast, certainly. Here he lies now, dead at our feet, not even a good hand with a rapier. He is smaller and paler than, and defeated by, that son of the handsome, broad-chested Montague, Montague who is so close to me now that if I put out my hand I could lay it upon his round arm. He meets my eyes across the bodies of the dead children. All here do look on me now, but he does not appear to hear the friar's insults. He thinks, perhaps, on something else. His own white nightshirt only partially covers his shoulders, hard and
190 firm as they are, and sharp and yet youthful. His jewels are about his neck, his dressing gown shimmering red and green and gold— he was perhaps on his way to bed, not freshly roused out of it. Yet he breaks his look from mine to whisper to the stained red stones we tread upon, where lies his son. He whispers, "What manners is in this, to press before thy father to a grave?" Any might take him for a loving family man, not one who is less in his own bed than a courtesan's, which is what he is. He who left his son to wander the city unchecked and encounter my daughter.

    I make no sound. I am the highest-ranking woman in Verona,
200 the highest-ranking personage after the prince and my husband, and though the friar may rant, none other dare do me any open disrespect. My neck is straight. My eyes are level.

    Juliet, child, wretched fool! Paris would have been grateful to her for being beautiful, would have petted and worshiped her. I said I would she were wedded to her grave when she refused him, and so she is. Why under heaven would she believe she might marry where she would, an unsuitable boy? Who told her such a thing? Not I. I was far too mindful a mother. How could she? Well, she has found her deserved punishment. May she revel in it. She has paid for her
210 one night with her love, a thing I never had, a thing I was denied, denied *myself,* and what harm would it have done me? None might ever have known.

APPLYING ACADEMIC VOCABULARY

commit	underlie

As you discuss the character of Lady Capulet, incorporate the Collection 4 academic vocabulary words: *commit* and *underlie*. Ask students to describe how deeply and on what terms Lady Capulet thinks Juliet should have **committed** to marry Paris. Discuss what feelings **underlie** her description of what is required in marriage in lines 169–179.

TEACH

CLOSE READ

Determine Theme   RL 2
(LINES 169–179)

Remind students that a **theme** is the author's comment upon a larger topic. Shakespeare explored the theme of the power of romantic love in *Romeo and Juliet*.

K **CITE TEXT EVIDENCE** Have students reread lines 169–179 and identify lines that indicate Lady Capulet's views on love and marriage. Discuss how this view compares to that of her daughter. *(Lady Capulet indicates in lines 174–176 that she sees no need for romantic love in marriage and that the actions associated with marriage can be done by rote, "like saying one's rosary." This idea is the opposite of the view of love and marriage that brought Juliet to her death.)*

Author's Choices: Point of   RL 5
View (LINES 180–198)

By using a first-person narrator, Berkman can add new information and a new perspective to the source material. These lines are the first indications that Lady Capulet has any relationship with Lord Montague.

L **CITE TEXT EVIDENCE** Have students reread lines 180–196. Ask them to identify lines that indicate Lady Capulet's thoughts about Lord Montague. *(She describes him as "handsome, broad-chested" in line 184; she describes his appearance as attractive in lines 188–192; and then she notes his behavior is not that of a "loving family man" in lines 195–197. Her final judgment in lines 197–198 is that his careless behavior with women was somehow to blame for the relationship between Romeo and Juliet.)*

Analyze Source Material   RL 9

(LINES 216–223)

Berkman takes some events from the source but uses the first-person narrator to add new information.

 ASK STUDENTS to reread lines 216–223 and identify actions that are taken directly from *Romeo and Juliet* and new information provided by the first-person narrator. *(The two fathers indicating that all is forgiven and that they will build golden statues of their children is taken directly from the play. Lady Capulet adds new information through her observation of Montague in lines 216–218 and in her petulant response to the fathers' declaration of peace. She also indicates hidden feelings for Montague with her focus on his shirt and "the soft, curling dark hair of his chest."*

Author's Choices: Point of View   RL 5

(LINES 224–229)

Berkman brings the entire story into focus by letting the narrator directly address the theme in these lines.

 ASK STUDENTS to reread lines 224–229. Have them comment on this revelation and say how it reflects the story's title and Lady Capulet's previous observations on love and marriage. *(When Lady Capulet relates the events of fourteen years ago, the reader sees possible motivations for her actions toward Juliet and her responses to her husband and Montague. She establishes that "duty" to her family was important fourteen years ago but indicates she may have erred in her choice by suggesting that she "knew nothing" then. Her marriage was one of duty; she participated in it by going through the motions as she would have advised Juliet to on the morning of her marriage to Paris.)*

COLLABORATIVE DISCUSSION Have pairs discuss the narrator of "Duty" and how Shakespeare's play influenced the short story. Students should support their opinions with lines from the text. Call on volunteers to share their conclusions with the class.

ASK STUDENTS to share any questions they generated in the course of reading and discussing the selection.

I stare at Montague. He feels it, brings his eyes back to mine. My heart softens, only a moment, as I see the anguish. Only a moment.

"Do you remember?" I say. That is all, but he knows what I mean. All those about us think I am merely cruelly taunting him, reminding him of when his son yet lived, and sharpen their sneers at me. My husband reaches across bodies to him, they

220 grip each other's right arms, they kiss, they embrace. They vow statues of these children raised in pure gold, peace evermore. None consult *me*. None ask if I want peace evermore. I watch Montague's white shirt falling over the soft, curling dark hair of his chest.

He knows that I ask if he remembers the night fourteen years ago of my father's Christmas revels. The night I pushed him away, pushed away his warm kisses in the cold, silent garden, his hands hot on me. The night long ago when I knew nothing. I thought my worth was in my worth to my family. Soiled, I had no price.

Him I loved. Him I did not marry.

COLLABORATIVE DISCUSSION What did you notice about the narrator of the story? With a partner, discuss how *The Tragedy of Romeo and Juliet* influenced Berkman's "Duty." Cite specific textual evidence to support your ideas.

ENGLISH LANGUAGE SUPPORT

Language: Personal Pronoun Referents Explain that **personal pronouns** are used in place of proper names and other nouns for simplicity and refer to the last person or thing mentioned (the referent). Point out the use of *his* in the sentences from line 180, "I did not know, of course, about his son. Montague's." The narrator explains who *his* refers to because Montague was not the most recent person mentioned.

ASK STUDENTS to identify the personal pronouns and referents in the following lines:

- Line 182 "Here he lies now, dead at our feet…" (*pronoun:* he, *referent:* Paris; *pronoun:* our, *referent:* group at the tomb)

- Lines 186–187 "He meets my eyes across the bodies of the dead children." (*pronoun:* He, *referent:* Montague)

Analyze Source Material: Interpretations of Shakespeare

RL 9

The brilliant works of William Shakespeare have inspired writers and other artists for hundreds of years. In his play *The Tragedy of Romeo and Juliet*, Shakespeare explores the ideas of youthful love, family rivalry, a woman's duty to her family, and the role of fate in one's life. It is one of Shakespeare's best-known and most-beloved plays, especially among young people. In "Duty," contemporary author Pamela Rafael Berkman transforms Shakespeare's familiar tale of "star-crossed lovers" by exploring the story from an unexpected angle.

When authors interpret the work of other artists, they often choose to highlight a particular aspect of the original work. For example, they may borrow the setting or plot of the original work and use it to introduce new characters and situations. Or they may focus on a theme or character from the original and use that as a springboard to initiate a new story. Such new interpretations may deepen the reader's understanding and appreciation of the original work.

Author's Choices: Point of View

RL 5

An author's choice of **point of view,** or the perspective from which a story is told, has an enormous impact on how readers experience and interpret the story's events. In "Duty," Berkman retells the last scene from *The Tragedy of Romeo and Juliet* through Lady Capulet's eyes. The chart shows how a shift in perspective can affect a reader's interpretation of a story.

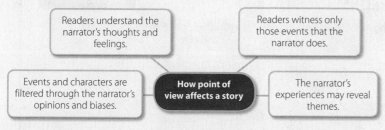

By presenting events from Lady Capulet's powerful, first-person point of view, the author invites readers to develop new opinions about Shakespeare's story of young love. As you analyze "Duty," keep these questions in mind:

- How does the point of view expose readers to additional facts about Lady Capulet?
- What is surprising about Lady Capulet's perspective on events and on other characters in the story?
- Does retelling the story from Lady Capulet's point of view affect your interpretation of the source material, *Romeo and Juliet*?

Duty **297**

CLOSE READ

Analyze Source Material: Interpretations of Shakespeare

RL 9

ASK STUDENTS to identify the elements of Shakespeare's play that Berkman borrowed for "Duty." *(basic plot, setting, and characters)* Discuss how her focus on one character, Lady Capulet, does not change the story of *Romeo and Juliet* but instead creates a new one. Have students discuss whether Lady Capulet's actions, thoughts, and background in "Duty" are consistent with the same character in *Romeo and Juliet*. *(Students may say that her actions in* Romeo and Juliet *and "Duty" are consistent and her apparent hardness of heart in both might be explained by the added background in "Duty." Others may feel that the story of her history in "Duty" is not plausible.)*

Author's Choices: Point of View

RL 5

Tell students that an effective author provides a strong sense of a first-person narrator's personality and voice. Ask students to provide an example from the story of these points from the graphic organizer.

- Understanding narrator's thought and feelings *(her feelings about Montague)*
- Events and characters filtered through narrator's opinions/biases *(her opinions of Paris and Romeo)*
- Narrator's experiences reveal themes *(Example: her view of the importance of duty to family)*

Strategies for Annotation   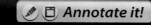 Annotate it!

Analyze Source Material and Author's Choices

RL 5, RL 9

Share these strategies for guided or independent analysis:

- Highlight in blue any words or actions that are taken directly from the source, *Romeo and Juliet*.
- Highlight in yellow words or actions that are markedly different from *Romeo and Juliet* and unique to "Duty."
- Highlight in pink words that are especially revealing in developing the character of the first-person narrator.

he breaks his look from mine to whisper to the stained red stones we tread upon, where lies his son. He whispers, "What manners is in this, to press before thy father to a grave?" Any might take him for a loving family man, not one who is less in his own bed than a courtesan's, which is what he is. He who left his son to wander the city unchecked and encounter my daughter.

Duty   **297**

PRACTICE & APPLY

Analyzing the Text

RL 2, RL 3, RL 5, RL 9

Possible answers:

1. Lady Capulet has tender feelings toward Juliet ("My own little poppet, my bean."), but regrets the girl's attraction to the "unsuitable" (line 207) Romeo ("She was too young to know there was little more useless than a boy!").

2. Berkman opens with a reference to "people in the street" calling out the names of the dead couple. In the play, both Lady Capulet and Montague refer to their old age, but in the story they are just twenty-seven and thirty, respectively. In the play, the Prince remarks that Montague is "early up;" Berkman expands upon this detail by having Lady Capulet admire Montague's shoulders beneath his nightshirt. In the play, after Friar Laurence explains his role in the tragedy, the Prince says, "We still have known thee for a holy man." Here Lady Capulet blames him (lines 103–107). Lady Capulet's perspective as a cynical, clear-eyed observer transforms details from the play.

3. Lady Capulet is only twenty-seven but married to an old man ("gray and cantankerous, like my husband") and she loved Lord Montague when she was Juliet's age ("Him I loved. Him I did not marry.").

4. The narrator reflects on the duty of her own loveless marriage (lines 68–71). Duty requires her to suppress emotion (lines 54–55), which explains cynicism and her reaction to the scene in the tomb.

5. Her perspective as a cold, disappointed, regretful woman enhances their idealism (lines 203–212).

6. Duty kept Lady Capulet from following her own heart; to her, duty is more important than love (225–227). Her point of view prompts the reader to address such themes.

7. The first-person perspective makes the characters more complex and the story more believable. Readers connect emotionally to Lady Capulet's response, some with sympathy, others with anger. Within the context of Shakespeare's great love story, her perspective on love creates a surprising mood.

8. Lady Capulet views the tragedy through the lens of her own experience—a woman who fulfilled her duties and denied her own heart. Juliet has paid the price for her "one night of love" and "has no age now." But Lady Capulet lives on, a young woman with a husband who "smells of decay" and without her beloved daughter to bring her comfort. Some might think that Lady Capulet's tragedy is greater.

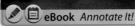 **eBook** *Annotate It!*

Analyzing the Text

RL 2, RL 3,
RL 5, RL 9, W 3

Cite Text Evidence Support your responses with evidence from the selection.

1. **Infer** "Duty" is told from Lady Capulet's point of view. What is her opinion of Juliet and Romeo?

2. **Identify** Identify several specific details from Shakespeare's play that Berkman incorporates in her story. How does she transform each one?

3. **Identify** What surprising facts do readers learn about the characters from the play when Lady Capulet tells the story? What hints about the surprise ending does Berkman provide throughout the story?

4. **Analyze** How does the author reveal the narrator's views on duty? Describe the importance of these views to the story.

5. **Analyze** In what ways does the narrator's point of view influence the reader's opinions of the characters of Romeo and Juliet?

6. **Interpret** Lady Capulet observes that Juliet "was too young to know that there is little more useless than a boy." What themes about love and duty are revealed through her point of view?

7. **Analyze** How does the author's use of first-person point of view affect the **mood,** or emotional atmosphere, of the story? In what way is this mood surprising?

8. **Compare** Whose story is more tragic, Juliet's or Lady Capulet's? Explain.

PERFORMANCE TASK

Writing Activity: Journal Entries Use characters from *Romeo and Juliet*, as presented in "Duty," to explore how point of view can be used to transform source material.

1. In the character of Lady Capulet, create a journal entry in which she delivers her opinions on the responsibilities of children to their parents and their families.

2. In the character of Juliet's nurse, create another journal entry in which the nurse delivers her opinion on how Lady Capulet raised her daughter, Juliet.

In both pieces of writing, include evidence from the text and use the conventions of standard English.

Assign this performance task.

PERFORMANCE TASK

W 3

Writing Activity: Journal Entries Explain that students should adopt the characters' attitudes and language. While Lady Capulet's opinions promote familial duty, a reader might detect an undertone of regret. The nurse's entry might describe her love for Juliet, perhaps by explaining how she poured her heart into her after losing her own daughter. It might also convey her anger at Lord and Lady Capulet for compelling Juliet to marry without love.

Critical Vocabulary

bereaved   afflict   succumb   delude   repulse

Practice and Apply Choose which of the two sentences best fits the meaning of each Critical Vocabulary word. Then write a sentence to explain your answer.

bereaved:
1. A boy sobs over the death of his favorite dog.
2. A boy demands a new dog when his old dog dies.

afflict:
1. A girl quickly brushes an insect off of her arm.
2. A girl scratches at the bug bites covering her arms and legs.

succumb:
1. The boy stared at the bowl of candy, then licked his lips.
2. The boy stared at the bowl of candy, then grabbed a handful.

delude:
1. A student thinks he made the best science project in the school's history.
2. A student thinks he could have worked harder on his science project.

repulse:
1. A shopkeeper refuses to wait on a poorly dressed customer.
2. A shopkeeper hangs a sign on the door that reads CLOSED.

Vocabulary Strategy: Context Clues

> The meaning of unfamiliar words can often be determined based on **context**, or how words are used within a text. Ask yourself the following questions:
> - What is the overall meaning of the sentence, paragraph, or text?
> - How does the unfamiliar word function in the sentence?
> - Does my guess match the word's dictionary meaning?

For example, the word *bereaved* in this story is used as an adjective to modify *parents*, and the "bereaved parents" are in a tomb. Later in the paragraph, the narrator describes a day that is a "still, dead dawn." The mood evoked is one of intense sadness. Therefore, you may guess that *bereaved* means "saddened." To verify if a guess is correct, check a dictionary.

Practice and Apply Determine the meanings of these four words from the story: *crypt* (line 11), *pallets* (line 22), *contortion* (line 48), *apothecary* (line 84).

1. Identify the function of the word in the sentence: Is it a noun, a verb, or an adjective?
2. Infer the word's meaning based on the context.
3. Look up the word in a dictionary to check your inference.

PRACTICE & APPLY

Critical Vocabulary

Possible answers:

bereaved: A boy who is bereaved over the loss of his dog would sob due to his sadness.

afflict: A girl who is afflicted by bug bites would scratch them because they itch.

succumb: The boy who succumbs would grab a handful of candy because he could not resist temptation.

delude: Only a student who deludes himself would believe that no other science project has ever been as good as his.

repulse: A shopkeeper who is repulsed by a shabbily dressed customer might refuse to wait on him or her.

Vocabulary Strategy: Context Clues

- *crypt* (n.) a vault or chamber that is used as a burial place
- *pallet* (n.) a platform, in this case for holding a body
- *contortion* (n.) a twisted, misaligned shape
- *apothecary* (n.) someone who prepares or dispenses drugs or medicine

---

Strategies for Annotation   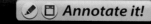 Annotate it!

Using Context Clues

Have students locate the sentences containing *crypt, pallets, contortion,* and *apothecary* in the text. Encourage them to use their eBook annotation tools to do the following:

- Highlight each vocabulary word.
- Reread the surrounding sentences, looking for clues to the word's meaning. Underline any clues you find, such as examples, synonyms, or antonyms.
- Review your annotations and try to infer the word's meaning.

of our <u>tomb</u>, the <u>tomb</u> of our family, the great yawning maw[1] of death. It had been newly fed.

When we came we found the stone rolled away, like that which covered Our Savior's <u>grave</u>.[2] Now I stand over the bodies of my girl and my enemy's boy, here in the dusty crypt. They are coiled like

Language and Style: Independent and Dependent Clauses

L 1b, L 3

Review the examples to make sure students understand that using dependent clauses along with independent clauses is a way to show connections between ideas and to add variety to writing.

Review these examples from the story and ask students to practice using clauses by breaking the sentences into two separate sentences and noticing how combining them with dependent clauses improves the writing.

1. Lines 35–38 "When she was alive…no roses in their skins." *(I wondered if she had greensickness. Greensickness makes girls her age very white.)*

2. Lines 55–56 "But she cries out to her husband…or action." *(She cries out to her husband. He stands amazed without comprehension or action.)*

3. Lines 96–98 "The friar nods…some sense and order." *(The friar nods. He acts as if he knows how to make order of the events in the crypt.)*

Answers: *Students should use the conventions of standard English grammar to include dependent and independent clauses in order to vary their sentences and to make them more interesting. Invite volunteers to share with the class some of the sentences they edited to combine or separate and how they help show connections between ideas and events and add variety to their writing.*

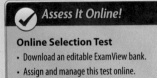

✓ Assess It Online!

Online Selection Test
- Download an editable ExamView bank.
- Assign and manage this test online.

Language and Style: Independent and Dependent Clauses

L 1b, L 3

A **clause** is a group of words with a subject and a verb. There are two types of clauses: **independent clauses** can stand alone as a sentence; **dependent clauses** cannot. Instead, dependent clauses act as modifiers by adding meaning to independent clauses. Dependent clauses often begin with these words: *as if, as, since, than, that, though, until, whenever, where, while, who,* and *why*. These words are conjunctions that clarify the connection between clauses.

Read the following sentence from the story.

When we came we found the stone rolled away, like that which covered Our Savior's grave.

This sentence contains one independent clause and two dependent clauses. Notice how the independent clause *we found the stone rolled away* forms a complete thought and can stand alone as a sentence. The two dependent clauses, which are underlined, provide additional information about the independent clause, but they cannot stand alone.

The two types of clauses function together effectively to convey the author's meaning. Without the clauses, the author's ideas might be presented this way:

We came. We found the stone rolled away. It resembled Our Savior's grave.

These simple sentences are choppy and less interesting to read. Here are more examples of effective independent and dependent clauses from "Duty." The dependent clauses are underlined.

Crumpled beside him is that fool Paris, who no less than Romeo died for love of my daughter.

I was not so afflicted myself, though many of my cousins and sisters were so.

Practice and Apply Return to the journal entries you created for this selection's Performance Task. Revise each entry to include two sentences that are independent clauses and two sentences that contain dependent clauses. Share your work with a partner and discuss how the clauses help show connections between ideas and events and add variety to your writing.

Analyze Representations in Different Mediums

TEACH

Review the idea that authors may draw on source material and transform it to create a new story, as Shakespeare did with *Romeo and Juliet* and Berkman did with "Duty." Tell students that in the same way, different mediums may present a story based on the same source material but transform it in subtle or obvious ways.

Discuss the idea that today, there are many movies that are listed as "based on true events" or "based on the novel" that significantly alter events, characters, etc., from an original text of a story to achieve an author's purpose. Because of this approach, it is necessary to judge each as a new fictional work rather than as a factual account of the original work.

PRACTICE AND APPLY

Note that *Romeo and Juliet* has been made into a film many times since the early 1900s. Ask students to locate a copy of a film version of *Romeo and Juliet* on the Internet or through other sources. Their task will be to write a short comparison of the movie depiction of the final scene in the tomb with the account in "Duty." They can focus on the following issues:

- **Characters:** Are all of the same characters present? Are the characters' appearances the same, as well as their manner and importance in the scene?
- **Setting:** How does the movie present the setting compared to the text version in "Duty"?
- **Mood or Tone:** Is the mood and tone presented in "Duty" the same or different in the movie version? Explain.
- **Point of View:** How is the point of view and focus on different characters similar or different in "Duty" and the movie version?

Author's Choices: Point of View

RETEACH

LEVEL UP TUTORIALS Assign the following *Level Up* tutorial: **Point of View**

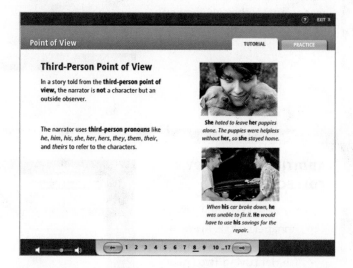

Review the concepts of a third-person and first-person narrator. Discuss the idea that a narrator may be unreliable—providing an account that is not factual or that is heavily influenced by a person's fears, attitude, etc. Have students review the following sentences and determine if they have a first-person or third-person narrator. Ask if the first-person narrator seems reliable or unreliable.

- Their bus broke down in the middle of rush-hour traffic. *(third person)*
- I thought about buying a new phone, but the price was more than I could afford. *(first person, probably reliable)*
- Clara panicked, wondering where to turn next. *(third person)*
- I've never seen such a pitiful dance routine, even though the judges thought it was better than mine. *(first person, probably unreliable)*

INDEPENDENT READING

Students can apply the skill to other pieces of literature. They should select two other books or stories they have read and identify the point of view. If the narration is first-person, they should state if the narrator is reliable or not and why. Have students work in small groups to explain their reasoning.

SWEET SORROW

The FYI site provides links to online articles from a variety of magazines and newspapers. Help students choose a few articles to read to further their exploration of the topic Sweet Sorrow.

NOVELWISE

Students can unlock the power of novels with this unique resource. Help students read through longer works with these tips:

- Find a Book
- Before You Read
- As You Read
- After You Read

Each book includes introductory material, worksheets, graphic organizers, and discussion guides.

ADDITIONAL TEXTS BY COLLECTION

Suggest students read these:

- "Annabel Lee": E. A. Poe
- "Barbara Allan" : Anonymous
- "On Her Loving Two Equally": Aphra Behn

After students read the selections, have them to recast each as news stories that state who, what, where, when, why and how.

NONFICTION CONNECTIONS

Suggest that students increase their reading of informational texts. The nonfiction connections include

- speeches
- diaries
- true-life accounts
- newspaper articles
- political cartoons

Creating an Independent Reading Program

PARENT AND FAMILY COMMUNICATION

Regular communication with families will help gain support for independent reading. Encourage student involvement.

- Send home short progress notes at regular intervals. Have your students draft the notes to include what they read, what they learned, some new words, and what they liked about the book.
- Include a parent form with the student note so that the parents can record the number of minutes or hours their student reads at home, as well as any questions or comments they may have. Ask them to sign, date, and return both parts of the note.
- Encourage students to read a few pages from their book to family members. Also encourage family members to read the book aloud with their student and to ask them questions.

RECORDING BOOKS AND TEXTS READ

Using a system for recording materials read will help students remember and analyze their choices.

- Prepare a reading log or digital spreadsheet for students to use. Have them keep the logs in their reading folders or on their digital device. If you are partnering with school or municipal librarians, give them a copy of the log.
- In addition to recording the title and author of the books read, ask students to record when they started and finished the book, whether it was easy or difficult, and what they liked or disliked.
- Remind students to log their progress whenever they finish reading a book. Go over the log with students during their individual reading conferences.

Write an Analytical Essay

This collection explores the many facets of love—joy, pain, passion, and conflict, to name just a few. Look back at the anchor text, *Romeo and Juliet*, and at the other texts in the collection. Consider the attributes or characteristics of love that are represented in each text. Synthesize your ideas by writing an analytical essay.

An effective analytical essay

- includes a clear thesis statement
- develops a comparison using examples from the texts
- organizes central ideas in a logically structured body
- uses transitions to create cohesion between sections of the essay
- has a concluding section that relates back to the introduction and leaves the reader with a thought-provoking statement about love

W 2a–f Write informative/explanatory texts.
W 4 Produce clear and coherent writing.
W 5 Develop and strengthen writing.
W 9a–b Draw evidence from literary or informational texts.

Visit hmhfyi.com to explore your topic and enhance your research.

PLAN

Analyze the Texts Review *Romeo and Juliet* to identify several aspects of love that Shakespeare explores in the play. Then look for connections between the play and other texts.

- What aspect of love is explored in both Shakespeare's play and two other texts? Choose three texts, including *Romeo and Juliet*, that explore the same characteristic of love.
- Examine all three texts and take notes on how the portrayal of love is similar and different in each. In your notes, list details, examples, and quotations that support your conclusions.

Gather Evidence Use the annotation tools in your eBook to find evidence from your chosen texts. Save each piece of evidence to *my*Notebook, in a folder titled *Collection 4 Performance Task*.

ACADEMIC VOCABULARY

As you share your ideas about how love is portrayed, be sure to use these words.

attribute
commit
expose
initiate
underlie

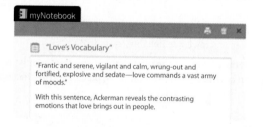

📄 "Love's Vocabulary"

"Frantic and serene, vigilant and calm, wrung-out and fortified, explosive and sedate—love commands a vast army of moods."

With this sentence, Ackerman reveals the contrasting emotions that love brings out in people.

Collection Performance Task **301**

WRITE AN ANALYTICAL ESSAY

W 2a-f, W 4, W 5, W 9a-b

Introduce students to the Performance Task by reading the introductory paragraph with them and reviewing the criteria for an effective analytical essay. Clarify that their essays will compare and contrast ideas about love in Shakespeare's play and in two other texts.

PLAN

ANALYZE THE TEXTS

Suggest that students can make the most effective use of their time by reviewing the notes they took while reading the selections to quickly identify relevant passages. Their answers to Analyzing the Text questions at the end of each selection may also point them to specific passages that they can reexamine.

▶ **View It!**

Professional Development Podcast:

Performance Task

WHEN STUDENTS STRUGGLE...

Analyze the Texts Have students work with partners to review the collection texts. Suggest that they answer these questions about each selection: *What does this text say about love? What events or details in the text support each idea about love?* Then have students work independently to gather more specific evidence from the three texts they want to write about. (Partners may decide to write about different texts.) When they have finished, have pairs meet again to discuss their evidence and the connections they see among the texts. Encourage them to ask clarifying questions to help each other strengthen their ideas.

PERFORMANCE TASK

PLAN

GET ORGANIZED

Emphasize the importance of having a clear thesis statement that states the central idea of the essay and ties together all the other ideas and evidence. Tell students that they should write a thesis statement before they start organizing their evidence in their outline. If the evidence does not fall into place, they should consider either revising the thesis statement or looking for additional evidence to support it.

PRODUCE

DRAFT YOUR ESSAY

Remind students that direct quotations from the selections must be identified with quotation marks. Students can proofread their quotations in the revising stage, but as they draft they should use quotation marks to remind themselves which text has been taken directly from another source.

LANGUAGE AND STYLE

Discuss the example and how Ackerman's language expresses her ideas clearly and memorably. Tell students that in their essays, they should use precise words to describe aspects of love (such as *passion, heartbreak,* and *euphoria*) as well as precise literary terms (*essay, poem, play, tragedy, myth, dialogue, description, metaphor,* and so on).

Get Organized Organize your details and evidence in an outline.

- Write a clear thesis statement about how a particular aspect of love is depicted in *Romeo and Juliet* and in other texts.
- Decide which organizational pattern you will use for your essay. You might present all your ideas about *Romeo and Juliet* first, then write about the second text, and finally write about the third text. Or, you could discuss the similar ideas in all three texts, followed by a discussion of their differences.
- Use your organizational pattern to sort the evidence you have gathered from the selections into a logical order.
- Search for an interesting quotation or detail to complement your thesis statement.
- Write down some ideas for your concluding section.

Interactive Lessons
To help you plan your essay, complete the following lesson:
- Organizing ideas

PRODUCE

Draft Your Essay Use your outline to write a draft of your essay.

- Introduce your thesis statement, the underlying idea on which your essay will be based. Be explicit and clear so readers will immediately understand your point of view on the topic.
- Present your details, quotations, and examples from the texts in logically ordered paragraphs. Each paragraph should have a central idea related to your thesis with evidence to support it.
- Use transitions to link sections of the text and to clarify the relationships among your ideas. Some transitions that are commonly used to compare and contrast ideas are *similarly, however, even though, on the one hand,* and *in the same way.*
- Write a concluding section that follows logically from the body of the essay. Leave your readers with an interesting statement about love that will give them something to think about.

my WriteSmart
Write your rough draft in *my*WriteSmart. Focus on getting your ideas down, rather than perfecting your choice of language.

Interactive Lessons
To help you draft your essay, complete the these lessons:
- Introductions and Conclusions
- Elaboration

Language and Style: Precise Language

Look for places in your essay where you can use precise language to describe something specifically rather than vaguely. Read this passage from Diane Ackerman's essay, "Love's Vocabulary."

> " Love is the white light of emotion. It includes many feelings which, out of laziness and confusion, we crowd into one simple word. "

Note how Ackerman uses the metaphor "the white light of emotion" and the vivid verb "crowd." Her language choices make the sentences more precise and interesting.

ENGLISH LANGUAGE SUPPORT

Use Precise Language Display or print out the Student Model for *Interactive Lessons:* Writing Informative Texts. Display this first draft of the writer's concluding paragraph:

Wells's use of repetition and figurative language creates a scary mood. In the shadowy house where the story takes place, Wells creates a feeling of fear.

Discuss the changes the writer made to create the final draft in the Student Model. If necessary, clarify the meanings of words such as *clever, threatening,* and *ominous,* and make sure students understand the figurative statements "shadows creep and stalk" and "Wells brings fear to life." Suggest that as students revise their own essays, they use a dictionary or thesaurus to find precise words they can use to replace vague ones.

REVISE

Improve Your Draft Have your partner or group of peers use the questions in the chart to review your draft.

✔ WriteSmart (*my* WriteSmart)

Have your partner or a group of peers review your draft in *my*WriteSmart. Ask your reviewers to note any reasons that do not support the thesis statement or that lack sufficient evidence.

Interactive Lessons
To help you revise your essay, complete these lessons:
· Precise Language and Vocabulary
· Formal Style

Questions	Tips	Revision Techniques
Does the thesis statement introduce readers to the subject and points of comparison?	**Underline** the subject. **Highlight** each point of comparison.	**Elaborate** on your thesis statement by identifying the aspect of love explored in each text.
Are key ideas presented logically and supported by textual evidence?	**Highlight** each key idea. **Underline** each piece of evidence that supports it.	**Add** evidence for any key idea that is not fully supported.
Are appropriate and varied transitions used to connect and contrast ideas?	**Underline** each transitional word or phrase.	**Add** transitions where needed to clarify the relationships between ideas.
Is a formal style maintained throughout the analysis?	**Highlight** slang and informal language.	**Reword** text to replace informal language with formal language.
Does the concluding section give the audience something to think about?	**Highlight** the concluding insight offered to readers.	**Add** a final thought-provoking statement about love.

PRESENT

Exchange Essays Exchange essays in a small group. Read your group members' essays. Use questions to provide feedback to your group members.

- Which aspects of the essay are particularly strong? Did any sections of the essay leave you feeling confused? How could they be clarified?

- Do you agree with your group members' analyses? Was there sufficient textual evidence to support his or her views?

REVISE

IMPROVE YOUR DRAFT

Let students form groups of five in which each member focuses on one question from the revision chart and reviews all the essays with that question in mind. Then, the "expert" on thesis statements can report on each essay (including his or her own), followed by the expert on textual evidence, and so on. Remind students to comment on each other's work in a respectful and helpful tone.

PRESENT

EXCHANGE ESSAYS

Students may share their essays with a wider audience by creating a display in the school library or by posting the essays on the school website. If the essays are posted online, students may choose to record audio or video clips of their text evidence and embed them in the text.

TO CHALLENGE STUDENTS...

Create a Performance Have students work with partners or in small groups to develop their essays as performances. Students should discuss where brief performance pieces could be inserted in a reading of each essay. For example, these might include dramatic readings from the selection texts or video presentations that illustrate ideas in the essay. Students may revise and shorten the text of their essays to better suit the performance format, but they should maintain a focus on supporting their thesis statement. Let students present their performances to an audience.

PERFORMANCE TASK

USE THE SCORING RUBRIC

Have partners use the rubric to evaluate each other's essay. Suggest that they focus on the organization of key points and supporting evidence. Are the connections between ideas clear and logical? If not, could these connections be clarified by adding transitional words or changing the order of sentences? Encourage students to give their partners concrete suggestions for improving the organization of their essays, as well as other criteria covered in the rubric.

REFLECT ON THE PROCESS

Tell students that thinking about their work on the analytical essay will help them complete other performance tasks. Have them answer the following questions:

- Was it difficult to choose which selections to write about? If so, how could you make this process go more smoothly the next time?
- Were you able to maintain a formal style and an objective tone throughout your essay? How will you apply what you've learned about style and tone to your next writing assignment?
- Did writing your essay give you a deeper understanding of the texts? If so, what did you learn?

PERFORMANCE TASK RUBRIC
ANALYTICAL ESSAY

	Ideas and Evidence	Organization	Language
4	• The introduction is appealing; the thesis statement clearly identifies the subjects and sets up points for comparison and contrast. • Concrete, relevant details and examples from the texts skillfully support each key point. • The concluding section summarizes the points of comparison and contrast, and leaves the reader with a thought-provoking idea.	• Key points and supporting textual evidence are organized logically, effectively, and consistently throughout the essay. • Transitions are well crafted and successfully connect related ideas.	• The writing reflects a formal style and an objective, knowledgeable tone. • Language is vivid and precise. • Sentence beginnings, lengths, and structures vary and have a rhythmic flow. • Spelling, capitalization, and punctuation are correct. If handwritten, the analysis is legible. • Grammar and usage are correct.
3	• The introduction could be more engaging; the thesis statement identifies the subjects and sets up one or two points for comparison and contrast. • One or two key points need more textual support. • The concluding section synthesizes most of the ideas and summarizes most points of comparison and contrast, but offers no new insight.	• The organization of key points and supporting textual evidence is confusing in a few places. • A few more transitions are needed to connect ideas.	• The style is inconsistent in a few places, and the tone is subjective at times. • Vague language is used in a few places. • Sentence beginnings, lengths, and structures vary somewhat. • Some spelling, capitalization, and punctuation mistakes occur. If handwritten, the analysis is mostly legible. • Some grammatical and usage errors are repeated in the essay.
2	• The thesis statement identifies the subjects and only hints at the points of comparison and contrast. • Evidence from the texts supports some key points but is often too general. • The concluding section gives an incomplete summary of the points of comparison and contrast and restates the controlling idea.	• Some key points are organized logically, but many supporting details from the texts are out of place. • More transitions are needed throughout the comparison to connect ideas.	• The style is too informal; the tone conveys subjectivity and a lack of understanding of the topic. • Vague, general language is used in many places. • Sentence structures barely vary, and some fragments or run-on sentences are present. • Spelling, capitalization, and punctuation are often incorrect but do not make comprehending the essay difficult. If handwritten, the analysis may be partially illegible. • Grammar and usage are incorrect in many places, but the writer's ideas are still clear.
1	• The appropriate elements of an introduction are missing. • Evidence from the texts is irrelevant or missing. • An identifiable concluding section is missing.	• A logical organization is not used; ideas are presented randomly. • Transitions are not used, making the comparison-contrast essay difficult to understand.	• The style and tone are inappropriate for the essay. • Language is too vague or general to convey the information. • Repetitive sentence structure, fragments, and run-on sentences make the writing monotonous and difficult to follow. • Spelling, capitalization, and punctuation are incorrect throughout. If handwritten, the analysis may be partially or mostly illegible. • Many grammatical and usage errors change the meaning of the writer's ideas.

Image Credits: ©The Asahi Shimbun/Getty Images

A Matter of Life or Death

❝To endure what is unendurable is true endurance.**❞**

—Japanese proverb

STREAM TO START

Motivate students to read the collection texts, and spark their curiosity about the collection by watching the video together in class. After students view the video, ask them to identify two things they hope to learn from reading about how people face adversity.

PERFORMANCE TASK PREVIEW

Point out to students that they will complete two performance tasks at the end of the collection. The performance tasks will require them to further analyze the selections in the collections and to synthesize ideas about these analyses. They will present their findings in a variety of products.

ACADEMIC VOCABULARY

Students can acquire facility with the academic vocabulary words through frequent, repeated exposure as they analyze and discuss the selections in the collection. Academic vocabulary can be used in the following instructional contexts. This will enable students to incorporate the academic vocabulary words into their working vocabulary.

View It!

Professional Development Podcast:
Academic Vocabulary

- Collaborative Discussion at the end of each selection
- Analyzing the Text questions for each selection
- Selection-level Performance Task
- Vocabulary Instruction (for Critical Vocabulary and/or for Vocabulary Strategy)
- Language and Style
- End-of-collection Performance Task for all selections in the collection

ASK STUDENTS to review the Academic Vocabulary word list for this collection. You may wish to pronounce each word aloud, so students hear the correct pronunciation. Then discuss the definitions and the related forms for each word. Remind students that they will encounter these five academic vocabulary words throughout the collection.

This collection provides a wide-ranging look at how humans endure in the face of adversity.

Stream to Start

hmhfyi.com

Channel One News®

COLLECTION

PERFORMANCE TASK Preview

At the end of this collection, you will have the opportunity to complete two tasks:

- Write an argument about the personal qualities necessary for survival.

- Participate in a panel discussion about how people adapt in order to survive.

ACADEMIC VOCABULARY

Study the words and their definitions in the chart below. You will use these words as you discuss and write about the texts in this collection.

Word	Definition	Related Forms
dimension (dĭ-mĕn´shən) *n.*	a feature, scale, or measurement of something	dimensional, dimensionality
external (ĭk-stûr´nəl) *adj.*	related to, part of, or from the outside	externalize, externally
statistic (stə-tĭs´tĭk) *n.*	a piece of numerical data	statistical, statistician
sustain (sə-stān´) *v.*	to support or cause to continue	sustainable, unsustainable
utilize (yōōt´l-īz´) *v.*	to make use of	utility, utilization

▤ myNotebook

As students read, analyze, and discuss the texts in this collection, encourage them to use the *my*WordList folder in *my*Notebook to build their own personal word lists.

- **Annotate** Students can highlight vocabulary terms and other unfamiliar words and save each highlighted word to *my*Notebook.
- **Organize** Within *my*Notebook, students can drag each word into the *my*WordList folder.
- **Elaborate** Ask students to add details to the entry for each word, such as a definition, other forms of the word, and a sample sentence.

English Language Support

ENGAGE WITH THE COLLECTION TOPIC

Draw students' attention to the title of the collection: *A Matter of Life or Death*. Clarify that in this case, *matter* refers to a subject of concern or feeling. Restate the collection title as *Concerns with Life or Death* to help students understand. Explain that the texts in this collection explore how and why people survive in life-or-death situations.

ACCESS PRIOR KNOWLEDGE Ask students to think about emergency situations. Discuss several scenarios, such as a fire, an accident, or getting lost in the wilderness. What things might be most important to one's survival? Why might some things be more important than others? How do students think they might react in these situations and why?

GIVE ONE, GET ONE

Use this strategy to deepen students' understanding of the texts in this collection and to encourage discussion.

- **First,** pose an open-ended question about a text that can generate a range of responses, or provide a list of questions for students to discuss.
- **Then,** give students a limited time (about 5 minutes) to develop a list of brief answers to the question(s) and find a classmate with whom to share ideas. Partners should ask each other for clarification about any details in the texts and comment on anything of interest. Have students select one idea from their partner's responses

and add it to their own, with their partner's name written next to it. Once this exchange is completed, let students move on to a new partner.
- **Next,** facilitate a class discussion by asking a volunteer to share a new idea he or she learned from a partner.
- **Finally,** ask the student whose idea has just been cited to share an idea gleaned from another conversation partner. Continue the process until everyone has shared an idea.

> Collection 5 Digital Resources for English Language Support

INTERACTIVE WHITEBOARD LESSONS

Use the Interactive Whiteboard Lessons to provide additional support on

- author's purpose and perspective
- evaluating arguments
- synthesizing information

LEVEL UP TUTORIALS

Students can access *Level Up* Tutorials from their eBooks to get additional help on analyzing literature, analyzing informational text, reading skills, vocabulary skills, and language conventions.

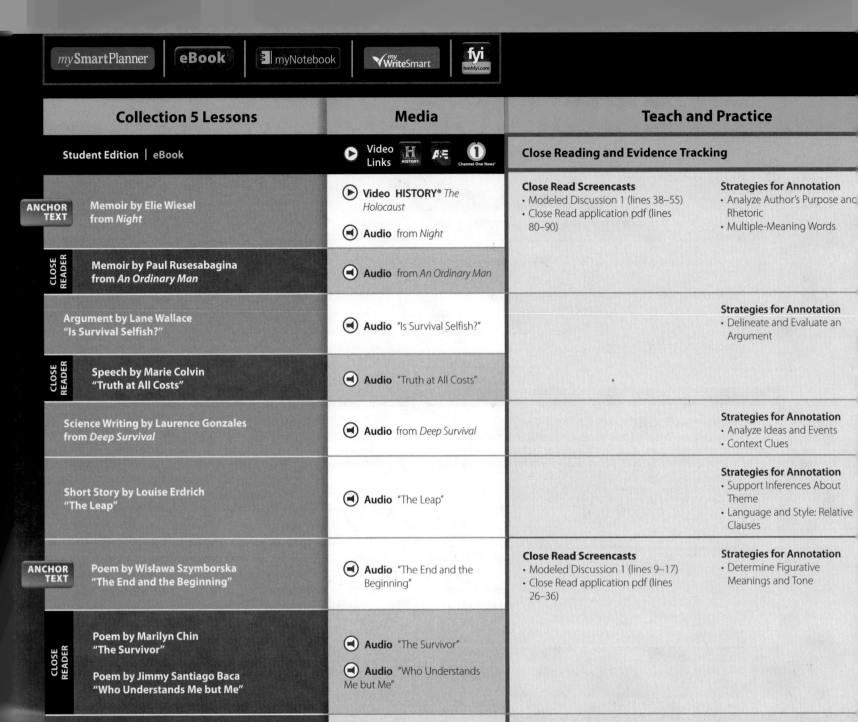

Collection 5 Lessons	Media	Teach and Practice
**Student Edition	eBook**	**Video Links** (HISTORY, A&E, Channel One News)	**Close Reading and Evidence Tracking**
ANCHOR TEXT Memoir by Elie Wiesel from *Night*	▶ Video **HISTORY®** *The Holocaust* ◀ Audio from *Night*	**Close Read Screencasts** • Modeled Discussion 1 (lines 38–55) • Close Read application pdf (lines 80–90)	**Strategies for Annotation** • Analyze Author's Purpose and Rhetoric • Multiple-Meaning Words
CLOSE READER Memoir by Paul Rusesabagina from *An Ordinary Man*	◀ Audio from *An Ordinary Man*		
Argument by Lane Wallace "Is Survival Selfish?"	◀ Audio "Is Survival Selfish?"		**Strategies for Annotation** • Delineate and Evaluate an Argument
CLOSE READER Speech by Marie Colvin "Truth at All Costs"	◀ Audio "Truth at All Costs"		
Science Writing by Laurence Gonzales from *Deep Survival*	◀ Audio from *Deep Survival*		**Strategies for Annotation** • Analyze Ideas and Events • Context Clues
Short Story by Louise Erdrich "The Leap"	◀ Audio "The Leap"		**Strategies for Annotation** • Support Inferences About Theme • Language and Style: Relative Clauses
ANCHOR TEXT Poem by Wisława Szymborska "The End and the Beginning"	◀ Audio "The End and the Beginning"	**Close Read Screencasts** • Modeled Discussion 1 (lines 9–17) • Close Read application pdf (lines 26–36)	**Strategies for Annotation** • Determine Figurative Meanings and Tone
CLOSE READER Poem by Marilyn Chin "The Survivor" Poem by Jimmy Santiago Baca "Who Understands Me but Me"	◀ Audio "The Survivor" ◀ Audio "Who Understands Me but Me"		
Collection 5 Performance Tasks: **A** Write an Argument **B** Participate in a Panel Discussion	**fyi** hmhfyi.com	**Interactive Lessons** **A** Writing an Argument **A** Writing as a Process **A** Using Textual Evidence	**B** Using Textual Evidence **B** Participating in Collaborative Discussions

For Systematic Coverage of Writing and Speaking & Listening Standards

Interactive Lessons
Writing a Narrative
Producing and Publishing with Technology

Assess		Extend	Reteach
Performance Task	✓ *Assess It Online!*	**Teacher eBook**	**Teacher eBook**
Writing Activity: Analysis	Selection Test	**Analyze Language**	**Analyze Author's Purpose > *Level Up* Tutorial >** Audience
Speaking Activity: Debate	Selection Test	**Conduct a Debate**	**Delineate and Evaluate an Argument > *Level Up* Tutorial >** Analyzing Arguments
Writing Activity: Argument	Selection Test	**Cite Textual Evidence > Interactive Whiteboard Lesson >** Cite Textual Evidence	**Summarize a Text > *Level Up* Tutorial >** Summarizing
Speaking Activity: Discussion	Selection Test	**Analyze Character > Interactive Whiteboard Lesson >** Character Development	**Support Inferences About Theme > *Level Up* Tutorial >** Theme
Writing Activity: Reflection	Selection Test	**Determine Theme > Interactive Whiteboard Lesson >** Determine Theme	**Determine Figurative Meanings and Tone > *Level Up* Tutorial >** Imagery
A Write an Argument **B** Participate in a Panel Discussion	Collection Test		

Lesson Assessments Writing a Narrative Producing and Publishing with Technology	**Standards Support and Enrichment**	For more instruction and practice in reading literary and informational texts, language, spelling, and speaking and listening, see Teacher Resources > Standards Support and Enrichment.

Collection 5 Lessons	Key Learning Objective	Performance Task
ANCHOR TEXT **Memoir by Elie Wiesel** **from *Night*, p. 307A** **Lexile 440L**	**The student will be able to…** analyze an author's purpose and his use of rhetoric and the impact of word choice on tone	Writing Activity: Analysis
Argument by Lane Wallace **"Is Survival Selfish?" p. 317A** **Lexile 1140L**	**The student will be able to…** delineate and evaluate an argument by examining a claim and the evidence provided to support that claim	Speaking Activity: Debate
Science Writing by Laurence Gonzales **from *Deep Survival*, p. 325A** **Lexile 960L**	**The student will be able to…** analyze ideas and events presented in the text, determine the central idea, and summarize the text	Writing Activity: Argument
Short Story by Louise Erdrich **"The Leap," p. 339A** **Lexile 1260L**	**The student will be able to…** analyze the impact of an author's choices and make inferences about theme	Speaking Activity: Discussion
ANCHOR TEXT **Poem by Wisława Szymborska** **"The End and the Beginning," p. 351A**	**The student will be able to…** determine the meanings of figurative language and how it influences tone in poetry	Writing Activity: Reflection

Collection 5 Performance Tasks:

A Write an Argument
B Participate in a Panel Discussion

Vocabulary Strategy	Language and Style	Differentiated Instruction	CLOSE READER Selection
Multiple-Meaning Words	Tone	**English Language Support:** Language: Phrasal Verbs and Verb Tenses **When Students Struggle:** Practice Fluency **To Challenge Students:** Compare Works	Memoir by Paul Rusesabagina from *An Ordinary Man*, p. 316b **Lexile 980L**
Synonyms	Indefinite Pronouns	**English Language Support:** Understand a Rhetorical Device **When Students Struggle:** • Examine Meaning of Language • Review Synonyms and Antonyms **To Challenge Students:** Explore Depths of Meaning	Speech by Marie Colvin "Truth at All Costs," p. 324b **Lexile 1080L**
Context Clues	Colons and Semicolons	**English Language Support:** • Comprehension: Time Sequence • Comprehension: Cause and Effect • Vocabulary: Phrasal Verbs • Vocabulary: Idioms **When Students Struggle:** • Determine Central Idea • Facilitate Comprehension • Practice Semicolons and Colons	
Prefixes	Relative Clauses	**English Language Support:** • Vocabulary: Sequence Words • Vocabulary: Homophones • Developing Reading Fluency **When Students Struggle:** • Visualize • Analyze Time Sequence **To Challenge Students:** Interpret Point of View	
		English Language Support: Language: Phrasal Verbs	Poem by Marilyn Chin "The Survivor," p. 354b Poem by Jimmy Santiago Baca "Who Understands Me but Me," p. 354b
	A. Transition Words	**A. English Language Support:** Justify Opinions **When Students Struggle:** Analyze the Texts **To Challenge Students:** Debate the Topic **B. English Language Support:** Plan a Panel Discussion **When Students Struggle:** Take Notes **To Challenge Students:** Gather Additional Evidence	

ANCHOR TEXT *from* **Night**

Memoir by Elie Wiesel

Why This Text?

Students often encounter memoirs that provide a unique perspective of a historical event. This lesson explores Elie Wiesel's use of rhetoric and word choice to provide a powerful account of his experiences as a victim of the Holocaust.

View It!

Professional Development Podcast:
Text-Dependent Analysis

Key Learning Objective: Students will be able to analyze an author's purpose and his use of rhetoric and the impact of word choice on tone.

For additional practice:

Close Reader selection
from "An Ordinary Man"
Memoir by Paul Rusesabagina

RI 1 Cite textual evidence.

RI 2 Determine a central idea; provide an objective summary.

RI 4 Determine the meaning of words and phrases.

RI 5 Analyze how claims are developed and refined.

RI 6 Determine an author's purpose and analyze how an author uses rhetoric to advance that purpose.

W 2 Write informative/explanatory texts.

L 3 Apply knowledge of language to make effective choices for meaning or style.

L 4 Determine the meaning of multiple-meaning words and phrases.

L 4c Consult reference materials.

▲ Text Complexity Rubric

Quantitative Measures	***from* Night** Lexile: 440L
Qualitative Measures	**Levels of Meaning/Purpose**  implied, but easy to infer
	Structure  organization of main ideas and details complex, but clearly stated and generally sequential
	Language Conventionality and Clarity  some unfamiliar or academic words
	Knowledge Demands specialized knowledge required
Reader/Task Considerations	• Teacher determined • Vary by individual reader and type of text • See the Text X-Ray for suggested Reader/Task Considerations.

English Language Support Before teaching, use the Text X-Ray below for an overview of the text's complexity. The Text X-Ray and the supports and scaffolds in the Teacher's Edition will help you guide students of different skill levels.

Text Complexity: Qualitative Measures

Levels of Meaning/Purpose

implied, but easy to infer

Help students analyze impact of word choice on tone.

- Teacher's Edition side notes, pp. 308, 309, 310, 311, 313
- Close Read Screencasts, p. 307
- Analyze Impact of Word Choice on Tone, p. 313

Guide students to identify an author's purpose.

- Teacher's Edition side notes, pp. 307, 308, 310, 311
- Performance Task, p. 314

To reteach analyzing author's purpose, see

- Analyze Author's Purpose, p. 316a

▶ *Use It! Level Up* **Tutorial:** Audience

Interactive Whiteboard Lesson: Word Choice and Tone

ZOOM IN ON **ANALYZING WORD CHOICE** After students have read the text, discuss its **tone**, or the author's attitude toward his subject. Point out that words with strong **connotations**, or associated ideas and feelings, can convey tone very powerfully. Read aloud lines 158–165, focusing on the last word, *inheritance*. Discuss its literal meaning, "the material possessions or wealth passed from one generation to the next." Ask students what feelings people have around the idea of an inheritance. *(Leaving an inheritance to one's children is often an act of love and pride, suggesting optimism for the family's future.)* Then discuss how the use of inheritance here creates a tone of despair. *(Wiesel's father has only a few pathetic items to share, and both father and son could easily die in the camp.)*

Structure

organization of main ideas and details complex, but clearly stated and generally sequential

Help students analyze the rhetorical devices that support the author's purpose.

- Teacher's Edition side notes, pp. 307, 308, 309, 310, 311, 312, 313
- Strategies for Annotation, p. 313
- Analyze Author's Purpose and Rhetoric, p. 313

ZOOM IN ON **ANALYZING RHETORICAL DEVICES** Read lines 121–127 aloud, emphasizing the sentences beginning with "We." Explain that this is an example of **parallel structure**, in which several sentences repeat the same grammatical structure. Then point out that by stringing together sentences with the same basic structure, rhythm, and length, Wiesel underscores the dull repetitiveness of the daily routine and the prisoners' numbness and resignation to it. Note that the first sentence that differs radically is the one that also introduces something new and unexpected: "The *Blockälteste* came running" (line 127). Read the lines aloud again to help students appreciate how the rhetoric mirrors the content.

Language Conventionality and Clarity

some unfamiliar or academic words

Teach unfamiliar vocabulary in context.

- Teacher's Edition Critical Vocabulary notes, pp. 308, 310, 311, 312, 315
- Applying Academic Vocabulary, p. 309
- Vocabulary Strategy: Multiple-Meaning Words, p. 315
- Strategies for Annotation, p. 315

Guide students to understand phrasal verbs.

- English Language Support, p. 308

Help students practice fluency.

- When Students Struggle, p. 310

Teach students to understand and use tone.

- Language and Style: Tone, p. 316

To teach students how to analyze language and style, see

- Analyze Language, p. 316a

ZOOM IN ON **PRETEACHING VOCABULARY** Before students read, preview the terms Wiesel uses to describe the setting of the prison camp, many of which are military terms. Share these definitions and encourage students to visualize what is described:

- *roll call* (line 4): reading names aloud to check who is there
- *block* (line 6): a group of barracks, or buildings for sleeping
- *inmates* (line 15): prisoners
- *crematorium* (line 16): an oven for burning dead bodies
- *bunks* (line 17): narrow, double-stacked beds
- *veterans* (line 17): people who have been through a war or other difficult experience
- *orders* (line 24): commands that must be obeyed
- *ration* (line 115): a fixed portion of food
- *form ranks* (line 143): stand in orderly lines

Knowledge Demands

some unfamiliar or academic words

specialized knowledge required

Support English Learners by providing some additional background information.

- Teacher's Edition Background note, p. 307

 For more context and historical background, students can view the video "The Holocaust" in their eBooks.

ZOOM IN ON **BUILDING KNOWLEDGE** Tell students that Wiesel was 15 years old when he and his family were deported to the Auschwitz concentration camp. He was just old enough to be kept alive as a worker. Elderly women and women with young children were often condemned to death upon arrival, and only Jews who were older than 14 years of age and deemed fit to work could survive to do hard labor.

Suggested Reader/Task Considerations

You might consider the following before assigning this memoir to students.

- Do students at this grade level have enough prior knowledge to grasp the impact of Wiesel's story?
- Might students have strong reactions to this account?

ZOOM IN ON **SUPPORTING COMPREHENSION**

- Ask the class to share what they know about European Jews, gypsies, and other populations seen as "other" during World War II. If necessary, provide resources or assign students targeted research tasks to fill in gaps in their knowledge before they read.
- Give students time to process their reactions to Wiesel's memoir, either in pair sharing, journal writing, or whole-class discussions. In addition, encourage motivated students to conduct additional research and share their findings with the class.

CLOSE READ

For more context and historical background, students can view the video "The Holocaust" in their eBooks.

Background Have students read the background and information about Elie Wiesel (ĕl´ē vē´səl). Tell them that during World War II millions of Jews and others (including prisoners of war and members of various religious groups) were sent to Nazi concentration camps, where most of them died. Although his parents and a younger sister perished in the camps, Wiesel's two older sisters survived. *Night* has been published in over thirty languages, and Wiesel was awarded the Nobel Prize for Peace in 1986. He continues to fight for human rights and freedom around the world.

AS YOU READ Direct students to use the As You Read suggestion to focus their reading.

Analyze Author's Purpose and Rhetoric (LINES 1–12)   RI 6

Tell students that authors write for various **purposes,** or reasons. They may write to inform, persuade, or entertain their readers.

A **ASK STUDENTS** what the first two paragraphs of the memoir reveal about the author's purpose. What details help them draw this conclusion? *(The author's purpose is to inform readers about his experiences as a prisoner in a concentration camp. Early on, the reader knows that the author is overworked and underfed. A "selection" is coming up.)*

Explain that a reader can determine an **author's purpose** by analyzing his or her **rhetoric,** or style. One element of rhetoric is **verbal irony.** This occurs when the author writes one thing but actually means the opposite.

B **ASK STUDENTS** to reread the first sentence of the excerpt, in which Wiesel says, "The SS offered us a beautiful present for the new year." How are these words ironic? What is the author really trying to say? *(The prisoners are facing a "selection"; some will die, and others will live. This is a grim, ugly prospect, not a beautiful gift.)*

Elie Wiesel (b. 1928) *is a teacher, writer, and Nobel Peace Prize winner. Born in Romania, Wiesel, along with his family, was among millions of European Jews deported to concentration camps during the Holocaust. In 1944, the Nazis sent the family to Auschwitz, where Wiesel's mother and sister perished. Months later, when Wiesel and his father were moved to Buchenwald concentration camp, his father also died. Buchenwald was eventually liberated, and Wiesel went on to write about his experience. His many works include* Dawn *and* The Accident, *both sequels to* Night.

from
Night

Memoir by Elie Wiesel

AS YOU READ Pay attention to how the descriptions of life in the concentration camp compare to what you already know about the topic. Write down any questions you generate during reading.

myNotebook
As you read, save new words to *myWordList.*

The SS[1] offered us a beautiful present for the new year. **B** We had just returned from work. As soon as we passed the camp's entrance, we sensed something out of the ordinary in the air. The roll call was shorter than usual. The evening soup was distributed at great speed, swallowed as quickly. We were anxious.

I was no longer in the same block as my father. They had transferred me to another Kommando,[2] the construction one, where twelve hours a day I hauled heavy slabs of stone. The head of my new block was a German Jew, small with piercing eyes. That
10 evening he announced to us that henceforth no one was allowed to leave the block after the evening soup. A terrible word began to circulate soon thereafter: selection.

A

Image Credits: (bc) ©Beau Lark/Corbis; (c) ©Julian Kumar/Godong/Corbis; (tr) ©Paul Zimmerman/Getty Images

---

[1] **SS:** abbreviation of *Schutzstaffel*, German for "defense force"; an armed unit of the Nazi Party that controlled concentration camps.
[2] **Kommando (kə-măn´dō):** German for "command," a small-group organization for laborers in the camps.

Night **307**

Close Read Screencasts   Close Read

Modeled Discussions

Have students click the *Close Read* icons in their eBooks to access a screencast in which readers discuss and annotate the following key passage:

- the advice by the block leader that will increase the prisoners' chance for survival *(lines 38–55)*

As a class, view and discuss this video. Then have students pair up to do an independent close read of an additional passage—a description of the author's behavior during the selection process *(lines 80–90).*

Night **307**

TEACH

Analyze Impact of Word Choice on Tone (LINES 38–40)   RI 4

Explain that **tone** is the author's attitude toward his reader or subject. It is created by the author's choice of words and examples.

E **ASK STUDENTS** to reread lines 38–40. Point out the word *slaughterhouses* and the phrase *factories of death* (lines 39–40). What tone do these words create? *(despair, horror, fear)*

Analyze Author's Purpose and Rhetoric (LINES 38–52)   RI 1, RI 6

Tell students that authors often reveal their purpose through **details** in the text.

F **CITE TEXT EVIDENCE** An important person in the block is the *Blockälteste*. Ask students what they learn about this person from the author's description. *(The Blockälteste understands how the selection process works because "he had already been through all the slaughterhouses, all the factories of death" [lines 39–40]. He gives the prisoners advice about how to escape selection: "'[T]ry to move your limbs, give yourself some color. Don't walk slowly, run!'" [lines 48–49].)* What does this description reveal about the author's purpose? *(The author wants to show that even people like the* Blockälteste, *who had spent so many years in the camps, were able to retain some kindness and compassion for their fellow prisoners.)*

CRITICAL VOCABULARY

reprieve: The author shows how the prisoners might escape immediate punishment.

ASK STUDENTS why the author used the word *reprieve* instead of a word like *salvation*. *(A reprieve is a temporary cancellation. Wiesel knows that another selection will happen eventually.)*

We knew what it meant. An SS would examine us. Whenever he found someone extremely frail—a "Muselman" was what we called those inmates—he would write down his number: good for the crematorium.

After the soup, we gathered between the bunks. The veterans told us: "You're lucky to have been brought here so late. Today, this is paradise compared to what the camp was two years ago. Back
20 then, Buna[3] was a veritable hell. No water, no blankets, less soup and bread. At night, we slept almost naked and the temperature was thirty below. We were collecting corpses by the hundreds every day. Work was very hard. Today, this is a little paradise. The Kapos[4] back then had orders to kill a certain number of prisoners every day. And every week, selection. A merciless selection . . . Yes, you are lucky."

"Enough! Be quiet!" I begged them. "Tell your stories tomorrow, or some other day."

They burst out laughing. They were not veterans for nothing.
30 "Are you scared? We too were scared. And, at that time, for good reason."

The old men stayed in their corner, silent, motionless, hunted-down creatures. Some were praying.

One more hour. Then we would know the verdict: death or **reprieve.**

And my father? I first thought of him now. How would he pass selection? He had aged so much. . . .

Our *Blockälteste*[5] had not been outside a concentration camp since 1933. He had already been through all the slaughterhouses, all
40 the factories of death. Around nine o'clock, he came to stand in our midst:

"*Achtung!*"[6]

There was instant silence.

"Listen carefully to what I am about to tell you." For the first time, his voice quivered. "In a few moments, selection will take place. You will have to undress completely. Then you will go, one by one, before the SS doctors. I hope you will all pass. But you must try to increase your chances. Before you go into the next room, try to move your limbs, give yourself some color. Don't walk slowly, run!
50 Run as if you had the devil at your heels! Don't look at the SS. Run, straight in front of you!"

He paused and then added:

reprieve
(rĭ-prēv´) *n.* The cancellation or postponement of punishment.

---

[3] **Buna (bŌŌ´nə):** a section of the concentration camp at Auschwitz.
[4] **Kapos (kä´pōs):** prisoners who performed certain duties for the guards.
[5] **Blockälteste (blŏk´ĕl´tɑs-tə):** a rank of Kapos; a prisoner designated by the Nazis to be the leader or representative of a block, or group of barracks.
[6] **Achtung! (ăk´tŌŌng):** German command for "Attention!"

ENGLISH LANGUAGE SUPPORT

Language: Phrasal Verbs and Verb Tenses Explain that a **phrasal verb** is a verb and another word (often a preposition) that function together as one verb. Point out the phrase "he would *write down* his number" (line 15). Explain that the two words together form a phrasal verb. In this sentence, it means "to record."

Point out that the phrasal verb is used in various **tenses** throughout the selection, including the past tense: *"Did they write me down?"* (line 88) and *"They did write me down"* (line 101). Write these sentences on the board and underline the verb parts.

ASK STUDENTS to use context clues to define these phrasal verbs: *burst out* (line 29), *look(ed) over* (line 77), *taken down* (line 79), *run(ning) out* (line 158), *catch up* (line 177), and *call out* (line 183). Have them recast the sentences by changing each verb's tense.

"And most important, don't be afraid!"

That was a piece of advice we would have loved to be able to follow.

I undressed, leaving my clothes on my cot. Tonight, there was no danger that they would be stolen.

Tibi and Yossi, who had changed Kommandos at the same time I did, came to urge me:

60 "Let's stay together. It will make us stronger."

Yossi was mumbling something. He probably was praying. I had never suspected that Yossi was religious. In fact, I had always believed the opposite. Tibi was silent and very pale. All the block inmates stood naked between the rows of bunks. This must be how one stands for the Last Judgment.

"They are coming!"

Three SS officers surrounded the notorious Dr. Mengele,[7] the very same who had received us in Birkenau. The *Blockälteste* attempted a smile. He asked us:

70 "Ready?"

Yes, we were ready. So were the SS doctors. Dr. Mengele was holding a list: our numbers. He nodded to the *Blockälteste*: we can begin! As if this were a game.

---

[7] **Dr. Mengele (mĕn-gə´lə):** Josef Mengele (1911–1979), Nazi physician at Auschwitz known for conducting cruel experiments on prisoners.

Night **309**

APPLYING ACADEMIC VOCABULARY

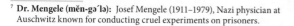

| dimension | sustain |

As you discuss the excerpt from Wiesel's memoir, incorporate the following Collection 5 academic vocabulary words: *dimension* and *sustain*. Discuss how the **dimension** of the Holocaust is hard to comprehend; this small piece of one memoir conveys only a tiny part of the larger horror. Ask students how they think the prisoners were able to **sustain** themselves—not only physically, but also emotionally and mentally.

CLOSE READ

Analyze Author's Purpose and Rhetoric (LINES 61–65)   RI 6

Tell students that there are a number of rhetorical devices that can suggest an author's purpose. One of these is **allusion**—a reference to a famous person, place, event, or work outside of the text.

E **ASK STUDENTS** to look at the reference to the Last Judgment in line 65. Explain that this refers to God's final judgment of a person's thoughts and actions. Ask students to explain why this is an especially strong comparison under these circumstances. *(In this scene, Yossi is praying and the prisoners are standing—naked and vulnerable—to see if they are next to be killed. The allusion also reminds the reader that the Nazis will be judged as well.)*

Analyze Impact of Word Choice on Tone (LINES 67–73)   RI 4

Tell students that, in order to convey tone, authors use words with particular **connotations**, or shades of meaning. Connotations can be positive or negative.

F **CITE TEXT EVIDENCE** Have students reread lines 67–73. Then ask them to find a word in the passage with a negative connotation. What tone is created by the use of this word? *(The word* notorious *[line 67] has a negative connotation. The word helps to create a tone of fear and anxiety, as the prisoners know that Dr. Mengele has a reputation for cruelty. The author reinforces the tone when he writes that the Blockälteste only "attempted a smile" when Dr. Mengele entered the barrack (lines 68–69)* What word with a similar meaning might have a positive connotation? *(well-known, famous)*

Analyze Impact of Word Choice on Tone (LINES 83–86) RI 4

Tell students that an author sometimes repeats a word with a specific connotation in order to reinforce the **tone**.

 ASK STUDENTS to reread lines 83–86 and ask them what words or phrases are repeated. *("You are too skinny" is repeated three times; "You are too weak" is repeated twice.)* Have students explain the different connotations of *thin* and *skinny*. What effect does the repetition of *skinny* have? *(Thin has a positive connotation, but* skinny *has a negative connotation of deprivation. Repetition of the word serves to underscore the author's despair, hunger, weakness, and fear.)*

Analyze Author's Purpose and Rhetoric (LINES 89–94) RI 6

Explain that authors often use the rhetorical device of **contrast,** or showing difference, to convey their purpose.

 ASK STUDENTS to reread lines 89–94. How does Wiesel describe Yossi and himself? *(smiling, laughing, and happy)* Then ask them how he describes those who have been selected. *("…standing apart, abandoned by the whole world. Some were silently weeping.")* Finally, ask students why Wiesel might have chosen to depict this contrast. *(He cannot truly feel happy when he sees that his fellow prisoners have been doomed. The contrast also reminds the reader how fine the line is between death and survival, every day.)*

CRITICAL VOCABULARY

emaciated: The author shows that the prisoners are thin and weak.

ASK STUDENTS to explain how being emaciated was dangerous to the prisoners. *(They were too thin and weak to work and would likely be killed.)*

The first to go were the "notables" of the block, the *Stubenälteste*,[8] the Kapos, the foremen, all of whom were in perfect physical condition, of course! Then came the ordinary prisoners' turns. Dr. Mengele looked them over from head to toe. From time to time, he noted a number. I had but one thought: not to have my number taken down and not to show my left arm.

80 In front of me, there were only Tibi and Yossi. They passed. I had time to notice that Mengele had not written down their numbers. Someone pushed me. It was my turn. I ran without looking back. My head was spinning: you are too skinny . . . you are too weak . . . you are too skinny, you are good for the ovens . . . The race seemed endless; I felt as though I had been running for years . . . You are too skinny, you are too weak . . . At last I arrived. Exhausted. When I had caught my breath, I asked Yossi and Tibi:

"Did they write me down?"

"No," said Yossi. Smiling, he added, "Anyway, they couldn't
90 have. You were running too fast . . ."

I began to laugh. I was happy. I felt like kissing him. At that moment, the others did not matter! They had not written me down.

Those whose numbers had been noted were standing apart, abandoned by the whole world. Some were silently weeping.

THE SS OFFICERS left. The *Blockälteste* appeared, his face reflecting our collective weariness.

"It all went well. Don't worry. Nothing will happen to anyone. Not to anyone . . ."

He was still trying to smile. A poor **emaciated** Jew questioned
100 him anxiously, his voice trembling:

"But . . . sir. They *did* write me down!"

At that, the *Blockälteste* vented his anger: What! Someone refused to take his word?

"What is it now? Perhaps you think I'm lying? I'm telling you, once and for all: nothing will happen to you! Nothing! You just like to wallow in your despair, you fools!"

The bell rang, signaling that the selection had ended in the entire camp.

With all my strength I began to race toward Block 36; midway,
110 I met my father. He came toward me:

"So? Did you pass?"

"Yes. And you?"

"Also."

emaciated
(ĭ-māʹshē-āt´id) *adj.*
made extremely thin and weak.

---

[8] **Stubenälteste (shtyōōʹbə-nĭl-tŭsʹ-tə):** a rank of Kapos; prisoners designated by the Nazis to be the leaders of their barracks, or rooms.

WHEN STUDENTS STRUGGLE . . .

Practice Fluency Tell students that when they read a text aloud, they should pay close attention to print cues, which can suggest pacing. Point out that punctuation, such as commas and periods, and, in this memoir, the line breaks, tell them when to pause and when to stop. Question marks and exclamation points also tell them when to vary their intonation.

Model reading a passage, such as lines 27–43. Then assign pairs to practice fluent reading. Tell students to read lines 95–113 aloud. Have each partner read one section of the passage, while the other reads the second section. Then have them switch sections. Remind them to pay attention to punctuation and line breaks as they read. Finally, have students discuss how reading the text aloud gives them a better understanding of the events and emotions being described.

We were able to breathe again. My father had a present for me: a half ration of bread, bartered for something he had found at the depot, a piece of rubber that could be used to repair a shoe.

The bell. It was already time to part, to go to bed. The bell regulated everything. It gave me orders and I **executed** them blindly. I hated that bell. Whenever I happened to dream of a better world, I imagined a universe without a bell.

A FEW DAYS passed. We were no longer thinking about the selection. We went to work as usual and loaded the heavy stones onto the freight cars. The rations had grown smaller; that was the only change.

We had risen at dawn, as we did every day. We had received our black coffee, our ration of bread. We were about to head to the work yard as always. The *Blockälteste* came running:

"Let's have a moment of quiet. I have here a list of numbers. I shall read them to you. All those called will not go to work this morning; they will stay in camp."

Softly, he read some ten numbers. We understood. These were the numbers from the selection. Dr. Mengele had not forgotten.

The *Blockälteste* turned to go to his room. The ten prisoners surrounded him, clinging to his clothes:

"Save us! You promised . . . We want to go to the depot, we are strong enough to work. We are good workers. We can . . .we want . . ."

He tried to calm them, to reassure them about their fate, to explain to them that staying in the camp did not mean much, had no tragic significance: "After all, I stay here every day . . ."

The argument was more than flimsy. He realized it and, without another word, locked himself in his room.

The bell had just rung.

"Form ranks!"

Now, it no longer mattered that the work was hard. All that mattered was to be far from the block, far from the crucible[9] of death, from the center of hell.

I saw my father running in my direction. Suddenly, I was afraid.

"What is happening?"

He was out of breath, hardly able to open his mouth.

"Me too, me too . . . They told me too to stay in the camp."

They had recorded his number without his noticing.

"What are we going to do?" I said anxiously.

But it was he who tried to reassure me:

---

[9] **crucible:** a vessel used for melting materials at high temperatures.

execute
(ĕk´sĭ-kyo͞ot´) v.
to carry out, or accomplish.

CLOSE READ

Analyze Author's Purpose and Rhetoric (LINES 117–120)   RI 6

Tell students that authors often use the rhetorical device of **repetition,** or repeating specific words and phrases, to convey their purpose.

I ASK STUDENTS what word the author repeats four times in lines 117–120. *(bell)* What effect does this repetition cause? What does it suggest about the author's purpose in this passage and overall in the memoir? *(The repetition of bell sounds like the tolling of a dirge-like bell, reinforcing the author's purpose of recreating the reality of life in the camps for the readers.)*

Analyze Impact of Word Choice on Tone (LINES 131–141)   RI 4

Tell students that authors convey their attitude about a character by using specific words to describe that character's actions.

J CITE TEXT EVIDENCE How does the author create a complex picture of the *Blockälteste*? What impact does Wiesel's word choice have on tone in this passage? Cite examples from the text. *(Wiesel uses the word* softly, *which has a gentle connotation, to describe how the* Blockälteste *reads the list. However, the* Blockälteste *is unable to reassure the prisoners:* "The argument was more than flimsy. He realized it, and without another word, locked himself in his room" [lines 131–141]. *This shows that the Blockälteste knows he cannot help the prisoners and shuts himself in his room to avoid facing them.)*

CRITICAL VOCABULARY

execute: A bell signals when the prisoners should carry out every action throughout the day.

ASK STUDENTS what the word *execute* tells them about life in the camp. *(Every moment of the prisoners' lives is about obeying, or executing, orders.)*

TO CHALLENGE STUDENTS . . .

Compare Works How do different people cope with fear? Most students will have read *Anne Frank: Diary of a Young Girl.* If not, briefly review the circumstances of the diary and explain that it has been one of the most widely read works on the Holocaust. *Night* is another. Ask students to make notes comparing and contrasting the two works. Then have small groups discuss the works, based on their notes and the following questions:

• How is a diary different from a memoir?

• What does each genre reveal that the other cannot?

Analyze Author's Purpose and Rhetoric (LINES 158–161)

RI 6

Another rhetorical device is **parallelism,** or **parallel structure,** which is the repetition of words, phrases, and sentences that have similar grammatical structures.

K **ASK STUDENTS** to reread lines 158–161, and identify the parallel structures. *(He felt, he was, he wanted, he knew, he was; His speech, his voice)* Ask students to explain the effect the parallelism creates. *(The parallel structure creates suspense and helps convey the pressure and panic that the author's father is feeling.)*

CRITICAL VOCABULARY

decisive: The first selection wasn't decisive because there were no consequences.

ASK STUDENTS to explain why another selection would prove decisive. *(The author's father suggests that a final review of the prisoners is the one upon which a firm choice would be made.)*

din: A din is usually a deafening noise.

ASK STUDENTS to explain why the din must have been so extreme. *(Military music can be very loud.)*

COLLABORATIVE DISCUSSION Have students reread the selection, noting details that they found surprising during their first reading. In their discussion, partners should share their ideas. Then have them explain what they had expected to happen, and why. Make sure they cite examples from the text.

ASK STUDENTS to share any questions they generated in the course of reading and discussing the selection.

"It's not certain yet. There's still a chance. Today, they will do another selection . . . a **decisive** one . . ."

I said nothing.

He felt time was running out. He was speaking rapidly, he wanted to tell me so many things. His speech became confused, his
160　voice was choked. He knew that I had to leave in a few moments. He was going to remain alone, so alone . . .

"Here, take this knife," he said. "I won't need it anymore. You may find it useful. Also take this spoon. Don't sell it. Quickly! Go ahead, take what I'm giving you!"

My inheritance . . .

"Don't talk like that, Father." I was on the verge of breaking into sobs. "I don't want you to say such things. Keep the spoon and knife. You will need them as much as I. We'll see each other tonight, after work."

170　He looked at me with his tired eyes, veiled by despair. He insisted:

"I am asking you . . . Take it, do as I ask you, my son. Time is running out. Do as your father asks you . . ."

Our Kapo shouted the order to march.

The Kommando headed toward the camp gate. Left, right! I was biting my lips. My father had remained near the block, leaning against the wall. Then he began to run, to try to catch up with us. Perhaps he had forgotten to tell me something… But we were marching too fast . . . Left, right!

180　We were at the gate. We were being counted. Around us, the **din** of military music. Then we were outside.

ALL DAY, I PLODDED AROUND like a sleepwalker. Tibi and Yossi would call out to me, from time to time, trying to reassure me. As did the Kapo who had given me easier tasks that day. I felt sick at heart. How kindly they treated me. Like an orphan. I thought: Even now, my father is helping me.

I myself didn't know whether I wanted the day to go by quickly or not. I was afraid of finding myself alone that evening. How good it would be to die right here!

190　At last, we began the return journey. How I longed for an order to run! The military march. The gate. The camp. I ran toward Block 36.

Were there still miracles on this earth? He was alive. He had passed the second selection. He had still proved his usefulness . . . I gave him back his knife and spoon.

COLLABORATIVE DISCUSSION With a partner, discuss two unexpected details from Wiesel's description of life in the concentration camp. Explain why they were surprising, citing specific passages in your discussion.

decisive
(dĭ-sī′sĭv) *adj.* final or concluding.

din
(dĭn) *n.* loud noise.

Analyze Author's Purpose and Rhetoric

_{RI 6}

Purpose is an author's reason for writing a text. Authors may write to persuade, to inform, or to entertain. They may even write for more than one purpose, but their purpose is rarely stated directly. Instead, readers infer, or draw conclusions about, the purpose based on the author's **rhetoric,** or style, and other clues in the text.

To advance their purpose, authors must engage the reader with a compelling style that includes thoughtful ideas and interesting details. Elie Wiesel chose to write in the form of a **memoir**—an autobiographical account of his personal experiences and observations of a significant event. Use these questions to help you think about Wiesel's reason for writing *Night*.

- What is the historical context for this memoir? About what significant event and people is Wiesel sharing memories?
- What perspective do you understand from reading this first-person account?
- Think about other nonfiction books or articles that you have read about Wiesel's topic. How does Wiesel's first-person account differ from these?
- What insight do you gain into the effect this historical event had on people?

Analyze Impact of Word Choice on Tone

_{RI 4}

The **tone** of a work is the author's attitude toward the subject and audience. A writer's tone might be formal and serious, angry, or lighthearted. There could even be several tones reflected in a single work. Writers shape tone through **word choices.** Words with particular connotations subtly change the meaning of a sentence and help to create the tone of a passage. Look at the examples from the selection. Which words help create the tone?

Tone	Example from *Night*
Fear and dread	"One more hour. Then we would know the verdict: death or reprieve."
Despair	"He felt time was running out. He was speaking rapidly, he wanted to tell me so many things. His speech became confused, his voice was choked."
Upbeat and encouraging	"Were there still miracles on this earth? He was alive. He had passed the second selection. He had still proved his usefulness."

CLOSE READ

Analyze Author's Purpose and Rhetoric

_{RI 6}

Review the definitions of purpose and rhetoric, and make sure that students understand that analyzing rhetoric can help them determine an author's purpose. Review some of the rhetorical devices in *Night:* parallelism, repetition, allusion, and verbal irony. Have students look for more examples of these in the selection.

Analyze Impact of Word Choice on Tone

_{RI 4}

Review connotations and denotations: A word's **connotation** is a shade of meaning, positive or negative; and **denotation** is its literal, dictionary definition.

Have students work with a partner to find the following words in the selection: *piercing* (line 10), *crucible* (line 145), and *inheritance* (line 165). Have students use context to determine each word's connotation. Then have them use a dictionary to determine each word's literal meaning. Finally, have partners discuss the effects of each word on the tone of the passage.

Strategies for Annotation  *Annotate it!*

Analyze Author's Purpose and Rhetoric

_{RI 6}

Have students review what they have learned about analyzing rhetoric to determine an author's purpose. Then share these strategies for guided or independent analysis:

- Highlight in blue rhetorical devices.
- Underline key words that offer more clues to the writer's purpose.
- On notes, identify the types of rhetorical devices and explain how the clues reveal the author's purpose.

After the soup, we gathered between the bunks. The veterans told us: "You're lucky to have been brought here so late. Today, this is paradise compared to what the camp was two years ago. Back then, Buna was a veritable hell. No water, no blankets, less soup

PRACTICE & APPLY

Analyzing the Text
RI 1, RI 2, RI 4, RI 5, RI 6

Possible answers:

1. *The words* silent, motionless, hunted-down, *and* creatures *have strong connotations. They convey a tone of desperation that reflects the inhumanity of the situation.*

2. *They barter for materials and for food. They often support each other, as when Yossi and Tibi supported Elie when he thought his father would be killed. They also attempt to sustain morale by offering words of hope in a hopeless situation.*

3. *The author wants the reader to understand and feel the fear and uncertainty that he experienced. He also indicates that he used feelings of inadequacy to goad himself to go beyond his limit of endurance in order to survive.*

4. *The style helps the author convey the sense that each item presented an obstacle to getting back to his block. The periods represent delays in his progress to check on his father.*

5. *The veterans tell Wiesel that the camp used to be much worse, and that many more people died (line 17). They laugh at Wiesel's reaction. The reader senses that they have been hardened by their experiences. Wiesel reveals that when the Blockälteste announces the selection, his voice quivers (line 45), but that when the prisoners who were selected ask him to save them (line 135), he yells at them. The reader infers that the Blockälteste feels both responsible for the prisoners and resentful of this sense of responsibility. After all, there is nothing he can do to help them. Wiesel also reveals that the prisoners who are selected wept and then clung to the head of the block. Though they at first seem resigned, they try to fight for their lives.*

6. *The word* obviously *represents a dark period in his life and in human history. As the unrelenting horror of his tale progresses, the term takes on an ominous, evil tone.*

Analyzing the Text
RI 1, RI 2, RI 4, RI 5, RI 6, W 2

Cite Text Evidence   Support your responses with evidence from the selection.

1. **Infer** In lines 32–33, Wiesel writes, "The old men stayed in their corner, silent, motionless, hunted-down creatures. Some were praying." Which words in this quotation have strong connotations? How do these words convey the tone of Wiesel's narrative?

2. **Cite Evidence** What evidence does Wiesel provide to support the idea that though beaten down, the prisoners had creative ways of coping with their confinement and of sustaining themselves?

3. **Analyze** Look back at the scene in which Wiesel must run before the SS doctors during selection (lines 83–86). Why does Wiesel repeat his thoughts, "you are too skinny, you are too weak"? How does the repetition help readers understand his experience?

4. **Interpret** Wiesel sometimes uses punctuation and sentence structure to convey meaning. Reread the second to last paragraph in the text. Why does he use short, incomplete sentences? How does this stylistic approach affect meaning?

5. **Analyze** Wiesel includes statements and reactions from other prisoners, the head of the block, and the veterans of the camp that reveal different perspectives about life in the concentration camp. Identify examples of these different perspectives and explain what they reveal about the prisoners' ordeal.

6. **Draw Conclusions** Why do you think Wiesel chose to call his memoir *Night*? What might be the significance of that title?

PERFORMANCE TASK

Writing Activity: Analysis Elie Wiesel's account of the concentration camp is deeply personal. Think about what he wrote and what he may have wanted to achieve with his account. Then write a brief analysis in which you answer the following questions:

- Why did Wiesel write *Night*? What did he hope to accomplish? Did he succeed?
- Did his descriptions of life in the camp connect with you, the reader? How?
- Elie Wiesel's account of the Holocaust was written years after the events took place. How might *Night* be different if it had been written as a diary, a first-person account of events immediately after they happened?
- Would you recommend this memoir to others? Why?

In your writing, include evidence from the text to support your analysis and use the conventions of standard English.

Assign this performance task.

PERFORMANCE TASK
W 2

Writing Activity: Analysis Before students draft their essay, have them review the points they must cover: Wiesel's purpose for writing the memoir, how the descriptions connected with the reader, how *Night* might have been different had it been written as a diary, and whether students would recommend it to others. Have partners exchange and evaluate each other's drafts. Then have them revise their essays and share them in small groups.

Critical Vocabulary

reprieve	emaciated	execute	decisive	din

Practice and Apply Use your knowledge of the Critical Vocabulary words to respond to each question.

1. Wiesel describes one of the prisoners as **emaciated.** What did the prisoner look like?

2. When Wiesel's father passed the second **decisive** selection, Wiesel was relieved. Explain why.

3. While a prisoner, Wiesel would **execute** his orders in the camp. Did the guards likely have a complaint about his work? Explain.

4. The narrator could hear the **din** of military music in the background. What did the music sound like?

5. The prisoners at the concentration camp hoped for a **reprieve** from death. What were they hoping for?

Vocabulary Strategy: Multiple-Meaning Words

The Critical Vocabulary word *execute* means "to accomplish or carry out fully." *Execute* has another definition, "to put to death." Like *execute*, many words have **multiple meanings.** Use the strategies below to determine or clarify the meaning of multiple-meaning words.

- Use context, or the way the word is used in a sentence or paragraph, to determine meaning. This strategy requires looking at the words and sentences around the unknown word to clarify meaning. For example, look at the following sentence: *Mountain climbing was her passion, and she wanted to scale every peak.* The context tells you that *scale* refers to climbing.
- Consult general and specialized reference materials, particularly glossaries and dictionaries, to determine or clarify a word's precise meaning. Dictionary entries provide all the definitions of a word, as well as its part of speech, so select the definition that makes sense.

Practice and Apply Work in a group to locate these words in the selection: *present* (line 1), *block* (line 6), *bunks* (line 17), *reflecting* (line 96). Use context clues or reference materials to determine the precise meaning for each word.

PRACTICE & APPLY

Critical Vocabulary

Possible answers:

1. *He looked extremely thin and unhealthy.*

2. *He knew there would not be another one.*

3. *No, because he performed his work properly and efficiently.*

4. *It sounded more like loud noise than music.*

5. *They hoped to avoid death and live another day.*

Vocabulary Strategy: Multiple-Meaning Words

Answers:

1. ***present:*** (n.): *a gift.*

2. ***block:*** (n.): *a row of structures.*

3. ***bunks:*** (n.): *rudimentary, vertically stacked beds.*

4. ***reflecting:*** (n.): *showing or representing something.*

Strategies for Annotation

Multiple-Meaning Words

Ask students to find the following words in the selection: *concentration* (line 38), *quivered* (line 45), *matter* (line 92), and *rung* (line 142). Encourage them to use their eBook annotation tools to do the following:

- Highlight the word in yellow.
- Look for clues to the word's meaning in the surrounding words. Underline examples, synonyms, or antonyms.
- On a note, write a definition of the word as it is used in the passage.
- Verify the word's precise meaning in a dictionary.

"Listen carefully to what I am about to tell you." For the first time, his voice quivered. "In a few moments, selection will take place. You will have to undress completely. Then you will go, one by

Language and Style: Tone

L 3

After reviewing the examples of formal and informal language, assign students 10–20 lines each of the selection. Have them "translate" the passages from formal into informal language. Then invite them to share their revisions in small groups. Students should discuss the difference in tone between the informal and formal versions.

Answers:

Students' revisions should reflect an understanding of formal and informal language and should also include at least two instances of strong imagery.

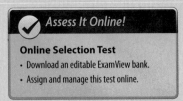

Assess It Online!

Online Selection Test
- Download an editable ExamView bank.
- Assign and manage this test online.

Language and Style: Tone

L 3

An author's attitude toward a subject or an audience helps create the overall feeling that a selection conveys. Authors establish **tone** by making effective word choices for meaning and style.

Read the following sentences from the selection:

> Those whose numbers had been noted were standing apart, abandoned by the whole world. Some were silently weeping.

Wiesel might have written the sentence like this:

> The prisoners whose numbers had been called were standing by themselves crying.

How is the second sentence different from the first? Look again at the first sentence. Notice that Wiesel uses words with strong connotations. Words like *apart, abandoned, silently,* and *weeping* create strong imagery for the reader, which in turn shapes a tone of tragedy and despair. Wiesel's use of formal language also adds to the weight and seriousness of the memoir's tone. Note the difference in the use of formal versus informal language in these passages.

Formal	Informal
"Listen carefully to what I am about to tell you." For the first time, his voice quivered. "In a few moments, selection will take place. You will have to undress completely. Then you will go, one by one, before the SS doctors. I hope you will all pass."	"Listen, everyone," he said as his voice shook. "Selection's going to start soon. You'll have to take your clothes off, then walk by the SS doctors one at a time. I hope everyone passes."
"What is it now? Perhaps you think I'm lying? I'm telling you, once and for all: nothing will happen to you! Nothing! You just like to wallow in your despair, you fools!"	"What? Do you think I'm lying? Nothing's going to happen to you! You're just feeling sorry for yourselves!"

Practice and Apply Look back at the analysis you wrote in response to this selection's Performance Task. Revise it to include formal, rather than informal, language and at least two sentences that contain strong imagery. Then discuss with a partner how formal language and strong imagery improve the meaning and tone of your work.

Analyze Language

L 3

TEACH

Tell students that **style** is the way in which an author uses language. Authors have individual styles that distinguish them from each other. All authors, however, may use a variety of rhetorical devices to help them convey their most important ideas and feelings. Tell students that elements of style may include the following:

- sentence length
- dialogue
- parallel structure
- punctuation
- word choice
- repetition
- formal or informal language

Draw students' attention to lines 107–114. Point out the short sentences in the excerpt—both dialogue and narrative—and very brief paragraphs, some with only one or two words. Ask volunteers to read the following excerpt aloud:

> The bell rang, signaling that the selection had ended in the entire camp.
> With all my strength I began to race toward Block 36; midway, I met my father. He came toward me:
> "So? Did you pass?"
> "Yes. And you?"
> "Also."
> We were able to breathe again.

Ask students to explain what effect the author's style creates, and to give examples. *(The staccato dialogue shows that they are breathless with fear. And then, "we were able to breathe again" [line 114]. The effect is to give the reader a feeling of the terror—and then relief—felt by the father and son.)*

COLLABORATIVE DISCUSSION

Have students form small groups and ask them to read aloud and then analyze the style of the following sections: lines 31–38, lines 58–73, lines 95–98, lines 144–157, and lines 158–179. Have them discuss the effect of the author's style in these passages.

Analyze Author's Purpose

RI 6

RETEACH

Tell students that when they analyze an author's purpose, they should also think about the author's intended audience. Determining the audience can help a reader evaluate a writer's choices. A reader should keep the following in mind:

- how an author's word choice, purpose, and main idea relate to the audience
- the relationship between the type of writing—the formality of the language—and the audience

 LEVEL UP TUTORIALS Assign the following *Level Up* tutorial: **Audience**

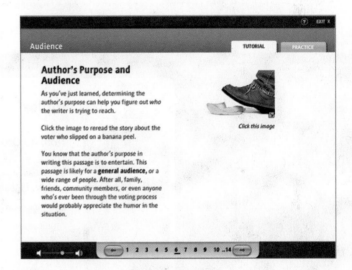

INDEPENDENT READING

Have students write a description of the audience that they think Elie Wiesel hopes to reach with his memoir. Is his purpose to inform, persuade, or share thoughts and feelings? Or does he have a combination of purposes? Is the language formal or informal? What is the central idea of his memoir?

from An Ordinary Man

Memoir by Paul Rusesabagina

Why This Text

Students do not always take the time to analyze how an author's rhetoric or style advances his or her point of view. *An Ordinary Man* is an account of one man's personal observations of a significant historical event: the 1994 genocidal slaughter in Rwanda. With the help of the close-reading questions, students will analyze Rusesabagina's rhetoric. This close reading will help students understand Rusesabagina's purpose for writing this memoir.

Background Have students read the background and the information about the author. Introduce the selection by telling students that the seeds for the 1994 violence in Rwanda were planted in 1916, when Belgian colonists devised a class system that divided the Tutsis and Hutus. In this class system, Tutsis were educated and Hutus were not. However, when Rwanda became free of Belgium in 1962, Hutus took power. From that point on, ethnic hatred between Tutsis and Hutus escalated.

AS YOU READ Ask students to pay attention to Rusesabagina's choices regarding content and word choice. How soon can they analyze his attitude toward the situation he describes?

Standards Support

- cite strong and thorough textual evidence
- determine the meaning of words and phrases as they are used in a text
- determine an author's purpose
- analyze how an author uses rhetoric to advance his or her purpose

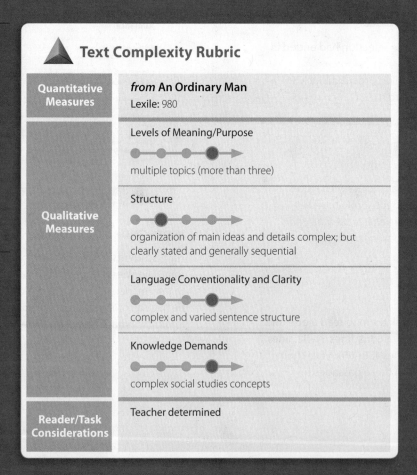

▲ **Text Complexity Rubric**

Quantitative Measures

from **An Ordinary Man**
Lexile: 980

Qualitative Measures

Levels of Meaning/Purpose

multiple topics (more than three)

Structure

organization of main ideas and details complex; but clearly stated and generally sequential

Language Conventionality and Clarity

complex and varied sentence structure

Knowledge Demands

complex social studies concepts

Reader/Task Considerations

Teacher determined

Analyze Author's Purpose and Rhetoric

Students should read this text carefully all the way through. Close-reading questions at the bottom of the page will help them focus on a thorough analysis of the text. As they read, students should jot down comments or questions about the excerpt in the side margins.

WHEN STUDENTS STRUGGLE . . .

To help students analyze Rusesabagina's purpose, have them work in a small group to fill out a chart, such as the one shown below, as they analyze the text.

CITE TEXT EVIDENCE For practice analyzing an author's purpose, ask students to cite evidence of the author's rhetorical choices that advanced his purpose.

Title	"An Ordinary Man"
Language	"just how little I was able to accomplish" (line 65), "I am nothing more or less than a hotel manager" (lines 172–173), "Very simple: words" (line 129), "like a sports event" (lines 144–145)
Word Choice	"poisonous stream of rhetoric" (line 133), "avalanche of words" (line 146), "sea of fire" (line 175)
Tone	"hacked to death with machetes" (line 16), "butchered" (line 24), "looking at their own severed limbs" (line 58)
Parallel structure	"Rwanda was a failure . . . It started as a failure . . . It was the failure . . . It was a failure . . . It was a failure . . . It was the failure . . ." (lines 150–156), "Not the liquor, not money, not the UN." (line 162), "I was slippery . . . I acted friendly . . . I put cartons . . . I flattered them . . . I said whatever . . ." (lines 165–167)
Author's Purpose:	to show that an "ordinary man" can make a difference through simple humanity

---

Background In 1994, a mass genocide took place in the East African state of Rwanda when Hutus killed 800,000 men, women, and children over a period of 100 days. Although tensions existed between the Hutus and Tutsis (the two main ethnic groups in Rwanda) for hundreds of years, things came to a head on April 6, 1994, when a plane carrying the President of Rwanda, a Hutu, was shot down. Many perceived this as an attack by Tutsis, and the tensions between the two groups escalated into full-blown violence. **Paul Rusesabagina** lived through the genocide and wrote about the horrors in his memoir An Ordinary Man (from which this excerpt comes), which later became the film Hotel Rwanda.

from An Ordinary Man

Memoir by Paul Rusesabagina

CLOSE READ
Notes

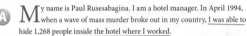

1. **READ ▷** As you read lines 1–43, begin to cite text evidence.

• Underline the actions Rusesabagina took when the genocide broke out.
• In the margin, explain what Rusesabagina has trouble understanding (lines 4–24).
• Circle words and phrases that convey a tone of disgust and horror.

(A) My name is Paul Rusesabagina. I am a hotel manager. In April 1994, when a wave of mass murder broke out in my country, I was able to hide 1,268 people inside the hotel where I worked.

When the militia and the Army came with orders to kill my guests, I took them into my office, treated them like friends, offered them beer and cognac, and then persuaded them to neglect their task that day. And when they came back, I poured more drinks and kept telling them they should leave in peace once again. It went on like this for seventy-six days. I was not

10 particularly **eloquent** in these conversations. They were no different from the words I would have used in saner times to order a shipment of pillowcases, for example, or tell the shuttle van driver to pick up a guest at the airport. I still don't understand why those men in the militias didn't just put a bullet in my head and execute every last person in the rooms upstairs but they didn't. None of the refugees in my hotel were killed. Nobody was beaten. Nobody was taken away and made to disappear. People were being hacked to death with machetes all over Rwanda, but that five-story building

eloquent:
well-spoken, moving

77

---

1. READ AND CITE TEXT EVIDENCE

(A) **ASK STUDENTS** to use their underlined and circled text to explain what Paul Rusesabagina did in response to the violence that erupted in Rwanda in 1994. *Students should cite evidence that Rusesabagina saved people's lives by hiding them in a hotel (lines 2–3), negotiated with the militia to save lives (lines 5–8), and survived a genocide (lines 15–16).*

Critical Vocabulary: eloquent (line 9) Have students define *eloquent* as Rusesabagina uses it here. *Students should explain that Rusesabagina is humble in his explanation of his conversations with the militia. The words were "no different from the words I would have used in saner times to order a shipment of pillowcases, for example" (lines 9–11).*

prevailed:

triumphed

became a refuge for anyone who could make it to our doors. The hotel could offer only an illusion of safety, but for whatever reason, the illusion **prevailed** and I survived to tell the story, along with those I sheltered. There
20 was nothing particularly heroic about it. My only pride in the matter is that I stayed at my post and continued to do my job as manager when all other aspects of decent life vanished. I kept the Hotel Mille Collines open, even as the nation descended into chaos and eight hundred thousand people were butchered by their friends, neighbors, and countrymen.

It happened because of racial hatred. Most of the people hiding in my hotel were Tutsis, descendants of what had once been the ruling class of Rwanda. The people who wanted to kill them were mostly Hutus, who were traditionally farmers. The usual stereotype is that Tutsis are tall and thin with delicate noses, and Hutus are short and stocky with wider noses, but
30 most people in Rwanda fit neither description. This divide is mostly artificial, a leftover from history, but people take it very seriously, and the two groups have been living uneasily alongside each other for more than five hundred years.

You might say the divide also lives inside me. I am the son of a Hutu farmer and his Tutsi wife. My family cared not the least bit about this when I was growing up, but since bloodlines are passed through the father in Rwanda, I am technically a Hutu. I married a Tutsi woman, whom I love with a fierce passion, and we had a child of mixed descent together. This type of blended family is typical in Rwanda, even with our long history of
40 racial prejudice. Very often we can't tell each other apart just by looking at one another. But the difference between Hutu and Tutsi means everything in Rwanda. In the late spring and early summer of 1994 it meant the difference between life and death.

He has trouble understanding how he wasn't killed along with his hotel guests. He doesn't see anything he did as "particularly heroic."

B 30

2. **REREAD** Reread lines 25–43. How do Rusesabagina's words convey his feelings about the division between Hutus and Tutsis? What is his purpose in describing his family when explaining these differences? Support your answer with explicit textual evidence.

He thinks the divisions are artificial, as he himself is married to a
Tutsi whom he loves "with a fierce passion." He uses his family as an
example of a blended family—one comprised of both Tutsis and
Hutus—and explains that most Rwandan families are blended.

78

Between April 6, when the plane of President Juvenal Habyarimana was shot down with a missile, and July 4, when the Tutsi rebel army captured the capital of Kigali, approximately eight hundred thousand Rwandans were slaughtered. This is a number that cannot be grasped with the rational mind. It is like trying—all at once—to understand that the earth is surrounded by billions of balls of gas just like our sun across a vast
50 blackness. You cannot understand the magnitude. Just try! Eight hundred thousand lives snuffed out in one hundred days. That's eight thousand lives a day. More than five lives per *minute*. Each one of those lives was like a little world in itself. Some person who laughed and cried and ate and thought and felt and hurt just like any other person, just like you and me. A mother's child, every one irreplaceable.

And the way they died . . . I can't bear to think about it for long. Many went slowly from slash wounds, watching their own blood gather in pools in the dirt, perhaps looking at their own severed limbs, oftentimes with the screams of their parents or their children or their husbands in their cars.
60 Their bodies were cast aside like garbage, left to rot in the sun, shoveled into mass graves with bulldozers when it was all over. It was not the largest genocide in the history of the world, but it was the fastest and most efficient.

At the end, the best you can say is that my hotel saved about four hours' worth of people. Take four hours away from one hundred days and you have an idea of just how little I was able to accomplish against the grand design.

C

D 50

The tone is of shock and disbelief.

sad; then angry and disgusted

despairing

3. **READ** As you read lines 44–73, continue to cite evidence.
   - Underline words or phrases that convey Rusesabagina's tone.
   - In the margin, describe the tone of each paragraph.
   - Circle the resources Rusesabagina used to save the people hiding at the hotel.

4. **REREAD** Reread lines 44–55. What is Rusesabagina's purpose in these lines?

His purpose is to explain how the genocide happened and to impress
upon us the enormity of the horror involved and the sheer numbers
killed.

79

---

2. **REREAD AND CITE TEXT EVIDENCE**

B **ASK STUDENTS** to read their answer aloud to a partner. Then, have them read aloud the specific text that supports their answer. Finally, have them rewrite their response after receiving a peer review. *Students should explain that Rusesabagina uses his family as evidence (lines 37–39) and that the separation between Tutsis and Hutus is based on habit and stereotypes, not on reason or reality (lines 30–31).*

Critical Vocabulary: prevailed (line 19) Have students explain Rusesabagina's use of *prevailed*. What are the illusion and the reality, and which one prevailed? *Students should explain that the illusion of safety was the opposite of the reality of the genocide. Despite the odds, the illusion of safety prevailed. No one was killed in the hotel.*

3. **READ AND CITE TEXT EVIDENCE**

C **ASK STUDENTS** to cite evidence for each description of Rusesabagina's tone. *"This is a number that cannot be grasped with the rational mind" (lines 47–48); "I can't bear to think about it" (line 56); "how little I was able to accomplish" (line 65).*

4. **REREAD AND CITE TEXT EVIDENCE**

D **ASK STUDENTS** to add text evidence to their responses. *Students may cite evidence from lines 50–55 to show that Rusesabagina wants readers to understand the events and the enormity of the horror.*

resigned

What did I have to work with? I had a five-story building. I had a cooler full of drinks. I had a small stack of cash in the safe. And I had a working telephone and I had my tongue. It wasn't much. Anybody with a gun or a machete could have taken these things away from me quite easily. My
70 disappearance—and that of my family—would have barely been noticed in the torrents of blood coursing through Rwanda in those months. Our bodies would have joined the thousands in the east-running rivers floating toward Lake Victoria, their skins turning white with water rot.

I wonder today what exactly it was that allowed me to stop the killing clock for four hours.

There were a few things in my favor, but they do not explain everything. I was a Hutu because my father was Hutu, and this gave me a certain amount of protection against immediate execution. But it was not only Tutsis who were slaughtered in the genocide; it was also the thousands of
80 moderate Hutus who were suspected of sympathizing with or even helping the Tutsi "cockroaches." I was certainly one of these cockroach-lovers. Under the standards of mad extremism at work then I was a prime candidate for a beheading.

"Image" is important because the hotel really wasn't safe or protected.

Another surface advantage: I had control of a luxury hotel, which was one of the few places during the genocide that had the image of being protected by soldiers. But the important word in that sentence is *image*. In the opening days of the slaughter, the United Nations had left four unarmed soldiers staying at the hotel as guests. This was a symbolic gesture. I was also able to bargain for the service of five Kigali policemen. But I
90 knew these men were like a wall of tissue paper standing between us and a flash flood.

Yet another of my advantages was a very strange one. I knew many of the architects of the genocide and had been friendly with them. It was, in a way, part of my job. I was the general manager of a hotel called the Diplomates, but I was eventually asked to take charge of a sister property, the nearby Hotel Mille Collines, where most of the events described in this book took place. The Mille Collines was *the* place in Kigali where the power

E

F

classes of Rwanda came to meet Western businessmen and dignitaries. Before the killing started I had shared drinks with most of these men,
100 served them complimentary plates of lobster, lit their cigarettes. I knew the names of their wives and their children. I had stored up a large bank of favors. I cashed them all in—and then borrowed heavily—during the genocide. My preexisting friendship with General Augustin Bizimungu in particular helped save the Mille Collines from being raided many times over. But **alliances** always shift, particularly in the chaos of war, and I knew my supply of liquor and favors would run dry in some crucial quarters. Before the hundred days were over a squad of soldiers was dispatched to kill me. I survived only after a desperate half hour during which I called in even more favors.
110 All these things helped me during the genocide. But they don't explain everything.

Let me tell you what I think was the most important thing of all.

I will never forget walking out of my house the first day of the killings. There were people in the streets who I had known for seven years, neighbors of mine who had come over to our place for our regular Sunday cookouts. These people were wearing military uniforms that had been handed out by the militia. They were holding machetes and were trying to get inside the houses of those they knew to be Tutsi, those who had Tutsi relatives, or those who refused to go along with the murders.

alliance:
relationship;
association

5. **READ** ▶ As you read lines 74–109, continue to cite textual evidence.

• Underline the advantages Rusesabagina had at the time of the genocide.
• In the margin, explain why the word "image" is important in line 85.
• Circle two instances in which Rusesabagina mentions being at risk.

6. ◀ **REREAD AND DISCUSS** Reread lines 76–109. In a small group, discuss what else might have helped Rusesabagina survive the genocide.

7. **READ** ▶ As you read lines 110–145, continue to cite textual evidence.

• In the margin, explain why Rusesabagina included the story about Peter.
• Underline text describing the "words" people had heard causing them to go "mad."

---

5. **READ AND CITE TEXT EVIDENCE**

E **ASK STUDENTS** to explain Rusesabagina's advantages and risks during the genocide. *Students should cite evidence from lines 81–83 to show that Rusesabagina was in danger. They should cite evidence from lines 84–86, 89, 92–93, and 101–102 to show Rusesabagina's advantages. Lines 107–109 are evidence of Rusesabagina's life being threatened.*

FOR ELL STUDENTS Encourage students to decipher the meaning of the noun *rot* (line 73). If they are having difficulty, help them by guiding them to the adjectival form, *rotten*.

6. **REREAD AND DISCUSS USING TEXT EVIDENCE**

F **ASK STUDENTS** to be prepared to share the results of their group discussions and to cite evidence to support their conclusions. *Rusesabagina describes his advantages as being on the "surface" in line 84. He credits his "large bank of favors" (lines 101–102) for saving his life and the lives of others in the hotel.*

7. **READ AND CITE TEXT EVIDENCE**

G **ASK STUDENTS** to cite text evidence to support their explanation of why Rusesabagina included the story about Peter. *Students should cite lines 121–122 as evidence that Peter was ordinary, lines 122–124 as evidence that Peter was gentle, and lines 125–126 as evidence that ordinary, gentle people had become murderers.*

Critical Vocabulary: alliance (line 105) Ask students to explain Rusesabagina's use of the word *alliance*.

Peter's story is an example of how seemingly normal people turned "mad" and violent.

120   There was one man in particular whom I will call Peter, though that is not his real name. He was a truck driver, about thirty years old, with a young wife. The best word I can use to describe him is an American word: *cool.* Peter was just a cool guy; so nice to children, very gentle, kind of a kidder, but never mean with his humor. I saw him that morning wearing a military uniform and holding a machete dripping in blood. Watching this happen in my own neighborhood was like looking up at a blue summer sky and seeing it suddenly turning to purple. The entire world had gone mad around me.

    What had caused this to happen? Very simple: words.

130   The parents of these people had been told over and over again that they were uglier and stupider than the Tutsis. They were told they would never be as physically attractive or as capable of running the affairs of the country. It was a poisonous stream of rhetoric designed to reinforce the power of the elite. When the Hutus came to power they spoke evil words of their own, fanning the old resentments, exciting the hysterical dark places in the heart.

exhortation:

urging by argument or appeal

    The words put out by radio station announcers were a major cause of the violence. There were explicit **exhortations** for ordinary citizens to break into the homes of their neighbors and kill them where they stood. Those 140 commands that weren't direct were phrased in code language that everybody understood: "Cut the tall trees. Clean your neighborhood. Do your duty." The names and addresses of targets were read over the air. If a person was able to run away his position and direction of travel were broadcast and the crowd followed the chase over the radio like a sports event.

8.   ◄ REREAD   Reread lines 137–145. How does calling the hunt for Tutsis a "sports event" convey the tone of the narrative?

It conveys Rusesabagina's shock and disgust at his countrymen's behavior. To imagine people viewing the life or death battle of Tutsis as entertainment is horrifying. Small details like this make Rusesbagina's writing very compelling.

82

> " *Words . . . can also be powerful tools of life.* "

    The avalanche of words celebrating racial supremacy and encouraging people to do their duty created an alternate reality in Rwanda for those three months. It was an atmosphere where the insane was made to seem normal and disagreement with the mob was fatal.

150   Rwanda was a failure on so many levels. It started as a failure of the European colonists who exploited trivial differences for the sake of a divide-and-rule strategy. It was the failure of Africa to get beyond its ethnic divisions and form true coalition governments. It was a failure of Western democracies to step in and avert the catastrophe when abundant evidence was available. It was a failure of the United States for not calling a genocide by its right name. It was the failure of the United Nations to live up to its commitments as a peacemaking body.

    All of these come down to a failure of words. And this is what I want to tell you: Words are the most effective weapons of death in man's **arsenal.** 160 But they can also be powerful tools of life. They may be the only ones.

arsenal:

weapons

    Today I am convinced that the only thing that saved those 1,268 people in my hotel was words. Not the liquor, not money, not the UN. Just ordinary words directed against the darkness. They are so important. I used words in many ways during the genocide—to plead, intimidate, coax, cajole, and negotiate. I was slippery and evasive when I needed to be. I acted friendly toward despicable people. I put cartons of champagne into their car trunks. I flattered them shamelessly. I said whatever I thought it would take to keep the people in my hotel from being killed. I had no cause to advance, no ideology to promote beyond that one simple goal. Those words were my 170 connection to a saner world, to life as it ought to be lived.

    I am not a politician or a poet. I built my career on words that are plain and ordinary and concerned with everyday details. I am nothing more or

9.   READ ►   As you read lines 146–179, continue to cite textual evidence.
- Underline the reasons given for Rwanda's failure.
- Circle the biggest failure that led to the genocide.
- Underline the reasons Rusesabagina gives for his actions.

83

---

8.   **REREAD AND CITE TEXT EVIDENCE**

H   **ASK STUDENTS**   to cite the specific text that supports their answer. *Students should cite evidence of the shock and disgust Rusesabagina felt at his countrymen's behavior and directions to kill their neighbors in lines 137–145.*

Critical Vocabulary: exhortation   (line 138) Ask volunteers to explain why *exhortation* is a good choice here.

FOR ELL STUDENTS   Clarify that the word *stream* (line 133) in this context is not a body of running water. In this text it means "a steady succession."

9.   **READ AND CITE TEXT EVIDENCE**

I   **ASK STUDENTS**   to explain what Rusesabagina credits with the saving of the 1,268 people in his hotel. *He credits words.*

Critical Vocabulary: arsenal   (line 159) Ask students to explain Rusesabagina's figurative use of *arsenal. Students should explain that Rusesabagina is using* arsenal *as a metaphor for the life-or-death power words can have.*

less than a hotel manager, trained to negotiate contracts and charged to give
shelter to those who need it. My job did not change in the genocide, even
though I was thrust into a sea of fire. I only spoke the words that seemed
normal and sane to me. I did what I believed to be the ordinary things that
an ordinary man would do. I said no to outrageous actions the way I
thought that anybody would, and it still mystifies me that so many others
could say yes.

10. **◄ REREAD** Reread lines 158–160. What does Rusesabagina mean
when he says that words are powerful tools of life, that they "may be the
only ones"?

*He explains how he used words to convince the militias to leave the
people in the hotel unharmed. He also explained how words had a
part in causing the racial hatred and fanning the flames of the
genocide. Words can save lives and also persuade others to kill.*

SHORT RESPONSE

Cite Text Evidence What is Rusesabagina's purpose in writing his book?
What is the significance of the book's title, *An Ordinary Man*? Be sure to
review your reading notes and **cite text evidence** in your response.

*Rusesabagina wants people to know what happened in Rwanda, and
what he did. He is humble, and reluctant to take credit for his deeds:
"There was nothing particularly heroic about it." His language is
plain but conveys the immensely horrific situation he lived through:
"I can't bear to think about it for long . . . the best you can say is
that my hotel saved about four hours' worth of people." The book's
title echoes what Rusesabagina says. Readers know that his actions
were extraordinary, but he doesn't think so. His only goal was to save
as many lives as possible.*

84

---

10. REREAD AND CITE TEXT EVIDENCE

Ⓙ ASK STUDENTS to sum up Rusesabagina's belief about the
power of words. *Students should cite evidence of his belief that only
words saved the people in his hotel (lines 160–162), and
strengthened his "connection to a saner world" (line 170).*

SHORT RESPONSE

Cite Text Evidence Student responses will vary, but they
should cite evidence from the article to support their analysis of
Rusesabagina's purpose. Students should:

- determine Rusesabagina's purpose.
- explain the significance of the memoir's title.
- cite evidence from the text to support their explanation.

TO CHALLENGE STUDENTS . . .

For additional context on the historical origins of the Rwandan
genocide, students can do research online.

ASK STUDENTS to cite evidence from "An Ordinary Man" and
their online research to make a statement about the destructive
power of stereotypes. What are the consequences of classifying a
group of people as "a problem"?

DIG DEEPER

With the class, return to Question 4, Reread. Have students share
their responses.

ASK STUDENTS to reread lines 44–55 to analyze how
Rusesabagina uses rhetoric to support his purpose.

- What similes does Rusesabagina use to express his point?
  *"It is like trying—all at once—to understand that the earth is
  surrounded by billions of balls of gas just like our sun . . ." (lines
  48–49). "Each one of those lives was like a little world in itself"
  (lines 52–53).* How do these examples support the author's
  purpose? *The first example demonstrates just how difficult it is
  to grasp the scale of the slaughter. The second example expresses
  that even a single death is a massive event.*

- How does Rusesabagina try to make the scale of the slaughter
  understandable to the reader? *He uses the total number of dead
  and the total amount of time, explaining first that it amounts
  to "eight thousand lives a day" (lines 51–52) and then to "more
  than five lives per minute" (line 52).* How does Rusesabagina's
  "math" support his purpose? *It allows the reader to grasp the
  enormity of the killing: more than 5 people a minute murdered
  continuously for one hundred days.*

ASK STUDENTS to return to the Short Response question and
to revise it based on the class discussion.

Is Survival Selfish?

Argument by Lane Wallace

Why This Text?

An argument is a vehicle for presenting a point of view and persuading an audience to agree with that point of view. This lesson examines whether people who act to ensure their own survival instead of helping others are selfish or not.

▶ **View It!**

Professional Development Podcast:

Teaching Argument

Key Learning Objective: The student will be able to delineate and evaluate an argument by examining a claim and the evidence provided to support that claim.

For additional practice :

Truth at All Costs

Close Reader selection
"Truth at All Costs"
Speech by Marie Colvin

RI 2 Determine a central idea and analyze its development.

RI 4 Determine the meaning of words and phrases.

RI 6 Determine an author's point of view or purpose.

RI 8 Delineate and evaluate the argument and specific claims in a text.

SL 1a Come to discussions prepared.

SL 1d Respond thoughtfully to diverse perspectives and justify views.

SL 4 Present information, findings, and supporting evidence.

L 3 Apply knowledge of language to make effective choices for meaning or style.

L 4c Consult general and specialized reference materials.

▲ Text Complexity Rubric

Quantitative Measures

Is Survival Selfish?
Lexile: 1140L

Qualitative Measures

Levels of Meaning/Purpose

more than one purpose; implied, easily identified from context

Structure

organization of main ideas and details complex but mostly explicit; may exhibit disciplinary traits

Language Conventionality and Clarity

some unfamiliar, academic, or domain-specific words

Knowledge Demands

some specialized knowledge required

Reader/Task Considerations

- Teacher determined
- Vary by individual reader and type of text
- See the Text X-Ray for suggested Reader/Task Considerations.

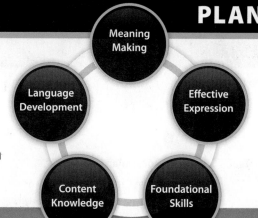

English Language Support Before teaching, use the Text X-Ray below for an overview of the text's complexity. The Text X-Ray and the supports and scaffolds in the Teacher's Edition will help you guide students of different skill levels.

Text Complexity: Qualitative Measures

Levels of Meaning/Purpose

more than one purpose; implied, easily identified from context

Help students evaluate an argument.

- Teacher's Edition side notes, pp. 319, 320, 321
- Strategies for Annotation, p. 321
- Delineate and Evaluate an Argument, p. 321

Guide students to determine purpose and point of view.

- Teacher's Edition side note, p. 319

To reteach delineating and evaluating an argument, see

- Delineate and Evaluate an Argument, p. 324a

▶ **Use It!** *Level Up* Tutorial: Analyzing Arguments
Interactive Whiteboard Lessons: Elements of an Argument, Evaluating Arguments

***ZOOM IN ON* EVALUATING AN ARGUMENT** Before students read the argument, review the Evaluating Evidence Checklist on page 321. Make sure they understand what it means for evidence to be **valid, relevant,** and **sufficient.** Then have pairs discuss the statements or reasons below. For each one, they should answer the question *What evidence could persuade me that this is true?* After they read the text, have students return to the list and discuss whether the author provided adequate evidence for each reason.

- People's instincts do not always help them survive.
- People who stay calm are more likely to survive.
- People who survive may be criticized for acting selfishly.
- In an emergency, people often act without really thinking.

Structure

organization of main ideas and details complex but mostly explicit; may exhibit disciplinary traits

Help students delineate an argument.

- Teacher's Edition side notes, pp. 317, 318, 319, 320, 321
- When Students Struggle, p. 318
- Strategies for Annotation, p. 321
- Delineate and Evaluate an Argument, p. 321

Prompt students to engage in a debate.

- Performance Task, p. 322

To teach students how to conduct a debate, see

- Conduct a Debate, p. 324a

***ZOOM IN ON* DELINEATING AN ARGUMENT** Have a volunteer define the term **claim** (in arguments, the idea or opinion that the author wants to prove). To help students identify the claim, have students make a two-column chart with these headings:

- Survivors act selfishly and may not help others.
- Survivors act smarter than others in the same situation.

As they read, students should note evidence for each statement. When they have finished reading, ask them if the argument answers the question *Is survival selfish?* with a simple yes-or-no position. *(No; the answer is more complex.)* If necessary, have them reread lines 18–21 to focus on Wallace's claim. Then work with the class to restate the claim in simpler terms. *(Survival is not simply selfish or smart, because every person and every situation is different.)*

Language Conventionality and Clarity

some unfamiliar, academic, or domain-specific words

Teach unfamiliar vocabulary in context.
- Teacher's Edition Critical Vocabulary notes, pp. 317, 318, 323
- Applying Academic Vocabulary, p. 319

Guide students to understand rhetorical devices.
- English Language Support, p. 317

Help students analyze the impact of word choice.
- Teacher's Edition side note, p. 320

Help students use synonyms.
- Vocabulary Strategy: Synonyms, p. 323
- When Students Struggle, p. 323

Teach students to use indefinite pronouns.
- Language and Style: Indefinite Pronouns, p. 324

***ZOOM IN ON* USING INDEFINITE PRONOUNS** Review the sentences with **indefinite pronouns** quoted on page 324. Point out that people often use indefinite pronouns when they want to cite a convincing fact but can't recall the specifics. For example, someone might say, "Some people think" instead of "Seventy-eight percent of adults think." Another common construction is "They say that _____." In this case, the pronoun *they* is used as an indefinite pronoun to refer to unnamed authorities on a subject. Tell students that when they cite evidence in an argument, it is almost always more convincing to use specific nouns than indefinite pronouns.

Knowledge Demands

some specialized knowledge required

Support English Learners by providing some background on key concepts introduced in the text.

***ZOOM IN ON* BUILDING KNOWLEDGE** Explain what the author means by the following phrases:
- *"women and children first" protocol* (line 13): a code of behavior in which men ensure that women and children are rescued from an emergency before they act to save themselves
- *"fight or flight" impulse* (line 92): a reflexive reaction to danger or stress in which the body automatically produces hormones that enhance strength and speed so that a person or animal can either fight an attacker or flee from danger

Suggested Reader/Task Considerations

You might consider the following before assigning this argument to students.
- Have any students in the class experienced a disaster or survived a life-threatening event?
- What connections can students make between this article and their studies in other classes?

***ZOOM IN ON* SUPPORTING COMPREHENSION**
- Be aware that students may not wish to share their personal stories of survival. Rather than eliciting accounts of personal traumas, allow students to offer their stories. If they do not, it is best to respect their privacy.
- Encourage interested students to research the history of the "women and children first" protocol and how it has been applied in actual disasters. Other students may wish to discuss with their science teachers animals' instincts, particularly the topic of altruistic behaviors in animals that relate to survival.

CLOSE READ

AS YOU READ Direct students to use the As You Read note to focus their reading.

Delineate and Evaluate an Argument (LINES 1–17)   RI 8

In an **argument,** an author must decide the most effective way to present ideas and present support for a claim. Remind students that a **claim** is an author's position on an issue. Tell students that when an author develops a claim, it may or may not be stated directly. Often, an author will use details and ideas at the beginning of an argument to get the audience thinking about an issue.

A **ASK STUDENTS** to reread lines 1–12. What topic is the author introducing? *(The author introduces the topic of someone acting to save themselves and being criticized by society for doing so.)* Ask them how this idea is supported in lines 13–17. *(The author summarizes the idea in these lines, saying that people who save themselves are not looked on "kindly," while those who "sacrifice themselves to save others" are praised.)* Have students discuss why the author begins her essay by using an **anecdote,** or a short account of an incident. *(Using an anecdote helps draw the reader into the ideas that the author wants to present. In this case, the author is pushing the reader to think about the question presented in the title, "Is Survival Selfish?" The anecdote shows how society can judge a person even when that person did help others before helping himself.)*

CRITICAL VOCABULARY

laud: People who work to save others and risk themselves are highly thought of and praised by our society.

ASK STUDENTS what the author is implying by saying that society lauds people who risk themselves for others. *(The author is implying that society sometimes judges people who survive more harshly than it should. Laud is a word with a positive connotation. People who sacrifice themselves are praised very highly.)*

LEVEL UP TUTORIALS For additional support, assign the following *Level Up* tutorial: **Analyzing Arguments.**

Is Survival Selfish?

Argument by Lane Wallace

AS YOU READ Think about whether you would use the word *selfish* to describe someone who survives a disaster. Write down any questions you generate during reading.

When the ocean liner *Titanic* sank in April of 1912, one of the few men to survive the tragedy was J. Bruce Ismay, the chairman and managing director of the company that owned the ship. After the disaster, however, Ismay was savaged by the media and the general public for climbing into a lifeboat and saving himself when there were other women and children still on board. Ismay said he'd already helped many women and children into lifeboats and had only climbed in one himself when there were no other women or children in the area and the boat was ready

10 to release. But it didn't matter. His reputation was ruined. He was labeled an uncivilized coward and, a year after the disaster, he resigned his position at White Star.

The "women and children first" protocol of the *Titanic* may not be as strong a social stricture[1] as it was a century ago. But we still tend to **laud** those who risk or sacrifice themselves to save others in moments of danger or crisis and look less kindly on those who focus on saving themselves, instead.

laud
(lôd) *v.* to praise.

But is survival really selfish and uncivilized? Or is it smart? And is going in to rescue others always heroic? Or is it sometimes

20 just stupid? It's a complex question, because there are so many factors involved, and every survival situation is different.

Self-preservation is supposedly an instinct. So one would think that in life-and-death situations, we'd all be very focused on whatever was necessary to survive. But that's not always true. In July

Image Credits: ©John Lund/Stone/Getty Images

---

[1] **social stricture:** behavioral restriction placed on society.

Is Survival Selfish? **317**

ENGLISH LANGUAGE SUPPORT

Understand a Rhetorical Device Tell students that authors use different techniques to help enhance their arguments and communicate effectively. These devices can include **rhetorical questions,** or questions that do not require a reply.

- Ask students to look at lines 18–21. Have a volunteer read the paragraph aloud.
- Point out that this paragraph contains many rhetorical questions and that these questions do not require responses. Explain that the author is using the questions to push readers to think about how they would answer them.

ASK STUDENTS how these questions affect how they think about survival. *(Answers will vary, but students may mention that these questions make them think about how every situation that involves survival is different and that it is difficult to judge what might be best.)*

CLOSE READ

Delineate and Evaluate an Argument (LINES 22–39)

RI 8

Remind students that **reasons** are explanations that support a claim and that **evidence,** such as personal experiences or anecdotes, supports the reasons.

B **CITE TEXT EVIDENCE** Ask students to explain how the author presents a reason and supporting evidence in lines 22–39. How does this pattern help them understand the claim and support? *(The author presents a reason in line 22, "Self-preservation is supposedly an instinct." Then the author uses an anecdote in lines 24–37 to question whether self-preservation is an instinct in people. This anecdote supports the author's claim that this is a complex question with different answers. Finally, the author draws a conclusion as in lines 38–39. Recognizing the pattern helps the reader follow the logical presentation of the author's argument.)*

CRITICAL VOCABULARY

transfixed: The author and her friend saw people standing still and watching a problem. **ASK STUDENTS** why the author was surprised that people were transfixed. *(It was an emergency and people should have been moving away.)*

consumed: The fire and smoke destroyed the inside of the plane. **ASK STUDENTS** why the woman had to act quickly to get off as the plane was consumed. *(The fire and smoke were intense and consumed the inside of the plane faster than most people were able to get out.)*

berate: People who survive often criticize themselves for not doing more to help others. **ASK STUDENTS** why people berate themselves for surviving a crisis. *(People feel guilty and question whether they should have done things differently.)*

edicts: There are often rules of behavior that are in place to help people survive. **ASK STUDENTS** why society has a positive view about people who ignore the edicts about safety procedures to help others. *(Society praises as heroes people who break rules to save others.)*

2007, I was having a drink with a friend in Grand Central Station[2] when an underground steam pipe exploded just outside. From where we sat, we heard a dull "boom!" and then suddenly, people were running, streaming out of the tunnels and out the doors.

30 My friend and I walked quickly and calmly outside, but to get any further, we had to push our way through a crowd of people who were staring, **transfixed,** at the column of smoke rising from the front of the station. Some people were crying, others were screaming, others were on their cell phones . . . but the crowd, for the most part, was *not* doing the one thing that would increase everyone's chances of survival, if in fact a terrorist bomb with god knows what inside it had just gone off—namely, moving away from the area.

We may have an instinct for survival, but it clearly doesn't always kick in the way it should. A guy who provides survival 40 training for pilots told me once that the number one determining factor for survival is simply whether people hold it together in a crisis or fall apart. And, he said, it's impossible to predict ahead of time who's going to hold it together, and who's going to fall apart.

So what is the responsibility of those who hold it together? I remember reading the account of one woman who was in an airliner that crashed on landing. People were frozen or screaming, but nobody was moving toward the emergency exits, even as smoke began to fill the cabin. After realizing that the people around her were too paralyzed to react, she took direct action, crawling over 50 several rows of people to get to the exit. She got out of the plane and survived. Very few others in the plane, which was soon **consumed** by smoke and fire, did. And afterward, I remember she said she battled a lot of guilt for saving herself instead of trying to save the others.

Could she really have saved the others? Probably not, and certainly not from the back of the plane. If she'd tried, she probably would have perished with them. So why do survivors **berate** themselves for not adding to the loss by attempting the impossible? Perhaps it's because we get very mixed messages about survival 60 ethics.

On the one hand, we're told to put our own oxygen masks on first, and not to jump in the water with a drowning victim. But then the people who ignore those **edicts** and survive to tell the tale are lauded as heroes. And people who do the "smart" thing are sometimes criticized quite heavily after the fact.

In a famous mountain-climbing accident chronicled in the book and documentary *Touching the Void*, climber Simon Yates was

transfix
(trăns-fĭks´) *v.* to captivate or make motionless with awe.

consume
(kən-sōōm´) *v.* to completely destroy or eradicate.

berate
(bĭ-rāt´) *v.* to criticize or scold.

edict
(ē´dĭkt´) *n.* an official rule or proclamation.

---

[2] **Grand Central Station:** a large commuter-rail and subway terminal in New York City.

WHEN STUDENTS STRUGGLE . . .

To help students manage the ambiguities of Wallace's argument, have students consider the question that the author poses in line 44. Have students form groups and ask each group to reread lines 44–60 and formulate an answer to the question, "So what is the responsibility of those who hold it together?"

Remind students to review the evidence that the author provides in the anecdote and to think about what the woman could have done to save others if she had not worked to save herself. Have each group write a conclusion that reflects the groups' thinking.

Have all the groups gather to discuss their ideas. Have students discuss how their group decided on its answer and what evidence the author provided to help in drawing that conclusion.

> "It's impossible to predict ahead of time who's going to hold it together, and who's going to fall apart."

attempting to rope his already-injured friend Joe Simpson down a mountain in bad weather when the belay[3] went awry. Simpson ended up hanging off a cliff, unable to climb up, and Yates, unable to lift him up and losing his own grip on the mountain, ended up cutting the rope to Simpson to save himself. Miraculously, Simpson survived the 100 foot fall and eventually made his way down the mountain. But Yates was criticized by some for his survival decision, even though the alternative would have almost certainly led to both of their deaths.

In Yates' case, he had time to think hard about the odds, and the possibilities he was facing, and to realize that he couldn't save anyone but himself. But what about people who have to make more instantaneous decisions? If, in fact, survivors are driven by instinct not civilization, how do you explain all those who choose otherwise? Who would dive into icy waters or onto subway tracks or disobey orders to make repeat trips onto a minefield to bring wounded to safety? Are they more civilized than the rest of us? More brave? More noble?

It sounds nice, but oddly enough, most of the people who perform such impulsive rescues say that they didn't really think before acting. Which means they weren't "choosing" civilization

---

[3] **belay:** the securing of a rope to a cleat or another object.

APPLYING ACADEMIC VOCABULARY

external	statistic

As you discuss Wallace's argument, incorporate the following Collection 5 academic vocabulary words: *external* and *statistic*. Ask students to explain why people's judgments about survivors might be influenced by **external** factors. Then have them discuss whether the use of **statistics** might provide relevant evidence to support Wallace's claim. Why would statistics be appropriate or not?

CLOSE READ

Determine Purpose and Point of View (LINES 70–76)   RI 6

Explain to students that an author has a specific **purpose** when writing an argument. Remind students that an author conveys his or her purpose and point of view through choice of language and details.

C CITE TEXT EVIDENCE Ask students why the author includes this anecdote. How does she convey her perspective and support her claim through this detail? *(She includes this anecdote because it supports her claim that survival situations are complex and that people face tough decisions that don't necessarily make them selfish or not selfish. In lines 74–76, the author states that "Yates was criticized by some for his survival decision…." This statement reinforces the idea that even when a person makes the most logical decision in a situation, the person may be criticized for not sacrificing their own life for the other person.)*

Delineate and Evaluate an Argument (LINES 79–85)   RI 8

Tell students that as they analyze an argument, they need to assess if the **evidence** being offered by the author is **valid, relevant,** and **sufficient.** Review the idea that authors need to provide reliable evidence that pertains to the topic or issue.

D ASK STUDENTS how the author uses the rhetorical questions in lines 79–85 as evidence to support her claim. *(The author uses the questions to not only encourage readers to think about the answers, but to provide further support for the idea that in survival situations people may or may not rely on instinct or civilization to guide their decisions.)* What information does the author provide in the questions about the kinds of decisions people make in survival situations? *(In lines 80–84, the author talks about survivors who "are driven by instinct not civilization," people who "dive into icy waters or onto subway tracks," people who "disobey orders to make repeat trips onto a minefield to bring wounded to safety." These questions provide the evidence that people frequently do not act for their own survival even though the logical decision might be to do as Yates did by "cutting the rope.")*

Delineate and Evaluate an Argument (LINES 104–108)

RI 8

An author needs to provide both reasons and evidence to support a claim. Remind students that in order for evidence to be sufficient, the author needs to provide enough of it and use a variety of sources.

(E) CITE TEXT EVIDENCE Ask students to explain whether the statement in lines 89–91 is a claim, a reason, or evidence. *(This statement is a reason because the author is explaining that instinct pushes us to run from and run to danger.)* What evidence does the author provide to support the statement? *(In lines 92–99, the author explains that because people have the impulse called "fight or flight" in dangerous situations, they sometimes act for their own survival and at other times are pulled to help others.)*

Analyze Impact of Word Choice (LINES 100–103)

RI 4

Remind students that authors choose specific words and phrases to support their claims.

(F) ASK STUDENTS to identify the phrase the author repeats in lines 100–101. *(The author repeats the phrase "some people.")* How does this phrase support her claim? *(Using "some people" rather than citing a specific person supports her claim that it is difficult for anyone to know how he or she will act in a life-or-death situation.)*

COLLABORATIVE DISCUSSION Have students reread the argument, looking for relevant passages. Remind them to consider the claim the author is trying to support as they decide whether the people in the stories have been selfish.

ASK STUDENTS to share any questions they generated in the course of reading and discussing the selection.

(E)

90 over instinct. If survival is an instinct, it seems to me that there must be something equally instinctive that drives us, sometimes, to run into danger instead of away from it.

Perhaps it comes down to the ancient "fight or flight" impulse. Animals confronted with danger will choose to attack it, or run from it, and it's hard to say which one they'll choose, or when. Or maybe humans are such social herd animals, dependent on the herd for survival, that we feel a pull toward others even as we feel a contrary pull toward our own preservation, and the two impulses battle it out within us . . . leading to the mixed messages we send each other on which impulse to follow.

100 Some people hold it together in a crisis and some people fall apart. Some people might run away from danger one day, and toward it the next. We pick up a thousand cues in an instant of crisis and respond in ways that even surprise ourselves, sometimes.

(F)

But while we laud those who sacrifice themselves in an attempt to save another, there is a fine line between brave and foolish. There can also be a fine line between smart and selfish. And as a friend who's served in the military for 27 years says, the truth is, sometimes there's no line at all between the two.

COLLABORATIVE DISCUSSION With a partner, review the various stories of survivors and discuss whether you would describe each person's actions as *selfish*. Is being selfish always bad? Cite textual evidence as well as your own reasoning in your discussion.

TO CHALLENGE STUDENTS . . .

Explore Depths of Meaning Does every question have a right answer? Discuss the concept of ambiguity. Tell students that an ambiguous situation is open to more than one interpretation. Have pairs discuss these questions:

- Reread lines 18–21 and 104–108. Is the author saying the same thing in these passages, or are there slight differences?
- Why does the author say in lines 102–103 that people surprise themselves sometimes? How does this statement support the author's claim?
- What would the author say about people who judge others who have survived an event in which they could have died?

Have pairs come together in groups to share and discuss their answers.

Delineate and Evaluate an Argument

RI 8

In an **argument,** the author expresses a position on an issue and then attempts to support that position. A successful argument persuades readers to agree with the author's position. To **evaluate** whether an argument is successful, you must first **delineate,** or outline, its basic parts. The diagram shows a simplified outline.

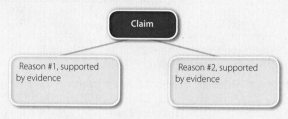

- The **claim** is the author's position on the topic or issue. It is the central idea around which the argument is structured.
- **Reasons** are explanations that support the claim by answering the question *Why does the author hold that opinion?* An author's reasoning must be clear and logical to create a valid argument.
- **Evidence** includes facts, statistics, personal experiences, statements by experts, and other information. The evidence supports the reasons and, ultimately, the author's claim.

Most arguments begin by stating a claim and then present reasons and evidence for the claim. To be convincing, an argument must include evidence that is valid, relevant, and sufficient. Use this checklist to evaluate evidence presented in "Is Survival Selfish?"

Evaluating Evidence Checklist
Evidence is valid if
• it is well known or common knowledge
• the author identifies the source
• the source appears to be trustworthy
• research shows the source to be reliable
Evidence is relevant if
• it is closely related to the topic or issue
• it supports the claim
Evidence is sufficient if
• there is enough of it
• it comes from a variety of sources

CLOSE READ

Delineate and Evaluate an Argument

RI 8

Review the Evaluating Evidence Checklist with students. Have them think about the evidence that the author has presented in "Is Survival Selfish?" Ask them to discuss whether they feel the evidence is valid, relevant, and sufficient citing at least three details from the text to support their ideas. *(Sample answers: The evidence provided in this text appears to be valid since the author cites the source of each supporting anecdote. The evidence seems relevant and tied to the argument. The evidence does come from a variety of sources.)*

Strategies for Annotation   *Annotate it!*

Delineate and Evaluate an Argument

RI 8

Have students use their eBook annotation tools to trace the reasons and evidence that are provided to support the author's claim. Have them do the following:

- Highlight in blue evidence where the author expresses reasons to support the claim.
- Highlight in green evidence that supports the reasons.
- On a note, explain the reasons and evidence that are most compelling and persuasive.

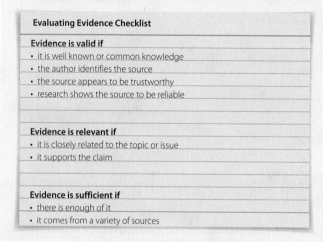

over instinct. If survival is an instinct, it seems to me that there must be something equally instinctive that drives us, sometimes, to run into danger instead of away from it.…

…Animals confronted with danger will choose to attack it, or run from it, and it's hard to say which one they'll choose, or

PRACTICE & APPLY

Analyzing the Text
RI 2, RI 8

Possible answers:

1. The author's claim may be stated as, "Survivors cannot be labeled as either selfish or not selfish because there are many factors that influence human behavior and because every survival situation is unique."

2. This is an example of a reason. It explains one of the factors that influences human behavior. As evidence for this reason, in the next paragraph the author describes how a woman who stayed calm after a plane crash survived while many others did not.

3. The author offers evidence based on personal experience—she witnessed an explosion at a train station, where much of the crowd subsequently gathered right outside, although it would have been safer for them to move away from the scene. The evidence is relevant because it involves instinct and decision-making in a crisis. Although the evidence is sufficient to support the author's smaller point about focus in a crisis, by itself it is not sufficient to support the author's main point that instinct drives our actions.

4. The author says "We get very mixed messages about survival ethics," and her tone implies that any resulting feelings of guilt are unwarranted. As evidence she offers an anecdote of the remorse felt by a survivor of an airplane accident. This example is relevant because it supports the immediate point about survivor guilt.

5. This paragraph addresses the author's claim because it adds support to the idea that instinct drives our actions. It discusses the fact that people who perform rescues instead of ensuring their own survival don't actually choose their actions. They simply act before thinking. This responds to the question in the previous paragraph about whether people are more civilized if they choose to help others, rather than "selfishly" saving themselves. It supports the idea that survivors can't be labeled selfish or not selfish because they act instinctively.

6. She means that in a life-threatening situation, the same action on the part of a survivor could be interpreted as either selfish or smart, but more likely it is both. This restates her initial claim that the actions of people in crisis result from a complex set of factors and cannot be neatly categorized as selfish or heroic.

eBook *Annotate It!*

Analyzing the Text
RI 2, RI 8,
SL 1a, SL 4

Cite Text Evidence Support your responses with evidence from the selection.

1. **Summarize** Lane Wallace begins her argument with a series of questions to get her readers thinking about what is selfish and what is heroic. In your own words, state the claim that she expresses in lines 18–21. Take into account the information she presents in the rest of her argument, including her conclusions at the end.

2. **Analyze** Wallace writes that "the number one determining factor for survival is simply whether people hold it together in a crisis or fall apart" (lines 40–42). Is this an example of a claim, a reason, or evidence? Explain.

3. **Critique** In lines 24–37 what evidence does Wallace offer to support her idea that people are not always focused on doing "whatever [is] necessary to survive" in a crisis? Is the evidence relevant and sufficient? Explain.

4. **Evaluate** In lines 44–60, Wallace notes that survivors often suffer from feelings of guilt. Does she think these feelings are justified? Does she support her reasoning with relevant and sufficient evidence? Explain your response.

5. **Evaluate** Reread lines 86–91. As evidence for Wallace's claim, is this paragraph valid and relevant? Explain.

6. **Interpret** In the final paragraph, Wallace writes that there is "a fine line between smart and selfish," and that "sometimes there's no line at all." What does she mean by this, and how does her conclusion restate her claim?

PERFORMANCE TASK

Speaking Activity: Debate In the selection, Lane Wallace explores whether survivors are selfish for trying to save their own lives while rescuers are heroic for trying to save others. Review the author's argument before completing this activity.

1. Divide the class into two teams. One team should take the position that survivors are selfish and uncivilized and that rescuers are heroic; the other team should take the position that survivors are smart and that rescuers are foolish.

2. Work with your team to gather evidence and use it to build a well-reasoned argument.

3. Hold a debate in which members from each team take turns stating the reasons and evidence for their claim, as well as responding to the other team's argument. Use appropriate eye contact and adequate volume to emphasize ideas.

4. After the debate, write a brief evaluation of each team's argument and explain which argument was more convincing.

Assign this
performance task.

PERFORMANCE TASK
SL 1a, SL 4

Speaking Activity: Debate Explain that debate participants should maintain a friendly and respectful tone toward their opponent. Arguments are won or lost on the basis of evidence and presentation, not on the denigration of the opposition. Have teams collect logical reasons and examples that draw on or expand upon ideas from the selection.

Critical Vocabulary

laud   transfix   consume   berate   edict

Practice and Apply Each of these word pairs contains one Critical Vocabulary word. Describe what is different and alike about the words in each pair. Use a dictionary or thesaurus as needed.

1. laud/welcome
2. transfix/stare
3. consume/fill
4. berate/battle
5. edict/tale

Vocabulary Strategy: Synonyms

Words that share the same or nearly the same meaning are called **synonyms.** Authors sometimes use synonyms to vary word choice and make their writing more interesting. For example, in line 49 of "Is Survival Selfish?" the author uses the word *paralyzed*. The synonym *transfixed* might also have worked, but the author had already used it in line 31.

If you come across an unfamiliar word in a text, try to think of another word that would make sense in the context of the sentence. Then check a dictionary or a thesaurus to see if your word is truly a synonym for the unfamiliar word. Note any subtle differences between the synonyms and try to understand why the author chose that precise word. Ask yourself whether the context sentence has the same or a slightly different meaning with your synonym as with the author's original word.

Practice and Apply Use a print or online thesaurus to complete this activity.

1. Create a two-column chart. In the first column, write the Critical Vocabulary words. In the second column, write at least two synonyms for each word.
2. Write a sentence using each Critical Vocabulary word.
3. For each sentence you write, exchange the Critical Vocabulary word for one of its synonyms. Work together with a partner to choose the best synonym for each sentence. Discuss whether using a synonym changes the meaning of each original sentence.

WHEN STUDENTS STRUGGLE...

Remind students that a thesaurus contains synonyms and antonyms. Writers use thesaurii to find a word, replace one used too frequently, or find a word that has a precise connotation. Read aloud the following:

"His **reputation** was ruined. He was labeled an **uncivilized** coward and, a year after the disaster, he resigned his position at White Star."

Have students use a thesaurus to find synonyms for *reputation (character, esteem, prestige, distinction)* and *uncivilized (cruel, unrefined, savage).* Discuss which synonyms would be appropriate for *reputation* and *uncivilized,* keeping in mind the nuances of the synonyms' meanings.

PRACTICE & APPLY

Critical Vocabulary

Possible answers:

1. *They are alike in that they both refer to an approval of something. They are different in that while* laud *means "to praise,"* welcome *means "to receive gladly."*

2. *They are alike in that they both refer to holding one's attention. They are different in that* stare *refers to looking fixedly for a prolonged moment, while* transfix *has to do with being awed or captivated.*

3. *They are alike in that they both refer to taking. They are different in that* consume *refers to something devoured or eaten, while* fill *refers to the taking up of all available space.*

4. *They are alike in that they both imply aggression. They are different in that* berate *means "to scold or criticize angrily," while* battle *means "to fight."*

5. *They are alike in that they both refer to something expressed or communicated. They are different in that* edicts *are pronouncements or rules, while* tales *are stories.*

Vocabulary Strategy: Synonyms

Possible answers:

Sentences will vary but should convey an understanding of critical-vocabulary definitions.

Critical Vocabulary	Synonyms
transfix	*paralyze, fascinate*
berate	*scold, reprimand*
consume	*deplete, devour*
edict	*rule, law*
laud	*praise, honor*

Language and Style: Indefinite Pronouns

L 3

As a class, review the indefinite pronouns in the chart. Remind students to consider how they use indefinite pronouns in their own writing. Lane Wallace uses indefinite pronouns carefully for meaning and for effect.

Answers:

Answers will vary. Students should write five sentences that correctly use each of the following indefinite pronouns: others, one, nobody, whatever, *and* another.

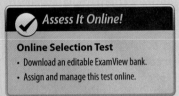

Assess It Online!

Online Selection Test
- Download an editable ExamView bank.
- Assign and manage this test online.

Language and Style: Indefinite Pronouns

L 3

When authors want to refer to a specific person, they use personal pronouns, such as *he, she,* or *I* ("She got out of the plane and survived"). To refer to one or more people or things that are not specifically mentioned, authors use **indefinite pronouns,** such as *anyone, all,* or *some.* In "Is Survival Selfish?" Lane Wallace uses a variety of indefinite pronouns.

Read this sentence from the selection:

But Yates was criticized by <u>some</u> for his survival decision . . . .

The indefinite pronoun *some* refers to the people who criticized Yates. It would be awkward—and probably impossible—to mention by name all of those who criticized the climber, so the author's use of *some* makes sense.

This chart lists other indefinite pronouns found in "Is Survival Selfish?"

Indefinite Pronoun	Example
others	". . . sacrifice themselves to save others . . ."
one	". . . one would think that in life-and-death situations . . ."
whatever	". . . whatever was necessary to survive."
nobody	". . . nobody was moving toward the emergency exits . . ."
another	". . . in an attempt to save another . . ."

Some words that can function as indefinite pronouns can also function as adjectives. For example, read this sentence from the selection:

<u>Some</u> people hold it together in a crisis and <u>some</u> people fall apart.

Here, *some* is used as an adjective because it describes the plural noun *people.*

Indefinite pronouns are sometimes used in pairs. Consider the following examples from the selection:

. . . the mixed messages we send <u>each other</u> . . .

Very <u>few others</u> in the plane . . .

In these examples, *each other* and *few others* may be considered compound indefinite pronouns because the words in each pair act together as a pronoun.

Practice and Apply Using the topic of survival ethics, write one sentence for each of the indefinite pronouns listed in the chart above. When you are finished, discuss your sentences with a partner.

Conduct a Debate

SL 1d

TEACH

Explain that a **debate** is an argument that covers both sides of an issue. A debate is made up of two teams that are presenting the reasons and evidence for their claim to gain the support of the audience.

A formal debate is set up so that each side consists of a team with two members. Each team argues either for or against a proposition. Each debater must think about the proposition and consider the evidence for both sides of it because it is more effective to argue if the debater knows both sides of the issue.

Review the format that the debate will take in the class. Have students assign roles within their group, and remind them to go back into the text to look for evidence to support their side of the argument.

Explain that while they are listening to the debate, students who are not presenting should be evaluating the debate using the following questions:

- Does the team prove that their side of the proposition is correct using a thorough analysis of the text?
- How effectively does the team present their reasons and evidence? Is their evidence valid, relevant, and sufficient?
- Does the team structure their responses to the opposing team with accurate reasons and evidence?
- Does each speaker use an appropriate rate and volume when speaking? Is each speaker able to maintain eye contact with the audience?
- Are the speakers polite to each other, listening carefully when debaters from the other team are speaking?

PRACTICE AND APPLY

Ask students in each team to work together to create a two-column For/Against chart to delineate, or outline, the basic parts of their argument. At the top of each column, they should write the claim or opposing claim. Then they should search the text for appropriate support for the claims. Encourage students to use the chart to help them consider the best way to present their side of the argument and refute the opposing claim.

Delineate and Evaluate an Argument

RI 8

RETEACH

Remind students that to evaluate whether an **argument** is successful, they must delineate (outline) its basic parts, which include the claim, reasons, and evidence. The evidence presented in an argument must be **valid, relevant,** and **sufficient.** Help students identify appropriate types of evidence:

1. An author provides only one source of evidence in an argument. Is this sufficient? *(No, evidence should come from a variety of sources.)*
2. An author creates a chart of population statistics in China to support the claim that the population of China is increasing. Is this evidence relevant? *(Yes, the statistics are related to the topic about which the author is writing.)*
3. An author includes a story about an uncommon event without citing a source. Is this evidence valid? *(No, a source is required if the evidence is not common knowledge.)*

 LEVEL UP TUTORIALS Assign the following *Level Up* tutorial: **Analyzing Arguments.**

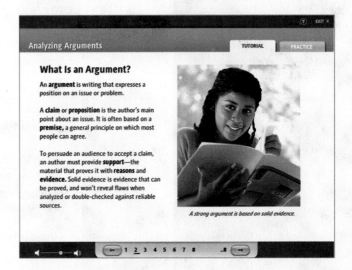

A strong argument is based on solid evidence.

INDEPENDENT READING

Have small groups of students look through some editorials in a local print or online newspaper. Ask them to evaluate one editorial to determine whether the argument is successful. Have each group write notes about or highlight the claim and some reasons and evidence. Ask them to share their analysis of the argument with another group.

Truth at All Costs

Speech by Marie Colvin

Why This Text

Students may have difficulty analyzing an argument without a thorough understanding of the writer's claims and evidence. Arguments such as this one, addressed in a speech by Marie Colvin, may use complex reasoning that becomes clear only with careful study. With the help of the close-reading questions, students will trace and evaluate Colvin's argument that being a war correspondent is worth the risk.

Background Have students read the background information about Marie Colvin, an American journalist who was killed in a Syrian attack while covering the siege of Homs for a British newspaper. Introduce the speech by pointing out that in her last television news broadcast, given on the day before she died, Colvin described the bombardment of Homs as the worst conflict she had ever encountered. Colvin believed that a war correspondent had to accept the risk to tell the truth about war, stating, "My job is to bear witness."

AS YOU READ Ask students to pay attention to the reasons Colvin gives to support her position that the job of a war correspondent is worth the risk. How soon into her speech can students begin to identify Colvin's point of view?

Standards Support

- cite strong and thorough textual evidence to support text analysis
- analyze how the author unfolds a series of ideas and how they are developed
- delineate and evaluate an argument
- assess an author's claims and reasoning

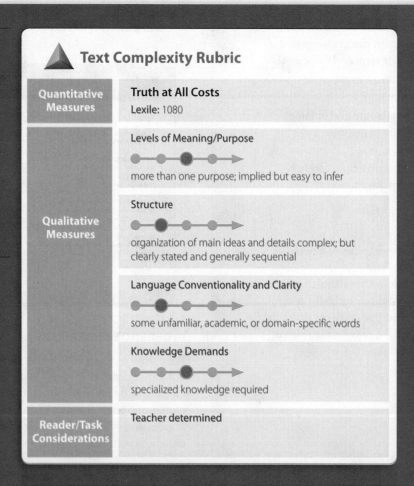

Text Complexity Rubric

Quantitative Measures	**Truth at All Costs** Lexile: 1080
Qualitative Measures	**Levels of Meaning/Purpose** more than one purpose; implied but easy to infer
	Structure organization of main ideas and details complex; but clearly stated and generally sequential
	Language Conventionality and Clarity some unfamiliar, academic, or domain-specific words
	Knowledge Demands specialized knowledge required
Reader/Task Considerations	Teacher determined

Strategies for CLOSE READING

Delineate and Evaluate an Argument

Students should read this speech carefully all the way through. Close-reading questions at the bottom of the page will help them focus on a thorough analysis of the argument. As they read, students should record comments or questions about the text in the side margins.

WHEN STUDENTS STRUGGLE . . .

To help students analyze the reasons Colvin gives to support her claim that the job of a war correspondent is worth the risk, have students work in a small group to fill out a chart such as the one shown below as they analyze the speech.

CITE TEXT EVIDENCE For practice in tracing an argument, ask students to cite the evidence Colvin uses to support her claim.

CLAIM: The job of a war correspondent is worth the risk.

SUPPORT:

Reason 1: The war correspondent's mission is to give an accurate, unbiased report of the horrors of war—"to find the truth . . . in propaganda."

Reason 2: Combat journalists have great responsibilities to report on the horrors of war despite the huge risk to themselves and others.

Reason 3: War correspondents must report on humanitarian disasters and civilian atrocities to bring awareness to others.

Reason 4: War correspondents can make a difference in that they "speak the truth to power," and make the public aware of the dangers of war.

Reason 5: Although war reporting has changed technologically over the years, it still serves the same purpose—journalists need to bear witness to war.

Background *The award-winning journalist* **Marie Colvin** *(1956–2012) spent most of her professional life as the Middle East war correspondent for the British newspaper* The Sunday Times. *A fearless reporter, Colvin reported directly from war zones. In Tamil-Tiger-held Sri Lanka, she was hit by shrapnel and lost the use of her left eye. In 2012, while reporting on the shelling of civilians in Syria, Colvin and a French photojournalist were killed in a rocket attack. At her memorial, she was called "the bravest of the brave." She gave the following speech in 2010 to honor journalists who had died in war zones.*

Truth at All Costs

Speech by Marie Colvin

CLOSE READ
Notes

1. **READ ▷** As you read lines 1–20, begin to collect and cite evidence.
   - Underline text explaining the reason for Colvin's speech.
   - Circle lines describing what it means to cover a war.
   - in the margin, paraphrase the claim Colvin makes about the "mission" of war correspondents (lines 12–20).

Your Royal Highness, ladies and gentlemen, I am honoured and humbled to be speaking to you at this service tonight to remember the journalists and their support staff who gave their lives to report from the war zones of the 21st century. I have been a war correspondent for most of my professional life. It has always been a hard calling. But the need for frontline, objective reporting has never been more compelling.

Covering a war means going to places torn by chaos, destruction and death, and trying to bear witness. It means trying to find the truth in a sandstorm of **propaganda** when armies, tribes or terrorists clash. And yes,
10 it means taking risks, not just for yourself but often for the people who work closely with you.

propaganda:
biased
information

85

---

1. **READ AND CITE TEXT EVIDENCE**

Ⓐ ASK STUDENTS to share their responses and then write one response that best states Colvin's claim in lines 12–20 about the basic "mission" of war correspondents. *Colvin believes the mission of a war correspondent is to report on the horrors of war accurately and without bias. They should cite lines 18–20 as evidence.*

Critical Vocabulary: propaganda (line 9) Have students share their definitions of *propaganda*. What does Colvin say is a war correspondent's role concerning propaganda? *She says that covering a war means trying to find the truth through all the biased information.*

FOR ELL STUDENTS Ask your ELL students to analyze the compound word *frontline* (line 6), identifying its two base words (*front + line*) and their meanings, and by defining the compound word. *It is the place where two armies face each other and fight during a war.*

The mission is
to report
accurately and
objectively on
war.

Despite all the videos you see from the Ministry of Defence or the
Pentagon, and all the sanitised language describing smart bombs and
pinpoint strikes, the scene on the ground has remained remarkably the
same for hundreds of years. Craters. Burned houses. Mutilated bodies.
Women weeping for children and husbands. Men for their wives, mothers
children.

bravado:
a showy
display of
courage

Our mission is to report these horrors of war with accuracy and
without prejudice. We always have to ask ourselves whether the level of risk
20 is worth the story. What is bravery, and what is **bravado**?

Journalists covering combat shoulder great responsibilities and face
difficult choices. Sometimes they pay the ultimate price. Tonight we honour
the 49 journalists and support staff who were killed bringing the news to
our shores. We also remember journalists around the world who have been
wounded, maimed or kidnapped and held hostage for months. It has never
been more dangerous to be a war correspondent, because the journalist in
the combat zone has become a prime target.

I lost my eye in an ambush in the Sri Lankan civil war.[1] I had gone to
the northern Tamil area from which journalists were banned and found an
30 unreported humanitarian disaster. As I was smuggled back across the
internal border, a soldier launched a grenade at me and the shrapnel sliced
into my face and chest. He knew what he was doing.

[1] **Sri Lankan civil war:** A 26-year civil war (1983–2009) between government troops and
the Tamil Tigers, a minority separatist group, who fought to establish an independent
state in Sri Lanka.

NATO forces guard the scene of a suicide bomb attack against British soldiers
Wednesday, January 28, 2004, in the snow in Kabul, Afganistan.

Just last week, I had a coffee in Afghanistan with a photographer friend,
Joao Silva. We talked about the terror one feels and must contain when
patrolling on an embed[2] with the armed forces through fields and villages
in Afghanistan . . . putting one foot in front of the other, steeling yourself
each step for the blast. The expectation of that blast is the stuff of
nightmares. Two days after our meeting, Joao stepped on a mine and lost
both legs at the knee.

40 Many of you here must have asked yourselves, or be asking yourselves
now, is it worth the cost in lives, heartbreak, loss? Can we really make a
difference?

[2] **embed:** traveling with an army.

2. ◀ REREAD Reread lines 18–20. Explain the question that Colvin is
asking. What idea is she emphasizing?

She is explaining that there is a difference between courage and
boldness. She emphasizes the idea that part of the war reporter's job
is to weigh the risks against the benefits of the story.

3. READ ▶ Read lines 21–39. Circle Colvin's claim about the danger war
correspondents face today. Underline the evidence she cites to support
her opinion.

4. ◀ REREAD Reread lines 33–39. How does the information Colvin gives
in these lines support her argument about the danger of war reporting?

Colvin tells an anecdote about a conversation she had with a
photographer about the difficulties of war reporting. She uses
loaded language ("the stuff of nightmares") to support her point
about the terror reporters feel, ending with the shocking news that
this photographer has since lost both his legs.

5. READ ▶ As you read lines 40–52, continue to cite evidence.
- Circle the questions Colvin asks (lines 40–42).
- Underline the question raised by the newspaper.
- In the margin, explain the newspaper's point of view (lines 43–45).

---

2. **REREAD AND CITE TEXT EVIDENCE**

B **ASK STUDENTS** what distinction Colvin is making between
bravery and bravado in lines 18–20. *Colvin is emphasizing that a
war correspondent should weigh the level of risk against the benefits
of getting a story to consider the difference between demonstrating
real bravery and making a showy display of courage.*

3. **READ AND CITE TEXT EVIDENCE**

C **ASK STUDENTS** to determine how Colvin supports her
opinion about the dangers faced by combat journalists today. *She
relates the story of how she lost an eye in the Sri Lankan civil war
(lines 28–32) and of how her photographer-friend Joao Silva stepped
on a land mine and lost both his legs (lines 33–39).*

Critical Vocabulary: bravado (line 20) Have students compare
their definitions of *bravado*, and ask for examples of people
acting with bravado.

4. **REREAD AND CITE TEXT EVIDENCE**

D **ASK STUDENTS** to cite examples of Colvin's choice of words
that support her argument. *The use of the word* steeling, *in
"steeling yourself each step for the blast" (lines 36–37), creates the
image of strength in the face of danger. The use of loaded language
such as "the stuff of nightmares" (lines 37–38) appeals to her
audience's emotions, and helps provide strong support for her
argument.*

5. **READ AND CITE TEXT EVIDENCE**

E **ASK STUDENTS** to explain the newspaper's point of view
concerning the risk Colvin took and the injury that resulted.
*Students should cite evidence from lines 43–45 to explain that one
newspaper suggested that Colvin took too great a risk in trying to get
a story.*

The paper suggested that Colvin's injury was her own fault.

E   I faced that question when I was injured. In fact one paper ran a headline saying, has Marie Colvin gone too far this time? My answer then, and now, was that it is worth it.

    Today in this church are friends, colleagues and families who know exactly what I am talking about, and bear the cost of those experiences, as do their families and loved ones.

50   Today we must also remember how important it is that news organisations continue to invest in sending us out at great cost, both financial and emotional, to cover stories.

G   We go to remote war zones to report what is happening. The public have a right to know what our government, and our armed forces, are doing in our name. Our mission is to speak the truth to power. We send home that first rough draft of history. We can and do make a difference in exposing the horrors of war and especially the atrocities that befall civilians.

60   The history of our profession is one to be proud of. The first war correspondent in the modern era was William Howard Russell[3] of the Times, who was sent to cover the Crimean conflict[4] when a British-led coalition fought an invading Russian army.

    Billy Russell, as the troops called him, created a firestorm of public indignation back home by revealing inadequate equipment, scandalous treatment of the wounded, especially when they were **repatriated**—does this sound familiar?—and an incompetent high command that led to the folly of the Charge of the Light Brigade.[5] It was a breakthrough in war

repatriate:

to send back to one's country

[3] **William Howard Russell:** known as "Billy" Russell (1820–1907), Russell was a reporter who gained renown for his reporting on the Crimean War.
[4] **Crimean conflict:** a war (1853–1856) between the Russian Empire and an alliance of several European empires, including the British Empire; it was known as the first "modern" war.
[5] **Charge of the Light Brigade:** an ill-fated charge of British light cavalry against Russian forces during the Crimean War.

6.   **REREAD AND DISCUSS**   Reread lines 40–52. With a small group, discuss the questions Colvin asks and the answers she gives.

7.   **READ**   As you read lines 53–90, continue to cite text evidence.
- Underline what Colvin says the public have a right to know.
- Circle text that explains how war reporters make a difference (lines 53–57).
- Circle text that describes what Colvin calls "the real difficulty."

88

> ## Our mission is to speak the truth to power.

reporting. Until then, wars were reported by junior officers who sent back dispatches to newspapers. Billy Russell went to war with an open mind, a
70 telescope, a notebook and a bottle of brandy. I first went to war with a typewriter, and learned to tap out a telex tape. It could take days to get from the front to a telephone or telex machine.

H   War reporting has changed greatly in just the last few years. Now we go to war with a satellite phone, laptop, video camera and a flak jacket. I point my satellite phone to south southwest in Afghanistan, press a button and I have filed.

    In an age of 24/7 rolling news, blogs and Twitters, we are on constant call wherever we are. But war reporting is still essentially the same— someone has to go there and see what is happening. You can't get that
80 information without going to places where people are being shot at, and others are shooting at you. The real difficulty is having enough faith in humanity to believe that enough people be they government, military or the man on the street, will care when your file reaches the printed page, the website or the TV screen.

8.   **REREAD**   Reread lines 73–79. Explain the contradiction Colvin introduces when she discusses how war reporting has changed.

When Colvin says war reporting has changed, she is talking primarily about changes in technology and protection. In other ways, war reporting hasn't changed because correspondents still need to go to dangerous places and see what's happening.

89

6.   REREAD AND DISCUSS USING TEXT EVIDENCE

F   **ASK STUDENTS** to cite evidence from the text about the questions Colvin asks and answers. *Students should cite evidence from lines 40–42, 43–45, and 50–52.*

7.   READ AND CITE TEXT EVIDENCE

G   **ASK STUDENTS** to explain how Colvin answers the question she asks in lines 53–57. How does it support the idea that a reporter is an eyewitness to history? *She says war journalists make a difference by telling people what is happening in a war (lines 53–55), by speaking "the truth to power" (line 55), and by exposing war atrocities (lines 56–58).*

Critical Vocabulary: repatriate (line 65) Have students explain *repatriate* and use it in a sentence.

8.   REREAD AND CITE TEXT EVIDENCE

H   **ASK STUDENTS** to cite evidence to support Colvin's contradictory claim in lines 73–79. *By citing the more sophisticated devices that journalists bring to the front today, such as a satellite phone, laptop, and video camera, which are far faster for filing a report than dispatches or telex machines, she is supporting her claim that war reporting has changed (lines 73–76). By recognizing that war journalists still have to go to the war-torn area to see what is happening (lines 78–79), she is supporting the contradictory claim.*

CLOSE READ
Notes

We do have that faith because we believe we do make a difference. And we could not make that difference—or begin to do our job—without the fixers, drivers and translators, who face the same risks and die in appalling numbers. Today we honour them as much as the front line journalists who have died in pursuit of the truth. They have kept the faith as

90   we who remain must continue to do.

9.   **REREAD**   Reread lines 81–90. What is Colvin's idea of faith? What does she say reporters need to believe in?

Colvin believes that war correspondents must have faith that their reporting makes a difference to someone who reads it.

SHORT RESPONSE

Cite Text Evidence   Explain whether or not Colvin convinced you that being a war correspondent is worth the risk. Review your reading notes, and evaluate the effectiveness of her argument. **Cite text evidence** in your response.

Possible response: Yes, it's worth the risk because war correspondents expose aspects of war that no other group does. They bear witness to the chaos and destruction of war and report on what their own governments and armies are doing in their name. Colvin cites the case of Billy Russell, who reported on the "inadequate equipment" and "scandalous treatment of the wounded" in the Crimean War, to bolster her case that the public needed to know this information. She also uses examples from her own life to show the dangers and the reasons behind the risk.

90

TO CHALLENGE STUDENTS . . .

For more context about war reporters and photographers, students can conduct print or online research into other men and women who have followed these careers.

ASK STUDENTS to research other people who have reported on wars. Have each student pick one such person, conduct research, and present findings to the rest of the class.

- Point out that there have been people reporting from the battlefield for centuries. Students may find it rewarding to choose a person who lived during a period they themselves find interesting.
- Students should try to learn what got the person interested in reporting on wars. They should find out who the reporter or photographer worked for and what wars he or she covered.
- Encourage students to find out interesting details about the person they have picked. They might present quotes that offer insight into the person's world or photographs that show the person's work.

---

9.   **REREAD AND CITE TEXT EVIDENCE**

 ASK STUDENTS how Colvin's last paragraph adds power to her argument. *Colvin believes that correspondents must have faith in the idea that their war reporting will make a difference to people. Her last paragraph, in which she pays tribute to those who help war journalists do their job and who have died in the process, makes a strong emotional appeal to her audience about the need to take risks for the sake of telling the truth about the horrors of war.*

SHORT RESPONSE

Cite Text Evidence   Students should:

- explain whether or not they agree with Colvin's argument.
- give reasons for their point of view.
- cite specific evidence from the text to support their reasons.

DIG DEEPER

With the class, return to Question 6, Reread and Discuss. Have students share the results of their discussion.

ASK STUDENTS whether they were satisfied with the outcome of their small-group discussions. Have each group share what their majority opinion was concerning the sufficiency of Colvin's evidence to support her conclusion—that being a war correspondent is worth the risk. What compelling evidence did the groups cite from the speech to support this opinion?

- Guide students to tell whether there was any convincing evidence cited by members holding the opposite opinion.
- Encourage groups to explain how they decided whether or not they had found sufficient evidence in the text to support their opinion. Did everyone in the group agree?
- After students have shared the results of their group's discussion, ask whether another group shared any findings they wish they had considered.

ASK STUDENTS to return to their Short Response answer and revise it based on the class discussion.

CLOSE READING NOTES

from Deep Survival

Science Writing by Laurence Gonzales

Why This Text?

Students may hear or read stories about survival and wonder how they would react in such a situation. This selection explores the qualities that are the key to survival in many life-threatening situations.

Key Learning Objective: The student will be able to analyze ideas and events presented in the text, determine the central idea, and summarize the text.

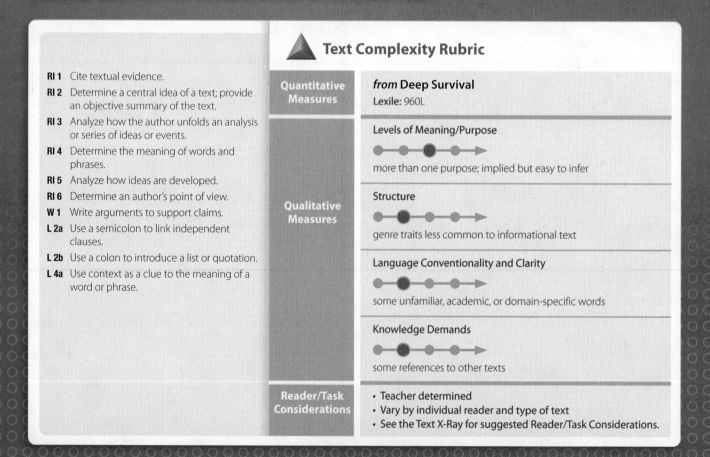

RI 1 Cite textual evidence.
RI 2 Determine a central idea of a text; provide an objective summary of the text.
RI 3 Analyze how the author unfolds an analysis or series of ideas or events.
RI 4 Determine the meaning of words and phrases.
RI 5 Analyze how ideas are developed.
RI 6 Determine an author's point of view.
W 1 Write arguments to support claims.
L 2a Use a semicolon to link independent clauses.
L 2b Use a colon to introduce a list or quotation.
L 4a Use context as a clue to the meaning of a word or phrase.

▲ Text Complexity Rubric

Quantitative Measures

from **Deep Survival**
Lexile: 960L

Qualitative Measures

Levels of Meaning/Purpose

more than one purpose; implied but easy to infer

Structure

genre traits less common to informational text

Language Conventionality and Clarity

some unfamiliar, academic, or domain-specific words

Knowledge Demands

some references to other texts

Reader/Task Considerations

- Teacher determined
- Vary by individual reader and type of text
- See the Text X-Ray for suggested Reader/Task Considerations.

English Language Support Before teaching, use the Text X-Ray below for an overview of the text's complexity. The Text X-Ray and the supports and scaffolds in the Teacher's Edition will help you guide students of different skill levels.

Meaning Making

Language Development

Effective Expression

Content Knowledge

Foundational Skills

Text Complexity: Qualitative Measures

Levels of Meaning/Purpose

more than one purpose; implied but easy to infer

Help students determine the central idea and summarize the text.

- Teacher's Edition side notes, pp. 326, 327, 328, 329, 331, 333, 334, 335
- When Students Struggle, pp. 328–329, 332
- Determine Central Idea and Summarize the Text, p. 335

To reteach summarizing a text, see

- Summarize a Text, p. 338a

▶ *Use It! Level Up* Tutorial: Summarizing

ZOOM IN ON SUMMARIZING Tell students that this text contains many ideas about survival, supported by stories of people who have survived. Explain that a **summary** of the whole text would focus on the **main ideas** and leave out details from the stories. Have students read the selection in pairs, pausing at intervals to discuss what they have read. Give them the following line references and ask them to summarize each passage in one or two sentences: lines 67–89 *(Survivors think for themselves instead of following rules)*; lines 90–113 *(Survivors don't need to be brave, but they must have a special kind of inner strength)*; lines 198–230 *(Survivors know how to conserve their energy)*; lines 249–261 *(Helping others is key to survival)*. After reading, have pairs share their summaries and work together to write a summary of the text as a whole.

Structure

genre traits less common to informational text

Help students analyze how an author develops ideas through anecdotes and other information.

- Teacher's Edition side notes, pp. 325, 326, 327, 328, 330, 332, 333, 334, 335
- English Language Support, pp. 325, 327
- Strategies for Annotation, p. 335
- Analyze Ideas and Events, p. 335

To teach students how to cite textual evidence in preparation for their Performance Task, see

- Cite Textual Evidence, p. 338a

▶ *Use It!* Interactive Whiteboard Lesson: Citing Textual Evidence

ZOOM IN ON ANALYZING STRUCTURE Read aloud lines 1–18. Explain that while the text begins with two **anecdotes**, or real-life accounts, the author's purpose is not merely to tell what happened to Juliane Koepcke and Bill Garleb. Instead, he uses the anecdotes to support and explain his ideas about survival. Read aloud lines 67–76 and discuss how this paragraph differs from the previous ones. *(It refers to Juliane's story but in the context of broader ideas or conclusions about the topic of survival.)*

Language Conventionality and Clarity

some unfamiliar, academic, or domain-specific words

Teach unfamiliar vocabulary in context.

- Teacher's Edition Critical Vocabulary notes, pp. 325, 326, 327, 328, 329, 337
- Applying Academic Vocabulary, pp. 326, 330
- English Language Support, pp. 331, 334
- Vocabulary Strategy: Context Clues, p. 337
- Strategies for Annotation, p. 337

Guide students to determine figurative meanings.

- Teacher's Edition side notes, pp. 329, 330, 331

Teach students to use colons and semicolons.

- Language and Style: Colons and Semicolons, p. 338
- When Students Struggle, p. 338

 Use It! **GrammarNotes:** Lesson 20: Using Semicolons, Lesson 21: Using Colons

ZOOM IN ON **USING CONTEXT CLUES** Reinforce how students can often find **context clues** in the surrounding text to help them figure out the meaning of an unfamiliar word. Review the four steps in using context clues outlined on page 337. Then model for students how you would apply these steps to figure out the meaning of *strategy* in line 35: The word is a noun; the sentence includes a possible synonym, *plan*; previous sentences describe Juliane's plan to head downhill to find water and then follow the water to civilization. Therefore, *strategy* means "a plan or a series of steps to achieve a goal." Assign pairs to apply the steps to the words *fatal* (line 40), *deliberately* (line 48), and *knottiest* (line 67). Have pairs share their results and then continue to apply the steps to other unknown words they encounter in the text.

Knowledge Demands

some references to other texts

Support English Learners by providing background information about a reference made in the text.

ZOOM IN ON **BUILDING KNOWLEDGE** Point out the author's reference to the Sand Pile Effect in line 201. Explain that this is a concept from physics. Have students imagine slowly pouring sand onto a surface to build a pile. As the pile gets taller, tiny avalanches or slides start to occur, maintaining relatively smooth slopes on all sides. However, there is no way to predict where the next avalanche will occur. Similarly, author Gonzales says, it is impossible to predict when or why a person will suddenly be overcome with fatigue.

Suggested Reader/Task Considerations

You might consider the following before assigning this science text to students.

- Do students have the visualization skills to appreciate the various survival stories described in the text?
- Might students develop an interest in the topic of survival training?

ZOOM IN ON **SUPPORTING COMPREHENSION**

- Encourage students to slow down when reading descriptive passages and use details in the text to visualize settings and events. Explain that this will help them understand the experiences of the survivors and their reactions to danger.
- Suggest that interested students research the kind of training people receive in survival schools and report back to the class. Discuss how these programs are similar to and different from the one led by Byron Kerns.

AS YOU READ Direct students to use the As You Read directions to focus their reading.

Analyze Ideas and Events

RI 1, RI 3, RI 5

(LINES 1–15)

Explain to students that Gonzales uses **anecdotes,** or brief stories, to introduce and develop ideas. These anecdotes of different people's survival experiences are combined with his observations.

Ⓐ **CITE TEXT EVIDENCE** Ask students to reread lines 1–15 and identify statements Gonzales uses to signal which part of Juliane's story is most important. *("To someone who knows about survival, that statement is telling" [lines 11–12]. "Amazing and also characteristic of a true survivor" [line 15].)* Discuss what part of Juliane's story sparked these observations. *(Gonzales points out Juliane's calm while she was falling, which allowed her to notice details about the world around her.)*

> **CRITICAL VOCABULARY**
>
> **disintegration**: Lightning caused Juliane's plane to come apart in pieces.
>
> **ASK STUDENTS** to describe what happened after the disintegration of Juliane's plane. *(After the plane broke into pieces in midair, Juliane and the other passengers fell into the jungle.)*

---

from
Deep Survival

Science Writing by Laurence Gonzales

AS YOU READ Think about the title of the selection and consider what the term *deep survival* means to the author. Write down any questions you generate during reading.

Juliane Koepcke was flying with her mother and ninety other passengers on Christmas Eve, 1971, when lightning struck, causing an extensive structural failure of the Lockheed Electra. Juliane fell out of the broken airplane into the Peruvian jungle. She was seventeen years old, wearing her Catholic confirmation dress and white high heels. Miraculously, she suffered only cuts and a broken collarbone from the crash. Later, she reported feeling "a hefty concussion." Then she was falling toward the jungle.

10 As she recalled, "I remember thinking that the jungle trees below looked just like cauliflowers." To someone who knows about survival, that statement is telling. She wasn't screaming; she wasn't in a panic. She was in wonder at the world in which she found herself. She was taking it all in, touching her new reality. Checking out her environment while falling. Amazing cool.

Amazing and also characteristic of a true survivor. Bill Garleb, an American GI who survived the Bataan Death March[1] in the Philippines, found his senses increasingly sharp as he experienced a deep wonder at the birds and colors and smells of the jungle.

A dozen other passengers survived the midair **disintegration**
20 of Juliane's plane, and their attitude, and hence their behavior and fate, were quite different from hers.

Juliane awoke alone on the floor of the jungle, still strapped into her seat. There was no sign of her mother, who'd been beside her in the plane. She spent the night trying to keep out of the rain

disintegration
(dĭs-ĭn′tĭ-grā′shən) *n.* the process of a whole coming apart in pieces.

---

[1] **Bataan Death March:** the forced transfer of captured American and Filipino soldiers by the Japanese after the World War II Battle of Bataan. Thousands died during the ordeal in April 1942.

Image Credits: (c) ©Aquila/Shutterstock; (cr) ©Outcaster

Deep Survival **325**

SCAFFOLDING FOR ELL STUDENTS

Comprehension: Time Sequence Help students analyze the anecdotes throughout the selection by understanding time sequence.

- Read aloud lines 1–9 and point out words and phrases that signal time sequences: *Christmas Eve, 1971; when; later; then.*

- Explain that following the events in order will allow them to understand the point the author is making.

ASK STUDENTS to answer these questions: What happened first? What happened next? Then what happened to Juliane? What did she say later? Have pairs read the selection and take turns asking and answering questions about the sequence of events in anecdotes.

CLOSE READ

Determine Central Idea and Summarize the Text (LINES 30–36)

RI 2

Explain that determining the main idea of individual paragraphs is a step toward determining the **central idea** of an entire selection, or the main point that the author is trying to communicate. The main idea of a paragraph may be stated or implied. When it is implied, readers must make **inferences,** or logical guesses, based on the supporting details presented in the paragraph.

 ASK STUDENTS to reread lines 30–36 and state the main idea of the paragraph in their own words. *(Juliane's survival plan was to walk downhill until she found water that would lead her to help.)* Discuss what details support that idea. *(Juliane's "father had told her that if she went downhill, she'd find water" and that "rivers usually led to civilization" [lines 33–34]; "she had a plan that she believed in" [line 36].)*

Analyze Ideas and Events (LINES 37–44)

RI 3, RI 5

Explain that Gonzales chooses his anecdotes carefully to make particular points.

 ASK STUDENTS to reread lines 37–44 and explain why Gonzales includes the anecdote from *Alive.* (*He wants to reinforce the idea that waiting for rescue can be a very bad idea. He is providing evidence to support the idea that the others who survived Juliane's plane crash made a bad decision by not taking responsibility for their own well-being.*)

CRITICAL VOCABULARY

deduce: Juliane concluded that rescue planes and helicopters would not be able to see her.

ASK STUDENTS how Juliane deduced that rescue planes and helicopters would not be able to see her. *(She observed that the jungle canopy was very thick and reasoned that it hid her from view.)*

---

under her seat. The next day, she **deduced** that even the helicopters and airplanes she could hear wouldn't be able to see her through the jungle canopy.[2] She'd have to get herself out. It was another important moment: She didn't spend time bemoaning her fate. She looked to herself, took responsibility, made a plan.

30   Her parents were researchers who worked in the jungle, and she was familiar with that environment. But Juliane had had no survival training. She didn't know where she was or which way she ought to go, but her father had told her that if she went downhill, she'd find water. He'd said that rivers usually led to civilization. And while that strategy can just as easily lead into a swamp, at least she had a plan that she believed in. She had a task.

Meanwhile, the others who had lived through the fall decided to await rescue, which is not necessarily a bad idea either. But expecting someone else to take responsibility for your well-being

40   can be fatal. In *Alive*, Piers Paul Read tells the story of the survivors of another airplane crash, this one in the Andes.[3] Everyone who survived the crash stayed put, assuming that they'd be rescued. Many died; the others wound up eating each other to keep from starving before someone finally walked out and found help.

Juliane had nothing except a few pieces of candy and some small cakes. She had no survival equipment, no tools, no compass or map—none of the things I'd been taught to use in survival school. But she very deliberately set up a program for herself. She set off, resting through the heat of the day and traveling during the

50   cooler periods. She walked for eleven days through dense jungle while being literally eaten alive by leeches and strange tropical insects, which bored into her, laid their eggs, and produced worms that hatched and tunneled out through her skin.

Eventually, she came to a hut along the banks of the river she'd been following. She staggered and collapsed inside. There is always a lot of chance involved in a survival situation, both good luck and bad. It was Juliane's good fortune that three hunters turned up the next day and delivered her to a local doctor. But, as Louis Pasteur[4] said, "Luck favors the prepared mind."

60   Tough and clearheaded, this teenage girl, who had lost her shoes (not to mention her mother) on the first day, saved herself; the other survivors took the same eleven days to sit down and die.

The forces that put them there were beyond their control. But the course of events for those who found themselves alive on the

deduce
(dĭ-dōōs´) *v.* to know through reason or logical conclusion.

---

[2] **jungle canopy:** the dense layer formed by the leaves and branches of the tallest trees.

[3] **Andes:** a mountain range in western South America running from Venezuela to Argentina.

[4] **Louis Pasteur:** (1822–1895) French chemist and biologist.

APPLYING ACADEMIC VOCABULARY

sustain	utilize

As you discuss the selection, incorporate the Collection 5 academic vocabulary words: *sustain* and *utilize*. Invite students to discuss how Juliane was able to **sustain** herself for a long period in the jungle. Ask them to explain what prevents some people from **utilizing** the survival tools they have at their disposal.

ground were the result of deep and personal individual reactions to a new environment.

The knottiest mystery of survival is how one unequipped, ill-prepared seventeen-year-old girl gets out alive and a dozen adults in similar circumstances, better equipped, do not. But the deeper I've gone into the study of survival, the more sense such outcomes make. Making fire, building shelter, finding food, signaling, navigation— none of that mattered to Juliane's survival. Although we cannot know what the others who survived the fall were thinking and deciding, it's possible that they knew they were supposed to stay put and await rescue. They were rule followers, and it killed them.

In the World Trade Center disaster,[5] many people who were used to following the rules died because they did what they were told by authority figures. An employee of the Aon Insurance Company on the ninety-third floor of the south tower had begun his escape but returned to his office after the security guards made a general announcement that the building was safe and that people should stay inside until they were told to leave. Before he died, he spoke to his father on the phone: "Why did I listen to them—I shouldn't have." Another man, an employee of Fuji Bank, actually reached the ground-floor lobby, only to be sent back in by a security guard. A third worker called a family member and recorded a final message on the answering machine: "I can't go anywhere because they told us not to move. I have to wait for the firefighters."

In thinking for herself, Juliane wasn't even particularly brave. Survival is not about bravery and heroics. Heroes can be perfect heroes and wind up dead. By definition, survivors must live. Juliane was afraid most of the time (of everything from piranhas when she had to wade in the water to the worms that were crawling around under her skin to the real or imagined creatures of the forest). Survivors aren't fearless. They *use* fear: they turn it into anger and focus.

Conversely, searchers are always amazed to find people who have died while in possession of everything they needed to survive. John Leach writes that "Victims have been recovered from life rafts with a survival box (containing flares, rations, first-aid kit and so on) unopened and the necessary contents unused."

"Some people just give up," Ken Hill told me, referring to his search and rescue operations in Nova Scotia. "Fifteen years I've been studying this, and I can't figure out why."

What saved Juliane was an inner resource, a state of mind. She certainly didn't have any physical equipment. But she'd been

conversely
(kən-vûrs´lē) *adv.* in a way that contradicts or reverses something.

---

[5] **World Trade Center disaster:** the destruction of New York office buildings by hijacked airplanes on September 11, 2001.

ENGLISH LANGUAGE SUPPORT

Comprehension: Cause and Effect Define **cause** as an event or action that directly results in another event or action. An **effect** is the result of a cause. Tell students that a cause always happens before an effect, but an author does not always present the events in that order. Read these sentences and have students identify the cause and the effect in each one:

- "They were rule followers *[cause]* and it killed them *[effect]*." (lines 75–76)
- "In the World Trade Center disaster, many people who were used to following the rules died *[effect]* because they did what they were told by authority figures *[cause]*." (lines 77–79)

CLOSE READ

Determine Central Idea and Summarize the Text (LINES 67–89)
RI 1, RI 2

Explain that more than one paragraph may develop the same main idea. Also point out that the main idea may be stated in a topic sentence that is often the first or last sentence in a paragraph.

D **CITE TEXT EVIDENCE** Ask students to reread lines 67–89 and identify any topic sentences. *("They were rule followers and it killed them" [lines 75–76]; "In the World Trade Center…died because they did what they were told by authority figures" [lines 77–79].)* Discuss how these topic sentences are related and what details support the main idea. *(Both sentences reflect the main idea that people who rely on rules or authority are often not the ones who survive. Supporting details include an inference about the other people in Juliane's plane and three different examples of people at the World Trade Center.)*

Analyze Ideas and Events (LINES 98–105)
RI 3, RI 5

Explain that Gonzales supports his use of anecdotes and personal observations with other kinds of evidence to develop his ideas.

E **ASK STUDENTS** to reread lines 98–105 and identify the types of evidence that Gonzales presents. Why might he use such evidence? *(He quotes two experts who have experience with people who fail to survive even when they have the resources that would allow them to do so. By citing these experts, he strengthens his ideas by showing that they are based on a large number of examples from people with firsthand knowledge about the topic.)*

CRITICAL VOCABULARY

conversely: Unlike Juliane, people with survival tools sometimes die.

ASK STUDENTS why Gonzales uses the term *conversely* to describe the phenomenon of people dying even though they have survival tools. *(He wants to show the reverse of Juliane's survival with no tools.)*

Analyze Ideas and Events

RI 3, RI 5

(LINES 108–113)

Explain that authors choose certain details to engage readers and to reinforce their central idea.

 ASK STUDENTS to reread lines 108–113 and explain why Gonzales might have chosen the details that he includes in the paragraph. (*By including a number of challenges that ordinary people face, such as divorce, career problems, illness, and accidents, alongside the extreme examples of war, prison camp, and being stranded in the jungle, he introduces the idea that all people need survival skills. These details are intended to engage readers who might feel that Juliane's story is not relevant to them.*)

Determine Central Idea and Summarize the Text

RI 1, RI 2

(LINES 114–123)

Remind students that readers must make **inferences,** or logical guesses, to understand ideas that are not directly stated in a text. Explain that making inferences is something that people do in their daily lives.

 CITE TEXT EVIDENCE Ask students to reread lines 114–123 and identify the inference that Gonzales makes about Byron Kerns. (*He infers that Kerns is a tough guy who is going to put them through a difficult training [lines 122–123].*) Discuss what details support that inference. (*Kerns is a "big, macho-looking guy" who wears a large machete on his belt and who has "twelve years of military experience" [lines 118–121].*)

CRITICAL VOCABULARY

distill: Gonzales learned to make water from the vapor in the air.

ASK STUDENTS to explain why it would be valuable to know how to distill water from the air. (*In a survival situation, a person could distill drinking water from the air when there is no other source of water available.*)

---

prepared mentally, somehow. A lifetime of experience shapes us to meet or be crushed by such challenges as a bad divorce, the

110 shattering of a career, a terrible illness or accident, a collapsing economy, a war, prison camp, the death of a loved one, or being stranded in the jungle. I went to survival school to try to understand that mystery and see if I could master my own journey. . . .

We took off from Pittsfield, Massachusetts, sharing the flying duties, and landed in Lynchburg, Virginia. As I climbed out of the cockpit and onto the wing, I caught my first glimpse of our instructor. Byron Kerns runs the Mountain Shepherd Survival School. He swaggered across the fueling ramp toward us wearing an 18-inch Panamanian machete on his belt, a big, macho-looking

120 guy with twelve years of military experience, including a stint with the Marines. He had worked at the famous Air Force Survival School in Washington State. When I saw him, I thought, We're in for it now.

That night, Byron explained that we were going to head off into the Virginia woods the next morning, early, and we'd be drilling for several days on such matters as map and compass work, firecraft, shelter, and signaling. We'd learn to find water or **distill** it from the air. We would not think about food, because it wasn't necessary. The Air Force plan was that you'd be found within three days.

130 "Your job," he said, "is to stay alive for seventy-two hours." When he left, Jonas[6] said, "This guy's going to whip you like a redheaded stepchild."[7]

Early the next morning, as we moved up a rocky river drainage through the mountains, I noticed that Kerns would stop frequently to point out something of beauty or interest. He spoke softly, as if we were in a church. He laughed a lot. He liked to be still and just think or smoke a cigarette. I saw no sign of the drill sergeant I'd expected. In our first exercise, Kerns asked me and Jonas to make a fire, and in a matter of minutes we had a roaring blaze going. Kerns

140 had turned away to get something from his pack. When he turned back, the flames were leaping several feet off the ground. "Whoa," he said, laughing, "easy, easy. I just wanted to know if you could start a fire. Some people can't." Then he gently separated the pile of wood and put it out.

Byron Kerns turned out to be soft-spoken, polite, cheerfully earnest, and gentle to a fault. He moved slowly, never hurried, and was always carefully assessing himself and his environment. He wasn't prone to high emotional states. He carried with him a

distill
(dĭ-stĭl´) *v.* to transform vapor into liquid.

---

[6] **Jonas Dovydenas:** (b. 1939) Lithuanian-born photographer.
[7] **a redheaded stepchild:** a person who is mistreated because he or she is unwanted.

WHEN STUDENTS STRUGGLE . . .

Encourage students to approach the task of determining a central idea and summarizing the text in small steps.

- Have students read the selection in pairs. Tell them to take turns reading aloud each paragraph. At the end of the paragraph, the reading partner asks the listening partner to state the main idea and two or three supporting details.

- Have students record their ideas in a chart like the one shown.

- When they have completed the selection, have them review their chart and look for the ideas that are most strongly supported to determine the central idea of the selection. They can also use the chart to help them write an objective summary of the text.

contagious air of calm. He reminded me of my father, actually.
150 Like so many retired pilots, my father wore soft shoes, talked softly,
and walked slowly. (As a pilot, you want to wear soft shoes so that
you can feel the rudder pedals. You don't want to make sudden,
unplanned motions in a combat aircraft cockpit, where the controls
are sensitive and lots of things can explode.) That **demeanor**, once
learned under penalty of death, is carried through the rest of your
life. Kerns also had that quiet, dark, and private humor.

Even after a lifetime in the wilderness, Kerns entered the woods
with a deep sense of respect and humility, like a man approaching
a magnificent, dangerous, and unpredictable creature. It's the same
160 way a good pilot approaches his aircraft.

As we worked in the wilderness, learning technical skills, Kerns
kept talking about Positive Mental Attitude. It was the number one
item on the checklist he'd given us, and that checklist was from
the Big Daddy of all checklist writers, the U.S. Air Force. Positive
Mental Attitude.

"It must be important," I told Jonas.

"Yeah, but what is it?" he asked.

"Think good thoughts and you'll be saved?"

"I'd rather have a chain saw and a cheeseburger," Jonas said. "A
170 cell phone and a GPS would be nice, too."

demeanor
(dĭ-mē′nər) *n.*
attitude or perceived
behavior.

Deep Survival **329**

Main Idea	Key Details
Lines 133–144: Kerns was gentle and relaxed in the woods.	*He spoke softly, often paused to think, encouraged Gonzales to take it easy.*
Lines 145–156: Kerns was calm, like Gonzales's father.	*They both walked and talked softly, did not make sudden moves, understood the need to be careful.*

LEVEL UP TUTORIALS For additional support, assign the
following *Level Up* tutorial: **Summarizing.**

CLOSE READ

Determine Figurative Meanings (LINES 157–160)   RI 4

Explain that figurative language is the use of language in nonliteral ways to help readers understand unfamiliar situations or ideas. Point out that Gonzales uses a **simile,** a figure of speech that compares two things using the word *like* or *as*, in lines 157–160.

Ⓗ ASK STUDENTS to interpret the simile and explain why Gonzales might have used it in this passage. *(He wants to make Kerns's "deep sense of respect and humility" more concrete for readers and to emphasize that surviving in nature requires people to understand that it can be "dangerous and unpredictable.")*

Determine Central Idea and Summarize the Text (LINES 161–170)   RI 1, RI 2

Explain that authors can use other clues besides topic sentences to signal when they are introducing an important idea.

Ⓘ CITE TEXT EVIDENCE Ask students to identify a main idea introduced in lines 161–170 and explain what clues they used to identify it. *(Positive Mental Attitude is the most important tool for survival. Gonzales repeats the phrase twice and uses capital letters to treat it like a proper noun. He also says it's "number one" on the checklist from the "Big Daddy of all checklist writers, the U.S. Air Force.")* Discuss the possible purpose of including the dialogue in lines 166–170. *(Gonzales uses the dialogue to show in an engaging way how he and Jonas reacted to the concept. Jonas's preference for "a chain saw and a cheeseburger" and "A cell phone and a GPS" also reveals that it may be hard to believe that something intangible like a positive attitude could be the most important survival tool.)*

CRITICAL VOCABULARY

demeanor: Gonzales thinks his father and Byron Kerns share certain attitudes and behavioral traits. **ASK STUDENTS** to explain what kind of demeanor Kerns exhibits. *(His behavior is calm and careful, and he moves deliberately in the woods.)*

Analyze Ideas and Events
(LINES 171–197)

RI 3, RI 5

Explain that once an author has introduced a central idea, he may use a variety of techniques to develop it so that readers get a fuller understanding of it.

J **ASK STUDENTS** to reread lines 171–197 and explain how Gonzales develops the idea he introduced in lines 161–165. *(He first describes how Kerns has a hard time explaining what Positive Mental Attitude is; Kerns can only say it's something inside you, not something physical you carry. Then Gonzales describes how Kerns acquired the trait, using an anecdote about an early training mission with a group of pilots in the mountains in winter. Gonzales adds to the anecdote by explaining the consequences of giving into apathy so that readers can fully grasp the seriousness of the situation. In this way he reinforces the importance of Positive Mental Attitude.)*

Determine Figurative Meanings (LINES 208–217)

RI 1, RI 4

Encourage students to continue to notice and analyze examples of similes as they read.

K **CITE TEXT EVIDENCE** Ask students to identify a simile in lines 208–217 and explain its meaning and purpose in the text. *(He says someone who's expended a tremendous amount of energy in a survival situation is "like a woman who's just given birth to a baby" [lines 210–211]. Since readers are likely to have some familiarity with the process of childbirth, Gonzales is helping them understand the kind of fatigue that people in survival situations face. He also makes it clear that in both situations it is important to take care of oneself in order to recover and avoid a psychological collapse on top of physical depletion.)*

As we slogged through the woods, practicing firecraft, shelter making, knots, and navigation . . . I kept asking Kerns, but he couldn't explain it. Nobody could. It meant the difference between life and death; he could tell me that. He had an adult portion of it; he assured me of that. "It's not what's in your pack," he'd say. "It's what's in here." He'd tap his chest. No wonder Tom Wolfe had called it *The Right Stuff*.[8] You couldn't exactly title a book *Positive Mental Attitude*, now, could you?

Kerns didn't always have it, though. He'd had to acquire it.
180 Early on in his Air Force days, he took a group of pilots into the mountains near Spokane for survival training maneuvers. "I was a greenhorn and just misjudged our situation," he told us. Back then, he was pretending to be the macho drill instructor I'd expected: Go, go, go, push, push, push. He was not yet cool. He was acting cool.

His class had been crossing a vast field of slushy snow, which made the going rough. The pilots began to suffer from fatigue, but Kerns kept driving them. "I now realize that was a mistake," he said. As the temperature dropped, darkness came down like a curtain. "Suddenly everybody wanted to give up. They just sat
190 down and lost all their will." Apathy is a typical reaction to any sort of disaster, and if you're exhausted in a field of snow at sundown in the mountains, you're pretty much about to witness the simple disaster of nature separating you permanently from everything you know and love in this world. That apathy can rapidly lead to complete psychological deterioration. Then you sit down and hypothermia[9] sets in, which produces more apathy, a more profound psychological deterioration, and ultimately, death.

Fatigue almost always comes as a surprise. It is as much a psychological condition as a physical one, and scientists have
200 struggled without success to understand it. It's like the difficulty of studying sand in order to understand the Sand Pile Effect. There's nothing in the muscles or nerves or even the biochemistry of the body that would seem to predict or explain fatigue. Once fatigue sets in, though, it is almost impossible to recover from it under survival conditions. It is not just a matter of being tired. It's more like a spiritual collapse, and recovery requires more than food and rest.

Following the explosive burst of activity that is sometimes required for survival, or in the panic stage when you're running
210 or climbing or swimming, you're like a woman who's just given birth to a baby. You're depleted and wide open to fatigue. It may take weeks to recover; and if you're not taking care of yourself, that

---

[8] **Tom Wolfe . . . The Right Stuff:** the title of Wolfe's 1979 book about the Mercury space program refers to the personal qualities required in astronauts.

[9] **hypothermia:** abnormally low body temperature.

APPLYING ACADEMIC VOCABULARY

dimension	external

As you discuss the selection, incorporate the Collection 5 academic vocabulary words: *dimension* and *external*. Discuss with students how Kerns misjudged the **dimension** of the situation when he took the Air Force pilots into the mountains for survival training in the snow. Then invite students to explain how both internal and **external** factors are important in survival.

fatigue can lead to an inability to sleep, which in turn can result in a sudden psychological collapse. The physical and psychological factors rapidly erode each other, which is why it is so important to pace yourself, rest frequently, and stay hydrated. That's why Kerns's pushing the pilots so hard had been a mistake.

220 A survival situation is a ticking clock: You have only so much stored energy (and water), and every time you exert yourself, you're using it up. The trick is to become extremely stingy with your scarce resources, balancing risk and reward, investing only in efforts that offer the biggest return.

In survival situations, people greatly underestimate the need for rest. While Kerns, Jonas, and I were doing map and compass exercises, he would frequently stop and look around at the woods, chatting with us. I'd be thinking: *Let's go, let's go, I know the way.* And he'd just stand there. Now I understand why. You should operate at about 60 percent of your normal level of activity, he explained, and rest and rehydrate frequently. If the weather is cool 230 and you're sweating, you're working too hard. . . .

When Kerns at last realized how serious his situation was with his fatigued Air Force pilots, he recounted, "I fell to my knees and I prayed. Faith is a very important thing in your will to survive."

As Peter Leschak put it, "Whether a deity is actually listening or not, there is value in formally announcing your needs, desires, worries, sins, and goals in a focused, prayerful attitude. Only when you are aware can you take action." Survival psychologists have observed the same thing.

Kerns added, "All at once, it hit me that I might actually lose 240 them. Those million-dollar pilots could die."

By chance, he found a fence and used the cedar post to start a fire. (Chance is nothing more than opportunity, and it is all around at every turn; the trick lies in recognizing it.) "It's amazing to see what fire can do. You're out in the woods, you're cold, you're lost, you're lonely. But the minute you light that fire, you're home, the lights are on, and supper's cooking. It made a world of difference going from complete darkness to light and warmth. It just turned everybody around."

Kerns learned many lessons that night. His mastery and 250 confidence turned the pilots around even more than the fire. It showed them the way, and it made Kerns more able to save himself. That lesson was driven home again and again: Helping someone else is the best way to ensure your own survival. It takes you out of yourself. It helps you to rise above your fears. Now you're a rescuer, not a victim. And seeing how your leadership and skill buoy others up gives you more focus and energy to persevere. The cycle reinforces itself: You buoy them up, and their response buoys you

Deep Survival **331**

ENGLISH LANGUAGE SUPPORT

Vocabulary: Phrasal Verbs Explain that a **phrasal verb** is a verb and another word (a preposition or an adverb) that together make up a verb. Point out the sentence "Suddenly everybody wanted to give up" (line 189). Explain that *give* and *up* have multiple meanings and that *up* can represent several parts of speech. Together the words form a phrasal verb that can have many meanings. In this case, it means "to stop doing what one is doing."

ASK STUDENTS to use context clues to define these phrasal verbs in the selection: *wound up/wind up* (lines 43, 92), *set up* (line 48), *set off* (line 49), *turned up* (line 57), *gets out* (line 68), *took off* (line 114), *head off* (line 124), *sets in* (line 196), *got up* (line 270), *shot down* (line 319), and *go on* (line 343).

Determine Figurative Meanings (LINES 218–222) RI 4

Tell students that another type of figurative language is a **metaphor,** which compares two things without the use of *like* or *as.*

L ASK STUDENTS to interpret the metaphor Gonzales uses in lines 218–222 and explain how it develops his central idea. *(He compares a survival situation to "a ticking clock" to make the point that resources are limited and that it is important to use them in the way that will bring the greatest benefit. This reinforces the importance of having a plan and the mental strength to use resources wisely.)*

Determine Central Idea and Summarize the Text (LINES 231–248) RI 2

Explain that an **objective summary** of a text is always shorter than the original text and that it requires readers to restate the most important ideas in their own words. To be objective, the summary must reflect only the author's ideas.

M ASK STUDENTS to reread lines 231–248 and write a two- or three-sentence objective summary of the passage. *(When Kerns realized that the Air Force pilots might die, he prayed for help and then built a fire from a fence post. Heat and light provided the physical and psychological support the pilots needed to survive.)* Then call on volunteers to share their summaries with the class and discuss how they are similar and different. Clarify the need to include only central ideas and crucial details.

Analyze Ideas and Events
RI 3, RI 5

(LINES 262–271)

Remind students that Gonzales combines anecdotes with general principles to develop his central idea.

 ASK STUDENTS to reread lines 262–271 and explain what general principle is illustrated by the anecdote. *(Ronald DiFrancesco's story illustrates the general principle that thinking of other people is a strong motivator for survival.)* How does this anecdote also illustrate the pull quote at the top of the page, "Plan the flight and fly the plan. But don't fall in love with the plan"? *(DiFrancesco had a plan, to go up the stairs to find air, but he changed his plan when he saw that it was not working out for others. He decided to go down the stairs, and as a result, he survived.)*

"Plan the flight and fly the plan. But don't fall in love with the plan."

up. Many people who survive alone report that they were doing it for someone else (a wife, boyfriend, mother, son) back home. When

260   Antoine de Saint-Exupéry was lost in the Lybian Desert, it was the thought of his wife's suffering that kept him going. . . .

In the 84th-floor offices of the World Trade Center's south tower, and an hour before the collapse, Ronald DiFrancesco was one of the people who met Brian Clark, the fire warden with the flashlight who was asking people: "Up or down?" DiFrancesco went up, hoping to find air. But after ten or so floors, he encountered people who were succumbing to fatigue and smoke. The people, all of whom would die, were just giving up and falling asleep. DiFrancesco, too, was collapsing, but then he said to himself, "I've

270   got to see my wife and kids again." And with that, he got up and bolted down the stairs to safety.

Doctors and nurses often survive better than others because they have someone to help. They have a well-defined purpose. Purpose is a big part of survival, but it must be accompanied by work. Grace without good works is not salvation. The survivor plans by setting small, manageable goals and then systematically achieving them. Hence the Air Force checklist and the notion, which my father drilled into me: Plan the flight and fly the plan. But don't fall in love with the plan. Be open to a changing world

280   and let go of the plan when necessary so that you can make a new

WHEN STUDENTS STRUGGLE . . .

Tell students that when they have a question about a particular sentence, their query may be clarified as they continue reading. If not, suggest they reread earlier paragraphs and consider how the difficult sentence relates to main ideas.

ASK STUDENTS to reread lines 272–282 and identify two main ideas. *(Purpose and work are both needed for survival. Make a survival plan but be open to changing it as needed.)* Discuss how these two ideas are related. *(Having a purpose is similar to having a plan. Work means following the plan and adjusting it.)* Then call on volunteers to explain how the sentence "Grace without good works is not salvation" relates to these ideas. *(Students may not be familiar with the religious allusion but should understand that Gonzales is restating the idea that purpose and work are both necessary to survival.)*

plan. Then, as the world and the plan both go through their book of changes, you will always be ready to do the next right thing.

People are animals with animal instincts, but they lack many of the other survival mechanisms animals possess, such as fur to keep them warm, fangs and claws, and flight or speed. Culture creates a collective survival mechanism for the species. People survive better in numbers. They survive because they use cognition to organize, say, for a hunt, and to make things, even as cognition inhibits their animalness, including strength. That's why, when

290 cognition is turned off, people are amazed by their own strength: because cognition continuously inhibits it. That is the whole secret to cognition: It is a mechanism for modulating emotional (physical) responses.

Every culture evolves survival rituals. Some, especially nontechnical ones, are devoted to not much more than survival. In Native American cultures, one ritual is the vision quest, in which a young person goes into the wild and fasts in search of a vision. It can be seen as a type of survival training, for if there is no food, no water, no way, a person has already practiced sitting still and

300 making the best of the situation. He'll have confidence in his ability to survive it.

The survival lessons that apply today are ancient. The *Tao Te Ching* is broken into two parts, "Integrity," and "The Way," which can be thought of as the two halves of surviving anything. Lao-tzu's[10] book is a handbook for a ruler, but it is also a handbook for the brain. An imbalance of the brain's functions leads us into trouble, and a triumph of balance gets us out. I've found similar lessons in Epictetus, Herodotus, Thucydides, the Bible, the Bhagavad Gītā.[11] "Is there any thing whereof it may be said, See,

310 this is new?" says Ecclesiastes. But there are always new people who haven't heard that there's nothing new under the sun. And there's always someone who doesn't get the word.

I had always wondered where our American survival rituals were. I think now that they're everywhere around us. The Boy Scouts in its original conception was a survival school. Sports are survival training in that they teach strength, agility, strategy, and the endurance of pain. But our culture is filled with survival stories as well. Cool is the ultimate American conception of the survival model. James Stockdale, a fighter pilot who was shot down over

320 Vietnam in 1965, spoke many times about how he survived seven

---

[10] *Tao Te Ching* . . . **Lao-tzu's (dao dé jīng . . . lou´dzŭ´):** a classic sixth-century B.C. Chinese text describing the way of seeing and behaving that forms the basis of the Taoist religion.

[11] **Epictetus, Herodotus, Thucydides, the Bible, the Bhagavad Gītā:** an ancient Greek philosopher, two ancient Greek historians, the Christian book of scripture, and a section of the Mahabharata, or Hindu scripture.

CLOSE READ

Analyze Ideas and Events (LINES 283–293)

RI 1, RI 3, RI 5

Explain that authors may develop ideas through comparison and contrast.

O CITE TEXT EVIDENCE Ask students to reread lines 283–293 and identify the two things that are contrasted. What does this contrast suggest about survival situations? (*Gonzales contrasts the survival mechanisms of humans and other animals. Cognition is the key to collective human survival even as it "inhibits their animalness" [line 289]. He points out that humans are stronger when their cognition is turned off. This contrast suggests that when humans face an extreme survival situation, they may need to turn off the cognitive habits that normally help them survive in human society.*)

Determine Central Idea and Summarize the Text (LINES 302–312)

RI 2

Encourage students to continue to look for topic sentences and to make inferences about the main ideas of individual paragraphs.

P ASK STUDENTS to reread lines 302–312 and state the central idea of the paragraph in their own words. (*Basic survival lessons have been known for centuries.*) Discuss Gonzales's purpose in referring to so many ancient texts. (*He cites the texts as authorities and explains that they all present some version of the idea that balance between purpose and work is essential to survival.*)

Determine a Central Idea and Summarize the Text

RI 1, RI 2

(LINES 339–349)

Explain that making inferences requires drawing on previous knowledge, which includes information that the author has presented earlier in the selection, not just the information presented in a particular paragraph.

Q **CITE TEXT EVIDENCE** Ask students to reread lines 339–349 and make inferences about why survivors describe their experience as "beautiful." *(Survivors likely use the term "beautiful" because the experience was one of heightened sensation and because it revealed their own inner strengths.)* Invite students to share earlier evidence that supports their inferences. *(Students may cite anecdotes involving Juliane [lines 9–13], the survivor of the Bataan Death March [lines 15–18], the survivor from the World Trade Center disaster who walked downstairs to survive [lines 262–271], and the pilot shot down in Vietnam [lines 319–334].)*

Analyze Ideas and Events

RI 3, RI 5

(LINES 350–358)

Remind students that Gonzales used the phrase "mystery of survival" in line 67.

R **ASK STUDENTS** to reread lines 350–358 and connect that earlier phrase to this passage. *(Gonzales says that it's a mystery why some people survive when others who seemed better equipped do not. He now thinks that it's the "mysterious quality" called Positive Mental Attitude that accounts for the difference. It sounds rather dull and abstract, but it's a personal quality that combines having a purpose or plan with the mental and emotional strength to carry it out.)*

COLLABORATIVE DISCUSSION Have students pair up to discuss the meaning of the title and how well it relates to the selection. Then have them share their conclusions with the class as a whole. Accept all reasonable responses.

ASK STUDENTS to share any questions they generated in the course of reading and discussing the selection.

---

and a half years in prison camp. "One should include a course of familiarization with pain," he said.

Stockdale observed, "You have to practice hurting. There is no question about it. . . . You have to practice being hazed. You have to learn to take a bunch of junk and accept it with a sense of humor."

He's talking about being cool, just as he was when his F-8 fighter-bomber was hit with 57-millimeter fire. He had been on a relaxed bomb run at the time. He'd even taken off his uncomfortable oxygen mask. "I could barely keep that plane from 330 flying into the ground while I got that damned oxygen mask to my mouth so I could tell my wingman that I was about to eject. What rotten luck. And on a milk run! My mind was clear, and I said to myself, 'five years.' I knew we were making a mess of the war in Southeast Asia, but I didn't think it would last longer than that." The Spartan practice of enduring the bite of the fox is "a course of familiarization with pain." Then there are the schools like Kerns's, which attempt to teach wilderness survival by directly meeting the problem head-on with Yankee ingenuity.

Q
340 Like being lost, survival is a transformation; being a leader can ensure that, when you reach the final stage of that metamorphosis, it is with an attitude of commitment, not resignation. The transformation of survival is permanent. People who have had the experience often go on to become the best search and rescue professionals. They have come to understand, perhaps unconsciously, that they can only live fully by helping others through that same transformation. All the survivors I've talked to have told me how horrible the experience was. But they have also told me, often with deep puzzlement, how beautiful it was. They wouldn't trade the experience for anything in the world.

R
350 It gradually dawned on me that only by researching and dissecting the mysterious quality the Air Force so dully called Positive Mental Attitude would I ever understand survival.

And I thought: Wait a minute. My father was in the Army Air Corps. Maybe that's what he had that allowed him to live.[12] If so, he'd certainly never talked about it. But what pilot would? I felt as if I'd stepped to the edge of the very thing I'd been after all my life. Here, concealed in the most unimaginative phrase possible, was the deep mystery I'd been trying to unravel.

COLLABORATIVE DISCUSSION With a partner, discuss whether the title *Deep Survival* is a good fit for the selection. Cite specific evidence from the text to support your answer.

---

[12]**My father . . . allowed him to live:** During World War II, the author's father fell from a plane without a parachute and miraculously survived.

ENGLISH LANGUAGE SUPPORT

Vocabulary: Idioms Explain that an **idiom** is a common expression that is often hard to figure out from the literal meanings of the words. An example is "take a bunch of junk" (line 325). The context clue is in the paragraph: "being hazed" is a synonym, and *accept* means the same as *take*. Help students understand that the pilot being held prisoner had to undergo some painful situations without showing he was upset.

ASK STUDENTS to work in pairs and use context clues to determine the meanings of these additional idioms:

- *being cool* (line 326)
- *it dawned on me* (line 350)
- *on a milk run* (line 332)
- *stepped to the edge* (line 356)

Determine Central Idea and Summarize the Text

RI 1, RI 2

When you **summarize** a text, you give a brief, objective account of the central idea the author presents in the work. The **central idea** is the main point that the author wants you to understand. To keep your summary **objective,** include only the author's ideas; do not include your responses or ideas about the text. Follow these steps to determine the central idea of the excerpt from *Deep Survival* and create an objective summary of the text:

1. Read the complete text without taking any notes.

2. Reread the text, focusing on the main ideas and the most important details. This time take notes, listing key words, main ideas with their supporting details, and quotations that make strong points.

3. Make an inference, or logical assumption, about the central idea of the text. Ask yourself: What do most of the ideas and details have in common? What does Gonzales want his readers to know?

4. In your own words, write a brief, objective summary of the text, focusing on the author's central idea only and omitting the supporting details.

Analyze Ideas and Events

RI 3, RI 5

Laurence Gonzales introduces and develops his ideas on the topic of survival through the use of **anecdotes,** or brief stories. He alternates the anecdotes with his own ideas and observations, as well as with information from experts. As you analyze the text, consider how the author utilizes particular sentences and paragraphs to communicate his ideas and how they build on one another. Consider this example:

Portion of Text	Type	Questions for Analysis
Lines 1–59	Anecdote (Juliane Koepcke's plane crash)	In lines 15–18, the author steps outside of the anecdote to present information from another survivor. How does this information clarify the point the author is making in the anecdote about Juliane?

Deep Survival **335**

TEACH

CLOSE READ

Determine Central Idea and Summarize the Text

RI 1, RI 2

Point out that text features such as the boldface terms and numbered list can help students grasp the main points about this skill.

- Call on volunteers to restate each definition of a boldface term in their own words. Clarify understanding as needed.

- Ask students to read the four steps to determine a central idea and summarize a text. Then call on volunteers to summarize the steps in one or two sentences.

- Discuss the difference between an objective summary and a critique or an evaluation. *(The latter would include a reader's responses to a text.)*

Analyze Ideas and Events

RI 3, RI 5

Review the three ways that Gonzales develops his ideas *(anecdotes, his own ideas and observations, information from experts)*. Invite volunteers to say what makes the ideas different from one another. Then have students reread lines 1–44 and identify examples of Gonzales's inserting his own ideas and observations into an anecdote. *(lines 10–14, 15, 27–29, 38–40)*

Strategies for Annotation 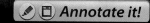 Annotate it!

Analyze Ideas and Events

RI 3, RI 5

Have students reread the selection to notice how Gonzales develops his ideas. Encourage them to use their eBook annotation tools to do the following:

- Highlight in yellow each detail from an anecdote.
- Highlight in green each of Gonzales's ideas or observations.
- Highlight in pink each example of information from an expert.
- Review your annotations and notice how the different techniques work together to develop ideas.

Eventually, she came to a hut along the banks of the river she'd been following. She staggered and collapsed inside. There is always a lot of chance involved in a survival situation, both good luck and bad. It was Juliane's good fortune that three hunters turned up the next day and delivered her to a local doctor. But, as Louis Pasteur said, "Luck favors the prepared mind."

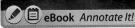

PRACTICE & APPLY

Analyzing the Text

RI 1, RI 2, RI 3, RI 4, RI 5, RI 6

Possible answers:

1. *He focuses on the fact that Juliane didn't panic; instead she was "taking it all in, touching her new reality." Gonzales signals his interest in this detail by using the phrase "Amazing cool."*

2. *The author compares Juliane's course of action to that of her fellow crash survivors. She acted to save herself; they "followed the rules" and waited for rescue—and died as a result. The comparison illustrates the point that following the rules is not always the key to survival.*

3. *The author connects the decision to follow rules—which, in the case of the World Trade Center, led to death— with following one's instincts, illustrated by Juliane's determination to save herself.*

4. *The author cites evidence of people failing to help themselves even though they had the means to do so. Examples include the following: The other people who survived Juliane's plane crash decided to await rescue although it was possible (as Juliane's experience proves) to find help (lines 60–62). The survivors of the Andes crash who stayed on the mountain would have died had others not gone down the mountain in search of help (lines 40–44). The author quotes John Leach, who wrote that victims have been recovered from life rafts on which the survival box has not even been opened (lines 100–102).*

5. *The anecdote shows that Positive Mental Attitude can be acquired, or learned; it also shows that faith is an important element in a person's will to survive.*

6. *Cultural survival rituals and the author's use of the word cool to describe the American survival model are simply different ways of describing Positive Mental Attitude. All involve having confidence in one's ability to survive and therefore stay calm.*

7. *Gonzales concludes, based on anecdotal evidence and information from experts, that Positive Mental Attitude— a quality of calm confidence—is the most important factor in determining a person's ability to survive.*

---

eBook *Annotate It!*

Analyzing the Text

RI 1, RI 2, RI 3, RI 4, RI 5, RI 6, W 1

Cite Text Evidence   Support your responses with evidence from the selection.

1. **Cite Evidence** In lines 1–14, what detail does Gonzales focus on when he describes Juliane's fall from the airplane? How can you tell that he finds this detail interesting?

2. **Analyze** What comparison does Gonzales make in lines 60–76? How does this comparison support one of his main points?

3. **Connect** Reread lines 67–89. What connection does Gonzales make between the experience of passengers in the plane and the anecdote about the World Trade Center disaster?

4. **Cite Evidence** What evidence does Gonzales cite to prove the point that survival is not always a matter of luck or preparation?

5. **Interpret** Gonzales relates an anecdote about pilots who undergo survival training and get stranded in the snow (lines 179–190, 231–261). What important truths about survival are revealed by the anecdote?

6. **Connect** Gonzales provides information on survival rituals in different cultures (lines 294–312). How does this relate to Kerns's ideas about Positive Mental Attitude? How does it relate to Gonzales's statement that "Cool is the ultimate American conception of the survival model"?

7. **Draw Conclusions** What does Gonzales's analysis of survival lead him to conclude about why some people seem to have an amazing ability to survive life-threatening situations against all odds, while others seem to just give up? In other words, what is his central idea?

PERFORMANCE TASK

Writing Activity: Argument What quotation from the text best supports Laurence Gonzales's central idea—his most important message about survival? Write an argument explaining why you agree or disagree with Gonzales's ideas about survival.

1. Sum up what the author wants you to know about survival. Then, write a claim stating your position about what it takes to survive a life-threatening event.

2. Make notes about reasons that support your claim. Then, collect evidence that supports your reasons. Consider an opposing claim and list valid counterarguments.

3. Write a draft of your argument. Be sure to present your reasons and evidence in a logical order.

4. Revise your draft to eliminate unrelated or illogical evidence. Finally, check your work to make sure you have used the conventions of standard English.

Assign this performance task.

PERFORMANCE TASK

W 1

Writing Activity: Argument Help students with these suggestions:

- Review the terms *claim, reasons, evidence,* and *counterarguments.*
- Have students identify a quotation and complete steps 1–2 on their own. Then have them present their ideas to a partner and solicit feedback on the strengths and weaknesses of their argument. Have students incorporate the feedback into their work, revising and editing as needed.

Critical Vocabulary

disintegration   deduce   conversely   distill   demeanor

Practice and Apply Complete the sentences to demonstrate your comprehension of each Critical Vocabulary word.

1. The **disintegration** of an airplane in flight would cause . . .

2. Juliane **deduced** that rescue planes would not find her because . . .

3. Some people who have no survival equipment can survive life-threatening situations through wits alone; **conversely**, some people who have survival equipment . . .

4. In survival school, people learn how to **distill** water from air so that . . .

5. A calm **demeanor** is an important asset in a military pilot because . . .

Vocabulary Strategy: Context Clues

If you are uncertain of the meaning of a word, you can often figure out its meaning by using **context clues,** or information in the surrounding sentences or paragraphs. For example, the Critical Vocabulary word *disintegration* (line 19) is used in the description of a plane crash. The context includes the phrases "extensive structural failure" and "broken airplane." These clues tell you that *disintegration* means "breaking up into pieces."

Practice and Apply Find each of these words in the selection: *canopy* (line 27), *apathy* (line 190), *buoy* (line 255), *bolted* (line 271), *metamorphosis* (line 340). With a partner, discuss the context clues that can help you figure out each word's meaning. Follow these steps:

1. Determine the word's function in the sentence. For example, is it a noun that names a person, place, or thing, or is it a verb that describes an action?

2. Read the sentence in which the word appears. Does the overall meaning of the sentence allow you to guess the word's meaning?

3. If the sentence does not provide enough information, read the paragraph in which the word appears. If necessary, reread the previous paragraph and the one that follows to look for clues.

4. If you still do not have enough clues, think about the larger context of the selection. How does the word fit with what you know about the subject?

PRACTICE & APPLY

Critical Vocabulary   L 4a

Possible answers:

1. *. . .its falling parts to scatter over a wide area.*

2. *. . .rescuers would not be able to see her through the dense cover of jungle trees.*

3. *. . .perish because they lack the wits to use it.*

4. *. . .they can drink the condensed liquid and not die of thirst.*

5. *. . .the instruments in a combat aircraft cockpit are very sensitive, so sudden, uncontrolled actions could lead to a crash.*

Vocabulary Strategy: Context Clues

Possible answers:

Students' success in determining meaning from context will vary with their vocabulary and prior knowledge. Word functions are as follows: canopy: *noun;* apathy: *noun;* buoy: *verb;* bolted: *verb;* metamorphosis: *noun.*

Strategies for Annotation   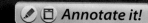 Annotate it!

Context Clues   L 4a

Have students locate the sentences containing the words *canopy, apathy, buoy, bolted,* and *metamorphosis* in the selection. Encourage them to use their eBook annotation tools to do the following:

- Highlight each assigned word.

- Reread the surrounding sentences, looking for clues to the word's meaning. Underline any clues you find, such as examples, synonyms, or antonyms.

- Review your annotations and try to infer the word's meaning.

under her seat. The next day, she **deduced** that even the helicopters and airplanes she could hear wouldn't be able to see her through the jungle canopy. She'd have to get herself out.

Language and Style: Colons and Semicolons

L 2a–b

Call on volunteers to read aloud each example in the charts showing the uses of colons and semicolons. Discuss how the pauses and connections signaled by each punctuation mark help readers understand the author's ideas.

Possible answers:

Answers will vary. Using the conventions of standard English grammar and punctuation, students should combine ideas and sentences from their original arguments with colons and semicolons in ways that add clarity.

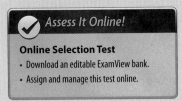

Assess It Online!

Online Selection Test
- Download an editable ExamView bank.
- Assign and manage this test online.

L 2a–b

Language and Style: Colons and Semicolons

When used correctly, punctuation helps clarify meaning for readers by linking ideas and by showing places to pause. In the excerpt from *Deep Survival*, Laurence Gonzales uses both **colons** and **semicolons** to add clarity and interest to the text.

A colon is used to introduce a sentence, a quotation, or a list. A complete sentence that follows a colon usually begins with a capital letter.

Uses of Colons	
Purpose	**Example**
illustrate or provide an example of what was just stated	It was another important moment: She didn't spend time bemoaning her fate. (lines 27–28)
introduce a quotation	Before he died, he spoke to his father on the phone: "Why did I listen to them—I shouldn't have." (lines 83–85)
introduce a list	The Survival School provides training in the following skills: using maps and compasses, building and tending a fire, and signaling.

A semicolon is used to connect closely related ideas. It is stronger than a comma but less abrupt than a period. It indicates that the statement that follows will add explanation.

Uses of Semicolons	
Purpose	**Example**
separate independent clauses and add explanation	She wasn't screaming; she wasn't in a panic. (lines 11–12)
precede a conjunctive adverb that joins two clauses	Juliane had no survival training; nevertheless, she managed to survive a dangerous jungle journey without external help.
separate parallel phrases that contain commas	A survival box should contain flares, for signaling rescuers; rations, for keeping up strength; and a first-aid kit, for medical emergencies.

Practice and Apply Look back at the argument you wrote for this selection's Performance Task. Revise your argument to include at least one colon and one semicolon. Then discuss with a partner how each punctuation mark you added improved or clarified your meaning.

WHEN STUDENTS STRUGGLE...

To provide students with extra instruction and practice in the correct use of semicolons and colons, use these **GrammarNotes** lessons:

GRAMMAR NOTES PRESENTATIONS
Lesson 20: Using Semicolons; Lesson 21: Using Colons

INTERACTIVE WHITEBOARD LESSON
Cite Textual Evidence

RI 1

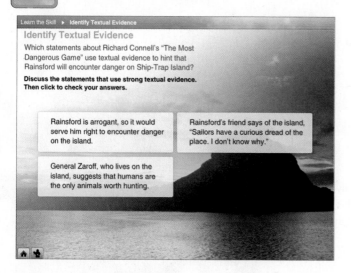

Learn the Skill ▶ Identify Textual Evidence

Identify Textual Evidence

Which statements about Richard Connell's "The Most Dangerous Game" use textual evidence to hint that Rainsford will encounter danger on Ship-Trap Island?

Discuss the statements that use strong textual evidence. Then click to check your answers.

> Rainsford is arrogant, so it would serve him right to encounter danger on the island.

> Rainsford's friend says of the island, "Sailors have a curious dread of the place. I don't know why."

> General Zaroff, who lives on the island, suggests that humans are the only animals worth hunting.

TEACH

To help students prepare for writing the Performance Task argument, explain that strong evidence includes quotations, facts, and details rather than unsupported opinions. Then review the steps for citing textual evidence.

- **Step 1: Mark Up Details in the Text** Remind students that they will be looking for details that support their claim or position about what it takes to survive a life-threatening event.

- **Step 2: Identify Directly Stated Evidence** Explain that some evidence is directly stated by the author. Such evidence can be cited through direct quotations from the text; through **paraphrasing,** which means restating information in one's own words; or through **summarizing,** which is briefly retelling the main ideas in one's own words.

- **Step 3: Make Logical Inferences** Explain that sometimes students will need to make logical guesses about the text based on details in the text and their own prior knowledge. All inferences must be supported by the details in the text.

COLLABORATIVE DISCUSSION

Have students work in pairs to apply the sentence starters in Screen 9 to analyze the selection. Encourage them to use these models when citing textual evidence in writing their Performance Task argument.

Summarize a Text

RI 2

RETEACH

Remind students that a **summary** is a brief retelling of the main ideas of a piece of writing in one's own words. Present these two summaries of a familiar tale.

- A young girl is going to visit her grandmother in the woods. A mean wolf gets to the grandmother's house first and swallows the grandmother. The wolf tries to eat the girl, too, but she is rescued by a hunter, who then cuts the wolf open and releases the grandmother unharmed.

- A girl wearing a red cloak is walking through the woods carrying a basket of food for her grandmother when she meets a wolf. The wolf suggests she stop to pick flowers for the grandmother. Later the girl is puzzled by her grandmother's deep voice and sharp teeth.

ASK STUDENTS which summary is better. Why? *(The first description is a better summary because it recounts the most important ideas from the story. The second focuses on minor details.)*

 LEVEL UP TUTORIALS Assign the following *Level Up* tutorial: **Summarizing**

Summarizing

What Is a Summary?

When you tell people about a movie you just saw or a book you've just read, you are probably giving them a **summary**.

When you summarize a text, you briefly retell the main ideas or key events using your own words.

Let me tell you about this great movie I saw!

INDEPENDENT READING

Students can apply the skill to a magazine or newspaper article or a textbook passage. Have them work independently to determine the central idea and most important supporting details in the piece. Ask: What is the main point that the author wants you to understand? What details help you know this is the main point?

The Leap

Short Story by Louise Erdrich

Why This Text?

To get the most from what they read in fiction, students must analyze an author's choices and make valid inferences about the work's theme. This lesson explores the impact of Erdrich's use of flashback and tension, as well as the story's theme, or underlying message.

Key Learning Objective: The student will be able to analyze the effects of an author's choices and make inferences about theme.

RL 1 Cite textual evidence.

RL 2 Determine a theme and analyze its development over the course of the text.

RL 3 Analyze how complex characters develop over the course of the text and advance the theme.

RL 4 Determine the meaning of words and phrases as they are used in the text.

RL 5 Analyze an author's choices concerning how to structure a text.

SL 1a Come to discussions prepared.

L 1b Identify and use word changes that indicate different meanings or parts of speech.

L 4c Consult reference materials to find the pronunciation of a word.

Text Complexity Rubric

	The Leap
Quantitative Measures	**The Leap** Lexile: 1260L

	Levels of Meaning/Purpose
Qualitative Measures	 multiple levels of meaning (multiple themes)
	Structure several shifts in chronology; use of flashback and flash-forward
	Language Conventionality and Clarity  some figurative language
	Knowledge Demands moderately complex theme

| **Reader/Task Considerations** | • Teacher determined
 • Vary by individual reader and type of text
 • See the Text X-Ray for suggested Reader/Task Considerations. |

English Language Support Before teaching, use the Text X-Ray below for an overview of the text's complexity. The Text X-Ray and the supports and scaffolds in the Teacher's Edition will help you guide students of different and skill levels.

Meaning Making

Language Development

Effective Expression

Content Knowledge

Foundational Skills

Text Complexity: Qualitative Measures

Levels of Meaning/Purpose

multiple levels of meaning (multiple themes)

Help students support inferences about theme.

- Teacher's Edition side notes, pp. 339, 340, 341, 343, 344, 345, 347
- Strategies for Annotation, p. 347
- Support Inferences About Theme, p. 347

Guide students in comprehending the text through visualizing.

- When Students Struggle, p. 340

Help students comprehend the text by having them read difficult passages aloud.

- English Language Support, p. 344

Prompt students to discuss inferences about the narrator.

- Teacher's Edition side note, p. 346

To reteach supporting inferences about theme, see

- Support Inferences About Theme, p. 350a

 Use It! Level Up Tutorial: Theme

***ZOOM IN ON* INFERRING THEME** Before students read, have them look out for references to leaps that the characters make in this story. After they read, have students discuss both literal and figurative leaps. List them on the board. *(The narrator moves back home after her "failed life"; the narrator mentally leaps back in time to recall how she owes her life to her mother; the mother leaps toward the wire to save her life; the mother learns to read and write; the mother remarries and settles in a small town; the mother tears off her dress to leap onto the roof; mother and daughter leap from the burning house.)* Then have small groups discuss **themes** or messages suggested by the story. Prompt them with this question: Why do people make leaps in life, and what do these leaps reveal about them? *(Possible theme: When people make sudden, life-changing decisions, they often reveal what they value most, such as life or love.)*

Structure

several shifts in chronology; use of flashback and flash-forward

Help students analyze the use of flashback to create tension.

- Teacher's Edition side notes, pp. 340, 341, 342, 344, 346, 347
- English Language Support, p. 339
- When Students Struggle, p. 345
- Analyze Author's Choices: Flashback and Tension, p. 347

To teach students to analyze how authors develop characters, see

- Analyze Character, p. 350a

 Use It! **Interactive Whiteboard Lesson:** Character Development

***ZOOM IN ON* ANALYZING FLASHBACK** Explain that a **flashback** describes events that happened before a story's main action. Read aloud lines 1–9. Guide students to recognize the story's present time through the use of present-tense verbs. Then draw students' attention to lines 22–23: "I owe her my existence three times. The first was when she saved herself." Ask students what they can predict from these sentences about the flashbacks in this story. *(There will be three flashbacks. The words* first, second, *and* third *may be used to introduce them. They will be described in the past tense.)* Have students continue reading. Direct them to raise their hands when they discover each flashback *(line 38).*

Language Conventionality and Clarity

some figurative language

Teach unfamiliar vocabulary in context.
- Teacher's Edition Critical Vocabulary notes, pp. 339, 342, 343, 345, 346, 349
- Applying Academic Vocabulary, p. 341
- English Language Support, p. 342

Guide students to recognize sequence words.
- English Language Support, p. 339

Help students determine figurative meanings.
- Teacher's Edition side note, p. 342

Help students use prefixes to clarify the meanings of words.
- Vocabulary Strategy: Prefixes, p. 349

Teach students to use relative clauses.
- Language and Style: Relative Clauses, p. 350
- Strategies for Annotation, p. 350

***ZOOM IN ON* USING PREFIXES** Help students understand that recognizing **prefixes**, or word parts added to the beginnings of words, can help them define unfamiliar words. Review the meanings of *en-*, *ex-*, *con-*, and *com-* on page 349 and discuss what they contribute to the meanings of the Critical Vocabulary words. Point out that *col-* is another spelling of *con-/com-*. Then divide these words among pairs to locate and define: *commemorates* (line 24), *collide* (line 35), *concentrate* (line 76), *except* (line 107), *collapsed* (line 109), *confined* (line 112), *complicated* (line 136), *exchange* (line 151), *exhausted* (line 175), *containers* (line 177), *extension* (line 188). Have them look up the words to clarify meanings as needed.

Knowledge Demands

moderately complex theme

Support English Learners in understanding more about the author.
- Teacher's Edition Background note, p. 339

***ZOOM IN ON* BUILDING KNOWLEDGE** Tell students that a *gale* (line 32) is a strong wind. On the Beaufort Wind Scale, a breeze becomes a *near gale* when it reaches speeds of 28–33 knots, or 32–38 mph. This wind is strong enough to make trees sway. When the speed increases to 34–40 knots (39–46 mph), the wind is called a *gale*. Small branches are blown off trees, and people struggle to walk into the wind. At 41–47 knots (47–54 mph), the wind becomes a *strong gale*, powerful enough to blow tiles off roofs.

Suggested Reader/Task Considerations

You might consider the following before assigning this story to students.
- Do all the students have the necessary background knowledge about the kind of circus described in the text?
- Might students have difficulty visualizing the details of the Flying Avalons' trapeze act and how Anna saved herself when it went wrong?

***ZOOM IN ON* SUPPORTING COMPREHENSION**
- Discuss circus performances students have seen in person, on TV, or in movies. Review the circus descriptions in the text: dancing Arabian horses, contortionists, and trapeze acts.
- If students have trouble envisioning exactly what happened during the fatal trapeze performance, review lines 74–100 together. Have two volunteers pantomime what the narrator describes.

TEACH

CLOSE READ

Louise Erdrich Have students read the information about the author. Tell students that although Erdrich grew up in North Dakota, she attended Dartmouth College in New Hampshire, the state where this story is set. "The Leap" was first published in 1990.

AS YOU READ Direct students to use the As You Read note to focus their reading. Remind them to write down any questions they generate during reading.

Support Inferences About Theme (LINES 1–3)   RL 1, RL 2

Tell students that the **theme,** or underlying message, of a work of fiction can be communicated in many ways throughout the story. In this story, the title and the opening lines hint at one theme.

Ⓐ **ASK STUDENTS** to keep in mind the title as they reread lines 1–3. What can you infer about the story's theme from these lines? *(Since the narrator opens the story talking about her mother, readers can infer that one theme might have to do with her relationship with her mother. Based on the title and the fact that the mother was part of a blindfolded trapeze act, readers may also infer that the mother's experience as a trapeze performer may be important to the story's theme.)*

CRITICAL VOCABULARY

encroaching: The narrator describes how cataracts have gradually intruded up on her mother's sight.

ASK STUDENTS how the mother has adapted to her loss of sight due to encroaching cataracts. *(Although the cataracts have robbed her of sight, the mother appears to be able to navigate well in her own home.)*

Louise Erdrich (b. 1954) *is best known for exploring the Native American experience in her novels, poetry, and children's books. Born in Little Falls, Minnesota, she grew up in North Dakota. Of German American and Ojibwa (Chippewa) descent, her writing reflects a fascination with the influence of family and heritage on individuals and community. She lives in Minneapolis, Minnesota, where she owns a bookstore and continues to write. Her best-known works include the novels* Love Medicine, The Beet Queen, *and* The Round House.

The Leap

Short Story by Louise Erdrich

AS YOU READ Pay attention to how the narrator conveys her feelings about her mother as the story unfolds. Write down any questions you generate during reading.

Ⓐ My mother is the surviving half of a blindfold trapeze act, not a fact I think about much even now that she is sightless, the result of **encroaching** and stubborn cataracts. She walks slowly through her house here in New Hampshire, lightly touching her way along walls and running her hands over knickknacks, books, the drift of a grown child's belongings and castoffs. She has never upset an object or as much as brushed a magazine onto the floor. She has never lost her balance or bumped into a closet door left carelessly open.

10   It has occurred to me that the catlike precision of her movements in old age might be the result of her early training, but she shows so little of the drama or flair one might expect from a performer that I tend to forget the Flying Avalons. She has kept no sequined costume, no photographs, no fliers or posters from that part of her youth. I would, in fact, tend to think that all memory of double somersaults and heartstopping catches had left her arms and legs were it not for the fact that sometimes, as I sit sewing in

encroach
(ĕn-krōch´) *v.* to gradually intrude upon or invade.

The Leap **339**

ENGLISH LANGUAGE SUPPORT

Vocabulary: Sequence Words To help students understand the shifts in time, review signal words and phrases that will alert them to changes in time sequence. Words and phrases that may indicate a change in time include *once, when, then, that day (week, year, etc.).* Have students keep a list of sequence words and phrases that they encounter in the text along with line numbers. Guide students to list only the signal words that show a time change from present to past or from past to present. *(Examples: now, line 2;* first, *line 22;* now, *line 25;* that afternoon, *line 60;* once, *line 90;* at that time, *line 91)*

Support Inferences About Theme (LINES 22–24)

RL 1, RL 2

Discuss with students the way the narrator gradually reveals her mother's history and how it relates to her. Readers can continue to make inferences about the story's theme as it unfolds.

B **CITE TEXT EVIDENCE** Have students reread lines 22–24. Ask them what is revealed about the narrator's feelings about her mother in these lines, and how this might relate to the story's theme. *(Based on these lines, readers can infer that the narrator feels gratitude toward her mother. This is clear in the words "I owe her my existence three times." This is further evidence that the story's theme has to do with mother-daughter relationships.)*

Analyze Author's Choices: Flashback and Tension

RL 5

(LINES 33–43)

Tell students that pacing is one way a writer can build tension in a work of fiction. This can be done by using flashbacks or by using descriptive passages to slow down the unfolding of a suspenseful story.

C **ASK STUDENTS** what techniques are being used to build tension in lines 33–43. *(The narrator pauses in her account of the disaster to reflect on weather patterns, explaining how a storm can arrive without much warning. This slows down the telling of the story, building suspense. When she returns to the flashback, she continues drawing out the story by imagining what it was like for the audience that day, before the storm hit. By describing the audience filling the tent, buying peanuts, and waiting for the show to start, she paints a picture of a day that seemed normal and pleasant, with no hint of the disaster that would occur.)*

---

20 the room of the rebuilt house in which I slept as a child, I hear the crackle, catch a whiff of smoke from the stove downstairs and suddenly the room goes dark, the stitches burn beneath my fingers, and I am sewing with a needle of hot silver, a thread of fire.

I owe her my existence three times. The first was when she saved herself. In the town square a replica tent pole, cracked and splintered, now stands cast in concrete. It commemorates the disaster that put our town smack on the front page of the Boston and New York tabloids. It is from those old newspapers, now historical records, that I get my information. Not from my mother, Anna of the Flying Avalons, nor from any of her in-laws, nor certainly from the other half of her particular act, Harold Avalon, 30 her first husband. In one news account it says, "The day was mildly overcast, but nothing in the air or temperature gave any hint of the sudden force with which the deadly gale would strike."

I have lived in the West, where you can see the weather coming for miles, and it is true that out here we are at something of a disadvantage. When extremes of temperature collide, a hot and cold front, winds generate instantaneously behind a hill and crash upon you without warning. That, I think, was the likely situation on that day in June. People probably commented on the pleasant air, grateful that no hot sun beat upon the striped tent 40 that stretched over the entire center green. They bought their tickets and surrendered them in anticipation. They sat. They ate caramelized popcorn and roasted peanuts. There was time, before the storm, for three acts. The White Arabians of Ali-Khazar rose on their hind legs and waltzed. The Mysterious Bernie folded himself into a painted cracker tin, and the Lady of the Mists made herself appear and disappear in surprising places. As the clouds gathered outside, unnoticed, the ringmaster cracked his whip, shouted his introduction, and pointed to the ceiling of the tent, where the Flying Avalons were perched.

50 They loved to drop gracefully from nowhere, like two sparkling birds, and blow kisses as they threw off their plumed helmets and high-collared capes. They laughed and flirted openly as they beat their way up again on the trapeze bars. In the final vignette[1] of their act, they actually would kiss in midair, pausing, almost hovering as they swooped past one another. On the ground, between bows, Harry Avalon would skip quickly to the front rows and point out the smear of my mother's lipstick, just off the edge of his mouth. They made a romantic pair all right, especially in the blindfold sequence.

---

[1] **vignette:** a brief scene.

WHEN STUDENTS STRUGGLE . . .

Visualization is a technique that can aid struggling students' comprehension of a text. After students have read the description of the circus scene, have them turn to a partner and describe the tent, the audience, the trapeze performance, and what happened to the Flying Avalons when lightning struck. Partners should help each other classify events and add any missing details.

"I owe her my existence three times."

⁶⁰ That afternoon, as the anticipation increased, as Mr. and Mrs. Avalon tied sparkling strips of cloth onto each other's face and as they puckered their lips in mock kisses, lips destined "never again to meet," as one long breathless article put it, the wind rose, miles off, wrapped itself into a cone, and howled. There came a rumble of electrical energy, drowned out by the sudden roll of drums. One detail not mentioned by the press, perhaps unknown—Anna was pregnant at the time, seven months and hardly showing, her stomach muscles were that strong. It seems incredible that she would work high above the ground when any fall could be so ⁷⁰ dangerous, but the explanation—I know from watching her go blind—is that my mother lives comfortably in extreme elements. She is one with the constant dark now, just as the air was her home, familiar to her, safe, before the storm that afternoon.

From opposite ends of the tent they waved, blind and smiling, to the crowd below. The ringmaster removed his hat and called for silence, so that the two above could concentrate. They rubbed their hands in chalky powder, then Harry launched himself and swung once, twice, in huge calibrated² beats across space. He hung from his knees and on the third swing stretched wide his

---
² **calibrated:** checked or determined by comparison with a standard.

The Leap **341**

CLOSE READ

Analyze Author's Choices: Flashback and Tension   RL 5

(LINES 60–64)

Discuss with students how the author uses flashback to create tension throughout the story. One way she does this is by revealing the end before she relates the details of the story.

D CITE TEXT EVIDENCE Have students reread lines 60–64 and identify the "ending" the author reveals in this passage. (*By mentioning that Mr. and Mrs. Avalon's lips were "never again to meet," readers can infer that Mr. Avalon will be killed in the disaster that is about to unfold.*)

Support Inferences about Theme   RL 1, RL 2
(LINES 70–74)

Remind students that they should be looking for evidence of the story's theme as they read.

E CITE TEXT EVIDENCE Ask students to read lines 70–74. Then ask students to explain what is revealed about the daughter's feelings about her mother in this passage. (*The daughter appears to admire her mother's ability to "live comfortably in extreme elements," noting how she has adapted to being in "constant dark.")*

APPLYING ACADEMIC VOCABULARY

external	utilize

As you discuss the narrator's account of the circus disaster, incorporate the following Collection 5 academic vocabulary words: *external* and *utilize*. Ask students to notice how the narrator **utilized external** sources (*newspaper articles, historical records*) to learn the details of the Flying Avalon act and the disaster itself.

Analyze Author's Choices: Flashback and Tension

RL 5

(LINES 90–95)

Explain to students that authors often move back and forth from flashbacks to the present to provide context and perspective on a story the narrator is telling.

F ASK STUDENTS why they think the author chose to move back to the present so the narrator could relate a childhood memory in the middle of the story about the circus disaster. *(This passage shows that despite the daughter's assertion early in the story that her mother showed no evidence of her life as a trapeze performer, those experiences did influence her as a parent.)*

Determine Figurative Meanings (LINES 100–102)

RL 4

Discuss with students that authors often use **figurative language** to help convey meaning. Figurative language is language that communicates meaning beyond the literal meanings of the words.

G ASK STUDENTS what the author intends to convey with the phrase "only the blank scar tissue of a quieter future" in lines 101–102. How does this relate to what the reader already knows about the mother? *(This phrase foreshadows the fact that the mother will no longer be a trapeze artist. At this point in the story, the reader already knows that the mother has lived a quieter life away from the circus ring.)*

CRITICAL VOCABULARY

extricating: The narrator describes how her mother had to be removed from the tent wreckage.

ASK STUDENTS the connotative difference between the words *extricate* and *removed*. Why did the author choose the word *extricate* here instead of *removed*? *(Extricate implies that the mother was entangled or trapped and that it took some work to release her. Removed doesn't give the reader any information about how difficult it was to get her out of the tent.)*

---

80 arms, held his hand out to receive his pregnant wife as she dove from her shining bar.

It was while the two were in midair, their hands about to meet, that lightning struck the main pole and sizzled down the guy wires, filling the air with a blue radiance that Harry Avalon must certainly have seen through the cloth of his blindfold as the tent buckled and the edifice toppled him forward, the swing continuing and not returning in its sweep, and Harry going down, down into the crowd with his last thought, perhaps, just a prickle of surprise at his empty hands.

90 My mother once said that I'd be amazed at how many things a person can do within the act of falling. Perhaps, at the time, she was teaching me to dive off a board at the town pool, for I associated the idea with midair somersaults. But I also think she meant that even in that awful doomed second one could think, for she certainly did. When her hands did not meet her husband's, my mother tore her blindfold away. As he swept past her on the wrong side, she could have grasped his ankle, the toe-end of his tights, and gone down clutching him. Instead, she changed direction. Her body twisted toward a heavy wire and she managed to hang on to the braided

100 metal, still hot from the lightning strike. Her palms were burned so terribly that once healed they bore no lines, only the blank scar tissue of a quieter future. She was lowered, gently, to the sawdust ring just underneath the dome of the canvas roof, which did not entirely settle but was held up on one end and jabbed through, torn, and still on fire in places from the giant spark, though rain and men's jackets soon put that out.

Three people died, but except for her hands my mother was not seriously harmed until an overeager rescuer broke her arm in **extricating** her and also, in the process, collapsed a portion of the

110 tent bearing a huge buckle that knocked her unconscious. She was taken to the town hospital, and there she must have hemorrhaged,[3] for they kept her, confined to her bed, a month and a half before her baby was born without life.

Harry Avalon had wanted to be buried in the circus cemetery next to the original Avalon, his uncle, so she sent him back with his brothers. The child, however, is buried around the corner, beyond this house and just down the highway. Sometimes I used to walk there just to sit. She was a girl, but I rarely thought of her as a sister or even as a separate person really. I suppose you could call it the

120 egocentrism[4] of a child, of all young children, but I considered her a less finished version of myself.

extricate
(ĕk´strĭ-kāt´) *v.* to release or disentangle from.

---

[3] **hemorrhaged:** bled heavily.
[4] **egocentrism:** belief in the primary or sole importance of the self.

ENGLISH LANGUAGE SUPPORT

Vocabulary: Homophones Explain that homophones are words that sound alike but have different spellings. Have students look at lines 82–89 as you read them aloud and write the homophones on the board. Review the meaning of each word from the text and discuss the homophones. Have pairs write sentences using each homophone. Challenge them to write sentences with complete sets of homophones.

two (line 82)	to	too	**seen** (line 85)	scene
meet (line 82)	meat		**through** (line 85)	threw
their (line 82)	there	they're	**not** (line 87)	knot

I can easily pick hers out from the road, for it is bigger than the others and in the shape of a lamb at rest, its legs curled beneath. The carved lamb looms larger as the years pass, though it is probably only my eyes, the visions shifting, as what is close to me blurs and distances sharpen. In odd moments, I think it is the edge drawing near, the edge of everything, the unseen horizon we do not really speak of in the eastern woods. And it also seems to me, although this is probably an idle fantasy, that the statue is growing more sharply etched, as if, instead of weathering itself into a porous mass, it is hardening on the hillside with each snowfall, perfecting itself.

It was during her confinement in the hospital that my mother met my father. He was called in to look at the set of her arm, which was complicated. He stayed, sitting at her bedside, for he was something of an armchair traveler and had spent his war quietly, at an air force training grounds, where he became a specialist in arms and legs broken during parachute training exercises. Anna Avalon had been to many of the places he longed to visit—Venice, Rome, Mexico, all through France and Spain. She had no family of her own and was taken in by the Avalons, trained to perform from a very young age. They toured Europe before the war, then based themselves in New York. She was illiterate.

It was in the hospital that she finally learned to read and write, as a way of overcoming the boredom and depression of those weeks, and it was my father who insisted on teaching her. In return for stories of her adventures, he graded her first exercises. He bought her her first book, and over her bold letters, which the pale guides of the penmanship pads could not contain, they fell in love.

I wonder if my father calculated the exchange he offered: one form of flight for another. For after that, and for as long as I can remember, my mother has never been without a book. Until now, that is, and it remains the greatest difficulty of her blindness. Since my father's recent death, there is no one to read to her, which is why I returned, in fact, from my failed life where the land is flat. I came home to read to my mother, to read out loud, to read long into the dark if I must, to read all night.

Once my father and mother married, they moved onto the old farm he had inherited but didn't care much for. Though he'd been thinking of moving to a larger city, he settled down and broadened his practice in this valley. It still seems odd to me, when they could have gone anywhere else, that they chose to stay in the town where the disaster had occurred, and which my father in the first place had found so **constricting.** It was my mother who insisted upon it,

constrict
(kən-strĭkt´) *v.* to limit or impede growth.

The Leap   **343**

Support Inferences About Theme (LINES 155–158)

RL 2

Tell students that writers often try to show how their characters feel through their actions, rather than telling readers outright. Remind students that characters' actions can help develop a story's theme.

H ASK STUDENTS what they can infer about the narrator's feelings about her mother from lines 155–158. *(The narrator's actions show her devotion and gratitude toward her mother. By committing her life to caring for and reading to her mother, she demonstrates her love and willingness to sacrifice.* How do the feelings convey the story's theme? *(The feelings described underscore the theme of a strong and lifelong bond between mother and daughter.)*

CRITICAL VOCABULARY

constricting: The narrator describes how her father felt that the town limited his growth.

ASK STUDENTS to explain why a small town might have felt constricting to her father while her mother felt at home there. *(Her father didn't have the chances to travel that her mother did. He probably felt there was less diversity and culture than in a city. He may have expected that an urban area might provide more opportunities to learn and grow than a small town might offer.)*

Support Inferences about Theme (LINES 169–172) **RL 2**

Tell students that works of fiction often have multiple themes.

 ASK STUDENTS to reread lines 169–172. Given what they know about the mother and daughter so far, what themes does this paragraph support? *(Gratitude and love between a mother and daughter and the human will to survive are two important themes in this story that are supported in this paragraph.)*

Analyze Author's Choices: Flashback and Tension **RL 5**

(LINES 173–180)

Explain that Erdrich builds tension by flashing back to different periods in time. The story moves from the present, to the distant past before the narrator was born, and to her own childhood.

 ASK STUDENTS to identify the cues that let the reader know that the paragraph starting with line 173 is a flashback. *(The tense shifts from present to past.)* Then ask how this event was hinted at earlier in the story. *(The narrator hints at the fire when she talks about smelling smoke and the room going dark while sewing in her childhood room earlier in the story.)*

after her child did not survive. And then, too, she loved the sagging farmhouse with its scrap of what was left of a vast acreage of woods and hidden hay fields that stretched to the game park.

170   I owe my existence, the second time then, to the two of them and the hospital that brought them together. That is the debt we take for granted since none of us asks for life. It is only once we have it that we hang on so dearly.

    I was seven the year the house caught fire, probably from standing ash. It can rekindle, and my father, forgetful around the house and perpetually exhausted from night hours on call, often emptied what he thought were ashes from cold stoves into wooden or cardboard containers. The fire could have started from a flaming box, or perhaps a buildup of creosote[5] inside the chimney was the culprit. It started right around the stove, and the heart of the house

180 was gutted. The baby-sitter, fallen asleep in my father's den on the first floor, woke to find the stairway to my upstairs room cut off by flames. She used the phone, then ran outside to stand beneath my window.

    When my parents arrived, the town volunteers had drawn water from the fire pond and were spraying the outside of the

---

[5] **creosote:** a flammable, oily byproduct of burning carbon-based fuels like coal, peat, and wood.

344   Collection 5

ENGLISH LANGUAGE SUPPORT

Developing Reading Fluency Reading difficult passages aloud can help with comprehension, especially with longer harder-to-parse sentences. Have students work in pairs to read lines 173–183 aloud to one another. They should use the punctuation to guide their pacing and expression. After each member of a pair has read the passage aloud, they should summarize the paragraph in their own words to confirm comprehension.

house, preparing to go inside after me, not knowing at the time that there was only one staircase and that it was lost. On the other side of the house, the superannuated⁶ extension ladder broke in half. Perhaps the clatter of it falling against the walls woke me, for I'd 190 been asleep up to that point.

As soon as I awakened, in the small room that I now use for sewing, I smelled the smoke. I followed things by the letter then, was good at memorizing instructions, and so I did exactly what was taught in the second-grade home fire drill. I got up, I touched the back of my door before opening it. Finding it hot, I left it closed and stuffed my rolled-up rug beneath the crack. I did not hide under my bed or crawl into my closet. I put on my flannel robe, and then I sat down to wait.

Outside, my mother stood below my dark window and saw 200 clearly that there was no rescue. Flames had pierced one side wall, and the glare of the fire lighted the massive limbs and trunk of the vigorous old elm that had probably been planted the year the house was built, a hundred years ago at least. No leaf touched the wall, and just one thin branch scraped the roof. From below, it looked as though even a squirrel would have had trouble jumping from the tree onto the house, for the breadth of that small branch was no bigger than my mother's wrist.

Standing there, beside Father, who was preparing to rush back around to the front of the house, my mother asked him to unzip her 210 dress. When he wouldn't be bothered, she made him understand. He couldn't make his hands work, so she finally tore it off and stood there in her pearls and stockings. She directed one of the men to lean the broken half of the extension ladder up against the trunk of the tree. In surprise, he **complied**. She ascended. She vanished. Then she could be seen among the leafless branches of late November as she made her way up and, along her stomach, inched the length of a bough that curved above the branch that brushed the roof.

Once there, swaying, she stood and balanced. There were plenty 220 of people in the crowd and many who still remember, or think they do, my mother's leap through the ice-dark air toward that thinnest extension, and how she broke the branch falling so that it cracked in her hands, cracked louder than the flames as she vaulted with it toward the edge of the roof, and how it hurtled down end over end without her, and their eyes went up, again, to see where she had flown.

I didn't see her leap through air, only heard the sudden thump and looked out my window. She was hanging by the backs of her

comply
(kəm-plī´) *v.* to obey an instruction or command.

---
⁶ **superannuated:** obsolete; ready for retirement.

CLOSE READ

Support Inferences About Theme (LINES 208–214)   RL 1, RL 2

Point out that in this part of the story, readers are learning about the third time the narrator "owes her existence" to her mother.

Ⓚ CITE TEXT EVIDENCE Ask students to read lines 208–214. What can readers infer about the mother's feelings about her daughter from this passage? How does this relate to some of the themes in this text? Have students cite specific evidence for their inferences. *(Readers can see that the mother is extremely devoted to her daughter and will do anything she needs to do to protect her life. This is evident in the fact that she took charge of the situation, removed her dress without shame, and took risky action to get her daughter out of the house. This relates to the mother-daughter relationship theme, as well as the will to survive theme.)*

CRITICAL VOCABULARY

complied: The narrator describes how the fire fighters obeyed her mother's request to lean the broken ladder against the tree for her.

ASK STUDENTS why it is important to the story that we know the fire fighter complied with the narrator's mother without question. *(It shows how her mother must have taken charge in her determination to save her daughter. The men understood that she was in control and was ready for action.)*

WHEN STUDENTS STRUGGLE...

This story's time sequence moves back and forth frequently, but each event is important to ushering in the next one. To help struggling students follow the sequence of events and understand their significance, have them write each major event on a note card. When they are finished reading, they should arrange the note cards to reflect chronological order, creating a flowchart as shown.

Circus disaster ▸▸ *Mother meets narrator's father* ▸▸ *Mother and father marry* ▸▸ *Mother saves daughter from house fire* ▸▸ *Daughter moves back in with mother*

 LEVEL UP TUTORIALS For additional support, assign the following *Level Up* tutorial: **Theme.**

Analyze Author's Choices: Tension and Flashback

RL 5

(LINES 242–252)

Tell students that sometimes past events can be alluded to in less overt ways.

Ⓛ ASK STUDENTS what past events are alluded to in the language the author uses to describe the mother and daughter's descent from the window. *(The narrator alludes to the mother's experience as a trapeze performer several times. The mother points her toes as they leap from the window, as if she were performing in the circus again. Then as they fall, the narrator describes her mother's heartbeat as sounding "loud as thunder, long as the roll of drums," which alludes to the earlier image of the circus drums drowning out the sound of thunder.)*

CRITICAL VOCABULARY

tentative: The narrator describes how her mother knocked on the window to get her attention.

ASK STUDENTS how this detail contrasts with the mother's other actions during the rescue. *(The mother is bold and determined in gaining access to her daughter's window, not at all cautious until she sees her daughter.)*

COLLABORATIVE DISCUSSION Have students form pairs to discuss the narrator's feelings about her mother and the ways the author reveals the mother's character. Have them share their conclusions with the class as a whole. Accept all reasonable responses.

ASK STUDENTS to share any questions they generated in the course of reading and discussing the selection.

---

heels from the new gutter we had put in that year, and she was
230 smiling. I was not surprised to see her, she was so matter-of-fact.
She tapped on the window. I remember how she did it, too. It
was the friendliest tap, a bit **tentative**, as if she was afraid she had
arrived too early at a friend's house. Then she gestured at the latch,
and when I opened the window she told me to raise it wider and
prop it up with the stick so it wouldn't crush her fingers. She swung
down, caught the ledge, and crawled through the opening. Once
she was in my room, I realized she had on only underclothing, a
bra of the heavy stitched cotton women used to wear and step-in,
lace-trimmed drawers. I remember feeling light-headed, of course,
240 terribly relieved, and then embarrassed for her to be seen by the
crowd undressed.

  I was still embarrassed as we flew out the window, toward
earth, me in her lap, her toes pointed as we skimmed toward the
painted target of the fire fighter's net.

  I know that she's right. I knew it even then. As you fall, there
is time to think. Curled as I was, against her stomach, I was not
startled by the cries of the crowd or the looming faces. The wind
roared and beat its hot breath at our back, the flames whistled.
I slowly wondered what would happen if we missed the circle or
250 bounced out of it. Then I wrapped my hands around my mother's
hands. I felt the brush of her lips and heard the beat of her heart in
my ears, loud as thunder, long as the roll of drums.

tentative
(tĕn′tə-tĭv) *adj.* with caution and without confidence.

COLLABORATIVE DISCUSSION How does the narrator feel about her mother? With a partner, discuss how the author reveals the character of the mother through the narrator. Cite specific evidence from the text to support your ideas.

TO CHALLENGE STUDENTS . . .

Interpret Point of View What is a former trapeze artist thinking in an emergency that threatens the survival of a family member? Tell students that first-person narration limits the reader's knowledge of what other characters experience. Invite them to rewrite the scene of the mother rescuing the daughter from the house either in first-person with the mother narrating or using a third-person omniscient voice. They should consider how the mother felt when she came home and realized her daughter was trapped in the burning house, and what she saw and experienced as she acted to rescue her. Have students share and compare their finished products.

Analyze Author's Choices: Flashback and Tension

RL 5

The ability to create **tension,** or suspense, is central to the author's craft. Tension propels a story forward and keeps the reader wondering what will happen next. One effective technique for creating tension is the **flashback—**a literary device used to manipulate time by inserting an earlier event into the present action, often by having a character recall something that happened in the past. As a flashback is introduced, the verb tense will shift from the present to the past or past perfect tense. Signal words, such as *once* (as in, *once upon a time*) and *remember* (as in, *I remember when*) might be used to alert the reader that a shift in time is about to occur. They also remind the reader that a flashback is still in effect.

The chart tracks some shifts in time and tension in "The Leap." By following the action, you can see how shifts in the story's **chronology,** or order, help to sustain or build tension. Complete your own chart as you analyze the story.

Tension Tracker		
Example	**Flashback Clues** (verb tense; signal words)	**Action Summary**
"I owe her my existence three times. The first was when..."	shift from present to past tense	narrator begins to explain her debt to her mother
"I have lived in the West ..."	shift to past perfect tense	narrator provides information about her own adult life

Support Inferences About Theme

RL 1, RL 2

In a short story, the **theme,** or the underlying message, usually develops and emerges through **inference.** An inference is a logical conclusion based on clues in the text as well as on your own experience. To uncover the theme, begin by analyzing the story's title. Then, look for clues in the text that indicate what the title might mean. Be aware of the possibility that the title may have multiple meanings. By keeping a list of clues, you can create a summary of supporting inferences that will help you to determine the story's theme. For example, you might note that the word *leap* is in the title, and because the narrator's mother was a trapeze artist, she was probably able to make dangerous leaps. Ask yourself, what might be the figurative meaning of a *leap*? Look for these kinds of clues to determine the theme the author wants to convey.

CLOSE READ

Analyze Author's Choices: Flashback and Tension

RL 5

Tell students that the author creates tension by starting in the present and hinting at dramatic events in the narrator's and her mother's past. In this way readers first see the results of these events, and then, through flashbacks, gradually learn what lead to the present circumstances.

Support Inferences About Theme

RL 1, RL 2

To help students make text-supported inferences about the story's theme, discuss with them the literal and figurative meanings of the word *leap.* For example, a person can make a "leap of faith" in deciding to trust or love someone. You can also guide students to think about the theme by asking:

- Who is the main focus of the story?
- What challenges does the mother face in her life, and how does she overcome them?
- How does the narrator feel toward her mother?

By answering these questions with evidence from the text, students will be able to make inferences about the story's theme, which is about courage, overcoming challenges, and love.

Strategies for Annotation   ✏️ 🗇 *Annotate it!*

Support Inferences About Theme

RL 1, RL 2

Share these strategies for guided or independent analysis:

- Underline literal references to "leaping."
- Highlight in blue figurative references to leaping.
- On notes, record your interpretation of the figurative references, noting how they convey a theme.

do, my mother's 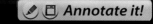 leap through the ice-dark air toward that thinnest extension, and how she broke the branch falling so that it cracked in her hands, cracked louder than the flames as she vaulted with it toward the edge of the roof, and how it hurtled down end over end.

Analyzing the Text

RL 1, RL 2, RL 3, RL 5

Possible answers:

1. *In lines 15–21, the narrator drifts into a reverie of her mother's past career as a trapeze artist. The narrator also mentions a rebuilt house, a "crackle" and "whiff of smoke" that suggest a fire may have occured.*

2. *Reaching for her husband would mean choosing to die with him as he fell to the ground. By reaching for the wire, Anna chooses life, which shows her fierce devotion to living. One can infer that the "leap" may refer to a lunge toward life.*

3. *The first is the literal leap to the hot wire during the circus accident. A second may be the figurative leap of falling in love with the doctor, followed by the literal leaps from the tree to the rooftop and from the window to the firefighters' net.*

4. *1. Her mother saves herself from falling off the trapeze. 2. After the tragedy, her mother opens her heart, falls in love, marries, and has a child (the narrator). 3. Her mother risks her life to save her daughter from the house fire. Each instance is revealed through flashback and each flashback offers a closer connection to the narrator, increasing the story's tension.*

5. *In both instances, Anna bravely attempts to save her child: an unborn child the first time, and then the narrator as a young child. Both scenes offer evidence of the mother's bravery and devotion to her daughter.*

6. *The daughter feels gratitude toward her mother for ensuring her existence and saving her life. She shows her love for her mother by returning to her childhood home to help her mother in her old age. The mother "lives comfortably in extreme elements." Through her heroic acts, we see that the mother loves her daughter and believes in survival and in the power of love.*

7. *As the daughter waits calmly to be rescued and the mother skillfully brings her to safety, she learns the value of love and trust and faith, especially in extreme circumstances. These lines express a theme that life and love require us to take a blind leap. We risk getting hurt, but if we approach life with an open heart, things will likely turn out for the best.*

Cite Text Evidence   Support your responses with evidence from the selection.

1. **Interpret** How do lines 15–21 act as a flashback? What clues do they give about the rest of the story? Provide specific evidence in your response.

2. **Infer** In lines 98–100, Anna decides to reach for the hot braided metal rather than for her husband as he falls. What does this reveal about her character? What inferences can you make about the story's title in this passage?

3. **Interpret** Identify the leaps in the story. Which leaps are literal? Which are figurative?

4. **Analyze** The narrator speaks of the three ways that she owes her existence to her mother. Identify the three ways and the literary techniques used to reveal them. How does each revelation affect the story's tension?

5. **Compare** What do these scenes reveal about the mother's character?
   - Anna saves herself during the trapeze accident.
   - Anna saves her daughter from the house fire.

6. **Draw Conclusions** Based upon what the narrator reveals, draw conclusions about the mother and her relationship with her daughter. Cite evidence from the text to support your response.

7. **Infer** Reread lines 227–252. What does the narrator learn? What inferences can you make about the story's theme?

PERFORMANCE TASK

Speaking Activity: Discussion Imagery about circuses occurs throughout "The Leap." Explore the author's use of circus imagery in a writing exercise and in discussion groups.

1. Reread the story, jotting down notes on specific references to the circus. Beside each reference, note whether each image contributes to character, theme, setting, or any other aspect of the story.

2. In small discussion groups, use your notes to respond to this question: In what ways does circus imagery contribute to the story? Write a brief summary of your discussion.

Assign this performance task.

PERFORMANCE TASK

SL 1a

Speaking Activity: Discussion Before students form groups, have them create a two-column chart that cites story elements in one column and specific examples from the text in the other. (Examples that develop *characterization*: the absence of sequined costumes, fliers, and other memorabilia [lines 14–15]; *setting*: the description of the performers [lines 43–59] and tent-pole replica [lines 23–24]; allusions to *theme*: the blindfold sequence [lines 60–61])

Critical Vocabulary

encroach   extricate   constrict   comply   tentative

Practice and Apply Answer these questions, using a dictionary or thesaurus as needed. Make sure your answers reflect your understanding of each Critical Vocabulary word's meaning.

1. Should rescue crews provide a **tentative** response to **encroaching** forest fires? Why or why not?

2. Would it feel **constricting** if one always **complied** with the wishes of others? Explain.

3. Why would you **extricate** yourself from a planned road trip upon learning of an **encroaching** blizzard?

Vocabulary Strategy: Prefixes

The Critical Vocabulary words *encroach, extricate, constrict,* and *comply* all contain **prefixes,** an affix added to the beginning of a base word. Knowing the meaning of common prefixes, such as *en-, ex-, con-,* and *com-,* will help you clarify the meaning of unknown words. Here are the meanings of some common prefixes and examples of other words that contain the prefixes:

Prefixes	Meanings	Examples
en-	to go into or onto	energy, entire
ex-	out of or away from	exchange, extend
com-, con-	together, with, jointly	comfort, contain, condition

If a base word is unfamiliar, use your knowledge of the word's prefix and how the word is used in context to clarify its meaning. If necessary, consult a dictionary to determine the precise meaning of a word.

Practice and Apply Identify a new word, either from the selection or on your own, that contains each of the prefixes in the chart. For each word you choose, follow these steps:

1. Identify the base word, the main word part. For example, the base word for *exchange* is *change.*

2. Write a definition for each word that incorporates the prefix meaning and the base word meaning. Use a dictionary to check your definition. Make changes if needed.

3. Finally, write a sample sentence for each word you chose.

PRACTICE & APPLY

Critical Vocabulary

Possible answers:

1. *Rescue crews should not be hesitant when responding to a fire that may be closing in on nearby homes or they might arrive too late in order to save the home.*

2. *To always go along with someone else's wishes would probably feel very confining because it would limit your opportunities to express your own ideas.*

3. *You would want to free yourself from having to drive in the dangerous conditions that the approaching storm might cause.*

Vocabulary Strategy: Prefixes

Possible answers:

Word choices and the resulting definitions will vary, but each should correctly combine a prefix and a base word. Students' sentences should convey a clear understanding of the words they chose. Sentences should be original and not found in the selection or in a dictionary.

Language and Style: Relative Clauses

L 1b

Review the examples in the chart and make sure students understand how each one illustrates the use of relative clauses. Invite students to tell which question each example relative clause answers.

Possible answers:

Students should apply the conventions of standard English to incorporate relative clauses into the summaries of their discussions. Examples of additional relative clauses appear on lines 103 (which), 220 (who), and 225 (where).

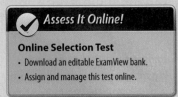

Assess It Online!

Online Selection Test
· Download an editable ExamView bank.
· Assign and manage this test online.

Language and Style: Relative Clauses

L 1b

A **clause** is a group of words that contains a subject and a predicate.
Relative clauses describe nouns and function as adjectives. Here are the characteristics of a relative clause:

· It begins with a signal word: a relative pronoun *(that, which, who, whom, whose)* or a relative adverb *(when, where,* or *why).*
· It follows a noun or a noun phrase.
· It provides extra information about a noun or a noun phrase, or it answers the questions *What kind? How many?* or *Which one?*

Authors use relative clauses not only to convey specific meanings but also to add interest and variety to their work. Read this sentence from "The Leap":

> It commemorates the disaster <u>that put our town smack on the front page of the Boston and New York tabloids.</u>

The clause fulfills all the elements of a relative clause: it begins with a relative pronoun—*that*; it follows a noun—*disaster*; it answers the question *Which one?*—the disaster that put the town in the tabloids.

Erdrich could have expressed the same ideas this way:

> It commemorates the disaster. The disaster put our town smack on the front page of the Boston and New York tabloids.

Notice how the sentence with the relative clause is smoother and easier to read. Here are some other examples of relative clauses from the "The Leap":

Relative Clauses		
Signal Word	**Relative Clause**	**Words Modified**
which	He was called in to look at the set of her arm, <u>which was complicated.</u>	"the set of her arm"
who	. . . and it was my father <u>who insisted on teaching her.</u>	"father"
where	. . . they chose to stay in the town <u>where the disaster had occurred . . .</u>	"town"

Practice and Apply Look back at the summary you created in response to this selection's Performance Task. Revise the summary to include at least three relative clauses. With a partner, discuss your revised summaries. Then work together to identify at least five more relative clauses in "The Leap" that are not included as examples in this lesson.

Strategies for Annotation

Annotate it!

Language and Style: Relative Clauses

L 1b

Share these strategies for identifying relative clauses in the selection:
· Underline the relative clauses.
· Highlight in yellow the words the clause is modifying.
· Highlight in blue the signal word.

> I have lived in the West, where you can see the weather coming
> for miles, and it is true that out here we are a something of a
> disadvantage. When extremes of temperature collide, a hot

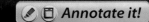

Analyze Character

TEACH

Explain that authors use various techniques to develop **characters** in fiction. Readers get to know characters through:

- **Speech**—The way a character speaks can reveal things about a character such as what part of the country or world they are from. The words a character says can reveal feelings and personality.

- **Thoughts**—Depending on the story's point of view, readers can learn about a character based on his or her thoughts. In "The Leap," the first-person narrator reveals her admiration for her mother through her thoughts.

- **Actions**—Characters reveal whether they are selfish or generous, brave or cowardly, kind or unkind, loyal or disloyal, and much more through their actions. Their reactions to other characters and to events in a story are equally revealing. Erdrich uses actions to develop the mother's character in "The Leap."

PRACTICE AND APPLY

Have students reread the descriptions of the mother saving herself during the trapeze accident (lines 60–106) and her daughter from the fire (lines 199–244). Explain that the author reveals the mother's character through her actions instead of thoughts. Have students list several adjectives and phrases that describe the mother based on her actions as a starting point for answering item 5 in Analyzing the Text. *(Sample answers: brave, loving, calm in a crisis, determined to survive, protective, agile)*

 INTERACTIVE WHITEBOARD LESSON If students need further instruction, use this *Interactive Whiteboard Lesson:* **Character Development.**

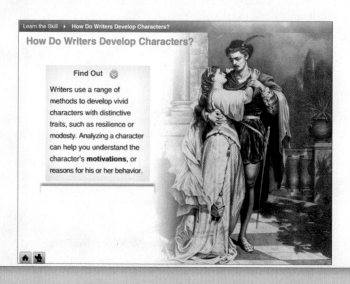

Support Inferences About Theme

RETEACH

Review the term *theme*. In a work of fiction, **theme** is the central idea or message in the story. In fables and fairy tales, the theme is often the lesson and given directly at the end of the story. In literature, however, the theme is usually not obvious, and is revealed through the events and actions of the characters. Readers can make **inferences**, or assumptions, about the theme based on evidence in the text. Tell students that to determine the theme in "The Leap" or any other work of fiction, they can:

- Look at the title for clues. In "The Leap," the title alludes to the various real and symbolic leaps in the story.

- Be alert for ideas or symbols that are repeated. In "The Leap," the narrator describes the three times she owes her life to her mother, a key element of the story's theme.

- Pay attention to the story's details and events, and the characters' reactions to them. In "The Leap," the author uses three dramatic events to reveal the mother's character and her daughter's feelings about her.

 LEVEL UP TUTORIALS Assign the following *Level Up* tutorial: **Theme**

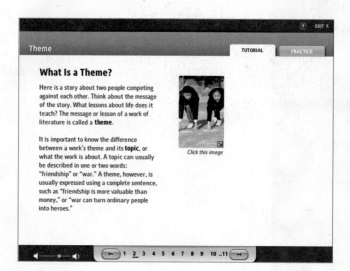

INDEPENDENT READING

Students can apply the skill to another story they have read. Have them analyze a story's theme and support their inferences with textual evidence. Students may share their analyses in pairs or small groups.

The End and the Beginning

Poem by Wisława Szymborska   Translated by Joanna Trzeciak

Why This Text?

Students may encounter poetry that seeks to make sense of an experience by describing it in terms of vivid imagery and figurative language. This lesson explores how figurative language influences tone by examining Szymborska's poem about the aftermath of war.

View It!

Professional Development Podcast:

Text Complexity

Key Learning Objective: The student will be able to determine the meanings of figurative language and how it influences tone in poetry.

For additional practice:

Poems About **Survival**

Close Reader selections
"The Survivor,"
Poem by Marilyn Chin
"Who Understands Me but Me
Poem by Jimmy Santiago Baca

RL 1 Cite textual evidence.

RL 2 Determine a theme.

RL 4 Determine figurative and connotative meanings and analyze the impact on tone.

RL 5 Analyze structure.

RL 6 Analyze point of view or cultural experience from outside the United States.

W 3d Use precise words, phrases, and sensory language.

W 9a Apply Reading standards to literature.

SL 1a Come to discussions prepared.

L 5a Interpret figures of speech in context.

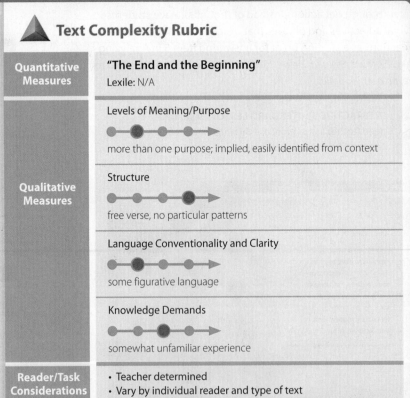

▲ Text Complexity Rubric

Quantitative Measures	"The End and the Beginning" Lexile: N/A
Qualitative Measures	**Levels of Meaning/Purpose** more than one purpose; implied, easily identified from context
	Structure free verse, no particular patterns
	Language Conventionality and Clarity some figurative language
	Knowledge Demands somewhat unfamiliar experience
Reader/Task Considerations	• Teacher determined • Vary by individual reader and type of text • See the Text X-Ray for suggested Reader/Task Considerations.

English Language Support
Before teaching, use the Text X-Ray below for an overview of the text's complexity. The Text X-Ray and the supports and scaffolds in the Teacher's Edition will help you guide students of different skill levels.

Text Complexity: Qualitative Measures

Levels of Meaning/Purpose

more than one purpose, implied, easily identified from context

Help students analyze the tone of a poem.
- Teacher's Edition side notes, pp. 351, 352, 353
- Close Read Screencasts, p. 351
- Strategies for Annotation, p. 353
- Determine Figurative Meanings and Tone, p. 353

To teach determining theme, see
- Teacher's Edition side note, p. 352
- Determine Theme, p. 354a

To reteach determining tone, see
- Determine Figurative Meanings and Tone, p. 354a

 Use It! Level Up Tutorials: Theme, Imagery

ZOOM IN ON ANALYZING TONE Remind students that a poem's **tone** is the speaker's attitude or feeling toward the subject—in this case, what happens after a war. Read aloud lines 1–17, using your voice to emphasize the dull, repetitive nature of the cleanup tasks. Ask: How does the speaker feel about cleaning up? Is it fun and exciting? Guide students to identify the tone as weary. Then read aloud the last two stanzas, lines 37–47. Emphasize the change in tone as the focus shifts from those who are cleaning up to someone who is relaxing in a field. Discuss words that could describe this new tone, such as *carefree* and *optimistic*.

Structure

free verse, no particular patterns

Help students analyze structural elements such as repetition and parallelism.
- Teacher's Edition side note, p. 351
- Strategies for Annotation, p. 353

ZOOM IN ON ANALYZING STRUCTURE Using the side note on page 351, help students understand how the rhetorical devices of **repetition** and **parallelism** lend structure to the poem. Point out that the repetition of "someone has to" in lines 1–17 creates a string of sentences with parallel grammatical structures. The repetition emphasizes that all the statements are related—they all describe tasks associated with cleaning up after a war. It also mirrors the almost ordinary, day-after-day nature of the chores. Ask pairs to practice reading this section of the poem aloud to each other to hear the effect of the repetition.

Language Conventionality and Clarity

some figurative language

Help students analyze the connotative meanings of words.
- Determine Figurative Meanings and Tone, p. 353

Guide students in understanding phrasal verbs.
- English Language Support, p. 352

Support students' discussion of a poem.
- Teacher's Edition side note, p. 352

ZOOM IN ON **PREVIEWING VOCABULARY** Display lines 9–13 and have students consider the use of *mired* in line 9. Point out the items in which "someone has to get mired": scum, ashes, sofa springs, splintered glass, bloody rags. *Mired* literally means "stuck in mud," but what kind of miring could this be? Explain that poets often use words to mean more than their literal definition. How else could someone be "mired"? Display line 14-17 and ask students to work together to come up with definitions for the following terms: *girder* and *glaze*.

Knowledge Demands

somewhat unfamiliar experience

Support English Learners in understanding the historical context of this poem.
- Teacher's Edition Background note, p. 351

ZOOM IN ON **BUILDING KNOWLEDGE** Tell students that since the poet was born in western Poland and was about 17 when World War II began, she is almost certainly drawing upon her postwar experiences in Krakow, Poland. Szymborska lived there both during and after the war. Where there once stood a notorious slave labor camp called Plaszow, today there is a grassland eerily reminiscent of the image at the poem's end.

Suggested Reader/Task Considerations

You might consider the following before assigning this poem to students.
- Might the poem spark students' curiosity about the impact of World War II on Krakow, Poland?
- Can this poem be used to develop students' questioning skills as they discuss its perspective on the aftermath of war?

ZOOM IN ON **SUPPORTING COMPREHENSION**

- Suggest that students conduct research to learn more about Krakow and, in particular, the Krakow Ghetto. (This place is central to the story and 1993 film *Schindler's List.*) Ask students to share their findings with the class.
- If students have already read the excerpt from *Night,* discuss Elie Wiesel's fierce conviction that he must bear witness to all that happened and not allow anyone to forget the Holocaust, because forgetting is what allows terrible things to happen all over again. Then have students contrast Wiesel's position with the theme of this poem.

Wisława Szymborska (vēs-wä´wä shĭm-bôr´skə)
Have students read the biographical information about the poet. Explain that although Ms. Szymborska lived through turbulent times in Europe and though she saw her country turned upside down by war, she did not think of herself as a political poet. She wrote about the individual, and it is through that lens that she viewed the world. She did acknowledge, however, that politics and its consequences—not the least of which is war—have a profound impact on the individual.

AS YOU READ Direct students to use the As You Read question to focus their reading

Determine Figurative Meanings (LINES 1–13)   RL 4

Tell students that poets use precise words and phrases, including **sensory language,** to create powerful images that appeal to the reader's sense of sight, sound, smell, touch, and taste.

A **ASK STUDENTS** to reread lines 1–13 and point out words and phrases that appeal to their senses. *(rubble, sofa spring, bloody rags, ashes, splintered glass, etc.)* Ask students what general picture these words or phrases create in their minds. *(Possible answer: a ruined city destroyed by war.)*

Explain that poets use techniques such as repetition and parallelism to convey meaning. Point out that **repetition** is the use of a word or phrase again and again. **Parallelism** is the repetition of the same grammatical structure to show that two or more ideas are similar or equally important. Explain that repetition and parallelism may be used together.

B **CITE TEXT EVIDENCE** Have students identify an example of repetition and parallelism. *(lines 2, 5, and 9)* Ask students what ideas the poet suggests are of similar or equal importance. *(cleaning up, pushing the rubble, and getting mired in scum and ashes)* Ask students how these acts contrast with the poet's refrain of "someone has to…" *(The pronoun emphasizes how war has depersonalized individuals as they perform drab yet often grisly mundane tasks.)*

Wisława Szymborska (1923–2012) *was born in western Poland and spent most of her life in Krakow, Poland. Her first two published volumes of poetry, written in post–World War II Communist-dominated Poland, were written in the style of Socialist Realism. Szymborska later disowned these works. Her disillusionment with communism was reflected in Calling Out to Yeti, published in 1957. Her poems, noted for their unique, ironic tone, have been translated into many languages. Szymborska was awarded the Nobel Prize in Literature in 1996.*

The End and the Beginning

Poem by Wisława Szymborska   translated by Joanna Trzeciak

AS YOU READ Think about all the aspects of daily life that are disrupted by war. Write down any questions you generate during reading.

> After every war
> **someone has to clean up.**   **A**
> Things won't
> straighten themselves up, after all.
>
> 5 **Someone has to push the rubble**   **B**
> to the side of the road,
> so the corpse-filled wagons
> can pass.
>
> **Someone has to get mired**
> 10 in scum and ashes,
> sofa springs,
> splintered glass,
> and bloody rags.

Image Credits: (c) ©A. Majeed/AFP/Getty Images; (tr) ©Forum/Universal Images Group/Getty Images

---

Close Read Screencasts

Modeled Discussions

Have students click the *Close Read* icons in their eBooks to access the screencast in which readers discuss and annotate the following key passage:

- The third through fourth stanzas (lines 9–17), which begin "Someone has to get mired…" and end "Someone has to glaze a window, / rehang a door."

As a class, view and discuss the video. Then have students work in pairs to perform a close read of an additional passage—the seventh through eighth stanzas (lines 26–36).

Determine Figurative Meanings and Analyze Tone

RL 4

(LINES 14–21)

Explain that **tone** refers to an author's attitude toward the subject. Authors shape a work's tone through word choices, images they create, and topics they explore. An author may feel angry or disappointed about a topic, or perhaps excited and hopeful. As a result, word choices would reflect that attitude.

C **ASK STUDENTS** to explain the images the poet creates in lines 14–17. (*She creates images of people rebuilding.*) Then refer students to lines 18–21 and ask them why the poet does not think these images are photogenic. (*They are drab and ugly, and they lack drama.*) Ask students to define the poet's attitude toward her subject, based on her word choice and images. (*Possible answer: weary, sad, ironic*)

Analyze Theme and Tone

RL 2, RL 4

(LINES 26–42)

Remind students that a poem's **theme** is its central message or idea. A poem may contain more than one theme. Explain that we determine a theme by analyzing language, tone, and imagery.

D **CITE TEXT EVIDENCE** Have students reread lines 26–42. Ask them to explain what, people might be figuratively throwing on garbage piles, along with the rubble of war. (*the arguments and attitudes that led to war*) Ask what the poet suggests will happen to those traumatized by war. (*lines 37–42: People who suffered will yield way for those who did not.*) Ask what tone the poet uses and how it informs the theme. (*Possible answer: A weary, jaded tone suggests healing only comes to those who haven't witnessed the violence.*)

COLLABORATIVE DISCUSSION Have pairs discuss the speaker's observations about the aftermath of war. Remind them that the poet wrote about mundane chores as well as extraordinarily emotional tasks. Have partners share their conclusions with the class.

ASK STUDENTS to share any questions they generated in the course of reading and discussing the selection.

Someone has to drag in a girder
15 to prop up a wall.
Someone has to glaze a window,
rehang a door.

Photogenic it's not,
and takes years.
20 All the cameras have left
for another war.

We'll need the bridges back,
and new railway stations.
Sleeves will go ragged
25 from rolling them up.

Someone, broom in hand,
still recalls the way it was.
Someone else listens
and nods with unsevered[1] head.
30 But already there are those nearby
starting to mill about[2]
who will find it dull.

From out of the bushes
sometimes someone still unearths
35 rusted-out arguments
and carries them to the garbage pile.

Those who knew
what was going on here
must make way for
40 those who know little.
And less than little.
And finally as little as nothing.

In the grass that has overgrown
causes and effects,
45 someone must be stretched out
blade of grass in his mouth
gazing at the clouds.

COLLABORATIVE DISCUSSION What part of cleaning up after a war is the most difficult? With a partner, discuss the speaker's observations about this. Cite specific evidence from the text to support your answer.

---

[1] **unsevered:** not cut off; not separated.
[2] **mill about:** move idly or aimlessly.

ENGLISH LANGUAGE SUPPORT

Language: Phrasal Verbs Explain to students that a **phrasal verb** is a verb and another word that function as one. Together they convey a slightly different meaning than the verb does by itself. Point out the verb *clean up* in line 2. Explain that *clean up* implies cleaning and putting things in order.

ASK STUDENTS to use context clues to define the following phrasal verbs from the poem: *straighten up* (line 4), *rolling up* (line 25), *stretched out* (line 45).

Determine Figurative Meanings and Tone

RL 4, L 5a

In poetry, an author's word choices, and the images that those words create, help convey the speaker's meaning and set the **tone,** or attitude toward the subject. Analyzing the precise meanings of words and phrases that a poet uses can deepen your understanding of the poem. You can analyze the significance of Wisława Szymborska's word choices in "The End and the Beginning" by looking at the elements outlined in this chart.

Imagery	Connotation	Tone
Poets often use **imagery,** or descriptive words and phrases that re-create sensory experiences for the reader. Imagery usually appeals to one or more of the five senses—sight, hearing, smell, taste, and touch—to help readers imagine exactly what is being described. For example, the striking image of "corpse-filled wagons" passing through rubble-lined roads calls to mind photographs that most readers will have seen of war-torn, bombed out cities. The image helps the reader identify with what the speaker is observing. Look for other images in the poem that engage your senses and evoke a strong emotional response.	Poets choose words and expressions not only for their **denotative,** or dictionary, meanings, but also for their **connotative,** or subjective, meanings. Connotative meanings suggest feelings or ideas that go beyond the dictionary definitions. For example, look at these three possible word choices: • "someone has to clean up" • "someone has to tidy up" • "someone has to reorganize" In line 2, Szymborska chose to use *clean up*. This phrase suggests dirtiness and also casts blame on those who made the mess. The words *tidy up* and *reorganize* would not have conveyed the same precise meaning.	A poet's choice of language conveys his or her **tone,** or attitude. Elements to consider when evaluating tone include • words with positive or negative connotations • use of informal language such as idioms or colloquial expressions • repetition of significant words or ideas Szymborska repeats the word *someone* throughout this poem. The use of this indefinite pronoun adds an impersonal quality to the poem, yet the effect of war is intensely personal.

The End and the Beginning **353**

CLOSE READ

Determine Figurative Meanings and Tone

RL 4, L 5a

Explain that poets are economical yet very precise about their use of words. They generally use few words, so they choose each word very carefully to convey meanings that are sometimes both literal and figurative. Point out that poets use figurative and sensory language to appeal to readers' senses and allow them to experience the poem. Review with students the elements in the chart and the corresponding examples from the poem.

Point out that recognizing tone in literature is essential to gaining meaning, just as recognizing a person's tone of voice is essential to understanding what they are actually saying. Explain that tone is shaped by figurative language and imagery, as well as by the topic.

Strategies for Annotation   🖋 📱 *Annotate it!*

Determine Figurative Meanings and Tone

RL 4, L 5a

Share these strategies for guided or independent analysis:

• Highlight in blue descriptive words and phrases that create images for the reader.
• Underline instances of repetition or parallelism that serve to emphasize words or ideas.
• On notes, explain how the images and the repetition help express the poet's attitude toward the subject, or tone.

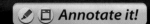

Someone, broom in hand,

still recalls the way it was.

Someone else listens and nods with unsevered₁ head.

But already there are those nearby

starting to mill about₂ who will find it dull.

The End and the Beginning **353**

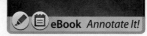
PRACTICE & APPLY

Analyzing the Text   RL 1, RL 2, RL 4, RL 6, L 5a

Possible answers:

1. The poet may be commenting on what those who survived the war have lost—including their past selves. Along with their innocence, their individual identities have been erased. The use of "someone" also emphasizes that war is a universal tragedy, not contained to just one country or generation.

2. The language is informal, which helps the reader identify with the speaker. (Examples include "clean up," "straighten themselves out," "get mired," "drag in a girder," "photogenic it's not.") The speaker is focused on the immediate task at hand, but is also jaded, aware that somewhere "another war" is inevitable. Beginning in line 30, the speaker recognizes the possibility of a gradual healing and a future for a younger generation unscarred by war.

3. The phrase refers to the arduous, dirty work necessary to rebuild the country. Images such as "corpse-filled wagons," "scum and ashes, sofa springs, splintered glass, and bloody rags" reinforce the horror, and the mention of a need for new girders, bridges, and railways stations shows the enormous scope of the destruction.

4. The grass symbolizes regeneration and growth. The idle person in line 45, not burdened with reconciling the past, and has never experienced the horrors of war.

5. Rather than moving from the beginning to the end, the title refers to the passage of time between the end of the war and the beginning of a life free from its effects. It "takes years," but eventually the aftermath "must make way for those" who no longer labor under its influence.

6. World War II and its aftermath inform Szymborska's war-weary, matter-of-fact tone. Poland suffered significant losses of life and property during the war, and the ruined infrastructure, the presence of Auschwitz and other abandoned death camps, and the buried shells and the material that "sometimes someone still unearths" provide constant reminders to "those who knew." Only those who know "as little as nothing" of such strife have the capacity to escape its oppressive psychological effects.

Analyzing the Text   RL 1, RL 2, RL 4, RL 6, W 9a, SL 1a, L 5a

Cite Text Evidence   Support your responses with evidence from the selection.

1. **Infer** Notice how the speaker repeats the word "someone" throughout the poem. What statement about war is she making by using an indefinite pronoun rather than referring to a specific person?

2. **Analyze** Answer these questions to explore how Szymborska creates the tone of the poem. Cite words and phrases from the poem to support your answers.
   - Does the speaker use formal or informal language? What is the effect of this choice?
   - What is the speaker's attitude toward the situation he or she is describing?
   - How does the tone of the poem change beginning with line 30?

3. **Interpret** In line 18, the speaker says the aftermath of war is not "photogenic." What images in the poem reinforce this idea about war? How does she show the dimensions of the devastation?

4. **Interpret** Reread the last stanza of the poem. What does the grass **symbolize,** or represent? What does the speaker mean when she describes someone as being "stretched out / blade of grass in his mouth / gazing at the clouds"?

5. **Draw Conclusions** Consider why Szymborska titled her poem "The End and the Beginning" rather than using the more common order "The Beginning and the End." How does the title reflect the message of the poem? Reread stanzas 5 and 10 and explain how they reflect this message.

6. **Connect** Poland experienced great political unrest and upheaval during Szymborska's lifetime: Nazi and Soviet occupations during World War II, postwar repressive Communist control, decades-long resistance of workers against the Communist regime, and, in 1989, the election of a new, non-Communist government. How does Poland's political situation inform Szymborska's choice of subject and her tone in "The End and the Beginning"?

PERFORMANCE TASK

Writing Activity: Reflection Szymborska uses vivid images that, on a literal level, describe the physical activity of recovering from a war. Think about how the images also have a figurative meaning, related to the work of rebuilding a government and a society that have been destroyed by war.

1. Select two examples of imagery from the poem and analyze the meaning of the images as they relate to rebuilding a government or a society.

2. Write a brief explanation of the figurative meaning of each image that you chose.

3. Share and discuss your findings with a partner.

Assign this performance task.

PERFORMANCE TASK   W 9a, SL 1a, L 5a

Writing Activity: Reflection Have students gather or recall photos that depict destruction caused by war. Have them think of words that convey those images and evoke figurative meanings. As they analyze the text, have them consider how Szymborska followed a similar process when writing the poem. Have them explore the literal and figurative meanings of the images they chose from the poem, and then work in pairs to compare and contrast interpretations.

Determine Theme

RL 2

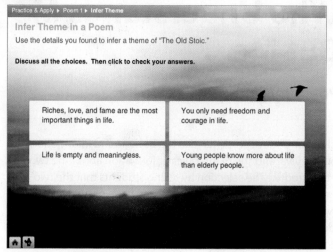

TEACH

Remind students that Wisława Szymborska was a Polish poet who lived through the invasion and occupation of Poland by Nazi Germany during World War II. Then explain the following concepts:

- A poem's **theme** is its central message or insight about life.
- A theme is different from the **topic** of a poem. Topic refers to the general subject that the poem is about, for example, war. Theme refers to a message or point the author wants to make about war.
- Poets use their own experiences, as well as world events, to inform their poetry and develop their themes.
- Understanding a poet's background and the circumstances under which he or she lived and wrote helps readers determine the messages and insights the poet wants to share with readers.

PRACTICE AND APPLY

Tell students that many poems have been written about war. Ask students to browse poetry anthologies or poetry web sites on the Internet to select one poem that has war or the after effects of war as its topic. Ask students to research the poem's context by finding out about the author and where and when the poem was written. Then have them present their poems to the class, explaining the poem's theme and its historical context.

Determine Figurative Meanings and Tone

RL 4, L 5a

RETEACH

Remind students that **figurative meanings** are words that let readers picture what the author says beyond the words' literal meaning. Figurative meanings shape the tone of a literary work. Explain that **tone** is the writer's attitude toward the subject and that tone influences meaning. Select a poem that exemplifies this effect of tone, such as Edgar Allan Poe's "The Raven."

- If the poem is short enough, read it in its entirety. In the case of "The Raven," read the first four or five stanzas.
- Ask students to point out images that stand out in the poem, for example, in "The Raven," they might point to the dying ember that "wrought its ghost upon the floor" or the "sad uncertain rustling of each purple curtain." Have students note words that stand out or are repeated, e.g. *rapping, chamber door,* and *Lenore* in "The Raven."
- Have students think of what feelings or attitudes (tone) an author conveys through figurative language and repetition.

 LEVEL UP TUTORIALS Assign the following *Level Up* tutorial: **Imagery**

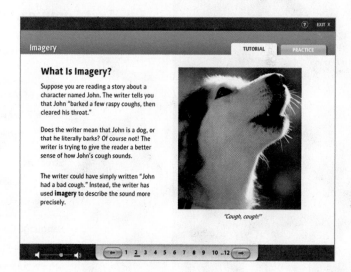

INDEPENDENT READING

Students can apply the skill to a poem in a book or magazine, or to song lyrics, which are poems set to music. Have them identify figurative language and determine tone. Ask: What images does the author conjure up? What feelings do these images convey?

Poems About Survival

The Survivor

Who Understands Me But Me

Poem by Marilyn Chin

Poem by Jimmy Santiago Baca

Why These Texts

Readers of poetry may have trouble analyzing how poets use figurative language to create the poem's tone, or the poet's attitude toward the subject. With the help of the close-reading questions, students will identify words in the texts that create and convey the tone in each poem. They will also analyze how the tone can change within a poem.

Background Have students read the background information about survival and the biographical information about the two poets. Introduce the selection by telling students that the two poems they are about to read address the issue of survival. "The Survivor" explores how to survive in an unfriendly culture. "Who Understands Me But Me" explores the issue of surviving physical and mental imprisonment.

AS YOU READ Tell students to pay close attention to the figurative language in each poem and to think about the poet's attitude toward the subject.

Standards Support

- cite strong and thorough textual evidence
- determine the meaning of words and phrases, including figurative and connotative meanings
- analyze the cumulative impact of specific word choices on meaning and tone

▲ Text Complexity Rubric

	The Survivor Lexile: N/A	Who Understands Me But Me Lexile: N/A
Quantitative Measures		
Qualitative Measures	Levels of Meaning/Purpose single level of complex meaning	Levels of Meaning/Purpose multiple levels of complex meanings
	Structure free verse, no particular patterns	Structure free verse, no particular patterns
	Language Conventionality and Clarity some figurative language	Language Conventionality and Clarity ambiguous language requiring inferences
	Knowledge Demands some cultural and literary knowledge useful	Knowledge Demands fairly complex theme
Reader/Task Considerations	Teacher determined	Teacher determined

Strategies for CLOSE READING

Determine Figurative Meanings and Tone

Students should read each poem closely, noting the poet's word choices and thinking about the positive or negative connotations of those words. Close-reading questions will help students identify the words and images that create the tone of each poem. As they read, students should jot down in the margins notes or comments on each poem.

WHEN STUDENTS STRUGGLE . . .

To help students understand how figurative meanings create tone in a poem, have them work in small groups to fill out a chart like the one shown below.

CITE TEXT EVIDENCE For practice analyzing figurative meanings and the tone such language conveys, ask students to analyze this line from "The Survivor," identifying words that create tone.

Line from the Poem:
"All the tempests will render still; seas will calm, horses will retreat, voices to surrender."
Phrases with Figurative or Connotative Meanings That Convey the Tone:
"tempests will render still," "calm," "retreat," "surrender"
Description of the Tone:
The speaker is relieved that things will calm down.

Background *Someone once said, "It is not the strongest or the most intelligent who will survive but those who can best manage change." Adapting to new surroundings and learning how to survive in them is challenging, be it a new school, a new house, or even a new culture. In the selections below, poets* **Marilyn Chin** *and* **Jimmy Santiago Baca** *explore the theme of survival.*

Poems About
Survival

The Survivor. . . . . Marilyn Chin
Who Understands Me But Me . . . . Jimmy Santiago Baca

Marilyn Chin *was born in Hong Kong and grew up in Portland, Oregon. Known as an "activist" poet, Chin frequently confronts themes of cultural assimilation and feminism. In an essay about American poetry, she writes, "My poetry both laments and celebrates my 'hyphenated' identity. . . My work is seeped with the themes and travails of exile, loss and assimilation. What is the loss of country if not the loss of self?"*

Jimmy Santiago Baca *has said, "I don't know if I would have lived had I not found poetry." He was born in New Mexico, of Apache and Chicano ancestry. Raised at first by a grandmother, he was a runaway at the age of 13. Convicted of drug charges, he was sentenced to a maximum security prison, where he began to turn his life around. He learned to read and write, and discovered his love of poetry. Since his release, he has published poetry, memoirs, and a screenplay.*

91

1. **READ ▶** As you read lines 1–16 of "The Survivor," begin to collect and cite text evidence.

• Circle repeating words in lines 1–4.
• Underline text that describes the "you" in the poem.
• In the margin, explain what must be relinquished in lines 15–16.

3. **READ ▶** As you read lines 1–38 of "Who Understands Me But Me," begin to collect and cite text evidence.

• Underline each thing the speaker lives without in lines 1–16.
• In the margin, explain what setting the speaker evokes in lines 1–16.
• In the margin, explain what the speaker finds when he follows the tracks (lines 30–38).

The Survivor
Marilyn Chin

B Don't tap your chopsticks against your bowl.
Don't throw your teacup against the wall in anger.
Don't suck on your long black braid and weep.
Don't tarry around the big red sign that says
5 "danger!"
All the tempests will **render** still; seas will calm,
horses will retreat, voices to surrender.
That you have this way and not that,
that your skin is yellow, not white, not black,
10 that you were born not a boychild but a girl,
that this world will be forever puce-pink are just as well.
Remember, the survivor is not the strongest or
most clever;
merely, the survivor is almost always the youngest.
A 15 And you shall have to relinquish that title
before long.

render:
to cause to become

The title of "youngest" must be relinquished

2. **◀ REREAD** Reread lines 6–7 of "The Survivor." Determine how the tone of these lines differs from the preceding lines (1–5). Support your answer with explicit textual evidence.

In lines 6–7, the tone changes from one of rebellion and harshness to one of resolve and relief. Phrases such as "seas will calm, / horses will retreat" offer solace from the reprimands in the previous lines that begin with "Don't."

Who Understands Me But Me
Jimmy Santiago Baca

C They turn the water off, so I live without water,
they build walls higher, so I live without treetops,
they paint the windows black, so I live without sunshine,
they lock my cage, so I live without going anywhere,
5 they take each last tear I have, I live without tears,
they take my heart and rip it open, I live without heart,
they take my life and crush it, so I live without a future,
they say I am beastly and fiendish, so I have no friends,
they stop up each hope, so I have no passage out of hell,
10 they give me pain, so I live with pain,
they give me hate, so I live with my hate,
they have changed me, and I am not the same man,
they give me no shower, so I live with my smell,
they separate me from my brothers, so I live without brothers,
15 who understands me when I say this is beautiful?
who understands me when I say I have found other freedoms?

I cannot fly or make something appear in my hand,
I cannot make the heavens open or the earth tremble,
I can live with myself, and I am amazed at myself, my love,
20 my beauty,
I am taken by my failures, astounded by my fears,
I am stubborn and childish,
in the midst of this wreckage of life they **incurred**,
I practice being myself,
25 and I have found parts of myself never dreamed of by me,

These images of higher walls, black windows, and a locked cage evoke a prison setting.

incur:
become liable or subject to

92

93

---

1. **READ AND CITE TEXT EVIDENCE** Encourage students to use a dictionary to define any unfamiliar words such as *tarry* ("linger" or "hang around"), *puce* ("a dark red"), and *relinquish* ("give up").

A **ASK STUDENTS** to identify what is meant by "that title" (line 15) that the speaker is told she will have to relinquish. *Being the youngest; presumably the speaker will soon no longer be the youngest.*

2. **REREAD AND CITE TEXT EVIDENCE**

B **ASK STUDENTS** to describe the tone of lines 1–5 and to identify words that help create that tone. *The tone is one of anger and derision. The repetition of the word* Don't *and the phrase* in anger *help create the tone.*

Critical Vocabulary: render (line 6) Have students share their definitions of *render*.

3. **READ AND CITE TEXT EVIDENCE** Have students think of a place that might have windows painted black, high walls, and locks on the doors. *jail, prison*

C **ASK STUDENTS** to identify details in lines 1 through 4 that help them understand that people other than the speaker are controlling what he can and cannot do. *"they turn the water off," "they build walls higher," "they paint the windows black," "they lock my cage"*

Critical Vocabulary: incur (line 23) Point out that *incur* can also mean "to bring down something upon oneself." Ask students to cite the details in line 23 that describe what "they" incurred. *"wreckage of life"*

FOR ELL STUDENTS Tell students that a fiend is an evil or wicked person. Have students explain the meaning of *fiendish*.

goad:

to urge or prod

they were **goaded** out from under rocks in my heart
when the walls were built higher,
when the water was turned off and the windows painted black.
I followed these signs

D 30   like an old tracker and followed the tracks deep into myself,
followed the blood-spotted path,
deeper into dangerous regions, and found so many parts of myself,
who taught me water is not everything,
and gave me new eyes to see through walls,

35   and when they spoke, sunlight came out of their mouths,
and I was laughing at me with them,
we laughed like children and made pacts to always be loyal,
who understands me when I say this is beautiful?

The speaker finds "so many parts of myself" and "new eyes to see through walls"

4. ◀ **REREAD**   Reread lines 29–38 of "Who Understands Me But Me."
Interpret the tone, and support your answer with textual evidence.

Baca's tone is triumphant. The inward journey, "I followed these signs like an old tracker and followed the tracks deep into myself," ends in triumph and joy as parts of the self are found: "sunlight came out of their mouths" and "we laughed like children."

SHORT RESPONSE

Cite Text Evidence   How do the two writers use figurative language to convey contrasting tones within their poems? **Cite textual evidence** in your response.

Both writers use powerful imagery to convey an experience of being confined by the expectations or actions of others. Chin's line, "Don't suck on your long black braid and weep," and Baca's line, "They turn the water off, so I live without water," are examples of this confinement. As Chin's poem finds resolve, "seas will calm," Baca's contrasting imagery is ecstatic: "new eyes to see through walls, and when they spoke, sunlight came out of their mouths." With the change of tone in each poem, we witness survival.

94

---

4. ⬛ REREAD AND CITE TEXT EVIDENCE

D **ASK STUDENTS** to find details in lines 29–38 that have figurative meanings that help them visualize the inward journey that the speaker made. *Possible responses: "deep into myself," "deeper into dangerous regions," "found so many parts of myself," "gave me new eyes to see through walls," "sunlight came out of their mouths," "I say this is beautiful."*

Critical Vocabulary: goad (line 26) Have students compare their definitions and use *goad* in a sentence. *For example: We had to goad her to write the essay.*

SHORT RESPONSE

Cite Text Evidence   Students' responses will vary, but they should cite evidence from the text to support their answers. Students should:

- describe the contrasting tones in each poem.
- explain how the tone of each poem changes.
- cite specific evidence from the text to support their ideas.

TO CHALLENGE STUDENTS . . .

The poems of Marilyn Chin and Jimmy Santiago Baca were written partly to explain how they managed to survive—and still manage to survive—under harsh circumstances. Everyone has difficulties to endure, and what might seem minor to one person can be a huge obstacle to another.

ASK STUDENTS to write a short poem about a person successfully struggling against adversity. The poem can be about themselves, someone they know, a fictitious character, or about a general situation. Encourage students to use language that suits the tone they want to communicate. Volunteers can share their completed poems with the rest of the class.

DIG DEEPER

With the class, return to Question 4, Reread. Have students share and discuss their answers.

ASK STUDENTS to work in small groups to describe the tone in the beginning of the poem. Have students cite evidence from the text to support their thinking.

- Have students identify the point at which the tone of defiance in the beginning of the poem begins to change. *(line 16)*
- Have students describe the tone of lines 16–25. *They may describe the tone as one of determination.*
- After students have traced the development of the tone throughout the poem, have volunteers from each group use their findings to read aloud for the class all or part of the poem "Who Understands Me But Me."

ASK STUDENTS to return to their response to Question 4, Reread, and expand it to include a discussion about how the tone changes as the poem progresses.

A MATTER OF LIFE OR DEATH

The FYI site provides links to online articles from a variety of magazines and newspapers. Help students choose a few articles to read to further their exploration of the topic A Matter of Life or Death.

NOVELWISE

Students can unlock the power of novels with this unique resource. Help students read through longer works with these tips:

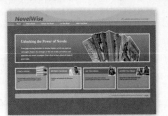

- Find a Book
- Before You Read
- As You Read
- After You Read

Each book includes introductory material, worksheets, graphic organizers, and discussion guides.

ADDITIONAL TEXTS BY COLLECTION

Suggest students read the following:

- "The Lady, or the Tiger?" by Frank R. Stockton
- "The Interlopers" by Saki
- from *A Journal of the Plague Year* by Daniel Defoe
- "The Lady of Shalott" by Alfred, Lord Tennyson

Ask students to choose a work, read it, and analyze the characters. What motivates the protagonist to act the way he or she does? How are other characters affected by his or her actions?

NONFICTION CONNECTIONS

Suggest that students increase their reading of informational texts. The nonfiction connections include

- speeches
- diaries
- true-life accounts
- newspaper articles
- political cartoons

Creating an Independent Reading Program

TEACHER GUIDANCE AND FEEDBACK REGARDING TEXT SELECTION AND PROGRESS

Students can benefit from the teacher's knowledge of literary and informational texts as teachers evaluate students' progress.

- As students delve into their books, ask them if the selection seems easy, hard, or about right. If it's about right, is it holding the student's interest?
- In private, have each student read one to three pages aloud. Keep track of miscues, and ask a few comprehension questions.
- Make recommendations based on your assessment. If the student is struggling, suggest easier texts. If the student isn't challenged, suggest other selections that require more effort.
- Have students set a goal: for example, learning a certain number of new words. They can track their goals in their progress reports.

STUDENT-TEACHER CONFERENCING

One-on-one conferencing helps teachers keep track of students' progress and reactions. The individual conference helps students evaluate their progress and get suggestions for further reading.

- Ask students why they chose the work and how they reacted to it. Did they enjoy it and if so, why? What new information did they learn? What did they do when they got to a word they didn't know? What relevance did the book have to their experiences?
- Listen carefully to their responses and give feedback where appropriate. Make additional recommendations to encourage further reading. If a student likes a selection, suggest works in the same series or by the same author.
- Before students begin their post-reading logs or activities, ask them if they have questions or need clarification before they start.

Write an Argument

Based on the evidence from at least three selections, would you say that survival requires selfishness? Synthesize your ideas by writing an argument in support of your position.

An effective argument

- makes a persuasive claim and develops it with valid reasons and relevant evidence from the texts
- anticipates counterclaims and addresses them
- establishes clear, logical relationships among claims, counterclaims, reasons, and evidence
- includes a logically structured body, including transitions
- has a satisfying conclusion that effectively summarizes the claim

W 1a–e Write arguments to support claims in an analysis.
W 4 Produce clear and coherent writing.
W 5 Develop and strengthen writing.
W 9a–b Draw evidence from literary or informational texts.

Mentor Text See how this example from "Is Survival Selfish?" makes smooth transitions from one idea to the next.

> " In Yates' case, he had time to think hard about the odds, and the possibilities he was facing, and to realize that he couldn't save anyone but himself. But what about people who have to make more instantaneous decisions? "

PLAN

Analyze the Texts Reread *Night*, taking notes about survival. Is it necessary to be selfish in order to survive a selection? Then choose two other texts from the collection and make notes about survival in those texts, too.

Use the annotation tools in your eBook to find evidence from your chosen texts. Save each piece of evidence to *my*Notebook, in a folder titled *Collection 5 Performance Task*.

ACADEMIC VOCABULARY

As you build your argument about survival, be sure to use these words.

dimension
external
statistic
sustain
utilize

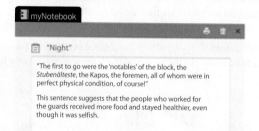

myNotebook

"Night"

"The first to go were the 'notables' of the block, the *Stubenälteste*, the Kapos, the foremen, all of whom were in perfect physical condition, of course!"

This sentence suggests that the people who worked for the guards received more food and stayed healthier, even though it was selfish.

WRITE AN ARGUMENT

W 1a–e, W 4, W 5, W 9a–b

Introduce students to the Performance Task by reading the introductory paragraph with them and reviewing the criteria for an effective argument. Clarify that their claim will answer the question *Does survival require selfishness?* and that they will support the claim with evidence from *Night* and two other selections. Students may complete this Performance Task in connection with their studies of survival instinct or survival struggles in their science or social studies classes. Coordinate with other teachers as appropriate.

PLAN

ANALYZE THE TEXTS

Suggest that students consider the most effective way to use the annotation tools in their eBooks as they take notes and gather evidence. For example, they might organize their evidence into categories—the central ideas in their argument—and use a different color of highlighting for each category. They can also use color coding to organize handwritten notes.

WHEN STUDENTS STRUGGLE

Analyze the Texts Explain to students that understanding both sides of an argument can help them develop claims and counterclaims fairly. Let students work in small groups to analyze the collection texts. For each text, have them identify the survival situations addressed and then discuss their thoughts about whether selfishness was necessary in each situation. Suggest that they use a chart like the one shown to take notes during the discussion.

Text	Survival Situation	Was Selfishness Necessary?
Night		
"Is Survival Selfish?"		
Deep Survival		

PERFORMANCE TASK A

PLAN

DEVELOP COUNTERARGUMENTS

To identify counterclaims, students might share their claims with a partner and discuss possible objections to them. Emphasize that a counterclaim should be a serious position that a person who has thought about the issue of survival might take. Once each partner has one or two counterclaims to work with, suggest that students help each other brainstorm keywords that they can use to search for more information online.

PRODUCE

DRAFT YOUR ESSAY

Remind students that their purpose is to be persuasive. As they draft their arguments, they should keep in mind the people who will be reading their essays. What will persuade these readers to accept their claim about survival? Point out that the crucial element in any argument is logic: every idea must be supported by evidence, and each sentence must follow logically from the one before it.

LANGUAGE AND STYLE

Have students work with partners to identify places in their drafts where they can use transitions to link ideas. In addition to emphasizing similarities or differences, point out that transitions also introduce examples or additional details (*in addition, moreover, for instance*) and show cause-and-effect relationships (*consequently, as a result, therefore*).

Make a Claim Write a claim that clearly and concisely states your position. Your claim is effective if

- it makes your position on the issue clear to readers
- you have reasons that will persuade your readers to agree
- you can support the claim with sufficient evidence from the texts

Develop Counterarguments What might your readers say to oppose your claim? Think of at least two counterclaims that a reader might make. Decide how you would respond to each counterclaim. You may need to conduct further research. Outline the reasons and evidence for your counterarguments.

Get Organized Organize your ideas in an outline, using the notes from your analysis. Be sure to include a clearly stated claim supported by sufficient reasons and evidence. Present counterclaims and refute them with counterarguments supported by additional evidence.

PRODUCE

Draft Your Essay Write a well-organized draft of your argument. Think about your purpose and audience as you write.

- Introduce your argument in a memorable way that will grab the attention of your readers. Clearly state your claim.
- Present your reasons, evidence, and counterarguments in logically ordered paragraphs.
- Explain how the evidence from the texts supports your ideas.
- Use transitions to connect reasons and evidence to your claim.
- Use formal language and a respectful tone.
- Write a persuasive conclusion that summarizes your position.

Language and Style: Transition Words

Look for places in your argument where you can use transition words to link ideas, events, or reasons. Read this passage from *Deep Survival*.

> " Survivors aren't fearless. They *use* fear: they turn it into anger and focus. Conversely, searchers are always amazed to find people who have died while in possession of everything they needed to survive. "

Note how Gonzales uses *conversely* to show that the ideas about survivors and people who give up are being contrasted. His use of the word makes the relationship between the ideas clearer.

Interactive Lessons
To help you plan your essay, complete the following lesson:
- Writing Arguments: What Is a Claim?

my WriteSmart

Write your rough draft in *myWriteSmart*. Focus on getting your ideas down, rather than perfecting your choice of language.

Interactive Lessons
To help you draft your essay, complete the following lessons in *Writing Arguments:*
- Creating a Coherent Argument
- Formal Style

ENGLISH LANGUAGE SUPPORT

Justify Opinions Help students understand that arguments are organized around reasons and evidence. Explain that each reason should answer a *Why* question about their claim. The evidence may include relevant facts, details, examples, or quotations from the collection texts, additional research, or their own background knowledge. Ask partners to share their reasons and evidence. Suggest that they ask their each other the following questions:

- Have I listed my reasons in a logical order, or would my argument be more convincing if I rearranged them?

- What questions do you have about how my reasons and evidence are related?
- What are my strongest and weakest pieces of evidence? Why?
- How could I strengthen my counterarguments?

Students should use their partner's feedback to help them organize their ideas into an outline and draft their essays.

Improve Your Draft Have your partner or group of peers use the questions in the chart to review your draft.

Have your partner or a group of peers review your draft in *my*WriteSmart. Ask your reviewers to note any reasons that do not support the claim or that lack sufficient evidence.

Interactive Lessons
To help you revise your essay, complete the following lesson:
· Writing as a Process: Revising and Editing

Questions	Tips	Revision Techniques
Does the introduction grab the audience's attention and include a clearly stated claim?	**Underline** the attention-grabbing text. **Highlight** the claim.	**Add** an attention-grabber. **Add** a claim or **rework** the existing one to make it clearer.
Do at least two valid reasons support the claim? Is each reason supported by relevant and sufficient evidence?	**Highlight** each reason. **Underline** each piece of evidence.	**Add** reasons or revise existing ones to make them more valid. **Insert** relevant evidence to ensure that your support is sufficient.
Do transitions connect reasons and evidence to the claim?	**Underline** each transition.	**Add** words, phrases, or clauses to connect related ideas that lack transitions.
Do I maintain a formal style throughout the argument?	**Highlight** slang and informal language.	**Reword** text to replace informal language with formal language.
Are counterclaims acknowledged and refuted with counterarguments?	**Underline** any sentence that addresses a counterclaim. **Highlight** the sentences that refute them.	**Add** sentences that identify audience concerns, and address those opposing claims.
Does the conclusion effectively summarize the argument?	**Highlight** the summary of the argument.	**Add** sentences to restate your argument.

PRESENT

Share with a Group Read your argument to a small group. Your classmates should listen and take notes. Do they understand your position? Have you persuaded them to agree with your argument? Be prepared to respond to any comments or questions.

PERFORMANCE TASK A

REVISE

EXCHANGE ESSAYS

Instruct peer reviewers to focus their feedback on two or three techniques from the chart so that they do not overwhelm their partners with too many details. Remind students that they will be sharing their arguments in small groups. Suggest that they practice reading their essays aloud as a final revision tool. As they listen to themselves read, they may realize that some logical connections are not clear or that they need to state their ideas more persuasively.

PRESENT

SHARE WITH A GROUP

Other options for sharing students' essays include
· posting them on the school's website
· hosting another class for a panel discussion of ideas raised in the essays

TO CHALLENGE STUDENTS...

Debate the Topic Challenge students to argue opposing viewpoints in a timed formal debate. Students may adapt their arguments to present opening statements, rebuttal arguments, and closing statements. Instruct students to take notes on their opponents' opening statements to help them prepare their rebuttals.

PERFORMANCE TASK A

USE THE SCORING RUBRIC

Have students exchange the final draft of their arguments with a partner. Then ask them to use the rubric to score their partner's argument. They should write a paragraph explaining their reasons for the scores they give in each category.

REFLECT ON THE PROCESS

Tell students that taking the time to reflect on the writing process in this task will help them apply what they learned in future assignments. Ask students to think about how well their arguments persuaded the audience. Then have them answer the following questions:

- What strategies did you use to engage readers in your introduction?
- How well did you connect your claims, counterclaims, reasons, and evidence?
- How did writing your argument affect your views about survival and selfishness?

PERFORMANCE TASK A RUBRIC
ARGUMENT

	Ideas and Evidence	Organization	Language
4	• The introduction is memorable and persuasive; the claim clearly states a position on a substantive topic. • Valid reasons and relevant evidence from the texts convincingly support the writer's claim. • Counterclaims are anticipated and effectively addressed with counterarguments. • The concluding section effectively summarizes the claim.	• The reasons and textual evidence are organized consistently and logically throughout the argument. • Varied transitions logically connect reasons and textual evidence to the writer's claim.	• The writing reflects a formal style and an objective, or controlled, tone. • Sentence beginnings, lengths, and structures vary and have a rhythmic flow. • Spelling, capitalization, and punctuation are correct. If handwritten, the argument is legible. • Grammar and usage are correct.
3	• The introduction could do more to capture the reader's attention; the claim states a position on an issue. • Most reasons and evidence from the texts support the writer's claim, but they could be more convincing. • Counterclaims are anticipated, but the counterarguments need to be developed more. • The concluding section restates the claim.	• The organization of reasons and textual evidence is confusing in a few places. • A few more transitions are needed to connect reasons and textual evidence to the writer's claim.	• The style is informal in a few places, and the tone is defensive at times. • Sentence beginnings, lengths, and structures vary somewhat. • Several spelling and capitalization mistakes occur, and punctuation is inconsistent. If handwritten, the argument is mostly legible. • Some grammatical and usage errors are repeated in the argument.
2	• The introduction is ordinary; the claim identifies an issue, but the writer's position is not clearly stated. • The reasons and evidence from the texts are not always logical or relevant. • Counterclaims are anticipated but not addressed logically. • The concluding section includes an incomplete summary of the claim.	• The organization of reasons and textual evidence is logical in some places, but it often doesn't follow a pattern. • Many more transitions are needed to connect reasons and textual evidence to the writer's position.	• The style becomes informal in many places, and the tone is often dismissive of other viewpoints. • Sentence structures barely vary, and some fragments or run-on sentences are present. • Spelling, capitalization, and punctuation are often incorrect but do not make comprehending the argument difficult. If handwritten, the essay may be partially illegible. • Grammar and usage are incorrect in many places, but the writer's ideas are still clear.
1	• The introduction is missing. • Significant supporting reasons and evidence from the texts are missing. • Counterclaims are neither anticipated nor addressed. • The concluding section is missing.	• An organizational strategy is not used; reasons and textual evidence are presented randomly. • Transitions are not used, making the argument difficult to understand.	• The style is inappropriate, and the tone is disrespectful. • Repetitive sentence structure, fragments, and run-on sentences make the writing monotonous and hard to follow. • Spelling and capitalization are often incorrect, and punctuation is missing. If handwritten, the argument may be partially or mostly illegible. • Many grammatical and usage errors change the meaning of the writer's ideas.

Participate in a Panel Discussion

This collection focuses on the ways people endure devastating experiences. Look back at the anchor text, "The End and the Beginning," and at the other texts in the collection. How do individuals and communities adapt to radically different situations in order to survive? Synthesize your ideas by holding a panel discussion about how each selection shows people adapting for survival.

An effective participant in a panel discussion

- makes a clear, logical, and well-defended generalization about the ways people adapt for survival in one of the selections
- uses quotations and specific examples to illustrate ideas
- responds thoughtfully and politely to the ideas of the moderator and other panel members
- evaluates other panel members' contributions
- summarizes the discussion by synthesizing ideas

SL 1a–d Initiate and participate effectively in a range of collaborative discussions.

SL 3 Evaluate a speaker's point of view, reasoning, and use of evidence.

SL 4 Present information, findings, and supporting evidence.

SL 6 Adapt speech to a variety of contexts and tasks.

PLAN

Get Organized Work with your classmates to prepare for a panel discussion.

- Join a group of four classmates and select one student to be the moderator for your discussion.
- As a group, choose three texts from the collection, including "The End and the Beginning," for your group to discuss. Each student who is not the moderator will be the expert on one of these texts. Decide which student will focus on each text.
- Create a format for your discussion—a schedule that shows the order in which members of the panel will speak and for how long. It will be the moderator's job to keep the discussion on schedule.
- Set rules regarding the appropriate times for the moderator or the audience (your classmates) to ask panel members questions.

 myNotebook

Use the annotation tools in your eBook to find evidence that supports your ideas about how people adapt for survival. Save each piece of evidence to your notebook.

ACADEMIC VOCABULARY

As you share what you learned from your assigned text, try to use these words.

dimension
external
statistic
sustain
utilize

PARTICIPATE IN A PANEL DISCUSSION

SL 1a–d, SL 3, SL 4, SL 6

Introduce the Performance Task by reading the introductory paragraph with students and reviewing the criteria for effective participation in a panel discussion. If students have not held a panel discussion before, explain that in this format, several experts on a topic hold a discussion in front of an audience. Panel members take turns sharing what they know about the topic, and then the audience is invited to ask questions.

Students may complete this Performance Task in connection with their studies of natural disasters or other devastating events in history. Coordinate with other teachers as appropriate.

PLAN

GET ORGANIZED

Tell students to be sure to complete all the steps under "Get Organized," since they lay the groundwork for the rest of the task. Let students know the total amount of time each group will have for their panel discussion so that they can plan accordingly.

As groups decide which texts to discuss, remind them to keep in mind the topic of the discussion: How do individuals and groups adapt in order to survive? They should select the texts they believe will give them the best material to explore this topic.

PERFORMANCE TASK B

PLAN

GATHER EVIDENCE

Point out that, during the discussion, panel members will mostly be summarizing or paraphrasing evidence from the texts. However, students should look for a few brief, pithy quotations in each selection that they can weave into the conversation. Well-chosen quotations will demonstrate their familiarity with the texts and will also help engage the audience's interest.

PRODUCE

WRITE AND PRACTICE

Advise students to organize their notes in a way that allows them to quickly locate any information they need to make a point or answer a question. Also emphasize that panel members will make their opening remarks based on an outline instead of reading word-for-word from a written statement. They should be familiar enough with their topic to speak directly to the panel and to the audience, glancing down at their notes only as needed.

Gather Evidence Analyze your assigned text. Gather evidence that you will use to discuss adaptation and survival. Note specific details, examples, and quotations. Ask yourself these questions as you take notes:

- How do the people in your text adapt to their situation in order to survive?
- What aspects of a person's character allow some people to adapt more easily to devastating situations?
- What kinds of external forces affect a person's ability to adapt to a devastating experience?
- What generalization, or broad conclusion, can you make about how people adapt to devastating events in order to survive?

During this time, the moderator should make a list of relevant questions to be asked during the panel discussion.

Interactive Lessons
To help you prepare for your discussion, complete these lessons:
- Participating in Collaborative Discussions: Preparing for Discussion
- Using Textual Evidence: Synthesizing Information

Write and Practice Work individually to outline your ideas about your assigned text. Then practice with your group.

- State a clear generalization about the ways people adapt to devastating experiences.
- Write several central ideas that support your generalization. Each idea should relate your generalization to the text.
- Match each piece of evidence with the central idea it most clearly supports. Provide clear examples.
- Present your ideas to your group, using vocabulary that is specific to the domain of your assigned text. The moderator will ask questions about your ideas and examples, preparing you to "think on your feet" during the real discussion.
- If you are the moderator, use this time to decide how to introduce and conclude the discussion. Write a statement that tells the audience the topic and format. Write notes for a concluding statement. Be ready to modify your remarks if new ideas emerge from the discussion.

Write your outline in *myWriteSmart.* Focus on getting your ideas down, rather than perfecting your choice of language.

Interactive Lessons
To help you practice your discussion, complete the following lesson:
- Speaking Constructively

ENGLISH LANGUAGE SUPPORT

Plan a Panel Discussion Note that in a collaborative discussion, precise language and verbal and nonverbal techniques can help participants engage and inform an audience. Remind students their outlines will serve as a general road map that they can refer to during the discussion; however, they may not have time to present every piece of evidence. Before students practice, suggest the following strategies as they review their outlines:

- Make sure your main ideas and evidence are ordered logically. Highlight your strongest quotations and examples to remind you to refer to them.

- Circle any words that you're unsure how to pronounce. Consult a dictionary to confirm the pronunciation.
- Jot down phrases you might use when responding to other panelists, such as *I see your point about _____, but _____* and *I heard you say _____, and I haven't thought about that before. However _____.*

REVISE

Reinforce Your Ideas Based on the practice session and the rubric on the following page, make changes to your outline. Consider the following questions:

- Were you able to defend your generalization? If not, revise your statement so that it better reflects your textual evidence and your central ideas.

- Were you able to answer the moderator's questions clearly and without hesitation? If not, you may need to reorganize your outline so that you can find the information you need more quickly and easily.

- Did the moderator's questions help you see your text in a new light? If so, add new evidence to your outline that you can share during the real discussion.

myWriteSmart

Have your partner or a group of peers review your outline in *my*WriteSmart. Ask your reviewers to note any evidence that does not support your generalization about how people adapt for survival.

Interactive Lessons
To help you revise your outline, complete the following lesson:
· Participating in Collaborative Discussions: Listening and Responding

PRESENT

Have the Discussion Now it's time to present your panel discussion before the rest of the class. Have your outline at hand for reference during the discussion.

- Begin by having the moderator introduce the topic, the panelists, and the basic format for the discussion. The moderator will then ask the first question and continue to facilitate the discussion in the agreed-upon format.

- Use your outline to remind you of your main points, but try to speak directly to the panel and to the audience. Don't just read from your paper. Use domain-specific vocabulary.

- Listen closely to what all speakers say so that you can respond appropriately.

- Sustain a respectful tone toward your fellow panel members, even when you disagree with their ideas.

- When all the panelists have made their statements and discussed ideas amongst themselves, the moderator should invite audience members to ask questions.

- Conclude by having the moderator summarize the discussion and thank the panelists for their participation.

Summarize Write a summary of the main points from the discussion. Then explain whether the discussion made you rethink your generalization, and why.

PERFORMANCE TASK B

REVISE

REINFORCE YOUR IDEAS

Students' outlines provide a written record of their work that you may use, along with their participation in the panel discussion and their summaries, to assess their performance on this task. If you plan to collect the outlines for this purpose, let students know in advance.

PRESENT

HAVE THE DISCUSSION

If possible, give students the option of videotaping their panel discussions. They can use the videos to review and critique their own performance later. Groups might also select clips to post on the school's website.

WHEN STUDENTS STRUGGLE...

Take Notes Explain that listening carefully during the discussion will help students evaluate others' points of view and respond thoughtfully to each panelist. As students prepare their final outlines, suggest that they fold their papers lengthwise and write their ideas and evidence in the left column. Students can then use the right column to take notes on other panelists' points during the discussion. Remind students to look for and highlight connections between other panelists' points and their own ideas and evidence.

My Points	Other Panelists' Points

PERFORMANCE TASK B

USE THE SCORING RUBRIC

Have student audience members use the rubric to score discussion panelists. Assign a different student to score each panelist. Students should use the language of the rubric to explain the reasons for the score they gave.

REFLECT ON THE PROCESS

Explain to students that taking the time to reflect on their performance in this task will help them apply what they learned and improve their skills. Ask them to think about how effectively they prepared for and contributed to their discussions. Then have groups answer and discuss the following questions:

- How effective was the organization and the format of our discussion? What would you do differently in a future discussion?

- What connections did you make between the different ideas and evidence presented?

- What insights did you gain from the discussion? How did the discussion influence your views about how people adapt for survival?

PERFORMANCE TASK B RUBRIC
PANEL DISCUSSION

	Ideas and Evidence	Organization	Language
4	• The panelist clearly states a valid generalization and supports it with strong, relevant ideas and well-chosen evidence from the texts. • The panel member carefully evaluates others' evidence and reasoning and responds with insightful comments and questions. • The panelist synthesizes the analysis of the texts to help listeners understand the generalization.	• The panelist's remarks are based on a well-organized outline that clearly identifies the generalization and the supporting ideas and evidence. • The panelist concludes with a statement that reinforces the generalization and includes the ideas that have emerged from the discussion.	• The panelist adapts speech to the context of the discussion, using appropriately formal English to discuss the texts and ideas. • The panelist consistently quotes accurately from the texts to support ideas. • The panelist uses domain-specific language throughout the discussion. • The panel member consistently maintains a polite and thoughtful tone throughout the discussion.
3	• The panelist states a generalization and supports it with relevant ideas and evidence from the texts. • The panel member evaluates others' evidence and reasoning and responds with appropriate comments and questions. • The panelist synthesizes some ideas and links to the generalization.	• The panelist's remarks are based on an outline that identifies the generalization, supporting ideas, and evidence. • The panelist concludes with a statement that reinforces the generalization.	• The panelist mostly uses formal English to discuss literature and ideas. • The panelist mostly quotes accurately from the texts to support ideas. • The panelist uses domain-specific language a few times during the discussion. • The panel member maintains a polite and thoughtful tone throughout most of the discussion.
2	• The panelist states a reasonably clear generalization and supports it with some ideas and evidence. • The panel member's response to others' comments shows limited evaluation of the evidence and reasoning. • The panelist does not synthesize ideas but simply repeats the generalization in a vague way.	• The panelist's remarks reflect an outline that may identify the generalization but does not organize ideas and evidence very effectively. • The panelist makes a weak concluding statement that does little to reinforce the generalization.	• The panelist uses some formal and some informal English to discuss the texts and ideas. • The panelist's quotations and examples sometimes do not accurately reflect the texts. • The panelist rarely uses domain-specific language. • The panel member occasionally forgets to maintain a polite tone when responding to others' comments and questions.
1	• The panelist's generalization is unclear; ideas and evidence are not coherent. • The panel member does not evaluate others' evidence and reasoning. • The panelist does not synthesize ideas.	• The panelist does not follow an outline that organizes ideas and evidence. • The panelist's remarks lack any kind of conclusion or summary.	• The panelist uses informal English and/or slang, resulting in a lack of clarity. • The panelist's quotations and examples do not accurately reflect the texts. • The panelist does not use domain-specific language. • The panel member does not maintain a polite tone when responding to others' comments and questions.

TO CHALLENGE STUDENTS...

Gather Additional Evidence Challenge students to research additional details, examples, and quotations that relate to insights they gained from their discussions. Encourage them to gather information from sources outside of the collection texts. Ask students to add a section to their discussion summaries that reflects this additional evidence.

Image Credits: ©Oliver Burston/Ikon Images/Getty Images

Heroes and Quests

"If a journey doesn't have something to teach you about yourself, then what kind of journey is it?"

—Kira Salak

PLAN

STREAM TO START

Motivate students to read the collection texts and spark their curiosity about the collection by watching the video in class. After students watch the video, ask them to think about two things they hope to learn from reading about the journeys people make for knowledge, curiosity, necessity, or a combination of reasons. Call on volunteers to share their responses.

PERFORMANCE TASK PREVIEW

Point out to students that they will complete a performance task at the end of the collection. The performance task will require them to further analyze the selections in the collection and to synthesize ideas about these analyses. They will present their findings in a variety of products.

ACADEMIC VOCABULARY

Students can acquire facility with the academic vocabulary words through frequent, repeated exposure as they analyze and discuss the selections in the collection. Academic vocabulary can be used in the following instructional contexts. This will enable students to incorporate the academic vocabulary words into their working vocabulary.

- Collaborative Discussion at the end of each selection
- Analyzing the Text questions for each selection
- Selection-level Performance Task
- Vocabulary instruction (for Critical Vocabulary and/or for Vocabulary Strategy)
- Language and Style
- End-of-collection Performance Task for all selections in the collection

ASK STUDENTS to review the Academic Vocabulary word list for this collection. You may wish to pronounce each word aloud, so students hear the correct pronunciation. Then discuss the definitions and the related forms for each word. Remind students that they will encounter these five academic vocabulary words throughout the collection.

Heroes and Quests

The hero's journey takes many forms, from traveling through forbidding places to exploring the mind.

Stream to Start   hmhfyi.com   Channel One News®

COLLECTION
PERFORMANCE TASK Preview

At the end of this collection, you will have the opportunity to complete a task:

- Write an analytical essay about why people undertake arduous journeys.

ACADEMIC VOCABULARY

Study the words and their definitions in the chart below. You will use these words as you discuss and write about the texts in this collection.

Word	Definition	Related Forms
motivate (mō′tə-vāt′) *v.*	to provide a cause for doing something	motivation, motivational
objective (əb-jĕk′tĭv) *n.*	an intention, purpose, or goal	objectively, subjective
pursuit (pər-sōot′) *n.*	the action of chasing or following something	pursue, pursuer
subsequent (sŭb′sĭ-kwĕnt′) *adj.*	coming after or following	subsequently, sequential
undertake (ŭn′dər-tāk′) *v.*	to assume responsibility for or take on a job or course of action	undertaking, undertook

364

▤ myNotebook

- As students read, analyze, and discuss the texts in this collection, encourage them to use the *my*WordList folder in *my*Notebook to build their own personal word lists.
- **Annotate** Students can highlight vocabulary terms and other unfamiliar words and save each highlighted term to *my*Notebook.
- **Organize** Within *my*Notebook, students can drag each word into the *my*WordList folder.
- **Elaborate** Ask students to add details to the entry for each word, such as a definition, other forms of the word, and a sample sentence.

English Language Support

▶ **View It!**
Professional Development Podcast:
English Language Learners

ENGAGE WITH THE COLLECTION TOPIC

Draw students' attention to the collection title: Heroes and Quests. Clarify that a quest is a journey taken to search for or to accomplish something. Explain that the texts in the collection explore why and how people undertake different quests. The collection also presents truths that the people and characters learn.

ACCESS PRIOR KNOWLEDGE Ask students to explain what heroes are and why quests are important. What do heroes represent, or mean, to people? Are heroes always good or positive, or can heroes cause bad things to happen? Why do people go on quests? What are they looking for? Is a physical journey the only way to learn about yourself or the people around you?

THIS IS ABOUT/THIS IS REALLY ABOUT

Use this strategy to help students determine the central idea of the texts in this collection.

- **First,** direct students to read a specific passage in a text and to be ready to explain what the passage is about. Once they've read it, have them report their findings. Record and display their ideas. Have the class compare ideas, distinguish main ideas from details, and highlight the main ideas. Explain that the highlighted phrases represent the group's initial thoughts about the passage.
- **Then,** have students work individually to determine which highlighted idea best expresses all or part of the

main idea. Form small groups to compare conclusions and to agree on the idea that best captures the passage's main idea. Record and display the groups' ideas.
- **Next,** facilitate a class discussion about editing the list. For each idea, ask, "This says the passage is about ____, but what is the passage really about?"
- **Finally,** have students rejoin their groups and use what they've learned to write a complete and accurate summary of the passage.

Collection 6 Digital Resources for English Language Support

INTERACTIVE WHITEBOARD LESSONS

Use the Interactive Whiteboard Lessons to provide additional support on:

- theme/central idea
- citing textual evidence
- plot and conflict

LEVEL UP TUTORIALS

Students can access *Level Up* Tutorials from their eBooks to get additional help with analyzing literature, analyzing informational text, reading skills, vocabulary skills, and language conventions.

COLLECTION 6 DIGITAL OVERVIEW

| my SmartPlanner | eBook | myNotebook | my WriteSmart | fyi hmhfyi.com |

Collection 6 Lessons	Media	Teach and Practice

Student Edition | eBook

▶ Video Links HISTORY A&E Channel One News

Close Reading and Evidence Tracking

ANCHOR TEXT — Epic Poem by Homer from the *Odyssey*	◀ **Audio** from the *Odyssey* ▶ **Video HISTORY®** *Odysseus: Curse of the Sea*	**Close Read Screencasts** • Modeled Discussion 1 (Book 1, lines 5–15) • Modeled Discussion 2 (Book 17, lines 9–20) • Close Read application pdf (Book 23, lines 54–67) — **Strategies for Annotation** • Analyze Figurative Meanings
CLOSE READER — Excerpt from Epic Poem by Homer "The Cyclops" from the *Odyssey*	◀ **Audio** "The Cyclops" from the *Odyssey* ▶ **Video HISTORY®** *Odysseus: Curse of the Sea*	
Travel Writing by Kira Salak from *The Cruelest Journey: 600 Miles to Timbuktu*	◀ **Audio** from *The Cruelest Journey: 600 Miles to Timbuktu*	**Strategies for Annotation** • Analyze Ideas and Events • Denotation and Connotation
CLOSE READER — Nonfiction by David Finkel from *The Good Soldiers*	◀ **Audio** from *The Good Soldiers*	
Argument by Michael Griffin "The Real Reasons We Explore Space"	◀ **Audio** "The Real Reasons We Explore Space"	**Strategies for Annotation** • Delineate and Evaluate an Argument • Transitions
Poem by Mary Oliver "The Journey"	◀ **Audio** "The Journey"	**Strategies for Annotation** • Interpret Figurative Language
Collection 6 Performance Task: Research and Write an Analytical Essay	fyi **hmhfyi.com**	**Interactive Lessons** **A** Writing an Informative Text **B** Conducting Research **A** Writing as a Process **B** Using Textual Evidence

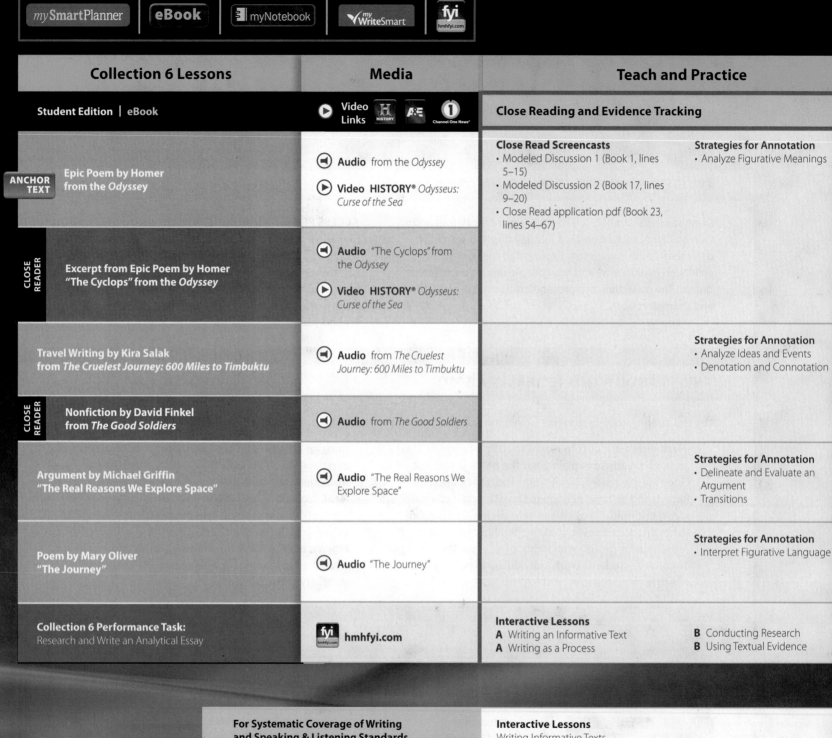

For Systematic Coverage of Writing and Speaking & Listening Standards	**Interactive Lessons** Writing Informative Texts Giving a Presentation

Assess		Extend	Reteach
Performance Task	✓ *Assess It Online!*	**Teacher eBook**	**Teacher eBook**
Writing Activity: Narrative	Selection Test	**Analyze Character**	**Analyze Author's Choices > *Level Up* Tutorial >** Universal and Recurring Themes
Writing Activity: Analysis	Selection Test	**Write an Analysis > Interactive Whiteboard Lesson >** Write an Analysis	**Analyze Ideas and Events > *Level Up* Tutorial >** Reading for Details
Writing Activity: Editorial	Selection Test	**Determine Meaning and Analyze Ideas**	**Delineate and Evaluate an Argument > *Level Up* Tutorial >** Analyzing Arguments
Speaking Activity: Discussion	Selection Test	**Analyze a Free Verse Poem > Interactive Whiteboard Lessons >** Poetry: Language and Form	**Interpret Figurative Language > *Level Up* Tutorial >** Figurative Language
Research and Write an Analytical Essay	Collection Test		

Lesson Assessments Writing Informative Texts Giving a Presentation	**Standards Support and Enrichment**	For more instruction and practice in reading literary and informational texts, language, spelling, and speaking and listening, see Teacher Resources > Standards Support and Enrichment.

Collection 6 Lessons	Key Learning Objective	Performance Task
ANCHOR TEXT EXEMPLAR **Epic Poem by Homer** from the *Odyssey*, p. 365A	**The student will be able to…** analyze elements of an epic poem, such as plot, setting, theme, and character as well as its figurative language	Writing Activity: Narrative
Travel Writing by Kira Salak from *The Cruelest Journey: 600 Miles to Timbuktu*, p. 421A **Lexile 1030L**	**The student will be able to…** determine the central idea of a text, analyze the ideas and events presented, and cite text evidence	Writing Activity: Analysis
Argument by Michael Griffin "The Real Reasons We Explore Space," p. 433A **Lexile 1170L**	**The student will be able to…** delineate and evaluate an argument	Writing Activity: Editorial
Poem by Mary Oliver "The Journey," p. 441A	**The student will be able to…** interpret figurative language	Speaking Activity: Discussion

Collection 6 Performance Task:

Research and Write an Analytical Essay

Vocabulary Strategy	Language and Style	Differentiated Instruction	CLOSE READER Selection
Words from Latin	Absolute Phrases	**English Language Support:** 366, 370, 372, 377, 381, 382, 386, 391, 396, 400, 405, 406, 407, 411 **When Students Struggle:** 365, 367, 374, 378, 383, 384, 387, 390, 392, 398, 403, 408, 410, 414, 416 **To Challenge Students:** 373, 380, 385, 388, 395, 402, 409, 415	Excerpt from Epic Poem by Homer "The Cyclops" from the *Odyssey*, p. 420b
Denotation and Connotation	Sentence Length	**English Language Support:** • Identify Present Participles as Different Parts of Speech • Language: Conjunctions **When Students Struggle:** • Drawing Conclusions • Vocabulary: Context Clues **To Challenge Students:** • Infer Reasons • Investigate Additional Details	Nonfiction by David Finkel from *The Good Soldiers*, p. 432b **Lexile 1050L**
Synonyms and Antonyms	Transitions	**English Language Support:** • Vocabulary: Multiple-Meaning Words • Vocabulary: Synonyms and Antonyms **When Students Struggle:** Reasons and Evidence **To Challenge Students:** Analyze Language	
		English Language Support: Comprehension Support	
	Cite Sources	**English Language Support:** Understand Text Structure **When Students Struggle:** Analyze the Texts **To Challenge Students:** Hold a Discussion	

ANCHOR TEXT EXEMPLAR

from the Odyssey

Epic Poem by Homer   Translated by Robert Fitzgerald

Why This Text?

Students encounter references to the characters, plot, and themes of the *Odyssey* in literary works and in other contexts. This lesson explores some of the hero Odysseus's best-known adventures as well as his homecoming.

Key Learning Objective: The student will be able to analyze elements of an epic poem, such as plot, setting, theme, and character, as well as its figurative language.

For additional practice:

Close Reader selection
from the Odyssey, The Cyclops
Epic Poem by Homer

RL 1 Cite textual evidence.

RL 2 Determine a theme of a text.

RL 3 Analyze how complex characters develop over the course of a text.

RL 4 Determine the meaning of words and phrases used in the text.

RL 5 Analyze an author's choices concerning how to structure a text, order events, and manipulate time.

RL 6 Analyze a particular cultural experience reflected in literature from outside the United States.

W 3a Write narratives to engage and orient the reader.

W 3d Use precise words and phrases, telling details, and sensory language.

L 1b Use various types of phrases.

L 4c Consult reference materials to determine meaning.

L 5a Interpret figures of speech in context.

▲ Text Complexity Rubric

Quantitative Measures	***from the* Odyssey** Lexile: N/A
Qualitative Measures	**Levels of Meaning/Purpose** multiple levels of meaning (multiple themes)
	Structure complex structures
	Language Conventionality and Clarity many unfamiliar, academic, or domain-specific words
	Knowledge Demands increased amount of cultural and literary knowledge useful
Reader/Task Considerations	• Teacher determined • Vary by individual reader and type of text • See the Text X-Ray for suggested Reader/Task Considerations.

English Language Support

Before teaching, use the Text X-Ray below for an overview of the text's complexity. The Text X-Ray and the supports and scaffolds in the Teacher's Edition will help you guide students of different skill levels.

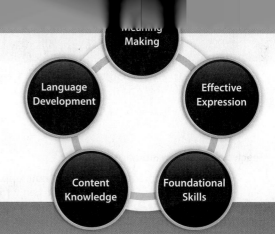

Meaning Making

Language Development

Effective Expression

Content Knowledge

Foundational Skills

Text Complexity: Qualitative Measures

Levels of Meaning/Purpose

multiple levels of meaning (multiple themes)

Help students analyze character and the epic hero.

- Teacher's Edition side notes, pp. 365, 368, 370–377, 379, 381, 383, 390–391, 394–399, 402–403, 405, 410
- English Language Support, p. 370
- When Students Struggle, pp. 383–384, 390, 403, 410, 414
- Close Read Screencasts, pp. 371, 401
- Analyze Character: Epic Hero, p. 399

Guide students to determine theme and support inferences.

- Teacher's Edition side notes, pp. 384, 387, 389, 404, 414

To teach analyzing archetypal characters, see

- Analyze Character, p. 420a

ZOOM IN ON **ANALYZING CHARACTER** Point out to students that in Greek literature, the **epic hero** has human flaws as well as extreme bravery, intelligence, and strength. Use these questions to help students **infer** Odysseus' traits in Book 9.

- What can you infer about Odysseus from his description of the "Cyclops" in lines 56–67? *(He values law and community, because he calls the giants "rough" and "indifferent," "without a law to bless them." He considers farming a sign of civilization, because he criticizes the ignorant giants for not plowing or sowing the ground.)*
- What character traits does Odysseus show in lines 111–115? *(He shows cunning and preparedness by bringing drink and food to subdue the giant.)*
- What does the recollection in lines 125–132 reveal about Odysseus? *(He is humble enough to show regret for the mistake he made by endangering his men.)*

Structure

complex structures

Help students analyze the structure of the epic poem.

- Teacher's Edition side notes, pp. 365, 367, 371, 373, 375–378, 381–382, 384–388, 392, 393, 401–414, 416, 417
- When Students Struggle, pp. 365, 367, 374–375, 378–379, 387, 392, 398, 408, 416
- Analyze Author's Choices: Epic Poem, p. 417

To reteach analyzing the author's choices in structuring the epic poem, see

- Analyze Author's Choices: Epic Poem, p. 420a

Guide students to analyze representations in different mediums.

- Teacher's Edition side note, p. 369

▶ *Use It!* *Level Up* Tutorial: Universal and Recurring Themes

ZOOM IN ON **ANALYZING AUTHOR'S CHOICES** Divide the text among small groups. Have each group read their section and discuss the following questions:

- Where does the action take place?
- What events happen in this section? How do these events reveal Greek values, such as courage, loyalty, intelligence, and love of home?

Have groups share their answers in a whole-class discussion. Then have students read the entire selection with these ideas in mind.

Language Conventionality and Clarity

many unfamiliar, academic, or domain-specific words

Teach unfamiliar vocabulary in context.

- Teacher's Edition Critical Vocabulary notes, pp. 371, 378, 379, 382, 387, 388, 393, 396, 400, 404, 405, 408, 409, 410, 414, 419
- English Language Support, pp. 372, 381, 382, 391, 405
- Applying Academic Vocabulary, pp. 376, 389, 412

Help students analyze figurative meanings.

- Teacher's Edition side notes, pp. 366, 374, 378, 380, 386, 396, 407, 408, 413, 415, 417
- English Language Support, pp. 396, 407
- Strategies for Annotation, pp. 393, 413, 417
- Analyze Figurative Meanings, p. 417

Support students in analyzing language.

- English Language Support, pp. 366, 377, 386, 400, 406, 411, 419
- Vocabulary Strategy: Prefixes, p. 400; Words from Latin, p. 419
- Language and Style: Absolute Phrases, p. 420

ZOOM IN ON ANALYZING FIGURATIVE LANGUAGE Before reading, tell students that the poem includes several types of **figurative language.** Preview the figurative language by sharing the following examples:

- An **allusion** is an indirect reference to a well-known person, place, event, or literary work. The selection opens with an allusion to the Muses, daughters of Zeus who devoted themselves to the arts. "Sing in me, Muse" refers to Calliope, the Muse of epic storytelling.
- A **simile** is a comparison using *like* or *as*: "Like pipes his nostrils jetted." A **metaphor** is a direct comparison, as in these metaphors for flowing blood: "crimson runnels, a river of mortal red" (Book 22, lines 17–18).
- An **epithet** is a phrase used to describe someone. One epithet for Odysseus is "the master of battle" (Book 22, line 118).

Knowledge Demands

increased amount of cultural and literary knowledge useful

Support English Learners in understanding the historical and cultural context of the epic poem.

- Teacher's Edition side note, p. 368
- Teacher's Edition Background note, p. 369

 For more context and historical background, students can view the video "Odysseus: Curse of the Sea" in their eBooks.

ZOOM IN ON BUILDING CULTURAL KNOWLEDGE Tell students that references to Homer's characters and stories abound not only in literature and the arts, but also in everyday English language. For example, someone with "the patience of Penelope" has the ability to wait a long while, referring to Penelope's long wait for Odysseus. Likewise, a "siren song" is an attractive but false promise, referring to the beautiful songs of the Sirens that led sailors to their death.

Suggested Reader/Task Considerations

You might consider the following before assigning this epic poem to students.

- Will the text inspire students to develop an interest in Greek mythology or other mythologies?
- Will students struggle to comprehend the vocabulary used in the poem?

ZOOM IN ON SUPPORTING COMPREHENSION

- Inform students that mythologies provide windows into the values and beliefs of other cultures. Encourage students to share what they know about Greek mythology or other mythologies.
- Have students listen to an audio recording and focus on understanding the major events. Then, have pairs read closely, identifying and defining unfamiliar text as they go.

The Epic

*Extraordinary heroes in pursuit of hideous monsters. Brutal battles fought and perilous quests undertaken. Spectacular triumphs and crushing defeats. The epic, still very much alive in today's novels and movies, began thousands of years ago in the oral tradition of ancient Greece. There, listeners gathered around poet-storytellers to hear the daring exploits of the hero Odysseus. Across storm-tossed seas, through wild forests, amid countless dangers and subsequent narrow escapes, the hero, motivated by a singular focus on his objective, prevails against all odds. It's no wonder that Homer's **Odyssey** remains one of the most beloved epics in Western literature. It captivates us and carries us off into a time and place quite different from—yet somehow similar to—our own.*

Characteristics of the Epic

An **epic** is a long narrative poem. It recounts the adventures of an epic hero, a larger-than-life figure who undertakes great journeys and performs deeds requiring remarkable bravery and cunning. As you begin your own journey through Homer's epic, you can expect to encounter the following elements.

Elements of the Epic	
Epic Hero • Possesses superhuman strength, craftiness, and confidence • Helped or harmed by gods or fate • Embodies qualities valued by the culture • Overcomes perilous situations	**Archetypes** Characters and situations recognizable across times and cultures • brave hero • evil temptress • sea monster • loyal servant • suitors' contest • buried treasure
Epic Plot Depicts a long, strange journey filled with such complications as • strange creatures • divine intervention • treacherous weather • large-scale events	**Epic Themes** Reflect universal concerns, such as • courage • the fate of a nation • loyalty • life and death • beauty • a homecoming
Epic Setting • Includes fantastic or exotic lands • Involves more than one nation or culture	

CLOSE READ

The Epic

Epic Hero, Plot, and Setting Call on volunteers to read the bullet points that describe the epic hero, the plot, and the setting. Tell students that an epic is more than an adventure story; it has an outcome that significantly affects the destiny of a nation or group of people.

Explain that the epic hero has extraordinary abilities but also human frailties. He moves with confidence through a world fraught with uncertainties. Even with his flaws, the ideal qualities he embodies create an image to which others might aspire.

Point out that an epic hero's journey includes many challenges, often supernatural in origin. These obstacles in the way of his goals provide him with the opportunity to prove that he possesses the traits of a true hero. In the Greek and Roman epics, various gods intercede on behalf of the hero, helping him to overcome his enemies.

Epic Archetypes and Themes Read the descriptions of archetypes and epic themes aloud as students follow along in their books. Ask students to identify other archetypes with which they are familiar, such as the warrior princess or traitorous friend.

Tell students that they can expect more than one theme to be developed in the epic. Remind them that theme is the message about life that the poet conveys through the characters and plot.

WHEN STUDENTS STRUGGLE . . .

Draw a web on the board with the five elements of the epic surrounding the center oval labeled "Epic." Brainstorm with students a list of stories from literature or film that seem to fit the description of an epic.

Then organize students into small groups. Assign each group a story from the list with which all group members are familiar.

ASK STUDENTS to list examples from their assigned story for each element in the web that help explain whether or not the story is an epic. Discuss the epic characteristics that groups believe their stories have.

The Language of Homer

Similes Remind students that they have encountered similes in other literary works. Make sure they understand that an epic simile is more elaborate than a simile in a short poem. Explain that a simile does more than make a comparison; it also conveys an idea about what is being described. For example, a writer might compare someone's voice to the melody of an angelic harp or the wailing of an emergency siren. Discuss the differences between each comparison.

Epithets Clarify that the word *epithet* has multiple meanings. It can also refer to "an abusive or nasty phrase." To ensure that students understand the epithets that they will find in the epic, have them make up one or more that they would like used to describe themselves, such as "Nadia, player of soccer" or "Carlos, master of computers." Ask how epithets would influence the opinions formed about the person being described.

Allusions Write the words *allusions* and *illusions* on the board. Call on volunteers to define each. Explain that allusions refer to something or someone outside of the work itself. While writers may expect their audience to be familiar with the allusions they use, allusions in classic works of literature help provide historical context from the period in which they were written.

The Language of Homer

Since Homer's work originated as ancient Greek verse, you will read an English translation. Many translations of the *Odyssey* have appeared over the years, and each translator has interpreted it differently. Consider, for example, these two passages from Book 2. The first adopts a formal tone that is much closer to the original. The second version employs a more conversational voice.

Translation 1	Translation 2
When Primal Dawn spread on the eastern sky her fingers of pink light, Odysseus's true son stood up, drew on his tunic and mantle, slung on a sword-belt and a new-edged sword, tied his smooth feet into good rawhide sandals, and left his room, a god's brilliance upon him. —translated by Robert Fitzgerald (1961)	Dawn came, showing her rosy fingers through the early mists, and Telemachus leapt out of bed. He dressed himself, slung a sharp sword over his shoulder, strapt a stout pair of boots on his lissom feet, and came forth from his chamber like a young god. —translated by W.H.D. Rouse (1937)

The people of ancient Greece who first experienced the *Odyssey* heard it sung in a live performance. The poet, or another performer, used epic similes, epithets, and allusions to help keep the audience enthralled.

- A **simile** is a comparison between two unlike things, using the word *like* or *as*. Homer often employs the **epic simile**, a comparison developed at great length over several lines. For example, the epic simile in the following passage compares an angry Odysseus to a roasting sausage.

> His rage
> held hard in leash, submitted to his mind,
> while he himself rocked, rolling from side to side,
> as a cook turns a sausage, big with blood
> and fat, at a scorching blaze, without a pause,
> to broil it quick: so he rolled left and right, . . .

- An **epithet** renames a person or thing with a descriptive phrase. To maintain the meter of the poem or complete a line of verse, the poet would often use an epithet containing the necessary number of syllables. For example, Homer often refers to Odysseus by such epithets as "son of Laertes" and "raider of cities."
- An **allusion** is a reference to a literary or historical person, place, event, or composition. For example, when Telemachus, Odysseus' son, beholds the palace of Menelaus, he exclaims, "This is the way the court of Zeus must be." Every listener in Greece immediately understood the allusion to Zeus, the ruler of the gods.

ENGLISH LANGUAGE SUPPORT

Comprehend Poetry Project on the board the first translation of the passage from Book 2 on this page. Point out to students that these lines make up one sentence.

- Explain that when they read a complicated sentence such as this one, they need to break it down into its simpler parts.
- Guide students to identify first the subject and then the compound verbs with their objects and modifiers. Mark these on the board.
- Point out the subordinate clause. Ask a volunteer to summarize the information this adds to the sentence.
- Ask for a volunteer to express the basic idea of these lines of poetry. (*At dawn, Odysseus's son got dressed and left his room.*)

Reading the Epic

Any journey through the *Odyssey* offers the reader a complex experience. On one level, Homer provides an action-packed narrative that makes us eagerly anticipate each thrilling step in the adventure. On another level, readers can analyze and appreciate the poem as a work of art. The following strategies can help you navigate your own voyage.

Reading the Epic as Narrative

- Pay close attention to the changing narrators. Who is telling the story at a given point? Consider the ways in which different narrators deepen your understanding of characters and events.
- Visualize the setting and the action by observing key details in the text.
- Note major events and conflicts and try to predict their outcomes. Use a chart like the one shown to track characters, including gods and goddesses. Categorize characters as friends or foes, and explain how they help or hinder Odysseus's efforts.

Characters Who Help	Characters Who Hinder
Goddess Athena pleads with Zeus to help Odysseus escape from Calypso's island.	The god Poseidon stirs up powerful storms that cause problems for Odysseus and his crew.

Reading the Epic as Poetry

- Read the epic aloud. Listen for sound devices, such as **alliteration, meter,** and **rhyme,** and notice how they reflect and enhance meaning.
- Follow punctuation closely, and remember that the end of a line does not indicate the end of a thought.
- Consider how imagery and figurative language, including epic similes, reveal characters and events. Note allusions and epithets.

Reading the Epic within the Context of Its Time

- Look closely at how Odysseus behaves. What character traits does he display? What do these traits tell you about the values of the time?
- Draw upon your own prior knowledge of ancient Greek civilization and history. What events and customs would have influenced Homer?
- Remember that the Greeks of Homer's time believed the gods took an active interest in human affairs. (In fact, the gods themselves behaved very much like humans.) How do such religious beliefs influence the epic?

CLOSE READ

Reading the Epic

Reading the Epic as Narrative Have a volunteer read the text aloud. Make sure students understand the meanings of these terms: *narrator, setting, conflict.* Review the types of conflicts that students might expect to find as Odysseus journeys home.

Reading the Epic as Poetry Read the bulleted points aloud as students follow along. Remind students that the meter is the rhythm, or beat, of the poem. Then define each of these terms: *alliteration, rhyme, imagery.* Ask volunteers to give examples of each.

Remind students that in figurative language, words are not always used in their literal sense but may instead be used to convey ideas and to evoke emotions in listeners. Have them discuss why imagery would be so useful in a poem spoken aloud to a group.

Reading the Epic within the Context of Its Time After students have read this section independently, discuss how heroes reflect the values, or what is important, to a particular society. Ask students to name modern heroes, real-life or fictional. Discuss what each shows about what is important to our society.

WHEN STUDENTS STRUGGLE . . .

On the board, list the italicized terms below. Write the examples in a second column in random order. Have pairs work to match each example.

- *alliteration:* sailing the seven seas
- *rhyme:* night of fright
- *imagery:* the sea exploded onto the rocky shore
- *simile:* jewels sparkled like stars in the night sky
- *character traits:* bravery, intelligence, thoughtfulness, loyalty

ASK STUDENTS to compare their answers with those of another student pair before going over them as a class.

Examining the Homeric Epics

The Trojan War Tell students that Troy, also known as Ilium, was an ancient seaport on the Aegean Sea in present-day Turkey. In the 1870s and 1880s, Heinrich Schliemann, a wealthy German businessman, excavated the site of ancient Troy. His findings suggest that the story of the Trojan War may be based on fact.

Have students reread the account of the Trojan horse. Ask them what this scheme suggests about the character of Odysseus. *(He was a clever, intelligent leader.)*

Heroism Tell students that Tell students that the name of the tendon in the back of the heel came from the story of Achilles. According to one version of the myth, his mother dipped him into the River Styx to make him immortal. But, because she was holding him by the heel, he could be injured there, and, in fact, died as a result of being hit by an arrow in that spot. A person's particular point of weakness is alluded to as his or her Achilles' heel.

The Intervention of Gods Tell students that Homer's epics are the earliest written record of ancient Greece. Make sure students understand that Greek mythology was not an organized system of religion; rather, some Greek myths explain natural occurrences or physical features; others tell entertaining stories; others pass down values, beliefs, and customs.

Examining the Homeric Epics

Considered the greatest masterpieces of the epic form, the *Iliad* and the *Odyssey* present high drama and intense emotions. In both books, important plot elements include the interference of gods in human affairs, the epic heroism of the central characters, and the saga of the Trojan War and its aftermath.

The Trojan War

The legendary conflict between Greece (or Achaea) and Troy began around 1200 BC. Paris, a Trojan prince, kidnapped Helen, the wife of Menelaus, king of Sparta. Menelaus recruited the armies of allied kingdoms to attack Troy and recover his wife. For ten years the Greek forces held Troy under siege, but they could not penetrate the walls of the city.

Finally, Odysseus, king of Ithaca, came up with a plan to break the stalemate. He ordered his men to build a giant wooden horse. One morning the people of Troy awoke to find that horse outside the city gates—and no Greeks in sight. Assuming the Greeks had retreated and had left the horse as a peace offering, they brought the horse inside the gates. They soon discovered, too late, that the horse was filled with Greek soldiers and that their city was doomed.

Heroism

Great heroes play key roles in Homer's epics. The *Iliad* tells the story of Achilles, the mightiest Greek warrior, and of his bitter quarrel with Agamemnon, brother of Menelaus and commander of the Greek forces at Troy. The tale climaxes in a fierce battle between Achilles and Hector, Paris's brother, and Hector's subsequent funeral.

The *Odyssey* recounts Odysseus' adventures as he struggles to make his way home from post-war Troy, along with the conflicts that arise in Ithaca just before and after his return. He prevails against gruesome monsters, enchanting women, and greedy rivals intent on preventing him from reaching his objective. Although Odysseus lacks the superhuman martial abilities of Achilles, he employs great cleverness and guile to get out of difficult situations.

The Intervention of Gods

Adding to the heroes' struggles are the residents of Mount Olympus, bickering gods who like nothing better than influencing and manipulating human affairs. For example, Athena, goddess of wisdom, supports the Greeks in the Trojan War; Aphrodite, goddess of love, sides with Troy. Further, the heroes often displease other gods who place additional obstacles in their paths. The Olympians display human shortcomings and petty jealousies, and people become pawns as the gods pursue advantages in their internal quarrels.

For more context and historical background, students can view the video "Odysseus: Curse of the Sea" in their eBooks.

Background Have students read the background information on Homer and the *Odyssey*. Explain that although Homer may have composed the *Odyssey* in the eighth century BC scholars believe that the epic recreates Greece's Bronze Age, an era that had ended approximately 500 years earlier, during which warrior chieftains lived in elaborate palaces and led colonizing expeditions to expand trade and territory. Display a map of the Aegean Sea area. Point out the location of Greece and the region in Turkey believed to be the site of the Trojan War. Explain that scholars have tried to correlate the places along Odysseus' route to places in the Mediterranean Sea.

Analyze Representations in Different Mediums
RL 7

Remind students that a subject can be represented in different mediums. Review that a medium is a vehicle for artistic expression. Examples include poems, stories, paintings, or films. Since each medium offers its own particular strengths and limitations, different artists often emphasize different aspects of the subject. The HISTORY video "Odysseus: Curse of the Sea" dramatizes key episodes from the Odyssey. After students have read Part 1, have them view the video. Ask these questions to compare how Homer presents Odysseus' encounter with the Cyclops to how it is depicted in the video:

How does the video present the story of the Cyclops? What parts of the story does it emphasize, and which parts does it withhold? *(By having the Cyclops make animal-like noises and repeatedly showing close-ups of his eye, the video makes him seems even more savage than in the text. The video also makes his eating of the men seem even more savage than in the text. The video does not leave out any parts of the story as told by Homer.)* How does the video portray the character of Odysseus? How is this portrayal similar to or different from Homer's portrayal? *(Odysseus' portrayal in the video is similar to Homer's characterization. Both versions emphasize that Odysseus is a clever and strong leader.)*

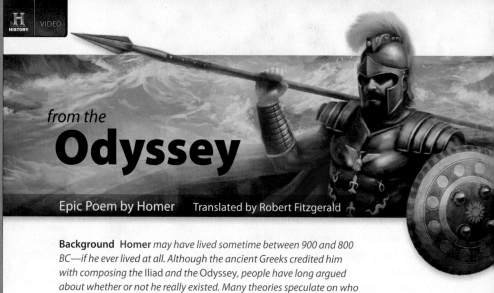

from the
Odyssey

Epic Poem by Homer   Translated by Robert Fitzgerald

Background Homer *may have lived sometime between 900 and 800 BC—if he ever lived at all. Although the ancient Greeks credited him with composing the* Iliad *and the* Odyssey, *people have long argued about whether or not he really existed. Many theories speculate on who Homer may have been and where he may have lived. Details in the stories suggest that he was born and lived in the eastern Aegean Sea, either on the islands of Chios or Smyrna, and that he was blind.*

Whatever position modern scholars take on the debate, most believe that one or two exceptionally talented individuals created the Homeric epics. The Iliad *and the* Odyssey *each contain 24 books of verse, but they probably predate the development of writing in Greece. The verses, which were originally sung, gradually became part of an important oral tradition. Generations of professional reciters memorized and performed the poems at festivals throughout Greece. By 300 BC, several versions of the books existed, and scholars undertook the job of standardizing the texts.*

Homer's poems profoundly influenced Greek culture and, as a result, contributed to the subsequent development of Western literature, ideas, and values. The Roman poet Virgil wrote a related poem, the Aeneid, *in Latin, and Odysseus appears in Dante's* Inferno. *Poets throughout English literature, from Geoffrey Chaucer in the Middle Ages to William Shakespeare in the Renaissance to John Keats in the Romantic era, have found inspiration in Homer. James Joyce's 1922 novel* Ulysses *(the Latin form of Odysseus' name) transforms one ordinary Dublin day into an Odyssean journey. Dozens of movies have retold the saga of the Trojan War and the long journey home, both directly and symbolically. For thousands of years people have taken the tales of a wandering Greek bard and made them their own.*

TEACH

CLOSE READ

Important Characters in the Odyssey

Display a three-column chart on the board similar to the one shown. For each book, read the names of the characters, allowing time for students to repeat them. Discuss the information given and then have students classify each character as a god/goddess; human; or other.

Record students' classifications in the chart. Ask them for a word or phrase to help identify the character. Have them copy the charts to keep as a reference throughout their reading.

Gods/ Goddesses	Humans	Other
Helios: sun god *Zeus:* ruler of gods and goddesses	*Telemachus:* son of Odysseus *Penelope:* wife of Odysseus	

Important Characters in the *Odyssey (in order of mention)*

Book 1

Helios (hē′lē-ŏs′)—the sun god, who raises his cattle on the island of Thrinacia (thrĭ-nā′shə)

Zeus (zo͞os)—the ruler of the Greek gods and goddesses; father of Athena and Apollo

Telemachus (tə-lĕm′ə-kəs)—Odysseus' son

Penelope (pə-nĕl′ə-pē)—Odysseus' wife

Book 9

Alcinous (ăl-sĭn′ō-əs)—the king of the Phaeacians (fē-ā′shənz)

Circe (sûr′sē)—a goddess and enchantress who lives on the island of Aeaea (ē-ē′ə)

Cicones (sĭ-kō′nēz)—allies of the Trojans, who live at Ismarus (ĭs-măr′əs)

Lotus Eaters—inhabitants of a land Odysseus visits

Cyclopes (sī-klō′pēz)—a race of one-eyed giants; an individual member of the race is a Cyclops (sī′klŏps)

Apollo (ə-pŏl′ō)—the god of music, poetry, prophecy, and medicine

Poseidon (pō-sīd′n)—the god of the seas, earthquakes, and horses; father of the Cyclops who battles Odysseus

Athena (ə-thē′nə)—the goddess of war, wisdom, and cleverness; goddess of crafts

Book 10

Aeolus (ē′ə-ləs)—the guardian of the winds

Laestrygones (lĕs′trĭ-gō′nēz)—cannibal inhabitants of a distant land

Eurylochus (yo͝o-rĭl′ə-kəs)—a trusted officer of Odysseus

Persephone (pər-sĕf′ə-nē)—the wife of Hades, ruler of the underworld

Tiresias (tī-rē′sē-əs) of Thebes (thēbz)—a blind prophet whose spirit Odysseus visits in the underworld

Book 11

Elpenor (ĕl-pē′nôr)—one of Odysseus' crew, killed in an accident

Book 12

Sirens (sī′rənz)—creatures, part woman and part bird, whose songs lure sailors to their death

Scylla (sĭl′ə)—a six-headed sea monster who devours sailors

Charybdis (kə-rĭb′dĭs)—a dangerous whirlpool personified as a female sea monster

Book 17

Argos (är′gŏs)—Odysseus' dog

Eumaeus (yo͞o-mē′əs)—a servant in Odysseus' household

Books 21–23

Antinous (ăn-tĭn′ō-əs)—a suitor of Penelope's

Eurymachus (yo͝o-rĭm′ə-kəs)—a suitor of Penelope's

Philoetius (fĭ-lē′shəs)—a servant in Odysseus' household

Amphinomus (ăm-fĭn′ə-məs)—a suitor of Penelope's

Eurynome (yo͝o-rĭn′ə-mē)—a female servant in Odysseus' household

Eurycleia (yo͝or′ĭ-klē′ə)—an old female servant, still loyal to Odysseus

---

ENGLISH LANGUAGE SUPPORT

Clarify Pronunciation Create a set of flashcards with the names of the characters on them. Then organize students into mixed language-ability groups.

- Have students take turns pronouncing each character's name, using the list and
- phonetic spellings on this page.
- Circulate around the room to check and correct the pronunciation.
- Then hold up each flashcard. Have the class chorally pronounce the names.
- Ask volunteers to explain who each character is.

PART ONE: THE WANDERINGS OF ODYSSEUS

AS YOU READ Pay attention to details that tell how Odysseus confronts the various challenges of his journey. Write down any questions you generate during reading.

BOOK 1:

A Goddess Intervenes

Sing in me, Muse, and through me tell the story
of that man skilled in all ways of contending,
the wanderer, **harried** for years on end,
after he plundered the stronghold
5 on the proud height of Troy.

                  He saw the townlands
and learned the minds of many distant men,
and weathered many bitter nights and days
in his deep heart at sea, while he fought only
to save his life, to bring his shipmates home.
10 But not by will nor valor could he save them,
for their own recklessness destroyed them all—
children and fools, they killed and feasted on
the cattle of Lord Helios, the Sun,
and he who moves all day through heaven
15 took from their eyes the dawn of their return.

Of these adventures, Muse, daughter of Zeus,
tell us in our time, lift the great song again. . . .

The story of Odysseus begins with the goddess Athena's appealing to Zeus to help Odysseus, who has been wandering for ten years on the seas, to find his way home to his family on Ithaca. While Odysseus has been gone, his son, Telemachus, has grown to manhood and his wife, Penelope, has been besieged by suitors wishing to marry her and gain Odysseus' wealth. The suitors have taken up residence in her home and are constantly feasting on the family's cattle, sheep, and goats. They dishonor Odysseus and his family. Taking Athena's advice, Telemachus travels to Pylos for word of his father. Meanwhile, on Ithaca, the evil suitors plot to kill Telemachus when he returns.

myNotebook

As you read, mark up the text. Save your work to *myNotebook*.
- Highlight details
- Add notes and questions
- Add new words to *myWordList*

1 Muse: a daughter of Zeus, credited with divine inspiration.

harried (hăr´ēd) *adj.* tormented; harassed **harry** *v.*

11–13 their own recklessness . . . the Sun: a reference to an event occurring later in the poem—an event that causes the death of Odysseus' entire crew.

Close Read Screencasts ▶ View It!

Modeled Discussions

Have students click the *Close Read* icons in their eBooks to access the screencast in which readers discuss and annotate the following key passage:

- the explanation of what happened to Odysseus' crew (Book 1, lines 5–15)

As a class, view and discuss the video.

TEACH

CLOSE READ

AS YOU READ Direct students to use the As You Read note to focus their reading.

Analyze Character: Epic Hero (LINES 1–17)   RL 3

Tell students that the epic opens with an invocation, or plea that the Muse help the speaker tell the story of Odysseus worthily. These lines also briefly introduce the plot and the **epic hero** Odysseus.

Ⓐ ASK STUDENTS why the details about the way in which Odysseus' men were lost are included in this invocation. *(It is made clear that the men perished because of their own recklessness; it is not the fault of Odysseus.)*

Analyze Author's Choices: Epic Poem (SYNOPSIS)   RL 5, RL 6

Tell students that the italicized text summarizes the parts of the poem not included in this excerpt. Point out that this synopsis is about the events occurring in Ithaca as Odysseus tries to make his way home. Remind students that when two plots happen at the same time, they are called **parallel plots.**

Ⓑ ASK STUDENTS to describe the conflicts faced by Odysseus' family. *(His wife Penelope must fend off suitors who want Odysseus' wealth and property. Meanwhile, they are also conspiring to kill Telemachus, his son.)*

> **CRITICAL VOCABULARY**
>
> **harried:** After the war in Troy ended, Odysseus spends ten years being harassed as he tries to get home to Ithaca.
>
> **ASK STUDENTS** to describe how Odysseus would feel after ten years of being harried. *(He would be frustrated and perhaps angry; he would be homesick.)*

Analyze Character:
Epic Hero (LINES 1–7; 17–25)

RL 3

Explain that epics are often characterized by long speeches made by the hero and other major characters. These speeches reveal important ideas about the hero's culture as well as his own character.

C **CITE TEXT EVIDENCE** Ask students to reread lines 1–6. How will Odysseus repay the hospitality shown by Alcinous? Why is this vow important? *(He promises that they will be friends or allies if he survives the rest of his journey home. In an era characterized by wars, this kind of alliance would be politically significant.)*

Make sure students understand that Odysseus fought for ten years in the Trojan War; he has spent ten more years trying to get home.

D **ASK STUDENTS** what the details in lines 17–25 reveal about Odysseus' feelings. *(He is homesick; he says that he will not see "a place more dear" than Ithaca. "Where shall a man find more sweetness to surpass / his own home and his parents?")*

BOOK 9:

New Coasts and Poseidon's Son

For seven of the ten years Odysseus has spent wandering the Mediterranean Sea, he has been held captive by the goddess Calypso on her island. In Book 5, Zeus sends the god Hermes to tell Calypso to release Odysseus; she helps him build a raft on which he can sail to his next destination. He must sail for 20 days before landing on the island of Scheria, where he will be helped in his effort to return home. In Books 6–8, Odysseus is welcomed by King Alcinous, who gives a banquet in his honor. That night the king begs Odysseus to tell who he is and what has happened to him. In Books 9–12, Odysseus relates to the king his adventures.

"I AM LAERTES' SON"

"What shall I
say first? What shall I keep until the end?
The gods have tried me in a thousand ways.
But first my name: let that be known to you,
5   and if I pull away from pitiless death,
friendship will bind us, though my land lies far.

I am Laertes' son, Odysseus.
                  Men hold me
formidable for guile in peace and war:
this fame has gone abroad to the sky's rim.
10 My home is on the peaked sea-mark of Ithaca
under Mount Neion's wind-blown robe of leaves,
in sight of other islands—Dulichium,
Same, wooded Zacynthus—Ithaca
being most lofty in that coastal sea,
15 and northwest, while the rest lie east and south.
A rocky isle, but good for a boy's training;
I shall not see on earth a place more dear,
though I have been detained long by Calypso,
loveliest among goddesses, who held me
20 in her smooth caves, to be her heart's delight,
as Circe of Aeaea, the enchantress,
desired me, and detained me in her hall.
But in my heart I never gave consent.
Where shall a man find sweetness to surpass
25 his own home and his parents? In far lands

7–8 hold me formidable for guile: consider me impressive for my cunning and craftiness.

11–13 Mount Neion's (nē´ŏnz´); **Dulichium** (dōō-lǐk´ē-əm); **Same** (sā´mē); **Zacynthus** (zə-sǐn´thəs).

18–26 Odysseus refers to two beautiful goddesses, Calypso and Circe, who have delayed him on their islands. (Details about Circe appear in Book 10.)

ENGLISH LANGUAGE SUPPORT

Vocabulary: Multiple-Meaning Words Remind students that some words have more than one meaning. Explain that the context in which a word is used can help them to understand which meaning is intended. Point out the word *tried* in line 3. Tell students that this verb has several meanings including "attempted," "sampled," and "tested or put under a great strain." By using the context, readers can determine that *tried* means "tested."

ASK STUDENTS to use context clues and a dictionary to determine the meanings of these words: *bind* (line 6) ; *long* (line 18) ; *held* (line 19). Review their meanings and remind students to use both context and the dictionary for other words that may be confusing.

he shall not, though he find a house of gold.
What of my sailing, then, from Troy?

What of those years
of rough adventure, weathered under Zeus? . . .”

Odysseus explains that soon after leaving Troy, he and his crew land near Ismarus, the city of the Cicones. The Cicones are allies of the Trojans and therefore enemies of Odysseus. Odysseus and his crew raid the Cicones, robbing and killing them, until the Ciconian army kills 72 of Odysseus’ men and drives the rest out to sea. Delayed by a storm for two days, Odysseus and his remaining companions then continue their journey.

THE LOTUS EATERS

“I might have made it safely home, that time,
30 but as I came round Malea the current
took me out to sea, and from the north
a fresh gale drove me on, past Cythera.
Nine days I drifted on the teeming sea
before dangerous high winds. Upon the tenth
35 we came to the coastline of the Lotus Eaters,
who live upon that flower. We landed there
to take on water. All ships’ companies
mustered alongside for the mid-day meal.
Then I sent out two picked men and a runner
40 to learn what race of men that land sustained.
They fell in, soon enough, with Lotus Eaters,
who showed no will to do us harm, only
offering the sweet Lotus to our friends—
but those who ate this honeyed plant, the Lotus,
45 never cared to report, nor to return:
they longed to stay forever, browsing on
that native bloom, forgetful of their homeland.
I drove them, all three wailing, to the ships,
tied them down under their rowing benches,
50 and called the rest: ‘All hands aboard;
come, clear the beach and no one taste
the Lotus, or you lose your hope of home.’
Filing in to their places by the rowlocks
my oarsmen dipped their long oars in the surf,
55 and we moved out again on our sea faring.

30 Malea (mä-lē´ä).

32 Cythera (sĭ-thîr´ə).

38 mustered: assembled; gathered.

Analyze Character: Epic Hero (SYNOPSIS)

RL 3

Tell students that an **archetypal hero** conforms to a pattern seen in heroes from other cultures and times.

E ASK STUDENTS how Odysseus displays the characteristics of an archetypal hero in his encounter with the Cicones. *(He uses physical force to subdue his enemies.)*

Analyze Author’s Choices: Epic Poem (LINES 29–55)

RL 5, RL 6

Explain that the poet **flashes back** in the next books of the poem. Although Odysseus is presently at the court of King Alcinous, he narrates events that have happened in the past.

F ASK STUDENTS how the Lotus Eaters pose a threat to Odysseus and his men. *(Those who eat the Lotus blossom never want to leave and become “forgetful of their homeland.”)* What does the description of the incident with the Lotus Eaters add to the epic? Ask why Odysseus does not elaborate further on his description of this incident. *(The incident shows Odysseus’ firm leadership. The brief description helps show how quickly and decisively he dealt with yet another situation that could have had much more dire consequences.)* How does this encounter with the Lotus Eaters contrast with Odysseus’ approach to the Cicones? *(Because the Lotus Eaters are peaceful, there is no need for violence. Odysseus leaves them alone.)*

TO CHALLENGE STUDENTS . . .

Determine Theme Are the Lotus Eaters harmless? Odysseus is very forceful when he speaks to the crew and drags back the three who succumbed to the effects of the lotus flower. Ask students to discuss the threat the Lotus Eaters pose to Odysseus and his men. What theme is revealed through Odysseus’ reactions? *(The Lotus Eaters relinquish all responsibility and conscious action. To Odysseus, a man of action who comes from a society that admires those who seek knowledge and take on responsibility, this state of inertia would be abhorrent. The message here is that life cannot be all pleasure; it is important to carry out one’s responsibilities to society and to others as well.)*

TEACH

CLOSE READ

Analyze Figurative Meanings (LINES 68–70) RL 4, L 5a

Remind students that **epithets** are descriptive phrases that rename a person or a thing. Point out that epithets are used by the poet to convey descriptive information.

 ASK STUDENTS to identify the epithet in lines 68–70 and explain what they learn from it. (*The epithet describes dawn as "young Dawn with finger tips of rose." This phrase shows the time of day and the conditions. It is a beautiful sunrise.*)

Analyze Character: Epic Hero (LINES 71–75) RL 3

Tell students that an **epic hero** has some very human traits as well as those that define him as extraordinary. Direct students to note how the characteristics of Odysseus are seen through his decisions and actions.

 ASK STUDENTS why they think Odysseus wants to visit the land of the Cyclops. What does this action reveal about his character? (*Odysseus is both curious and daring. He is willing to risk danger by going to a place that may be inhospitable.*)

THE CYCLOPS

In the next land we found were Cyclopes,
giants, louts, without a law to bless them.
In ignorance leaving the fruitage of the earth in mystery
to the immortal gods, they neither plow
60   nor sow by hand, nor till the ground, though grain—
wild wheat and barley—grows untended, and
wine-grapes, in clusters, ripen in heaven's rain.
Cyclopes have no muster and no meeting,
no consultation or old tribal ways,
65   but each one dwells in his own mountain cave
dealing out rough justice to wife and child,
indifferent to what the others do. . . ."

Across the bay from the land of the Cyclopes is a lush, deserted island. Odysseus and his crew land on the island in a dense fog and spend days feasting on wine and wild goats and observing the mainland, where the Cyclopes live. On the third day, Odysseus and his company of men set out to learn if the Cyclopes are friends or foes.

"When the young Dawn with finger tips of rose
came in the east, I called my men together
70   and made a speech to them:

                    'Old shipmates, friends,
the rest of you stand by; I'll make the crossing
in my own ship, with my own company,
and find out what the mainland natives are—
for they may be wild savages, and lawless,
75   or hospitable and god fearing men.'

At this I went aboard, and gave the word
to cast off by the stern. My oarsmen followed,
filing in to their benches by the rowlocks,
and all in line dipped oars in the gray sea.

80   As we rowed on, and nearer to the mainland,
at one end of the bay, we saw a cavern
yawning above the water, screened with laurel,
and many rams and goats about the place
inside a sheepfold—made from slabs of stone
85   earthfast between tall trunks of pine and rugged
towering oak trees.

56 Cyclopes (sī-klō´pēz): refers to the creatures in plural; *Cyclops* is singular.

77 stern: the rear end of a ship.

82 screened with laurel: partially hidden by laurel trees.

374 Collection 6

WHEN STUDENTS STRUGGLE . . .

Discuss flashback with students, explaining that writers use this device to give listeners and readers background information about characters and tell about events in the past.

To guide students' comprehension of how flashbacks affect the sequence of events, have them fill in a sequence chart. Prompt them as needed by completing the first and last boxes or any others with which they struggle. Remind them to use the italicized synopses as well as the actual poem.

Encourage students to add boxes to their sequence chart as they read further and learn about the other adventures Odysseus has after he leaves the land of the Cyclops.

A prodigious man
slept in this cave alone, and took his flocks
to graze afield—remote from all companions,
knowing none but savage ways, a brute
90 so huge, he seemed no man at all of those
who eat good wheaten bread; but he seemed rather
a shaggy mountain reared in solitude.
We beached there, and I told the crew
to stand by and keep watch over the ship;
95 as for myself I took my twelve best fighters
and went ahead. I had a goatskin full
of that sweet liquor that Euanthes' son,
Maron, had given me. He kept Apollo's
holy grove at Ismarus; for kindness
100 we showed him there, and showed his wife and child,
he gave me seven shining golden talents
perfectly formed, a solid silver winebowl,
and then this liquor—twelve two-handled jars
of brandy, pure and fiery. Not a slave
105 in Maron's household knew this drink; only
he, his wife and the storeroom mistress knew;
and they would put one cupful—ruby-colored,
honey-smooth—in twenty more of water,
but still the sweet scent hovered like a fume
110 over the winebowl. No man turned away
when cups of this came round.

97–98 Euanthes (yōō-ăn´thēz); **Maron** (mâr´ŏn´).

101 talents: bars of gold or silver of a specified weight, used as money in ancient Greece.

CLOSE READ

Analyze Author's Choices: Epic Poem (LINES 86–92)   RL 5, RL 6

Tell students that another narrative device used in the poem is **foreshadowing.** Remind students that by giving clues to what will happen in the future, the poet keeps the audience interested.

I **ASK STUDENTS** what is foreshadowed by the description of the Cyclops. *(The Cyclops is described as "a shaggy mountain reared in solitude." He appears to be so savage that there is little resemblance to humans. These details foreshadow that the Cyclops may be dangerous.)*

Analyze Character: Epic Hero (LINES 93–111)   RL 3

Remind students that they can make inferences about Odysseus' motives and even the wisdom of his actions from the details he presents.

J **ASK STUDENTS** why Odysseus takes the wine as well as his twelve best fighting men. *(Odysseus anticipates trouble, which is why he takes his most skilled soldiers. He may use the wine to disarm the Cyclops or perhaps to show that he comes in friendship.)* Have students use the details to draw conclusions about whether or not this expedition is a good idea. *(Odysseus obviously anticipates trouble, yet he goes anyway. He is putting his men and himself at risk, so it is probably not a good decision.)*

| Odysseus leaves Troy. | → | He raids the Cicones and loses 72 men. | → | He visits the Lotus Eaters. | → | He goes to the island of the Cyclopes. | → | | → | |

Odysseus arrives at the island of King Alcinous and tells his story.

Analyze Character: RL 3
Epic Hero (LINES 125–132)

Clarify for students that **dialogue** advances plot and also reveals character.

(K) ASK STUDENTS what they learn from the dialogue between Odysseus and his crew. *(The crew members are uneasy and want to leave, taking what they need for their continued voyage. Odysseus refuses, driven by a desire to learn more about the Cyclops and what he might give them.)* Ask students what is foreshadowed by the line "no pretty sight, it turned out for my friends." *(Odysseus will survive this encounter, but some of those he brought with him will not.)*

Analyze Author's Choices: RL 5, RL 6
Epic Poem (LINES 140–153)

Tell students that often in narratives the **setting** has an impact on the action. Direct them to look carefully at the details the poet includes about the Cyclops's cave.

(L) ASK STUDENTS to reread lines 140–153. Ask them what impression this description provides of the Cyclops and his cave. What potential conflict is foreshadowed by these details? *(The Cyclops appears quite domestic as he follows his routine. His cave is vast; the description of the doorway slab and the fact that two dozen wagons could not move it suggest that Odysseus and his men are trapped unless the giant chooses to let them out.)*

A wineskin full
I brought along, and victuals in a bag,
for in my bones I knew some towering brute
would be upon us soon—all outward power,
115 a wild man, ignorant of civility.

We climbed, then, briskly to the cave. But Cyclops
had gone afield, to pasture his fat sheep,
so we looked round at everything inside:
a drying rack that sagged with cheeses, pens
120 crowded with lambs and kids, each in its class:
firstlings apart from middlings, and the 'dewdrops,'
or newborn lambkins, penned apart from both.
And vessels full of whey were brimming there—
bowls of earthenware and pails for milking.
125 My men came pressing round me, pleading:
                                        'Why not
take these cheeses, get them stowed, come back,
throw open all the pens, and make a run for it?
We'll drive the kids and lambs aboard. We say
put out again on good salt water!'
                                        Ah,
130 how sound that was! Yet I refused. I wished
to see the caveman, what he had to offer—
no pretty sight, it turned out, for my friends.
We lit a fire, burnt an offering,
and took some cheese to eat; then sat in silence
135 around the embers, waiting. When he came
he had a load of dry boughs on his shoulder
to stoke his fire at suppertime. He dumped it
with a great crash into that hollow cave,
and we all scattered fast to the far wall.
140 Then over the broad cavern floor he ushered
the ewes he meant to milk. He left his rams
and he-goats in the yard outside, and swung
high overhead a slab of solid rock
to close the cave. Two dozen four-wheeled wagons,
145 with heaving wagon teams, could not have stirred
the tonnage of that rock from where he wedged it
over the doorsill. Next he took his seat
and milked his bleating ewes. A practiced job
he made of it, giving each ewe her suckling;
150 thickened his milk, then, into curds and whey,
sieved out the curds to drip in withy baskets,
and poured the whey to stand in bowls

112 victuals (vĭt´lz): food.

121–122 The Cyclops has separated his lambs into three age groups.

123 whey: the watery part of milk, which separates from the curds, or solid part, during the making of cheese.

129 good salt water: the open sea.

133 burnt an offering: burned a portion of the food as an offering to secure the gods' goodwill. (Such offerings were frequently performed by Greek sailors during difficult journeys.)

151 withy baskets: baskets made from twigs.

APPLYING ACADEMIC VOCABULARY

motivate	subsequent

As you discuss the events that take place in the Cyclops's cave, incorporate the following Collection 6 academic vocabulary words: *motivate* and *subsequent*. To analyze the cause-and-effect relationship between events, ask students to explain what **motivates** Odysseus to explore and then stay in the Cyclops's cave. Have them summarize the **subsequent** effects of that decision.

cooling until he drank it for his supper.
When all these chores were done, he poked the fire,
155 heaping on brushwood. In the glare he saw us.

'Strangers,' he said, 'who are you? And where from?
What brings you here by sea ways—a fair traffic?
Or are you wandering rogues, who cast your lives
like dice, and ravage other folk by sea?'

157 fair traffic: honest trading.

160 We felt a pressure on our hearts, in dread
of that deep rumble and that mighty man.
But all the same I spoke up in reply:

'We are from Troy, Achaeans, blown off course
by shifting gales on the Great South Sea;
165 homeward bound, but taking routes and ways
uncommon; so the will of Zeus would have it.
We served under Agamemnon, son of Atreus—
the whole world knows what city
he laid waste, what armies he destroyed.
170 It was our luck to come here; here we stand,
beholden for your help, or any gifts
you give—as custom is to honor strangers.
We would entreat you, great Sir, have a care
for the gods' courtesy; Zeus will avenge
175 the unoffending guest.'

172–175 It was a sacred Greek custom to honor strangers with food and gifts. Odysseus is reminding the Cyclops that Zeus will punish anyone who mistreats a guest.

                              He answered this
from his brute chest, unmoved:

                              'You are a ninny,
or else you come from the other end of nowhere,
telling me, mind the gods! We Cyclopes
care not a whistle for your thundering Zeus
180 or all the gods in bliss; we have more force by far.
I would not let you go for fear of Zeus—
you or your friends—unless I had a whim to.
Tell me, where was it, now, you left your ship—
around the point, or down the shore, I wonder?'

185 He thought he'd find out, but I saw through this,
and answered with a ready lie:

                              'My ship?
Poseidon Lord, who sets the earth a-tremble,
broke it up on the rocks at your land's end.
A wind from seaward served him, drove us there.
190 We are survivors, these good men and I.'

CLOSE READ

Analyze Author's Choices: Epic Poem (LINES 176–184)   RL 5, RL 6

Remind students that an **epic** is a long narrative poem that includes many **conflicts** involving various mortals and immortals.

(M) ASK STUDENTS to describe the Cyclops's attitude toward his guests. What does this attitude suggest about the possible conflict between the Cyclops and Odysseus? *(He has no time for the laws of hospitality and thinks his guests are fools for having found themselves in this situation. He most likely has plans to harm them.)*

Analyze Character: Epic Hero (LINES 185–190)   RL 3

Tell students that a character's reaction to conflict may reveal important qualities.

(N) ASK STUDENTS why Odysseus lies to the Cyclops about the ship. What traits does Odysseus show in this exchange with the Cyclops? *(He does not want the Cyclops to find the ship and destroy their means of escape from this island. Odysseus shows through this reply that he is quick-witted, shrewd, and tricky.)*

ENGLISH LANGUAGE SUPPORT

Language: Phrasal Verbs Tell students that a **phrasal verb** is a verb and another word that function together as one verb. Point out "But all the same I spoke up in reply" in line 162. Explain that *up* usually functions as a preposition, but in this sentence it does not introduce a prepositional phrase. Instead, it forms a phrasal verb with *spoke*. To speak up is to increase the volume of one's voice or to speak boldly.

ASK STUDENTS to use context clues to define these phrasal verbs on this page: *find out* (line 185), *saw through* (line 185), *broke up* (line 188).

Analyze Figurative Meanings (LINES 191–197)

RL 4, L 5a

Remind students that **epic similes** are comparisons developed at length that create a vivid image in the audience's mind and reinforce important ideas.

O CITE TEXT EVIDENCE Ask students how the epic simile in lines 194–197 intensifies the impression of the strength of the Cyclops and the helplessness of Odysseus and his men. (*The men are compared to "squirming puppies" that the giant picks up and dashes against the floor. The Cyclops is compared to a mountain lion, "gaping and crunching."*)

Analyze Author's Choices: Epic Poem (LINES 198–210)

RL 5, RL 6

Tell students that to make the epic exciting and suspenseful, events occur that complicate the hero's attempts to resolve the conflict.

P ASK STUDENTS why Odysseus refrains from killing the giant. What does this mean for the resolution of the conflict? (*He doesn't kill the Cyclops because he and his men could never move the heavy doorway slab. They would die in the cave. This is a complication because they will have to find another way to escape from the Cyclops.*)

CRITICAL VOCABULARY

ponderous: The door is a massive slab of stone that is far too heavy and bulky for the Greeks to move aside.

ASK STUDENTS to explain how the ponderous door makes their situation almost impossible to escape. (*Because the men cannot move the slab, they cannot escape while the Cyclops is sleeping or while he is gone.*)

Neither reply nor pity came from him,
but in one stride he clutched at my companions
and caught two in his hands like squirming puppies
to beat their brains out, spattering the floor.
195   Then he dismembered them and made his meal,
gaping and crunching like a mountain lion—
everything: innards, flesh, and marrow bones.
We cried aloud, lifting our hands to Zeus,
powerless, looking on at this, appalled;
200   but Cyclops went on filling up his belly
with manflesh and great gulps of whey,
then lay down like a mast among his sheep.
My heart beat high now at the chance of action,
and drawing the sharp sword from my hip I went
205   along his flank to stab him where the midriff
holds the liver. I had touched the spot
when sudden fear stayed me: if I killed him
we perished there as well, for we could never
move his **ponderous** doorway slab aside.
210   So we were left to groan and wait for morning.

When the young Dawn with fingertips of rose
lit up the world, the Cyclops built a fire
and milked his handsome ewes, all in due order,
putting the sucklings to the mothers. Then,
215   his chores being all dispatched, he caught
another brace of men to make his breakfast,
and whisked away his great door slab
to let his sheep go through—but he, behind,
reset the stone as one would cap a quiver.
220   There was a din of whistling as the Cyclops
rounded his flock to higher ground, then stillness.
And now I pondered how to hurt him worst,
if but Athena granted what I prayed for.
Here are the means I thought would serve my turn:

225   a club, or staff, lay there along the fold—
an olive tree, felled green and left to season
for Cyclops' hand. And it was like a mast
a lugger of twenty oars, broad in the beam—
a deep-sea-going craft—might carry:
230   so long, so big around, it seemed. Now I
chopped out a six foot section of this pole
and set it down before my men, who scraped it;
and when they had it smooth, I hewed again
to make a stake with pointed end. I held this

ponderous (pŏn′dər-əs) *adj.* heavy in a clumsy way; bulky.

216 brace: pair.

218–219 The Cyclops reseals the cave with the massive rock as easily as an ordinary human places the cap on a container of arrows.

226 left to season: left to dry out and harden.

228 lugger: a small, wide sailing ship.

WHEN STUDENTS STRUGGLE . . .

Tell students that a conflict is a struggle between two opposing forces. Explain that some conflicts are external. These conflicts happen between two or more characters, between a character and nature, or between a character and society. Other conflicts are internal. They take place within a character as he or she tries to make a decision or solve a problem.

To help students understand the conflicts that Odysseus experiences in this book of the poem, have them work with a partner to fill out a web or similar diagram. Remind them to look closely at lines 191–273 to make sure they identify all of the conflicts.

235 in the fire's heart and turned it, toughening it,
     then hid it, well back in the cavern, under
     one of the dung piles in **profusion** there.
     Now came the time to toss for it: who ventured
     along with me? whose hand could bear to thrust
240 and grind that spike in Cyclops' eye, when mild
     sleep had mastered him? As luck would have it,
     the men I would have chosen won the toss—
     four strong men, and I made five as captain.

     At evening came the shepherd with his flock,
245 his woolly flock. The rams as well, this time,
     entered the cave: by some sheep-herding whim—
     or a god's bidding—none were left outside.
     He hefted his great boulder into place
     and sat him down to milk the bleating ewes
250 in proper order, put the lambs to suck,
     and swiftly ran through all his evening chores.
     Then he caught two more men and feasted on them.
     My moment was at hand, and I went forward
     holding an ivy bowl of my dark drink,
255 looking up, saying:
                    'Cyclops, try some wine.
     Here's liquor to wash down your scraps of men.
     Taste it, and see the kind of drink we carried
     under our planks. I meant it for an offering
     if you would help us home. But you are mad,
260 unbearable, a bloody monster! After this,
     will any other traveller come to see you?'

     He seized and drained the bowl, and it went down
     so fiery and smooth he called for more:

     'Give me another, thank you kindly. Tell me,
265 how are you called? I'll make a gift will please you.
     Even Cyclopes know the wine-grapes grow
     out of grassland and loam in heaven's rain,
     but here's a bit of nectar and ambrosia!'

     Three bowls I brought him, and he poured them down.
270 I saw the fuddle and flush come over him,
     then I sang out in cordial tones:
                              'Cyclops, ®
     you ask my honorable name? Remember
     the gift you promised me, and I shall tell you.

profusion
(prə-fyōō′zhən) *n.*
abundance.

268 nectar (nĕk′tər) **and
ambrosia** (ăm-brō′zhə):
the drink and food of the
gods.

270 fuddle and flush:
the state of confusion
and redness of the face
caused by drinking
alcohol.

CLOSE READ

Analyze Character: RL 3
Epic Hero (LINES 238–275)

Tell students that some cultures admired courage
and strength above all other qualities. Point out that
Odysseus' **traits** reveal that the Greeks also revered
the ability to reason.

Q **CITE TEXT EVIDENCE** Ask students to explain
the good luck that Odysseus has. Then have them
discuss how he takes advantage of the good luck
and what that reveals about him. *(He finds the olive
tree in the cave. The four men he would have chosen
win the toss. The rams come into the cave as well as the
ewes. He has the wine from Maron. He takes advantage
of this good luck by forming a plan based on what he
has. This reveals his intelligence and ability to think
under pressure.)*

Have students speak aloud the name that Odysseus
gives the Cyclops.

R **ASK STUDENTS** what the sound of the name
suggests about what Odysseus might be planning.
*(The name sounds like "Nobody," which suggests that
Odysseus is planning some kind of trick or trap. He
thinks ahead.)*

CRITICAL VOCABULARY

profusion: The cave has an abundance of dung
piles scattered all around it.

ASK STUDENTS what idea about the Cyclops is
reinforced by the profusion of dung around his
living quarters as well as the animals sharing it
with him. *(The Cyclops is bestial and subhuman,
willing to live in squalor as his animals do.)*

The Cyclops is too strong for Odysseus to overcome.	He cannot kill the Cyclops while he is sleeping or they will be trapped in the cave.

Odysseus' conflicts

Odysseus has to watch his men being eaten and is powerless to help them.	Odysseus has to think of a plan to defeat the Cyclops.

Analyze Figurative Meanings (LINES 276–277)

RL 4, L 5a

Remind students that earlier Odysseus had requested that the Cyclops give him the gift due a guest according to Greek laws of hospitality.

 ASK STUDENTS to explain the irony of the gift the Cyclops says he will give to Odysseus. *(He will give Odysseus the gift of being the last one eaten. This is ironic because it will be anything but a gift to have to see his comrades die first.)*

Point out that to make this event more vivid to the audience, the poet uses an **epic simile,** or extended comparison.

T ASK STUDENTS to identify the epic simile in lines 295–303 that describes how the Cyclops's eye is affected. How does this simile impact the audience's ability to visualize the action? *(The effect on the eyeball is compared to the reaction created when a white-hot piece of metal is plunged into cold water. That is how the eye hissed and steamed. The comparison would be very familiar to the audience and enable them to know exactly what sights and sounds accompanied Odysseus' actions.)*

My name is Nohbdy: mother, father, and friends,
275 everyone calls me Nohbdy.'

And he said:

'Nohbdy's my meat, then, after I eat his friends.
Others come first. There's a noble gift, now.'

Even as he spoke, he reeled and tumbled backward,
his great head lolling to one side: and sleep
280 took him like any creature. Drunk, hiccupping,
he dribbled streams of liquor and bits of men.

Now, by the gods, I drove my big hand spike
deep in the embers, charring it again,
and cheered my men along with battle talk
285 to keep their courage up: no quitting now.
The pike of olive, green though it had been,
reddened and glowed as if about to catch.
I drew it from the coals and my four fellows
gave me a hand, lugging it near the Cyclops
290 as more than natural force nerved them; straight
forward they sprinted, lifted it, and rammed it
deep in his crater eye, and I leaned on it
turning it as a shipwright turns a drill
in planking, having men below to swing
295 the two-handled strap that spins it in the groove.
So with our brand we bored that great eye socket
while blood ran out around the red hot bar.
Eyelid and lash were seared; the pierced ball
hissed broiling, and the roots popped.

In a smithy

300 one sees a white-hot axehead or an adze
plunged and wrung in a cold tub, screeching steam—
the way they make soft iron hale and hard—:
just so that eyeball hissed around the spike.
The Cyclops bellowed and the rock roared round him,
305 and we fell back in fear. Clawing his face
he tugged the bloody spike out of his eye,
threw it away, and his wild hands went groping;
then he set up a howl for Cyclopes
who lived in caves on windy peaks nearby.
310 Some heard him; and they came by divers ways
to clump around outside and call:

286 the pike: the pointed stake.

299 smithy: blacksmith's shop.

300 adze (ădz): an axlike tool with a curved blade.

310 divers: various.

TO CHALLENGE STUDENTS . . .

Compare and Contrast What was important to the ancient Greeks? Point out that the Cyclopes are different in almost every way from Odysseus and his men. Explain to students that these differences and the attitude with which Odysseus views them reveal a great deal about what was important to the ancient Greeks.

Have students work with a partner to contrast Polyphemus and Odysseus, using a chart or other graphic organizer. Make sure students consider lifestyle, character traits, behaviors, values, and physical characteristics in their comparison.

Have pairs discuss their findings. As a class, make inferences about Greek society based on these differences.

'What ails you,
Polyphemus? Why do you cry so sore
in the starry night? You will not let us sleep.
Sure no man's driving off your flock? No man
315 has tricked you, ruined you?'

312 **Polyphemus**
(pŏl´ə-fē´məs): the name
of the Cyclops.

Out of the cave
the mammoth Polyphemus roared in answer:

'Nohbdy, Nohbdy's tricked me, Nohbdy's ruined me!'

To this rough shout they made a sage reply:

318 **sage:** wise.

'Ah well, if nobody has played you foul
320 there in your lonely bed, we are no use in pain
given by great Zeus. Let it be your father,
Poseidon Lord, to whom you pray.'

319–322 Odysseus'
lie about his name has
paid off.

So saying
they trailed away. And I was filled with laughter
to see how like a charm the name deceived them.
325 Now Cyclops, wheezing as the pain came on him,
fumbled to wrench away the great doorstone
and squatted in the breach with arms thrown wide
for any silly beast or man who bolted—
hoping somehow I might be such a fool.
330 But I kept thinking how to win the game:
death sat there huge; how could we slip away?
I drew on all my wits, and ran through tactics,
reasoning as a man will for dear life,
until a trick came—and it pleased me well.
335 The Cyclops' rams were handsome, fat, with heavy
fleeces, a dark violet.

327 **breach:** opening.

Three abreast
I tied them silently together, twining
cords of willow from the ogre's bed;
then slung a man under each middle one
340 to ride there safely, shielded left and right.
So three sheep could convey each man. I took
the woolliest ram, the choicest of the flock,
and hung myself under his kinky belly,
pulled up tight, with fingers twisted deep
345 in sheepskin ringlets for an iron grip.
So, breathing hard, we waited until morning.

The Wanderings of Odysseus: Book 9 **381**

ENGLISH LANGUAGE SUPPORT

Vocabulary: Idiomatic Expressions Remind students that **idiomatic expressions** do not mean what the words say. Explain that examining how an idiom is used in context can help students interpret the meaning. Direct students' attention to the phrase *played you foul* in line 319. Guide students to use context clues to define the phrase as "done something bad to you."

ASK STUDENTS to use context clues to define these additional phrases: *like a charm* (line 324); *win the game* (line 330); *drew on all my wits* (line 332); *for dear life* (line 333). Remind students to apply this strategy when they encounter idiomatic phrases in future reading.

CLOSE READ

Analyze Author's Choices: RL 5, RL 6
Epic Poem (LINES 311–322)

Explain to students that a **foil** is a character that provides a striking contrast with another character. This contrast highlights the characters' differences.

Ⓤ ASK STUDENTS to explain how Odysseus and the Cyclops show their differences in lines 311–322. *(Odysseus relies on his intelligence to solve most conflicts; the Cyclops uses brute strength. In this part of the poem, Odysseus' cunning saves what is left of his crew. Because the Cyclops is saying that "Nobody" is hurting him, the other Cyclopes are kept out of the conflict. Their suspicions are allayed. If they had banded together against the Greeks, Odysseus and his men would have had no hope.)*

Analyze Character: RL 3
Epic Hero (LINES 322–346)

Remind students that Odysseus was the mastermind behind the plan that brought the ten-year Trojan War to an end. Presenting a large, wooden horse as an offering to the people of Troy provided the Greeks a hiding place from which to launch a surprise attack against the city.

Ⓥ ASK STUDENTS to reread lines 322–346 and explain how Odysseus' plan to escape the Cyclops is similar to his plan to win the Trojan War. *(As in the Trojan War, there is a stalemate between the two enemies. Odysseus has to deceive the Cyclops somehow in order to win the conflict. As with the Trojan horse, he uses the innocent appearance of one thing to disguise another. In this case, he uses the rams to disguise the escape of his crew.)*

Analyze Author's Choices: Epic Poem (LINES 358–373)

RL 5, RL 6

Remind students that **suspense** is the excitement or tension readers feel as they wait to find out what happens.

(W) CITE TEXT EVIDENCE Ask students how the poet creates suspense in this part of the poem. *(The Cyclops holds back the ram to which Odysseus is clinging, questioning why it is lagging behind. The audience wonders if he suspects something or if Odysseus will be able to hang on.)*

CRITICAL VOCABULARY

adversary: When Odysseus judges the ship is safely away, he taunts his enemy the Cyclops.

ASK STUDENTS whether Odysseus' victory over his adversary is completely admirable. Why or why not? *(It is not completely admirable. He shows great ingenuity, but he should never have been in the situation to begin with. He shows poor leadership in placing his crew in that position.)*

When Dawn spread out her finger tips of rose
the rams began to stir, moving for pasture,
and peals of bleating echoed round the pens
350   where dams with udders full called for a milking.
Blinded, and sick with pain from his head wound,
the master stroked each ram, then let it pass,
but my men riding on the pectoral fleece
the giant's blind hands blundering never found.
355   Last of them all my ram, the leader, came,
weighted by wool and me with my meditations.
The Cyclops patted him, and then he said:

'Sweet cousin ram, why lag behind the rest
in the night cave? You never linger so,
360   but graze before them all, and go afar
to crop sweet grass, and take your stately way
leading along the streams, until at evening
you run to be the first one in the fold.
Why, now, so far behind? Can you be grieving
365   over your Master's eye? That carrion rogue
and his accurst companions burnt it out
when he had conquered all my wits with wine.
Nohbdy will not get out alive, I swear.
Oh, had you brain and voice to tell
370   where he may be now, dodging all my fury!
Bashed by this hand and bashed on this rock wall
his brains would strew the floor, and I should have
rest from the outrage Nohbdy worked upon me.'

He sent us into the open, then. Close by,
375   I dropped and rolled clear of the ram's belly,
going this way and that to untie the men.
With many glances back, we rounded up
his fat, stiff-legged sheep to take aboard,
and drove them down to where the good ship lay.
380   We saw, as we came near, our fellows' faces
shining; then we saw them turn to grief
tallying those who had not fled from death.
I hushed them, jerking head and eyebrows up,
and in a low voice told them: 'Load this herd;
385   move fast, and put the ship's head toward the breakers.'
They all pitched in at loading, then embarked
and struck their oars into the sea. Far out,
as far off shore as shouted words would carry,
I sent a few back to the **adversary**:

353 pectoral fleece: the wool covering a sheep's chest.

385 put...the breakers: turn the ship around so that it is heading toward the open sea.

adversary (ăd′vər-sĕr′ē) *n.* an opponent; enemy.

ENGLISH LANGUAGE SUPPORT

Use Context Clues Remind students that if they encounter unfamiliar words as they read, they should look for context clues, or surrounding words and phrases, to help them determine meaning. Point out *lag* in line 358. Model using context clues to figure out that it means "to fall behind." Then have students verify their definitions by substituting them for the word or words in the line to check for sense. On the board, write: *afar* (line 360); *carrion rogue* (line 365); *should have rest* (line 372).

ASK STUDENTS to work in pairs to define the words and phrases using context clues. *(far away; rotten, dishonest person; I would be free)* Review the definitions together. Ask volunteers to identify other words on these pages that are unfamiliar. As a class, use context to figure out their meanings.

390 'O Cyclops! Would you feast on my companions?
Puny, am I, in a Caveman's hands?
How do you like the beating that we gave you,
you damned cannibal? Eater of guests
under your roof! Zeus and the gods have paid you!'

395 The blind thing in his doubled fury broke
a hilltop in his hands and heaved it after us.
Ahead of our black prow it struck and sank
whelmed in a spuming geyser, a giant wave
that washed the ship stern foremost back to shore.

400 I got the longest boathook out and stood
fending us off, with furious nods to all
to put their backs into a racing stroke—
row, row, or perish. So the long oars bent
kicking the foam sternward, making head

405 until we drew away, and twice as far.
Now when I cupped my hands I heard the crew
in low voices protesting:

'Godsake, Captain!

Why bait the beast again? Let him alone!'
'That tidal wave he made on the first throw
410 all but beached us.'

390–394 Odysseus assumes that the gods are on his side.

395–403 The hilltop thrown by Polyphemus lands in front of the ship, causing a huge wave that carries the ship back to the shore. Odysseus uses a long pole to push the boat away from the land.

406 cupped my hands: put his hands on either side of his mouth in order to magnify his voice.

Analyze Character:
Epic Hero (LINES 390–405)   RL 3

Discuss with students how Odysseus, as the narrator of the story, has the ability to choose what he does and does not tell.

X ASK STUDENTS to consider why Odysseus would include his taunting of the Cyclops and the consequence. How does Odysseus view his own actions? *(His inclusion of these details shows that he is not at all ashamed of his actions and considers them to be proof of courage and daring. He may think that escaping destruction a second time makes the story more admirable. Or, he may be an honest narrator who feels the story should be complete.)*

WHEN STUDENTS STRUGGLE...

Remind students that summarizing what they have read can help them to remember important ideas. Explain that when they summarize, they restate the major points and most significant details in their own words.

Have students work with a partner to write a short summary of how Odysseus tricks the Cyclops into letting him and his men escape. Tell students their summaries should be two or three sentences long.

ASK STUDENTS to take turns reading their summaries aloud.

Analyze Author's Choices: Epic Poem (LINES 420–436)

RL 5, RL 6

Tell students that often in Greek literature, a prophecy, or prediction about the future, is fulfilled but not in the way anticipated by the person receiving it.

Ⓨ ASK STUDENTS why Polyphemus is surprised by the fulfillment of the prophecy. *(He believed that Odysseus would be a giant.)* What does the Cyclops's characterization of Odysseus as "small, pitiful and twiggy" suggest about the value of "brawn versus brain" in a conflict? *(It suggests that intelligence will win out over sheer strength.)*

Determine Theme (LINES 437–446)

RL 2

Explain to students that the consequences of a person's actions often help to reveal an important **theme,** or message, about life.

Ⓩ ASK STUDENTS what theme is conveyed by Odysseus' behavior in this part of the poem. *(Excessive pride will lead to the person's downfall and perhaps those of others as well. Odysseus cannot resist flaunting his victory over the Cyclops. As a result, he will endure great suffering, brought about by his own arrogance. His crew will lose their lives.)*

'All but stove us in!'

'Give him our bearing with your trumpeting,
he'll get the range and lob a boulder.'

'Aye

He'll smash our timbers and our heads together!'

I would not heed them in my glorying spirit,
415   but let my anger flare and yelled:

'Cyclops,

if ever mortal man inquire
how you were put to shame and blinded, tell him
Odysseus, raider of cities, took your eye:
Laertes' son, whose home's on Ithaca!'

420   At this he gave a mighty sob and rumbled:

'Now comes the weird upon me, spoken of old.
A wizard, grand and wondrous, lived here—Telemus,
a son of Eurymus; great length of days
he had in wizardry among the Cyclopes,
425   and these things he foretold for time to come:
my great eye lost, and at Odysseus' hands.
Always I had in mind some giant, armed
in giant force, would come against me here.
But this, but you—small, pitiful and twiggy—
430   you put me down with wine, you blinded me.
Come back, Odysseus, and I'll treat you well,
praying the god of earthquake to befriend you—
his son I am, for he by his avowal
fathered me, and, if he will, he may
435   heal me of this black wound—he and no other
of all the happy gods or mortal men.'

Few words I shouted in reply to him:
'If I could take your life I would and take
your time away, and hurl you down to hell!
440   The god of earthquake could not heal you there!'

At this he stretched his hands out in his darkness
toward the sky of stars, and prayed Poseidon:
'O hear me, lord, blue girdler of the islands,
if I am thine indeed, and thou art father:
445   grant that Odysseus, raider of cities, never
see his home: Laertes' son, I mean,

421 Now comes . . . of old: Now I recall the destiny predicted long ago.

421–430 Now comes . . . you blinded me: Polyphemus tells of a prophecy made long ago by Telemus, a prophet who predicted that Polyphemus would lose his eye at the hands of Odysseus.

432 the god of earthquake: Poseidon.

433 avowal: honest admission.

WHEN STUDENTS STRUGGLE . . .

To guide students' comprehension of the text, have them work in pairs to read lines 437–446 and identify the cause-and-effect relationship. Next, have them answer the following questions:

- What is Odysseus' attitude toward the Cyclops?
- What is the result of what he says to the Cyclops?
- What could he have done instead to achieve a better result? Explain.

ASK STUDENTS to share their answers to the questions.

who kept his hall on Ithaca. Should destiny
intend that he shall see his roof again
among his family in his father land,
450 far be that day, and dark the years between.
Let him lose all companions, and return
under strange sail to bitter days at home.'

In these words he prayed, and the god heard him.
Now he laid hands upon a bigger stone
455 and wheeled around, titanic for the cast,
to let it fly in the black-prowed vessel's track.
But it fell short, just aft the steering oar,
and whelming seas rose giant above the stone
to bear us onward toward the island.   There
460 as we ran in we saw the squadron waiting,
the trim ships drawn up side by side, and all
our troubled friends who waited, looking seaward.
We beached her, grinding keel in the soft sand,
and waded in, ourselves, on the sandy beach.
465 Then we unloaded all the Cyclops' flock
to make division, share and share alike,
only my fighters voted that my ram,
the prize of all, should go to me. I slew him
by the sea side and burnt his long thighbones
470 to Zeus beyond the stormcloud, Cronus' son,
who rules the world. But Zeus disdained my offering;
destruction for my ships he had in store
and death for those who sailed them, my companions.

Now all day long until the sun went down
475 we made our feast on mutton and sweet wine,
till after sunset in the gathering dark
we went to sleep above the wash of ripples.

When the young Dawn with finger tips of rose
touched the world, I roused the men, gave orders
480 to man the ships, cast off the mooring lines;
and filing in to sit beside the rowlocks
oarsmen in line dipped oars in the gray sea.
So we moved out, sad in the vast offing,
having our precious lives, but not our friends."

455 **titanic for the cast:** drawing on all his enormous strength in preparing to throw.

457 **aft:** behind.

459 **the island:** the deserted island where most of Odysseus' men had stayed behind.

470 **Cronus' son:** Zeus' father, Cronus, was a Titan, one of an earlier race of gods.

483 **offing:** the part of the deep sea visible from the shore.

A2

Analyze Author's Choices: RL 5, RL 6
Epic Poem (LINES 465–484)

Remind students that they can read an epic to learn more about the culture from which it arose. Tell them to use the actions of the characters to understand important customs and beliefs.

A2 **CITE TEXT EVIDENCE** Ask students to identify details that reveal the religious beliefs of the ancient Greeks. *(The Greeks sacrificed animals to the gods to win their favor. Odysseus burns parts of the ram to Zeus, but Zeus does not accept them, meaning they may have burned incompletely or irregularly. This foreshadows misfortune for Odysseus.)* Have students discuss what the phrase "share and share alike" reveals about the relationship between Odysseus and his men. *(The spoils of any raid or war are shared equally among them. This suggests that the crew is considered as important as Odysseus in many ways.)*

TO CHALLENGE STUDENTS . . .

Analyze Author's Choices Is it better to know or not know what the future holds? This is a question that people have debated through the years. The Cyclops's words foreshadow the trouble that lies ahead for Odysseus. Organize students into small groups to discuss these questions:

- What effect does the Cyclops's curse have on the poem?
- Why does the poet include this information when it could easily have been left out?
- What ideas about destiny are suggested by the Cyclops's curse and the circumstances that led to it?

ASK STUDENTS to share their group's insights in a whole-class discussion.

Analyze Author's Choices: Epic Poem (SYNOPSIS)

RL 5, RL 6

Direct students to read the synopsis to find out what has happened since Odysseus and his men left the island of the Cyclopes.

B2 **ASK STUDENTS** how the Cyclops's curse is already being fulfilled. *(Odysseus now only has one ship of men remaining. The rest have perished as a result of their encounter with the Laestrygones.)*

Analyze Figurative Meanings (LINES 1–11)

RL 4, L 5a

Remind students that **epic similes** can help them gain insight into setting, characters, and events in the poem.

C2 **CITE TEXT EVIDENCE** Have students explain what is being compared in lines 1–11. What ideas about the character of Circe and future plot events are suggested by this simile? *(This simile compares wolves and mountain lions, normally fierce creatures, to tame dogs that fawn on their masters. This abnormal behavior foreshadows the powerful control that Circe can exert and suggests that she will keep Odysseus' men in her thrall.)*

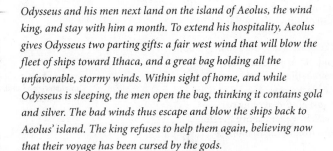

BOOK 10:

Circe, the Grace of the Witch

B2 *Odysseus and his men next land on the island of Aeolus, the wind king, and stay with him a month. To extend his hospitality, Aeolus gives Odysseus two parting gifts: a fair west wind that will blow the fleet of ships toward Ithaca, and a great bag holding all the unfavorable, stormy winds. Within sight of home, and while Odysseus is sleeping, the men open the bag, thinking it contains gold and silver. The bad winds thus escape and blow the ships back to Aeolus' island. The king refuses to help them again, believing now that their voyage has been cursed by the gods.*

The discouraged mariners next stop briefly in the land of the Laestrygones, fierce cannibals who bombard the fleet of ships with boulders. Only Odysseus, his ship, and its crew of 45 survive the shower of boulders. The lone ship then sails to Aeaea, home of the goddess Circe, who is considered by many to be a witch. There, Odysseus divides his men into two groups. Eurylochus leads one platoon to explore the island, while Odysseus stays behind on the ship with the remaining crew.

"In the wild wood they found an open glade,
around a smooth stone house—the hall of Circe—
and wolves and mountain lions lay there, mild
in her soft spell, fed on her drug of evil.
5 None would attack—oh, it was strange, I tell you—
but switching their long tails they faced our men
like hounds, who look up when their master comes
with tidbits for them—as he will—from table.
Humbly those wolves and lions with mighty paws
10 fawned on our men—who met their yellow eyes
and feared them.
                                        In the entrance way they stayed
to listen there: inside her quiet house
they heard the goddess Circe.
                                        Low she sang
in her beguiling voice, while on her loom
15 she wove ambrosial fabric sheer and bright,
by that craft known to the goddesses of heaven.
No one would speak, until Polites—most
faithful and likable of my officers, said:

10 fawned on: showed affection for.

15 ambrosial: fit for the gods.

17 Polites (pə-lī'tēz).

ENGLISH LANGUAGE SUPPORT

Analyze Epic Similes Using a whiteboard, project lines 1–11. Invite volunteers to mark the text:

- Highlight in blue the nouns in line 3 that form the first part of the epic simile.
- Underline the noun in line 7 to which they are compared.
- Highlight in green the descriptive phrases that develop this comparison.

ASK STUDENTS to explain how this simile conveys a feeling of strangeness and evil.

but switching their long tails they faced our men

like hounds, who look up when their master comes

'Dear friends, no need for stealth: here's a young weaver
20   singing a pretty song to set the air
a-tingle on these lawns and paven courts.
Goddess she is, or lady. Shall we greet her?'

So reassured, they all cried out together,
and she came swiftly to the shining doors
25   to call them in. All but Eurylochus—
who feared a snare—the innocents went after her.
On thrones she seated them, and lounging chairs,
while she prepared a meal of cheese and barley
and amber honey mixed with Pramnian wine,
30   adding her own vile pinch, to make them lose
desire or thought of our dear father land.
Scarce had they drunk when she flew after them
with her long stick and shut them in a pigsty—
bodies, voices, heads, and bristles, all
35   swinish now, though minds were still unchanged.
So, squealing, in they went. And Circe tossed them
acorns, mast, and cornel berries—fodder
for hogs who rut and slumber on the earth.

Down to the ship Eurylochus came running
40   to cry alarm, foul magic doomed his men!
But working with dry lips to speak a word
he could not, being so shaken; blinding tears
welled in his eyes; **foreboding** filled his heart.
When we were frantic questioning him, at last
45   we heard the tale: our friends were gone. . . ."

*Eurylochus tells Odysseus what has happened and begs him to sail
away from Circe's island. Against this advice, however, Odysseus
rushes to save his men from the enchantress. On the way, he meets
the god Hermes, who gives him a magical plant called moly to protect
him from Circe's power. Still, Hermes warns Odysseus that he must
make the goddess swear she will play no "witches' tricks." Armed with
the moly and Hermes' warning, Odysseus arrives at Circe's palace.*

    *Circe gives Odysseus a magic drink, but it does not affect
him and he threatens to kill her with his sword. Circe turns the pigs
back into men but puts them all into a trance. They stay for one year,
until Odysseus finally begs her to let them go home. She replies that
they must first visit the land of the dead and hear a prophecy from
the ghost of Tiresias.*

foreboding
(fôr-bō′dĭng) *n.* a sense
of approaching evil.

The Wanderings of Odysseus: Book 10 **387**

WHEN STUDENTS STRUGGLE . . .

To help students keep track of the plot, have them return to their sequence chains
and insert the events described on these pages. Review them as a class.

| Odysseus and his men escape from the Cyclops. | ▶ | They stay with Aeolus, who helps them once but refuses a second time. | ▶ | The Laestrygones destroy all the ships but one. | ▶ | They are trapped by Circe. | ▶ | They travel to the land of the dead. |

CLOSE READ

Support Inferences   RL 1
(LINES 19–38)

Direct students to use details from the text to help
them understand characters' motivations and
feelings.

D2 **ASK STUDENTS** why Polites feels that Circe poses
no threat. *(She is young, her voice is "beguiling," and
she appears to be innocently weaving.)* What makes
Eurylochus fear "a snare"? *(The odd behavior of the
wolves and mountain lions might have made him
suspicious that Circe is not as innocent as she seems.)*

Analyze Author's Choices: RL 5, RL 6
Epic Poem (SYNOPSIS)

Discuss with students how the structure of an epic
includes **multiple plots** that create an action-packed
story.

E2 **ASK STUDENTS** why Odysseus must go to the
land of the dead. What does his willingness to do
this show about his character? *(Circe will not let
them go unless they visit the land of the dead first.
Odysseus' courage is shown by his willingness to visit the
underworld to hear the prophecy.)*

> **CRITICAL VOCABULARY**
>
> **foreboding**: Eurylochus feels such a sense of evil
> from Circe that he is doubtful whether his friends
> can ever be rescued.
>
> **ASK STUDENTS** how Eurylochus reacts to this
> sense of foreboding. What does his solution to the
> problem suggest about his feelings? *(He is so scared
> that he wants to leave the island and abandon the
> other crew members. He has a very strong sense that
> none of them will escape Circe's evil.)*

Analyze Author's Choices: Epic Poem (LINES 1–23)

RL 5, RL 6

Discuss with students what Odysseus does initially and why. Then explain that details of **setting** can create a certain **mood,** or atmosphere, in a work.

 CITE TEXT EVIDENCE Ask students to identify details that describe what Odysseus experiences as he waits by the pit. *(He sees "men grown old in pain," spirits "torn by brazen lanceheads, / battle-slain, bearing still their bloody gear." He hears "rustling cries" from the spirits crowding to get to the blood.)* **What mood is evoked by these details?** *(These sights and sounds instill fear in Odysseus and in the audience. It is eerie and ominous.)*

CRITICAL VOCABULARY

assuage: In order to get what he wants, Odysseus must keep the dead happy by promising and performing sacrifices.

ASK STUDENTS to explain what Odysseus' efforts to assuage the dead reveal about the Greek view of the afterlife. *(The Greeks saw the underworld as the place where people's souls gathered and drifted in a kind of half-life existence, drawn to the blood of once-living animals.)*

BOOK 11:

The Land of the Dead

Odysseus and his crew set out for the land of the dead. They arrive and find the place to which Circe has directed them.

"Then I addressed the blurred and breathless dead,
vowing to slaughter my best heifer for them
before she calved, at home in Ithaca,
and burn the choice bits on the altar fire;
5   as for Tiresias, I swore to sacrifice
a black lamb, handsomest of all our flock.
Thus to assuage the nations of the dead
I pledged these rites, then slashed the lamb and ewe,
letting their black blood stream into the wellpit.
10 Now the souls gathered, stirring out of Erebus,
brides and young men, and men grown old in pain,
and tender girls whose hearts were new to grief;
many were there, too, torn by brazen lanceheads,
battle-slain, bearing still their bloody gear.
15 From every side they came and sought the pit
with rustling cries; and I grew sick with fear.
But presently I gave command to my officers
to flay those sheep the bronze cut down, and make
burnt offerings of flesh to the gods below—
20 to sovereign Death, to pale Persephone.
Meanwhile I crouched with my drawn sword to keep
the surging phantoms from the bloody pit
till I should know the presence of Tiresias.

One shade came first—Elpenor, of our company,
25 who lay unburied still on the wide earth
as we had left him—dead in Circe's hall,
untouched, unmourned, when other cares compelled us.
Now when I saw him there I wept for pity
and called out to him:

                    'How is this, Elpenor,
30 how could you journey to the western gloom
swifter afoot than I in the black lugger?'

He sighed, and answered:

                    'Son of great Laertes,
Odysseus, master mariner and soldier,
bad luck shadowed me, and no kindly power;

assuage (ə-swāj´) *v.* to calm or pacify

10 Erebus (ĕr´ə-bəs): a region of the land of the dead, also known as the underworld or Hades. Hades is also the name of the god of the underworld.

18 flay: to strip off the outer skin of.

TO CHALLENGE STUDENTS . . .

Examine Symbolism Tell students that a theme running through many epics involves the hero's descent to the underworld. Ask students to think about the significance of this journey for a true hero. Have them consider these questions:

- What does the underworld represent?
- By returning from the underworld, what has the hero overcome?

ASK STUDENTS to write a paragraph explaining the symbolism of the hero's visit to the underworld. Have them share their paragraphs in small groups.

"Do not abandon me unwept, unburied, to tempt the gods' wrath, while you sail for home."

35 ignoble death I drank with so much wine.
I slept on Circe's roof, then could not see
the long steep backward ladder, coming down,
and fell that height. My neck bone, buckled under,
snapped, and my spirit found this well of dark.
40 Now hear the grace I pray for, in the name
of those back in the world, not here—your wife
and father, he who gave you bread in childhood,
and your own child, your only son, Telemachus,
long ago left at home.

          When you make sail
45 and put these lodgings of dim Death behind,
you will moor ship, I know, upon Aeaea Island;
there, O my lord, remember me, I pray,
do not abandon me unwept, unburied,
to tempt the gods' wrath, while you sail for home;
50 but fire my corpse, and all the gear I had,
and build a cairn for me above the breakers—
an unknown sailor's mark for men to come.
Heap up the mound there, and implant upon it
the oar I pulled in life with my companions.'

**50–51 fire my corpse
. . . cairn:** Elpenor wants
Odysseus to hold a
funeral for him.

Support Inferences: Draw Conclusions (LINES 36–54) RL 1

Point out that every culture has certain rituals and customs for treating the dead.

G2 ASK STUDENTS what Elpenor's request suggests about the Greek view of the dead. *(Elpenor asks that Odysseus hold a funeral for him. This ritual suggests the respect that the Greeks had for the dead and their belief that a civilized society should honor them.)*

APPLYING ACADEMIC VOCABULARY

objective	undertake

As you discuss Odysseus' actions in this part of the poem, incorporate the following Collection 6 academic vocabulary words: *objective* and *undertake*. Have students explain Odysseus' **objective** in traveling to the underworld and filling a pit with blood. Then have them describe the task that Elpenor wants Odysseus to **undertake** for him.

Analyze Character: Epic Hero (LINES 77–117)

RL 3

Remind students that an epic hero's fate is often of great importance to the gods and to the hero's homeland. Direct students to the prophecy that Odysseus hears from Tiresias, the blind prophet.

H2 ASK STUDENTS to explain whether or not this prophecy will come true. Why or why not? (*Possible answer: Yes, that is why Circe sent Odysseus there; also, prophecies in epics often come true.*) Ask students to discuss which parts of the prophecy depend on the actions of Odysseus and his men. (*When they go through the strait, they must restrain themselves. When they land on Thrinacia, they must not touch the herds of Helios. When Odysseus finally arrives home, he must travel and make a sacrifice to Poseidon as well as sacrifices of one hundred cattle to the gods once he returns to Ithaca. If he and his men do not heed these instructions, then they will suffer the consequences.*) What does the prophecy's structure reveal about the Greek view of fate? (*In this prophecy, a person's actions and decisions play a part, indicating that the Greeks believed in free will. They believed that people could influence the direction of their lives to a certain extent.*)

---

55 He ceased, and I replied:

'Unhappy spirit,
I promise you the barrow and the burial.'

So we conversed, and grimly, at a distance,
with my long sword between, guarding the blood,
while the faint image of the lad spoke on.
60 Now came the soul of Anticlea, dead,
my mother, daughter of Autolycus,
dead now, though living still when I took ship
for holy Troy. Seeing this ghost I grieved,
but held her off, through pang on pang of tears,
65 till I should know the presence of Tiresias.
Soon from the dark that prince of Thebes came forward
bearing a golden staff; and he addressed me:

'Son of Laertes and the gods of old,
Odysseus, master of land ways and sea ways,
70 why leave the blazing sun, O man of woe,
to see the cold dead and the joyless region?
Stand clear, put up your sword;
let me but taste of blood, I shall speak true.'

At this I stepped aside, and in the scabbard
75 let my long sword ring home to the pommel silver,
as he bent down to the sombre blood. Then spoke
the prince of those with gift of speech:

'Great captain,
 a fair wind and the honey lights of home
are all you seek. But anguish lies ahead;
80 the god who thunders on the land prepares it,
not to be shaken from your track, implacable,
in rancor for the son whose eye you blinded.
One narrow strait may take you through his blows:
denial of yourself, restraint of shipmates.
85 When you make landfall on Thrinacia first
and quit the violet sea, dark on the land
you'll find the grazing herds of Helios
by whom all things are seen, all speech is known.
Avoid those kine, hold fast to your intent,
90 and hard seafaring brings you all to Ithaca.
But if you raid the beeves, I see destruction
for ship and crew. Though you survive alone,
bereft of all companions, lost for years,
under strange sail shall you come home, to find

58 with my long sword ...blood: the ghosts are attracted to the blood of the sacrifice; Odysseus must hold them at bay with his sword.

66 prince of Thebes: Tiresias, the blind seer, comes from the city of Thebes (thēbz).

89–91 kine; beeves: two words for cattle.

WHEN STUDENTS STRUGGLE...

To make sure students understand Tiresias's prophecy, have small groups paraphrase these sections: lines 77–90, 91–104, and 105–116.

Remind them that when they paraphrase, they restate the ideas in their own words. Suggest that students write *or* between the first and second section paraphrases and *then* between the second and third paraphrases to show the relationships between the ideas.

ASK STUDENTS to take turns sharing their paraphrases. Write a class version on the board for students to use to correct their own.

95 your own house filled with trouble: insolent men
eating your livestock as they court your lady.
Aye, you shall make those men atone in blood!
But after you have dealt out death—in open
combat or by stealth—to all the suitors,
100 go overland on foot, and take an oar,
until one day you come where men have lived
with meat unsalted, never known the sea,
nor seen seagoing ships, with crimson bows
and oars that fledge light hulls for dipping flight.
105 The spot will soon be plain to you, and I
can tell you how: some passerby will say,
"What winnowing fan is that upon your shoulder?"
Halt, and implant your smooth oar in the turf
and make fair sacrifice to Lord Poseidon:
110 a ram, a bull, a great buck boar; turn back,
and carry out pure hekatombs at home
to all wide heaven's lords, the undying gods,
to each in order. Then a seaborne death
soft as this hand of mist will come upon you
115 when you are wearied out with rich old age,
your country folk in blessed peace around you.
And all this shall be just as I foretell.' . . ."

Odysseus speaks to the shade of his mother. She tells him that
Penelope and Telemachus are still grieving for him and that his
father, Laertes, has moved to the country, where he, too, mourns his
son. Odysseus' mother explains that she died from a broken heart.
Odysseus also speaks with the spirits of many great ladies and men
who died, as well as those who were being punished for their earthly
sins. Filled with horror, Odysseus and his crew set sail.

101–102 where men have lived with meat unsalted: refers to an inland location where men do not eat salted (preserved) meat as sailors do aboard a ship.

CLOSE READ

Analyze Character: Epic Hero (SYNOPSIS)   RL 3

12 **ASK STUDENTS** how Odysseus' conversation with his mother might affect his desire to return home. (*Odysseus might be more anxious to return home after hearing about his wife, son, and father.*)

ENGLISH LANGUAGE SUPPORT

Vocabulary: Compound Words Tell students that **compound words** are formed by putting two or more words together. Project lines 95–116 on the whiteboard. Invite volunteers to mark the text:

- Highlight each compound word. (*livestock, overland, seagoing, passerby, seaborne*)
- Put a slash between the words that form the compound.

ASK STUDENTS to work in pairs to define the compound words using the meanings of each individual word. Model the strategy using the word *livestock*.

Analyze Author's Choices: Epic Poem (LINES 1–25)

RL 5, RL 6

Have students read this passage to find out what additional struggles await Odysseus after he leaves Circe's island.

J2 **ASK STUDENTS** to describe the threat posed by the Sirens. (*They bewitch those passing by with their beautiful songs, enticing sailors to their island to become the Sirens' victims.*) Have students predict whether Odysseus will choose to hear the song. Why or why not? (*He will. He is curious and will not want to miss out on this opportunity.*) Why might Circe not want to advise Odysseus which route to take next? (*As a true epic hero, it is up to him to use his abilities to meet the challenges of his journey. Part of his test is to make hard decisions as well.*)

BOOK 12:

The Sirens; Scylla and Charybdis

Odysseus and his men return to Circe's island. While the men sleep, Circe takes Odysseus aside to hear about the underworld and to offer advice.

"Then said the Lady Circe:
'So: all those trials are over.

                  Listen with care

to this, now, and a god will arm your mind.
Square in your ship's path are Sirens, crying
5 beauty to bewitch men coasting by;
woe to the innocent who hears that sound!
He will not see his lady nor his children
in joy, crowding about him, home from sea;
the Sirens will sing his mind away
10 on their sweet meadow lolling. There are bones
of dead men rotting in a pile beside them
and flayed skins shrivel around the spot.

                       Steer wide;

keep well to seaward; plug your oarsmen's ears
with beeswax kneaded soft; none of the rest
15 should hear that song.

                      But if you wish to listen,

let the men tie you in the lugger, hand
and foot, back to the mast, lashed to the mast,
so you may hear those harpies' thrilling voices;
shout as you will, begging to be untied,
20 your crew must only twist more line around you
and keep their stroke up, till the singers fade.
What then? One of two courses you may take,
and you yourself must weigh them. I shall not
plan the whole action for you now, but only
25 tell you of both.

                  Ahead are beetling rocks

and dark blue glancing Amphitrite, surging,
roars around them. Prowling Rocks, or Drifters,
the gods in bliss have named them—named them well.
Not even birds can pass them by. . . .

30   A second course

lies between headlands. One is a sharp mountain
piercing the sky, with stormcloud round the peak
dissolving never, not in the brightest summer,

2–3 In Circe, Odysseus has found a valuable ally. In the next hundred lines, she describes in detail each danger that he and his men will meet on their way home.

14 kneaded (nĕ´dĭd): squeezed and pressed.

18 those harpies' thrilling voices: the delightful voices of those horrible female creatures.

25 beetling: jutting or overhanging.

26 glancing Amphitrite (ăm´fĭ-trī´tē): sparkling seawater. (Amphitrite is the goddess of the sea and the wife of Poseidon. Here, Circe uses the name to refer to the sea itself.)

31 headlands: points of land jutting out into the sea; promontories.

WHEN STUDENTS STRUGGLE . . .

To clarify plot events, have students return to their sequence chain. Have them work in pairs to identify the events that will happen after Odysseus and his men leave Circe's island. Have students review what Tiresias told Odysseus as well as what Circe says here.

ASK STUDENTS to identify the next obstacles that Odysseus and his men will face in sequential order. (*the Sirens, Scylla and Charybdis, the island of Helios*) Remind them that Odysseus is still telling King Alcinous his story. Ask students where these events would be placed on the sequence chain. (*before the last box, which is his arrival at the court of King Alcinous*)

to show heaven's azure there, nor in the fall.
35 No mortal man could scale it, nor so much
as land there, not with twenty hands and feet,
so sheer the cliffs are—as of polished stone.
Midway that height, a cavern full of mist
opens toward Erebus and evening. Skirting
40 this in the lugger, great Odysseus,
your master bowman, shooting from the deck,
would come short of the cavemouth with his shaft;
but that is the den of Scylla, where she yaps
abominably, a newborn whelp's cry,
45 though she is huge and monstrous. God or man,
no one could look on her in joy. Her legs—
and there are twelve—are like great tentacles,
unjointed, and upon her serpent necks
are borne six heads like nightmares of ferocity,
50 with triple serried rows of fangs and deep
gullets of black death. Half her length, she sways
her heads in air, outside her horrid cleft,
hunting the sea around that promontory
for dolphins, dogfish, or what bigger game
55 thundering Amphitrite feeds in thousands.
And no ship's company can claim
to have passed her without loss and grief; she takes,
from every ship, one man for every gullet.

The opposite point seems more a tongue of land
60 you'd touch with a good bowshot, at the narrows.
A great wild fig, a shaggy mass of leaves,
grows on it, and Charybdis lurks below
to swallow down the dark sea tide. Three times
from dawn to dusk she spews it up
65 and sucks it down again three times, a whirling
maelstrom; if you come upon her then
the god who makes earth tremble could not save you.
No, hug the cliff of Scylla, take your ship
through on a racing stroke. Better to mourn
70 six men than lose them all, and the ship, too.'

So her advice ran; but I faced her, saying:

'Only instruct me, goddess, if you will,
how, if possible, can I pass Charybdis,
or fight off Scylla when she raids my crew?'

75 Swiftly that loveliest goddess answered me:

34 heaven's azure
(ăzh´ər): the blue sky.

abominably
(ə-bŏm´ə-nə-blē) *adv.* in a
hateful way; horribly.

66 maelstrom
(māl´strəm): a large,
violent whirlpool.

The Wanderings of Odysseus: Book 12   **393**

CLOSE READ

Analyze Author's Choices: RL 5, RL 6
Epic Poem (LINES 35–70)

Tell students that Greek myths sometimes explained natural phenomena. As a seafaring people, the Greeks would be affected by hazards on the sea.

K2 ASK STUDENTS to evaluate each of the three options that Circe describes for getting past Scylla and Charybdis. Are they all equal? Why or why not? *(No one, not even a bird, can pass the Prowling Rocks. Charybdis will destroy the boat and everyone on it. Scylla will take some men, but the others will survive.)* What course will Odysseus most likely choose? Why? *(The only sensible course is to pass by Scylla. That is the only route that will get any of them home again.)* Have students discuss what dangers of the sea are represented by Scylla and Charybdis. *(possibly an octopus and a whirlpool)*

CRITICAL VOCABULARY

abominably: The sound that Scylla makes is a horrible yapping noise.

ASK STUDENTS to contrast the behavior of Circe in this book with the sailors' first encounter with her, in which she behaved abominably. *(She is helpful, presenting Odysseus' options and advising him on what to do to successfully overcome each obstacle. Earlier, she turned his men into pigs and kept them prisoners.)*

Strategies for Annotation   🖉 📱 Annotate it!

Analyze Figurative Meanings   RL 4, L 5a

Have students use their eBook tools to analyze the description of Scylla and Charybdis in lines 38–70.

- Highlight similes and metaphors in pink.
- Highlight sensory language in yellow.
- Review your annotations. On a note, explain why this part of the journey will be an especially difficult test of Odysseus' leadership and courage.

no one could look on her in joy. Her legs—
and there are twelve—are like great tentacles,
unjointed, and upon her serpent necks
are borne six heads like nightmares of ferocity,
with triple serried rows of fangs and deep
gullets of black death.

Analyze Character: Epic Hero (LINES 76–85)

RL 3

Tell students that epic heroes often act consistently when confronted with certain situations.

 ASK STUDENTS to summarize Circe's advice to Odysseus here. *(Circe warns Odysseus not to try to fight Scylla. It will give her time to take more men.)* Based on Odysseus' actions in other episodes, will he follow her advice? Why or why not? *(Since Odysseus has ignored warnings in the past, most likely he will follow his own plan here too.)*

Analyze Character: Epic Hero

RL 3

(LINES 101–107)

M2 ASK STUDENTS whether Odysseus has the power to control his fate. Have them explain. *(He can control his own actions but cannot control those of his men. His role in this is to make sure that his men know the possible consequences of their actions.)*

'Must you have battle in your heart forever?
The bloody toil of combat? Old contender,
will you not yield to the immortal gods?
That nightmare cannot die, being eternal
80   evil itself—horror, and pain, and chaos;
there is no fighting her, no power can fight her,
all that avails is flight.
                              Lose headway there
along that rockface while you break out arms,
and she'll swoop over you, I fear, once more,
85   taking one man again for every gullet.
No, no, put all your backs into it, row on;
invoke Blind Force, that bore this scourge of men,
to keep her from a second strike against you.

Then you will coast Thrinacia, the island
90   where Helios' cattle graze, fine herds, and flocks
of goodly sheep. The herds and flocks are seven,
with fifty beasts in each.
                              No lambs are dropped,
or calves, and these fat cattle never die.
Immortal, too, their cowherds are—their shepherds—
95   Phaethusa and Lampetia, sweetly braided
nymphs that divine Neaera bore
to the overlord of high noon, Helios.
These nymphs their gentle mother bred and placed
upon Thrinacia, the distant land,
100   in care of flocks and cattle for their father.

Now give those kine a wide berth, keep your thoughts
intent upon your course for home,
and hard seafaring brings you all to Ithaca.
But if you raid the beeves, I see destruction
105   for ship and crew.
                              Rough years then lie between
you and your homecoming, alone and old,
the one survivor, all companions lost.' . . ."

At dawn, Odysseus and his men continue their journey. Odysseus decides to tell the men only of Circe's warnings about the Sirens, whom they will soon encounter. He is fairly sure that they can survive this peril if he keeps their spirits up. Suddenly, the wind stops.

                              "The crew were on their feet
briskly, to furl the sail, and stow it; then,

82 all . . . flight: all you can do is flee.

87 invoke . . . men: pray to the goddess Blind Force, who gave birth to Scylla.

89 coast: sail along the coast of.

95–96 Phaethusa (fā´ə-thoo´sə); **Lampetia** (lăm-pē´shə); **Neaera** (nē-ē´rə).

101–105 Circe warns Odysseus not to steal Helios' fine cattle because Helios will take revenge.

110   each in place, they poised the smooth oar blades
     and sent the white foam scudding by. I carved
     a massive cake of beeswax into bits
     and rolled them in my hands until they softened—
     no long task, for a burning heat came down
115   from Helios, lord of high noon. Going forward
     I carried wax along the line, and laid it
     thick on their ears. They tied me up, then, plumb
     amidships, back to the mast, lashed to the mast,
     and took themselves again to rowing. Soon,
120   as we came smartly within hailing distance,
     the two Sirens, noting our fast ship
     off their point, made ready, and they sang. . . .

     The lovely voices in ardor appealing over the water
     made me crave to listen, and I tried to say
125   'Untie me!' to the crew, jerking my brows;
     but they bent steady to the oars. Then Perimedes
     got to his feet, he and Eurylochus,
     and passed more line about, to hold me still.
     So all rowed on, until the Sirens
130   dropped under the sea rim, and their singing
     dwindled away.

                      My faithful company
     rested on their oars now, peeling off
     the wax that I had laid thick on their ears;
     then set me free.

                    But scarcely had that island
135   faded in blue air than I saw smoke
     and white water, with sound of waves in tumult—
     a sound the men heard, and it terrified them.
     Oars flew from their hands; the blades went knocking
     wild alongside till the ship lost way,
140   with no oarblades to drive her through the water.
     Well, I walked up and down from bow to stern,
     trying to put heart into them, standing over
     every oarsman, saying gently,

                      'Friends,
     have we never been in danger before this?
145   More fearsome, is it now, than when the Cyclops
     penned us in his cave? What power he had!
     Did I not keep my nerve, and use my wits
     to find a way out for us?

117–118 plumb amidships: exactly in the center of the ship.

126 Perimedes (pĕr´ĭ-mē´dēz).

134–139 The men panic when they hear the thundering surf.

CLOSE READ

Analyze Character: Epic Hero (LINES 117–131)   RL 3

Remind students that an epic hero is characterized by extraordinary traits. Have students revisit their predictions from page 392 about how Odysseus might react to the Sirens. Then have them reread lines 117–131.

N2 ASK STUDENTS how, once again, Odysseus reveals his character through his decisions and actions. (*Odysseus, forewarned by Circe that he might succumb to the sound and message of the Sirens, asks his crew to tie him up so that he can resist the Sirens' lure. As an epic hero, he understands that the Sirens are a test of his resolve, and he uses his abilities to meet the challenges of his journey.*)

(LINES 134–148)

Point out that the audience and Odysseus know what is coming next, but the sailors have no idea.

D2 CITE TEXT EVIDENCE Have students identify details that describe the men's reaction to the uproar of the sea. In what way does Odysseus show himself to be an able leader? (*"Oars flew from their hands; the blades went knocking / wild alongside till the ship lost way." When Odysseus sees this reaction, he walks up and down calming the men and reminding them that he has steered them safely through other conflicts.*)

TO CHALLENGE STUDENTS . . .

Support a Claim Ask students what they think the Sirens would sing to them. Why? Then explain that the symbolism of these creatures is frequently discussed. One view is that they represent temptation; their song is whatever the person desires most in the world to hear.

Have students discuss their ideas about what the Sirens represent in the poem and what they may be singing to Odysseus. Have them cite details from the text to support their view or research the question using valid sources. Ask groups to share their insights with the class.

Analyze Character: Epic Hero (LINES 160–172)   RL 3

Have students recall Circe's warning from earlier in Book 12 about what Odysseus should not do.

P2 ASK STUDENTS to evaluate Odysseus' actions in this passage. Is his decision not to inform his men of Scylla's danger justified? Explain. *(Most likely the men would have balked at going through the strait if they had known of the danger, so Odysseus is probably right to keep it from them.)* Ask students to consider what is revealed by Odysseus' statement that "Circe's / bidding against arms had slipped" his mind. *(His first instinct is to fight. He sees himself as a warrior. He ignores warnings because in his heart he believes he knows more or can meet the threat.)*

Analyze Figurative Meanings (LINES 172–187)   RL 3, L 5a

Direct students to read the description of Charybdis, noting the poet's language.

Q2 CITE TEXT EVIDENCE Ask students which aspect of Charybdis frightens the men more. How does the poet's language convey this fearfulness? *(The men are most frightened when the sea swallows the water to reveal the dark bottom below. The phrases "funnel of the maelstrom," "rock bellowing," "dark / sand raged on the bottom far below," and "yawning mouth in fear / of being devoured" help the audience to envision what the sailors are seeing.)*

CRITICAL VOCABULARY

travail: The men are rowing laboriously and with great effort to try to get through this strait as quickly and safely as possible.

ASK STUDENTS why the sailors might be motivated to keep going in spite of the travail. *(They face certain death if they stop rowing. No matter how much pain they are in, the alternative is much worse.)*

Now I say

by hook or crook this peril too shall be
150   something that we remember.

Heads up, lads!

We must obey the orders as I give them.
Get the oarshafts in your hands, and lay back
hard on your benches; hit these breaking seas.
Zeus help us pull away before we founder.   **154 founder:** sink.
155   You at the tiller, listen, and take in
all that I say—the rudders are your duty;
keep her out of the combers and the smoke;   **157 combers:** breaking waves.
steer for that headland; watch the drift, or we
fetch up in the smother, and you drown us.'   **158–159 watch . . . smother:** keep the ship on course, or it will be crushed in the rough water.

160   That was all, and it brought them round to action.
But as I sent them on toward Scylla, I
told them nothing, as they could do nothing.
They would have dropped their oars again, in panic,
to roll for cover under the decking. Circe's
165   bidding against arms had slipped my mind,
so I tied on my cuirass and took up
two heavy spears, then made my way along
to the foredeck—thinking to see her first from there,
the monster of the gray rock, harboring
170   torment for my friends. I strained my eyes
upon that cliffside veiled in cloud, but nowhere
could I catch sight of her.

And all this time,

in **travail**, sobbing, gaining on the current,   **travail** (trə-vāl´) *n.* painful effort.
we rowed into the strait—Scylla to port
175   and on our starboard beam Charybdis, dire
gorge of the salt sea tide. By heaven! when she   **176 gorge:** throat; gullet.
vomited, all the sea was like a cauldron
seething over intense fire, when the mixture
suddenly heaves and rises.

The shot spume   **179 shot spume:** flying foam.
180   soared to the landside heights, and fell like rain.

But when she swallowed the sea water down
we saw the funnel of the maelstrom, heard
the rock bellowing all around, and dark
sand raged on the bottom far below.
185   My men all blanched against the gloom, our eyes   **185 blanched:** became pale.
were fixed upon that yawning mouth in fear
of being devoured.

ENGLISH LANGUAGE SUPPORT

Analyze Figurative Meanings Project lines 172–187 on the whiteboard. Read aloud the lines. Tell students that **personification** is a figure of speech in which human qualities are given to a nonhuman thing, such as an object or animal.

- Ask students what pronoun the poet uses to refer to the whirlpool. *(she)*
- Explain that the poet is giving human characteristics to the whirlpool Charybdis to help create a vivid picture in the listeners' minds of what is happening. Discuss how the verb "vomited" is also associated with a human activity.
- Help students find and interpret the other examples of personification in this passage.
- Discuss what each example helps them to visualize.

Then Scylla made her strike,
whisking six of my best men from the ship.
I happened to glance aft at ship and oarsmen
190 and caught sight of their arms and legs, dangling
high overhead. Voices came down to me
in anguish, calling my name for the last time.

A man surfcasting on a point of rock
for bass or mackerel, whipping his long rod
195 to drop the sinker and the bait far out,
will hook a fish and rip it from the surface
to dangle wriggling through the air:

                 so these
were borne aloft in spasms toward the cliff.

She ate them as they shrieked there, in her den,
200 in the dire grapple, reaching still for me—
and deathly pity ran me through
at that sight—far the worst I ever suffered,
questing the passes of the strange sea.

           We rowed on.

The Rocks were now behind; Charybdis, too,
205 and Scylla dropped astern. . . ."

189 aft: toward the rear of the ship.

198 borne aloft in spasms: lifted high while struggling violently.

200 grapple: grasp.

CLOSE READ

Analyze Character: Epic Hero (LINES 187–203)   RL 3

R2 **ASK STUDENTS** why Odysseus does not fight Scylla even though he is armed. *(He realizes that he would be helpless against her. He would be lost as well as others.)* What human emotions does Odysseus reveal in this passage? *(He feels terrible when the men call his name as they are borne up to Scylla's cliff. He says that "deathly pity ran me through / at that sight.")*

TEACH

CLOSE READ

COLLABORATIVE DISCUSSION Have students first review the major events in the poem. Then suggest that they skim those passages to find evidence of Odysseus' heroism. After they have organized their responses, have them share their ideas with the class as a whole. Accept all reasonable responses.

ASK STUDENTS to share any questions they generated in the course of reading and discussing the selection.

Odysseus tries to persuade his men to bypass Thrinacia, the island of the sun god, Helios, but they insist on landing. Driven by hunger, they ignore Odysseus' warning not to feast on Helios' cattle. This disobedience angers the sun god, who threatens to stop shining if payment is not made for the loss of his cattle. To appease Helios, Zeus sends down a thunderbolt to sink Odysseus' ship. Odysseus alone survives. He eventually drifts to Ogygia, the home of Calypso, who keeps him on her island for seven years. With this episode, Odysseus ends the telling of his tale to King Alcinous.

COLLABORATIVE DISCUSSION In what instances does Odysseus demonstrate his greatest acts of heroism? Discuss your ideas with a partner. Cite specific textual evidence to support your ideas.

WHEN STUDENTS STRUGGLE . . .

Review students' sequence chains with them, adding Odysseus' sojourn on Calypso's island before the last box. Then organize students into groups of three.

- Have them divide up the entries in their charts so that each member of the group has approximately the same number of events.
- Have them write brief summaries of the important ideas connected with each of their events.
- Have group members present their summaries in sequential order.

Analyze Character: Epic Hero

RL 3

Odysseus is an **epic hero**—a larger-than-life character who embodies the ideals of a nation or race. Epic heroes take part in long, dangerous adventures and accomplish great deeds. They are considered **archetypes** because they can be found in many works from different cultures throughout the ages.

Although epic heroes may have superhuman abilities, they still have human flaws. These flaws make them more complex and appealing. For example, Odysseus demonstrates extraordinary strength and courage, but his overconfidence results in a tendency to dismiss warnings. His imperfections help make him more likable than a perfect character, and the audience can relate to his mistakes. These questions can help you analyze how the complex character of Odysseus develops over the course of the epic:

- What do you learn about Odysseus' character through how he faces various conflicts?
- What traits, or qualities, does Odysseus show through his interactions with other characters?
- What do Odysseus' character traits tell you about what the ancient Greeks found admirable?

Analyzing the Text

RL 1, RL 2, RL 3

Cite Text Evidence   Support your responses with evidence from the selection.

1. **Infer** What do you learn about the character of Odysseus through the poet's introduction in Book 1 (lines 1–17)?

2. **Summarize** How does Odysseus regard the Cyclopes, based on the description in lines 56–67 of Book 9? What does this description reveal about Odysseus' values as well as the values of the ancient Greeks?

3. **Interpret** As Odysseus recalls his men's pleas to flee the Cyclops' cave, he remarks, "Ah, / how sound that was! Yet I refused. I wished / to see the caveman, what he had to offer." What qualities of an epic hero does Odysseus reveal in this comment?

4. **Analyze** What strengths does Odysseus demonstrate in his encounter with the Cyclops? Explain.

5. **Summarize** Why does Odysseus continue to taunt the Cyclops as he pulls away from the shore? What traits does he demonstrate through this behavior, and what are the consequences?

6. **Analyze** A **foil** is a character who contrasts with another character. How does the character of Eurylochus serve as a foil to Odysseus in Book 10?

7. **Infer** What does the audience learn about Odysseus from his encounters with his shipmate Elpenor and his mother Anticlea in Book 11?

The Odyssey   **399**

PRACTICE & APPLY

Analyze Character: Epic Hero

RL 3

Review the ideas about epic heroes. Have students form three groups. Have each group discuss answers to one of the questions and report on their discussion to the class.

Analyzing the Text

RL 1, RL 2, RL 3

Possible answers:

1. The passage reveals Odysseus' talent, wisdom, determination, and courage. Telling phrases are "that man skilled in all ways contending," "harried for years on end," and "while he fought only to save his life, to bring his shipmates home."

2. Odysseus views the Cyclopes as barbaric. Their lack of government, knowledge, work ethic, traditions, and compassion for others clearly conflicts with Odysseus' values and the values of the Greeks.

3. His comment reveals his ability to critique his behavior and recognize his own faults.

4. Odysseus demonstrates his courage, forethought, cleverness, and carefulness through the following actions: taking his twelve best men to the cave and leaving the rest to guard the ship, carrying Maron's drink as a potential weapon, telling the Cyclops that he and his men had been shipwrecked, realizing that if he kills the Cyclops in the cave he and his men will be trapped, making the stake to stab the Cyclop's eye, telling the Cyclops that his name is Nohbdy, and hiding under the rams to escape from the cave.

5. Odysseus wants the Cyclops to know who outwitted him because the Cyclops killed his men and insulted him. This shows his excessive pride and his tendency to dismiss potential dangers. In response to Odysseus' taunts, the Cyclops prays to his father Poseidon to take revenge.

6. By advising Odysseus to sail away from the island after Circe turns the other men into pigs, Eurylochus serves as a foil to Odysseus through his conservative, less impulsive style of leadership and through his reluctance to risk his life in order to save his comrades.

7. Odysseus' encounter with Elpenor's ghost shows that he is a well-respected, dutiful, and gracious leader who feels loyalty and responsibility for his crew. His encounter with his mother's soul reveals that he is a loving, devoted son. In both encounters Odysseus shows patience, respect, and grace.

The Odyssey   **399**

Critical Vocabulary

L 4c

Answers:

1. *adversary*

2. *foreboding*

3. *harried*

4. *abominably*

5. *profusion*

6. *assuage*

7. *travail*

8. *ponderous*

Vocabulary Strategy: Prefixes

Students' discussions should accurately reflect each word's etymology and meaning.

Possible example words and sentences:

1. adolescent: *The agency will not allow an adolescent to rent a car.*

2. prophecy: *The oracle uttered a prophecy that made the crew quite afraid.*

3. abstract: *Mortimer, refusing to offer any practical advice, spoke about the problem only in abstract terms.*

4. submarine: *Miguel, fishing just outside the harbor, was shocked to see a submarine surface alongside his skiff.*

5. obsolete: *Ramona could not open the downloaded file on her obsolete laptop.*

Critical Vocabulary

L 4c

| harried | ponderous | profusion | adversary |
| foreboding | assuage | abominably | travail |

Practice and Apply   Use the Critical Vocabulary words to answer the questions. Then, with a partner, take turns providing evidence to support your answers.

1. Which word is an antonym, or a word with the opposite meaning, of *friend*?

2. Which word most closely relates to *prediction*?

3. Which word is an antonym of *calm*?

4. Which word most closely relates to *atrociously*?

5. Which word is an antonym of *shortage*?

6. Which word most closely relates to *soothe*?

7. Which word most closely relates to *struggle*?

8. Which word most closely relates to *awkward*?

Vocabulary Strategy: Prefixes

Recognizing **prefixes** can help you understand the meanings of unfamiliar words. For example, in the Critical Vocabulary word *foreboding*, the prefix *fore-*, meaning "beforehand," combines with the verb *bode*, meaning "to give signs of something." This can help you understand the definition "a sense of impending doom." Here are some more examples.

Prefixes	Meanings	Examples
ad-, as-	to, toward, before	adversary, assuage
pro-	in place of, in favor of, forward	profusion, proceed
ab-	away from	abominably, abject
sub-	below, almost, close after	subsequent, subordinate
ob-	before, toward, inversely	objective, obligate

Practice and Apply   Consult a dictionary to determine the meaning of each example word in the chart. Then, discuss with a partner how each word's prefix relates to its meaning. Finally, identify another example word for each prefix, and use the word in a sentence.

ENGLISH LANGUAGE SUPPORT

To facilitate students' understanding of the Vocabulary Strategy activity, write the definitions of each example word on the board.

Have students work in mixed language-ability groups to match the words with the definitions, using their knowledge of the prefixes. Have them explain how the prefix relates to the word's meaning.

ASK STUDENTS to take turns using each example word in a sentence.

TEACH

CLOSE READ

AS YOU READ Direct students to use the As You Read note to focus their reading.

Analyze Author's Choices: Epic Poem (LINES 1–14) RL 5, RL 6

Explain that a **symbol** is a person, place, object, or activity that stands for something other than itself. Tell students that an epic may contain symbols to deepen the meaning or convey an important idea.

 ASK STUDENTS to look closely at the description of Odysseus' faithful dog Argos. In what way might Argos symbolize Ithaca since Odysseus has been gone? *(Argos has deteriorated just as Ithaca has in the twenty years that Odysseus has been gone. The dog has been neglected and poorly treated; Penelope and Telemachus too have suffered at the hands of the suitors.)*

PART TWO: THE HOMECOMING

AS YOU READ Pay attention to how the events in the epic build toward a resolution. Write down any questions you generate during reading.

BOOK 17:

The Beggar at the Manor

In Books 13–15, King Alcinous and his friends send Odysseus on his way home. Odysseus sleeps while the rowers bring him to Ithaca. When he awakens, he fails to recognize his homeland until Athena appears and tells him that he is indeed home. She disguises him as an old man, so that he can surprise the suitors, and then urges him to visit his faithful swineherd, Eumaeus. Athena goes to Telemachus and tells him to return home. She warns him of the suitors' plot to kill him and advises him to stay with the swineherd for a night. Telemachus does as she bids.

    In Book 16, Odysseus reveals his identity to Telemachus, and a tearful reunion ensues. Telemachus lets Odysseus know that they face more than 100 suitors. Odysseus tells Telemachus to return home. He will follow, and Telemachus must pretend not to know him. He must also lock away Odysseus' weapons and armor. Telemachus returns home, and Odysseus and the swineherd soon follow. Odysseus is still diguised as a beggar.

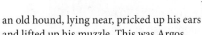
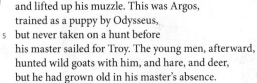

                                   While he spoke

 an old hound, lying near, pricked up his ears
and lifted up his muzzle. This was Argos,
trained as a puppy by Odysseus,
5 but never taken on a hunt before
his master sailed for Troy. The young men, afterward,
hunted wild goats with him, and hare, and deer,
but he had grown old in his master's absence.
Treated as rubbish now, he lay at last
10 upon a mass of dung before the gates—
manure of mules and cows, piled there until
fieldhands could spread it on the king's estate.
Abandoned there, and half destroyed with flies,
old Argos lay.

Close Read Screencasts

Modeled Discussions

Have students click the *Close Read* icons in their eBooks to access the screencast in which readers discuss and annotate the following key passage:

• Argos's recognition of Odysseus (Book 17, lines 9–20)

As a class, view and discuss the video. Then have students pair up to do an independent close read of an additional passage—Penelope's realization of Odysseus' true identity (Book 23, lines 54–67).

CLOSE READ

Analyze Character: Epic Hero (LINES 14–27)

RL 3

Remind students that they know a great deal about Odysseus from the first part of the poem; however, he may reveal additional **traits** as he faces new challenges.

B **ASK STUDENTS** to note how Odysseus hides his emotions in this scene. Why might this trait be important later in the poem? (*In order to carry off his disguise successfully, Odysseus will have to control his emotions when he sees his wife and others to whom he is close.*)

Analyze Author's Choices: Epic Poem (LINES 27–41)

RL 5, RL 6

Remind students that **dramatic irony** is when the audience knows something that the characters do not. This device is used by authors to heighten suspense and intensify the impact of an event or scene.

C **ASK STUDENTS** to explain the dramatic irony of this scene. (*Eumaeus is talking about Odysseus, unaware that it is Odysseus he is speaking to.*) Have students explain what this dramatic irony suggests about future events in the poem. (*No one else, including Penelope and the suitors, will know that the old beggar is Odysseus in disguise. Odysseus will be able to execute his plan.*)

> But when he knew he heard
>
> **B** 15 Odysseus' voice nearby, he did his best
> to wag his tail, nose down, with flattened ears,
> having no strength to move nearer his master.
> And the man looked away,
> wiping a salt tear from his cheek; but he
> 20 hid this from Eumaeus. Then he said:
>
> "I marvel that they leave this hound to lie
> here on the dung pile;
> he would have been a fine dog, from the look of him,
> though I can't say as to his power and speed
> 25 when he was young. You find the same good build
> in house dogs, table dogs landowners keep
> all for style."
>
> And you replied, Eumaeus:
>
> **C** "A hunter owned him—but the man is dead
> in some far place. If this old hound could show
> 30 the form he had when Lord Odysseus left him,
> going to Troy, you'd see him swift and strong.
> He never shrank from any savage thing
> he'd brought to bay in the deep woods; on the scent
> no other dog kept up with him. Now misery
> 35 has him in leash. His owner died abroad,
> and here the women slaves will take no care of him.
> You know how servants are: without a master
> they have no will to labor, or excel.
> For Zeus who views the wide world takes away
> 40 half the manhood of a man, that day
> he goes into captivity and slavery."
>
> Eumaeus crossed the court and went straight forward
> into the mégaron among the suitors;
> but death and darkness in that instant closed
> 45 the eyes of Argos, who had seen his master,
> Odysseus, after twenty years. . . .
>
> *Odysseus enters his home as a beggar, and the suitors mock and abuse him. Penelope asks to speak with the beggar, but Odysseus puts her off until nightfall.*

43 mégaron: the main hall of a palace or house

TO CHALLENGE STUDENTS . . .

Analyze Rhetoric and Details What adjectives describe your feelings throughout the first part of the *Odyssey*? Have students reread lines 1–46. Would they use the same adjectives or different ones? Elicit from students the idea that this scene is touching and poignant unlike those in the first part of the poem.

Have students work in small groups to explore the ways in which the poet communicates these feelings. Have them consider the use of dialogue, the symbolism of the dog, the qualities shown by the dog, and Odysseus' own feelings.

Ask groups to share their analyses with the class. Together, discuss the purpose of this scene in the poem.

BOOK 21:

The Test of the Bow

In Books 18–20, Odysseus observes the suitors and finds that two in particular, Antinous and Eurymachus, are rude and demanding. Penelope asks Odysseus the beggar for news of her husband. He says he has heard that Odysseus is on his way home. Penelope, however, has given up hope for Odysseus' return. She proposes an archery contest to the suitors, with marriage to her as the prize. She enters the storeroom and takes down the heavy bow that Odysseus left behind.

Now the queen reached the storeroom door and halted.
Here was an oaken sill, cut long ago
and sanded clean and bedded true. Foursquare
the doorjambs and the shining doors were set
5   by the careful builder. Penelope untied the strap
around the curving handle, pushed her hook
into the slit, aimed at the bolts inside
and shot them back. Then came a rasping sound
as those bright doors the key had sprung gave way—
10 a bellow like a bull's vaunt in a meadow—
followed by her light footfall entering
over the plank floor. Herb-scented robes
lay there in chests, but the lady's milkwhite arms
went up to lift the bow down from a peg
15 in its own polished bowcase.

                                    Now Penelope

sank down, holding the weapon on her knees,
and drew her husband's great bow out, and sobbed
and bit her lip and let the salt tears flow.
Then back she went to face the crowded hall,
20 tremendous bow in hand, and on her shoulder hung
the quiver spiked with coughing death. Behind her
maids bore a basket full of axeheads, bronze
and iron implements for the master's game.
Thus in her beauty she approached the suitors,
25 and near a pillar of the solid roof
she paused, her shining veil across her cheeks,
her maids on either hand and still,
then spoke to the banqueters:

15–18 Notice that Penelope still grieves for Odysseus, even after 20 years.

21 quiver (kwĭv´ər): a case in which arrows are carried.

22–23 axeheads . . . game: metal heads of axes (without handles) that Odysseus employs in a display of archery skill.

Analyze Author's Choices:
Epic Poem (LINES 8–12)   RL 5, RL 6

Remind students that an **archetype** is a pattern in literature that is found in a variety of works from different cultures and time periods.

D **ASK STUDENTS** to identify the archetypal image in these lines. Have them explain how this image builds suspense. *(The image of a bull bellowing in a field is an archetypal male image which suggests strength, anger, and power. The bellowing indicates both a warning and a challenge. The bull represents Odysseus and reminds the audience that he is preparing to defend his home and family.)*

Analyze Character   RL 3

(LINES 16–23)

Point out to students that Penelope is an important **character** in her own right, although much of the poem so far has focused on Odysseus. Direct them to read this passage to learn more about her.

E **ASK STUDENTS** what Penelope's actions here reveal about her. *(As she takes down Odysseus' bow, she begins to sob. This shows that even after twenty years, she still misses him. She is a faithful and loving wife.)*

WHEN STUDENTS STRUGGLE . . .

To guide students' comprehension of the text, have them work in pairs to make a list of words and short phrases used to describe Penelope in lines 5–25. One partner should read aloud the passage while the other student takes notes. Have them review the notes and then use them to answer the following questions.

- What words describe Penelope's physical appearance?
- What words and phrases show that she is strong?
- What is her purpose in going to the storeroom?
- What is her conflict?

ASK STUDENTS to share their responses.

Analyze Author's Choices: Epic Poem (LINES 28–40)

RL 5, RL 6

Explain that the first four books of the *Odyssey* which are not included in these excerpts, develop the plot of Penelope, Telemachus, and the suitors. Point out that this speech helps to summarize what has occurred over the past twenty years.

F **CITE TEXT EVIDENCE** Have students identify the details that explain Penelope's conflict. (*The suitors "commandeered this house/to feast and drink in, day and night." They "found/no justification" for themselves except their "lust" to marry her.*) Ask students what can be inferred from the requirements of the contest. (*Penelope wants to make it as difficult as she can in the hopes that no one will be able to accomplish it.*)

Support Inferences

RL 1

(LINES 41–59)

Remind students that Odysseus' disguise gives him the opportunity to observe the reactions of those around him.

G **ASK STUDENTS** why the swineherd and cowherd are described as "downcast." (*They may fear that one of the suitors will win the contest. They do not think any of them worthy to take Odysseus' place.*) What does their reaction lead Odysseus to do? (*He further tests their loyalty to see if they would support him.*)

CRITICAL VOCABULARY

commandeer: Once they thought Odysseus was safely out of the way, the suitors took over his house by force.

ASK STUDENTS what kind of characters would commandeer someone else's house. What impression of the suitors does this word create? (*The suitors are bullies and opportunists taking advantage of a helpless woman.*)

F

30

35

"My lords, hear me:
suitors indeed, you **commandeered** this house
to feast and drink in, day and night, my husband
being long gone, long out of mind. You found
no justification for yourselves—none
except your lust to marry me. Stand up, then:
we now declare a contest for that prize.
Here is my lord Odysseus' hunting bow.
Bend and string it if you can. Who sends an arrow
through iron axe-helve sockets, twelve in line?
I join my life with his, and leave this place, my home,
my rich and beautiful bridal house, forever

40

to be remembered, though I dream it only.". . .

Despite heating and greasing the bow, the lesser suitors prove unable to string it. The most able suitors, Antinous and Eurymachus, hold off. While the suitors are busy with the bow, Odysseus—still disguised as an old beggar—goes to enlist the aid of two of his trusted servants, Eumaeus, the swineherd, and Philoetius, the cowherd.

G

45

Two men had meanwhile left the hall:
swineherd and cowherd, in companionship,
one downcast as the other. But Odysseus
followed them outdoors, outside the court,
and coming up said gently:

"You, herdsman,
and you, too, swineherd, I could say a thing to you,
or should I keep it dark?

No, no; speak,
my heart tells me. Would you be men enough

50

to stand by Odysseus if he came back?
Suppose he dropped out of a clear sky, as I did?
Suppose some god should bring him?
Would you bear arms for him, or for the suitors?"

The cowherd said:

"Ah, let the master come!
Father Zeus, grant our old wish! Some courier

55

guide him back! Then judge what stuff is in me
and how I manage arms!"

Likewise Eumaeus
fell to praying all heaven for his return,
so that Odysseus, sure at least of these,
told them:

commandeer
(kŏm´ən-dîr´) *v.* to take
control of by force.

35–37 Note that the
contest has two parts:
first the suitor must
bend the heavy bow
and string it—a task
that requires immense
strength and skill—and
then he must shoot an
arrow straight through
the holes in 12 axe
heads set up in a row.

"I am at home, for I am he.

60 I bore **adversities**, but in the twentieth year
I am ashore in my own land. I find
the two of you, alone among my people,
longed for my coming. Prayers I never heard
except your own that I might come again.

65 So now what is in store for you I'll tell you:
If Zeus brings down the suitors by my hand
I promise marriages to both, and cattle,
and houses built near mine. And you shall be
brothers-in-arms of my Telemachus.

70 Here, let me show you something else, a sign
that I am he, that you can trust me, look:
this old scar from the tusk wound that I got
boar hunting on Parnassus. . . ."

                                    Shifting his rags

75 he bared the long gash. Both men looked, and knew,
and threw their arms around the old soldier, weeping,
kissing his head and shoulders. He as well
took each man's head and hands to kiss, then said—
to cut it short, else they might weep till dark—

80 "Break off, no more of this.
Anyone at the door could see and tell them.
Drift back in, but separately at intervals
after me.
                              Now listen to your orders:
when the time comes, those gentlemen, to a man,

85 will be dead against giving me bow or quiver.
Defy them. Eumaeus, bring the bow
and put it in my hands there at the door.
Tell the women to lock their own door tight.
Tell them if someone hears the shock of arms

90 or groans of men, in hall or court, not one
must show her face, but keep still at her weaving.
Philoetius, run to the outer gate and lock it.
Throw the cross bar and lash it.". . .

*Odysseus the beggar asks the suitors if he might try the bow. Worried
that the old man may show them up, they refuse, but Penelope urges
them to let Odysseus try. At Telemachus' request, Penelope leaves the
men to settle the question of the bow among themselves. Two trusted
servants lock the doors of the room, and Telemachus orders the bow
be given to Odysseus.*

adversity
(ăd-vûr′sĭ-tē) *n.* hardship;
misfortune.

73 Parnassus
(pär-năs′əs): a mountain
in central Greece.

The Homecoming: Book 21   **405**

ENGLISH LANGUAGE SUPPORT

Define Idioms Remind students that when they encounter **idioms,**
or phrases meaning something different from their words, they should
use context clues to help them understand the expressions. Project lines
59–85. Ask for volunteers to mark the text, prompting them as needed:

- Highlight idioms in yellow. *("in store for you" [line 65]; "to cut it short"*
  [line 79]; "to a man" [line 84]; "dead [set] against" [line 85])
- Underline words that give clues to the meaning of each expression.

ASK STUDENTS to define each expression using the context clues. *(line*
65: what your future will be; line 79: to conclude what otherwise might
continue; line 84: every one; line 85: completely opposed to the idea of)

Analyze Character   RL 3
(LINES 59–79)

Tell students that **archetypal characters** such
as Eumaeus and Philoetius appear frequently in
literature and films.

H **ASK STUDENTS** what trait these two servants
embody. *(They are loyal.)* Have students explain why
this trait is valued by Odysseus especially at this
particular time. *(He needs allies to help him execute*
his plan.)

Analyze Author's Choices: RL 5, RL 6
Epic Poem (LINES 80–93)

Remind students that because an epic poem is a
narrative, it is structured to include the major parts of
a **plot.** Review these terms with students: exposition,
rising action, climax, falling action, resolution.

I **ASK STUDENTS** to explain what they think
is going to happen. What stage of the plot is
approaching? *(With these instructions and the*
revelation of his identity, the action rises and the climax
approaches. Odysseus is planning to confront the suitors
with his two servants and his son once he has the bow
and arrows.)

> **CRITICAL VOCABULARY**
>
> **adversity:** Odysseus tells his two servants that
> he endured many hardships before arriving back
> safely in Ithaca.
>
> **ASK STUDENTS** to explain how Odysseus will
> overcome the adversity with which he struggles
> now. *(He must reestablish his authority over his*
> *kingdom. He will do this by defeating the suitors.)*

Analyze Author's Choices: Epic Poem (LINES 94–102)

RL 5, RL 6

Point out to students that the poet heightens the suspense in this part of the poem.

J **ASK STUDENTS** to identify the primary conflict in lines 94–102. *(The conflict is between Odysseus and the suitors.)* In what way does dramatic irony add to the suspense of this scene for the audience? *(The audience knows who the beggar is and what he is capable of. The suitors continue to make fun of him, believing him to be a helpless old man.)*

And Odysseus took his time,
95 turning the bow, tapping it, every inch,
    for borings that termites might have made
    while the master of the weapon was abroad.
    The suitors were now watching him, and some
    jested among themselves:

                              "A bow lover!"

100 "Dealer in old bows!"

                        "Maybe he has one like it
at home!"

                  "Or has an itch to make one for himself."

"See how he handles it, the sly old buzzard!"

ENGLISH LANGUAGE SUPPORT

Understand Conversational Patterns Explain to students that words are sometimes omitted in conversation. Read aloud the dialogue on this page. Point out that in line 80 (page 405), Odysseus leaves out the words "We must," but they are understood by the listeners.

Have students work with a partner to identify the lines of dialogue on this page that have missing words.

ASK STUDENTS to rewrite each line, inserting the missing words. Call on pairs to read their completed sentences.

And one disdainful suitor added this:

"May his fortune grow an inch for every inch he bends it!"
105 But the man skilled in all ways of contending,
satisfied by the great bow's look and heft,   **106 heft:** weight.
like a musician, like a harper, when
with quiet hand upon his instrument
he draws between his thumb and forefinger
110 a sweet new string upon a peg: so effortlessly
Odysseus in one motion strung the bow.
Then slid his right hand down the cord and plucked it,
so the taut gut vibrating hummed and sang
a swallow's note.

       In the hushed hall it smote the suitors   **114 smote:** struck;
115 and all their faces changed. Then Zeus thundered affected sharply.
overhead, one loud crack for a sign.
And Odysseus laughed within him that the son   **115–116** The thunder, a
of crooked-minded Cronus had flung that omen down. sign from Zeus, indicates
He picked one ready arrow from his table   that the gods are on
120 where it lay bare: the rest were waiting still   Odysseus' side.
in the quiver for the young men's turn to come.
He nocked it, let it rest across the handgrip,   **118 Cronus** (krō´nəs):
and drew the string and grooved butt of the arrow, Zeus' father.
aiming from where he sat upon the stool.
         Now flashed   **122 nocked it:** placed
125 arrow from twanging bow clean as a whistle   the arrow's feathered
through every socket ring, and grazed not one, end against the
to thud with heavy brazen head beyond.   bowstring.
       Then quietly
Odysseus said: **127 brazen:** made of
               brass.
     "Telemachus, the stranger
you welcomed in your hall has not disgraced you.
130 I did not miss, neither did I take all day
stringing the bow. My hand and eye are sound,
not so **contemptible** as the young men say.   **contemptible**
The hour has come to cook their lordships' mutton— (kən-tĕmp´tə-bəl) *adj.*
supper by daylight. Other amusements later,   deserving of scorn;
135 with song and harping that adorn a feast."   despicable.

He dropped his eyes and nodded, and the prince
Telemachus, true son of King Odysseus,
belted his sword on, clapped hand to his spear,
and with a clink and glitter of keen bronze
140 stood by his chair, in the forefront near his father.

ENGLISH LANGUAGE SUPPORT

Vocabulary: Analyze Epic Similes Explain that epic similes appeal to multiple senses. Project lines 105–114. Have volunteers mark the text:

- Underline the action being described. *(Odysseus strung the bow.)* Then highlight in blue what Odysseus is compared to. *(a musician, a harper)*

- Highlight in green words and phrases that appeal to the sense of sight. *(he draws between . . . upon a peg)* Then highlight in yellow words and phrases that appeal to the sense of touch. *(slid his right . . . plucked it, taut gut vibrating)*

ASK STUDENTS to describe the overall impression of Odysseus' action that is created by this simile.

CLOSE READ

Analyze Figurative Meanings (LINES 105–114) RL 4, L 5a

Remind students that an **epic simile** is a comparison that is developed at length.

K CITE TEXT EVIDENCE Ask students to explain the epic simile found in this passage. *(Odysseus' action of stringing his bow is compared to a musician putting a new string in his instrument. When he is finished, he "plucked it, / so the taut gut vibrating hummed and sang / a swallow's note.")* Ask students to think about why the simile is appropriate. *(Odysseus will make his bow sing as he sends arrows through the air; he is as skilled as a musician in playing his bow.)*

Analyze Author's Choices: Epic Poem (LINES 114–140) RL 5, RL 6

Discuss with students how the poet sets the scene with the single crack of thunder. Remind them that it is only with the gods' help that Odysseus was able to get home safely.

L ASK STUDENTS to reread lines 124–127. Have them discuss why so few lines are devoted to Odysseus' actual winning of the contest. *(Winning the contest is not a challenge for Odysseus. This shows him to be a true hero, since the others could not even string the bow, let alone think of sending the arrow straight through. It is also unimportant to Odysseus to win it. The contest was a means to an end.)*

Point out that the book ends with the father and son standing side by side facing more than one hundred enemies.

M ASK STUDENTS why the scene described in lines 136–140 might be considered an epic moment. *(Odysseus is making a stand against an enemy that greatly outnumbers him in order to defend home, hearth, and honor against those who have scorned and abused him and his family. He must bring to bear all of his heroic traits—bravery, strength, determination, and cunning—in order to vanquish this enemy.)*

Analyze Figurative Meanings (LINES 1–4)   RL 4, L 5a

Remind students that **epithets** are phrases that point out traits associated with a particular person, giving the audience a deeper understanding of character.

 ASK STUDENTS to identify the epithet in these lines. What ideas are conveyed by this phrase? *(Odysseus is called "the wiliest fighter of the islands." Someone who is wily is tricky and cunning. This describes Odysseus' cleverness and ability to think his way out of a problem.)*

Analyze Author's Choices: Epic Poem (LINES 4–20)   RL 5, RL 6

Explain that this passage contains **epic conventions** such as calling on the gods to assist the hero. Apollo is the god of archers and the bow is his weapon.

O ASK STUDENTS why Odysseus invokes the name of Apollo. *(Odysseus needs to accurately shoot Antinous. He won't get a second chance.)* Have students discuss the strategy behind Odysseus' first shot. *(Antinous is a leader of the suitors. With him gone, it will be more difficult for them to organize and defend themselves.)*

Remind students that epics convey universal themes related to love, honor, and death.

P ASK STUDENTS what idea about death is suggested in lines 9–13. *(Death comes unexpectedly and in the middle of life.)* What words describe the forcefulness of Odysseus' shot? What is the purpose of this description? *(The arrow "punched up to the feathers through his throat." "His nostrils jetted/crimson runnels." This description helps the audience to experience the shock felt by the suitors.)*

CRITICAL VOCABULARY

revelry: Antinous, confident that there is no threat from the beggar, continues to party with his friends. **ASK STUDENTS** what Antinous's continued revelry and his action of drinking out of Odysseus' golden cup suggest about his character. *(He is arrogant.)*

BOOK 22:

Death in the Great Hall

Now shrugging off his rags the wiliest fighter of the islands
leapt and stood on the broad door sill, his own bow in his hand.
He poured out at his feet a rain of arrows from the quiver
and spoke to the crowd:

5   "So much for that. Your clean-cut game is over.
Now watch me hit a target that no man has hit before,
if I can make this shot. Help me, Apollo."

He drew to his fist the cruel head of an arrow for Antinous
just as the young man leaned to lift his beautiful drinking cup,
embossed, two-handled, golden: the cup was in his fingers:
10   the wine was even at his lips: and did he dream of death?
How could he? In that **revelry** amid his throng of friends
who would imagine a single foe—though a strong foe indeed—
could dare to bring death's pain on him and darkness on his
        eyes?
Odysseus' arrow hit him under the chin
15   and punched up to the feathers through his throat.

Backward and down he went, letting the winecup fall
from his shocked hand. Like pipes his nostrils jetted
crimson runnels, a river of mortal red,
and one last kick upset his table
20   knocking the bread and meat to soak in dusty blood.

Now as they craned to see their champion where he lay
the suitors jostled in uproar down the hall,
everyone on his feet. Wildly they turned and scanned
the walls in the long room for arms; but not a shield,
25   not a good ashen spear was there for a man to take and throw.
All they could do was yell in outrage at Odysseus:

"Foul! to shoot at a man! That was your last shot!"

"Your own throat will be slit for this!"

                "Our finest lad is down!

You killed the best on Ithaca."

                "Buzzards will tear your eyes out!"

P revelry (rĕv´əl-rē) *n.* noisy merrymaking; festivity.

18 runnels: streams.

23–25 Earlier, in preparation for this confrontation, Odysseus and Telemachus removed all the weapons and shields that were hanging on the walls.

WHEN STUDENTS STRUGGLE . . .

Tell students that when they read a passage that includes dialogue, they need to indicate the change in speaker by adjusting their voice expression, rate, and volume. Direct students' attention to lines 4–20. Read them aloud to model how to signal to listeners that the dialogue is finished and the narrative has resumed.

ASK STUDENTS to form pairs to practice fluent reading.

- One partner should read the passage while the other listens to hear how the reader accomplishes the shift from dialogue to narrative.
- Have them reverse roles.
- Then have pairs discuss strengths of each reading before taking turns to read a different passage of dialogue and narrative aloud.

30 For they imagined as they wished—that it was a wild shot,
    an unintended killing—fools, not to comprehend
    they were already in the grip of death.
    But glaring under his brows Odysseus answered:

    "You yellow dogs, you thought I'd never make it
35 home from the land of Troy. You took my house to plunder,
    twisted my maids to serve your beds. You dared
    bid for my wife while I was still alive.
    Contempt was all you had for the gods who rule wide heaven,
    contempt for what men say of you hereafter.
40 Your last hour has come. You die in blood."

    As they all took this in, sickly green fear
    pulled at their entrails, and their eyes flickered
    looking for some hatch or hideaway from death.
    Eurymachus alone could speak. He said:

45 "If you are Odysseus of Ithaca come back,
    all that you say these men have done is true.
    Rash actions, many here, more in the countryside.
    But here he lies, the man who caused them all.
    Antinous was the ringleader; he whipped us on
50 to do these things. He cared less for a marriage
    than for the power Cronion has denied him
    as king of Ithaca. For that
    he tried to trap your son and would have killed him.
    He is dead now and has his portion. Spare
55 your own people. As for ourselves, we'll make
    restitution of wine and meat consumed,
    and add, each one, a tithe of twenty oxen
    with gifts of bronze and gold to warm your heart.
    Meanwhile we cannot blame you for your anger."

60 Odysseus glowered under his black brows
    and said:
                "Not for the whole treasure of your fathers,
    all you enjoy, lands, flocks, or any gold
    put up by others, would I hold my hand.
    There will be killing till the score is paid.
65 You forced yourselves upon this house. Fight your way out,
    or run for it, if you think you'll escape death.
    I doubt one man of you skins by."

    They felt their knees fail, and their hearts—but heard
    Eurymachus for the last time rallying them.

42 entrails: internal organs.

47 rash: foolish; thoughtless.

51 Cronion (krō´nē-ŏn´): Zeus, the son of Cronus.

restitution (rĕs´tĭ-tōō´shən) *n.* a making good for loss or damage; repayment.

57 tithe: payment.

67 skins by: sneaks away.

Analyze Author's Choices: RL 5, RL 6
Epic Poem (LINES 30–59)

Remind students to look for characters' **motivations** as revealed through their dialogue.

Q CITE TEXT EVIDENCE Ask students to explain Odysseus' success in taking the suitors by surprise. *(They believe that the killing of Antinous is "a wild shot, / an unintended killing.")* What is the purpose of Odysseus' speech in lines 34–40? *(He wants the suitors to know why they are going to die. Now that the element of surprise is over, he wants them to realize that he is back and that they have gravely insulted him and his family.)* Have students explain why Eurymachus responds to Odysseus. *(He wants to save himself and his friends by shifting the responsibility onto Antinous, who is already dead. He also hopes to take away Odysseus' anger by apologizing and promising restitution of wine and meat consumed as well as twenty oxen and gifts of bronze and gold. He reminds Odysseus that the suitors are his own people.)*

> **CRITICAL VOCABULARY**
>
> **restitution:** In his desperation, Eurymachus promises a generous repayment to make up for the suitors' wrongdoing.
>
> **ASK STUDENTS** why Odysseus refuses to accept Eurymachus's offer of restitution. *(He is too deeply angry. He doesn't feel that "things" can repair the damage done to his household and family.)*

TO CHALLENGE STUDENTS...

Compare and Contrast Remind students of the epithets that they might use to describe themselves. Point out that depending on where they are and what they are doing, those epithets might vary.

ASK STUDENTS to analyze, in groups, epithets used to describe Odysseus.

• Have them list the phrases from Part 1 and the context in which each appears.

• Then have them identify epithets used in this part of the poem.

• Have them discuss how the epithets are the same or different. Ask them to explain how these epithets foreshadow important scenes and fit the context of each part of the poem.

Analyze Character   RL 3

(LINES 70–79)

 ASK STUDENTS to reread lines 70–79. Then ask them to explain what they learn about Eurymachus based on his conduct and words in this situation. *(Although an enemy, he is courageous and makes a good leader. He rallies the suitors, saying "Fight, I say, let's remember the joy of it. Swords out!" He is a strategist as shown by his command to rush Odysseus where he stands.)*

Analyze Author's Choices: RL 5, RL 6
Epic Poem (LINES 80–106)

Explain that a major characteristic of an epic is a battle described with specific details.

S **ASK STUDENTS** how the battle with the suitors has taken on epic proportions. *(There are almost 100 suitors to Odysseus, Telemachus, and the two servants. The odds are not on the side of Odysseus, but the gods are, which heightens the epic proportions of the battle. Odysseus must use all of his skills to win this battle. If he does so, he will prove himself an epic hero in every sense of the phrase.)*

CRITICAL VOCABULARY

implacable: Eurymachus realizes that talking to Odysseus further is useless; Odysseus is unforgiving.

ASK STUDENTS how Eurymachus knows that Odysseus is implacable. *(Odysseus refuses his offer of restitution; he warns Eurymachus and the others that he is going to kill them all; he shows great anger in his last speech to Eurymachus.)*

---

70   "Friends," he said, "the man is **implacable**.
   Now that he's got his hands on bow and quiver
   he'll shoot from the big door stone there
   until he kills us to the last man.

                                        Fight, I say,
   let's remember the joy of it. Swords out!
75   Hold up your tables to deflect his arrows.
   After me, everyone: rush him where he stands.
   If we can budge him from the door, if we can pass
   into the town, we'll call out men to chase him.
   This fellow with his bow will shoot no more."

80   He drew his own sword as he spoke, a broadsword of fine
         bronze,
   honed like a razor on either edge. Then crying hoarse and loud
   he hurled himself at Odysseus. But the kingly man let fly
   an arrow at that instant, and the quivering feathered butt
   sprang to the nipple of his breast as the barb stuck in his liver.
85   The bright broadsword clanged down. He lurched and fell
         aside,
   pitching across his table. His cup, his bread and meat,
   were spilt and scattered far and wide, and his head slammed
         on the ground.
   Revulsion, anguish in his heart, with both feet kicking out,
   he downed his chair, while the shrouding wave of mist closed
         on his eyes.

90   Amphinomus now came running at Odysseus,
   broadsword naked in his hand. He thought to make
   the great soldier give way at the door.
   But with a spear throw from behind Telemachus hit him
   between the shoulders, and the lancehead drove
95   clear through his chest. He left his feet and fell
   forward, thudding, forehead against the ground.

   Telemachus swerved around him, leaving the long dark spear
   planted in Amphinomus. If he paused to yank it out
   someone might jump him from behind or cut him down with
         a sword
100   at the moment he bent over. So he ran—ran from the tables
   to his father's side and halted, panting, saying:

   "Father let me bring you a shield and spear,
   a pair of spears, a helmet.
   I can arm on the run myself; I'll give
105   outfits to Eumaeus and this cowherd.
   Better to have equipment."

implacable
(ĭm-plăk´ə-bəl) *adj.*
impossible to soothe;
unforgiving.

88–89 Eurymachus'
death is physically
painful, but he also has
"revulsion, anguish in his
heart."

90 Amphinomus
(ăm-fĭn´ə-məs): one of
the suitors.

WHEN STUDENTS STRUGGLE . . .

Remind students that they can use details from the text and their own knowledge to understand more than what is stated. Direct students to lines 80–89. Point out that as Eurymachus dies, he is described as having "anguish in his heart." Display this inference chart on the board. Have students work together to infer the cause of Eurymachus's anguish.

Details	Knowledge	Inference
has "anguish in his heart"; thinks that Odysseus has a right to be angry	Loyalty is prized highly by the ancient Greeks. Subjects are supposed to be loyal to their king.	He feels guilty for dishonoring his king and showing a lack of loyalty.

"Run then, while I hold them off with arrows as long as the arrows last."

Said Odysseus:

"Run then, while I hold them off with arrows
as long as the arrows last. When all are gone
if I'm alone they can dislodge me."

                                     Quick

110 upon his father's word Telemachus
ran to the room where spears and armor lay.
He caught up four light shields, four pairs of spears,
four helms of war high-plumed with flowing manes,
and ran back, loaded down, to his father's side.

115 He was the first to pull a helmet on
and slide his bare arm in a buckler strap.
The servants armed themselves, and all three took their stand
beside the master of battle.

                            While he had arrows
he aimed and shot, and every shot brought down

120 one of his huddling enemies.
But when all barbs had flown from the bowman's fist,
he leaned his bow in the bright entry way
beside the door, and armed: a four-ply shield
hard on his shoulder, and a crested helm,

125 horsetailed, nodding stormy upon his head,
then took his tough and bronze-shod spears. . . .

113 helms: helmets.

CLOSE READ

Analyze Author's Choices: RL 5, RL 6
Epic Poem (LINES 109–118)

Point out that this part of the epic reveals more about the character of Telemachus.

(T) ASK STUDENTS how Telemachus conducts himself in the conflict with the suitors. *(Telemachus shows that he is the son of Odysseus in character and action as well as in blood. He fights courageously in battle, shows initiative, and is able and competent.)*

ENGLISH LANGUAGE SUPPORT

Language: Phrasal Verbs Remind students that they have encountered **phrasal verbs** in other parts of the poem and have used context clues to define them. Review the strategy, using the context of the phrasal verb
yank [it] out in line 98 to define it as "remove."

ASK STUDENTS to work with a partner to apply the same strategy to define these phrasal verbs: *cut [him] down* (line 99); *hold off* (line 107); *brought down* (line 119). Discuss their responses and the clues they used to help them.

Analyze Author's Choices: Epic Poem (SYNOPSIS)

RL 5, RL 6

U **ASK STUDENTS** to note Athena's motive in not assisting Odysseus and Telemachus yet. What does this reasoning suggest about the Greek view of the relationship between the gods and humans? *(The Greeks knew that their own actions influenced whether or not the gods intervened on their behalf. They could make the gods angry as Odysseus did. They could make the gods look favorably upon them by honoring them and trying to live up to the ideals of the society. Odysseus and Telemachus have to prove that they are worthy of Athena's help.)*

U *The suitors make various unsuccessful attempts to expel Odysseus from his post at the door. Athena urges Odysseus on to battle, yet holds back her fullest aid, waiting for Odysseus and Telemachus to prove themselves. Six of the suitors attempt an attack on Odysseus, but Athena deflects their arrows. Odysseus and his men seize this opportunity to launch their own attack, and the suitors begin to fall. At last Athena's presence becomes known to all, as the shape of her shield becomes visible above the hall. The suitors, recognizing the intervention of the gods on Odysseus' behalf, are frantic to escape but to no avail. Odysseus and his men are compared to falcons who show no mercy to the flocks of birds they pursue and capture. Soon the room is reeking with blood. Thus the battle with the suitors comes to an end, and Odysseus prepares himself to meet Penelope.*

412 Collection 6

APPLYING ACADEMIC VOCABULARY

pursuit	subsequent

As you discuss the events in the climax of the poem, incorporate the Collection 6 academic vocabulary words *pursuit* and *subsequent*. Ask students to discuss Odysseus' **pursuit** of justice and the ways in which it is similar to or different from their concept of justice. Then ask students how his actions here might help or harm him in his **subsequent** return to his throne.

BOOK 23:

The Trunk of the Olive Tree

Greathearted Odysseus, home at last,
was being bathed now by Eurynome
and rubbed with golden oil, and clothed again
in a fresh tunic and a cloak. Athena

5　lent him beauty, head to foot. She made him
taller, and massive, too, with crisping hair
in curls like petals of wild hyacinth
but all red-golden. Think of gold infused
on silver by a craftsman, whose fine art

10　Hephaestus taught him, or Athena: one
whose work moves to delight: just so she lavished
beauty over Odysseus' head and shoulders.
He sat then in the same chair by the pillar,
facing his silent wife, and said:

　　　　　　　　　　　　"Strange woman,
15　the immortals of Olympus made you hard,
harder than any. Who else in the world
would keep aloof as you do from her husband
if he returned to her from years of trouble,
cast on his own land in the twentieth year?

20　Nurse, make up a bed for me to sleep on.
Her heart is iron in her breast."

　　　　　　　　　　　　　Penelope

spoke to Odysseus now. She said:

　　　　　　　　　　　　"Strange man,
if man you are . . . This is no pride on my part
nor scorn for you—not even wonder, merely.
25　I know so well how you—how he—appeared
boarding the ship for Troy. But all the same . . .
Make up his bed for him, Eurycleia.
Place it outside the bedchamber my lord
built with his own hands. Pile the big bed
30　with fleeces, rugs, and sheets of purest linen."

With this she tried him to the breaking point,
and he turned on her in a flash raging:

"Woman, by heaven you've stung me now!
Who dared to move my bed?

2　Eurynome
(yŏŏ-rĭn´ə-mē): a female
servant.

10　Hephaestus
(hĭ-fĕs´təs): the god of
metalworking.

11　lavished: showered.

**15　immortals of
Olympus:** the gods, who
live on Mount Olympus.

27–30 The bed, built
from the trunk of an
olive tree still rooted in
the ground, is actually
unmovable.

CLOSE READ

Analyze Figurative　　　　　RL 4, L 5a
Meanings (LINES 1–12)

Review the definition of **allusion** with students,
reminding them that it is an indirect reference to a
well-known figure or literary text.

Ⓥ ASK STUDENTS what the allusion to Hephaestus
in line 10 conveys about Odysseus' appearance.
*(This allusion heightens the impression of Odysseus'
magnificent transformation.)*

Analyze Author's Choices:　　　RL 5, RL 6
Epic Poem (LINES 14–30)

Discuss with students how a character's attitude is
revealed through his or her words.

Ⓦ ASK STUDENTS to explain the conflict that
Odysseus faces in this book. Why is this conflict
different from his other struggles? *(He must win his
wife's trust. He cannot do this through battle or guile.)*
Have them describe Penelope's attitude toward
Odysseus. What words and phrases reveal this
attitude? *(Penelope is skeptical. She calls him "strange
man" and questions whether he is a man, suspecting
he might be a god or something else.)* Have students
explain why she feels this way. *(She has been taken
advantage of and dishonored so many times that she
no longer trusts anyone. She may also not want to be
disappointed if he turns out to be a fraud.)*

Strategies for Annotation

✎ 🖺 Annotate it!

Analyze Figurative Meanings　　　RL 4, L 5a

Have students use their eBook annotation tools to analyze the language
that describes Odysseus in lines 1–14.

- Underline words with strongly positive connotations. On a note,
  explain what ideas about Odysseus they convey.
- Highlight similes in yellow. On a note, analyze the feeling and idea
  brought out by the comparison.
- Highlight images that appeal to the senses in blue.
- Discuss in a small group the purpose of Odysseus' transformation.

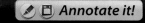

lent him beauty, head to foot. She made him

taller, and massive, too, with crisping hair

in curls like petals of wild hyacinth

but all red-golden. Think of gold infused

on silver by a craftsman, whose fine art

Hephaestus taught him, or Athena: one

Determine Theme RL 2

(LINES 40–51)

Remind students that symbols often help to convey **theme**.

X **ASK STUDENTS** to describe the features of the bed. In what way might this bed symbolize the marriage of Odysseus and Penelope? *(The bed is built around an olive tree that cannot be moved. This bed represents the stability and inability of anyone to harm the marriage of Penelope and Odysseus. It also symbolizes Penelope's faithfulness during the years that Odysseus was gone.)*

Analyze Author's Choices: RL 5, RL 6
Epic Poem (LINES 51–74)

Explain that after the climax, the narrative moves to a resolution of the remaining conflicts.

Y **ASK STUDENTS** how Penelope has resolved her conflict. In what way does her solution show her to be well matched with Odysseus? *(Penelope has proved that Odysseus is her husband by getting him to reveal what he knows about their bed, which no one else would. In this way, she proves that she is as clever as he is and a good match for him.)*

> #### CRITICAL VOCABULARY
>
> **tremulous:** Penelope is shaking with emotion as she realizes that her husband truly has returned to her.
>
> **ASK STUDENTS** to think about the result of the contest. What emotions other than joy are causing her to be tremulous? *(She is feeling relief that she doesn't have to marry a stranger.)*

---

35   No builder had the skill for that—unless
a god came down to turn the trick. No mortal
in his best days could budge it with a crowbar.
There is our pact and pledge, our secret sign,
built into that bed—my handiwork
40   and no one else's!

                   An old trunk of olive
grew like a pillar on the building plot,
and I laid out our bedroom round that tree,
lined up the stone walls, built the walls and roof,
gave it a doorway and smooth-fitting doors.
45   Then I lopped off the silvery leaves and branches,
hewed and shaped that stump from the roots up
into a bedpost, drilled it, let it serve
as model for the rest. I planed them all,
inlaid them all with silver, gold and ivory,
50   and stretched a bed between—a pliant web
of oxhide thongs dyed crimson.

                      There's our sign!
I know no more. Could someone else's hand
have sawn that trunk and dragged the frame away?"

Their secret! as she heard it told, her knees
55   grew **tremulous** and weak, her heart failed her.
With eyes brimming tears she ran to him,
throwing her arms around his neck, and kissed him,
murmuring:

                   "Do not rage at me, Odysseus!
No one ever matched your caution! Think
60   what difficulty the gods gave: they denied us
life together in our prime and flowering years,
kept us from crossing into age together.
Forgive me, don't be angry. I could not
welcome you with love on sight! I armed myself
65   long ago against the frauds of men,
impostors who might come—and all those many
whose underhanded ways bring evil on!
Helen of Argos, daughter of Zeus and Leda,
would she have joined the stranger, lain with him,
70   if she had known her destiny? known the Achaeans
in arms would bring her back to her own country?
Surely a goddess moved her to adultery,
her blood unchilled by war and evil coming,
the years, the **desolation**; ours, too.

50–51 a pliant web . . . crimson: a network of ox-hide straps, dyed red, stretched between the sides of the bed to form a springy base for the bedding.

tremulous
(trĕm´yə-ləs) *adj.* marked by trembling or shaking.

68 Argos (är´gŏs); **Leda** (lē´də).

desolation
(dĕs´ə-lā´shən) *n.* lonely grief; misery.

WHEN STUDENTS STRUGGLE . . .

To help students review what they know about the characters of both Odysseus and Penelope, have them compare their qualities. Write these traits on the board: *courage, cleverness, patience, caution.* Discuss the meaning of each and how it would be shown.

- Organize students into four groups. Assign each group one of the traits.
- Have them review the poem to find an example of how both Odysseus and Penelope show that quality.
- Ask students to share their examples. Record them in a chart on the board.

ASK STUDENTS to discuss why Penelope is a good match for Odysseus.

Analyze Figurative Meanings (LINES 81–89)

RL 4, L 5a

Ⓩ ASK STUDENTS to explain the epic simile in lines 81–89. Why is this simile apt considering Odysseus' experiences? *(Penelope is compared to a safe shore where a tired, shipwrecked swimmer arrives after a monumental struggle for survival in tumultuous seas. This simile is apt because of Odysseus' many adventures on the sea and the many times he had to battle for his life.)*

75　But here and now, what sign could be so clear
　　as this of our own bed?
　　No other man has ever laid eyes on it—
　　only my own slave, Actoris, that my father
　　sent with me as a gift—she kept our door.
80　You make my stiff heart know that I am yours."

　　Now from his breast into his eyes the ache
　　of longing mounted, and he wept at last,
　　his dear wife, clear and faithful, in his arms,
　　longed for
　　　　　　　　　as the sunwarmed earth is longed for by a swimmer
85　spent in rough water where his ship went down
　　under Poseidon's blows, gale winds and tons of sea.
　　Few men can keep alive through a big surf

78 Actoris (ăk-tôr´ĭs).

The Homecoming: Book 23　**415**

TO CHALLENGE STUDENTS . . .

Analyze Connections Would Homer have ever dreamed that his characters and story would be the source of inspiration for countless writers? Share examples of works based on the *Odyssey*, such as these poems: "Ulysses" by Alfred Lord Tennyson; "Penelope" by Dorothy Parker; "Ithaka" by C.P. Cavafy; and "An Ancient Gesture" by Edna St. Vincent Millay.

Have students choose one of the poems and analyze its connection to the characters, themes, and events in Homer's poem. They should write a paragraph or two to support their ideas with details from both literary works.

Have students discuss their poems in groups, explaining how the poem gave them a new perspective on Homer's work or added to their understanding.

COLLABORATIVE DISCUSSION Have students review the second part of the poem, jotting down notes on the events and the details that create suspense and tension. Have partners then compare notes before sharing their conclusions with the class as a whole. Accept all reasonable responses.

ASK STUDENTS to share any questions they generated in the course of reading and discussing the selection.

to crawl, clotted with brine, on kindly beaches
in joy, in joy, knowing the abyss behind:
90 and so she too rejoiced, her gaze upon her husband,
her white arms round him pressed as though forever. . . .

Odysseus and Penelope tell each other about all that happened to them while Odysseus was away. Then Odysseus visits his father, Laertes, to give him the good news of his safe return. Meanwhile, the townspeople, angry about the deaths of the young suitors, gather to fight Odysseus. In the end, Athena steps in and makes peace among them all.

COLLABORATIVE DISCUSSION What are the moments of greatest tension in Part 2? With a partner, discuss what details in the text help build tension. Cite specific textual evidence to support your ideas.

WHEN STUDENTS STRUGGLE . . .

To increase students' comprehension of Part 2 of the poem, have them review the elements of plot.

- Display a two-column chart on the board with the headings "Conflict" and "Resolution."
- Organize students into small groups and have them work together to identify the major conflicts that Odysseus must overcome in this part of the poem and the way in which those conflicts are resolved. Remind them to refer to the italicized text in addition to the lines of the poem.
- Have groups take turns contributing their conflicts and resolutions to the class chart.

Analyze Author's Choices: Epic Poem

In the simplest terms, an epic is a long adventure story. An **epic** plot spans many years and involves a long journey. Often, the fate of an entire nation is at stake. An epic **setting** spans great distances and foreign lands. Epic **themes** reflect timeless concerns, such as courage, honor, life, and death.

Consider these questions as you analyze how the author's choices about the structure of the *Odyssey* help create a compelling narrative:

- How are the characteristics of an epic reflected in the plot, setting, characters, and themes?
- In what ways does the *Odyssey* embody the qualities and ideals of ancient Greek culture?
- What themes are still applicable today?

Analyze Figurative Meanings

RL 4, L 5a

Epics are often rich with **figurative language,** or words used to symbolize ideas and evoke emotions rather than to convey literal meanings. As you analyze the figurative meanings in the *Odyssey*, consider the cumulative impact that this language has on the reader's ability to imagine the settings, characters, and events.

Figurative Language	Example
An **epic simile** (also called a Homeric simile) is a long, elaborate comparison that often continues for a number of lines.	Odysseus compares gouging out the Cyclops's eye to turning a huge drill: "I leaned on it / turning it as a shipwright turns a drill / in planking, having men below to swing / the two-handled strap that spins it in the groove. / So with our brand we bored that great eye socket. . . ."
An **epithet** is a brief phrase that reflects traits associated with a particular person or thing.	Odysseus is referred to as "son of Laertes," "raider of cities," and "that man skilled in all ways of contending".
An **allusion** is an indirect reference to a famous person, place, event, or literary work.	The poet calls upon a daughter of Zeus, often credited with inspiration: "Sing in me, Muse, and through me tell the story".
A **metaphor** directly compares two things by saying that one thing *is* another.	Odysseus comments on Penelope's aloofness: "Her heart is iron in her breast".

The Odyssey **417**

TEACH

CLOSE READ

Analyze Author's Choices: Epic Poem

RL 5, RL 6

Help students to understand the various elements of an epic poem. Explain that everything happens on a grand scale in the *Odyssey*. The journey takes ten years, the monsters are supernatural, and the hero has abilities beyond most humans as well as help from the gods. Point out that although elements of the epic may be unrealistic, its messages about how to live honorably and courageously are relevant and the hero's ideal traits serve as a model for inspiration.

Analyze Figurative Meanings

RL 4, L 5a

Review the examples in the chart. Then organize students into small groups and ask them to find one additional example of each type of figurative language. Have them note the book and line numbers for each example and discuss the meaning of each example in their groups. Finally, have each group share their examples with the class.

Strategies for Annotation

Annotate it!

Analyze Figurative Meanings

RL 4, L 5a

Have students use their eBook annotation tools to help them identify and analyze the figurative language in the poem.

- Using different colors, highlight an example of a metaphor, an epic simile, an allusion, and an epithet.
- On a note, identify each example and explain what it adds to your understanding of the characters or events.
- Share your examples in small groups.

He dropped his eyes and nodded, and the prince

Telemachus, 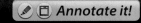 true son of King Odysseus,

belted his sword on, clapped hand to his spear,

PRACTICE & APPLY

Analyzing the Text

RL 1, RL 2, RL 4, RL 5, RL 6, L 5a

Possible answers:

1. *Divine intervention is one characteristic of an epic. Both Athena and Zeus support Odysseus' efforts to reclaim his home and reunite with his wife. Athena disguises him as a beggar, shows her shield, and later beautifies him. Zeus' crack of thunder terrifies the suitors.*

2. *Homer explores universal themes such as courage and honor, the nature of good and evil, life and death, and the importance of family and home. Odysseus' triumph expresses the idea that good wins over evil. The mass killing of the suitors conveys the message that people have little control over life and death.*

3. *Penelope is wary of being tricked. The way in which she tests Odysseus reveals that she too is clever and sly; she has also grown distrustful and may feel resigned to disappointments.*

4. *Odysseus must remain in disguise until he can challenge his enemies openly. He first reveals himself to Telemachus, then Eumaeus and Philoetius. He declares his identity to the suitors upon taking a stand against them, and finally shows himself to Penelope after they have been defeated. The gradual series of revelations dramatically heightens the tension for each event in the sequence.*

5. *Both characters endure extreme hardship, although Penelope's struggles are more mental than physical. Both characters possess the ideal traits of heroes: strength, intelligence, courage, honor, loyalty, and devotion.*

6. *The epithet's use in Book 21 (line 105) has greater impact and meaning because it appears within the context of Odysseus preparing to fight against considerable odds. The epithet also foreshadows Odysseus' inevitable triumph over his enemies.*

7. *The metaphor compares the falling arrows to pouring rain, illustrating that Odysseus is an able warrior who knows how to prepare for battle and foreshadowing that arrows will fall on his opponents like water from the sky.*

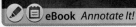

Analyzing the Text

RL 1, RL 2, RL 4, RL 5, RL 6, W 3a, W 3d, L 5a

Cite Text Evidence   Support your responses with evidence from the selection.

1. **Summarize** In what ways does the role of the gods in Part Two reflect the characteristics of an epic?

2. **Identify** What universal themes does Homer explore in the *Odyssey*? Choose two events from either Part One or Part Two, and explain how Homer conveys a **theme**, or central message, in each.

3. **Analyze** What motivates Penelope to test Odysseus' identity? What does this reveal about her character and how she has been affected by her husband's absence?

4. **Interpret** How does the order in which Odysseus reveals himself to his friends and loved ones build suspense? Explain.

5. **Compare** In what ways are Penelope's struggles similar to and different from those of Odysseus? What ideal traits do both characters possess?

6. **Analyze** The epithet "that man skilled in all ways of contending" first appears in Book 1 and subsequently in Book 21 as Odysseus strings his bow in front of the suitors. How does this epithet have greater impact and meaning in Book 21 in the epic?

7. **Interpret** Determine the meaning of the figurative language in this line: "He poured out at his feet a rain of arrows from the quiver" (Book 22, line 3). What impact does this metaphor have on the description of Odysseus as a warrior?

PERFORMANCE TASK

Writing Activity: Narrative The point of view in the *Odyssey* rarely wavers from Odysseus' perspective. Nevertheless, other characters' words and actions hint at what they are thinking. Explore the epic from another point of view through this brief writing task:

- Narrate an event from the *Odyssey* from the point of view one of the following characters: Polyphemus, Circe, Eurylochus, Tiresias, Scylla, Athena, Eumaeus, Telemachus, Eurymachus, or Penelope.

- Engage and orient the reader using techniques such as dialogue and description to set up the situation and create a smooth progression of events.
- Use precise words and phrases, telling details, and sensory language to convey a vivid picture of the events.

Assign this performance task.

PERFORMANCE TASK

W 3a, W 3d

Writing Activity: Narrative Have students draft narratives on their own. Suggest they decide which event they would like to narrate and then note details that would reflect the perspective of the character they choose to narrate it. Explain that the character should be involved in the incident, and that details in the text should support his or her perspective. Have partners exchange drafts and provide constructive feedback.

Critical Vocabulary

| commandeer | adversity | contemptible | revelry |
| restitution | implacable | tremulous | desolation |

Practice and Apply Use your knowledge of the Critical Vocabulary words to answer each question. Then, take turns explaining your answers to a partner.

1. Would it be effective for a person trying to **commandeer** a situation to speak in a **tremulous** voice? Why?

2. Why might people who have survived some kind of **adversity** engage in **revelry?**

3. Is it always possible to make **restitution** after doing something **contemptible?** Why?

4. How might an **implacable** assault on a city lead to **desolation?**

Vocabulary Strategy: Words from Latin

Recognizing **word roots** can help you determine the meanings of unfamiliar words. For example, the Critical Vocabulary word *desolation*, meaning "a feeling of loneliness," contains the Latin root *sol*, which means "alone." This root is found in numerous other English words. Study the Latin roots and their meanings in the chart, along with example words that contain each root.

Latin Root	Meaning	Examples
sol-	alone	soliloquy, solo
trem-	tremble	tremor, tremulous
plac-	calm	implacable, placate
vers-	turn	adversity, versatile

Practice and Apply For each Latin root in the chart, follow these steps:

1. Look online or in print resources for one additional example of a word that uses the Latin root.

2. Use your knowledge of the root's meaning to write a definition for each example word.

3. Consult a dictionary to confirm each example word's meaning.

4. Use each example word in a sentence.

PRACTICE & APPLY

Critical Vocabulary

Possible answers:

1. *No; a person trying to take control should speak in a strong, assertive voice, not a shaky one.*

2. *Because they are so happy and relieved that their hardship has ended, they might want to celebrate with a party.*

3. *No; sometimes an action is so terrible and disgusting that the person who did it cannot make amends.*

4. *Such an assault would show no pity for the people of the city, ending with utter devastation and grief.*

Vocabulary Strategy: Words from Latin

Possible answers:

- **sole:** *alone, or one and only. Ishmael was the shipwreck's sole survivor.*

- **tremolo:** *a vibrating musical effect caused by the rapid repetition of a note. By tapping their bows to produce a tremolo effect, the violinists created the impression of falling rain.*

- **placid:** *peaceful, with little movement or activity. A pebble, tossed into the placid water, sent rings rippling across the pond.*

- **reverse:** *turn in an opposite direction or inside out. We hiked two miles into the blind canyon, then had to reverse our course.*

ENGLISH LANGUAGE SUPPORT

Vocabulary: Word Roots Organize students into same-language groups. Assign each group one of the Latin roots.

- Have them create a web for their root word, including as many words from their home language that contain the root as possible.

- Have them then write the English equivalent for each word they have identified.

- Have groups share their webs with the class.

Language and Style: Absolute Phrases

L 1b

Explain that authors use **absolute phrases** to add details or imagery to their sentences. An absolute phrase describes the entire main clause of the sentence and is always set off by commas. Write one of the example phrases on the board and work together as a class to identify and understand the absolute phrase and its purpose in the sentence. Ask students to explain how the absolute phrase adds detail to the sentence.

For practice, divide students into pairs and have them work together to write three sentences with absolute phrases. When they are finished, have them share their work with the class.

Answers:

Students' revisions of their narratives should demonstrate an ability to give additional information by incorporating absolute phrases and show an understanding of proper usage and punctuation.

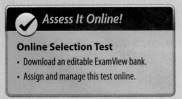

Assess It Online!

Online Selection Test
- Download an editable ExamView bank.
- Assign and manage this test online.

Language and Style: Absolute Phrases

L 1b

An **absolute phrase** consists of a noun and a participle, a verb form ending in -*ed* or -*ing* that acts as an adjective. Absolute phrases must be set off with commas and may also contain objects of the participle and any modifiers. Rather than modifying a specific word in a sentence, absolute phrases describe the main clause of a sentence. Absolute phrases are a helpful way to add information to a sentence.

Look at this example of an absolute phrase from the *Odyssey*.

> I drove them, <u>all three wailing</u>, to the ships,
> tied them down under their rowing benches,
> and called the rest.

In this sentence, the absolute phrase *all three wailing* is also an example of imagery. The phrase adds information and helps evoke a sense of what it was like for Odysseus to drag his men from the land of the Lotus Eaters.

This chart shows two other examples of absolute phrases.

Absolute Phrase	What It Modifies
<u>Arrows soaring past them,</u> the suitors scanned the room looking for weapons and shields.	The noun *arrows* is modified by the participle *soaring* and the additional modifiers *past them*. The absolute phrase modifies, or describes, the rest of the sentence, *the suitors scanned the room looking for weapons and shields.*
Odysseus dreamed only of his return to Ithaca, <u>his mind focused on his reunion with Penelope.</u>	The noun *mind* is modified by the participle *focused* and the additional modifiers *his* and *on his reunion with Penelope*. The absolute phrase modifies the rest of the sentence, *Odysseus dreamed only of his return to Ithaca.*

Practice and Apply Look back at the narrative you wrote in response to this selection's Performance Task. Revise your narrative to include at least two absolute phrases. Share your revised narrative with a partner and discuss how your revisions add variety and interest.

Analyze Character

RL 3

TEACH

Point out that the *Odyssey*, like other epics, includes a variety of **archetypal characters** that conform to certain patterns. Ask students to list examples, such as the faithful servants, the treacherous enemies, the loyal son, the devoted wife, and the courageous hero.

Explain that several of these characters are archetypes only. They are not developed into full-fledged characters; they are there to serve a particular purpose in the epic. Tell students that others, however, such as the hero Odysseus and his wife Penelope, are more completely imagined. They are characters in their own right; just as importantly, they stand as a representation of what the particular culture held to be ideal for a person of that gender and position.

Clarify that to understand what is revealed about the ancient Greek culture through Odysseus and Penelope, it is necessary to keep these ideas in mind:

- The ways in which they differ from other heroes and "devoted wives" give insight into the specific traits valued by the Greeks.
- In Odysseus' case, the characteristics of his personality that lead to trouble for himself or others are the opposite of the Greek ideal.

PRACTICE AND APPLY

Ask students to recall Odysseus' behavior with the Cyclops. What does this episode show about the traits that the Greeks did not admire? *(Odysseus is not ideal in the way that he taunts the Cyclops out of pride and puts his men in danger to satisfy his own arrogance. He and his men are punished for this behavior.)* Ask students to think about the qualities of Odysseus that are emphasized in his dealings with his enemies. What in addition to courage and strength helps him to overcome these foes? *(intelligence, cunning, the ability to reason)* Have students consider Penelope. What qualities beyond faithfulness does she show? *(She is able to hold off the suitors for twenty years by a variety of tricks, showing her own cleverness. She is strong in spirit.)* In what ways are the ideal man and woman of the ancient Greeks, as embodied in Odysseus and Penelope, similar to or different from the ideal man and woman of today? *(They share the qualities of strength, courage, and intelligence. They are different in that the ideal man and woman today share a balance of domestic and worldly pursuits undreamed of in ancient Greek culture.)*

Analyze Author's Choices: Epic Poem

RL 5, RL 6

RETEACH

Review an **epic poem's** elements, ensuring students grasp the characteristics of the plot, setting, hero, and themes.

- Have students tell how the *Odyssey's* plot conforms to an epic plot. *(The hero takes a ten-year journey and overcomes many obstacles on his quest. He must use his strength and wits to fight supernatural creatures and mortal enemies. He must battle to regain his throne and restore order to Ithaca.)*
- Have students volunteer the ways in which the setting of the *Odyssey* is epic in nature. *(Odysseus visits exotic and unknown lands and even descends to the underworld.)*
- Have students identify universal themes brought out by the poem and cite evidence to support their interpretation. *(The* Odyssey *shows there is no place like home through Odysseus' intense efforts to return to Ithaca. It celebrates the importance of knowledge as a means of discovering one's place in the world and conveys the idea that one must face conflict with courage and intelligence. It presents the truth that humans cannot avoid death, but can embrace life while alive.)*

 LEVEL UP TUTORIALS Assign the following *Level Up* tutorial: **Universal and Recurring Themes.**

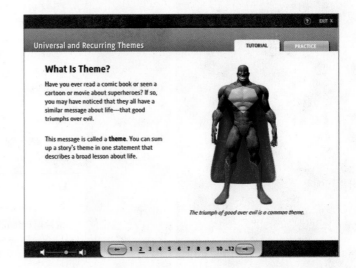

INDEPENDENT READING

Have students read one of the books of the *Odyssey* not included in this selection. Ask: How does the book contribute to the epic nature of the plot, setting, or theme?

from the Odyssey
The Cyclops

Epic Poem by Homer

For more context and historical background, students can view the video "Odysseus: Curse of the Sea" in their eBooks.

Why This Text

Students may have difficulty reading epic poetry. This excerpt from the *Odyssey* provides an opportunity to analyze how Odysseus faces conflict and interacts with other characters. With the help of close-reading questions, students will analyze the way Odysseus resolves a conflict when his men are trapped in a cave with a Cyclops. This close reading will lead students to analyze the character traits of an epic hero.

Background Have students read the background and the information about Homer. Introduce the selection by telling students that the speaker is Odysseus. He is going home after leading his army to victory in the Trojan War. For more background, students can view the video "Odysseus: Curse of the Sea" which provides background on the Trojan War and the start of Odysseus's journey.

AS YOU READ Ask students to note how Odysseus overcomes challenges. What will he learn when he faces the Cyclops?

Standards Support

- cite strong and thorough textual evidence
- analyze how complex characters develop over the course of a text
- analyze how characters interact with other characters, advance the plot, and develop the theme
- determine the meaning of words and phrases as they are used in the text

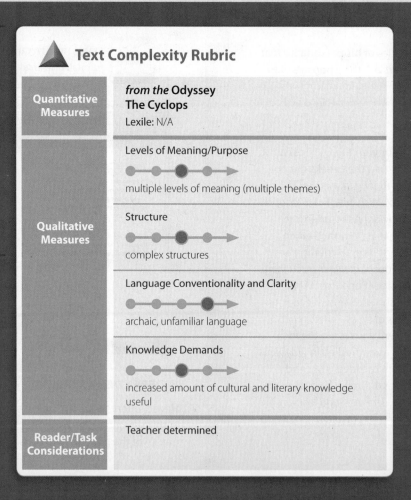

Text Complexity Rubric

Quantitative Measures

from the Odyssey
The Cyclops
Lexile: N/A

Qualitative Measures

Levels of Meaning/Purpose

multiple levels of meaning (multiple themes)

Structure

complex structures

Language Conventionality and Clarity

archaic, unfamiliar language

Knowledge Demands

increased amount of cultural and literary knowledge useful

Reader/Task Considerations

Teacher determined

Strategies for CLOSE READING

Analyze Character: Epic Hero

Students should read this epic poetry carefully all the way through. Close-reading questions at the bottom of the page will help them focus on a thorough analysis of the text. As they read, students should jot down comments or questions about the poem in the side margins.

WHEN STUDENTS STRUGGLE . . .

To help students analyze Odysseus, have them work in a small group to fill out a chart, such as the one shown below, as they analyze the text.

CITE TEXT EVIDENCE For practice analyzing an epic hero, ask students to cite evidence of Odysseus's strengths and flaws.

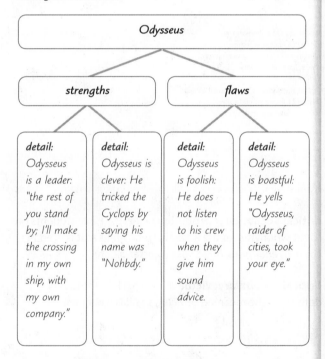

Odysseus

strengths

flaws

detail:
Odysseus is a leader: "the rest of you stand by; I'll make the crossing in my own ship, with my own company."

detail:
Odysseus is clever: He tricked the Cyclops by saying his name was "Nohbdy."

detail:
Odysseus is foolish: He does not listen to his crew when they give him sound advice.

detail:
Odysseus is boastful: He yells "Odysseus, raider of cities, took your eye."

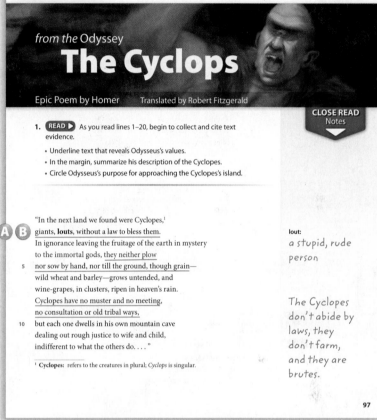

Background No one knows for sure who **Homer** was, though the later Greeks believed he was a blind minstrel, or singer, who went from town to town. He is commonly credited with composing the Iliad (the story of the Trojan War) and the Odyssey. The Odyssey tells of the many adventures of a soldier named Odysseus on his ten-year journey home from the Trojan War. As this passage begins, Odysseus tells the story of encountering Polyphemus, the Cyclops.

from the Odyssey
The Cyclops

Epic Poem by Homer   Translated by Robert Fitzgerald

CLOSE READ
Notes

1. **READD** As you read lines 1–20, begin to collect and cite text evidence.

- Underline text that reveals Odysseus's values.
- In the margin, summarize his description of the Cyclopes.
- Circle Odysseus's purpose for approaching the Cyclopes's island.

"In the next land we found were Cyclops,[1]
giants, **louts**, without a law to bless them.
In ignorance leaving the fruitage of the earth in mystery
to the immortal gods, they neither plow
5 nor sow by hand, nor till the ground, though grain—
wild wheat and barley—grows untended, and
wine-grapes, in clusters, ripen in heaven's rain.
Cyclops have no muster and no meeting,
no consultation or old tribal ways,
10 but each one dwells in his own mountain cave
dealing out rough justice to wife and child,
indifferent to what the others do. . . ."

---
[1] **Cyclops:** refers to the creatures in plural; Cyclops is singular.

lout:
a stupid, rude person

The Cyclopes don't abide by laws, they don't farm, and they are brutes.

97

---

1. **READ AND CITE TEXT EVIDENCE** Explain to students that they can find Odysseus's values not only by looking at positive things he says about himself and his culture, but also by looking at negative things he says about the Cyclopes.

A ASK STUDENTS to cite text that reveals Odysseus's values. *Students should cite evidence from lines 2, 4–5, and 8–9.* Ask them to use their circled text as evidence to draw a conclusion about Odysseus's character. Answers will vary. *They might say he is brave, or a leader.*

Critical Vocabulary: lout (line 2) How does this use of the word *lout* reveal Odysseus's values? *It is an insulting word, so readers can infer that Odysseus values the opposite of whatever is represented by the Cyclopes. For example, when Odysseus says the Cyclopes are "without a law to bless them" (line 2), readers can infer that Odysseus values law.*

Across the bay from the land of the Cyclopes was a lush, deserted island. Odysseus and his crew landed on the island in a dense fog and spent days feasting on wine and wild goats and observing the mainland, where the Cyclopes lived. On the third day, Odysseus and his company of men set out to learn if the Cyclopes were friends or foes.

"When the young Dawn with finger tips of rose
came in the east, I called my men together
15 and made a speech to them:

'Old shipmates, friends,
the rest of you stand by; I'll make the crossing
in my own ship, with my own company,
and find out what the mainland natives are—
for they may be wild savages, and lawless,
20 or **hospitable** and god fearing men.'

hospitable:
generous

At this I went aboard, and gave the word
to cast off by the stern. My oarsmen followed,
filing in to their benches by the rowlocks,
and all in line dipped oars in the gray sea.

25 As we rowed on, and nearer to the mainland,
at one end of the bay, we saw a cavern
yawning above the water, screened with laurel,
and many rams and goats about the place
inside a sheepfold—made from slabs of stone

---

2. ◀ REREAD Reread lines 1–20. Based on the text, what inferences can you make about the values of Odysseus and his audience?

His criticism of the Cyclopes ("giants, louts, without a law to bless them") shows that he values agriculture and community. He and his audience also value friendship, hospitality, and respect for the gods.

3. READ ▶ As you read lines 21–60, continue to cite textual evidence.
• Underline text describing what Odysseus sees as he approaches land.
• Circle words Odysseus uses to describe the Cyclops.
• In the margin, explain what Odysseus brings with him to the island (lines 41–60).

---

30 earthfast[2] between tall trunks of pine and rugged
towering oak trees.

A **prodigious** man

slept in this cave alone, and took his flocks
to graze afield—remote from all companions,
knowing none but savage ways, a brute
35 so huge, he seemed no man at all of those
who eat good wheaten bread; but he seemed rather
a shaggy mountain reared in solitude.
We beached there, and I told the crew
to stand by and keep watch over the ship;
40 as for myself I took my twelve best fighters
and went ahead. I had a goatskin full
of that sweet liquor that Euanthes'[3] son,
Maron, had given me. He kept Apollo's
holy grove at Ismarus; for kindness
45 we showed him there, and showed his wife and child,
he gave me seven shining golden talents[4]
perfectly formed, a solid silver winebowl,
and then this liquor—twelve two-handled jars
of brandy, pure and fiery. Not a slave
50 in Maron's household knew this drink; only
he, his wife and the storeroom mistress knew;
and they would put one cupful—ruby-colored,
honey-smooth—in twenty more of water,
but still the sweet scent hovered like a fume
55 over the winebowl. No man turned away
when cups of this came round.

A wineskin full

I brought along, and **victuals** in a bag,
for in my bones I knew some towering brute
would be upon us soon—all outward power,
60 a wild man, ignorant of civility.

We climbed, then, briskly to the cave. But Cyclops
had gone afield, to pasture his fat sheep,
so we looked round at everything inside:

prodigious:
very big; huge

He brings liquor that was given to him as a gift and a bag of food.

victuals:
food

---

[2] **earthfast:** firmly grounded.
[3] **Euanthes:** a god in Greek mythology.
[4] **talents:** bars of gold or silver of a specified weight, used as money in ancient Greece.

---

2. **REREAD AND CITE TEXT EVIDENCE**

B **ASK STUDENTS** to cite evidence to support their inferences about the values of Odysseus and his audience. *Students may cite evidence that Odysseus values "law" (line 2), agriculture (lines 4–5), and community (lines 8–9). They may cite evidence that Odysseus values friendship (line 12) as well as hospitality and fear of god (line 20).*

3. **READ AND CITE TEXT EVIDENCE**

C **ASK STUDENTS** to cite text evidence to support their explanation of what Odysseus brings with him to the island. *Students should cite evidence that he took a "goatskin full of that sweet liquor" (lines 41–42) and "victuals in a bag" (line 57).*

Critical Vocabulary: hospitable (line 20) Have students explain how the word *hospitable* reveals a value of the ancient Greeks. *They considered hospitality a quality of refined people.*

Critical Vocabulary: prodigious (line 32) Have students give some synonyms for the adjective *prodigious* as it is used in this context. *enormous, huge, vast, colossal, gigantic, massive*

Critical Vocabulary: victuals (line 57) Have students determine the meaning of *victuals* as it is used here.

a drying rack that sagged with cheeses, pens
65 crowded with lambs and kids, each in its class:
    firstlings apart from middlings, and the 'dewdrops,'
    or newborn lambkins, penned apart from both.
    And vessels full of whey⁵ were brimming there—
    bowls of earthenware and pails for milking.
70 My men came pressing round me, pleading:

E   'Why not
    take these cheeses, get them stowed, come back,
    throw open all the pens, and make a run for it?
    We'll drive the kids and lambs aboard. We say
    put out again on good salt water!'

                                             Ah,
75 how sound that was! Yet I refused. I wished
    to see the caveman, what he had to offer—
    no pretty sight, it turned out, for my friends.
    We lit a fire, burnt an offering,
    and took some cheese to eat; then sat in silence
80 around the embers, waiting. When he came
    he had a load of dry boughs on his shoulder
    to stoke his fire at suppertime. He dumped it
    with a great crash into that hollow cave,
    and we all scattered fast to the far wall.

⁵ **whey:** the watery part of milk, which separates from the curds, or solid part, during the
  making of cheese.

4. ◀ REREAD Reread lines 55–60. Why does Odysseus bring the liquor
    with him? Cite text evidence in your response.

    He brings the liquor because he had a hunch that he might need to
    incapacitate the Cyclops. The liquor was so good "No man turned
    away when cups of this came round."

5. READ ▶ As you read lines 61–135, continue to cite textual evidence.
    • Underline text describing the "sound" request that Odysseus's men make.
    • Circle text that shows heroic qualities of Odysseus.
    • In the margin, explain the ancient Greek custom "to honor strangers"
      described in lines 115–120.

100

85 Then over the broad cavern floor he ushered
    the ewes he meant to milk. He left his rams
    and he-goats in the yard outside, and swung
    high overhead a slab of solid rock
    to close the cave. Two dozen four-wheeled wagons,
90 with heaving wagon teams, could not have stirred
    the tonnage of that rock from where he wedged it
    over the doorsill. Next he took his seat
    and milked his bleating ewes. A practiced job
    he made of it, giving each ewe her suckling;
95 thickened his milk, then, into curds and whey,
    sieved out the curds to drip in withy baskets,⁶
    and poured the whey to stand in bowls
    cooling until he drank it for his supper.
    When all these chores were done, he poked the fire,
100 heaping on brushwood. In the glare he saw us.

    'Strangers,' he said, 'who are you? And where from?
    What brings you here by sea ways—a fair traffic?⁷
    Or are you wandering rogues, who cast your lives
    like dice, and **ravage** other folk by sea?'

105 We felt a pressure on our hearts, in dread
    of that deep rumble and that mighty man.
    But all the same I spoke up in reply:

    'We are from Troy, Achaeans, blown off course
    by shifting gales on the Great South Sea;
110 homeward bound, but taking routes and ways
    uncommon; so the will of Zeus would have it.
    We served under Agamemnon,⁸ son of Atreus—
    the whole world knows what city
    he laid waste, what armies he destroyed.
115 It was our luck to come here; here we stand,
    beholden for your help, or any gifts
    you give—as custom is to honor strangers.
    We would entreat you, great Sir, have a care
    for the gods' courtesy; Zeus will avenge
120 the unoffending guest.'

⁶ **withy baskets:** baskets made from twigs.
⁷ **fair traffic:** honest trade.
⁸ **Agamemnon:** Commander of the Greek armed forces in the Trojan War.

101

ravage:
destroy
violently; ruin

It was a Greek
custom to
honor
strangers with
food and gifts.
Odysseus is
reminding the
Cyclops that
Zeus will
punish anyone
who mistreats
a guest.

He answered this
from his brute chest, unmoved:

'You are a ninny,
or else you come from the other end of nowhere,
(F) telling me, mind the gods! We Cyclopes
care not a whistle for your thundering Zeus
125   or all the gods in bliss; we have more force by far.
I would not let you go for fear of Zeus—
you or your friends—unless I had a whim to.
Tell me, where was it, now, you left your ship—
around the point, or down the shore, I wonder?'

130   He thought he'd find out, but I saw through this,
and answered with a ready lie:

'My ship?
Poseidon Lord, who sets the earth a-tremble,
broke it up on the rocks at your land's end.
A wind from seaward served him, drove us there.
135   We are survivors, these good men and I.'

Neither reply nor pity came from him,
but in one stride he clutched at my companions
and caught two in his hands like squirming puppies
to beat their brains out, spattering the floor.
140   Then he dismembered them and made his meal,
gaping and crunching like a mountain lion—
everything: innards, flesh, and marrow bones.
We cried aloud, lifting our hands to Zeus,
powerless, looking on at this, appalled;

6.   ◀ REREAD AND DISCUSS Reread lines 122–127. With a small group,
discuss the Cyclops's response to Odysseus's reminder to be hospitable
and not anger Zeus. What does this response tell you about the
Cyclops's attitude toward the gods?

7.   READ ▶ As you read lines 136–244, continue to cite text evidence.
• In the margin, explain Odysseus's reasoning in lines 148–154.
• Circle the epithet, or repeated descriptive phrase, in line 156. Explain the
  meaning of these words in the margin.
• Underline text that outlines Odysseus's plan in lines 170–244.

102

---

145   but Cyclops went on filling up his belly
with manflesh and great gulps of whey,
then lay down like a mast among his sheep.
My heart beat high now at the chance of action,
and drawing the sharp sword from my hip I went
150   along his flank to stab him where the midriff
holds the liver. I had touched the spot
when sudden fear stayed me: if I killed him
we perished there as well, for we could never
move his **ponderous** doorway slab aside.
155   So we were left to groan and wait for morning.

When the young Dawn with fingertips of rose
lit up the world, the Cyclops built a fire
and milked his handsome ewes, all in due order,
putting the sucklings to the mothers. Then,
160   his chores being all dispatched, he caught
another brace of men to make his breakfast,
and whisked away his great door slab
to let his sheep go through—but he, behind,
reset the stone as one would cap a quiver.
165   There was a din of whistling as the Cyclops
rounded his flock to higher ground, then stillness.
And now I pondered how to hurt him worst,
if but Athena granted what I prayed for.
Here are the means I thought would serve my turn:

170   a club, or staff, lay there along the fold—
an olive tree, felled green and left to season
for Cyclops' hand. And it was like a mast
a lugger[9] of twenty oars, broad in the beam—
a deep-sea-going craft—might carry:
(G) 175   so long, so big around, it seemed. Now I
chopped out a six foot section of this pole
and set it down before my men, who scraped it;
and when they had it smooth, I hewed again
to make a stake with pointed end. I held this
180   in the fire's heart and turned it, toughening it,
then hid it, well back in the cavern, under
one of the dung piles in profusion there.

---

[9] **lugger:** a small, wide sailing ship.

If Odysseus
kills the
Cyclops, he
and his men
would be
trapped and
eventually die.

ponderous:
heavy and
massive

The reddish
rays of sunrise
brighten the
horizon.

103

---

6.   REREAD AND DISCUSS USING TEXT EVIDENCE

(F) **ASK STUDENTS** to cite evidence to support their inferences
in their discussion. Their evidence should be specific, and should
include line numbers. *Students should cite lines 123–124, "We
Cyclopes care not a whistle for your thundering Zeus."*

7.   READ AND CITE TEXT EVIDENCE

(G) **ASK STUDENTS** to use their underlined text as evidence,
and explain Odysseus's plan. *Students should find evidence that
Odysseus crafted a weapon (lines 175–181), with which he planned
to blind the Cyclops (lines 184–186). He offered the Cyclops liquor
(lines 198–199), and got him drunk (lines 214–215). Then he said his
name was "Nohbdy" (line 219), and he used his weapon to blind the
Cyclops (lines 227–228, 233–237, and 241–242).*

Critical Vocabulary: ponderous (line 154) Discuss
denotations and connotations of *ponderous*. Remind students
that Homer wrote in Greek, and this is a translation. The
translator, Robert Fitzgerald, had to choose the best English
word to communicate Homer's description of the door.
Fitzgerald had to make choices that communicated Homer's
tone and poetry, not only his literal meaning. Why might
Fitzgerald have chosen this word? *The word* ponderous *has
several meanings: "having great weight," "awkward and unwieldy,"
"monotonous and tiresome." Each meaning can apply to the
doorway slab and the impression it makes on the men. The sound
of the word itself also adds to the feeling of the line.*

Now came the time to toss for it: who ventured
along with me? whose hand could bear to thrust
185 and grind that spike in Cyclops' eye, when mild
sleep had mastered him? As luck would have it,
the men I would have chosen won the toss—
four strong men, and I made five as captain.

At evening came the shepherd with his flock,
190 his woolly flock. The rams as well, this time,
entered the cave: by some sheep-herding whim—
or a god's bidding—none were left outside.
He hefted his great boulder into place
and sat him down to milk the bleating ewes
195 in proper order, put the lambs to suck,
and swiftly ran through all his evening chores.
Then he caught two more men and feasted on them.
My moment was at hand, and I went forward
holding an ivy bowl of my dark drink,
200 looking up, saying:

            'Cyclops, try some wine.
Here's liquor to wash down your scraps of men.
Taste it, and see the kind of drink we carried
under our planks. I meant it for an offering
if you would help us home. But you are mad,
205 unbearable, a bloody monster! After this,
will any other traveller come to see you?'

He seized and drained the bowl, and it went down
so fiery and smooth he called for more:

'Give me another, thank you kindly. Tell me,
210 how are you called? I'll make a gift will please you.
Even Cyclopes know the wine-grapes grow
out of grassland and loam in heaven's rain,
but here's a bit of nectar and ambrosia!'[10]

  Three bowls I brought him, and he poured them down.
215 I saw the fuddle and flush[11] come over him,
then I sang out in cordial tones:

---

[10] **ambrosia:** food of the gods.
[11] **fuddle and flush:** the state of confusion and redness of the face caused by drinking alcohol.

         'Cyclops,
you ask my honorable name? Remember
the gift you promised me, and I shall tell you.
My name is Nohbdy: mother, father, and friends,
220 everyone calls me Nohbdy.'

            And he said:
'Nohbdy's my meat, then, after I eat his friends.
Others come first. There's a noble gift, now.'

Even as he spoke, he reeled and tumbled backward,
his great head lolling to one side: and sleep
225 took him like any creature. Drunk, hiccupping,
he dribbled streams of liquor and bits of men.

Now, by the gods, I drove my big hand spike
deep in the embers, charring it again,
and cheered my men along with battle talk
230 to keep their courage up: no quitting now.
The **pike** of olive, green though it had been,
reddened and glowed as if about to catch.
I drew it from the coals and my four fellows
gave me a hand, lugging it near the Cyclops
235 as more than natural force nerved them; straight
forward they sprinted, lifted it, and rammed it
deep in his crater eye, and I leaned on it
turning it as a shipwright turns a drill
in planking, having men below to swing
240 the two-handled strap that spins it in the groove.
So with our brand we bored that great eye socket
while blood ran out around the red hot bar.
Eyelid and lash were seared; the pierced ball
hissed broiling, and the roots popped.

pike:
pointed stake

---

8. ◀ REREAD AND DISCUSS Reread lines 214–244. In a small group, discuss why Odysseus tells the Cyclops his name is "Nohbdy" (line 219). What is Odysseus planning?

9. READ ▶ As you read lines 245–339, continue to cite textual evidence.

- In the margin, explain the action in lines 245–269.
- Underline text that describes Odysseus's escape plan.
- In the margin, explain how Odysseus and his men escape (lines 319–334).

FOR ELL STUDENTS Draw students' attention to the phrase *to toss for it* (line 183). Then have them read the rest of the stanza and use the context clues to infer the meaning: "to flip a coin to make a decision."

8. **REREAD AND DISCUSS USING TEXT EVIDENCE**

H **ASK STUDENTS** to cite text evidence to support their predictions about what Odysseus is planning. Have small groups discuss what has happened to the Cyclops, and what he is likely to do next. How might the name Nohbdy be part of Odysseus's plan? *Students may conclude that when the Cyclops says "Nohbdy," it will put the other Cyclopes off Odysseus's track.*

9. **READ AND CITE TEXT EVIDENCE**

I **ASK STUDENTS** to cite evidence to support their explanation of the action in lines 245–269. *Students should cite evidence that the Cyclops called for help (line 253), that he roars "Nohbdy's tricked me" (line 262), and that the Cyclopes leave, thinking there is nobody to fight (lines 264–268).*

Critical Vocabulary: pike (line 231) Ask students to explain the meaning of *pike* as it is used here.

from the Odyssey: The Cyclops **420g**

In a smithy[12]

245 one sees a white-hot axehead or an adze
plunged and wrung in a cold tub, screeching steam—
the way they make soft iron hale and hard—:
just so that eyeball hissed around the spike.
The Cyclops bellowed and the rock roared round him,
250 and we fell back in fear. Clawing his face
he tugged the bloody spike out of his eye,
threw it away, and his wild hands went groping;
then he set up a howl for Cyclopes
who lived in caves on windy peaks nearby.
255 Some heard him; and they came by divers[13] ways
to clump around outside and call:

'What ails you,
Polyphemus? Why do you cry so sore
in the starry night? You will not let us sleep.
Sure no man's driving off your flock? No man
260 has tricked you, ruined you?'

Out of the cave
the mammoth Polyphemus roared in answer:
'Nohbdy, Nohbdy's tricked me, Nohbdy's ruined me!'
To this rough shout they made a sage reply:
'Ah well, if nobody has played you foul
265 there in your lonely bed, we are no use in pain
given by great Zeus. Let it be your father,
Poseidon Lord, to whom you pray.'

So saying
they trailed away. And I was filled with laughter
to see how like a charm the name deceived them.
270 Now Cyclops, wheezing as the pain came on him,
fumbled to wrench away the great doorstone
and squatted in the breach with arms thrown wide
for any silly beast or man who bolted—
hoping somehow I might be such a fool.
275 But I kept thinking how to win the game:
death sat there huge; how could we slip away?

Polyphemus calls for the Cyclopes, but when they arrive, he explains that "Nohbdy" tricked him. Thinking there is nobody to fight, the Cyclopes leave.

[12] **smithy:** blacksmith's shop.
[13] **divers:** diverse; various.

106

I drew on all my wits, and ran through tactics,
reasoning as a man will for dear life,
until a trick came—and it pleased me well.
280 The Cyclops' rams were handsome, fat, with heavy
fleeces, a dark violet.

Three abreast

I tied them silently together, twining
cords of willow from the ogre's bed;
then slung a man under each middle one
285 to ride there safely, shielded left and right.
So three sheep could convey each man. I took
the woolliest ram, the choicest of the flock,
and hung myself under his kinky belly,
pulled up tight, with fingers twisted deep
290 in sheepskin ringlets for an iron grip.
So, breathing hard, we waited until morning.

When Dawn spread out her finger tips of rose
the rams began to stir, moving for pasture,
and peals of bleating echoed round the pens
295 where dams with udders full called for a milking.
Blinded, and sick with pain from his head wound,
the master stroked each ram, then let it pass,
but my men riding on the pectoral fleece[14]
the giant's blind hands blundering never found.
300 Last of them all my ram, the leader, came,
weighted by wool and me with my **meditations.**
The Cyclops patted him, and then he said:

'Sweet cousin ram, why lag behind the rest
in the night cave? You never linger so,
305 but graze before them all, and go afar
to crop sweet grass, and take your stately way
leading along the streams, until at evening

meditations: *serious, reflective thought*

[14] **fleece:** wool covering a sheep's chest.

10. ◀ REREAD AND DISCUSS Reread lines 275–315. With a small group, discuss how Odysseus exemplifies an epic hero in these lines. Cite text evidence in your discussion.

107

FOR ELL STUDENTS Explain to students that the adjective *hale* (line 247) means "healthy."

10. **REREAD AND DISCUSS USING TEXT EVIDENCE**

ASK STUDENTS to be prepared to share the results of their small-group discussions with the class. Students should be prepared to cite specific text evidence to support their analysis of Odysseus's heroism. *Students should cite Odysseus's use of his wits (line 277) to develop a plan to defeat his enemy.*

Critical Vocabulary: meditations (line 301) Have students determine the meaning of *meditations* as it is used here. What might the content of Odysseus's meditations have been? *Odysseus is probably thinking about whether or not his plan will work and if he and his men will escape from the Cyclops.*

you run to be the first one in the fold.
Why, now, so far behind? Can you be grieving
310　over your Master's eye? That carrion rogue
and his accurst companions burnt it out
when he had conquered all my wits with wine.
Nohbdy will not get out alive, I swear.
Oh, had you brain and voice to tell
315　where he may be now, dodging all my fury!
Bashed by this hand and bashed on this rock wall
his brains would strew the floor, and I should have
rest from the outrage Nohbdy worked upon me.'

He sent us into the open, then. Close by,
320　I dropped and rolled clear of the ram's belly,
going this way and that to untie the men.
With many glances back, we rounded up
his fat, stiff-legged sheep to take aboard,
and drove them down to where the good ship lay.
325　We saw, as we came near, our fellows' faces
shining; then we saw them turn to grief
tallying those who had not fled from death.
I hushed them, jerking head and eyebrows up,
and in a low voice told them: 'Load this herd;
330　move fast, and put the ship's head toward the breakers.'
They all pitched in at loading, then embarked
and struck their oars into the sea. Far out,
as far off shore as shouted words would carry,
I sent a few back to the adversary:

335　'O Cyclops! Would you feast on my companions?
Puny, am I, in a Caveman's hands?
How do you like the beating that we gave you,
you damned cannibal? Eater of guests
under your roof! Zeus and the gods have paid you!'

Odysseus ties his men under the bellies of the Cyclops's sheep. The blind Cyclops cannot see the men. In addition, he does not feel them, because the sheep are tied together.

11. **READ ▶** As you read lines 340–404, continue to cite textual evidence.
 • Underline text describing what Polyphemus does when he realizes Odysseus and his men have escaped and explain it in the margin (lines 340–352).
 • Circle the protests made by Odysseus's crew.
 • In the margin, paraphrase lines 366–375.

108

" The blind thing in his doubled fury broke a hilltop in his hands and heaved it after us. "

K 340　The blind thing in his doubled fury broke
a hilltop in his hands and heaved it after us.
Ahead of our black prow it struck and sank
whelmed in a spuming geyser, a giant wave
that washed the ship stern foremost back to shore.
345　I got the longest boathook out and stood
fending us off, with furious nods to all
to put their backs into a racing stroke—
row, row, or perish. So the long oars bent
kicking the foam sternward, making head
350　until we drew away, and twice as far.
Now when I cupped my hands I heard the crew
in low voices protesting:

'Godsake, Captain!
Why bait the beast again? Let him alone!'
'That tidal wave he made on the first throw
355　all but beached us.'

'All but stove us in!'
'Give him our bearing with your trumpeting,
he'll get the range and lob a boulder.'

'Aye
He'll smash our timbers and our heads together!'
I would not heed them in my glorying spirit,
360　but let my anger flare and yelled:

'Cyclops,
if ever mortal man inquire

The Cyclops throws the top of a hill at Odysseus's ship. The wave it creates sends his ship back to the shore.

109

---

11. READ AND CITE TEXT EVIDENCE

K **ASK STUDENTS** to cite their underlined and circled text as evidence, and explain one or more flaws in Odysseus's character. *Students should cite evidence from lines 340–344 to show that Odysseus's taunts resulted in great danger to himself and his crew. They should cite lines 352–361, and explain that Odysseus ignored good advice from his crew.*

WHEN STUDENTS STRUGGLE . . .

To help students understand Odysseus's character, have small groups work together to read aloud lines 335–397 as a script. Assign students to read the parts of Odysseus, the Cyclops, and the crewmen. Assign a narrator to read the lines that are not Odysseus's direct speech. Then, have students discuss what character strengths and character flaws Odysseus shows in these lines.

ASK STUDENTS to cite specific text evidence with line numbers to support their analysis of Odysseus's strengths and flaws. *Odysseus cannot control his temper—he endangers himself and his men when he taunts the Cyclops and calls out "How do you like the beating we gave you, you damned cannibal?" (lines 337–338) He is, however, a good leader: "I got the longest boathook out and stood fending us off" (lines 345–346) and encouraging his men to "row, row, or perish" (line 348).*

how you were put to shame and blinded, tell him
Odysseus, raider of cities, took your eye:
Laertes'[15] son, whose home's on Ithaca!'

365   At this he gave a mighty sob and rumbled:

'Now comes the weird upon me, spoken of old.
A wizard, grand and wondrous, lived here—Telemus,[16]
a son of Eurymus; great length of days
he had in wizardry among the Cyclopes,
370   and these things he foretold for time to come:
my great eye lost, and at Odysseus' hands.
Always I had in mind some giant, armed
in giant force, would come against me here.
But this, but you—small, pitiful and twiggy—
375   you put me down with wine, you blinded me.
Come back, Odysseus, and I'll treat you well,
praying the god of earthquake to befriend you—
his son I am, for he by his avowal[17]
fathered me, and, if he will, he may
380   heal me of this black wound—he and no other
of all the happy gods or mortal men.'

Few words I shouted in reply to him:
'If I could take your life I would and take
your time away, and hurl you down to hell!
385   The god of earthquake could not heal you there!'

At this he stretched his hands out in his darkness
toward the sky of stars, and prayed Poseidon:
'O hear me, lord, blue girdler of the islands,
if I am thine indeed, and thou art father:
390   grant that Odysseus, raider of cities, never
see his home: Laertes' son, I mean,
who kept his hall on Ithaca. Should destiny
intend that he shall see his roof again
among his family in his father land,
395   far be that day, and dark the years between.

A prophet once told Polyphemus he would lose his eye, but he imagined "some giant" would take him down, not someone as small as Odysseus.

---

[15]**Laertes:** King of Ithaca, an island in the Ionian Sea.
[16]**Telemus:** a prophet in Greek mythology.
[17]**avowal:** honest admission.

110

Let him lose all companions, and return
under strange sail to bitter days at home.'
In these words he prayed, and the god heard him.
Now he laid hands upon a bigger stone
400   and wheeled around, titanic for the cast,
to let it fly in the black-prowed vessel's track.
But it fell short, just aft the steering oar,
and whelming seas rose giant above the stone
to bear us onward toward the island.

                     There
405   as we ran in we saw the squadron waiting,
the trim ships drawn up side by side, and all
our troubled friends who waited, looking seaward.
We beached her, grinding keel in the soft sand,
and waded in, ourselves, on the sandy beach.
410   Then we unloaded all the Cyclops' flock
to make division, share and share alike,
only my fighters voted that my ram,
the prize of all, should go to me. I slew him
by the sea side and burnt his long thighbones
415   to Zeus beyond the stormcloud, Cronus' son,
who rules the world. But Zeus disdained my offering;
destruction for my ships he had in store
and death for those who sailed them, my companions.

Now all day long until the sun went down
420   we made our feast on mutton and sweet wine,

Zeus's dissatisfaction signals further suffering for Odysseus. He will lose his ships and his companions.

---

12.   ◀ REREAD   Reread ines 386–404. Explain Polyphemus's curse in your own words.

The Cyclops asks Poseidon to prevent Odysseus from returning home. If this cannot happen, he asks that the journey home take a long time, that Odysseus lose his crew, and that his home life be unhappy.

13.   READ ▶   Read lines 405–429. Underline text foreshadowing future events. In the margin, explain how the text "Zeus disdained my offering" furthers the plot (line 416).

111

FOR ELL STUDENTS The clause "Now comes the weird upon me" (line 366) may confuse students. Explain that the word *weird* means "very strange, or relating to the supernatural." Challenge students to analyze the clause and rewrite it in their own words. *Possible response: Now I am aware of something very strange.*

12.   REREAD AND CITE TEXT EVIDENCE

L   **ASK STUDENTS** to cite text evidence to support their explanation of Polyphemus's curse. *Students should explain that the Cyclops asks Poseidon to prevent Odysseus from returning home (lines 390–391). If this cannot happen, he asks that the journey home take a long time (lines 392–395), that he lose his crew (line 396), and that his home life be unhappy: "bitter days at home" (line 397).*

13.   READ AND CITE TEXT EVIDENCE

M   **ASK STUDENTS** how the foreshadowed future events—"destruction for my ships . . . death for those who sailed them . . ." (lines 417–418)—relate to the prayer the Cyclops made to Poseidon in the previous section. *The Cyclops pleaded that if Odysseus did manage to return to his home, "far be that day, and dark the years between" (line 395).*

till after sunset in the gathering dark
we went to sleep above the wash of ripples.

When the young Dawn with finger tips of rose
touched the world, I roused the men, gave orders
425   to man the ships, cast off the mooring lines;
and filing in to sit beside the rowlocks
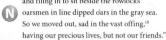 oarsmen in line dipped oars in the gray sea.
So we moved out, sad in the vast offing,[18]
having our precious lives, but not our friends."

[18]**offing:** the part of the deep sea seen from the shore.

14. **◀ REREAD AND DISCUSS** Reread lines 423–429. With a small group,
discuss why Odysseus and his men have mixed feelings as they leave
the land of the Cyclopes.

SHORT RESPONSE

Cite Text Evidence   In what ways is Odysseus an epic hero? Discuss his
strengths and his flaws. Review your reading notes, and **cite text evidence**
in your response.

*Odysseus embodies Greek ideals: He is a military hero who "served
under Agamemnon"; he is of royal lineage—"Laertes' son"—and he
respects and remembers the gods. He has undertaken a long and
difficult journey and defeated a formidable opponent using his
intelligence: "I drew on all my wits, and ran through tactics,
reasoning as a man will for dear life, until a trick came." The
audience may identify with Odysseus's flaws: He is stubborn and
refuses to take other people's advice. He is also prone to taking rash
actions that endanger the lives of others.*

112

---

14. REREAD AND DISCUSS USING TEXT EVIDENCE

ASK STUDENTS to cite specific text evidence with line
numbers to support their explanation of why Odysseus and his
men have mixed feelings as they leave the land of the Cyclopes.
*Students should cite lines 428–429 as evidence that Odysseus and his
crew are happy to be alive, but sad about the friends that were killed
by the Cyclops.*

SHORT RESPONSE

Cite Text Evidence   Student responses will vary, but they should
cite evidence from the text to support their analysis of Odysseus as an
epic hero. Students should:

- analyze ways in which Odysseus's character fits the definition of an
  epic hero.
- provide a text-based analysis of Odysseus's character traits.
- cite strong textual evidence to support their response.

TO CHALLENGE STUDENTS . . .

For more context and interviews with historians about Odysseus
and his adventures, students can view the video "Odysseus: Curse
of the Sea" in their eBooks.

ASK STUDENTS to pay special attention to the interviews with
the various historians. What insights do they offer about Odysseus
and the customs of the ancient Greeks? *Students might say that the
historians emphasize Odysseus's curiosity (which is also attributed to
the Greek sense of adventure and exploration), the Greek tradition of
giving gifts to strangers, and the gruesomeness of the cannibalism of
the Cyclops.*

DIG DEEPER

With the class, return to Question 10, Reread and Discuss. Have
students share the results of their discussion.

ASK STUDENTS whether they were satisfied with the outcome
of their small-group discussions. Have each group share their
understanding of what made Odysseus a hero. What compelling
evidence did the groups cite from the text to support their
analysis?

- Ask students whether their understanding of what traits in
  Odysseus were heroic was unanimous, or whether group
  members had different ideas about what made Odysseus a
  hero.
- Ask students to talk about how their group worked together
  to identify text evidence. Was there agreement about which
  evidence was the strongest? Was there some evidence that
  was not included because it did not seem strong enough?
- Now that students have read the entire text, ask small groups
  to rejoin to locate additional evidence of Odysseus's heroic
  qualities. Does the additional evidence found in the text
  support the conclusions students made in their work on
  Question 10?

ASK STUDENTS to return to their Short Response answer and
revise it based on the class discussion.

from The Cruelest Journey: 600 Miles to Timbuktu

Travel Writing by Kira Salak

Why This Text?

Students may find travel narratives especially fascinating. These accounts of explorers and adventurers expose them to different cultures, places, and ways of thinking about the world. In this lesson, students will read a travel narrative that questions the very nature and purpose of exploration. They will encounter a variety of narrative techniques that get readers involved in the author's journey and help point to the narrative's central idea.

Key Learning Objective: The student will be able to determine the central idea of a text, analyze the ideas and events presented, and cite text evidence.

For additional practice:

Close Reader selection
from The Good Soldiers
Nonfiction by David Finkel

RI 1 Cite textual evidence.
RI 2 Determine a central idea; analyze its development over the course of the text.
RI 3 Analyze how the author unfolds a series of ideas or events.
RI 5 Analyze how an author's ideas are developed and refined.
RI 6 Determine author's point of view and how an author uses rhetoric to advance that point of view.
W 2 Write informative/explanatory texts.
L 3 Apply knowledge of language to make effective choices for meaning or style.
L 5b Analyze nuances in the meaning of words with similar denotations.

▲ Text Complexity Rubric

Quantitative Measures	*from* **The Cruelest Journey: 600 Miles to Timbuktu** Lexile: 1030L
Qualitative Measures	**Levels of Meaning/Purpose** ●━●━●━●━▶ more than one purpose; implied, easily identified from context
	Structure ●━●━●━●━▶ clearly stated, sequential organization of main ideas and details
	Language Conventionality and Clarity ●━●━●━●━▶ figurative, less accessible language
	Knowledge Demands ●━●━●━●━▶ more difficult social studies concepts
Reader/Task Considerations	• Teacher determined • Vary by individual reader and type of text • See the Text X-Ray for suggested Reader/Task Considerations.

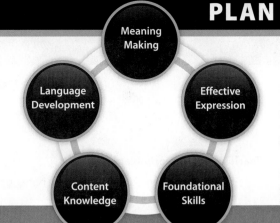

 English Language Support Before teaching, use the Text X-Ray below for an overview of the text's complexity. The Text X-Ray and the supports and scaffolds in the Teacher's Edition will help you guide students of different skill levels.

Text Complexity: Qualitative Measures

Levels of Meaning/Purpose

more than one purpose; implied, easily identified from context

Help students determine the central idea of the text and cite supporting evidence.

- Teacher's Edition side notes, pp. 422, 423, 425, 426, 427, 428, 429
- When Students Struggle, p. 423
- Determine Central Idea and Cite Evidence, p. 429

To teach students to write an analysis of the central idea, see

- Performance Task, p. 430
- Write an Analysis, p. 432a

 Use It! Interactive Whiteboard Lesson: Citing Textual Evidence

ZOOM IN ON DETERMINING CENTRAL IDEA Tell students that **paraphrasing** the text— restating the author's thoughts in their own words—may help them determine the narrative's **central idea**. After students have read the selection, have pairs paraphrase the passages below. Next, ask each pair to form a sentence stating the text's central idea. Have pairs share their sentences with the class. *(Possible central idea: A journey is worthwhile if you challenge yourself and learn something.)*

- "Rain or no rain . . . whether I'll get to the end." (lines 14–16)
- "Still, when a person tells me I cannot do something, I'll want to do it all the more." (lines 26–27)
- "And so I've told the world . . . my teacher." (lines 123–125)
- "I see the weeks . . . a stagnant life." (lines 217–225)

Structure

clearly stated, sequential organization of main ideas and details

Help students analyze ideas and events in a travel narrative.

- Teacher's Edition side notes, pp. 421, 422, 423, 424, 425, 426, 427, 428, 429
- Strategies for Annotation, p. 429
- Analyze Ideas and Events, p. 429

Guide students to determine author's point of view.

- Teacher's Edition side note, p. 424

To reteach analyzing ideas and events, see

- Analyze Ideas and Events, p. 432a

 Use It! *Level Up* Tutorial: Reading for Details

ZOOM IN ON ANALYZING NARRATIVE TECHNIQUES Explain to students that travel narratives include storytelling techniques such as **description, imagery, pacing,** and **dialogue**. Review the terms' definitions. Then use these questions to discuss the techniques:

- What is the purpose of including the French phrase for "How are you, madam?" (line 164)? *(Dialogue helps break up passages and speeds up the pace. French reflects the region's culture and history.)*
- What narrative techniques are used in lines 185–191? *(imagery and description)*

Language Conventionality and Clarity

figurative, less accessible language

Teach unfamiliar vocabulary in context.

- Teacher's Edition Critical Vocabulary notes, pp. 422, 423, 424, 427, 431
- Applying Academic Vocabulary, pp. 422, 426
- English Language Support, p. 428

Help students analyze language and style.

- English Language Support, pp. 421, 425
- Language and Style: Sentence Length, p. 432

Support students in understanding denotations and connotations.

- Vocabulary Strategy: Denotation and Connotation, p. 431
- Strategies for Annotation, p. 431

ZOOM IN ON **USING CONTEXT CLUES** Tell students that **context clues** can be used to determine the meanings of unfamiliar words. Use the following examples to demonstrate how to use context clues. Then have small groups determine the meanings of other unfamiliar words in the text.

- What context clues hint at the meaning of *harbinger* in lines 156–159? *(The author predicts the "distant" building is a sign that she's approaching the city, so harbinger must mean "a sign of something to come.")*
- What surrounding words or phrases in lines 223–225 help to define *stagnant*? *("Nothing seemed to change" suggests that stagnant means "unchanging.")*

Knowledge Demands

more difficult social studies concepts

Support English Learners in understanding the author's background.

- Teacher's Edition Background note, p. 421

ZOOM IN ON **BUILDING BACKGROUND KNOWLEDGE** Students may benefit from knowing more about these references.

- "El Dorado" (line 159) refers to a legendary city of gold in South America. Beginning in the 1500s, Spanish conquistadors and other Europeans unsuccessfully tried to locate the mythical city.
- The kayak's thigh straps (lines 150, 192) attach to the boat and wrap over the paddler's legs, keeping the kayak more stable in rough water.

Suggested Reader/Task Considerations

You might consider the following before assigning this selection to students.

- Is the text useful for developing **visualization** and **inferencing** skills?
- Will students make connections between the content of the text and other subject areas?

ZOOM IN ON **SUPPORTING COMPREHENSION**

- Read aloud the first paragraph. Ask volunteers to **paraphrase,** or restate in their own words, the author's description. Help them make **inferences.** Ask: What might the author be feeling at this moment?
- Alert teachers in other subject areas that students will be reading content related to adventure travel in Mali. Social studies teachers can help students understand the history and geography of Mali and West Africa.

CLOSE READ

Background Have students read the information about the author. Tell them that Salak began traveling on her own when she was nineteen, and, at the age of twenty, she went on a solo backpacking trip to Africa. In addition to her travels in Mali, the Democratic Republic of Congo, Papua New Guinea, and Alaska, she has traveled to many other places including Mozambique, Iran, Rwanda, Uganda, Bhutan, Mexico, and Peru.

Salak's taste for adventure and challenge is not limited to travel. She also finds time for martial arts, primitive camping, and mountain climbing.

AS YOU READ Direct students to use the As You Read note to focus their reading.

Analyze Ideas and Events
RI 1, RI 3

(LINES 1-11)

Explain that **travel narratives** are nonfiction, but they can include many elements that also make fiction compelling. One of these is the use of **imagery.** Imagery is language that appeals to the senses of sight, hearing, taste, touch, and smell.

Ⓐ CITE TEXT EVIDENCE Have students reread lines 1–11 and identify the imagery Salak uses to communicate the tension she feels at the beginning of her trip. *(She vividly describes a violent, "apocalyptic" [line 6] thunderstorm, and uses words like* pierces *and* slices *to describe lightning, and* racks *and* pounds *to describe thunder [lines 8–9]. This imagery helps the reader see, hear, and feel what she is experiencing.)*

Kira Salak (b. 1971) *wrote* The Cruelest Journey *to document her 600-mile solo kayak trip on the Niger River. The first person to ever achieve this feat, she traveled through a remote and dangerous region in Africa. Salak is an adventurer, an explorer, and a journalist. She has covered the civil war in the Democratic Republic of Congo, traveled across Papua New Guinea, and biked across Alaska. In 2005, she received a National Geographic Emerging Explorer Award, which recognizes people who are helping build world knowledge through exploration.*

from
The Cruelest Journey
600 Miles to Timbuktu

Travel Writing by Kira Salak

AS YOU READ What does Salak think and feel about her journey? Make note of her thoughts, comments, and any telling details you notice. Write down any questions you generate during reading.

from Chapter One

In the beginning, my journeys feel at best ludicrous, at worst insane. This one is no exception. The idea is to paddle nearly 600 miles on the Niger River in a kayak, alone, from the Malian town of Old Ségou to Timbuktu. And now, at the very hour when I have decided to leave, a thunderstorm bursts open the skies, sending down apocalyptic rain, washing away the very ground beneath my feet. It is the rainy season in Mali, for which there can be no comparison in the world. Lightning pierces trees, slices across houses. Thunder racks the skies and pounds the earth like mortar
10 fire, and every living thing huddles in tenuous shelter, expecting the world to end. Which it doesn't. At least not this time. So that we all give a collective sigh to the salvation of the passing storm as it rumbles its way east, and I survey the river I'm to leave on this morning. Rain or no rain, today is the day for the journey to begin.

Ⓐ

ENGLISH LANGUAGE SUPPORT

Identify Present Participles as Different Parts of Speech In their reading, students will encounter words with *-ing* endings that could be nouns, adjectives, or verbs. Review the basic definitions of these parts of speech. Then read lines 26–30 aloud while students follow along in the text. Ask them to identify the words with *-ing* endings *(something, failing, melting, huddling, cooking, peering)*. Help students determine the part of speech for each word by examining the context. For example, words with *-ing* endings that describe nouns, such as *"huddling goats"* and *"cooking fires,"* are adjectives.

ASK STUDENTS to find more examples of *-ing* words as they read, and to determine whether they are nouns, verbs, or adjectives by examining the context.

CLOSE READ

Analyze Ideas and Events
RI 1, RI 3

(LINES 17-25)

Point out that travel narratives include a variety of characters. An author can convey information about the characters in the narrative—including herself—by using the narrative technique of **dialogue.**

B **ASK STUDENTS** what the dialogue between Salak and Modibo reveals about each person. (*Salak's statement, "Let's do it" [line 17], shows that she is fearless, practical, and determined. Modibo, who says he "will pray" for her [line 19] and that he "thinks [she is] crazy" [line 22], shows that he is a cautious person who is aware of the dangers involved in her journey and is concerned for her safety.*)

Determine Central Idea and Cite Evidence
RI 1, RI 2
(LINES 36-39)

Explain that authors of travel narratives, like those of other nonfiction works, want to communicate a **central idea.** To determine the central idea, a reader can look for details such as descriptions or the author's thoughts about the experience. In an analysis of the central idea, one way that supporting **evidence** can be cited is by quoting the text.

C **CITE TEXT EVIDENCE** Have students identify the text that shows how Salak feels at the beginning of her journey. How does she react to being called "crazy"? (*One explanation that Salak gives about why she is determined to go on the journey, no matter how "crazy" people think it might be, is that her inspiration Mungo Park did it, "If he could travel down the Niger, then so can I" [lines 38–39].*)

CRITICAL VOCABULARY

circuitously: The river flows and turns in many directions over a long distance.

ASK STUDENTS to explain what details Salak provides to show that the river flows circuitously. (*The Niger does not flow directly to the Atlantic, but indirectly through desert, swamps, and jungle.*)

And no one, not even the oldest in the village, can say for certain whether I'll get to the end.

"Let's do it," I say, leaving the shelter of an adobe hut. My guide from town, Modibo, points to the north, to further storms. He says he will pray for me. It's the best he can do. To his knowledge, no
20 man has ever completed such a trip, though a few have tried. And certainly no woman has done such a thing. This morning he took me aside and told me he thinks I'm crazy, which I understood as concern and thanked him. He told me that the people of Old Ségou think I'm crazy too, and that only uncanny[1] good luck will keep me safe.

Still, when a person tells me I can't do something, I'll want to do it all the more. It may be a failing of mine. I carry my inflatable kayak through the narrow passageways of Old Ségou, past the small adobe huts melting in the rains, past the huddling goats and
30 smoke of cooking fires, people peering out at me from the dark entranceways. It is a labyrinth[2] of ancient homes, built and rebuilt after each storm, plastered with the very earth people walk upon. Old Ségou must look much the same as it did in Scottish explorer Mungo Park's time when, exactly 206 years ago to the day, he left on the first of his two river journeys down the Niger to Timbuktu, the first such attempt by a Westerner. It is no coincidence that I've planned to leave on the same day and from the same spot. Park is my benefactor of sorts, my guarantee. If he could travel down the Niger, then so can I. And it is all the guarantee I have for this trip—
40 that an obsessed 19th-century adventurer did what I would like to do. Of course Park also died on this river, but I've so far managed to overlook that.

I gaze at the Niger through the adobe passageways, staring at waters that began in the mountainous rain forests of Guinea and traveled all this way to central Mali—waters that will journey northeast with me to Timbuktu before cutting a great circular swath through the Sahara and retreating south, through Niger, on to Nigeria, passing **circuitously** through mangrove swamps and jungle, resting at last in the Atlantic in the Bight of Benin.[3] But the
50 Niger is more than a river; it is a kind of faith. Bent and plied by Saharan sands, it perseveres more than 2,600 miles from beginning to end through one of the hottest, most desolate regions of the world. And when the rains come each year, it finds new strength of purpose, surging through the sunbaked lands, giving people the boons of crops and livestock and fish, taking nothing, asking nothing. It humbles all who see it.

circuitously
(sər-kyōōˊĭ-təs-lē) *adv.* in an indirect and lengthy manner.

---

[1] **uncanny:** mysterious or impossible to explain.
[2] **labyrinth:** a complex collection of paths, such as a maze.
[3] **Bight of Benin:** a gulf on Africa's west coast between Ghana and Nigeria.

APPLYING ACADEMIC VOCABULARY

undertake	motivate

As you discuss Salak's travel narrative, incorporate the following Collection 6 academic vocabulary words: *undertake* and *motivate*. Have students discuss why Salak decided to **undertake** such a dangerous journey. What does she say **motivates** her to choose this journey down the Niger? Is she clear about her motivation?

If I were to try to explain why I'm here, why I chose Mali and the Niger for this journey—now that is a different matter. I can already feel the resistance in my gut, the familiar clutch of fear.
I used to avoid stripping myself down in search of motivation, scared of what I might uncover, scared of anything that might suggest a taint of the pathological.[4] And would it be enough to say that I admire Park's own trip on the river and want to try a similar challenge? That answer carries a whiff of the **disingenuous**; it sounds too easy to me. Human motivation, itself, is a complicated thing. If only it was simple enough to say, "Here is the Niger, and I want to paddle it." But I'm not that kind of traveler, and this isn't that kind of trip. If a journey doesn't have something to teach you about yourself, then what kind of journey is it? There is one thing I'm already certain of: Though we may think we choose our journeys, they choose us.

Hobbled donkeys cower under a new onslaught of rain, ears back, necks craned. Little children dare each other to touch me, and I make it easy for them, stopping and holding out my arm. They stroke my white skin as if it were velvet, using only the pads of their fingers, then stare at their hands to check for wet paint.

Thunder again. More rain falls. I stop on the shore, near a centuries-old kapok tree under which I imagine Park once took shade. I open my bag, spread out my little red kayak, and start to pump it up. I'm doing this trip under the sponsorship of *National Geographic Adventure,* which hopes to run a magazine story about it. This means that they need photos, lots of photos, and so a French photographer named Rémi Bénali feverishly snaps pictures of me. I don't know what I hate more—river storms or photo shoots. I value the privacy and **integrity** of my trips, and I don't want my journey turning into a circus. The magazine presented the best compromise it could: Rémi, renting a motor-driven pirogue,[5] was given instructions to find me on the river every few days to do his thing.

My kayak is nearly inflated. A couple of women nearby, with colorful cloth wraps called *pagnes* tied tightly about their breasts, gaze at me cryptically, as if to ask: *Who are you and what do you think you're doing?* The Niger churns and slaps the shore, in a surly mood. I don't pretend to know what I'm doing. Just one thing at a time now, kayak inflated, kayak loaded with my gear. Paddles fitted together and ready. Modibo is standing on the shore, watching me.

"I'll pray for you," he reminds me.

I balance my gear, adjust the straps, get in. And, finally, irrevocably, I paddle away. . . .

---

[4] **taint of the pathological:** trace of mental illness.
[5] **pirogue (pĭ-rōg´):** a canoe made from a hallowed tree trunk.

disingenuous
(dĭs´ĭn-jĕn´yōō-əs)
adj. insincere, deceitful.

integrity
(ĭn-tĕg´rĭ-tē) *n.* consistency and strength of purpose.

WHEN STUDENTS STRUGGLE . . .

Ask pairs of students to reread lines 33–79 and identify the three references to the explorer Mungo Park. Have them explain to each other how each reference supports Salak's motivation to take the dangerous journey. *(In lines 33–42, Salak tells the reader that Park attempted the same journey she is about to take, and that he is an inspiration that such a trip might be successful. In lines 62–65, Salak notes that it is clear she cannot imitate Park exactly—she has to take her own journey, for her own reasons. In lines 77–79, Salak imagines that she is embarking on her own journey, but one parallel to Park's.)*

LEVEL UP TUTORIALS For additional support, assign the following *Level Up* tutorial: **Reading for Details.**

CLOSE READ

Determine Central Idea and Cite Evidence (LINES 68-71)   RI 2

Tell students that another way to cite evidence is to **paraphrase** the text. Paraphrasing a text means restating it in your own words.

D ASK STUDENTS what idea Salak is trying to support in lines 68–71. Have them paraphrase the passage to explain the evidence that Salak provides for her central idea. *(Salak is supporting the central idea that journeys should be learning experiences. As she thinks about the purpose of her trip, Salak concludes that the only journeys worth taking are those that teach us about ourselves; those are the journeys we must take.)*

Analyze Ideas and Events (LINES 72-79)   RI 1, RI 3

Tell students that the author of a travel narrative can create tension by including vivid details.

E CITE TEXT EVIDENCE Have students identify the details in lines 72–79 that contribute to the underlying tension of the scene as Salak prepares to depart. *(The description of "[h]obbled donkeys cower under a new onslaught of rain, ears back, necks craned" [lines 72–73] shows that these creatures are at the mercy of the elements, as Salak herself will soon be; the brief statements "Thunder again. More rain falls" [line 77] are vivid details that allow the reader to experience the ominous weather along with Salak.)*

CRITICAL VOCABULARY

disingenuous: An insincere person often tries to deceive others. **ASK STUDENTS** why Salak thinks her answer to why she has chosen to take this journey is disingenuous. *(The truth is usually complicated—not as simple as her answer would make it seem.)*

integrity: Someone whose words and actions are consistent is able to keep focused on what is important. **ASK STUDENTS** to explain why Salak uses the word *integrity* to describe her trips. *(She takes the trips on her own terms, establishing the conditions that will assure her privacy and singleness of purpose.)*

Analyze Ideas and Events

RI 1, RI 3

(LINES 100-114)

Remind students that in a travel narrative, every detail contributes to the story. Details about conflicts and obstacles help readers get involved in the adventure.

F **CITE TEXT EVIDENCE** Have students cite the details in lines 100–114 that describe the obstacles Salak faces in the first moments of her journey. (*"The wind drives the current in reverse" [line 102], "crashing and driving forward" [line 104], "arm muscles smarting and rebelling against this journey" [lines 105–106], "I crawl . . . fighting the Niger" [line 106], "The people know something I don't" [line 109], "a screech of pain. My right arm lurches from a ripped muscle" [lines 111–112], "pulses of pain as I fight the river" [line 114]*)

Determine Author's Point of View (LINES 111-115)

RI 6

G **ASK STUDENTS** to reread 111–115 to identify how Salak uses rhetoric or language to support her point of view. (*Salak says, "There is only one direction to go: forward. Stopping has become anathema" [lines 114–115]. Salak is expressing these ideas because she feels that the journey must go on. She is determined to overcome all obstacles, however dangerous, to complete the journey.*)

> **CRITICAL VOCABULARY**
>
> **embark**: Setting out on a trip, a traveler has many expectations.
>
> **ASK STUDENTS** what kinds of expectations Salak says we often express when we embark on a trip. (*When we set out on a journey, we say it is to see a place and learn about its people.*)

---

100   The storm erupts into a new overture. Torrential rains. Waves higher than my kayak, trying to capsize me. But my boat is self-bailing[6] and I stay afloat. The wind drives the current in reverse, tearing and ripping at the shores, sending spray into my face. I paddle madly, crashing and driving forward. I travel inch by inch, or so it seems, arm muscles smarting and rebelling against this journey. I crawl past New Ségou, fighting the Niger for more distance. Large river steamers rest in jumbled rows before cement docks, the town itself looking dark and deserted in the downpour. No one is out in their boats. The people know something I don't:
110 that the river dictates all travel.

     A popping feeling now and a screech of pain. My right arm lurches from a ripped muscle. But this is no time and place for such an injury, and I won't tolerate it, stuck as I am in a storm. I try to get used to the pulses of pain as I fight the river. There is only one direction to go: forward. Stopping has become anathema.[7]

I wonder what we look for when we **embark** on these kinds of trips. There is the pat answer that you tell the people you don't know: that you're interested in seeing a place, learning about its people. But then the trip begins and the hardship comes, and hardship is

embark
(ĕm-bärk´) *v.* to set out on a course or a journey (often aboard a boat).

---

6 **self-bailing:** the boat has holes, or scuppers, that allow water to drain from the cockpit.
7 **anathema:** something hated or despised.

TO CHALLENGE STUDENTS . . .

Infer Reasons Why do we do what we do? Remind students about the information they have learned about Salak. Based on that information, and her discussion of her reasons for taking this trip, have students write a short story with Salak as the main character, that takes place before she embarks on the journey. The story could be set in the United States, in Africa, or elsewhere. It could be set several years in the past, or the day before this excerpt begins. Encourage students to include in their story a suggestion of the purpose of Salak's journey and what her journey (and/or her general future) will be like.

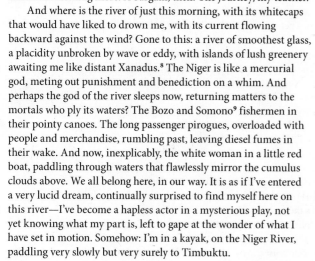

120 more honest: it tells us that we don't have enough patience yet, nor humility, nor gratitude. And we thought that we did. Hardship brings us closer to truth, and thus is more difficult to bear, but from it alone comes compassion. And so I've told the world that it can do what it wants with me during this trip if only, by the end, I have learned something more. A bargain, then. The journey, my teacher.

And where is the river of just this morning, with its whitecaps that would have liked to drown me, with its current flowing backward against the wind? Gone to this: a river of smoothest glass, a placidity unbroken by wave or eddy, with islands of lush greenery
130 awaiting me like distant Xanadus.[8] The Niger is like a mercurial god, meting out punishment and benediction on a whim. And perhaps the god of the river sleeps now, returning matters to the mortals who ply its waters? The Bozo and Somono[9] fishermen in their pointy canoes. The long passenger pirogues, overloaded with people and merchandise, rumbling past, leaving diesel fumes in their wake. And now, inexplicably, the white woman in a little red boat, paddling through waters that flawlessly mirror the cumulus clouds above. We all belong here, in our way. It is as if I've entered a very lucid dream, continually surprised to find myself here on
140 this river—I've become a hapless actor in a mysterious play, not yet knowing what my part is, left to gape at the wonder of what I have set in motion. Somehow: I'm in a kayak, on the Niger River, paddling very slowly but very surely to Timbuktu.

As Salak continues on her journey, she encounters raging storms, dangerous hippos, and unrelenting heat. Because she is traveling in a small kayak and unable to carry many supplies, she comes ashore each night, seeking shelter and food from the locals, who live along the banks of the river. The locals are very curious about a woman undertaking such a dangerous journey alone. Some of them greet her warmly and generously; others with hostility. Finally, weak from dysentery, she approaches her final destination—Timbuktu.

from Chapter Thirteen

"This river will never end," I say out loud, over and over again, like a mantra. My map shows an obvious change to the northeast, but that turn hasn't come for hours, may never come at all. To be so close to Timbuktu, and yet so immeasurably far away. All I know is that I must keep paddling. I *have* to be close. Determined still to get

---

[8] **Xanadus (zăn´ə-dōoz´):** Xanadu, the summer palace of Kublai Khan; connotes an elaborate, ideal paradise.
[9] **Bozo and Somono:** ethnic groups native to Mali and the Niger River delta.

The Cruelest Journey: 600 Miles to Timbuktu **425**

ENGLISH LANGUAGE SUPPORT

Language: Conjunctions Explain that a **conjunction** is a word or words that connect the two parts of a sentence. A **coordinating conjunction** connects words used in the same way, such as *and, but, yet,* and *so.* Example:

- To be so close. . . *and yet so . . .* far away. *(lines 146–147)*

Explain that coordinating conjunctions are sometimes used at the beginnings of sentences to connect with previous sentences:

- *But* then the trip begins . . . *(line 119)*
- *And* we thought that we did. *(line 121)*

ASK STUDENTS to find more examples of conjunctions in the text.

Determine Central Idea and Cite Evidence
RI 2

(LINES 119-125)

Tell students that to learn more about an author's thoughts and motivations in writing a text, it is important to think about the evidence the author provides in the form of details about life and people.

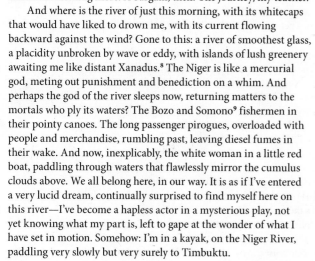 **ASK STUDENTS** why they think people take journeys. How does Salak show that she dismisses the idea that people take journeys only to see a place and learn about people? Ask them to paraphrase the passage as part of their answer. *(After saying that people commonly say that the reason for a journey is to see new places and learn about people, Salak talks about how the hardship of a journey makes us realize that there are other more important reasons for journeys. She says that difficult experiences help us find the truth about ourselves; this can be painful but in the end they make us better human beings.)*

Analyze Ideas and Events
RI 1, RI 3

(LINES 128-138)

Tell students that **mood,** or the emotional response a work creates in readers, is created by details. An author uses words to bring readers closer to the most important ideas in a text.

ASK STUDENTS what mood Salak creates in lines 128–138 with the words that she uses to describe the river. Have them cite specific words and phrases that help create the mood. *(The mood is one of calmness, restfulness, and peace. Having just survived the storm, Salak finds herself on a much calmer river. She uses phrases such as "smoothest glass" [line 128], "placidity unbroken" [line 129], "islands of lush greenery" [line 129], and "waters that flawlessly mirror the cumulous clouds above" [lines 137–138] to ease the tension that had built up.)*

Analyze Ideas and Events

RI 1, RI 3

(LINES 152–175)

Tell students that the author of a travel narrative frequently adjusts the **pacing,** speeding up or slowing down events, by varying sentence length.

 ASK STUDENTS to describe the pace of the narrative in lines 152–175. *(Salak is struggling to reach the port. Most sentences in lines 152–175 are fairly long, showing a regular pace, almost as if the words are mimicking the rhythm of her paddling. She repeats the phrase "I paddle" several times, and then "Timbuktu, Timbuktu" [line 161] also shows the rhythm of her progress.)* How does the pace in lines 174–175 change? *(When she is "yanked back" [line 174], the choppy sentences reflect the author's feelings: She is frustrated, temporarily stopped in her tracks, just short of reaching her goal.)* Why is it significant that Salak varies the pacing at this point in the narrative? *(The pacing helps the reader comprehend the extraordinary effort that Salak is making to finish the journey. The change in pace punctuates how close to her limit of endurance she has come.)*

Determine Central Idea and Cite Evidence

RI 1, RI 2

(LINES 176-177)

Remind students that quoting or paraphrasing evidence in the text is a way to support an analysis of the selection's central idea.

 CITE TEXT EVIDENCE Have students cite the part of the text that tells how Salak feels about the last obstacle she encounters as she nears the shore. *(Salak is frustrated that her rudder is tangled with the fishnets, and that she has to stop to fix it. Even so, she is able to have a positive attitude when she writes, "The universe surely has a sense of humor" [lines 176–177].)*

---

to Timbuktu's port of Korioumé by nightfall, I shed the protection
150 of my long-sleeved shirt, pull the kayak's thigh straps in tight, and
prepare for the hardest bout of paddling yet.

I paddle like a person possessed. I paddle the hours away, the
sun falling aside to the west but still keeping its heat on me. I keep
up a cadence in my head, keep my breaths regular and deep, in
synch with my arm movements. The shore passes by slowly, but it
passes. As the sun gets ominously low, burning a flaming orange,
the river turns almost due north and I can see a distant, square-
shaped building made of cement: the harbinger of what can only
be Korioumé. Hardly a tower of gold, hardly an El Dorado, but I'll
160 take it. I paddle straight toward it, ignoring the pains in my body,
my raging headache. *Timbuktu, Timbuktu!* Bozo fishermen ply
the river out here, and they stare at me as I pass. They don't ask for
money or *cadeaux*[10]—can they see the determination in my face,
sense my fatigue? All they say is, *"Ça va, madame?"*[11] with obvious
concern. One man actually stands and raises his hands in a cheer,
urging me on. I take his kindness with me into the final stretch,
rounding the river's sharp curve to the port of Korioumé.

I see Rémi's boat up ahead; he waits for me by the port, telephoto
lens in hand. It's the first time during this trip that I'm not fazed by
170 being photographed. I barely notice him. I barely notice anything
except the port ahead of me. All I can think about is stopping. Here
is the ending I've promised myself for weeks. Here I am, 600 miles of
river covered, with the port of Timbuktu straight ahead.

Something tugs at my kayak. I'm yanked back: fishnets,
caught in my rudder. To be this close, within sight of my goal, and
thwarted by yet one more thing. The universe surely has a sense of
humor. I jump into the water, fumbling at the nylon netting tangled
around the screws holding the rudder to the inflatable rubber. It's
shallow here, and my bare feet sink into river mud full of sharp
180 pieces of rock that cut instantly into my soles. I try to ignore the
pain, working fast, pulling the netting off until I free my kayak.
When I get inside, the blood from my feet mixes with gray river
water like a final offering to the Niger. I maneuver around the nets,
adjust my course for the dock of Korioumé, and paddle hard.

Just as the last rays of the sun color the Niger, I pull up beside
a great white river steamer, named, appropriately, the *Tombouctou.*
Rémi's boat is directly behind me, the flash from his camera
lighting up the throng of people gathering on shore. There is no
more paddling to be done. I've made it. I can stop now. I stare up
190 at the familiar crowd waiting in the darkness. West African pop
music blares from a party on the *Tombouctou.*

---

[10] **cadeaux (kə-dō´):** French word meaning "gifts."
[11] **Ça va, madame? (sävä, mä-däm´):** French for "How are you, madam?"

APPLYING ACADEMIC VOCABULARY

pursuit	objective

As students continue to read and discuss the travel narrative, incorporate the following Collection 6 academic vocabulary words: *pursuit* and *objective*. Discuss how Salak's **pursuit** of her goal makes her willing to undergo such discomfort and danger. As her **objective**—the end of the 600-mile journey on the river—nears, how does Salak cope with the difficulties she meets in the final stretch? What can you conclude about what kind of person she is?

Slowly, I undo my thigh straps and get out of my kayak, hauling it from the river and dropping it onshore for the last time. A huge crowd has gathered around me, children squeezing in to stroke my kayak. People ask where I have come from and I tell them, "Old Ségou." They can't seem to believe it.

"Ségou?" one man asks. He points down the Niger. His hand waves and curves as he follows the course of the river in his mind.

"Oui," I say.

200   "Ehh!" he exclaims.

"Ségou, Ségou, Ségou?" a woman asks.

I nod. She runs off to tell other people, and I can see passersby rushing over to take a look at me. What does a person look like who has come all the way from Ségou? They stare down at me in my sweat-stained tank top, my clay-smeared skirt, my sandals both held together with plastic ties.

I unload my things to the clamor of their questions, but even speaking seems to pain me now. Such a long time getting here. And was the journey worth it? Or is it blasphemy to ask that now? I can

210   barely walk, have a high fever. I haven't eaten anything for more than a day. How do you know if the journey is worth it? I would give a great deal right now for silence. For stillness.

My exhaustion and sickness begin to alter this arrival, numbing the sense of finish and self-congratulation and replacing it with only the most important of questions. I've found that illness does this to me, quiets the busy thoughts of the mind, gives me a rare clarity that I don't usually have. I see the weeks on the river, the changing tribal groups, the lush shores down by Old Ségou metamorphosing[12] slowly into the treeless, sandy spread near

220   Timbuktu. I'm wishing I could explain it to people—the subtle yet certain way the world has altered over these past few weeks. The inevitability of it. The grace of it. Grace, because in my life back home every day had appeared the same as the one before. Nothing seemed to change; nothing took on new variety. It had felt like a **stagnant** life.

I know now, with the utter conviction of my heart, that I want to avoid that stagnant life. I want the world to always be offering me the new, the grace of the unfamiliar. Which means—and I pause with the thought—a path that will only lead through my fears.

230   Where there are certainty and guarantees, I will never be able to meet that unknown world.

Night settles on the shore, and Rémi pulls his boat up alongside the cement dock. I deflate my kayak for the last time and pack it up, carrying it and my things onto the boat. Heather[13] and Rémi

stagnant
(stăg′nənt) *adj.*
unchanging; without activity or development.

---

[12]**metamorphosing:** completely changing into another form.

[13]**Heather:** photographer Rémi Bénali's girlfriend, who is traveling with him.

TO CHALLENGE STUDENTS . . .

Investigate Additional Details Suggest that students read more of *The Cruelest Journey* to learn more about Salak's journey to Timbuktu. If the book is not available, a number of excerpts from her other books, as well as articles, can be found on the Internet. Have students read various articles and excerpts; then, in small groups, have them summarize what they have read.

As they read and discuss Salak's work, encourage students to consider the following question: By describing their travels, can explorers make the world a better place? Can they help us become better people?

CLOSE READ

Analyze Ideas and Events (LINES 197-212)   RI 1, RI 3

Remind students that authors use dialogue to help show what people are thinking and to advance the action and message of the text.

(L) **ASK STUDENTS** how the dialogue in lines 197 and 201 is similar to the thinking of Modibo in lines 17–25. *(The repetition of the word Ségou? with the question mark shows that like Modibo in Old Ségou, the people in Timbuktu are having difficulty in believing that such a journey is possible, or why it would be necessary.)* How does this dialogue also support Salak's own thinking in lines 207–212? *(In her depleted state, Salak is, like Modibo at the beginning of the journey and the people in Timbuktu, wondering why she pushed forward and continued through the journey.)*

Determine Central Idea and Cite Evidence   RI 1, RI 2
(LINES 226-231)

Explain that sometimes an author's words are so precise that it is better to quote rather than paraphrase them.

(M) **CITE TEXT EVIDENCE** Have students cite evidence that reveals what Salak has learned about herself by the time she reaches Timbuktu. What are the consequences she will have to face? *(When Salak reaches her destination, she understands the following: "I want to avoid that stagnant life. I want the world to always be offering me the new, the grace of the unfamiliar" [lines 226–228]. As a consequence of this choice, Salak says that, "Where there are certainty and guarantees, I will never be able to meet that unknown world" [lines 230–231].)*

CRITICAL VOCABULARY

stagnant: A life that consists of routine and unchanging patterns doesn't provide a fulfilling experience. **ASK STUDENTS** why Salak believes her life was stagnant before she embarked on her journey. How is it different now? *(Her life was unchanging, without variety. Now she wants to have more new experiences even though she realizes that she might have to give up some things to achieve her goals.)*

Analyze Ideas and Events

RI 1, RI 3

(LINES 257-261)

Remind students that **mood** is the emotional response a work creates in readers.

(N) ASK STUDENTS why Salak struggles to celebrate the end of her journey. What mood does she create with her description of crossing to the opposite shore? *(The stars, like Salak herself, are "dazed" [line 259]. Salak is exhausted and sick—"too sick to fully acknowledge the end of my trip" [line 261]. The mood is one of confusion and distress.)*

Determine Central Idea and Cite Evidence

RI 2

(LINES 266-270)

(O) ASK STUDENTS to reread the last five lines of the narrative and paraphrase the final sentence. *(Salak feels that she is still on the river—the Niger will always be part of her, and part of her will always belong to the Niger.)* How does this conclusion relate to her central idea? *(Her connection to the river will carry her onward through the journey of her life.)*

COLLABORATIVE DISCUSSION Have students pair up and discuss Salak's thoughts about her journey at the beginning of her trip. Their responses to the question about whether or not they were surprised by Salak's feelings at the end of the trip should be supported by details in the narrative.

ASK STUDENTS to share any questions they generated in the course of reading and discussing the selection.

---

both give me a hug of congratulation, but I'm still too numb to really comprehend that I've done it yet. To celebrate, Rémi offers me my choice of their onboard selection of soft drinks. I take an Orange Fanta. Outside, barely discernible in the darkness, the crowd of onlookers continues to discuss what I've done. I can hear
240 them exchanging the word "Ségou" and I wonder if they believe that I've paddled this far. But it doesn't matter. I lie down on one of the benches. My head feels hot, and it aches to the metronome-like beating[14] of my heart.

Rémi has gone onshore and tries valiantly to get us a taxi into Timbuktu, but the driver of the only car available at this late hour demands an exorbitant sum of more than $150 to drive 30 kilometers. It is the first time I've seen Rémi get so blustering and assertive, and he argues passionately for a lower sum. We are all hoping for what we've promised ourselves tonight—a hotel room
250 in Timbuktu with blessed air-conditioning—but the driver won't budge his price, thinking he has us. As we're all nearly out of our magazine expense money, I suggest we camp and go to Timbuktu the next morning, when there are sure to be plenty of taxis to take us there at a reasonable price. For the first time, I see this disappointment as just another uncontrollable part of life, like the storms that arose on the Niger. Nothing personal.

I point to the opposite shore as a place to camp away from the crowds. Rémi and Heather agree, and so the great boat is started up and we speed over the Niger beneath a sky dazed with stars. We
260 ground the boat on the opposite shore, and I go about setting up my tent. I'm too sick to fully acknowledge the end of my trip. Rémi offers me a drink to celebrate, but I know I wouldn't be able to keep it down. I do manage to swallow some antibiotics and antinausea pills, which quiet my stomach enough to allow me to eat a mango and some of the noodles Rémi's cook has made for us. As I sit to eat, I'm swaying back and forth in my mind, as if I were still careering over the waves of the Niger. I've heard that this happens to sailors, that they get so attached to being tossed by the waves that they have trouble readjusting to solid ground. For me, it is as if the Niger still
270 keeps a part of me, as if to tell me that I finally belong to it.

COLLABORATIVE DISCUSSION Were you surprised by how Salak felt at the end of her trip? With a partner, discuss Salak's thoughts on beginning the trip and details that may have led to her feelings at the end of the trip. Cite specific evidence from the text to support your ideas.

[14] **metronome-like beating:** steady, rhythmic pulsing.

FOR STRUGGLING READERS...

Vocabulary: Context Clues Some students may have trouble with challenging vocabulary in the selection, such as *discernible* (line 238), *valiantly* (line 244), and *exorbitant* (line 246). Using a whiteboard, project lines 244–247. Show students that they can use **context clues** to figure out the meanings of the words. For example, "more than $150 to drive 30 kilometers" suggests that an *"exorbitant sum"* means that it is too much money.

ASK STUDENTS to work in pairs to review the text and use context clues to define and discuss any words that they found difficult. Remind them that they can use a dictionary while reading a text if they find that context clues don't provide enough support to clearly understand the meaning of the word or the author's ideas.

Analyze Ideas and Events

RI 3

A **travel narrative** is a type of nonfiction that records an author's experiences exploring new places. Travel writers don't just present a series of facts; they tell a story that includes characters, a conflict to be resolved, and themes about life. In this excerpt, Kira Salak uses narrative techniques to reveal her own reflections on her journey. She doesn't just tell you what she sees, she shows you how she feels. By including vivid details and imagery to describe people, places, and events, Salak builds tension and gets readers involved in her adventure. In addition to description and imagery, Salak uses other techniques in her narrative:

- The **mood** of a work is the emotional response it creates in readers. What details does Salak include to create the mood of her narrative?
- **Pacing** refers to the passage of time in a written work. Short, choppy sentences can speed up a narrative, while longer sentences slow it down. The use of the present tense adds immediacy, giving readers the sense that events are unfolding right now. How does Salak vary the pacing in her narrative?
- Writers of nonfiction may use **dialogue** to show what people are like and to advance the action of the story. How does Salak use dialogue in her narrative?

Determine Central Idea and Cite Evidence

RI 1, RI 2

The author of a travel narrative aims to tell a good story full of interesting people, places, and events. In most cases, the author also wants to communicate a **central idea** about life and people. To determine the central idea, ask yourself what purpose the author has for sharing certain details—including descriptions of the journey as well as the author's reflections on what happens.

As you think about the central idea of this selection, consider how Salak feels at the beginning of her journey and what she has learned about herself by the end. Look for specific evidence in the text to support your analysis. Two methods you can use to **cite textual evidence** are quoting the text and paraphrasing the text.

Quoting	Paraphrasing
Quoting the text means using the author's exact words to support an analysis of the text. Use a quotation when the author's specific words are critical to making your point. Always use quotation marks to show that you are using the author's words rather than your own. *Kira Salak begins her narrative by writing, "In the beginning, my journeys feel at best ludicrous, at worst insane."*	**Paraphrasing** the text is restating something in your own words. Paraphrasing helps you clarify the author's meaning, because you must understand it before you can rephrase it. For example, the first sentence of the selection could be paraphrased this way: *The author says that early on, her journeys always feel foolish or crazy.*

TEACH

CLOSE READ

Analyze Ideas and Events

Review the terms *description, imagery, mood, pacing,* and *dialogue*. Have students discuss how using these narrative techniques helps an author involve her readers in the story she wants to tell.

Organize students in groups and have them find one example of each of the above techniques in the travel narrative. Have them complete a sentence about each technique like the one shown below:

"Salak uses the technique of _____ to help readers _____."

Determine Central Idea and Cite Evidence

Have students write a paragraph about Salak's expectations as she sets out on the journey, and another about the lessons she has learned. In each paragraph, have them paraphrase and quote from the text.

Strategies for Annotation 🖉 📖 *Annotate it!*

Analyze Ideas and Events

Share these strategies for guided or independent analysis:

- Highlight in blue details that help you visualize the scene.
- Underline words and phrases that make the description especially vivid.
- On a note, explain what mood is created with this description.
- Encourage students to use their eBook annotation tools to analyze other narrative techniques in the selection.

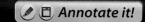

kayak through the narrow passageways of Old Ségou, past the small adobe huts melting in the rains, past the huddling goats and smoke of cooking fires, people peering out at me from the dark entranceways. It is a labyrinth of ancient homes, built and rebuilt after each storm, plastered with the very earth people walk upon.

> The mood created is one of wonder at how people have endured.

PRACTICE & APPLY

Analyzing the Text

Possible answers:

1. *The writer sets out on a journey and wonders what she will learn. Her journey is rife with challenges and doubts (though much of the rising action is omitted from the selection and summarized). Ultimately, she discovers that she does not want a stagnant life—that she will charge directly into her fears.*

2. *The mood conveys tedium and exhaustion. The narrator struggles to complete the final leg of the journey. ("This river will never end.") With determination she paddles "like a possessed person," ignoring her pain. Her tunnel vision remains fixed on the port ahead. When she becomes ensnared in the fishing net, she feels as though she will never reach shore.*

3. *Salak says she might be doing it because she admired Park's voyage on this river and wanted the challenge, or that because the Niger is there, she just wants to paddle it. But really she embarks on this trip to learn something about herself, and she believes that the trip has chosen her in order to teach her something.*

4. *The first passage moves at a faster pace than does the second. Short sentences and fragments ("The storm erupts into a new overture. Torrential rains.") describe the author's struggle as she embarks on her journey. Quick bursts of information are appropriate for an action-packed scene. In the second passage, sentences grow longer and the pace slows as the author shifts to describe her reflections on the journey.*

5. *Responses will vary. Students may agree that the trip was ill-advised, given the storm, the fact that nobody else was on the river, and Salak's early injury. Later she becomes quite ill but pushes on. Others may say that Salak's journey isn't crazy, and that it is worthwhile to face danger and discomfort to escape a "stagnant" life and to learn something about oneself.*

6. *The dialogue illustrates public reactions to the author's accomplishment: people cannot believe that she has paddled all the way from Old Ségou. While most of the narrative recounts solitary actions and private thoughts, the dialogue offers another perspective and provides some variation.*

7. *Salak is driven, determined, and somewhat obstinate. She says, "when a person tells me I can't do something, I'll want to do it all the more." She shows a preference for privacy by traveling alone and grumbling about the photographer. She loves adventure and is motivated by facing physical challenges and overcoming fears and obstacles.*

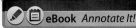 **eBook** *Annotate It!*

Analyzing the Text

RI 1, RI 2,
RI 3, RI 5, W 2

Cite Text Evidence   Support your responses with evidence from the selection.

1. **Identify Patterns** Many travel narratives follow an arc similar to the plot of a story—a conflict is introduced, intensifies, comes to a climax, and is resolved. Outline the arc of the story told in this travel narrative.

2. **Analyze** The mood at the beginning of Chapter One is ominous. What is the mood as the excerpt from Chapter Thirteen begins? What details create this mood?

3. **Interpret** Reread lines 57–71. What reasons does Salak give for making this trip? Why does she really undertake this journey? What does she expect to learn from this experience?

4. **Compare** Compare the pacing in lines 100–115 to that in lines 116–143. Which section seems to move faster, and why? How does the pacing help convey what the author is saying in each passage?

5. **Evaluate** Salak writes, "In the beginning, my journeys feel at best ludicrous, at worst insane." Do you think Salak's journey to Timbuktu was either of these things? Use quotations and paraphrases of the text to support your response.

6. **Analyze** What does the dialogue in lines 197–201 add to the narrative? How does the dialogue contribute to the central idea of the selection?

7. **Summarize** Briefly describe the author. What seems to motivate Salak to undertake these journeys? Support your description with details about her actions, words, and thoughts.

PERFORMANCE TASK

Writing Activity: Analysis At first glance, you might think this selection is about travel on the Niger River, an adventure in Mali, or a long journey. What central idea gives meaning to all the details about Salak's adventure?

- Write a brief essay that analyzes the central idea of this selection. State the central idea and then use quotations and paraphrases to support your analysis.

- Remember to follow the conventions of standard English in your writing.

- Exchange essays with a partner and give each other feedback. Did you both use quotation marks to indicate the author's words? Are your paraphrases accurate? Does your evidence support the central idea you identified?

Assign this
performance task.

PERFORMANCE TASK

Writing Activity: Analysis Have students draft the essay on their own. Student analyses should define the selection's central idea in terms of the self-realization the narrator gains by exploring and challenging herself. Have partners exchange drafts and evaluate them for thoroughness. The feedback should reflect what they have learned about quoting and paraphrasing text, and identifying and providing strong supporting evidence.

Critical Vocabulary

circuitously	disingenuous	integrity	embark	stagnant

Practice and Apply Answer each question in a way that demonstrates your comprehension of the Critical Vocabulary word.

1. What might be the benefits of traveling **circuitously** to an unfamiliar destination?

2. Have you ever given a **disingenuous** answer? Explain.

3. When have you acted with **integrity?** Explain.

4. What would you do to get ready to **embark** on a trip around the world?

5. What would you do if you felt your life was **stagnant?**

Vocabulary Strategy: Denotation and Connotation

The **denotation,** or dictionary meaning, of the Critical Vocabulary word *embark* is "to start something." *Embark* also has certain **connotations,** or associations that are suggested by the word but that go beyond the literal meaning of the word.

embark	
Denotation	**Connotation**
To start something	To start something long or challenging

You wouldn't *embark* on a quick errand, but you would *embark* on a long voyage.

Practice and Apply The words in each pair have similar denotations. Write sentences that demonstrate differences in the connotations of the words in each pair.

1. *still* and *stagnant*

2. *leave* and *embark*

3. *purity* and *integrity*

4. *dishonest* and *disingenuous*

5. *indirectly* and *circuitously*

PRACTICE & APPLY

Critical Vocabulary

Possible answers:

1. *Traveling in a meandering, roundabout fashion is not the quickest way to travel, but you might see something along the way that you otherwise would have missed.*

2. *Once, when I didn't want to admit something, I answered insincerely and withheld some information.*

3. *I regularly act with integrity when I take exams and write reports, because I never cheat or plagiarize.*

4. *Before setting off on a trip around the world, I'd probably pack, get somebody to take care of my pets, and say goodbye to family and friends.*

5. *If I were stuck in an unchanging, monotonous life, I would make an abrupt change in the way I live.*

Vocabulary Strategy: Denotation and Connotation

Tell students that authors choose words with precise connotations in order to suggest a mood and convey meaning.

Possible answers:

1. *Being still suggests choosing not to move; being stagnant suggests an inability to do so.*

2. *To leave connotes exiting a place; but to embark suggests setting off on an extended journey.*

3. Purity *means "not affected or uncontaminated," while* integrity *can mean "whole and undivided."*

4. *Both dishonest and disingenuous answers do not provide the whole truth, but* dishonest *implies an intentional falsehood, while* disingenuous *indicates withheld information.*

5. *Neither indirect nor circuitous routes follow straight courses, but a circuitous route connotes travel in an arc or curve.*

Strategies for Annotation

Denotation and Connotation

Have students locate *cower* (line 72), *velvet* (line 75), *lush* (line 129), *raging* (line 161), *throng* (line 188), and *clay-smeared* (line 205). Encourage them to use their eBook annotation tools to do the following:

- Highlight the word in yellow and on a note, write its denotation.
- Underline words that suggest a positive or negative connotation.
- Think of a word with a similar denotation but different connotation. Explain how using it might have affected the mood of the description.

a placidity unbroken by wave or eddy, with islands of lush greenery awaiting me like distant Xanadus. The Niger is like a mercurial god

PRACTICE & APPLY

Language and Style: Sentence Length

Have partners find more examples of passages with long sentences in the narrative and read them aloud to each other. Encourage them to find examples that mirror the description of the landscape or the actions the author is performing. Then suggest that they shorten the sentences. Have them compare the two versions and evaluate the effect that sentence length has on pacing and the overall impact of the description.

Possible answers:

Answers will vary. Students' revisions of their analyses should demonstrate an ability to vary short and long sentences appropriately in order to add interest and avoid choppy writing.

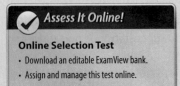

Assess It Online!

Online Selection Test
- Download an editable ExamView bank.
- Assign and manage this test online.

Language and Style: Sentence Length

L 3

Authors vary **sentence length** and style to keep a piece from becoming monotonous. Authors also use sentence length to achieve a specific effect. For example, long sentences tend to slow readers down, while short sentences are read more quickly. A series of short, choppy sentences can also add tension.

> Read this sentence from the selection:

> I gaze at the Niger through the adobe passageways, staring at waters that began in the mountainous rain forests of Guinea and traveled all this way to central Mali—waters that will journey northeast with me to Timbuktu before cutting a great circular swath through the Sahara and retreating south, through Niger, on to Nigeria, passing circuitously through mangrove swamps and jungle, resting at last in the Atlantic in the Bight of Benin.

Salak could have written the passage this way:

> I gaze at the Niger through the adobe passageways. I stare at waters that began in the mountainous rain forests of Guinea and traveled all this way to central Mali. These waters will journey northeast with me to Timbuktu. Then they will cut a great circular swath through the Sahara and retreat south, through Niger, on to Nigeria. Along the way, they will pass circuitously through mangrove swamps and jungle. They will rest at last in the Atlantic in the Bight of Benin.

By using a long, winding sentence, the author mirrors the flow of the river she is describing.

> Later, Salak changes her sentence style as shown in this example:

> Just one thing at a time now, kayak inflated, kayak loaded with my gear. Paddles fitted together and ready.

Here, Salak uses shorter phrases and sentences to mirror the sequence of quick actions she is performing.

> Authors also use breaks in sentences for effect. Consider this sentence:

> Which means—and I pause with the thought—a path that will only lead through my fears.

The use of dashes to offset Salak's side comment causes readers to pause with her and think carefully about the insight she is sharing.

Practice and Apply Go back to the analysis you wrote in response to this selection's Performance Task. Find at least three places where you can enhance your essay by using different sentence lengths.

Write an Analysis

RI 2, W 2

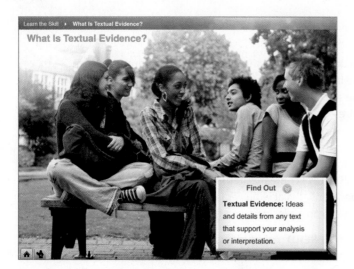

TEACH

Before students write their essays for the Performance Task, review the main considerations for citing text evidence with quotations and paraphrases.

- **Identify strong evidence**. Make sure the quotations and paraphrases you use in your analysis are relevant to the central idea that you have determined.
- **Determine whether the evidence is more effectively presented with a quotation or paraphrase**. At times, the author's exact wording will clearly support your analysis as it is; in such cases, quoting is preferable to paraphrasing.
- **A paraphrase should be in your own words.** In general, long sentences should be shortened. Especially when paraphrasing a longer excerpt, make sure to keep the ideas in the same order as in the selection.

COLLABORATIVE DISCUSSION

Encourage students to keep the above suggestions in mind as they write their essays. As they evaluate each other's work, have partners refer to these suggestions as well. Ask them to discuss how using quotations and paraphrases strengthens their essays.

Analyze Ideas and Events

RI 1, RI 3

RETEACH

Review the following questions students should ask themselves as they analyze **ideas** and **events** in the narrative.

- What details—appearance, actions, thoughts, and feelings—does the author use to describe the people in the narrative, including herself?
- What details show the obstacles the author encounters?
- Does the author interrupt the flow of events? If so, what details does she include to explain the interruption?
- Do the details appeal to any of the five senses? If so, what details does she include to show why the events were interrupted?

Encourage students to reread the entire narrative if they have trouble making connections between the author's ideas and the events. They should look for details that they might have missed the first time they read the narrative.

 LEVEL UP TUTORIALS Assign the following *Level Up* tutorial: **Reading for Details**

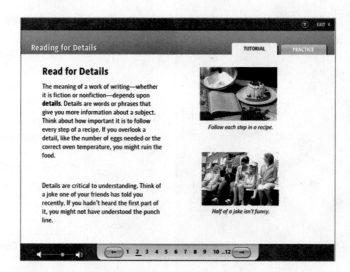

INDEPENDENT READING

Have students apply the skill to another travel narrative and share their analysis of one or two passages in a small group discussion. They should select a passage that includes at least some of the kinds of details described above: people, obstacles, and sensory details. Encourage them to consider how their analysis gives them a better appreciation for Salak's travel narrative.

from The Good Soldiers

Nonfiction by David Finkel

Why This Text

Students may finish reading a work of nonfiction without a complete understanding of the author's main points. Nonfiction selections such as this excerpt from the book *The Good Soldiers* by David Finkel may have more than one complex central idea. With the help of the close-reading questions, students will determine the central ideas by examining the specific details and other supporting evidence in the text.

Background Have students read the background and the information about the author David Finkel. Introduce the selection by telling students that Finkel is a Pulitzer Prize–winning journalist at the *Washington Post* and also a recipient of the MacArthur "genius grant" for his long-form narrative journalism. In awarding him the prize, the MacArthur Foundation singled out his book *The Good Soldiers*, published in 2009. Finkel compares getting a good news story to his camera's zoom lens. "I'm at wide angle," he says, "and I'm trying to get as close as possible and stay as long as I can."

AS YOU READ Ask students to pay close attention to the central ideas in this nonfiction selection and to the interactions among ideas or events in the text. How soon into the selection can students begin to identify a central idea?

Standards Support

- cite multiple pieces of textual evidence
- determine a central idea and analyze its development over the course of the text, including how it is introduced, shaped, and refined by specific details
- analyze how the author unfolds a series of ideas or events
- explain how a series of ideas or events is developed in a text, and the connections that are drawn between them

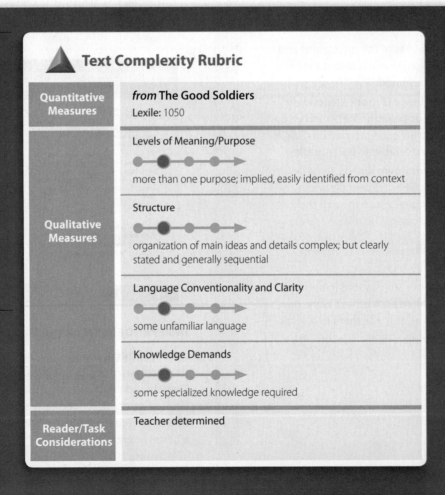

Text Complexity Rubric

| Quantitative Measures | *from* The Good Soldiers
Lexile: 1050 |

Levels of Meaning/Purpose

more than one purpose; implied, easily identified from context

Structure

organization of main ideas and details complex; but clearly stated and generally sequential

Language Conventionality and Clarity

some unfamiliar language

Knowledge Demands

some specialized knowledge required

Reader/Task Considerations Teacher determined

Strategies for CLOSE READING

Determine Central Idea and Cite Evidence

Students should read this text carefully all the way through. Close-reading questions at the bottom of the page will help them focus on a thorough analysis of the central idea of the selection and on how it is supported by specific details and evidence in the text. As they read, students should record comments or questions about the text in the side margins.

WHEN STUDENTS STRUGGLE . . .

To help students follow the selection's central idea, have them work in small groups to fill out a chart such as the one shown as they analyze this work of nonfiction.

CITE TEXT EVIDENCE For practice finding the central idea of an entire selection, ask students to examine how the central idea is developed over the course of the text, including how it emerges and is shaped and refined by specific details.

Central Idea	Supporting Details
Decency can be found even in war, and rules can be broken for the sake of doing what's right.	Line 35: Author's reflection, "How did moments of decency occur in this war?"
	Line 36: Cummings tells Izzy to bring his injured daughter to the base.
	Lines 60–65: Cummings decides to save Izzy's daughter, despite the rules.
	Lines 68–101: Cummings makes and receives phone calls to try to get Izzy's daughter treated at an American aid facility.
	Lines 117–122: Even though Cummings knows he has guessed wrong about which daughter is wounded, he has her taken into the American facility.
	Line 134: Author's reflection, "What do the rules say?"
	Lines 135–152: Neither Cummings nor anyone else cared what the rules said; all that mattered was saving the girl's life.

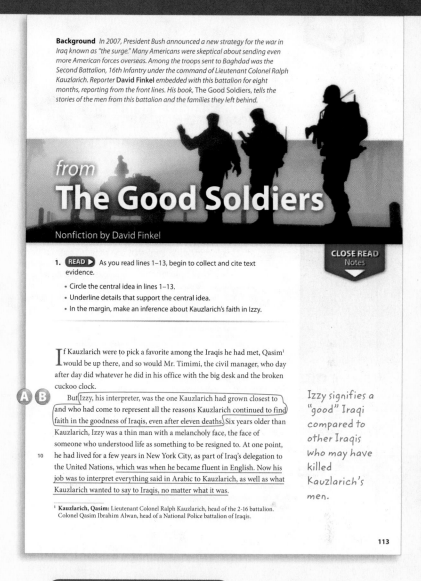

Background In 2007, President Bush announced a new strategy for the war in Iraq known as "the surge." Many Americans were skeptical about sending even more American forces overseas. Among the troops sent to Baghdad was the Second Battalion, 16th Infantry under the command of Lieutenant Colonel Ralph Kauzlarich. Reporter **David Finkel** embedded with this battalion for eight months, reporting from the front lines. His book, The Good Soldiers, tells the stories of the men from this battalion and the families they left behind.

from
The Good Soldiers

Nonfiction by David Finkel

CLOSE READ
Notes

1. **READ ▶** As you read lines 1–13, begin to collect and cite text evidence.

 - Circle the central idea in lines 1–13.
 - Underline details that support the central idea.
 - In the margin, make an inference about Kauzlarich's faith in Izzy.

If Kauzlarich were to pick a favorite among the Iraqis he had met, Qasim[1] would be up there, and so would Mr. Timimi, the civil manager, who day after day did whatever he did in his office with the big desk and the broken cuckoo clock.

Ⓐ Ⓑ But Izzy, his interpreter, was the one Kauzlarich had grown closest to and who had come to represent all the reasons Kauzlarich continued to find faith in the goodness of Iraqis, even after eleven deaths. Six years older than Kauzlarich, Izzy was a thin man with a melancholy face, the face of someone who understood life as something to be resigned to. At one point,
10 he had lived for a few years in New York City, as part of Iraq's delegation to the United Nations, which was when he became fluent in English. Now his job was to interpret everything said in Arabic to Kauzlarich, as well as what Kauzlarich wanted to say to Iraqis, no matter what it was.

[1] **Kauzlarich, Qasim:** Lieutenant Colonel Ralph Kauzlarich, head of the 2-16 battalion. Colonel Qasim Ibrahim Alwan, head of a National Police battalion of Iraqis.

Izzy signifies a "good" Iraqi compared to other Iraqis who may have killed Kauzlarich's men.

113

1. READ AND CITE TEXT EVIDENCE

Ⓐ ASK STUDENTS to examine the details to identify the central idea in the first two paragraphs. *Students should cite text evidence in lines 5–7 to state the central idea—that of all the Iraqis Kauzlarich had met, Izzy, his interpreter, was the one he "had grown closest to," also citing lines 9–13 to show how the specific details about Izzy support the central idea.*

FOR ELL STUDENTS Some students may not understand *pick a favorite* in line 1. Ask a student who may know to explain what it means here. Then have students tell how the phrase suggests the central idea of lines 1–13. *Students should recognize that it sets up the central idea that of all the Iraqis he had met, Izzy was the one Kauzlarich liked best.*

> ## He was standing on a street with his bleeding daughter at his side.

Some Iraqis resented the Americans being there, and didn't like people who helped the Americans.

C   There were times when Iraqis would look at Izzy in obvious disgust, as if he were nothing more than a tool of the Americans. But he did his job enthusiastically, partly because of his affection for the United States—his older daughter, now seventeen, was born in New York City—and partly because of something that had happened over the summer when he had gone home to spend a few days with his family in central Baghdad.

20   Late one afternoon, a bomb had exploded just outside of his apartment building. Even by Baghdad standards it was a monstrous explosion. Twenty-five people died and more than one hundred others were injured, but seven miles away, no one on the FOB[2] knew anything about it until Brent Cummings's[3] cell phone rang and Izzy was on the other end, in a panic.

D   There had been an explosion, he said. His apartment was in ruins, his building was on fire, and one of his daughters had been badly injured by

---

[2] **FOB:** an abbreviation for Forward Operations Base, a base set up in special operations to support training or tactical operations.
[3] **Brent Cummings:** Major Brent Cummings, Kauzlarich's second in command.

2. ◀ REREAD   Reread lines 5–13. What is the author's purpose in explaining Kauzlarich's feelings about Izzy? Support your answer with explicit text evidence.

By stating that Izzy is the reason Kauzlarich still has "faith in the goodness of Iraqis," we can infer that Kauzlarich blames Iraqis for the "eleven deaths" of his men.

3. READ ▶   As your read lines 14–31, continue to cite text evidence.
- Underline the text in lines 14–19 that hints at an important event.
- In the margin, make an inference about some Iraqi attitudes toward Americans (lines14–19).
- Circle the central idea that describes Izzy's situation in lines 25–31.

114

---

something that had pierced her head. He had taken her to a hospital, but there were so many other injured people that doctors had said there was nothing they could do, that she needed more help than they could give, and 30 so he was standing on a street with his bleeding daughter at his side, afraid that she was going to die.

    "The only hope you have is to get her to an American hospital?" Cummings asked, repeating what Izzy had just said. Izzy started to answer. The cell phone went dead. "Izzy?" Cummings said. "Izzy?"

E How did moments of decency occur in this war?

    "Izzy," Cummings said, calling him back. "Bring your daughter here." That was how.

F   "Oh thank you, sir. Thank you, sir," Izzy said.

    And that's when things got complicated. Even this war had its rules, 40 and one of them covered who could be treated at an American aid facility. Americans could, of course, but Iraqis could not, unless they were injured by the American military, and only if the injury was life-threatening. Since the car bomb had been an Iraqi bomb, none of the injured was entitled to American care, including, it seemed, Izzy's daughter.

Cummings tells Izzy to bring his daughter to the base.

Even though terrible things happen in war, some acts of decency still occurred.

4. ◀ REREAD   Reread lines 20–31. How does the author develop the sense that events are unfolding quickly? Support your answer with explicit textual evidence.

By using reported dialogue, the author advances the action and adds immediacy. The blow-by-blow description of events—"his building was on fire" and "so he was standing on a street with his bleeding daughter at his side"—speeds up the pacing of the narrative.

5. READ ▶   As you read lines 32–49, continue to cite textual evidence.
- In the margin, explain what Cummings tells Izzy to do.
- Circle the author's reflections in lines 31–39.
- In the margin, explain the reasoning behind the author's thoughts.

115

---

2. REREAD AND CITE TEXT EVIDENCE

B **ASK STUDENTS** to analyze the author's reason for explaining how Kauzlarich feels about Izzy. *Students should include specific references to lines 5–7 to explain the author's purpose. By admitting that Izzy is the reason Kauzlarich has retained his "faith in the goodness of Iraqis," students can infer that Kauzlarich blames the Iraqis for the death of eleven of his troops.*

3. READ AND CITE TEXT EVIDENCE

C **ASK STUDENTS** to work with a partner to write one response that infers what some Iraqis felt about the American troops. *Students should cite evidence from lines 14–19 to infer that some Iraqis felt contempt for the American troops and despised the Iraqis who helped the Americans.*

4. REREAD AND CITE TEXT EVIDENCE

D **ASK STUDENTS** to analyze how the author uses reported dialogue to convey the idea that events are unfolding at a rapid pace. *By having Cummings report what Izzy is saying on the phone (lines 25–31), students should recognize that the author is presenting a blow-by-blow description of the horrific events taking place and that the use of the run-on sentence in lines 27–31 adds a breathless pace to the narrative.*

5. READ AND CITE TEXT EVIDENCE

E **ASK STUDENTS** to work with a partner to write one response that explains the reasoning behind the author's rhetorical question to himself in line 35. *Students should cite evidence from lines 32–37 to explain that because Cummings tells Izzy to bring his daughter to the base for treatment, the author realizes that even in amid the horrors of war, some acts of decency can occur.*

But Cummings had in mind Izzy's previous life, before he was an interpreter. If the daughter who was injured had been born in New York City, did that make her eligible? Could an American-born Iraqi who was injured by a non-American bomb receive medical care in an American military medical facility?

50   Cummings didn't know the answer. He phoned some doctors at the aid station, but they didn't know, either. He tried the FOB legal representative, but couldn't get through. He wasn't even sure which of the daughters had been injured—the one born in New York, or the eight-year-old who was born in Baghdad. He called Izzy back. The connection was terrible. He dialed again and again.

H   "Izzy . . . okay . . . where is your daughter that is from the United States?"

    Again the phone went dead.

    He called again. The connection kept breaking up. "Is your daughter
60 from the United States with you right now? . . . Is she hurt? . . . Which daughter is hurt? . . . Is she on the street with you? . . . You can't what? . . . What?"

G   Again the phone went dead, and at that point Cummings made a decision not to ask any more questions, just to assume what the answer would be. He was making a guess. He understood that. But with Kauzlarich

away for a few hours on another FOB to attend a memorial ceremony, there was no one else to ask what to do.

I   He telephoned an officer in another battalion who controlled access to the FOB and whose approval would be needed for someone not in the
70 military to get through the gate without being turned away, detained, or shot. "Yes," he said. "I'm sure we can produce a birth certificate." He wondered whether such a certificate, if it even existed, had burned up in the fire. He checked the time. The sun was going down. A curfew would be in effect soon, at which point Izzy and his daughter wouldn't be allowed outside until sunrise. The officer kept asking questions. "We'll figure that piece out," Cummings said impatiently. "Right now, I just want to help the guy."

    Next he called the battalion's physician and told him to be ready to treat one female, age unknown, in a matter of minutes. "A U.S. citizen," he
80 added, and then to that added, "maybe."

    Next he tried Izzy again, to see how close he was to the FOB, and Izzy, his voice more panicked than before, said he wasn't close at all, that he was still on the street, still next to his daughter, trying to find a taxi. "Thank you, sir," he kept saying. "Thank you, sir. Thank you, sir."

    There was nothing to do but wait. It wasn't as if a convoy could go pick up Izzy. He would have to get here on his own. The sun was almost down

---

6. **◀ REREAD**   Reread lines 32–49. Explain Izzy's dilemma. Why does the author pose two questions in lines 45–49?

Izzy's daughter is badly injured and the Iraqi doctors said they couldn't help her. The author poses the questions to show the uncertainty of the situation. Even though Cummings has offered help, he does not know if he has the authority to do so.

7. **READ ▶**   As you read lines 50–67, continue to cite textual evidence.

- Circle each use of "didn't know" in lines 50–55. In the margin, explain how this repetition highlights the conflict.
- Underline the decision Cummings makes in lines 63–67. In the margin, draw an inference as to why he makes that decision.

116

---

8. **◀ REREAD**   Reread lines 56–62. How do the short, choppy lines of dialogue affect the pacing of the narrative? Support your answer with explicit textual evidence.

They speed up the narrative adding urgency ("Is she hurt?"), and indicate Cummings's growing frustration ("You can't what? . . . What?").

9. **READ ▶**   As you read lines 68–129, continue to cite textual evidence.

- Underline every mention of a call made by or answered by Cummings.
- Circle statements Cummings makes that may not be true.
- Underline text explaining what Cummings knows when he sees Izzy and his family.

117

---

6. **REREAD AND CITE TEXT EVIDENCE**

F **ASK STUDENTS** what the author means when he says in line 39, "And that's when things got complicated." How do his two questions in lines 45–49 "flesh out" the complications of the situation? *Students should cite specific evidence in lines 39–44 to restate the complications and recognize that the two questions the author poses in lines 45–49 illustrate the uncertainty of the issue as to whether or not Izzy's daughter could be treated at an American medical facility.*

7. **READ AND CITE TEXT EVIDENCE**

G **ASK STUDENTS** what the central idea is in lines 63–67. Then have partners share their margin notes to infer why Cummings makes the decision he does. *Students should note that the central idea is that Cummings decides not to ask any more questions but "just to assume what the answers would be." They should infer from lines 63–67 that he feels that Izzy's daughter might die if he doesn't decide to have her treated at the base.*

8. **REREAD AND CITE TEXT EVIDENCE**

H **ASK STUDENTS** how the choppy dialogue in lines 56–62 and the use of ellipses affect the pace of the narrative. *Students should cite evidence in lines 56–62 to note that the short, choppy lines of dialogue and ellipses, which indicate that the cell phone connection is breaking up, indicate the urgency of the situation, while speeding up the action and the narrative pace.*

9. **READ AND CITE TEXT EVIDENCE**

I **ASK STUDENTS** to find and cite examples of each phone call made or received by Cummings in lines 68–101. How do the calls highlight the confusion of the situation while speeding up the narrative account? *Students should cite specific textual evidence in lines 68, 78, 81, 87, 89, 90, 95, 97, and 100 to indicate how the phone calls amplify the confusion since no one, including Cummings, has any answers, and how they highlight the immediacy and the frantic pace of the situation.*

now. A call came from an officer in another battalion who said he'd heard that the 2-16 had lost some soldiers somewhere. "No," Cummings said. Then another officer called saying he'd heard some soldiers had been
90 injured in an apartment bombing. Then another: the rumor was that some 2-16 soldiers had died in an EFP[4] attack.

"No, there are no injured Coalition Forces,"[5] Cummings kept saying. "It is an Iraqi—an Iraqi American—who was hurt. It is the interpreter's daughter."

He phoned Izzy again.

Still trying to find a taxi.

Another call, from the doctor: "I don't know the extent of the injuries . . . I don't know if he's even in a cab yet . . . I don't know if they're going to make it here before curfew."
100 Another call. It was Izzy. They were in a taxi. They were on the bridge, two minutes from the base.

Cummings hurried to the gate. It was dark now. The FOB's ambulance pulled up to receive the girl. Five minutes had gone by. Where was the taxi? Now the guards said they had stopped it in the distance and that there was no way it would be allowed any closer than it had gotten, which was somewhere out of sight. "Get a litter," Cummings yelled to the ambulance crew. Sprinting, he went out the gate, passing coils of razor wire and blast walls, and then stopping when he saw Izzy walking toward him, illuminated by the headlights of the ambulance.
110 Izzy's clothing was filthy.

Next to him was his wife, who was crying.

On his other side was one of his daughters, the one born in New York, who appeared to be uninjured.

And in front of them all, wobbly but walking, was a young girl with shiny purple sandals, blood all over her blue jeans, and a bandage covering the left side of her face.

 It was the eight-year-old, the daughter born in Baghdad, the one who according to the rules had no standing whatsoever to be treated on the FOB. "Izzy," Cummings called out, knowing right then that he had guessed
120 wrong. He ran toward the family as other soldiers reached the girl. They lifted her up. She began crying. They carried her through the gate without stopping. They ran with her into the aid station, and as the doors swung

---

[4] **EFP:** Explosively Formed Penetrator, also known as Explosively Formed Projectile, a warhead designed to penetrate armor.
[5] **Coalition Forces:** military command led by the United States and its allies during the Iraq War.

> " . . . when he was unable to say anything else, he bowed his head, and then wiped his eyes . . . "

shut she cried out in Arabic for her father, who'd been told to remain in the lobby.

Izzy took a seat in a corner. Cummings stood nearby. "Was it a car bomb?" he asked after a while.

"No, sir," Izzy said. "It was two car bombs."

And then he said nothing more, not until one of the doctors came into the lobby to tell him that his daughter was going to be all right.

130 "Thank you, sir," he managed to say, and when he was unable to say anything else, he bowed his head, and then wiped his eyes, and then followed the doctor into the treatment area, where he saw his Iraqi daughter surrounded by American doctors and medics.

What do the rules say?

At that moment, anyway, no one seemed concerned one way or another: not the doctors, not the family, and not Cummings, who stood at the very same spot he'd stood at as he watched Crow[6] die, watching once again.

The injuries to the girl were serious. There was a deep cut across her cheek, and worse, something had gone into the left side of her forehead,
140 near her temple, and was deeply embedded in bone. Izzy held her hand as the doctors wrapped her in a sheet, making sure to secure her arms tightly.

Sometimes it's okay to break the rules.

---

[6] **Crow:** Sergeant William Crow died from an EFP hit on his convoy in June 2007.

---

10. ◀ **REREAD AND DISCUSS** With a small group, discuss whether or not you think Cummings made the right decision.

11. **READ** ▶ As you read lines 130–152, continue to cite textual evidence.
   - Circle the question the author asks.
   - Underline text describing similarities between the Americans and the Iraqis.
   - In the margin, explain a possible theme of lines 130–137.

WHEN STUDENTS STRUGGLE . . .

To help students understand how the central idea is shaped and refined by specific details, ask them to reread lines 117–120 and 134–136. Have small groups discuss the idea that Cummings's guess about the daughter had been wrong (the injured daughter was the one who had been born in Baghdad, not in New York), but that it was less important to him (and to the girl's family and doctors) than the idea that rules can be broken for the sake of doing the right thing— the central idea.

FOR ELL STUDENTS Point out that the word *litter* (line 106) is a multiple-meaning word and that in this context it means "a stretcher (or board) for carrying a sick or injured person." Ask students to give the other meanings of the word, such as "trash" or "offspring," and to use each meaning of the word in its own sentence.

10. REREAD AND DISCUSS USING TEXT EVIDENCE

J ASK STUDENTS to appoint a reporter for each group to cite specific textual evidence and line numbers to support their position about whether or not Cummings made the right decision to save Izzy's daughter in spite of the rules. *Students should cite lines 34–36, 39–44, 46–49, 63–67, 71, 79–80, 93, 117–20, 134–136, 138–141, 143–145, and 148–152.*

11. READ AND CITE TEXT EVIDENCE

K ASK STUDENTS to work with a partner or a small group to write the central idea in lines 130–137. What key point about life and people is the author communicating? *Students may cite specific textual evidence in lines 134–136 to state that the central idea is that sometimes it's okay to break the rules for the sake of doing what's right.*

The sound in Baghdad is of mourning; on the FOB the sound is joy and relief.

Her mother closed her eyes. The doctors leaned in. It took a while, and at the worst of it the little girl couldn't remain quiet, but then the doctors were showing her what they had pulled out—a thick piece of glass nearly two inches long.

The glass had been part of an apartment that no longer existed, in a section of Baghdad where the sounds that night were of mourning.

(L) But here on the FOB, the sounds were of a mother whose home was ruined kissing her daughter's face, and a father whose home was ruined
150 kissing his daughter's hand, and a little girl whose home was ruined saying something in Arabic that caused her family to smile, and Cummings saying quietly in English, "Man, I haven't felt this good since I got to this hellhole."

12. ◀ **REREAD** Reread lines 146–152. In the margin, compare the sounds described in these lines. What mood does each create?

SHORT RESPONSE

Cite Text Evidence   What is the central idea of this piece? Explain how the author introduces and develops that idea over the course of the text. Review your reading notes and **cite text evidence**.

The central idea of this selection is that decency can be found even
during war, and rules can be broken for the sake of doing what is right.
The idea is introduced by the author's reflection, a rhetorical
question: "How did moments of decency occur in this war?" The
response is in Cummings's decision to save Izzy's daughter's life, despites
the rules. The central idea is shaped and refined by description and
dialogue. It is reiterated by the author at the end of the text, when he
asks, "What do the rules say?" He responds by saying that no one is
concerned with the rules in the face of the larger fact that a girl's life
has been saved.

120

12. REREAD AND CITE TEXT EVIDENCE

(L) **ASK STUDENTS** how the author manages to intensify the feeling of joy and relief on the FOB. *In lines 148–152, the author contrasts the happy sounds of the family members with the information that they have lost their home, and still they are happy. Cummings's commenting quietly adds to the depth of feeling.*

SHORT RESPONSE

Cite Text Evidence   Student responses will vary, but students should cite textual evidence to support their positions about the central idea of the selection. Students should:

• explain what the central idea is of the piece.

• give reasons for their point of view.

• cite specific textual evidence to support their reasons.

TO CHALLENGE STUDENTS . . .

For more context and a deeper understanding about American troops in the Iraq war, students can do research online.

ASK STUDENTS what they discovered about some of the difficulties American troops faced in Iraq. *Most of the people did not care who was in control—the insurgents or the coalition forces. They did not help the Americans, who, in Corporal Payne's view, were putting their lives on the line for the benefit of Iraq. Not speaking each other's language could make communication difficult, but Americans and the few Iraqis who joined forces with them managed to overcome that problem.*

DIG DEEPER

With the class, return to Question 10, Reread and Discuss. Have students share the results of their discussion.

ASK STUDENTS whether they were satisfied with the outcome of their small-group discussions. Have each group share what the majority opinion was of the group concerning whether or not Cummings had made the right decision to save Izzy's daughter despite what the rules said. What compelling evidence did the groups cite from the text to support this opinion?

• Encourage students to tell whether there was any convincing textual evidence cited by group members holding the minority opinion. If so, why didn't it sway the group's position?

• Have groups explain how they decided whether or not they had found sufficient evidence to support their opinion. Did everyone in the group agree as to what made the evidence sufficient? How did the group resolve any conflict or difference of opinion?

• After each group has shared the results of its discussion, ask whether another group shared any ideas they wished they had brought to the table.

ASK STUDENTS to return to their Short Response answer and to revise it based on the class discussion.

The Real Reasons We Explore Space

Poem by Mary Oliver

Why This Text?

Students regularly encounter formal and informal arguments in media, in conversations, and in text materials. This lesson explores the argument developed in Michael Griffin's article about the value of the space program.

▶ **View It!**

Professional Development Podcast:

Teaching Argument

Key Learning Objective: The student will be able to interpret figurative language.

RL 1 Cite textual evidence.

RL 2 Determine a theme of a text.

RL 4 Determine the meaning of words and phrases as they are used in the text, including figurative meanings.

RL 5 Analyze an author's choices concerning text structure.

SL 1 Participate effectively in a range of collaborative discussions.

SL 1a Come to discussions prepared; draw on that preparation to stimulate a thoughtful, well-reasoned exchange of ideas.

L 5a Interpret figures of speech.

▲ Text Complexity Rubric

Quantitative Measures	**The Real Reasons We Explore Space** Lexile: 1170L
Qualitative Measures	**Levels of Meaning/Purpose**  single purpose, explicitly stated
	Structure  clearly stated, sequential organization of main ideas and details
	Language Conventionality and Clarity  increased unfamiliar language
	Knowledge Demands  somewhat complex science and civics concepts
Reader/Task Considerations	• Teacher determined • Vary by individual reader and type of text • See the Text X-Ray for suggested Reader/Task Considerations.

English Language Support Before teaching, use the Text X-Ray below for an overview of the text's complexity. The Text X-Ray and the supports and scaffolds in the Teacher's Edition will help you guide students of different skill levels.

Meaning Making

Language Development

Effective Expression

Content Knowledge

Foundational Skills

Text Complexity: Qualitative Measures

Levels of Meaning/Purpose

single purpose, explicitly stated

To teach analyzing analogies to understand ideas and meaning in a text, see

- Determine Meaning and Analyze Ideas, p. 440a

***ZOOM IN ON* ANALYZING IDEAS** Explain that an **analogy** is a comparison that often helps readers understand an unfamiliar thing by comparing it to something familiar. Have students reread the author's conclusion (lines 118–128). Ask students to use the following sentence frames to discuss the conclusion and analyze the ideas it contains.

- The analogy "as cavemen learned to harness fire" compares ___ to ___.
- The analogy "as people two centuries ago learned to harness electricity" compares ___ to ___.
- The "new things" people will harness in the future might include ___.
- Confirming the existence of dark matter is one benefit to come from ___.

Structure

clearly stated, sequential organization of main ideas and details

Help students delineate and evaluate an argument.

- Teacher's Edition side notes, pp. 433, 434, 435, 436, 437
- When Students Struggle, p. 435
- Strategies for Annotation, p. 437
- Delineate and Evaluate an Argument, p. 437

To reteach delineating and evaluating an argument, see

- Delineate and Evaluate an Argument, p. 440a

 Use It! *Level Up* tutorial: Analyzing Arguments

***ZOOM IN ON* EVALUATING AN ARGUMENT** Establish with students that writers use evidence, logic, and **emotional appeals**—ideas or statements that arouse strong feelings—to persuade their readers. Have small groups use the following questions to discuss the use of logic and emotion in the text.

- What is the emotional appeal made in the first paragraph? *(Saying that Americans would feel "distraught" and "diminished" by the loss of the space program may appeal to familiar emotions that readers might feel when faced with a big change.)*
- What might be the purpose of using an emotional appeal to begin the argument? *(It hooks the reader into reading more of the text.)*
- Is it logical to state that people are naturally curious *(line 42)*? Explain. *(It is logical because curiosity is a well-known human trait; curiosity about space is evidence of human curiosity.)*

Language Conventionality and Clarity

increased unfamiliar language

Teach unfamiliar vocabulary in context.

- Teacher's Edition Critical Vocabulary notes, pp. 433, 434, 435, 439
- English Language Support, p. 433
- Applying Academic Vocabulary, p. 434

Help students analyze rhetorical language.

- Teacher's Edition side notes, pp. 434, 436

Support students in understanding synonyms and antonyms.

- Vocabulary Strategy: Synonyms and Antonyms, p. 439
- English Language Support, p. 439

Guide students in understanding transition words and phrases.

- Language and Style: Transitions, p. 440
- Strategies for Annotation, p. 440

ZOOM IN ON **ANALYZING CONTEXT CLUES** Before reading, display the Critical Vocabulary word *contemplate* (line 15). Display and read aloud the paragraph that includes the word (lines 12–19). A context clue, *dismiss* in line 16, is an **antonym,** a word that means the opposite of *contemplate*. Read aloud the definition of *contemplate* in the side margin and compare it with *dismiss*. Then have students form small groups to locate these words and identify clues in the surrounding text that help them guess the definitions: *vital*, line 65 *(synonym: crucial)*; *harmful*, line 73 *(antonym: safe)*; *followership*, line 111 *(antonym: leadership)*.

Knowledge Demands

somewhat complex science and civics concepts

Support English Learners in understanding the author's background.

- Teacher's Edition Background note, p. 433

For more context and historical background, students can view the video "Space Shuttle: The Last Mission" in their eBooks.

ZOOM IN ON **BUILDING CULTURAL KNOWLEDGE** Students may benefit from knowing more about these references.

- The author has a Ph.D. in aerospace engineering. Aerospace engineers design and manage the building of spacecraft, aircraft, missiles, and defense systems.
- The Hubble Space Telescope (line 2) orbits Earth, offering views of our galaxy, stars, and distant galaxies.
- Charles Lindbergh's transatlantic solo flight was celebrated as a historic milestone of the early 20th century. His feat sparked further exploration that contributed to the development of commercial aviation.

Suggested Reader/Task Considerations

You might consider the following before assigning this argument to students.

- Will students have any difficulty with the vocabulary used in the essay?
- Will students be interested in the way ideas are presented within the essay?

ZOOM IN ON **SUPPORTING COMPREHENSION**

- Have students highlight or note any unfamiliar words and phrases as they read. Pair English learners with more experienced English speakers to define highlighted words and phrases. Have them use reference works to confirm meanings.

TEACH

CLOSE READ

 For more context and historical background, students can view the video "Space Shuttle: The Last Mission" in their eBooks.

Background Have students read the background and information about the author. Tell students that Michael Griffin wrote this article for *Air and Space/Smithsonian* magazine in July 2007. As NASA Administrator, it was his job to further the U.S. Vision for Space Exploration plan. Griffin has a Ph.D. in aerospace engineering as well as five master's degrees covering several fields of engineering as well as business administration. In addition to NASA, he has worked in academia and at several space-related businesses.

AS YOU READ Direct students to use the As You Read note to focus their reading.

Delineate and Evaluate an Argument (LINES 1–17)

RI 8

Explain that in an **argument,** the speaker or writer presents one or more **claims,** or positions, on a specific issue and supports them with reasons and evidence.

Ⓐ ASK STUDENTS to reread lines 1–17 and interpret Griffin's position on the issue of space exploration. *(He believes that NASA and space exploration are extremely important to the American people and their identity.)*

CRITICAL VOCABULARY

contemplate: Griffin says Americans think carefully about investing money in large projects such as space exploration.

ASK STUDENTS why logical reasons have been most important when Americans contemplate the future of space exploration. *(People tend to think carefully about investing a large amount of money in a project like space exploration, and logical reasons seem to be the best justification for such decisions.)*

Background Michael Griffin *served as the administrator of the National Aeronautics and Space Administration (NASA) from 2005 to 2009. President Eisenhower founded NASA in 1958 soon after the Soviet Union launched the first artificial satellite. NASA has sent Americans into space, created the space shuttle as a reusable spacecraft, worked on the International Space Station, and landed rovers to learn about the conditions on Mars. NASA works to learn more about space, find ways to get to and explore space, and determine how our knowledge of space affects us on Earth.*

The Real Reasons We Explore Space

Argument by Michael Griffin

AS YOU READ Notice which reasons Griffin examines before he outlines the real reason he thinks we explore space. Write down any questions you generate during reading.

Image Credits: (t) ©Rick Fowler/X01020/Reuters/Corbis; (cr) ©Andrea Crisante/Shutterstock; (c) ©Victor Habbick Visions/Science Photo Library/Getty Images

I am convinced that if NASA were to disappear tomorrow, if we never put up another Hubble Space Telescope, never put another human being in space, people in this country would be profoundly distraught. Americans would feel that we had lost something that matters, that our best days were behind us, and they would feel themselves somehow diminished. Yet I think most would be unable to say why.

Ⓐ There are many good reasons to continue to explore space, which most Americans have undoubtedly heard. Some have been 10 debated in public policy circles and evaluated on the basis of financial investment. . . .

But these are not reasons that would make Americans miss our space program. They are merely the reasons we are most comfortable discussing. I think of them as "acceptable reasons" because they can be logically defended. When we **contemplate** committing large sums of money to a project, we tend to dismiss reasons that are emotional or value-driven or can't be captured on a

contemplate
(kŏn´təm-plāt´) *v.*
think carefully about.

The Real Reasons We Explore Space **433**

ENGLISH LANGUAGE SUPPORT

Vocabulary: Multiple-Meaning Words Explain that some English words have acquired additional meanings over time that are based on the original meaning. Students can use context clues to figure out the particular meaning intended in a given sentence or consult a dictionary as needed. Have pairs reread lines 1–17 and ask volunteers to explain the meaning of these words:

- *feel* (lines 4 and 5)
- *lost* (line 4)
- *circles* (line 10)
- *miss* (line 12)
- *value* (lines 17, 82, 84, 100, 102, and 109)

Encourage students to continue using context clues to define other multiple-meaning words they encounter in the text.

CLOSE READ

Delineate and Evaluate an Argument (LINES 30–49)

RI 8

Explain that to support a claim, authors must provide **reasons** (a person's beliefs or actions) and **evidence** (facts, quotations, or anecdotes to support reasons). Authors may manipulate readers' emotions by using loaded language or suggesting that readers agree because everyone else does (bandwagon).

B **CITE TEXT EVIDENCE** Have students reread lines 30–49 to identify the reasons Griffin gives to support his claim. *(1. "to be . . . the first or the best" [lines 35–36]; 2. "curiosity" [line 42]; 3. to show future generations what we did [lines 45–48]).* Have students summarize the supporting evidence. *(1. The desire to be the best is part of our basic make-up. [lines 37–38]; 2. All of us have experienced the urge to explore at some time in our lives. [lines 42–44]; 3. Humans have built monuments from the time of the pyramids to today's museums. [lines 45–49])* Discuss the strength of the evidence. *(It is largely anecdotal or based on personal generalizations. The building of monuments is a fact.)*

Language and Style: Rhetorical Questions

RI 4, L 3

(LINES 42–44)

Point out Griffin's use of **rhetorical questions,** or questions that do not require a reply, in this passage.

C **ASK STUDENTS** why Griffin uses rhetorical questions as evidence. *(to suggest that curiosity is a universal experience)* Are these questions valid support for his approach in lines 30–49? *(Lines 42–43: "who among us has not had the urge;" and lines 43–44: "what child has not been drawn" manipulate the reader's emotions. This is not evidence.)*

CRITICAL VOCABULARY

intuitive: Griffin believes that Americans have an instinctive feeling about why people want to accomplish great things. **ASK STUDENTS** to explain the difference between intuitive reasons and logical reasons for doing something. *(Intuitive reasons are based on instinct; logical reasons are based on facts and a rational mental process.)*

---

spreadsheet.[1] But in space exploration those are the reasons—what I think of as "real reasons"—that are the most important.

20 When Charles Lindbergh[2] was asked why he crossed the Atlantic, he never once answered that he wanted to win the $25,000 that New York City hotel owner Raymond Orteig offered for the first nonstop aircraft flight between New York and Paris. Burt Rutan and his backer, Paul Allen, certainly didn't develop a private spacecraft to win the Ansari X-Prize for the $10 million in prize money. They spent twice as much as they made. Sergei Korolev and the team that launched Sputnik[3] were not tasked by their government to be the first to launch an artificial satellite; they had to fight for the honor and the resources to do it.

30 I think we all know why people strive to accomplish such things. They do so for reasons that are **intuitive** and compelling to all of us but that are not necessarily logical. They're exactly the opposite of acceptable reasons, which are eminently logical but neither intuitive nor emotionally compelling.

First, most of us want to be, both as individuals and as societies, the first or the best in some activity. We want to stand out. This behavior is rooted in our genes. We are today the descendants of people who survived by outperforming others. Without question that drive can be carried to an unhealthy extreme; we've all seen

40 more wars than we like. But just because the trait can be taken too far doesn't mean that we can do without it completely.

A second reason is curiosity. Who among us has not had the urge to know what's over the next hill? What child has not been drawn to explore beyond the familiar streets of the neighborhood?

Finally, we humans have, since the earliest civilizations, built monuments. We want to leave something behind to show the next generation, or the generations after that, what we did with our time here. This is the impulse behind cathedrals and pyramids, art galleries and museums.

50 Cathedral builders would understand what I mean by real reasons. The monuments they erected to the awe and mystery of their God required a far greater percentage of their gross domestic product[4] than we will ever put into the space business, but we look back across 600 or 800 years of time, and we are still awed by what

intuitive
(ĭn-tōō′ĭ-tĭv) *adj.* known or understood without reasoning; instinctive.

---

[1] **spreadsheet:** a computer program, often used in accounting, that calculates data entered into its rows and columns.

[2] **Charles Lindbergh:** (1902–1974) an American pilot who in 1927 became the first person to successfully fly alone across the Atlantic.

[3] **Sergei Korolev . . . *Sputnik* (sûr′gā kô-rô′lĕv . . . spŏŏt′nĭk):** Korolev (1907–1966), a Russian engineer, designed the rocket that carried the first satellite (*Sputnik*) into space in 1957.

[4] **gross domestic product:** the monetary value of all the goods and services that a country produces during a certain time period.

APPLYING ACADEMIC VOCABULARY

motivate	undertake	pursuit

As you discuss Griffin's article, incorporate the following Collection 6 academic vocabulary words: *motivate, undertake,* and *pursuit.* To probe Griffin's argument ask students to discuss what he thinks **motivates** individuals or societies to **undertake** difficult challenges in **pursuit** of their dreams.

the builders accomplished. Those buildings, therefore, also stand as monuments to the builders.

The return the cathedral builders made on their investment could not have been summarized in a cost/benefit analysis. They began to develop civil engineering, the core discipline for
60 any society if it wishes to have anything more than thatched huts. They gained societal advantages that were probably even more important than learning how to build walls and roofs. For example, they learned to embrace deferred gratification, not just on an individual level, where it is a crucial element of maturity, but on a societal level, where it is equally vital. The people who started the cathedrals didn't live to finish them. The society as a whole had to be dedicated to the completion of those projects. We owe Western civilization as we know it today to that kind of thinking: the ability to have a constancy of purpose across years and decades.

70 It is my **contention** that the products of our space program are today's cathedrals. The space program satisfies the desire to compete, but in a safe and productive manner, rather than in a harmful one. It speaks abundantly to our sense of human curiosity, of wonder and awe at the unknown. Who can watch people assembling the greatest engineering project in the history of mankind—the International Space Station—and not wonder at the ability of people to conceive and to execute the project? And it also addresses our need for leaving something for future generations.

Of course the space program also addresses the acceptable
80 reasons, and in the end this is **imperative**. Societies will not succeed in the long run if they place their resources and their efforts in enterprises that, for whatever reason, don't provide concrete value. But I believe that projects done for the real reasons that motivate humans also serve the acceptable reasons. In that sense, the value of space exploration really is in its spinoffs, as many have argued. But it's not in spinoffs like Teflon and Tang and Velcro, as the public is so often told—and which in fact did not come from the space program. And it's not in spinoffs in the form of better heart monitors or cheaper prices for liquid oxygen for hospitals, although
90 the space program's huge demand for liquid oxygen spurred fundamental improvements in the production and handling of this volatile substance. The real spinoffs are, just as they were for cathedral builders, more fundamental.

Anyone who wants to build spacecraft, who wants to be a subcontractor, or who even wants to supply bolts and screws to the space industry must work to a higher level of precision than human beings had to do before the space industry came along. And that standard has influenced our entire industrial base, and therefore our economy.

contention
(kən-tĕn′shən) *n.*
argued assertion.

imperative
(ĭm-pĕr′ə-tĭv) *adj.*
crucial, necessary.

The Real Reasons We Explore Space **435**

WHEN STUDENTS STRUGGLE...

To help students get a complete picture of Griffin's argument, have them work in pairs to fill out a chart such as the one shown. For additional help, suggest that they look for signal words such as *first, second,* and *finally* (lines 35, 42, and 45). Point out that each signal word is followed by a reason.

Reasons	Evidence
To be first or best	Charles Lindbergh; Sputnik; "behavior is rooted in our genes"
Curiosity	Everyone wants to explore.
Leave something behind	pyramids, cathedrals, museums

CLOSE READ

Delineate and Evaluate an Argument (LINES 70–93)   RI 8

Explain that to prove a claim, writers must provide credible reasons and evidence related to the claim.

D ASK STUDENTS to reread lines 70–78 and explain how this passage relates to the reasons Griffin has put forth to prove his claim. (*Griffin restates his three reasons and says that the space program meets these criteria for why people undertake great projects.*)

Stress the importance of noting when writers introduce new reasons or evidence into an argument.

E CITE TEXT EVIDENCE Have students reread lines 79–93 to identify the reasons and evidence Griffin presents. (*He shifts his focus to "acceptable reasons," i.e., return on investment and "concrete value" and provides evidence of valuable spinoffs, notably "better heart monitors or cheaper prices for liquid oxygen." [lines 88–89]*) Have them explain how the passage relates to his "real reasons." (*Griffin contends that even though the space program provides these tangible results, the "real spinoffs are . . . more fundamental." [lines 92–93] It is his contention that the "real reasons" are the most important and the "acceptable reasons" will also be satisfied [lines 83–84] by the program, which provides "societal advantages" [line 61] as the cathedrals did.*)

CRITICAL VOCABULARY

contention: Griffin asserts that "the products of our space program are today's cathedrals." **ASK STUDENTS** to explain Griffin's contention about the connection between cathedrals and the space program. (*As part of his argument, Griffin states the space program serves the same purpose in our society that cathedrals did in earlier societies.*)

imperative: Griffin explains that it is necessary for the space program to address financial concerns as well as the more intuitive reasons he has outlined.

ASK STUDENTS why it is imperative that the space program provide concrete values to society. (*It is necessary for the space program to provide concrete values in order to justify the investment of resources made by society.*)

Delineate and Evaluate an Argument (LINES 100–107) RI 8

Tell students that speakers and writers often include multiple reasons and evidence to strengthen an argument.

F ASK STUDENTS to infer the reason that Griffin introduces in this passage and explain how it relates to the earlier reasons he has cited. *(He implies that a strong space program is important for national security. Although this could be considered an "acceptable reason," the way he frames the argument makes it more closely linked to the "real reason" of being best at something that then inspires others and appeals to the universal human desires outlined in his three reasons.)*

Analyze Author's Purpose and Rhetoric (LINES 108–117) RI 4, RI 6

Explain that **parallelism** is the use of similar grammatical constructions to express ideas that are related or of equal importance. The **repetition,** or repeated use, of parallel structures creates emphasis and unity.

G CITE TEXT EVIDENCE Ask students to reread lines 108–117 and identify examples of repetition and parallelism. *(Griffin answers the rhetorical question posed in lines 108–109 with sentences that begin with the phrase "You have to . . .")* Discuss the purpose of using this technique here and explore how it relates to Griffin's overall purpose in writing the article. *(These sentences tell Americans what they have to do not just to "do space projects" but to be a strong, competitive society. The rhetoric is a strong summation of Griffin's argument and supports his purpose of making a case for further space exploration.)*

COLLABORATIVE DISCUSSION Encourage students to jot down their own thoughts about Griffin's reasons and how good they are before discussing the questions with a partner. Then have them share their conclusions with the class as a whole. Accept reasonable responses.

ASK STUDENTS to share any questions they generated in the course of reading and discussing the selection.

---

100 As for national security, what is the value to the United States of being involved in enterprises which lift up human hearts everywhere? What is the value to the United States of being a leader in such efforts, in projects in which every technologically capable nation wants to take part? The greatest strategy for national security, more effective than having better guns and bombs than everyone else, is being a nation that does the kinds of things that make others want to do them with us.

What do you have to do, how do you have to behave, to do space projects? You have to value hard work. You have to live 110 by excellence, or die from the lack of it. You have to understand and practice both leadership and followership. You have to build partnerships; leaders need partners and allies, as well as followers.

You have to accept the challenge of the unknown, knowing that you might fail, and to do so not without fear but with mastery of fear and a determination to go anyway. You have to defer gratification because we work on things that not all of us will live to see—and we know it.

We now believe that 95 percent of the universe consists of dark energy or dark matter, terms for things that we as yet know nothing 120 about. Is it even conceivable that one day we won't learn to harness them? As cavemen learned to harness fire, as people two centuries ago learned to harness electricity, we will learn to harness these new things. It was just a few years ago that we confirmed the existence of dark matter, and we would not have done so without the space program. What is the value of knowledge like that? I cannot begin to guess. A thousand years from now there will be human beings who don't have to guess; they will know, and they will know we gave this to them.

COLLABORATIVE DISCUSSION With a partner, discuss the various reasons Griffin cites for exploring space. Are they good reasons? Cite specific textual evidence to support your ideas.

TO CHALLENGE STUDENTS . . .

Analyze Language Does Griffin use language successfully? Invite students to do a detailed analysis of Griffin's rhetoric, or the effectiveness and persuasiveness of his use of language. Encourage them to reread the selection and note where the language is particularly strong and where it seems weaker. Tell them to consider how the rhetoric advances Griffin's purpose for writing the article.

ASK STUDENTS to write a one-page critique of Griffin's rhetoric, citing specific textual evidence from the selection. Then allow them to share their writing in small groups and discuss the similarities and differences among the critiques.

Delineate and Evaluate an Argument

To **delineate,** or outline, an **argument,** first identify the author's claim. Look at the introduction, where the author often states the claim, and at the conclusion, where the author often restates the claim, sums up key points, or suggests actions based on conclusions. Then identify the specific reasons and evidence the author uses to support that position.

Consider whether the tone of the argument is objective or biased. Is the author supporting the claim with evidence including facts, statistics, personal experiences, statements by experts, and other information? Can the facts be verified? Are the author's sources reliable? Then assess whether the author's reasoning is valid. Look for false statements and fallacious reasoning, such as the examples in the chart.

Technique	Example	Explanation
False Cause and Effect	I ate shrimp last night and feel sick today. The shrimp must have been bad.	A connection between two ideas doesn't always mean that one causes the other.
Circular Reasoning	Ms. Vasquez is a great teacher because she does a great job teaching.	Circular reasoning restates the argument as a reason to support it.
Overgeneralization	I saw three shooting stars this past winter. Shooting stars appear in winter.	Generalizations based on limited data may not be accurate. Stereotypes are a form of generalization.

Evaluate whether the author plays on readers' emotions with words and phrases. While authors often appeal to emotions, they should also offer evidence and logical thinking. As a reader, be aware of ways authors may try to manipulate your emotions:

- **Bandwagon** (everyone is doing it)
- **Personal attack** (discrediting an idea by attacking the person who expressed it)
- **Transfer** (connecting feelings about one thing to something else)
- **Loaded language** (choosing words that elicit strong feelings)

TEACH

CLOSE READ

Delineate and Evaluate an Argument

Explain the difference between delineating and evaluating an argument.

- Delineating an argument means understanding the claim and following how the claim is supported by reasons and evidence.
- Evaluating an argument means determining whether the reasons and evidence are strong enough to prove the claim.

Explain that there must be a clear and reasonable connection between the claim and its support. Then explain that arguments based on logical fallacies, or errors in logic, are not sound. Conclusions arrived at through logical fallacies are not valid, no matter how appealing they may seem. Review the examples in the chart and explain that there are other types of logical fallacies as well.

Then review the list of possible misuses of emotional appeals. Emphasize that emotional appeal in persuasion is not always wrong or illogical but that arguments that are based only on emotions are generally weaker than those that also include hard evidence and rational appeals.

Strategies for Annotation ✏️ 🖥️ *Annotate it!*

Delineate and Evaluate an Argument

Share these strategies for guided or independent analysis:

- Highlight in yellow the claims that Griffin makes.
- Underline each reason and the evidence that supports it.
- Reread the phrases you underlined, noting the types of evidence that Griffin relies on.

It is my contention that the products of our space program are today's cathedrals. The space program satisfies the desire to compete, but in a safe and productive manner, rather than in a harmful one. It speaks abundantly to our sense of human curiosity, of wonder and awe at the unknown. Who can watch

PRACTICE & APPLY

Analyzing the Text

RI 1, RI 2, RI 3, RI 5, RI 6, RI 8

Possible answers:

1. *Griffin claims that the space program is an important, valuable enterprise. He cites the intuitive, emotional response the space program elicits in Americans. He appeals to their cultural values, including the desire to be the best, to explore and tame the unknown, and to leave something valuable for posterity.*

2. *For Griffin, "acceptable reasons . . . can be logically defended" or "evaluated on the basis of financial investment." Real reasons are "emotional or value-driven." He emphasizes real reasons in support of his claim, but he also cites valuable "spinoffs" from the space program as examples of acceptable reasons.*

3. *Griffin appeals to both. He appeals to emotion by offering "intuitive and compelling" reasons that connect to cultural values and accomplishments. He employs logic by tangentially citing valuable products derived from the space program, along with the "higher level of precision" and quality standards it fosters in "our entire industrial base, and therefore our economy."*

4. *An example of the bandwagon technique appears in line 30: ". . . we all know why people strive to accomplish such things." Griffin encourages the reader to support an idea because "everyone" does.*

5. *They were all inquisitive and driven to excel and accomplish things that had never been done. Rutan, Allen, and Korolev wanted to make lasting contributions. Their motivation connects to the three intuitive reasons Griffin cites in his claim: to be the best, to satisfy curiosity, and to build something lasting.*

6. *Griffin identifies cathedrals as lasting contributions to future generations. Like the space program, cathedrals exude a sense of awe and mystery, require significant expense and effort, and yield positive returns that cannot be tallied on a spreadsheet.*

7. *Griffin wants to rally public support for the space program. He appeals to Americans to recognize its value and support its continuation. His argument may inspire some, but he may not convince others who require more "acceptable" reasons for its funding at the expense of other programs.*

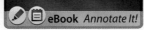

Analyzing the Text

RI 1, RI 2, RI 3, RI 5, RI 6, RI 8, W 1

Cite Text Evidence   Support your responses with evidence from the selection.

1. **Summarize** Identify Griffin's claim, or central idea, and delineate the key ideas of his argument.

2. **Evaluate** Griffin makes a distinction between "acceptable" reasons and "real" reasons for exploring space. Explain what he means by each type of reason. Which type of reason does he use to support his claim?

3. **Analyze** Does Griffin appeal to logic, emotion, or both in this piece? Cite examples that support your response.

4. **Interpret** In what part of the argument does Griffin make use of a bandwagon approach to convince readers of the validity of his claim? Explain.

5. **Analyze** Why does Griffin include Charles Lindbergh, Burt Rutan and Paul Allen, and Sergei Korolev in this selection? How does their motivation provide supporting evidence for Griffin's claim?

6. **Interpret** How does the analogy in Griffin's statement, "It is my contention that the products of our space program are today's cathedrals," connect to his claim?

7. **Evaluate** What purpose might Griffin have had for writing this piece? Given that purpose, how effective is Griffin's argument? Why?

PERFORMANCE TASK

Writing Activity: Editorial Michael Griffin argues that exploring space is important and provides both "acceptable" and "real" value. However, space exploration comes with a large price tag. Is that price tag worth it? Should exploring space be part of our national budget?

Write an editorial for or against continuing the space program. In your editorial,

- state a clear claim for your argument and present at least three supporting reasons
- use evidence consisting of examples, questions, and facts
- avoid faulty logic
- include a conclusion restating your claim
- use the conventions of standard English

Assign this performance task.

PERFORMANCE TASK

W 1

Writing Activity: Editorial Have students work in groups to conduct a "cost-benefit analysis" of the space program. Have them research the cost of space exploration, particularly in relation to the total federal budget. Then have them brainstorm a list of real and potential benefits of such an exploration. They can draw on information from the exercise to write. The editorials should contain a clearly stated claim, supporting reasons, evidence, and a forceful conclusion.

Critical Vocabulary

contemplate   intuitive   contention   imperative

Practice and Apply   Choose which of the two situations best fits each vocabulary word's meaning.

1. **Contemplate**
   a. You carefully consider the options before making a decision.
   b. You choose carelessly without considering the consequences.

2. **Intuitive**
   a. You weigh the advantages and disadvantages of a situation.
   b. You follow your instincts when making an important decision.

3. **Contention**
   a. You come to a decision after evaluating evidence.
   b. You assert an opinion about a specific issue.

4. **Imperative**
   a. You take a class that is required for graduation.
   b. You fill your schedule with electives.

Vocabulary Strategy: Synonyms and Antonyms

Synonyms are words that have the same or similar meanings. **Antonyms** are words with opposite meanings. As a reader, recognizing synonyms and antonyms can help you understand new vocabulary words. For example, the word *necessary* is a synonym for the Critical Vocabulary word *imperative*, while *optional* is an antonym. You can use an online or print thesaurus to find synonyms and antonyms.

Practice and Apply   Use a thesaurus to find a synonym and antonym for the remaining Critical Vocabulary words. Then write sentences using the synonym and the antonym as shown in this example:

imperative
synonym: *necessary*
Eating well is <u>necessary</u> to good health, but it is <u>imperative</u> that you exercise, too.
antonym: *optional*
Many people think that space exploration is <u>optional</u>, but I argue it is <u>imperative</u>.

Critical Vocabulary

Answers:

1. *a*
2. *b*
3. *b*
4. *a*

Vocabulary Strategy: Synonyms and Antonyms

Possible answers:

Students' sentences will vary. Possible synonyms and antonyms include the following:

contemplate—synonym: *consider;* antonym: *disregard*

intuitive—synonym: *innate;* antonym: *reasoned*

contention—synonym: *argument;* antonym: *accord*

ENGLISH LANGUAGE SUPPORT

Vocabulary: Synonyms and Antonyms   Explain that a thesaurus may include synonyms or antonyms that reflect conversational or informal English language patterns. In addition, synonyms may have different **connotations,** or emotional shades of meaning. Tell students that it takes practice to choose the best synonym or antonym to convey a precise meaning.

Allow students to work in pairs with a native-English speaker to complete the Practice and Apply activity.

Language and Style: Transitions

_{L 3}

Review the examples of different types of transitions in the chart and tell students that there are other transition words as well. Explain that transitions allow readers to follow an author's thinking process. Display lines 8–13 of the selection on the board or on a device and ask students to read the passage without the transition word *But* at the beginning of line 12. Discuss with students how the transition makes the connection between the ideas in the two paragraphs clearer.

Possible answers:

Answers will vary. Students' revisions of their editorials should demonstrate an ability to employ strong, appropriate transitions in order to connect ideas and to improve clarity.

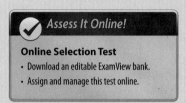

✓ Assess It Online!

Online Selection Test
- Download an editable ExamView bank.
- Assign and manage this test online.

Language and Style: Transitions

_{L 3}

Transitions are words or phrases that help connect ideas in a piece of writing. Read the following sentence from the selection:

> **But** these are not reasons that would make Americans miss our space program.

The word *but* lets the reader know that the author is shifting ideas. This statement as a whole leads the reader from the reasons Americans have heard to what the author thinks are the real reasons to explore space.

Later, the author identifies three reasons people strive to accomplish things. In the paragraphs that follow, he begins with these words and phrases: *First, A second reason*, and *Finally*. These transitions make it clear that the author is moving from one idea to another and then another. They also show that these three ideas are examples of the intuitive reasons the author wants to explain.

Given these examples, you can see that transitions are able to create a contrast between ideas, or they can link ideas. However, transitions can also

- introduce a sequence
- help orient readers in time or space
- identify examples, causes, or effects
- indicate conclusions

The chart below contains examples of transitional words and phrases related to a specific purpose.

Common Transitional Words and Phrases	
Purpose	**Examples**
Contrast ideas	but, however, although, on the other hand, while
Connect ideas	also, in addition, furthermore, too, first, second, finally
Introduce sequence	first, second, finally, initially, next, then, later
Orient readers in time or space	while, before, after, then, so far, meanwhile, here, nearby, above, below, next to
Identify examples, causes, or effects	for example, for instance, as a result, therefore, consequently
Indicate a conclusion	in conclusion, in summary

Practice and Apply Look back at the editorial you wrote in response to this selection's Performance Task. Identify the transitions that you used and revise your essay to add appropriate or stronger transitions. Then discuss with a partner how these transitions affect the flow of your essay and the connections between ideas.

Strategies for Annotation ✎ 🖉 *Annotate it!*

Language and Style: Transitions _{L 3}

Share these strategies for guided or independent analysis:

- Highlight in blue any examples of transition words or phrases.
- On a note, record the purpose of the transition.

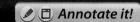

But these are not reasons that would make Americans miss our space program. They are merely the reasons we are most comfortable discussing. I think of them as "acceptable reasons" because they can be logically defended. When we contemplate

Determine Meaning and Analyze Ideas

RI 4

TEACH

Michael Griffin uses an extended analogy between medieval cathedrals and the space program as a key part of his argument. Explain that an **analogy** is a comparison between two things that are similar in some way but otherwise dissimilar. Analogies help to introduce unfamiliar subjects by comparing them to ones already known. An analogy often includes certain terms that signal the comparison (like, as, in the same way, similarly).

Tell students that Griffin is referring to the building of the great Gothic cathedrals in Europe beginning in the twelfth century. These giant cathedrals reflected the central importance of the Roman Catholic religion in people's lives. Taller than the Egyptian pyramids, some contained a hundred million pounds of stone. Several engineering innovations allowed builders to reach new heights and seemingly defy gravity by creating walls mostly of stained glass windows that supported roofs of stone. Building a cathedral employed the entire labor force in a town, often over several generations, as some cathedrals took a hundred years to build. Cathedrals also sparked competition between cities as they strove to outdo one another.

PRACTICE AND APPLY

Display lines 50–78 of the selection on the board or on a device. Call on volunteers to explain the analogy, point by point. *(Building the cathedrals required a greater proportional financial investment than the space program has done. Both the cathedrals and the space program bring benefits beyond those that can be explained by financial rewards alone. Both provide "societal advantages" in terms of advancing technology and in teaching "deferred gratification" that encourages people to follow a vision over a long period of time before all the results are seen. Both provide healthy competition, a way to satisfy curiosity and wonder, and a lasting legacy for the future.)*

Then invite students to evaluate how successful the analogy is. Ask: Are there fundamental differences between cathedrals and the space program that weaken the analogy? *(Many students may say the analogy is mostly successful for the similarities previously cited. Others may point out that our society is more diverse and complex than medieval society; it is not possible now to focus people on a single vision like building a cathedral. In addition, some may say that the space program provides less tangible benefit than a physical building that was part of the community where people lived.)*

Delineate and Evaluate an Argument

RI 8

RETEACH

Review examples of fallacious reasoning and manipulative emotional appeals. Then read these examples of reasons and evidence in support of this claim: *Stores should eliminate the use of plastic shopping bags.*

* Plastic shopping bags harm the environment. Research shows that plastic bags may take hundreds of years to decompose in landfills. They also harm wildlife when they end up as trash in the oceans.

* Plastic shopping bags should be eliminated because they are not a good idea. People who use plastic bags are wasteful and don't care about their effect on the environment.

Ask students to identify examples of fallacious reasoning. *(The second example uses circular reasoning and personal attacks.)*

 LEVEL UP TUTORIALS Assign the following *Level Up* tutorial: **Analyzing Arguments**

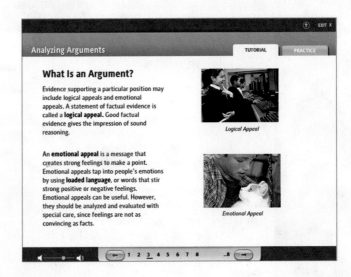

INDEPENDENT READING

Students can apply the skill to a current magazine or newspaper editorial. Have them work independently to outline the claim, reasons, and evidence. Ask: Does the writer include enough support to prove the claim? Does he or she use any fallacious reasoning?

hmhfyi.com

The Journey

Poem by Mary Oliver

Why This Text?

Stories involving a journey are often about emotional or spiritual growth as much as they are about moving from one geographical location to another. This poem uses the simple act of leaving the house as an extended metaphor for taking control of one's own destiny.

Key Learning Objective: The student will be able to interpret figurative language.

RL 1   Cite textual evidence.

RL 2   Determine a theme of a text.

RL 4   Determine the meaning of words and phrases as they are used in the text, including figurative meanings.

RL 5   Analyze an author's choices concerning text structure.

SL 1   Participate effectively in a range of collaborative discussions.

SL 1a Come to discussions prepared; draw on that preparation to stimulate a thoughtful, well-reasoned exchange of ideas.

L 5a   Interpret figures of speech.

 Text Complexity Rubric

Quantitative Measures	The Journey **Lexile:** N/A
Qualitative Measures	**Levels of Meaning/Purpose**  multiple levels of meaning (multiple themes)
	Structure  free verse, no particular patterns
	Language Conventionality and Clarity some figurative language
	Knowledge Demands  fairly complex theme
Reader/Task Considerations	• Teacher determined • Vary by individual reader and type of text • See the Text X-Ray for suggested Reader/Task Considerations.

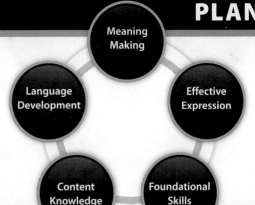

 English Language Support Before teaching, use the Text X-Ray below for an overview of the text's complexity. The Text X-Ray and the supports and scaffolds in the Teacher's Edition will help you guide students of different skill levels.

Text Complexity: Qualitative Measures

Levels of Meaning/Purpose

multiple levels of meaning (multiple themes)

Help students interpret figurative language to determine levels of meaning.

- Teacher's Edition side notes, pp. 442, 443
- English Language Support, p. 441
- Strategies for Annotation, p. 443
- Interpret Figurative Language, p. 443

To reteach interpreting figurative language, see

- Interpret Figurative Language, p. 444a

 Use It! *Level Up* Tutorial: Figurative Language

ZOOM IN ON DETERMINING LEVELS OF MEANING Remind students that **figurative language** conveys a meaning beyond the literal meaning of the words. Have pairs read the poem and discuss the questions below before sharing their answers with the class.

- On a literal level, what happens to "you" in the poem? *(You decide to leave the house and walk out into a storm, even though voices are telling you to stay.)*
- What might be the figurative meaning of the voices and the journey? In other words, what is the deeper meaning of the story? *(The journey represents taking charge of your own life even when it is scary and others try to hold you back.)*
- What **theme**, or message, can readers take from this poem? *(Each person must choose his or her own path in life and have the courage to follow it.)*

Structure

free verse, no particular patterns

Help students analyze the poem's structure.

- Teacher's Edition side note, p. 442

To teach students how to identify and analyze free verse, see

- Analyze a Free Verse Poem, p. 444a

 Use It! Interactive Whiteboard Lesson: Poetry: Language and Form

ZOOM IN ON ANALYZING TEXT STRUCTURE Point out that the poem has a **narrative** structure—it tells a story. Use these questions in a class discussion or in small-groups to help students analyze the poem.

- Who are the **characters** in the poem? *("you," "the voices around you," the personified wind "with its stiff fingers," and the "new voice . . . that kept you company")*
- What **conflict** do "you" face in the poem? *(You want to leave the house, but the voices try to stop you, and outside it is "late . . . and a wild night.")* How is the conflict resolved at the end of the poem? *(You leave the house and walk "deeper and deeper / into the world," determined to save your own life.)*

Language Conventionality and Clarity

some figurative language

Teach unfamiliar vocabulary in context.

- Applying Academic Vocabulary, p. 442
- English Language Support, p. 441

***ZOOM IN ON* APPLYING ACADEMIC VOCABULARY** To help students use the academic vocabulary words in discussion, provide these sentence frames:

- In the poem, "you" are **motivated** to leave the house because you know you must ___.
- It can be frightening to **undertake** the kind of journey described in the poem because ___.
- The poem suggests that the **pursuit** of happiness is both ___ and ___.

Knowledge Demands

fairly complex theme

Support English Learners in understanding more about the poet and her work.

- Teacher's Edition Background note, p. 441

***ZOOM IN ON* BUILDING BACKGROUND KNOWLEDGE** As students have read on page 441, Mary Oliver is well known for her close attention to details in the natural world. In her book *Our World*, published after the death of her partner of over 40 years, photographer Molly Malone Cook, Oliver credits Malone with showing her a deeper way of paying attention.

Suggested Reader/Task Considerations

You might consider the following before assigning this poem to students.

- Do students have the **inferencing skills** needed to understand the poem's levels of meaning?
- What **comprehension strategies** might help students read and understand the poem?

***ZOOM IN ON* SUPPORTING COMPREHENSION**

- Remind students that this poem "The Journey" is the last selection in this collection about heroes and quests. Ask students to keep in mind the quest described in this poem.
- Tell students to use the poem's natural breaks to stop and analyze what the poet is trying to say. Punctuation marks, such as dashes or periods, indicate good places for pausing to **summarize** ideas.

CLOSE READ

Mary Oliver Have students read the information about the author. Tell them that Oliver is known for being a very private person. At the time she won the Pulitzer Prize, many people had no idea who she was. Her earlier poems have a decided focus on the natural world and reveal little about her personal life. However, like any artist, Oliver has been on a journey throughout her career. Her prize-winning collection *American Primitive* was followed in 1986 by *Dream Work*, which includes this lesson's poem, "The Journey." In *Dream Work*, Oliver's attention shifts to include the problems of human life. Her later works reflect more of the poet's life and personality, as well as her lifelong attitude of amazement at the natural world.

AS YOU READ Direct students to use the As You Read note to focus their reading.

The Journey

Poem by Mary Oliver

Mary Oliver (b.1935) *is known for observing the natural world in a way that is both romantic and unflinchingly honest. Oliver's poems often draw attention to small details—a bird calling, a still pond, a grasshopper. Her vivid imagery of the natural world opens a window for her to explore larger issues, such as love, loss, wonder, and grief.*

Oliver published her first book of poetry, No Voyage and Other Poems, *in 1963. She has published numerous other collections, including* American Primitive, *which won the Pulitzer Prize for Poetry in 1984. She has also won the National Book Award. But Oliver is not just an award-winning poet; she is also a popular poet whose work appeals to many readers.*

Besides writing poetry, Oliver has taught at colleges and universities including Bennington College in Vermont. She has also written many essays, as well as two books about the craft of writing poetry. Her former residence in Provincetown, Massachusetts, has inspired much of her writing with its natural beauty.

AS YOU READ Pay attention to details that describe barriers to the journey in the poem. Write down any questions you generate during reading.

ENGLISH LANGUAGE SUPPORT

Comprehension Support Share these points with students:

- "The Journey" is told from the second-person point of view. The pronouns *you* and *your* engage the reader but imply that the poem's message applies to everyone.
- The poem has two levels of meaning, literal and metaphorical. Suggest that students read the poem once to understand the events described. During their second reading, they should ask themselves what deeper message the story conveys.

- Help students interpret the idiomatic phrases "little by little" in line 23 *(slowly)* and "kept you company" in line 30 *(stayed with you so that you would not be lonely).*

LEVEL UP TUTORIALS For additional support, assign the following *Level Up* tutorials: **Figurative Language.**

CLOSE READ

Analyze Text Structure

RL 5

(LINES 1–36)

Tell students that some poems are structured as a **narrative,** or events that tell a story. Others present images and ideas without a narrative structure.

 A **CITE TEXT EVIDENCE** Ask students whether this poem has a narrative structure, and have them support their answer. (*Yes. It describes a sequence of events in which a person faces a conflict—wanting to leave but being discouraged from doing so by "voices" and by the windy, "wild night" outside. The person eventually overcomes the obstacles and leaves the house, walking "deeper and deeper/into the world."*)

Interpret Figurative Language (LINES 10–11; 27–32)

RL 4, L 5a

Explain that the poem is a **metaphor;** that is, the poet compares the events to some aspect of human life. Each element in the poem has a deeper, figurative meaning.

B **ASK STUDENTS** to interpret the figurative meaning of the voices that cry, "Mend my life!" (*The voices represent other people in one's life who expect to be taken care of.*)

Explain that an **extended metaphor** shows many points of comparison and may be developed over the course of an entire work.

C **ASK STUDENTS** how the "new voice" and the act of striding "deeper and deeper/into the world" fit into the poem's extended metaphor. (*The "new voice" represents the person's learning to trust his or her own instincts. Striding into the world represents the person's living life as he or she wants to.*)

COLLABORATIVE DISCUSSION Call on pairs to share their ideas about the journey with the class. Accept all reasonable responses.

ASK STUDENTS TO share any questions they generated in the course of reading and discussing the selection.

The Journey

A
One day you finally knew
what you had to do, and began,
though the voices around you
kept shouting
5   their bad advice—
though the whole house
began to tremble
and you felt the old tug
at your ankles.
10 "Mend my life!" **B**
each voice cried.
But you didn't stop.
You knew what you had to do,
though the wind pried
15 with its stiff fingers
at the very foundations—
though their melancholy
was terrible.
It was already late
20 enough, and a wild night,
and the road full of fallen
branches and stones.
But little by little,
as you left their voices behind,
25 the stars began to burn
through the sheets of clouds,
and there was a new voice,
which was slowly
recognized as your own, **C**
30 that kept you company
as you strode deeper and deeper
into the world,
determined to do
the only thing you could do—
35 determined to save
the only life you could save.

COLLABORATIVE DISCUSSION What kind of journey do *you* take in this poem? With a partner, discuss what obstacles need to be overcome to complete this journey. Is the journey worth the effort? Cite specific textual evidence to support your ideas.

APPLYING ACADEMIC VOCABULARY

motivate	pursuit	undertake

While discussing "The Journey," incorporate the Collection 6 academic vocabulary words *motivate, pursuit,* and *undertake.* Discuss what **motivates** the person in the poem to **undertake** the journey, even in the face of so many obstacles. When you discuss the poem's theme, have students consider what the poem has to say about the **pursuit** of happiness.

Interpret Figurative Language

RL 4, L 5a

Figurative language is language that communicates meanings beyond the literal meanings of words. In figurative language, words are often used to represent ideas and concepts they would not otherwise be associated with. Poets use figurative language to make interesting comparisons and to help readers see subjects in a new light.

In "The Journey," Mary Oliver uses two types of figurative language—personification and metaphor.

Personification	Metaphor
Authors use **personification** to give human qualities to an object, animal, or idea. For example, an author might describe what a beach looks like during a storm by giving the sea human qualities: *"The angry sea took hungry bites from the shore."*	Authors use **metaphors** to compare two things that are basically unlike but have something in common. Unlike similes, metaphors do not use the words *like* or *as*. The author describing the storm might instead use a metaphor: *"The sea was a wild animal attacking the shore."* An **extended metaphor** is a longer metaphor that continues the comparison at length, even throughout an entire poem or literary work.

You probably noticed some examples of figurative language and imagery during your first reading of "The Journey." In subsequent readings, analyze Oliver's use of these devices more closely. Ask yourself how the devices make her poem more vivid and powerful.

CLOSE READ

Interpret Figurative Language

RL 4, L 5a

Review the instruction and make sure students understand the terms *figurative language, personification,* and *metaphor.* Explain that an extended metaphor includes many points of comparison between the two items. For example, the sample metaphor compares the sea to a wild animal that is attacking. This compares the action of the sea to the action of a wild animal. The metaphor could be extended by comparing the sea's waves to the animal's claws:

The sea was a wild animal attacking the shore. Its claws tore into the sand, leaving behind wet gashes.

Tell students that when they analyze an extended metaphor, they should look for all the different points of comparison to appreciate the author's full meaning.

Strategies for Annotation   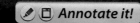 *Annotate it!*

Interpret Figurative Language   RL 4, L 5a

Encourage students to use their eBook annotation tools to analyze the extended metaphor in the poem:

- Highlight in blue words and phrases that indicate how other people inhibit the person's freedom.
- Highlight in green words and phrases that describe other obstacles to the person's freedom.
- Underline examples of personification.
- On notes, explain the figurative meanings of the highlighted words.

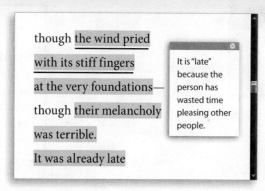

Analyzing the Text

RL 1, RL 2, RL 4, RL 5, L 5a

Possible answers:

1. The "voices around you" represent forces that prevent a person from taking control of his or her own life. In particular, they represent other people whose "bad advice" and demands for time and attention ("'Mend my life!' / each voice cried") can make it difficult for a person to do what is best for him- or herself.

2. "[T]he wind pried / with its stiff fingers / at the very foundations" (lines 14–16). The personification creates a vivid visual and tactile image of the wind as a giant person trying to pull the house apart. The figurative meaning of the wind is the uncertainty of change. The person in the poem wants to make a journey, but leaving the security of the house is scary.

3. The metaphor of the person summoning his or her strength to leave the house (make a major life change in the face of many obstacles) is carried throughout the stanza. By not breaking the poem into shorter stanzas, the poet creates the impression that the person does not pause to take a breath, because to hesitate would be to risk losing his or her resolution.

4. Images of the wind prying "with its stiff fingers," the "wild night," and "the road full of fallen / branches and stones" all suggest obstacles for the person who wants to set out on a journey. The stars that "began to burn/through the sheets of clouds" suggest hope and strength; they confirm that the person has made the right decision.

5. The branches and stones symbolize obstacles that make it more difficult for a person to accomplish important tasks in life.

6. The theme is that a person must follow his or her own path in life and not be held back by the opinions of other people or any other factors that stand in the way. The title suggests that life itself is a journey, and the extended metaphor, which unfolds throughout the poem, implies that getting past one's fears and doubts and taking the first few steps may be the hardest part.

Assess It!

Online Selection Test
- Download an editable ExamView bank.
- Assign and manage this test online.

eBook *Annotate It!*

Analyzing the Text

RL 1, RL 2, RL 4,
RL 5, SL 1a, SL 4, L 5a

Cite Text Evidence   Support your responses with evidence from the selection.

1. **Interpret**   In line 3, who are "the voices around you"? What might the voices represent?

2. **Analyze**   How does Oliver personify the wind? What is the figurative meaning of this strong wind outside the home of a person who is undertaking a journey?

3. **Interpret**   Notice that the poem is written in one long stanza, not broken into smaller stanzas. How does Oliver use this structure to develop an extended metaphor?

4. **Analyze**   Trace the nature images that occur throughout the poem. How does Oliver use each image to develop the extended metaphor in the poem?

5. **Interpret**   What do the branches and stones on the road **symbolize,** or represent?

6. **Infer**   What is the **theme,** or underlying message, of the poem? How do the title and structure of the poem help convey the theme?

PERFORMANCE TASK

Speaking Activity: Response to Literature   Think about the journey portrayed in this poem and the journey Kira Salak undertakes in *The Cruelest Journey: 600 Miles to Timbuktu* (also in this collection). What similarities and differences are there between the journeys?

- Review both selections and consider how you might answer the question. Cite text evidence from both selections that support your ideas.
- Think about how you can best present your ideas in a clear, concise way. You might discuss the poem first, and then the travel writing. Alternately, you might discuss one similarity or difference between the journeys at a time.

- Write a summary of the similarities and differences between the two journeys to present to the class.
- Note on your summary where you might adjust the volume or make eye contact to emphasize important points. Then deliver your presentation to the class.

Assign this performance task.

PERFORMANCE TASK

SL 1a

Speaking Activity: Response to Literature   To prepare for the discussion, have students review the selections and take notes on their own. *(Discussions and summaries may address these points: The person in "The Journey" makes a figurative journey; Kira Salak makes a literal one. Both face barriers [Salak faces injury, illness, and storms; "you" face people tugging at your ankles, wind, and rubble-filled streets—suggestive of the uncertainty of change.] Both learn something from their journey.)*

Analyze a Free Verse Poem

RL 4

TEACH

Ask students what makes a poem different from a work of prose such as a story or an essay. *(Possible answers: A poem looks different on the page because the lines are broken at specific points. Often, each line is quite short. A poem may be broken into stanzas, as opposed to paragraphs. Poetry often includes rhyming words and has a predictable rhythm. Poets tend to use more imagery and figurative language than prose writers. Most poems are shorter than a story or an essay.)* Then discuss these terms:

- **Traditional poetry** has a well-defined structure. Depending on the specific form, such as a sonnet or a ballad, a traditional poem follows a fixed pattern of line lengths, stanza lengths, and rhyming words.
- **Organic poetry** has no fixed rules. The poet is free to use poetic devices such as line breaks, stanza breaks, rhyme, and rhythm however he or she wants to create a particular effect or to convey a message.
- **Free verse** is a kind of organic poetry. A poem written in free verse may sound like everyday speech. The poet's ideas dictate where line breaks occur and whether or not the poem is divided into stanzas.

Ask students to identify the form of "The Journey." *(It is an organic, free verse poem.)*

PRACTICE AND APPLY

Have students review the poetic techniques used in "The Journey" and use a chart to record their ideas.

Technique	How It Is Used in "The Journey"
Line breaks	
Stanza breaks	
Rhyme	
Figurative language	

Have students share their ideas in small groups. Ask groups to evaluate whether Oliver's use of free verse is appropriate for her message. *(Possible answer: Free verse makes sense for a poem about a person breaking free from constraints. The form also creates an intimate, conversational tone appropriate for the kind of advice the poem offers to readers.)*

 INTERACTIVE WHITEBOARD LESSON If students need further instruction, use this *Interactive Whiteboard Lesson:* **Poetry: Language and Form**

Interpret Figurative Language

RL 5

RETEACH

Review that **figurative language** contains statements not meant to be taken literally. Figurative language describes something in a fresh way, often by comparing it to something else that seems to be completely different. Share these examples:

- **Personification** gives human qualities to a non-human entity. An example is "As the snowstorm progressed, the trees showed their respect by bowing deeply, their top branches brushing the ground." Showing respect and bowing are human actions, but here they describe how the trees bend under the weight of heavy snow.
- A **metaphor** compares two dissimilar things by saying that one is the other. An example is "The snow was a champion wrestler and soon had all the trees pinned to the ground."
- An **extended metaphor** adds points of comparison and may be developed throughout an entire work. It might compare aspects of a snowstorm to several different parts of a wrestling match and conclude by telling whether the snow or the trees eventually win.

 LEVEL UP TUTORIALS Assign the following *Level Up* tutorial: **Figurative Language**

INDEPENDENT READING

Have students work with partners to locate poems with examples of personification, metaphor, and extended metaphor. Ask pairs to share their examples with the class.

HEROES AND QUESTS

The *FYI* site provides links to online articles from a variety of magazines and newspapers. Help students choose a few articles to read to further their exploration of the topic Heroes and Quests.

NOVELWISE

Students can unlock the power of novels with this unique resource. Help students read through longer works with these tips:

- Find a Book
- Before You Read
- As You Read
- After You Read

Each book includes introductory material, worksheets, graphic organizers, and discussion guides.

ADDITIONAL TEXTS BY COLLECTION

Suggest students read the following:

- *from* Childe Harold's Pilgrimage by George Gordon, Lord Byron
- "Ulysses" by Alfred, Lord Tennyson

Have students read both poems and compare the themes, form, figurative language, and point of view.

NONFICTION CONNECTIONS

Suggest that students increase their reading of informational texts. The nonfiction connections include

- speeches
- diaries
- true-life accounts
- newspaper articles
- political cartoons

Creating an Independent Reading Program

OPPORTUNITIES FOR SOCIAL INTERACTION

Discussing books with classmates allows students to share what they know and to learn about other books.

- Give students time for small group discussions. Have them show the book, give the title and author, and then summarize it.
- If students read the same book, have them sit together and take turns reading aloud and discussing paragraphs or pages that made an impression on them.
- If students read different books on a similar topic, have them compare and contrast the books. One student should act as moderator to make sure everyone has an opportunity to share.
- At the end of the discussions, students should say whether they'd
- recommend their books. Set aside space in your class library to call out the books they think others will like.

WRITING IN RESPONSE TO BOOKS AND TEXTS READ

Writing in response to texts gives students the opportunity to think more deeply about the text.

- Before group discussions, allow time for students to write notes about the book they'd like to present.
- After the group discussions, encourage students to create a magazine-style review of books, possibly to post on a class social media page. They might also create and record commercials.
- Suggest students retell the book they read in a different format, such as a graphic novel, a dramatic presentation, or a limerick.
- During the school year, ask students to compare books they are reading and others they have read. What characters or genres attract them? How relevant are their book choices to their own lives? How do the different books grab and hold their interest?

Research and Write an Analytical Essay

Review the journeys taken in three texts in this collection, including the *Odyssey*. What compels characters or real people to set off on a journey—physical, mental, or spiritual—and what do they learn? Synthesize your ideas in an analytical essay. Use evidence from the texts and from additional sources to support your conclusions.

An effective analytical essay

- includes a clear thesis statement about how and why people gain insights from their travel or their mental/spiritual journeys
- engages the reader in the introduction with an interesting observation, quotation, or detail from one of the selections
- organizes central ideas in a logically structured body
- smoothly integrates source information that avoids plagiarism, with correctly cited sources
- uses transitions to show how ideas are related
- includes quotations or examples to illustrate central ideas
- has a concluding section that sums up the central ideas

W 2a–f Write informative/explanatory texts.
W 6 Use technology to produce, publish, and update writing products.
W 7 Conduct short research projects.
W 8 Gather relevant information.
W 9a–b Draw evidence from literary or informational texts to support analysis.

Visit hmhfyi.com to explore your topic and enhance your research.

PLAN

Analyze the Texts Review and take notes on the *Odyssey* and two other texts. Note details, examples, and relevant quotations from all three texts that support your central idea about journeys.

Use the annotation tools in your eBook to find evidence from your chosen texts. Save each piece of evidence to *my*Notebook, in a folder titled *Collection 6 Performance Task*.

myNotebook

"The Real Reasons We Explore Space"

"Who among us has not had the urge to know what's over the next hill? What child has not been drawn to explore beyond the familiar streets of the neighborhood?"

This passage argues that people go on journeys to satisfy their curiosity about the world.

ACADEMIC VOCABULARY

As you share your ideas about journeys, be sure to use these words.

motivate
objective
pursuit
subsequent
undertake

RESEARCH AND WRITE AN ANALYTICAL ESSAY

W 2a–f, W 6, W 7, W 8, W 9a–b

Introduce the Performance Task by reading the introductory paragraph with students and reviewing the criteria for an effective analytical essay. Ask students to recall the collection quotation by Kira Salak: "If a journey doesn't have something to teach you about yourself, then what kind of journey is it?" Discuss and clarify its meaning: an experience that doesn't add to a person's self awareness is not worth the effort. Emphasize that students will be synthesizing ideas from at least three texts about why people embark on journeys and what they learn about themselves by the end. Students may benefit from additional information about how and why people feel that journeys are a source of change and insight. You may want to ask a history teacher or school psychologist to provide information from the point of view of their disciplines.

PLAN

ANALYZE THE TEXTS

Remind students that their central idea should answer the question *What compels characters or people to set off on a journey, and what do they learn from their experiences?* Point out that students don't need to have a perfectly defined answer to this question yet. As they review the texts and identify relevant details and examples, their central idea will come into focus. They will also see which three texts, including the *Odyssey*, will provide the best material for their essay.

WHEN STUDENTS STRUGGLE ...

Analyze the Texts Divide students into groups of three and have each group choose three texts (including the *Odyssey*) to analyze. Let each group member analyze one text, then have the group review their notes and the texts as they discuss and answer these questions:

- Why were these journeys undertaken?
- In what ways are these journeys similar or different?
- What did the characters/people learn through their physical, mental, or spiritual journeys?

Then have the group members brainstorm possible thesis statements for their individual essays. Encourage them to help each other think of unique and interesting approaches to the essay topic.

PERFORMANCE TASK

PLAN

CONDUCT FURTHER RESEARCH

Suggest that students search the Web for well-written travel blogs that explore what the bloggers learn from their journeys. Students might also conduct interviews with people they know who have taken interesting journeys or had other life-changing experiences. Remind them to take careful notes or record the interviews so that they can quote their subjects accurately as they support their thesis statements.

PRODUCE

DRAFT YOUR ESSAY

Tell students to keep their audience in mind as they draft their essay. While their language should be appropriately formal, they also want to engage their readers with interesting ideas, examples, and quotations. Suggest that they pause periodically to read aloud what they have written. They should ask themselves: Are my ideas clear? Will my readers want to keep reading? What should I write next to keep my ideas flowing logically?

LANGUAGE AND STYLE: CITE SOURCES

Review the meaning of plagiarism and discuss how paraphrasing text without crediting the source may also lead to inadvertent plagiarism. Then review the citation format preferred in your classroom. Help students write and display several models of correctly formatted citations, either parenthetical or footnotes/endnotes, for students to use as they develop their essays.

Conduct Further Research Search for additional evidence in print and digital sources to support your thesis statement. Be sure to include source information so that you can accurately cite your sources.

Interactive Lessons
To help you research your essay, complete the following lesson:
• Conducting Research: Taking Notes

Get Organized Prioritize your ideas in a graphic organizer.

- Write a thesis statement about the journeys people take and subsequent effects on the traveler.
- Decide what organizational pattern you will use to develop your essay. Will you begin your essay with your strongest reason or save it for last?
- Use a graphic organizer to prioritize your reasons and evidence.
- Write down some ideas for your conclusion.

Interactive Lessons
To help you plan your essay, complete the following lesson:
• Writing an Informative Text: Organizing Ideas

PRODUCE

Draft Your Essay Write a draft of your essay. Consider your purpose and audience and remember that essay writing requires formal language and a respectful tone. Essays that analyze texts are expected to be appropriate for an academic context.

Write your rough draft in *my*WriteSmart. Focus on getting your ideas down, rather than perfecting your choice of language.

- Introduce a clear and concise thesis statement.
- Present your details, quotations, and examples from the selections and additional sources in logically ordered paragraphs.
- Each paragraph should have a central idea related to your thesis statement with evidence to support it. Explain how each piece of evidence supports the central idea.
- Use transitions to connect the main sections of your essay and to clarify the relationships among your ideas.
- Write a conclusion that summarizes your analysis and presents a final synthesis of your central ideas.

Language and Style: Cite Sources

When you use text, ideas, or information from a source, avoid plagiarism by giving credit to that source. One way to cite a source is to use a parenthetical citation in which you give the author's name and a page number in parentheses at the end of the sentence where the idea is found. See the following example.

> " As Kira Salak says in *The Cruelest Journey: 600 Miles to Timbuktu*, 'There is one thing I'm already certain of: Though we may think we choose our journeys, they choose us.' (Salak, quoted in *Collections* 423) "

ENGLISH LANGUAGE SUPPORT

Understand Text Structure Display the Student Model that accompanies *Interactive Lessons:* Writing Informative Texts. Read the first paragraph aloud and ask students to identify the thesis statement. *("He uses repetition . . . (or who once lived there).")* As you continue reading, pause at the end of each paragraph to discuss how the central idea supports the thesis and how the evidence presented supports the central idea. Point out the writer's use of direct quotations from the text to bolster her argument. Ask if students notice anything missing from the Student Model. Explain that the model references the source text and author, but because the model does not include information from other sources, additional citations are not required.

Use footnotes or endnotes when you quote or paraphrase a text, to direct your readers to the sources you used to develop your essay. Both are linked to sources through a superscript number. Your teacher will guide you to follow a standard format for citation, such as *The Chicago Manual of Style*.

REVISE

Improve Your Draft Have your partner or group of peers use the questions in the chart to review your draft.

Questions	Tips	Revision Techniques
Does the introduction include a clear thesis statement?	**Underline** the thesis statement.	**Add** a thesis statement that states the topic and main idea.
Are paragraphs organized logically, with clear central ideas?	**Highlight** the central idea of each paragraph.	**Add** central ideas to paragraphs. **Reorder** paragraphs so that the sequence makes sense.
Do details, quotations, and examples support each central idea?	**Underline** each piece of evidence that supports a central idea.	**Insert** details, quotations, and examples to support central ideas. **Delete** any that do not support an idea.
Are all sources cited correctly?	**Highlight** the citations for anything that came from sources.	**Add** source citations for any text, ideas, and information.
Do appropriate and varied transitions connect ideas?	**Underline** each transitional word or phrase.	**Add** transitions to clarify the relationships between ideas.
Does the conclusion synthesize the central ideas of the essay?	**Highlight** the phrases that synthesize the central ideas.	**Add** a synthesis that connects the central ideas.

WriteSmart

Have your partner or a group of peers review your draft in *my*WriteSmart. Ask your reviewers to note any ideas or evidence that does not support your controlling idea.

Interactive Lessons
To help you revise your essay, complete the following lesson:
• Writing as a Process: Revising and Editing

PRESENT

Share Your Essay When your final draft is completed, read your essay aloud to a small group. Your audience should listen, take notes, and be prepared to comment or ask questions.

Publish Online Create a class blog about journeys. Upload your essays to allow your classmates and other readers to comment on the ideas expressed in your analyses. You may also want to share your own travel experiences and what you learned about yourself.

PERFORMANCE TASK

REVISE

IMPROVE YOUR DRAFT

Encourage peer reviewers to read their partner's essay at least twice. The first reading should focus on whether the essay is clear and logical. In the second reading, have them answer the questions in the chart to identify places where the logic breaks down. This information will help them prepare feedback on how the writer can improve the draft.

PRESENT

PUBLISH ONLINE

Encourage students to make their blog as appealing as possible for readers. They might format their essays with pull quotes, photographs, and other graphics. Video or audio clips of students reading from their essays can also enhance the blog.

TO CHALLENGE STUDENTS...

Hold a Discussion The collection texts all focus on physical journeys: Odysseus trying to get home, Kira Salak traveling on the Niger, space travel, and leaving home to find a place in the world. Challenge students to review the reasons for each journey and to discuss whether or not they were necessary. Ask the following question:

• Could the people or characters have learned the same things by remaining where they were? Why or why not?

Encourage students to go back into the collection to collect evidence during their discussion. For example, point out lines 116–125 in *The Cruelest Journey*, and ask students if Kira Salak could have learned patience, humility, and gratitude without navigating the Niger in a kayak.

PERFORMANCE TASK

USE THE SCORING RUBRIC

Have students use the rubric to assess a partner's essay. In particular, have students evaluate the concluding section of the essay. Does it synthesize the most important ideas and summarize the analysis? If not, have them write a list of specific suggestions for strengthening the conclusion and providing readers with a review of ideas.

REFLECT ON THE PROCESS

Tell students that thinking about how they analyzed selections and used outside sources to develop an essay can help them plan and complete future writing assignments. Ask students if their thesis statements were finely tuned and adequately supported. Encourage them to answer the following questions as they reflect on their analytical essays.

- What did you find challenging about writing a thesis statement? What would you do differently to make writing a strong thesis easier?

- What part of your analytical essay provided the most support for your thesis? What type of evidence did you use in that section?

- What did you learn by integrating several sources into your an essay? How could you have organized your notes more effectively?

PERFORMANCE TASK RUBRIC
ANALYTICAL ESSAY

	Ideas and Evidence	Organization	Language
4	• An eloquent introduction includes the titles and authors of the selections; the thesis statement describes the view of journeys presented in the selections. • Specific, relevant details support the central ideas. • A satisfying concluding section synthesizes the ideas and summarizes the analysis.	• Central ideas and supporting evidence are organized logically throughout the essay. • Varied transitions show the relationships between ideas. • Sources for all details, ideas, and evidence are credited.	• The analysis has an appropriately formal style and a knowledgeable, objective tone. • Language is precise and captures the writer's thoughts with originality. • Sentence beginnings, lengths, and structures vary and have a rhythmic flow. • Spelling, capitalization, and punctuation are correct. If handwritten, the analysis is legible. • Grammar and usage are correct.
3	• The introduction identifies the titles and authors of the selections but could be more engaging; the thesis statement encompasses the view of journeys in at least two selections. • One or two central ideas need more support. • The concluding section synthesizes most of the ideas and summarizes most of the analysis.	• The organization of central ideas and supporting evidence is confusing in a few places. • A few more transitions are needed to clarify the relationships between ideas. • One or two details, ideas, and evidence from sources are not credited.	• The style becomes informal in a few places, and the tone does not always communicate confidence. • Most language is precise. • Sentence beginnings, lengths, and structures vary somewhat. • Several spelling, capitalization, and punctuation mistakes occur. If handwritten, the analysis is mostly legible. • Some grammatical and usage errors are repeated in the essay.
2	• The introduction identifies the titles and the authors of the selections; the thesis statement only hints at the main idea of the analysis. • Details support some central ideas but are often too general. • The concluding section gives an incomplete summary of the analysis and merely restates the controlling idea.	• Most central ideas are organized logically, but many supporting details are out of place. • More transitions are needed throughout the essay to connect ideas. • Most details, ideas, and evidence are not clearly credited.	• The style is informal in many places, and the tone reflects a superficial understanding of the selections. • Language is repetitive or vague at times. • Sentence structures barely vary, and some fragments or run-on sentences are present. • Spelling, capitalization, and punctuation are often incorrect but do not make comprehending the essay difficult. If handwritten, the analysis may be partially illegible. • Grammar and usage are incorrect in many places, but the writer's ideas are still clear.
1	• The appropriate elements of an introduction are missing. • Details and evidence are irrelevant or missing. • The analysis lacks a concluding section.	• A logical organization is not used; ideas are presented randomly. • Transitions are not used, making the essay difficult to understand. • Credit for sources is missing.	• The style and tone are inappropriate. • Language is inaccurate, repetitive, and vague. • Repetitive sentence structure, fragments, and run-on sentences make the writing monotonous and difficult to follow. • Spelling, capitalization, and punctuation are incorrect throughout. If handwritten, the analysis may be partially or mostly illegible. • Many grammatical and usage errors change the meaning of the writer's ideas.

TEACHER NOTE:
The page numbers to the left indicate pages in the Student Edition. Except for the two entries below, the page numbers in the Student Edition and the Teacher's Edition correspond.

Writing Arguments

Many of the Performance Tasks in this book ask you to craft an argument in which you support your ideas with text evidence. Any argument you write should include the following sections and characteristics.

Introduce Your Claim

Clearly state your **claim**—the point your argument makes. As needed, provide context or background information to help readers understand your position. Note the most common opposing views as a way to distinguish and clarify your ideas. From the very beginning, make it clear for readers why your claim is strong; consider providing an overview of your reasons or a quotation that emphasizes your view in your introduction.

EXAMPLES

Vague claim: We need more recreational facilities.	**Precise claim:** The city should build a new skate park downtown.
Not distinguished from opposing view: There are plenty of people who consider skate parks unsafe.	**Distinguished from opposing view:** While some people consider skate parks unsafe, the facts say differently.
Confusing relationship of ideas: Teens need more to do. Skate parks are enjoyed by people of all ages.	**Clear relationship of ideas:** By providing a safe activity not only for teens but for people of all ages, a skate park would benefit the entire community.

Develop Your Claim

The body of your argument must provide strong, logical reasons for your claim and must support those reasons with relevant evidence. A **reason** tells why your claim is valid; **evidence** provides specific examples that illustrate a reason. In the process of developing your claim, you should also refute **counterclaims,** or opposing views, with equally strong reasons and evidence. To demonstrate that you have thoroughly considered your view, provide a

well-rounded look at both the strengths and limitations of your claim and opposing claims. The goal is not to undercut your argument but rather to answer your readers' potential objections to it. Be sure, too, to consider how much your audience may already know about your topic in order to avoid boring or confusing your readers.

EXAMPLES

Claim lacking reasons: A skate park would be a good thing.	**Claim developed by reasons:** Among the benefits of a skate park are a potential reduction in petty crimes committed by bored teens and improved physical fitness across the community.
Omission of limitations: The people opposed to this idea wouldn't use a skate park.	**Fair discussion of limitations:** We should not dismiss safety concerns. Planning for the park should include safe ramp designs, first aid facilities, and ongoing maintenance.
Inattention to audience's knowledge: A kick-flip ollie can be executed just about anywhere, but with a half-pipe more advanced tricks are possible.	**Awareness of audience's knowledge:** Readers unfamiliar with skateboarding may be surprised to learn that most injuries happen to beginners in their driveways, not in well-planned skate parks.

Link Ideas

Even the strongest reasons and evidence will fail to sway readers if it is unclear how the reasons relate to the central claim of an argument. Make the connections clear for your readers, using not only transitional words and phrases, but also clauses and even entire sentences as bridges between ideas you have already discussed and ideas you are introducing.

EXAMPLES

Transitional word linking claim and reason: The entire community will benefit from a skate park downtown. <u>First,</u> health care and law enforcement costs may be reduced if bored or sedentary teens spend their free time there instead of in less productive activities.

Transitional phrase linking reason and evidence: Skating in a planned park would actually reduce injuries. <u>In fact,</u> the American Academy of Pediatrics states that "communities should be encouraged to develop safe skateboarding areas away from pedestrian and motor vehicle traffic."

Transitional clause linking claim and counter-claim: The health benefits of the park are clear. <u>Those opposed to the park plan, though, would say otherwise:</u> They feel that there is too much potential for injuries from falls.

Use Appropriate Style and Tone

An effective argument is most often written in a direct and formal style. The style and tone you choose in an argument should not be an afterthought—the way you express your argument can either drive home your ideas or detract from them. Even as you argue in favor of your viewpoint, take care to remain objective in tone—avoid using loaded language when discussing opposing claims.

EXAMPLES

Informal style: The park will help out the whole city, so they should be the ones to fork out for it.

Formal style: Because the benefits of the park include everyone in the city, it is logical for the city to provide the funding for the project.

continued

Biased tone: It doesn't make any sense to be against this plan.

Objective tone: Arguments opposing this plan have been refuted by statistics from many sources.

Inattention to conventions: We need to make this dream a reality!

Attention to conventions: This proposal, which will greatly benefit the community at little cost, deserves City Council attention.

Conclude Your Argument

Your conclusion may range from a sentence to a full paragraph, but it must wrap up your argument in a satisfying way; a conclusion that sounds tacked-on helps your argument no more than providing no conclusion at all. A strong conclusion is a logical extension of the argument you have presented. It carries forth your ideas through an inference, question, quotation, or challenge.

EXAMPLES

Inference: Support for a safe and enjoyable city begins with our youth.

Question: Who doesn't want to live in an active city with engaged young people?

Quotation: As the First Lady's Let's Move campaign points out, "community leaders can promote physical fitness by . . . revitalizing parks, playgrounds, and community centers; and by providing fun and affordable sports and fitness programs."

Challenge: Facilities of this type make the difference between an average city and a truly great one.

Writing
Informative Essays

Most of the Performance Tasks in this book ask you to write informational or explanatory essays in which you present a topic and examine it thoughtfully, through a well-organized analysis of relevant content. Any informative or explanatory essay that you create should include the following parts and features.

Introduce Your Topic

Develop a strong **thesis statement.** That is, clearly state your **topic** and the **organizational framework** through which you will connect or distinguish elements of your topic. For example, you might state that your essay will compare ideas, examine causes and effects, or explore a problem and its solutions.

EXAMPLES

Topic: animal shelters
Sample Thesis Statements
Compare-contrast: To decide whether to adopt a pet from a shelter or buy one from a breeder, consider the costs and then benefits of each source.
Cause-effect: While the causes of overcrowding in community animal shelters aren't difficult to guess at, the results are often hidden from the public eye.
Problem-solution: Our town's animal shelter faces a growing problem with overcrowding, but through community action we can manage the issue.

Clarifying the organizational framework up front will help you organize the body of your essay, suggest **headers** you can use to guide your readers, and help you identify **graphics** that you may need to clarify information. For example, if you compare and contrast the costs and benefits of adopting versus buying a pet, you might create a chart like the one shown to guide your writing. You could include the same chart in your essay as a graphic for readers. The row or column headings serve as natural paragraph headings.

	Animal Shelter	Reputable Breeding Facility
Costs	Minimal fee to cover spay/neuter and immunization costs	Usually several hundred dollars
Benefits	Knowledge that you have rescued a pet from a crowded kennel and probably euthanasia	Getting a specific pedigree with predictable traits

Develop Your Topic

In the body of your essay, flesh out the organizational framework you established in your introduction with strong supporting paragraphs. Include only support directly relevant to your topic. Don't rely on a single source, and make sure the sources you do use are reputable and current. The following table illustrates types of support you might use to develop aspects of your topic. It also shows how transitions link text sections, create cohesion, and clarify the relationships among ideas.

Types of Support in Informative Essays	Uses of Transitions in Informative Essays
Facts and examples: One cause of overcrowding is economic hardship; for example, when home foreclosures increase, the population of animal shelters also rises.	*One cause* signals the shift from the introduction to the body text in a cause-and-effect essay. *For example* introduces the support for the cause being cited.

continued

Types of Support in Explanatory/ Informative Essays	Uses of Transitions in Explanatory/ Informative Essays
Concrete details: <u>On the other hand</u>, if you want to choose from among a wide variety of dogs, visit your local shelter. Our shelter currently lists German shepherds, a labradoodle, a Pomeranian, and dozens more on its Website.	*On the other hand* transitions the reader from one point of comparison to another in a compare-contrast essay.
Statistics: <u>Turn to the Humane Society of the United States if you doubt the scope of the problem.</u> The HSUS estimates that shelters euthanize 3 to 4 million cats and dogs annually.	The entire transitional sentence introduces the part of a problem-solution essay that demonstrates the existence of a problem.

You can't always include all of the information you'd like to in a short essay, but you can plan to point readers directly to useful **multimedia links** either in the body of or at the end of your essay.

Use Appropriate Style and Tone

Use **formal English** to establish your credibility as a source of information. To project authority, use the language of the domain, or field, that you are writing about. However, be sure to define unfamiliar terms to avoid using jargon your audience may not know. Provide extended definitions when your audience is likely to have limited knowledge of the topic. Using quotations from reputable sources can also give your text authority; be sure to credit the source of quoted material. In general, keep the tone objective, avoiding using slang or biased expressions.

Informal, jargon-filled, biased language: Puppy mill owners should be forced to live as horribly as the animals they raise. They have no feelings for the pooches they proliferate except maybe greed for the coin these cash cows create.

Extended definition in formal style and objective tone: A "puppy mill" refers to a large-scale dog breeding operation that places profit before the well-being of its dogs, often housing them in tight quarters, forcing them to breed continuously, and neglecting their emotional, physical, and genetic health. According to Melanie Kahn, an HSUS spokesperson, "Many people don't realize that when they buy a puppy from a pet store or online they are likely supporting a puppy mill."

Conclusion

Wrap up your essay with a concluding statement or section that sums up or extends the information in your essay.

EXAMPLES

Articulate implications: Twenty-five percent of dogs in shelters are purebred. If we can encourage people who would normally seek a purebred dog from a breeder to adopt a shelter pet instead, we can significantly reduce the number of animals euthanized each year.

Emphasize significance: The number of pets languishing in shelters each year is small compared to the number of pets owned by U.S. households; a fractional increase in household pet ownership could save these animals from euthanasia.

Writing Narratives

When you are writing a fictional tale, an autobiographical incident, or a firsthand biography, you write in the narrative mode. That means telling a story with a beginning, a climax, and a conclusion. Though there are important differences between fictional and nonfiction narratives, you use similar processes to develop them.

Identify a Problem, Situation, or Observation

For a nonfiction **narrative,** dig into your memory bank for a problem you dealt with or an observation you've made about your life. For fiction, try to invent a problem or situation that can unfold in interesting ways.

EXAMPLES

Problem (nonfiction)	Last year I wanted to raise money to participate in a class trip to Washington, D.C.
Situation (fiction)	A social media website user periodically notices mysterious changes to his "status."

Establish a Point of View

Decide who will tell your story. If you are writing a reflective essay about an important experience or person in your own life, you will be the **narrator** of the events you relate. If you are writing a work of fiction, you can choose to create a first person narrator or tell the story from the third-person point of view. In that case, the narrator can focus on one character or reveal the thoughts and feelings of all the characters. These examples show the differences between a first- and third-person narrator.

EXAMPLES

First-person narrator (nonfiction)	Seven hundred fifty dollars: That's what it would cost me to go on the class trip to Washington D.C., but it might as well have been a million dollars.

Third-person narrator (fiction)	Peter's fingers froze over the "What's new with you" prompt of his status page. The box was already filled out, waiting for him to press the Update key. "My mom found a new job!" said the box. Peter hadn't written those words. And, as far as he knew, his mother had stopped looking for work months ago.

Gather Details

To make real or imaginary experiences come alive on the page, you will need to use **narrative techniques** like description and dialogue. Use the questions in the left column of the following chart to help you search your memory or imagination for the details that will form the basis of your narrative. You don't have to respond in full sentences, but try to capture the sights, sounds, and feelings that bring your narrative to life.

Who, What, When, Where?	Narrative Techniques
People: Who are the people or characters involved in the experience? What did they look like? What did they do? What did they say?	**Description:** Mr. Maguire, social studies teacher. Wears funny ties and cracks jokes but doesn't get to know students personally, in my opinion. **Dialogue:** He once said, "The families in this town are completely removed from the problems of two-thirds of the world." I said under my breath, "You don't know my family."

continued

Who, What, When, Where?	Narrative Techniques
Experience: What led up to or caused the event? What is the main event in the experience? What happened as a result of the event?	**Description:** A big deposit for the class trip—$200—would be due by Thanksgiving; I knew my family didn't have the cash. I would have to figure out a way to raise it myself. When schools were closed after a blizzard, I got my chance. After stoking up the courage to knock on doors, I shoveled until my blistered hands were numb, my back ached, and my clothes were wet with freezing perspiration.
Places: When and where did the events take place? What were the sights, sounds, and smells of this place?	**Description:** Fall of eighth grade—it was the last year of middle school and we felt special—top of the heap. The smell of autumn filled the air—decaying leaves, wood-burning stoves. Local farmers were predicting an early and rough winter.

Sequence Events

Before you begin writing, list the key events of the experience or story in **chronological,** or time, order. Place a star next to the point of highest tension—for example, the point at which a key decision determines the outcome of events. In fiction, this point is called the **climax,** but a gripping nonfiction narrative will also have a climactic event.

To build **suspense**—the uncertainty a reader feels about what will happen next—you'll want to think about the **pacing** or rhythm of your narrative. Consider disrupting the chronological order of events by beginning at the end and then starting over. Or interrupt the forward progression or flow of events with a **flashback,** which takes the reader to an earlier point in the narrative.

Another way to build suspense is with **multiple plot lines.** For example, the personal narrative about the class trip involves a second plot line in which a snowstorm is bearing down on the narrator's hometown. Both plot lines intersect when the narrator shovels snow for a week and as a result raises money for the class trip.

First Draft	Revision
My father, who is an incurable optimist, said the storm could be the break I needed.	Wiggling his eyebrows, my father said, "When life gives you a snowstorm, invest in a snow shovel!" [telling details]
Piles of snow were everywhere, and people couldn't get out of their driveways.	Snow banks three feet high lined the streets, and neighbors batted kitchen brooms at the snow around their cars. [precise words and phrases]
Peter felt weirded out by the mysterious post on his "What's new with you" page.	As Peter read the mysterious post, the tiny hairs at the base of his scalp rose and his palms sweated. [sensory details]

Conclude Your Narrative

At the conclusion of the narrative, you or your narrator will reflect on the meaning of the events. The conclusion should follow logically from the climactic moment of the narrative. The narrator of a personal narrative usually reflects on the significance of the experience—the lessons learned or the legacy left.

EXAMPLE

The school steps were piled with luggage that balmy Friday as excited students waited to board the buses. I stood by, remembering the tingle of frostbite in my fingertips and the ache in my back from that marathon week of shoveling snow. This scene, the one before me now, is what had kept me going. Straightening my back and flexing my fingers, I reached down and picked up my bag. With a satisfied smile, I joined my friends on the bus.

SEQUENCE EVENTS
Remind students to write legibly as they develop their lists of experiences.

Conducting Research

The Performance Tasks in this book will require you to complete research projects related to the texts you've read in the collections. Whether the topic is stated in a Performance Task or is one you generate, the following information will guide you through your research project.

Focus Your Research and Formulate a Question

Some topics for a research project can be effectively covered in three pages; others require an entire book for a thorough treatment. Begin by developing a topic that is neither too narrow nor too broad for the time frame of the assignment. Also check your school and local libraries and databases to help you determine how to choose your topic. If there's too little information, you'll need to broaden your focus; if there's too much, you'll need to limit it.

With a topic in hand, formulate a **research question**; it will keep you on track as you conduct your research. A good research question cannot be answered in a single word and should be open-ended. It should require investigation. You can also develop related research questions to explore your topic in more depth.

EXAMPLES

Possible topics for the *Odyssey*	The hero Odysseus—too broad The monster the Cyclops—too narrow Settings and events—fact or fiction?
Possible research question	To what degree are settings and events in the *Odyssey* based on fact?
Related questions	If any of the events are real, where did they take place? To what extent do historians agree or disagree on which aspects of the *Odyssey* are real?

Locate and Evaluate Sources

To find answers to your research question, you'll need to investigate primary and secondary sources, whether in print or digital formats. **Primary sources** contain original, firsthand information, such as diaries, autobiographies, interviews, speeches, and eyewitness accounts. **Secondary sources** provide other people's versions of primary sources in encyclopedias, newspaper and magazine articles, biographies, and documentaries.

Your search for sources begins at the library and on the Internet. Use advanced search features to help you find things quickly. Add a minus sign (-) before a word that should not appear in your results. Use an asterisk (*) in place of unknown words. List the name of and location of each possible source, adding comments about its potential usefulness. Assessing, or evaluating, your sources is an important step in the research process. Your goal is to use sources that are **credible**, or reliable and trustworthy.

Criteria for Assessing Sources	
Relevance: It covers the target aspect of my topic.	• How will the source be useful in answering my research question?
Accuracy: It includes information that can be verified by more than one authoritative source.	• Is the information up-to-date? Are the facts accurate? How can I verify them? • What qualifies the author to write about this topic? Is he or she an authority?
Objectivity: It presents multiple viewpoints on the topic.	• What, if any, biases can I detect? Does the writer favor one view of the topic?

Incorporate and Cite Sources

When you draft your research project, you'll need to include material from your sources. This material can be **direct quotations**, **summaries**, or **paraphrases** of the original source material. Two well-known **style manuals** provide information on how to cite a range of print and digital sources: the *MLA Handbook for Writers of Research Papers* (published by the Modern Language Association) and Kate L. Turabian's *A Manual for Writers of Research Papers, Theses, and Dissertations* (published by The University of Chicago Press). Both style manuals provide a wealth of information about conducting, formatting, drafting, and presenting your research, including guidelines for citing sources within the text (called parenthetical citations) and preparing the list of Works Cited, as well as correct use of the mechanics of writing. Your teacher will indicate which style manual you should use. The following examples use the format in the *MLA Handbook*.

Any material from sources must be completely documented, or you will commit **plagiarism**, the unauthorized use of someone else's words or ideas. Plagiarism is not honest. As you take notes for your research project, be sure to keep complete information about your sources so that you can cite them correctly in the body of your paper. This applies to all sources, whether print or digital. Having complete information will also enable you to prepare the list of Works Cited. The list of Works Cited, which concludes your research project, provides author, title, and publication information for both print and digital sources. The following pages show the *MLA Handbook's* Works Cited citation formats for a variety of sources.

EXAMPLES

Direct quotation [The writer is citing the poet Homer's word in the *Odyssey*, page 74.]	In Book Four of the *Odyssey,* Menelaus describes the island of Pharos as "as far out as the distance a hollow ship can make in a whole day's sailing" (Homer 74).
Summary [The writer is summarizing the conclusion of Tim Severin on page 75 of *The Ulysses Voyage: Sea Search for the Odyssey*.]	Severin was unable to trace Odysseus' journey exactly and found many parts of Homer's tale puzzling. He concluded that the geographies of folklore and navigation overlapped (245).
Paraphrase [The writer is paraphrasing, or stating in her own words, material from page 25 of Bernard Knox's book and from the *Brittanica Student Encyclopedia* on the Homeric Legend.]	The third-century-B.C. geographer Eratosthenes, for example, thought that Homer's story was completely imaginary (Knox 25; "Homeric Legend").

W 7, W 8

INCORPORATE AND CITE SOURCES
Remind students to write legibly as they take notes.

MLA Citation Guidelines

Today, you can find free websites that generate ready-made citations for research papers, using the information you provide. Such sites have some time-saving advantages when you're developing a Works Cited list. However, you should always check your citations carefully before you turn in your final paper. If you are following MLA style, use these guidelines to evaluate and finalize your work.

Books

One author

Severin, Tim. *The Ulysses Voyage: Sea Search for the Odyssey.* London: Hutchinson, 1987. Print.

Two authors or editors

Steiner, George, and Robert Fagles, eds. *Homer: A Collection of Critical Essays.* Englewood Cliffs: Prentice, 1962. Print.

Three authors

Heubeck, Alfred, Stephanie West, and J. B. Hainsworth. *A Commentary on Homer's Odyssey.* New York: Oxford UP, 1988. Print.

Four or more authors

The abbreviation et al. means "and others." Use et al. instead of listing all the authors.

Melick, Peter, et al. *The Odyssey Explained.* New York: Garden UP, 1997. Print.

No author given

Greek Literature: An Overview. New York: Sunrise, 1993. Print.

An author and a translator

Homer. *The Odyssey of Homer: A Modern Translation.* Trans. Richmond Lattimore. New York: Harper, 1967. Print.

An author, a translator, and an editor

La Fontaine, Jean de. *Selected Fables.* Trans. Christopher Wood. Ed. Maya Slater. New York: Oxford UP, 1995. Print.

Parts of Books

An introduction, a preface, a foreword, or an afterword written by someone other than the author(s) of a work

Knox, Bernard. Introduction. *The Odyssey of Homer.* Trans. Robert Fagles. New York: Penguin, 1996. 3–64. Print.

A poem, a short story, an essay, or a chapter in a collection of works by one author

Sappho. "He Is More Than a Hero." *The Works of Sappho.* Trans. Edward Osmond. New York: Garden UP, 1990. 53. Print.

A poem, a short story, an essay, or a chapter in an anthology of works by several authors

Solonos, Costa. "Journeys." Trans. Carl Foreman. *Greek Voices.* Ed. Katharine Greene and Gerald Spencer. London: Greenwood, 1985. 83–85. Print.

A novel or a play in a collection

Sophocles. *Antigone. The Three Theban Plays.* Trans. Robert Fagles. New York: Penguin, 1984. Print.

Magazines, Newspapers, and Encyclopedias

An article in a newspaper

Wilford, John Noble. "Was Troy a Metropolis? Homer Isn't Talking." *New York Times* 22 Oct. 2002: D1+. Print.

An article in a magazine

Severin, Tim. "The Quest for Ulysses." *National Geographic* Aug. 1986: 194–225. Print.

An article in an encyclopedia

"Homer." *The World Book Encyclopedia.* 2000 ed. Print.

Miscellaneous Nonprint Sources

An interview

Baldwin, Richard. Personal interview. 13 Mar. 2011.

A video recording

The Odyssey of Troy. A&E Home Video, 1994. DVD.

Electronic Publications

A CD-ROM

"Homeric Legend." *Britannica Student Encyclopedia.* 2004 ed. Chicago: Encyclopaedia Britannica, 2004. CD-ROM.

A document from an Internet site

Entries for online sources should contain as much of the information shown as available.

Author or compiler | Title or description of document | Title of website

Fagles, Robert. | Reply to query of Terry J. Keely. | Online NewsHour.

Site sponsor | Date of document | Medium of publication

Public Broadcasting Service. | 13 Mar. 1997. | Web.

Date of access

10 Apr. 2015.

Struck, Peter. "Map of Odysseus' Journey." Mythology. Course pages. Dept. of Classical Studies, U of Pennsylvania. 2004. Web. 9 Mar. 2011.

Participating in a Collaborative Discussion

Often, class activities, including the Performance Tasks in this book, will require you to work collaboratively with classmates. Whether your group will analyze a work of literature or try to solve a community problem, use the following guidelines to ensure a productive discussion.

Prepare for the Discussion

A productive discussion is one in which all the participants bring useful information and ideas to share. If your group will discuss a short story the class read, first re-read and annotate a copy of the story. Your annotations will help you quickly locate evidence to support your points.

Participants in a discussion about an important issue should first research the issue and bring notes or information sources that will help guide the group. If you disagree with a point made by another group member, your case will be stronger if you back it up with specific evidence from your sources.

EXAMPLES

Disagreeing without evidence: It doesn't make sense to be concerned about the school's environmental footprint.

Providing evidence for disagreement: I disagree about the relevance of environmental concerns to our school community. Several national environmental organizations point out that schools can play an important role in reducing the community's environmental footprint.

Set Ground Rules

The rules your group needs will depend on what your group is expected to accomplish. A discussion of themes in a poem will be unlikely to produce a single consensus; however, a discussion aimed at developing a solution to a problem should result in one strong proposal that all group members support. Answer the following questions to set ground rules that fit your group's purpose:

- What will this group produce? A range of ideas, a single decision, a plan of action, or something else?
- How much time is available? How much of that time should be allotted to each part of our discussion (presenting ideas, summarizing or voting on final ideas, creating a product such as a written analysis or a speech)?
- What roles need to be assigned within the group? Do we need a leader, a note-taker, a timekeeper, or other specific roles?
- What is the best way to synthesize our group's ideas? Should we take a vote, list group members as "for" or "against" in a chart, or use some other method to reach consensus or sum up the results of the discussion?

Move the Discussion Forward

Everyone in the group should be actively involved in synthesizing ideas. To make sure this happens, ask questions that draw out ideas, especially from less-talkative members of the group. If an idea or statement is confusing, try to paraphrase it or ask the speaker to explain more about it. If you disagree with a statement, say so politely and explain in detail why you disagree.

SAMPLE DISCUSSION

EFFECTIVE BEHAVIOR	WHAT IT LOOKS LIKE
Support others' contributions. In this example, Raul realizes that Kenisha's views are different from his. Instead of interrupting, he listens carefully to make sure he understands her evidence and what she thinks it means.	Raul listens to Kenisha while she presents her research and views on how to calculate their school's environmental footprint. "I read that article, too," Raul thinks to himself. "Then I read a more recent article that included a much longer list of considerations than those that were in the first article. I'll make a note about it and let Kenisha finish."
State your own views thoughtfully. As the discussion continues, Raul explains how his research turned up different results. He shows that he has used a reliable source.	"I read the same article Kenisha did," Raul begins, "but I found a more recent and I think more useful article on sustainable building in the journal *Architectural Engineering and Construction*. It describes how one high school calculated its environmental footprint before building a new addition."

Respond to Ideas

In a diverse group, everyone may have a different perspective on the topic of discussion, and that's a good thing. Consider what everyone has to say, and don't resist changing your view if other group members provide convincing evidence for theirs. If, instead, you feel more strongly than ever about your view, don't hesitate to say so and provide reasons related to what those with opposing views have said. Before wrapping up the discussion, try to sum up the points on which your group agrees and disagrees.

SAMPLE DISCUSSION

EFFECTIVE BEHAVIOR	WHAT IT LOOKS LIKE
Summarize agreements and disagreements. Cecilia compares the key points. She notices that Raul and Kenisha agree except for one point.	Cecilia is going to speak next, but rather than silently rehearsing her views, she compares Raul's views with Kenisha's. "Raul listed the same five considerations that Kenisha did. The only difference between them is how water consumption is calculated."
Justify your views or consider new ones. Considering Cecilia's comments, Raul sees that he and Kenisha differ on one point. He can justify his view but is willing to combine his approach with Kenisha's and Cecilia's.	Cecilia points out that Kenisha's and Raul's views differ in only one important respect. As Raul listens to Cecilia's summary, he thinks, "Cecilia is right. Kenisha's view and mine are almost the same except for one issue." He makes a mental note of this and continues to listen to Cecilia for more information and insight.

Debating an Issue

The selection and collection Performance Tasks in this text will direct you to engage in debates about issues relating to the selections you've read. Use the guidelines that follow to have a productive and balanced argument about both sides of an issue.

The Structure of a Formal Debate

In a debate, two teams compete to win the support of the audience about an issue. In a **formal debate,** two teams, each with three members, present their arguments on a given **proposition** or **policy statement.** One team argues for the proposition or statement and the other team argues against it. Each debater must consider the proposition closely and must research both sides of it. To argue convincingly either for or against a proposition, a debater must be familiar with both sides of the issue.

Plan the Debate

The purpose of a debate is to allow participants and audience members to consider both sides of an issue. Use these planning suggestions to hold a balanced and productive debate:

- **Identify Debate Teams** Form groups of six members based on the issue presented in the Performance Task. Three members of the team will argue for the **affirmative side** of the issue—that is, they support the issue. The other three members will argue for the **negative side** of the issue—that is, they do not support the issue.
- **Appoint a Moderator** The moderator will present the topic and goals of the debate, keep track of the time, and introduce and thank the participants.
- **Research and Prepare Notes** Search the texts you've read as well as print and online sources for **valid reasons** and **evidence** to support your team's claim. As with argument, be sure to anticipate possible opposing claims and compile evidence to counter those claims. You will use notes from your research during the debate.

- **Assign Debate Roles** One team member will introduce the team's **claim** and supporting evidence. Another team member will respond to questions and **opposing claims** in an exchange with a member of the opposing team. The last member will present a strong closing argument.

Hold the Debate

A formal debate is not a shouting match—rather, a well-run debate is an excellent forum for participants to express their viewpoints, build on others' ideas, and have a thoughtful, well-reasoned exchange of ideas. The moderator will begin by stating the topic or issue and introducing the participants. Participants should follow the moderator's instructions concerning whose turn it is to speak and how much time each speaker has.

FORMAL DEBATE FORMAT

SPEAKER	ROLE	TIME
Affirmative Speaker 1	Present the claim and supporting evidence for the affirmative ("pro") side of the argument.	5 minutes
Negative Speaker 1	Ask probing questions that will prompt the other team to address flaws in the argument.	3 minutes
Affirmative Speaker 2	Respond to the questions posed by the opposing team and counter any concerns.	3 minutes

continued

SPEAKER	ROLE	TIME
Negative Speaker 2	Respond to any questions posed by the opposing team, and counter any concerns.	5 minutes
Affirmative Speaker 3	Summarize the claim and evidence for the affirmative side, and explain why your reasoning is more valid.	3 minutes
Negative Speaker 3	Summarize the claim and evidence for the negative side, and explain why your reasoning is more valid.	3 minutes

Evaluate the Debate

Use the following guidelines to evaluate a team in a debate:

- Did the team prove that the issue is significant? How thorough was the analysis?
- How did the team effectively argue that you should support their affirmative or negative side of the proposition or issue?
- How effectively did the team present reasons and evidence, including evidence from the texts, to support the proposition?
- How effectively did the team rebut, or respond to, arguments made by the opposing team?
- Did the speakers maintain eye contact and speak at an appropriate rate and volume?
- Did the speakers observe proper debate etiquette—that is, did they follow the moderator's instructions, stay within their allotted time limits, and treat their opponents respectfully?

PRACTICE AND APPLY

Possible answers:
Students should create a chart like the one on page R16. The chart should include details similar to the ones below. Remind students to write legibly as they create their charts.
Claim: We need to look more closely at what Christopher Columbus actually did and his place in our history.
Reason: We honor Columbus as the first European to set foot in the Americas when he may not have been the first.
Evidence: Archaeologists found Norse ruins in Greenland and in what is now Newfoundland, dating from A.D. 1000. This evidence seems to prove that Vikings reached North America almost 500 years before Columbus.
Evidence: Although Columbus did reach the Americas, he did not discover them. Millions of people were already living here when he arrived.
Counterargument: Even though he may not have been the first European to set foot on American soil, Columbus' voyages made the rest of the world aware of the Americas.

Reading Arguments

An **argument** expresses a position on an issue or problem and supports it with reasons and evidence. Being able to analyze and evaluate arguments will help you distinguish between claims you should accept and those you should not.

Analyzing an Argument

A sound argument should appeal strictly to reason. An argument includes the following elements:

- A **claim** (or **thesis** or **controlling idea**) is the writer's position on an issue or problem.
- **Support** is any material that serves to prove a claim. In an argument, support usually consists of reasons and evidence.
- **Reasons** are declarations made to justify an action, decision, or belief.
- **Evidence** is the specific references, quotations, facts, examples, and opinions that support a claim. Evidence may also consist of statistics, reports of personal experience, or the views of experts.
- **Counterarguments** and **counterclaims** are arguments made to oppose other arguments. A good argument anticipates opposing counterclaims by providing counterarguments to answer them.

Claim	My curfew should be extended from 11 P.M. to midnight on Saturday night.
▼	
Reason	I don't have enough time to spend with my friends on weekdays because of homework and my job.
▼	
Evidence	On weekends I spend four hours doing homework and four hours at my job.
▼	
Counter-argument	I know that it's difficult for you to sleep when I'm out late, but you need to trust that I'll be home by midnight and give me a chance to prove it.

Practice and Apply

Identify the claim, reason, evidence, and counterargument used in this argument.

On the second Monday in October, Americans celebrate Columbus Day. We honor the Italian explorer who has been credited with discovering the Americas in 1492. Some people, however, think that we need to look more closely at what Christopher Columbus actually did and at his place in our history. I am one of those people.

First of all, although we honor Columbus as the first European to set foot in the Americas, he may not have been the first. Archaeologists have found Norse ruins in Greenland and what is now Newfoundland, dating from around AD 1000. This evidence seems to prove that Vikings actually reached the North American continent nearly 500 years before Columbus ever left the shores of Spain.

Second, although Columbus did reach the Americas, he did not discover them. Millions of people were already living here when he arrived.

Defenders of Columbus argue that, in a way, he did discover the Americas. Even if he wasn't the first European to set foot on the land, his voyages made the rest of the world aware of the Americas. In the years following Columbus' voyages, Europeans came to establish colonies and to explore the land.

I argue that this spread of culture brought great harm as well as great good to the Americas. The Europeans who came to the Americas brought deadly diseases with them. The native people had no immunity to such diseases as mumps, measles, smallpox, and typhus. As a result, hundreds of thousands of people died.

In conclusion, I don't suggest that people should boycott their local Columbus Day parades. I do think, though, that we should create a more balanced picture of the man we're honoring.

Recognizing Persuasive Techniques

Argumentative texts typically rely on more than just the logical appeal of an argument to be convincing. They also rely on **persuasive techniques**—devices that can sway you to adopt a position or take an action. Persuasive techniques are used in advertising, political speeches, films, and fundraisers. The chart shown here explains several ways a writer may attempt to sway you to adopt his or her position. Learn to recognize these techniques, and you will be less likely to be influenced by them.

Persuasive Technique	Example
Appeals by Association	
Bandwagon appeal Uses the argument that a person should believe or do something because "everyone else" does	More and more people are making the switch to Discountline long-distance service.
Testimonial Relies on endorsements from well-known people or satisfied customers	Pierre DuPont, world-class rock climber, would be left hanging without DuraTwine rope.
Snob appeal Taps into people's desire to be special or part of an elite group	Treat yourself to Tropical Paradise because, after all, you deserve the best under the sun.
Transfer Connects a product, candidate, or cause with a positive emotion or idea	Freedom . . . you can feel it the instant you put your hands on the wheel of a Farnsworth 4 × 4 SL.
Appeal to loyalty Relies on people's affiliation with a particular group	This car is made in America by Americans.
Emotional Appeals	
Appeals to pity, fear, or vanity Use strong feelings, rather than facts, to persuade	Without more police, we'll be at the mercy of thieves.

Word Choice

Glittering generality Makes a generalization that includes a word or phrase with positive connotations, such as freedom and honor, to promote a product or idea.	A vote for Evan Smith is a vote for democracy.

Practice and Apply

Identify the persuasive techniques used in the model.

Indiana and Issun Boshi— Building Another Great Team

Indiana is basketball country. Names like Bobby Knight, Larry Bird, and Isaiah Thomas have added greatness to the game for over a quarter century.

That's why Issun Boshi, Japan's leading automobile company, chose Indiana as its U.S. teammate. The new plant will produce 150,000 new vehicles a year, built by 25,000 hard-working Hoosiers just like you. In addition, many of those workers will be driving the cars they make at a special discount—that's only fair; that's the American way. It's how we play the game.

Just ask Indiana sportscaster Wally Elliot, who says, "Issun Boshi and Hoosier pride— now that's what I call an expansion team."

Analyzing Logic and Reasoning

When you evaluate an argument, you need to look closely at the writer's logic and reasoning. To do this, it is helpful to identify the type of reasoning the writer is using.

The Inductive Mode of Reasoning

When a writer leads from specific evidence to a general principle or generalization, that writer is using **inductive reasoning.** Here is an example of inductive reasoning.

Specific Facts

Fact 1 The American Society of Composers, Authors, and Publishers (ASCAP) was formed on Friday, February 13, 1914, to collect royalties on copyrighted music.

RI 6

PRACTICE AND APPLY
Answers:
Appeals by Association: snob appeal; appeal to loyalty; testimonial
Emotional Appeals: appeal to vanity, appeal to patriotism
Word Choice: glittering generality

PRACTICE AND APPLY
Answer:
Deductive reasoning

continued

Specific Facts

Fact 2 The licensing of the first female flight instructor took place on Friday, October 13, 1939.

Fact 3 On Friday, February 13, 1948, Orville Wright announced that he was giving the famous flying machine *Kitty Hawk* to the Smithsonian Institution.

Generalization

Good things can happen on Friday the 13th.

Strategies for Evaluating Inductive Arguments

Ask yourself the following questions to evaluate an inductive argument:

- **Is the evidence valid and sufficient support for the conclusion?** Inaccurate facts lead to inaccurate conclusions.

- **Does the conclusion follow logically from the evidence?** From the facts listed in the previous example, the conclusion that good things happen only on Friday the 13th would be too broad a generalization.

- **Is the evidence drawn from a large enough sample?** Even though there are only three facts listed above, the sample is large enough to support the claim. If you wanted to support the conclusion that only good things happen on Friday the 13th, the sample is not large enough.

The Deductive Mode of Reasoning

When a writer arrives at a conclusion by applying a general principle to a specific situation, the writer is using **deductive reasoning.** Here's an example.

Journalism that stretches the truth is deceptive.	General principle or premise
▼	
Hollywood Snoop Magazine **stretches the truth.**	Specific situation
▼	
Hollywood Snoop Magazine **practices deceptive journalism.**	Specific conclusion

Strategies for Evaluating Deductive Arguments

Ask yourself the following questions to evaluate a deductive argument:

- **Is the general principle actually stated, or is it implied?** Note that writers often use deductive reasoning in an argument without stating the general principle. They just assume that readers will recognize and agree with the principle. So you may want to identify the general principle for yourself.

- **Is the general principle sound?** Don't just assume the general principle is sound. Ask yourself whether it is really true.

- **Is the conclusion valid?** To be valid, a conclusion in a deductive argument must follow logically from the general principle and the specific situation.

The following chart shows two conclusions drawn from the same general principle.

All team members wore school colors on Friday.	
Accurate Deduction	**Inaccurate Deduction**
Mara is on the volleyball team; therefore, Mara wore school colors on Friday.	Jaime wore school colors on Friday; therefore, Jaime is on a school team.

Jaime could have worn school colors in support of a team without being a member.

Practice and Apply

Identify the mode of reasoning used in the following paragraph.

> Preteens and teenagers have access to a range of technology that their parents didn't have. Information that was once hard to find can now be obtained easily on the Internet. Smart phones provide many ways to communicate—text messages, social media sites, and decreasingly, old-fashioned phone calls. The effect is a childhood different than that experienced in the past.

R18   Student Resources

Identifying Faulty Reasoning

Sometimes an argument at first appears to make sense but isn't valid because it is based on a fallacy. A fallacy is an error in logic. Learn to recognize these common **rhetorical** and **logical fallacies.**

Type of Fallacy	Definition	Example
Circular reasoning	Supporting a statement by simply repeating it in different words	Teenagers should avoid fad diets, because it is important for **adolescents to stay away from popular weight-loss plans.**
Either/or fallacy	A statement that suggests that there are only two choices available in a situation that really offers more than two options	**Either** students should be allowed to leave school to have lunch at nearby fast-food restaurants, **or** they should be allowed to choose the cafeteria menu.
Oversimplification	An explanation of a complex situation or problem as if it were much simpler than it is	Making the team depends on **whether the coach likes you.**
Overgeneralization	A generalization that is too broad. You can often recognize overgeneralizations by the use of words such as *all, everyone, every time, anything, no one,* and *none.*	**No one** cares that there is not enough parking downtown.
Stereotyping	A dangerous type of overgeneralization. Stereotypes are broad statements about people on the basis of their gender, ethnicity, race, or political, social, professional, or religious group.	The only thing **the members of that political party** care about is big business.
Attacking the person or name-calling	An attempt to discredit an idea by attacking the person or group associated with it. Candidates often engage in name-calling during political campaigns.	**My opponent is not smart enough** to be mayor.
Evading the issue	Refuting an objection with arguments and evidence that do not address its central point	Yes, I broke my campaign promise not to raise taxes, **but higher taxes have led to increases in police patrols, paved highways, and smaller class size in schools.**
Non sequitur	A statement that uses irrelevant "proof" to support a claim. A non sequitur is sometimes used to win an argument by diverting the reader's attention to proof that can't be challenged.	I know I'll pass math. **Mr. Gray is my math teacher and my football coach.**
False cause	The mistake of assuming that because one event occurred after another event in time, the first event caused the second one to occur	The mayor declared a get-tough crime policy, and sure enough, **crime rates dropped.**

PRACTICE AND APPLY

Possible answers:

1. *Oversimplification: "Watching television causes a child's grades to drop." Explanation: The explanation for the problem, a drop in children's grades, is oversimplified. Not all children's grades drop.*

2. *Attacking the person or name-calling: "Money-hungry media moguls produce horrible programming." Explanation: The writer is attempting to discredit media moguls by attacking them and using harsh language.*

3. *False analogy: "If you say television isn't bad for children, you would probably say the earth is flat." Explanation: The writer compares two subjects that have nothing in common.*

4. *Either/or fallacy and Stereotyping: "They can either unplug the TV or expect their children to become uneducated slugs." Explanation: The either/or fallacy suggests that there is only one alternative to watching television (unplugging the TV). The term uneducated slug is a stereotype of children who watch television.*

---

continued

Type of Fallacy	Definition	Example
False analogy	A comparison that doesn't hold up because of a critical difference between the two subjects	She walks to the store and back every day, **so surely she can walk in the 10K race**.
Hasty generalization	A conclusion drawn from too little evidence or from evidence that is biased	That corner must be dangerous. **There were two car accidents there last week**.

Practice and Apply

Look for examples of logical fallacies in the following argument. Identify each one and explain why you identified it as such.

> Watching television causes a child's grades to drop. What other conclusion can be drawn? Money-hungry media moguls produce horrible programming just to sell advertising time. These programs interfere with children's thinking. If you say television isn't bad for children, you would probably say the earth is flat. Parents who care should at least limit their children's viewing. The most responsible parents should turn off the TV—permanently. They can either unplug the TV or expect their children to become uneducated slugs.

Evaluating Arguments

Learning how to evaluate a text's arguments and identify bias will help you become more selective when doing research and also help you improve your own reasoning and arguing skills. **Bias** is an inclination for or against a particular opinion or viewpoint. A writer may reveal a strongly positive or negative opinion on an issue by presenting only one way of looking at it or by heavily weighting the evidence on one side of the argument. Additionally, the presence of either of the following is often a sign that a writer is biased:

Loaded language consists of words with strongly positive or negative connotations that are intended to influence a reader's attitude.

EXAMPLE

The safety of our children depends on our driving the savage criminals out of this horrible neighborhood. (*Savage* and *horrible* have very negative connotations.)

Propaganda is any form of communication that is so distorted that it conveys false or misleading information. Some politicians create and distribute propaganda. Logical fallacies are often used in propaganda. For instance, the following example shows an oversimplification. The writer uses one fact to support a particular point of view but does not reveal another fact that does not support that viewpoint.

EXAMPLE

Since the new park opened, vandalism in the area has increased by 10 percent. Clearly, the park has had a negative impact on the area. (The writer does not include the fact that the vandalism was caused by people who were not drawn into the area by the park.)

Strategies for Evaluating Evidence

It is important to have a set of standards by which you can evaluate arguments. Use the questions below to help you critically assess an argument.

- **Are the facts presented credible and thus verifiable?** Facts can be proved by eyewitness accounts, authoritative sources such as encyclopedias and almanacs, experts, or research.

- **Are the opinions presented well substantiated?** Any opinions offered should be supported by facts, be based on research or eyewitness accounts, or be the opinions of experts on the topic.

- **Is the evidence relevant and sufficient?** Relevant evidence applies to the conclusion, and sufficient evidence leaves no reasonable questions unanswered. If a choice is offered, background for making the choice should be provided. If taking a side is called for, all sides of the issue should be presented.

- **Is the evidence biased?** Be alert to evidence that contains loaded language or other signs of bias.
- **Is the evidence authoritative?** The people, groups, or organizations that provided the evidence should have credentials that support their authority.
- **Is it important that the evidence be current?** Where timeliness is crucial, as in the areas of medicine and technology, the evidence should reflect the latest developments in the areas.

Practice and Apply

Read the argument below. Identify the facts, opinion, and elements of bias.

Why are students who show up late for tests, fill in answers randomly, and then snooze for the rest of the period allowed to jeopardize school test scores and reduce the quality of instruction for motivated kids? The answer is simple—compulsory attendance laws. These laws say that kids must be in school. But a study by economists William Landes and Lewis Solomon found little evidence that such laws increase attendance rates at all. Why not tell poor attenders, who are almost always failing too, "You're done. You don't belong here." Private schools do it, and the ability to expel students contributes to a positive climate.

Strategies for Determining a Strong Argument

Make sure that all or most of the following statements are true:

- The argument presents a claim or controlling idea.
- The claim is connected to its support by a general principle that most readers would readily agree with. Valid general principle: *It is the job of a school to provide a well-rounded physical education program.* Invalid general principle: *It is the job of a school to produce healthy, physically fit people.*
- The reasons make sense.
- The reasons are presented in a logical and effective order.
- The claim and all reasons are adequately supported by sound evidence.
- The evidence is sufficient, credible, and relevant.

- The logic is sound. There are no instances of faulty reasoning.
- The argument adequately anticipates and addresses reader concerns and counterclaims with counterarguments.

Practice and Apply

Use the preceding criteria to evaluate the strength of the following editorial.

According to veterinarian and animal-rights advocate Dr. Michael W. Fox, more than 100 million animals are used each year in laboratory tests. These animals are used to study such things as the causes and effects of illnesses and to test drugs. This unnecessary and cruel animal testing must be stopped.

The most important reason to stop this testing is that it's wrong to make living creatures suffer. Even though they can't talk or use tools as people do, animals have feelings. Zoologist Ann Speirs says that animals may suffer even more than people do, because they can't understand what's happening to them.

People who favor animal research argue that the medical advances gained justify animal experimentation. They also say that the suffering experienced by the animals is minor. People like that are dumber than any guinea pig or rat.

Another important reason to stop this testing is that everybody knows it isn't reliable. Many drugs that help animals are harmful to people. One example is the drug thalidomide. After it was tested in animals in the 1950s and early 1960s, it was given to pregnant women. More than 10,000 of these women gave birth to handicapped babies. The process works the other way, too. Many drugs that help people kill animals. Two common examples are penicillin and aspirin.

Animal testing also affects the environment. The Animal Protection Service says that a quarter of a million chimpanzees, monkeys, and baboons are taken from their natural homes and used in laboratory experiments every year. Those animals will never be able to reproduce, and whole species may become extinct.

A final reason for not using animals in experiments is that there are other research methods available. Two examples are using bits of animal tissue and cells and using computer models.

In conclusion, animal testing has to stop because it just can't go on.

RI 5, RI 6, RI 8

PRACTICE AND APPLY
Possible answers
Facts: A study by economists William Landes and Lewis Solomon found little evidence to show that compulsory attendance laws increase attendance rates.

Opinions: Kids who are forced to be in school because of attendance laws are to blame for the reduced quality of instruction in school. Poor attenders are almost always failing. The ability to expel students contributes to a positive climate in schools.

Elements of bias: "Why are students who show up late for tests, fill in answers randomly, and then snooze for the rest of the period allowed to jeopardize school test scores and reduce the quality of instruction for motivated kids?" "Why not tell poor attenders . . . 'You're done. You don't belong here.'"

PRACTICE AND APPLY
Students' responses will vary, but they should evaluate the strength of the claim, the evidence supporting the claim, and the counterclaims:
Possible answer: Overall, the editorial does not illustrate a very strong argument. The claim—that animal testing is unnecessary and cruel and that it must be stopped—reveals a heavily biased opinion. The writer uses words and phrases with a negative connotation and emotional or biased tone (for example, "unnecessary," "cruel," and "must be stopped"). In addition, many of the statements presented as facts are inappropriate and not supported by sufficient evidence. Finally, the author does not adequately refute opposing claims with logical arguments or evidence. Instead, the writer engages in name-calling and faulty reasoning.

Grammar

Writing that is full of mistakes can confuse or even annoy a reader. A business letter with a punctuation error might lead to a miscommunication and delay a reply. Or a sentence fragment might lower your grade on an essay. Paying attention to grammar, punctuation, and capitalization rules can make your writing clearer and easier to read.

Quick Reference: Parts of Speech

Part of Speech	Function	Examples
Noun	names a person, a place, a thing, an idea, a quality, or an action	
Common	serves as a general name, or a name common to an entire group	poet, novel, love, journey
Proper	names a specific, one-of-a-kind person, place, or thing	Lewis, Jackson, Pleasant Street, Stanley Cup
Singular	refers to a single person, place, thing, or idea	child, park, flower, truth
Plural	refers to more than one person, place, thing, or idea	children, parks, flowers, truths
Concrete	names something that can be perceived by the senses	roof, flash, Dublin, battle
Abstract	names something that cannot be perceived by the senses	intelligence, fear, joy, loneliness
Compound	expresses a single idea through a combination of two or more words	haircut, father-in-law, Christmas Eve
Collective	refers to a group of people or things	army, flock, class, species
Possessive	shows who or what owns something	Strafford's, Bess's, children's, witnesses'
Pronoun	takes the place of a noun or another pronoun	
Personal	refers to the person making a statement, the person(s) being addressed, or the person(s) or thing(s) the statement is about	I, me, my, mine, we, us, our, ours, you, your, yours, she, he, it, her, him, hers, his, its, they, them, their, theirs
Reflexive	follows a verb or preposition and refers to a preceding noun or pronoun	myself, yourself, herself, himself, itself, ourselves, yourselves, themselves
Intensive	emphasizes a noun or another pronoun	(same as reflexives)
Demonstrative	points to one or more specific persons or things	this, that, these, those

continued

Part of Speech	Function	Examples
Interrogative	signals a question	who, whom, whose, which, what
Indefinite	refers to one or more persons or things not specifically mentioned	both, all, most, many, anyone, everybody, several, none, some
Relative	introduces an adjective clause by relating it to a word in the clause	who, whom, whose, which, that
Reciprocal	refers to individual parts of a plural antecedent	each other, one another
Verb	expresses an action, a condition, or a state of being	
Action	tells what the subject does or did, physically or mentally	run, reaches, listened, consider, decides, dreamed
Linking	connects the subject to something that identifies or describes it	am, is, are, was, were, sound, taste, appear, feel, become, remain, seem
Auxiliary	precedes the main verb in a verb phrase	be, have, do, can, could, will, would, may, might
Transitive	directs the action toward someone or something; always has an object	The storm **sank** the ship.
Intransitive	does not direct the action toward someone or something; does not have an object	The ship **sank.**
Adjective	modifies a noun or pronoun	**strong** women, **two** epics, **enough** time
Adverb	modifies a verb, an adjective, or another adverb	walked **out, really** funny, **far** away
Preposition	relates one word to another word	at, by, for, from, in, of, on, to, with
Conjunction	joins words or word groups	
Coordinating	joins words or word groups used the same way	and, but, or, for, so, yet, nor
Correlative	used as a pair to join words or word groups used the same way	both . . . and, either . . . or, neither . . . nor
Subordinating	introduces a clause that cannot stand by itself as a complete sentence	although, after, as, before, because, when, if, unless
Interjection	expresses emotion	wow, ouch, hurrah

Quick Reference: The Sentence and Its Parts

The diagrams that follow will give you a brief review of the essentials of a sentence and some of its parts.

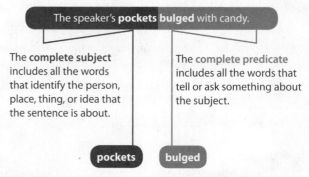

The speaker's pockets bulged with candy.

The **complete subject** includes all the words that identify the person, place, thing, or idea that the sentence is about.

The complete predicate includes all the words that tell or ask something about the subject.

pockets

bulged

The **simple subject** tells exactly whom or what the sentence is about. It may be one word or a group of words, but it does not include modifiers.

The simple predicate, or verb, tells what the subject does or is. It may be one word or several, but it does not include modifiers.

Every word in a sentence is part of a complete subject or a complete predicate.

At the drugstore, an understanding clerk had given the speaker a chocolate bar.

A **prepositional phrase** consists of a preposition, its object, and any modifiers of the object. In this phrase, *at* is the preposition and *drugstore* is its object.

subject

A direct object is a word or group of words that tells who or what receives the action of the verb.

An indirect object is a word or group of words that tells to whom or for whom or to what or for what the verb's action is performed. A sentence can have an indirect object only if it has a direct object. The indirect object always comes before the direct object.

Verbs often have more than one part. A verb may be made up of a **main verb,** like *given,* and one or more **auxiliary,** or **helping, verbs,** like *had*.

Quick Reference: Punctuation

Mark	Function	Examples
End Marks period, question mark, exclamation point	ends a sentence	We can start now. When would you like to leave? What a fantastic hit!
period	follows an initial or abbreviation **Exception:** postal abbreviations of states	Mrs. Dorothy Parker, C. P. Cavafy, p.m., lb., oz., Blvd., Dr., NE (Nebraska), NV (Nevada)
period	follows a number or letter in an outline	I. Volcanoes A. Central-vent 1. Shield
Comma	separates part of a compound sentence	I had never liked poetry, but now I really love it.
	separates items in a series	She is brave, loyal, and kind.
	separates adjectives of equal rank that modify the same noun	The slow, easy route is best.
	sets off a term of address	Maria, how can I help you? You must do something, soldier.
	sets off a parenthetical expression	Hard workers, as you know, don't quit. I'm not a quitter, believe me.
	sets off an introductory word, phrase, or dependent clause	Yes, I forgot my key. At the beginning of the day, I feel fresh. While she was out, I was here. Having finished my chores, I went out.
	sets off a nonrestrictive, or nonessential, phrase or clause	Ed Pawn, the captain of the chess team, won. Ed Pawn, who is the captain, won. The two leading runners, sprinting toward the finish line, finished in a tie.
	sets off parts of dates and addresses	Mail it by May 14, 2015, to the Hauptman Company, 321 Market Street, Memphis, Tennessee.
	follows the salutation and closing of a letter	Dear Jim, Sincerely yours,
	separates words to avoid confusion	By noon, time had run out. What the minister does, does matter. While cooking, Jim burned his hand.

continued

Mark	Function	Examples
Semicolon	separates items that contain commas in a series	We spent the first week of summer vacation in Chicago, Illinois; the second week in St. Louis, Missouri; and the third week in Albany, New York.
	separates parts of a compound sentence that are not joined by a coordinating conjunction	The last shall be first; the first shall be last. I read the Bible; however, I have not memorized it.
	separates parts of a compound sentence when the parts contain commas	After I ran out of money, I called my parents; but only my sister was home, unfortunately.
Colon	introduces a list	Those we wrote were the following: Dana, John, and Will.
	introduces a long quotation	Abraham Lincoln wrote: "Four score and seven years ago, our fathers brought forth on this continent a new nation. . . ."
	follows the salutation of a business letter	To Whom It May Concern: Dear Leonard Atole:
	separates certain numbers	1:28 p.m., Genesis 2:5
Dash	emphasizes parenthetical information or indicates an abrupt break in thought	I was thinking of my mother—who is arriving tomorrow—just as you walked in.
Parentheses	enclose less-important material	It was so unlike him (John is always on time) that I began to worry. The last World Series game (did you see it?) was fun.
Hyphen	joins parts of a compound adjective before a noun	The not-so-rich taxpayer won't stand for this!
	joins part of a compound with *all-*, *ex-*, *self-*, or *-elect*	The ex-firefighter helped rescue him. Our president-elect is self-conscious.
	joins part of a compound number (to ninety-nine)	Today, I turned twenty-one.
	joins part of a fraction	My cup is one-third full.
	joins a prefix to a word beginning with a capital letter	Which Pre-Raphaelite painter do you like best? It snowed in mid-October.
	indicates that a word is divided at the end of a line	How could you have any reason-able expectations of getting a new computer?
Apostrophe	used with *s* to form the possessive of a noun or an indefinite pronoun	my friend's book, my friends' books, anyone's guess, somebody else's problem

continued

Mark	Function	Examples
	replaces one or more omitted letters in a contraction or numbers in a date	don't (omitted *o*), he'd (omitted *woul*), the class of '99 (omitted *19*)
	used with *s* to form the plural of a letter	I had two A's on my report card.
Quotation Marks	set off a speaker's exact words	Sara said, "I'm finally ready." "I'm ready," Sara said, "finally." Did Sara say, "I'm ready"? Sara said, "I'm ready!"
	set off the title of a story, article, short poem, essay, song, or chapter	I liked McLean's "Marine Corps Issue" and Oliver's "The Journey." I like Joplin's "Me and Bobby McGee."
	indicate sarcasm or irony	Chris is a real "friend." He always shows up when he needs help but never when I do.
Ellipses	replace material omitted from a quotation	"When in the course of human events . . . and to assume among the powers of the earth. . . ."
Italics	indicate the title of a book, play, magazine, long poem, opera, film or TV series, or the name of a ship	*The Hunger Games, Hamlet, People,* the *Odyssey, Madama Butterfly, Gone with the Wind, The Big Bang Theory, USS Constitution*

Quick Reference: Capitalization

Category	Examples
People and Titles	
Names and initials of people	Amy Tan, W. H. Auden
Titles used before names	Professor Holmes, Senator Long
Deities and members of religious groups	Jesus, Allah, Buddha, Zeus, Baptists, Roman Catholics
Names of ethnic and national groups	Hispanics, Jews, African Americans
Geographical Names	
Cities, states, countries, continents	Philadelphia, Kansas, Japan, Europe
Regions, bodies of water, mountains	the South, Lake Baikal, Mount Everest
Geographic features, parks	Great Basin, Yellowstone National Park
Streets and roads, planets	318 East Sutton Drive, Charles Court, Jupiter, Pluto
Organizations, Events, Etc.	
Companies, organizations, teams	Ford Motor Company, Boy Scouts of America, St. Louis Cardinals

continued

Category	Examples
Buildings, bridges, monuments	Empire State Building, Eads Bridge, Washington Monument
Documents, awards	Declaration of Independence, Stanley Cup
Special named events	Mardi Gras, World Series
Government bodies, historical periods and events	U.S. Senate, House of Representatives, Middle Ages, Vietnam War
Days and months, holidays	Thursday, March, Thanksgiving, Labor Day
Specific cars, boats, trains, planes	Porsche, *Mississippi Queen*, *Stourbridge Lion*, Concorde
Proper Adjectives	
Adjectives formed from proper nouns	French cooking, Freudian psychology, Edwardian age, Midwestern university
First Words and the Pronoun *I*	
First word in a sentence or quotation	This is it. He said, "Let's go."
First word of sentence in parentheses that is not within another sentence	The spelling rules are covered in another section. (Consult that section for more information.)
First words in the salutation and closing of a letter	Dear Madam, Very truly yours,
First word in each line of most poetry Personal pronoun *I*	Then am I A happy fly If I live Or if I die.
First word, last word, and certain parts of speech in a title	*A Tale of Two Cities,* "The World Is Too Much with Us"

Grammar Handbook

1 Nouns

A **noun** is a word used to name a person, a place, a thing, an idea, a quality, or an action. Nouns can be classified in several ways.

1.1 COMMON NOUNS

Common nouns are general names, common to entire groups.

1.2 PROPER NOUNS

Proper nouns name specific, one-of-a-kind people, places, and things.

Common	Proper
guitarist, museum, lake, month	B.B. King, Rock and Roll Hall of Fame, Lake Pontchartrain, February

1.3 SINGULAR AND PLURAL NOUNS

A noun may take a **singular form** (*city, foot*) or a **plural form** (*cities, feet*), depending on whether it names a single person, place, thing, or idea or more than one. Be sure to spell plural forms correctly.

For more information, see **Forming Plural Nouns**, page R54.

1.4 POSSESSIVE NOUNS

A **possessive noun** shows who or what owns something.

2 Pronouns

A **pronoun** is a word that is used in place of a noun or another pronoun. The word or word group to which the pronoun refers is called its **antecedent.**

2.1 PERSONAL PRONOUNS

Personal pronouns change their form to express person, number, gender, and case. The forms of these pronouns are shown in the following chart.

	Nominative	Objective	Possessive
Singular			
First person	I	me	my, mine
Second person	you	you	your, yours
Third person	she, he, it	her, him, it	her, hers, his, its
Plural			
First person	we	us	our, ours
Second person	you	you	your, yours
Third person	they	them	their, theirs

2.2 AGREEMENT WITH ANTECEDENT

Pronouns should agree with their antecedents in number, gender, and person.

If an antecedent is singular, use a singular pronoun.

> EXAMPLE: *I lost my new **cell phone**. I may have left it on the bus.*

If an antecedent is plural, use a plural pronoun.

> EXAMPLES: *Take the **snacks** out of the grocery bag, and put them in the pantry. **Delores and Arnetta** rode their bikes to the park.*

The gender of a pronoun must be the same as the gender of its antecedent.

> EXAMPLE: *The **man** thought he left his hat in the **room**. He ran back to it to look for the hat.*

The person (first, etc.) of the pronoun must be the same as the person of its antecedent.

> EXAMPLE: *You folks will have to go to the stadium to buy your tickets for the concert.*

PRACTICE AND APPLY

Remind students to write legibly as they compose their responses to the Practice and Apply activities.

Answers:

1. *The story "A Sound of Thunder" tells about a man who travels back in time and his adventures.*

2. *Eckels panics at the size of the dinosaur and its enormous teeth.*

3. *Travis looks at Eckels's shoes and notices dirt on them.*

4. *Travis feels he has to kill Eckels, so he shoots him.*

PRACTICE AND APPLY

Answers:

1. *she; nominative*

2. *they; nominative*

3. *its; possessive*

4. *her; possessive*

5. *him; objective*

Practice and Apply

Rewrite each sentence so that the underlined pronoun agrees with its antecedent.

1. The story "A Sound of Thunder" tells about a man who travels back in time and <u>its</u> adventures.

2. Eckels panics at the size of the dinosaur and <u>his</u> enormous teeth.

3. Travis looks at Eckels's shoes and notices dirt on <u>it</u>.

4. Travis feels <u>they</u> has to kill Eckels, so he shoots him.

2.3 PRONOUN CASE

Personal pronouns change form to show how they function in sentences. Different functions are shown by different **cases: nominative, objective,** and **possessive.** For examples, see Section 2.1.

A **nominative pronoun** is used as a subject or a predicate nominative in a sentence.

An **objective pronoun** is used as a direct object, an indirect object, or the object of a preposition.

SUBJECT   OBJECT   OBJECT OF PREPOSITION

He will lead them to us.

A **possessive pronoun** shows ownership. The pronouns *mine, yours, hers, his, its, ours,* and *theirs* can be used in place of nouns.

EXAMPLE: *This horse is mine.*

The pronouns *my, your, her, his, its, our,* and *their* are used before nouns.

EXAMPLE: *This is my horse.*

WATCH OUT! Many spelling errors can be avoided if you watch out for *its* and *their.* Don't confuse the possessive pronouns *its* and *their* with the contractions *it's* and *they're.*

TIP To decide which pronoun to use in a comparison, such as "She works harder than (I or me)," fill in the missing word(s): *She works harder than I work.*

Practice and Apply

Replace the underlined words with an appropriate pronoun, and identify the pronoun's case.

1. In "The Necklace," <u>Mme. Loisel</u> was not happy about her life.

2. Mme. Loisel married a clerk but wished <u>the couple</u> could be wealthy.

3. She hated <u>the apartment's</u> dirty walls.

4. One evening <u>Mme. Loisel's</u> husband said, "I have something for you."

5. Mme. Loisel's reaction to the party invitation was puzzling to <u>M. Loisel.</u>

2.4 REFLEXIVE AND INTENSIVE PRONOUNS

These pronouns are formed by adding -*self* or -*selves* to certain personal pronouns. Their forms are the same, and they differ only in how they are used.

A **reflexive pronoun** follows a verb or preposition and reflects back on an earlier noun or pronoun.

EXAMPLES: *He likes himself too much. She is now herself again.*

Intensive pronouns intensify or emphasize the nouns or pronouns to which they refer.

EXAMPLES: *They themselves will educate their children. You did it yourself.*

WATCH OUT! Avoid using *hisself* or *theirselves.* Standard English does not include these forms.

NONSTANDARD: *The sniper kept hisself hidden behind a chimney.*

STANDARD: *The sniper kept himself hidden behind a chimney.*

2.5 RECIPROCAL PRONOUNS

The **reciprocal pronouns** *each other* and *one another* refer to the individual members of a plural antecedent. These pronouns express mutual actions or relationships between the members they represent. Reciprocal pronouns can also take the possessive forms *each other's* and *one another's.*

EXAMPLES: *The ducks on the pond quacked at* one another.
John and Pedro borrowed each other's *favorite book.*

TIP Some authorities hold that *each other* should be used in reference to two things or people and that *one another* should be used in reference to more than two. Following traditional usage guidelines such as this can give your writing a more formal tone.

2.6 DEMONSTRATIVE PRONOUNS

Demonstrative pronouns point out things and persons near and far.

	Singular	Plural
Near	this	these
Far	that	those

2.7 INDEFINITE PRONOUNS

Indefinite pronouns do not refer to specific persons or things and usually have no antecedents. The chart shows some commonly used indefinite pronouns.

Singular	Plural	Singular or Plural	
another	both	all	most
anybody	few	any	none
no one	many	more	some
neither	several		

TIP Indefinite pronouns that end in *one, body,* or *thing* are always singular.

INCORRECT: *Did* everybody play their *part well?*

CORRECT: *Did* everybody play his or her *part well?*

If the indefinite pronoun might denote either a male or a female, *his or her* may be used to refer to it, or the sentence may be recast.

EXAMPLES: *Did everybody play his or her part well?*
Did all the students play their parts well?

2.8 INTERROGATIVE PRONOUNS

An **interrogative pronoun** tells a reader or listener that a question is coming. The interrogative pronouns are *who, whom, whose, which,* and *what.*

EXAMPLES: Who *is going to rehearse with you?*
From whom *did you receive the script?*

TIP *Who* is used as a subject; *whom,* as an object. To find out which pronoun you need to use in a question, change the question to a statement.

QUESTION: *(Who/Whom) did you meet there?*

STATEMENT: *You met (?) there.*

Since the verb has a subject (you), the needed word must be the object form, whom.

EXAMPLE: *Whom did you meet there?*

WATCH OUT! A special problem arises when you use an interrupter, such as *do you think,* within a question.

EXAMPLE: *(Who/Whom) do you think will win?*

If you eliminate the interrupter, it is clear that the word you need is *who.*

2.9 RELATIVE PRONOUNS

Relative pronouns relate, or connect, adjective clauses to the words they modify in sentences. The noun or pronoun that a relative clause modifies is the antecedent of the relative pronoun. Here are the relative pronouns and their uses.

	Subject	Object	Possessive
Person	who	whom	whose
Thing	which	which	whose
Thing/Person	that	that	whose

Often short sentences with related ideas can be combined by using a relative pronoun to create a more effective sentence.

SHORT SENTENCE: *Poe wrote "The Raven."*

RELATED SENTENCE: *"The Raven" is one of the most famous poems in American literature.*

COMBINED SENTENCE: *Poe wrote "The Raven," which is one of the most famous poems in American literature.*

Practice and Apply

Write the correct form of each incorrect pronoun.
1. Whom has read "The Gift of the Magi"?
2. Jim needs money for a present for Della, so he takes his watch to the pawnshop hisself.
3. Would anybody else sell their watch to buy a Christmas present?
4. He chooses a beautiful pair of them jeweled combs for Della's hair.
5. Della sells her long hair to buy a watch chain for himself.

2.10 PRONOUN REFERENCE PROBLEMS

The referent of a pronoun should always be clear. Avoid problems by rewriting sentences.

An **indefinite reference** occurs when the pronoun *it, you,* or *they* does not clearly refer to a specific antecedent.

UNCLEAR: *In the new production of Romeo and Juliet, you have more experienced actors.*

CLEAR: *The new production of Romeo and Juliet has more experienced actors.*

A **general reference** occurs when the pronoun *it, this, that, which,* or *such* is used to refer to a general idea rather than a specific antecedent.

UNCLEAR: *Jenna takes acting lessons. This has improved her chances of getting a part in the school play.*

CLEAR: *Jenna takes acting lessons. The lessons have improved her chances of getting a part in the school play.*

Ambiguous means "having more than one possible meaning." An **ambiguous reference** occurs when a pronoun could refer to two or more antecedents.

UNCLEAR: *Odysseus escaped from Cyclops, and he blinded him.*

CLEAR: *Odysseus escaped from Cyclops, and he blinded Cyclops.*

Practice and Apply

Rewrite the following sentences to correct indefinite, ambiguous, and general pronoun references.
1. In Miss Lottie's yard you don't have any grass.
2. Miss Lottie plants marigolds. This makes her barren yard look strange.
3. Lizabeth and her brother throw stones at the marigolds, which ends Miss Lottie's planting.
4. Miss Lottie stares at Lizabeth as if she is strange.

3 Verbs

A **verb** is a word that expresses an action, a condition, or a state of being.

3.1 ACTION VERBS

Action verbs express mental or physical activity.

EXAMPLE: *Mr. Cho slept with the window open.*

3.2 LINKING VERBS

Linking verbs join subjects with words or phrases that rename or describe them.

EXAMPLE: *When he awoke the next morning, his bed was wet from the rain.*

3.3 PRINCIPAL PARTS

Action and linking verbs typically have four principal parts, which are used to form verb tenses. The principal parts are the **present,** the **present participle,** the **past,** and the **past participle.**

Action verbs and some linking verbs also fall into two categories: regular and irregular. A **regular verb** is a verb that forms its past and past participle by adding *-ed* or *-d* to the present form.

Present	Present Participle	Past	Past Participle
risk	(is) risking	risked	(has) risked
solve	(is) solving	solved	(has) solved
drop	(is) dropping	dropped	(has) dropped
carry	(is) carrying	carried	(has) carried

An **irregular verb** is a verb that forms its past and past participle in some other way than by adding -ed or -d to the present form.

Present	Present Participle	Past	Past Participle
begin	(is) beginning	began	(has) begun
break	(is) breaking	broke	(has) broken
go	(is) going	went	(has) gone

3.4 VERB TENSE

The **tense** of a verb indicates the time of the action or state of being. An action or state of being can occur in the present, the past, or the future. There are six tenses, each expressing a different range of time.

The **present tense** expresses an action or state that is happening at the present time, occurs regularly, or is constant or generally true. Use the present part.

NOW: *That snow looks deep.*

REGULAR: *It snows every day.*

GENERAL: *Snow falls.*

The **past tense** expresses an action that began and ended in the past. Use the past part.

EXAMPLE: *The storyteller finished his tale.*

The **future tense** expresses an action or state that will occur. Use *shall* or *will* with the present part.

EXAMPLE: *They will attend the next festival.*

The **present perfect tense** expresses an action or state that (1) was completed at an indefinite time in the past or (2) began in the past and continues into the present. Use *have* or *has* with the past participle.

EXAMPLE: *Poetry has inspired many readers.*

The **past perfect tense** expresses an action in the past that came before another action in the past. Use *had* with the past participle.

EXAMPLE: *He had built a fire before the dog ran away.*

The **future perfect tense** expresses an action in the future that will be completed before another action in the future. Use *shall have* or *will have* with the past participle.

EXAMPLE: *They will have read the novel before they see the movie version of the tale.*

An auxiliary verb is not used with a past-tense irregular verb, but it is always used with a past-participle irregular verb.

INCORRECT: *I have saw her before.* (*Saw* is the past tense form and shouldn't be used with *have*.)

CORRECT: *I have seen her somewhere before.*

INCORRECT: *I seen her before.* (*Seen* is the past participle form of an irregular verb and shouldn't be used without an auxiliary verb.)

3.5 PROGRESSIVE FORMS

The progressive forms of the six tenses show ongoing actions. Use forms of *be* with the present participles of verbs.

PRESENT PROGRESSIVE: *She is rehearsing her lines.*

PAST PROGRESSIVE: *She was rehearsing her lines.*

FUTURE PROGRESSIVE: *She will be rehearsing her lines.*

PRESENT PERFECT PROGRESSIVE: *She has been rehearsing her lines.*

PAST PERFECT PROGRESSIVE: *She had been rehearsing her lines.*

PRACTICE AND APPLY

Answers:

1. *Many people benefited from the civil rights movement. (past tense)*
2. *Martin Luther King Jr. remains a towering figure in the history of nonviolent protest. (present tense)*
3. *King became the leader of the Montgomery bus boycott. (past tense)*
4. *When he spoke to the crowds in Washington, D.C., more than 200,000 people heard his words. (past tense)*
5. *Our class read his speech "I Have a Dream." (past tense)* **Alternate answer:** *Our class is reading his speech "I Have a Dream." (present progressive)*
6. *It was a chilly morning as Rosa Parks went to work.*
7. *She left her job early and prepared to go out of town.*
8. *She boarded the bus and took a seat in the "colored" section.*
9. *After several more stops, there were no more seats at the front of the bus.*
10. *Rosa Parks refused to give up her seat and was arrested.*

FUTURE PERFECT PROGRESSIVE: *She will have been rehearsing her lines.*

WATCH OUT! Do not shift from tense to tense needlessly. Watch out for these special cases.

- In most compound sentences and in sentences with compound predicates, keep the tenses the same.

  INCORRECT: *His boots freeze, and he shook with cold.*

  CORRECT: *His boots freeze, and he shakes with cold.*

- If one past action happens before another, do shift tenses.

  INCORRECT: *They wished they started earlier.*

  CORRECT: *They wished they had started earlier.*

Practice and Apply

Rewrite each sentence, using a form of the verb in parentheses. Identify each form that you use.

1. Many people (benefit) from the civil rights movement.
2. Martin Luther King Jr. (remain) a towering figure in the history of nonviolent protest.
3. King (become) the leader of the Montgomery bus boycott.
4. When he (speak) to the crowds in Washington, D.C., more than 200,000 people heard his words.
5. Our class (read) his speech "I Have a Dream."

Rewrite each sentence to correct an error in tense.

6. It is a chilly morning as Rosa Parks went to work.
7. She leaves her job early and was preparing to go out of town.
8. She boarded the bus and is taking a seat in the "colored" section.
9. After several more stops, there are no more seats in the front of the bus.
10. Rosa Parks refused to give up her seat and is arrested.

3.6 ACTIVE AND PASSIVE VOICE

The voice of a verb tells whether its subject performs or receives the action expressed by the verb. When the subject performs the action, the verb is in the **active voice.** When the subject is the receiver of the action, the verb is in the **passive voice.**

Compare these two sentences:

ACTIVE: *Richard Wilbur wrote "The Writer."*

PASSIVE: *"The Writer" was written by Richard Wilbur.*

To form the passive voice, use a form of *be* with the past participle of the verb.

WATCH OUT! Use the passive voice sparingly. It can make writing awkward and less direct.

AWKWARD: *"The Writer" is a poem that was written by Richard Wilbur.*

BETTER: *Richard Wilbur wrote the poem "The Writer."*

There are occasions when you will choose to use the passive voice because

- you want to emphasize the receiver: *The king was shot.*
- the doer is unknown: *My books were stolen.*
- the doer is unimportant: *French is spoken here.*

4 Modifiers

Modifiers are words or groups of words that change or limit the meanings of other words. Adjectives and adverbs are common modifiers.

4.1 ADJECTIVES

Adjectives modify nouns and pronouns by telling which one, what kind, how many, or how much.

WHICH ONE: *this, that, these, those*

EXAMPLE: *That bird is a scarlet ibis.*

WHAT KIND: *small, sick, courageous, black*

EXAMPLE: *The sick bird sways on the branch.*

HOW MANY: *some, few, ten, none, both, each*

EXAMPLE: *Both brothers stared at the bird.*

HOW MUCH: *more, less, enough, fast*

EXAMPLE: *The bird did not have enough strength to remain perched.*

4.2 PREDICATE ADJECTIVES

Most adjectives come before the nouns they modify, as in the examples above. A **predicate adjective,** however, follows a linking verb and describes the subject.

EXAMPLE: *My friends are very intelligent.*

Be especially careful to use adjectives (not adverbs) after such linking verbs as *look, feel, grow, taste,* and *smell.*

EXAMPLE: *The bread smells wonderful.*

4.3 ADVERBS

Adverbs modify verbs, adjectives, and other adverbs by telling where, when, how, or to what extent.

WHERE: *The children played outside.*

WHEN: *The author spoke yesterday.*

HOW: *We walked slowly behind the leader.*

TO WHAT EXTENT: *He worked very hard.*

Adverbs may occur in many places in sentences, both before and after the words they modify.

EXAMPLES: *Suddenly the wind shifted.*

The wind suddenly shifted.

The wind shifted suddenly.

4.4 ADJECTIVE OR ADVERB?

Many adverbs are formed by adding *-ly* to adjectives.

EXAMPLES: *sweet, sweetly; gentle, gently*

However, *-ly* added to a noun will usually yield an adjective.

EXAMPLES: *friend, friendly; woman, womanly*

4.5 COMPARISON OF MODIFIERS

Modifiers can be used to compare two or more things. The form of a modifier shows the degree of comparison. Both adjectives and adverbs have **comparative** and **superlative** forms.

The **comparative form** is used to compare two things, groups, or actions.

EXAMPLES: *His father's hands were stronger than his own.*

His father was more courageous than the other man.

The **superlative form** is used to compare more than two things, groups, or actions.

EXAMPLES: *His father's hands were the strongest in the family.*

His father was the most courageous of them all.

4.6 REGULAR COMPARISONS

Most one-syllable and some two-syllable adjectives and adverbs have comparatives and superlatives formed by adding *-er* and *-est.* All three-syllable and most two-syllable modifiers have comparatives and superlatives formed with *more* or *most.*

Modifier	Comparative	Superlative
small	smaller	smallest
thin	thinner	thinnest
sleepy	sleepier	sleepiest
useless	more useless	most useless
precisely	more precisely	most precisely

WATCH OUT! Note that spelling changes must sometimes be made to form the comparatives and superlatives of modifiers.

EXAMPLES: *friendly, friendlier* (Change *y* to *i,* and add the ending.)

sad, sadder (Double the final consonant, and add the ending.)

4.7 IRREGULAR COMPARISONS

Some commonly used modifiers have irregular comparative and superlative forms. They are listed in the following chart. You may wish to memorize them.

Modifier	Comparative	Superlative
good	better	best
bad	worse	worst
far	farther *or* further	farthest *or* furthest
little	less *or* lesser	least
many	more	most
well	better	best
much	more	most

4.8 PROBLEMS WITH MODIFIERS

Study the tips that follow to avoid common mistakes:

Farther and Further Use *farther* for distances; use *further* for everything else.

Double Comparisons Make a comparison by using *-er/-est* or by using *more/most*. Using *-er* with *more* or using *-est* with *most* is incorrect.

> INCORRECT: *I like her more better than she likes me.*

> CORRECT: *I like her better than she likes me.*

Illogical Comparisons An illogical or confusing comparison results when two unrelated things are compared or when something is compared with itself. The word *other* or the word *else* should be used when comparing an individual member to the rest of a group.

> ILLOGICAL: *The narrator was more curious about the war than any student in his class.* (implies that the narrator isn't a student in the class)

> LOGICAL: *The narrator was more curious about the war than any other student in his class.* (identifies that the narrator is a student)

Bad vs. Badly *Bad*, as an adjective, is used before a noun or after a linking verb. *Badly*, always an adverb, never modifies a noun. Be sure to use the right form after a linking verb.

> INCORRECT: *Ed felt badly after his team lost.*

> CORRECT: *Ed felt bad after his team lost.*

Good vs. Well *Good*, as an adjective, is used before a noun or after a linking verb. *Well* is often an adverb meaning "expertly" or "properly." *Well* can also be used as an adjective after a linking verb when it means "in good health."

> INCORRECT: *Helen writes very good.*

> CORRECT: *Helen writes very well.*

> CORRECT: *Yesterday I felt bad; today I feel well.*

Double Negatives If you add a negative word to a sentence that is already negative, the result will be an error known as a double negative. When using *not* or *-n't* with a verb, use *any-* words, such as *anybody* or *anything*, rather than *no-* words, such as *nobody* or *nothing*, later in the sentence.

> INCORRECT: *We haven't seen nobody.*

> CORRECT: *We haven't seen anybody.*

Using *hardly*, *barely*, or *scarcely* after a negative word is also incorrect.

> INCORRECT: *They couldn't barely see two feet ahead.*

> CORRECT: *They could barely see two feet ahead.*

Misplaced Modifiers Sometimes a modifier is placed so far away from the word it modifies that the intended meaning of the sentence is unclear. Place modifiers as close as possible to the words they modify.

> MISPLACED: *We found the child in the park who was missing.* (The child was missing, not the park.)

> CLEARER: *We found the missing child in the park.*

Dangling Modifiers Sometimes a modifier doesn't appear to modify any word in a sentence. Most dangling modifiers are participial phrases or infinitive phrases.

> DANGLING: *Looking out the window, his brother was seen driving by.*

> CLEARER: *Looking out the window, Josh saw his brother driving by.*

Practice and Apply

Choose the correct word or words from each pair in parentheses.

1. *The House on Mango Street* gives (better, more better) insight into Mexican-American culture than any other book I've read.
2. Sandra Cisneros's family moved so often that she hardly had (any, no) friends.
3. She felt (bad, badly) that she didn't live in a perfect house like the ones she saw on TV.
4. At one time Cisneros didn't think (nothing, anything) was positive about belonging to a different culture.

Practice and Apply

Rewrite each sentence that contains a misplaced or dangling modifier. Write "correct" if the sentence is written correctly.

1. The house on Loomis Street belongs to Esperanza's family with the broken water pipes.
2. Esperanza has to carry water from the house in empty milk jugs.
3. A nun asks Esperanza from the convent where she lives.
4. Feeling bad about the nun's reaction, the house is no longer good enough for Esperanza.

5 The Sentence and Its Parts

A **sentence** is a group of words used to express a complete thought. A complete sentence has a subject and a predicate.

5.1 KINDS OF SENTENCES

There are four basic types of sentences.

Type	Definition	Example
Declarative	states a fact, a wish, an intent, or a feeling	Joan Bauer understands youths.

continued

Type	Definition	Example
Interrogative	asks a question	Did you read "Pancakes"?
Imperative	gives a command or direction	Read the story.
Exclamatory	expresses strong feeling or excitement	The story is funny!

5.2 COMPOUND SUBJECTS AND PREDICATES

A compound subject consists of two or more subjects that share the same verb. They are typically joined by the coordinating conjunction *and* or *or*.

> EXAMPLE: *A short story or novel will keep you engaged.*

A compound predicate consists of two or more predicates that share the same subject. They too are typically joined by a coordinating conjunction, usually *and, but,* or *or*.

> EXAMPLE: *The class finished all the poetry but did not read the short stories.*

5.3 COMPLEMENTS

A **complement** is a word or group of words that completes the meaning of the sentence. Some sentences contain only a subject and a verb. Most sentences, however, require additional words placed after the verb to complete the meaning of the sentence. There are three kinds of complements: direct objects, indirect objects, and subject complements.

Direct objects are words or word groups that receive the action of action verbs. A direct object answers the question *what* or *whom*.

> EXAMPLES: *The students asked many questions.* (Asked what?)
>
> *The teacher quickly answered the students.* (Answered whom?)

L1

PRACTICE AND APPLY
Answers:
1. *better*
2. *any*
3. *bad*
4. *anything*

PRACTICE AND APPLY
Answers:
1. *The house with the broken water pipes on Loomis Street belongs to Esperanza's family.*
2. *correct*
3. *A nun from the convent asks Esperanza where she lives.*
4. *Feeling bad about the nun's reaction, Esperanza no longer thinks the house is good enough.*

PRACTICE AND APPLY
Possible answers:

1. *The man who lives next door hit another car on his drive to work.*

2. *The extremely spicy gumbo set my mouth on fire.*

3. *A loud crashing noise awakened her in the middle of the night.*

4. *My cousin borrowed my aunt's brand new car without asking for permission to use it.*

5. *Before he left for Europe, my best friend called me from the airport.*

Indirect objects tell to whom or what or for whom or what the actions of verbs are performed. Indirect objects come before direct objects. In the examples that follow, the indirect objects are highlighted.

> EXAMPLES: *My sister usually gave her friends good advice.* (Gave to whom?)
>
> *Her brother sent the store a heavy package.* (Sent to what?)

Subject complements come after linking verbs and identify or describe the subjects. A subject complement that names or identifies a subject is called a **predicate nominative**. Predicate nominatives include **predicate nouns** and **predicate pronouns.**

> EXAMPLES: *My friends are very hard workers.*
>
> *The best writer in the class is she.*

A subject complement that describes a subject is called a predicate adjective.

> EXAMPLE: *The pianist appeared very energetic.*

6 Phrases

A **phrase** is a group of related words that does not contain a subject and a predicate but functions in a sentence as a single part of speech.

6.1 NOUN PHRASES

A **noun phrase** includes a noun and the modifiers that distinguish it. Modifiers might come before or after the noun.

> EXAMPLES: *The record-breaking quarterback led his team to the state championship game.*
>
> *The quarterback who threw four interceptions in one game was traded to another team.*

In these examples, the noun *quarterback* is modified by *record-breaking* and *who threw four interceptions in one game.* The noun and its modifiers form the noun phrase.

Practice and Apply

Add a modifier to at least one noun in each of the following sentences to create a noun phrase.

1. The man hit another car on his drive to work.
2. The gumbo set my mouth on fire.
3. A noise awakened her in the middle of the night.
4. My cousin borrowed my aunt's car without asking for permission to use it.
5. Before he left for Europe, my friend called me from the airport.

6.2 VERB PHRASES

A **verb phrase** consists of at least one main verb and one or more helping verbs. A helping verb (also called an auxiliary verb) helps the main verb express action or state of being.

Besides all forms of the verb *be,* some common helping verbs are *can, could, did, do, does, had, have, may, might, must, shall, should, will,* and *would.*

> EXAMPLE: *She should think about her future.*

Sometimes the parts of a verb phrase are interrupted by other parts of speech.

> EXAMPLE: *She had always been thinking about her future.*

In this example, the adverb *always* interrupts the verb phrase *had been thinking.*

The word *not* is an adverb. It is never part of a verb phrase, even when it is joined to a verb as the contraction *–n't.*

> EXAMPLES: *She should not have lifted that rock.*
>
> *She shouldn't have lifted that rock.*

Rewrite each sentence to include a helping verb.

1. His physical therapist designed an exercise program for him.
2. Before exercising he spends at least five minutes warming up.
3. When lifting heavy objects, he wears a back brace.
4. The doctor reminds him of proper lifting techniques at every check-up.
5. Without physical therapy, healing is often difficult.

6.3 PREPOSITIONAL PHRASES

A **prepositional phrase** is a phrase that consists of a preposition, its object, and any modifiers of the object. Prepositional phrases that modify nouns or pronouns are called **adjective phrases.** Prepositional phrases that modify verbs, adjectives, or adverbs are **adverb phrases.**

> ADJECTIVE PHRASE: *The central character of the story is a villain.*

> ADVERB PHRASE: *He reveals his nature in the first scene.*

Remember that adjectives modify nouns by telling which one, what kind, how much, or how many. Adverbs modify verbs, adjectives, and other adverbs by telling where, when, how, or to what extent. The same is true of prepositional phrases that act as adjective phrases or adverb phrases.

Practice and Apply

Identify the prepositional phrases and the words they modify in the following sentences. State whether the prepositional phrase is an adjective phrase or an adverb phrase.

1. A daily newspaper has something for almost everyone.
2. Our entire family reads the newspaper in the morning.
3. Dad always begins with the sports page; Mom prefers the national news.

continued

Practice and Apply

4. My sister's favorite part of the newspaper is the lifestyle section.
5. She enjoys features like "How-to Hints."

6.4 APPOSITIVES AND APPOSITIVE PHRASES

An **appositive** is a noun or pronoun that identifies or renames another noun or pronoun. An **appositive phrase** includes an appositive and modifiers of it.

An appositive can be either **essential** or **nonessential.** An **essential appositive** provides information that is needed to identify what is referred to by the preceding noun or pronoun.

> EXAMPLE: *The book is about the author Richard Wright.*

A **nonessential appositive** adds extra information about a noun or pronoun whose meaning is already clear. Nonessential appositives and appositive phrases are set off with commas.

> EXAMPLE: *The book, an autobiography, tells how he began writing.*

7 Verbals and Verbal Phrases

A **verbal** is a verb form that is used as a noun, an adjective, or an adverb. A **verbal phrase** consists of a verbal along with its modifiers and complements. There are three kinds of verbals: **infinitives, participles,** and **gerunds.**

7.1 INFINITIVES AND INFINITIVE PHRASES

An **infinitive** is a verb form that usually begins with *to* and functions as a noun, an adjective, or an adverb. An **infinitive phrase** consists of an infinitive plus its modifiers and complements. The examples that follow show several uses of infinitive phrases.

> NOUN: *To know her is my only desire.* (subject)

> I'm *planning to walk with you.* (direct object)

L 1b

PRACTICE AND APPLY
Possible answers:
1. *His physical therapist has designed an exercise program for him.*
2. *Before exercising he should spend at least five minutes warming up.*
3. *When lifting heavy objects, he does wear a back brace.*
4. *The doctor will remind him of proper lifting techniques at every check-up.*
5. *Without physical therapy, healing would be difficult.*

PRACTICE AND APPLY
Answers:
1. *"for almost everyone"; modifies "something"; adjective phrase*
2. *"in the morning"; modifies "reads"; adverb phrase*
3. *"with the sports page"; modifies "begins"; adverb phrase*
4. *"of the newspaper"; modifies "part"; adjective phrase*
5. *"like 'How-to Hints'" modifies "features"; adjective phrase*

PRACTICE AND APPLY

Answers:

1. *"standing tall"; modifies "skyscrapers"*
2. *"supporting the walls and floors"; modifies "skeleton"*
3. *"destroyed by fire"; modifies "Chicago"*
4. *"constructed on a metal frame"; modifies "skyscraper"*
5. *"using the latest material"; modifies "architects"*

ADJECTIVE: *We saw his need to be loved.* (adjective modifying need)

ADVERB: *She wrote to voice her opinions.* (adverb modifying wrote)

Because *to,* the sign of the infinitive, precedes infinitives, it is usually easy to recognize them. However, sometimes *to* may be omitted.

EXAMPLE: *Let no one dare [to] enter this shrine.*

7.2 PARTICIPLES AND PARTICIPIAL PHRASES

A **participle** is a verb form that functions as an adjective. Like adjectives, participles modify nouns and pronouns. Most participles are present-participle forms, ending in *-ing,* or past-participle forms ending in *-ed* or *-en.* In the examples below, the participles are highlighted.

MODIFYING A NOUN: *The dying man had a smile on his face.*

MODIFYING A PRONOUN: *Frustrated, everyone abandoned the cause.*

Participial phrases are participles with all their modifiers and complements.

MODIFYING A NOUN: *The dogs searching for survivors are well trained.*

MODIFYING A PRONOUN: *Having approved your proposal, we are ready to act.*

Practice and Apply

Identify the participial phrases in the following sentences, and indicate which word each phrase modifies.

1. How are skyscrapers created, and what keeps them standing tall?
2. From this foundation rises a steel skeleton, supporting the walls and floors.
3. Chicago, nearly destroyed by fire in 1871, was later rebuilt with innovative designs.
4. The first skyscraper constructed on a metal frame was built there during this period.
5. Architects, using the latest materials, were glad to design in new ways.

7.3 DANGLING AND MISPLACED PARTICIPLES

A participle or participial phrase should be placed as close as possible to the word that it modifies. Otherwise the meaning of the sentence may not be clear.

MISPLACED: *The boys were looking for squirrels searching the trees.*

CLEARER: *The boys searching the trees were looking for squirrels.*

A participle or participial phrase that does not clearly modify anything in a sentence is called a dangling participle. A **dangling participle** causes confusion because it appears to modify a word that it cannot sensibly modify. Correct a dangling participle by providing a word for the participle to modify.

DANGLING: *Running like the wind, my hat fell off.* (The hat wasn't running.)

CLEARER: *Running like the wind, I lost my hat.*

7.4 GERUNDS AND GERUND PHRASES

A gerund is a verb form ending in *-ing* that functions as a noun. Gerunds may perform any function nouns perform.

SUBJECT: *Running is my favorite pastime.*

DIRECT OBJECT: *I truly love running.*

INDIRECT OBJECT: *You should give running a try.*

SUBJECT COMPLEMENT: *My deepest passion is running.*

OBJECT OF PREPOSITION: *Her love of running keeps her strong.*

Gerund phrases are gerunds with all their modifiers and complements.

SUBJECT: *Wishing on a star never got me far.*

OBJECT OF PREPOSITION: *I will finish before leaving the office.*

APPOSITIVE: *Her avocation, flying airplanes, finally led to full-time employment.*

Rewrite each sentence, adding the phrase shown in parentheses.

1. "Daughter of Invention" was written by Julia Alvarez. (a short story)
2. The narrator loves writing. (to record her experiences)
3. She will appear at an assembly. (to give a speech)
4. She finally finishes her speech. (working feverishly for hours)
5. She reads her speech to her parents. (feeling proud)

7.5 ABSOLUTE PHRASES

An **absolute phrase** is a noun or pronoun, its participle, and any modifiers. It modifies an entire sentence, or independent clause, rather than just one word.

> EXAMPLE: *The theater buzzing with excitement, the crowd waited for the band to take the stage.*

In this example, *The theater buzzing with excitement* is an absolute phrase that modifies the sentence *the crowd waited for the band to take the stage.* The noun *theater* is modified by the participle *buzzing* and by the prepositional phrase *with excitement.* Notice that a comma separates the absolute phrase from the sentence, or independent clause.

Add an absolute phrase to modify each sentence. With a partner, discuss how the additions improve the original sentences.

1. The kids ate the entire bowl of oranges.
2. The sun set beyond the sparkling lake.
3. The board of directors rejected her proposal.
4. He decided to join the drama club.
5. We ran through the field of tall grass.

8 Clauses

A **clause** is a group of words that contains a subject and a predicate. There are two kinds of clauses: independent clauses and subordinate clauses.

8.1 INDEPENDENT AND SUBORDINATE CLAUSES

An **independent clause** can stand alone as a sentence, as the word *independent* suggests.

> INDEPENDENT CLAUSE: *Taos is famous for its Great Bank Robbery.*

A sentence may contain more than one independent clause.

> EXAMPLE: *Many people remember the robbery, and they will tell you all about it.*

In the preceding example, the coordinating conjunction *and* joins two independent clauses.

Two independent clauses can also be joined with a **conjunctive adverb,** such as *consequently, finally, furthermore, however, moreover,* or *nevertheless.* To separate the two independent clauses, a semicolon is used before the conjunctive adverb.

> EXAMPLE: *The painter decided to take up sculpture; however, his studio was not big enough for large projects using granite.*

A **subordinate clause,** or dependent clause, cannot stand alone as a sentence. It is subordinate to, or dependent on, an independent clause.

> EXAMPLE: *Although the two men needed cash, they didn't get it from the bank.*

The highlighted clause cannot stand by itself.

Identify each italicized clause in the following sentences as independent or subordinate (dependent). Then explain your answers.

1. The fire started *because someone did not smother a campfire.*
2. *The family that bought our house* is moving next week.
3. *Since she had practiced diligently,* she won the golf match.
4. Wherever Maggie goes, *her golden retriever Hopper follows her.*
5. According to our math teacher, *the binary system is important to know.*

L 1b

PRACTICE AND APPLY
Answers:

1. *"Daughter of Invention," a short story, was written by Julia Alvarez.*
2. *The narrator loves writing to record her experiences.*
3. *She will appear at an assembly to give a speech.*
4. *Working feverishly for hours, she finally finishes her speech.*
5. *Feeling proud, she reads her speech to her parents.*

PRACTICE AND APPLY
Possible answers:

6. *With soccer practice over for the day, the kids ate the entire bowl of oranges.*
7. *The sun set beyond the sparkling lake, the storm having passed over the area.*
8. *The board of directors, stating its budget had been cut, rejected her proposal.*
9. *The semester having just started, he decided to join the drama club.*
10. *We ran through the field of tall grass, our bare feet crushing the blades beneath us.*

PRACTICE AND APPLY
Answers:

1. *subordinate; cannot stand alone*
2. *subordinate; cannot stand alone*
3. *subordinate; cannot stand alone*
4. *independent; is a complete sentence by itself*
5. *independent; is a complete sentence by itself*

PRACTICE AND APPLY

Possible answers:

1. *As I entered the building, a painting, which was full of vibrant reds and blues, caught my eye.*

2. *The photographer, who was used to waiting for the dolphins to appear in the waves, sat on a small ledge all day.*

3. *The two attorneys argued over the contract that could change their clients' lives forever.*

4. *At the assembly, Ms. Baily made two announcements about the junior prom that surprised everyone.*

5. *Saburo and his friends cautiously entered the cave, which was dark and full of spiders.*

PRACTICE AND APPLY

Answers:

1. *"through the newspapers from the first half of the twentieth century"; tells where*

2. *"wherever he went"; tells where*

3. *"because he viewed spinning as a symbol of the peaceful, traditional Indian lifestyle"; tells why*

4. *"so that they would not have to depend on British industries"; tells why*

5. *"until the government met his demands"; tells under what condition*

8.2 ADJECTIVE CLAUSES

An **adjective clause,** or relative clause, is a subordinate clause used as an adjective. It usually follows the noun or pronoun it modifies.

> EXAMPLE: *Tony Hillerman is someone whom millions know as a mystery writer.*

Adjective clauses are typically introduced by the relative pronoun *who, whom, whose, which,* or *that.*

For more information, see **Relative Pronouns**, page R31.

> EXAMPLES: *A person who needs money should get a job.*
>
> *The robbers, whose names were Gomez and Smith, entered the bank.*

An adjective clause can be either essential or nonessential. An **essential adjective clause** provides information that is necessary to identify the preceding noun or pronoun.

> EXAMPLE: *One robber wore a disguise that was meant to fool Taos's residents.*

A **nonessential adjective clause** adds additional information about a noun or pronoun whose meaning is already clear. Nonessential clauses are set off with commas.

> EXAMPLE: *The suspects, who drove away in a pickup truck, sideswiped a car driven by a minister.*

TIP The relative pronouns *whom, which,* and *that* may sometimes be omitted when they are objects in adjective clauses.

> EXAMPLE: *Hillerman is a writer [whom] millions enjoy.*

Practice and Apply

Revise the following sentences by substituting an adjective clause (relative clause) for each italicized adjective. Add specific details to make the sentences more interesting.

1. As I entered the building, a *colorful* painting caught my eye.
2. The *patient* photographer sat on a small ledge all day.

---

continued

Practice and Apply

3. The two attorneys argued over the *important* contract.
4. At the assembly, Ms. Bailey made two *surprising* announcements.
5. Saburo and his friends cautiously entered the *dark* cave.

8.3 ADVERB CLAUSES

An **adverb clause** is a subordinate clause that is used to modify a verb, an adjective, or an adverb. It is introduced by a subordinating conjunction.

Adverb clauses typically occur at the beginning or end of sentences.

> MODIFYING A VERB: *When we need you, we will call.*
>
> MODIFYING AN ADVERB: *I'll stay here where there is shelter from the rain.*
>
> MODIFYING AN ADJECTIVE: *Roman felt as good as he had ever felt.*

Practice and Apply

Identify each adverb clause in the following sentences. Then write what the clause tells: *when, where, why, how, to what extent,* or *under what condition.*

1. If you look through the newspapers from the first half of the twentieth century, you will see many pictures of Mohandas K. Gandhi.
2. This man led India to independence from Britain, and he took his spinning wheel wherever he went.
3. He did so because he viewed spinning as a symbol of the peaceful, traditional Indian lifestyle.
4. He also hoped to encourage the Indian people to make their own clothes so that they would not have to depend on British industries.
5. As a form of protest, Gandhi led marches or fasted until the government met his demands.

8.4 NOUN CLAUSES

A **noun clause** is a subordinate clause that is used as a noun. A noun clause may be used as a subject, a direct object, an indirect object, a predicate nominative, or the object of a preposition. Noun clauses are introduced either by pronouns, such as *that, what, who, whoever, which,* and *whose,* or by subordinating conjunctions, such as *how, when, where, why,* and *whether.*

TIP Because the same words may introduce adjective and noun clauses, you need to consider how a clause functions within its sentence. To determine if a clause is a noun clause, try substituting *something* or *someone* for the clause. If you can do it, it is probably a noun clause.

EXAMPLE: *I know whose woods these are.* ("I know *something*." The clause is a noun clause, direct object of the verb *know.*)

Practice and Apply

Identify the noun clause in each sentence. Then tell how the clause is used: as a subject, a predicate nominative, a direct object, an indirect object, or an object of a preposition.

1. We moved to Massachusetts and did not know what we would find there.
2. What surprised me first were the yellowish green fire engines.
3. Our neighbors explained that this color keeps the fire engines from being confused with other large red trucks.
4. Write your research paper about whomever you admire most.
5. The small grapefruit-sized bowling balls with no finger holes were not what she usually used.

Practice and Apply

Add descriptive details to each sentence by writing the type of clause indicated in parentheses.

1. My aunt has an interesting hobby. (adjective clause)
2. She works on her craft at night. (adverb clause)

continued

Practice and Apply

3. She writes. (noun clause)
4. She has written several books. (adjective clause)
5. I asked her to write a story about me. (adverb clause)

9 The Structure of Sentences

When classified by their structure, there are four kinds of sentences: simple, compound, complex, and compound-complex.

9.1 SIMPLE SENTENCES

A **simple sentence** is a sentence that has one independent clause and no subordinate clauses. The fact that such a sentence is called simple does not mean that it is uncomplicated. Various parts of simple sentences may be compound, and simple sentences may contain grammatical structures such as appositive and verbal phrases.

EXAMPLES: *Ray Bradbury, a science fiction writer, has written short stories and novels.* (appositive and compound direct object)

The narrator, recalling the years of his childhood, tells his story. (participial phrase)

9.2 COMPOUND SENTENCES

A **compound sentence** consists of two or more independent clauses. The clauses in compound sentences are joined with commas and coordinating conjunctions (*and, but, or, nor, yet, for, so*) or with semicolons. Like simple sentences, compound sentences do not contain any subordinate clauses.

EXAMPLES: *I enjoyed Bradbury's story "The Utterly Perfect Murder," and I want to read more of his stories.*

The narrator has lived a normal, complete life; however, he decides to kill his childhood playmate.

L 1b

PRACTICE AND APPLY
Answers:

1. *"what we would find there"; direct object*
2. *"what surprised me first"; subject*
3. *"that this color keeps the trucks from being confused with other large red trucks"; direct object*
4. *"about whomever you admire most"; object of a preposition*
5. *"what she usually used"; predicate nominative*

PRACTICE AND APPLY
Answers:

1. *My aunt who lives in Denver has an interesting hobby.*
2. *She works on her craft at night after her children have gone to bed.*
3. *She writes about how the American West was settled.*
4. *She has written several books that have been published.*
5. *I asked her to write a story about me while she is visiting us.*

WATCH OUT! Do not confuse compound sentences with simple sentences that have compound parts.

> EXAMPLE: *A subcommittee drafted a document and immediately presented it to the entire group.* (Here *and* joins parts of a compound predicate, not a compound sentence.)

9.3 COMPLEX SENTENCES

A **complex sentence** consists of one independent clause and one or more subordinate clauses. Each subordinate clause can be used as a noun or as a modifier. If it is used as a modifier, a subordinate clause usually modifies a word in the independent clause, and the independent clause can stand alone. However, when a subordinate clause is a noun clause, it is a part of the independent clause; the two cannot be separated.

> MODIFIER: *One should not complain unless one has a better solution.*

> NOUN CLAUSE: *We sketched pictures of whomever we wished.* (The noun clause is the object of the preposition *of* and cannot be separated from the rest of the sentence.)

9.4 COMPOUND-COMPLEX SENTENCES

A **compound-complex sentence** contains two or more independent clauses and one or more subordinate clauses. Compound-complex sentences are, simply, both compound and complex. If you start with a compound sentence, all you need to do to form a compound-complex sentence is add a subordinate clause.

> COMPOUND: *All the students knew the answer, yet they were too shy to volunteer.*

> COMPOUND-COMPLEX: *All the students knew the answer that their teacher expected, yet they were too shy to volunteer.*

9.5 PARALLEL STRUCTURE

When you write sentences, make sure that coordinate parts are equivalent, or **parallel,** in structure.

> NOT PARALLEL: *Erin loved basketball and to play hockey.* (*Basketball* is a noun; *to play hockey* is a phrase.)

> PARALLEL: *Erin loved basketball and hockey.* (*Basketball* and *hockey* are both nouns.)

> NOT PARALLEL: *He wanted to rent an apartment, a new car, and traveling around the country.* (*To rent* is an infinitive, *car* is a noun, and *traveling* is a gerund.)

> PARALLEL: *He wanted to rent an apartment, to drive a new car, and to travel around the country.* (*To rent, to drive,* and *to travel* are all infinitives.)

10 Writing Complete Sentences

Remember, a sentence is a group of words that expresses a complete thought. In writing that you wish to share with a reader, try to avoid both sentence fragments and run-on sentences.

10.1 CORRECTING FRAGMENTS

A **sentence fragment** is a group of words that is only part of a sentence. It does not express a complete thought and may be confusing to a reader or listener. A sentence fragment may be lacking a subject, a predicate, or both.

> FRAGMENT: *Waited for the boat to arrive.* (no subject)

> CORRECTED: *We waited for the boat to arrive.*

> FRAGMENT: *People of various races, ages, and creeds.* (no predicate)

> CORRECTED: *People of various races, ages, and creeds gathered together.*

> FRAGMENT: *Near the old cottage.* (neither subject nor predicate)

> CORRECTED: *The burial ground is near the old cottage.*

In your writing, fragments may be a result of haste or incorrect punctuation. Sometimes fixing a fragment will be a matter of attaching it to a preceding or following sentence.

FRAGMENT: *We saw the two girls. Waiting for the bus to arrive.*

CORRECTED: *We saw the two girls waiting for the bus to arrive.*

10.2 CORRECTING RUN-ON SENTENCES

A **run-on sentence** is made up of two or more sentences written as though they were one. Some run-ons have no punctuation within them. Others may have only commas where conjunctions or stronger punctuation marks are necessary. Use your judgment in correcting run-on sentences, as you have choices. You can make a run-on two sentences if the thoughts are not closely connected. If the thoughts are closely related, you can keep the run-on as one sentence by adding a semicolon or a conjunction.

RUN-ON: *We found a place for the picnic by a small pond it was three miles from the village.*

MAKE TWO SENTENCES: *We found a place for the picnic by a small pond. It was three miles from the village.*

RUN-ON: *We found a place for the picnic by a small pond it was perfect.*

USE A SEMICOLON: *We found a place for the picnic by a small pond; it was perfect.*

ADD A CONJUNCTION: *We found a place for the picnic by a small pond, and it was perfect.*

WATCH OUT! When you form compound sentences, make sure you use appropriate punctuation: a comma before a coordinating conjunction, a semicolon when there is no coordinating conjunction. A very common mistake is to use a comma alone instead of a comma and a conjunction. This error is called a **comma splice.**

INCORRECT: *He finished the apprenticeship, he left the village.*

CORRECT: *He finished the apprenticeship, and he left the village.*

11 Subject-Verb Agreement

The subject and verb in a clause must agree in number. Agreement means that if the subject is singular, the verb is also singular, and if the subject is plural, the verb is also plural.

11.1 BASIC AGREEMENT

Fortunately, agreement between subjects and verbs in English is simple. Most verbs show the difference between singular and plural only in the third person of the present tense. In the present tense, the third-person singular form ends in *-s.*

Present-Tense Verb Forms	
Singular	**Plural**
I sleep	we sleep
you sleep	you sleep
she, he, it sleeps	they sleep

11.2 AGREEMENT WITH *BE*

The verb *be* presents special problems in agreement, because this verb does not follow the usual verb patterns.

Forms of *Be*			
Present Tense		**Past Tense**	
Singular	**Plural**	**Singular**	**Plural**
I am	we are	I was	we were
you are	you are	you were	you were
she, he, it is	they are	she, he, it was	they were

11.3 WORDS BETWEEN SUBJECT AND VERB

A verb agrees only with its subject. When words come between a subject and a verb, ignore them when considering proper agreement. Identify the subject, and make sure the verb agrees with it.

EXAMPLES: *A story in the newspapers tells about the 1890s.*

Dad as well as Mom reads the paper daily.

11.4 AGREEMENT WITH COMPOUND SUBJECTS

Use plural verbs with most compound subjects joined by the word *and*.

EXAMPLE: *My father and his friends read the paper daily.*

To confirm that you need a plural verb, you could substitute the plural pronoun *they* for *my father and his friends.*

If a compound subject is thought of as a unit, use a singular verb. Test this by substituting the singular pronoun *it.*

EXAMPLE: *Peanut butter and jelly [it] is my brother's favorite sandwich.*

Use a singular verb with a compound subject that is preceded by *each, every,* or *many a.*

EXAMPLE: *Each novel and short story seems grounded in personal experience.*

When the parts of a compound subject are joined by *or, nor,* or the correlative conjunctions *either . . . or* or *neither . . . nor,* make the verb agree with the noun or pronoun nearest the verb.

EXAMPLES: *Cookies or ice cream is my favorite dessert.*

Either Cheryl or her friends are being invited. Neither ice storms nor snow is predicted today.

11.5 PERSONAL PRONOUNS AS SUBJECTS

When using a personal pronoun as a subject, make sure to match it with the correct form of the verb **be.** (See the chart in Section 11.2.) Note especially that the pronoun *you* takes the forms *are* and *were,* regardless of whether it is singular or plural.

WATCH OUT! *You is* and *you was* are nonstandard forms and should be avoided in writing and speaking. *We was* and *they was* are also forms to be avoided.

INCORRECT: *You was a good student.*

CORRECT: *You were a good student.*

INCORRECT: *They was starting a new school.*

CORRECT: *They were starting a new school.*

11.6 INDEFINITE PRONOUNS AS SUBJECTS

Some indefinite pronouns are always singular; some are always plural.

Singular Indefinite Pronouns			
another	either	neither	one
anybody	everbody	nobody	some-body
anyone	everyone	no one	some-one
anything	every-thing	nothing	some-thing
each	much		

EXAMPLES: *Each of the writers was given an award. Somebody in the room upstairs is sleeping.*

Plural Indefinite Pronouns			
both	few	many	several

EXAMPLES: *Many of the books in our library are not in circulation.*

Few have been returned recently.

Still other indefinite pronouns may be either singular or plural.

Singular or Plural Indefinite Pronouns		
all	more	none
any	most	some

The number of the indefinite pronoun *any* or *none* often depends on the intended meaning.

EXAMPLES: *Any of these topics has potential for a good article.* (any one topic)

Any of these topics have potential for good articles. (all of the many topics)

The indefinite pronouns *all, some, more, most,* and *none* are singular when they refer to quantities or parts of things. They are plural when they refer to numbers of individual things. Context will usually give a clue.

EXAMPLES: *All of the flour is gone.* (referring to a quantity)

All of the flowers are gone. (referring to individual items)

11.7 INVERTED SENTENCES

Problems in agreement often occur in inverted sentences beginning with *here* or *there*; in questions beginning with *how, when, why, where,* or *what*; and in inverted sentences beginning with phrases. Identify the subject—wherever it is—before deciding on the verb.

> EXAMPLES: *There clearly are far too many cooks in this kitchen.*
>
> *Far from the embroiled cooks stands the master chef.*

Practice and Apply

Locate the subject of each verb in parentheses in the sentences below. Then choose the correct verb form.

1. Many Greeks sail home from Troy, but few (struggles, struggle) as hard as Odysseus to get there.
2. Neither Odysseus nor his men (know, knows) what dangers lie ahead.
3. There (is, are) more dangers awaiting him than there (is, are) gods to save him.
4. Everybody who has read about Odysseus' trials (knows, know) what he endured.
5. There (is, are) few friends who can help him during his ten-year odyssey.

11.8 SENTENCES WITH PREDICATE NOMINATIVES

When a predicate nominative serves as a complement in a sentence, use a verb that agrees with the subject, not the complement.

> EXAMPLES: *The speeches of Martin Luther King Jr. are a landmark in American civil rights history.* (*Speeches* is the subject and it takes the plural verb *are.*)
>
> *One landmark in American civil rights history is the speeches of Martin Luther King Jr.* (The subject is *landmark* and it takes the singular verb *is.*)

11.9 *DON'T* AND *DOESN'T* AS AUXILIARY VERBS

The auxiliary verb *doesn't* is used with singular subjects and with the personal pronouns *she, he,* and *it.* The auxiliary verb *don't* is used with plural subjects and with the personal pronouns *I, we, you,* and *they.*

> SINGULAR: *She doesn't know Martin Luther King's famous "I Have a Dream" speech.*
>
> *Doesn't the young woman read very much?*
>
> PLURAL: *We don't have the speech memorized. Don't speakers usually memorize their speeches?*

11.10 COLLECTIVE NOUNS AS SUBJECTS

Collective nouns are singular nouns that name groups of persons or things. *Team,* for example, is the collective name of a group of individuals. A collective noun takes a singular verb when the group acts as a single unit. It takes a plural verb when the members of the group act separately.

> EXAMPLES: *Our team usually wins.* (The team as a whole wins.)
>
> *Our team vote differently on most issues.* (The individual members vote.)

11.11 RELATIVE PRONOUNS AS SUBJECTS

When the relative pronoun *who, which,* or *that* is used as a subject in an adjective clause, the verb in the clause must agree in number with the antecedent of the pronoun.

> SINGULAR: *I didn't read the **poem** about fireworks that was assigned.*

The antecedent of the relative pronoun *that* is the singular **poem**; therefore, *that* is singular and must take the singular verb *was.*

> PLURAL: ***William Blake and Amy Lowell**, who are very different from each other, are both outstanding poets.*

The antecedent of the relative pronoun *who* is the plural compound subject *William Blake and Amy Lowell.* Therefore *who* is plural, and it takes the plural verb *are.*

L 1b

PRACTICE AND APPLY
Answers:
1. *struggle*
2. *know*
3. *are; are*
4. *knows*
5. *are*

Vocabulary and Spelling

The key to becoming an independent reader is to develop a toolkit of vocabulary strategies. By learning and practicing the strategies, you'll know what to do when you encounter unfamiliar words while reading. You'll also know how to refine the words you use for different situations—personal, school, and work.

Being a good speller is important when communicating your ideas in writing. Learning basic spelling rules and checking your spelling in a dictionary will help you spell words that you may not use frequently.

1 Using Context Clues

The context of a word is made up of the punctuation marks, words, sentences, and paragraphs that surround it. A word's context can give you important clues about its meaning, including both its denotation and connotation.

1.1 GENERAL CONTEXT

Sometimes you need to infer the meaning of a word by reading all the information in a passage.

After twelve hours without food, I was so ravenous that I ate seven slices of pizza.

You can figure out from the context that *ravenous* means "extremely hungry."

1.2 SPECIFIC CONTEXT CLUES

Sometimes writers help you understand the meanings of words by providing specific clues such as those shown in the chart.

Specific Context Clues		
Type of Clue	**Key Words/Phrases**	**Example**
Definition or restatement of the meaning of the word	or, which is, that is, in other words, also known as, also called	His first conjecture, **or guess,** was correct.
Example following an unfamiliar word	such as, like, as if, for example, especially, including	She loved macabre stories, **such as those by Edgar Allan Poe and Stephen King.**
Comparison with a more familiar word or concept	as, like, also, similar to, in the same way, likewise	Despite his physical suffering, his mind was as **lucid** as any **rational** person's.
Contrast with a familiar word or experience	unlike, but, however, although, on the other hand, on the contrary	Unlike her **clumsy** partner, she was an **agile** dancer.
Cause-and-effect relationship in which one term is familiar	because, since, when, consequently, as a result, therefore	Because this perfume has such a **sharp** scent, I will buy the one with a **subtle** fragrance.

1.3 IDIOMS, SLANG, AND FIGURATIVE LANGUAGE

An **idiom** is an expression whose overall meaning is different from the meaning of the individual words. **Slang** is informal language in which made-up words and ordinary words are used to mean something different from their meanings in formal English. **Figurative language** is language that communicates meaning beyond the literal meaning of the words. Use context clues to figure out the meanings of idioms, slang, and figurative language.

> The mosquitoes *drove us crazy* on our hike through the woods. (idiom; means "bothered")
>
> That's a really *cool* backpack that you're wearing. (slang; means "excellent" or "first-rate")
>
> I was angry. *Heat rose under my skin* until I felt as if *searing flames* were threatening to engulf my whole body. (figurative language; hot skin and flames symbolize anger)

2 Analyzing Word Structure

Many words can be broken into smaller parts. These word parts include base words, roots, prefixes, and suffixes.

2.1 BASE WORDS

A **base word** is a word part that by itself is also a word. Other words or word parts can be added to base words to form new words.

2.2 ROOTS

A **root** is a word part that contains the core meaning of the word. Many English words contain roots that come from older languages such as Greek, Latin, Old English (Anglo-Saxon), and Norse. Knowing the meaning of the word's root can help you determine the word's meaning.

Root	Meaning	Examples
bi (Greek)	life	biography
gramm (Greek)	letter, something written	grammar
grad (Latin)	step, degree	graduate
man (Latin)	hand	manual
hēadfod (Old English)	head, top	headfirst

2.3 PREFIXES

A **prefix** is a word part attached to the beginning of a word. Most prefixes come from Greek, Latin, or Old English.

Prefix	Meaning	Examples
pre-	before	**pre**school
ex-	out, from	**ex**tend
re-	again, back	**re**turn

2.4 SUFFIXES

A **suffix** is a word part that appears at the end of a root or base word to form a new word. Some suffixes do not change word meaning. These suffixes are

- added to nouns to change the number of persons or objects
- added to verbs to change the tense
- added to modifiers to change the degree of comparison

Suffix	Meaning	Examples
-s, -es	to change the number of a noun	snack + s = snacks
-d, -ed, -ing	to change verb tense	walk + ed = walked
-er, -est	to change the degree of comparison in modifiers	wild + er = wilder fast + est = fastest

Other suffixes can be added to a root or base to change the word's meaning. These suffixes can also determine a word's part of speech.

Suffix	Meaning	Examples
-age	action or process	pilgrimage
-able	ability	enjoyable
-ize	to make	criticize

Strategies for Understanding Unfamiliar Words

- Look for any prefixes or suffixes. Remove them to isolate the base word or the root.
- See if you recognize any elements—prefix, suffix, root, or base—of the word. You may be able to guess its meaning by analyzing one or two elements.
- Consider the way the word is used in the sentence. Use the context and the word parts to make a logical guess about the word's meaning.
- Consult a dictionary to see whether you are correct.

3 Understanding Word Origins

3.1 ETYMOLOGIES

Etymologies show the origin and historical development of a word. When you study a word's history and origin, you can find out when, where, and how the word came to be.

dra•ma (drä´mə) *n.* **1.** A work that is meant to be performed by actors. **2.** Theatrical works of a certain type or period in history. [Late Latin *drāma*, *drāmat-*, from Greek *drān*, to do or perform.]

for•mi•car•y (fôr´mǐ-kěr´ē) *n., pl.* **-ies** A nest of ants; an anthill. [Medieval Latin *formīcārium*, from Latin *formīca*, ant.]

lock² (lŏk) *n.* **1a.** A length or curl of hair; a tress. **b.** The hair of the head. Often used in the plural. **2.** A small wisp or tuft, as of wool or cotton. [Middle English *lok* from Old English *loc, locc*.]

3.2 WORD FAMILIES

Words that have the same root make up a word family and have related meanings. The chart shows a common Greek and a common Latin root. Notice how the meanings of the example words are related to the meanings of their roots.

Latin Root	*vid, vis:* "see"
English	**vision** eyesight **video** visual portion of a televised broadcast **visible** possible to see

Greek Root	*phonē:* "sound"
English	**homophone** word that sounds like another word **phonetics** the study of speech sounds **telephone** a device that converts voice into a form that can be transmitted as sound waves

3.3 WORDS FROM CLASSICAL MYTHOLOGY

The English language includes many words from classical mythology. You can use your knowledge of Greek, Roman, and Norse myths to understand the origins and meanings of these words. For example, *herculean task* refers to the strongman Hercules. Thus *herculean task* probably means "a job that is large or difficult." The chart shows a few common words from mythology.

Greek	Roman	Norse
Achilles' heel	cereal	Thursday
aegis	volcano	berserk
muse	cupid	rune
Midas touch	floral	valkyrie

3.4 FOREIGN WORDS

The English language has grown to include words from diverse languages such as French, Dutch, Spanish, Italian, Portuguese, and Chinese. Many of these words stayed the way they were in their original languages.

French	Dutch	Spanish	Italian
ballet	boss	canyon	diva
beret	caboose	rodeo	carnival
mirage	dock	salsa	spaghetti

4 Synonyms and Antonyms

4.1 SYNONYMS

A **synonym** is a word with a meaning similar to that of another word. You can find synonyms in a thesaurus or a dictionary. In a dictionary, synonyms are often given as part of the definition of the word. The following word pairs are synonyms:

happy/joyful   sad/unhappy

angry/mad   beautiful/lovely

4.2 ANTONYMS

An **antonym** is a word with a meaning opposite that of another word. The following word pairs are antonyms:

best/worst   well/ill

light/dark   happy/sad

5 Denotation and Connotation

5.1 DENOTATION

A word's dictionary meaning is called its **denotation.** For example, the denotation of the word *rascal* is "an unethical, dishonest person."

5.2 CONNOTATION

The images or feelings you connect to a word add a finer shade of meaning, called **connotation.** The connotation of a word goes beyond its basic dictionary definition. Writers use connotations of words to communicate positive or negative feelings.

Positive	Neutral	Negative
gaze	look	glare
slender	thin	scrawny
playful	active	rowdy

Make sure you understand the denotation and connotation of a word when you read it or use it in your writing.

6 Analogies

An analogy is a comparison between two things that are similar in some way. Analogies are sometimes used in writing when unfamiliar objects or ideas are described or explained in terms of familiar ones. Analogies often appear on tests as well, usually in a format like this:

bird : fly :: A) boat : water

B) bear : cave

C) fish : scales

D) fish : swim

E) sparrow : wings

Follow these steps to determine the correct answer:

- Read the first half of the analogy as "*bird* is to *fly* as. . . ."
- Read the answer choices as "*boat* is to *water*," "*bear* is to *cave*," and so on.
- Ask yourself how the words *bird* and *fly* are related. (A bird can fly.)
- Ask yourself which of the choices shows the same relationship. (A boat can't water and a bear can't cave, but a fish can swim. Therefore, the answer is D.)

7 Homonyms and Homophones

7.1 HOMONYMS

Homonyms are words that have the same spelling and sound but have different meanings.

The girl had to stoop to find her ball under the stoop.

Stoop can mean "a small porch," but an identically spelled word means "to bend down." Because the words have different meanings, each word has its own dictionary entry.

The lawyer argued the case of the missing jewelry case.

Case can mean "evidence in support of a claim." However, another identically spelled word means "container." Each word has a different meaning and its own dictionary entry.

Sometimes only one of the meanings of a homonym may be familiar to you. Use context clues to help you figure out the meaning of an unfamiliar word.

7.2 HOMOPHONES

Homophones are words that sound alike but have different meanings and spellings. The following homophones are frequently misused:

it's/its	they're/their/there
to/too/two	stationary/stationery

Many misused homophones are pronouns and contractions. Whenever you are unsure whether to write *your* or *you're* and *who's* or *whose*, ask yourself if you mean *you are* or *who is/has*. If you do, write the contraction. For other homophones, such as *fair* and *fare*, use the meaning of the word to help you decide which one to use.

8 Words with Multiple Meanings

Some words have acquired additional meanings over time that are based on the original meaning.

Thinking of the horror movie made my skin creep. I saw my little brother creep around the corner.

These two uses of *creep* have different meanings, but both of them have the same origin. You will find all the meanings of *creep* listed in one entry in the dictionary.

9 Specialized Vocabulary

Specialized vocabulary is special terms suited to a particular field, or domain, of study or work. For example, science, mathematics, and history all have their own domain-specific technical or specialized vocabularies. To figure out specialized terms, you can use context clues; your knowledge of Latin, Greek, and Old English roots and affixes; and reference sources, such as dictionaries on specific subjects, atlases, or manuals.

10 Using Reference Sources

10.1 DICTIONARIES

A **general dictionary** will tell you not only a word's definitions but also its pronunciation, parts of speech, and history and origin. A **specialized dictionary** focuses on terms related to a particular field of study or work. Use a dictionary to check the spelling of any word you are unsure of in your English class and for other subjects as well.

10.2 THESAURI

A **thesaurus** (plural, thesauri) is a dictionary of synonyms. A thesaurus can be especially helpful when you find yourself using the same modifiers over and over again.

10.3 SYNONYM FINDERS

A **synonym finder** is often included in word processing software. It enables you to highlight a word and be shown a display of its synonyms.

10.4 GLOSSARIES

A **glossary** is a list of specialized terms and their definitions. It is often found in the back of a book and sometimes includes pronunciations. Many textbooks contain glossaries. In fact, this textbook has three glossaries: the **Glossary of Literary and Informational Terms**, the **Glossary of Academic Vocabulary** and the **Glossary of Critical Vocabulary**. Use these glossaries to help you understand how terms are used in this textbook.

11 Spelling Rules

11.1 WORDS ENDING IN A SILENT *E*

Before adding a suffix beginning with a vowel or *y* to a word ending in a silent *e*, drop the *e* (with some exceptions).

amaze + -ing = amazing

love + -able = lovable

create + -ed = created

nerve + -ous = nervous

Exceptions: *change + -able = changeable; courage + -ous = courageous*

When adding a suffix beginning with a consonant to a word ending in a silent *e*, keep the *e* (with some exceptions).

late + -ly = lately

spite + -ful = spiteful

noise + -less = noiseless

state + -ment = statement

Exceptions: *truly, argument, ninth, wholly, awful,* and others.

When a suffix beginning with *a* or *o* is added to a word with a final silent *e*, the final *e* is usually retained if it is preceded by a soft *c* or a soft *g*.

bridge + -able = bridgeable

peace + -able = peaceable

outrage + -ous = outrageous

advantage + -ous = advantageous

When a suffix beginning with a vowel is added to words ending in *ee* or *oe*, the final silent *e* is retained.

agree + -ing = agreeing   free + -ing = freeing

hoe + -ing = hoeing   see + -ing = seeing

11.2 WORDS ENDING IN *Y*

Before adding most suffixes to a word that ends in *y* preceded by a consonant, change the *y* to *i*.

easy + -est = easiest

crazy + -est = craziest

silly + -ness = silliness

marry + -age = marriage

Exceptions: *dryness, shyness,* and *slyness.* However, when you add *-ing,* the *y* does not change.

empty + -ed = emptied but

empty + -ing = emptying

When adding a suffix to a word that ends in *y* preceded by a vowel, the *y* usually does not change.

play + -er = player

employ + -ed = employed

coy + -ness = coyness

pay + -able = payable

11.3 WORDS ENDING IN A CONSONANT

In one-syllable words that end in one consonant preceded by one short vowel, double the final consonant before adding a suffix beginning with a vowel, such as *-ed* or *-ing*. These are sometimes called 1+1+1 words.

dip + -ed = dipped   set + -ing = setting

slim + -est = slimmest   fit + -er = fitter

The rule does not apply to words of one syllable that end in a consonant preceded by two vowels.

feel + -ing = feeling   peel + -ed = peeled

reap + -ed = reaped   loot + -ed = looted

In words of more than one syllable, double the final consonant when (1) the word ends with one consonant preceded by one vowel and (2) the word is accented on the last syllable.

be·gin´   per·mit´   re·fer´

In the following examples, note that in the new words formed with suffixes, the accent remains on the same syllable:

be·gin´ + -ing = be·gin´ning = beginning

per·mit´ + -ed = per·mit´ted = permitted

In some words with more than one syllable, though the accent remains on the same syllable when a suffix is added, the final consonant is nevertheless not doubled, as in the following examples:

tra´vel + er = tra´vel·er = traveler

mar´ket + er = mar´ket·er = marketer

In the following examples, the accent does not remain on the same syllable; thus, the final consonant is not doubled:

re·fer´ + -ence = ref´er·ence = reference

con·fer´ + -ence = con´fer·ence = conference

11.4 PREFIXES AND SUFFIXES

When adding a prefix to a word, do not change the spelling of the base word. When a prefix creates a double letter, keep both letters.

dis- + approve = disapprove

re- + build = rebuild

ir- + regular = irregular

mis- + spell = misspell

anti- + trust = antitrust

il- + logical = illogical

When adding -ly to a word ending in l, keep both l's. When adding -ness to a word ending in n, keep both n's.

careful + -ly = carefully

sudden + -ness = suddenness

final + -ly = finally

thin + -ness = thinness

11.5 FORMING PLURAL NOUNS

To form the plural of most nouns, just add -s.

prizes   dreams   circles   stations

For most singular nouns ending in o, add -s.

solos   halos   studios   photos   pianos

For a few nouns ending in o, add -es.

heroes   tomatoes   potatoes   echoes

When the singular noun ends in s, sh, ch, x, or z, add -es.

waitresses   brushes   ditches

axes   buzzes

When a singular noun ends in y with a consonant before it, change the y to i and add -es.

army—armies   candy—candies

baby—babies   diary—diaries

ferry—ferries   conspiracy—conspiracies

When a vowel (a, e, i, o, u) comes before the y, just add -s.

boy—boys   way—ways

array—arrays   alloy—alloys

weekday—weekdays   jockey—jockeys

For most nouns ending in f or fe, change the f to v and add -es or -s.

life—lives   calf—calves   knife—knives

thief—thieves shelf—shelves loaf—loaves

For some nouns ending in f, add -s to make the plural.

roofs   chiefs   reefs   beliefs

Some nouns have the same form for both singular and plural.

deer   sheep   moose   salmon   trout

For some nouns, the plural is formed in a special way.

man—men   goose—geese

ox—oxen   woman—women

mouse—mice   child—children

For a compound noun written as one word, form the plural by changing the last word in the compound to its plural form.

stepchild—stepchildren   firefly—fireflies

If a compound noun is written as a hyphenated word or as two separate words, change the most important word to the plural form.

brother-in-law—brothers-in-law

life jacket—life jackets

11.6 FORMING POSSESSIVES

If a noun is singular, add 's.

mother—my mother's car Ross—Ross's desk

Exception: The s after the apostrophe is dropped after *Jesus', Moses',* and certain names in classical mythology *(Zeus')*. These possessive forms can thus be pronounced easily.

If a noun is plural and ends with s, just add an apostrophe.

parents—my parents' car

the Santinis—the Santinis' house

If a noun is plural but does not end in s, add 's.

people—the people's choice

women—the women's coats

11.7 SPECIAL SPELLING PROBLEMS

Only one English word ends in -sede: supersede. Three words end in -ceed: exceed, proceed, and succeed. All other verbs ending in the sound "seed" (except for the verb seed) are spelled with -cede.

concede	precede	recede	secede

In words with ie or ei, when the sound is long e (as in she), the word is spelled ie except after c (with some exceptions).

i before *e*	thief	relieve	field
	piece	grieve	pier
except after *c*	conceit	perceive	ceiling
	receive	receipt	
Exceptions:	either	neither	weird
	leisure	seize	

12 Commonly Confused Words

words	definitions	examples
accept/except	The verb *accept* means "to receive or believe"; *except* is usually a preposition meaning "excluding."	**Except** for some of the more extraordinary events, I can **accept** that the *Odyssey* recounts a real journey.
advice/advise	*Advise* is a verb; *advice* is a noun naming that which an *adviser* gives.	I **advise** you to take that job. Whom should I ask for **advice**?
affect/effect	As a verb, *affect* means "to influence." *Effect* as a verb means "to cause." If you want a noun, you will almost always want *effect*.	Did Circe's wine **affect** Odysseus' mind? It did **effect** a change in Odysseus' men. In fact, it had an **effect** on everyone else who drank it.
all ready/already	*All ready* is an adjective meaning "fully ready." *Already* is an adverb meaning "before or by this time."	He was **all ready** to go at noon. I have **already** seen that movie.
allusion/illusion	An *allusion* is an indirect reference to something. An *illusion* is a false picture or idea.	There are many **allusions** to the works of Homer in English literature. The world's apparent flatness is an **illusion**.
among/between	*Between* is used when you are speaking of only two things. *Among* is used for three or more.	**Between** *Hamlet* and *King Lear*, I prefer the latter. Emily Dickinson is **among** my favorite poets.
bring/take	*Bring* is used to denote motion toward a speaker or place. *Take* is used to denote motion away from such a person or place.	**Bring** the books over here, and I will **take** them to the library.

continued

words	definitions	examples
fewer/less	*Fewer* refers to the number of separate, countable units. *Less* refers to bulk quantity.	We have **less** literature and **fewer** selections in this year's curriculum.
leave/let	*Leave* means "to allow something to remain behind." *Let* means "to permit."	The librarian will **leave** some books on display but will not **let** us borrow any.
lie/lay	To *lie* is "to rest or recline." It does not take an object. *Lay* always takes an object.	Rover loves to **lie** in the sun. We always **lay** some bones next to him.
loose/lose	*Loose* (lo͞os) means "free, not restrained"; *lose* (lo͞oz) means "to misplace or fail to find."	Who turned the horses **loose**? I hope we won't **lose** any of them.
precede/proceed	*Precede* means "to go or come before." Use *proceed* for other meanings.	Emily Dickinson's poetry **precedes** that of Alice Walker. You may **proceed** to the next section of the test.
than/then	Use *than* in making comparisons; use *then* on all other occasions.	Who can say whether Amy Lowell is a better poet **than** Denise Levertov? I will read Lowell first, and **then** I will read Levertov.
their/there/they're	*Their* means "belonging to them." *There* means "in that place." *They're* is the contraction for "they are."	**There** is a movie playing at 9 p.m. **They're** going to see it with me. Sakara and Erin drove away in **their** car after the movie.
two/too/to	*Two* is the number. *Too* is an adverb meaning "also" or "very." Use *to* before a verb or as a preposition.	Meg had **to** go **to** town, **too**. We had **too** much reading **to** do. **Two** chapters is **too** many.

Glossary of Literary and Informational Terms

Act An act is a major division within a play, similar to a chapter in a book. Each act may be further divided into smaller sections, called scenes. Plays can have as many as five acts, or as few as one.

Allegory An allegory is a work with two levels of meaning—a literal one and a symbolic one. In such a work, most of the characters, objects, settings, and events represent abstract qualities. Personification is often used in traditional allegories. As in a fable or a parable, the purpose of an allegory may be to convey truths about life, to teach religious or moral lessons, or to criticize social institutions.

Alliteration Alliteration is the repetition of consonant sounds at the beginning of words. Note the repetition of the *d* sound in these lines: The <u>d</u>are <u>d</u>evil <u>d</u>ove into the <u>d</u>eep sea.

See also Consonance.

Allusion An allusion is an indirect reference to a famous person, place, event, or literary work.

Almanac *See* Reference Works.

Analogy An analogy is a point-by-point comparison between two things that are alike in some respect. Often, writers use analogies in nonfiction to explain unfamiliar subjects or ideas in terms of familiar ones.

See also Extended Metaphor; Metaphor; Simile.

Antagonist An antagonist is a principal character or force in opposition to a **protagonist,** or main character. The antagonist is usually another character but sometimes can be a force of nature, a set of circumstances, some aspect of society, or a force within the protagonist.

Archetype An archetype is a pattern in literature that is found in a variety of works from different cultures throughout the ages. An archetype can be a plot, a character, an image, or a setting. For example, the association of death and rebirth with winter and spring is an archetype common to many cultures.

Argument An argument is speech or writing that presents a claim about an issue or problem and supports it with reasons and evidence. An argument often takes into account other points of view, anticipating and answering objections that opponents of the position might raise.

See also Claim; Counterargument; Evidence.

Argumentative Essay *See* Essay.

Aside In drama, an aside is a short speech directed to the audience, or another character, that is not heard by the other characters on stage.

See also Soliloquy.

Assonance Assonance is the repetition of vowel sounds within nonrhyming words. An example of assonance is the repetition of the *u* sound in the following line: I made my <u>u</u>sual man<u>eu</u>ver on my snowboard.

Assumption An assumption is an opinion or belief that is taken for granted. It can be about a specific situation, a person, or the world in general. Assumptions are often unstated.

Author's Message An author's message is the main idea or theme of a particular work.

See also Main Idea; Theme.

Author's Perspective An author's perspective, or point of view, is a unique combination of ideas, values, feelings, and beliefs that influences the way the writer looks at a topic. **Tone,** or attitude, often reveals an author's perspective.

See also Author's Purpose; Tone.

Author's Position An author's position is his or her opinion on an issue or topic.

See also Claim.

Author's Purpose A writer usually writes for one or more of these purposes: to express thoughts or feelings, to inform or explain, to persuade, to entertain.

See also Author's Perspective.

Autobiography An autobiography is a writer's account of his or her own life. In almost every case, it is told from the first-person point of view. Generally, an autobiography focuses on the most significant events and people in the writer's life over a period of time. Shorter autobiographical narratives include **journals, diaries,** and **letters.** An **autobiographical essay,** another type of short autobiographical work, focuses on a single person or event in the writer's life.

See also Memoir.

Ballad A ballad is a type of narrative poem that tells a story and was originally meant to be sung or recited. Because it tells a story, a ballad has a setting, a plot, and characters. **Traditional ballads** are written in four-line stanzas with regular rhythm and rhyme. **Folk ballads** were composed orally and handed down by word of mouth. These ballads usually tell about ordinary people who have unusual adventures or perform daring deeds. A **literary ballad** is a poem written by a poet in imitation of the form and content of a folk ballad.

Bias Bias is an inclination toward a particular judgment on a topic or issue. A writer often reveals a strongly positive or strongly negative opinion by presenting only one way of looking at an issue or by heavily weighting the evidence. Words with intensely positive or negative connotations are often a signal of a writer's bias.

Bibliography A bibliography is a list of books and other materials related to the topic of a text. Bibliographies can be good sources of works for further study on a subject.

See also Works Consulted.

Biography A biography is the true account of a person's life, written by another person. As such, a biography is usually told from a third-person point of view. The writer of a biography usually researches his or her subject in order to present accurate information. The best biographers strive for honesty and balance in their accounts of their subjects' lives.

Blank Verse Blank verse is unrhymed poetry written in **iambic pentameter.** That is, each line of blank verse has five pairs of syllables. In most pairs, an unstressed syllable is followed by a stressed syllable. The most versatile of poetic forms, blank verse imitates the natural rhythms of English speech. Much of Shakespeare's drama is in blank verse.

See also Iambic Pentameter.

Business Correspondence Business correspondence includes all written business communications, such as business letters, e-mails, and memos. In general, business correspondence is brief, to the point, clear, courteous, and professional.

Cast of Characters In the script of a play, a cast of characters is a list of all the characters in the play, usually in order of appearance. It may include a brief description of each character.

Cause and Effect A **cause** is an event or action that directly results in another event or action. An **effect** is the direct or logical outcome of an event or action. Basic **cause-and-effect relationships** include a single cause with a single effect, one cause with multiple effects, multiple causes with a single effect, and a chain of causes and effects. The concept of cause and effect also provides a way of organizing a piece of writing. It helps a writer show the relationships between events or ideas.

Central Idea *See* Main Idea; Theme.

Character Characters are the individuals who participate in the action of a literary work. Like real people, characters display certain qualities, or **character traits;** they develop and change over time; and they usually have **motivations,** or reasons, for their behaviors. Complex characters can have multiple or conflicting motivations.

Main characters: Main characters are the most important characters in literary works. Generally, the plot of a short story focuses on one main character, but a novel may have several main characters.

Minor characters: The less prominent characters in a literary work are known as minor characters. Minor characters support the plot. The story is not centered on them, but they help carry out the action of the story and help the reader learn more about the main character.

Dynamic character: A dynamic character is one who undergoes important changes as a plot unfolds. The changes occur because of his or her actions and experiences in the story. The change is usually internal and may be good or bad. Main characters are usually, though not always, dynamic.

Static character: A static character is one who remains the same throughout a story. The character may experience events and have interactions with other characters, but he or she is not changed because of them.

Round character: A round character is one who is complex and highly developed, having a variety of traits and different sides to his or her personality. Some of the traits may create conflict in the character. Round characters tend to display strengths, weaknesses, and a full range of emotions. The writer provides enough detail for the reader to understand their feelings and emotions.

Flat character: A flat character is one who is not highly developed. A flat character is one-sided: he or she usually has one outstanding trait, characteristic, or role. Flat characters exist mainly to advance the plot, and they display only the traits needed for their limited roles. Minor characters are usually flat characters.

See also Characterization.

Characterization The way a writer creates and develops characters' personalities is known as characterization. There are four basic methods of characterization:

- The writer may make direct comments about a character's personality or nature through the voice of the narrator.
- The writer may describe the character's physical appearance.
- The writer may present the character's own thoughts, speech, and actions.
- The writer may present thoughts, speech, and actions of other characters in response to a character.

See also Character.

Chorus In early Greek tragedy, the chorus commented on the actions of the characters in a drama. In some Elizabethan plays, such as Shakespeare's *Romeo and Juliet,* the role of the chorus is taken by a single actor who serves as a narrator and speaks the lines in the **prologue** (and sometimes in an **epilogue**). The chorus serves to foreshadow or summarize events.

Chronological Order Chronological order is the arrangement of events in their order of occurrence. This type of organization is used in both fictional narratives and in historical writing, biography, and autobiography.

Claim In an argument, a claim is the writer's position on an issue or problem. Although an argument focuses on supporting one claim, a writer may make more than one claim in a work.

See also Argument; Thesis Statement.

Clarify Clarifying is a reading strategy that helps a reader to understand or make clear what he or she is reading. Readers usually clarify by rereading, reading aloud, or discussing.

Classification Classification is a pattern of organization in which objects, ideas, or information is presented in groups, or classes, based on common characteristics.

Cliché A cliché is an overused expression. "Better late than never" and "hard as nails" are common examples. Good writers generally avoid clichés unless they are using them in dialogue to indicate something about characters' personalities.

Climax In a plot, the climax is the point of maximum interest or tension. Usually the climax is a turning point in the story, which occurs after the reader has understood the **conflict** and become emotionally involved with the characters. The climax sometimes, but not always, points to the **resolution** of the conflict.

See also Plot.

Comedy A comedy is a dramatic work that is light and often humorous in tone, usually ending happily with a peaceful resolution of the main conflict. A comedy differs from a farce by having a more believable plot, more realistic characters, and less boisterous behavior.

Comic Relief Comic relief consists of humorous scenes, incidents, or speeches that are included in a serious drama to provide a reduction in emotional intensity. Because comic relief breaks the tension, it allows an audience to prepare emotionally for events to come. Shakespeare often uses this device in his tragedies.

Compare and Contrast To compare and contrast is to identify similarities and differences in two or more subjects. Compare-and-contrast organization can be used to structure a piece of writing, serving as a framework for analyzing the similarities and differences in two or more subjects.

Complex Character *See* Character.

Complication A complication is an additional factor or problem introduced into the rising action of a story to make the conflict more difficult. Often, a plot complication makes it seem as though the main character is getting farther away from the thing he or she wants.

Conclusion A conclusion is a statement of belief based on evidence, experience, and reasoning. A **valid conclusion** is a conclusion that logically follows from the facts or statements upon which it is based. A **deductive conclusion** is one that follows from a particular generalization or premise. An **inductive conclusion** is a broad conclusion or generalization that is reached by arguing from specific facts and examples.

Conflict A conflict is a struggle between opposing forces. Almost every story has a main conflict—a conflict that is the story's focus. An **external conflict** involves a character pitted against an outside force, such as nature, a physical obstacle, or another character. An **internal conflict** is one that occurs within a character.

See also Plot.

Connect Connecting is a reader's process of relating the content of a text to his or her own knowledge and experience.

Connotation A connotation is an attitude or a feeling associated with a word, in contrast to the word's **denotation,** which is its literal, or dictionary, meaning. The connotations of a word may be positive or negative. For example, *enthusiastic* has positive associations, while *rowdy* has negative ones. Connotations of words can have an important influence on style and meaning and are particularly important in poetry.

Consonance Consonance is the repetition of consonant sounds within and at the end of words, as in "lonely afternoon." Consonance is unlike rhyme in that the vowel sounds preceding or following the repeated consonant sounds differ. Consonance is often used together with **alliteration, assonance,** and **rhyme** to create a musical quality, to emphasize certain words, or to unify a poem.

See also Alliteration.

Consumer Documents Consumer documents are printed materials that accompany products and services. They are intended for the buyers or users of the products or services and usually provide information about use, care, operation, or assembly. Some common consumer documents are applications, contracts, warranties, manuals, instructions, package inserts, labels, brochures, and schedules.

Context Clues When you encounter an unfamiliar word, you can often use context clues as aids for understanding. Context clues are the words and phrases surrounding the word that provide hints about the word's meaning.

Controlling Idea *See* Main Idea.

Counterargument A counterargument is an argument made to answer an opposing argument, or **counterclaim.** A good argument anticipates opposing viewpoints and provides counterarguments to refute (disprove) or answer them.

Counterclaim *See* Counterargument.

Couplet A couplet is a rhymed pair of lines. A couplet may be written in any rhythmic pattern, for example:

Follow your heart's desire
And good things may transpire.

See also Stanza.

Credibility Credibility refers to the believability or trustworthiness of a source and the information it contains.

Critical Essay *See* Essay.

Critical Review A critical review is an evaluation or critique by a reviewer or critic. Different types of reviews include film reviews, book reviews, music reviews, and art show reviews.

Critique *See* Critical Review.

Database A database is a collection of information that can be quickly and easily accessed and searched and from which information can be easily retrieved. It is frequently presented in an electronic format.

Debate A debate is basically an argument—but a very structured one that requires a good deal of preparation. In academic settings, debate usually refers to a formal argumentation contest in which two opposing teams defend and attack a proposition.

See also Argument.

Deductive Reasoning Deductive reasoning is a way of thinking that begins with a generalization, presents a specific situation, and then advances with facts and evidence to a logical conclusion. The following passage has a deductive argument embedded in it: "All students in the drama class must attend the play on Thursday. Since Ava is in the class, she had better show up." This deductive argument can be broken down as follows: generalization—all students in the drama class must attend the play on Thursday; specific situation—Ava is a student in the drama class; conclusion—Ava must attend the play.

Denotation *See* Connotation.

Dénouement *See* Falling Action.

Dialect A dialect is a form of language that is spoken in a particular geographic area or by a particular social or ethnic group. A group's dialect is reflected in its pronunciations, vocabulary, expressions, and grammatical structures. Writers use dialects to capture the flavors of locales and to bring characters to life, re-creating the way they actually speak.

Dialogue Dialogue is written conversation between two or more characters. Writers use dialogue to bring characters to life and to give readers insights into the characters' qualities, traits, and reactions to other characters. Realistic, well-paced dialogue also advances the plot of a narrative. In fiction, dialogue is usually set off with quotation marks. In drama, stories are told primarily through dialogue. Playwrights use stage directions to indicate how they intend the dialogue to be interpreted by actors.

Diary A diary is a daily record of a writer's thoughts, experiences, and feelings. As such, it is a type of autobiographical writing. The terms *diary* and *journal* are often used synonymously.

Diction A writer's or speaker's choice of words and way of arranging the words in sentences is called diction. Diction can be broadly characterized as formal or informal. It can also be described as technical or common, abstract or concrete, and literal or figurative. A writer for a science journal would use a more formal, more technical, and possibly more abstract diction than would a writer for the science section of a local newspaper.

See also Style.

Dictionary *See* Reference Works.

Drama Drama is literature in which plots and characters are developed through dialogue and action; in other words, it is literature in play form. Drama is meant to be performed. Stage plays, radio plays, movies, and television programs are types of drama. Most plays are divided into acts, with each act having an emotional peak, or climax. Certain modern plays have only one act. Most plays contain stage directions, which describe settings, lighting, sound effects, the movements and emotions of actors, and the ways in which dialogue should be spoken.

Dramatic Irony *See* Irony.

Dramatic Monologue A dramatic monologue is a lyric poem in which a speaker addresses a silent or absent listener in a moment of high intensity or deep emotion, as if engaged in private conversation. The speaker proceeds without interruption or argument, and the effect on the reader is that of hearing just one side of a conversation. This technique allows the poet to focus on the feelings, personality, and motivations of the speaker.

See also Lyric Poetry; Soliloquy.

Draw Conclusions To draw a conclusion is to make a judgment or arrive at a belief based on evidence, experience, and reasoning.

Dynamic Character *See* Character.

Editorial An editorial is an opinion piece that usually appears on the editorial page of a newspaper or as part of a news broadcast. The editorial section of a newspaper presents opinions rather than objective news reports.

See also Op-Ed Piece.

Either/Or Fallacy An either/or fallacy is a statement that suggests that there are only two possible ways to view a situation or only two options to choose from. In other words, it is a statement that falsely frames a dilemma, giving the impression that no options exist but the two presented —for example, "Either we stop the construction of a new airport, or the surrounding suburbs will become ghost towns."

Elegy An elegy is an extended meditative poem in which the speaker reflects on death—often in tribute to a person who has died recently—or on an equally serious subject. Most elegies are written in formal, dignified language and are serious in tone.

Emotional Appeals Emotional appeals are messages that evoke strong feelings—such as fear, pity, or vanity—in order to persuade instead of using facts and evidence to make a point. An **appeal to fear** is a message that taps into people's fear of losing their safety or security. An **appeal to pity** is a message that taps into people's sympathy and compassion for others to build support for an idea, a cause, or a proposed action. An **appeal to vanity** is a message that attempts to persuade by tapping into people's desire to feel good about themselves.

Encyclopedia *See* Reference Works.

Epic An epic is a long narrative poem on a serious subject, presented in an elevated or formal style. It traces the adventures of a great hero whose actions reflect the ideals and values of a nation or race. Epics address universal concerns, such as good and evil, life and death, and sin and redemption. The *Odyssey* is an epic.

Epic Hero An epic hero is a larger-than-life figure who embodies the ideals of a nation or race. Epic heroes take part in dangerous adventures and accomplish great deeds. Many undertake long, difficult journeys and display great courage and superhuman strength.

Epic Simile An epic simile (also called a Homeric simile) is a long, elaborate comparison that often continues for a number of lines. Homer uses epic similes in the *Odyssey*.

See also Simile.

Epilogue An epilogue is a short addition at the end of a literary work, often dealing with the future of the characters. The concluding speech by Prince Escalus in *Romeo and Juliet* serves as an epilogue.

Epithet An epithet is a brief phrase that points out traits associated with a particular person or thing. In the *Odyssey*, Odysseus is often called "the master strategist."

Essay An essay is a short work of nonfiction that deals with a single subject. Some essays are **formal**—that is, tightly structured and written in an impersonal style. Others are **informal,** with a looser structure and a more personal style. Generally, an **informative** or **expository essay** presents or explains information and ideas. A **personal essay** is typically an informal essay in which the writer expresses his or her thoughts and feelings about a subject, focusing on the meaning of events and issues in his or her own life. In a **reflective essay,** the author makes a connection between a personal observation or experience and a universal idea, such as love, courage, or freedom. A **critical essay** evaluates a situation, a course of action, or a work of art. In an **argumentative** or **persuasive essay,** the author attempts to convince readers to adopt a certain viewpoint or to take a particular stand.

Evaluate To evaluate is to examine something carefully and judge its value or worth. Evaluating is an important skill for gaining insight into what you read. A reader can evaluate the actions of a particular character, for example, or can form an opinion about the value of an entire work.

Evidence Evidence is the specific pieces of information that support a claim. Evidence can take the form of facts, quotations, examples, statistics, or personal experiences, among others.

Exposition Exposition is the first stage of a plot in a typical story. The exposition provides important background information and introduces the setting and the important characters. The conflict the characters face may also be introduced in the exposition, or it may be introduced later, in the rising action.

See also Plot.

Expository Essay *See* Essay.

Extended Metaphor An extended metaphor is a figure of speech that compares two essentially unlike things at some length and in several ways. It does not contain the words *like* or *as*.

See also Metaphor.

External Conflict *See* Conflict.

Fable A fable is a brief tale told to illustrate a moral or teach a lesson. Often the moral of a fable appears in a distinct and memorable statement near the tale's beginning or end.

See also Moral.

Fact versus Opinion A fact is a statement that can be proved or verified. An opinion, on the other hand, is a statement that cannot be proved because it expresses a person's beliefs, feelings, or thoughts.

See also Inference; Generalization.

Fallacy A fallacy is an error in reasoning. Typically, a fallacy is based on an incorrect inference or a misuse of evidence. Some common logical fallacies are **circular reasoning, either/or fallacy, oversimplification, overgeneralization,** and **stereotyping.**

See also Either/Or Fallacy, Logical Appeal, Overgeneralization.

Falling Action In a plot, the falling action follows the climax and shows the results of the important action that happened at the climax. Tension eases as the falling action begins; however, the final outcome of the story is not yet fully worked out at this stage. Events in the falling action lead to the **resolution,** or **dénouement,** of the plot.

See also Climax; Plot.

Fantasy Fantasy is a type of fiction that is highly imaginative and portrays events, settings, or characters that are unrealistic. The setting might be a nonexistent world, the plot might involve magic or the supernatural, and the characters might employ superhuman powers.

Farce Farce is a type of exaggerated comedy that features an absurd plot, ridiculous situations, and humorous dialogue. The main purpose of a farce is to keep an audience laughing. The characters are usually stereotypes, or simplified examples of individual traits or qualities. Comic devices typically used in farces include mistaken identity, deception, physical comedy, wordplay—such as puns and double meanings—and exaggeration.

Faulty Reasoning *See* Fallacy.

Feature Article A feature article is a main article in a newspaper or a cover story in a magazine. A feature article is focused more on entertaining than informing. Features are lighter or more general than hard news and tend to be about human interest or lifestyles.

Fiction Fiction is prose writing that consists of imaginary elements. Although fiction can be inspired by actual events and real people, it usually springs from writers' imaginations. The basic elements of fiction are plot, character, setting, and theme. The novel and short story are forms of fiction.

See also Character; Novel; Plot; Setting; Short Story; Theme.

Figurative Language Figurative language is language that communicates meanings beyond the literal meanings of words. In figurative language, words are often used to symbolize ideas and concepts they would not otherwise be associated with. Writers use figurative language to create effects, to emphasize ideas, and to evoke emotions. Simile, metaphor, extended metaphor, hyperbole, and personification are examples of figurative language.

See also Hyperbole; Metaphor; Personification; Simile.

Figure of Speech *See* Figurative Language; Hyperbole; Metaphor; Personification; Simile; Understatement.

First-Person Point of View *See* Point of View.

Flashback A flashback is an account of a conversation, an episode, or an event that happened before the beginning of a story. Often, a flashback interrupts the chronological flow of a story to give the reader information needed to understand a character's present situation. Flashbacks also help create such effects as mystery, tension, or surprise.

Foil A foil is a character who provides a striking contrast to another character. By using a foil, a writer can call attention to certain traits possessed by a main character or simply enhance a character by contrast. In Shakespeare's *Romeo and Juliet,* Mercutio serves as a foil to Romeo.

Foreshadowing Foreshadowing is a writer's use of hints or clues to suggest events that will occur later in a story. The hints and clues might be included in a character's dialogue or behavior, or they might be included in details of description. Foreshadowing creates suspense, mystery, and surprise, and makes readers eager to find out what will happen.

Form Form refers to the principles of arrangement in a poem—the ways in which lines are organized. Form in poetry includes the following elements: the length of lines, the placement of lines, and the grouping of lines into stanzas.

See also Stanza.

Frame Story A frame story exists when a story is told within a narrative setting, or "frame"; it creates a story within a story. This storytelling technique has been used for over one thousand years and was employed in famous works such as *One Thousand and One Arabian Nights* and Geoffrey Chaucer's *The Canterbury Tales.*

Free Verse Free verse is poetry that does not contain regular patterns of rhythm or rhyme. The lines in free verse often flow more naturally than do rhymed, metrical lines and thus achieve a rhythm more like that of everyday speech. Although free verse lacks conventional meter, it may contain various rhythmic and sound effects, such as repetitions of syllables or words. Free verse can be used for a variety of subjects.

See also Meter; Rhyme.

Functional Documents *See* Consumer Documents; Public Documents; Workplace Documents.

Generalization A generalization is a broad statement about a class or category of people, ideas, or things, based on a study of only some of its members.

See also Overgeneralization.

Genre The term *genre* refers to a category in which a work of literature is classified. The major genres in literature are fiction, nonfiction, poetry, and drama.

Government Publications Government publications are documents produced by government organizations. Pamphlets, brochures, and reports are just some of the many forms these publications may take. Government publications can be reliable resources for a wide variety of topics.

Graphic Aid A graphic aid is a visual tool that is printed, handwritten, or drawn. Text features such as charts, diagrams, graphs, photographs, and maps can all be graphic aids. Sometimes captions are included with a graphic aid to convey information.

Graphic Organizer A graphic organizer is a "word picture"—that is, a visual illustration of a verbal statement—that helps a reader understand a text. Charts, tables, webs, and diagrams can all be graphic organizers. Graphic organizers and graphic aids can look the same. For example, a table in a science article will not be constructed differently from a table that is a graphic organizer. However, graphic organizers and graphic aids do differ in how they are used. Graphic aids are the visual representations that people encounter when they read informational texts. Graphic organizers are visuals that people construct to help them understand texts or organize information.

Haiku Haiku is a form of Japanese poetry in which 17 syllables are arranged in three lines of 5, 7, and 5 syllables each. The rules of haiku are strict. In addition to the syllabic count, the poet must create a clear picture that will evoke a strong emotional response in the reader. Nature is a particularly important source of inspiration for Japanese haiku poets, and details from nature are often the subjects of their poems.

Hero A hero is a main character or protagonist in a story. In older literary works, heroes tend to be better than ordinary humans. They are typically courageous, strong, honorable, and intelligent. They are protectors of society who hold back the forces of evil and fight to make the world a better place. In modern literature, a hero may simply be the most important character in a story. Such a hero is often an ordinary person with ordinary problems.

Historical Documents Historical documents are writings that have played a significant role in human events or are themselves records of such events. The Declaration of Independence, for example, is a historical document.

Historical Fiction A short story or novel can be classified as historical fiction when the settings and details of the plot include real places and real events of historical importance. Historical figures may appear as major or minor characters. In historical fiction, the setting generally influences the plot in important ways.

Horror Fiction Horror fiction contains strange, mysterious, violent, and often supernatural events that create suspense and terror in the reader. Edgar Allan Poe and Stephen King are famous authors of horror fiction.

How-To Writing A how-to book or article explains how to do something—usually an activity, a sport, or a household project.

Humor In literature, there are three basic types of humor, all of which may involve exaggeration or irony. **Humor of situation** arises out of the plot of a work. It usually involves exaggerated events or **situational irony,** which arises when something happens that is different from what was expected. **Humor of character** is often based on exaggerated personalities or on characters' failure to recognize their own flaws, a form of dramatic irony. **Humor of language** may include sarcasm, exaggeration, puns, or verbal irony, in which what is said is not what is meant.

See also Irony.

Hyperbole Hyperbole is a figure of speech in which the truth is exaggerated for emphasis or humorous effect.

Iambic Pentameter Iambic pentameter is a metrical pattern of five feet, or units, each of which is made up of two syllables, the first unstressed and the second stressed. Iambic pentameter is the most common meter used in English poetry; it is the meter used in blank verse and in the sonnet. Shakespeare used iambic pentameter in his plays.

See also Blank Verse; Sonnet.

Idiom An idiom is a common figure of speech whose meaning is different from the literal meaning of its words. For example, the phrase "raining cats and dogs" does not literally mean that cats and dogs are falling from the sky; the expression means "raining heavily."

Imagery Imagery consists of descriptive words and phrases that re-create sensory experiences for the reader. Imagery usually appeals to one or more of the five senses— sight, hearing, smell, taste, and touch—to help the reader imagine exactly what is being described.

Implied Controlling Idea An implied controlling idea is one that is suggested by details rather than stated explicitly.

See also Main Idea.

Implied Main Idea *See* Main Idea.

Index The index of a book is an alphabetized list of important topics and details covered in the book and the page numbers on which they can be found. An index can be used to quickly find specific information about a topic.

Inductive Reasoning Inductive reasoning is the process of logically reasoning from specific observations, examples, and facts to arrive at a general conclusion or principle.

Inference An inference is a logical assumption that is based on observed facts and one's own knowledge and experience.

Informational Nonfiction Informational nonfiction is writing that provides factual information. It often explains ideas or teaches processes. Examples include news reports, science textbooks, software instructions, and lab reports.

Informative Essay *See* Essay.

Internal Conflict *See* Conflict.

Internet The Internet is a global, interconnected system of computer networks that allows for communication through e-mail, listserves, and the World Wide Web. The Internet connects computers and computer users throughout the world.

Interview An interview is a conversation conducted by a writer or reporter, in which facts or statements are elicited from another person, recorded, and then broadcast or published.

Irony Irony is a special kind of contrast between appearance and reality—usually one in which reality is the opposite of what it seems. One type of irony is **situational irony,** a contrast between what a reader or character expects and what actually exists or happens. Another type of irony is **dramatic irony,** in which the reader or viewer knows something that a character does not know. **Verbal irony** exists when someone knowingly exaggerates or says one thing and means another.

Journal A journal is a periodical publication issued by a legal, medical, or other professional organization. Alternatively, the term may be used to refer to a diary or daily record.
See also Diary.

Legend A legend is a story handed down from the past, especially one that is popularly believed to be based on historical events. Though legends often incorporate supernatural or magical elements, they claim to be the story of a real human being and are often set in a particular time and place. These characteristics separate a legend from a myth.
See also Myth.

Limited Point of View *See* Point of View.

Line The line is the core unit of a poem. In poetry, line length is an essential element of the poem's meaning and rhythm. **Line breaks,** where a line of poetry ends, may coincide with grammatical units. However, a line break may also occur in the middle of a grammatical or syntactical unit, creating a meaningful pause or emphasis. Poets use a variety of line breaks to manipulate sense, grammar, and syntax and thereby create a wide range of effects.

Literary Criticism *See* Text Criticism.

Literary Nonfiction Literary nonfiction is nonfiction that is recognized as being of artistic value or that is about literature. Autobiographies, biographies, essays, and eloquent speeches typically fall into this category.

Loaded Language Loaded language consists of words with strongly positive or negative connotations intended to influence a reader's or listener's attitude.

Logical Appeal A logical appeal relies on logic and facts, appealing to people's reasoning or intellect rather than to their values or emotions. Flawed logical appeals—that is, errors in reasoning—are considered logical fallacies.
See also Fallacy.

Logical Argument A logical argument is an argument in which the logical relationship between the support and the claim is sound.

Lyric Poetry A lyric poem is a short poem in which a single speaker expresses personal thoughts and feelings. Most poems other than dramatic and narrative poems are lyric poems. In ancient Greece, lyric poetry was meant to be sung. Modern lyrics are usually not intended for singing, but they are characterized by strong melodic rhythms. Lyric poetry has a variety of forms and covers many subjects, from love and death to everyday experiences.

Magical Realism Magical realism is a literary genre that combines fantastic or magical events with realistic occurrences in a matter-of-fact way to delight or surprise the reader. A famous example of magical realism is Gabriel García Márquez's novel *One Hundred Years of Solitude*.

Main Idea A main idea, or controlling idea, is the most important idea or impression about a topic that a writer or speaker conveys. It can be the central idea of an entire work or of just a paragraph. Often, the main idea of a paragraph is expressed in a topic sentence. However, a main idea may just be implied, or suggested, by details. A main idea and supporting details can serve as a basic pattern of organization in a piece of writing, with the central idea about a topic being supported by details.

Make Inferences *See* Inference.

Memoir A memoir is a form of autobiographical writing in which a writer shares his or her personal experiences and observations of significant events or people. Often informal or even intimate in tone, memoirs usually give readers insight into the impact of historical events on people's lives.

See also Autobiography.

Metaphor A metaphor is a figure of speech that makes a comparison between two things that are basically unlike but have something in common. Unlike similes, metaphors do not contain the word *like* or *as*.

See also Extended Metaphor; Figurative Language; Simile.

Meter Meter is a regular pattern of stressed and unstressed syllables in a poem. The meter of a poem emphasizes the musical quality of the language. Each unit of meter, known as a **foot,** consists of one stressed syllable and one or two unstressed syllables. In representations of meter, a stressed syllable is indicated by the symbol ´; an unstressed syllable, by the symbol ˘. The four basic types of metrical feet are the **iamb,** an unstressed syllable followed by a stressed syllable (˘ ´); the **trochee,** a stressed syllable followed by an unstressed syllable (´ ˘); the **anapest,** two unstressed syllables followed by a stressed syllable (˘ ˘ ´); and the **dactyl,** a stressed syllable followed by two unstressed syllables (´ ˘ ˘).

See also Rhythm.

Mise en Scène *Mise en scène* is a term from the French that refers to the various physical aspects of a dramatic presentation, such as lighting, costumes, scenery, makeup, and props.

Monitor Monitoring is the strategy of checking your comprehension as you are reading and modifying the strategies you are using to suit your needs. Monitoring may include some or all of the following strategies: questioning, clarifying, visualizing, predicting, connecting, and rereading.

Mood In a literary work, mood is the feeling or atmosphere that a writer creates for the reader. Descriptive words, imagery, and figurative language contribute to the mood of a work, as do the sound and rhythm of the language used.

See also Tone.

Moral A moral is a lesson taught in a literary work, such as a fable. For example, the moral "Do not count your chickens before they are hatched" teaches that one should not count on one's fortunes or blessings until they appear.

See also Fable.

Motivation *See* Character.

Myth A myth is a traditional story, usually concerning some superhuman being or unlikely event, that was once widely believed to be true. Frequently, myths were attempts to explain natural phenomena, such as solar and lunar eclipses or the cycle of the seasons. For some peoples, myths were both a kind of science and a religion. In addition, myths served as literature and entertainment, just as they do for modern-day audiences.

Greek mythology forms much of the background in Homer's *Odyssey*. For example, the myth of the judgment of Paris describes events that led to the Trojan War. The goddesses Athena, Hera, and Aphrodite asked a mortal—Paris—to decide which of them was the most beautiful. Paris chose Aphrodite and was rewarded by her with Helen, wife of the Greek king Menelaus.

Narrative Nonfiction Narrative nonfiction is writing that reads much like fiction, except that the characters, setting, and plot are real rather than imaginary. Its purpose is usually to entertain or to express opinions or feelings. Narrative nonfiction includes, but is not limited to, autobiographies, biographies, memoirs, diaries, and journals.

Narrative Poetry Narrative poetry tells a story or recounts events. Like a short story or a novel, a narrative poem has the following elements: plot, characters, setting, and theme.

Narrator The narrator of a story is the character or voice that relates the story's events to the reader.

See also Persona; Point of View.

News Article A news article is a piece of writing that reports on a recent event. In newspapers, news articles are usually written concisely and report the latest news, presenting the most important facts first and then more detailed information. In magazines, news articles are usually more elaborate than those in newspapers because they are written to provide both information and analysis. Also, news articles in magazines do not necessarily present the most important facts first.

Nonfiction Nonfiction is writing that tells about real people, places, and events. Unlike fiction, nonfiction is mainly written to convey factual information, although writers of nonfiction shape information in accordance with their own purposes and attitudes. Nonfiction can be a good source of information, but readers frequently have to examine it carefully in order to detect biases, notice gaps in the information provided, and identify errors in logic. Nonfiction includes a diverse range of writing—newspaper articles, letters, essays, biographies, movie reviews, speeches, true-life adventure stories, advertising, and more.

Novel A novel is an extended work of fiction. Like a short story, a novel is essentially the product of a writer's imagination. Because a novel is considerably longer than a short story, a novelist can develop a wider range of characters and a more complex plot.

Novella A novella is a work of fiction that is longer than a short story but shorter than a novel. A novella differs from a novel in that it concentrates on a limited cast of characters, a relatively short time span, and a single chain of events. The novella is an attempt to combine the compression of the short story with the development of the novel.

Ode An ode is a complex lyric poem that develops a serious and dignified theme. Odes appeal to both the imagination and the intellect, and many commemorate events or praise people or elements of nature.

Omniscient Point of View *See* Point of View.

Onomatopoeia Onomatopoeia is the use of words whose sounds echo their meanings, such as *buzz, whisper, gargle,* and *murmur.* Onomatopoeia as a literary technique goes beyond the use of simple echoic words, however. Skilled writers, especially poets, choose words whose sounds intensify images and suggest meanings.

Op-Ed Piece An op-ed piece is an opinion piece that usually appears opposite ("op") the editorial page of a newspaper. Unlike editorials, op-ed pieces are written and submitted by named writers.

Organization *See* Pattern of Organization.

Overgeneralization An overgeneralization is a generalization that is too broad. You can often recognize overgeneralizations by the appearance of words and phrases such as *all, everyone, every time, any, anything, no one,* and *none.* Consider, for example, this statement: "None of the sanitation workers in our city really care about keeping the environment clean." In all probability, there are many exceptions; the writer can't possibly know the feelings of every sanitation worker in the city.

Overview An overview is a short summary of a story, a speech, or an essay. It orients the reader by providing a preview of the text to come.

Oxymoron An oxymoron is a special kind of concise paradox that brings together two contradictory terms. "Deafening silence" and "original copy" are examples of oxymorons.

Paradox A paradox is a seemingly contradictory or absurd statement that may nonetheless suggest an important truth.

Parallelism Parallelism is the use of similar grammatical constructions to express ideas that are related or equal in importance. Martin Luther King Jr. uses parallelism in his "I Have a Dream" speech.

Parallel Plot A parallel plot is a particular type of plot in which two stories of equal importance are told simultaneously. The story moves back and forth between the two plots.

Paraphrase Paraphrasing is the restating of information in one's own words.

See also Summarize.

Parody A parody is an imitation of another work, a type of literature, or a writer's style, usually for the purpose of poking fun. It may serve as an element of a larger work or be a complete work in itself. The purpose of parody may be to ridicule through broad humor, deploying such techniques as exaggeration or the use of inappropriate subject matter. Such techniques may even provide insights into the original work.

Pastoral A pastoral is a poem presenting shepherds in rural settings, usually in an idealized manner. The language and form of a pastoral tends to be formal. English Renaissance poets were drawn to the pastoral as a means of conveying their own emotions and ideas, particularly about love.

Pattern of Organization A pattern of organization is a particular arrangement of ideas and information. Such a pattern may be used to organize an entire composition or a single paragraph within a longer work. The following are the most common patterns of organization: cause-and- effect, chronological order, compare-and-contrast, classification, deductive, inductive, order of importance, problem-solution, sequential, and spatial.

See also Cause and Effect; Chronological Order; Classification; Compare and Contrast; Problem-Solution Order; Sequential Order.

Periodical A periodical is a publication that is issued at regular intervals of more than one day. For example, a periodical may be a weekly, monthly, or quarterly journal or magazine. Newspapers and other daily publications generally are not classified as periodicals.

Persona A persona is a voice that a writer assumes in a particular work. A persona is like a mask worn by the writer, separating his or her identity from that of the speaker or the narrator. It is the persona's voice—not the writer's voice—that narrates a story or speaks in a poem.

See also Narrator; Speaker.

Personal Essay *See* Essay.

Personification Personification is a figure of speech in which human qualities are given to an object, animal, or idea, for example: The night wind sings an eerie song.

See also Figurative Language.

Persuasion Persuasion is the art of swaying others' feelings, beliefs, or actions. Persuasion normally appeals to both the intellect and the emotions of readers. **Persuasive techniques** are the methods used to influence others to adopt certain opinions or beliefs or to act in certain ways. Types of persuasive techniques include emotional appeals, logical appeals, and loaded language. When used properly, persuasive techniques can add depth to writing that's meant to persuade. Persuasive techniques can, however, be misused to cloud factual information, disguise poor reasoning, or unfairly exploit people's emotions in order to shape their opinions.

See also Emotional Appeals; Loaded Language; Logical Appeal.

Persuasive Essay *See* Essay.

Play *See* Drama.

Plot The sequence of events in a story is called the plot. A plot focuses on a central **conflict** or problem faced by the main character. The actions that the characters take to resolve the conflict build toward a climax. In general, it is not long after this point that the conflict is resolved and the story ends. A plot typically develops in five stages: exposition, rising action, climax, falling action, and resolution.

See also Climax; Exposition; Falling Action; Rising Action.

Poetry Poetry is a type of literature in which words are carefully chosen and arranged to create certain effects. Poets use a variety of sound devices, imagery, and figurative language to express emotions and ideas.

See also Alliteration; Assonance; Ballad; Free Verse; Imagery; Meter; Rhyme; Rhythm; Stanza.

Point of View Point of view refers to the method of narration used in a short story, novel, narrative poem, or work of nonfiction. In a work told from a **first-person** point of view, the narrator is a character in the story. In a work told from a **third-person** point of view, the narrative voice is outside the action, not one of the characters. If a story is told from a **third-person omniscient,** or all-knowing, point of view, the narrator sees into the minds of all the characters. If events are related from a **third-person limited** point of view, the narrator tells what only one character thinks, feels, and observes.

See also Narrator.

Predict Predicting is a reading strategy that involves using text clues to make a reasonable guess about what will happen next in a story.

Primary Source *See* Sources.

Prior Knowledge Prior knowledge is the knowledge a reader already possesses about a topic. This information might come from personal experiences, expert accounts, books, films, or other sources.

Problem-Solution Order Problem-solution order is a pattern of organization in which a problem is stated and analyzed and then one or more solutions are proposed and examined. Writers use words and phrases such as *propose, conclude, reason for, problem, answer,* and *solution* to connect ideas and details when writing about problems and solutions.

Procedural Texts Procedural texts are functional texts that were created to communicate instructions, rules, processes, or other detailed, step-by-step information.

See also Consumer Documents; Public Documents; Workplace Documents.

Prologue A prologue is an introductory scene in a drama. Some Elizabethan plays include prologues that comment on the theme or moral point that will be revealed in the play. The prologue is a feature of all Greek drama.

Prop The word *prop,* originally an abbreviation of the word *property,* refers to any physical object that is used in a drama.

Propaganda Propaganda is a form of communication that may use distorted, false, or misleading information. It usually refers to manipulative political discourse.

Prose Generally, prose refers to all forms of written or spoken expression that are not in verse. The term, therefore, may be used to describe very different forms of writing— short stories as well as essays, for example.

Protagonist A protagonist is the main character in a work of literature—the character who is involved in the central conflict of the story. Usually, the protagonist changes after the central conflict reaches a climax. He or she may be a hero and is usually the one with whom the audience tends to identify.

Public Documents Public documents are documents that were written for the public to provide information that is of public interest or concern. They include government documents, speeches, signs, and rules and regulations.

See also Government Publications.

Pun A pun is a joke that comes from a play on words. It can make use of a word's multiple meanings or of a word's sound.

Quatrain A quatrain is a four-line stanza, or group of lines, in poetry. The most common stanza in English poetry, the quatrain can have a variety of meters and rhyme schemes.

Realistic Fiction Realistic fiction is fiction that is a truthful imitation of ordinary life.

Recurring Theme *See* Theme.

Reference Works General reference works are sources that contain facts and background information on a wide range of subjects. More specific reference works contain in-depth information on a single subject. Most reference works are good sources of reliable information because they have been reviewed by experts. The following are some common reference works: encyclopedias, dictionaries, thesauri, almanacs, atlases, chronologies, biographical dictionaries, and directories.

Reflective Essay *See* Essay.

Refrain A refrain is one or more lines repeated in each stanza of a poem.

See also Stanza.

Repetition Repetition is a technique in which a sound, word, phrase, or line is repeated for emphasis or unity. Repetition often helps to reinforce meaning and create an appealing rhythm. The term includes specific devices associated with both prose and poetry, such as alliteration and parallelism.

See also Alliteration; Parallelism; Sound Devices.

Resolution *See* Falling Action.

Review *See* Critical Review.

Rhetorical Devices Rhetorical devices are techniques writers use to enhance their arguments and communicate more effectively. Rhetorical devices include analogy, parallelism, rhetorical questions, and repetition.

See also Analogy; Repetition; Rhetorical Questions.

Rhetorical Questions Rhetorical questions are those that do not require a reply. Writers use them to suggest that their arguments make the answer obvious or self-evident.

Rhyme Rhyme is the occurrence of similar or identical sounds at the end of two or more words, such as *suite, heat,* and *complete.* Rhyme that occurs within a single line of poetry is **internal rhyme.** Rhyme that occurs at the ends of lines of poetry is called **end rhyme.** End rhyme that is not exact but approximate is called **slant rhyme,** or **off rhyme.** Notice the following example of slant rhyme involving the words *care* and *dear:*

> You act like you don't care,
> But I know you do, my dear.

Rhyme Scheme A rhyme scheme is a pattern of end rhymes in a poem. A rhyme scheme is noted by assigning a letter of the alphabet, beginning with *a,* to each line. Lines that rhyme are given the same letter.

Rhythm Rhythm is a pattern of stressed and unstressed syllables in a line of poetry. Poets use rhythm to bring out the musical quality of language, to emphasize ideas, to create moods, and to heighten emotional responses. Devices such as alliteration, rhyme, assonance, consonance, and parallelism create rhythm.

See also Meter.

Rising Action Rising action is the stage in a plot in which the conflict develops and story events build toward a climax. During this stage, complications arise that make the conflict more intense. Tension grows as the characters struggle to resolve the conflict.

See also Plot.

Romance A romance refers to any imaginative story concerned with noble heroes, chivalric codes of honor, passionate love, daring deeds, and supernatural events. Writers of romances tend to idealize their heroes as well as the eras in which the heroes live. Medieval romances include stories of kings, knights, and ladies who are motivated by love, religious faith, or simply a desire for adventure.

Sarcasm Sarcasm is a kind of particularly cutting irony. Generally, sarcasm is the taunting use of praise to mean its opposite—that is, to insult someone or something.

Satire Satire is a literary technique in which ideas, customs, behaviors, or institutions are ridiculed for the purpose of improving society. Satire may be gently witty, mildly abrasive, or bitterly critical, and it often involves the use of irony and exaggeration to force readers to see something in a critical light.

Scanning Scanning is the process of searching through writing for a particular fact or piece of information. When you scan, your eyes sweep across a page, looking for key words that may lead you to the information you want.

Scansion Scansion is the notation of stressed and unstressed syllables in poetry. A stressed syllable is indicated by the symbol ´; an unstressed syllable, by the symbol ˘. Using scansion can help you determine the rhythm and meter of a poem.

See also Meter.

Scene In drama, the action is often divided into acts and scenes. Each scene presents an episode of the play's plot and typically occurs at a single place and time.

See also Act.

Scenery Scenery is a painted backdrop or other structures used to create the setting for a play.

Science Fiction Science fiction is fiction in which a writer explores unexpected possibilities of the past or the future, using known scientific data and theories as well as his or her creative imagination. Most science fiction writers create believable worlds, although some create fantasy worlds that have familiar elements.

See also Fantasy.

Screenplay A screenplay is a play written for film.

See also Teleplay.

Script The text of a play, film, or broadcast is called a script.

Secondary Source *See* Sources.

Sensory Details Sensory details are words and phrases that appeal to the reader's senses of sight, hearing, touch, smell, and taste. For example, the sensory detail "a fine film of rain" appeals to the senses of sight and touch. Sensory details stimulate the reader to create images in his or her mind.

See also Imagery.

Sequential Order A pattern of organization that shows the order in which events or actions occur is called sequential order. Writers typically use this pattern of organization to explain steps or stages in a process.

Setting Setting is the time and place of the action of a story.

See also Fiction.

Setting a Purpose The process of establishing specific reasons for reading a text is called setting a purpose.

Short Story A short story is a work of fiction that centers on a single idea and can be read in one sitting. Generally, a short story has one main conflict that involves the characters, keeps the story moving, and stimulates readers' interest.

See also Fiction.

Sidebar A sidebar is additional information set in a box alongside or within a news or feature article. Popular magazines often make use of sidebar information.

Signal Words Signal words are words and phrases that indicate what is to come in a text.

Readers can use signal words to discover a text's pattern of organization and to analyze the relationships among the ideas in the text.

Simile A simile is a figure of speech that makes a comparison between two unlike things, using the word *like* or *as,* for example: Her blue-eyed stare was like ice.

See also Epic Simile; Figurative Language; Metaphor.

Situational Irony *See* Irony.

Soliloquy In drama, a soliloquy is a speech in which a character speaks his or her thoughts aloud. Generally, the character is on the stage alone, not speaking to other characters and perhaps not even consciously addressing an audience. At the beginning of Act Two, Scene 3, of *Romeo and Juliet,* Friar Laurence has a long soliloquy. Shakespeare makes use of soliloquies in many of his plays.

See also Aside; Dramatic Monologue.

Sonnet A sonnet is a lyric poem of 14 lines, commonly written in **iambic pentameter.** Sonnets are often classified as Petrarchan or Shakespearean. The Shakespearean, or Elizabethan, sonnet consists of three quatrains, or four-line units, and a final couplet. The typical rhyme scheme is *abab cdcd efef gg.*

See also Iambic Pentameter; Rhyme Scheme.

Sound Devices Sound devices, or uses of words for their auditory effect, can convey meaning and mood or unify a work. Some common sound devices are alliteration, assonance, consonance, meter, onomatopoeia, repetition, rhyme, and rhythm.

See also Alliteration; Assonance; Consonance; Meter; Onomatopoeia; Repetition; Rhyme; Rhythm.

Sources A source is anything that supplies information. **Primary sources** are materials written by people who were present at events, either as participants or as observers. Letters, diaries, autobiographies, speeches, and photographs are primary sources. **Secondary sources** are records of events that were created sometime after the events occurred; the writers were not directly involved or were not present when the events took place. Encyclopedias, textbooks, biographies, most newspaper and magazine articles, and books and articles that interpret or review research are secondary sources.

Spatial Order Spatial order is a pattern of organization that highlights the physical positions or relationships of details or objects. This pattern of organization is typically found in descriptive writing. Writers use words and phrases such as *on the left, to the right, here, over there, above, below, beyond, nearby,* and *in the distance* to indicate the arrangement of details.

Speaker In poetry the speaker is the voice that "talks" to the reader, similar to the narrator in fiction. The speaker is not necessarily the poet.

See also Persona.

Speech A speech is a talk or public address. The purpose of a speech may be to entertain, to explain, to present a claim, to inspire, or any combination of these aims. "I Have a Dream" by Martin Luther King Jr. was written and delivered in order to inspire an audience.

Stage Directions A play typically includes instructions called stage directions, which are usually printed in italic type. They serve as a guide to directors, set and lighting designers, performers, and readers. When stage directions appear within passages of dialogue, parentheses are usually used to set them off from the words spoken by characters.

Stanza A stanza is a group of two or more lines that form a unit in a poem. A stanza is comparable to a paragraph in prose. Each stanza may have the same number of lines, or the number of lines may vary.

See also Couplet; Form; Poetry; Quatrain.

Static Character *See* Character.

Stereotype In literature, a simplified or stock character who conforms to a fixed pattern or is defined by a single trait is known as a stereotype. Such a character does not usually demonstrate the complexity of a real person. Familiar stereotypes in popular literature include the absentminded professor and the busybody.

Stereotyping Stereotyping is a type of overgeneralization. Stereotypes are broad statements made about people on the basis of their gender, ethnicity, race, or political, social, professional, or religious group.

Stream of Consciousness Stream of consciousness is a literary technique developed by modern writers, in which thoughts, feelings, moods, perceptions, and memories are presented as they randomly flow through a character's mind.

Structure Structure is the way in which the parts of a work of literature are put together. In poetry, structure involves the arrangement of words and lines to produce a desired effect. A common structural unit in poetry is the stanza, of which there are numerous types. In prose, structure is the arrangement of larger units or parts of a work. Paragraphs, for example, are basic units in prose, as are chapters in novels and acts in plays. The structure of a poem, short story, novel, play, or nonfictional work usually emphasizes certain important aspects of content.

See also Act; Stanza.

Style Style is the particular way in which a work of literature is written—not *what* is said but *how* it is said. It is the writer's unique way of communicating ideas. Many elements contribute to style, including word choice, sentence structure and length, tone, figurative language, and point of view. A literary style may be described in a variety of ways, such as formal, informal, journalistic, conversational, wordy, ornate, poetic, or dynamic.

Summarize To summarize is to briefly retell, or encapsulate, the main ideas of a piece of writing in one's own words.

See also Paraphrase.

Support Support is any material that serves to prove a claim. In an argument, support typically consists of reasons and evidence. In persuasive texts and speeches, however, support may include appeals to the needs and values of the audience.

Supporting Detail *See* Main Idea.

Surprise Ending A surprise ending is an unexpected plot twist at the end of a story. The surprise may be a sudden turn in the action or a piece of information that gives a different perspective to the entire story.

Suspense Suspense is the excitement or tension that readers feel as they wait to find out how a story ends or a conflict is resolved. Writers create suspense by raising questions in readers' minds about what might happen next. The use of **foreshadowing** and **flashback** are two ways in which writers create suspense.

See also Foreshadowing; Flashback.

Symbol A symbol is a person, a place, an object, or an activity that stands for something beyond itself. For example, a flag is a colored piece of cloth that stands for a country. A white dove is a bird that represents peace.

Synthesize To synthesize information is to take individual pieces of information and combine them with other pieces of information and with prior knowledge or experience to gain a better understanding of a subject or to create a new product or idea.

Tall Tale A tall tale is a humorously exaggerated story about impossible events, often involving the supernatural abilities of the main character. Stories about folk heroes such as Pecos Bill and Paul Bunyan are typical tall tales.

Teleplay A teleplay is a play written for television. In a teleplay, scenes can change quickly and dramatically. The camera can focus the viewer's attention on specific actions. The camera directions in teleplays are much like the stage directions in stage plays.

Text Criticism Text criticism is writing in which literary works, including their various elements, are analyzed, interpreted, evaluated, or compared.

Text Features Text features are design elements that indicate the organizational structure of a text and help make the key ideas and supporting information understandable. Text features include headers, boldface type, italic type, bulleted or numbered lists, sidebars, captions, and graphic aids such as charts, tables, timelines, illustrations, and photographs.

Theme A theme, or central idea, is an underlying message about life or human nature that a writer wants the reader to understand.

It is a perception about life or human nature that the writer shares with the reader. In most cases, themes are not stated directly but must be inferred. A theme may imply how a person should live but should not be confused with a **moral.**

Recurring themes are themes found in a variety of works. For example, authors from varying backgrounds might convey similar themes having to do with the importance of family values. **Universal themes** are themes that are found throughout the literature of all time periods. For example, the *Odyssey* contains a universal theme relating to the hero's search for truth, goodness, and honor.

See also Moral.

Thesaurus *See* Reference Works.

Thesis Statement In an argument, a thesis statement is an expression of the claim that the writer or speaker is trying to support. In an essay, a thesis statement is an expression, in one or two sentences, of the main idea or purpose of the piece of writing.

See also Claim.

Third-Person Point of View *See* Point of View.

Tone Tone is the attitude a writer takes takes toward a subject. Unlike mood, which is intended to shape the reader's emotional response, tone reflects the feelings of the writer. A writer communicates tone through choice of words and details. Tone may often be described by a single word, such as *serious, humorous, formal, informal, somber, sarcastic, playful, ironic, bitter,* or *objective.*

See also Author's Perspective; Mood.

Topic Sentence The topic sentence of a paragraph states the paragraph's central idea. All other sentences in the paragraph provide supporting details.

Tragedy A tragedy is a dramatic work that presents the downfall of a dignified character (**tragic hero**) or characters who are involved in historically or socially significant events. The events in a tragic plot are set in motion by a decision that is often an error in judgment (**tragic flaw**) on the part of the hero. Succeeding events are linked in a cause-and-effect relationship and lead inevitably to a disastrous conclusion, usually death. Shakespeare's *Romeo and Juliet* is a tragedy.

Tragic Flaw *See* Tragedy.

Tragic Hero *See* Tragedy.

Traits *See* Character.

Turning Point *See* Climax.

Understatement Understatement is a technique of creating emphasis by saying less than is actually or literally true. It is the opposite of **hyperbole,** or exaggeration. One of the primary devices of irony, understatement can be used to develop a humorous effect, to create satire, or to achieve a restrained tone.

See also Hyperbole; Irony.

Universal Theme *See* Theme.

Verbal Irony *See* Irony.

Visualize Visualizing is the process of forming a mental picture based on written or spoken information.

Voice Voice is a writer's unique use of language that allows a reader to "hear" a human personality in the writer's work. Elements of style that contribute to a writer's voice include sentence structure, diction, and tone. Voice can reveal much about the author's personality, beliefs, and attitudes.

Website A website is a collection of "pages" on the World Wide Web that is usually devoted to one specific subject. Pages are linked together and are accessed by clicking hyperlinks or menus, which send the user from page to page within the site. Web sites are created by companies, organizations, educational institutions, branches of the government, the military, and individuals.

Word Choice *See* Diction.

Workplace Documents Workplace documents are materials that are produced or used within a work setting, usually to aid in the functioning of the workplace. They include job applications, office memos, training manuals, job descriptions, and sales reports. Workplace documents often include text features, such as captions, graphics, and headers, that make key ideas and supporting information understandable.

Works Cited A list of works cited lists names of all the works a writer has referred to in his or her text. This list often includes not only books and articles but also nonprint sources.

Works Consulted A list of works consulted names all the works a writer consulted in order to create his or her text. It is not limited just to those works cited in the text.

See also Bibliography.

Using the Glossaries

The following glossaries list the Academic Vocabulary and Critical Vocabulary words found in this book in alphabetical order. Use these glossaries just as you would a dictionary—to determine the meanings, parts of speech, pronunciation, and syllabication of words. (Some technical, foreign, and more obscure words in this book are not listed here but are defined for you in the footnotes that accompany many of the selections.)

Many words in the English language have more than one meaning. These glossaries give the meanings that apply to the words as they are used in the selections in this book. Words closely related in form and meaning are listed together in one entry (for instance, *consumption* and *consume*), and the definition is given for the first form.

The following abbreviations are used to identify parts of speech of words:

adj. adjective *adv.* adverb *n.* noun *v.* verb

Each word's pronunciation is given in parentheses. A guide to the pronunciation symbols appears in the Pronunciation Key below. The stress marks in the Pronunciation Key are used to indicate the force given to each syllable in a word. They can also help you determine where words are divided into syllables.

For more information about the words in these glossaries or for information about words not listed here, consult a dictionary.

Pronunciation Key

Symbol	Examples	Symbol	Examples	Symbol	Examples
ă	pat	m	mum	ûr	urge, term, firm, word, heard
ā	pay	n	no, sudden* (sud'n)		
ä	father	ng	thing	**Symbol**	**Examples**
âr	care	ŏ	pot	v	valve
b	bib	ō	toe	w	with
ch	church	ô	caught, paw	y	yes
d	deed, milled	ôr	core	z	zebra, xylem
ĕ	pet	oi	noise	zh	vision, pleasure, garage
ē	bee	ŏŏ	took	ə	about, item, edible, gallop, circus
f	fife, phase, rough	oor	lure		
g	gag	ōō	boot	ər	butter
h	hat	ou	out		
hw	which	p	pop	**Sounds in Foreign Words**	
ĭ	pit	r	roar	KH	*German* ich, ach; *Scottish* loch
ī	pie, by	s	sauce		
îr	pier	sh	ship, dish	N (bôn)	*French,* bon, fin
j	judge	t	tight, stopped	œ	*French* feu, oeuf; *German* schön
k	kick, cat, pique	th	thin		
l	lid, needle* (nēd'l)	*th*	this	ü	*French* tu; *German* über
		ŭ	cut		

* In English the consonants *l* and *n* often constitute complete syllables by themselves.

Stress Marks

The relevant emphasis with which the syllables of a word or phrase are spoken, called stress, is indicated in three different ways. The strongest, or primary, stress is marked with a bold mark ('). An intermediate, or secondary, level of stress is marked with a similar but lighter mark ('). The weakest stress is unmarked. Words of one syllable show no stress mark.

Glossary of Academic Vocabulary

attribute (ăt´rə-byoot´) *n.* a characteristic, quality, or trait.

capacity (kə-păs´ĭ-tē) *n.* the ability to contain, hold, produce, or understand.

commit (kə-mĭt´) *v.* to carry out, engage in, or perform.

confer (kən-fûr´) *v.* to grant or give to.

decline (dĭ-klīn´) *v.* to fall apart or deteriorate slowly.

dimension (dĭ-měn´shən) *n.* a feature, scale, or measurement of something.

emerge (ĭ-mûrj´) *v.* to come forth, out of, or away from.

enable (ĕ-nā´bəl) *v.* to give the means or opportunity.

enforce (ĕn-fôrs´) *v.* to compel observance of or obedience to.

entity (ĕn´tĭ-tē) *n.* a thing that exists as a unit.

expose (ĭk-spōz´) *v.* to make visible or reveal.

external (ĭk-stûr´nəl) *adj.* related to, part of, or from the outside.

generate (jĕn´ə-rāt´) *v.* to produce or cause something to happen or exist.

impose (ĭm-pōz´) *v.* to bring about by force.

initiate (ĭ-nĭsh´ē-āt´) *v.* to start or cause to begin.

integrate (ĭn´tĭ-grāt´) *v.* to pull together into a whole; unify.

internal (ĭn-tûr´nəl) *adj.* inner; located within something or someone.

motivate (mō´tə-vāt´) *v.* to provide a cause for doing something.

objective (əb-jĕk´tĭv) *n.* an intention, purpose, or goal.

presume (prĭ-zoom´) *v.* to take for granted as being true; to assume something is true.

pursuit (pər-soot´) *n.* the action of chasing or following something.

resolve (rĭ-zŏlv´) *v.* to decide or become determined.

reveal (rĭ-vēl´) *v.* to show or make known.

statistic (stə-tĭs´tĭk) *n.* a piece of numerical data.

subsequent (sŭb´sĭ-kwĕnt´) *adj.* coming after or following.

sustain (sə-stān´) *v.* to support or cause to continue.

trace (trās) *v.* to discover or determine the origins or developmental stages of something.

underlie (ŭn´dər-lī´) *v.* to be the cause or support of.

undertake (ŭn´dər-tāk´) *v.* to assume responsibility for or take on a job or course of action

utilize (yoot´l-īz) *v.* to make use of.

Glossary of Critical Vocabulary

abominably (ə-bŏm´ə-nə-blē) *adv.* in a hateful way; horribly.

adversary (ăd´vər-sĕr´ē) *n.* an opponent; enemy.

adversity (ăd-vûr´sĭ-tē) *n.* hardship; misfortune.

afflict (ə-flĭkt´) *v.* to cause pain to; to trouble.

allocate (ăl´ə-kāt´) *v.* to assign or designate for.

assail (ə-sāl´) *v.* attack, disturb.

assess (ə-sĕs´) *v.* to evaluate.

assuage (ə-swāj´) *v.* to calm or pacify.

audacious (ô-dā´shəs) *n.* bold, rebellious.

autonomy (ô-tŏn´ə-mē) *n.* independent self-governance.

berate (bĭ-rāt´) *v.* to criticize or scold.

bereaved (bĭ-rēvd´) *adj.* having suffered the loss of a loved one; grieving.

cadence (kād´ns) *n.* lyrical rhythm.

circuitously (sər-kyōō´ĭ-təs-lē) *adv.* in an indirect and lengthy manner.

civic (sĭv´ĭk) *adj.* related to community and citizenship.

cognition (kŏg-nĭsh´ən) *n.* the process or pattern of gaining knowledge.

commandeer (kŏm´ən-dir´) *v.* to take control of by force.

commemorate (kŏ-mĕm´ə-rāt´) *v.* to celebrate or honor.

compatriot (kəm-pā´trē-ət) *n.* a fellow citizen or person from same country.

comply (kəm-plī´) *v.* to obey an instruction or command.

concede (kən-sēd´) *v.* to surrender or acknowledge defeat.

conceive (kən-sēv´) *v.* to form or develop in the mind; devise.

constitute (kŏn´stĭ-tōōt´) *v.* to form or comprise.

constrict (kən-strĭkt´) *v.* to limit or impede growth.

consume (kən-sōōm´) *v.* to completely destroy or eradicate.

contagion (kən-tā´jən) *n.* the spreading from one to another.

contemplate (kŏn´təm-plāt´) *v.* think carefully about.

contemptible (kən-təmp´tə-bəl) *adj.* deserving of scorn; despicable.

contention (kən-tĕn´shən) *n.* argued assertion.

conversely (kən-vûrs´lē) *adv.* in a way that contradicts or reverses something.

convert (kən-vûrt´) *v.* to change one's system of beliefs.

decisive (dĭ-sī´sĭv) *adj.* final or concluding.

deduce (dĭ-dōōs´) *v.* to know through reason or logical conclusion.

default (dĭ-fôlt´) *v.* to fail to keep a promise to repay a loan.

degenerate (dĭ-jĕn´ər-āt´) *v.* to decline morally.

delude (dĭ-lōōd´) *v.* to deceive or instill a false belief in.

demeanor (dĭ-mē´nər) *n.* attitude or perceived behavior.

derive (dĭ-rīv´) *v.* to obtain or extract from.

desolate (dĕs´ə-lĭt) *adj.* unhappy; lonely.

desolation (dĕs´ə-la´shən) *n.* lonely grief; misery.

detract (dĭ-trăkt´) *v.* to take away from.

din (dĭn) *n.* loud noise.

discernible (dĭ-sûr´nə-bəl) *adj.* recognizable or noticeable.

discordant (dĭ-skôr´dnt) *adj.* conflicting or not harmonious.

disingenuous (dĭs´ĭn-jĕn´yōō-əs) *adj.* insincere, deceitful.

disintegration (dĭs-ĭn'tĭ-grā'shən) *n.* the process of a whole coming apart in pieces.

distend (dĭ-stĕnd') *v.* to bulge or expand.

distill (dĭ-stĭl') *v.* to transform vapor into liquid.

diversity (dĭ-vûr'sĭ-tē) *n.* having varied social and/or ethnic backgrounds.

edict (ē'dĭkt') *n.* an official rule or proclamation.

emaciated (ĭ-mā'shē-āt'id) *adj.* made extremely thin and weak.

emanate (ĕm'ə-nāt') *v.* to emit or radiate from.

embark (ĕm-bärk') *v.* to set out on a course or a journey (often aboard a boat).

empathy (ĕm'pə-thē) *n.* the ability to understand and identify with another's feelings.

encroach (ĕn-krōch') *v.* to gradually intrude upon or invade.

execute (ĕk'sĭ-kyōot') *v.* to carry out or accomplish.

exhort (ĭg-zôrt') *v.* to strongly urge or encourage.

expanse (ĭk-spăns') *n.* a large area.

extricate (ĕk'strĭ-kāt') *v.* to release or disentangle from.

foremost (fôr'mōst') *adv.* most importantly.

foreboding (fôr-bō'dĭng) *n.* a sense of approaching evil.

gradation (gră-dā'shən) *n.* a slight, successive change in color, degree, or tone.

guise (gīz) *n.* form or outward appearance; outfit.

harried (hăr'ēd) *adj.* tormented; harassed.

immerse (ĭ-mûrs') *v.* to absorb or involve deeply.

impeccably (ĭm-pĕk'ə-blē) *adv.* perfectly.

imperative (ĭm-pĕr'ə-tĭv) *adj.* crucial, necessary.

imperceptible (ĭm'pər-sĕp'tə-bəl) *adj.* unnoticeable.

implacable (ĭm'plăk'ə-bəl) *adj.* impossible to soothe; unforgiving.

implication (ĭm'plĭ-kā'shən) *n.* consequence or effect.

increment (ĭn'krə-mənt) *n.* an addition or increase by a standard measure of growth.

inextricably (ĭn-ĕk'strĭ-kə-blē) *adv.* in a way impossible to untangle.

innate (ĭ-nāt') *adj.* inborn; existing at birth.

intangible (ĭn-tăn'jə-bəl) *n.* something that is difficult to grasp or explain.

integrity (ĭn-tĕg'rĭ-tē) *n.* consistency and strength of purpose.

intention (ĭn-tĕn'shən) *n.* purpose or plan.

intermittent (ĭn'tər-mĭt'nt) *adj.* occurring at erratic or irregular intervals.

interwoven (ĭn'tər-wō'vən) *adj.* blended or laced together.

intrusion (ĭn-trōo'zhən) *n.* act of trespass or invasion.

intuitive (ĭn-tōo'ĭ-tĭv) *adj.* known or understood without reasoning; instinctive.

invocation (ĭn'və-kā'shən) *n.* a formal appeal, often used in prayer.

invoke (ĭn-vōk') *v.* to refer or call attention to.

irrelevant (ĭ-rĕl'ə-vənt) *adj.* insignificant, unimportant.

laud (lôd) *v.* to praise.

loiter (loi'tər) *v.* to stand or wait idly.

lozenge (lŏz'ĭnj) *n.* a diamond-shaped object.

momentous (mō-mĕn'təs) *adj.* very important; fateful.

negligence (nĕg'lĭ-jəns) *n.* carelessness or failure to take normal precautions.

nullify (nŭl'ə-fī') *v.* to make of no value or consequence.

opaque (ō-pāk') *adj.* clouded; difficult to see through.

parallel (păr'ə-lĕl') *adj.* related; corresponding.

perish (pĕr´ĭsh) *v.* to die or come to an end.

pluralistic (plŏŏr´ə-lĭs´tĭc) *adj.* consisting of many ethnic and cultural groups.

ponderous (pŏn´dər-əs) *adj.* heavy in a clumsy way; bulky.

prism (prĭz´əm) *n.* a transparent, light-refracting object which figuratively refers to an individual's viewpoint.

profusion (prə-fyōō´zhən) *n.* abundance.

reclaim (rĭ-klām´) *v.* to retake possession; reform.

redemptive (rĭ-dĕmp´tiv) *adj.* causing freedom or salvation.

reiteration (rē-ĭt´ə-rā´shən) *n.* restatement or repetition.

reprieve (rĭ-prēv´) *n.* the cancellation or postponement of punishment.

repulsed (rĭ-pŭlsd´) *adj.* disgusted.

resolve (rĭ-zŏlv´) *v.* to decide or become determined.

restitution (rĕs´tĭ-tōō´shən) *n.* a making good for loss or damage; repayment.

revelry (rĕv´əl-rē) *n.* noisy merrymaking; festivity.

revile (rĭ-vīl´) *v.* to condemn or insult.

segregate (sĕg´rĭ-gāt´) *v.* to cause people to be separated based on gender, race, or other factors.

serrate (sĕr´āt´) *adj.* having a jagged, saw-toothed edge.

sheepish (shē´pĭsh) *adj.* showing embarrassment.

stagnant (stăg´nənt) *adj.* unchanging; without activity or development.

staidness (stād´nĭs) *n.* the quality of being steady, calm, and serious.

subversive (səb-vûr´sĭv) *adj.* intended to undermine or overthrow those in power.

succession (sək-sĕsh´ən) *n.* sequence; ordered arrangement.

succumb (sə-kŭm´) *v.* to surrender or fall victim to.

supple (sŭp´əl) *adj.* flexible or easily adaptable.

synchronization (sĭng´krə-nĭ-zā´shən) *n.* coordinated, simultaneous action.

tangible (tăn´jə-bəl) *n.* something that can be touched.

tentative (tĕn´tə-tĭv) *adj.* with caution and without confidence.

transfix (trăns-fĭks´) *v.* to captivate or make motionless with awe.

travail (trə-vāl´) *n.* painful effort.

tremulous (trĕm´yə-ləs) *adj.* marked by trembling or shaking.

validate (văl´ĭ-dāt´) *v.* to establish the value, truth, or legitimacy of.

Index of Skills

Key:

Teacher's Edition page numbers and subject entries are printed in **boldface** type.
Subject entries and page references that apply to both the Student Edition and the Teacher's Edition appear in lightface type.
There is no content from the Close Reader in this index.

Index of Titles and Authors

Key:

Authors and titles that appear in the Student Edition are in lightface type.

Authors and titles that appear in the Close Reader are in **boldface** type.

Names of authors who appear in both the Student Edition and the Close Reader are lightface. For these authors, Student Edition page references are lightface and Close Reader page references are **boldface**.

Student Edition Acknowledgments

Close Reader Acknowledgments

"And of Clay Are We Created" from *The Stories of Eva Luna* by Isabel Allende. Text copyright © 1989 by Isabel Allende. English translation copyright © 1991 by Macmillan Publishing Company. Reprinted by permission of Simon & Schuster, Inc. and Agencia Literaria Carmen Balcells.

Excerpt from *Animals in Translation: Using the Mysteries of Autism to Decode Animal Behavior* by Temple Grandin and Catherine Johnson. Text copyright © 2005 by Temple Grandin and Catherine Johnson. Reprinted by permission of Simon & Schuster, Inc. and Betsy Lerner.

Excerpt from *The Good Soldiers* by David Finkel. Text copyright © 2009 by David Finkel. Reprinted by permission of Farrar, Straus and Giroux, LLC, The Melanie Jackson Agency and Atlantic Books.

Excerpt from "Introduction: Love's Vocabulary" from *A Natural History of Love* by Diane Ackerman. Text copyright © 1994 by Diane Ackerman. Reprinted by permission of Random House, Inc. Any third party use of this material, outside of this publication, is prohibited. Interested parties must apply directly to Random House, Inc. for permission.

"Making the Future Better Together" (retitled from "After September 11, 2011, Focus on the Next 10 Years") by Eboo Patel from The Washington Post, September 12, 2011. Text copyright © 2011 by Eboo Patel. Reprinted by permission of Eboo Patel.

"Marie Colvin: 'Our mission is to report these horrors of war with accuracy and without prejudice'" by Marie Colvin from *The Guardian*, February 22, 2012, www.guardian.co.uk. Text copyright © by Marie Colvin. Reprinted by permission of the Estate of Marie Colvin.

"My Ceremony for Taking" by Lara Mann from *www.drunkenboat.com*, November 15, 2012. Text copyright © 2012 by Lara Mann. Reprinted by permission of Drunken Boat.

"Night Calls" by Lisa Fugard from Outside, Vol. xx, No. 5, May 1995. Text copyright © 1995 by Lisa Fugard. Reprinted by permission of Lisa Fugard.

Excerpts from *The Odyssey* by Homer, translated by Robert Fitzgerald. Translation copyright © 1961, 1963 by Robert Fitzgerald, renewed © 1989 by Benedict R.C. Fitzgerald on behalf of the Fitzgerald children. Reprinted by permission of Farrar, Straus and Giroux, LLC and Benedict Fitzgerald.

Excerpt from "Introduction" from *An Ordinary Man: An Autobiography* by Paul Rusesabagina, with Tom Zoellner. Text copyright © 2006 by Paul Rusesabagina. Reprinted by permission of Viking Penguin, a division of Penguin Group (USA) Inc.

"The Prisoner Who Wore Glasses" from *Tales of Tenderness and Power* by Bessie Head. Text copyright © 1989 by The Estate of Bessie Head. Reprinted by permission of Johnson & Alcock.

"The Stayer" from *Palm* Crows by Virgil Suárez. Text copyright © 2001 by Virgil Suárez. Reprinted by permission of The University of Arizona Press.

"The Survivor" from *The Phoenix Gone, The Terrace Empty* by Marilyn Chin. Text copyright © 1994 by Marilyn Chin. Reproduced with permission of Milkweed Editions.

Excerpt from "What Can I Do to Make Things Better" by Kofi Annan from *Parade Magazine*. Text copyright © by Kofi Annan. Reprinted by permission of Kofi Annan.

"Who Understands Me But Me" from *Immigrants in Our Own Land* by Jimmy Santiago Baca. Text copyright © 1977, 1979, 1981, 1982, 1990 by Jimmy Santiago Baca. Reprinted by permission of New Directions Publishing Corporation.